SOCIAL RESEARCH METHODS

edition 2

To Carole, Elyssa, and Sharyn, for everything.

SOCIAL RESEARCH METHODS

edition **2**

Qualitative and Quantitative Approaches

H. RUSSELL BERNARD

University of Florida

Los Angeles | London | New Delhi
Singapore | Washington DC

Los Angeles | London | New Delhi
Singapore | Washington DC

FOR INFORMATION:

SAGE Publications, Inc.
2455 Teller Road
Thousand Oaks, California 91320
E-mail: order@sagepub.com

SAGE Publications Ltd.
1 Oliver's Yard
55 City Road
London EC1Y 1SP
United Kingdom

SAGE Publications India Pvt. Ltd.
B 1/I 1 Mohan Cooperative Industrial Area
Mathura Road, New Delhi 110 044
India

SAGE Publications Asia-Pacific Pte. Ltd.
3 Church Street
#10-04 Samsung Hub
Singapore 049483

Publisher: Vicki Knight
Senior Associate Editor: Lauren Habib
Editorial Assistant: Kalie Koscielak
Production Editor: Libby Larson
Copy Editor: Carole M. Bernard
Typesetter: C & M Digitals (P) Ltd.
Proofreader: Stefanie Storholt
Indexer: Molly Hall
Cover Designer: Anupama Krishnan
Marketing Manager: Nicole Elliot
Permissions Editor: Adele Hutchinson

Copyright © 2013 by SAGE Publications, Inc.

Printed in Great Britain

Library of Congress Cataloging-in-Publication Data

Bernard, H. Russell (Harvey Russell), 1940-
Social research method : qualitative and quantitative approaches / H. Russell Bernard.—2nd ed.

p. cm.
Includes bibliographical references and index.

ISBN 978-1-4129-7854-5 (cloth)

1. Social sciences—Research—Methodology. I. Title.

H62.B439 2013
300.72—dc23   2011049881

This book is printed on acid-free paper.

12 13 14 15 16 10 9 8 7 6 5 4 3 2 1

Brief Contents

Detailed Contents

PART III: Data Collection   179

Preface

GOALS AND PHILOSOPHY

When I wrote the first edition of this book, between 1996 and 1998, the subtitle, *Qualitative and Quantitative Approaches*, announced something relatively new. At the time, the mixed-methods movement was just getting underway in the social sciences. Indeed, of the 1,350 citations in January 2012 to the term "mixed methods" in the *Social Science Citation Index*, 21 of them were earlier than 2000. I'm happy to report that mixed methods is no longer innovative in the least. There is a successful *Journal of Mixed Methods Research* (http://mmr.sagepub.com/), a *Handbook of Mixed Methods Research* (Tashakkori and Teddlie 2003), and several excellent books on designing and carrying out mixed-methods research (Creswell 2009; Creswell and Plano Clark 2007).

I can hardly contain my enthusiasm for all this.

There is, of course, an irreducible difference between those of us for whom the first principle of inquiry is that reality is constructed uniquely by each person and those of us who start from the principle that external reality awaits our discovery through a series of approximations. There is also an important (though not incompatible) difference between those of us who seek to *understand* human phenomena in relation to differences in beliefs and values and those of us who seek to *explain* human thought and behavior as the consequence of external forces.

But, while the boundaries between the disciplines remain strong, those boundaries are no longer about methods—if they ever were. Whatever our epistemological differences, the actual methods by which we collect and analyze our data belong to everyone across the social sciences.

In short, all the methods belong to all of us.

WHAT'S IN THIS BOOK

There are 22 chapters in this book, organized into four sections: (1) background to research; (2) designing research; (3) collecting data; and (4) analyzing data.

Section I, on the background to research, comprises three chapters: Chapter 1 covers the history of social science and introduces the competing philosophical positions in the field; Chapter 2 is about the logical foundations of social science research—the concepts of variables, measurement, and units of analysis; and Chapter 3 is about choosing research problems and searching the literature.

Chapter 1 addresses these questions: (1) What are the social sciences? (2) What are the intellectual roots of the social sciences? (3) What good are the social sciences? Chapter 1 also introduces the complex issue of ethics in the social sciences.

There is no chapter devoted to ethics in this book because ethics is too important to deal with that way. It's part of *everything* we do in social science, and the topic of ethics is dealt with, at length, in several chapters. Look for references to those discussions under "ethics" in the index.

Chapter 2 introduces the vocabulary of social research. There's a lot of jargon, but it's the good kind. Important concepts deserve words of their own, and Chapter 2 is full of important concepts like reliability, validity, levels of measurement, covariation, and the controversial idea of operationism.

Chapter 3 is about choosing research problems and the literature in preparation for collecting data. There is a profound difference between a *social problem* and a social *research problem*. Child abuse, infant mortality, the spread of HIV, teens carrying guns to school—these are social problems, and serious ones. Politicians, activists, members of the clergy, and social researchers can all contribute to solving these problems. But in my view, the most important contribution a social scientist can make to solving a social problem is to be right about what causes it. This requires ideas for research and familiarity with what has been done before. Learning the difference between a social problem and a social research problem is, I think, one of the most difficult tasks that social researchers face.

Selecting a research topic always involves an ethical issue. The operational test of whether a particular piece of research is ethical is whether social norms tolerate it, but this relativistic position has a serious flaw, which I address in Chapter 3.

Section II, on designing research, comprises four chapters. Chapter 4 is about the concepts and principles of experimental design, and Chapters 5, 6, and 7 are about sampling. The experimental method is as much a part of the foundation of survey research in sociology as it is of laboratory research in psychology. The principle of random assignment in experiments, for example, has its analog in the principle of random sampling in survey research. Experiments on people involve special ethical issues, which I explore in Chapter 4 as well.

Chapter 5 is about the basics of sampling: what samples are and why we need them and various methods for getting samples. Chapter 6 is an introduction to sampling theory, including the central limit theorem, and determining the size of representative samples. Chapter 7 is on nonprobability sampling, including quota sampling, snowball and respondent driven sampling, purposive sampling, and convenience sampling. Together, Chapters 4, 5, 6, and 7 address two big questions in social research: (1) How can I be sure that my findings are valid? (2) Given that my findings are valid, how far can I generalize them beyond the people (or countries, or court cases) I actually studied?

Including chapters on sampling as part of research design reflects my own teaching style, but some instructors may assign Chapters 5 and 6 with Chapters 20, 21, and 22 on analyzing quantitative data and Chapter 7 with Chapters 16, 17, 18, and 19 on analyzing qualitative data.

Section III is about the real how-to of collecting social science data. There are seven chapters in this section: Chapter 8 deals with unstructured and semistructured interviewing; Chapter 9 is on questionnaires and survey research; Chapter 10 is on collecting relational data; Chapter 11 covers the development and use of scales; Chapter 12 is about the elusive, yet highly effective method of participant observation; Chapter 13 covers the taking and managing of field notes; and Chapter 14 is about methods of direct and indirect observation.

Unstructured and semistructured interviewing, covered in Chapter 8, involve a minimum of control. In unstructured interviewing, the idea is to get people to open up and to let them express themselves in their own terms and at their own pace. Semistructured interviewing follows a written list of questions and topics that need to be covered in a particular order.

Focus groups—a kind of semistructured interview—are recruited to discuss a particular topic—like people's reaction to a television commercial or their attitudes toward a social service program. Survey researchers may use focus groups to help design a questionnaire and also to help interpret the results of surveys.

Response effects are measurable differences in interview data that are predictable from characteristics of respondents, interviewers, and environments—and they are a problem in all interviewing, from unstructured hanging-out interviews to questionnaire-based telephone or Internet interviews. Chapter 8 ends with a review of this important problem.

In structured interviews, people are asked to respond to as nearly identical a set of stimuli as possible. Chapter 9 covers questionnaire design, improving response rates, the use of open-ended versus closed-ended questions, asking questions about sensitive topics, using several interviewers in team research, and translating questionnaires from one language to another.

Questionnaires are one kind of structured interview, but other fully structured interview methods include free listing, pile sorting, triad tests, sentence frames, paired comparisons, rankings, and ratings. These are covered in Chapter 10.

Chapter 11 is about the development and use of scales. A single question on a questionnaire is technically a scale if it lets you assign the people you're studying to categories of a variable. Many interesting variables in social science, however, are complex and can't easily be assessed with single indicators. Chapter 11 covers methods for developing and testing composite measures of complex concepts. Methods covered include Guttman scales, Likert scales, semantic differential scales, and direct magnitude scales.

Participant observation, covered in Chapter 12, is one of the four strategic methods of the social sciences, along with experiments, surveys, and archival research. Participant observation turns fieldworkers into instruments of data collection and data analysis. This requires certain skills, which include learning the local language, dialect, or jargon; developing explicit awareness; building memory; maintaining naiveté; learning to hang out and build rapport; maintaining objectivity; and learning to write clearly.

Participant observation fieldwork produces field notes—lots of them. Chapter 13 describes how to write and manage field notes.

Chapter 14 covers direct and indirect observation. Direct observation involves watching people and recording their behavior on the spot; indirect observation involves gathering the archeological residue of people's behavior. Some methods of direct observation include continuous monitoring (associated with behavioral assessment), spot observation (associated with time allocation studies), and experience sampling (for assessing moods and emotions as well as behaviors). Direct observation is reactive when people know that you are watching them (people can play to the observer), so some researchers use unobtrusive observation. This involves deception, which raises obvious ethical issues.

Section IV comprises eight chapters about analyzing data. Chapter 15 is an overview of the whole analysis enterprise. Different kinds of data—qualitative and quantitative data—require different analytic methods, but analysis is always the same thing: the search for patterns in data and for ideas that help explain why those patterns are there in the first place. One of the most important concepts in all data analysis—whether we're working with quantitative or qualitative data—is the data matrix. This concept is introduced in Chapter 15.

Chapter 16 covers methods for analyzing the kinds of data described in Chapter 10—that is, data on the content and structure of cultural domains and social networks. Data of this kind are often qualitative, but they are collected in structured interviews.

Chapters 17, 18, and 19 cover the analysis of unstructured qualitative data. Most of the recoverable information about human thought and behavior is naturally occurring text—diaries, property transactions, recipes, correspondence, song lyrics, billboards, books, magazines, newspapers, artifacts, images, advertisements. . . . Text analysis is not a single method. It includes interpretive analysis, narrative analysis, discourse analysis, the grounded theory approach, and content analysis. As in so many areas of social research, text analysis often involves a sensible blend of qualitative and quantitative methods.

Chapter 17 covers ethnographic decision modeling (including flow chart models, IF-THEN charts, and decision tables), the elicitation and display of folk taxonomies (including componential analysis), and analytic induction (including Boolean tests, which are a formalization of analytic induction). What these methods have in common is that they are based on some principles of systematic logic applied to qualitative data.

Chapter 18 covers "grammar beyond the sentence"—that is, the analysis of various forms of discourse, including conversation, narrative, and performance—including schema analysis.

Chapter 19 covers the two most widely known kinds of text analysis: grounded theory and content analysis. The two methods reflect the two great epistemological approaches for all research: induction and deduction.

Finally, Chapters 20, 21, and 22 are an introduction to the basics of statistical reasoning and data analysis—methods that are used across the social sciences. Chapter 20 deals with univariate statistics—that is, statistics that describe a *single variable*, without making any comparisons among variables. Chapters 21 and 22 are discussions of bivariate and multivariate statistics—statistics that describe *relationships among variables* and let you test hypotheses about what causes what.

If you want to become comfortable with statistical analysis, you need more than a basic course; you need a course in regression and applied multivariate analysis and a course (or a lot of hands-on practice) in the use of one of the popular statistical packages, like SPSS®, SAS®, STATA®, and SYSTAT®. Neither the material in this book nor a course in the use of statistical packages is a replacement for taking statistics from professional instructors of that subject. Nevertheless, after working through the materials in Chapters 20, 21, and 22, students should be able to use basic statistics to describe their data and be able to take their data to a professional statistical consultant—and understand what she or he suggests.

Some Features of the Book

1. *Opening objectives and introductions to the chapters.* Each chapter begins with a page called "In This Chapter" that lays out all the major headings. This page repeats the material in the detailed Table of Contents for each chapter and makes it easier to understand, at a glance, what's coming. Right after this opening page, each chapter has an introduction that provides a quick review of the major issues.

2. *Boxes.*

Box Preface.1: Boxes are important

You'll see some boxes, like this, throughout the book. These boxes are not asides. I use this device when I want to expand on and highlight some important material. For example, Box 2.1 notes that every research question has an ethical component; Box 16.3 highlights the difference between a similarity matrix and a dissimilarity matrix; Box 19.1 explains the theory of ethnopoetics; Box 19.4 highlights problems with measuring reliability in coding text; Box 12.1 highlights the issue of whether participant observation is science; Box 20.7 explains the concept of degrees of freedom; and so on.

3. *Numbered steps*. Methods like experiments, questionnaires, and participant observation are complex processes, not just techniques. I've broken down these methods into a series of numbered, highlighted steps to make it easier to locate them for review.

4. *Key concepts*. All new terms appear in bold-faced type like this—but only the first time they appear. Then, as a study aid, there is a section at the end of each chapter titled "Key Concepts in This Chapter." That section has all the bold-faced terms in the chapter and all these terms are listed in the index as well.

5. *Summary and exercises*. Following the Key Concepts section, there are two more study aids: a summary of the main points of the chapter and a series of exercises for illustrating and nailing down some of the main points.

6. *Further reading*. Finally, each chapter ends with recommendations for further reading. Some of these recommendations are classics in the literature on social science methods; others are recent examples that further illustrate some of the key points in each chapter. All the extra readings are pointed to in the text with a bold reference to Further Reading.

WHAT'S NEW IN THIS EDITION

The **Further Reading** section at the end of each chapter is expanded and the result is that the bibliography is about 60% larger than in the last edition. People ask me why there are so many references to really, really old stuff. The reason is that I want students to know that the literature on research methods is very rich and I want them to know about many of the classics. Many examples have been updated, including new information about some of the classics.

The separate chapter on searching the literature is gone from this edition because students are universally aware of the databases. Chapter 3 retains the information about the databases that I think are most important for students to control and instructions on how to use the databases effectively.

Sampling takes up three chapters in this edition, up from one in the first edition. A lot of progress has been made in the development of nonprobability methods of sampling, for example, so these are treated in a separate chapter. In the first edition, I treated consensus analysis in the chapter on participant observation and on choosing informants. Consensus analysis has become much more widely used in the last 15 years. It is now described in greater detail in Chapter 16, on cultural domain analysis. Choosing both key informants and specialized informants, however, remains in the chapter on nonprobability methods of sampling.

Interviewing takes up three chapters in this edition, up from two in the first edition. In Chapter 8, on unstructured and semistructured interviewing, the sections on recording equipment and on voice recognition software (VRS) have been updated, and examples have been added or updated. Chapters 9 and 10 are on two very different kinds of structured interviewing. Chapter 9 focuses on questionnaires and surveys. I've updated the material on computer-based methods and on Internet-based surveys and added material on the list experiment. Chapter 10 introduces methods used in cognitive science, including free lists, pile sorts, triad tests, and paired comparisons. Methods for analyzing these data are in Chapter 16.

In Chapter 11, on scaling, I've updated material on the various instruments. In Chapter 12, on participant observation, I've updated several examples and added bibliography. In Chapter 13, on taking and managing field notes, I've updated or added examples and added information on using word processors as text managers. In Chapter 14, the bibliography has been updated.

Chapter 15 is unchanged from the first edition. Chapter 16 contains new material on analyzing data from the systematic ethnographic methods described in Chapter 10: free lists, pile sorts, and so on. The section on network analysis in Chapter 16 is new to this edition. Multidimensional scaling and cluster analysis are described in Chapter 16, as is cultural consensus analysis and cultural consonance analysis. Chapter 17 continues with methods in this cognitive science tradition of social science, including decision modeling and taxonomic analysis, and it covers new methods for analytic induction.

The chapter on text analysis in the last edition is now two chapters. Chapters 18 and 19 owe much to my work with Gery Ryan (Bernard and Ryan 2010; Ryan and Bernard 2000, 2003). Chapter 18 focuses on methods for analyzing whole texts; Chapter 19 deals with methods that involve finding themes in texts and analyzing the distribution of themes.

Chapters 20, 21, and 22 are updated versions of Chapters 14, 15, and 16 in the first edition.

What's Not in This Book

A word about some things that are not in this book. Easy-to-carry, easy-to-use cameras that produce high-quality still and moving images and synchronized sound are making it easier than ever to do visual research. I treat a few visual methods here, including cinema verité of family life (see Chapter 14 in the section on video monitoring of behavior) and the use of photographs in interviews (see the section on photovoice in Chapter 8), but for overviews of visual methods in social research see El Guindi (2004) and Spencer (2011), and see *Visual Studies*, the journal of the International Visual Sociology Association, and *Visual Anthropology Review*, the journal of the Society for Visual Anthropology. See Appendix E for information on software for analyzing photographs and video as text.

For methods in the study of online communities, see Boellstorff (2008), Constable (2003), Hine (2000), and Kozinets (2010).

In Chapter 12, I describe several rapid assessment methods that come from applications research, incuding participatory mapping and participatory transects. For more on methods in community-based, participatory research, see Israel et al. (2005), Reason and Bradbury (2001), and Viswanathan (2004).

Those interested in geospatial analysis should consult De Smith et al. (2007) and various online tutorials (e.g., http://www.spatialanalysisonline.com).

ACKNOWLEDGMENTS

Anyone who has ever written a textbook knows that I really, really mean it when I say I'm grateful to a lot of people who have helped along the way—students, colleagues, editors, reviewers, and production staff.

I've received so much help from students over the years, particularly Clarence Gravlee, Christopher McCarty, and Gery Ryan. Continuing discussions with Gravlee and McCarty have sharpened my focus on the methods for analyzing relational data. Ryan's influence will be evident in Chapters 17, 18, and 19 in the discussions about ethnographic decision models, conversation analysis, and coding themes. He is also the coauthor with me of a book on analyzing qualitative data (Bernard and Ryan 2010).

Other students who have been keen critics of my writing include: Kenneth Adams, Nanette Barkey, Bryan Byrne, Domenick Dellino, Michael Evans, Louis Forline, Stacey Giroux, Harold Green, Camilla Harshbarger, Fred Hay, Scott Hill, Mark House, Shepherd Iverson, Aryeh Jacobsohn, David Kennedy, Adam Kiš, Oliver Kortendick, Barbara Marriott, Mason Mathews, Chad Maxwell, George Mbeh, Rosalyn Negrón, Isaac Nyamongo, Julia Pauli, David Price, Jorge Rocha, Michael Schnegg, Gene Ann Shelley,

Fatma Soud, Susan Stans, Amanda Stronza, Elli Sugita, Kenneth Sturrock, Tracy Van Holt, Holly Williams, and Amber Wutich.

Over 45 years of teaching research methods, I have benefited from the many textbooks on the subject in psychology (e.g., Kerlinger 1973; Murphy et al. 1937), sociology (e.g., Babbie 1983; Goode and Hatt 1952; Lundberg 1964; Nachmias and Nachmias 1976), and anthropology (e.g., Brim and Spain 1974; A. Johnson 1978; Pelto and Pelto 1978). The scholars whose works most influenced my thinking about research methods were Paul Lazarsfeld (1954, 1982; Lazarsfeld and Rosenberg 1955; Lazarsfeld et al. 1972) and Donald Campbell (1957, 1974, 1975; Campbell and Stanley 1966; Cook and Campbell 1979).

Over those same 45 years, I've profited from discussions about research methods with Michael Agar, Stephen Borgatti, James Boster, Devon Brewer, Michael Burton, Michael Chibnik, Joel Cohen, Ronald Cohen, Roy D'Andrade, Don Dillman, William Dressler, Carol Ember, the late Melvin Ember, Michael Fischer, Linton Freeman, Sue Freeman, John Gatewood, Christina Gladwin, Ricardo Godoy, Raymond Hames, the late Marvin Harris, Penn Handwerker, Carole Hill, Jeffrey Johnson, Willett Kempton, Hartmut Lang, Gary Martin, John Omohundro, Michael Paolisso, Pertti Pelto, Aaron Podolefsky, Douglas Raybeck, the late Jack Roberts, A. Kimball Romney, Lee Sailer, Paula Sabloff, the late Thomas Schweizer, J. Richard Stepp, Lynn Thomas, Roger Trent, Susan Weller, Douglas White, Oswald Werner, Harry Wolcott, and Alvin Wolfe.

Other colleagues who have influenced my thinking about research methods include Ronald Burt, Patrick Doreian, Linda Garro, Theodore Graves, Eugene Hammel, Allen Johnson, Charles Kadushin, Maxine Margolis, Stuart Plattner, Ronald Rice, the late Peter Rossi, James Short, Harry Triandis, the late Charles Wagley, and Eben Weitzman. Most of them knew that they were helping me talk and think through the issues presented in this book, but some may not have, so I take this opportunity to thank them all.

I am much indebted to W. Penn Handwerker. He and I collaborated on a book for teaching students the basics of statistical data analysis, and he has helped me over the years with many questions about research problems. Whether it was just to talk about how to present this or that method or to discuss the subtleties of multicollinearity, Penn never complained and never let up.

In 1987, Pertti Pelto, Lee Sailer, and I taught the first National Science Foundation Summer Institute on Research Methods in Cultural Anthropology—known as "methods camp." Stephen Borgatti joined Pelto and me in 1988 and the three of us taught together for 8 years, from 1988 to 1995. My intellectual debt to those two colleagues is profound. Pelto (1970) wrote the pioneering methods text in cultural anthropology, and I've long been influenced by his sensible combination of ethnographic and numerical data in field research. Borgatti tutored me on the measurement of similarities and dissimilarities and has greatly influenced my thinking about the formal study of emically defined cultural domains. Borgatti's influence is evident in my discussion of domain analysis (Chapters 10 and 16). Teachers of these methods will want to consult Borgatti's web pages and his chapter in the *Ethnographer's Tool Kit* (Borgatti 1999).

When the original methods camp ended in 1995, Jeffrey Johnson initiated a new, NSF-supported program, the Summer Institute on Research Design in Cultural Anthropology (the SIRD)—this one for PhD students. Johnson invited Susan Weller and me to join him in that program and I've benefited every year since then from long discussions with these colleagues—and the more than 200 students who have participated—about the pedagogy of research methods.

In 2005, we initiated another program, the Short Courses on Research Methods in Cultural Anthropology (the SCRM)—again, supported by NSF. These 5-day courses have been run in parallel to the SIRD at the Duke University Marine Laboratories, in Beaufort, North Carolina. Here again, I have benefited from the wisdom of the faculty who teach in this program, including Eduardo Brondizio, Elizabeth Cartwright, Jerome Crowder, William Dressler, Clarence Gravlee, Raymond Hames, Jeffrey Johnson, Gary Martin, Christopher McCarty, Justin Nolan, Kathryn Oths, Michael Paolisso, J. Richard Stepp, Tracy Van Holt, and Amber Wutich.

My closest colleague, and the one to whom I am most intellectually indebted, was Peter Killworth, with whom I worked from 1972 until his death in 2008. Peter was a geophysicist at the University of Southampton and was accustomed to working with data that had been collected by deep-sea current meters, satellite weather scanners, and the like. He shared my vision of an effective science of humanity and he showed an appreciation for the difficulties a naturalist like me encounters in collecting real-life data, in the field, about human behavior and thought. Most importantly, he helped me see the possibilities for overcoming those difficulties through the application of scientific research practices. The results are never perfect, but the process of trying is always exhilarating. That's the central lesson of this book, and I hope it comes through.

Textbook authors have special debts to editors and to members of the production staff. Those debts start accumulating even before the writing starts and continue to mount after the book is published. The first edition of this book was written under the editorship of C. Deborah Laughton (now at Guilford Press). My current editor at Sage, Vicki Knight, and her assistant, Lauren Habib, have been a constant source of support. And Mitch Allen (first at Sage, then at AltaMira, and now at Left Coast Press, Inc.) has been there for me for a very, very long time.

Production editors are the unsung heroes of textbook publishing. My great thanks to Libby Larson, the production editor for this book. I've never worked with anyone better.

I'm indebted to the seven colleagues who reviewed the manuscript of this book anonymously and offered such helpful criticism. I'm especially grateful that, after the whole process was over, they allowed me to thank them publicly: Monika Ardelt, University of Florida; Coye Cheshire, University of California, Berkeley; Benedict J. Colombi, University of Arizona; Erica B. Gibson, University of South Carolina; Julian Kilker, University of Nevada, Las Vegas; Iris Phillips, University of Southern Indiana; and Jenny Trinitapoli, Arizona State University.

I save for last the people who deserve my thanks more than any others. It's not just authors who give up vacations and weekends to write books. Whole families are brought into the art of abnegation. Thanks to Elyssa, Sharyn, Matthew, Zoë, and Dylan for their support and love and for understanding when I'd show up to visit with a laptop in tow and closet myself. And thanks to Carole Bernard for—well, for everything. Carole worked with me on this book through all its incarnations. Her editorial advice and deadly eye for detail has saved me from so many embarrassments that I've stopped counting. No one can possibly know, without firsthand experience, what it's like to live with someone who is writing a book like this one. I only know that I wouldn't want to do it.

HRB
Gainesville, Florida
June 30, 2011

About the Author

H. Russell Bernard received his PhD from the University of Illinois and is Professor Emeritus of Anthropology at the University of Florida. He has done research in Greece, Mexico, and the United States and has taught or done research at universities in the United States, Greece, Japan, and Germany. Bernard's areas of research include technology and social change, language death, and social network analysis. Since 1987, Bernard has participated in summer courses, sponsored by the U.S. National Science Foundation, on research methods and research design. He is former editor of *Human Organization* and the *American Anthropologist* and is the current editor of *Field Methods*. Bernard's books include *Research Methods in Anthropology: Qualitative and Quantitative Approaches* (5th edition, AltaMira Press, 2011), *Native Ethnography*, with Jesús Salinas Pedraza (SAGE Publications 1989) and *Analyzing Qualitative Data: Systematic Approaches*, with Gery Ryan (SAGE Publications 2009). Bernard was the 2003 recipient of the Franz Boas Award from the American Anthropological Association and is a member of the National Academy of Sciences. When he isn't writing or doing research, he enjoys cooking, playing at guitar, traveling with Carole, and spending time with his grandchildren Zoë and Dylan.

PART I
Background to Research

1

About
Social Science

THE SOCIAL SCIENCE SUCCESS STORY

This book is about research in the social sciences—that is, the sciences of human thought and human behavior. Our lives are profoundly affected by the social sciences: Our public schools are scenes of one experiment after another, as we search for better ways to help children learn. Those experiments are part of social science at work. Our cities are scenes of hundreds of programs designed, we hope, to help people develop their employment skills or gain access to health care or find shelter. . . .

All these programs are part of social science at work. We are bombarded with ads to buy this or that thing, to vote for this or that candidate, to give to this or that charity. Those ads, too, are part of social science at work.

We are always on the lookout for ways to extend and make more comfortable our own lives and the lives of our children. In the absence of any hard information about how to do that, we quite naturally mystify the forces that make some people rich and some poor, make some people sick and others healthy, and make some people die young and others live a long time. From its beginnings in the sixteenth century, modern science has been demystifying those forces. Science is about the systematic creation of knowledge that provides us with the kind of control over nature—from the weather to disease to our own buying habits—that we have always sought.

Some people are very uncomfortable with this "mastery over nature" metaphor. When all is said and done, though, few people—not even the most outspoken critics of science—would give up the material benefits of science. For example, one of science's great triumphs over nature is antibiotics. We know that overprescription of those drugs eventually sets the stage for new strains of drug-resistant bacteria, but we also know perfectly well that we're not going to stop using antibiotics. We'll rely (we hope) on *more* science to come up with better bacteria fighters.

Air conditioning is another of science's triumphs over nature. In Florida, where I live, there is constant criticism of overdevelopment. But try getting middle-class people in my state to give up air conditioning for just one day in the summer and you'll find out in a hurry about the weakness of ideology compared to the power of creature comforts. If running air conditioners pollutes the air or uses up fossil fuel, we'll rely (we hope) on *more* science to solve those problems, too.

TECHNOLOGY AND SCIENCE

Ask 500 people, as I did in a telephone survey, to list "the major contributions that science has made to humanity" and there is strong consensus: Cures for diseases, space exploration, computers, nuclear power, satellite telecommunications, television, automobiles, artificial limbs, and transplant surgery head the list. Not one person—not one—mentioned the discovery of the dual helix structure of DNA. Just one out of 500 mentioned Einstein's theory of relativity. In other words, the contributions of science are, in the public imagination, technologies—the things that provide the mastery over nature I mentioned.

We are accustomed to thinking about the success of the physical and biological sciences, but not about that of the social sciences. Ask those same 500 people to list "the major contributions that the social and behavioral sciences have made to humanity" and you get a long silence on the phone, followed by a raggedy list, with no consensus.

I want you to know, right off the bat, that social science is serious business and that it has been a roaring success, contributing mightily to humanity's global effort to control nature. Everyone in science today, from astronomy to zoology, uses probability theory and the array of statistical tools that have developed from that theory. It is all but forgotten that probability theory was applied social science from the start. It was developed in the seventeenth century by mathematicians Pierre Fermat (1601–1665) and Blaise Pascal (1623–1662) to help people do better in games of chance, and it was well established a century later when two other mathematicians, Daniel Bernoulli (1700–1782) and Jean D'Alambert (1717–1783), debated publicly the pros and cons of large-scale inoculations in Paris against smallpox.

In those days (before Edward Jenner's breakthrough in 1798 in the development of safe vaccinations), inoculations against small-pox involved injecting small doses of the live disease. There was a substantial risk of death from the inoculation (about 1-in-200), but the disease was ravaging cities in Europe and killing people by the tens of thousands. The problem was to assess the probability of dying from smallpox versus dying from the vaccine.

This is one of the earliest uses I have found of social science and probability theory in the making of state policy, but there were soon to be more. One of them was social security.

In 1889, Otto von Bismarck came up with a pension plan for retired German workers. Based on sound social science data, Bismarck's minister of finance suggested that 70 would be just the right age for retirement. At that time, the average life expectancy in Germany was closer to 50, and just 30% of children born then could expect to live to 70. Germany lowered the retirement age to 65 in 1916, by which time, life expectancy had edged up a bit—to around 55 (Max-Planck Institute 2002). In 1935, when the Social Security system was signed into law in the United States, Germany's magic number 65 was adopted as the age of retirement. White children born that year in the United States had an average life expectancy of about 63; for Black children it was about 51 (SAUS 1947:Table 88).

Today, life expectancy in the highly industrialized nations is close to 80—fully 30 years longer than 100 years ago—and social science data are being used more than ever in the development of public policy. How much leisure time should we have? What kinds of tax structures are needed to support a medical system that caters to the needs of 80-somethings when birth rates are low and there are fewer working adults to support the retirement of the elderly?

The success of social science is not all about probability theory and risk assessment. Fundamental breakthroughs by psychologists in understanding the stimulus-response mechanism in humans have made possible the treatment and management of phobias, bringing comfort to untold millions of people. Unfortunately, the same breakthroughs have brought us wildly successful attack ads in politics and millions of adolescents becoming hooked on cigarettes. I never said you'd *like* all the successes of social science (see Box 1.1).

Box 1.1 Life insurance: Betting on dying

Beginning in the 1840s, fundamental knowledge in the social sciences have given us great understanding of how economic and political forces impact demography. One result is life insurance. Suppose I'm the life insurance company. You bet me that you will die within 365 days. I ask you a few questions: How old are you? Do you smoke? What do you do for a living? Do you fly a private plane? Then, depending on the answers (I've got all that fundamental knowledge, remember?), I tell you that the bet is your $235 against my promise to pay your heirs $100,000 if you die within 365 days.

If you *lose the bet* and stay alive, I keep your $235. Next year, we go through this again, except that now I set your bet at $300.

This is simply spectacular human engineering at work, and it's all based on scientifically developed knowledge about risk assessment. Another product of this knowledge is state lotteries—taxes on people who are bad at math (Petty 1899 [1690]:64).

Failures in Science and Social Science

If the list of successes in the social sciences is long, so is the list of failures. School busing in the late 1960s to achieve racial integration was based on scientific findings in a report by James Coleman (1966). Those findings were achieved in the best tradition of careful scholarship. They just happened to be wrong because the scientists involved in the study didn't anticipate "White flight"—a phenomenon in which Whites abandoned cities for suburbs, taking much of the urban tax base with them and driving the inner cities into poverty.

On the other hand, the list of failures in the physical and biological sciences is just as spectacular. In the Middle Ages, alchemists tried everything they could to turn lead into gold. They had lots of people investing in them, but it just didn't work. Cold fusion is still a dream that attracts a few hardy souls. And no one who saw the explosion of the Challenger on live television in 1986 will ever forget it.

There are some really important lessons from all this. (1) Science isn't perfect but it isn't going away because it's too successful at doing what people everywhere want it to do. (2) The sciences of human thought and human behavior are much, much more powerful than most people understand them to be. (3) The power of social science, like that of the physical and biological sciences, comes from the same source: the scientific method in which ideas, based on hunches or on formal theories, are put forward, tested publicly, and replaced by ideas that produce better results. (4) Social science knowledge, like that of any science, can be used to enhance our lives or to degrade them.

WHAT ARE THE SOCIAL SCIENCES?

The social science landscape is pretty complicated. The main branches, in alphabetical order, are anthropology, economics, history, political science, psychology, social psychology, and sociology. Each of these fields has many subfields, and there are, in addition, many other disciplines in which social research is done. These include communications, criminology, demography, education, epidemiology, geography, journalism, leisure studies, nursing, indigenous studies, and social work, to name just a few.

Over time, methods for research have been developed within each of these fields, but no discipline owns any method. You may not agree with my out-front, positivist epistemology, my enthusiasm for science as mastery over nature, but the methods for collecting and analyzing data about human thought, human feelings, and human behavior belong to everyone.

Sociologists developed the questionnaire survey. People still associate sociology with that method, but questionnaire surveys are used in all the social sciences today.

Anthropologists developed the method of participant observation. It continues to be the hallmark of that discipline, but today participant observation is used in all the social sciences.

Direct observation of behavior was developed in psychology. It's still used more in psychology (and animal ethology) than in other disciplines, but now that method belongs to the world, too.

No one is expert in all the methods available for research. But seasoned social scientists all know about the array of methods available to them for collecting and analyzing data. By the time you get through this book, you should have a pretty good idea of the range of methods used in the social sciences and what kinds of research problems are best addressed by the various methods (see Box 1.2).

Box 1.2 Research is a craft

Research is a craft. I'm not talking *analogy* here. Research isn't *like* a craft. It *is* a craft. If you know what people have to go through to become skilled carpenters or makers of clothes, you have some idea of what it takes to learn the skills for doing research. It takes practice and more practice.

Have you ever known a professional seamstress? My wife and I were doing fieldwork in Ixmiquilpan, a small town in the state of Hidalgo, Mexico, in 1962 when we met Florencia. She made dresses for little girls—Communion dresses, mostly. Mothers would bring their girls to Florencia's house. Florencia would look at the girls and say "Turn around . . . turn again . . . OK." And that was that. The mother and daughter would leave, and Florencia would start making a dress. No pattern, no elaborate measurement. There would be one fitting to make some adjustments, but that was it.

I was amazed at Florencia's ability to pick up scissors and start cutting fabric without a pattern. Then, in 1964, Carole and I went to Greece and met Irini. She made dresses for women on the island of Kalymnos where I did my doctoral fieldwork. Women would bring Irini a catalog or a picture—from Sears or from some Paris fashion show—and Irini would make the dresses. Irini was more cautious than Florencia. She made lots of measurements and took notes. But there were no patterns. She just looked at her clients, made the measurements, and started cutting fabric.

How do people learn that much? With lots of practice. And that's the way it is with research. Don't expect to do perfect research the first time out. In fact, don't ever expect to do perfect research. Just expect that each time you do a research project, you will bring more and more experience to the effort and that your abilities to gather and analyze data and write up the results will get better and better.

SOME HISTORY OF METHODS IN SOCIAL RESEARCH

In the 1830s, when modern social science began, all the practitioners thought of themselves as belonging to one large enterprise: the application of the scientific method to the study of human thought and human behavior. By the 1930s, the social sciences had divided and formed separate departments in universities and it was easy to distinguish all the disciplines from one another.

Partly, the distinctions were based on the kinds of questions people asked. Psychologists asked questions about the mind; anthropologists asked questions about culture; sociologists asked questions about society; and so on. But, to a large extent, distinctions among the social sciences were based on the methods people used in trying to answer research questions. Psychologists used laboratory experiments; sociologists used survey questionnaires; anthropologists trekked to the field to do something they called participant observation; economists built mathematical models; historians hung out in archives and used special methods for assessing the credibility of documents.

Today, despite the proliferation of departments and journals and professional organizations, we are coming full circle. More and more, social scientists recognize that we are part of the same enterprise. We continue to ask different questions about the same set of phenomena, but we now all have access to the same methods. *The theme of this book is that methods—all methods—belong to all of us.* Whatever our theoretical orientation, whatever our discipline, a sound mix of qualitative and quantitative data is inevitable in any study of human thought and behavior. Whether we use words or numbers, we might as well use them right.

I use the term "social sciences" and not "social and behavioral sciences" because the latter is too big a mouthful. Actually, *all* of the social science disciplines are social *and* behavioral: They all deal with human behavior and thought at both the individual and group levels.

Some psychologists, for example, focus on individual thought and behavior, while others study group processes. Many sociologists and political scientists study groups of people (labor unions, firms, hospitals, churches, nations) and how those groups are organized and connected to one another, but many also study individual behavior (sexual preferences, consumer choices, responses to illness). They aggregate their data to understand societies, but they ask their questions of individual people. Anthropologists focus on cultures—a supremely aggregate phenomenon—but many are concerned with individuals. In-depth interviews produce rich data about the experiences that real people have being labor migrants, or living with AIDS, or making it as a single parent, or being a surgeon, a cop, or an intravenous drug user.

EPISTEMOLOGY— DIFFERENT WAYS OF KNOWING

The problem with trying to write a book about research methods (beside the fact that there are so *many* of them) is that the word "method" has at least three meanings. At the most general level, it means epistemology, or the study of how we know things. At a still-pretty-general level, it's about strategic choices, like whether to do participant observation fieldwork, dig up information from libraries and archives, or run an experiment. These are **strategic methods**, which means that they comprise lots of methods at once.

At the specific level, method is about technique—what kind of sample to use, whether to do face-to-face interviews or use the telephone, whether to use an interpreter or learn the local language well enough to do your own interviewing, whether to use a Solomon four-group design or a static-group comparison design in running an experiment, and so on.

When it comes to epistemology, there are several key questions. One is whether you subscribe to the philosophical principles of **rationalism** or **empiricism**. Another is whether you buy the assumptions of the scientific method, often called **positivism** in the social sciences, or favor the competing method, often called **humanism** or **interpretivism**. These are tough questions, with no easy answers. I discuss them in turn.

Rationalism, Empiricism, and Kant

The clash between rationalism and empiricism is at least as old as ancient Greek philosophy. It is still a hotly debated topic in the philosophy of knowledge.

Rationalism is the idea that human beings achieve knowledge because of their capacity to reason. From the rationalist perspective, there are a priori truths, which, if we just prepare our minds adequately, will become evident to us. From this perspective, progress of the human intellect over the centuries has resulted from reason. Many great thinkers, from Plato (428–327 BCE) to Leibnitz (Gottfried Wilhelm Baron von Leibniz, 1646–1716) subscribed to the rationalist principle of knowledge. "We hold these truths to be self-evident . . ." is an example of assuming a priori truths.

The competing epistemology is empiricism. For empiricists, the only knowledge that human beings acquire is from sensory experience. For empiricists, like John Locke (1632–1704), human beings are born **tabula rasa**—with a "clean slate." What we come to know is the result of our experience written on that slate. David Hume (1711–1776) elaborated the empiricist philosophy of knowledge: We see and hear and taste things, and, as we accumulate experience, we make generalizations. We come, in other words, to understand what is true from what we are exposed to.

This means, Hume held, that we can never be absolutely sure that what we know is true. (By contrast, if we reason our way to a priori truths, we can be certain of whatever knowledge we have gained.) Hume's brand of skepticism is a fundamental principle of modern science. The scientific method, as it's understood today, involves making incremental improvements in what we know, edging toward truth but never quite getting there—and always being ready to have yesterday's truths overturned by today's empirical findings.

Immanuel Kant (1724–1804) proposed a way out, a third alternative. A priori truths exist, he said, but if we see those truths it's because of the way our brains are structured. The human mind, said Kant, has a built-in capacity for ordering and organizing sensory experience. This was a powerful idea that led many scholars to look to the human mind itself for clues about how human behavior is ordered.

Noam Chomsky, for example, proposed that human beings can learn any language because humans have a universal grammar already built into their minds. This would account, he said, for the fact that material from one language can be translated into any other language.

A competing theory was proposed by B. F. Skinner, a radical behaviorist. Humans learn their language, Skinner said, the way all animals learn everything, by operant conditioning, or reinforced learning. Babies learn the sounds of their language, for example, because people who speak the language reward babies for making the "right" sounds. A famous debate between Skinner (1957) and Chomsky (1959) more than 50 years ago has been a hot topic for partisans on both sides ever since (Palmer 2006; Stemmer 2004; Virués-Ortega 2006).

The intellectual clash between empiricism and rationalism creates a dilemma for all social scientists. Empiricism holds that people learn their values and therefore that values are relative. I consider myself an empiricist, but I accept the rationalist idea that there are universal truths about right and wrong.

I'm not in the least interested, for example, in transcending my disgust with, or taking a value-neutral stance about genocide in Germany of the 1940s, or in Cambodia of the 1970s, or in Bosnia and Rwanda of the 1990s, or in Sudan in 2010. I can never say that the Aztec practice of sacrificing thousands of captured prisoners was just another religious practice that one has to tolerate to be a good cultural relativist. No one has ever found a satisfactory way out of this dilemma. As a practical matter, I recognize that both rationalism and empiricism have contributed to our current understanding of the diversity of human behavior.

Modern social science has its roots in the empiricists of the French and Scottish

Enlightenment. The early empiricists of the period, like David Hume, looked outside the human mind, to human behavior and experience, for answers to questions about human differences. They made the idea of a mechanistic science of humanity as plausible as the idea of a mechanistic science of other natural phenomena (**Further Reading:** epistemology).

In the rest of this chapter, I outline the assumptions of the scientific method and how they apply to the study of human thought and behavior in the social sciences today.

THE NORMS OF SCIENCE: THE RULES AND ASSUMPTIONS OF SCIENCE

The norms of science are clear. Science is "an objective, logical, and systematic method of analysis of phenomena, devised to permit the accumulation of reliable knowledge" (Lastrucci 1963:6). Three words in Lastrucci's definition—"objective," "method," and "reliable"—are especially important.

1. *Objective*. The idea of truly objective inquiry has long been understood to be a delusion. Scientists do hold, however, that *striving* for objectivity is useful. In practice, this means being explicit about our measurements (whether we make them in words or in numbers), so that others can more easily find the errors we make. We constantly try to improve measurement, to make it more precise and more accurate, and we submit our findings to peer review—what Robert Merton called the "organized skepticism" of our colleagues (1938:334–36).

2. *Method*. Each scientific discipline has developed a set of techniques for gathering and handling data, but there is, in general, a single scientific method. The method is based on three assumptions: (1) reality is "out there" to

be discovered; (2) direct observation is the way to discover it; and (3) material explanations for observable phenomena are always sufficient, and metaphysical explanations are never needed. Direct observation can be done with the naked eye or enhanced with various instruments (like microscopes); and human beings can be improved by training as instruments of observation. (I'll say more about that in Chapters 12 and 14 on participant observation and direct observation.)

Metaphysics refers to explanations of phenomena by any nonmaterial force, such as the mind or spirit or a deity—things that, by definition, cannot be investigated by the methods of science. This does not deny the existence of metaphysical knowledge, but scientific and metaphysical knowledge are quite different. There are time-honored traditions of metaphysical knowledge—knowledge that comes from introspection, self-denial, and spiritual revelation—in cultures across the world.

In fact, science does not reject metaphysical knowledge—though individual scientists may do so—only the use of metaphysics to explain natural phenomena. The great insights about the nature of existence, expressed throughout the ages by poets, theologians, philosophers, historians, and other humanists may one day be understood as biophysical phenomena, but so far, they remain tantalizingly metaphysical.

3. *Reliable*. Something that is true in Detroit is just as true in Vladivostok and Nairobi. Knowledge can be kept secret by nations, but there can never be such a thing as "Venezuelan physics," "American chemistry," or "Kenyan geology."

Not that it hasn't been tried. From around 1935–1965, T. D. Lysenko, with the early help of Josef Stalin, succeeded in gaining absolute power over biology in what was then the Soviet Union. Lysenko developed a Lamarckian theory of genetics, in which human-induced changes in seeds would, he claimed, become inherited. Despite public rebuke from the entire non-Soviet scientific world, Lysenko's "Russian genetics" became official Soviet policy—a policy that nearly ruined agriculture in the Soviet Union and its European satellites well into the 1960s (Joravsky 1970) (**Further Reading**: the norms of science).

THE DEVELOPMENT OF SCIENCE AS AN INSTITUTION IN MODERN SOCIETIES

Early Ideas

The scientific method is barely 400 years old and its systematic application to human thought and behavior is less than half that. Aristotle insisted that knowledge should be based on experience and that conclusions about general cases should be based on the observation of more limited ones. But Aristotle did not advocate disinterested, objective accumulation of reliable knowledge. Moreover, like Aristotle, all scholars until the seventeenth century relied on metaphysical concepts, like the soul, to explain observable phenomena. Even in the nineteenth century, biologists still talked about "vital forces" as a way of explaining the existence of life.

Early Greek philosophers, like Democritus (460–370 BCE) who developed the atomic theory of matter, were certainly materialists, but one ancient scholar stands out for the kind of thinking that would eventually divorce science from studies of mystical phenomena. In his single surviving work, a poem entitled *On the Nature of the Universe* (1998), Titus Lucretius Carus (98–55 BCE) suggested that everything that existed in the world had to be made of some material substance. Consequently, if the soul and the

gods were real, they had to be material, too (see Minadeo 1969). But Lucretius' work did not have much impact on the way knowledge was pursued, and even today his work is little appreciated in the social sciences (see Harris [1968] and Carneiro [2010] for exceptions).

The Age of Exploration, Printing, and Modern Science

Skip to around 1400, when a series of revolutionary changes began in Europe—some of which are still going on—that transformed Western society and other societies around the world. In 1413, the first Spanish ships began raiding the coast of West Africa, hijacking cargo and acquiring slaves from Islamic traders. New tools of navigation (the compass and the sextant) made it possible for adventurous plunderers to go farther and farther from European shores in search of booty.

These breakthroughs were like those in architecture and astronomy by the ancient Mayans and Egyptians. They were based on systematic observation of the natural world but they were not generated by the social and philosophical enterprise we call science. That required several other revolutions.

Johannes Gutenberg completed the first edition of the Bible on his newly invented printing press in 1455. (Printing presses had been used earlier in China, Japan, and Korea, but lacked movable type.) By the end of the fifteenth century, every major city in Europe had a press. Printed books provided a means for the accumulation and distribution of knowledge. Eventually, printing would make organized science possible, but it did not by itself guarantee the objective pursuit of reliable knowledge any more than the invention of writing had done four millennia before (N. Z. Davis 1981; Eisenstein 1979).

Martin Luther was born just 15 years after Gutenberg died. No historical figure is more associated with the Protestant Reformation, which began in 1517, and the Reformation added much to the history of modern science. It challenged the authority of the Roman Catholic Church to be the sole interpreter and disseminator of theological doctrine. The Protestant affirmation of every person's right to interpret scripture required literacy on the part of everyone, not just the clergy. The printing press made it possible for every family of some means to own (and read) its own Bible. This promoted widespread literacy in Europe and later in the United States, and this, along with the ability of scholars to publish their work at relatively low cost, helped make possible the development of science as an organized activity.

Galileo

The direct philosophical antecedents of modern science came at the end of the sixteenth century. If I had to pick one single figure on whom to bestow the honor of founding modern science, it would have to be Galileo Galilei (1564–1642). His best-known achievement was his thorough refutation of the Ptolemaic geocentric (Earth-centered) theory of the heavens. But he did more than just insist that scholars *observe* things rather than rely on metaphysical dogma to explain them. He developed the idea of the experiment by causing things to happen (rolling balls down differently inclined planes, for example, to see how fast they go) and measuring the results.

Galileo became professor of mathematics at the University of Padua when he was 28. He developed a new method for making lenses and used the new technology to study the motions of the planets. He concluded that the sun (as Copernicus claimed), not the Earth (as the ancient scholar Ptolemy had claimed) was at the center of the solar system.

This was one more threat to their authority that Roman church leaders didn't need at the time. They already had their hands full, what with breakaway factions in the Reformation and other political problems. The church reaffirmed its official support for the Ptolemaic theory, and in 1616 Galileo was ordered not to espouse either his refutation of it or his support for the Copernican heliocentric (sun-centered) theory of the heavens.

Galileo waited 16 years and published the book that established science as an effective method for seeking knowledge. The book's title was *Dialogue Concerning the Two Chief World Systems, Ptolemaic and Copernican*, and it still makes fascinating reading (Galilei 1997 [1632]). Between the direct observational evidence that he had gathered with his telescopes and the mathematical analyses that he developed for making sense of his data, Galileo hardly had to espouse anything. The Ptolemaic theory was simply rendered obsolete.

In 1633, Galileo was convicted by the Inquisition for heresy and disobedience. He was ordered to recant his sinful teachings and was confined to house arrest until his death in 1642. He nearly published *and* perished. In 1992, Pope John Paul II reversed the Roman Catholic Church's 1616 ban on teaching the Copernican theory and apologized for its condemnation of Galileo.

Bacon and Descartes

Two other figures are often cited as founders of modern scientific thinking: Francis Bacon (1561–1626) and René Descartes (1596–1650). Bacon is known for his emphasis on induction, the use of direct observation to confirm ideas and the linking together of observed facts to form theories or explanations of how natural phenomena work. Bacon correctly never told us how to get ideas or how to accomplish the linkage of empirical facts. Those activities remain essentially humanistic—you think hard (Box 1.3).

Box 1.3 On induction and deduction

There are two great epistemological approaches in all research: **induction** and **deduction**. In its idealized form, inductive research involves the search for pattern from observation and the development of explanations—theories—for those patterns through a series of hypotheses. The hypotheses are tested against new cases, modified, retested against yet more cases, and so on, until saturation occurs—that is, new cases stop requiring more testing.

By contrast, in its idealized form, deductive research starts with theories (derived from common sense, from observation, or from the literature) and hypotheses derived from theories, and then moves on to observations—which either confirm or falsify the hypotheses. (We'll see examples of these two approaches in Chapter 19 on grounded theory and content analysis.)

Real research is never purely inductive or purely deductive. In general, the less we know about a research problem, the more inductive we'll be—the more we let observation be our guide—and the more we know about a problem, the more deductive we'll be. **Exploratory research** is, therefore, likely to be pretty inductive, while **confirmatory research** is likely to be deductive.

When I started working with the Ñähñu Indians of central Mexico, for example, I wondered why so many parents wanted their children *not* to learn how to read and write Ñähñu in school. As I became aware of the issue, I started asking everyone I talked to about it. With each new interview, pieces of the puzzle fell into place. This was a really, really inductive approach. After a while, I came to understand the problem: It's a long, sad story, repeated across the world by indigenous people who have learned to devalue their own cultures and reject their own languages in the hope that this will help their children do better economically. After that, I started right off by asking people about my hunches—for example, about the economic penalty of speaking Spanish in Mexico with an identifiable Indian accent. In other words, I switched to a really, really deductive approach.

It's messy, but this paradigm for building knowledge—the continual combination of inductive and deductive research—is used by scholars across the humanities and the sciences alike and has proved itself, over thousands of years. If we know anything about how and why stars explode or about how HIV is transmitted or about why women lower their fertility when they enter the labor market, it's because of this combination of effort. Human experience—the way real people experience real events—is endlessly interesting because it is endlessly unique, and so, in a way, the study of human experience is always exploratory and is best done inductively.

On the other hand, we also know that human experience is patterned. A migrant from Mexico who crosses the U.S. border one step ahead of the authorities lives through a unique experience and has a unique story to tell, but twenty such stories will almost certainly reveal similarities.

To Bacon goes the dubious honor of being the first "martyr of empiricism." In March 1626, at the age of 65, Bacon was driving through a rural area north of London. He had noticed earlier that both cold and fire impeded putrefaction (Bacon 1902 [1620]:137). To test his observation, he stopped his carriage, bought a hen from a local resident, killed the hen, and stuffed it with snow. Bacon was right—the cold snow did keep the bird from rotting—but he himself caught bronchitis and died a month later (Lea 1980).

Descartes didn't make any systematic, direct observations—he did neither fieldwork nor experiments—but in his *Discourse on Method* (1960 [1637]), and particularly in his monumental *Meditations* (1993 [1641]), he distinguished between the mind and all external material phenomena. He also outlined clearly his vision of a universal science of nature based on direct experience and the application of reason—that is, observation and theory.

Newton

Isaac Newton (1643–1727) pressed the scientific revolution at Cambridge University. Along with Leibniz, he invented calculus and used it to develop celestial mechanics and other areas of physics. Just as important, he devised the **hypothetico-deductive** model of science that combines both induction (empirical observation) and deduction (reason) into a single, unified method (Toulmin 1980).

In this model, which more accurately reflects how scientists actually conduct their work, it makes no difference where you get an idea: from data, from a conversation with your brother-in-law, or from just plain, hard, reflexive thinking. What matters is whether you can *test* your idea against data in the real world. This model seems rudimentary to us now, but it is of fundamental importance and was quite revolutionary in the late seventeenth century (**Further Reading**: history of science).

Science, Money, and War

The scientific approach to knowledge was established just as Europe began to experience the growth of industry and the development of large cities. Those cities were filled with uneducated factory laborers. This created a need for increased productivity in agriculture among those not engaged in industrial work.

Optimism for science ran high, as it became obvious that the new method for acquiring knowledge about natural phenomena promised bigger crops, more productive industry, and more successful military campaigns. The Royal Society in England has its roots in meetings among a group of philosophers in London in 1644 who did experiments (much like a club . . . they paid dues for the experiments).

One of the leaders of that group was John Wilkins. In 1648, he published *Mathematicall Magick*, a book about the benefit of science in developing new technology, "particularly for such Gentlemen as employ their Estates in those chargeable Adventures of Draining Mines, Coalpits, etc." The organizing mandate for the French Academy of Science academy (1666) included a modest proposal to study "the explosive force of gunpowder enclosed (in small amounts) in an iron or very thick copper box" (Easlea 1980:216).

As the potential benefits of science became evident, political support increased across Europe. More scientists were produced. More university posts were created for them to work in. More laboratories were established at academic centers. Journals and learned societies developed as scientists sought more outlets for publishing their work. Sharing knowledge through journals made it easier for scientists to do their own work and to advance through the university ranks. Publishing and sharing knowledge became a material benefit, and the behaviors were soon supported by a value, a norm.

The norm was so strong that European nations at war allowed enemy scientists to cross their borders freely in pursuit of knowledge. In 1780, Reverend Samuel Williams of Harvard University applied for and received a grant from the Massachusetts legislature to observe a total eclipse of the sun predicted for 27 October. The perfect spot, he said, was an island off the coast of Massachusetts.

Unfortunately, Williams and his party would have to cross Penobscot Bay. The American Revolutionary War was still on, and the bay was controlled by the British. The speaker of the Massachusetts House of Representatives, John Hancock, wrote a letter to the commander of the British forces, saying "Though we are politically enemies, yet with regard to Science it is presumable we shall not dissent from the practice of civilized people in promoting it" (Rothschild 1981, quoted in Bermant 1982:126). The appeal of one "civilized" person to another worked. Williams got his free passage.

THE DEVELOPMENT OF SOCIAL SCIENCE

Locke

It is fashionable these days to say that social science should not imitate physics. As it turns out, physics and social science were developed at about the same time, and on the same philosophical basis, by two friends, Isaac Newton and John Locke (1632–1704). It would not be until the nineteenth century that a formal program of applying the scientific method to the study of humanity would be proposed by Auguste Comte, Claude-Henri de Saint-Simon, Adolphe Quételet, and John Stuart Mill (more about them in a bit). But Locke understood that the rules of science applied equally to the study of celestial bodies (what Newton was interested in) and to human behavior (what Locke was interested in).

In his *Essay Concerning Human Understanding* (1996 [1690]), Locke reasoned that since we cannot see everything, and since we cannot even record perfectly what we do see, some knowledge will be closer to the truth than other knowledge. Prediction of the behavior of planets might be more accurate than prediction of human behavior, but both predictions should be based on better and better observation, measurement, and reason (see Nisbet 1980; Woolhouse 1996).

Voltaire, Condorcet, and Rousseau

The legacy of Descartes, Galileo, and Locke was crucial to the eighteenth-century Enlightenment and to the development of social science. Voltaire (François Marie Arouet, 1694–1778) was an outspoken proponent of Newton's nonreligious approach to the study of all natural phenomena, including human behavior (Voltaire 1967 [1738]). In several essays, Voltaire introduced the idea of a science to uncover the laws of history. This was to be a science that could be applied to human affairs and *enlightened* those who governed so that they might govern better.

Other Enlightenment figures had quite specific ideas about the progress of humanity. Marie Jean de Condorcet (1743–94) described all of human history in 10 stages, beginning with hunting and gathering, and moving up through pastoralism, agriculture, and several stages of Western states. The 9th stage, he reckoned, began with Descartes and ended with the French Revolution and the founding of the republic. The last stage was the future, reckoned as beginning with the French Revolution.

Jean-Jacques Rousseau (1712–1778), by contrast, believed that humanity had started out in a state of grace, characterized by equality of relations, but that civilization, with its agriculture and commerce, had corrupted humanity and led to slavery, taxation, and other inequalities. Rousseau was not, however, a raving romantic, as is sometimes supposed. He did not advocate that modern people abandon civilization and return to hunt their food in the forests. Rousseau held that the state embodied humanity's efforts, through a social contract, to control the evils brought about by civilization. In his classic work *On the Social Contract*, Rousseau (1988 [1762]) laid out a plan for a state-level society based on equality and agreement between the governed and those who govern.

The Enlightenment philosophers, from Bacon to Rousseau, produced a philosophy that focused on the use of knowledge in service to the improvement of humanity, or, if that weren't possible, at least to the amelioration of its pain. The idea that science and reason could lead humanity toward perfection may seem naive to some people these days, but the ideas of John Locke, Jean Jacques Rousseau, and other Enlightenment figures were built into the writings of Thomas Paine (1737–1809) and Thomas Jefferson (1743–1826), and were incorporated into the rhetoric surrounding rather sophisticated events—like the American and French Revolutions (**Further Reading:** history of social science).

THE VARIETIES OF POSITIVISM

Early Positivism: Quételet, Saint-Simon, and Comte

The person most responsible for laying out a program of mechanistic social science was Auguste Comte (1798–1857). In 1824, he wrote: "I believe that I shall succeed in having it recognized . . . that there are laws as well defined for the development of the human species as for the fall of a stone" (quoted in Sarton 1935:10).

Comte could not be bothered with the empirical research required to uncover the Newtonian laws of social evolution that he believed existed. Comte was content to deduce the social laws and to leave "the verification and development of them to the public" (1875–1877, III:xi; quoted in Harris 1968).

Not so Adolphe Quételet (1796–1874), a Belgian astronomer who turned his skills to both fundamental and applied social research. He developed life expectancy tables for insurance companies and, in his book *A Treatise on Man* (1969 [1842]), he presented statistics on crime and mortality in Europe. The first edition of that book (1835) carried the audacious subtitle "Social Physics," and, indeed, Quételet extracted some very strong generalizations from his data. He showed that, for the Paris of his day, it was easier to predict the proportion of men of a given age who would be in prison than the proportion of those same men who would die in a given year. "Each age [cohort]" said Quételet, "paid a more uniform and constant tribute to the jail than to the tomb" (1969 [1842]:viii).

Despite Quételet's superior empirical efforts, he did not succeed in building a following around his ideas for social science. But Claude-Henri de Saint-Simon (1760–1825) did, and he was apparently quite a figure. He fought in the American Revolution, became a wealthy man in land speculation in France, was imprisoned by Robespierre, studied science after his release, and went bankrupt living flamboyantly.

Saint-Simon had the audacity to propose that scientists become priests of a new religion that would further the emerging industrial society and would distribute wealth equitably. The idea was taken up by industrialists after Saint-Simon's death in 1825, but the movement broke up in the early 1830s, partly because its treasury was impoverished by paying for some monumental parties (see Durkheim 1958).

Saint-Simon was the originator of the so-called **positivist school** of social science, but Comte developed the idea in a series of major books. Comte tried to forge a synthesis of the great ideas of the Enlightenment—the ideas of Kant, Hume, Voltaire—and he hoped that the new science he envisioned would help to alleviate human suffering. Between 1830 and 1842, Comte published a six-volume work, *The System of Positive Philosophy*, in which he proposed his famous "law of three stages" through which knowledge developed (see Comte 1974 [1855], 1975).

In the first stage of human knowledge, said Comte, phenomena are explained by invoking the existence of capricious gods whose whims can't be predicted by human beings. Comte and his contemporaries proposed that religion itself evolved, beginning with the worship of inanimate objects (fetishism) and moving up through polytheism to monotheism. But any reliance on supernatural forces as explanations for phenomena, said Comte, even a modern belief in a single deity, represented a primitive and ineffectual stage of human knowledge.

Next came the metaphysical stage, in which explanations for observed phenomena are given in terms of "essences," like the "vital forces" commonly invoked by biologists of the time. The so-called positive stage of human knowledge is reached when people come to rely on empirical data, reason, and the development of scientific laws to explain phenomena. Comte's program of positivism, and his development of a new science he called "sociology," is contained in his four-volume work *System of Positive Polity*, published between 1875 and 1877.

I share many of the sentiments expressed by the word "positivism," but I've never liked the word itself. I suppose we're stuck with it. Here is John Stuart Mill (1866) explaining the sentiments of the word to an English-speaking audience: "Whoever regards all events as parts of a constant order, each one being the invariable consequent of some antecedent condition, or combination of conditions, accepts fully the Positive mode of thought" (p. 15) and "All theories in which the ultimate standard of institutions and rules of actions was the happiness of mankind, and observation and experience the guides . . . are entitled to the name Positive" (p. 69).

Mill thought that the word "positive" was not really suited to English and would have preferred to use phenomenal or experiential in his translation of Comte. I wish Mill had trusted his gut on that one.

Comte's Excesses

Comte wanted to call the new positivistic science of humanity "social physiology," but Saint-Simon had used that term. Comte tried out the term "social physics," but apparently dropped it when he found that Quételet was using it, too. The term "sociology" became somewhat controversial; language puritans tried for a time to expunge it from the literature on the grounds that it was a bastardization—a mixture of both Latin (*societas*) and Greek (*logo*) roots. Despite the dispute over the name of the discipline, Comte's vision of a scientific discipline that both focused on and served society found wide support.

Unfortunately, Comte, like Saint-Simon, had more in mind than just the pursuit of knowledge for the betterment of humankind. Comte envisioned a class of philosophers who, with support from the state, would direct all education. They would advise the government, which would be composed of capitalists "whose dignity and authority," explained John Stuart Mills, "are to be in the ratio of the degree of generality of their conceptions and operations—bankers at the summit, merchants next, then manufacturers, and agriculturalists at the bottom" (1866:122).

It got worse. Comte proposed his own religion; condemned the study of planets that were not visible to the naked eye; advocated burning most books except for a hundred or so of the ones that people needed to become best educated; and opposed women working. "As his thoughts grew more extravagant," Mill tells us, "Comte's self-confidence grew more outrageous. The height it ultimately attained must be seen, in his writings, to be believed" (1866:130).

Comte attracted a coterie of admirers who wanted to implement the master's plans. Mercifully, they are gone (we hope), but for many scholars, positivism still carries the taint of Comte's outrageous ego.

The Activist Legacy of Comte's Positivism

Despite Comte's excesses, there were three fundamental ideas in his brand of positivism that captured the imagination of many scholars in the nineteenth century and continue to motivate many social scientists, including me. The first is the idea that the scientific method is the surest way to produce knowledge about the natural world. The second is that scientifically produced knowledge is effective—it lets us control nature, whether we're talking about the weather, or disease, or our own fears, or buying habits. And the third is that effective knowledge can be used to improve human lives. As far as I'm concerned, those ideas haven't lost any of their luster.

These days, positivism is often linked to support for whatever power relations happen to be in place. It's an astonishing turnabout, because historically, positivism was linked to social activism. *The Subjection of Women* (1869), by John Stuart Mill, advocated full equality for women. Adolphe Quételet, the Belgian astronomer, demographer, and criminologist, was a committed social reformer.

The legacy of positivism as a vehicle for **social activism** is clear in Jane Addams's work with destitute immigrants at Chicago's Hull House (1926); in Sidney and Beatrice Webb's attack on the British medical system (1910); in Charles Booth's account of the conditions under which the poor lived in London (1902); and in Florence Nightingale's (1871) assessment of death rates in maternity hospitals (see McDonald [1993] for an extended account of Nightingale's long-ignored work).

The central position of positivism as a philosophy of knowledge is that experience is the foundation of knowledge. We record what we experience—what we see others do, what we hear others say, what we feel others feel. The quality of the recording, then, becomes the key to knowledge. Can we, in fact, record what others experience? Yes, of course we can. Are there pitfalls in doing so? Yes, of course there are. To some social researchers, these pitfalls are evidence of natural limits to social science; to others, like me, they are a challenge to extend the current limits by improving measurement. The fact that knowledge is tentative is something we all learn to live with.

Later Positivism I: The Vienna Circle

Positivism has taken some interesting turns. Ernst Mach (1838–1916), an Austrian physicist, took Hume's arch-empiricist stance further than even Hume might have done himself: If you could not verify something, insisted Mach, you should question its existence. If you can't see it, it isn't there. This extreme stance led Mach to reject the atomic theory of physics because, at the time, atoms could not be seen.

The discussion of Mach's ideas was the basis of a seminar group that met in Vienna and Berlin during the 1920s and 1930s. The group, composed of mathematicians, philosophers, and physicists, came to be known as the **Vienna Circle** of logical positivists. They were also known as logical empiricists, and when social scientists today discuss positivism, it is often this particular brand that they have in mind (see Mach 1976).

The term **logical empiricism** better reflects the philosophy of knowledge of the members of the Vienna Circle than does **logical positivism**. Unfortunately, Feigl and Blumberg used logical positivism in the title of their 1931 article in the *Journal of Philosophy* in which they laid out the program of their movement, and the name positivism stuck—again (L. D. Smith 1986).

The fundamental principles of the Vienna Circle were that knowledge is based on experience and that metaphysical explanations of phenomena were incompatible with science. Science and philosophy, they said, should attempt to answer only scientifically answerable questions. A question like "Was Mozart or Brahms the better composer?" can only be addressed by metaphysics and should be left to artists.

In fact, the logical positivists of the Vienna Circle did not see art—painting, sculpture, poetry, music, literature, and literary criticism—as conflicting with science. The arts, they said, allow people to express personal visions and emotions and are legitimate unto themselves. Since poets do not claim that their ideas are testable expressions of reality, their ideas can be judged on their own merits as evocative and insightful, or not. Therefore, any source of wisdom (like poetry) that generates ideas, and science, which tests ideas, are mutually supportive and compatible (Feigl 1980). I find this eminently sensible. Sometimes, when I read a really great line of poetry, like Robert Frost's line from *The Mending Wall*, "Good fences make good neighbors," I think "How could I *test* that? Do good fences *always* make good neighbors?" When sheep herders fenced off grazing lands in nineteenth-century Texas, keeping cattle out of certain regions, it started range wars.

Listen to what Frost had to say about this in the same poem: "Before I built a wall I'd ask to know/ What I was walling in or walling out./ And to whom I was like to give offence." The way I see it, the search for understanding is a human activity, no matter who does it and no matter what epistemological assumptions they follow.

Understanding begins with questions and with ideas about how things work. When *do* fences make good neighbors? Why do women make less money, on average, for the same work as men in most industrialized countries? Why is Barbados's birth rate falling faster than Saudi Arabia's? Why is there such a high rate of alcoholism on Native American reservations? Why do nation states, from Italy to Kenya, almost universally discourage people from maintaining minority languages? Why do public housing programs often wind up as slums? If advertising can get children hooked on cigarettes, why is public service advertising so ineffective in lowering the incidence of high-risk sex among adolescents?

Later Positivism II: Instrumental Positivism

The practice that many researchers today love to hate, however, is neither the positivism of Auguste Comte nor that of the Vienna Circle. It is, instead, what Christopher Bryant (1985:137) called **instrumental positivism**.

In his 1929 presidential address to the American Sociological Society, William F. Ogburn laid out the rules. In turning sociology into a science, he said, "it will be necessary to crush out emotion." Further, "it will be desirable to taboo ethics and values (except in choosing problems); and it will be inevitable that we shall have to spend most of our time doing hard, dull, tedious, and routine tasks" (Ogburn 1930:10). Eventually, he said, there would be no need for a separate field of statistics because "all sociologists will be statisticians" (p. 6).

THE REACTIONS AGAINST POSITIVISM

That kind of rhetoric just begged to be reviled. In *The Counter-Revolution of Science*, Friedrich von Hayek (1952) laid out the case against the possibility of what Ogburn imagined would be a science of humanity. In the social sciences, Hayek said, we deal with mental phenomena, not with material facts. The data of the social sciences, Hayek insisted, are not susceptible to treatment as if they were data from the natural world. To pretend that they are is what he called "scientism."

Furthermore, said Hayek, scientism is more than just foolish. It is evil. The ideas of Comte and of Marx, said Hayek, gave people the false idea that governments and economies could be managed scientifically and this, he concluded, had encouraged the development of the communism and totalitarianism that seemed to be sweeping the world when he was writing in the 1950s (Hayek 1952:110, 206).

I have long appreciated Hayek's impassioned and articulate caution about the need to protect liberty, but he was wrong about positivism and even about scientism. Science did not cause Nazi or Soviet tyranny any more than religion caused the tyranny of the Crusades or the burning of witches in seventeenth-century Salem, Massachusetts. Tyrants of every generation have used any means, including any convenient epistemology or cosmology, to justify and further their despicable behavior. Whether tyrants seek to justify their power by claiming that they speak to the gods or to scientists, the awful result is the same. But the *explanation* for tyranny is surely neither religion nor science.

It is also apparent that an effective science of human behavior exists, no matter whether it's called positivism or scientism or human engineering or anything else. However distasteful it may be to some, John Stuart Mill's simple formula for a science applied to the study of human phenomena has been very successful in helping us understand (and control) human thought and behavior. Whether we like the outcomes is a matter of conscience, but no amount of moralizing diminishes the fact of success.

Today's truths are tomorrow's rubbish, in the social sciences just as in physics, and no epistemological tradition has a patent on interesting

questions or on good ideas about the answers to such questions. Several competing traditions offer alternatives to positivism in the social sciences. These include humanism, hermeneutics, and phenomenology (**Further Reading: positivism**).

Hermeneutics

The ancient Greek god Hermes (known as Mercury in the Roman pantheon—he of the winged hat) had the job of delivering and interpreting for humans the messages of the other gods. From this came the Greek word *hermeneus*, or interpreter, and from that comes our word hermeneutics, the continual interpretation and reinterpretation of texts.

Modern hermeneutics in social science is an outgrowth of the Western tradition of biblical exegesis. In that tradition, the Old and New Testaments are assumed to contain eternal truths, put there by an omnipotent creator through some emissaries—prophets, writers of the gospels, and the like. The idea is to continually interpret the words of those texts to understand their original meaning and their directives for living in the present (see Box 1.4).

Box 1.4 Hermeneutics and holy writ

Rules for reconciling contradictions in scripture were developed by early Talmudic scholars, about a hundred years after the death of Jesus of Nazareth. For example, one of the rules was that "the meaning of a passage can be derived either from its context or from a statement later on in the same passage" (Jacobs 1995:236). Another was that "when two verses appear to contradict one another, a third verse can be discovered which reconciles them" (Jacobs 1995:236). Today, the thirteen Talmudic rules for interpreting scripture remain part of the morning service among Orthodox Jews, and Talmudic hermeneutics continues to be central to Jewish theology.

Scholars of the New Testament have used hermeneutic reasoning since the time of Augustine (354–430) to determine the order in which the three synoptic gospels (Mark, Mathew, and Luke) were written. They are called synoptic gospels because they are all synopses of the same events and can be lined up and compared for details. Whenever there is a discrepancy about the order of events, Mark and Mathew agree or Mark and Luke agree, but Mathew and Luke almost never agree against Mark. There are many theories about what

(Continued)

(Continued)

caused this—including some that involve one or more of the gospels being derived from an undiscovered source. Research on this problem continues to this day (for a review, see Stein 1987).

Today, in the United States, constitutional law is a form of biblical hermeneutics. Jurists take it as their task to consider what the writers of each phrase in the U.S. Constitution meant when they wrote the phrase, and to interpret that meaning in light of current circumstances. It is exegesis on the U.S. Constitution that has produced entirely different interpretations across time about the legality of slavery, abortion, women's right to vote, the government's ability to tax income, and so on.

Although they have not influenced Western social science, there are long exegetical traditions in Islam (Abdul-Rahman 2003; Abdul-Raof 2010; Calder 1993), Hinduism (Sherma and Sharma 2008; Timm 1992), Buddhishm (Sharf 2002), and other religions.

The hermeneutic tradition has come into the social sciences with the close and careful study of all free-flowing texts, including political speeches, folktales and myths, life histories, letters from soldiers in battle to their families at home, transcriptions of doctor-patient interactions, sitcoms. . . . Think, for example, of the stories taught in U.S. schools about Columbus's voyages. The hermeneutic approach would stress that: (1) the stories contain some underlying meaning, at least for the people who tell them; and (2) it is our job to discover that meaning, knowing that the meaning can change over time and can also be different for subgroups within a society—like Americans of northern and central European descent, African Americans, Chicanos, and Navajos, for example.

The idea that culture is "an assemblage of texts" is the basis for the interpretive scholarship of Clifford Geertz (1973). And Paul Ricoeur, arguing that action, like the written word, has meaning to actors, extended the hermeneutic approach even to free-flowing behavior itself (1981, 2007).

Today, hermeneutic method is practiced across the social sciences and is applied to the study of all kinds of texts, including jokes, sermons, songs, and actions. For a hermeneutic analysis of African American sermons, for example, see Hamlet (1994) (**Further Reading:** hermeneutics and social science).

Phenomenology

Like positivism, phenomenology is a philosophy of knowledge that emphasizes observation of phenomena. Unlike positivists, however, phenomenologists emphasize the experience of phenomena to determine their essences, the things that make them what they are. Gold, for example, has been a universal currency for centuries, but variations in its price are accidents of history and do not reflect its essence. This distinction between essential and accidental properties of things was first made by Aristotle in his *Metaphysics* (especially Book VII) and has influenced philosophy ever since. Phenomenologists seek to *sense* reality and to describe it in words, rather than numbers—words that reflect consciousness and perception.

The philosophical foundations of phenomenology were developed by Edmund Husserl (1859–1938), who argued that the scientific method, appropriate for the study of physical phenomena, was inappropriate for the study of human thought and action (1964 [1907], 1999). Husserl was no antipositivist. What was needed, he said, was an approach that, like positivism, respects the data that we acquire through our senses but is appropriate for understanding how human beings experience the world (Spiegelberg 1980:210). To do this requires putting aside—or bracketing—our biases so that we don't filter other people's experiences through our own cultural lens and can understand experiences as others experience them (Giorgi 1986; McNamara 2005:697; Moustakas 1994).

Husserl's ideas were elaborated by Alfred Schutz, and Schutz's version of phenomenology has had a major impact in social science, particularly in psychology and in anthropology. When you study molecules, Schutz said, you don't have to worry about what the world "means" to the molecules (1962:59). But when you try to understand the reality of a human being, it's a different matter entirely. The only way to understand social reality, said Schutz, was through the meanings that people give to that reality.

A phenomenological study, then, involves trying to: (1) see reality through another person's eyes; and (2) writing convincing descriptions of what those people experience rather than explanations and causes. Good ethnography—a narrative that describes a culture or a part of a culture—is usually good phenomenology. There is still no substitute for a good story, well told, especially if you're trying to make people understand how the people you've studied think and feel about their lives (**Further Reading:** phenomenology).

Humanism

Humanism is an intellectual tradition that traces its roots to Protagoras' (490–420 BCE) dictum that "Man is the measure of all things," which means that truth is not absolute but is decided by human judgment. Humanism has been historically at odds with the philosophy of knowledge represented by science (Box 1.5).

Box 1.5 Humanism and science

We are all free to identify ourselves as humanists or as positivists, but it's much more fun to be both. The scientific component of social science demands that we ask whether our measurements are meaningful—"it is certainly desirable to be precise," said Robert Redfield (1948:148), "but it is quite as needful to be precise about something worth knowing"—but the humanistic component forces us to ask if we are pursuing worthwhile ends and doing so with worthwhile means.

In the end, the tension between science and humanism is wrought by the need to answer practical questions with evidence and the need to understand ourselves—that is, the need to measure carefully and the need to listen hard.

Ferdinand C. S. Schiller (1864–1937), for example, was a leader of the European humanist revolt against positivism. He argued that since the method and contents of science are the products of human thought, reality and truth could not be "out there" to be found, as positivists assume, but must be made up by human beings (Schiller 1969 [1903]).

Wilhelm Dilthey (1833–1911) was another leader of the revolt against positivism in the social sciences. He argued that the methods of the physical sciences, while undeniably effective for the study of inanimate objects, were inappropriate for the study of human beings. There were, he insisted, two distinct kinds of sciences: the Geisteswissenschaften and the Naturwissenschaften—that is, the human sciences and the natural sciences. Human beings live in a web of meanings that they spin themselves. To study humans, he argued, we need to understand those meanings (1989 [1883]).

Humanists, then, do not deny the effectiveness of science for the study of nonhuman objects, but emphasize the uniqueness of humanity and the need for a different (that is, nonscientific) method for studying human beings. Similarly, scientists do not deny the inherent value of humanistic knowledge. To explore whether King Lear is to be pitied or admired as a pathetic leader or as a successful one is an exercise in seeking humanistic knowledge. The answer to the question cannot possibly be achieved by the scientific method. In any event, finding *the* answer to the question is not important. Carefully *examining* the question of Lear, however, and producing many possible answers, leads to insight about the human condition. And that *is* important.

Just as there are many competing definitions of positivism, so there are for humanism as well. Humanism is often used as a synonym for humanitarian or compassionate values and a commitment to the amelioration of suffering. The problem is that died-in-the-wool positivists can also be committed to humanitarian values. Counting the dead *accurately* in Darfur is a really good way to preserve outrage. We need more, not less, science, lots and lots more, and more humanistically informed science, to contribute more to the amelioration of suffering and the weakening of false ideologies—racism, sexism, ethnic nationalism—in the world.

Humanism sometimes means a commitment to subjectivity—that is, to using our own feelings, values, and beliefs to achieve insight into the nature of human experience. In fact, trained subjectivity is the foundation of clinical disciplines, like psychology, as well as the foundation of participant observation ethnography. It isn't something apart from social science. (See Berg and Smith [1985] for a review of clinical methods in social research.)

Humanism sometimes means an appreciation of the unique in human experience. Writing a story about the thrill or the pain of giving birth, about surviving hand-to-hand combat, about living with AIDS, about winning or losing a long struggle with illness—or writing someone else's story for them, as ethnographers often do—are not activities *opposed* to a natural science of experience. They *are* the activities of a natural science of experience (**Further Reading**: humanities and the sciences).

ABOUT NUMBERS AND WORDS: THE QUALITATIVE/QUANTITATIVE SPLIT

The split between the positivistic approach and the interpretive-humanistic approach pervades the human sciences. In psychology and social psychology, most *research* is in the positivistic tradition, while much *clinical* work is in the interpretivist tradition because, as its practitioners cogently point out, it works. In sociology, there is a growing tradition of interpretive research, but most sociology is done from the positivist perspective.

Notice the use of words like "approach," "perspective," and "tradition" in that last paragraph. Not once did I say that "Research in X is mostly quantitative" or that "Research in Y is mostly qualitative." That's because a commitment to a humanistic or a positivist epistemology is independent of any commitment to, or skill for, quantification. Searching the Bible for statistical evidence to support the subjugation of women doesn't turn the enterprise into science.

By the same token, at the early stages of its development, any science relies primarily on qualitative data. Long before the application of mathematics to describe the dynamics of avian flight, fieldworking ornithologists did systematic observation and recorded (in words) data about such things as wing movements, perching stance, hovering patterns, and so on. Qualitative description is a kind of measurement, an integral part of the complex whole that comprises scientific research.

As sciences mature, they come naturally to depend more and more on quantitative data and on quantitative tests of qualitatively described relations. But this never, ever lessens the need for or the importance of qualitative research at every stage of science, from identifying interesting problems to explaining why things happen.

For example, qualitative research—say, talking to a few key informants—might lead us to say that "Most of the land in Centerville is controlled by a minority." Later, quantitative research—say, examining property records—might result in our saying "76% of the land in Centerville is controlled by 14% of the inhabitants." The first statement is not wrong, but its sentiment is confirmed and made stronger by the second statement. If it turned out that "54% of the land is controlled by 41% of the inhabitants," then the first part of the qualitative statement would still be true—more than 50% of the land is owned by less than 50% of the people, so most of the land is, indeed controlled by a minority—but the sentiment of the qualitative assertion would be rendered weak by the quantitative observations.

Suppose the relation is strong—that, in fact, 76% of the land in Centerville is controlled by 14% of the inhabitants. We still need qualitative research to explore the causes and consequences of this fact.

For social scientists whose work is in the humanistic tradition, quantification is inappropriate. And for those whose work is in the positivist tradition, it is important to remember that numbers do not automatically make any inquiry scientific. Never use the distinction between quantitative and qualitative as cover for talking about the difference between science and humanism. Lots of scientists do their work without numbers, and many scientists whose work is highly quantitative consider themselves humanists.

ETHICS AND SOCIAL SCIENCE

The biggest problem in conducting a science of human behavior is not selecting the right sample size or making the right measurement. It's doing those things ethically, so you can live with the consequences of your actions. I'm not exaggerating about this. Ethics is part of method in science, just as it is in medicine or business, or any other part of life. For while scholars discuss the fine points about whether a true science of human behavior is really possible, effective social science is being done all the time and with rather spectacular, if sometimes disturbing, success.

Since the eighteenth century, every phenomenon to which the scientific method has been systematically applied, over a sustained period of time, by a large number of researchers, has yielded its secrets, and the knowledge has been turned into more effective human control of events. And that includes human thought and behavior. When Quételet and Comte were laying down the program for a science of human affairs in the mid-nineteenth century, no one could predict the outcome of elections, or help people through crippling phobias with behavior modification, or engineer the increased consumption of a particular brand of cigarettes. We may question the wisdom of engineering cigarette purchases in the first place, but the fact remains, we *can* do these things, we *are* doing these things, and we're getting better and better at it all the time.

It hardly needs to be pointed out that the increasing effectiveness of science over the past few centuries has also given human beings the ability to cause greater environmental degradation, to spread tyranny, and even to cause the ultimate, planetary catastrophe through nuclear war. This makes a science of humanity even more important now than it has ever been before (**Further Reading:** ethics and social science).

Consider this: Marketers in a midwestern city, using the latest supercomputers, found that if someone bought disposable diapers at 5 p.m., the next thing he or she was likely to buy was a six-pack of beer. So they set up a display of chips next to the disposable diapers and increased snack sales by 17% (Wilke 1992). At the time, 20 years ago, that was a breakthrough in the monitoring of consumer behavior. Today, every time you buy something on the Internet or download a computer program or a piece of music, you leave a trail of information about yourself and your consumer preferences. By tracking your purchases over time and by sharing information about your buying behavior across websites, market researchers develop ads that are targeted just for you.

We need to turn our skills in the production of such effective knowledge to important problems: hunger, disease, poverty, war, environmental pollution, family and ethnic violence, and racism, among others. Social scientists can play important roles in social change by predicting the consequences of ethically mandated programs and by refuting false notions (such as various forms of racism) that are inherent in most popular ethical systems.

Don't get me wrong here. The people who discovered that fact about the six packs and the diapers are darned good social scientists, as are the people who design all those automated data-collection mechanisms for monitoring your behavior on the Internet. I'm not calling for rules to make all those scientists work on problems that I think are important. Scientists choose to study the things that industry and government pay for, and those things change from country to country and from time to time in the same country. Science has to earn its support by producing useful knowledge. What "useful" means, however, changes from time to time even in the same society, depending on all sorts of historical circumstances.

Suppose we agreed that "useful" meant to save lives. AIDS is a terrible disease, but over three times as many people died in motor vehicle accidents in the United States in 2006 as died of AIDS—about 40,000 and 12,000 respectively (SAUS 2010:Tables 116, 123). Should we spend three times more money teaching safe driving than we do teaching safe sex?

I think the answer is pretty clear. In a democracy, researchers and activists want the freedom to put their skills and energies to work on what they think is important. That's just how it is, and, personally, I hope it stays that way. In the rest of this book, I deal with some of the methods we can use to make useful contributions. But *you* have to decide what those contributions will be, and for whom they will be useful.

Key Concepts in This Chapter

epistemology	humanism	deduction
strategic methods	interpretivism	exploratory research
technique	tabula rasa	confirmatory research
rationalism	skepticism	hypothetico-deductive
empiricism	metaphysics	model of science
positivism	induction	Enlightenment

social contract
positivist school
social activism
Vienna Circle
logical empiricism

logical positivism
hermeneutics
phenomenology
bracketing
instrumental positivism

humanism
Geisteswissenschaften
Naturwissenschaften
trained subjectivity

Summary

- The social and behavior sciences include psychology, social psychology, sociology, political science, economics, and anthropology.
  - In addition, many applied disciplines today use knowledge from all the social sciences and contribute fundamental knowledge to the social sciences. Some of these applied disciplines include criminology and penology, nursing, social work, and education.
- The intellectual foundations of modern social sciences come from eighteenth-century Enlightenment philosophy, which included an activist commitment to knowledge as the basis for human progress and a commitment to empiricism in the pursuit of knowledge.
  - This led to the intellectual position known as positivism. The alternative to positivism is humanism.
- Many social scientists today are asking legitimate questions about the scientific norms of objectivity and the universality of knowledge. Nevertheless, the social sciences have participated in the general success of science in the production of effect technologies that people want.
  - Opinion polls, auto and life insurance, marketing, product design, and behavioral therapy are among the many successes of modern social science.
- As with all science, there is no guarantee that effective knowledge will be used for benign and not for malignant purposes, so effective knowledge—whether in the physical, biological, or social sciences—creates an ethical imperative that is the focus of continuing discussion.

Exercises

1. Some people say that social science has little effect in the real world. Is there evidence to contradict this critique?

2. Explain the difference between the goals of humanists and those of positivists. Describe what you think might be the common ground for scholars in these camps. Is there common ground in their goals? In their epistemology? In their behavior as researchers?

3. Describe the difference between induction and deduction and the difference between rationalism and empiricism.

4. What does the saying "There's no such thing as value-free research" mean? Some scholars argue that, although value-free research is not possible, value-*neutral* research is. What do you think?

Further Reading

Epistemology and philosophy of science. Original sources: Descartes (1993 [1641]), Hume (1978 [1739–40]), Kant (1966 [1787]), Locke (1996 [1690]).

BonJour (1985), Campbell (1988), Campbell and Overman (1988), Cottingham (1988), Dancy (1985), Fuller (2004), Grayling (1996), Hollinger (1994), Hollis (1996), Kuhn (1970), Papineau (1996), Popper (1966, 1968), Rosenau (1992), Schweizer (1998).

The norms of science. Anderson, Ronning et al. (2010), Ben-David and Sullivan (1975), Jasanoff et al. (1995), Merton (1970, 1973), Resnik (2007), Storer (1966).

History of science. The definitive reference is the Cambridge History of Science (8 volumes [Porter 2003–2009]). See also Asimov (1989), Christianson (1984), Cottingham (1999), de Solla Price (1975), Drake (1978), Fermi and Bernardini (1961), Finocchiaro (2005), Hausman and Hausman (1997), Jacob and Stewart (2004), Machamer (1998), Markie (1986), Sarton (1952–1959), Schuster (1977), Selin (2008), Silver (1998), Weinberger (1985), Westfall (1993), M. D. Wilson (1991), Wormald (1993).

History of social science. Fisher (1993), Gordon (1993), McDonald (1993, 1994), Porter and Ross (2003), R. Smith (1997).

Positivism. Comte (1988), Giddens (1974), Neurath (1973), Richardson and Uebel (2007), Steinmetz (2005).

Hermeneutics and social science. Dilthey (1989 [1883], 1996), Jemielniak and Mikłaszewicz (2010), Mantzavinos (2005), Ormiston and Schrift (1990), Ricoeur (1981, 2007), Seebohm (2004).

Phenomenology. Creswell (1998), Giorgi (1986), McNamara (2005), Petoto et al. (1999).

Humanities and the sciences. Dilthey (1989 [1883]), Geertz (1973), Jones (1965), Kearney (1996), Rabinow and Sullivan (1987), Ricoeur (1981, 2007), Snow (1964), Weber (1978).

Ethics and social science. Becker (2004), Bosk (2004), Fielding (2008), Haggerty (2004), Hoeyer (2006), Keith-Spiegel and Koocher (2005), Mumford et al. (2009), Shrader-Frechette (1994). See also, Ethics of Social Research, in Chapter 3, Further Reading on deception and debriefing at the end of Chapter 4, and Further Reading on deception in field studies, Chapter 14.

2

The Foundations of Social Research

THE LANGUAGE AND LOGIC OF SOCIAL RESEARCH

This chapter is about the fundamental concepts of social research: variables, measurement, validity, reliability, cause and effect, and theory. When you finish this chapter, you should understand the crucial role of measurement in science and the mutually supportive roles of data and ideas in the development of theory.

You should also have a new skill: You should be able to operationalize any complex human phenomenon, like "being modern" or "anomie" or "alienation" or "readiness to learn research methods." You should, in other words, be able to reduce any complex variable to a set of measurable traits.

By the end of this chapter, though, you should also become very critical of your new ability at operationalizing. Just because you *can* make up measurements doesn't guarantee that they'll be useful or meaningful. The better you become at concocting clever measurements for complex things, the more critical you'll become of your own concoctions and those of others (**Further Reading:** the language of social research).

VARIABLES

A **variable** is something that can take more than one value, and those *values can be words or numbers*. If you ask a woman how old she was at her first pregnancy, the answer will be a number (16 or 40, or whatever), but if you ask her about her religion, the answer will be a word ("Muslim" or "Methodist").

The most common variables in social research are age, sex, ethnic affiliation, "race" (more about why that word is in quotes in a minute), education, income, marital status,

and occupation. Others that you might see include blood pressure (in medical social science), number of children (lots of studies use this one), number of times married, distance from an airport (or a hospital, or a welfare agency, or a public library, or a bus stop), level of support for various causes (a woman's right to an abortion, the distribution of clean needles to drug addicts, sex education for fifth graders, etc.).

Social research, whether it's based on questionnaires, field observations, or experiments, is based on defining variables, looking for associations among them, and trying to understand whether—and how—variation in one thing causes variation in another. Research affects people, though, so all research has an ethical component. I'll have more to say about this throughout the book.

Dimensions of Variables

Variables can be **unidimensional** or **multidimensional**. The distance from Chicago to Albuquerque can be expressed in driving time or in miles, but no matter how you measure it, distance is expressed as a straight line and straight lines are one dimensional. You can see this in Figure 2.1.

If we add Miami, we have three distances: Chicago-Miami, Chicago-Albuquerque, Albuquerque-Miami. One dimension isn't enough to express the relation among three cities. We have to use two dimensions. Look at Figure 2.2.

The two dimensions in Figure 2.2 are up-down and right-left, or North-South and East-West. If we add Nairobi to the exercise, we'd have to add a third dimension (straight through the paper at a slight downward angle from Albuquerque) or do what Gerardus Mercator (1512–1594) did to force a three-dimensional object (the Earth) into a two-dimensional picture. He managed to portray a sphere in two dimensions, but at the cost of distortion at the edges. This is why, on a map of the world,

Figure 2.1 Two Ways to Measure Distance

Figure 2.2 Three Points Create Two Dimensions

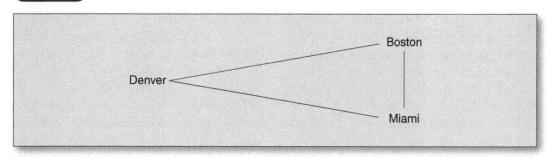

Greenland (an island of 840,000 square miles), looks the same size as China (a land mass of about 3.7 *million* square miles).

Unidimensional variables, like height, weight, birth order, age, and marital status, are relatively easy to measure. By contrast, stress, wealth, and political orientation are all multidimensional and more difficult to measure. We often talk about political orientation as if it were unidimensional, with people lying somewhere along a line between conservative and liberal. But if you think about it, people can be liberal about some dimensions of life and conservative about others. For example, you might agree strongly with the statement that "Men and women should get equal pay for equal work" and also with the statement that "A strong military is necessary to defend freedom in America." These statements test political orientation about domestic economic policy and foreign policy—two of the many dimensions of political orientation.

Even something as seemingly straightforward as income is multidimensional. To measure the annual income of various Americans, for example—cab drivers in St. Louis, Haitians in New York, retired people in Tampa, sociologists in Seattle—you may have to account for salaries, social security, private pension funds, gifts, gambling winnings, tax credits, interest on savings, wages paid entirely in cash (including tips), food stamps, contributions from extended kin, and so on.

In Chapter 11, I'll discuss the building of scales and how to test for unidimensionality of variables.

Simplifying Variables: Race and Gender

Race and gender are examples of variables that are really complex but that appear to be simple. Their complexity is hard to measure so we measure them simply, as dichotomous variables, with two values each: Black/White, female/male.

Actually, we've learned a lot by making the measurement simple. For example, any man in the United States who is labeled "Black" is about seven times more likely to be the victim of homicide than is any man labeled "White."

Black babies are about two-and-a-half times more likely to die in infancy than are White babies, and people labeled "Black" are two-and-a-half times more likely as people labeled "White" to be poor (which meant $21,203 for a family of four in 2007) (SAUS 2010:Tables 300, 107, 694, 695).

But we've missed a lot, too. We know that there are gradations of skin color besides Black and White, so it's reasonable to ask whether people who are *more* Black are *more* likely to be a victim of homicide, to die in infancy, to be poor, etc. Around 1970, medical researchers began to find a relation in the United States between darkness of skin color and blood pressure among people labeled "Blacks" (see Boyle 1970; Harburg et al. 1978). The darker the skin, the higher the blood pressure was likely to be.

Later, researchers began to find that education and social class were more important predictors of high blood pressure among Blacks than was darkness of skin color (see Keil, Sandifer et al. 1981; Keil, Tyroler et al. 1977). This meant that darker-skinned people were more likely to be the victims of discrimination and, as a consequence, uneducated and poor. Poverty causes stress and poor diet, both of which are direct causes of high blood pressure.

But suppose we treated skin color as the continuous variable it really is rather than as a dichotomous variable? Clarence Gravlee (2002b; Gravlee et al. 2005) did this in his study of race and blood pressure in Puerto Rico. He measured skin color in two ways. First, he showed people a line with nine numbers on it and asked them to rate themselves from light to dark by telling him which number best described their skin color. Then he measured the color of people's inner arm with a photospectrometer. The first measure is emic (what people think, themselves, about their color) and the second is etic (an objective, external measurement that doesn't depend on what people think).

Now, etic skin color—the amount of melanin that people have in their skin, as measured by that photospectrometer—by itself didn't account for variation in blood pressure. But the *difference* between etic skin color and what people *say* their color is was strongly associated with people's blood pressure (Gravlee 2002b:182). The relationship between these variables is anything but simple. Poor people who rate themselves as having darker skin than they really have are likely to have higher blood pressure. For middle-class people, it's the other way around: They are likely to have lower blood pressure when they rate their skin color as darker than it really is. The puzzle requires a lot more work, but this much is clear: Variation in blood pressure is not caused by melanin (Gravlee and Dressler 2005) (Box 2.1).

Box 2.1 Every research question has an ethical component

It may not be possible for everyone who uses skin color as an independent variable to measure it with a photospectrometer (the gadgets are very expensive), but if we did this, we could assess whether White schoolteachers react more negatively to darker-skinned Black children than they do to lighter-skinned Black children, and if so, by how much. This would help us account for some of the variation in Black children's school scores as a function of teacher reaction to skin color. This, in turn, would show *how* skin color leads to discrimination in education, *how* discrimination in education leads to poverty, and *how* all this leads to lowered life expectancy.

We already know that Whites live longer than Blacks. Making skin color a continuous variable would help us learn how racism actually works, not just its consequences.

If the benefits of such research are attractive, though, consider the risks. Racists might claim that our findings support their despicable ideas about the genetic inferiority of African Americans. Life insurance companies might start charging premiums based on amount of skin pigmentation. Even if the Supreme Court ruled against this practice, how many people would be hurt before the matter was adjudicated? As you can see, every research question has an ethical component.

Gender is another dichotomous variable (male and female) that is more complex than it seems. We usually measure gender according to the presence of male or female sexual characteristics. Then we look at the relation between the presence of those characteristics and things like income, level of education, IQ score, amount of labor migration, attitudes about various social issues, aptitude for math, success in certain jobs, and so on.

But we're not interested in whether differences in human anatomy predict any of these things. What we really want to know is how being *more* male or *more* female (socially and psychologically) predicts things like the ability to cope with widowhood, health status in old age, effectiveness in running a business, and so on.

Bem (1974, 1979) and Spence (1991, Spence and Helmreich 1978, and Spence et al. 1974) developed scales that measure sex-role identity. The scales are called the BSRI (Bem Sex Role Inventory) and the PAQ (Personality Attribute Questionnaire).

The BSRI consists of 60 words or phrases: 20 that represent what Americans in the early 1970s generally thought of as masculine traits (like independent and assertive); 20 that represented generally accepted feminine traits (like affectionate and sympathetic); and 20 that represented generally accepted gender-neutral traits (like tactful and happy). Respondents rate themselves on a scale of 1 to 7 on how much they think each trait applies to them. Depending on your score, you are either sex typed (displaying stereotyped feminine traits or masculine traits) or androgynous (getting a high score on both feminine and masculine traits) or undifferentiated (getting a low score on both feminine and masculine traits).

The BSRI has been used in hundreds of studies across many societies and, although ideas about typically masculine or feminine traits have changed in four decades, the work has produced many interesting results. In Finland, Sundvik and Lindeman (1993) applied the BSRI to 257 managers (159 men and 98 women) of a government-controlled transportation company. Each manager had rated a subordinate on 30 dimensions—things like the ability to get along with others, independence in getting the job done, willingness to implement innovations, and so on. The sex-typed female managers (the women who scored high on femaleness, according to the BSRI) rated their male subordinates more favorably than they rated their female subordinates. Similarly, the sex-typed male managers rated their female subordinates more favorably than they rated their male subordinates.

The bottom line, according to Sundvik and Lindeman: "Among persons whose self-concepts are formed on the basis of gender, both the queen bee and the king ape syndromes are alive and well" (1993:8). Sex-typed managers discriminate against subordinates of the same sex.

Traits thought to be masculine in one culture might be thought of as feminine in another. Aggressiveness is a trait widely viewed across many cultures to be desirable for men and boys and undesirable for women and girls. In Zimbabwe, however, 488 schoolteachers, half of whom were men, gave this trait their lowest desirability rating of the 20 masculine items in the BSRI (Wilson et al. 1990).

In Japan, Katsurada and Sugihara (1999) found that all 20 masculine traits in the BSRI were culturally appropriate, but that three of the classically 20 feminine traits in the scale ("sensitive to the needs of others," "understanding," and "loyal") were inappropriate. (Loyalty, for example, is considered a highly desirable trait for everyone in Japan, so it can't be used in a test to distinguish between men and women.) Based on tests with 300 college students, Katsurada and Sugihara recommend substituting "conscientious," "tactful," and "happy" in the list of feminine adjectives when the BSRI is used in Japan. After nearly 40 years of research with the BSRI, we've learned a lot about the differences between men and women.

One thing we've learned is that those differences are much more complex than a biological dichotomy would make them appear to be. We've also learned that gender role differences are even more complex than Bem imagined. Choi and Fuqua (2003) looked at 23 validation studies of the BSRI and found that Bem's inventory doesn't fully capture the complexity of masculinity and femininity. But that just means that we're learning more with each generation of researchers— exactly what we expect from a cumulative science (**Further Reading:** measuring gender across cultures).

Dependent and Independent Variables

Recall the life insurance problem: The company predicts how long you will live, given your sex, age, education, weight, blood pressure, and a few other variables. They bet that you will *not die* this year. You take the bet. If you lose (and remain alive), the company takes your annual premium and banks it. If you win the bet (and die), the company pays your beneficiary.

For insurance companies to turn a profit, they have to win more bets than they lose. They can make mistakes at the individual level, but in the *aggregate* (that is, averaging over all people) they have to predict longevity from things they can measure.

Longevity, then, is the dependent variable, because it *depends on* sex, education, occupation, etc. These are called independent variables because they are logically prior to—and therefore, independent of—the dependent variable of longevity. How long you live doesn't have any effect on your sex. Similarly, in our earlier example, blood pressure was the dependent variable. There is no way skin color depends on a person's blood pressure.

It's not always easy to tell whether a variable is independent or dependent. Do inner-city adolescent girls get pregnant because they are poor, or is it the other way around? Does the need for litigation stimulate the production of attorneys, or is it the other way around?

A lot of mischief is caused by failure to understand which of two variables depends on the other. One of my teachers, Oscar Lewis (1961, 1965), described what he called a "culture of poverty" among slum dwellers in cities around the world. People who live in a culture of poverty, said Lewis, are not very future oriented. This plays out, he said, in their shopping for food every day and in never buying large economy sizes of anything. Lewis's point was that truly poor people can't invest in soap futures by buying large boxes of it. He saw a low level of expressed orientation toward the future, then, as the dependent variable and poverty as the independent variable. (On Lewis's ideas about the culture of poverty, see Harvey and Reed [1996] and Morris [1996].)

Many people interpreted Lewis's work as meaning exactly the opposite: that poverty is caused by a low level of future orientation. According to this topsy-turvy, victim-blaming reasoning, if poor people—Native Americans, inner-city African Americans, rural Appalchians, slum dwellers in Delhi— would just learn to save their money and invest in the future, then they could break the poverty cycle. This educational model of social change may serve to create pointless programs to teach poor people how to save money they don't have, but it doesn't do much else (Box 2.2).

Box 2.2 The educational model of social change

The educational model of social change is based on the attractive idea that, because the last thing that happens before an action is a thought, if you want to create better actions then you need to create better thoughts. In other words, if you want to change people's behavior, you have to change how they think: Teach women in India the value of small families so they'll use birth control to prevent unwanted pregnancies; teach teenagers the importance of safe sex so they'll use condoms; and so on.

In rural West Virginia, for example, there is a lot of teen pregnancy and many adolescents drop out of high school. State policymakers there commonly blame these behaviors on the culture of poverty (Bickel et al. 1997). The behaviors that policymakers want so much to change, however, are caused by the continuing deterioration of economic and social conditions in rural communities. No amount of "educating" poor people about their bad habits will change the material circumstances that cause the so-called culture of poverty.

The educational model is the basis for one of the world's biggest industries—social change and development—but the model is mostly ineffective because behavioral change (the supposed dependent variable) doesn't usually depend on education (the supposed independent variable). In fact, across the developing world, when women have access to well-paying jobs outside the home, they tend to lower their fertility. Once that happens, they encourage their daughters to stay in school longer (Handwerker 1989). Education doesn't just cause jobs to happen. Instead, jobs for women in one generation cause education in the next. (I'll have more to say on fertility control and the educational model of behavioral change in Chapter 3, when I discuss the role of theory in the development of research questions.)

MEASUREMENT AND CONCEPTS

Variables are measured by their indicators, and indicators are defined by their values. Some variables, and their indicators, are easily observed and measured. Others are more conceptual. The difference is important.

Consider the variables race and gender again. If skin color can take one of two values (Black or White), then to *measure* race you simply look at a person and decide which value to record. If you use secondary sexual characteristics as an indicator of gender, then to *measure* gender you look at a person and decide whether they are female or male.

In other words, *measurement is deciding which value to record*. That decision is prone to error. Some people whom you classify as White or Black might be classified as Black or White by another observer. And gender is even worse. Many people, both men and women, have ambiguous secondary sexual characteristics and many women wear what were once considered to be men's clothes. Is Pat a man's name or a woman's? What about Chris? Leslie? Any of these indicators may lead you into making the wrong measurement—marking down a man or boy as a woman or girl, or vice versa.

Improving measurement in science means lowering the probability of and the amount of error. Light-skinned African Americans who cease to identify themselves ethnically as Black persons count on those errors for what they hope will be upward economic mobility. Dark-skinned Whites, like some Americans of Mediterranean descent, sometimes complain that they are being mistaken for Blacks and discriminated against.

Race and gender are concepts, or mental constructions. We have to make them up to study them. All variables are concepts, but some concepts, like height and weight, are easier to measure than others. Concepts like religious intensity, dedication to public service, willingness to accept new agricultural technologies, tolerance for foreign fieldwork, desire for an academic job, compassion, and jealousy are complex and much more difficult to measure.

Complex concepts are often called constructs. We are led to defining constructs by our experience: Some people just seem more religiously intense than others, more jealous than others, more tolerant of foreign fieldwork than others, etc. We verify our intuition about conceptual variables by measuring them, or by measuring their results.

Suppose you put an ad in the paper that says: "Roommate wanted. Easy-going, non-smoker preferred." When people answer the ad you can look at their fingers and smell their clothes to see if they smoke. But you have to ask people a series of indicator *questions* to gauge their easy-goingness.

Similarly, to predict who among a group of prisoners is predisposed to return to crime after release, you will want to measure that predisposition with a series of indicators. The indicators can be answers to questions on formal tests, or answers to open-ended questions about plans for the future, or even directly observable facts—like whether someone has a strong family to which they will return after release from prison.

It may be easier to measure some concepts than others, but the fact is, all measurement is difficult. People have worked for centuries to develop good instruments for measuring things like temperature. And if it's difficult to measure temperature (a concept, after all, backed up by time-tested theories), how do you measure worker alienation or machismo? Measuring variables like these, which lack concrete indicators, is one of our biggest challenges in social science because these variables are mostly what we're interested in.

One of the most famous variables in social science is **socioeconomic status** (SES). Measuring it is no easy task. You can use income as one indicator, but there are many wealthy people who have low SES (the so-called nouveau riche), and many relatively low-income people who have high SES (think of those down-at-the-heels nobles in England who have to open their castles to tourists to make ends meet). You can add level of education to income as an indicator, but that still won't be enough in most societies of the world to get at something as multidimensional as SES. You can add occupation, father's occupation, number of generations in a community, and so on, depending on the group you are studying, and you still might wind up dissatisfied with the result if your measure fails to predict some dependent variable of interest.

And, as you saw with the Bem androgyny scale earlier, indicators of any concept may vary from culture to culture. This doesn't mean that measurement is impossible. It means that if you decide to use a scale that was developed and tested in one culture on a new culture, you need to adapt and test the scale for the new culture. More about test scales in Chapter 11.

CONCEPTUAL AND OPERATIONAL DEFINITIONS

While most of the interesting variables in social science are concepts, some of our most important concepts are not variables. The concept of "love" is not a variable, but the concept of "being in love or not" *is* one. The concept of "culture" is not a variable, but the concept of "intensity of feeling of belonging to a particular culture" *is* one. The concept of attitude is not a variable, but the concept of "supporting or not supporting the right of adults in the United States to own hand guns" implies a variable with at least two attributes: support and nonsupport.

Conceptual Definitions

There are two ways to define variables—conceptually and operationally. **Conceptual definitions** are abstractions, articulated in words, that facilitate understanding. They are the sort of definitions we see in dictionaries, and we use them in everyday conversation to tell people what we mean by some term or phrase. Operational definitions consist of a set of instructions on how to measure a variable that has been conceptually defined.

Suppose I tell you that "Alice and Fred just moved to a spacious house." Nice concept. You ask: "What do you mean by 'spacious'?" and I say "You know, big rooms, high ceilings."

If that isn't enough for you, we'll have to move from a conceptual definition of "spacious" to an operational one. We'll have to agree on what to measure: Do we count the screened-in porch and the garage or just the interior living space? Do we count the square footage or the cubic footage? That is, do we get a measure of the living surface, or some measure of the "feeling of spaciousness" that comes from high ceilings? Do we measure the square footage of open space before or after the furniture and appliances go in? If we had to agree on things like this for every concept, ordinary human discourse would come to a grinding halt.

Science is not ordinary human discourse, however, and this, in my view, is the most important difference between the humanistic and the scientific (positivistic) approaches to social science. Humanistic researchers seek to maintain the essential feel of human discourse. Positivists focus more on specific measurement. I do not see these two styles as inimical to one another, but as complementary.

To get a feel for how complementary the two styles can be, ask some 50 year olds and some 20 year olds—men and women of both ages—to tell you how old you have to be in order to be middle aged. You'll see immediately how volatile the conceptual definition of "middle age" is. If you ask people about what it *means* to "be middle aged," you'll get plenty of material for an interesting paper on the subject. If you want to *measure* the differences between men and women and between older and younger people on this variable, you'll have to do more than just ask them. Figure 2.3 shows an instrument for measuring this variable.

Many concepts that we use in social research have volatile definitions: "power," "social class," "machismo," "alienation," "willingness to change," and "fear of retribution." If we are to talk sensibly about such things, we need clear, **intersubjective** definitions of them. In other words, although there can be no objective definition of middle age, we can at least agree on what we mean by "middle age" for a particular study and on how to measure the concept.

Figure 2.3   An Instrument for Measuring What People Think "Middle Age" Means

1 5 10 15 20 25 30 35 40 45 50 55 60 65 70 75 80 85 90 95 100

Here is a line that represents age. Obviously, a person 1 year of age is a baby, and a person 100 years of age is old. Put a mark on the line where you think middle age begins and another mark where you think middle age ends.

Complex variables are conceptually defined by reducing them to a series of simpler variables. The concept of "ethnic identity" is very complex. But if you state clearly that you mean to measure: (1) varying levels of overt expression of pride in ethnic heritage; (2) varying levels of knowledge about ethnic foods; and (3) varying levels of financial commitment to participation in ethnic heritage activities in your conceptual definition, then at least others will understand what you're talking about when you say that people are "high" or "low" on ethnic identity.

Similarly, "machismo" might be characterized by "a general feeling of male superiority," accompanied by "insecure behavior in relationships with women." Intelligence might be conceptually defined as "the ability to think in abstractions and to generalize from cases." These definitions have something important in common: They have no external reality against which to test their truth value.

Conceptual definitions are at their most powerful when they are linked together to build theories that explain research results. When the United Nations was founded in 1945, the hope was that trade between industrialized and nonindustrialized countries of the world would result in economic development for everyone. The economies of the developed countries would expand and the benefits of an expanding economy would be seen in the underdeveloped countries. A decade later, it was obvious that this wasn't happening. The rich countries were getting richer and the poor countries were getting poorer.

Raul Prebisch, an Argentinian economist who worked at the UN, argued that under colonialism, rich countries were importing raw materials from poor countries to produce manufactured goods and that poor countries had come to depend economically on the rich countries. Prebisch's dependency theory links the concept of "control of capital" with those of "mutual security" and "economic dependency," and the linkage helps explain why economic development often results in some groups winding up with less access to capital than they had before a development program (Prebisch 1984, 1994).

Conceptual definitions are at their weakest in the conduct of research itself because concepts have no empirical basis. To repeat: We have to make them up to study them.

There is nothing wrong with this. There are three things one wants to do in any science: (1) describe a phenomenon of interest; (2) explain what causes it; and (3) predict what it causes. The existence of a conceptual variable is inferred from what it predicts—how well it makes theoretical sense out of a lot of data.

The Concept of Intelligence

The classic example of a conceptual variable is intelligence. Intelligence is anything we say it is. There is no way to tell whether it is really: (1) the ability to think in abstractions and to generalize from cases; (2) the ability to remember long strings of unconnected facts; or (3) the ability to recite all of Shakespeare from memory. The value of the concept of intelligence is that it allows us to predict, *with varying success*, things like job success, grade-point average, likelihood of having healthy children, and likelihood of being arrested for a felony.

The key to understanding the last statement is the phrase "with varying success." It is by now well known that measures of intelligence are culture bound; the standard U.S. intelligence tests are biased in favor of Whites and against African Americans because of differences in access to education and differences in life experiences. Further afield, intelligence tests that are designed for Americans or Canadians or other Western societies may not have any meaning at all to people in radically different cultures.

There is an apocryphal story about some American researchers who were determined to develop a culture-free intelligence test based on manipulation and matching of shapes and colors. With an interpreter along for guidance, they administered the test to a group of Bushmen in the Kalahari Desert of South Africa. The first Bushman they tested listened politely to the instructions about matching the colors and shapes and then excused himself.

He returned in a few minutes with half a dozen others, and they began an animated discussion about the test. The researchers asked the interpreter to explain that each man had to take the test himself. The Bushmen responded by saying how silly that was; they solve problems together, and they would solve this one, too. So, although the content of the test might have been culture free, the testing procedure itself was not.

This critique of intelligence *testing* in no way lessens the importance or usefulness of the *concept* of intelligence. The concept is useful, in certain contexts, because its measurement allows us to predict other things we want to know. And it is to actual measurement that we now turn.

Operational Definitions

Conceptual definitions are limited because, while they point us toward measurement, they don't really give us any recipe for measurement. Without measurement, we cannot make useful comparisons. We cannot tell whether Spaniards are more flamboyant than the British, or whether Catholicism is more authoritarian than Buddhism. We cannot evaluate the level of anger in an urban community over perceived abuses by the police of their authority, or compare the level of that anger to the anger found in another community in another city.

Operational definitions specify exactly what you have to do to measure something that has been defined conceptually. Here are four examples of operational definitions:

1. Intelligence: Take the Wechsler Adults Intelligence Scale (WAIS) and administer it to a person. Count up the score. Whatever score the person gets is his or her intelligence.

2. Machismo: Ask a man if he approves of women working outside the home, assuming the family doesn't need the money; if he says "no," then give him a score of 1, and if he says "yes," then score him 0. Ask him if he thinks women and men should have the same sexual freedom before marriage; if he says "no," score 1 and score 0 for "yes." Ask him if a man should be punished for killing his wife and her lover; if he says "no," score 1; score 0 for "yes." Add the scores. A man who scores 3 has more machismo than a man who scores 2, and a man who scores 2 has more machismo than a man who scores 1.

3. Ethnic identity: Ask a sample of third-generation Chinese Americans who were born in San Francisco if they speak the language of their grandparents fluently. If "yes," score 1. If "no," score 0. Ask them if they eat at non-Chinese restaurants at least once a week. Score 1 for "no," and 0 for "yes." Ask them eight other questions of this type, and give them a score of 1 for each answer that signifies self-identification with their parents' heritage. Anyone who scores at least 6 out of 10 is an "identifier." Anyone with a score of 5 or less is a "rejecter" of Chinese heritage or identity.

4. Support for trade barriers against China: Ask workers in a factory to complete the Support of Trade Barriers against China Scale. Add the four parts of the scale together to produce a single score. Record that score.

These definitions sound pretty boring, but think about this: If you and I use the same definitions for variables, *and if we stick to those definitions in making measurements*, then our data are strictly comparable:

1. We can tell if adults in city A have higher intelligence scores than do adults in city B.

2. We can tell if members of one Hispanic group have higher machismo scores than members of another Hispanic group.

3. We can tell if members of an ethnic minority in city A have higher cultural identity scores than do members of the same ethnic minority in city B.

4. We can tell whether the average scores indicating level of support for trade barriers against China is greater among workers in the factory you studied than it is among workers in the factory I studied.

I find the ability to make such comparisons exciting and not at all boring. But did you notice that I *never* said anything in those comparisons about ethnic identity per se, or intelligence per se, or machismo or support for trade barriers per se. In each case, all I said was that we could tell if the *scores* were bigger or smaller (**Further Reading:** operationism).

What's So Good About Operationism

Operational definitions are *strictly limited to the content of the operations specified*. That's why I also didn't say anything about whether it was a good idea or a stupid one to make any of these measurements or comparisons. *If the content of an operational definition is bad, then so are all conclusions you draw from using it to measure something*.

This is *not* an argument against operationism in science. Just the opposite. Operationism is the best way to expose bad measurement. By defining measurements operationally, we can tell if one measurement is better than another. If the operational measurement of, say, machismo, seems silly or offensive, it may be because the concept is not very useful to begin with. No amount of measurement or operationism bails out bad concepts. The act of trying, though, usually *exposes* bad concepts and helps you jettison them (Box 2.3).

Box 2.3 Improving measurement

Adhering to bad measurements is bad science and can have some bad consequences for people. In the 1960s, I was a consultant on a project that was supposed to help Chicano high schoolers develop good career aspirations. Studies had been conducted in which Chicano and Anglo high schoolers were asked what they wanted to be when they reached 30 years of age. Chicanos expressed, on average, a lower occupational aspiration than did Anglos. This led some social scientists to advise policymakers that Chicano youth needed reinforcement of career aspirations at home. (There's that educational model again.)

Contrary to survey findings, ethnographic research showed that Chicano parents had very high aspirations for their children. The parents were frustrated by two things: (1) despair over the cost of sending their children to college; and (2) high-school counselors who systematically encouraged Chicana girls to become housewives and Chicano boys to learn a trade or go into the armed services.

The presumed relation between the dependent variable (level of career aspiration) and the independent variable (level of aspiration by parents for the careers of their children) was backwards. The parents' level of career aspiration for their children didn't cause the children to have low aspirations. The children were driven to low aspirations by structural features of their environment. The parents of those children reflected this reality—they said explicitly to interviewers who bothered to ask—so as not to give their children false hopes.

The operational definition of the variable "parents' career aspirations for their children" was useless. Here's the operational definition that should have been used in the study of Chicano parents' aspirations for their children's careers:

Go to the homes of the respondents. Using the native language of the respondents (Spanish or English as the case may be), talk to parents about what they want their high school age children to be doing in 10 years. Explore each answer in depth and find out why parents give each answer.

Ask specifically if the parents are telling you what they think their children *will* be doing or what they *want* their children to be doing. If parents hesitate, say: "Suppose nothing stood in the way of your [son] [daughter] becoming anything they wanted to be. What would you like them to be doing 10 years from now?"

Write down what the parents say and code it for the following possible scores: 1 = unambivalently in favor of children going into high-status occupations; 2 = ambivalent about children going into high-status occupations; 3 = unambivalently in favor of children going into low- or middle-status occupations.

Use the Nam-Powers-Boyd occupation scale (Nam and Boyd 2004) to decide whether the occupations selected by parents as fitting for their children are high, middle, or low status. Be sure to take and keep notes on what parents say are the reasons for their selections of occupations.

Notice in this example that taking a qualitative approach did not stop us from being operational.

Operationism is often crude and simplistic, and that, too, can be a strength. Robert Wuthnow (1976) operationalized the concept of religiosity in 43 countries using UNESCO data on the number of books published in those countries and the fraction of those books classified as religious literature. Now *that's* crude. Still, Wuthnow's measure of "average religiosity" correlates with seven of eight indicators of modernity. For example, the higher the literacy rate in 1952, the lower the religiosity in 1972.

I have no idea what that means, but I think following up Wuthnow's work with more refined measurements—to test hypotheses about the societal conditions that support or weaken religiosity—is a lot more exciting than dismissing it because it was so audaciously crude.

The Problem With Operationism

Strict operationism creates a knotty philosophical problem. Measurement turns abstractions (concepts) into reality. Since there are many ways to measure the same abstraction, the reality of any concept hinges on the device you use to measure it. So, sea temperature is different if you measure it from a satellite (you get an answer based on radiation) or with a thermometer (you get an answer based on a column of mercury). Intelligence is different if you measure it with a Stanford-Binet test or the Wechsler scales. If you ask a person in any of the industrialized nations "How old are you?" or "How many birthdays have you had?" you will probably retrieve the same number. But the very concept of age in the two cases is different because different "instruments" (queries are instruments) were used to measure it.

This principle was articulated in 1927 by Percy Bridgman in *The Logic of Modern Physics* and has become the source of an enduring controversy. The bottom line on strict operational definitions is this: No matter how much you insist that intelligence is really more than what is measured by an intelligence test, that's all it can ever be. Whatever you think intelligence is, it is exactly and only what you measure with an intelligence test and nothing more.

If you don't like the results of your measurement, then build a better test, where better means that the outcomes are more useful in building theory, in making predictions, and in engineering behavior.

I see no reason to waffle about this, or to look for philosophically palatable ways to soften the principle here. The science that emerges from a strict operational approach to understanding variables is much too powerful to water down with backpedaling. It is obvious that "future orientation" is more than my asking someone "Do you buy large or small boxes of soap?" The problem is, *you* might not include that question in your interview of the same respondent, unless I specify that I asked that question in that particular way (Box 2.4).

Box 2.4 Operational definitions permit scientists to talk to one another using the same language

Operational definitions permit replication of research and the accumulation of knowledge. The **Attitudes Toward Women Scale (AWS)**, for example, was developed by Janet Spence and Robert Helmreich in 1972 (Spence and Helmreich 1972, 1978) and has been used in about 400 studies since then, including some seventy dissertations. Many of those studies involved American college students and, as you'd guess, attitudes toward women have became more liberal/feminist over the years. By 1990, men's average score on the AWS was about the same as women's average score in 1975 (Twenge 1997). In other words, men's attitudes changed, but lagged those of women by 15 years. (These data, remember, reflect the attitudes of college students—the quarter of the population whom we expect to be at the vanguard of social change.)

Some of the items on the AWS seem pretty old-fashioned today. For example, in one item, people are asked how much they agree or disagree with the idea that "women should worry less about their rights and more about becoming good wives and mothers." You probably wouldn't use that item if you were building an attitudes-toward-women scale today, but keeping the original, 1972 AWS intact over all this time lets us track attitudes toward women over time (**Further Reading:** the AWS).

LEVELS OF MEASUREMENT

Whenever you define a variable operationally, you do so at some level of measurement. Most social scientists recognize the following four levels of measurement, in ascending order: nominal, ordinal, interval, and ratio. The general principle in research is: Always use the highest level of measurement that you can. (This principle will be clear by the time you get through the next couple of pages.)

Nominal Variables

A variable is something that can take more than one value. The values of a nominal variable comprise a list of names. You can list religions, occupations, and ethnic groups; you can also list fruits, emotions, body parts, things to do on the weekend, baseball teams, rock stars . . . the list of things you can list is endless.

Think of nominal variables as *yes-no questions, the answers to which tell you nothing about degree or amount*. What's your name? In what country were you born? Are you healthy? On the whole, do you think the economy is in good shape? Is Mexico in Latin America? Is Bangladesh a poor country? Is Switzerland a rich country? What is your gender?

For gender, you can assign the numeral 1 to men and 2 to women, but gender will still be a qualitative, nominal variable. The number 2 happens to be twice as big as the number 1, but this fact is meaningless with nominal variables. You can't add up all the 1s and 2s and calculate average sex any more than you can add up all the telephone numbers in the Chicago phone book and get the average phone number.

Assigning numbers to things does make it easier to do certain kinds of statistical analysis on

qualitative data—more on this in Chapters 19 (on coding text) and 21 (on regression).

The following survey item is an operationalization of the nominal variable called "religious affiliation":

26a. Do you identify with any religion? (check one)

☐ Yes ☐ No

If you checked "yes," then please answer question 26b.

26b. What is your religion (check one):

☐ Protestant

☐ Catholic

☐ Jewish

☐ Muslim

☐ Other religion

This operationalization of the variable religious affiliation has two important characteristics: It is *exhaustive* and *mutually exclusive*. The famous "other" category in nominal variables makes the list exhaustive—that is, all possible categories have been named in the list—and the instruction to "check one" makes the list mutually exclusive. (More on this in Chapter 9 when we discuss questionnaire design.)

Mutually exclusive means that things can't belong to more than one category of a nominal variable at a time. We assume, for example, that people who say they are Catholic generally don't say they are Muslim. I say generally because life is complicated and variables that seem mutually exclusive may not be. Some citizens of Lebanon have one Catholic and one Muslim parent and may think of themselves as both Muslim and Catholic.

Most people think of themselves as either male or female, but not everyone does. The prevalence of transsexuals in human populations is not known precisely, but worldwide, it is likely to be between 1 in 10,000 and 1 in 100,000 for male-to-female transsexuals (biological males whose gender identity is female) and between 1 in 100,000 and 1 in 400,000 for female-to-male transsexuals (Cohen-Kettenis and Gooren 1999).

Most people in Western countries think of themselves as a member of one so-called race or another, but more and more people think of themselves as belonging to two or more races. In Brazil, 38.5% of the population checked "parda" (a cover term for mixed race) as their race in the 2000 census (http://tinyurl.com/2btbhrc). In 2000, the U.S. Census offered people the opportunity to check off more than one so-called race from six choices: White, Black or African American, American Indian or Alaska Native, Asian, Native Hawaiian and other Pacific islander, and Other. Nearly seven million people (2.4% of the 281 million in the United States in 2000) checked more than one of the six options (Grieco and Cassidy 2001).

And when it comes to ethnicity, the requirement for mutual exclusivity is just hopeless. There are Chicano African Americans, Chinese Cuban Americans, Filipino Cherokees, and so on. This just reflects the complexity of real life, but it does make analyzing data more complicated because each *combination of attributes* has to be treated as a separate category of the variable "ethnicity" or collapsed into one of the larger categories. More about this in Chapters 20 and 21 when we get to data analysis.

Occupation is a nominal variable, but lots of people have more than one occupation. People can be pediatric oncology nurses and antique car salespeople at the same time. A list of occupations is a measuring instrument at the nominal level: You hold each person up against the list and see which occupation(s) he or she has (have).

The attributes of nominal variables can change over time. In the 1970s, surveys done in the United States, typically asked people: "Are you (check one): Protestant, Catholic, Jewish, other religion, no religion." In the 1970s, there were very few people in the

United States who considered themselves Muslims. By 2008, about 1.3 million people in the United States described themselves as Muslims, about half as many who identified themselves as Jews (SAUS 2010:Table 75).

Ordinal Variables

Like nominal-level variables, ordinal variables are generally exhaustive and mutually exclusive, but they have one additional property: Their values can be rank ordered. Any variable measured as high, medium, or low, like socioeconomic class, is ordinal. The three classes are, in theory, mutually exclusive and exhaustive. In addition, a person who is labeled "middle class" is lower in the social class hierarchy than someone labeled "high class" and higher in the same hierarchy than someone labeled "lower class." What ordinal variables do not tell us is *how much* more.

Scales of opinion—like the familiar "strongly agree," "agree," "neutral," "disagree," "strongly disagree" found on so many surveys—are ordinal measures. They measure an internal state, agreement, in terms of *less* and *more*, but not in terms of *how much* more.

This is the most important characteristic of ordinal measures: There is no way to tell how far apart the attributes are from one another. A person who is middle class might be twice as wealthy and three times as educated as a person who is lower class. Or they might be three times as wealthy and four times as educated. A person who "agrees strongly" with a statement may agree twice as much as someone who says they "agree"—or eight times as much, or half again as much. There is no way to tell.

Interval and Ratio Variables

Interval variables have all the properties of nominal and ordinal variables. They are an exhaustive and mutually exclusive list of attributes, and the attributes have a rank-order structure. They have one additional property, as well: The distances between the attributes are meaningful. Interval variables, then, involve true **quantitative measurement**.

The difference between 30° Centigrade and 40° is the same 10° as the difference between 70° and 80°, and the difference between an IQ score of 90 and 100 is (assumed to be) the same as the difference between one of 130 and 140. On the other hand, 80° Fahrenheit is not twice as hot as 40°, and a person who has an IQ of 150 is not 50% smarter than a person with an IQ of 100.

Ratio variables are interval variables that have a true zero point—that is, a 0 that measures the absence of the phenomenon being measured. The Kelvin scale of temperature has a true zero: It identifies the absence of molecular movement, or heat.

The consequence of a true zero point is that measures have ratio properties. A person who is 40 years old is 10 years older than a person who is 30, and a person who is 20 is 10 years older than a person who is 10. The 10-year intervals between the attributes (years are the attributes of age) are identical. That much is true of an interval variable. In addition, however, a person who is 20 is twice as old as a person who is 10; and a person who is 40 is twice as old as a person who is 20. These, then, are true ratios.

Although temperature (in Fahrenheit or Celsius) and IQ are nonratio interval variables, most interval-level variables in the social sciences are also ratio variables. In fact, it has become common practice in the social sciences to refer to ratio-level variables as interval variables and vice versa. This is not technically pure, but the confusion of the terms "interval" and "ratio" doesn't cause much real damage.

Some examples of ratio variables include: age, number of years of education, number of times a person has changed residence, income in dollars or other currency, years married, years spent migrating, population size, distance in meters from a house to a well, number of violent crimes per hundred thousand population, number of dentists per million population, number of months since last employment, number of kilograms of fish caught per week, number of hours per week spent in food preparation. Number of years of education is usually treated as a ratio variable, even though a year of grade school is hardly worth the same as a year of graduate school.

In general, concepts (like alienation, political orientation, level of assimilation) are measured at the ordinal level. People get a high score for being "very assimilated," a low score for being "unassimilated," and a medium score for being "somewhat assimilated." When a concept variable like intelligence is measured at the interval level, it is likely to be the focus of a lot of controversy regarding the validity of the measuring instrument.

Concrete observables—things you can actually see—are often measured at the interval level. But not always. Observing whether a woman has a job outside her home is nominal, **qualitative measurement** based on direct observation.

A Rule About Measurement

Remember this rule: Always measure things at the highest level of measurement possible. Don't measure things at the ordinal level if you can measure them as ratio variables.

If you really want to know the price that people paid for their homes, then ask the price. Don't ask them whether they paid "less than $150,000, between $150,000 and $300,000, or more than $300,000." If you really want to know how much education people have had, ask them how many years they went to school. Don't ask "Have you completed grade school, high school, some college, four years of college?" This kind of packaging just throws away information by turning interval-level variables into ordinal ones. As we'll see in Chapter 9, survey questions are pretested before going into a questionnaire. If people won't give you straight answers to straight questions, you can back off and try an ordinal scale. But why start out crippling a perfectly good interval-scale question by making it ordinal when you don't know that you have to?

During data analysis you can lump interval-level data together into ordinal or nominal categories. If you know the ages of your respondents on a survey, you can divide them into old and young; if you know the number of calories consumed per week for each family in a study, you can divide the data into low, medium, and high. But you cannot do this trick the other way around. If you collect data on income by asking people whether they earn "up to $75,000 per year" or "more than $75,000 per year," you cannot go back and assign actual numbers of dollars to each informant.

Notice that "up to $75,000" and "more than $75,000" is an ordinal variable that *looks like* a nominal variable because there are only two attributes. If the attributes are rankable, then the variable is ordinal. "A lot of fish" is more than "a small amount of fish," and "highly educated" is greater than "poorly educated." Ordinal variables can have any number of ranks. For purposes of statistical analysis, though, ordinal scales with five or more ranks are often treated as if they were interval level variables. More about this in Chapter 21 on bivariate analysis.

UNITS OF ANALYSIS

One of the first things to do in any research project is decide on the unit of analysis. In a case study, there is exactly one unit of analysis—the school, the hospital, the police squad, the sports team, the community, the church, the nation. Research designed to test hypotheses requires many units of analysis, usually a sample from a large population—organic farmers, Puerto Ricans living in Baltimore, women in the Teamsters Union, runaway children who are living on the street, children in Head Start programs, maternity nurses in private hospitals, people who go to chiropractors, Hispanic patrol officers in the U.S. Immigration and Naturalization Service who work on the border between the United States and Mexico.

How many units of analysis do you need in a sample? That depends on several things, which we'll get to in Chapter 6 on sampling theory and in Chapter 7 on nonrandom samples. Here's a hint, though: Good research samples can be much smaller than you might think (take a peek at Table 16.13).

Although most research in social science is about populations of people, many other things can be the units of analysis. You can focus on farms instead of farmers, or on unions instead of union members, or on wars instead of warriors. You can study marriage contracts and building permits; folk tales, songs, and myths; and countries, cultures, cities, and neighborhoods. Countries are the focus of much research in political science, for example, and neighborhoods are the focus of much research on crime.

A Rule About Units of Analysis

Remember this rule: No matter what you are studying, always collect data on the lowest level unit of analysis possible.

Household economics can only be understood by studying . . . well, households (Wilk 1990). Collect data, though, on individuals within households. You can always package your data about individuals into data about households during analysis, but if you want to examine the association between female income and child spacing and you collect income data on households in the first place, then you are locked out. You can always aggregate data collected on individuals, but you can never disaggregate data collected on groups.

This rule applies whether you're studying people or countries. If you are studying relations among trading blocs in major world regions, then collect trade data on countries and pairs of countries, not on regions of the world.

The Ecological Fallacy

Once you select your unit of analysis, remember it as you go through data analysis, or you're likely to commit the dreaded ecological fallacy. This fallacy (also known as the Nosnibor effect, after W. S. Robinson [1950] who described it) comes from drawing conclusions about the wrong units of analysis—making generalizations about people, for example, from data about groups or places.

For example, in 1930, 11% of foreign-born people in the United States were illiterate, compared with 3% of those born in the United States. The correlation between these two variables was 0.118. In other words, across 97 million people (the population of the United States at the time), being foreign born was a moderately strong predictor of being illiterate. But when Robinson looked at the data for the (then) 48 states in the United States, he got an entirely different result. The correlation between the percent illiterate and the percent of foreign-born people was –0.526. That minus sign means that the more foreign born, the *less* illiteracy.

What's going on? Well, as Jargowsky (2005) observes, immigrants went mostly to the big industrial states where they were more likely to find jobs. Those northern and midwestern states had better schools and higher literacy—along with a lot of immigrants, many of whom were illiterate. And that was Robinson's point: If you only looked at the state-by-state averages (the aggregated units of analysis) instead of at the individual data, you'd draw the wrong conclusion about the relationship between the two variables.

Here's an example closer to home. In a consumer survey across a city you notice that the neighborhoods that have the lowest average age also have the highest average dollar value of recent purchases of consumer electronics.

You are tempted to conclude that young people are more interested in, and purchase, consumer electronics more frequently than do older people.

But you could be completely wrong. The *neighborhoods* with lower average age may spend more on smart phones and such, but it may be the *older people* who are doing most of the spending. It is usually not valid to take data gathered about *neighborhoods* and draw conclusions about *neighbors* (**Further Reading:** the ecological inference problem).

And this brings us to the crucial issue of validity.

VALIDITY, RELIABILITY, ACCURACY, AND PRECISION

Validity refers to the accuracy and trustworthiness of instruments, data, and findings in research. Nothing in research is more important than validity.

The Validity of Instruments and Data

Does the question "How long does it take you to drive to work each day?" have **instrument validity**? In other words, is it a valid instrument for measuring the amount of time it takes people to drive to work each day? That depends on how accurate you want the data to be. If you want the data to be accurate to within, say, 20 minutes on, say 70% of occasions, then the instrument is probably valid. If you want the data to be accurate to, say, within 5 minutes on, say, 90% of occasions, then the instrument is probably not valid because people just can't dredge up the information you want at that level of accuracy.

Is the question "Do you practice polytheistic fetishism?" a valid instrument for measuring religious practices? If people don't understand the question—if you're asking them to think in categories that are alien to their culture—then it's not a valid instrument for measuring anything.

Data validity is tied to instrument validity. If questions asking people to recall their behavior are not valid instruments for tapping into informants' past behavior, then the data retrieved by those instruments are not valid, either.

The Validity of Findings

Once we have valid instruments and valid data, we can ask about **finding validity** or **conclusion validity**. Asian Americans (mostly an aggregate of Chinese Americans, Japanese Americans, and Vietnamese Americans) get higher average scores on the math part of the Scholastic Aptitude Tests (SAT) than do other ethnic groups in the United States—581 versus 515 for all ethnic groups combined (College Board 2008). Suppose that the SAT math test is a valid instrument for measuring the general math ability of 18 year olds in the United States. Is it valid to conclude that "Asians are better at math" than other people are? No, it isn't. That conclusion can only be reached by invoking an unfounded, racist assumption about the influence of certain genes—like the ones responsible for epicanthic eye folds—on the ability of people to do math.

Reliability

Reliability refers to whether or not you get the same answer by using an instrument to measure something more than once. If you insert a thermometer into boiling water at sea level, it should register 212° Fahrenheit each and every time. Instruments can be things like thermometers and scales, or they can be questions that you ask people.

Like all other kinds of instruments, some questions are more reliable for retrieving information than others. "How many brothers and sisters do you have?" is a pretty reliable instrument—you almost always get the same response when you ask a person that question a second time as you get the first time—but "How much is your parents' house worth?" is much less reliable. And "How old were you when you were toilet trained?" is just hopeless.

We'll take up the measurement of interrater reliability—where more than one observer records a measurement—in Chapter 19.

Precision

Precision is about the number of decimal points in a measurement. When you stand on an old-fashioned scale, the spring is compressed. As the spring compresses, it moves a pointer to a number that signifies how much weight is being put on the scale. Let's say that you really, truly weigh 156.625 pounds, to the nearest thousandth of a pound.

If you have a predigital bathroom scale like mine, there are five little marks between each pound reading; that is, the scale registers weight in 5ths of a pound. In terms of precision, then, your scale is somewhat limited. The best it could possibly do would be to announce that you weigh "somewhere between 156.6 and 156.8 pounds, and closer to the former figure than to the latter." In this case, you might not be too concerned about the error introduced by lack of precision.

Whether you care or not depends on the needs you have for the data. If you are concerned about losing weight, then you're probably not going to worry too much about the fact that your scale is only precise to the nearest 5th of a pound. But if you're measuring the weights of pharmaceuticals, and someone's life depends on your getting the precise amounts into a compound, that's another matter.

Accuracy

Finally, **accuracy**. Assume that you are satisfied with the level of precision of the scale.

What if the spring were not calibrated correctly (there was an error at the factory where the scale was built, or last week your overweight house guest bent the spring a little too much) and the scale were off? Now we have the following interesting situation: The data from this instrument are valid (it has already been determined that the scale is measuring weight—exactly what you think it's measuring); they are reliable (you get the same answer every time you step on it); and they are precise enough for your purposes. But they are not *accurate*. What next?

You could see if the scale were always inaccurate in the same way. You could stand on it 10 times in a row, without eating or doing exercise in between. That way, you'd be measuring the same thing 10 different times with the same instrument. If the reading were always the same, then the instrument would at least be reliable, even though it wasn't accurate. Suppose it turned out that your scale was always incorrectly lower by 5 pounds.

This is called **systematic bias**. Then, a simple correction formula would be all you'd need to feel confident that the data from the instrument were pretty close to the truth. The formula would be:

$$\text{True Weight} = \text{Your Scale Weight} + 5 \text{ pounds}$$

The scale might be off in more complicated ways, however. It might be that for every 10 pounds of weight put on the scale, an additional half pound correction has to be made. Then the **recalibration** formula would be

$$\text{True Weight} = (\text{Your Scale Weight}) + (\text{Scale Weight}/10)(.5)$$

or

$$(\text{Your scale weight}) \times (1.05)$$

That is, take the scale weight, divide by 10, multiply by half a pound, and add the result to the reading on your scale.

If an instrument is not precise enough for what you want to do with the data, then you simply have to build a more precise one. There is no way out. If it is precise enough for your research and reliable but inaccurate in known ways, then a formula can be applied to correct for the inaccuracy.

The real problem is when instruments are inaccurate in unknown ways. The bad news is that this happens a lot. If you ask people how long it takes them to drive to work, they'll tell you. If you ask people what they ate for breakfast, they'll tell you that, too. Answers to both questions may be dead on target, or they may bear no useful resemblance to the truth. The good news is that respondent accuracy is one of the methodological questions that social scientists have been investigating for years and on which real progress continues to be made (**Further Reading:** respondent accuracy).

Tests for Reliability

There are several tests of reliability:

1. **Interobserver (or interrater) reliability.** Suppose you set up an experiment to see whether 5-year-old children act more aggressively or more cooperatively in same-sex play groups or in mixed-sex play groups. You'll have several observers code the behavior of the children and you'll want them to achieve consistency in what they see and write down.

Or suppose you have a set of open-ended interviews about what it's like to break up after a relationship that's lasted more than a year. You'll want several people coding those interviews. In both cases—whether you're coding behavior or the content of text—you'll want your coders to achieve a high interobserver reliability score. I'll have more to say in Chapter 19 (on text analysis) about how to calculate that score.

2. **Test-retest reliability.** A reliable test of, say, ability in math or of interest in a particular occupation should give you more or less the

same results each time you use it on the same person. When tests are developed, they are typically tested for reliability by giving them to a group of people then calling back those same people a week later to take the test again.

Many standardized tests have two parallel test forms. When both forms are given to the same person, they should produce more or less the same results. "More or less" here means at least 0.80. Another test for reliability is the split-half test. This is used in the development of scales, about which *much* more in Chapter 11.

Determining Validity

You may have noticed a few paragraphs back that I casually slipped in the statement that some scale had *already been determined* to be a valid instrument. How do we know that a scale is measuring weight? Maybe it's measuring something else. How can we be sure? We have to make concepts up to study them, so there is no direct way to evaluate the validity of an instrument for measuring a concept. Ultimately, we are left to decide, on the basis of our best judgment, whether an instrument is valid or not.

We are helped in making that judgment by some tests for face validity, content validity, construct validity, and criterion validity.

Face Validity

Establishing face validity involves simply looking at the operational indicators of a concept and deciding whether or not, *on the face of it*, the indicators make sense. The indicators might be items on an opinion survey or they might be tests of knowledge and ability.

On the face of it, asking people "How old were you when you were toilet trained?" is not a valid way to get at this kind of information. A paper-and-pencil test about the rules of the road is not, on the face of it, a valid indicator of whether someone knows how to drive a car. But the paper-and-pencil test is probably a valid test for determining if an applicant for a driver's license can read road signs. These different instruments—the road test and the paper-and-pencil test—have face validity for measuring different things.

Face validity is based on consensus among researchers: If everyone agrees that asking people "How old are you" is a valid instrument for measuring age, then, until proven otherwise, that question is a valid instrument for measuring age.

Content Validity

Content validity is achieved when an instrument has appropriate content for measuring a complex concept, or construct. If you walk out of a test and feel that it was unfair because it tapped too narrow a band of knowledge, your complaint is that the test lacked content validity. Achievement tests—for assessing whether pilots are ready to fly solo and for assessing whether family therapists are ready to be licensed—are judged on their content validity.

Content validity is very, very tough to achieve, particularly for complex, multidimensional constructs. A test to measure the strength of "ethnic identity" among, say, second-generation Mexican Americans has to have content that deals with religion, language, political and economic values, sense of history, and gastronomy.

Religion: Mexican Americans tend to be mostly Roman Catholic, but a growing number of Mexicans are now Protestants. The migration of a few million of these converts to the United States over the next decade will have an impact on ethnic politics—and ethnic identity—within the Mexican American population.

Language: Some second-generation Mexican Americans speak almost no Spanish; others are completely bilingual. Some use Spanish only in the home; others use it with their friends and business associates.

Socioeconomic status: Many Mexican Americans are poor (about 31% of Hispanic households in the United States have incomes below $25,000 a year), but many others are well off (about 20% have incomes above $75,000 a year) (SAUS 2010:Table 674). People with radically different incomes tend to have different political and economic values.

Sense of history: Some so-called Mexican Americans have roots that go back to before the British Pilgrims landed at Plymouth Rock. The Hispanos (as they are known) of New Mexico were Spaniards who came north from the Spanish colony of Mexico. Their self-described ethnic identity is quite different from recent immigrants from Mexico.

Gastronomy: The last refuge of ethnicity is food. When language is gone (Spanish, Yiddish, Polish, Gaelic, Greek, Chinese . . .), and when ties to the "old country" are gone, burritos, bagels, pirogis, corned beef, moussaka, and lo mein remain. For some second-generation Mexican Americans, cuisine is practically synonymous with identity; for others , it's just part of a much larger complex of traits.

A valid measure of ethnic identity, then, has to get at all these areas. People's use of Spanish inside and outside the home and their preference for Mexican or Mexican American foods are good measures of *some* of the content of Mexican American ethnicity. But if these are the only questions you ask, then your measure of ethnicity has low content validity. (See Cabassa [2003] and Cruz et al. [2008] on acculturation scales for Hispanics in the United States.)

"Life satisfaction" is another very complex variable, composed of several concepts like "having sufficient income," "a general feeling of well-being," and "satisfaction with level of personal control over one's life." In fact, most of the really interesting things that social scientists study are complex constructs, things like "quality of life," "socioeconomic class," "ability of teenagers to resist peer pressure to smoke," and so on.

Construct Validity

An instrument has high construct validity if there is a close fit between the construct it supposedly measures and actual observations made with the instrument. An instrument has high construct validity, in other words, if it allows you to infer that a unit of analysis (a person, a country, whatever) has a particular complex trait and if it supports predictions that are made from theory.

Scholars have offered various definitions of the construct of ethnicity, based on different theoretical perspectives. Does a particular measure of Mexican American ethnicity have construct validity? Does it somehow "get at" the various components of this complex idea?

Asking people "How old are you?" has so much face validity that you hardly need to ask whether the instrument has construct validity—whether it gets at the construct of chronological age. Giving people an IQ test, by contrast, is controversial because there is so much disagreement about what the construct of intelligence is. Lots of constructs in which we're interested—intelligence, ethnicity, machismo, alienation, acculturation, liberal—are controversial and so are the measures for them. Getting people to agree that a particular *measure* has high construct validity requires that they agree that the construct is valid in the first place.

Suppose you test the hypothesis that uneducated and unskilled women who have steady, if low-paying, jobs are more likely to leave physically abusive relationships than are women who have no income other than welfare. This hypothesis comes from the theory that lower-class women in industrial (or industrializing) societies who are financially independent of men will, among other things, lower their fertility and get out of abusive situations. You gather the data and the results are mixed. Some women do leave those abusive relationships, some don't.

Now the problem is: Do you question the measure of financial independence (the construct), or do you question the hypothesis and the theory it comes from? Perhaps the theory was wrong. Or perhaps the measure had low construct validity.

Criterion Validity

An instrument has high criterion validity if there is a close fit between the measures it produces and the measures produced by some other instrument that is known to be valid. This is the gold standard test.

A tape measure, for example, is known to be an excellent instrument for measuring height. If you knew that a man in the United States wore shirts with 35″ sleeves, and pants with 34″ cuffs, you could bet that he was over 6' tall and be right more than 95% of the time. On the other hand, you might ask: "Why should I measure his cuff length and sleeve length to know *most of the time, in general*, how tall he is when I could use a tape measure and know *all of the time, precisely* how tall he is?"

Indeed. If you want to measure someone's height, then use a tape measure. Don't substitute a lot of fuzzy proxy variables for something that's directly measurable by known, valid indicators. But if you want to measure things like quality of life, and socioeconomic class—things that don't have well-understood, valid indicators—then a complex measure will just have to do until something simpler comes along (Box 2.5).

Box 2.5 The principle of Ockham's razor

The preference in science for simpler explanations and measures over more complicated ones is called the principle of **parsimony**. It is also known as **Ockham's razor**, after William of Ockham (1285–1349), a medieval philosopher who argued *entia non sunt multiplicanda praeter necessitatem*, or "Don't make things more complicated than they need to be."

You can tap the power of criterion validity for complex constructs with the **known group comparison technique**. If you develop a scale to measure political ideology, you could try it out on members of the American Civil Liberties Union and on members of the Christian Coalition of America. Members of the ACLU should get high "left" scores, and members of the CC should get high "right" scores. If they don't, then there's probably something wrong with the scale. In other words, the known-group scores are the criteria for the validity of your instrument.

A particularly strong form of criterion validity is predictive validity—whether an instrument lets you predict accurately something else you're interested in. "Stress" is a complex construct. It occurs when people interpret events as threatening to their lives. Some people interpret a bad grade on an exam as a threat to their whole life, while others just blow it off. Now, stress is widely thought to produce a lowered immune response and increase the chances of getting sick. A really good *measure* of stress, then, ought to predict the likelihood of getting sick.

Remember the life insurance problem? You want to predict whether someone is likely to die in the next 365 days to know how much to charge them in premiums. Age and sex tell you a lot. But if you know their weight, whether they smoke, whether they exercise regularly, what their blood pressure is, whether they have ever had any of a list of diseases, and whether they test-fly experimental aircraft for a living, then you can predict—with a higher and higher degree of accuracy—whether they will die within the next 365 days. Each piece of data—each component of a construct you might call "lifestyle"—adds to your ability to predict something of interest.

The Bottom Line

The bottom line on all this is that although various forms of validity can be demonstrated,

Truth, with a capital T, is never final. We are never dead sure of anything in science. We try to get closer and closer to the truth by better and better measurement. All of science relies on concepts whose existence must ultimately be demonstrated by their effects. You can ram a car against a cement wall at 50 miles an hour and account for the amount of crumpling done to the radiator by referring to a concept called "force." You can't see force, but you can sure see its effects. The greater the force, the more crumpled the radiator. You demonstrate the existence of intelligence by showing how it predicts school achievement or monetary success (**Further Reading**: validity).

The Problem With Validity

If you suspect that there is something deeply, desperately wrong with all this, you're right. The whole argument for the validity (indeed, the very existence) of something like intelligence is, frankly, circular: How do you know that intelligence exists? Because you see its effects in achievement. And how do you account for achievement? By saying that someone has achieved highly because they're intelligent. How do you know machismo exists? Because men dominate women in some societies. And how do you account for dominance behavior, like wife beating? By saying that wife beaters are acting out their machismo.

In the hierarchy of construct reality, force ranks way up there (after all, it's got several hundred years of theory and experimentation behind it), while things like intelligence and machismo are pretty weak by comparison. And yet, as I made clear in Chapter 1, the social and behavioral sciences are roaring successes, on a par with the physical sciences in terms of the effects they have on our lives every day. This is possible because social scientists have refined and tested many useful concepts and measurements for those concepts.

Ultimately, the validity of any concept—force in physics, the self in psychology, modernization in sociology and political science, acculturation in anthropology—depends on two things: (1) the utility of the device that measures it and (2) the collective judgment of the scientific community that a concept and its measure are valid. In the end, we are left to deal with the effects of our judgments, which is just as it should be. Valid measurement makes valid data, but validity itself depends on the collective opinion of researchers.

CAUSE, EFFECT, AND THEORY

Cause and effect is among the most highly debated issues in the philosophy of knowledge. (See Hollis [1996] for a review.) We can never be absolutely certain that variation in one thing causes variation in another. Still, if measurements of two variables are valid, you can be reasonably confident that one variable causes another if four conditions are met.

1. The two variables co-vary—that is, as scores for one variable increase or decrease, scores for the other variable increase or decrease as well.

2. The covariation between the two variables is not **spurious**.

3. There is a **logical time order** to the variables. The presumed causal variable must always precede the other in time.

4. A mechanism is available that explains *how* an independent variable causes a dependent variable. There must, in other words, be a theory.

Condition 1: Covariation

When two variables are related they are said to co-vary. Covariation is also called **correlation** or simply **association**.

Association is not a **sufficient condition** for claiming a causal relation between two variables, but it is a **necessary condition**. Whatever else may be needed to establish cause and effect, you can't claim that one thing causes another if they aren't related in the first place.

Here are a few interesting covariations:

1. Sexual freedom for women tends to increase with the amount that women contribute to subsistence (Schlegel and Barry 1986).

2. Ground-floor, corner apartments occupied by students at big universities have a much higher chance of being burglarized than other units in the same apartment bloc (M. B. Robinson and C. E. Robinson 1997).

3. When married men and women are both employed full time, they spend the same amount of time in the various rooms of their house—except for the kitchen (Ahrentzen et al. 1989).

4. When eyewitnesses are pressured, they are more likely to pick a suspect out of a police line-up than if they are left alone to make their decision (Steblay 1997).

5. The more people of all ages are exposed to violence on television the more likely they are to show aggressive or antisocial behavior (Paik and Comstock 1994).

You might think that to establish cause, independent variables would have to be strongly related to the dependent variable. Not always. People all over the world make decisions about whether or not to use (or demand the use of) a condom as a part of sexual relations. These decisions are based on many factors, all of which may be weakly but causally related to the ultimate decision. These factors include: the education level of one or both partners; the level of income of one or both partners; the availability and cost of condoms; the amount of time that partners have been together; the amount of previous sexual experience of one or both partners; whether either or both partners know anyone personally who has died of AIDS; and so on.

Each independent variable may contribute only a little to the outcome of the dependent variable (the decision that is finally made), but the contribution may be quite direct and causal.

Condition 2: Lack of Spuriousness

Just as weak correlations can be causal, strong correlations can turn out not to be. When this happens, the original correlation is said to be spurious. There is a correlation between the number of firefighters at a fire and the amount of damage done: the more firefighters, the higher the insurance claim. You could easily conclude that firefighters cause fire damage.

We know better: Both the amount of damage and the number of firefighters is caused by the size of the blaze. We need to control for this third variable—the size of the blaze—to understand what's really going on.

Young and Minai (2001) found that the number of clinics available, per 100,000 people, in Japan was *positively* and significantly correlated with the rate of mortality for men. It turns out that newly industrialized prefectures attracted lots of doctors who opened clinics *and* lots of male migrants from the countryside in search of jobs. It also turns out that being alone, as a migrant, away from the social support of rural communities, raises the probability of male mortality. In other words, the rise in the number of clinics was simultaneous with a rise in the rate of men dying, but the relationship between these variables was spurious.

Dellino (1984) found an inverse relation between perceived quality of life and involvement with the tourism industry on the island of Exuma in the Bahamas. When he controlled for the size of the community (he studied several on the island), the original correlation disappeared. People in the more congested areas were more likely to score low on the perceived-quality-of-life index whether or not they were involved with tourism, while those in the small, outlying communities were more likely to score high on the index. People in the congested areas were also more likely to be involved in tourism-related activities, because that's where the tourists go.

The list of spurious relations is endless, and it is not always easy to detect them for the frauds that they are. A higher percentage of men get lung cancer than women, but when you control for the length of time that people have smoked, the gender difference in carcinomas vanishes. Pretty consistently, young people accept new technologies more readily than older people. But in many societies, the relation between age and readiness to adopt innovations disappears when you control for level of education. Urban migrants from tribal groups often give up polygyny in Africa and Asia, but both migration *and* abandonment of polygyny are often caused by a third factor: lack of wealth.

Your only defense against spurious covariations is vigilance. No matter how obvious a covariation may appear, discuss it with disinterested colleagues—people who have no stake at all in telling you what you want to hear. Present your initial findings in class seminars at your university or where you work. Beg people to find potentially spurious relations in your work. You'll thank them for it if they do.

Condition 3: Precedence, or Time Order

Besides a nonspurious association, something else is required to establish a cause-and-effect relation between two variables: a logical time order. Firefighters don't cause fires—they show up *after* the blaze starts. African Americans have higher blood pressure, on average, than Whites do, but high blood pressure does not cause people to be African American.

Unfortunately, things are not always so clear cut. Does adoption of new technologies cause wealth, or is it the other way around? Does urban migration cause dissatisfaction with rural life, or the reverse? Does consumer demand cause new products to appear, or vice versa? Does the growth in the number of lawsuits cause more people to study law so that they can cash in, or does overproduction of lawyers cause more lawsuits?

What about the increase in elective surgery in the United States? Does the increased supply of physicians cause an increase in elective surgery, or does the demand for surgery create a surfeit of surgeons? Or are both caused by one or more external variables, like an increase in discretionary income in the upper middle class, or the fact that insurance companies pay more and more of Americans' medical bills?

Figure 2.4 shows several forms of time order between two variables. Read Figure 2.4(a) as "*a* is antecedent to *b*." Read Figure 2.4(b) as "*a* and *b* are antecedent to *c*." And read Figure 2.4(c) as "*a* is antecedent to *b* which is an intervening variable antecedent to *c*." A lot of data analysis in social science is about understanding and controlling for antecedent and intervening variables—about which more in Chapter 21.

Condition 4: Theory, or Mechanism

Finally, even when you have established nonspurious covariation and a logical time sequence for two or more variables, you need a theory—a mechanism—that *explains* the association. Theories are ideas about how things work. Good theories are good ideas about how things work—that is, ideas that have held up against challenges and that explain new cases of things as they come up.

One of my favorites is called cognitive dissonance theory (Festinger 1957). It's based on the insight that: (1) people can tell when their beliefs about what *ought* to be don't match their perception of how things really are; and

Figure 2.4   Time Order Between Two or Three Variables

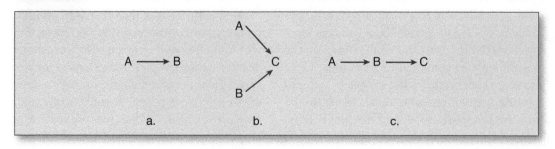

(2) this causes an uncomfortable feeling. The feeling is called cognitive dissonance. People then have a choice: They can live with the dissonance (be uncomfortable); change the external reality (fight city hall); or change their beliefs (usually the path of least resistance, but not necessarily the easy way out).

Cognitive dissonance theory helps explain why some people accept new technologies that they initially reject out of fear for their jobs: Once a technology is entrenched, and there is no chance of getting rid of it, it's easier to change your ideas about what's good and what's bad than it is to live with dissonance (Bernard and Pelto 1987). Dissonance theory helps explain why men in countries across the world are increasingly accepting of women working outside the home: When economic necessity drives women into the work force, it's painful to hold onto the idea that that's the wrong thing for women to do.

On the other hand, some people do actually quit their jobs rather than accept new technologies, and some men continue to argue against women working outside the home, even when those men depend on their wives' income to make ends meet. This is an example of a general theory that fails to predict local phenomena. It leads us to seek more data and more understanding to predict when cognitive dissonance theory is insufficient as an explanation.

The literature is filled with good ideas for how to explain covariations. There is a well-known correlation between average daily temperature and the number of violent crimes reported to police (C. A. Anderson 1989; Cohn 1990). The association between temperature and violence, however, is neither as direct nor as simple as the correlational evidence might make it appear. **Routine activity theory** (Cohen and Felson 1979) states that if you want to understand what people are doing, start with what they usually do. **Social contact theory** (Allport 1979 [1954]) states that if you want to understand the probability for any event that involves human interaction, start by mapping activities that place people in contact with one another. Both of these theories are examples of Ockham's famous razor (see Box 2.5, above).

Following routine activity theory, we find out that people are likely to be indoors, working, or going to school in air-conditioned comfort, during the hottest part of the day from Monday through Friday. Following social contact theory, we find that on very hot days, people are more likely to go out during the evening hours—which places them in more contact with one another. People also drink more alcohol during the evening hours. These facts, not temperature per se, may account for violence. Applying these theories, Cohn and Rotton (1997) found that more crimes of violence *are* reported to police on hot days than on cool days, but those crimes are, in fact, more likely to occur during the cooler evening hours than during the hottest part of the day.

Many theories are developed to explain a purely local phenomenon and then turn out to have wider applicability. Anthropologists have noticed that when men from polygynous African societies move to cities, they often give up polygyny. This consistent covariation is explained by the fact that men who move away from tribal territories in search of wage labor must abandon their land, their houses, and the shared labor of their kinsmen. Under those conditions, they simply cannot afford to provide for more than one wife, much less the children that multiple wives produce. The relation between urbanization and changes in marriage customs is explained by antecedent and intervening variables.

If you read the literature across the social sciences, you'll see references to something called contagion theory. This one invokes a copycat mechanism to explain why suicides are more likely to come in batches when one of them is widely publicized in the press (Romer et al. 2006) and why more women candidates stand for election in districts that already have women legislators in office (Matland and Studlar 1996).

Relative deprivation theory is based on the insight that people compare themselves to specific peer groups, not to the world at large (Martin 1981; Stouffer et al. 1949). It explains why sociology professors don't feel all that badly about engineering professors earning a lot of money, but hate it if psychologists or anthropologists in their university get significantly higher salaries. World systems theory proposes that the world's economies and political bodies are part of a single capitalist system that has a core and a periphery and that each nation can be understood in some sense by examining its place in that system.

All such theories start with one or two primitive axioms—things that are simply defined and that you have to take at face value. The definition of cognitive dissonance is an example: When people have inconsistent beliefs, or when they perceive things in the real world to be out of whack with their ideas of how things *should* be, they feel discomfort. This discomfort leads people to strive naturally toward cognitive consonance. Neither the fact of dissonance, nor the discomfort it produces, nor the desire for consonance is ever explained. They are primitive axioms. *How* people deal with dissonance and *how* they try to achieve consonance are areas for empirical research. As empirical research accumulates, the theory is tested and refined (Box 2.6).

Box 2.6 Cultural consonance theory

William Dressler developed his theory of **cultural consonance** based on cognitive dissonance theory. Cultural consonance is the degree to which people's lives mirror a widely shared set of beliefs about what lives should look like. What's a successful life? This differs from culture to culture, but in many cultures, the list of things that indicate success is widely shared. Dressler and his colleagues have found that people who have more of these things (whose lives are in consonance with the cultural model) have lower stress and fewer blood pressure problems than do people whose lives lack cultural consonance (Dressler et al. 1997, 2002; Dressler, Balieiro et al. 2007; Dressler, Ribeiro et al. 2004, and see Chapter 16 on measuring cultural consensus).

In relative deprivation theory, the fact that people have reference groups to which they compare themselves doesn't get explained, either. It, too, is a primitive axiom, an assumption, from which you deduce some results. The results are predictions, or hypotheses, that you then go out and test. The ideal in science is to deduce a prediction from theory and to test the prediction. That's the culture of science. The way social science really works much of the time is that you don't predict results, you postdict them. You analyze your data, come up with findings, and explain the findings after the fact.

There is nothing wrong with this. Knowledge and understanding can come from good ideas before you collect data or after you collect data. You must admit, though, there's a certain panache in making a prediction, sealing it in an envelope, and testing it. Later, when you take the prediction out of the envelope and it matches your empirical findings, you get a lot of points (**Further Reading:** theory and causal analysis in the social sciences).

THE KALYMNIAN CASE: EXPLAINING WHY PEOPLE RISK THEIR LIVES

Here's an example of explaining findings after the fact. In my experience, it's pretty typical of how social scientists develop, refine, and change their minds about theories.

In my work in 1964–1965 on the island of Kalymnos, Greece, I noticed that young sponge divers (in their 20s) were more likely to get the bends than were older divers (those over 30). (The bends is a crippling malady that affects divers who come up too quickly after a long time in deep water.) I also noticed that younger divers were more productive than very old divers (those over 45), but not more productive than those in their middle years (30–40).

As it turned out, younger divers were subject to much greater social stress to demonstrate their daring and to take risks with their lives—risks that men over 30 had already put behind them. The younger divers worked longer under water (gathering more sponges), but they came up faster and were consequently at higher risk of bends. The middle group of divers made up in experience for the shortened time they spent in the water, so they maintained their high productivity at lower risk of bends. The older divers were feeling the effects of infirmity brought on by years of deep diving, hence their productivity was lowered, along with their risk of death or injury from bends.

The real question was: What caused the young Kalymnian divers to engage in acts that placed them at greater risk?

My first attempt at explaining all this was pretty lame. I noticed that the men who took the most chances with their lives had a certain rhetoric and swagger. They were called *levédhis* (Greek for a brave young man) by other divers and by their captains. I concluded that these men had more *levedhiá* (the quality of being brave and young) and that this made them higher risk takers. In fact, this is what many of my informants told me. Young men, they said, feel the need to show their manhood, and that's why they take risks by staying down too long and coming up too fast.

The problem with this cultural explanation was that it just didn't explain anything. Yes, the high risk takers swaggered and exhibited something we could label "machismo" or "*levedhiá.*" But what good did it do to say that lots of machismo caused people to dive deep and come up quickly? Where did young men get this feeling, I asked? "That's just how young men are," my informants told me. I reckoned that there might be something to this testosterone-poisoning theory, but it didn't seem adequate.

Eventually, I saw that the swaggering behavior and the values voiced about manliness were cultural ways to ratify, not explain, the high-risk diving behavior. Both the diving behavior and the ratifying behavior were the product of a third variable, an economic distribution system called *plátika*.

Divers traditionally took their entire season's expected earnings in advance, before shipping out in April for the 6-month sponge fishing expedition in North Africa. By taking their money (*plátika*) in advance, they placed themselves in debt to the boat captains. Just before they shipped out, the divers would pay off the debts that their families had accumulated during the preceding year. By the time they went to sea, the divers were nearly broke and their families started going into debt again for food and other necessities.

In the late 1950s, synthetic sponges began to take over the world markets, and young men on Kalymnos left for overseas jobs rather than go into sponge fishing. As divers left the island, the remaining divers demanded higher and higher *plátika*. They said that it was to compensate them for increases in the cost of living, but their demand for more money was a pure response by the divers to the increasing scarcity of their labor.

The price of sponges, however, was dropping over the long term, due to competition with synthetics, so the higher *plátika* for the divers meant that the boat captains were losing profits. The captains put more and more pressure on the divers to produce more sponges, to stay down longer, and to take greater risks. This resulted in more accidents on the job (Bernard 1967, 1987).

Note that in all the examples of theory I've just given, the predictions and the post hoc explanations, I didn't have to quote a single statistic—not even a percentage score. That's because theories are qualitative. Ideas about cause and effect are based on insight; they are derived from either qualitative or quantitative observations and are initially expressed in words. *Testing* causal statements—finding out *how much* they explain rather than *whether* they seem to be plausible explanations—requires quantitative observations. But theory construction—explanation itself—is the quintessential qualitative act.

Key Concepts in This Chapter

variable	intersubjective	ecological fallacy
unidimensional variables	Attitudes Toward Women	validity
multidimensional variables	Scale (AWS)	reliability
dichotomous variables	levels of measurement	precision
dependent variables	nominal variables	accuracy
independent variables	ordinal variables	systematic bias
educational model of social	interval variables	instrument validity
change	quantitative measurement	data validity
indicators of variables	ratio variables	finding, or conclusion
values of variables	zero point	validity
concepts	observables	recalibration
constructs	qualitative measurement	interobserver reliability
socioeconomic status (SES)	unit of analysis	test-retest reliability
conceptual definitions	aggregate data	parallel test forms
operational definitions	disaggregated data	split-half reliability

face validity

content validity

construct validity

criterion validity

parsimony, or Ockham's
    razor

known group comparisons

predictive validity

covariation, or correlation,
    or association

spurious correlations

logical time order of
    variables

sufficient condition

necessary condition

controlling for a third
    variable

antecedent variables

intervening variables

theory, or mechanism

cognitive dissonance theory

routine activity theory

social contact theory

contagion theory

relative deprivation theory

primitive axioms

cultural consonance

postdiction

Summary

- Social research is about variables—that is, about characteristics of people, countries, organizations, or other units of analysis and how variables are related to one another.
- A controversial foundation of modern social research is operationism, which involves making absolutely explicit how variables are measured.
  - The main advantage of operationism is that researchers can replicate one another's work and build cumulative knowledge.
  - The main disadvantage of operationism is that it forces us to measure complex variables—like compassion, religiosity, political orientation, and the like—using simple tools. There is, then, the risk of trivializing the process of research.
  - On balance, more social scientists rely on operationism than criticize it, but this varies across the social science disciplines.
- Measurement in the social sciences can be at the nominal, ordinal, or interval/ratio level.
  - Ratio-level variables have a true zero point.
  - The rule is always to measure at the highest level of measurement possible. You can turn a variable measured at the ratio level into an ordinal or a nominal variable, but you can't go the other way.
- In developing measures for variables, researchers are concerned with the problems of reliability, validity, precision, and accuracy.
  - Reliability is a necessary but insufficient condition for validity. Validity is never proven absolutely, but is a goal toward which we strive.
  - Theory is explanation, which involves establishing an association between variables, eliminating the possibility that the association is spurious, establishing a logical time order, and developing a real-life mechanism that links the variables in a cause-effect relation.

Exercises

1. Ask 20 people a question that requires a self-report of behavior. For example, ask "How many times during the last month have you cut class?" Then, ask the same people "How many times during the last week have you cut class?" At the end of the interview, ask people to explain how they figured out what to say in answering your question. Did people think about and count up the actual incidents, or did they estimate the number of incidents? If they

estimated, then ask them how they did that and try to understand the rules of inference they used.

Calculate the per-week average for the one-month question and the average for the one-week question. Are the two averages the same?

2. Common wisdom has it that as people grow older, their idea of how old you have to be in order to be middle aged changes. To test this hypothesis, produce a copy of Figure 2.3 on a blank sheet of paper and use that instrument to collect some data from people of different ages.

3. Here is a list of adjectives, each of which is a concept that is of interest to social researchers. Try to conceptualize and operationalize these concepts that describe characteristics of individual people: poor, religious, macho, affluent, abusive. Suppose we want to array the countries of the world according to how much economic freedom and how much political freedom their citizens have. How can we conceptualize and operationalize economic and political freedom?

4. Using concrete examples, explain the characteristics of nominal, ordinal, and interval/ratio measurements. How would you measure each of the following, using at least two different levels of measurement: (a) age; (b) income; (c) family size.

5. Discuss the difference between validity and reliability. Why is it so hard to establish validity?

6. Ask some people if they consider themselves to be politically liberal or politically conservative. Some people will find the question unanswerable, but some people will answer the question. Repeat this until you have data from 20 people. This question will create data at the nominal level of measurement. In the same interview, ask those 20 people whether they consider themselves very liberal (or very conservative), somewhat liberal (conservative), or mildly liberal (conservative). This will create some data at the ordinal level of measurement.

Finally, ask those same 20 people a series of focused issue questions. Here are a few examples: (a) Are you in favor of an adult woman's right to an abortion, entirely at her own discretion, or are you opposed to women having that right? (b) Are you in favor of the death penalty for premeditated murder or are you opposed to the death penalty for that crime? (c) Are you in favor of sending our troops to [fill in whatever country of is in the news at the moment] to fight a ground war or are you opposed to sending troops?

These questions, or questions like them, will create data at the nominal level of measurement. Keep careful track of the reactions of your respondents and write up your findings. Among other things, you may find that people who say they are very conservative or very liberal fail to answer specific issue questions in ways you might expect. Why is that?

Further Reading

The language and logic of social research. Campbell and Overman (1988), Campbell and Stanley (1963), T. D. Cook and Campbell (1979), Gubrium and Holstein (1997), Lazarsfeld (1993), Lazarsfeld and Rosenberg (1955), Merton and Lazarsfeld (1950).

Measuring gender across cultures. Belansky and Boggiano (1994), Gaziolglu (2008), Green and Kenrick (1994), Lippa (1991), Ozkan and Lajunen (2005), Peng (2006), Ruffing-Rahal et al. (1998), Wark and Krebs (1996), Zoccali et al. (2008).

Measurement in the social sciences. Blalock (1974), Coombs (1964), Lester and Bishop (1997), Miller and Salkind (2002), Nunnally (1978), Stevens (1946).

Operationism. Bridgman (1927), Lundberg (1942, 1964). For a critique: Lincoln and Guba (1985).

The AWS. Loo and Thorpe (1998, 2005), Spence and Hahn (1997), Twenge (1997).

The ecological inference problem. Clancy et al. (2003), Dunier (2006), King (1997), King et al. (2004), van Poppel and Day (1996).

Respondent accuracy. Bernard, Killworth et al. (1984), Brewer (2000), Brewer and Yang (1994), Freeman et al. (1987), Frenk et al. (2011), Godoy et al. (1998), Jackson and Nuttall (1997), Poulin (2010), Ricci et al. (1995), Roberts et al. (2005), Romney et al. (1986), Tanur (1992), Schwarz (1999), Sudman et al. (1996), Vadez et al. (2003), Wutich (2009).

Validity. Campbell and Fiske (1959), Fiske (1982).

Theory and causal analysis in the social sciences. Abbot (1998), Baert (1998), Barnes (1995), Bell (2009), Cambell and Stanley (1963), T. D. Cook et al. (2008), Craib (1997), Cullen and Wilcox (2010), DiMaggio (1995), Harris (1979), Kaufman and Poole (2000), Kincaid (1996), Rubin (1974), Shadish et al. (2002), Stinchcombe (1968), Sutton and Staw (1990), Swaen and van Amelsvoort (2009), Weik (1995), Winch (1990).

3

Preparing
for Research

SETTING THINGS UP

This chapter is about some of the things that go on *before* data are collected and analyzed. First, I'll take you through the ideal research process and compare that to how research really gets done. I'll discuss the problem of choosing problems—how do I know what to study?—and I'll give you some pointers on how to scour the literature so you can benefit from the work of others when you start a research project.

The Ideal Research Process

Despite all the myths about how research is done, it's actually a messy process that's cleaned up in the reporting of results. Figure 3.1 shows how the research process is supposed to work in the ideal world:

1. First, a theoretical problem is formulated.

2. Next, an appropriate site and method are selected.

3. Then, data are collected and analyzed.

4. Finally, the theoretical proposition with which the research was launched is either challenged or supported.

In fact, all kinds of practical and intellectual issues get in the way of this neat scheme. In the end, research papers are written so that the chaotic aspects of research are not emphasized, and the orderly inputs and outcomes are.

I see nothing wrong with this: It would be a monumental waste of precious space in books and journals to describe the *real* research process for every project that's reported. Besides, every seasoned researcher knows just how messy it all is, anyway. On the other hand, you shouldn't have to become a highly experienced researcher before you're let into the secret of how it's really done.

A Realistic Approach

There are five questions to ask yourself about every research question you are thinking about pursuing. Most of these can also be asked about potential research sites and research methods. If you answer these questions honestly (at least to yourself), chances are you'll do good research every time. If you cheat on this test, even a teeny bit, chances are you'll regret it. The questions, in no particular order, are

1. Does this topic (or research site, or data collection method) really interest me?

2. Is this a problem that is amenable to scientific inquiry?

3. Are adequate resources available to investigate this topic? To study this population at this particular research site? To use this particular data collection method?

Figure 3.1 How Research Is Supposed to Work

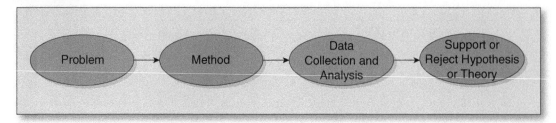

4. Will my research question, or the methods I want to use, lead to unresolvable ethical problems?

5. Is the topic of theoretical and/or practical interest?

Personal Interest

The first thing to ask about any potential research question is: Am I really excited about this? Researchers do their best work when they are genuinely having fun, so don't do boring research when you can choose any topic you like.

You can't always choose any topic you like. In contract research, you sometimes have to take on a research question that a client finds interesting but that you find deadly dull. The most boring research I've ever done was on a contract where my coworkers and I combined ethnographic and survey research of rural homeowners' knowledge of fire prevention and their attitudes toward volunteer fire departments. This was in 1973. I had young children at home and the research contract paid me a summer salary. It was honest work and I delivered a good product to the agency that supported the project. But I never wrote up the results for publication.

By comparison, that same year I did some contract research on the effects of coed prisons on homosexuality among male and female inmates. I was very interested in that study and it was much easier to spend the extra time and effort polishing the contract reports for publication (Killworth and Bernard 1974).

I've seen many students doing research for term projects, M.A. theses, and even doctoral dissertations simply out of convenience and with no enthusiasm for the topic. If you are not interested in a research question, then no matter how important other people tell you it is, don't bother with it. If others are so sure that it's a dynamite topic of great theoretical significance, let *them* study it.

The same goes for research populations. If you select a topic of interest, and then try to test it on a population in which you have no interest, your research will probably suffer. Some nursing researchers enjoy working in the maternity ward, while others are drawn to pediatric oncology. The maternity ward is filled with children being born, and the oncology ward with children who are facing death. It doesn't take much to imagine that some people who love working around newborns are going to be less than enthusiastic about doing research in pediatric oncology.

It doesn't matter whether you're going to do experiments, conduct a telephone survey, or do in-depth ethnographic interviews: Enthusiasm counts for a lot in research. Federal prisons and Wall Street banking firms are both complex organizations. But they are very, very different kinds of places to spend time in, so if you are going to study a complex organization, check your gut first and make sure you're excited about where you're going. It's really hard to conduct penetrating, in-depth interviews over a period of a several weeks to a year if you aren't interested in the lives of the people you're studying.

And if you think it's tough to run personal interviews on a topic you're bored with, try making up and administering a 10-page questionnaire on a topic of no interest to you. Or try designing an experiment in which you have to run subjects for months on end and where you have no personal stake in the results. It's not just deadly dull, it's a recipe for bad research.

You don't need any justification for your interest in studying a particular group of people or a particular topic. Personal interest is . . . well, personal. So ask yourself: Will my interest be sustained there? If the answer is "no," then reconsider. Accessibility of a research site or the availability of funds for the conduct of a survey are pluses, but by themselves they're not enough to make good research happen.

Science Versus Nonscience

If you're really excited about a research topic, then the next question is: Is this a topic that can be studied by the methods of science? If the answer is "no," then no matter how much fun it is, and no matter how important it seems, don't even try to make a scientific study of it. Either let someone else do it, or use a different approach.

Consider this empirical question: How often do derogatory references to women occur in the Old Testament? If you can come up with a good, operational definition of "derogatory," then you can answer this question by looking through the corpus of data and counting the instances that turn up. Pretty straightforward, descriptive science.

But consider this question: Does the Old Testament offer support for unequal pay for women today? This is simply not answerable by the scientific method. It is no more answerable than the question: Is Rachmaninoff's music better than Tchaikovsky's? Or: Is it morally correct to mainstream slightly retarded children in grades K–6? Or: Is Britain's parliamentary system or the U.S.'s presidential system a better form of democracy? Or: Should the remaining hunting-and-gathering bands of the world be preserved just the way they are and kept from being spoiled by modern civilization?

Whether or not a study is a scientific one depends first on the nature of the question being asked and *then* on the methods used.

I can't stress too often or too strongly that when I talk about using the scientific method I'm *not* talking about numbers. In science, whenever a research problem can be investigated with quantitative measurement, numbers are more than just desirable, they're required. On the other hand, there are many intellectual problems for which quantitative measures are not yet available. Those problems require qualitative measurement.

First-pass descriptions of processes (preparing for surgery, putting on makeup, setting the table for Thanksgiving), or of events (weddings, football games, art shows), or of systems of nomenclature (kinds of trucks, ways to avoid getting AIDS) require words, not numbers. Dorothy Holland and Debra Skinner (1987) asked some university women to list the kinds of guys there are. They got a list of words like "creep," "hunk," "nerd," "jerk," "sweetie pie," and so on. Then they asked some women, for each kind: "Is this someone you'd like to date?" The yes-no answers are nominal—that is, qualitative—measurement.

We'll get back to this kind of systematic collection of qualitative data in Chapter 10.

Resources

The next question to ask is whether adequate resources are available for you to conduct your study. There are three major kinds of resources: time, money, and people. What may be adequate for some projects may be inadequate for others. Be totally honest with yourself about this issue.

Time

Some social research projects can be completed in just a few days, while others take years. It takes a year or more to do an ethnographic study of a culture that is very different from your own, but a lot of focused ethnography can be done much more quickly. Gwendolyn Dordick (1996) spent 3 months studying a homeless shelter for 700 men in New York City. She visited the shelter four times a week for 3 hours or more each time, and spent 4 days at the shelter from morning until lights-out at 10 p.m. This was enough time for her to understand a great deal about life in the shelter, including how a group of just 15 men had coalesced into a ruling elite and how some men had formed faux marriages (that could, but did not necessarily, involve sex) to protect themselves and their few possessions from violence and thievery.

Some experiments in social psychology can also take months or years to set up, especially in evaluation studies. By contrast, the data-collection phase of surveys and of some types of experiments might be completed in a matter of weeks.

If you are doing research for a term project, the topic has to be something you can look at in a matter of a few months—and squeezing the research into a schedule of other classes, at that. It makes no sense to select a topic that requires two semesters' work when you have one semester in which to do the research. This effort to cram 10 gallons of water into a 5-gallon can is futile and quite common. Don't do it.

Money

Many things come under the umbrella of money. Equipment is essentially a money issue, as is salary or subsistence for you and other persons involved in the research. Funds for assistants, supplies, and travel all have to be calculated before you can actually conduct a major research project. No matter how interesting it is to you, and no matter how important it may seem theoretically, if you haven't got the resources to use the right methods, skip it for now.

Naturally, most people do not have the money it takes to mount a major research effort. That's why there are granting agencies. Writing proposals is a special craft. It pays to learn it early. Research grants for MA research are typically between $1,000 and $5,000. Grants for doctoral research are typically between $10,000 and $40,000. If you spend 100 hours working on a grant proposal that brings you $10,000 to do your research, that's $100/hr for your time. If you get turned down and spend another 100 hours rewriting the proposal, that's still $50 an hour for your time if you're successful. Pretty good pay for interesting work.

If your research requires the comparison of two panels of respondents using face-to-face interviews and you have only enough money to do telephone interviews, ask yourself if you can accomplish your research goal by using telephone interviews. If you can't, then can

you accomplish it by cutting out the comparison and running the more expensive interviews on just one group? Ask yourself whether it's worthwhile pursuing your research if it has to be scaled down to fit available resources. If the answer is "no," then find another topic.

People

"People" includes you and others involved in the research, as well as those whom you are studying. Does the research require that you do logistic regression? If it does, then are you prepared to acquire that skill? Does the research require access to or acceptance by a particular group of people, like ambulance paramedics? Do you have access to that group?

Does the research require that you speak Haitian Creole? If so, are you willing to put in the time and effort to learn that language? If the research can be done with interpreters, are competent people available at a cost that you can handle?

Will the research require that you interview elite members of the society you are studying—like medical malpractice lawyers, plastic surgeons, Lutheran priests? Do you have access to these populations? Will you be able to gain their cooperation? Or will they tell you to get lost or, even worse, provide you with perfunctory answers to your questions. Better not do the study in the first place than wind up with useless data.

THE ETHICS OF SOCIAL RESEARCH

I wish I could give you a list of criteria against which you could measure the "ethicalness" of every research idea you ever come up with. Unfortunately, it's not so simple. The fact is, what is popularly ethical research today may become popularly unethical tomorrow, and vice versa. (This does *not* mean that all ethics are relative. But more on that later.)

During World War II, many social scientists worked for what would today be called the Department of Defense and they were applauded as patriots for lending their expertise to the war effort. Twenty-five years later, during the Vietnam War, social scientists who worked for the Department of Defense were excoriated. Today, social scientists are participating in U.S. military programs for studying local culture in battle zones. This, too, has produced intense debate about the proper role, if any, of social scientists in military and intelligence operations (Rohde 2007) (**Further Reading:** social science in the military and in intelligence).

Milgram's Obedience Experiment

It's because popular ethics change that Stanley Milgram was able to conduct his famous experiment on obedience in the 1960s. Milgram (1963, 1965) duped people into thinking that they were taking part in an experiment on how well human beings learn under conditions of punishment. The subjects in the experiment were "teachers." The "learners" were Milgram's accomplices. The idea was to see how obedient people would be—how much electrical shock they would administer to a "learner" when told to do so by someone in authority, like an experimenter in a lab coat.

Milgram varied the conditions in his experiments to test for gender differences, for differences in locale (the Yale University campus vs. a run-down building in downtown Bridgeport, Connecticut), and for differences the proximity of the experimenter and the victim to the subject (in the same room, in different rooms), but in all the experiments, the basics were the same. The subjects sat at a panel of 30 switches, labeled from 15 volts to 450 volts. There was a label every fourth switch (that is, every 60 volts), from "Slight Shock" (15 volts) all the way up to "Danger: Severe Shock" (375 volts) and XXX (435 volts and 450 volts). Each time the learner made a mistake on a word-recall test, the subject was told to give the learner a bigger shock.

Milgram paid each participant $4.50 up front (about $35 in 2012), to make them feel obligated to go through with the experiment. He also gave them a little test shock—45 volts (the second lever on the 30-lever panel)—to make them believe that the punishment they'd be delivering to the so-called learners was for real.

In many of the experiments, the learner grunted at 75 volts. The reaction escalated as the putative voltage increased. At 150 volts, learners began pleading to be let out of the experiment. At 285 volts, the learner's response, as Milgram reported it, could "only be described as an agonizing scream" (1974:4). All those reactions by the learners were actually played back from tape so that subjects would hear exactly the same things. The experimenter, in an official-looking lab coat, kept telling the subject to administer the shocks—saying things like: "You have no choice. You must go on."

Most of those who dropped out of Milgram's experiments did so after administering 150-volt shocks. But 65% of the subjects in the original experiment (where, by the way, the learner didn't complain until the subject supposedly gave him a 300-volt shock and then pounded on the wall of the room separating him from the subject) obeyed orders and administered what they thought were shocks beyond the XXX level. Many subjects protested but were convinced by the researchers that it was all right to follow orders.

Milgram's full experiment probably wouldn't get by any committee for the protection of human subjects now, but Jerry Burger (2009) was able to replicate Milgram's original experiment up to the crucial 150-volt limit. The bottom line: 28 of Burger's 40 subjects agreed to continue after the 150-volt limit.

Were Milgram's experiments unethical? Did Milgram cause his subjects emotional harm when they thought about what they'd done? If you were among Milgram's subjects who obeyed to the end, would you be haunted by this? The literature on this is mixed (see Murray [1980] and Herrera [2001] for contrasting views), but we do know this: Milgram's make-believe experiment was less costly and more ethical than the natural experiments carried out at My Lai, and Shatila, and Srebenica—the Vietnamese village (in 1968), the Lebanese refugee camp (in 1982), and the Bosnian village (in 1995)—whose civilian inhabitants were wiped out by American, Lebanese, and Serbian soldiers, respectively, "under orders."

Those experiments, too, showed what ordinary people are capable of doing—except that in those cases, real people really got killed. Until Milgram did his experiments, it had been easy to scoff at Nazi war criminals whose defense was that they were "just following orders." In 1979, Milgram was asked on CBS's show, *Sixty Minutes*, if that sort of thing could happen again. His answer: "Having observed a thousand people in the experiment . . . if a system of death camps were set up in the United States of the sort we had seen in Nazi Germany, one would be able to find sufficient personnel for those camps in any medium-sized American town" (quoted in Blass 1999:955).

Zimbardo's Stanford Prison Experiment

In 1971, Philip Zimbardo and his colleagues built a mock prison in the basement of the psychology building at Stanford University. They put an ad in the newspaper, asking for college-student volunteers to participate in a study of prison life. They screened 75 young men and chose 21 whom they felt were the most mature and stable—people who could take the planned 2 weeks of role playing in the "Stanford County Prison."

These researchers had a rude shock ahead of them. "Most dramatic and distressing to us," they wrote at the end of the experiment, "was the ease with which sadistic behavior could be elicited from individuals who were not 'sadistic types' and the frequency with which acute emotional breakdowns could occur in men selected precisely for their emotional stability" (Haney et al. 1973:89).

The 21 recruits, all White men between 17 and 30, were told that if they were assigned to be prisoners, they should expect to go through a hard time for 2 weeks—no physical violence would be tolerated, but prisoners would give up privacy and other basic rights for the duration of the experiment. The participants would get $15 per day for their participation in the study (about $80 in 2012), and could quit at any time, but they would forfeit the money if they did so.

Once everyone was on board and fully briefed, the experimenters assigned 10 of the men randomly to be prisoners and 11 to be guards. The guards were issued uniforms, whistles, and night sticks and were told they would serve on three-man, 8-hour shifts around the clock. Then everyone went home to wait.

When the time came for the experiment to begin, the Palo Alto City Police Department sent real officers to the homes of the "prisoners." The police handcuffed the prisoners and hustled them off to jail, sometimes in full view of neighbors. The prisoners were fingerprinted, placed in a detention cell, and then taken to the makeshift prison at Stanford University, where the guards were waiting. There, they were stripped and sprayed with what they were told was a delousing solution (it was really deodorant). They were issued smocks, with a number painted on the front and back, and no underwear. They were made to stand for mug shots in the humiliating uniforms and were given work assignments, exercise periods, and movie rights. Then they were assigned, randomly, three at a time, to 6×9 ft. cells. The cell doors shut.

Though no physical violence was allowed, the guards quickly became verbally abusive and learned to use every bit of the power they had. Prisoners had to ask permission to light a cigarette, read a novel, write a letter, go to the toilet—permission that some of the guards arbitrarily denied. When the prisoners were allowed to go to the toilet, they were blindfolded and handcuffed and led, publicly, from their cells by some guards. Some guards called the prisoners "girls," referring to the smock uniforms.

The prisoners became docile and passive. During the debriefing, after the experiment, some prisoners said they thought that the roles had been defined by size, with the larger men assigned the role of guard. In fact, the roles had been assigned randomly and there was no difference in the average weight of the guards and prisoners.

Some guards tried not to get into this abusive behavior pattern. But they immediately bought into the norm of never interfering with another guard whose behavior they didn't approve. They went along to get along.

By the second day, the guards had defined eating and sleeping time as privileges, and four of the prisoners had gone into what the experimenters diagnosed as "extreme emotional depression . . . and acute anxiety," accompanied by crying and rage (Haney et al. 1973:81). These four were released from the experiment, as was a fifth who had to be treated for a psychosomatic rash that covered parts of his body. Three times a day, the guards took the prisoners out of the cells for a count. On the first day, the counts lasted a few minutes. By the fifth day, the counts were lasting hours.

Five prisoners stuck it out. The warden of the prison held a hearing and asked each of the five if they would forfeit the money they were due if they were paroled and released early from the experiment. Three of them said they would. By the time of the so-called parole hearing, the prisoners were owed $75 apiece— about $400 today. When they were told that any decision to parole them would have to be discussed with the staff, each prisoner went quietly back to his cell.

They didn't have to. They could have just quit what had become a very painful experience. "Yet, so powerful was the control which the situation had come to have over them, so much a reality had this simulated environment become . . . they returned to their cells to await a 'parole' decision by their captors" (Haney et al. 1973:93).

After 6 days, then, there were still two prisoners who wanted to continue, but the experiment was stopped. The researchers decided that they couldn't ethically continue. Besides, they had already learned enough to support Milgram's conclusion: Otherwise good people can be induced by circumstances to do evil things.

In a way, Zimbardo's experiment is even more frightening than Milgram's, something Zimbardo himself recognized immediately and has continued to talk about publicly (Zimbardo 1973, 2007, 2009). There were no men in white lab coats telling the guards that they had to harass their charges into acute anxiety, depression, and psychosomatic rashes. Everyone, guards and prisoners alike, knew at the outset that they could get out by just saying they *wanted* out.

Instead, the participants picked up the roles they were assigned and played them to the hilt. The guards had the freedom to define their role any way they wanted to—and did so by becoming abusive at the first opportunity they had. The prisoners who were emotionally disturbed in the first 2 days didn't ask to be released.

If you were assigned the role of guard in a replication of Zimbardo's experiment, would you become abusive? Before you answer, recall the pictures of American soldiers in 2003 laughing while psychologically torturing Iraqi prisoners of war at Abu Ghraib. And think about the title of Zimbardo's book (2007) summarizing 30 years of work: *The Lucifer Effect: Understanding How Good People Turn Evil* (**Further Reading:** Milgram's and Zimbardo's obedience experiments).

What Does It All Mean?

Just because times, and ethics, seem to change, does not mean that anything goes. Everyone agrees that scholars have ethical responsibilities, but not everyone agrees on what those responsibilities are. All the major scholarly societies have published their own code of ethics—all variations on the same theme, but all variations nonetheless. I've listed the Internet addresses for several of these codes of ethics in Appendix E.

These documents are not perfect, but they cover a lot of ground and are based on the accumulated experience of thousands of researchers who have grappled with ethical dilemmas over the past 60 years. Look at those codes of ethics regularly during the course of any research project, both to get some of the wisdom that has gone into them and to develop your own ideas about how the documents might be improved.

Don't get trapped into nihilistic relativism. Cultural relativism (the unassailable fact that people's ideas about what is good and beautiful are shaped by their culture) is a great antidote for overdeveloped ethnocentrism. But, as Merrilee Salmon makes clear (1997), ethical relativism (that all ethical systems are equally good since they are all cultural products) is something else entirely.

Can you imagine defending the human rights violations of Nazi Germany as just another expression of the richness of culture? Would you feel comfortable defending, on the basis of cultural relativism, the so-called ethnic cleansing in the 1990s of Bosnians and Kosovar Albanians by Serbs in the former Yugoslavia? Or the slaughter of Tutsis by Hutus in Rwanda? Or of American Indians by immigrant Europeans in the nineteenth century?

There is no value-free science. Everything that interests you as a potential research focus comes fully equipped with risks to you and to the people you study. Should social scientists do social marketing for a state lottery, knowing that poor people will be squandering their meager resources on false hopes of sudden riches? Or is social marketing only for getting people to use condoms and to wash their hands before preparing food?

How about working on projects that raise worker productivity in poverty zones if that means some workers will become redundant and lose their jobs? In each case, all you can do (and *must* do) is assess the potential human costs and the potential benefits. And when I say "potential benefits," I mean to you, personally, not just to humanity through the accumulation of knowledge.

Don't hide from the fact that you are interested in your own glory, your own career, your own advancement. It's a safe bet that your colleagues are interested in their career advancement, too. We have all heard of cases in which a scientist put his or her own career aggrandizement above the health and well-being of others. This is devastating to science, and to scientists, but it happens when otherwise good, ethical people (1) convince themselves that they are doing something noble for humanity, rather than for themselves; and (2) consequently fool themselves into thinking that *that* justifies their hurting others. (See Hudson [2004] for more on fraud in science.)

When you make these assessments of costs and benefits, be prepared to come to decisions that may not be shared by all your colleagues. Remember the problem of the relation between darkness of skin color and various measures of life success (including wealth, health, and longevity)? Would you, personally, be willing to participate in a study of this problem?

Suppose the study was likely to show that a small, but significant percentage of the variation in earning power in the United States was predictable from (*not* caused by) darkness of skin color. Some would argue that this would be useful evidence in the fight against racism and would jump at the chance to do the investigation. Others would argue that the evidence would be used by racists to do further damage in our society, so the study should simply not be done lest the information it produces fall into the wrong hands.

There is no answer to this dilemma. Above all, be honest with yourself. Ask yourself: Is this ethical? If the answer is "no," then skip it;

find another topic. Once again, there are plenty of interesting research questions that won't put you into a moral bind (**Further Reading:** ethical issues in social science).

Research and Institutional Review Boards

The key ethical issue in the conduct of all social research is whether those being studied are placed at risk by those doing the studying. This goes for field research—including surveys, ethnographies, and naturalistic experiments—as much as it does for laboratory studies. All universities in the United States have long had Institutional Review Boards, or IRBs. These are internal agencies whose members review and pass judgment on the ethical issues associated with all research on people, including biomedical and psychosocial.

With regard to the protection of human subjects, most social research in the United States is covered by the Code of Federal Regulations, Title 45, Part 46, from the Department of Health and Human Services. (See http://www.nsf.gov/bfa/dias/policy/human.jsp and http://ohsr.od.nih.gov/info/sheet5.html.) This set of regulations has been adopted by many agencies, including the National Science Foundation and the National Institutes of Health and is known as the Common Rule. Many American Indian tribes have their own IRBs. Social research on American Indians is often governed by those IRBs.

Here are some tips for getting your IRB application approved:

1. Learn the rules and learn them thoroughly. Read the literature—and the blogs—about the experiences that others have had in getting acceptance for projects that involved field research, for research with children or other vulnerable people, for research that was entirely inductive (like many grounded theory projects) or that had an inductive and confirmatory phase where the investigator had to

use unstructured interviewing at one stage and structured interviewing later (like many mixed-methods projects).

2. If you are doing ethnography to understand process and mechanism rather than outcomes, explain that. Participant observation is a strategic method, at the same level of generality as experiments or archival research or survey research. You wouldn't say that you will do survey research and let it go at that.

3. Get your IRB protocol in long, long before you plan to start your research. Don't make a lack of planning on your part anyone else's emergency. Some universities (but not all) will let you submit a grant proposal to an agency without having IRB approval for the work you propose. The agencies just can't release the money to your institution if your proposal is funded until you have the IRB approval. If your university allows this, you usually have at least 6 months after sending in the proposal to work with the IRB on appropriate methods. In any case, getting a proposal in for master's or doctoral-level funding 6 months before you want to do your work is not a burden. It's just part of time management.

4. If you are working overseas and using a language other than English, translate your informed consent document or oral presentation—into Swahili or Urdu or whatever language you'll be using in the field.

5. The IRB can use expedited review of minor changes in a previously approved protocol if you make the change within a year. Adding a survey to an ethnography is not a minor change, but outlining a survey as part of the research design means that you only have to submit the actual questions for review when you get beyond the inductive and into the hypothesis testing phase of your research. Some IRBs take this as appropriate for expedited review, since the protocol—ethnography, followed by a survey—has already been approved. But even if full review is required, you're less likely to run into problems since the

protocol, including methods of sampling and recruiting has already been approved.

6. Request permission to recruit and interview more people than you think you'll need in your study to cover all contingencies. What contingencies? Sample attrition is one, but you'll also find that you need to be flexible in recruiting people into in-depth interviews. This may mean changing not only the number of people you have to recruit, but the way you recruit, as well. And this means putting *all* the potential methods for recruiting into your proposal.

7. Don't settle for a short-term gain from the IRB that may cripple your research agenda later. Don't agree, for example, not to collect names if you may need them later.

8. Treat all this as part of normal training in how to do research. This will help make the relationship between researchers and those whose job it is to protect human subjects of social research from harm collaborative rather than confrontational.

Theory—Explanation and Prediction

All research is specific. Whether you conduct ethnographic or questionnaire research, do content analysis or run an experiment, the first thing you do is *describe a process* or *investigate a relation* among some variables in a population. Description is essential, but to get from description to theory is a big leap. It involves asking: "What causes the phenomenon to exist in the first place?" and "What does this phenomenon cause?" Theory, then, is about explaining and predicting things.

It may seem odd to talk about theory in a textbook on research methods, but you can't design research until you choose a research question, and research questions depend crucially on theory. A good way to understand what theory is about is to pick a phenomenon

that begs to be explained and to look at competing explanations for it. See which explanation you like best. Do that for a few phenomena and you'll quickly discover which paradigm you identify with. That will make it easier to pick research problems and to develop hypotheses that you can go off and test.

Here is an example of something that begs to be explained: Everywhere in the world, there is a very small chance that children will be killed or maimed by their parents. However, the chance that a child is killed by a parent is much higher if a child has one or more nonbiological parents than if the child has two biological parents (Daly and Wilson 1988, 1998; Lightcap et al. 1982). This "Cinderella effect," as it's known, means that those evil-step-parent folk tales are based on more than fantasy. Or are they? A lot depends on the paradigm you start with.

Alternative Paradigms for Building Theories

One explanation is that it's biological—in the genes, as it were. Male gorillas are known to kill off the offspring of new females they bring into their harem. Humans, the reasoning goes, have a bit of that instinct in them, too. They fight the impulse, and culture usually trumps biology, but over millions of cases, biology is bound to come out sometimes. This is an explanation based on assumptions from evolutionary theory. (There are several varieties of this, which you'll see under the label of sociobiology or evolutionary psychology or evolutionary anthropology.)

Another explanation is that it's cultural. Yes, it's more common for children to be killed or hurt by nonbiological than by biological parents, but this kind of mayhem is more common in some cultures than in others. Also, the deaths of some children at the hand of their biological parents may go unnoticed and unreported simply because we don't expect that, while the deaths of children at the hands of nonbiological parents get more notice simply because we're on the lookout for it (Crume et al. 2002). And, although killing and maiming of children is rare everywhere, in some cultures mothers are more likely than fathers to be the culprits, even when the woman's partner is the stepfather (Alexandre et al. 2010). Women and men learn different gender roles in different societies, and so, the theory goes, we have to look at cultural differences for a true explanation of the phenomenon. This is called an idealist (or ideational) theory because it is based on what people think—on their ideas.

Yet another explanation is that when adult men and women bring children to a second marriage, they know that their assets are going to be diluted by the claims the spouse's children have on those assets—immediate claims and claims of inheritance. This leads some of those people to harm their spouse's children from the former marriage. In a few cases, this causes death. This is a materialist theory, as is the idea that women who have children from a previous marriage may, on average, be forced to marry men who carry a higher risk of being abusive.

Sociobiology, idealism, and materialism are theoretical paradigms or theoretical perspectives. They contain a few basic *rules for finding theories* that explain observed events. The evolutionary paradigm stresses the primacy of biological features of humans as the basis for human behavior. Idealism stresses the importance of internal states—attitudes, preferences, ideas, beliefs, values—as the basis for human behavior. And materialism stresses structural and infrastructural forces—like the economy, the technology of production and reproduction, demography, and environmental conditions—as causes of human behavior (**Further Reading:** paradigms for research).

When you want to explain a specific phenomenon, you apply the principles of your favorite paradigm and come up with a specific explanation—a theory.

Why do women everywhere in the world tend to have nurturing roles? If you think that biology rules here, then you'll be inclined to support evolutionary theories about other phenomena as well. If you think economic and political forces cause values and behavior, then you'll be inclined to apply the materialist perspective in your search for explanations in general. If you think that culture—people's values—is of paramount importance, then you'll tend to apply the idealist perspective to come up with explanations.

The different paradigms are not so much in competition as they are complementary, for different levels of analysis. The evolutionary explanation for the battering of nonbiological children is appealing for aggregate, evolutionary phenomena—the big, big picture. An evolutionary explanation addresses the question: What is the reproductive advantage of this behavior happening at all?

We know that the behavior of hurting or killing step-children is not inevitable, so an evolutionary explanation can't account for why some step-parents hurt their children and others don't. A materialist explanation is more productive for addressing that question. Some step-parents who bring a lot of resources to a second marriage become personally frustrated by the possibility of having their wealth raided and diluted by their new spouse's children. The reaction would be strongest for step-parents who have competing obligations to support their biological children who are living with yet another family. These frustrations will cause *some* people to become violent, but not others.

But the materialist explanation doesn't tell us why a particular step-parent is supportive or unsupportive of his or her nonbiological children. At this level of analysis, we need a processual and psychological explanation, one that takes into account the particular historical facts of the case (Box 3.1).

Is there a sociobiological basis for powerful spouses to batter powerless ones? Or is this all something that gets stimulated by material conditions, like poverty? Lots more research is

Box 3.1 Intimate partner violence on Barbados

Handwerker (1996b) found that step-parents in Barbados were, overall, no more likely to treat children violently than were biological parents. But the presence of a *step-father* increased the likelihood that women battered their daughters and decreased the likelihood that women battered their sons. In homes with step-parents, women saw their daughters as potential competitors for resources available from their partner and they saw sons as potential sources of physical protection and income.

And there was more. Powerful women (those with their own sources of income) protected their children from violence, treated them affectionately, and elicited affection for them from their man. The probability that a son experienced an affectionate relationship with a biological father rose with the length of time the two lived together, but only for sons who had powerful mothers. Men battered powerless women and the children of powerless women, and powerless women battered their own children.

needed on this fascinating question, but I think the points here are clear: (1) different paradigms produce different answers to the same question; and (2) a lot of really interesting questions may have answers that are generated from several paradigms.

There is a long list of things that beg to be explained in the social world: Why does total fertility (the number of children born to women of childbearing age) decrease when societies move from agricultural to industrial production? Why does modernization result in a lower ratio of ascribed to achieved statuses? Why does romantic love become the basis for marriage in economically advanced societies?

The Consequences of Paradigms

Differences in theoretical paradigms have profound consequences. If you think that beliefs and attitudes are what make people behave as they do, then if you want to change people's behavior, the obvious thing to do is change their attitudes. This is the basis of the educational model of social change I mentioned in Chapter 2—the runaway best-seller model for change in our society.

Do you want to get students in American high schools to achieve more? Educate them about the importance of taking the most challenging courses. Want to get women in developing nations to have fewer children? Educate them about the importance of small families. Want to lower the rate of infectious disease in developing countries? Educate people about the importance of good hygiene. Want to get adolescents in Boston or Seattle or wherever to stop having high-risk sex? Educate them about the importance of abstinence or, if that fails, about how to take protective measures against sexually transmitted disease. Want to get people in the United States to use their cars less? Educate them about car pooling.

These kinds of programs often fail—but they do work sometimes. The closer a behavior is to the culture (or **superstructure**) of society, the easier it is to intervene culturally. Brand preferences are often superstructural, so advertising works to get people to switch brands—to change their behavior. But if people's behavior is rooted in the **structure** or **infrastructure** of society, then forget about changing their behavior by educating them to have better attitudes.

If you need a car because the only affordable housing is 30 miles from your job, no amount of rhetoric will convince you to take the bus. In poor countries, having many children may be the only security people have in their old age. You can educate people (through social advertising) about using the pill as opposed to less-effective methods of birth control, once people have decided to lower their fertility, but educational rhetoric doesn't influence the number of children that people want in the first place.

Idiographic and Nomothetic Theories

Theory comes in two basic sizes: elemental or idiographic theory and generalizing or nomothetic theory. An idiographic, or elemental, theory accounts for the facts in a single case. A nomothetic theory accounts for the facts in many cases. The more cases that a theory accounts for, the more nomothetic it is.

The distinction was first made by Wilhelm Windelband, a philosopher of science, in 1894. By the late 1800s, Wilhelm Dilthey's distinction between the Naturwissenschaften and Geisteswissenschaften—the sciences of nature and the sciences of the mind—had become quite popular. The problem with Dilthey's distinction, said Windelband, was that it couldn't accommodate the then brand-new science of psychology. The subject matter made psychology a Geisteswissenchaft, but the discipline relied on the experimental method, and this made it a Naturwissenschaft.

What to do? Yes, said Windelband, the search for reliable knowledge is, indeed, of two kinds: the sciences of law and the sciences of events, or, in a memorable turn of phrase, "the study of what always is and the study of what once was." Windelband coined the terms *idiographic* and *nomothetic* to replace Dilthey's Natur- and Geisteswissenschaften.

Organic evolution is governed by laws, Windelband observed, but the sequence of organisms on this planet is an event that is not likely to be repeated on any other planet. Languages are governed by laws, but any given language at any one time is an event in human linguistic life. The goal of the idiographic, or historical sciences, then, is to deliver "portraits of humans and human life with all the richness of their unique forms" (Windelband 1998 [1894]:16).

Windelband went further. Every causal explanation of an event—every idiographic analysis, in other words—requires some idea of how things happen at all. No matter how vague the idea, there must be nomothetic principles guiding idiographic analysis.

Windelband's formulation is a perfect description of what all natural scientists— vulcanologists, ornithologists, astronomers, ethnographers—do all the time. They describe things; they develop deep understanding of the cases they study; and they produce explanations for individual cases based on nomothetic rules. The study of *a* volcanic eruption, of *a* species' nesting habits, of *a* star's death is no more likely to produce new nomothetic knowledge than is the study of *a* society's adaptation to new circumstances. But the idiographic effort, based on the application of nomothetic rules, is required equally across all the sciences if induction is to be applied and greater nomothetic knowledge achieved.

Those efforts in the social and behavioral sciences are well known. Sigmund Freud (1962) based his theory of psychosexual development on just a few cases. Jean Piaget (1952) did the same in developing his universal theory of cognitive development, as did B. F. Skinner (1938) in developing the theory of operant conditioning. In anthropology, Lewis Henry Morgan (1877) and others made a brave, if ill-fated effort in the nineteenth century to create nomothetic theories about the evolution of culture from the study of cases at hand. The unilineal evolutionary theories they advanced were wrong, but the effort to produce nomothetic theory was *not* wrong. Leslie White (1949) and Julian Steward (1955) advanced more nuanced theories about how the process works.

Nomothetic Is Not Necessarily Better

When you first run into these concepts, it's easy to suppose that nomothetic is better than idiographic, but idiographic theories are often more immediately useful. The following examples showcase the contributions of both idealist and materialist perspectives as well as the importance of both idiographic and nomothetic theory.

The Gender Gap in Wages

Across the world, and although there are some exceptions, women tend to earn less than men do for the same work. In the United States, women earned about 77 cents in 2009 for every dollar men earned. A theory that explains this gender gap for wages in the United States is an idiographic theory. A theory that explains why women in all industrial societies earned less than men did in 2009 (controlling for currency differences, and differences in cost of living across countries) is more nomothetic. But suppose we are involved in developing legislation on the matter in, say, England or Sweden or Chile. Then, an idiographic theory—one that takes account of the political and economic realities of a particular country—is what we need.

The Gender Gap in Voting

In 1920, when women got the vote in the United States, politicians were afraid that women would swamp the polls and vote for things like child-support programs. For decades, neither of those fears materialized. By 1954, women were still only 34% of voters and they were not voting in blocs for so-called women's issues. Since 1980, though, the percentage of eligible female voters who have gone to the polls in U.S. presidential elections has exceeded the percentage of eligible male voters who turned out. In this voting gender gap, a greater proportion of women voters than men went for the Democratic candidate. Jeff Manza and Clem Brooks (1998) analyzed data from 11 presidential elections, from 1952 to 1992, to measure and explain the then emerging gender gap. Their theory is that since: (1) women are disadvantaged in the labor force (earning less than men do, hitting that glass ceiling in management, and so on); and (2) women depend more on public sector jobs than men do; and (3) women need more help with child care and with welfare than men do; then (4) women's increasing participation in the labor force would naturally drive them toward the Democratic Party and away from the Republican Party in national elections.

It turns out that the gender gap may be more complicated. Kellstedt et al. (2010) analyzed U.S. presidential election data and public policy data from 1980 through 2004 and found that the general tendency is for the U.S. electorate to become more conservative during periods of liberal policy and vice versa. This goes for both men and women, but men respond more quickly and in greater numbers than women do in making this shift. The result: The gender gap increases when public policy becomes more liberal because men become more conservative faster than do women. And conversely: the gender gap decreases when public policy turns conservative—again, because men react more quickly than do women in moving to the left.

Manza and Brooks's theory about the rise of the gender gap in U.S. presidential elections doesn't explain why it took women in the United States so long to use their political power in presidential elections, and it doesn't tell us why women don't consistently put Democrats into the U.S. House of Representatives and Senate. But Manza and Brooks's theory accounts for the facts on the ground in the case they deal with, and that's enough for a theory to do. In any science, a lot of the best work is at the idiographic level of theory making.

The Second Demographic Transition

Demographic transition theory accounts for variations in the average number of children born to women in a society. The first demographic transition happened at the end of the Paleolithic when people swapped hunting and gathering for agriculture as the main means of production. During the Paleolithic (from about 2.5 million to about 12,000 years ago), population growth was very, very slow. But across the world, as people switched from hunting and gathering to agriculture, as they settled down and accumulated surplus, their populations exploded.

The second demographic transition began in the late eighteenth century in Europe with industrialization and has been spreading around the world ever since. Today, Japan, Germany, Italy, and other highly industrialized countries have total fertility rates, or TFRs, in the neighborhood of 1.5 to 1.2—that's 29% to 43% below the 2.1 TFR needed in those countries just to replace the current population.

Demographic transition theory—explaining the link between economic development and lower TFR—is highly nomothetic. It accounts for why Japan, a fully industrialized nation, has such a low TFR. But it doesn't predict what the consequences of that low TFR will be. For the time being, at least (until even bigger nomothetic theories are developed), we still need an idiographic theory for this.

Japan has about 126 million people—about 40% of the population of the United States—living in an area the size of Montana. Japan has the world's second-largest economy, and the Japanese enjoyed a per capita income of about $34,000 in 2008 (IMF 2009). This is based on manufacturing products for export. The oil to run the factories that produce all those exports has to be imported. So does a lot of food to feed all those people who are working in the factories. The TFR of 1.3 in Japan makes it easy to predict that Japan's industries need to find lots of new workers to maintain productivity—and the lifestyle supported by that productivity.

Belgium and Italy—two other countries with low TFRs—solved this problem by opening their borders to people from the formerly communist countries of eastern Europe and by increasing female participation in the labor force. There was strong resistance to these solutions in Japan, but in 1990, the need for workers prevailed. Japan began offering Brazilians and Peruvians of Japanese descent special visas to resettle on the theory that it would be easy for people who looked Japanese to assimilate. Some 236,000 Brazilians and Peruvians took the offer, but in 2009, after nearly two decades of economic stagnation and the fact that the South Americans weren't becoming Japanese, the Japanese government was offering those hundreds of thousands of immigrants money to go home (Ducanes and Abella 2008:18; Tabuchi 2009).

The Japanese case shows that lower TFR in industrialized countries doesn't lead to the same response—at least not in the short run. But what about the long run? Japan's economy will recover and the need for workers will only get stronger. This will once again challenge the culture of ethnic nationalism in Japan. A nomothetic theory of how industrialized countries react to lower TFR requires a longer time frame, as does one that posits a change in culture (like ideas about ethnic nationalism) in accommodation to changes in the economy, in technology, and in fertility.

Dowry Deaths

In 1977, the New Delhi police reported 311 dowry deaths—deaths by kitchen fires of women, mostly young brides who were killed because their families had not delivered a promised dowry to the groom's family (Claiborne 1984). By 2005, the government of India reported 6,787 such dowry deaths of young women but this may be an underestimate (Sanghavi et al. 2009). The numbers are in dispute (for one thing, many cases apparently go unreported), but even if the incidence were a fraction of what's reported, the phenomenon demands an explanation.

Daniel Gross (1992) theorized that the phenomenon was the consequence of female hypergamy (marrying up) and dowry. Families that can raise a large dowry in India can marry off their daughter to someone of greater means. This created a bidding war as the families of wealthier sons demand more and more for the privilege of marrying those sons. Apparently, many families of daughters in India have gone into debt to accumulate the dowries. When they can't pay off the debt, some of the families of grooms have murdered the brides in faked "kitchen accidents," where kerosene stoves purportedly blow up. This gives the grooms' families a chance to get another bride whose families can deliver. (For more on dowry inflation, see S. Anderson [2003]. For more on dowry death, see Van Willigen and Chana [1991].) Gross's explanation for the kitchen fires in India doesn't explain why other societies that have escalating dowry don't have kitchen fires. Nor does it tell us why dowry persists in India despite its being outlawed since 1961, or why dowry—which, after all, only occurs in 7.5% of the world's societies—exists in the first place. But Gross's theory deals effectively with the facts of the case.

There is no list of research questions. You have to use your imagination and your curiosity about how things work and follow your hunches. Above all, never take anything at face value. Every time you read an article, ask yourself: "What would a study look like that would test whether the major assertions and conclusions of this article were really correct?" If someone says: "The only things students care about are sex, drugs, and twitter," the proper response is: "We can test that."

A GUIDE TO RESEARCH TOPICS, ANYWAY

There may not be a list of research topics, but there are some useful guidelines. First of all, there are very few big-theory issues—I call them research arenas—in all of social science.

Here are four of them: (1) the nature-nurture problem; (2) the evolution problem; (3) the internal-external problem; and (4) the social facts or emergent properties problem.

1. The nature-nurture problem. This is an age-old question: How much of our personality and behavior is determined by our genes and how much by our exposure to different environments? Many diseases (cystic fibrosis, Tay-Sachs, sickle-cell anemia) are greatly determined by our genes, but others (heart disease, diabetes, asthma) are at least partly the result of our cultural and physical environment.

Schizophrenia is a genetically inherited disease, but its expression is heavily influenced by our cultural environment. Hallucinations are commonly associated with schizophrenia but when Robert Edgerton (1966) asked over 500 people in four East African tribes to list the behavior of people who are severely mentally ill, less than 1% of them mentioned hallucinations (see also Edgerton and Cohen 1994; Jenkins and Barrett 2004).

Research on the extent to which differences in cognitive functions of men and women are the consequence of environmental factors (nurture) or genetic factors (nature) or the interaction between those factors is part of this research arena (Caplan et al. 1997; Coluccia and Louse 2004). So are studies of human response to signs of illness across cultures (Clark et al. 2009; Kleinman 1980).

2. The evolution problem. Studies of how groups change through time from one *kind* of thing to another kind of thing are in this arena. Societies change very slowly through time, but at some point we say that a village has changed into a town or a town into a city or that a society has changed from a feudal to an industrial economy. All studies of the differences between small societies—Gemeinschaften—and big societies—Gesellschaften—are in this arena. So are studies of inexorable bureaucratization as organizations grow.

3. The internal-external problem. Studies of the way in which behavior is influenced by

values and by environmental conditions are in this arena. Studies of **response effects** (how people respond differently to the same question asked by a woman or by a man, for example) are in this arena, too.

4. The social facts, or emergent properties problem. The name for this problem comes from Emile Durkheim's (1933 [1893]) argument that social facts exist outside of individuals and are not reducible to psychological facts. A great deal of social research is based on the assumption that people are influenced by social forces that *emerge* from the interaction of humans but that transcend individuals. Many studies of social networks and social support, for example, are in this arena, as are studies that test the influence of organizational forms on human thought and behavior.

GENERATING TYPES OF STUDIES

Now look at Table 3.1. I have divided research topics (not arenas) into classes, based on the relation among five kinds of variables.

1. Internal states. These include attitudes, beliefs, values, and perceptions. Cognition is an internal state.

2. External states. These include characteristics of people, such as age, wealth, health status, height, weight, gender, and so on.

3. Behavior. This covers what people eat, who they communicate with, how much they work and play—in short, everything that people do and much of what social scientists are interested in understanding.

4. Artifacts. This includes all the physical residue from human behavior—radioactive waste, tomato slicers, sneakers, arrowheads, computer disks, Viagra, skyscrapers—everything.

5. Environment. This includes physical, biological, and social environmental characteristics: the amount of rainfall, the amount of biomass per square kilometer, location on a river or ocean front—the physical and biological features that influence human thought and behavior. Living under a democratic versus an authoritarian regime or working in an organization that tolerates or does not tolerate sexual harassment are examples of social environments that have consequences for what people think and how they behave (Box 3.2).

Table 3.1   Types of Studies

	Internal States	External States	Reported Behavior	Observed Behavior	Artifacts	Environment
Internal States	I	II	IIIa	IIIb	IV	V
External States		VI	VIIa	VIIb	VIII	IX
Reported Behavior			Xa	Xb	XIa	XIIa
Observed Behavior				Xc	XIb	XIIb
Artifacts					XIII	XIV
Environment						XV

Box 3.2 Biological variables

A sixth kind of variable comprises **biological indicators**, like blood pressure and body mass index. We won't cover this kind of variable here, but biocultural research—the interaction among biological, cultural, and environmental factors in shaping human thought and human behavior—is a rapidly growing field in the social sciences. See Dressler (2005) for more on this.

Category (3) includes both reported behavior and **actual behavior**. A great deal of research has shown that about a third to a half of everything people report about their behavior is not true (Bernard and Killworth et al. 1984). If you ask children what they eat or how much they exercise, they'll tell you, but their report may have no useful resemblance to what they actually eat or how much they actually exercise (Johnson et al. 1996). If you ask people how many times a year they go to church, you're likely to get data that do not reflect actual behavior (Hadaway and Marler 2005).

Some of the difference between what people say they do and what they do is the result of out-and-out lying. Most of the difference, though, is because people can't hang on to the level of detail about their behavior that is called for when they are confronted by social scientists asking them how often they go to church, or eat beef, or whatever. What people *think* about their behavior may be precisely what you're interested in, but that's a different matter.

Matching Kinds of Variables and Kinds of Problems

Most social research focuses on internal states and on reported behavior. But the study of humanity can be much richer, once you get the hang of putting together these five kinds of variables and conjuring up potential relations. Here are some examples of possible studies for each of the cells in Table 3.1.

Cell I: The interaction of internal states, like perceptions, attitudes, beliefs, values, and moods.

Religious beliefs, authoritarianism, and prejudice against homosexuals (Tsang and Rowatt 2007).

Perceived gender role and attitudes about rape in Turkey (Gölge et al. 2003).

Religious beliefs and attitudes about gun control in the United States (Flanagan and Longmire 1996).

This cell is also filled with studies that compare internal states across groups. See, for example, Cooke's (2004) study of attitudes toward gun control among American, British, and Australian youth and Yarrow et al.'s (2006) study comparing the early development of implicit racial prejudice in rural Japan and urban United States.

Cell II: The interaction of internal states (perceptions, beliefs, moods, etc.) and external states (completed education, health status, organizational conditions).

Attitudes about the price of food among women of different socioeconomic and health statuses (Bowman 2006).

Variations in organizational structure correlate with employee satisfaction (Cummings and Berger 1976; Gregory et al. 2009).

Cell IIIa: The interaction between *reported* behavior and internal states.

Perception of how well the economy is doing and reported voting behavior (Kwon 2010).

Attitudes toward the environment and reported environment-friendly behavior (Bamberg and Moser 2007; Kahn and Morris 2009).

Reported rate of alcohol consumption and attitudes toward gender roles (Christie-Mizell and Peralta 2009).

Cell IIIb: The interaction between *observed* behavior and internal states.

Attitudes and beliefs about resources and actual behavior in the control of a household thermostat (Kempton 1987).

Behavioral indicators of nervousness among men at an STI clinic (Lichtenstein 2004).

Cell IV: The interaction of material artifacts and internal states.

The effects on Holocaust Museum staff in Washington, DC, of working with the physical reminders of the Holocaust (McCarroll et al. 1995).

How young children in New Zealand learn gender roles from pictures in early school readers (Jackson and Gee 2005).

Cell V: The interaction of social and physical environmental factors and internal states.

As homes become more crowded, parents are less responsive to their children (Evans et al. 2010).

Children in Africa who witness violence are likely to develop symptoms of stress, but a positive school climate reduces the effect (O'Donnell et al. 2011).

The design of memorials can help people recover from trauma and loss (Watkins et al. 2010).

Cell VI: How the interaction among external states relates to outcomes, like longevity or financial success.

The effect of where immigrant scientists in the United States get their college education (in the United States or in their native countries) on their earning power (Tong 2010).

The interaction of income and income inequality on low birth weight (Olson et al. 2010).

Cell VIIa: The relation between external states and *reported* behavior.

The impact of gender, area of residence, and religious affiliation on the likelihood of attending church as people get older (Schwadel 2010).

Factors affecting self-reported suicidal behavior among adolescents in Ireland (McMahon et al. 2010).

Cell VIIb: The relation between external states and *observed* behavior.

Ethnicity of clientele, gender of bartender, and other factors associated with smoking in bars, despite laws against smoking (Moore et al. 2009).

Cell VIII: The relation of physical artifacts and external states.

How age and gender differences relate to cherished possessions among children and adolescents from 6 to 18 years of age (Dyl and Wapner 1996).

Cell IX: The relation of external states and environmental conditions.

The effect of neighborhood street culture on violence among adolescents, beyond that predicted by individual values (Stewart and Simons 2010).

How poor physical and social conditions of poor neighborhoods contribute to bad health and early death (Cohen et al. 2003).

Cell Xa: The relation between behaviors, as *reported* by people to researchers.

The relation of self-reported level of church attendance and self-reported "hooking up" among American college women (Burdette et al. 2009).

Adolescents are more likely to drink alcohol regularly if they report that their same-sex twin or their friends are drinkers than if their parents report regular drinking (Scholte et al. 2008).

Cell Xb: The relation between behaviors, as *observed* by researchers.

The relation among various responsible environmental behaviors (REB), like recycling and turning off the light when leaving a room, and actual REB (Chao and Lam 2011).

Direct observation and comparison of behaviors is used in many fields, including psychology (in assessing behavioral disorders), in education (in assessing learning disabilities), in nursing (in assessing patients' dietary habits), in political science (in assessing the belicosity of nations toward one another), in occupational sociology (in assessing ergonomics and performance), and so on. I'll discuss direct observation at some length in Chapter 14.

Cell XIa: The relation of observed behavior to specific physical artifacts.

Content analysis of top-grossing films from 1950 to 2006 shows that the portrayal of tobacco use declined proportionate to the actual decline of smoking in the population (Jamieson and Romer 2010).

Cell XIb: The relation of reported behavior to specific physical artifacts.

People who are employed view prized possessions as symbols of their own personal history, while people who are unemployed see prized possessions as having utilitarian value (Dittmar 1991).

Cell XIIa: The relation of reported behavior to factors in the social or physical environment.

The relation of compulsive consumer behavior in young adults and whether they were raised in intact or disrupted families (Rindfleisch et al. 1997).

Cell XIIb: The relation of observed behavior to factors in the social or physical environment.

The influence of environmental factors (one-way vs. two-way traffic, the presence or absence of a specific pedestrian signal,

number of lanes in a road, and so on) on pedestrians obeying a traffic signal in Montreal (Cambon de Lavalette et al. 2009).

People spend more or less time in a store and spend more or less money, depending on factors in the store environment (Sherman et al. 1997).

Cell XIII: The association of physical artifacts to one another and what this predicts about human thought or behavior.

Comparing the favorite possessions of urban Indians (in India) and Indian immigrants to the United States to see whether certain sets of possessions remain meaningful among immigrants (Mehta and Belk 1991).

This is also an example of Cell IV. Note the difference between expressed *preferences* across artifacts and the coexistence of artifacts across places or times.

Cell XIV: The probability that certain artifacts (relating, for example, to subsistence) will be found in certain physical or social environments (rain forests, deserts, shoreline communities). This area of research is mostly the province of archeology.

Cell XV: How features of the social and physical environment interact and affect human behavioral and cognitive outcomes.

Environmental features of offices, like amount of cubicle privacy, lighting, and noise, affect job satisfaction and worker performance (Goins et al. 2010; Newsham et al. 2009).

Social and physical environmental features of retail stores interact to affect the buying behavior of consumers (Baker et al. 1992).

The above list is only meant to give you an idea of how to think about potential covariations and, consequently, about potential research topics. Always keep in mind that *covariation does not mean cause.* Covariation can be spurious, the result of an antecedent or an intervening variable. (Refer to Chapter 2 for a discussion of causality, spurious relations, and antecedent variables.)

And keep in mind that many of the examples in the list above are statements about possible bivariate correlations—that is, they are about possible covariation between two things. Social phenomena being the complex sorts of things they are, a lot of research involves multivariate relations—that is, covariation among three or more things at the same time.

For example, it's well known that people who call themselves religious conservatives in the United States are likely to support the National Rifle Association's policy on gun control (Cell I). But the association between the two variables (religious beliefs and attitudes toward gun control) is by no means perfect and is affected by many intervening variables.

I'll tell you about testing for bivariate relations in Chapter 21 and about testing for multivariate relations in Chapter 22. As in so many other things, you crawl before you run and you run before you fly.

THE LITERATURE SEARCH

The first thing to do after you get an idea for a piece of research is to find out what has already been done on it. Don't neglect this part of the research process and never say "little is known about . . ." any topic in any research paper or grant proposal you write. You need to make a heroic effort to uncover sources. Without that effort, you risk wasting a lot of time going over already-covered ground. Even worse, you risk having your colleagues ignore your work because you didn't do your homework. Fortunately, heroic efforts are pretty easy, what with all the documentation resources available for scouring the literature. Begin by looking through volumes of the *Annual Review*. There are *Annual Review* volumes for psychology (every year since 1950), anthropology (every two years from 1959 to 1971 and every year since 1972), sociology (since 1975), public health (since 1997), and political science (since 1998). Authors who are invited to publish in these volumes are experts in their fields; they have digested a lot of information and have packaged it in a way that gets you right into the middle of a topic in a hurry.

Also contact people on listservs and networking groups that deal with your research topic. If there are central figures in the field, contact them by e-mail and request a time when you can call them on the phone. Yes, by phone. E-mail and texting may be convenient for *you*, but many scholars are too busy to respond to requests for lists of articles and books. On the other hand, many scholars *will* talk to you on the phone if they think they can really help.

All you need are a few key references to get started. Don't worry about the key references being out of date. The *ISI Web of Knowledge*, and, in particular, the *Web of Science*, eliminates the problem of obsolescence in bibliographies.

The Web of Science

The *Thompson Reuters Web of Science* contains the *Science Citation Index*, the *Social Sciences Citation Index*, and the *Arts and Humanities Citation Index*. This set of indexes, available at most university libraries and in many small college libraries, covers about 10,000 journals, including about 2,500 in the social sciences. The title, author, journal, year, and page numbers for every article goes into the database, along with the e-mail address of the corresponding author, when it's available.

Most important is that all the references cited by each author of each article in each journal surveyed go into the database. Some articles have a handful of references, but review articles, like the ones in the *Annual Review* series, can have hundreds of citations. If you know the name of just one author whose work *should* be cited by anyone working in a particular field, you can find out, for any given year, who cited that author and where. In other words, you can search the literature *forward* in time; this means that older bibliographies, like those in the *Annual Review* series, are never out of date.

For example, anyone writing on locus of control (whether people feel that they are in charge of their own destinies or are pawns of external forces) is going to cite one of Julian Rotter's classic papers (1966, 1990). Anyone writing about urban gangs in the United States is likely to cite William Foote Whyte's *Street Corner Society* (1981 [1943]) or Gerald Suttles's *The Social Order of the Slum* (1968) (Box 3.3).

Box 3.3 About the citation indexes . . .

I want to make sure that you understand the power of this resource. Without the citation indexes, you can only search *backward in time*. If you have an article or book published in 2008, the references will only go up to, say, 2005 or 2006. Each of *those* references would also have a bibliography going back in time. But with the citation indexes, if you know of a single, classic article written in, say, 1978, you can find all the articles published *today* in which that article was cited and then work backward from those.

The *Social Science Citation Index* alone indexes about 150,000 articles a year. Ok, so 150,000 *sources* is only a good-sized fraction of the social science papers published in the world each year, but the *authors* of those articles read—and cited—about 3 *million* citations to references to the literature. That's 3 million citations every year, for decades. I used the paper versions of these indexes for 30 years before they went online. If the online versions vanished, I'd go back to the paper ones in a minute. They're that good.

Other Documentation Databases

These days, documentation is a robust business, and there are many indexing and abstracting resources. Besides the citation indexes, some important resources for social scientists are: ERIC, NTIS and FDsys, PsycINFO, PubMed, Cambridge Sociological Abstracts, ProQuest Dissertations and Theses Database, LEXIS-NEXIS, and OCLC (Box 3.4).

Box 3.4 Indexing and archiving: JSTOR and other full-text archives

There is an important distinction between indexing-abstracting services, like ERIC, NTIS, etc., and full-text archiving services. JSTOR, for example, archives complete runs of hundreds of journals in 55 disciplines, including the social sciences. The archive for sociology and political science alone comprises some 200 journals. Most of the journals in JSTOR have moving walls of between three and five years. A three-year moving wall means that articles published in 2012 will be available in JSTOR in 2015.

ERIC

ERIC is a federally funded product of the Educational Resources Information Center and is available free at http://www.eric.ed.gov/. It covers literature since 1966 of interest to researchers in education, but many of the 1,130 journals in the database are of interest to all social scientists. The ERIC database includes a lot of grey literature—government reports and reports from private foundations and industries that contain useful information but can be tough to find. The ERIC database contained 1.3 million records in 2011 and is continually updated.

NTIS and FDsys

NTIS, the National Technical Information Service, indexes and abstracts federally funded research reports in all areas of science. It's available free at http://www.ntis.gov/. The research that Peter Killworth and I did in the 1970s and 1980s testing our computer program for network analysis was supported by contracts from the Office of Naval Research. When you have a contract with a U.S. government agency, you generally produce a series of technical reports on the work you do as you go along. Those technical reports get logged in to the NTIS.

Many technical reports later get published as articles. But many don't. Some of the reports aren't published because they are too preliminary—"not ready for prime time," as it were. But lots of technical reports don't get published because they contain huge tables of basic data. That's not the stuff that journals can publish, but it may be treasure for another researcher. It used to be that reports on government contracts were filed and then shelved, never to be heard from again. But with the NTIS database, the public can now easily locate all that information.

The NTIS has technical reports from archeological digs, from voter registration surveys, from consumer behavior surveys, from focus groups on attitudes about unprotected sex, from evaluations of new designs for low-cost housing, from laboratory experiments on how much people might be willing to pay for gasoline, from natural experiments to test how long people can stay in a submerged submarine without going crazy—if the federal government has funded it under contract, there's probably a technical report of it.

Agencies of the U.S. government publish a vast array of reports and data on housing, the elderly, alcohol and drug abuse, violence against women, Native American health, prisons, and hundreds of other topics. These reports are available through FDsys, the Federal Digital System at http://www.gpo.gov/fdsys/.

PubMed

PubMed is a product of the National Library of Medicine (National Institutes of Health) and is available free at http://www.ncbi.nlm.nih.gov/pubmed/. This database covers about 5,400 journals in the medical sciences, including the medical social sciences. It contained over 20 million citations in 2011 and is continually updated.

If you are working on anything that has to do with health care, PubMed is a must. Ask PubMed for articles from 2005 to 2011 on "high-risk sexual behavior and adolescents" and it returns a list of over 700 items.

PsycINFO

PsycINFO is a product of the American Psychological Association. The Jurassic version of this database goes back to the seventeenth century. It indexes and abstracts about 2,500 journals in the behavioral and social sciences and contains over 3 million records.

CSA Sociological Abstracts

Sociological Abstracts is a product of CSA Illumina. It indexes and abstracts about 1,800 journals dating from 1952, with excellent coverage of research methods, the sociology of language, occupations and professions, health, family violence, poverty, and social control. It covers the sociology of knowledge and the sociology of science as well as the sociology of the arts, religion, and education.

ProQuest Dissertations and Theses Database

This database indexes and abstracts dissertations and theses back to 1997. Around 2 million of those dissertation and theses are available in full text. Much of the best and most up-to-date research is done by graduate students. If your institution subscribes to this database, be sure to check it out when you do the background reading for your own project.

LEXIS/NEXIS

If your library has LEXIS/NEXIS, don't consider any literature search complete until you've used this database. The system began in 1973 as a way to help lawyers find information on cases. Today, the database contains the searchable text of over 5 billion documents from some 40,000 sources, including the major English-language newspapers in the world, law cases, transcripts of U.S. congressional hearings, and publications and reports of the U.S. Congress. (The congressional database is a product of ProQuest and is incorporated in the Lexis/Nexis database.)

OCLC

OCLC (Online Computer Library Center) is the world's largest library database. Over 71,000 libraries across the world catalog their holdings, in 479 languages, in OCLC's catalog, called WorldCat. The system had 190 million bibliographic records in 2011. If you find a book or a journal article in the SSCI or PsycINFO, etc. and your library doesn't have it, then OCLC will tell you which library *does*

have it. Interlibrary loans depend on OCLC. In addition, OCLC publishes a database called ArticleFirst. This leviathan, which is updated daily, covers 16,000 journals in all fields, including many in the social sciences. Coverage is only from 1990, but as the database grows—it was over 27 million records in 2011—it becomes more and more useful.

META-ANALYSIS

Meta-analysis involves piling up all the quantitative studies ever done on a particular topic to assess quantitatively what is known about the size of the effect. It is, as Hunt (1997) says, how science takes stock. The pioneering work on meta-analysis (M. L. Smith and Glass 1977) addressed the question: Does psychotherapy make a difference? That is, do people who get psychotherapy benefit, compared to people who have the same problems and who don't get psychotherapy? Since then, there have been thousands of meta-analyses on everything from gender differences in performance on math tests (Lindberg et al. 2010) to the influence of the Internet on citizen participation in public policy making (Yang and Zhiyong 2010).

Meta-analysis forces you to become familiar with the literature on a particular topic and it makes you aware of the research holes that need to be filled. Schutte and Hosch (1997), for example, did a meta-analysis of mock jury studies about rape or child sexual abuse. In a mock jury study, participants are shown evidence of a defendant's guilt and innocence in a particular crime. The jury deliberates and renders a verdict. It's an attractive method because it mimics a real-world situation and because you can manipulate the experimental treatment—the crime, the various kinds of evidence for the defendant's guilt or innocence, the demographics of the jurors, and so on.

Schutte and Hosch scoured the literature. They began by searching the PsycINFO database from 1967 on for articles that contained *any* of the terms "sexual abuse," "child abuse," "rape," "sex," and "juror." They also posted requests on PSYLAW, an Internet discussion group for people interested in law and psychology. They then used the bibliographies from the articles they turned up to hunt for further references and kept on doing this iterative search until no new studies turned up that fit their criteria.

And what were the criteria? First, they only used reports that were based on studies of jury-eligible people. That meant excluding studies of people under 18 years of age and excluding studies of non-U.S. citizens (so all studies of Canadians and Britons, for example, were excluded). Second, they excluded studies in which respondents (mock jurors) were asked to rate a mock defendant's guilt on a Likert-type of scale of, say, 1-to-5. In real jury cases, defendants are judged guilty or not guilty, not "somewhat guilty" or "very guilty."

Schutte and Hosch wound up with 36 studies, 19 involving accusations of rape, and 17 involving accusations of child sexual abuse. All these studies together comprise 9,813 participants (51% of whom were women) and a mean of 273 participants per study. This points to one of the strengths of meta-analysis: Even though the number of *studies* in such an analysis might be low, the number of *people* represented in those studies can be huge.

Across the 36 studies, women jurors were far more likely to vote for conviction than were men (58.5% compared to 41.5%). This was hardly surprising, but the study did turn up something very interesting: 29 out of the 36 studies involved female victims and male defendants. Of the seven studies in which females were the accused, every case was about child sexual abuse, and three of the seven studies reported no difference in the probability that male or female mock jurors would vote to convict. This is just the sort of finding that sharp-eyed researchers latch on to when they're out shopping for interesting research gaps to fill. Indeed, recently, there have been more mock-jury studies examining the effects of gender of both victim and defendant (Pozzulo et al. 2010; Quas et al. 2002) (**Further Reading:** meta-analysis).

Key Concepts in This Chapter

experiment on obedience
debriefing
evolutionary theory
evolutionary psychology
evolutionary anthropology
sociobiology
idealist (ideational) theory
materialist theory
theoretical paradigms
theoretical perspectives
levels of analysis
educational model of social
    change
superstructure
structure
infrastructure

idiographic theory
nomothetic theory
Naturwissenschaften and
    Geisteswissenschaften
gender gap
demographic transition
total fertility rate, or TFR
dowry death
research arenas
the nature-nurture
    problem
the evolution problem
Geminschaften
Gesellschaften
the internal-external
    problem

response effects
the social facts, or emergent
    properties problem
internal and
    external states
behavior
artifacts
environment
biological indicators
reported behavior
actual behavior
bivariate correlations
multivariate relations
documentation resources
locus of control
meta-analysis

Summary

- Research is idealized, but in the end, it gets done the way most things get done: by doing the best we can and by trying to do better next time.

  o Researchers choose their problems for many reasons, including personal interest, availability of research funds, contractual obligations, and to build sound explanations for social and behavioral phenomena.

- The ethics dilemma in social research is profound. The operational test of whether a particular piece of research is ethical is whether social norms tolerate it.

  o This relativistic position, however, does not encourage absolute moral judgments. Ultimately, the choice is left to researchers, and the researchers are responsible for the consequences of their actions.

  o It is unlikely that either Milgram's or Zimbardo's experiments on obedience would be funded today, yet the lessons from their experiments continue to provide guidance on the responsibility of the individual for her or his actions.

- There are quite different approaches, or paradigms, to theory building in the social sciences. These paradigms guide us to search for different *kinds* of answers—biological, ideational, and material—to the same question.

  o The three main paradigms for explanation are idealism, materialism, and sociobiology.

- All research projects begin with a literature search. The bibliographic tools available today make it much easier than in the past to cover the literature thoroughly.

  o The Social Science Citation Index, ERIC, NTIS and FDsys, PubMed, Sociological Abstracts, LEXIS-NEXIS, and OCLC are some of the documentation resources available.

  o Many topics of research have been the subject of meta-analysis. Begin your assessment of the literature by reading any meta-analyses that may be available.

Exercises

1. Building a database of references for a research topic of your choice is the best way to learn how to use the bibliographic tools in your college library. Choose any topic you like and try to make the literature search exhaustive. This is a great way to learn about narrowing down your research *interests* into manageable research *problems*.

   If you're interested in gender differences, for example, the initial search for the string "gender differences" in PsycINFO returns about 25,000 items between 1685 (yes, 1685) and 2011. Better focus it more. Asking for "gender differences" and "test taking" returns about 40 items, with the earliest at 1987. Asking for "human sex differences" and "test taking" returns about 90 items, beginning with 1966.

2. Use Table 3.1 to think up some research problems. Think about how you would operationalize the variables for each study you think up. Go to the library and see if you can find any studies on the research problems you come up with.

3. After reading this chapter, you should have more to say about the concepts of value-free science and research. The examples, though, have been experiments, not research based on questionnaires or on participant observation ethnography.

Does questionnaire research done over the telephone pose any ethical problems? How about online? How about ethnographic research? Use the bibliographic tools in your library to find articles on these issues in social research ethics. Look up the problem of informed consent and learn about the different requirements in social research and medical research. If you stop someone on the street to administer a questionnaire and they answer you, does that imply consent?

4. Use the bibliographic tools in your college library to find at least one example of social research that is based explicitly on the idealist paradigm. Then find an example of research based on the materialist paradigm and another based on the evolutionary paradigm. Be sure that the three articles are reports of research, not a theoretical discussion. Write a brief report describing the articles and then discuss the different approaches taken by the authors.

Further Reading

Social science in the military and in intelligence. For opposing views of social scientists' involvement in the wars in Iraq and Afghanistan, see Price (2003) and McFate (2005); see also González (2007) and Kilcullen (2007). For a summary of this debate, see Fluehr-Lobban (2008) and Forte (2011).

Milgram's and Zimbardo's obedience experiments. Benjamin and Simpson (2009), Blass (2004), Bocciaro and Zimbardo (2010), Packer (2008), Slater et al. (2006).

Ethical issues in social science. Boruch and Cecil (1983), Bosk (2004), Burgess (1989), Citro et al. (2003), Fluehr-Lobban (1996), Hammersley (2009), Herrera (1996), Keith-Spiegel and Koocher (2005), Lyman (1989), Mertens and Ginsberg (2009), van den Hoonaard (2002), Weisstub (1998), Weisstub and Diaz Pintos (2007).

Paradigms for research. On evolutionary perspectives, see Pinker (2003) and the online journal *Evolutionary Psychology* (http://www.epjournal.net/); for examples of cultural, or idealist approaches, see Geert (1973); on the materialist approach, see Harris (1979).

Meta-analysis. Cook et al. (1992), Cooper et al. (2009), Farley and Lehman (1986), Glass (1976), Guzzo et al. (1987), Hedges and Olkin (1985), Hunt (1997), Hunter and Schmidt (2004), Matt and Navarro (1997), Pan (2008), Rosenthal (1984), Wolf (1986).

PART II
Research Design

—————————————— ❧❧ ——————————————

—————————————— ❧❧ ——————————————

4

Research Design
Experiments and Experimental Thinking

INTRODUCTION

Early in the twentieth century, F. C. Bartlett, the pioneering psychologist who developed schema theory, went to Cambridge University to study with W. H. R. Rivers, an experimental psychologist. Rivers had been invited in 1899 to join the Torres Straits expedition and saw the opportunity to do comparative psychology studies of non-Western people (Tooker 1997:xiv). When Bartlett got to Cambridge, he asked Rivers for some advice. Bartlett expected a quick lecture on how to go out and stay out, about the rigors of fieldwork, and so on. Instead, Rivers told him: "The best training you can possibly have is a thorough drilling in the experimental methods of the psychological laboratory" (Bartlett 1937:416).

Bartlett found himself spending hours in the lab, "lifting weights, judging the brightness of lights, learning nonsense syllables, and engaging in a number of similarly abstract occupations" that seemed to be "particularly distant from the lives of normal human beings." In the end, though, Bartlett concluded that Rivers was right. Training in the experimental methods of psychology, said Bartlett, gives one "a sense of evidence, a realization of the difficulties of human observation, and a kind of scientific conscience which no other field of study can impart so well" (1937:417).

Whether you are doing questionnaire surveys, participant observation ethnography, or content analysis of texts, a solid grounding in the logic of the experimental method is one of the keys to good research skills. In this chapter, I discuss how experimental design and experimental thinking is used across the social sciences as a guide to better research on human thought and human behavior.

At the end of this chapter, you should understand the variety of research designs and how they are implemented in experiments, field research, and surveys. You should understand the concept of threats to validity and the various ways in which social scientists respond to those threats (**Further Reading:** research design).

EXPERIMENTS

There are several ways to categorize experiments. First of all, there is the distinction between randomized and nonrandomized assignment of participants, or true experiments versus quasi-experiments. In true experiments, participants (or subjects) are assigned randomly to either a treatment group or a control group. In quasi-experiments, subjects are selected rather than assigned.

Another way to categorize experiments is in terms of where they are done: in the laboratory or out in the world. Experiments in the lab offer greater control; field experiments offer greater realism. I distinguish two kinds of field experiments—natural experiments and naturalistic experiments—but the logic of experiments is the same no matter where they're done.

Randomized Experiments

Whether you're studying people or pigeons, doing research in the laboratory or in the wild, the rules for the design of any true experiment in the social sciences are the same as for experiments in physics or agriculture. There are, of course, differences in experiments with humans and experiments with objects or pigeons or plants. These differences, though, involve important ethical issues like deception, informed consent, and withholding of treatment, not logic. More on these ethical issues later.

THE LOGIC OF TRUE EXPERIMENTS

Steps in the Classic Experiment

There are five steps in a classic experiment:

1. Formulate a hypothesis.

2. Randomly assign participants to the intervention group or to the control group.

3. Measure the dependent variable(s) in one or both groups. This is called O_1 or "observation at time 1."

4. Introduce the treatment or intervention.

5. Measure the dependent variable(s) again. This is called O_2 or "observation at time 2."

Later, I'll walk you through some variations on this five-step formula, including one very important variation that does not involve Step 3 at all. But first, the basics.

Step 1.

Before you can do an experiment, you need a research question that can be studied using the experimental approach. In other words, you need a clear hypothesis about the relation between some independent variable (or variables) and some dependent variable (or variables). Experiments thus tend to be based on confirmatory rather than exploratory research questions (see Box 1.3).

The testing of new drugs can be a simple case of one independent and one dependent variable. The independent variable might be, say, "taking versus not taking" a drug. The dependent variable might be "getting better versus not getting better." The independent and dependent variables can be much more subtle. "Taking versus not taking" a drug might be "taking more of or less of" a drug and "getting better versus not getting better" might be "the level of improvement in high-density lipoprotein" (the so-called good cholesterol).

Move this logic to agriculture: *Ceteris paribus* (holding everything else—like amount of sunlight, amount of water, amount of weeding—constant), some corn plants get a new fertilizer and some don't. Then, the dependent variable might be the number of ears per corn stalk or the number of days it takes for the cobs to mature, or the number of grams of carbohydrates per cob.

Finally, move this same logic to human thought and human behavior: *Ceteris paribus*, police who take part in this new training program will be less aggressive in their arrests than will police who do not take part in it.

Things get more complicated when there are multiple independent (or dependent) variables. You might want to test two different training programs on police who come from three different ethnic backgrounds, for example. But the underlying logic for setting up experiments and for analyzing the results is similar across the sciences. When it comes to experiments, everything starts with a clear hypothesis.

Step 2.

You need at least two groups—the treatment group (also called the **intervention group** or the **stimulus group**) and the control group. One group gets the intervention (a new drug, for example, or exposure to a new method of teaching some subject), and the other group (the control group) doesn't. The treatment group (or groups) and the control group are involved in different experimental conditions.

In a true experiment, individuals are randomly assigned to either the intervention group or to the control group. This ensures that any differences between the groups are the consequence of chance and not of systematic bias. Some people in a population may be more religious, or more wealthy, or less sickly, or more prejudiced than others, but random assignment ensures that those traits are randomly distributed through the groups in an experiment.

Random assignment does not eliminate the possibility of selection bias altogether, but it makes differences between experimental conditions (groups) due solely to chance by taking the decision of who goes in what group out of your hands. The principle behind random assignment will become clearer after you work through Chapter 7 on probability sampling, but the bottom line is this: Whenever you *can* assign participants randomly in an experiment, do it.

Step 3.

One or both groups are measured on one or more dependent variables. This is called the pretest.

Dependent variables in humans can be physical things like weight, height, number of leucocytes per milliliter of blood, or resistance to malaria. They can also be attitudes, psychological states, knowledge, or mental and physical achievements. For example, in weight-loss programs, you might measure the ratio of body fat to body mass as the dependent variable. If you are trying to raise women's understanding of the benefits of breast-feeding by exposing them to a multimedia presentation on this topic, then a preliminary test of women's attitudes about breast-feeding before they see the presentation is an appropriate pretest for your experiment. A preliminary score on a vocabulary test might be the pretest in an experiment to raise students' scores on the verbal part of the SAT.

Here are some social and psychological dependent variables I've seen recently in literature on experiments: attitude toward abortion; knowledge of mathematics among sixth graders; ability to function outside a hospital despite being clinically depressed; level of expressed racism; amount of self-esteem; level of perceived stress; support for the distribution of needles to intravenous drug users. In short, the dependent variable in an experiment can be anything you think might change as a result of some intervention.

You don't always need a pretest. More on this in a bit, when we discuss threats to validity in experiments.

Step 4.

The intervention (the independent variable) is introduced.

Step 5.

The dependent variables are measured again. This is the posttest.

A Walk-Through of an Example

Here's a made-up example of a true experiment: Take 100 college women (18–22 years of age) and randomly assign 50 of them to each of two groups. Bring each woman to the lab and show her a series of flash cards. Let each card contain a single, three-digit random number. Measure how many three-digit numbers each woman can remember. Repeat the task, but let the members of one group hear the most popular rock song of the week playing in the background as they take the test. Let the other group hear nothing. Measure how many three-digit numbers people can remember and whether rock music improves or worsens performance on the task.

Do you think this is a frivolous experiment? It turns out that many college students, ages 18–22, study while listening to rock music. It also turns out that this drives their parents crazy. I'll bet that more than one reader of this book has been asked something like: "How can you learn anything with all that noise?" The experiment outlined here is designed to test whether students can, in fact, "learn anything with all that noise."

There is plenty to criticize about this experimental design. Only women are involved and there are no graduate students, or high school students, either. Furthermore, there is no test of whether classic rock helps or hinders learning more than, say, hip-hop, or rhythm and blues, or country music, or Beethoven, or. . . . In fact, the experiment, as designed, doesn't even test whether people can learn anything important or *useful* when they listen or don't listen to rock music. The experiment tests only whether college-age women learn to memorize more or fewer three-digit numbers when the learning is accompanied by a single rock tune. The learning task is artificial.

But a lot of what's really powerful about the experimental method is embodied in this example. Suppose that the rock-music group does better on the task. We can be pretty sure that it's not because of their gender or their age or their education, but because of the music. Just sticking in more independent variables (like expanding the group to include men, graduate students, or high school students; or playing different tunes; or making the learning task more realistic), without modifying the experiment's design to control for all those variables, creates what are called confounds to validity. They *confound* the experiment and make it impossible to tell if the intervention is what really caused any observed differences in the dependent variable.

Good experiments test narrowly defined questions. This is what gives them knowledge-making power. When you do a good experiment, you *know* something at the end of it. In this case, you know that women students at one school memorize or do not memorize three-digit numbers better when they listen to a particular rock tune.

I know this doesn't sound like much. Critics of experimental thinking in the social sciences say that it forces you to learn more and more about less and less, until finally you know everything there is to know about nothing.

Cute, but wrong. Think about it: The kind of knowledge you get from a well-designed experiment can be verified or falsified by another experiment. You can repeat the experiment at another school. If you get a different answer, then you need an explanation for this finding. Perhaps there is something about the student selection process at the two schools that produces the different results? Perhaps students at one school come primarily from working-class families, while students from the other school come from upper-middle-class families. Perhaps students from different socioeconomic classes grow up with different study habits, or prefer different kinds of music.

Conduct the experiment again, but include men this time. Conduct it again, and include two music conditions: a rock tune and a classical piece. Take the experiment on the road

and run it all over again at different-sized schools in different regions of the country. Then, on to Paraguay . . .

INTERNAL AND EXTERNAL VALIDITY

True experiments, with randomized assignment and full control by the researcher, produce knowledge that has high internal validity. This means that changes in the dependent variables were probably *caused by*—not merely related to or correlated with—the treatment. Continual replication and verification produce cumulative knowledge, with high external validity—that is, knowledge that you can generalize to people who were not part of your experiment.

Replication of knowledge is every bit as important as its production in the first place. In fact, in terms of usefulness, replicated knowledge is exactly what we're after.

Consider the following experiment, designed to test whether offering people money produces fewer errors in an arithmetic task. Take two groups of individuals and ask them to solve 100 simple arithmetic problems. Tell one group that they will be given a dollar for every correct answer. Tell the other group nothing. Be sure to assign participants randomly to the groups to ensure equal distribution of skill in arithmetic. See if the treatment group (the one that gets the monetary rewards) does better than the control group.

This experiment can be embellished to eliminate confounds that threaten internal validity. Conduct the experiment a second time, with the same people, reversing the control and treatment groups. In other words, tell the former treatment group that they will not receive any financial reward for correct answers and tell the former control group that they will receive a dollar for every correct answer. (Of course, give them a new set of problems to solve.)

This creates a whole new experiment. You're no longer testing whether financial incentives motivate people to try harder in solving a set of arithmetic problems. Now you're also testing whether pulling financial incentives away from people who are accustomed to getting them will affect their ability to solve those arithmetic problems.

Conduct the experiment many times, changing or adding independent variables. In one version of the experiment, you might keep the groups from knowing about each other. In another, you might let each group know about the other's efforts and rewards (or lack of rewards). Perhaps when people know that others are being rewarded for good behavior and that they themselves are not rewarded they will double their efforts to gain the rewards (this is called the "John Henry effect"). Perhaps they just become demoralized and give up.

By controlling the interventions and the group membership, you can build up a series of conclusions regarding cause and effect between various independent and dependent variables.

While controlled experiments like these have the virtue of high internal validity, they have the liability of low external validity. It may be true that a reward of a dollar per correct answer results in significantly more correct answers for the groups you tested in your laboratory. But you can't tell whether a dollar is sufficient reward for all groups, or whether a quarter would be enough to create the same experimental results in some groups. Worst of all, you don't know whether the laboratory results explain *anything* you want to know about in the real world.

To test external validity, you might propose some kind of monetary reward for teaching children in a dozen actual third-grade classrooms, to do arithmetic—six classrooms in which, say, children earn a penny per correct answer, and six in which there is no monetary incentive. If it turns out that the kids in the intervention classrooms get higher scores on arithmetic tests at the end of the year, then the next question is: How far do the results generalize? Just to the classrooms in the experiment? To all third graders in the school district? To all third graders in the state? In the country?

Kinds of Confounds: Threats to Validity

It's pointless to ask questions about external validity until you establish internal validity. In a series of influential publications, Donald Campbell and his colleagues identified the threats to internal validity of experiments (see Campbell 1957, 1979; Campbell and Stanley 1966; T. D. Cook and Campbell 1979). Here are seven of the most important confounds:

History

The history confound refers to any independent variable, other than the treatment, that (1) occurs between the pretest and the posttest in an experiment and (2) affects the experimental groups differently. Suppose you are doing a laboratory experiment, with two groups (experimental and control), and there is a power failure in the building. So long as the lights go out for both groups, there is no problem. But if the lights go out for one group and not the other, it's difficult to tell whether it was the treatment or the power failure that causes changes in the dependent variable.

In a laboratory experiment, history is controlled by isolating subjects as much as possible from outside influences. When we do experiments outside the laboratory, it is almost impossible to keep new independent variables from creeping in and confounding things.

Recall the example of testing whether monetary incentives help third graders do better in arithmetic. Suppose that right in the middle of the school term during which the experiment was being conducted, the Governor's Task Force on Elementary Education issues its long-awaited report and it contains the observation that arithmetic skills must be emphasized during the early school years. Furthermore, it says, teachers whose classes make exceptional progress in this area should be rewarded with 10% salary bonuses.

The governor accepts the recommendation and announces a request for a special legislative appropriation. Elementary teachers all over the state start paying extra attention to arithmetic skills. Even supposing that the students in the treatment classes do better than those in the control classes, how can we be certain that the magnitude of the difference would not have been greater had this historical confound not occurred?

Maturation

The maturation confound refers to the fact that people in any experiment grow older, or get more experienced while you are trying to conduct an experiment. Consider the following experiment: Start with a group of teenagers on a Native American reservation and follow them for the next 60 years. Some of them will move to cities, some will go to small towns, and some will stay on the reservation. Periodically, test them on a variety of dependent variables (their political opinions, their wealth, their health, their family size, and so on). See how the various experimental treatments (city vs. reservation vs. town living) affect these variables.

Here is where the maturation confound enters the picture. The people you are studying get older. Older people in many societies become more politically conservative. They are usually wealthier than younger people. Eventually, they come to be more illness-prone than younger people. Some of the changes you measure in your dependent variables will be the result of the various treatments and some of them may just be the result of maturation.

Maturation is sometimes taken too literally. Social service delivery programs "mature" by working out bugs in their administration. People "mature" through practice with experimental

conditions and they become fatigued. We see this all the time in new social programs where people start out being enthusiastic about innovations in organizations and eventually get bored or disenchanted.

Testing and Instrumentation

The testing confound occurs in laboratory and field experiments when subjects get used to being tested for indicators on dependent variables. This quite naturally changes their responses. Asking people the same questions again and again in a longitudinal study, or even in an ethnographic study done over six months or more, can have this effect.

The instrumentation confound results from changing measurement instruments. Changing the wording of questions in a survey is essentially changing instruments. Which responses do you trust: the ones to the earlier wording or the ones to the later wording? If you do a set of observations in the field—like children's behavior at recess or nurses' behavior in responding to patients in a hospital or cops' behavior in making arrests—and later send in someone else to continue the observations, you have changed instruments.

Which observations do you trust as closer to the truth: yours or those of the substitute instrument (the new field researcher)? In multi-researcher projects, this problem is usually dealt with by training all investigators to see and record things in more or less the same way. This is called increasing interrater reliability. (More on this in Chapter 19, on analyzing qualitative data.)

Regression to the Mean

Regression to the mean is a confound that can occur when you study groups that have extreme scores on a dependent variable. No matter what the treatment is, over time you'd expect the extreme scores to become more moderate, just because there's nowhere else for them to go. If men who are taller than 6'7" marry women who are taller than 6′3″, then their children are likely to be (1) taller than average and (2) closer to average height than either of their parents are. There are two independent variables (the height of each of the parents) and one dependent variable (the height of the children). We expect the dependent variable to "regress toward the mean," since it really can't get more extreme than the height of the parents.

I put that phrase "regress toward the mean" in quotes because it's easy to misinterpret this phenomenon—to think that the "regressing" toward the mean of an dependent variable is caused by the extreme scores on the independent variables. It isn't, and here's how you can tell that it isn't: Very, very tall children are likely to have parents whose height is more like the mean. One thing we know for sure is that the height of children doesn't cause the height of their parents. Regression to the mean is a statistical phenomenon—it happens in the aggregate and is not something that happens to individuals (Box 4.1).

Box 4.1 The problem of extreme values

Many social intervention programs make the mistake of using people with extreme values on dependent variables as subjects. Suppose you're asked to evaluate a new reading program for third graders. To give the program a real workout, you choose children who scored in the bottom 10% of their class and compare them to children in the top 10% of their class. You'll probably find that the bottom 10% shows improvement, but don't write home about this just yet. You'll also probably find that the top 10% shows some decrease in their performance.

What's going on? Well, those bottom 10-percenters have nowhere to go but up, and the top 10-percenters have nowhere to go but down. If you introduced no program at all, the kids at the extremes would have a statistical chance, just by random fluctuation, of getting scores that are more like the mean the next time you test them. By choosing groups that score at the extreme, you wind up not being able to tell if the new reading program caused the change in scores, or if the change was just a statistical regression to the mean.

Selection of Participants

Selection bias in choosing subjects is a major confound to validity in both quasi-experiments and natural experiments. In laboratory experiments, you assign subjects at random, from a single population, to both treatment groups and control groups. This distributes any differences among individuals in the population throughout the groups, making the groups equivalent. This reduces the possibility that differences among the groups will cause differences in outcomes on the dependent variables, so selection is not a threat to the internal validity of the experiment.

Random assignment of participants to experimental conditions *reduces* the possibility of selection bias, but it doesn't eliminate the possibility altogether. Random assignment, then, maximizes the chance for valid outcomes—outcomes that are not clobbered by hidden factors.

In natural experiments, we have *no control* over assignment of individuals to groups.

Question: Do victims of violent crime have less stable marriages than persons who have not been victims? Obviously, researchers cannot randomly assign subjects to the treatment (violent crime). It could turn out that people who are victims of violent crime are more likely to have unstable marriages anyway, even if they never experienced violence.

Question: Do migrants to cities from small towns engage in more entrepreneurial activities than stay-at-homes? If we could assign rural people randomly to the treatment group (those engaging in urban migration), we'd have a better chance of finding out. Since we cannot, selection is a threat to the internal validity of the experiment. Suppose that the answer to the question at the top of this paragraph were "yes." We still don't know the direction of the causal arrow: Does the treatment (migration) cause the outcome (greater entrepreneurial activity)? Or does having an entrepreneurial personality cause migration?

Mortality

The mortality confound refers to the fact that individuals may not complete their participation in an experiment. Suppose we follow two sets of married couples for five years. The couples in one group get free family counseling sessions once every three months. The other couples don't. During the first year of the experiment we have 200 couples in each group. By the fifth year, 30 couples have dropped out of the treatment group and 130 of the 170 remaining couples (76%) are still married. In the control group, 50 couples have dropped out and 75 of the 150 remaining couples (50%) are still married. One conclusion is that lack of counseling caused those in the control group to get divorced at a faster rate than those in the treatment group.

But what of those 30 couples in the treatment group and the 50 couples in the control group who left? It could be that they were mostly still married or mostly divorced. In either case, this would affect the results of the experiment, but we just don't know. Mortality can be a serious problem in natural experiments if it gets to be a large fraction of the group(s) under study.

Mortality also affects panel surveys. That's where you interview the same people more than once to track something about their lives. (More about panel studies in Chapter 9.)

Diffusion of Treatments

The diffusion of treatments threat to validity occurs when a control group cannot be prevented from receiving the treatment in an experiment. This is particularly likely in quasi-experiments where the independent variable is an information program.

In a project with which I was associated some years ago, a group of African Americans were given instruction on modifying their diet and exercise behavior to lower their blood pressure. Another group was randomly assigned from the population to act as controls—that is, they did not receive instruction. The evaluation team measured blood pressure in the treatment group and in the control group before the program was implemented. But when they went back after the program was completed, they found that control group members had also been changing their behavior. They had learned of the new diet and exercises from the members of treatment group.

CONTROLLING FOR THREATS TO VALIDITY

In what follows, I want to show you how the power of experimental logic is applied to real research problems. The major experimental designs are shown in Figure 4.1. The notation is pretty standard.

X stands for some intervention—a stimulus or a treatment of a subject.

R means that subjects are randomly assigned to experimental conditions—either to the intervention group that gets the treatment, or to the control group that doesn't.

Several designs include random assignment and several don't.

O stands for "observation." O_1 means that some observation is made at Time 1. O_2 means that some observation is made at Time 2, and so on.

Observation means "measurement of some dependent variable," but as you already know,

Figure 4.1 Some Research Designs

Figure 4.Ia The Classic Design: Two-Group Pretest-Posttest

	Time 1		Time 2	
	Assignment	Pretest	Intervention	Posttest
Group 1	R	O_1	X	O_2
Group 2	R	O_3		O_4

Figure 4.Ib The Solomon Four-Group Design

	Time 1		Time 2	
	Assignment	Pretest	Intervention	Posttest
Group 1	R	O_1	X	O_2
Group 2	R	O_3		O_4
Group 3	R		X	O_5
Group 4	R			O_6

Figure 4.Ic The Classic Design Without Randomization

	Time 1		Time 2	
	Assignment	Pretest	Intervention	Posttest
Group 1		O_1	X	O_2
Group 2		O_3		O_4

Figure 4.Id The Campbell and Stanley Posttest-Only Design

	Time 1		Time 2	
	Assignment	Pretest	Intervention	Posttest
Group 1	R		X	O_1
Group 2	R			O_2

Figure 4.Ie The One-Shot Case Study Design

	Time 1		Time 2	
	Assignment	Pretest	Intervention	Posttest
			X	O

Figure 4.If The One-Group Pretest-Posttest Design

	Time 1		Time 2	
	Assignment	Pretest	Intervention	Posttest
		O_1	X	O_2

Figure 4.Ig Two-Group Posttest-Only Design: Static Group Comparison

	Time 1		Time 2	
	Assignment	Pretest	Intervention	Posttest
			X	O_1
				O_2

Figure 4.Ih The Interrupted Time Series Design

	Time 1		Time 2	
	Assignment	Pretest	Intervention	Posttest
		OOO	X	OOO

the idea of measurement is pretty broad. It can be taking someone's temperature or testing their reading skill. It can also be just writing down whether they are smiling.

The Classic Design

We begin with the classic experimental design, the two-group pretest-posttest with random assignment. It is shown in Figure 4.1a. From a population of potential participants, some participants have been assigned randomly to a treatment group and a control group. Read across the top row of the table. An observation (measurement) of some dependent variable or variables is made at time 1 on the members of group 1. That is O_1. Then an intervention is made (the group is exposed to some treatment, X). Then, another observation is made at time 2. That is O_2.

Figure 4.1a   The Classic Design: Two-Group Pretest-Posttest

	Time 1		Time 2	
	Assignment	Pretest	Intervention	Posttest
Group 1	R	O_1	X	O_2
Group 2	R	O_3		O_4

Now look at the second row of the Figure 4.1a. A second group of people are observed, also at time 1. Measurements are made of the same dependent variable(s) that were made for the first group. The observation is labeled O_3. There is no X on this row, which means that no intervention is made on this group of people. They remain unexposed to the treatment or intervention in the experiment. Later, at time 2, after the first group has been exposed to the intervention, the second group is observed again. That's O_4.

Random assignment of participants ensures equivalent groups, and the second group, without the intervention, ensures that several threats to internal validity are taken care of. Most importantly, you can tell how often (how many times out of a hundred, for example) any differences between the pretest and posttest scores for the first group might have occurred anyway, even if the intervention hadn't taken place.

The classic experimental design is used widely across the social sciences to evaluate education programs—everything from teaching dental students in how to handle a mirror in a patient's mouth (it's not easy; everything you see is backward), to teaching Samoan women the value of getting a Pap smear (see Kunovich and Rashid [1992] and Mishra et al. [2009]).

Patricia Chapman and colleagues (Chapman et al. 1997) wanted to educate student athletes about sports nutrition. They had access to an eight-team girl's high school softball league in southern California. The participants were 14–18 years old on each team. Chapman et al. assigned each of 72 players randomly to one of two groups. The girls in the treatment group got two 45-minute lectures a week for six weeks about things like dehydration, weight loss, vitamin and mineral supplements, energy sources, and so on. The control group got no instruction.

Before the six-week program started, the researchers asked each participant to complete the Nutrition Knowledge and Attitude Questionnaire (Werblow et al. 1978) and to list the foods they'd consumed in the previous 24 hours. The nutrition knowledge-attitude test and the 24-hour dietary recall test were the pretests in this experiment. Then, when the six-week program was over, Chapman et al. gave the participants the same two tests. These were the posttests. The pretests provided baseline data and the posttests provided data for assessing whether the nutrition education program had made a difference.

The education intervention did make a difference—in knowledge, but not in reported behavior. The participants in both the treatment and control groups scored about the same on the knowledge/attitude test in the pretest. After they went through the lecture series, the participants in the treatment group scored about 18 points more (out of 200 possible points) than those in the control group. Before the program, the 36 girls in the control group reported an average 24-hour intake of 1,683 calories and those in the treatment group reported an average of 2,054 calories.

As Chapman et al. point out, though, even 2,054 calories is not enough for adolescent females who are involved in competitive sports. After the intervention—after all those lectures—the reported 24-hour average caloric intake was 1,793 for the control group and 1,892 for the treatment group. In other words, if the intervention had any effect on behavior, it was to lower (and hence, worsen) the intake of these young female athletes. Chapman et al. point out that the results confirm the findings of other studies: For many adolescent females, the attraction of competitive sports is the possibility of losing weight.

The Solomon Four-Group Design

The classic design has one important flaw: It is subject to testing bias. Differences between variable measurements at time 1 and time 2 might be the result of the intervention, but they also might be the result of people getting savvy about being watched and measured. Pretesting can, after all, sensitize people to the purpose of an experiment, and this, in turn, can change people's behavior. The Solomon four-group design, shown in Figure 4.1b, controls for this. Since there are no measurements at time 1 for groups 3 and 4, this problem is controlled for. (This design is named for Richard Solomon. See Solomon [1949] and Solomon and Lessac [1968].)

Larry Leith (1988) used the Solomon four-group design to study a phenomenon known to all sports fans as the "choke." That's when an athlete plays well during practice and then loses it during the real game, or plays well all game long and folds in the clutch when it really counts. It's not pretty.

Leith assigned 20 male students randomly to each of the four conditions in the Solomon four-group design. The pretest and the posttest were the same: Each participant shot 25 free throws on a basketball court. The dependent variable was the number of successful free throws out of 25 shots in the posttest. The independent variable—the treatment—was giving or not giving the following little pep talk to each participant just before he made those 25 free throws for the posttest:

Research has shown that some people have a tendency to choke at the free-throw line when shooting free throws. No one knows why some

Figure 4.1b The Solomon Four-Group Design

| | Time 1 | | Time 2 | |
	Assignment	Pretest	Intervention	Posttest
Group 1	R	O_1	X	O_2
Group 2	R	O_3		O_4
Group 3	R		X	O_5
Group 4	R			O_6

people tend to choking behavior. However, don't let that bother you. Go ahead and shoot your free throws. [Leith 1988:61]

What a wonderfully simple, utterly diabolic experiment. You can guess the result: There was a significantly greater probability of choking if you were among the groups that got that little pep talk, irrespective of whether they'd been given the warm-up pretest.

The Solomon four-group design is very useful in evaluation research. From New York to Nairobi, social workers, teachers, and researchers have been looking for ways to teach adolescents about the effective use of condoms in the prevention of sexually transmitted diseases and unwanted pregnancies. Interventions are usually some kind of teaching program administered in the classroom, and study after study shows that they don't work.

Kvalem et al. (1996) evaluated one of these in-school programs. They had 124 classes of 16–20 year olds, comprising a total of 2,411 students from Vestvold County in Norway. They assigned the classes randomly to the four conditions in the four-group design. I mention this study because the major finding was not that the program worked. It didn't. The major finding was a strong interaction effect between the pretest and the intervention on the reported use of condoms.

The pretest was an 80-item questionnaire about sexual behavior, use of condoms, and demographics. The posttest was the same questionnaire, sent six months and 12 months after the intervention. Of the four groups on the Solomon four-group design, the group that

had *both* the pretest *and* the intervention had a higher likelihood of reporting condom use six months after the intervention. Six months later, though, when the posttest was given again, the interaction effect had disappeared.

The study by Kvalem et al. is instructive. It shows clearly the importance of testing for the effects of pretesting in social and psychological experiments. And it shows clearly the importance of following up with a second posttest to make sure that any effects on the dependent variable have lasted. If Kvalem et al. had not done that second posttest, they might have been tempted to interpret the interaction effect as having policy implications: If you want to get adolescents to use condoms, combine a pretest with an educational intervention. Kvalem et al.'s second posttest questionnaire, sent to the participants after 12 months, stopped them from making that mistake.

The Two-Group Pretest-Posttest Without Random Assignment

Figure 4.1c shows the design for a two-group pretest-posttest without random assignment. In this quasi-experiment, participants are not assigned randomly to the control and the experimental condition. This compromise with design purity is often the best we can do.

Watkins et al. (2010) studied the healing power of the Vietnam Veterans Memorial (VVM). They had a population of 62 Vietnam vets who were in treatment at a VA hospital for post-traumatic stress syndrome (PTSD). Of those, 32 went on an annual excursion to the

| Figure 4.1c | The Classic Design Without Randomization |

| | Time 1 | | Time 2 | |
	Assignment	Pretest	Intervention	Posttest
Group 1		O_1	X	O_2
Group 2		O_3		O_4

VVM. All the vets had their PTSD symptoms tested regularly. A month after the trip to the VVM, those who went on the trip, and who had been on the trip at least twice before, has less severe symptoms.

Campbell and Boruch (1975) showed that lack of random assignment in quasi-experiments like this can lead to problems. Suppose you invent a technique for improving reading comprehension among third graders. You select two third-grade classes in a school district. One of them gets the intervention and the other doesn't. Students are measured before and after the intervention to see whether their reading scores improve.

Suppose the children in one class are from wealthier homes, on average, than are the children in the other class and suppose that the wealthier children test higher in reading comprehension at the end of the year than the poorer children. Would you (or the agency you're working for) be willing to bet, say, $300,000 on implementing the new reading comprehension program in all classes in the school district? Would you bet that it was the new program and not some confound, like socioeconomic class, that caused the differences in test scores?

If all the children, one at a time, were assigned randomly to the two groups (those who got the program and those who didn't), then this confound would disappear—not because socioeconomic status stops being a factor in how well children learn to read, but because children from poor and rich families would be equally likely to be in the treatment group or in the control group. Any bias that socioeconomic status causes in interpreting the results of the experiment would be distributed randomly and would, in theory, wash out.

But children come packaged in classrooms. It's physically impossible for a teacher to administer two separate programs in one classroom, so evaluation of these kinds of interventions are usually quasi-experiments because they have to be.

The Posttest-Only Design With Random Assignment

Look carefully at Figure 4.1d. It is the second half of the Solomon four-group design and is a posttest-only design with random assignment. This design—known also as the Campbell and Stanley posttest-only design—has a lot going for it. It retains the random assignment of participants in the classical design and in the Solomon four-group design, but it *eliminates pretesting*—and the possibility of a confound from pretest sensitization. When subjects are assigned randomly to experimental conditions (control or treatment group), a significant difference on O_1 and O_2 in the posttest-only design means that we can have a lot of confidence that the intervention, X, caused that difference (T. D. Cook and Campbell 1979).

Another advantage is the huge saving in time and money. There are no pretests in this design and there are only two posttests instead of the four in the Solomon four-group design.

McDonald and Bridge (1991) used this elegant design in their study of how gender stereotyping by nurses affects how nurses care for patients.

Figure 4.1d The Campbell and Stanley Posttest-Only Design

| | Time 1 | | Time 2 | |
	Assignment	Pretest	Intervention	Posttest
Group 1	R		X	O_1
Group 2	R			O_2

McDonald and Bridge asked 160 female medical-surgical nurses to read an information packet about a colostomy patient whom they would be attending within the next 8 hours. The nurses were assigned randomly to one of eight experimental conditions: (1) The patient was named Mary B. or Robert B. to produce *two patient-gender conditions*. (2) Half the nurses read just a synopsis of the condition of Mary B. or Robert B. and half read the same synopsis as the fourth one in a series of seven. This produced *two memory-load conditions*. (3) Finally, half the nurses read that the temperature of Mary B. or Robert B. had just spiked unexpectedly to 102°, and half did not. This produced *two patient stability conditions*.

The three binary conditions combined to form eight experimental conditions in a **factorial design** (more on factorial designs at the end of this chapter).

Next, McDonald and Bridge asked nurses to estimate, to the nearest minute, how much time they would plan for each of several important nursing actions. Irrespective of the memory load, nurses planned significantly more time for giving the patient analgesics, for helping the patient to walk around, and for giving the patient emotional support when the patient was a man (Box 4.2).

Box 4.2 Posttest-only: The underappreciated design

The Campbell and Stanley posttest-only design, with random assignment, is named for Donald Campbell and Julian Stanley (1963). It is not used as much as I think it should be, despite its elegance, its delightful simplicity, and its low cost. In a recent search of the literature, I found 1,110 examples of studies that used the pretest-posttest design, compared to 133 for studies that used the posttest-only design (with or without random assignment). This preference for the classic design is due partly to the appealing-but-mistaken idea that matching participants in experiments on key independent variables (age, ethnicity, etc.) is somehow better than randomly assigning participant to groups and partly to the nagging suspicion that pretests are essential to the experimental method.

That nagging suspicion—that we can do better than trust the outcome of events to randomness—has been the focus of a lot of research since a paper by Gilovich et al. in 1985 titled: "The Hot Hand in Basketball—On the Misperception of Random Sequences." The hot-hand phenomenon—the belief that streaks (in sports and in money management, for example) are the result of nonrandom forces—is hard to break. By the same token, so is the belief that small samples, if drawn randomly, are sufficient to warrant generalizing to a population. On this one, see the 600+ citations to Tversky and Kahneman (1971) and Chapters 6 and 7 on representative and nonrepresentative sampling

The One-Shot Case Study

The one-shot case study design is shown in Figure 4.1e. It is also called the ex post facto design because a single group of individuals is measured on some dependent variable *after* an intervention has taken place.

This is the most common design in culture change studies, where it is obviously impossible to manipulate the dependent variable. You arrive in a community and notice that something important has taken place. A new exit on the highway produces more tourist traffic or an interstate highway has bypassed a town and tourism revenues have plummeted. You try to evaluate the natural experiment by interviewing people (O) and by trying to assess the impact of the intervention (X).

Figure 4.1e   The One-Shot Case Study Design

| | Time 1 | | Time 2 | |
	Assignment	Pretest	Intervention	Posttest
			X	O

With neither a pretest nor a control group, you can't be sure that what you observe is the result of some particular intervention. Despite this apparent weakness, however, the intuitive appeal of findings produced by one-shot case studies can be formidable.

In the 1950s, physicians began general use of the Pap Test, a simple office procedure for determining the presence of cervical cancer. Figure 4.2 shows that since 1950, the death rate from cervical cancer in the United States has dropped steadily, from about 18 per 100,000 women to about 11 in 1970, to about 8.3 in 1980, to about 6.5 in 1995, and to about 2.4 in 2005. On the other hand, if you look only at the data *after* the intervention (the one-shot case study X O design) you might conclude that the intervention (the Pap Test) caused this drop in cervical cancer deaths. There is no doubt that the continued decline of cervical cancer deaths is due largely to the early detection provided by the Pap Test, but by 1950, the death rate had already declined by 36% from 28 per 100,000 women in 1930 (Williams 1978:16).

Never use a design of less logical power when one of greater power is feasible. If pretest data are available, use them. On the other hand, a one-shot case study is often the best you can do. Virtually all ethnography falls in this category, and as I have said before, nothing beats a good story, well told (**Further Reading:** case study methods).

The One-Group Pretest-Posttest

The one-group pretest-posttest design is shown in Figure 4.1f. Some variables are measured (observed), then the intervention takes place,

Figure 4.2   Death Rate From Cervical Cancer, 1930–2005

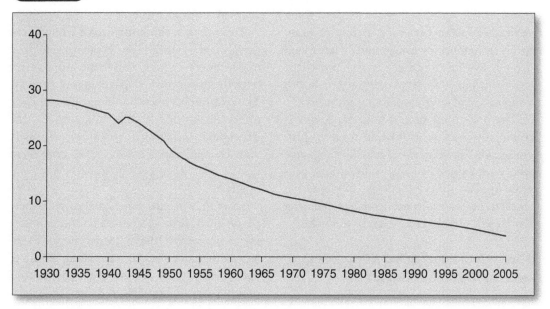

Source: Adapted from B. Williams, *A Sampler on Sampling,* Figure 2.1, p. 17. ©1978, Lucent Technologies.

Figure 4.1f   The One-Group Pretest-Posttest Design

	Time 1		Time 2	
Assignment	**Pretest**	**Intervention**	**Posttest**
	O_1	X	O_2

Figure 4.1g   Two-Group Posttest-Only Design: Static Group Comparison

		Time 1		Time 2	
	Assignment	**Pretest**	**Intervention**	**Posttest**
			X	O_1
				O_2

and then the variables are measured again. This takes care of some of the problems associated with the one-shot case study, but it doesn't eliminate the threats of history, testing, maturation, selection, and mortality. Most importantly, if there is a significant difference in the pretest and posttest measurements, we can't tell if the intervention made that difference happen.

M. Peterson and Johnstone (1995) studied the effects on 43 women inmates of a U.S. federal prison of an education program about drug abuse. The participants all had a history of drug abuse, so there is no random assignment here. Peterson and Johnstone measured the participants' health status and perceived well-being before the program began and after the program had been running for nine months. They found that physical fitness measures were improved for the participants as were self-esteem, health awareness, and health-promoting attitudes.

The one-group pretest-posttest design is commonly used in evaluating training programs. The question asked is: Did the people who were exposed to this skill-building program (police officers, nurses, kindergarten teachers, high school algebra students, etc.) get any benefit out of it, and if so, how much?

The Two-Group Posttest Only Design Without Random Assignment

The two-group posttest only design without random assignment design is shown in

Figure 4.1g. This design, also known as the static group comparison, improves on the one-shot *ex post facto* design by adding an untreated control group—an independent case that is evaluated only at time 2. In this design, however, the researcher has no control over assignment of participants to the intervention or control group. This creates an unresolvable validity threat.

There is no way to tell whether the two groups were comparable at time 1, before the intervention, even with a comparison of observations 1 and 3. Therefore, you can only guess whether the intervention caused any differences in the groups at time 2.

Despite this, the static-group comparison design is the best one for evaluating natural experiments, where you have no control over the assignment of participants anyway. The relation between smoking cigarettes (the intervention) and getting lung cancer (the dependent variable), for example, is easily seen by applying the humble *ex post facto* design with a control group for a second posttest.

In 1965, when the American Cancer Society (ACS) did its first big Cancer Prevention Study, men who smoked (that is, those who were subject to the intervention) were about 12 times more likely than nonsmokers (the control group) to die of lung cancer. At that time, relatively few women smoked and those who did had not been smoking very long. Their risk was just 2.7 times that for women nonsmokers of dying from lung cancer.

Once those first ACS data were gathered, however, they became the baseline for a later study and by 1988, things had changed dramatically. Male smokers were then about 23 times more likely than nonsmokers to die of lung cancer, and female smokers were 12.8 times more likely than female nonsmokers to die of lung cancer. Men's risk had doubled (from about 12 to about 23), but women's risk had more than quadrupled (from 2.7 to about 13) (National Cancer Institute 1997).

The death rate for lung cancer has continued to fall among men in the United States, while the death rate for women has increased (http://apps.nccd.cdc.gov/uscs/) (Box 4.3).

Box 4.3 Migration and gender roles: A static-group comparison design

Lambros Comitas and I wanted to find out if the experience abroad of Greek labor migrants had any influence on men's and women's attitudes toward gender roles when they returned to Greece. The best design would have been to survey a group before they went abroad, then again while they were away, and again when they returned to Greece. Since this was not possible, we studied one group of persons who had been abroad and another group of persons who had never left Greece. We treated these two groups as if they were part of a static-group comparison design (Bernard and Comitas 1978).

From a series of life histories with migrants and nonmigrants, we learned that the custom of giving dowry was under severe stress (Bernard and Ashton-Vouyoucalos 1976). Our survey confirmed this: Those who had worked abroad were far less enthusiastic about providing expensive dowries for their daughters than were those who had never left Greece. We concluded that this was in some measure due to the experiences of migrants in West Germany.

There were threats to the validity of this conclusion: Perhaps migrants were a self-selected bunch of people who held the dowry and other traditional Greek customs in low esteem to begin with. But we had those life histories to back up our conclusion. Surveys are weak compared to true experiments, but their power is improved if they are conceptualized in terms of testing natural experiments and if their results are backed up with data from open-ended interviews.

The Interrupted Time Series Design

The interrupted time series design, shown in Figure 4.1h, can be very persuasive. It involves getting data from a series of points before and after an intervention and evaluating statistically whether the intervention has had an impact.

Figure 4.3 shows the rate of alcohol deaths, per 100,000 population, in Russia, from 1956 to 2002 (Pridemore et al. 2007:281). The year 1992 marks the formal shift in Russia to a market economy from a centrally planned one.

As it turns out, homicide and suicide rates show very similar patterns—something that Pridemore et al. interpret as outcomes that are predictable from Durkheim's (1933 [1893], 1951 [1897]) theory of anomie.

The interrupted time series design is used to assess the effect of new laws. Until 1985, if two working spouses in Canada were married in January, then each of them paid full taxes on their own income. But if they married in December, one of them could claim the other as a dependent. The loophole was closed in

Figure 4.1h   The Interrupted Time Series Design

Time 1		Time 2	
Assignment	Pretest	Intervention	Posttest
	OOO	*X*	*OOO*

Figure 4.3   Alcohol Deaths in Russia, 1956–2002: An Interrupted Time Series

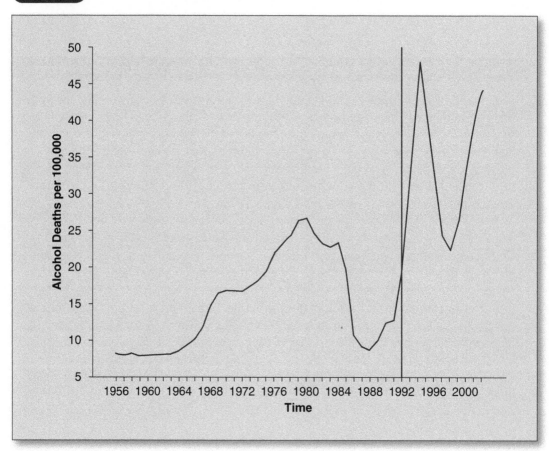

Source: W. A. Pridemore et al., "An Interrupted Time-Series Analysis of Durkeim's Social Deregulation Thesis: The Case of the Russian Federation." *Justice Quarterly* 24:272–90, p. 281, 2007.

1986. Gelardi (1996) treated the new law as an interruption in a time series and found, just as we'd predict, a significant decrease in the percentage of marriages in December immediately after the new law took effect.

Gelardi found the same result when he examined times series data from England and Wales, where a similar change in the law had occurred in 1968. Bonham et al. (1992) found that Hawaii's 1987 tax of 5.25% on hotel rooms had no effect on rentals. In that case, the state simply made money and the hotel industry didn't suffer any loss.

THOUGHT EXPERIMENTS

As you can see, it is next to impossible to eliminate threats to validity in natural experiments.

However, there is a way to understand those threats and to keep them as low as possible: Think about research questions as if it were possible to test them in *true* experiments. These are called **thought experiments**.

This wonderful device is part of everyday culture in the physical sciences. In 1972, I did an ethnographic study of scientists at Scripps Institution of Oceanography. Here's a snippet from a conversation I heard among some physicists there. "If we could only get rid of clouds, we could capture more of the sun's energy to run stuff on Earth," one person said. "Well," said another, "there are no clouds above the Earth's atmosphere. The sun's energy would be lots easier to capture out there."

"Yeah," said the first, "so suppose we send up a satellite, with solar panels to convert sunlight to electricity, and we attach a really long extension cord so the satellite was tethered to the Earth. Would that work?" The discussion got weirder from there, if you can imagine, but it led to a lot of really useful ideas for research.

Suppose you wanted to know if Americans who own hand guns are more likely to get shot than are Americans who don't own hand guns. The experiment you'd have to set up is pretty macabre, but do the thought experiment nonetheless (no ethical issues are at stake in thinking). What experimental conditions would be required for you to be sure that both owning a hand gun and having a high probability of getting shot were not caused by some third factor, like place of residence and exposure to violent crime?

Or suppose you wanted to know if small farms can produce organically grown food on a scale sufficiently large to be profitable. What would a true experiment to test this question look like? You might select some smallish farms with similar acreage and assign half of them randomly to grow vegetables organically. You'd assign the other half of the farms to grow the same vegetables using all the usual technology (pesticides, fungicides, chemical fertilizers, and so on). Then, after a while, you'd measure some things about the farms'

productivity and profitability and see which of them did better.

How could you be sure that organic or nonorganic methods of farming made the difference in profitability? Perhaps you'd need to control for access to the kinds of market populations that are friendly toward organically produced food (like university towns) or for differences in the characteristics of soils and weather patterns. Obviously, you can't do a true experiment on this topic, randomly assigning farmers to use organic or high-tech methods, but you *can* evaluate the experiments that real farmers are conducting every day in their choice of farming practices.

So, after you've itemized the possible threats to validity in your thought experiment, go out and look for natural experiments—societies, voluntary associations, organizations—that conform most closely to your ideal experiment. Then evaluate those natural experiments.

That's what Karen Davis and Susan Weller (1999) did in their study of the efficacy of condoms in preventing the transmission of HIV among heterosexuals. Here's the experiment you'd have to conduct. First, get 1,000 heterosexual couples. Make each couple randomly serodiscordant. That is, for each couple, randomly assign the man or the woman to be HIV-positive. Assign each couple randomly to one of three conditions: (1) they use condoms for each sexual act; (2) they sometimes use condoms; or (3) they don't use condoms at all. Let the experiment run a few years. Then see how many of the couples in which condoms are always used remain serodiscordant and how many become seroconcordant—that is, they are both HIV-positive. Compare across conditions and see how much difference it makes to always use a condom.

Clearly, no one could conduct such an experiment. But Davis and Weller scoured the literature on condom efficacy and found 25 studies that met three criteria: (1) the focus was on serodiscordant heterosexual couples who said they regularly had penetrative sexual intercourse; (2) the HIV status of the subjects in each study had been determined by a blood test; and (3) there was information on the use of condoms. The 25 studies involved thousands of subjects, and from this **meta-analysis** Davis and Weller established that consistent use of condoms reduced the rate of HIV transmission by over 85% (**Further Reading:** thought experiments).

TRUE EXPERIMENTS IN THE LAB

Laboratory experiments to test theories about how things work in the real world is the preeminent method in social psychology. It has long been observed that fraternity hazing is difficult, dangerous, and painful—and produces people who come out of it supporting their tormentors. Remember Festinger's cognitive dissonance theory? That theory predicts that people who come out of a tough initiation experience (marine recruits at boot camp, prisoners of war, girls and boys who go through genital mutilation, etc.) wind up as supporters of their tormentors.

In a classic experiment, Elliot Aronson and Judson Mills (1959) recruited 63 college women for a discussion group that ostensibly was being formed to talk about psychological aspects of sex. To make sure that only mature people—people who could discuss sex openly—would make it into this group, some of the women would have to go through a screening test. Or at least that's what they were *told*.

A third of the women were assigned randomly to a group that had to read a list of obscene words and some sexually explicit passages from some novels—aloud, in front of a man who was running the experiment. (It may be hard to imagine now, but those women who went through this in the 1950s must have been very uncomfortable.) Another third were assigned randomly to a group that had to recite some nonobscene words that had to do

with sex, and a third group went through no screening at all.

Then, each participant listened in on a discussion that was supposedly going on among the members of the group she was joining. The "discussion" was actually a recording and it was, as Aronson and Mills said, "one of the most worthless and uninteresting discussions imaginable" (Aronson and Mills 1959:179). The women rated the discussion, on a scale of 0–15, on things like dull-interesting, intelligent-unintelligent, and so on.

Those in the tough initiation condition rated the discussion higher than did the women in either the control group or the mild initiation group. Since all the women were assigned randomly to participate in one of the groups, the outcome was unlikely to have occurred by chance. The women in the tough initiation condition had gone through a lot to join the discussion. When they discovered how boringly nonprurient it was, what did they do? They convinced themselves that the group was worth joining.

Aronson and Mills's findings were corroborated by Gerard and Mathewson (1966) in an independent experiment. Those findings from the laboratory can now be the basis for a field test, across cultures, of the original hypothesis.

Conversely, events in the real world can stimulate laboratory experiments. In 1963, in Queens, New York, Kitty Genovese was stabbed to death in the street one night. There were reported to be 38 eye-witnesses who saw the whole grisly episode from their apartment windows, and not one of them called the police. The newspapers called it "apathy," but Bibb Latané and John Darley had a different explanation. They called it **diffusion of responsibility** and they did an experiment to test their idea (1968).

Latané and Darley invited ordinary people to participate in a "psychology experiment." While the subjects were waiting in an anteroom to be called for the experiment, the room filled with smoke. If there was a single subject in the room, 75% reported the smoke right away. If there were three or more subjects waiting together, they reported the smoke only 38% of the time. People in groups just couldn't figure out whose responsibility it was to do something. So they did nothing.

As it turns out, there probably weren't 38 witnesses to the murder; none of the witnesses could have seen the whole episode; and some of the witnesses did call the police (Manning et al. 2007). Nevertheless, hundreds of studies on what's known as the bystander effect have been published since Latané and Darley did their pioneering work. A real event gave two scientists an idea that they tested in an experiment, and that experiment opened a whole area of research (**Further Reading:** diffusion of responsibility).

TRUE EXPERIMENTS IN THE FIELD

When experiments are done outside the lab, they are called field experiments. Several researchers have been studying the effect of being touched on consumers' spending. In one experiment (Hornik 1992), as lone shoppers (no couples) entered a large bookstore, an "employee" came up and handed them a catalog. Alternating between customers, the employee-experimenter touched about half the shoppers lightly on the upper arm.

The results? Across 286 shoppers, those who were touched spent an average of $15.03; those who were not touched spent just $12.23. (That's $26 vs. $21 in 2011 dollars.) The difference was across the board, no matter what the sex of the toucher or the shopper.

In another of his experiments, Hornik enlisted the help of eight servers—four men and four women—at a large restaurant. At the end of the meal, the servers asked each of 248 couples (men and women) how the meal was. Right then, for half the couples, the servers touched the arm of either the male or the female in the couple for one second. The servers

didn't know it, but they had been selected out of 27 servers in the restaurant to represent two ends of a physical attractiveness scale. The results? Men and women alike left bigger tips when they were touched, but the effect was stronger for women patrons than for men. Overall, couples left about a 19% tip when the woman was touched, but only 16.5% when the man was touched. (See Seiter [2007] for more field experiments on tipping.)

Ronald Milliman (1986) tested the effects of slow and fast music on the behavior of customers in a restaurant. First, Milliman played a number of instrumental pieces as background music. He asked 227 randomly chosen customers "Do you consider the music playing right now as slow tempo, fast tempo, or in between?" From these data, he identified slow music as 72 beats per minute or fewer and fast music as 92 beats per minute or more.

Then, for eight consecutive weekends, Milliman played slow music and fast music on alternating nights. The first weekend, he played slow music on Friday night and fast music on Saturday night. The next weekend he reversed the order—just in case different kinds of people like to go out on Friday and Saturday night. This procedure simulated assigning customers randomly to the different conditions of slow or fast music. Milliman used only instrumental music in order not to confound the experiment with **exogenous variables** like gender of vocalist, popularity of vocalist, and so on.

Milliman looked at the effect of the two music tempos on six dependent variables. Music tempo had no effect on five of those variables. It had no effect on the time it took for employees to take, prepare, and serve customers' orders. It had no effect on the number of people who decided to leave the restaurant before being seated (it was a popular restaurant, and there was usually a wait on weekends for a table). And it had no effect on the total dollar amount of food purchased.

Music tempo had a significant effect, however, on the amount of time that customers spent at their tables. With slow music, customers spent 56 minutes eating; with fast music, they spent only 45 minutes. For tables that were occupied those extra 11 minutes, the average bar tab was $30.47, about $9 more than the average bar tab per table in the fast-music treatment. Since the amount of food purchased was the same under both conditions, and since profits are much higher on bar purchases, the total profit margin per table was dramatically higher in the slow music treatment.

Marvin Harris and his colleagues (1993) conducted a field experiment in Brazil to test the effect of substituting one word in the question that deals with race on the Brazilian census. The demographers who designed the census had decided that the term *parda* was a more reliable gloss than *morena* for what English speakers call "brown," despite overwhelming evidence that Brazilians prefer the term *morena*.

In the town of Rio de Contas, Harris et al. assigned 505 houses randomly to one of two groups and interviewed one adult in each house. All respondents were asked to say what *cor* (color) they thought they were. This was the free-choice option. Then they were asked to choose one of four terms that best described their *cor*. One group (with 252 respondents) was asked to select among *branca* (white), *parda* (brown), *preta* (black), and *amerela* (yellow). This was the "*parda* option"—the one used on the Brazilian census. The other group (with 253 respondents) was asked to select among *branca*, *morena* (brown), *preta*, and *amerela*. This was the "*morena* option," and is the intervention, or treatment in Harris's experiment.

Among the 252 people given the *parda* option, 131 (52%) identified themselves as *morena* in the free-choice option (when simply asked to say what color they were). But when given the *parda* option, only 80 of those people said they were *parda* and 41 said they were *branca* (the rest chose the other two categories). Presumably, those 41 people would have labeled themselves *morena* if they'd had the

chance; not wanting to be labeled *parda*, they said they were *branca*. The *parda* option, then, produces more Whites (*brancas*) in the Brazilian census and fewer Browns (*pardas*).

Of the 253 people who responded to the *morena* option, 160 (63%) said they were *morena*. Of those 160, only 122 had chosen to call themselves *morena* in the free-choice option. So, giving people the *morena* option actually increases the number of Browns (*morenas*) and decreases the number of Whites (*brancas*) in the Brazilian census.

Does this difference make a difference? Social scientists who study the Brazilian census have found that those who are labeled Whites live about seven years longer than do those labeled non-Whites in that country. If 31% of self-described *morenas* say they are Whites when there is no *morena* label on a survey and are forced to label themselves *parda*, what does this do to all the social and economic statistics about racial groups in Brazil? (Harris et al. 1993) (**Further Research:** field experiments).

NATURAL EXPERIMENTS

True experiments and quasi-experiments are *conducted* and the results are *evaluated* later. Natural experiments, by contrast, are going on around us all the time. They are not conducted by researchers at all—they are simply evaluated.

Here are four examples of common natural experiments: (1) Some employees in a company get expanded job responsibilities; some do not. (2) Some young people choose to migrate from small, isolated communities in northern Quebec to Montreal; others stay put. (3) Some second-generation, middle-class Mexican American students go to college; some do not. (4) Some cultures practice female infanticide; some do not.

Each of these situations constitutes a natural experiment that tests *something* about human behavior and thought. The trick is to ask "What hypothesis is being tested by what's going on here?"

To evaluate natural experiments—that is, to figure out what hypothesis is being tested—you need to be alert to the possibilities and collect the right data. There's a really important natural experiment going in an area of Mexico where I've worked over the years. A major irrigation system has been installed over the last 50 years in parts of a desert valley. Some of the villages affected by the irrigation system are populated entirely by Ñähñu (Otomí) Indians; other villages are entirely mestizo (as the majority population of Mexico is called).

Some of the Indian villages in the area are too high up the valley slope for the irrigation system to reach. I could not have decided to run this multimillion dollar system through certain villages and bypass others, but the instant the decision was made by others, a natural experiment on the effects of a particular intervention was set in motion. There is a treatment (irrigation), there are treatment groups (villages full of people who get the irrigation), and there are control groups (villages full of people who are left out).

Unfortunately, I can't evaluate the experiment because I simply failed to see the possibilities early enough. Several studies of the region show that the intervention is having profound effects, but no one thought to measure things at the village level like average wealth or rates of migration, alcoholism, literacy, diabetes . . . things that could easily have been affected by the coming of irrigation. Had anyone done so—if we had baseline data—we would be in a better position to ask "What hypotheses about human behavior are being tested by this experiment?" I can't reconstruct variables from 50 years ago. The logical power of the experimental model for establishing cause and effect between the intervention and the dependent variables is destroyed.

Some natural experiments, though, like the famous 1955 Connecticut speeding law, produce terrific data all by themselves for evaluation. In 1955, the governor of Connecticut ordered strict enforcement of speeding laws in the state. The object was to cut down on the alarming number of traffic fatalities. Anyone caught speeding had their driver's license suspended for at least 30 days. Traffic deaths fell from 324 in 1955 to 284 in 1956. A lot of people had been inconvenienced with speeding tickets and suspension of driving privileges, but 40 lives had been saved.

The question was whether the crackdown was the cause of the decline in traffic deaths. Campbell and Ross (1968) used the available data to find out. They plotted the traffic deaths for 1951 to 1959 in Connecticut, Massachusetts, New York, New Jersey, and Rhode Island. Each of those states has more or less the same weather, and they all produced good data on traffic fatalities. Four of the five states showed an increase in highway deaths in 1955, and all five states showed a decline in traffic deaths the following year, 1956. If that were all you knew, you couldn't be sure about the cause of the decline. However, traffic deaths continued to decline steadily in Connecticut for the next three years (1957, 1958, 1959). In Rhode Island and Massachusetts, they went up; in New Jersey, they went down a bit and then up again; and in New York, they remained about the same.

Connecticut was the only state that showed a consistent reduction in highway deaths for four years after the stiff penalties were introduced. Campbell and Ross treated these data as a series of natural experiments, and the results were convincing: Stiff penalties for speeders saves lives.

Natural Experiments Are Everywhere

If you think like an experimentalist, you eventually come to see the unlimited possibilities for research going on all around you. Across the United States, school boards set rigid cutoff dates for children who are starting school. Suppose the cutoff is August 1. Children born at the end of July start kindergarten at age 5. Children born at the beginning of August start at age 6. Since children from 5 to 7 are going through an intense period of cognitive development, Morrison et al. (1996) treat this situation as a natural experiment and ask: Are there short- and long-term impacts on cognitive skills of just missing or just making the cutoff?

Ever notice how people like to tell stories about the time they found themselves sitting next to a famous person on a plane? It's called BIRGing in social psychology—basking in reflected glory. Cialdini et al. (1976) evaluated the natural BIRGing experiment that is conducted on most big university campuses every weekend during football season. Over a period of eight weeks, professors at Arizona State, Louisiana State, Ohio State, Notre Dame, Michigan, the University of Pittsburgh, and the University of Southern California recorded the percentage of students in their introductory psychology classes who wore school insignias (buttons, hats, t-shirts, etc.) on the Monday after Saturday football games.

For 177 students per week, on average, over eight weeks, 63% wore some school insignia after wins in football versus 44% after losses or ties. The difference was statistically significant and the finding opened up a whole area of research that continues (Madrigal and Chen 2008).

Here's another one. On January 1, 2002, 12 of the then-15 members of the European Union gave up their individual currencies and adopted the euro (there are now 17 countries in the eurozone out of 27 in the European Union). Greece was one of the 12, Denmark wasn't. Some researchers noticed that many of the euro coins were smaller than the Greek drachma coins they'd replaced and thought that this might create a choking hazard for small children (Papadopoulos et al. 2004). The researchers compared the number of choking incidents reported in Danish and Greek hospitals in January through March from 1996 through 2002.

Sure enough, there was no increase in the rate of those incidents in Denmark (which hadn't converted to the euro), but the rate in Greece suddenly more than doubled in 2002 (Box 4.4).

Box 4.4 Case control and natural experiments

In a **case control design**, you compare naturally occurring cases of a criterion (like having a certain illness or injury, or attempting suicide, or being homeless) with people who match the cases on many criteria, but *not* on the case criterion.

This method is widely used in public health research. The first link between cigarette smoking and lung cancer, for example, was the result of a case-control study (Wynder and Graham 1950). A classic case-control study in the social sciences was done by Art Rubel and colleagues (1984) on the Latin American folk illness known as *susto*. Among Indian people, the symptoms of *susto*—anxiety, diarrhea, difficulty breathing, and others—are often said to result from a loss of soul, while among mestizo people the symptoms are often attributed to having experienced some fright (from the verb *asustarse*, to become frightened).

Rubel and his colleagues compared people in two Indian villages and one mestizo village in Mexico, all of whom suffered from *susto* (the **index cases**) with people in the same villages who did not (the **control cases**). There were no statistically significant differences between the 47 index cases and the 48 controls on tests of psychiatric symptoms. Seven years after the study was completed, however, 17% of the index cases had died—and *none* of the control cases had died. The design in this study makes it thoroughly convincing.

There is a well-known hypothesis in psychology called the "goal-gradient hypothesis" or "deadline hypothesis." In 1934, Clark Hull showed that the closer rats came to food, the faster they went. Since then, we've learned that the number of plays in a football game is highest in the second quarter, next highest in the fourth quarter, and lowest in the first and third quarters; trading goes up in the last two hours of the day at the New York Stock Exchange (Webb and Weick 1983); and when people get one of those "Buy ten coffees, get one free" cards, they buy coffees more frequently, the closer they get to the reward (Kivetz et al. 2006). Apparently, people, like rats, perform the most when they face a deadline.

Data for evaluating natural experiments can come from direct observation (counting up the t-shirts with school colors) or from archives (records of stock trades), but they can also come from survey questionnaires. Emotional pressures are among the predictors of alcoholism. Before 1975, all men 18 years old and older in the United States were subject to the military draft—a kind of lottery that determined who would spend at least two years in the armed services. Goldberg et al. (1991) reasoned that men who had been subject to the military draft were subject to more emotional pressures than those who weren't. Goldberg et al. evaluated this natural experiment with data on over 1,800 male respondents in the National Health Interview Surveys of 1977, 1983, and 1985.

As it turned out, men who had been eligible for the draft were *not* more likely to be heavy consumers of alcohol later in life than were men who had never been eligible for the draft. But the men who had been eligible for the draft were more likely to have served in the military, and those men were more likely than men who had not served to be heavy drinkers.

NATURALISTIC EXPERIMENTS

In a naturalistic experiment, you contrive to collect experimental data under natural conditions.

You make the data happen out in the natural world (not in the lab) and you evaluate the results.

In a memorable experiment, elegant in its simplicity of design, Doob and Gross (1968) had a car stop at a red light and wait for 15 seconds after the light turned green before moving again. In one experimental condition, they used a new car and a well-dressed driver. In another condition, they used an old, beat-up car and a shabbily dressed driver. They repeated the experiment many times and measured the time it took for people in the car behind the experimental car to start honking their horns. It won't surprise you to learn that people were quicker to vent their frustration at apparently low-status cars and drivers.

Piliavin et al. (1969) did a famous naturalistic experiment to test the "good Samaritan" problem. Students in New York City rode a particular subway train that had a 7.5-minute run at one point. At 70 seconds into the run, a researcher pitched forward and collapsed. The team used four experimental conditions: The "stricken" person was either Black or White and was either carrying a cane or a liquor bottle. Observers noted how long it took for people in the subway car to come to the aid of the supposedly stricken person, the total population of the car, whether bystanders were Black or White, and so on. You can conjure up the results. There were no surprises.

Harari et al. (1985) recruited drama majors to test whether men on a college campus would come to the aid of a woman being raped. They staged realistic-sounding rape scenes and found that there was a significant difference in the helping reaction of male passersby if those men were alone or in groups (**Further Reading:** naturalistic experiments).

The Small-World Experiment

Consider this: You're having coffee near the Trevi Fountain in Rome. You overhear two Americans chatting next to you and you ask where they're from. One of them says he's from Sioux City, Iowa. You say you've got a friend from Sioux City and it turns out to be your new acquaintance's cousin. The culturally appropriate reaction at this point is for everyone to say, "Wow, what a small world."

Stanley Milgram (1967) contrived an experiment to test how small the world really is. He asked a group of people in the midwestern United States to send a folder to a divinity student at Harvard University, but only if the subject *knew* the divinity student personally. Otherwise, he asked them to send the folders to an acquaintance whom they thought had a chance of knowing the "target" at Harvard.

The folders got sent around from acquaintance to acquaintance until they wound up in the hands of someone who actually knew the target—at which point the folders were sent, as per the instructions in the game, to the target. The average number of links between all the "starters" and the target was about five. It really *is* a small world.

No one expects this experiment to actually happen in real life. It's contrived as can be and lacks control. On the other hand, it's compelling because it says *something* about how the natural world works. The finding was so compelling that it was the basis for the Broadway play *Six Degrees of Separation*, as well as the movie of the same name that followed and the game *Six Degrees of Kevin Bacon*. It also provoked research, first by social scientists and then by physicists and mathematicians, on the structure of relations in everything from people to corporations to nations to neurons to sites on the Internet. Looking for the structure of relations is another way of saying network analysis (**Further reading:** small-world research).

The Lost-Letter Technique

Another of Milgram's contributions is a method for doing unobtrusive surveys of political opinion. The method is called the "lost-letter technique" and consists of "losing" a lot of letters that have addresses and stamps on them (Milgram et al. 1965).

The technique is based on two assumptions. First, people in many societies believe that they ought to mail a letter if they find one, especially if it has a stamp on it. Second, people will be less likely to drop a lost letter in the mail if it is addressed to someone or some organization that they don't like.

Milgram et al. (1965) tested this in an experiment in New Haven, Connecticut. They lost 400 letters in 10 districts of the city. They dropped the letters on the street; they left them in phone booths; they left them on counters at shops; and they tucked them under windshield wipers (after penciling "found near car" on the back of the envelope). Over 70% of the letters addressed to an individual or to a medical research company were returned. Only 25% of the letters addressed to either "Friends of the Communist Party" or "Friends of the Nazi Party" were returned. (The addresses were all the same post box that had been rented for the experiment.)

By losing letters in a sample of communities, and by calculating the different rates at which they are returned, you can test variations in sentiment. Two of Milgram's students distributed anti-Nazi letters in Munich. The letters did not come back as much from some neighborhoods as from others, and they were thus able to pinpoint the areas of strongest neo-Nazi sentiment (Milgram 1969:68).

Bushman and Bonacci (2004) extended the lost-letter technique to e-mail by purposely sending messages out that appeared to be intended for someone other than the recipient. The surname of the supposed recipient was clearly either European or Arabic. The message said that the recipient either had or had not been awarded a prestigious four-year scholarship and that a response was required within 48 hours. The recipients of these messages were 512 intro psych college students who had filled out a questionnaire two weeks prior to the experiment, so the researchers had a lot of information about those recipients, including scores on a scale of prejudice against various minorities (Asians, Hispanics, African Americans, and Arab Americans). Those with higher prejudice scores were less likely to return the message with good news for an Arab and more likely to return the message with bad news.

The lost-letter technique has sampling problems and validity problems galore associated with it. But you can see just how intuitively powerful the results can be (**Further Reading:** the lost-letter technique) (Box 4.5).

Box 4.5 Naturalistic experiments don't have to be complicated

Walker (2006) rode his bicycle 200 miles through Bristol and Salisbury England during regular working hours dressed as an ordinary commuter—sometimes wearing a helmet, sometimes not; sometimes wearing a woman's long-haired wig, sometimes not. Walker outfitted his bike with a hidden distance sensor and a tiny camera and then, systematically varying his distance from the curb, he measured how close cars came as they passed him. The further from the edge he rode, the closer drivers came; drivers stayed further from him when he appeared to be a woman; and drivers came closer to him when he wasn't wearing a helmet than when he was. Fortunately, both times he got hit doing this experiment, he was wearing the helmet.

Comparative Field Experiments

Naturalistic field experiments appeal to me because they are excellent for comparative research, and comparison is so important for developing theory. Feldman (1968) did five field experiments in Paris, Boston, and Athens to test whether people in those cities respond more kindly to foreigners or to members of their own culture.

In one experiment, the researchers simply asked for directions and measured whether foreigners or natives got better treatment. Parisians and Athenians gave help significantly more often to fellow citizens than to foreigners. In Boston, there was no difference.

In the second experiment, foreigners and natives stood at major metro stops and asked total strangers to do them a favor. They explained that they were waiting for a friend, couldn't leave the spot they were on, and had to mail a letter. They asked people to mail the letters for them (the letters were addressed to the experiment headquarters) and simply counted how many letters they got back from the different metro stops in each city. Half the letters were unstamped.

In Boston and Paris, between 32% and 35% of the people refused to mail a letter for a fellow citizen. In Athens, 93% refused. Parisians treated Americans significantly better than Bostonians treated Frenchmen on this task. In fact, in cases where Parisians were asked to mail a letter that was stamped, they treated Americans significantly better than they treated other Parisians. (So much for *that* stereotype.)

In the third experiment, researchers approached informants and said: "Excuse me, sir. Did you just drop this dollar bill?" (or other currency, depending on the city). It was easy to measure whether or not people falsely claimed the money more from foreigners than from natives. This experiment yielded meager results.

In the fourth experiment, foreigners and natives went to pastry shops in the three cities, bought a small item, and gave the clerk 25% more than the item cost. Then they left the shop and recorded whether the clerk had offered to return the overpayment. This experiment also showed little difference among the cities or between the way foreigners and locals are treated.

And in the fifth experiment, researchers took taxis from the same beginning points to the same destinations in all three cities. They measured whether foreigners or natives were charged more. In neither Boston nor Athens was a foreigner overcharged more than a local. In Paris, however, Feldman found that "the American foreigner was overcharged significantly more often than the French compatriot in a variety of ingenious ways" (1968:11).

Feldman collected data on more than 3,000 interactions and was able to draw conclusions about cultural differences in how various peoples respond to foreigners as opposed to other natives. Some stereotypes were confirmed; others were crushed. Since Feldman's pioneering work, dozens of studies have been done on cross-cultural differences in helping strangers (see Levine et al. [2001], for example).

Bochner's Field Experiments in Australia

Bochner did a series of interesting experiments on the nature of Aboriginal-White relations in urban Australia (see Bochner [1980:335–40] for a review). These experiments are clever, inexpensive, and illuminating, and Bochner's self-conscious critique of the limitations of his own work is a model for field experimentalists to follow. In one experiment, Bochner put two classified ads in a Sydney paper:

Young couple, no children, want to rent small unfurnished flat up to $25 per week. Saturday only. 759–6000.

Young Aboriginal couple, no children, want to rent small unfurnished flat up to $25 per week. Saturday only. 759–6161. [Bochner 1972:335]

Different people were assigned to answer the two phones, to ensure that callers who responded to both ads would not hear the same voice. Note that the ads were identical in every respect, except for fact that in one of the ads the ethnicity

of the couple was identified and in the other it was not. There were 14 responses to the ethnically nonspecific ad and two responses to the ethnically specific ad (three additional people responded to both ads).

In another experiment, Bochner exploited what he calls the "Fifi effect" (Bochner 1980:336). The Fifi effect refers to the fact that urbanites acknowledge the presence of strangers who pass by while walking a dog and ignore others. Bochner sent a White woman and an Aboriginal woman, both in their early 20s, and similarly dressed, to a public park in Sydney. He had them walk a small dog through randomly assigned sectors of the park, for 10 minutes in each sector.

Each woman was followed by two observers, who gave the impression that they were just out for a stroll. The two observers *independently* recorded the interaction of the women with passersby. The observers recorded the frequency of smiles offered to the women, the number of times anyone said anything to the women, and the number of nonverbal recognition nods the women received. The White woman received 50 approaches; the Aboriginal woman received only 18 (Bochner 1971:111).

There are many elegant touches in this experiment. Note how the age and dress of the experimenters were controlled so that only their ethnic identity remained as a dependent variable. Note how the time for each experimental trial (10 minutes in each sector) was controlled to ensure an equal opportunity for each woman to receive the same treatment by strangers. Bochner did preliminary observation in the park and divided it into sectors that had the same population density so that the chance for interaction with strangers would be about equal in each run of the experiment, and he used two independent observer-recorders.

As Bochner points out, however, there were still design flaws that threatened the internal validity of the experiment (1980:337). As it happens, the interrater reliability of the two observers in this experiment was nearly perfect. But suppose the two observers shared the same cultural expectations about Aboriginal-White relations in urban Australia. They might have quite reliably misrecorded the cues that they were observing.

Reactive and unobtrusive observations alike tell you *what* happened, not *why*. It is tempting to conclude that the Aboriginal woman was ignored because of active prejudice. But, says Bochner, "perhaps passersby ignored the Aboriginal . . . because they felt a personal approach might be misconstrued as patronizing" (Bochner 1980:338).

In Bochner's third study, a young White or Aboriginal woman walked into a butcher's shop and asked for 10 cents' worth of bones for her pet dog (about 50 cents in current Australian dollars). The dependent variables in the experiment were the weight and quality of the bones. (An independent dog fancier rated the bones on a three-point scale, without knowing how the bones were obtained, or why.) Each woman visited seven shops in a single middle-class shopping district.

In both amount and quality of bones received, the White woman did better than the Aboriginal, but the differences were not statistically significant—the sample was just too small so no conclusions could be drawn from that study alone. *Taken all together*, though, the three studies done by Bochner and his students comprise a powerful set of information about Aboriginal-White relations in Sydney. Naturalistic experiments like these have their limitations, but they often produce intuitively compelling results. And since Bochner's work, over 30 years ago, dozens of other field studies have been done testing for discrimination in housing, lending, and hiring (Ahmed and Hammarstedt 2008; Sharpe 1998).

ARE FIELD EXPERIMENTS ETHICAL?

Field experiments come in a range of ethical varieties, from innocuous to borderline to downright ugly. I see no ethical problems with the lost-letter technique. When people mail one of the lost letters, they don't know that they are taking part in a social science experiment, but that doesn't bother me. Personally, I see no harm in the experiment to test whether people vent their anger by honking their car horns more quickly at people they think are lower socioeconomic class. These days, however, with road rage an increasing problem, I do not recommend repeating Doob and Gross's experiment.

Randomized field experiments, used mostly in evaluation research, can be problematic. Suppose you wanted to know whether fines or jail sentences are better at changing the behavior of drunk drivers. One way to do that would be to randomly assign people who were convicted of the offense to one or the other condition and watch the results. Suppose one of subjects whom you didn't put in jail kills an innocent person?

The classic experimental design in drug testing requires that some people get the new drug, that some people get a placebo (a sugar pill that has no effect), and that neither the patients nor the doctors administering the drugs know which is which. This double-blind placebo design is responsible for great advances in medicine and the saving of many lives. But suppose that, in the middle of a double-blind trial of a drug you find out that the drug really works. Do you press on and complete the study? Or do you stop right there and make sure that you aren't withholding treatment from people whose lives could be saved? The ethical problems associated with withholding of treatment are under increasing scrutiny (Storosum et al. 2003; Walther 2005; Wertz 1987).

There is a long history of debate about the ethics of deception in psychology and social psychology (see Hertwig and Ortmann [2008] for a review). My own view is that, on balance, some deception is clearly necessary—certain types of research just can't be done without it. When you use deception, though, you run all kinds of risks—not just to research subjects, but to the research itself. These days, college students (who are the subjects for most social psych experiments) are very savvy about all this and are on the lookout for clues as to the "real" reason for an experiment the minute they walk in the door.

If you don't absolutely need deception in true behavioral experiments, that's one less problem you have to deal with. If you decide that deception is required, then understand that the responsibility for any bad outcomes is yours and yours alone.

The experiments by Piliavin et al. (1969) and Harari et al. (1985) on whether people will come to the aid of a stricken person or a woman being raped are real ethical problems. Some of the participants (who neither volunteered to be in an experiment nor were paid for their services) might still be wondering what happened to that poor guy on the subway whom they stepped over in their hurry to get away from an uncomfortable situation—or that woman whose screams they ignored. In laboratory experiments, at least, subjects are debriefed—told what the real purpose of the study was—to reduce emotional distress. In the guerrilla theater type of field experiment, though, no debriefing is possible (Box 4.6).

Box 4.6 Even debriefing has its dark side

Experiments with human subjects, both laboratory and field experiments, pose threats of harm that survey research or ethnographic research don't share. A great many experiments, as we have seen, involve deception—fooling subjects into thinking that an experiment is about one thing when it is really about something else entirely. Research subjects in these experiments may experience a loss of self-esteem when they find out that they've been duped.

If an experiment requires deception, make sure a debriefing session is a routine part of the design. At the debriefing, the true goal of the experiment is divulged. Subjects are told why deception was required, are thanked for their cooperation, and are given the opportunity to talk about any problems they may have with their participation in the experiment. The idea is to help people feel good about their cooperation in a scientific experiment rather than foolish about their having been hoodwinked. Some people may experience a loss of self-esteem if they conclude that they acted badly in an experiment.

How would *you* feel if you were one of the people who failed to respond to a rape victim, and then were told that you were just part of an experiment—that no real rape ever took place, and thank you very much for your help? (**Further Reading:** deception and debriefing).

If you think some of *these* cases are borderline, consider the study by West et al. (1975) on whether there is a little larceny in us all.

The Watergate Experiment

In the Watergate affair of 1974, men loyal to then President Richard Nixon broke into the headquarters of the Democratic Party at the Watergate Hotel in Washington, DC, to photograph documents pertinent to the 1972 election campaign. Their bungling of the job, and the subsequent cover-up by Nixon and his staff at the White House, led to the unprecedented resignation of the president of the United States from office in 1974. Soon after, West et al. conducted their experiment.

They confronted 80 different students with a proposition to burglarize a local advertising firm. Subjects were randomly assigned to one of four conditions. In the first condition, subjects were told that the job was to be done for the Internal Revenue Service. The IRS, it seemed, needed to get the goods on this company to bring them to trial for tax evasion. If the subjects were caught in the act, then the government would guarantee immunity from prosecution. In the second condition, subjects were told that there was no immunity from prosecution.

In the third condition, subjects were told that another advertising agency had paid $8,000 for the job, and that they (the subjects) would get $2,000 for their part in it. (Remember, that was $2,000 in 1975—about $9,000 today.) Finally, in the fourth condition, subjects were told that the burglary was being committed just to see if the plan would work. Nothing would be taken from the office.

Understand that this was not a "let's pretend" exercise. People were not brought into a laboratory and told to imagine that they were being asked to commit a crime. This was for real. Subjects met the experimenter at his home or at a restaurant. They were all criminology students at a university and knew the experimenter to be an actual local private investigator. The private eye arranged an elaborate and convincing plan for the burglary, including data on the comings and goings of police patrol cars, aerial photographs, blueprints of the building—the works.

The subjects of this experiment really believed that they were being solicited to commit a crime. Just as predicted by the researchers, a lot of them agreed to do it in the first condition, where they thought the crime was for a government agency and that they'd be free of danger from prosecution if caught. What do you suppose would happen to *your* sense of self-worth when you were finally debriefed and told that you were one of the 36 out of 80 (45%) who agreed to participate in the burglary in the first condition? (See S. W. Cook [1975] for a critical comment on the ethics of this experiment.)

FACTORIAL DESIGNS: MAIN EFFECTS AND INTERACTION EFFECTS

Most experiments involve analyzing the effects of several independent variables at once. A factorial design lays out all the combinations of all the categories of the independent variables. That way you know how many subjects you need, how many to assign to each condition, and how to run the analysis when the data are in.

It is widely believed that a good laugh has healing power. Rotton and Shats (1996) developed an experimental design to test this. They recruited 39 men and 39 women who were scheduled for orthopedic surgery. The patients were assigned randomly to one of nine groups—eight experimental groups and one control group. The patients in the eight treatment groups got to watch a movie in their room the day after their surgery.

There were three variables: choice, humor, and expectancy. The participants in the high-choice group got a list of 20 movies from which they chose four. The participants in the low-choice group watched a movie that one of the people in the high-choice group had selected. Half the subjects watched humorous movies, and half watched action or adventure movies. Before watching their movie, half the subjects read an article about the benefits of humor, while half read an article about the healthful benefits of exciting movies.

Figure 4.4 is a branching tree diagram that shows how these three variables, each with two attributes, create the eight logical groups for Rotton and Shats's experiment. Table 4.1 shows the same eight-group design, but in a format that is more common. The eight nodes at the bottom of the tree in Figure 4.4 and the sets of numbers in the eight boxes of

Figure 4.4 The Eight Conditions in Rotton and Shat's 2 × 2 × 2 Design

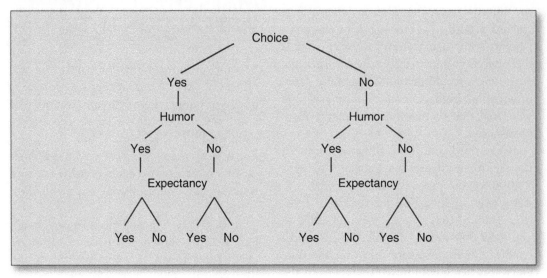

Source: J. Rotton and M. Shats, "Effects of State Humor, Expectancies, and Choice on Postsurgical Mood and Self-Medication: A Field Experiment," *Journal of Applied Social Psychology*, Vol. 26, pp.1775–94, 1996, Wiley-Blackwell.

Table 4.1 Three-Way, 2 × 2 × 2, Factorial Design

			Variable 3	
		Variable 2	Attribute 1	Attribute 2
Variable 1	Attribute 1	Attribute 1	1,1,1 Condition 1	1,1,2 Condition 2
		Attribute 2	1,2,1 Condition 3	1,2,2 Condition 4
	Attribute 2	Attribute 1	2,1,1 Condition 5	2,1,2 Condition 6
		Attribute 2	2,2,1 Condition 7	2,2,2 Condition 8

Table 4.1 are called the conditions in a factorial design.

The dependent variables in this study included a self-report by patients on the amount of pain they had and a direct measure of the amount of pain medication they took.

All the patients had an access device that let them administer more or less of the analgesics that are used for controlling pain after orthopedic surgery.

In assessing the results of a factorial experiment, researchers look for **main effects** and interaction effects. Main effects are the effects of each independent variable on each dependent variable. Interaction effects are effects on dependent variables that occur as a result of *interaction* between two or more independent variables. In this case, Rotton and Shats wanted to know the effects of humor on postoperative pain, but they wanted to know the effect *in different contexts*: in the context of choosing the vehicle of humor or not, in the context of being led to believe that humor has healing benefits or not, and so on.

As it turned out, being able to choose their own movie had no effect when patients saw action films. But patients who saw humorous films and who had not been able to make their own choice of film gave themselves more pain killer than did patients who saw humorous films and had been able to make the selection themselves (Rotton and Shats 1996).

We'll look at how to measure these effects when we take up ANOVA, or analysis of variance, in Chapter 21.

Key Concepts in This Chapter

logic of the experimental method
experimental thinking
research designs
threats to validity
randomized assignment
nonrandomized assignment
true experiments
quasi-experiments
treatment group
control group
field experiments
natural experiments
naturalistic experiments
classic experiment
confirmatory research
exploratory research
intervention group
stimulus group
experimental conditions
systematic bias
selection bias
pretest
posttest
confounds to validity
internal validity
cumulative knowledge

external validity
history confound
maturation confound
testing confound
instrumentation confound
interrater reliability
regression to the mean
mortality confound
diffusion of treatments
two-group pretest-posttest design
pretests
posttests
Solomon four-group design
interaction effect
two-group pretest-posttest design without random assignment
posttest-only design with random assignment
Campbell and Stanley posttest-only design
factorial design
one-shot case study
ex post facto design

one-group pretest-posttest design
two-group posttest only design without random assignment
static group comparison
interrupted time series design
thought experiments
meta-analysis
diffusion of responsibility
exogenous variables
diffusion of responsibility
baseline data
case control design
index cases
control cases
withholding of treatment
deception
debriefing
conditions in a factorial design
main effects
interaction effects

Summary

- The experimental method is not one single technique, but an approach to the development of knowledge. In experiments, researchers try to control the effects of confounds to understand the effects of particular independent variables on outcomes. In other words, they try to maximize the internal validity of experiments.

  ○ The well-known threats to validity include: history, maturation, testing, regression to the mean, selection bias, mortality of subjects (referring to the subjects of experiments dropping out), and diffusion of treatment.

- Different experimental designs control for various threats to validity. Among the widely used designs are: the two-group, pretest-posttest design with random assignment, the Solomon four-group design, the two-group pretest-posttest design without random assignment, the posttest only design with random assignment, the one-shot case study, the one-group pretest-posttest, two-group posttest only design (also called the static group comparison), and the interrupted time series.

  ○ Some designs are more effective than others, but it is not possible to use the most effective designs in all situations.

- You don't necessarily need a laboratory to carry out a true social science experiment. Many experiments are conducted in the field.

  ○ Natural experiments, quasi-experiments, and naturalistic experiments are based on field research rather than on laboratory research.

- Social and behavioral experiments raise particularly serious ethical problems. Even with proper debriefing, participants in experiments may experience loss of self-esteem. The need, or lack of need, for deception in social research is a matter of continuing debate.

- Most experiments involve analyzing the effects of several independent variables at once. A factorial design lays out all the combinations of all the categories of the independent variables. This sets up a blueprint for systematic data analysis.

  ○ In assessing the results of a factorial experiment, researchers look for main effects and interaction effects. Main effects are the effects of each independent variable on each dependent variable. Interaction effects are effects on dependent variables that occur as a result of interaction between two or more independent variables.

Exercises

1. For a random sample of students on your campus, count the number who are wearing school color—clothes, insignia, etc.—on Mondays following sports wins versus Mondays following sports losses. This replicates the study I discussed earlier by Cialdini et al. (1976). See Chapter 5 about taking a random sample.

2. Suppose you were designing an experiment to test whether a new diet plan, coupled with a motivational seminar, helped obese people lose weight. This is a plan developed by a major food manufacturer, so there's plenty of money behind it and you can design the experiment

with whatever resources you think are needed. For example, you can have a large number of participants and a control group; you can have random assignment; you can pay participants; and so on. Write up the design and discuss how you plan to address various threats to the validity of the experiment, including regression to the mean, the John Henry effect, maturation, history, and so on.

3. Look through your local newspaper and find a report of some innovative social program, such as prison reform, a program to provide jobs to young people during school vacations, or a proposal for a new welfare system. Describe how you would evaluate the success of the innovative program. First, briefly describe the innovative program. Next, specify the key dependent variable that the program seeks to affect. Finally, describe how you would measure the dependent variable and how you would assess whether the program had any effect on that variable.

4. A local government agency has awarded you a contract to evaluate a program it has had in place for two years. The program is a day-care center for children of working mothers in a predominantly Spanish-speaking area of a major city in the Southwest. When the program was proposed, its advocates claimed that the cost, in dollars, would be less than the cost of welfare payments to the women who couldn't work because they had no place to leave their children. Now, two years later, the data are in and the bottom line is that it costs much more to keep each child than it would cost to close the day-care center and return to the system of direct welfare payments to the mothers.

Advocates for the center claim that there are many more concerns than just "the bottom line," but they are having a hard time articulating those concerns. Design an evaluation research effort that addresses all the concerns, *except the fiscal ones*, of the parties in this situation.

5. Assume that you have developed a study technique that you believe will result in students scoring higher on this exam. You test the technique with the following design:

R $0_1 \times 0_2$

R 0_3 0_4

List *all* the predictions you can make. If it turns out that O_4 is greater than O_1, what will you conclude? Describe the confounds to internal validity in this experiment. Be sure to distinguish between internal and external validity.

Further Reading

Research design. Brink and Wood (1998), T. D. Cook and Campbell (1979), Glass et al. (1979), Kazdin (1998), Kirk (1995), Marczyk et al. (2005), Trochim (1986). On design in qualitative research: Creswell (2003), Lincoln and Guba (1985), Maxwell (2005).

Case study methods. Feagin et al. (1991), Gerring (2007), Gomm et al. (2000), Mills et al. (2009), Yin (2003).

Thought experiments. Brown (2010), Horowitz and Massey (1991), Sorensen (1992), Tindale and Vollrath (1992).

Diffusion of responsibility. Bandura et al. (1996), Corrion et al. (2009), Freeman et al. (1975), Henriksen and Dayton (2006), Shotland and Straw (1976).

Naturalistic experiments. McGarva et al. (2006), Ruback and Juieng (1997), van Straaten et al. (2008), Walker (2007).

Small-world research. Barabási (2002), Bernard and Killworth (1979), Cho and Fowler (2010), Crossley (2005), Kilduff et al (2008), Kochen (1989), Schnettler (2009), Shotland (1976), Watts and Strogatz (1998, 1999, 2003, 2004).

The lost-letter technique. Ahmed (2010), Bridges et al. (2002), Stern and Faber (1997), Waugh et al. (2000).

Deception and debriefing. Barchard and Williams (2008), Benham (2008), Broeder (1998), K. S. Cook and Yamagishi (2008), Fisher (2005), Kimmel (1998), F. G. Miller et al. (2008), Nicks et al. (1997), Ortmann and Hertwig (1997, 1998), Sharpe and Faye (2009), Sieber et al. (1995) Taylor and Shepperd (1996). See also: **Further Reading** on deception in field studies, Chapter 14.

5
Sampling
The Basics

WHAT ARE SAMPLES AND WHY DO WE NEED THEM?

Informant accuracy, data validity, and even ethical issues (like whether it's all right to deceive people in conducting experiments) are all measurement problems in research. The other big class of problems involves sampling: Given that your measurements are credible, how much of the world do they represent? How far can you generalize the results of your research?

The answer depends, first of all, on the kind of data in which you're interested. There are two kinds of data of interest to social scientists: individual data and cultural data. These two kinds require different approaches to sampling.

Individual data are about *attributes of individuals in a population*. Each person has an age, for example; each person has an income; and each person has preferences for things like products, political positions, and characteristics for a mate. If the idea in collecting data is to estimate the average age, or income, or preference in a larger population—that is, to estimate some population parameters—then a scientifically drawn, unbiased sample is a must. By scientifically drawn, I mean random selection of cases so that every unit of analysis in your study has an equal chance of being chosen for study.

Cultural data are different. Cultural data require experts. If you want to understand a process—like how people in a factory work group decide on whether to lodge a complaint to management, or how the police in a squad car determine whether to stop someone on the street—then you want people who can offer expert explanations about the cultural norm and about variations on that norm (Handwerker et al. 1997). It's one thing to ask: "How many people did you stop on the street for questioning last week?" This requires an answer about individual behavior. It's another thing to ask: "How do people in your squad decide whether to stop someone for questioning on a street patrol?" This requires cultural experts.

Individual attribute data requires probability sampling; cultural data require nonprobability sampling. This chapter is about the basics of probability sampling, which will take us into a discussion of probability theory, variance, and distributions in Chapter 6. We'll get to nonprobability sampling in Chapter 7 (**Further Reading:** general sampling).

WHY THE UNITED STATES STILL HAS A CENSUS

If samples were just easier and cheaper to study but failed to produce useful data, there wouldn't be much to say for them. A study based on a random sample, however, is often *better* than one based on the whole population.

Since 1790, the United States has conducted a census once every 10 years in which every person in the country is supposed to be counted in order to apportion seats in the House of Representatives to the states. Lots of things can go wrong with counting. Heads of households are responsible for filling out and returning the census forms, but in 1990, only 63% of the mailed forms were returned, and that was down from 78% in 1970. The Bureau of the Census had to hire and train half a million people to track down all the people who had not been enumerated in the mailed-back forms.

Even then, there were problems with the final numbers. Some college students were counted twice: Their parents had counted them on the mailed-back census form and then, on census day, some of those same students were tracked down again by enumerators who canvassed the dorms. Meanwhile, lots of other people (like illegal immigrants and people living in places to which the census takers would rather not go) were not being counted at all.

In 1997, the Bureau of the Census asked the U.S. Congress to allow sampling instead of counting for at least some parts of the 2000 Census. This caused a serious political problem: If sampling produced more accurate (and, presumably, higher) estimates of the number of citizens who are, say, homeless or who are migrant farm workers, this would benefit only certain states and might benefit the Democratic Party over the Republican Party. So, Congress rejected the proposal, citing Article 1, Section 2 of the Constitution, which refers to the Census as an "actual Enumeration" (with a capital E, no less).

No getting around it: Actually enumerating means counting, not estimating, and the U.S. Supreme Court agreed, in 1999. To deal with the inaccuracies of a head count, the Bureau of the Census publishes adjustment tables, based on samples. In 2000, for example, the bureau determined that it had undercounted American Indians who live off reservations by about 53,000 (see U.S. Bureau of the Census n.d.). In May 2009, at his confirmation hearing to head the bureau, Robert Groves assured Republican senators that he would not use sampling methods in the then upcoming 2010 Census (Herszenhorn 2009).

IT PAYS TO TAKE SAMPLES AND STICK WITH THEM

If you are doing all the work yourself, it's next to impossible to interview more than a few hundred people. Even a small county school system might have 500 employees, including teachers, administrators, and staff. You'd need several interviewers to reach all those people within a reasonable amount of time. Interviewers may not use the same wording of questions; they may not probe equally well on subjects that require sensitive interviewing; they may not be equally careful in recording data on field instruments and in coding data for analysis. And, as you'll see in the section on telephone interviewing, in Chapter 9, some interviewers actually falsify data.

Most important, you have no idea how much error is introduced by these problems. A well-chosen sample, interviewed by people who have similarly high skills in getting data, has a known chance of being incorrect on any variable. Furthermore, studying an entire population may pose a history threat to the internal validity of your data. If you *don't* add interviewers it may take you so long to complete your research that events intervene that make it impossible to interpret your data.

For example, suppose you're interested in how the nursing staff at a midsize, private hospital feels about a reorganization plan. You decide to survey *all* 210 nurses on the staff, using a structured, 10-minute personal interview. You know that it's tough to track some nurses down—they are very busy and sometimes don't have even

10 minutes to stop and chat; they change shifts, forcing you to find them at 4 a.m.—but you have three months for the research and you figure you can do the survey a little at a time.

Two months into your work, you've gotten 160 interviews on the topic—only 50 to go. Just about that time, the hospital announces that it has been bought out by a big health maintenance corporation—one that's traded on the New York Stock Exchange. All of a sudden the picture changes. Your "sample" of 160 is biased toward those people whom it was easy to find, and you have no idea what *that* means. And even if you could now get those remaining 50 respondents, their opinions may have been radically changed by the new circumstances. The opinions of the 160 respondents who already talked to you may have also changed.

Now you're really stuck. You can't simply throw together the 50 and the 160 interviews; you have no idea what *that* will do to your results. Nor can you compare the 160 and the 50 as representing the nursing staff's attitudes before and after the buy-out. Neither sample is unbiased with regard to what you are studying.

If you had taken a random sample of 60 people in a single week early in your project, you'd now be in much better shape because you'd know the potential sampling error in your study. If historical circumstances (the surprise buy-out, for example) require it, you could interview the same sample of 60 again (in what is known as a **panel study**) or take another representative sample of the same size and see what differences there are before and after the critical event. In either case, *you are better off with the sample than with the whole population.* There is no guarantee that a week is quick enough to avoid the problem described here. It's just less likely to be a problem. Less likely is better than more likely (Box 5.1).

Box 5.1 Probability samples are probably representative

Probability samples are based on taking a given number of units of analysis from a list, called a **sampling frame**, which represents some **population** under study. In a probability, or **unbiased sample**, each individual has exactly the same chance as every other individual of being selected. When this principle is violated, samples become biased.

A famous case of sampling bias occurred in 1970 while the United States was engaged in a very unpopular war in Vietnam. Men were selected to serve in the military by a supposedly random draw. Three hundred and sixty-six capsules (one for each day of the year, including leap year) were put in a drum and the drum was turned to mix the capsules. Then dates were pulled from the drum, one at a time. All the men whose birthdays fell on the days that were selected were drafted.

When enough men had been selected to fill the year's quota, the lottery stopped. Men whose birthdays hadn't been pulled were safe until the following year when the lottery would be run again. It turned out that men whose birthdays were in the later months had a better chance of being drafted than men whose birthdays were earlier in the year. This happened because the drum wasn't rotated enough to thoroughly mix the capsules (Williams 1978). Not a good sampling technique.

Sampling Frames

If you can get it, the first thing you need for a good sample is a good **sampling frame**. (I say "if you can get it" because a lot of social research is done on populations for which no sampling frame exists. More on this at the end of this chapter.) A sampling frame is a list of units of analysis, *from which* you take a sample and *to which* you generalize.

A sampling frame may be the tax rolls of a community or a geographic information system (GIS) map of housing units. Lists of local addresses may be available at libraries or at municipal buildings or online. (Careful: Lists of addresses can be out of date even before they are made public.) Telephone directories were used as sampling frames in the past, but are increasingly obsolete as sampling frames as more and more people across the world switch to cell-phone-only service. Professional survey researchers in the industrialized nations of the world often purchase samples from firms that keep up-to-date databases just for this purpose. For many projects, though, you just have to make your own census of the population you are studying. A census of a factory or a hospital or a small town gives you the opportunity to walk around a community and to talk with most of its members at least once. It lets you be seen by others and it gives you an opportunity to answer questions, as well as to ask them. It allows you to get information that official censuses don't retrieve. A list of the employees at a plant, for example, probably won't have information on all the variables that you need for your research.

A census of a community of actors gives you a sampling frame from which to take many samples during a research project. It also gives you a basis for comparison if you go back to the same population later.

Simple Random Sampling

To get a **simple random sample** of 200 out of 640 professors in a university, you number each individual from 1 to 640 and then take a random grab of 200 out of the numbers from 1 to 640. Most packages for statistical analysis have built in random-number generators, and you can create random samples by using one of the random-number generators on the Internet—like the one at http://www.rand omizer.org/form.htm.

When you have your list of random numbers, then whoever goes with each one is in the sample. Period. If there are 1,230 people in the population, and your list of random numbers says that you have to interview person #212, then do

it. No fair leaving out some people because they are members of the elite and probably wouldn't want to give you the time of day. No fair leaving out people you don't like or don't want to work with. None of that.

A common form of meddling with samples is when door-to-door interviewers find a sample selectee not at home and go to the nearest house for a replacement. This can have dramatically bad results (Box 5.2).

Box 5.2 The social research industry

In the real world of research, random samples are tampered with all the time. No snickering here about the "real world" of research. Social research is a major, worldwide industry. The American Community Survey of the U.S. Census surveys, by mail, around 250,000 people each month—that's around 3,000,000 interviews a year—plus telephone follow-ups with 85,000 people and face-to-face follow-ups with about 40,000 people each month (U.S. Bureau of the Census 2009:Ch. 2, p. 4). Over 300 firms are members of the Council of American Survey Research Organizations (Wright and Marsden 2010:17–19), and about $2 billion was spent in 2009 on online research alone (Baker et al. 2010:715). That's real enough for most people.

Suppose you go out to interview between 10 a.m. and 4 p.m. People who are home during these hours tend to be old, or sick, or mothers with small children. Those same people are home in the evening, too, but now they're joined by all the single people home from work, so the average family size goes down. As Tom Smith, director at the National Opinion Research Center, says, going to the nearest at-home household for a replacement interview introduces systematic bias to your data because you tend to replace nonrespondents with people who are like respondents rather than with people who are like nonrespondents (1989:53).

Telephone survey researchers typically call back from three to 10 times before replacing a member of a sample. When survey researchers suspect (from prior work) that, say, 25% of a sample won't be reachable within, say, three

call-backs, they increase their original sample size by 25% so the final sample will be both the right size and representative. The reason we know this is because researchers report these kinds of compromises when they publish their results. You should, too.

Systematic Random Sampling

If you have a big, unnumbered sampling frame, like the 51,413 students at the University of Florida in 2008, then simple random sampling is nearly impossible. You would have to number all those names first. Instead, you can do **systematic random sampling**. For this, you need a **random start** and a **sampling interval**, N. You enter the sampling frame at the random start and take every Nth person (or item) in the frame. If you have a printout of 51,413 names, listed 400 to a page, select a single random number between 1 and 51,413. If the random number is 9,857, the listing will be 257 names down from the top of page 25.

The sampling interval depends on the size of the population and the number of units in your sample. If there are 51,413 people in the population, and you are sampling 400 of them, then after you enter the sampling frame (the list of 51,413 names) you need to take every 128th person (400 × 128 = 51,200) to ensure that every person has *at least one chance* of being chosen. If there are 640 people in a population, and you are sampling 200 of them, then you would take every 4th person. If you get to the end of the list and you are at number 2 in an interval of 4, just go to the top of the list, start at 3, and keep on going (Box 5.3).

Box 5.3 Periodicity and systematic sampling

Systematic sampling *usually* produces a representative sample, but be aware of the **periodicity** problem. Suppose you're studying a big retirement community in South Florida. The development has 30 identical buildings. Each has six floors, with 10 apartments on each floor, for a total of 1,800 apartments. Now suppose that each floor has one big corner apartment that costs more than the others and attracts a slightly more affluent group of buyers.

If you do a systematic sample of every 10th apartment then, depending on where you entered the list of apartments, you'd have a sample of 180 corner apartments or no corner apartments at all.

David and Mary Hatch (1947) studied a sample of 413 wedding announcements taken from the Sunday society pages of the *New York Times* for June from 1932 to 1942. They found that 238, or about 58% of the announcements, were about weddings in an Episcopal church. They noted that only 2.5% of the population of New York City was Episcopalian at the time, and concluded that the Episcopalian church represented the elite of New York. Cahnman (1948) pointed out that the Hatches had studied only June issues of the *Times*. It seemed reasonable. After all, aren't most society weddings in June? Well, yes. Christian weddings. Upper-class Jews married in other months. The *Times* covered those weddings, but the Hatches missed them. The original article reported 25 weddings (6%) in a Catholic church. (At the time, Catholics were still mostly working-class Irish and Italians.) And Jews weren't on the Hatches' radar because they didn't even note the absence of Jewish weddings.

You can avoid the periodicity problem by doing simple random sampling, but if that's not possible, another solution is to make two systematic passes through the population using different sampling intervals. Then you can compare the two samples on a few independent variables, like age or years of education. Any differences should be attributable to sampling error. If they're not, then you might have a periodicity problem.

STRATIFIED SAMPLING

Stratified random sampling ensures that key subpopulations are included in your sample. You divide a population (a sampling frame) into subpopulations (subframes), based on key independent variables and then take a random (unbiased), sample from each of those subpopulations. You might divide the population into men and women, or into rural and urban subframes—or into key age groups (18–34, 35–49, etc.) or key income groups. As the main sampling frame gets divided by key *independent* variables, the subframes presumably get more and more homogeneous with regard to the key *dependent* variable in the study.

In 2009, for example, the Qunnipiac University Poll asked a representative sample of 2,041 registered voters in the United States the following question: Do you think abortion should be legal in all cases, legal in most cases, illegal in most cases or illegal in all cases? Across all voters, 52% said that abortion should be legal in all (15%) or most (37%) cases and 41% said it should be illegal in all (14%) or most (27%) cases. The remaining 7% had no opinion.

These facts hide some important differences across religious, political, and other subgroups. Among Catholic voters, 50% said that abortion should be legal in all (8%) or most (42%) cases; among Jewish voters, 86% said that abortion should be legal in all (33%) or most (53%) cases. Among registered Democrats, 66% favored legal abortion in all or most cases; among registered Republicans, 30% took that position (Quinnipiac University 2009). Sampling from smaller chunks (by age, gender, and so on) ensures not only that you capture the variation but that you also wind up understanding how that variation is distributed.

This is called maximizing the between-group variance and minimizing the within-group variance for the independent variables in a study. *It's what you want to do in building a sample* because it reduces sampling error and thus makes samples more precise.

This sounds like a great thing to do, but you have to *know what the key independent variables are.* Shoe size is almost certainly not related to what people think is the ideal number of children to have. Gender and generation, however, seem like plausible variables on which to stratify a sample for a study of ideal family size. So, if you are taking a poll to find this number, you might divide the adult population into, say, four generations: 15–29, 30–44, 45–59, and over 59.

With two genders, this creates a sampling design with eight strata: men 15–29, 30–44, 45–59, and over 59; women 15–29, 30–44, 45–59, and over 59. Then you take a random sample of people from each of the eight strata and run your poll. If your hunch about the importance of gender and generation is correct, you'll find the attitudes of men and the attitudes of women more homogeneous than the attitudes of men and women thrown together. Table 5.1 shows the distribution of gender and age cohorts for the United States in 2008. The numbers are in thousands. The numbers in parentheses are percentages of the total population 15 and older.

A proportionate stratified random sample of 2,400 respondents, 15 and older, would

Table 5.1 Gender and Age Cohorts for the U.S. in 2008

Age cohort	Males	Females	Total
15–29	33,132 (13%)	31,836 (13%)	64,968 (26%)
30–44	31,008 (13%)	30,668 (12%)	61,676 (25%)
45–59	31,442 (13%)	32,779 (13%)	64,221 (26%)
>59	25,316 (10%)	31,671 (13%)	56,987 (23%)
Total	120,898 (49%)	126,954 (51%)	247,852 (100%)

Source: Table 8, Statistical Abstract of the United States (2010).

include 312 men between the ages of 30 and 44 (13% of 2,400 = 312), but 288 women between the ages of 30 and 44 (12% of 2,400 = 288), and so on.

Watch out, though. We are accustomed to thinking in terms of gender on questions about family size, but gender-associated preferences are changing rapidly in late industrial societies, and we might be way off base in our thinking. Separating the population into gender strata might just be creating unnecessary work. Worse, it might introduce unknown error. If your guess about age and gender being related to desired number of children is wrong, then using Table 5.1 to create a sampling design will just make it harder for you to discover your error (Box 5.4).

Box 5.4 The rules on stratifying samples

Here are the rules on stratification: (1) If differences on a dependent variable are large across strata like age, sex, ethnic group, and so on, then stratifying a sample is a great idea. (2) If differences are small, then stratifying just adds unnecessary work. (3) If you are uncertain about the independent variables that could be at work in affecting your dependent variable, then leave well enough alone and don't stratify the sample. *You can always stratify the data* you collect and test various stratification schemes in the analysis instead of in the sampling.

Disproportionate Sampling

Disproportionate stratified random sampling is appropriate whenever an important sub-population is likely to be underrepresented in a simple random sample or in a stratified random sample. Native Americans (including American Indians and Alaska Natives) comprise just 1.3% of the population of the United States. If you take 1,000 samples of 1,000 Americans at random, you expect to run into about 13 Native Americans, *on average, across all the samples*. (Some samples will have no Native Americans and some may have 20, but on average you'll get about 13.) Without disproportionate sampling, Native Americans would be underrepresented in any national survey in the United States.

Bachman et al. (2010) wanted to estimate the problem of sexual assault and rape among Native Americans. The U.S. National Crime Victimization Survey canvasses between 67,000 and 100,000 people every year and includes questions for women about rape and sexual assault. But even this massive survey didn't have enough cases for reliable analysis,

so Bachman et al. aggregated all the surveys between 1992 and 2005.

Suppose you are doing a study of factors affecting grade-point averages among a population of 8,000 college students. You suspect that the independent variable called "race" is associated in some way with the dependent variable.

Suppose further that 5% of the student population is African American and that you have time and money to interview 400 students out of the population of 8,000. If you took 10,000 samples of 400 each from the population (replacing the 400 each time, of course), then the average number of African Americans in all the samples would approach 20—that is, 5% of the sample.

But you are going to take *one* sample of 400. It might contain exactly 20 (5%) African Americans; on the other hand, it might contain just five (1.25%) African Americans. To ensure that you have sufficient data on African American students and on White students, you put the African Americans and the Whites into separate *strata* and draw two random samples of 200 each. The African Americans are disproportionately sampled by a factor of 10 (200 instead of the expected 20).

This was the problem that Lieber and Fox (2005) faced in their study of how being African American in Iowa influences decisions in the juvenile courts system—from the decision to detain someone in the first place to the decision on length and type of sentence and the many decisions in between. The population of Iowa is 2.7% African American, compared to 13% in the United States as a whole. Lieber and Fox's sampling frame was all juvenile court referrals during a 21-year period, from 1980 to 2000. They selected 5,554 cases at random, of which 30% (1,666 cases) were African Americans.

This disproportionate random sampling procedure ensured that there would be a minimum number of African American cases for each of the decision stages. It also meant that there was a deliberately created, known source of bias—lack of proportionate representation in the subgroups—which had to be taken into account in data analysis. Which brings us to weighting of data.

Weighting Results

One popular method for collecting data about daily activities is called "experience sampling" (Csikszentmihalyi and Larson 1987; Hektner et al. 2007). You give a sample of people a beeper or a cell phone. They carry it around and you beep or call them at random times during the day. They fill out a little form (either on paper or on a smartphone or PDA that's been programmed with a form) about what they're doing at the time.

We'll look at these kinds of methods in Chapter 14. For now, suppose you want to contrast what people do on weekends and what they do during the week. If you beep people, say, eight times during each day, you'll wind up with 40 reports for each person for the five-day workweek but only 16 forms for each person for each two-day weekend because

you've sampled the two strata—weekdays and weekends—proportionately.

If you want more data points for the weekend, you might beep people 12 times on Saturday and 12 times on Sunday. That gives you 24 data points, but you've disproportionately sampled one stratum. The weekend represents 2/7, or 28.6% of the week, but you've got 64 data points and 24 of them, or 37.5%, are about the weekend. Before comparing any data across the strata, you need to make the weekend data and the weekday data statistically comparable.

This is where **weighting** comes in. Multiply each weekday data point by 1.50 so that the 40 data points become worth 60 and the 24 weekend data points are again worth exactly 2/7 of the total.

Known sources of bias also occur by accident, like when you have unequal response rates in a stratified sample. Suppose you sample 200 men and 200 women for a survey in a factory that employs 60% women and 40% men. Of the 400 potential respondents, 178 men and 163 women respond to your questions. If you compare the answers of men and women on a variable, first, weight each man's data by 178/163 = 1.09 times each woman's data on that variable.

That takes care of the unequal response rates. Then weight each woman's data as counting 1.5 times each man's data on the variable. That takes care of the fact that there are half again as many women employees as there are men.

This may seem complicated, but weighting is a simple procedure available in all major statistical analysis packages.

CLUSTER SAMPLING AND COMPLEX SAMPLING DESIGNS

Cluster sampling is based on the fact that people act out their lives in more or less natural groups, or clusters, like geographic areas (counties, precincts, states), and institutions (like schools, churches, brotherhoods, credit unions, and so on). By sampling from these clusters, we narrow the sampling field from large, heterogeneous chunks to small, homogeneous ones that are relatively easy to find. This minimizes travel time in reaching scattered units of data collection. It also lets you sample populations for which there are no convenient lists or frames.

For example, there are no lists of schoolchildren in large cities, but children cluster in schools. There *are* lists of schools, so you can take a sample of them, and then sample children within each school selected.

Laurent et al. (2003) wanted to assess the rate of sexually transmitted diseases among unregistered female sex workers in Dakar, Senegal. By definition, unregistered means no list, so the researchers used a two-stage cluster sample. They created a sampling frame of all registered and all clandestine bars in Dakar, plus all the unregistered brothels and all the nightclubs. They did this over a period of several months with the help of some women prostitutes, some local physicians who had treated those women, and two social workers, each of whom had worked with female sex workers for over 25 years. Laurent et al. calculated that they needed 94 establishments, so they chose a simple random sample of places from the list of 183. Then they went in teams to each of the 94 places and interviewed all the unregistered prostitutes who were there at the time of the visit.

Sampling designs can involve several stages. If you are studying Haitian refugee children in Miami, you could take a random sample of schools, but if you do that, you'll almost certainly select some schools in which there are no Haitian children. A three-stage sampling design is called for.

In the first stage, you would make a list of the neighborhoods in the city, find out which ones are home to a lot of refugees from Haiti,

and sample those districts. In the second stage, you would take a random sample of schools from each of the chosen districts. Finally, in the third stage, you would develop a list of Haitian refugee children in each school and draw your final sample.

Al-Nuaim et al. (1997) used multistage stratified cluster sampling in their national study of adult obesity in Saudi Arabia. In the first stage, they selected cities and villages from each region of the country so that each region's total population was proportionately represented. Then they randomly selected districts from the local maps of the cities and villages in their sample. Next, they listed all the streets in each of the districts and selected every third street. Then they chose every third house on each of the streets and asked each adult in the selected houses to participate in the study.

PROBABILITY PROPORTIONATE TO SIZE

The best estimates of a parameter are produced in samples taken from clusters of equal size. When clusters are not equal in size, then samples should be taken PPS—with probability proportionate to size.

Suppose you had money and time to do 800 household interviews in a city of 50,000 households. You intend to select 40 blocks, out of a total of 280, and do 20 interviews in each block. You want each of the 800 households in the final sample to have exactly the same probability of being selected.

Should each block be equally likely to be chosen for your sample? No, because census blocks never contribute equally to the total population from which you will take your final sample. A block that has 100 households in it *should* have twice the chance of being chosen for 20 interviews as a block that has 50 households, and half the chance of a block that has 200 households.

When you get down to the block level, each household on a block with 100 residences has a 20% (20/100) chance of being selected for the sample; each household on a block with 300 residences has only a 6.7% (20/300) chance of being selected.

Lené Levy-Storms wanted to talk to older Samoan women in Los Angeles County about mammography. The problem was not that women were reticent to talk about the subject. The problem was how do you find a representative sample of older Samoan women in Los Angeles County?

From prior ethnographic research, Levy-Storms knew that Samoan women regularly attend churches where the minister is Samoan. She went to the president of the Samoan Federation of America in Carson, California, and he suggested nine cities in L.A. County where Samoans were concentrated. There were 60 churches with Samoan ministers in the nine cities, representing nine denominations. Levy-Storms asked each of the ministers to estimate the number of female church members who were over 50 years old. Based on these estimates, she chose a PPS sample of 40 churches (so that churches with more or fewer older women were properly represented). This gave her a sample of 299 Samoan women over 50. This clever sampling strategy really worked: Levy-Storms contacted the 299 women and wound up with 290 interviews—a 97% cooperation rate (Levy-Storms and Wallace 2003).

PPS sampling is called for under three conditions: (1) when you are dealing with large, unevenly distributed populations (such as cities that have high-rise and single-family neighborhoods); (2) when your sample is large enough to withstand being broken up into a lot of pieces (clusters) without substantially increasing the sampling error; and (3) when you have data on the population of many small blocks in a population and can calculate their respective proportionate contributions to the total population.

PPS Samples in the Field— Space Sampling

What do you do when you don't have neat clusters and neat sampling frames printed out on a computer by a reliable government agency? The answer is to place your trust in randomness and *create* maximally heterogeneous clusters from which to take a random sample using space sampling or map sampling.

The map sampling method is adapted from transect sampling in wildlife biology (Burnham et al. 1980). Draw or get a map of the area you are studying. Place 100 numbered dots around the edge of the map. Try to space the numbers equidistant from one another, but don't worry if they are not. Select a pair of numbers at random and draw a line between them. Now select another pair of numbers (be sure to replace the first pair before selecting the second), and draw a line between them. In the unlikely event that you choose the same pair twice, simply choose a third pair. Keep doing this, replacing the numbers each time. After you've drawn about 50 lines, you can begin sampling.

Notice that the lines drawn across the map in Figure 5.1 create a lot of wildly uneven spaces. Since you don't know the distribution of population density in the area you are studying, this technique maximizes the chance that you will properly survey the population, more or less PPS. By creating a series of (essentially) random chunks of different sizes, you distribute the error you might introduce by not knowing the density, and that distribution lowers the possible error.

Number the uneven spaces created by the lines and choose some of them at random. Go to those spaces, number the households, and select an appropriate number at random. Remember, you want to have the same number of households from *each* made-up geographic cluster, no matter what its size. If you are doing 400 interviews, you would select 20 geographic chunks and do 20 interviews or behavioral observations in each.

Figure 5.1 Sampling Map

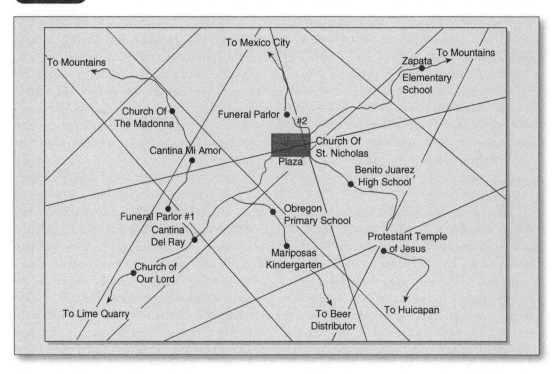

My colleagues and I used this method in 1986 to find out how many people in Mexico City knew someone who died in that city's monster earthquake the year before (Bernard, Johnson et al. 1989). Instead of selecting households, though, my interview team went to each geographic chunk we'd selected and stopped the first 10 people they ran into on the street at each point. This is called a street-intercept survey (Box 5.5).

Box 5.5 Street- and mall-intercept sampling

K. W. Miller et al. (1997) sampled blocks of streets in a city and did a street-intercept survey of African American men. They compared the results to a random-digit dialing telephone survey in the same city. The street-intercept survey did a better job of representing the population than did the telephone survey. For one thing, the response rate for the street intercept survey was over 80%.

Compare that to the typical telephone survey, where half or more of the respondents may refuse to be interviewed. Also, with telephone surveys, the socioeconomic profile of respondents is generally higher than in the population (partly because more affluent people agree more often to be interviewed on the telephone). A variant of this method is mall-intercept sampling, used widely in marketing (**Further Reading:** street and mall intercept surveys).

Handwerker (1993) used a map-sampling method in his study of sexual behavior on Barbados. In his variation of map sampling, you generate 10 random numbers between 0 and 360 (the degrees on a compass). Next, put a dot in the center of a map that you will use for the sampling exercise, and use a protractor to identify the 10 randomly chosen compass points. You then draw lines from the dot in the center of the map through all 10 points to the edge of the map and interview people (or observe houses, or whatever) along those lines. (See Duranleau [1999] for an empirical test of the power of map sampling.)

If you use this technique, you may want to establish a sampling interval (like every fifth case, beginning with the third case). If you finish interviewing along the lines and don't have enough cases, you can take another random start, with the same or a different interval and start again. Be careful of periodicity, though (Box 5.6).

Box 5.6 Combining map sampling and cluster sampling

In Chapter 4, I mentioned a study in which Lambros Comitas and I compared Greeks who had returned from what was then West Germany as labor migrants with Greeks who had never left their country (Bernard and Comitas 1978). There were no lists of returned migrants, but we thought we could do a cluster sample by locating the children of returned migrants in the Athens schools and then use the children to select a sample of their parents.

The problem was that we couldn't even get a list of schools in Athens. So we took a map of the city and divided it into small bits by laying a grid over it. Then we took a random sample of the bits and sent interviewers to find the school nearest each bit selected. The interviewers asked the principal of each school to identify the children of returned labor migrants. (It was easy for the principal to do, by the way. The principal said that all the returned migrant children spoke Greek with a German accent.) That way, we were able to make up two lists for each school: one of children who had been abroad, and one of children who had not. By sampling children randomly from those lists at each school, we were able to select a representative sample of parents.

Camilla Harshbarger (1995) used another variation of map sampling in her study of farmers in North West Province, Cameroon (1993). To create a sample of 400 farmers, she took a map of a rural community and drew 100 dots around the perimeter. She used a random number table to select 50 pairs of dots and drew lines between them. She numbered the points created by the crossing of lines and chose 80 of those points at random. Then Harshbarger and her field assistants interviewed one farmer in each of the five compounds they found closest to each of the 80 selected dots. (If you use this dot technique, remember to include the points along the edges of the map in your sample or you'll miss households on those edges.)

There are times when a random, representative sample is out of the question. After she did those interviews with 400 randomly selected farmers in North West Province, Cameroon, Harshbarger set out to interview Fulani cattle herders in the same area. Here's what Harshbarger wrote about her experience in trying to interview the herders:

It was rainy season in Wum and the roads were a nightmare. The graziers lived very far out of town and quite honestly, my research assistants were not willing to trek to the compounds because it would have taken too much time and we would never have finished the job. I consulted X and he agreed to call selected people to designated school houses on certain days. We each took a room and administered the survey with each individual grazier.

Not everyone who was called came for the interview, so we ended up taking who we could get. Therefore, the Wum grazier sample was not representative and initially that was extremely difficult for me to accept. Our team had just finished the 400-farmer survey of Wum that *was* representative, and after all that work it hit me hard that the grazier survey would not be. To get a representative sample, I would have needed a four-wheel drive vehicle, a driver, and more money to pay research assistants for a lengthy stay in the field. Eventually, I forgave myself for the imperfection. [personal communication]

The lessons here are clear. (1) If you are ever in Harshbarger's situation, you, too, can forgive yourself for having a nonrepresentative sample. (2) Even then, like Harshbarger, you should feel badly about it.

Maximizing Between-Group Variance: The Wichita Study

Whenever you do multistage cluster sampling, be sure to take as large a sample as possible from the largest, most heterogeneous clusters. The larger the cluster, the larger the between-group variance; the smaller the cluster, the higher the within-group variance.

Counties in the United States are more like each other on any variable (income, race, average age, whatever) than states are; towns within a county are more like each other than counties are; neighborhoods in a town are more like each other than towns are; blocks are more like each other than neighborhoods are. In sampling, the rule is: *maximize between-group variance*.

What does this mean in practice? The following is an actual example of multistage sampling from John Hartman's study of Wichita, Kansas (Hartman 1978; Hartman and Hedblom 1979:160ff.). At the time of the study, in the mid-1970s, Wichita had a population of about 193,000 persons over 16. This was the population to which the study team wanted to generalize. The team decided that they could afford only 500 interviews. There were 82 census tracts in Wichita, from which they randomly selected 20. These 20 tracts then became the actual population of their study. We'll see in a moment how well their actual study population simulated (represented) the study population to which they wanted to generalize.

Hartman and Hedblom added up the total population in the 20 tracts and divided the population of *each tract* by the total. This gave the percentage of people that each tract, or cluster, contributed to the new population total. Since the researchers were going to do 500 interviews, each tract was assigned that percentage of the interviews. If there were 50,000 people in the 20 tracts, and one of the tracts had a population of 5,000, or 10% of the total, then 50 interviews (10% of the 500) would be done in that tract.

Next, the team numbered the blocks in each tract and selected blocks at random until they had enough for the number of interviews that were to be conducted in that tract. When a block was selected it stayed in the pool, so that in some cases more than one interview was to be conducted in a single block. This did not happen very often, and the team wisely left it up to chance to determine this.

This study team made some excellent decisions that maximized the heterogeneity (and hence the representativeness) of their sample. As clusters get smaller and smaller (as you go from tract to block to household, or from village to neighborhood to household), the homogeneity of the units of analysis within the clusters gets greater and greater. People in one census tract or village are more like each other than people in different tracts or villages. People in one census block or barrio are more like each other than people across blocks or barrios. And people in households are more like each other than people in households across the street or over the hill.

This is very important. Most researchers would have no difficulty with the idea that they should only interview one person in a household because, for example, husbands and wives often have similar ideas about things and report similar behavior with regard to kinship, visiting, health care, child care, and consumption of goods and services. Somehow, the lesson becomes less clear when new researchers move into clusters that are larger than households.

But the rule stands: Maximize heterogeneity of the sample by taking as many of the biggest clusters in your sample as you can, and as many of the next biggest, and so on, always at the expense of the number of clusters at the bottom where homogeneity is greatest. Take more tracts or villages, and fewer blocks per tract or barrios per village. Take more blocks per tract or barrios per village, and fewer households per block or barrio. Take more households and fewer persons per household.

Many survey researchers say that, as a rule, you should have no fewer than five households in a census block. The Wichita group did not follow this rule but only had enough money and person power to do 500 interviews and they wanted to maximize the likelihood that their sample would represent faithfully the characteristics of the 193,000 adults in their city.

The Wichita study group drew two samples—one main sample and one alternate sample.

Whenever they could not get someone on the main sample, they took the alternate. That way, they maximized the representativeness of their sample because the alternates were chosen with the same randomized procedure as the main respondents in their survey. They were not forced to take next-door neighbors when a main respondent wasn't home. (This kind of "winging it" in survey research has a tendency to clobber the representativeness of samples. In the United States, at least, interviewing only people who are at home during the day produces results that represent women with small children, shut-ins, telecommuters, and the elderly—and not much else.)

Next, the Wichita team randomly selected the households for interview within each block. This was the third stage in this multistage cluster design. The fourth stage consisted of flipping a coin to decide whether to interview a man or a woman in households with both. Whoever came to the door was asked to provide a list of those in the household over 16 years of age. If there was more than one eligible person in the household, the interviewer selected one at random, conforming to the decision made earlier on sex of respondent.

Table 5.2 shows how well the Wichita team did. All in all, they did very well. In addition to the variables shown in the table here, the Wichita sample was a fair representation of marital status, occupation, and education, although there were some pretty large discrepancies on this last independent variable. For example, according to the 1970 census, 8% of the population of Wichita had less than eight years of schooling, but only 4% of the sample had this characteristic. Only 14% of the general population had completed one–three years of college, but 22% of the sample had that much education.

All things considered, though, the sampling procedure followed in the Wichita study was a model of technique, and the results show it. Whatever they found out about the 500 people they interviewed, the researchers could be very confident that the results were generalizable to the 193,000 adults in Wichita.

In sum: If you don't have a sampling frame for a population, try to do a multistage cluster sample, narrowing down to natural clusters that do have lists. Sample heavier at the higher levels in a multistage sample and lighter at the lower stages.

Table 5.2 Comparison of Survey Results and Population Parameters for the Wichita Study by Hartman and Hedblom

	Wichita in 1973	Hartman and Hedblom's Sample for 1973 (in Percentages)
White	86.8	82.8
African	9.7	10.8
Chicano	2.5	2.6
Other	1.0	2.8
Male	46.6	46.9
Female	53.4	53.1
Median age	38.5	39.5

Source: J. J. Hartman and J. H. Hedblom, *Methods for the Social Sciences: A Handbook for Students and Non-Specialists,* p. 165, 1979, Greenwood Publishing Company.

HOW BIG SHOULD A SAMPLE BE?

There are two things you can do to get good samples. You can ensure **sample accuracy** by making sure that every element in the population has an equal chance of being selected—that is, you can make sure the sample is unbiased. You can ensure **sample precision** by increasing the size of unbiased samples. We've already discussed the importance of how to make samples unbiased. The next step is to decide how big a sample needs to be.

Sample size depends on: (1) the heterogeneity of the population or chunks of population (strata or clusters) from which you choose the elements; (2) how many population subgroups (that is, independent variables) you want to deal with simultaneously in your analysis; (3) the size of the phenomenon that you're trying to detect; and (4) how precise you want your sample statistics (or parameter estimators) to be.

1. Heterogeneity of the population. When all elements of a population have the same score on some measure, a sample of 1 will do. Ask a lot of people to tell you how many days there are in a week and you'll soon understand that a big sample isn't going to uncover a lot of heterogeneity. But if you want to know what the average ideal family size is, you may need to cover a lot of social ground. People of different ethnicities, religions, incomes, genders, and ages may have very different ideas about this. (In fact, these independent variables may interact in complex ways. Multivariate analysis tells you about this interaction. We'll get to this in Chapter 22.)

2. The number of subgroups in the analysis. Remember the factorial design problem in Chapter 4 on experiments? We had three independent variables, each with two attributes, so we needed eight groups ($2^3 = 8$). It wouldn't do you much good to have, say, one experimental subject in each of those eight groups. If you're going to analyze all eight of the conditions in the experiment, you've got to fill each of the conditions with some reasonable number of subjects. If you have only 15 people in each of the eight conditions, then you need a sample of 120.

The same principle holds when you're trying to figure out how big a sample you need for a survey. If you have four age groups and two genders, you wind up with an eight-cell sampling design.

If all you want to know is a single proportion—like what percentage of people in a population approve or disapprove of something—then you need about 100 respondents to be 95% confident, within plus or minus three points, that your sample estimate is within two standard deviations of the population parameter (more about confidence limits, normal distributions, standard deviations, and parameters coming up in the next chapter). But if you want to know whether retired widowers who have less than $3,000 per month in total income have different opinions from, say, working, married mothers who have more than $3,000 per month in total income, then you'll need a bigger sample.

3. **The size of the subgroup.** If the population you are trying to study is rare and hard to find, and if you have to rely on a simple random sample of the entire population, you'll need a very large initial sample. A needs assessment survey of people over 75 in Florida took 72,000 phone calls to interviews—about 44 calls per interview (Henry 1990:88). This is because only 6.5% of Florida's population was over 75 at the time of the survey. By contrast, the monthly Florida survey of 600 representative consumers in that state takes about 5,000 calls (about eight per interview). That's because just about everyone in the state 18 and older is a consumer and is eligible for the survey (Christopher McCarty, personal communication).

The smaller the difference on any measure between two populations, the bigger the sample you need to detect that difference. Suppose you suspect that Blacks and Whites in a prison system have received different sentences for the same crime. Henry (1990:121) shows that a difference of 16 months in sentence length for the same crime would be detected with a sample of just 30 in each racial group (if the members of the sample were selected randomly, of course). To detect a difference of three months, however, you need 775 in each group.

4. **Precision.** This one takes us into sampling theory.

Key Concepts in This Chapter

individual data	periodicity	PPS-probability
cultural data	stratified random sapling	proportionate to size
population parameters	maximizing the between-	space sampling
probability sampling	group variance	map sampling
nonprobability sampling	minimizing the within-	street-intercept survey
random sample	group variance	between-group
panel study	sampling design	variance
sampling frame	age cohort	within-group variance
population	proportionate stratified	sample accuracy
unbiased sample	random sample	sample precision
simple random sample	disproportionate stratified	sample statistics
systematic random sample	random sample	parameter estimators
random start	weighting	population heterogeneity
sampling interval	cluster sampling	factorial design

Summary

- There are two kinds of data of interest to social scientists: individual data and cultural data. These two kinds of data require different approaches to sampling.
  - Individual data are about attributes of individuals in a population. To estimate the parameters of these attributes in a population requires probability sampling.
  - Cultural data requires experts, which means relying on nonprobability sampling.
- There are several ways to take probability samples.
  - Simple random sampling involves generating a list of random numbers and applying that list to a numbered sampling frame. (Most researchers actually take systematic, rather than simple random samples.)
  - Stratified random samples are used to ensure that key subpopulations are included in a study. Disproportionate stratified random sampling is used to ensure that important but relatively small subpopulations are included in a sample.
  - Cluster sampling is used when there is no overall sampling frame. Cluster sampling is based on the fact that people live in natural clusters (counties, states, etc.) and they participate in the activities of institutions (schools, churches, credit unions, etc.).
  - The best estimates of a parameter are produced in samples taken from clusters of equal size. When clusters are not equal in size, then samples should be taken PPS—with probability proportionate to size.
- Sample size depends on: (1) the heterogeneity of the population from which you choose the elements; (2) how many population subgroups you want to deal with simultaneously in your analysis; (3) the size of the phenomenon that you're trying to detect; and (4) how precise you want your parameter estimators to be. Precision involves sampling theory.

Exercises

1. Record in a spreadsheet, like Excel®, as many variables as you can about your contacts on a networking site, like Facebook—things like age, sex, ethnicity, region where they live, etc. This gives you a sampling frame and parameters for the variables you've recorded. Take a random sample of the friends in your spreadsheet and estimate the parameter values of the variables for which you have measures. Try to create other sampling frames—for businesses in your town or for members of a church or other organization, like a sorority or fraternity, to which you belong.

2. Consider a study in which we will do 150 interviews in a town of 23,000 inhabitants. There are neighborhoods in the town, and we want an unbiased sample that represents all of the neighborhoods. One of the neighborhoods, with 12,000 residents, is much larger than the other four. If we do a PPS sample (one that takes account of the different sizes of the neighborhoods), then what is the probability that any individual in the big neighborhood will wind up in our sample?

3. Answer the following questions about sampling:

   a. What is the danger in systematic random sampling?

   b. Why are telephone books usually poor sampling frames?

   c. What is a stratified, random disproportionate sample?

d. Why do we sample more heavily among hierarchically higher (more heterogeneous) units than among lower (more homogeneous) ones?

e. What is the relation among "parameter," "estimator," and "sampling error"?

f. What are the two ways in which sampling error are reduced?

4. A multinational corporation asks you to survey their 840 midlevel managers. There are 590 men and 250 women in the cohort of managers. You decide to take a stratified random sample of 100 from each of the gender groups. What is the sampling weight for each of the strata? Hint: Find the probability, p, of sampling each man and each woman, given that you are sampling 100 of each. The weight is the inverse of p, or $1/p$.

Further Reading

General sampling. Ardilly and Tillé (2006), Czaja and Blair (2005), Dattalo (2008, 2010), Handwerker (2003), Hoyle (1999), Nardi (2003), Onwuegbuzie and Collins (2007), Stine (1990), Teddlie and Yu (2007).

Street intercept and mall intercept sampling. Bruwer and Haydam (1996), Bush and Hair (1985), Choi et al. (2008), Daley et al. (2001), Gates and Solomon (1982), Hemphill et al. (2007), Hew and Wesley (2008), Oxford et al. (2004), Ross et al. (2006), WalterMaurer et al. (2003).

6
Sampling Theory

At the end of this chapter, you should understand why it's possible to estimate *very accurately, most of the time*, the average age of the
228 million adults in the United States by talking to just 1,600 of them. And you should
understand why you can also do this *pretty
accurately, much of the time*, by talking to just
400 of them.

PROBABILITY DISTRIBUTIONS

Sampling theory is partly about **probability
distributions**, which come in a variety of
shapes. Figure 6.1 shows four of those

shapes: (1) uniform, (2) exponential,
(3) bimodal, and (4) skewed. There is
another, very important shape: symmetrical.
We'll get to that next.

1. The **uniform distribution**. Suppose the
numbers from 1 to 100 are a population of
elements—things from which you want to
choose a sample. If you choose a number
from 1 to 100 at random, then each number
(or element) has a uniform probability of
being chosen. In other words, these elements
have a uniform probability distribution. The
characteristic shape of a uniform distribution is a rectangle, shown in Figure 6.1(a).
The items in the population (in this case, a
list of numbers from 1 to 100) are listed
along the *x*-axis. Each number has a 1/100

Figure 6.1 Four Kinds of Distributions

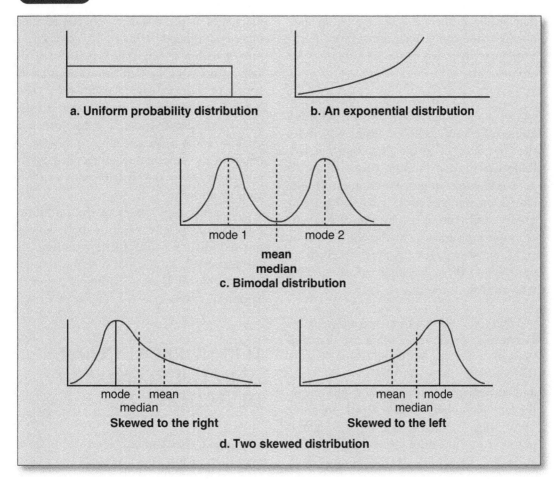

a. Uniform probability distribution

b. An exponential distribution

mode 1   mode 2

mean
median
c. Bimodal distribution

mode   mean
median
Skewed to the right

mean   mode
median
Skewed to the left

d. Two skewed distribution

(1%, or 0.01) probability of being selected. In throwing a fair die, each number, from 1 to 6, has a 1/6=0.167 chance of turning up. Flipping a fair coin and getting a heads has a uniform probability of 0.50.

2. The exponential distribution. This distribution describes many phenomena that happen through time. In some sports, games that are tied at the end of a certain amount of time are sent into sudden-death overtime. The number of minutes it takes for a team to score the winning goal in these sports forms an exponential distribution like the one in Figure 6.1(b). As the minutes drag on (the horizontal x-axis along the bottom), the probability of a team scoring a winning goal (the vertical y-axis) goes up. But the probability doesn't go up steadily . . . it goes up exponentially. The longer it takes, the faster the probability rises that one team will score in the next minute. The time, from right now, of your cell phone dying is part of an exponential distribution. The longer you wait, the likelier the event becomes.

3. The bimodal and multimodal distributions. Suppose the x-axis in Figure 6.1(c) is age and the y-axis is the probability of answering "yes" to the question "Did you like the beer

commercial shown during the Super Bowl yesterday?" The bimodal distribution shows that people in their 20s and people in their 60s liked the commercial, but others didn't. With more than two modes, distributions are multimodal.

4. **Skewed distributions.** A distribution can be skewed positively (with a long tail going off to the right) or negatively (with the tail going off to the left). Figure 6.1(d) looks like the distributions of scores in two very different university courses. In the course on the left, most students got low grades, and there is a long tail of students who got high grades. In the course on the right, most students got relatively high grades, and there is a long tail of students who got lower grades.

Figure 6.2 shows three variations of a symmetric distribution—that is, distributions for which the mean and the median are the same. (If you need to look up the mean and the median, see Chapter 20.) The one on the left is leptokurtic (from Greek, meaning "thin bulge") and the one on the right is platykurtic (meaning "flat bulge"). The curve in the middle is the famous bell-shaped, normal distribution.

The physical distance between marriage partners usually forms a leptokurtic distribution. People tend to marry people who live near them—even in modern, industrialized societies—and there are fewer and fewer marriages as the distance between partners increases (Sheets 1982). By contrast, if judges within a single jurisdiction use the same sentencing guidelines, we expect the length of sentences handed down by those judges for the same crime to form a more platykurtic distribution. If judges can take circumstances into account to reduce or lengthen the sentence recommended by the guidelines, then the distribution won't be entirely uniform.

The symmetric curve in the middle of Figure 6.2 is the famous bell-shaped, normal distribution. Understanding the properties of the normal distribution and of the central limit theorem is a key to sampling.

THE NORMAL CURVE AND THE STANDARD DEVIATION

The normal distribution is generated by a formula that can be found in many intro statistics texts. A detailed picture of the distribution, with its important features, is shown in Figure 6.3. One feature is that it has a mean of 0 and a standard deviation of 1.

Figure 6.2 Three Symmetric Distributions, Including the Normal Distribution

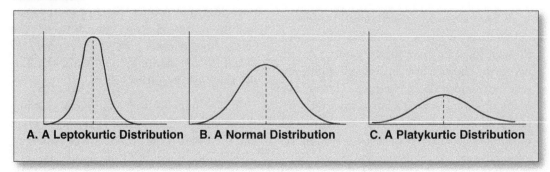

A. A Leptokurtic Distribution   B. A Normal Distribution   C. A Platykurtic Distribution

Figure 6.3 The Normal Curve and the First, Second, and Third Standard Deviations

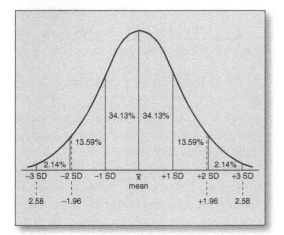

The standard deviation is a measure of how much the scores in a distribution vary from the mean score. The larger the standard deviation, the more dispersion around the mean. Here's the formula for the standard deviation, or *sd*. (The *sd* is the square root of the variance. We will take all this up again in Chapter 20.)

$$sd = \sqrt{\frac{\sum (x - \bar{x})^2}{n - 1}} \qquad \text{formula 6.1}$$

The symbol $\bar{x}$ in formula 6.1 is read "*x*–bar" and is used to signify the mean of a *sample*. The mean of a *population* (the parameter we want to estimate), is symbolized by μ (the Greek lower-case letter "mu," pronounced "myoo"). The standard deviation of a population is symbolized by σ (the Greek lower-case letter "sigma"), and the standard deviation of a sample is written as *SD* or *sd* or *s*. Read formula 6.1 as follows: The standard deviation is the square root of the sum of all the squared differences between every score in a set of scores and the mean, divided by the number of scores minus 1.

The standard deviation of a sampling distribution of means is the standard error of the mean, or *SEM*. The formula for calculating *SEM* is:

$$SEM = \frac{sd}{\sqrt{n}} \qquad \text{formula 6.2}$$

where *n* is the sample size. In other words, the standard error of the mean gives us an idea of how much a sample mean varies from the mean of the population that we're trying to estimate.

An example: Suppose that in a sample of 100 rural high-school teachers you find that the average income is $42,600 with an *sd* of $8,000. The standard error of the mean is:

$$42,600 \pm \frac{8,000}{\sqrt{100}} = 42,600 \pm 800$$

Do the calculation:

$$42,600 + 800 = 43,400$$

$$42,600 - 800 = 41,800$$

z-Scores

Appendix A is a table of *z*-scores, or standard scores. These scores are the number of standard deviations from the mean in a normal distribution, in increments of 1/100th of a standard deviation. For each *z*-score, beginning with 0.00 standard deviations (the mean) and on up to 3.09 standard deviations (on either side of the mean), Appendix A shows the *percentage of the physical area under the curve of a normal distribution*. That percentage represents the percentage of cases that fall within any number of standard deviations above and below the mean in a normally distributed set of cases.

We see from Appendix A that 34.13% of the area under the curve is 1 *sd* above the mean and another 34.13% is 1 *sd* below the mean. Thus, 68.26% of all scores in a normal distribution fall within 1 *sd* of the mean. We also see from Appendix A that 95.44% of all scores in a normal distribution fall within 2 *sd* and that 99.7% fall within 3 *sd*.

This is shown graphically in Figure 6.3. You can see why so many cases are contained within 1 *sd* above and below the mean: The normal curve is tallest and fattest around the mean and much more of the area under the curve is encompassed in the first *sd* from the mean than is encompassed between the first and second *sd* from the mean.

If 95.44% of the area under a normal curve falls within 2 *sd* from the mean, then 95% should fall within slightly less than 2 *sd*. Appendix A tells us that 1.96 *sd* above and below the mean accounts for 95% of all scores in a normal distribution. And, similarly, 2.58 *sd* account for 99% of all scores. This is also shown graphically in Figure 6.3.

THE CENTRAL LIMIT THEOREM

The normal distribution is an idealized form. In practice, many variables are not distributed in the perfectly symmetric shape we see in Figure 6.3. The fact that many variables are not normally distributed would make sampling a hazardous business, were it not for the central limit theorem. According to this theorem, if you take many samples of a population, and *if the samples are big enough*, then:

1. The mean and the standard deviation of the sample means will approximate the true mean and standard deviation of the population. (You'll understand why

this is so a bit later in the chapter, when we discuss confidence intervals.)

2. The distribution of sample means will approximate a normal distribution.

We can demonstrate both parts of the central limit theorem with some examples.

Part 1 of the Central Limit Theorem

Table 6.1 shows the per capita gross domestic product (PCGDP) for the 50 poorest countries in the world in 2007.

Here is a random sample of five of those countries: Uzbekistan, Senegal, Guinea, Rwanda, and Liberia. Consider these five as a population of units of analysis. In 2007, these countries had an annual per capita GDP, respectively of $704, $908, $452, $354, and $195 (U.S. dollars). These five numbers sum to $2,613 and their average, 2613/5, is $522.60.

There are 10 possible samples of two elements in any population of five elements. All 10 samples for the five countries in our example are shown in the left-hand column of Table 6.2. The middle column shows the mean for each sample. This list of means is the sampling distribution. And the right-hand column shows the cumulative mean.

Notice that the mean of the means for all 10 samples of two elements—that is, the mean of the sampling distribution—is $522.60, which is *exactly the actual mean* per capita GDP of the five countries in the population. In fact, it must be: *The mean of all possible samples of size 2 is equal to the parameter that we're trying to estimate.*

Figure 6.4a is a frequency polygon that shows the distribution of the five actual PCGDP values. A frequency polygon is just a histogram with lines connecting the tops of the bars so that the shape of the distribution is emphasized. Compare the shape of this distribution to the one in Figure 6.4b showing the distribution of the 10 sample means for the five

Table 6.1 The 50 Poorest Countries in the World, 2007

Country	PCGDP	Country	PCGDP
Burundi	118	Burkina Faso	483
DR-Congo	151	Mali	554
Zimbabwe	159	Tajikistan	555
Liberia	195	Comoros	556
Ethiopia	201	Cambodia	598
Guinea-Bissau	211	Haiti	612
Malawi	257	Benin	618
Eritrea	271	N. Korea	618
Niger	289	Ghana	647
Somalia	291	Chad	692
Sierra Leone	330	Kyrgyzstan	704
Afghanistan	345	Uzbekistan	704
Rwanda	354	Laos	711
Mozambique	362	Kiribati	762
Tanzania	368	Kenya	786
Gambia	377	Lesotho	797
Madagascar	377	Viet Nam	815
Myanmar	379	Mauritania	874
Togo	386	Senegal	908
Timor-Leste	393	São Tome and Principe	912
Central African Rep.	394	Papua New Guinea	953
Uganda	403	Yemen	967
Nepal	419	Zambia	974
Bangladesh	428	India	976
Guinea	452	Solomon Islands	978

Source: United Nations, Dept. of Economic and Social Affairs (2009).

Table 6.2 All Samples of Two From Five Elements

Sample	Mean	Cumulative Mean
Uzbekistan and Senegal	(704 + 908)/2 = 806.0	806.0
Uzbekistan and Guinea	(704 + 452)/2 = 578.0	1384.0
Uzbekistan and Rwanda	(704 + 354)/2 = 529.0	1913.0
Uzbekistan and Liberia	(704 + 195)/2 = 449.5	2362.5
Senegal and Guinea	(908 + 452)/2 = 680.0	3042.5
Senegal and Rwanda	(908 + 354)/2 = 631.0	3673.5
Senegal and Liberia	(908 + 195)/2 = 551.5	4225.0
Guinea and Rwanda	(452 + 354)/2 = 403.0	4628.0
Guinea and Liberia	(452 + 195)/2 = 323.5	4951.5
Liberia and Rwanda	(195 + 354)/2 = 274.5	5226.0
	$\bar{x} = 5226/10 = 522.6$	

Figure 6.4 Five Cases and the Distribution of Samples of Size 2 From Those Cases

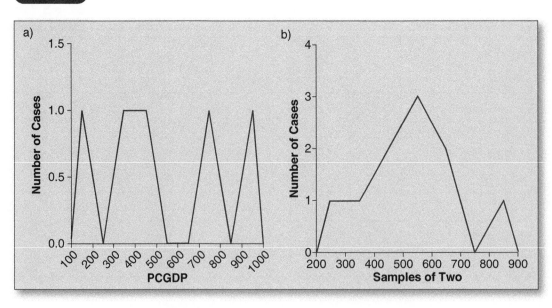

PCGDP values we're dealing with here. That distribution looks more like the shape of the normal curve: It's got that telltale bulge in the middle.

Part 2 of the Central Limit Theorem

Figure 6.5 shows the distribution of the 50 data points for GDP in Table 6.1. The range is quite broad, from $118 to $978 per year per person, and the shape of the distribution is multimodal.

The actual mean of the data in Table 6.1—that is, the parameter we want to estimate—is $533.28. There are 2,118,760 samples of size 5 that can be taken from 50 elements. Table 6.3 shows the means from 10 samples of five countries chosen at random from the data in Table 6.1.

Even in this small set of 10 samples, the mean is $504.72—quite close to the actual mean of $533.28. Figure 6.6a shows the distribution of these samples. It has the look of a normal distribution straining to happen. Figure 6.6b shows 20 samples of five from the 50 countries in Table 6.1. The strain toward the normal curve is unmistakable and the mean of those 20 samples is $505.18.

The problem is that in real research, we don't get to take 10 or 20 samples. We have to make do with one. The first sample of five elements that I took had a mean of $522.60—pretty close to the actual mean of $533.28. But it's very clear from Table 6.3 that any one sample of five elements from Table 6.1 could be off by a lot. The means in Table 6.3 range, after all, from $434.40 to $652.80. That's a big spread, when the average we're trying to estimate is $533.28. Still, as you can see from Figures 6.6a and 6.6b, as we add samples, the mean of the samples gets closer and closer to the parameter we're trying to estimate and the distribution of the means of the samples looks more and more like the normal distribution.

Figure 6.5 Distribution of 50 Cases From Table 6.1

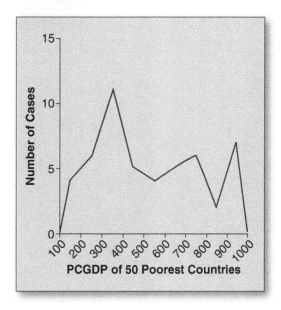

Table 6.3 10 Means From Samples of Size 5 Taken From the 50 Elements in Table 6.1

522.60
434.40
586.20
468.20
465.00
652.80
461.20
489.20
458.60
509.00
Mean = 504.72
Standard Deviation 67.51

Figure 6.6   Visualizing the Central Limit Theorem: The Distribution of Sample Means
Approximates a Normal Distribution

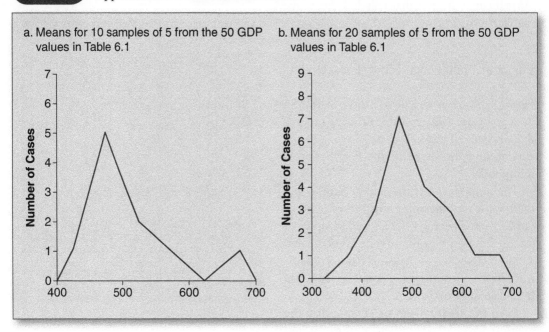

a. Means for 10 samples of 5 from the 50 GDP values in Table 6.1

b. Means for 20 samples of 5 from the 50 GDP values in Table 6.1

We are much closer to answering the question: How big does a sample have to be?

THE STANDARD ERROR AND CONFIDENCE INTERVALS

In the hypothetical example on page 149 we took a sample of 100 rural schoolteachers in the United States and found that the mean income was $42,600, standard error $800. We know from Figure 6.3 that 68.26% of all samples of size 100 from this population will produce an estimate that is between 1 standard error above and 1 standard error below the mean—that is, between $41,800 and $43,400. The 68.26% confidence interval, then, is $800.

We also know from Figure 6.3 that 95.44% of all samples of size 100 will

produce an estimate of 2 standard errors, or between $41,200 and $44,200. The 95.44% confidence interval, then, is $1,600. If we do the sums for the example, we see that the 95% confidence limits are:

$$\$42,600 \pm 1.96(\$800) = \$41,032 \text{ to } \$44,168$$

and the 99% confidence limits are:

$$\$42,600 \pm 2.58(\$800) = \$40,536 \text{ to } \$44,664$$

Our "confidence" in these 95% or 99% estimates comes from the power of a random sample and the fact that—by the central limit theorem—*sampling distributions are known to be normal irrespective of the distribution of the variable whose mean we are estimating* (Box 6.1).

Box 6.1 What confidence limits *are* and what they *aren't*

If you say that the 95% confidence limits for the estimated mean income are $41,032 and $44,168, this does *not* mean that there is a 95% chance that the true mean, μ, lies somewhere in that range. The true mean may or may not lie within that range and we have no way to tell. What we can say, however, is that:

1. if we take a very large number of suitably large random samples from the population (we'll get to what "suitably large" means in a minute); and
2. if we calculate the mean, $\bar{x}$, and the standard error, SE, for each sample; and
3. if we then calculate the confidence intervals for each sample mean, based on ±1.96 SE; then
4. 95% of these confidence intervals will contain the true mean, μ.

Calculating Sample Size for Estimating Means

Now we are *really* close to answering the question about sample size. Suppose we want to get the standard error down to $400 instead of $800. We need to solve the following equation:

$$SE = \frac{sd}{\sqrt{n}} = \frac{8,000}{\sqrt{n}} = 400$$

Solving for n:

$$\sqrt{n} = \frac{8,000}{400} = 20$$

$$n = 20^2 = 400$$

In other words, to reduce the standard error of the mean from $800 to $400—to cut it in half—we have to quadruple the sample size from 100 to 400 people. If we do this and get a mean of $42,600, sd $8000, the standard error would be $400 and we could estimate, with 95% confidence, that the true mean of the population was between $41,816 and $43,384. Compare that to the 95% confidence limits with 100 people in the sample: $41,032 to $44,168.

As the standard error goes down, we get narrower—that is, more precise—confidence limits. To cut the standard error in half again, we would need a sample of 1,600 people.

There is another pattern, too. If we want to increase our confidence from 95% to 99% that the true mean of the population is within a particular confidence interval, we can raise the multiplier in formula 6.2 from roughly 2 standard deviations to roughly 3. Using the confidence interval of $800, we would calculate:

$$\sqrt{n} = 3\left(\frac{8,000}{800}\right) = 30$$

$$n = 3^2 = 900$$

We need 900 people, not 400, to be about 99% confident that our sample mean is within $800, plus or minus, of the parameter.

SMALL SAMPLES: THE *t* DISTRIBUTION

In real research, even doing surveys, we often have no choice and have to use small samples. What we need is a distribution that is a bit more

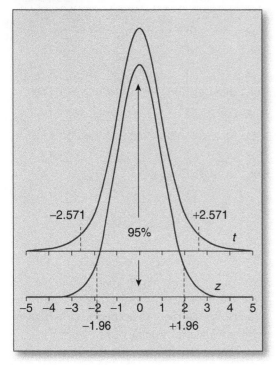

Figure 6.7 Variability in a *t* Distribution and a Normal Distribution

forgiving than the normal distribution. Fortunately, just such a distribution was discovered by W. S. Gossett, an employee of the Guiness brewery in Ireland. Writing under the pseudonym of "Student," Gossett described the distribution known as **Student's *t***. It is based on a distribution that takes into account the fact that statistics calculated on small samples vary more than do statistics calculated on large samples and so have a bigger chance of misestimating the parameter of a continuous variable.

The *t* distribution is found in Appendix B. Figure 6.7 shows graphically the difference in the *z* and *t* distributions. In a normal distribution, plus or minus 1.96 *sd* covers 95% of all sample means. In a *t*-distribution, with 5 degrees of freedom, it takes 2.571 *sd* to cover 95% of all sample means.

The confidence interval for small samples, using the *t* distribution is given in formula 6.3:

$$\text{Confidence Interval} = \bar{x} \pm \left(t_{a/2}\right)\left[\frac{sd}{\sqrt{n}}\right]$$

formula 6.3

where alpha (α) is the confidence interval you want. If you want to be 95% confident, then α = .05. Since half the scores fall above the mean and half below, we divide alpha by two and get .025.

Look up what's called the **critical value** of *t* in Appendix B. In the column for .025, we see that the value is 2.571 with 5 degrees of freedom. Degrees of freedom are one less than the size of the sample, so for a sample of six we need a *t* statistic of >2.571 to attain 95% confidence. (The concept of degrees of freedom is described further in Chapter 20 in the section on *t*-tests. And keep in mind that we're interested in the **modulus**, or absolute value of *t*. A value of –2.571 is just as statistically significant as a value of +2.571.)

So, with small samples—which, for practical purposes, means less than 30 units of analysis—we use Appendix B (for *t*) instead of Appendix A (for *z*) to determine the confidence limits around the mean of our estimate. You can see from Appendix B that for large samples—30 or more—the difference between the *t* and the *z* statistics is negligible. (The *t*-value of 2.042 for 30 degrees of freedom—which means a sample of 31—is very close to 1.96.)

The Catch

Suppose that instead of estimating the income of a population with a sample of 100, we use a sample of 10 and get the same result—$42,600 and a standard deviation of $8,000. For a sample this size, we use the *t* distribution. With 9 degrees of freedom and an alpha value of .025, we have a *t* value of 2.262. For a normal curve, 95% of all scores fall within 1.96 standard errors of the mean. The corresponding *t* value is 2.262 standard errors. Substituting in the formula, we get:

$$\$42,600 \pm 2.262\left(\frac{\$8,000}{\sqrt{10}}\right) = \$36,878 \text{ to } \$48,332$$

But there's a catch. With a large sample (greater than 30), we know from the central limit theorem that the sampling distribution will be normal even if the population isn't. Using the *t* distribution with a small sample, we can calculate the confidence interval around the mean of our sample *only under the assumption that the population is normally distributed.*

In fact, looking back at Figure 6.5, we know that the distribution of the real data is not perfectly normal. It is somewhat skewed (more about skewed distributions in Chapter 20). In real research, we'd never take a sample from a set of just 50 data points—we'd do our calculations on the full set of the actual data. When we take samples, it's because we don't know what the distribution of the data looks like. And that's why sample size counts.

ESTIMATING PROPORTIONS

And now for proportions. What we've learned so far about estimating the mean of continuous variables (like income and percentages) is applicable to the estimation of proportions as well.

In April 2009, the ABC News/Washington Post poll reported that 41% of Americans over 18 years of age said they had one or more guns in their home. The poll included 1,072 respondents and had, as the media say, a "margin of sampling error of plus-or-minus three percentage points." The point estimate of 41% means that 440 of the 1,072 people polled said that they had at least one gun in their house.

We can calculate the confidence interval around this point estimate. From the central limit theorem, we know that whatever the true proportion of people is who keep a gun in their home, the estimates of that proportion will be normally distributed if we take a large number of samples of 1,072 people. The formula for determining the 95% confidence limits of a point estimator is:

$$P(\text{the true proportion}) = \pm 1.96\sqrt{PQ/n}$$

$$\text{formula 6.4}$$

We use an italicized letter, *P*, to indicate the true proportion. Our estimate is the regular upper-case P and Q is 1–P. Table 6.4 shows what happens to the square root of PQ as the true value of *P* goes up from 10% to 90% of the population.

We can use our own estimate of *P* in the equation for the confidence limits. Substituting .41 for P and .59 (1–.41) for Q, we get:

$$P = P \pm 1.96\sqrt{(.41)(.59)/1072} = .02944$$

which, with rounding error, is the familiar "plus or minus three percentage points." This means that we are 95% confident that the true proportion of adults in the United States who had at least one gun in their home (or at least said they did) at the time this poll was conducted was between 38% and 44%.

Suppose we want to estimate *P* to within plus-or-minus 2 percentage points instead of 3 and we still want to maintain the 95% confidence level. We substitute in the formula as follows:

$$P = P \pm 1.96\sqrt{(.41)(.59)/n} = .02$$

and we solve for *n*:

$$n = \frac{1.96^2(.41)(.59)}{.02^2} = \frac{(3.8416)(.41)(.59)}{.0004}$$
$$= 2,323.21$$

Table 6.4 Relation of P and Q and $\sqrt{PQ}$

If the Value of P Is Really	Then PQ Is	and $\sqrt{PQ}$ Is
.10 or .90	.09	.30
.20 or .80	.16	.40
.30 or .70	.21	.46
.40 or .60	.24	.49
.50	.25	.50

which we round up to 2,324. Generalizing, then, the formula for sample size when estimating proportions in a large population is:

$$n = z^2(P)(Q)/(\text{Confidence Interval})^2$$

formula 6.5

where z is the area under the normal curve that corresponds to the confidence limit we choose. When the confidence limit is 95%, then z is 1.96. When the confidence limit is 99%, then z is 2.58. And so on.

If we start out fresh and have no prior estimate of P, we follow Table 6.4 and set P and Q to .5 each. This maximizes the size of the sample for any given confidence interval or confidence level. If we want a sample that produces an estimate of a proportion with a confidence interval of 2 percentage points and we want to be 95% confident in that estimate, we calculate:

$$n(\text{sample size}) = \frac{1.96^2(.5)(.5)}{.02^2} = 2,401$$

In time allocation studies, for example, we estimate the proportion of various behaviors (like eating, cooking, doing household chores, leisure) by observing a sample of behaviors. We'll deal with this in Chapter 14, on methods of direct observation (see especially Table 14.1).

Estimating Proportions in Samples for Smaller Populations

This general formula, 6.5, is *independent of the size of the population*. Florida has a population of about 18 million. A sample of 400 is .000022 of 18 million; a sample of 2,401 is .00013 of 18 million. Both proportions are microscopic. A random, representative sample of 400 from a population of 1 million gets you the same confidence level and the same confidence interval as

you get with a sample of 400 from a population of 18 million.

Often, though, we want to take samples from relatively small populations. The key word here is "relatively." When formula 6.4 or 6.5 calls for a sample that turns out to be 5% or more of the total population, we apply the finite population correction. The formula (from Cochran 1977) is:

$$n' = \frac{n}{1 + \dfrac{n-1}{N}}$$

formula 6.6

where n is the sample size calculated from formula 6.5; n' (read: n-prime) is the new value for the sample size; and N is the size of the total population from which n is being drawn.

Here's an example. Suppose you are sampling the 540 female students at a small college to determine how many have ever participated in extreme sports. How many of those women do you need to interview to ensure a 95% probability sample, with a 5% confidence interval?

Answer: Since we have no idea what the percentage is that we're trying to estimate, we set P and Q at 0.5 each in formula 6.5. Solving for n (sample size), we get:

$$n = \frac{1.96^2(.5)(.5)}{.05^2} = 384.16$$

which we round up to 385. Then we apply the finite population correction:

$$n' = \frac{385}{1 + \dfrac{384}{540}} = 225$$

This is still a hefty percentage of the 540 people in the population, but it's a lot smaller than the 385 called for by the standard formula (Box 6.2).

Box 6.2 Settling for bigger confidence intervals

If we were willing to settle for a 10% confidence interval, we'd need only 82 people in this example, but the trade-off would be substantial. If 65 out of 225, or 29%, reported that they had participated in extreme sports, we would be 68% confident that from 24% to 34% really did, and 95% confident that 19% to 39% did. But if 24 out of 82 (the same 29%) reported having participated in extreme sports, we'd be 68% confident that the true figure was between 19% and 39% and 95% confident that it was between 9% and 49%. With a spread like that, you wouldn't want to bet much on the sample statistic of 29%.

Epidemiologists, anthropologists, and others who work with small populations often face this problem. Anthropologists work around it by relying on long-term ethnography—combining qualitative and quantitative approaches. If you've been doing ethnography in a community of 540 people for six months, you may feel comfortable taking a confidence interval of 10% because you are personally (not statistically) confident that your intuition about the group will help you interpret the results of a small sample. Epidemiologists may use special statistical treatments appropriate to small samples.

Another Catch

All of this discussion has been about estimating single parameters, whether proportions or means. You will often want to measure the interaction among several variables at once. Suppose you study a population of wealthy, middle-class, and poor people. That's three kinds of people. Now add two sexes, male and female (that makes six kinds of people) and two colors, Black and White (that makes 12 kinds). If you want to know how all those independent variables combine to predict, say, average number of children desired, the sampling strategy gets more complicated.

Representative sampling is one of the trickiest parts of social research. I recommend strongly that you consult an expert in sampling if you are going to do complex tests on your data (**Further Reading:** sampling theory and sample design).

Key Concepts in This Chapter

probability distributions	normal distribution	cumulative mean
the uniform distribution	standard deviation	frequency polygon
the exponential distribution	standard error of the mean	confidence interval
bimodal and multimodal	z-scores	Student's t
distributions	standard scores	critical value
skewed distributions	central limit theorem	modulus
leptokurtic	population	finite population
platykurtic	sampling distribution	correction

Summary

- Sampling theory is based on the normal distribution and the central limit theorem.
  - o The normal distribution has a mean of 0 and a standard deviation of 1. The standard deviation is a measure of how much the scores in a distribution vary from the mean score.
  - o The larger the standard deviation, the more dispersion around the mean. The standard deviation of a sampling distribution of means is the standard error of the mean.
  - o In normal distributions, 34.135% of the area under the curve is contained in one standard deviation above and one standard deviation below the mean. And 68.26% of samples of size 100 produce an estimate that is between 1 standard error above and 1 standard error below the mean.
  - o To reduce the standard error of the mean by half requires quadrupling the sample size.
- A table of z-scores, or standard scores shows the number of standard deviations from the mean in a normal distribution, in increments of 1/100th of a standard deviation.
- According to the CLT, if you take many samples of a population, and if the samples are big enough, then: (1) the mean and the standard deviation of the sample means will approximate the true mean and standard deviation of the population; and (2) the distribution of sample means will approximate a normal distribution.
- Sample precision refers to the size of the standard error you are willing to tolerate.
  - o Sample size depends on: (1) the heterogeneity of the population from which you choose the elements; (2) how many population subgroups you want to deal with simultaneously in your analysis; (3) the size of the phenomenon that you're trying to detect; and (4) how precise you want your parameter estimators to be.
- Sampling theory for estimating the mean of continuous variables is applicable to the estimation of proportions as well.
  - o For small populations, adjust the sample size using the finite population correction if the sample is 5% or more of the total.

Exercises

1. Assume that in a sample of 400 respondents, chosen properly from a population of 300,000, 22% said that they came from a family in which at least one of their parents had been an immigrant, and 78% said that both of their parents had been born in this country. How closely do these data describe the population parameter?

2. Here's an experiment you can run to show that the mean of many samples of any given size approaches the true mean of a population. Collect 100 well-worn pennies and make a list of their dates of issue (1976, 1994, 2000, etc.). Add up the 100 dates and divide by 100 to get the average date of issue.

   Throw the pennies into a bag and shake well. (Use a *big bag*, like from the supermarket, so you can shake and mix the pennies really well.) Now reach into the bag and without looking, take a sample of five pennies each. Calculate the average date of issue of those five pennies and put them back in the bag. This is called sampling with replacement.

Repeat this nine more times and plot the 10 average dates, just as I plotted the scores in Figure 6.6a.

Run the experiment again, but this time don't put the pennies back in the bag after each grab. This is sampling without replacement. Compare the results of the two experiments. Consider the implication of these results for estimating parameters of populations of people with samples that are done with or without replacement.

Further Reading

Sampling theory and sample design. Agresti and Franklin (2007), Henry (1990), Jaeger (1984), Kish (1995 [1965]), Levy and Lemeshow (2009), Thompson (2002).

7

Nonprobability Sampling

INTRODUCTION

If your objective is to estimate a parameter or a proportion from a sample to a larger population, and if your research calls for the collection of data about attributes of individuals (whether those individuals are people or organizations or episodes of a sitcom), then the rule is simple: Collect data from a sufficiently large, randomly selected, unbiased sample. If you know that you *ought* to use a random, unbiased sample, and you have the means to *get* an unbiased sample, and you still choose to use a nonprobability sample, then expect to take a lot of flak.

There are, however, three quite different circumstances under which nonprobability samples are exactly what are called for:

1. Nonprobability samples are always appropriate for labor-intensive, in-depth studies of a few cases. Most studies of narratives are based on fewer than 50 cases, so every case has to count. This means choosing cases on purpose, not randomly. In-depth research on sensitive topics requires nonprobability sampling. It can take months of participant observation

fieldwork before you can collect narratives about topics like sexual and reproductive history or bad experiences with mental illness or use of illegal drugs.

Come to think of it, just about everything is a sensitive topic when you dig deeply enough. Sexual history is an obviously sensitive topic, but so is the management of household finances when you get into how people really allocate their resources. People love to talk about their lives, but when you get into the details of a life history, you quickly touch a lot of nerves. Really in-depth research requires informed informants, not just responsive respondents—that is, people whom you choose on purpose, not randomly.

2. Nonprobability samples are also appropriate for large surveys when, despite our best efforts, we just can't get a probability sample. In these cases, use a nonprobability sample and *document the bias*. That's all there is to it. No need to agonize about it.

3. And, as I said at the beginning of Chapter 5, when you are collecting cultural data, as contrasted with data about individuals, then expert informants, not randomly selected respondents, are what you really need. Think of the difference between asking someone "How old was your child when you first gave him an egg to eat?" versus "At what age do children here first eat eggs?" More about finding cultural experts (people who are likely to really know when most mothers introduce eggs around here) later in this chapter and in

Chapter 16. (**Further Reading:** nonprobability sampling for individual and cultural data).

The major nonprobability sampling methods are: **quota sampling, purposive sampling** (also called **judgment sampling**), **convenience sampling**, and **chain-referral (snowball) sampling**. A special kind of mixed method, that combines elements of probability and nonprobability sampling, is the **case control design** (see Box 4.4).

QUOTA SAMPLING

Quota sampling is stratified sampling without random selection. It is used widely in election polls as well as in studies that rely on qualitative data, like in-depth interviews.

The key to quota sampling is the development of a **sampling design**, or **sampling grid**. Suppose you are studying the lived experiences of Mexican labor migrants to the United States. You want to compare the experiences of people up to 30 years of age and those over 30; of mestizos (the dominant ethnic group in Mexico) and Indians; and of men and women. That's three binary independent variables. Figure 7.1 shows the eight cells in this design. If you want at least five informants in each cell, you'll need to do 40 interviews.

Tinsley et al. (2002) interviewed 437 elderly users of Lincoln Park in Chicago. They selected

Figure 7.1 Quota Sampling Grid With Three Binary Independent Variables

Labor migrants to the United States							
Up to 30 years of age				Over 30 years of age			
Mestizo		Indian		Mestizo		Indian	
Male	Female	Male	Female	Male	Female	Male	Female

quota samples of about 50 men and 50 women from each of the four major ethnic groups in the area: Blacks, Whites, Hispanics, and Asian Americans. Besides gender and ethnicity, Tinsley et al. stratified on place and time. They divided the park into three zones (north, south, and middle) and three time periods (6 a.m.–10 a.m., 11 a.m.–3 p.m., and 4 p.m.–8 p.m.). There were, then, nine zone-time strata in which interviewers selected respondents. The interviewers were also told to make sure they got some weekday and some weekend users of the park.

When it's done right, quota samples often do a good job of reflecting the population parameters of interest. In other words, quota sampling is an art that often approximates the results of probability sampling at less cost and less hassle than strict probability sampling (Box 7.1).

Box 7.1 Famous polling debacles from quota samples

Often, but not always. In 1948, pollsters predicted, on the basis of quota sampling, that Thomas Dewey would beat Harry Truman in the U.S. presidential election. The *Chicago Tribune* was so confident in those predictions that they printed an edition announcing Dewey's victory—while the votes were being counted that would make Truman president.

Skip to 1992. In the general election in Britain that year, four different polls published on the day of the election put the Liberal Party, on average, about 1 point ahead of the Conservative Party. All the polls were based on quota sampling. The Conservatives won by 8 points. In fact, from 1992 to 1997, political polls using quota samples in Britain systematically overestimated the support for the Liberals (Curtice and Sparrow 1997). A similar polling debacle happened in the 2002 presidential election in France. Twelve polls predicted that Jacques Chirac and Lionel Jospin would defeat the far-right candidate, Jean-Marie Le Pen in the first round of voting and face each other in a run-off. No one predicted that Le Pen would trounce Jospin and face Chirac in the run-off (Durand et al. 2004:277).

Quota samples are biased toward people you can find easily—which means, for example, that they're biased against really poor and really rich people and against single people who aren't home as much as homemakers or retired people are (Marsh and Scarborough 1990)—so quota sampling is dangerous when it comes to making predictions about close election outcomes—or estimating any population parameter, for that matter, if you need precise results.

On the other hand, quota sampling is appropriate in the study of cultural domains. If you want to know how junior sports—Little League Baseball, Pop Warner football, Youth Soccer, junior and senior high school football—function in small communities across the United States, you'd ask people who have children playing those sports. There will be some intracultural variation, but open-ended interviews with four or five really knowledgeable people will produce the relevant cultural data—including data on the range of ideas that people have about these institutions (**Further Reading:** quota sampling).

PURPOSIVE, OR JUDGMENT SAMPLING

In purposive sampling, you decide the purpose you want informants (or communities) to serve, and you go out to find some. This is somewhat like quota sampling, except that there is no overall sampling design that tells you how many of each type of informant you need for a study. You take what you can get.

I used purposive sampling in my study of the Kalymnian (Greek) sponge-fishing industry (1987). I knew I had to interview sponge merchants, boat owners, and divers, but my first interviews taught me that I had to interview people whom I had never considered: men who used to be divers but who had quit, gone to Australia as labor migrants, and returned to their island. It was very easy to find those returned migrants: Everyone on the island either had one in their family or knew people who did.

There are at least five good reasons for using purposive samples. They are used widely in (1) pilot studies, (2) intensive case studies, (3) critical case studies, (4) hard-to-find-population studies, and (5) studies of anything where no other method of sampling is available.

1. Pilot studies. These are studies done before running a larger study. Mhurchu et al. (2008) did a pilot study in New Zealand on the effect of video games on children's level of physical activity. Twenty 12-year olds who owned and were active users of PlayStation2® consoles were assigned randomly to receive or not receive a package of exer-games (games that involve doing physical exercise). The kids wore an accelerometer on their hip—to measure motion—for four days before the study began and for four days after week six and after week 12. At both week six and week 12, the kids who had the exer-games were doing more physical activity than the control group. Even with just 20 participants, these pilot results were taken as a strong hint that a larger project, with more participants and over a longer period of time would be productive.

2. In intensive case studies, the object is often to identify and describe a cultural phenomenon. Dickerson et al. (2000) studied the experiences of American Indian graduate nursing students and cultural barriers that might lead the students to drop out of their training. Dickerson et al. found and interviewed 11 students who were enrolled in an advanced nurse practitioner program. Samples don't get much more purposive than this, and they don't get much more appropriate, either.

Life history research and qualitative research on special populations (drug addicts, trial lawyers, shamans, elite athletes) rely on purposive sampling. Hays (1984) went through the obituary section of a local newspaper and interviewed a purposive sample of survivors. She found that three-fourths of those who died at age 65 or older had surviving children or siblings living close enough to provide support—and one-fourth didn't. Barroso (1997) studied a purposive sample of 14 men and six women in the Tampa, Florida area, all of whom had lived with AIDS for at least three years.

And researchers don't usually pull research sites—hospitals, school systems, police precincts—out of a hat. They rely on their judgment to find one that reflects the things they are interested in.

3. Critical case studies. These are done in all fields of science and have long been the basis, by deduction, for the development of theory. Freud based his theory of psychosexual development on a few critical cases from his practice. Political scientists study cases like the Orange Revolution in Ukraine for clues about the transition from autocracy to democracy (McFaul 2007). At the other end of the deduction-induction continuum, polling companies try to identify bellwether communities—towns and cities that have voted for the winner in the past, say, six presidential or parliamentary elections—and then poll those few communities.

Choosing key informants in ethnographic research is a form of critical-case sampling. It would be pointless to select a handful of people randomly from a population and try to turn them into trusted key informants. More about that later in this chapter.

4. We almost always have to rely on purposive sampling in studying hard-to-find populations.

Think about locating and interviewing refugees from Somalia and Ethiopia living in a large American city. Many of these people experienced torture and don't exactly welcome researchers who want to ask them a lot of questions. This was the problem facing researchers in Minneapolis (see Jaranson et al. 2004; Spring et al. 2003). The study design called for a quota sample of 1,200 respondents, including 300 Oromo women, 300 Oromo men, 300 Somali women, and 300 Somali men.

The study team recruited male and female interviewers from the community—people who shared ethnicity, language, and religion with the people they were trying to locate and interview. The project team sent out fliers, placed announcements in church bulletins, and made presentations at meetings of Oromo and Somali organizations. The interviewers also used their own social networks to locate potential respondents. Over 25 months, the team built trust in the community and wound up with 1,134 of the 1,200 interviews called for in the study.

Kimberly Mahaffy (1996) was interested in how lesbian Christians deal with the cognitive dissonance that comes from being rejected by mainstream Christian churches. Mahaffy sent letters to gay Christian organizations, asking them to put an ad for potential respondents in their newsletters. She sent flyers to women's bookstores and to lesbian support groups, asking for potential respondents to get in touch with her.

Eventually, Mahaffy got 163 completed questionnaires from women who fit the criteria she had established for her research, including 44 from women who self-identified as born-again or evangelical Christians. Mahaffy could not possibly have gotten an unbiased sample of lesbian Christians, but the corpus of data that she collected from her respondents had all the information she needed to answer her research questions.

5. Purposive sampling is often the best we can do in studies of any social issue or human behavior.

In the mid-1960s, in a movement known as "mainstreaming," publicly supported psychiatric hospitals across the United States were closed and their residents were released to live in their own communities. A private board-and-care industry grew up to accommodate these patients, as well as people who suffered from physical disorders. Shostack and Campagna (1991) were interested in the conditions and needs of these board-and-care homes in New Jersey and in the needs of the residents of those homes—things like whether residents had opportunities for recreation, whether residents were being prepared for life outside the home, and so on.

Working alone and without financial support, Shostack and Campagna were not able to cover the entire state. They approached the welfare boards of five New Jersey counties, and those boards arranged for interviews with the operators of 17 homes in their jurisdictions. Table 7.1 compares the age, sex, and racial distribution of the residents in Shostack and Campagna's purposive sample with that of the 450 homes in the entire state.

This is an interesting example of nonprobability cluster sampling. Shostack and Campagna identified appropriate board-and-care homes and then interviewed the operators of those homes. Shostack and Campagna are careful to note that theirs is a judgment sample, not an unbiased sample. They had a very good sample for an exploratory study, however, especially one that involved just two researchers. Their detailed findings about the institutional needs of the low-income frail elderly and the low-income mentally ill who live in privately run board-and-care homes deserve careful reading.

Most purposive samples are pretty small (ethnographic studies are often based on

| Table 7.1 | Characteristics of Residents in Shostack and Campagna's Sample Homes and All of the Homes in the State of New Jersey in 1988 | |

Characteristics	Residents in Sample Homes (Percent)	Residents in All 450 Homes (Percent)
Male	43	42
Female	57	58
Under 50 Years of Age	19	31
50 and Over	81	69
White	89	88
Nonwhite	11	12

Source: Adapted from A. E. Shostack and G. P. Campagna, *Adult Residential Care Journal 5.* Copyright © 1991. Reprinted by permission of Plenum Publishing Corporation.

30–60 interviews, plus participant observation), but purposive sampling is not *just* for small samples. Ackerman and Gondolf (1991) had some ideas they wanted to test about differences between ACOAs (adult children of alcoholics) and non-ACOAs. (ACOAs are said to be disproportionately represented in the human services field.) Ackerman and Gondolf went to 62 human development conferences in 38 states across the United States and handed out 50 questionnaires to anyone who was around after the keynote address. Ackerman and Gondolf got back 1,630 usable questionnaires—about half of the 3,275 questionnaires they handed out.

One of the questions they asked was: "When you were growing up, did you have a parent who drank too much?" Ackerman and Gondolf randomly selected 500 respondents who answered "yes" and 500 who answered "no" to construct their sample of ACOAs and non-ACOAs for data analysis. The adult children of alcoholics were much more likely to have witnessed child abuse and spouse abuse than were non-ACOAs, and, as adults, the ACOAs had a much higher divorce rate than did non-ACOAs. Ackerman and Gondolf concluded that the data from their purposive sample support the suggestion of clinicians that people who

have an alcoholic parent are more likely to have other indicators of a tough family life.

If you think Ackerman and Gondolf had a big purposive sample, consider the work of Kail et al. (1995). They studied female drug addicts who traded sex for money or drugs and female addicts who didn't. The team of researchers had a purposive sample of over 9,000 female drug addicts who were not in treatment. Prostitutes were more likely than nonprostitutes to share needles with others and were less likely to use new needles or to clean old needles before each episode. The sample of female drug addicts was not unbiased; it was, in fact, *intentionally* biased to get answers to questions of practical importance (**Further Reading:** purposive sampling).

CONVENIENCE, OR HAPHAZARD SAMPLING

Convenience sampling is a glorified term for grabbing whoever will stand still long enough to answer your questions. It is useful for exploratory research, to get a feel for "what's going on out there," and for pretesting questionnaires to make sure that the items are unambiguous and not too threatening. But convenience sampling is dangerous. If you ask students at the library how they feel about some current campus issue, you may get different answers than if you ask students who are playing cards in the cafeteria. If you only do interviews around noon, when it is convenient for you, you'll miss all those people for whom noon is not a convenient hour.

Sometimes convenience samples are all that are available, and you just have to make do. Studies of the homeless are usually done with convenience samples, for obvious reasons, as are studies of people who are in intensive care units in hospitals. All samples represent *something*. The trick is to make them representative of what *you* want them to be. That's what turns a convenience sample into a purposive one.

K. Miller et al. (1997) wanted to get a handle on sources of conflict between certified nurse-midwives and physicians who are in collaborative practices. Miller et al. posted a copy of their survey on an electronic bulletin board maintained by a school of nursing and got a convenience sample of 78 nurse-midwife respondents.

The data from these respondents produced a list of common sources of conflict in collaborative practices between nurse-midwives and physicians. We wouldn't put much stock in the fact that a specific *percentage* of the nurse-midwives report conflict with their physician partners over billing of insurance companies for services, but the *list* of conflicts is very instructive because it is the basis for more in-depth research (**Further Reading:** convenience sampling).

CHAIN REFERRAL, OR NETWORK SAMPLING: THE SNOWBALL AND RDS METHODS

Snowball sampling and respondent-driven sampling (RDS) (also known, generically, as chain referral sampling and network sampling) are two network sampling methods for studying hard-to-find or hard-to-study populations. Populations can be hard to find and study for at least four reasons:

1. They contain very few members who are scattered over a large area (think strict vegans in rural Georgia, bilingual deaf children in Texas who are fluent in signing English and Spanish), and/or:

2. They are stigmatized and reclusive (HIV-positive people who never show up at clinics until they are sick with AIDS) or even actively hiding (transgendered people who have been physically attacked, men who have battered their female partners), and/or:

3. They are people who really have something to hide (Richardson [1988], for example, used snowball sampling to locate single or divorced women who were in long-term relationships with married men), and/or:

4. They are members of an elite group (surgeons, professional athletes) and don't care about your need for data.

Snowball Sampling

Charles Kadushin (1968) laid out the snowball method in his study of elites in modern, complex societies, but elites can just as well be "teachers in this school district whose opinions really count" or "surgeons in this HMO whose work is respected." Using key informants and/or documents, you locate one or two people in a population. Then you ask those people to: (1) list others in the population; and (2) recommend someone from the list whom you might interview. You get handed from person to person and the sampling frame grows with each interview. Eventually, the sampling frame becomes saturated—that is, no new names are offered.

Ostrander (1980) used snowball sampling in her study of class consciousness among upper-class women in a midwestern U.S. city. She selected her first informant by looking for someone who had graduated from an elite women's college, was listed in the social register, was active in upper-class clubs—and who would talk to her. At the end of the interview, she asked the informant to "suggest another woman of your social group, with a background like yours, who might be willing to talk to me."

Thomas Weisner has been following 205 counterculture women and their families since 1974. Weisner built this sample by recruiting women in California who were in their third trimester of pregnancy. He used snowball sampling, but to ensure that participants came from all over the state and represented various kinds of families, he used no more than two referrals from any one source (Weisner 2002:277) (Box 7.2).

Box 7.2 Sometimes you just have to start over

David Griffith and his colleagues used *two* snowball samples in their study of food preferences in Moberly, Missouri. They chose an initial "seed" household in a middle-income neighborhood and asked a man in the house to name three people in town with whom he interacted on a regular basis. The first person cited by the respondent lived in a lower-income neighborhood across town. That person, in turn, named other people who were in the lower-income bracket.

After a while, the researchers realized that, though they'd started with a middle-income informant who had children at home, they were getting mostly lower-income, elderly people in the snowball sample. So they started again, this time with a seed from an elite, upper-middle-income neighborhood. By the time they got through, Griffith et al. had a well-balanced sample of 30 people with whom they did in-depth interviews (reported in J. C. Johnson 1990:78).

Respondent-Driven Sampling

Snowball sampling is popular and fun to do, but it does not produce a statistically representative sample in a large population. In a small community, like practitioners of alternative medicine in a town, the members are likely to be in contact with one another. Here, snowball sampling is an effective way to build an exhaustive sampling frame from which you can select people at random to interview—or elect to interview all of them.

In large communities, though—like all the practitioners of alternative medicine in a large city—the members who are well known have a better chance of being named in a snowball procedure than do members who are less well known. And in large populations, people who have large networks name more people than do people who have small networks. For large populations, then, snowball sampling can produce useful nonprobability samples, but every person does not have the same chance of being included. (For more on problems with snowball sampling, see Biernacki and Waldorf [1981] and Watters and Biernacki [1989].)

Douglas Heckathorn (1997) developed respondent-driven sampling to deal with this problem. Like snowball sampling, RDS begins with a few people who act as seeds. The respondents are paid for being interviewed and are then asked to recruit up to three members of their networks into the study. To move this process along, Heckathorn paid each of his seed respondents $10 (this might be $50 today, but you get the idea) and he gave them three coupons. Anyone who came to Heckathorn to be interviewed and who had one of those coupons was paid the same $10. (He upped the bounty to $15 for referring a female drug injector because they were harder to find.) Those respondents, in turn, got several coupons and recruited others into the study.

There are two improvements to snowball sampling here. (1) The people who a respondent names in a snowball interview may not want you even to know about their existence, much less be anxious to grant you an interview. In RDS, the initial members of the sample are volunteers as are the people they recruit. (2) When it's done right, the RDS method produces samples that are less biased than are traditional snowball samples (Salganik and Heckathorn 2004) (**Further Reading:** chain referral sampling) (Box 7.3).

Box 7.3 Gaming the RDS

RDS is now widely used in the study of injection drug users and other populations at high risk for HIV/AIDS. Scott (2008) interviewed 70 injection drug users in Chicago who had participated in the full entire RDS sequence: They had received $20 for completing an interview and had collected $30 more for bringing in three associates (at $10 each) who had also completed an interview. Forty-eight of the 70 had sold at least one of their coupons to someone else because they could not trust three people in their network to complete the interview. This may introduce some distortion to the samples, but RDS remains the best available method for locating and studying populations at risk for HIV/AIDS.

CHOOSING INFORMANTS

Across the social sciences, you'll see references to research participants as respondents, or subjects, or informants. Respondents respond to survey questions; subjects are the subject of some experiment; and informants . . . well, informants tell you *what they think you need to know* about their culture (Box 7.4).

Box 7.4 Ethnographic consultants

Most ethnographers call the people whom they interview informants. Some prefer the term **consultants**. Robert Garot (2007:54), for example, refers to the inner-city gang members he interviews as consultants because, he says, he uses their accounts to report events that he did not observe himself. Others point out that people who work with ethnographers are experts on some topic—how to move cattle from ranch to market, how to use local plants to heal cuts, how to hold a church supper. Experts are called consultants if they are employed temporarily by a business or a government agency, so why not give the same courtesy to ethnographic informants?

There are two kinds of ethnographic informants: key informants and specialized informants. Key informants are people who know a lot about their culture and are, for reasons of their own, willing to share all their knowledge with you. When you do long-term ethnography you develop close relationships with a few key informants—relationships that can last a lifetime. You don't choose these people. They and you choose each other, over time. Specialized informants have particular competence in some cultural domain. If you want to know the rules of Little League Baseball, or when to genuflect in a Roman Catholic Mass, or how police handle evidence at a crime scene, you need to talk to people who can speak knowledgeably about those things.

Key Informants

Good key informants are people whom you can talk to you easily, who understand the information you need, and who are glad to give it to you or get it for you. Pelto and Pelto (1978:72) advocate training informants "to conceptualize cultural data in the frame of reference" that you, the researcher, use. In some cases, you may want to just listen. But when you run into a really great informant, I see no reason to hold back. Teach the informant about the analytic categories you're developing and ask whether the categories are correct. In other words, encourage the informant to become the ethnographer. (For a thoughtful presentation of another perspective, see Wolcott [2008].)

I've worked with Jesús Salinas since 1962. In 1971, I was about to write an ethnography of his culture, the Ñähñu of central Mexico, when he mentioned that he'd be interested in writing an ethnography himself. I dropped my project and taught him to read and write Ñähñu. Over the next 15 years, Salinas produced four volumes about the Ñähñu people—volumes that I translated and from which I learned many things that I'd never have learned

had I written the ethnography myself. For example, Ñähñu men engage in rhyming duels, much like "playing the dozens" among African American men. I wouldn't have thought to ask about those duels because I had never witnessed one (see Bernard and Salinas Pedraza 1989).

Just as Salinas has influenced my thinking about Mexican Indian life, Salinas's ethnography was heavily influenced by his association with me. We've discussed and analyzed parts of Ñähñu culture over the years and we've even argued over interpretation of observed facts. Then I remember that I've been his informant as well, telling him what he wanted to know about anthropology and linguistics and about how people in my culture look at data about cultures.

Finding Key Informants

One of the most famous key informants in the ethnographic literature is Doc in William Foote Whyte's *Street Corner Society* (1981 [1943]). Whyte studied "Cornerville," an Italian American neighborhood in a place he called "Eastern City." (Cornerville was the North End of Boston.) Whyte asked some social workers if they knew anyone who could help Whyte with his study. One social worker told Whyte to come to her office and meet a man whom she thought could do the job. When Whyte showed up, the social worker introduced him to Doc and then left the room. Whyte nervously explained his predicament, and Doc asked him "Do you want to see the high life or the low life?" (Whyte 1989:72).

Whyte couldn't believe his luck. He told Doc he wanted to see all he could, learn as much as possible about life in the neighborhood. Doc told him:

> Any nights you want to see anything, I'll take you around. I can take you to the joints—the gambling joints. I can take you around to the street corners. Just remember that you're my

friend. That's all they need to know. I know these places and if I tell them you're my friend, nobody will bother you. You just tell me what you want to see, and we'll arrange it. . . . When you want some information, I'll ask for it, and you listen. When you want to find out their philosophy of life, I'll start an argument and get it for you. [Whyte 1989:72]

Doc was straight up. He told Whyte to rely on him and to ask him anything, and Doc was good to his word throughout Whyte's three years of fieldwork. Doc introduced Whyte to the boys on the corner; Doc hung out with Whyte and spoke up for Whyte when people questioned Whyte's presence. Doc was just spectacular.

Or was he? Boelen (1992) visited Cornerville 25 times between 1970 and 1989, sometimes for a few days, other times for several months. She tracked down and interviewed everyone she could find from *Street Corner Society*. Doc had died in 1967, but Boelen interviewed his two sons in 1970 (then in their late teens and early 20s). She asked them what Doc's opinion of Whyte's book had been and reports the elder son saying: "My father considered the book untrue from the very beginning to the end, a total fantasy" (Boelen 1992:29).

Whyte (1996a, 1996b) refuted Boelen's report, as did another of Whyte's key informants (Orlando 1992). We'll never know the whole truth. Whyte certainly made mistakes, but the same can be said for all ethnographers. For some scholars, mistakes invalidate a positivist stance in ethnography. For others, including me, it does not.

Doc May Be Famous, but He's Not Unique

All successful ethnographers will tell you that they eventually came to rely on one or two key people in their fieldwork. What was rare about Doc is how quickly and easily Whyte teamed up with him. It's not easy to find informants like Doc. When Jeffrey Johnson began fieldwork in a North Carolina fishing community, he went

to the local marine extension agent and asked for the agent's help. The agent, happy to oblige, told Johnson about a fisherman whom he thought could help Johnson get off on the right foot.

It turned out that the fisherman was a transplanted northerner; he had a pension from the Navy; he was an activist Republican in a thoroughly Democratic community; and he kept his fishing boat in an isolated moorage, far from the village harbor. He was, in fact, maximally different from the typical local fisherman. The agent had meant well, of course (J. C. Johnson 1990:56).

In fact, the first informants with whom you develop a working relationship in the field may be "deviant" members of their culture. Agar (1980b:86) reports that during his fieldwork in India he was taken on by the *naik*, or headman of the village. The *naik*, it turned out, had inherited the role but was not respected in the village and did not preside over village meetings. This did not mean that the *naik* knew nothing about village affairs and customs; he was what Agar called a "solid insider," yet somewhat of an outcast—a "marginal native," just like the ethnographer was trying to be (Freilich 1977). If you think about it, Agar said, you should wonder about the kind of person who would befriend an ethnographer.

In my own fieldwork (at sea, in Mexican villages, on Greek islands, in rural communities in the United States, and in modern American bureaucracies), I have consistently found the best informants to be people who are cynical about their own culture. They may not be outcasts (in fact, they are always solid insiders), but they say they *feel* somewhat marginal to their culture, by virtue of their intellectualizing of and disenchantment with their culture. They are always observant, reflective, and articulate. In other words, they invariably have all the qualities that I would like to have myself.

Don't choose key ethnographic informants too quickly. Allow yourself to go awash in data for a while and play the field. When you have several prospects, check on their roles and statuses in the community. Be sure that the key informants you select don't prevent you from gaining access to other important informants (i.e., people who won't talk to you when they find out you're so-and-so's friend). Good ethnography is, at its best, a good story, so find trustworthy informants who are observant, reflective, and articulate—who know how to tell good stories—and stay with them. In the end, ethnographic fieldwork stands or falls on building mutually supportive relations with a few key people (Box 7.5).

Box 7.5 Informants and sampling: Are a few informants enough?

The answer to this question is that it depends on what you want to know. When we conduct questionnaire surveys we know how to choose an unbiased sample of respondents. In any large aggregate of people, there are bound to be serious differences of opinion and behavior. A random sample increases the likelihood that these differences (even if you don't know what they might be) are represented in your data. (The logic for this was explored in Chapter 5.)

Ethnography, on the other hand, is about understanding people's lived experiences. This kind of information requires a few knowledgeable and articulate informants rather than an unbiased sample of people. Ethnography is also about **emic explanations** of how things work—why people think they are poor, why they think some ethnic groups are successful and others aren't, why they think women earn less for the same work than men do, what they think people can do to prevent or treat colds. This kind of information, too, requires a few key informants.

Are a few informants *really* capable of providing adequate information about a culture? Yes, if you ask them things they *really* know about. In other words, we select ethnographic informants for their *competence* rather than for their *representativeness*. More on this below and on measuring cultural competence in the section on cultural consensus analysis in Chapter 16.

Informants Sometimes Lie

Don't be surprised if informants lie to you. Jeffrey Johnson, a skilled boat builder, worked in an Alaskan boat yard as part of his field study of a fishing community. At one point in his fieldwork, two other ethnographers showed up, both women, to conduct some interviews with the men in the boat yard. Johnson reports:

> The two anthropologists had no idea I was one of *them* since I was dressed in carpenter's overalls, with all the official paraphernalia— hammer, tape measure, etc. I was sufficiently close to overhear the interview and, knowing the men being interviewed, recognized quite a few blatant lies. In fact, during the course of one interview, a captain would occasionally wink at me as he told a whopper of a lie. [personal communication]

This is not an isolated incident. A Comox Indian woman spent two hours narrating a text for Franz Boas. The text turned out to be nothing but a string of questions and answers. Boas didn't speak Comox well enough to know that he was being duped, but when he found out he noted it in his diary (Rohner 1969:61).

This sort of thing can happen to anyone who does participant observation ethnography, but some cultures are more tolerant of lying than are others. Nachman (1984) found that the most articulate informants among the Nissan of New Guinea were great truth tellers and accomplished liars at the same time. Among the Nissan, says Nachman, people expect big men to give speeches and to "manipulate others and to create socially acceptable meanings," even if that means telling outright lies (**Further Reading:** lying informants).

Selecting Culturally Specialized Informants

The search for formal and systematic ways to select focused ethnographic informants—people who can help you learn about particular areas of a culture—has been going on for a very long time. In 1957, Marc-Adelard Tremblay was involved in a Cornell University survey research project on poverty in Nova Scotia. He wanted to use ethnographic informants to help the team's researchers design a useful questionnaire, so he made a list of some roles in the community he was studying—things like sawmill owners, doctors, farmers, bankers—and chose informants who could talk to him knowledgeably about things in their area of expertise. Tremblay had no external test to tell him whether the informants he selected were, in fact, the most competent in their areas of expertise, but he felt that on-the-spot clues made the selection of informants valid.

Michael Robbins and his colleagues studied acculturation and modernization among the Baganda of Uganda, using a more formal method to select informants who might be competent on this topic (Robbins et al. 1969). First they ran a survey of households in a rural sector, asking about things that would indicate respondents' exposure to Western culture. Then they used the results of the survey to select appropriate informants.

Robbins et al. had 80 variables in the survey that had something to do with acculturation and they ran a factor analysis to find out which variables package together. More about factor analysis in Chapter 22. For now, think of it as a way to reduce those 80 variables to just a handful of underlying variables around which individual variables cluster. It turned out that 14 of the original 80 variables clustered together in one factor. Among those original variables were: being under 40 years of age, drinking European beer, speaking and reading English, having a Western job, and living in a house that has concrete floors and walls.

Robbins et al. called this cluster the "acculturation factor." They chose informants who had high scores on this factor and interviewed them about acculturation. Robbins et al. reversed Tremblay's method. Tremblay used key informants to help him build a survey instrument; Robbins et al. used a survey to find key informants. Today, this might be called mixed methods. It's a powerful way to conduct any scientific inquiry.

Poggie's Study of Ciudad Industrial

In any given domain of culture, some people are more competent than others. In our culture, some people know a lot about the history of baseball; some people can name the actors in every sitcom since the beginning of television in the 1940s. Some people are experts on medicinal plants; others are experts on cars and trucks. John Poggie (1972) did an early study of informant competence. He selected one informant in each of seven Mexican communities. The communities ranged in size from 350 to 3,000 inhabitants. The informants were village or town presidents, judges, or (in the case of agricultural communities) the local commissioners of communal land. Poggie asked these informants questions about life in the communities and compared the answers with data from a high-quality social survey.

For example, Poggie asked the seven informants: "How many men in this town are workers in Ciudad Industrial?" (Ciudad Industrial is a fictitious name of a city that attracted many labor migrants from the communities that Poggie studied.) In his survey, Poggie asked respondents if they had ever worked in Ciudad Industrial. The correlation between the answers given by Poggie's expert informants and the data obtained from the survey was 0.90.

Poggie also asked: "What percentage of the houses here are made of adobe?" This time, the correlation between the informants and the survey was only 0.71. Table 7.2 shows the seven questions Poggie asked, and how well his informants did when their answers were compared to the survey.

Overall, informants produced answers most like those in the survey when they were asked to respond to questions about things that are publicly observable. The survey data are not necessarily more *accurate* than the informants' data. But as the questions require informants to talk about things inside people's homes (such as what percentage of people eat eggs), or about what people think (what percentage of people would

like to work in Ciudad Industrial), informants' answers look less and less like those of the survey.

Poggie concluded: "There is little reason to believe that trust and rapport would improve the reliability and precision concerning what percentage sleep in beds, who would like to live in the new industrial city, or what percentage eat bread daily" (1972:29). (For more on selecting informants who have high competence in specialized domains, see the discussion of consensus analysis in Chapter 16.)

SAMPLE SIZE IN NONPROBABILITY SAMPLING

There is growing evidence that 10–20 knowledgeable people are enough to uncover and understand the core categories in any well-defined cultural domain or study of lived experience. Morse (1994) recommended a minimum of six interviews for phenomenological

Table 7.2 Agreement Between Informants and Survey Data in Seven Villages

Questions asked of informants	Correlation with questionnaire data
Number of men from this town who are workers in Ciudad Industrial	0.9
Percentage of houses made of adobe	0.71
Percentage of households that have radios	0.52
Percentage of people who eat eggs regularly	0.33
Percentage of people who would like to live in Ciudad Industrial	0.23
Percentage of people who eat bread daily	0.14
Percentage of people who sleep in beds	0.05

Source: "Toward Quality Control in Key Informant Data" by J. J. Poggie, 1972, *Human Organization* 31:26–29.

studies and 30–50 interviews for ethnographic studies and grounded theory studies. The data from two recent studies support Morse's experience-based guess.

M. G. Morgan et al. (2002:76) did in-depth interviews with four different samples of people about various risks in the environment. As they coded the interviews for concepts, Morgan et al. plotted the number of new concepts in each interview across the four samples. In all four cases, the first few interviews produce a lot of new data, but by 20 interviews, hardly any new information is retrieved.

Guest et al. (2006) interviewed 30 sex workers in Ghana and another 30 in Nigeria. They coded the transcripts in batches of six, working first on the interviews from Ghana and then on the ones from Nigeria, and plotted the number of new themes uncovered in the coding. Of the 114 themes identified in the entire corpus, 80 turn up in the first six interviews in both Ghana and Nigeria. Another 20 themes turned up in the second batch of six interviews. Only five new themes were added to the codebook to accommodate the 30 interviews from Nigeria.

And, as we'll see in Tables 16.13 and 16.14 (when we get to consensus analysis), Weller and Romney (1988:77) showed that just 10–13 knowledgeable informants are needed to understand the contents of a well-defined cultural domain. This is all very good news for ethnographers (and see Handwerker 2001:93–96).

AND FINALLY . . .

The credibility of research results comes from the power of the methods used in measurement and sampling. Good measurement is the key to internal validity and representative sampling is the key to *external* validity. Well-done nonprobability sampling is actually part of good measurement. It contributes to credibility by contributing to *internal* validity. When someone reads a research report based on really good measurement of a nonprobability sample, they come away thinking, "Yep, I believe those conclusions about the people who were studied in that piece of research."

That's plenty. If you want the credibility of your conclusions to extend beyond the group of people (or countries, or organizations, or comic books) you studied, then either: (1) repeat the study one or more times with nonprobability samples; or (2) use a probability sample. Remember: Every sample represents something. An unbiased sample represents a population with a known probability of error. A nonprobability sample lacks this one feature. For a very, very large number of research questions, this is simply not a problem.

Key Concepts in This Chapter

quota sampling
purposive sampling
judgment sampling
convenience sampling
chain-referral
    sampling
case control design
sampling design
sampling grid

pilot studies
intensive case studies
critical case studies
hard-to-find-population
    studies
critical-case sampling
snowball sampling
respondent-driven
    sampling (RDS)

network sampling
respondents
subjects
informants
consultants
key informants
specialized
    informants
emic explanations

Summary

- It is often impossible to do strict probability sampling under real research conditions. In these cases, use a nonprobability sample. Also, when you are collecting cultural data, rather than individual attribute data, random sampling is inappropriate. Some types of nonprobability sampling are: quota sampling, judgment sampling, convenience sampling, and snowball sampling.

  o In quota sampling, you decide on the subpopulations of interest and on the proportions of those subpopulations in the final sample. Quota sampling resembles stratified probability sampling, but respondents are not chosen randomly. Many commercial polling companies use quota samples that are fine tuned on the basis of decades of research.

  o In purposive, or judgment sampling, you decide the purpose you want the units of analysis (people, communities, countries) to serve. This is somewhat like quota sampling, except that there is no overall sampling design that tells you how many of each type of informant you need for a study.

  o Convenience or haphazard sampling means grabbing whoever will stand still long enough to answer your questions. It is useful for exploratory research, to get a feel for "what's going on out there," and for pretesting questionnaires to make sure that the items are unambiguous and not too threatening. Pilot studies are often done with convenience samples.

  o There are two kinds of chain-referral sampling: snowball sampling and respondent driven sampling. In snowball sampling, you locate one or more key individuals and ask them to name others who would be likely candidates for your research. Snowball sampling is used in studies of social networks, where the object is to find out who people know and how they know each other. Respondent-driven sampling is a form of snowball sampling and is particularly suited to studies of hard-to-find populations.

Exercises

1. What are the advantages and disadvantages of probability sampling, purposive sampling, quota sampling, and convenience sampling? When is a convenience sample called for in research?

2. Does the distinction between qualitative and quantitative data have any bearing on whether a probability or nonprobability sample is appropriate?

3. You are called on to study the reaction by students at your school to a program about binge drinking. You determine that the only way to get immediate reaction is to ask people coming out of the auditorium if they will answer your survey and, if they agree, to hand them a survey form to fill out on the spot. Develop a quota sampling grid for gender (male, female), freshman versus senior class, and ethnicity (White, African American, Hispanic, and other).

Further Reading

Nonprobability sampling for individual and cultural data. Handwerker and Wozniak (1997), Johnson (1990).

Quota sampling. Braunstein (1993), Curtice and Sparrow (1997), Feng et al. (2010), Marsh and Scarbrough (1990), Morrow et al. (2007), Palys (2008).

Purposive sampling. Barker et al. (2004), Palys (2008), Rhodes et al. (2008), Van Ryzin (1995).

Convenience sampling. Hultsch et al. (2002), Johnston et al. (2009), Pruchino et al. (2008), Schwarcz et al. (2008), Westermeyer (1996), Yang et al. (2009).

Chain referral. Elliott, Golinelli et al. (2006), Elliott, McCaffrey et al. (2009), Heckathorn (2002, 2007), Kalton (2009), Salganik and Heckathorn (2004), Scott (2008).

Lying informants. Bernard et al. (1984), Bleek (1987), Nachman (1984), Salamone (1977).

PART III
Data Collection

8

Interviewing I

Unstructured and Semistructured

THE BIG PICTURE

This is the first of three chapters on interviewing. The concept of "interviewing" covers a lot of ground, from totally unstructured interactions, through semistructured situations, to highly formal interactions with respondents. Interviewing is done on the phone, in person, by mail and—more and more—by computer or on the Internet. This chapter is about unstructured and semistructured face-to-face interviewing, including management of focus groups. Chapter 9 is about questionnaires; and Chapter 10 is about some of the important, specialized techniques for collecting survey data, including cultural domain analysis and network analysis.

Unstructured interviewing is used across the social sciences as the front end to the development of questionnaires and, in ethnographic research, as one of the main methods for collecting data. Unstructured interviewing goes on during the course of an ordinary day of participant observation: in office, in factories, in patrol cars, in hospital wards—just about anywhere. Semistructured, or in-depth interviewing, is another of the main data collection methods in ethnography and it's also one of the main methods for collecting household survey data. Semistructured interviews follow a general script and cover a list of topics but are also open ended.

There is a vast literature on how to conduct effective interviews: how to gain rapport, how to get people to open up, how to introduce an interview, and how to end one. You can't learn to interview by reading about it, but after you read this chapter and *practice some of the techniques* described, you should be well on your way to becoming an effective interviewer. You should also have a pretty good idea of how much more there is to learn and be on your way to exploring the literature (**Further Reading**: interviewing).

INTERVIEW CONTROL

There is a continuum of interview situations based on the **amount of control** we try to exercise over people's responses (Dohrenwend and Richardson 1965; Gorden 1975; Spradley 1979). These different *types of interviews* produce different *types of data* that are useful for *different types* of research projects and that appeal to *different types* of researchers. For convenience, I divide the continuum of interviews into four large chunks.

1. Informal Interviewing

At one end there is informal interviewing, characterized by a total lack of structure or control. The researcher just tries to remember conversations heard during the course of a day "in the field." This requires constant jotting and daily sessions in which you sit at a computer, typing away, unburdening your memory, and developing field notes. If you're doing participant observation fieldwork, then informal interviewing is the method of choice at the beginning, when you're just settling in and getting to know the lay of the land. It is also used throughout ethnographic fieldwork to build greater rapport and to uncover new topics of interest that might have been overlooked.

When it comes to interviewing, never mistake the adjective "informal" for "lightweight." This is hard, hard work. You have to remember a lot; you have to duck into private corners a lot (so you can jot things down); and you have to use a lot of deception (to keep people from knowing that you're really at work, studying them). Informal interviewing can get pretty tiring.

Still, in some kinds of research, like ethnography with street children, informal interviewing is all you've got. Mark Connolly (1990) studied street children in Guatemala City and Bogotá, Colombia. These children live, eat, and sleep on the street. Hanging out and talking informally with these children was the only way that Connolly could do this research.

2. Unstructured Interviewing

Next comes unstructured interviewing, one of the two types covered in this chapter. There is nothing at all informal about unstructured interviewing, and nothing deceptive, either. You sit down with another person and hold an interview. Period. Both of you know what you're doing, and there is no shared feeling that you're just engaged in pleasant chit-chat.

Unstructured interviews are based on a clear plan that you keep constantly in mind, but they are also characterized by a minimum of control over the respondent's responses. The idea is to get people to open up and let them express themselves in their own terms, and at their own pace. A lot of what is called ethnographic interviewing is unstructured. Unstructured interviewing is used in situations where you have lots and lots of time—like when you are doing long-term fieldwork and can interview people on many separate occasions (Box 8.1).

Box 8.1 Paying informants

Should field researchers pay their informants? If so, how much? I'm a firm believer in paying for people's time, but there are exceptions. If you are studying people who are worth millions of dollars, paying them is inappropriate. You can't possibly pay them enough to compensate them financially for their time. It's better to make a donation to a charity that they support.

Paying informants will vary from case to case, but the general rule, for me at least, is that if you want to interview people formally—sit down with them, voice recorder on the table and/or notebook in hand—they should be paid at least the local rate for their time. With key informants, the rule for me is that there's always a culturally appropriate way—money, job training, buying cement for a new school—to compensate people for their contribution to your career.

---

3. Semistructured Interviewing

In situations where you won't get more than one chance to interview someone, semistructured interviewing is best. It has much of the freewheeling quality of unstructured interviewing and requires all the same skills, but semistructured interviewing is based on the use of an interview guide. This is a written list of questions and topics that need to be covered in a particular order.

This is the kind of interview that most people write about—the kind done in professional surveys. The interviewer maintains discretion to follow leads, but the interview guide is a set of clear instructions—instructions like this one: "Probe to see if informants (men and women alike) who have daughters have different values about premarital sex than do people who have only sons."

Formal, written guides are an absolute must if you are sending out several interviewers to collect data. But even if you do all the interviewing on a project yourself, you should build a guide and follow it if you want reliable, comparable qualitative data.

Semistructured interviewing works very well in projects where you are dealing with managers, bureaucrats, and elite members of a community—people who are accustomed to efficient use of their time. It demonstrates that you are fully in control of what you want from an interview but lets both you and your respondent follow new leads. It shows that you are prepared and competent but that you are not trying to exercise excessive control over the respondent.

4. Structured Interviewing

Finally, in fully structured interviews, people are asked to respond to as nearly identical a set of stimuli as possible. One variety of structured interviews involves use of an interview schedule—an explicit set of instructions to interviewers who administer questionnaires orally. Instructions might read "If the informant says that she or he has at least one daughter over 10 years of age, then ask questions 26b and 26c. Otherwise, go on to question 27."

Self-administered questionnaires are a kind of structured interview. Other structured interviewing techniques include pile sorting, frame elicitation, triad sorting, and tasks that require people to rate or rank order a list of things. I'll deal with structured interviews in Chapters 9 and 10.

UNSTRUCTURED INTERVIEWING

Unstructured interviewing is truly versatile. It is used by scholars who identify with the hermeneutic tradition and by those who identify with the positivist tradition. It is used in studies that require only textual data and in studies that require both textual and numerical data. Field ethnographers may use it to develop formal guides for semistructured interviews or to learn what questions to include, in the native language, on a highly-structured questionnaire (see Werner and Schoepfle [1987] for a good discussion of this). I say that field

ethnographers *may* use unstructured interviewing in developing structured interview schedules because unstructured interviewing also stands on its own.

When you want to know about the lived experience of fellow human beings—what it's like to survive hand-to-hand combat, how you get through each day when you have a child dying of leukemia, how it feels to make it across the border into Texas from Mexico only to be deported 24 hours later—you just can't beat unstructured interviewing.

Unstructured interviewing is excellent for building initial rapport with informants before moving to more formal interviews, and it's perfect for talking to informants who would not tolerate a more formal interview. The personal rapport you build with close informants in long-term fieldwork can make highly structured interviewing—and even semistructured interviewing—feel somehow unnatural. In fact, really structured interviewing can get in the way of your ability to communicate freely with key informants.

But not always. Some people want very much to talk about their lives, but they really don't like the unstructured interview format. I once asked a fisherman in Greece if I could have a few minutes of his time to discuss the economics of small-scale fishing.

I was about five minutes into the interview, treading lightly—you know, trying not to get too quickly into his finances, even though that's exactly what I wanted to know about—when he interrupted me: "Why don't you just get to the point?" he asked. "You want to know how I decide where to fish, and whether I use a share system or a wage system to split the profits, and how I find buyers for my catch, and things like that, right?" He had heard from other fishermen that these were some of the topics I was interviewing people about. No unstructured interviews for him; he was a busy man and wanted to get right to it.

A Case Study of
Unstructured Interviewing

Once you learn the art of "probing" (which I'll discuss in a while), unstructured interviewing can be used for studying sensitive issues, like sexuality, racial or ethnic prejudice, or "hot" political topics. I find it particularly useful in studying conflict. In 1972–1973, for example, I went to sea on two different oceanographic research vessels (Bernard and Killworth 1973, 1974). In both cases, there was an almost palpable tension between the scientific personnel and the crew of the ship. Through both informal and unstructured interviewing on land between cruises, I was able to establish that the conflict was predictable and regular. Let me give you an idea of how complex the situation was.

In 1972–1973, it cost $5,000 a day to run a major research vessel, not including the cost of the science. (That would be about $28,000 in 2012.) The way oceanography works, at least in the United States, the chief scientist on a research cruise has to pay for both ship time and for the cost of any experiments he or she wants to run. To do this, ocean scientists compete for grants from institutions like the U.S. Office of Naval Research, NASA, and the National Science Foundation.

The spending of so much money is validated by publishing significant results in prominent journals. It's a tough, competitive game, and one that leads scientists to use every minute of their ship time. As one set of scientists comes ashore after a month at sea, the next set is on the dock waiting to set up their experiments and haul anchor.

The crew, consequently, might only get 24 or 48 hours shore leave between voyages. That can cause some pretty serious resentment toward scientists. And that can lead to disaster. I found many documented instances of sabotage of expensive research by crew members who were, as one of them said, "sick and tired of being treated like goddamn bus drivers." In one incident, involving a British research vessel, a freezer filled with Antarctic shrimp, representing two years of data collection, went overboard during the night. In another, the crew and scientists from a U.S. Navy oceanographic research ship got into a brawl while in port (*Science* 1972:1346).

The structural problem I uncovered began at the top. Scientists whom I interviewed felt they had the right to take the vessels wherever they wanted to go, within prudence and reason, in search of answers to questions they had set up in their proposals. The captains of the ships believed (correctly) that *they* had the last word on maneuvering their ships at sea. Scientists, said the captains, sometimes went beyond prudence and reason in what they demanded of the vessels.

For example, a scientist might ask the captain to take a ship out of port in dangerous weather because ship time is so precious. This conflict between crew and scientists has been known—and pretty much ignored—since Charles Darwin sailed with HMS *Beagle* and it will certainly play a role in the productivity of long-term space station operations.

Unraveling this conflict at sea required participant observation and unstructured (as well as informal) interviewing with many people. No other strategy for data collection would have worked. At sea, people live for long periods of time in close physical quarters, and there is a common need to maintain good relations for the organization to function well.

It would have been inappropriate for me to have used highly structured interviews about the source of tension between the crew and the scientists. Better to steer the interviews around the issue of interest and let informants teach me what I needed to know. In the end, no analysis was better than that offered by one engine room mechanic who told me "These scientist types are so damn hungry for data, they'd run the ship aground looking for interesting rocks if we let them."

Getting Started

There are some important steps to take when you start interviewing someone for the first time. First, assure people of anonymity and confidentiality. Explain that you simply want to know what *they* think and what *their* observations are. If you are interviewing someone whom you have come to know over a period of time, explain why you think their opinions and observations on a particular topic are important. If you are interviewing someone chosen from a random sample, and whom you are unlikely to see again, explain how they were chosen and why it is important that you have their cooperation to maintain representativeness.

If people say that they really don't know enough to be part of your study, assure them that their participation is crucial and that you are truly interested in what they have to say (and you'd better mean it, or you'll never pull it off). Tell everyone you interview that you are trying to learn from *them*. Encourage them to interrupt you during the interview with anything they think is important. And always ask for permission to *record* personal interviews *and to take notes*. This is vital. If you can't take notes, then, in most cases, the value of an interview plummets. (See below, on using a recorder and taking notes.)

Keep in mind that people who are being interviewed know that you are shopping for information. There is no point in trying to hide this. If you are open and honest about your intentions, and if you are genuinely interested in what people have to say, many people will help you.

This is not always true. A lot of social science research is done with people who are happy—even eager—to share their lives with you. But a lot of it is done with people who are poor, powerless, and marginalized—people in prison, sex workers, runaways, battered women, injecting drug users, illegal immigrants. . . . They aren't always happy to share their lives in interviews.

Letting the Informant or Respondent Lead

If you can carry on "unthreatening, self-controlled, supportive, polite, and cordial interaction in everyday life," then interviewing will come easy to you and informants will feel comfortable responding to your questions (Lofland 1976:90). No matter how supportive you are as a person, though, an interview is never really like a casual, unthreatening conversation in everyday life. In casual conversations, people take more or less balanced turns (Spradley 1979) and there is no feeling that somehow the discussion has to stay on track or follow some theme (see also Hyman and Cobb 1975; Merton et al. 1956). In unstructured interviewing, you keep the conversation focused on a topic, while giving the respondent room to define the content of the discussion.

The rule is: Get people on to a topic of interest and get out of the way. Let the informant provide information that he or she thinks is important.

During my research on the Kalymnian sponge fishermen in Greece, I spent a lot of time at Procopis Kambouris's *taverna*. (A Greek *taverna* is a particular kind of restaurant.) Procopis's was a favorite of the sponge fishermen. Procopis was a superb cook; he made his own wine every year from grapes that he selected himself; and he was as good a teller of sea stories as he was a listener to those of his clientele. At Procopis's *taverna* I was able to collect the work histories of sponge fishermen—when they'd begun their careers, the training they'd gotten, the jobs they'd held, and so on. The atmosphere was relaxed (plenty of retsina wine and good things to eat), and conversation was easy.

As a participant observer, I developed a sense of camaraderie with the regulars, and we exchanged sea stories with a lot of flourish. I had been to sea for three months on a Greek merchant ship a few years earlier and had stories of my own to swap, but still, no one at Procopis's ever made the mistake of thinking that I was there just for the camaraderie. They knew that I was writing about their lives and that I had lots of questions to ask. They also knew immediately when I switched from the role of participant observer to that of ethnographic interviewer.

One night, I slipped into just such an interview/conversation with Savas Ergas. He was 64 years old at the time and was planning to make one last six-month voyage as a sponge diver during the coming season in 1965. I began to interview Savas on his work history at about 7:30 in the evening, and we closed Procopis's place at about 3 a.m. During the course of the evening, several other men joined and left the group at various times, as they would on any night of conversation at Procopis's. Savas had lots of stories to tell (he was a living legend and he played well to a crowd), and we had to continue the interview a few days later, over several more liters of retsina.

At one point on that second night, Savas told me (almost offhandedly) that he had spent more than a year of his life walking the bottom of the Mediterranean. I asked him how he knew this, and he challenged me to document it. Savas had decided that there was something important that I needed to know, and he maneuvered the interview around to make sure I learned it.

This led to about three hours of painstaking work. We counted the number of seasons he'd been to sea over a 46-year career (he remembered that he hadn't worked at all during 1943 because of "something to do with the war"). We figured conservatively the number of days he'd spent at sea, the average number of dives per trip, and the average depth and time per dive. We joked about the tendency of divers to exaggerate their exploits and about how fragile human memory is when it comes to this kind of detail.

It was difficult to stay on the subject, because Savas was such a good raconteur and a perceptive analyst of Kalymnian life. The interview meandered off on interesting tangents, but after a while, either Savas or I would steer it back to the issue at hand. In the end, discounting heavily for both exaggeration and faulty recall, we reckoned that he'd spent at least 10,000 hours—about a year and a fourth, counting each day as a full 24 hours—under water and had walked the distance between Alexandria and Tunis at least three times.

The exact numbers really didn't matter. What did matter was that Savas Ergas had a really good sense of what *he* thought I needed to know about the life of a sponge diver. It was I, the interviewer, who defined the focus of the interview; but it was Savas, the respondent, who determined the content. And was I ever glad he did.

PROBING

The key to successful interviewing is learning how to probe effectively—that is, to stimulate a respondent to produce more information, without injecting yourself so much into the interaction that you only get a reflection of yourself in the data. Suppose you ask a suburban housewife "Have you ever worked outside the home?" and she says "Yes." The next question (the probe) is "What did you do?" Suppose the answer is "Oh, lots of different things." Your next response should not be "Waitress? Sales? Construction?" but "Like what, exactly? Could you tell me some of the places where you've worked?"

There are many kinds of probes that you can use in an interview. (In what follows, I will draw on the important work by Briggs [1986], Dohrenwend and Richardson [1965], Gorden [1987], Hyman and Cobb [1975], Kahn and Cannell [1957], Kluckhohn [1945], Merton et al. [1956], Reed and Stimson [1985],

Warwick and Lininger [1975], Whyte [1960], Whyte and Whyte [1984], and on my own experience and that of my students.)

The Silent Probe

The most difficult technique to learn is the silent probe, which consists of just remaining quiet and waiting for the person to continue. The silence may be accompanied by a nod or a mumbled "uh-huh" as you focus on your note pad. The silent probe sometimes produces more information than does direct questioning. At least at the beginning of an interview, informants look to you for guidance as to whether or not they're on the right track. They want to know whether they're "giving you what you want." Most of the time, especially in unstructured interviews, you want the informant to define the relevant information.

Some people are more glib than others and require very little prodding to keep up the flow of information. Others are more reflective and take their time. Inexperienced interviewers tend to jump in with verbal probes as soon as an informant goes silent. Meanwhile, the informant may be just reflecting, gathering thoughts, and preparing to say something important. You can kill those moments (and there are a lot of them) with your interruptions.

Glibness can be a matter of *cultural*, not just personal style. Gordon Streib reported that he had to adjust his own interviewing style radically when he left New York City to study the Navajo in the 1950s (Streib 1952). Streib, a New Yorker himself, had done studies based on semistructured interviews with subway workers in New York. Those workers uniformly maintained a fast, hard-driving pace during the interviews—a pace with which Streib, as a member of the culture, was comfortable.

But that style was entirely inappropriate with the Navajo, who were uniformly more reflective than the subway workers (Streib, personal communication). In other words, the

silent probe is sometimes not a probe at all; being quiet and waiting for an informant to continue may simply be appropriate cultural behavior.

On the other hand, the silent probe is a high-risk technique, which is why beginners avoid it. If an informant is genuinely at the end of a thought and you don't provide further guidance, your silence can become awkward. You may even lose your credibility as an interviewer. The silent probe takes practice to use effectively. But it's worth the effort.

The Echo Probe

Another kind of probe consists of simply repeating the last thing someone has said, and asking them to continue. This echo probe is particularly useful when an informant is describing a process or an event.

Here's an example of what *not* to do: "I see. The students walk across the stage and receive their diplomas from the principal. How about students who are out of town during graduation? Can they receive their diplomas by e-mail?" This redirects the interview and stops the informant from finishing a description. Better to jot a note to yourself to follow up later about students who are out of town and say: "I see. The students walk across the stage and receive their diplomas from the principal. Then what happens?"

This probe doesn't redirect the interview. It shows that you understand what's been said so far and encourages the informant to continue with the narrative. If you use the echo probe too often, though, you'll hear an exasperated informant asking "Why do you keep repeating what I just said?"

The Uh-Huh Probe

You can encourage an informant to continue with a narrative by just making affirmative comments, like "Uh-huh," or "Yes, I see," or "Right, uh-huh," and so on. Matarazzo (1964) showed how powerful this **uh-huh** probe or **neutral probe** can be. He did a series of identical, semistructured, 45-minute interviews with a group of informants. He broke each interview into three 15-minute chunks. During the second chunk, the interviewer was told to make affirmative noises, like "uh-huh," whenever the informant was speaking. Informant responses during those chunks were about a third longer than during the first and third periods.

The Tell-Me-More Probe

The tell-me-more probe may be the most common form of probe among experienced interviewers. Respondents give you an answer and you probe for more by saying: "Could you tell me more about that?" Other variations include "Why exactly do you say that?" and "Why exactly do you feel that way?" You have to be careful about using stock probes like these. As Converse and Schuman point out (1974:50), if you get into a rut and repeat these probes like a robot, don't be surprised to hear someone finishing up a nice long discourse by saying "Yeah, yeah, and why *exactly* do I feel like that?" (From personal experience, I can guarantee that the mortification factor allows this sort of thing to happen only once. The experience lasts a lifetime.)

The Long Question Probe

The long-question probe is another way to induce more continuous responses. Instead of asking "How do you plant a home garden?" ask "What are all the things you have to do to actually get a home garden going?" When I interviewed sponge divers on Kalymnos, instead of asking them "What is it like to make a dive into very deep water?" I said "Tell me about diving into really deep water. What do you do to get ready, and how do you descend and ascend? What's it like down there?"

Later in the interview, or on another occasion, I would home in on special topics. But to break the ice and get the interview flowing, there is nothing quite as useful as what Spradley (1979) called the **grand tour question**.

This does not mean that asking longer questions or using neutral probes necessarily produces *better* responses. They do, however, produce *more* responses, and, in general, more is better. Furthermore, the more you can keep an informant talking, the more you can express interest in what they are saying and the more you build rapport. This is especially important in the first interview you do with someone whose trust you want to build (see Spradley 1979:80). There is still a lot to be learned about how various kinds of probes affect what informants tell us.

Threatening questions—those asking for sensitive information—should be short but should be preceded by a long, rambling run-up: "We're interested in the various things that people do these days to keep from getting diseases when they have sex. Some people do different kinds of things, and some people do nothing special. Do you ever use condoms?" If the respondents says "Yes," or "No," or "Sometimes," *then* you can launch that series of questions about why, why not, when, with whom, and so on. The wording of sensitive questions should, in general, be supportive and nonjudgmental. (See below for more on threatening questions.)

Probing by Leading

After all this, you may be cautious about being really directive in an interview. Don't be. Many researchers caution against "leading" an informant. Lofland (1976), for example, warns against questions like "Don't you think that . . . ?" and suggests asking "What do you think about . . . ?" He is, of course, correct. On the other hand, any question an interviewer asks leads an informant. You might as well learn to do it well.

Consider this leading question that I asked a Ñähñu Indian: "Right. I understand. The compadre (godparent) is *supposed* to pay for the music for the baptism fiesta. But what happens if the compadre doesn't have the money? Who pays then?" This kind of question can stop the flow of an informant's narrative stone dead. It can also produce more information than the informant would otherwise have provided. At the time, I thought the informant was being overly "normative." That is, I thought he was stating an ideal behavioral custom (having a compadre pay for the music at a fiesta) as if it were never violated.

It turned out that all he was doing was relying on his own cultural competence— "abbreviating," as Spradley (1979:79) called it. The informant took for granted that the anthropologist knew what to him was the obvious answer: If the compadre didn't have enough money, well, then there might not be any music.

My interruption reminded the informant that I just wasn't up to his level of cultural competence; I needed him to be more explicit. He went on to explain other things that he considered obvious but that I would not have even known to ask about. For instance, someone who has committed himself to pay for the music at a fiesta might borrow money from *another* compadre to fulfill the obligation. In that case, he wouldn't tell the person who was throwing the fiesta. That might make the host feel bad, like he was forcing his compadre to go into debt.

In this interview, in fact, the informant eventually became irritated with me because I asked so many things that he considered obvious. He wanted to abbreviate a lot and provide a more general summary; I wanted details. I backed off and asked a different informant for the details. I have since learned to start some probes with "This may seem obvious, but . . ." (Box 8.2).

Box 8.2 Listen for what's left out

Informants abbreviate all the time, and this means that you have to listen carefully for what's *left out*, not just what's *in* the interview narrative. Laurie Price (1987) collected tales of misfortune from very poor people in Quito, Ecuador. In one story, Maria talks about her crippled 6-year-old daughter. As Price tells it, Maria does not mention that, for months, she carried her daughter every day "down a 200-step flight of public stairs and 4 blocks to the nearest bus stop so the girl could go to physical therapy" (p. 318). The child's father, it turns out, drives a bus that he parks every night next to their house, but during the herculean effort to help the daughter, the father never pitches in or rearranges his schedule. "Such efforts are the unmarked cases for mothers," says Price (p. 319).

Directive probes (leading questions) may be based on what an informant has just finished saying or on something an informant told you an hour ago or a week ago. As you progress in long-term research, you come to have a much greater appreciation for what you really want from an interview. It is perfectly legitimate to use the information you've already collected to focus your subsequent interviews.

This leads researchers from informal to unstructured to semistructured interviews and even to completely structured interviews like questionnaires. When you feel as though you have learned something important about a group and its culture, the next step to test that knowledge—to see if it is idiosyncratic to a particular informant or subgroup in the culture or if it can be reproduced in many informants.

Baiting: The Phased-Assertion Probe

A particularly effective probing technique is called phased assertion (Kirk and Miller 1986) or baiting (Agar 1996:142). This is when you act like you already know something to get people to open up.

I used this technique in a study of how Ñähñu Indian parents felt about their children learning to read and write Ñähñu. Bilingual (Spanish-Indian) education in Mexico is a politically sensitive issue (Heath 1972), and when I started asking about it, a lot of people were reluctant to talk freely.

In the course of informal interviewing, I learned from a schoolteacher in one village that some fathers had come to complain about the teacher trying to get the children to read and write Ñähñu. The fathers, it seems, were afraid that studying Ñähñu would get in the way of their children becoming fluent in Spanish. Once I heard this story, I began to drop hints that I knew the reason parents were against children learning to read and write Ñähñu. As I did this, the parents opened up and confirmed what I'd found out.

Every journalist (and gossip monger) knows this technique well. As you learn a piece of a puzzle from one informant, you use it with the next informant to get more information; and so on. The more you seem to know, the more comfortable people feel about talking to you and the less people feel they are actually divulging anything. *They* are not the ones who are giving away the "secrets" of the group.

Phased assertion also prompts some informants to jump in and correct you if they think you know a little, but that you've "got it all wrong." In some cases, I've purposely made wrong assertions to provoke a correcting response.

Highly Verbal and Nonverbal Respondents

Some people try to tell you *too much*. They are the kind of people who just love to have an audience. You ask them one little question and off they go on one tangent after another, until you become exasperated. Converse and Schuman (1974:46) recommend "gentle inattention"—putting down your pen, looking away, leafing through your papers. Nigel King (1994:23) recommends saying something like: "That's very interesting. Could we go back to what you were saying earlier about. . . ."

You may, however, have to be a bit more obvious. New interviewers, in particular, may be reluctant to cut off informants, afraid that doing so is poor interviewing technique. In fact, as William Foote Whyte observed, informants who want to talk your ear off are probably used to being interrupted. It's the only way their friends get a word in edgewise. But you need to learn how to cut people off without rancor. "Don't interrupt *accidentally* . . . ," Whyte said, "learn to interrupt *gracefully*" (1960:353; emphasis in the original). Each situation is somewhat different; you learn as you go in this business.

One of the really tough things you run into is someone telling you "I don't know" in answer to lots of questions. In qualitative research projects, where you choose respondents precisely because you think they know something of interest, the "don't know" refrain can be especially frustrating.

Converse and Schuman (1974:49) identified four kinds of don't-know response: (1) I don't know (and frankly I don't care); (2) I don't know (and it's none of your business); (3) I don't know (actually, I do know, but you wouldn't be interested in what I have to say about that); and (4) I don't know (and I wish you'd change the subject because this line of questioning makes me really uncomfortable). There is also (I wish I could help you but) I really don't know.

Sometimes you can get beyond this, sometimes you can't. You have to face the fact that not everyone who volunteers to be interviewed is a good respondent. Sometimes you just have to take "don't know" for an answer and cut your losses by going on to someone else.

The Ethics of Probing

Are these tricks of the trade ethical? Peter Collings (2009) asked Inuit hunters in Alaska: "Name all of the people you share country food with." The response was usually a very short list, so when informants stopped listing names, Collings would ask "What about your x? Surely you share food with your x," where x was a category of relative in Innuinaqtun, the local language. This, said Collings, reminded people that he had command of the kinship terminology and that he knew his informant had an x.

Later in the interview, Collings would refer to one of the people whom the informant had named and say "So-and-so is your older brother," using the Innuinaqtun term. "Just as the fieldworker is studying the community," says Collings, "so, too, is the community studying the fieldworker" to find out if he or she is culturally competent (pp. 149–50). By demonstrating cultural competence, Collings argues, phased assertion helps establish rapport—at least where *he* works (p. 139).

Still, getting people to open up creates responsibilities to your informants. First, there is no ethical imperative in social research more important than seeing to it that you do not harm innocent people who have provided you with information in good faith. Not all respondents are innocents, though. Some people commit wartime atrocities. Some practice infanticide. Some are HIV positive and, out of bitterness, are purposely infecting others. Do you protect them all? Are any of these examples more troublesome to you than others? These are not extreme cases, thrown in here to prepare you for the worst, "just in case." They are the sorts of ethical dilemmas that researchers confront all the time.

Second, the better you get at making people open up, the more responsible you become that they don't later suffer some emotional

distress for having done so. Informants who divulge *too* quickly what they believe to be secret information can later come to have real regrets and even loss of self-esteem. They may suffer anxiety over how much they can trust you to protect them in the community.

It is sometimes better to stop people from divulging privileged information in the first or second interview and to wait until both of you have built a mutually trusting relationship. If you sense that an informant is uncomfortable with having spoken too quickly about a sensitive topic, end the interview with light conversation and reassurances about your discretion. Soon after, look up the informant and engage in light conversation again, with no probing or other interviewing techniques involved. This will also provide reassurance of trust.

Remember: The first ethical decision you make in research is whether to collect certain kinds of information at all. Once that decision is made, *you* are responsible for what is done with that information, and *you* must protect people from becoming emotionally burdened for having talked to you.

LEARNING TO INTERVIEW

It's impossible to eliminate reactivity and subjectivity in interviewing, but, like any other craft, you will get better and better at interviewing the more you practice. It helps a lot to practice in front of others and to have an experienced interviewer monitor and criticize your performance. Even without such help, however, you can improve your interviewing technique just by paying careful attention to what you're doing. Harry Wolcott (1995:102) offers excellent advice on this score: Pay as much attention to your own words as you do to the words of your respondents.

Wolcott also advises: Keep interviews focused on a few big issues (1995:112). More good advice from an accomplished interviewer. Here's a guaranteed way to wreck rapport and ruin an interview: A respondent asks you "Why do you ask? What does that have to do with what we're talking about?" You tell her: "Well, it just seemed like an interesting question—you know, something I thought might be useful somehow down the road in the analysis."

Here you are, asking people to give you their time and tell you about their lives and you're treating that time with little respect. If you can't imagine giving a satisfactory answer to the question "Why did you ask *that*?" then leave *that* out.

Do *not* use your friends as practice informants. You cannot learn to interview with friends because there are role expectations that get in the way. Just when you're really rolling and getting into probing deeply on some topic that you both know about, they are likely to laugh at you or tell you to knock it off.

Practice interviews should *not* be just for practice. They should be done on topics you're really interested in and with people who are likely to know a lot about those topics. Every interview you do should be conducted as professionally as possible and should produce useful data (with plenty of notes that you can code and retrieve).

The Importance of Language

An increasing number of researchers across the social sciences these days do research that requires working in a second language. In the United States, for example, there at least 35 million people who speak Spanish as their primary language at home and about 15 million more who speak Spanish as a second language. More than two million people in the United States speak Chinese, and over a million speak Vietnamese or Tagalog. Perhaps half a million more speak Haitian Creole.

Among the most constructive things you can do in preparing for research in another language is to practice conducting unstructured and semistructured interviewing in that language. Find persons from the culture you are going to study and interview them on some topic of interest. If you are going to Turkey to study women's roles, find Turkish students (or the spouses of those students) at your university and interview them on some topic to your research interest. These practice interviews will help you sharpen your skills at interviewing in another language.

Pacing the Study

Two of the biggest problems faced by researchers who rely heavily on semistructured interviews are boredom and fatigue. Even small projects may require 30–40 interviews to generate sufficient data to be worthwhile. Asking the same questions over and over again can get pretty old. Gorden (1975) studied 30 interviewers who worked for 12 days doing about two tape-recorded interviews per day. Each interview was from one to two hours long.

The first interview on each day, over all interviewers, averaged about 30 pages of transcription. The second averaged only 25 pages. Furthermore, the first interviews, on average, got shorter and shorter during the 12-day period of the study. In other words, on any given day, boredom made the second interview shorter; and over the 12 days, boredom (and possibly fatigue) took its toll on the first interviews of each day.

Of course, in many projects you won't conduct all your interviews in 12 days. Nevertheless, the lesson is clear. Plan each project in advance and calculate the number of interviews you are going to get. Pace yourself. Don't try to bring in all your interview data in a short time. Spread the project out, if possible.

But not always. When you are studying patterns of behavior that have been stable for some time, spreading the interviews out is a good thing to do. If you are studying people's reactions to hot issues, spreading out a project over a long period of time creates a serious "history" confound (see Chapter 4).

Here's the tradeoff: The longer a project takes, the less likely that the first interviews and the last interviews will be valid indicators of the same things. In long-term participant observation fieldwork (about six months to a year), I recommend going back to your early informants and interviewing them a second time. See whether their observations and attitudes have changed, and if so, why.

PRESENTATION OF SELF

How should you present yourself in an interview? As a friend? As a professional? As someone who is sympathetic or as someone who is nonjudgmental? It depends on the nature of the project. When the object is to collect comparable data across respondents, it makes no difference whether you're collecting words or numbers—cordial-but-nonjudgmental is the way to go.

That's sometimes tough to do. You're interviewing someone on a project about what people do to help the environment and your respondent says: "All those eco-Nazis want is to make room for more owls. They don't give a damn about real people's jobs." (Yes, that happened on one of my projects.) That's when you find out whether you can probe without injecting your feelings into the interview. Professional interviewers (the folks who collect the data for the General Social Survey, for example) learn to maintain their equilibrium and move on (see Converse and Schuman 1974).

Some situations are so painful, however, that it's impossible to maintain a neutral façade. Gene Shelley interviewed 72 people in Atlanta who were HIV-positive (Shelley et al. 1995). Here's a typical comment by one of Shelly's informants: "I have a lot of trouble watching all my friends die. Sometimes my whole body shuts down inside. I don't want to know people who are going to die. Some of my friends, there are three or four people a week in the obits. We all watch the obits."

How would *you* respond? Do you say: "Uh-huh. Tell me more about that"? Do you let silence take over and force the respondent to go on? Do you say something sympathetic? Shelley reports that she treated each interview as a unique situation and responded as her intuition told her to respond—sometimes more clinically, sometimes less, depending on her judgment of what the respondent needed her to say. Good advice.

Sometimes you have to go even further, beyond sympathetic response, all the way to intervention. Christine Webb (1984) interviewed women who had been through a hysterectomy. Webb is a nurse/researcher who also has personal experience as a gynecology patient. As a nurse, she was bound by hospital regulations not to initiate treatments on her own. As a researcher, she was expected to remain neutral. But as she listened to women talk about how they were treated with indifference or arrogance by their male physicians, Webb couldn't justify keeping her knowledge and advice to herself. "I felt," she said, "that my responsibilities to the women justified the risk that the doctors might disapprove of what I was doing" (p. 255).

Webb reminds us that doctors "control not only nurses' more regular work with patients but also what nursing research is carried out, and how and by whom it is done" (p. 254), so disapproval by the doctors might have meant the end of her research.

There are times when you just have to make your choice and stand your ground.

On Just Being Yourself

In 1964, when we were working on the island of Kalymnos, my wife Carole would take our two-month-old baby for daily walks in a carriage. Older women would peek into the baby carriage and make disapproving noises when they saw our daughter sleeping on her stomach. Then they would reach into the carriage and turn the baby over, explaining forcefully that the baby would get the evil eye if we continued to let her sleep on her stomach.

Carole had read the latest edition of *The Commonsense Book of Baby and Child Care* (the classic baby book by Dr. Benjamin Spock). We carried two copies of the book with us—in case one fell out of a boat or something—and Carole was convinced by Dr. Spock's writings that babies who sleep on their backs risk choking on their own mucous or vomit. Since then, medical opinion—and all the baby books that young parents read nowadays—have flip-flopped about this issue several times. At the time, though, not wanting to offend anyone, Carole listened politely and tried to act nonjudgmental.

One day, enough was enough. Carole told off a woman who intervened and that was that. From then on, women were more eager to discuss child-rearing practices in general. So when we let our baby crawl around on the floor and didn't bundle her up when we took her out for walks, Greek mothers were unhesitant in telling us that they disapproved. The more we challenged them, the more they challenged us. There was no rancor involved, and we learned a lot more than if Carole had just kept on listening politely and had said nothing.

This was informal interviewing in the context of long-term participant observation. If we had offended anyone, there would have been time and opportunity to make amends—or at least come to an understanding about cultural differences.

Little Things Mean a Lot

Little things are important in interviewing, so pay attention to them. How you dress and where you hold an interview, for example, tell your respondent a lot about you and what you expect. The interviewing dress code is: Use common sense. Proper dress depends on the venue. Showing up with a backpack or an attaché case, wearing jeans or a business suit—these are choices that should be pretty easy to make, once you've made the commitment to accommodate your dress to different circumstances.

The same goes for venue. I've held interviews in bars, in business offices, in government offices, on ferry boats, on beaches, in homes. . . . I can't give you a rule for selecting the single *right* place for an interview, since there may be several right places. But some places are just plain wrong for certain interviews. Here again, common sense goes a long way.

USING A VOICE RECORDER

Don't rely on your memory in interviewing; use a voice recorder in all structured and semistructured interviews, except where people specifically ask you not to. If you sense some reluctance about the recorder, leave it on the table and don't turn it on right away. Start the interview with chit-chat and when things get warmed up, say something like "This is really interesting. I don't want to trust my memory on something as important as this; do you mind if I record it?" Charles Kadushin (personal communication) hands a microphone with a shut-off switch to respondents to hold. Rarely, he says, do respondents actually use the switch, but giving people control over the interview shows that you take them very seriously.

Sometimes you'll be recording an interview and things will be going along just fine and you'll sense that a respondent is backing off from some sensitive topic. Just reach over to the recorder and ask the respondent if she or he would like you to turn it off. Harry Wolcott (1995:114) recommends leaving the recorder on, if possible, when the formal part of an interview ends. Even though you've finished, Wolcott points out, your respondent may have more to say.

Recording Equipment

For simple recording and transcribing of interviews, in a language you understand well, you can get away with a basic audio recorder for under $50. (But buy two of them. When you skimp on equipment costs and don't have a spare, this almost guarantees that you'll need one at the most inconvenient moment.) Basic recorders, with 2 gigabytes (gb) of flash memory hold hundreds of hours of voice recording. You can also use your iPod® or other music recorder as a digital audio recorder with a plug-in microphone. A 160-gb Classic iPod® has plenty of room for both music and interviews.

Whatever kind of work you do, remember to upload your data regularly to a computer and to store your data in several places—external hard drives, or online. If you are in an isolated field site and don't have reliable power, take along a solar battery charger so you can get your data offline and stored on something—even an old CD.

Some of the better voice recorders come with up to four built-in microphones that capture 360-degree sound. If you use a low-end recorder, then use a good, separate microphone. Some people like wearing a lavalier microphone—the kind you clip to a person's lapel or shirt collar—but many people find them intrusive. I prefer omnidirectional microphones because they pick up voices from anywhere in a room.

Sometimes people get rolling on a topic and want to get up and pace the room as they talk. Want to kill a really great interview? Tell somebody who's on a roll to please sit down and speak directly into the mike. Good microphones come with stands that keep the head from resting on any surface, like a table. Surfaces pick up and introduce background noise into any recording. If you don't have a really good stand for the mike, you can make one easily with some rubbery foam (the kind they use in making mattresses).

Test your recorder before every interview. And do the testing at home. There's only one thing worse than a recorder that doesn't run at all. It's one that runs but doesn't record. Then your informant is sure to say at the end of the interview: "Let's run that back and see how it came out" (Yes, that happened to me. But only once. And it needn't happen to anyone who reads this.)

Pay attention to the battery indicator. Want another foolproof way to kill an exciting interview? Ask the informant to "Please hold that thought" while you change batteries. When batteries get slightly low, throw them out or recharge them. If you are working in places that have unstable current, you'll rely on batteries to ensure recording fidelity. Just make sure that you start out with fresh batteries for each interview. Use house current for all playback, fast forward, and rewind operations and keep batteries *only* for recording. If you prefer household current for recording, then carry along a couple of long extension cords so you have a choice of where to set up for the interview.

In voice activation mode, the recorder turns off during long pauses—while an informant is thinking, for example. Holly Williams (personal communication) recommends not using the voice activation feature for interviews. She finds that the long breaks without any sound make transcribing easier because you don't have to shut the machine off and on as many times while you're typing.

Transcribers and VR Software

It takes six–eight hours to transcribe one hour of a recorded interview, depending on how closely you transcribe (getting all the "uhs" and "ers" and throat clearings, or just capturing the main elements of speech), how clear the recording is, and how proficient you are in the language and in typing. If you have to transcribe interviews yourself, there are several choices for equipment.

Transcription software lets you control the recorder (start, stop, move forward and backward) using the keyboard. Transcriber machines let you do this using a foot pedal. This lets you listen to a couple of seconds of recording at a time, type everything into the computer, and then move on to the next chunk. The technology lets you go back and repeat chunks, all while keeping your hands on the keyboard.

With voice recognition (VR) software, you listen to an interview through a set of headphones and repeat the words—both your questions and your informant's responses—out loud, in your own voice. The software listens to your voice and types out the words across the screen. You go over each sentence to correct mistakes (tell it that the word "bloat" should be "float" for instance) and to format the text (tell it where to put punctuation and paragraph breaks).

The process is slow at first, but the software learns over time to recognize inflections in your voice, and it makes fewer and fewer mistakes as weeks go by. It also learns all the special vocabulary you throw at it. The built-in vocabularies of current VR software systems are enormous—something like 300,000 words—but, though they may be ready to recognize "organizational networks," for example, you'll probably have to teach it "intraorganizational" or "supraorganizational" networks. And if you say, "Nurses F. G. and R. M. both say that the shifts are getting longer and are understaffed," you'll have to spell out "F. G." and "R. M." and "understaffed" so the software can add these words to its vocabulary.

As the software gets trained, the process moves up to 95%–98% accuracy at about 100–120 word per minute. With a 2%–5% error rate, you still have to go over every line of your work to correct it, but the total time for transcribing interviews can be reduced by half or more. (More about VR software in Appendix E.)

Recording Is Not a Substitute for Taking Notes

Finally, never substitute recording for note taking. A lot of very bad things can happen to recordings, and if you haven't got backup notes, you're out of luck. Don't wait until you get home to take notes, either. Take notes during the interview *about* the interview. Did the informant seem nervous or evasive? Were there a lot of interruptions? What were the physical surroundings like? How much probing did you have to do? Take notes on the contents of the interview, even though you get every word on the machine.

A few people will let you use a recorder but will balk at your taking notes. Don't assume, however, that people will be offended if you take notes. Ask them. Most of the time, all you do by avoiding note taking is lose a lot of data. Informants are under no illusions about what you're doing. You're interviewing them. You might as well take notes and get people used to it, if you can.

USING PHOTOS IN INTERVIEWS

Many researchers have found that photographs provide good cues to get informants started and keep people focused on the topic of research. In principle, you can use almost any visual cue in interviews. I've used maps in villages in Mexico to get people talking about local landmarks. You can walk around an urban neighborhood and ask residents to interpret graffiti. You can drive people down a highway and ask them to tell you what they see in billboards. Mostly, though, when researchers use visual cues in interviews, it's photos.

You'll see the use of photos as interview props referred to in the literature as photo-interviewing (Collier 1957), photo-elicitation (Clark-Ibañez 2004), reflexive photography (Douglas 1998), participatory photography (Gotschi et al. 2009), auto-photography (Phoenix 2010), and photovoice (Wang and Burris 1997).

All of these take advantage of the fact that: (1) photos stimulate lots of information during interviews; and (2) they help keep people focused on the topic of interest. Collier (1957) asked people in Nova Scotia the same questions about working in a local mill—either with or without pictures of the mill. "The photographic interview," said Collier, "got considerably more concrete information" about the mill and about coworkers there. In contrast, "the non-photo interviews strayed from the course of the research to include more distantly related associations and data; the informant talked more about himself and much of the interview was semi-autobiographical" (p. 849).

The big difference across techniques is whether the images used in an interview are taken by the researcher or by the informants. Participatory methods are increasingly popular, especially in community-based applications research. The word "voice" in photovoice, for example, stands for "voicing our individual and collective experience" (Wang and Burris 1997:381). In developing the method, Caroline Wang and Mary Ann Burris trained 62 women farmers in China to use cameras and told the women to photograph things in their village that showed their everyday lives. Here is Jin Xian, a 40-year-old farmer talking about a picture she'd taken of a young girl doing household chores:

> I took this photograph in Luliang County. I asked the girl in the picture her age. She said she was not yet ten and in her third year of school. I asked her many questions. "Do you have homework at noontime?" "Yes." "What do you do after lunch?" "I have to collect and wash the bowls and chopsticks and feed the pigs, because my parents are working in the field." If the parents were educated, they wouldn't let the child do so much housework. Village women, because of heavy housework and field work, don't have time to look after their children's studying. "Can your parents read?" "No." I took this photo to make parents pay attention to the educational issue of children, and to influence them to reduce home chores and field work. [Wang and Burris 1997:373]

Keller and Rivera (2007) taught seven Mexican American women how to use 24-shot disposable cameras. They asked the women to shoot pictures about getting, preparing, and eating food. After two weeks, the pictures were developed (a set was given to the women) and used in interviews. Keller and Rivera used a semistructured interview protocol to make sure that the interviewer covered the same ground with each of the informants. For each photo, the woman was asked to describe what was going on in the image, why the image was important, how it related to diet, and so on. At the end of the interview, informants were asked to look over all the photos together and talk about any themes that seemed important.

Analyzing the data from these interviews involves the same methods that you'd apply to any set of texts. Lots more about this in Chapter 19 (**Further Reading:** photo-elicitation).

FOCUS GROUPS

Focus groups are recruited to: (1) discuss how people feel about products (like brands of beer or new electronic gadgets); (2) assess social programs (is the new day care center providing enough support for working mothers?); (3) get stakeholder reaction to proposed programs (how do parents, teachers, administrators, and school board members feel about the proposal to move the start of the school year up by a month?); (4) explore whether questions on a survey seem arrogant or naive or culturally inappropriate to respondents; and (5) help interpret the results of a survey or a program evaluation.

The focus group method derives from work by Paul Lazarsfeld and Robert Merton in 1941 at Columbia University's Office of Radio Research. A group of people listened to a recorded radio program that was supposed to raise public morale before America's entry into World War II. The listeners were told to push a red button whenever they heard something that made them react negatively. When they heard something that made them react positively, they were to push a green button. The reactions were recorded automatically by a primitive polygraph-like apparatus. When the program was over, an interviewer talked to the group of listeners to find out why they had felt positively or negatively about each message they'd reacted to (Merton 1987) (Box 8.3).

Box 8.3 Not all group interviews are *focus group* interviews

Small-group interviews are useful in many settings.

1. Interviews with small groups of people are widely used to provide context for questionnaire data. Healey et al. (2010) studied the experiences of students (senior undergraduates and graduates) with research at the University of Gloucestershire in England. The researchers collected responses to a questionnaire by e-mail from 196 students. Then they convened five small groups—between two and five students in each group—to discuss the findings from the questionnaire. These groups provided background for a richer analysis of the questionnaire data. For example, one finding from the questionnaire was that almost half the students weren't aware of the research in which their teachers were involved. In a discussion group, a graduate student in geography reported that she knew her dissertation advisor was writing a book but complained that there was no effort to publicize the research of the faculty.

2. Small-group interviews are perfect for collecting natural discourse about a topic of interest. Megan Barnard (2009) convened three small groups at Texas A&M University to talk about their identification—or lack of it—with feminism. One group comprised two women and one man and all of them were friends who'd known each other for at least six months. The second group comprised four women who knew each other but weren't friends. And the third group comprised four women who didn't know each other at all. This design produced a lot of free-flowing dialog. (We'll take up the analysis of natural discourse in Chapter 18.)

3. Interviewing children is often best done in small-groups. Robert Thornberg (2008) studied what children in Swedish primary schools think about how school rules—don't run in the halls; raise your hand if you want to speak—are made and enforced. During his two years of ethnography, Thornberg did 49 interviews with groups of two to four students each.

4. Sometimes you just find yourself in an interview situation with a lot of people. In any tightly knit community, expect people to just come up and insert themselves into what you think are private interviews. This happened to Rachel Baker (1996a, 1996b) when she interviewed homeless boys in temples and junkyards in Kathmandu. If you insist on privacy, you might find yourself with no interview at all. Better to take advantage of the situation and just let the information flow. Be sure to take notes—on who's there, who's dominant, who's just listening, and so on—in any group interview.

The commercial potential of Lazarsfeld and Merton's pioneering work was immediately clear. The method of real-time recording of people's reactions, combined with focused interviewing of a group, is today a mainstay in advertising research. In a classic case, MCI, the now defunct phone company, found that people in focus groups didn't blame AT&T for the high cost of their long-distance phone bills; they blamed themselves for talking too long on long distance-calls. MCI came out with the advertising slogan: "You're not talking too much, just spending too much." MCI captured a big chunk of AT&T's clientele with that one winning slogan (Krueger 1994:33).

Today, focus groups are used widely in basic and applied research. D. L. Morgan (1989) ran focus groups with widows to find the factors that made it easier for some to cope with bereavement than others; Martínez and Carter-Pokras (2006) used focus groups to assess the health care priorities of immigrants from 10 Latin American countries to Baltimore. Bloom et al. (2003) ran five focus groups with a total of 29 coaches of elite college sports teams in Canada to assess the components of team building and cohesion.

Focus groups on some topics—like teen smoking—are now so frequent that meta-analyses are possible. Goldman and Glantz (1998) analyzed the results of 186 focus groups, involving over 1,500 children, on the effectiveness of antismoking campaigns in Massachusetts and California and Sussman et al. (2006) analyzed the results of 48 actual programs to stop teen smoking.

Why Are Focus Groups So Popular?

The focus group method was a commercial success from the 1950s on, but it lay dormant in academic circles for more than 20 years. This is probably because the method is virtually devoid of statistics. Beginning in the late 1970s, however, the method made a comeback as researchers came to understand the benefits of combining qualitative and quantitative methods.

Focus groups do not replace surveys, but rather complement them. Many survey researchers today use focus groups as the front end to designing questionnaires. Do the questions seem arrogant to respondents? Appropriate? Naive? A focus group can discuss the wording of a particular question or offer advice on how the whole questionnaire comes off to respondents.

Focus groups are also used to help interpret the results of surveys. A representative sample of Californians might be asked what they think about the three-strike law (that's the law that, since 1994, has sent people to prison for life, without parole, if they are convicted of a third felony of any kind). Then a series of focus groups would be convened to find out *why* people feel as they do and *how* they arrive at these feelings.

But focus groups are not just adjuncts to surveys. If you want to know *why* people feel as they do about something, or the mental steps they went through to decide which candidate to support or which product to buy, or why they like or don't like some program (like their company's health plan), or the reasons behind some complex behavior, then a series of focus groups can provide a tremendous amount of credible information.

Are Focus Groups Valid?

Ward et al. (1991) compared focus group and survey data from three studies of voluntary sterilization (tubal ligation or vasectomy) in Guatemala, Honduras, and Zaire. Ward et al. report that, "Overall, for 28% of the variables the results were similar" in the focus group and survey data. "For 42% the results were similar but focus groups provided additional detail; for 17% the results were similar, but the survey provided more detail. And in only 12% of the variables were the results dissimilar" (p. 273).

In the Guatemala study, 97% of the women surveyed reported no regrets with their decision to have a tubal ligation. The vast majority of women in the focus groups also reported no regrets. This was counted as a "similar result." Ten percent of the women surveyed reported having had a tubal ligation for health reasons. In the focus groups, too, just a few women reported health factors in their decision to have the operation, but they provided more detail and context, citing such things as complications from previous pregnancies.

This is an example of where the focus group and survey provide similar results, but where the focus group offers more detail. Data from the focus groups and the survey confirm that women heard about the operation from similar sources, but the survey shows that 40% of the women heard about it from a sterilized woman, 26% heard about it from a health professional, and so on. Here, the survey provides more detail, though both methods produce similar conclusions.

In general, though, focus groups—like participant observation, in-depth interviews, and other systematic qualitative methods—should be used for the collection of data about content and process and should not be relied on for collecting data about personal attributes or for estimating population parameters of personal attributes. The belief that a woman has or does not have a right to an abortion is a personal attribute, like gender, age, annual income, or religion. If you want to estimate the proportion of people in a population who believe that a woman has a right to an abortion, then focus groups are not the method of choice.

A proportion is a number, and if you want a good number—a valid one, a useful one—then you need a method that produces exactly that. A survey, based on a representative sample, is the method of choice here. But if you want information about content—about *why* people think a woman should or should not have the right to an abortion—then that's just the sort of thing a focus group can illuminate.

Running a Focus Group

The group moderator gets people talking about whatever issue is under discussion. Leading a focus group requires the combined skills of an ethnographer, a survey researcher, and a therapist. You have to watch out for people who want to show off and close them down, without coming on too strongly. You have to watch out for shy people and draw them out, without being intimidating.

Tips on how to do all this, and a lot more, are in *The Focus Group Kit*, a series of six how-to books (D. L. Morgan and Krueger 1998). Don't even think about getting into focus group management without going through this kit (Box 8.4).

Box 8.4 Composition of a focus group

Focus groups typically have 6–12 members, plus a moderator. Seven or 8 people is a popular size. If a group is too small, it can be dominated by one or two loudmouths; if it gets beyond 10 or 12, it gets tough to manage. Smaller groups are better when you're trying to get really in-depth discussions going about sensitive issues (D. L. Morgan 1997 [1870]). Of course, this assumes that the group is run by a skilled moderator who knows how to get people to open up and how to keep them opened up.

The participants in a focus group should be more or less homogeneous and, in general, should not know one another. Richard Krueger, a very experienced focus group moderator, says that "familiarity tends to inhibit disclosure" (1994:18). It's easy to open up more when you get into a discussion with people whom you are unlikely ever to see again (sort of like what happens on long air flights). Obviously, what "homogeneous" means depends on what you're trying to learn. If you want to know why a smaller percentage of middle-class African American women over 40 get mammograms than do their White counterparts, then you need a group of middle-class African American women who are over 40.

In a focus group about sensitive issues like abortion or drug use, the leader works at getting the group to gel and getting members to feel that they are part of an understanding cohort of people. If the group is run by an accomplished leader, one or more members will eventually feel comfortable about divulging sensitive information about themselves. Once the ice is broken, others will feel less threatened and will join in. Moderators should not be known to the members of a focus group, and focus group members should not be employees of a moderator. Hierarchy is not conducive to openness.

In running a focus group, remember that people will disclose more in groups that are supportive and nonjudgmental. Tell people that there are no right or wrong answers to the questions you will ask and emphasize that you've invited people who are similar in their backgrounds and social characteristics. This, too, helps people open up (Krueger 1994:113).

Above all, don't lead too much and don't put words in people's mouths. In studying nutritional habits, don't ask a focus group why they eat or don't eat certain foods; do ask them to talk about what kinds of foods they like and dislike and why. In studying risky sexual behavior, don't ask, "Do you use condoms whenever you visit a prostitute?" Do ask people to talk about their experience with prostitutes and exactly what kind of sexual practices they prefer. In studying political preferences, don't ask "Why don't you like Senator X?" Do ask people to explain what they like or dislike about various politicians.

Your job is to keep the discussion on the topic. Eventually, people will hit on the nutritional habits or the sexual practices or the politicians that interest you, and you can pick up the thread from there.

Analyzing Data From Focus Groups

The responses that people give in focus groups are not independent of one another, so you can't treat those responses as units of analysis, like you would in a survey. Ask participants in focus groups to complete a short questionnaire about the topic you plan to discuss *before* you begin the discussion. This gets people thinking about the topic and provides data on the variation in people's beliefs and attitudes about the topic you're studying.

You *can* analyze focus group data with the same techniques you would use on any corpus of text: field notes, life histories, open-ended interviews, and so on. Like all large chunks of text, you have two choices for very different kinds of analysis. You can do formal content analysis or you can do qualitative analysis. See Chapters 18 and 19 for more about this.

As with in-depth interviews, it's best to record (or video) focus groups. This is tricky, though, because the audio of any focus group is hard to understand and transcribe when two or more people talk at once. A good moderator keeps people talking one at a time. Don't hide the recorder or the microphones. Someone is sure to ask if they're being recorded, and when you tell them "Yes"—which you must do—they're sure to wonder why they had to ask.

If you are just trying to confirm some ideas or to get a general notion of how people feel about a topic, you can simply take notes from the audio and work with your notes. Most focus groups, however, are transcribed. The real power of focus groups is that they produce ethnographically rich data. Only transcription captures a significant part of that richness. But be prepared to work with a lot of information. Any single hour-and-a-half focus group can easily produce 50 pages or more of text.

Many focus groups have two staff members: a moderator and a person who does nothing but jot down the name each person who speaks and the first few words they say. This makes it easier for a transcriber to identify the voices. If you can't afford this, or if you feel that people would be uncomfortable with someone taking down their names, you can call on people by name or mention their name when you respond to them. Things can get rolling in a focus group (that's what you want), and you'll have a tough time transcribing the audio if you don't know who's talking (**Further Reading:** focus groups).

RESPONSE EFFECTS

Response effects are measurable differences in the responses of people being interviewed that are predictable from characteristics of the interviewers and those being interviewed—like whether the sex or race or age of interviewer and of the respondent are the same or different—and dozens of other things (Box 8.5).

Box 8.5 The expectancy effect

In 1966, Robert Rosenthal and Lenore Jacobson (1968) conducted an experiment. At the beginning of the school year, they told some teachers at a school that the children they were about to get had tested out as "spurters." That is, according to tests, they said, those particular children were expected to make significant gains in their academic scores during the coming year. Sure enough, those children did improve dramatically—which was really interesting, because Rosenthal and Jacobson had matched the "spurter" children and teachers at random.

This experiment showed the power of the **expectancy effect**, or "the tendency for experimenters to obtain results they expect, not simply because they have correctly anticipated nature's response but rather because they have helped to shape that response through their expectations" (Rosenthal and Rubin 1978:377).

Strictly speaking, the expectancy effect is not a response effect at all, but it's an important effect to keep in mind. If you are studying a small community, or a neighborhood in a city, or a hospital or clinic for a month or more, interacting daily with a few key informants, your own behavior can affect theirs in subtle (and not so subtle) ways, and vice versa. Don't be surprised if you find your own behavior changing over time in relation to key informants.

As early as 1929, Stuart Rice showed that the political orientation of interviewers can have a substantial effect on what they report their respondents told them. Rice was doing a study of derelicts in flop houses and he noticed that the men contacted by one interviewer consistently said that their down-and-out status was the result of alcohol; the men contacted by the other interviewer blamed social and economic conditions and lack of jobs. It turned out that the first interviewer was a prohibitionist and the second was a socialist (cited in Cannell and Kahn 1968:549).

Katz (1942) found that middle-class interviewers got more politically conservative answers in general from lower-class respondents than did lower-class interviewers, and Robinson and Rhode (1946) found that interviewers who looked non-Jewish and had non-Jewish-sounding names were almost *four times more likely* to get anti-Semitic answers to questions about Jews than were interviewers who were Jewish looking and who had Jewish-sounding names.

Since these pioneering efforts, hundreds of studies have been conducted on the impact of things like race, sex, age, and accent of both the interviewer and the informant; the source of funding for a project; the level of experience respondents have with interview situations; whether there is a cultural norm that encourages or discourages talking to strangers; whether the question being investigated is controversial or neutral; features of the environment where the interview takes place (like whether the interview is done in private or in the presence of a third party); the nature of the task that people are asked to perform (like whether the respondent is asked to write out an answer, in text, or to just circle a number on a form); the mode of the interview (like comparing face-to-face, telephone, and Internet interviews about the same topic).

Sex-of-interviewer effects have been the focus of many studies. Hyman and Cobb (1975), for example, found that female interviewers who took their cars in for repairs themselves (as opposed to having their husbands do it) were more likely to have female respondents who reported getting their own cars repaired.

Zehner (1970) found that when women in the United States were asked by women interviewers about premarital sex, they were more inhibited than if they were asked by men. Male respondents' answers were not affected by the gender of the interviewer. McCombie and Anarfie (2002) found the same sex-of-interviewer effect 30 years later in Ghana: Young men (15–18 year olds) were equally likely to tell male or female interviewers that they had had sex, but young women were more likely to divulge this to male interviewers than to female interviewers.

In the Tamang Family Research Project in Nepal, demographer William Axinn (1991) found that women were simply better than men as interviewers: The female interviewers had significantly fewer "don't know" responses than did the male interviewers. Axinn supposes this might be because the survey dealt with marital and fertility histories.

In a multi-year study in Kenya of women's networks and their AIDS-related behavior, sociologist Alex Weinreb (2006) found that the most reliable data were collected by female-*insider* interviewers—that is, women from the local area who were trained to be interviewers for the project—compared to the *stranger*-interviewers who were brought in from the outside.

And Robert Aunger (1992, 2004:145–62), an anthropologist, found the insider-outsider effect in his studies of three societies in the Ituri forest of Zaire. The Lese and Budu are horticultural, and the Efe are foragers. Aunger wanted to know if they shared the same food avoidances. He and three assistants, two Lese men and one Budu man, interviewed a total of 65 people. Each of the respondents was interviewed twice and was asked the same 140 questions about a list of foods.

Aunger identified two types of errors in his data: forgetfulness and mistakes. If informants said in the first interview that they did not avoid a particular food but said in the second interview that they did avoid the food, Aunger counted the error as forgetfulness. If informants reported in interview two a different type of avoidance for a food than they'd reported in interview one, Aunger counted this as a mistake.

Even with some missing data, Aunger had over 8,000 pairs of responses in his data (65 *pairs* of interviews, each with up to 140 responses), so he was able to look for the causes of discrepancies between interview one and interview two. About 67% of the forgetfulness errors and about 79% of the mistake errors were correlated with characteristics of informants (gender, ethnic group, age, and so on). However, about a quarter of the variability in what informants answered to the same question at two different times was due to characteristics of the interviewers (ethnic group, gender, native language, etc.), and about 12% of variability in forgetting was explained by interviewer experience.

As the interviewers interviewed more and more informants, the informants were less likely to report "no avoidance" on interview one and some avoidance on interview two for a specific food. In other words, interviewers got better and better with practice at drawing out informants on their food avoidances.

Of the four interviewers, though, the two Lese and the Budu got much better, while the anthropologist made very little progress. Was this because of Aunger's interviewing style, or because informants generally told the anthropologist different things than they told local interviewers, or because there is something special about informants in the Ituri forest? We'll know when we add variables to Aunger's study and repeat it in many cultures, including our own (**Further Reading:** response effects).

The Deference Effect

When people tell you what they think you want to know, in order not to offend you, that's called the deference effect or the acquiescence effect. Aunger may have experienced this in Zaire.

In fact, it happens all the time, and researchers have long been aware of the problem. In 1958, Lenski and Leggett embedded two contradictory questions in a face-to-face interview, half an hour apart. Respondents were asked whether they agreed or disagreed with the following two statements: (1) it's hardly fair to bring children into the world, the way things look for the future; (2) children born today have a wonderful future to look forward to. Just 5% of Whites agreed with *both* statements compared to 20% of African Americans. Lenski and Leggett concluded that this was the

deference effect in action: Blacks were four times more likely than Whites to agree to anything, even contradictory statements, because the interviewers were almost all White and of higher perceived status than the respondents (Lenski and Leggett 1960).

Skip to 1984. In the National Black Election Study, 872 African Americans were polled before and after the presidential election that year. Since interviewers were assigned randomly to respondents, some people were interviewed by a White person before the election and an African American after the election. And vice versa: Some people were interviewed by an African American before the election and a White person on the second wave.

When African American interviewers in the preelection polls were replaced by White interviewers in the postelection surveys, African Americans were more likely to say that Blacks don't have the power to change things, that Blacks can't make a difference in local or national elections, that Blacks cannot form their own political party, and that Whites are not responsible for keeping Blacks down—very powerful evidence of a race-of-interviewer effect (D. W. Davis 1997) (Box 8.6).

Box 8.6 Barack Obama and the Bradley Effect

In 1982, Tom Bradley, the mayor of Los Angeles, ran against George Deukmejian for the office of governor of California. Bradley was ahead in the polls for the governorship of California right up to election day—and lost. Some voters had told pollsters that they were for Bradley, who is Black, and then voted for Deukmejian, who is White.

The so-called Bradley effect was at work in 1989, when Douglas Wilder, an African American, ran against Marshall Coleman, who is White, for the governorship of Virginia. Preelection polls showed that Wilder was far ahead, but in the end, he won by only a slim margin. White voters were more likely to claim Wilder as their choice if the interviewer was African American than if the interviewer was White (Finkel et al. 1991).

Barack Obama is widely credited with ending the Bradley Effect, but he lost the 2008 New Hampshire primary to Hillary Clinton by three points after being ahead in the polls by eight points—right up to election day (Kohut 2008).

Reese et al. (1986:563) tested the deference effect in a telephone survey of Anglo and Mexican American respondents. When asked specifically about their cultural preference, 58% of Hispanic respondents said they preferred Mexican American culture over other cultures, irrespective of whether the interviewer was Anglo or Hispanic. Just 9% of Anglo respondents said they preferred Mexican American culture when asked by Anglo interviewers, but 23% said they preferred Mexican American culture when asked by Hispanic interviewers.

Questions about gender and gender roles produce deference effects, too. When you ask people in the United States how most couples divide child care, men are more likely than women to say that men and women share this responsibility—if the interviewer is a man (Kane and McCaulay 1993:11). Do women have too much influence, just the right amount of influence, or too little influence in today's society? When asked *this* question by a male interviewer, men are more likely to say that women have *too much* influence; when asked the same question by a female interviewer, men are more likely to say that women have *too little* influence.

And similarly for women: When asked by a female interviewer, women are more likely to say that men have *too much* influence than when asked by a male interviewer (Kane and Macaulay 1993:14–15).

Lueptow et al. (1990) found that women gave more liberal responses to female interviewers than to male interviewers on questions about gender roles. Men's attitudes about gender roles were, for the most part, unaffected by the gender of the interviewer—except that highly educated men gave the *most* liberal responses about gender roles to female interviewers.

"It appears," said Lueptow et al., "that educated respondents of both sexes are shifting their answers toward the socially desirable positions they think are held by female interviewers" (p. 38).

Attitudes about gender roles sure are adaptable. That was in 1990. In 2008, about 26% of the American public was "angry or upset" at the prospect of a woman president, even though, at the time almost 90% of Americans told pollsters that they would vote for a qualified woman for president (Streb et al. 2008:77).

Questions that aren't race related, by the way, are not affected much by the race or the ethnicity of either the interviewer or the respondent. Still, whenever you have multiple interviewers, keep track of the race, ethnicity, and gender of the interviewer and test for response effects. Identifying sources of bias is better than not identifying them, even if you can't eliminate them (**Further Reading:** deference effect).

The Social Desirability Effect

When people tell you what they think will make them look good, especially according to prevailing standards of behavior and thought, that's the social desirability effect. Hadaway et al. (1998) went to a large Protestant church and found 115 people in attendance at the Sunday school. On Monday morning, when Hadaway et al. polled the whole church membership, 181 people claimed to have been in Sunday school the previous day. Head-count experiments like this one typically produce estimates of church attendance that are 55%–59% the size of what people report (T. W. Smith 1998).

The social desirability effect is influenced by the way you ask the question. Major surveys, like the Gallup Poll, ask something like: "How often do you attend religious services?" Then they give the people choices like "once a week, once a month, seldom, never." Presser and Stinson (1998) asked people on Monday to list everything they had done from "midnight Saturday to midnight last night." When they asked the question this way, 29% of respondents said that they had gone to church. Asking "How often do you go to church?" produced estimates of 37%–45%. This is a 28%–55% *difference* in reported behavior and is statistically very significant (**Further Reading**: social desirability effect).

The Third-Party-Present Effect

We sort of take it for granted that interviews are private conversations, conducted one on one, but in fact, many face-to-face interviews have at least one third party in the room, often the spouse or partner of the person being interviewed. Does this affect how people respond to questions? As with other response effects, the answer is yes, sometimes. Zipp and Toth (2002), for example, analyzed data from a household survey in Britain and found that when the spouses are interviewed together, they are much more likely to agree about many things—like who does what around the house—than when they are interviewed separately. Apparently, people listen to each other's answers and modify their own answers accordingly, which puts on a nice, unified face about their relationship.

As you'd expect, there is a social desirability effect when a third party is present. Casterline and Chidambaran (1984) examined data from 24 developing countries in the World Fertility Study and found that women in those countries are less likely to admit using contraception when a third party is present at the interview.

On the other hand, Aquilino (1993) found that when their spouse is in the room, people report more marital conflict than when they are interviewed alone. They are also more likely to report that they and their spouse lived together before marriage if their spouse is in the room. Perhaps, as Mitchell (1965) suggested over 45 years ago, people own up more to sensitive things like this when they know it will be obvious to their spouse that they are lying. Seems like a good thing to test (**Further Reading**: third-party-present effect).

Threatening Questions

In general, if you are asking someone a non-threatening question, like whether they have a library card, then response effects are minimal. But if you ask people about their alcohol consumption, or whether they ever shoplifted when they were children, or whether they have family members who have had mental illness, or how many sexual partners they've had, then response effects are really important.

One key finding on this problem is, intuitively, that disclosure of information about socially undesirable behavior increases with the perception people have of their anonymity (Tourangeau and Yan 2007). So, people open up more on questionnaires about illegal or embarrassing behavior that are self-administered, including in web-based surveys, than in surveys conducted face-to-face, and still more when they think that a survey is truly anonymous. In fact, the same goes for any information that people consider sensitive—like how they feel about their health insurance plans in the United States (Braunsberger et al. 2007).

Another useful finding is that people may be more willing to disclose undesirable behavior to interviewers who are *not* members of their own ethnic group. In The Netherlands, second-generation Moroccans and Turks were more likely to report consuming alcohol when interviewed by a Dutch researcher than when interviewed by an ethnically matched interviewer (Dotinga et al. 2005). (See the section on the randomized response technique and the section on computerized interviews—CATI, CASI, CAPI—in Chapter 9.)

Asking about other people increases reports about socially undesirable behavior. Katz and Naré (2002) asked 1,973 single Muslim women between the ages of 15 and 24 in Dakar, Senegal, if they had ever been pregnant. Three percent of the women said they had. But 25% of the same women said that at least one of their *three closest friends* had been pregnant—more than eight times what they reported about themselves. (See Sudman et al. [1977:147–51] on the three-closest-friends technique.)

Asking the interviewers on a project to record their interviews produces a higher response rate, particularly to sensitive questions about things like sexual behavior. Apparently, when interviewers know that their work can be scrutinized (from the recordings), they probe more and get informants to open up more (Billiet and Loosveldt 1988).

And if you give people choices that include a big number of *any* behavior, you'll probably get reports of more of that behavior. Tourangeau and Smith (1996) asked men and women: "During the last 12 months, that is, since August/September 1993, how many men [women], if any, have you had intercourse with?" Some people were asked simply to tell the interviewer a number. Others were asked to choose one of the following: 0, 1, 2, 3, 4, 5 or more. And still others were asked to choose one of the following: 1–4, 5–9, 10–49, 50–99, 100 or more. People reported more sex partners when given high-end choices than when given low-end choices or an open-ended question (Tourangeau and Smith 1996:292). In Germany, people reported watching more television when they were given choices that included a big number of hours (Schwarz et al. 1985).

You might be surprised, though, at what counts as a threatening question. R. A. Peterson (1984) asked 1,324 people one of the following questions: (1) How old are you? (2) What is your age? (3) In what year were you born? or (4) Are you 18–24 years of age, 25–34, 35–49, 50–64, 65 or older? Then Peterson got the true ages for all the respondents from reliable records. There was no significant difference in the accuracy of the answers obtained with the four questions, but almost 10% of respondents refused to answer question 1, while only 1% refused to answer question 4, and this difference *is* significant (**Further Reading:** asking threatening questions).

RESPONDENT/ INFORMANT ACCURACY

Even when respondents tell you the absolute truth, as they see it, in response to your questions, there is still the question of whether the information they give you is accurate.

A lot of social research is about mapping opinions and attitudes. When people tell you that they *approve of* the job a politician is doing, or when they tell you that they *support* sex education in public schools, or that they *prefer* a particular brand of beer to some other brand, they are talking about internal states, and you pretty much have to take their word for it.

When we ask people on a survey to report on their actual behavior, however (How long does it take you to drive to work? How many beers do you drink each day?), or about their environmental circumstances (How many acres of land do you currently have in soybeans? How many hours per day is the TV on in your house?), we can't just assume respondent accuracy.

We see reports of behavior in our local newspapers all the time: College students are binge drinking more than they did five years ago; Americans are going to church less often than they did a decade ago; single men and women in their 20s, especially college graduates, are using condoms more than they did five years ago.

In back of *findings* like these are *questions* like these:

Circle one answer:

How many times last month did you consume five or more beers or other alcoholic drinks in a single day?

Never

Once

Twice

Three times

More than three times

How often do you go to church?

Never

Occasionally—once a month or less

About once a week

More than once a week

How often do you use a condom when you have sex with someone for the first time?

Never

Occasionally

Usually

Always

LaPiere Discovers the Problem

We've known for a long time that we should be suspicious of this kind of data. From 1930 to 1932, Richard LaPiere, accompanied by a Chinese couple, crisscrossed the United States, twice, by car. The threesome covered about 10,000 miles, stopping at 184 restaurants and 66 hotels. And they kept records. There was a lot of prejudice against Chinese in those days, but they were not refused service in a single restaurant and just one hotel turned them away (LaPiere 1934).

Six months after the experiment ended, LaPiere sent a questionnaire to each of the 250 establishments where the group had stopped. One of the things he asked was: "Will you accept members of the Chinese race as guests?" Ninety-two percent—230 out of 250—replied "No."

By today's standards, LaPiere's experiment was crude. He could have surveyed a control group—a second set of 250 establishments that they hadn't patronized but that were in the same towns where they'd stopped. With self-administered questionnaires, he couldn't be sure that the people who answered the survey (and who claimed that they wouldn't serve Chinese) were the same ones who had actually served the threesome. And LaPiere didn't mention in his survey that the Chinese couple would be accompanied by a White man.

Still, LaPiere's experiment was terrific for its time. It made clear that what people say they do (or would do) is not a proxy for what they actually do or will do (see Deutscher 1973).

A long list of studies now shows that a fourth to a half of what informants say about their behavior is inaccurate (Bernard et al. 1984; Killworth and Bernard 1976). Johns (1994) did a meta-analysis of 11 studies in which: (1) respondents reported on the number of days they were absent from a job; and (2) the researcher was able to check the accuracy of those self-reports against actual job records. The correlation between respondent reports and job records ranged from 0.30 to 0.92, with an average of 0.57, which means that about a third of the variance in the job records ($0.57^2 = 0.32$) is predicted by the respondent reports.

This basic finding shows up in what you might think were the most unlikely places: In the 1961 census of Addis Ababa, Ethiopia, 23% of the women underreported the *number of their children*. Apparently, people there didn't count babies who die before reaching the age of 2 (Pausewang 1973:65). People in the United States often omit newborns when they fill out the Decennial Census form (Dillman et al. 2009b:225) and in China today, if a child dies soon after birth, couples may decide to report neither the birth nor the death and instead try to conceive again as quickly as possible. Under the one-child policy, the births of female babies may not be reported at all because of the desire by couples to have a son (Merli and Rafferty 2000:110).

Why People Are Inaccurate Reporters of Their Own Behavior

There are many reasons for people to report inaccurate data about matters of externally verifiable fact—like whether they were hospitalized in the last year—as opposed to matters of opinion—like whether they think that the monarchy in England should be abolished. Here are four:

1. Once people agree to be interviewed, they have a personal stake in the process and usually try to answer all your questions—whether they understand what you're after or not.

2. Human memory is fragile, although it's clearly easier to remember some things than others.

Cannell et al. (1961) found that the ability to remember a stay in the hospital is related to the length of the stay, the severity of the illness that lands you there, and whether or not surgery is involved. It's also strongly related to the length of time since discharge. Cannell and Fowler (1965) found that people report accurately 90% of all overnight hospital stays that happened six months or less before being interviewed.

It's easy for people to remember a rare event, like surgery, that occurred recently. But, as Sudman and Schwarz (1989) point out, if you ask people to think about some common behavior going back months at a time, they probably use estimation rules. When Sudman and Schwartz asked people "How many [sticks] [cans] of deodorant did you buy in the last six months?" they started thinking: "Well, I usually buy deodorant about twice a month in the summer, and about once a month the rest of the year. It's now October, so I suppose I must have bought 10 deodorants over the last

six months." And then they say, "10," and that's what you write down.

3. Interviews are social encounters. People manipulate those encounters to whatever they think is their advantage.

Adolescent boys tend to exaggerate, and adolescent girls tend to minimize, reports of their own sexual experience (see Catania et al. 1996). University professors surely report watching less TV than they actually watch.

4. People can't count a lot of behaviors, so they use rules of inference.

In some situations, they invoke D'Andrade's "what goes with what" rule (1974) and report what they *suppose* must have happened, rather than what they actually saw. Freeman et al. (1987) asked people in their department to report on who attended a particular colloquium. People who were *usually* at the department colloquium were mentioned as having attended the particular colloquium—even by those who hadn't attended (and see Shweder and D'Andrade 1980).

Reducing Errors: Jogging People's Memories

Sudman and Bradburn (1974) distinguish two types of memory errors. The first is simply forgetting things, like a visit to the city, the purchase of a product, attendance at an event, etc. The second type is called "forward telescoping." This is when someone reports that something happened a month ago when it really happened two months ago. (Backward telescoping is rare.)

There are five things you can do to increase the accuracy of self-reported behavior. These methods won't eliminate *all* the error, but they will definitely eliminate *some* error. Less error is better.

1. Cued recall. People are asked to consult records, such as bank statements, telephone bills, college transcripts, and so on. Having

people consult their records does not always produce the results you might expect. Horn (1960) asked people to report their bank balance. Of those who did not consult their records, 31% reported correctly. Those who consulted their records did better, but not by much. Only 47% reported correctly (reported in Bradburn 1983:309). Still, there is much psychological evidence that cuing stimulates greater recall of things like word pairs and the message content of television commercials (Gunter et al. 1997; Otani and Whiteman 1994), so cued recall *should* increase recall of behavior.

2. **Aided recall.** People are given a list of possible answers to a question and asked to choose among them. Aided recall increases the number of events recalled, but also appears to increase the telescoping effect (Bradburn 1983:309).

3. **Bounded recall.** In studies where you interview people more than once, you can correct for telescoping by reminding them what they said last time in answer to a question and then asking them about their behavior since their last report. Bounded recall corrects for telescoping but does not increase the number of events recalled, and, in any event, is only useful in studies where the same people are interviewed again and again.

4. **Landmarks.** This involves establishing a personal landmark—like being in an auto accident, having surgery, getting married, filing for bankruptcy, becoming a grandparent, graduating from college—and asking people to report on things that have happened since then. Loftus and Marburger (1983) found that

landmarks help reduce forward telescoping. The title of their article says it all: "Since the Eruption of Mt. St. Helens, Has Anyone Beaten You Up? Improving the Accuracy of Retrospective Reports with Landmark Events."

Note that if you ask people to recall incidents during, say, the last two years in which they were victims of crime, they are likely to mention incidents that happened three and four years ago. Being victimized by crime is something people remember rather well, but people are terrible at bracketing events during a two-year interval.

5. **Restricted time.** To increase the accuracy of recall, Sudman and Schwartz (1989) advocate keeping the recall period short. They asked people "How many times have you been out to a restaurant in the last three months?" and "How many times have you been out to a restaurant in the last month?" The per-month average for the one-month question was 55% greater than the per-month average for the three-month question.

Informant accuracy remains a major problem. Gary Wells and colleagues (2003) showed a video of a staged crime to 253 students. Then they showed the students a photo lineup of six people and asked the students to pick out the culprit. Every single student picked one of the six photos, but there was a small problem: The culprit wasn't in the six photos. We need a lot more research about the rules of inference that people use when they respond to questions about where they've been, who they were with, and what they were doing (**Further Reading:** respondent accuracy).

Key Concepts in This Chapter

unstructured interviewing	structured interviewing	ethnographic interviewing
semistructured interviewing	amount of control	interview guide
in-depth interviewing	informal interviewing	interview schedule

lived experience
silent probe
echo probe
uh-huh probe
neutral probe
tell-me-more probe
long-question probe
grand tour question

phased assertion
baiting
presentation of self
focus groups
response effects
expectancy effect
deference effect
acquiescence effect

social desirability effect
third-party-present effect
rules of inference
cued recall
aided recall
bounded recall
landmarks
restricted time

Summary

- There is a continuum of interview situations based on the amount of control we try to exercise over people's responses.

  o In informal interviewing, the researcher just tries to remember conversations heard during the course of a day. This requires constant jotting and daily sessions in which jottings are turned into extended field notes. Informal interviewing is used in ethnographic fieldwork to build rapport and to uncover new topics of interest.

  o Unstructured interviewing involves actual interviewing but is characterized by a minimum of control over the respondent's responses. The idea is to get people to open up and to let them express themselves in their own terms and at their own pace. A lot of what is called ethnographic interviewing is unstructured. Unstructured interviewing is used in situations where you have lots and lots of time and can interview people on more than one occasion.

  o Semistructured interviewing has much of the freewheeling quality of unstructured interviewing but is based on the use of an interview guide. This is a written list of questions and topics that need to be covered in a particular order.

  o In structured interviews, people are asked to respond to as nearly identical a set of stimuli as possible. Interview schedules and questionnaires are fully structured interviews.

- The key to successful interviewing is learning how to probe effectively—that is, to stimulate a respondent to produce more information, without injecting yourself so much into the interaction that you only get a reflection of yourself in the data. Learning the art of probing takes practice.

  o The most difficult technique to learn is the silent probe. Other forms of probing include the echo probe, the tell-me-more probe, the long question probe, the phased-assertion probe, and probing by leading.

  o The better you learn the art of probing, the better you get at making people "open up" and the more responsible you become that they don't later suffer some emotional distress for having done so.

  o Successful interviewing takes a variety of skills. It may require you learning a specialized vocabulary, or even a new language. You also have to learn to pace a set of interviews to avoid boredom and fatigue. Presentation of self is another important part of interviewing.

- Interviewing produces a huge amount of data. Whenever possible, record all structured and semistructured interviews, unless people specifically ask you not to.
  - A good, omnidirectional microphone helps keep the interview spontaneous.
  - It can take from six to eight hours to transcribe one hour of recorded speech. If you transcribe your interviews, invest in a transcription machine.
  - Voice recording software can cut the time it takes for transcription in half.
- Focus groups are recruited to discuss a particular topic—like people's reaction to a television commercial or their attitudes toward a social service program. Focus groups complement surveys. Survey researchers may use focus groups to help in designing a questionnaire. A focus group can discuss the wording of a particular question, for example, or offer advice on how the whole questionnaire comes off to respondents. Focus groups are also used to help interpret the results of surveys.
  - Focus groups typically have 6–12 members, plus a moderator. The participants in a focus group should be more or less homogeneous and, in general, should not know one another.
  - You can analyze focus group data with the same techniques you would use on any corpus of text: field notes, life histories, open-ended interviews, and so on.
- Response effects are measurable differences in interview data that are predictable from characteristics of informants, interviewers, and environments.
  - When people tell you what they think you want to know, in order not to offend you, that's called the deference effect or the acquiescence effect.
  - The expectancy effect involves creating the objective results we want to see.
  - An important but often overlooked response effect is inaccuracy in self-reports of behavior. This may come from people trying to answer questions even when they don't know the answer, from simple inaccurate memory, from the social desirability effect (wanting to project a desirable image of themselves), or even from simple lying.
  - Interviewers use cued recall, aided recall, bounded recall, landmarks, and time restriction to help respondents report behavior accurately.
- All research that relies on self-reports is subject to the problems of informant inaccuracy. Whether inaccuracy is the result of lying or forgetting, it is an important problem and remains the subject of research.

Exercises

1. The only way to learn how to interview is to do it. Interviewing has to have a purpose. You can't interview someone "just for practice." So pick a topic about which you'd really like to know more—something that you want to write up into a research paper—and interview several people about that topic.

   Some people like to start off with antiseptic, uncontroversial topics because they think it will be easier to get respondents to open up. I find that the opposite is true. It takes pretty high-level interviewing skills to get people to pour out details about things that are common, ordinary, and uncontroversial.

   To get an idea of how hard it is to get details in an interview, start by trying to get someone's life history. You can begin with a favorite aunt or uncle, or a family friend who is much older than you. As you set up your recorder, tell the person that you'd like them to start at the beginning and give you as much detail as possible about each event they describe in their life.

Once you get started, don't be surprised if the first thing your respondent says is something like: "I was born in Canton, Ohio, in 1940. I went to Manning High School and when I graduated I joined the army." That's about as bare-bones as it can get. Now it's your job to get the details.

Ask people to tell you about their earliest memories and follow the threads you get from that. Ask them to name their friends in grade school and high school and ask if they know what those friends are doing now. Follow *those* leads, too. Ask about their first date and movies and music they remember from when they were kids. Did they dance? If so, what were the names of the dances they did back then?

This is just the beginning, but you get the idea. Don't let a life history take less than two hours of solid interviewing. If it takes more than one sitting, then just go with the flow. If you're lucky, it will take you five hours, not two. By the time you repeat this exercise with your second respondent, you'll be asking questions you'd never thought of before and moving the interview along with some of the techniques I discussed earlier.

2. Get a team of five or six people together to learn about running a focus group. Have the team read up on how to run focus groups. Decide on a topic together. Focus groups about consumer products seem to work well, assuming that everyone in the group has experience with the products. Take turns being the moderator of the group. Try to keep the conversation going for an hour. Have one member of the group video each session so that you can all learn from the experience, no matter who is the moderator.

3. Do a computer bibliographic search for the term "response effect." What are gender-of-interviewer and race-of-interviewer effects? Are there differences in these effects for telephone interviews versus face-to-face interviews?

Further Reading

Interviewing. Bingham et al. (1959), Camp et al. (2001), Hyman (1975), Kadushin (1972), Kvale (2009), McCracken (1988), Rubin and Rubin (2005), Sommers-Flanagan and Sommers-Flanagan (2003), Willis (2005).

Photo-elicitation. Bukowski and Buetow (2011), Cahyanto et al. (2009), Harper (2002), Kamper and Steyn (2011), Oliffe and Botorff (2007).

Focus groups. Bloor et al. (2001), Goldman and McDonald (1987), Greenbaum (1998, 2000), Lee (2010), Stewart et al. (2007), Templeton (1994), Walden (2008), Weinberger et al. (1998).

Response effects. Aquilino (1994), Borgers et al. (2004), Bradburn, Sudman et al. (1979), Dijkstra and van der Zouwen (1982), Fowler et al. (1998), Narayan and Krosnick (1996), Schober and Conrad (1997), Schuman (2008, 2009), Schwarz (1999), Singer and Presser (1989), Sudman and Bradburn (1974, 1982), Tanur (1992), van der Vaart et al. (2006), Wentland and Smith (1993).

Deference effect. Hyman (1954), Miyazaki and Taylor (2008), Webster (1990).

Social desirability effect. Berinsky (2004), Holbrook and Krosnick (2010), Nederhof

(1985), Phillips and Clancy (1972), Press and Townsley (1998), van den Mortel (2007).

Third-party present effect. Aquilino et al. (2000), Blair (1979), Boeije (2004), Edwards et al. (1998), R. Smith (1997).

Asking threatening questions. Blair et al. (1977), Gerich (2008), Kim et al. (2010), Morris (1993), Rifon et al. (2005), Turner et al. (2009), Uriell and Dudley (2009), Villaroel et al. (2008), Wiederman et al. 1994, Ybarra et al. (2009).

Respondent accuracy. Bennett et al. (2009), Calabro et al. (2009), Cannell et al. (1979), Godoy et al. (2009), Harvey et al. (2009), Kubota et al. (2010), Marquis and Cannell (1969), Roberts et al. (2005), Stray (2009), van der Vaart (2009), Woodside and Wilson (2002), Wutich (2009).

9

Interviewing II
Questionnaires

INTRODUCTION

This is the first of two chapters about structured interviews. In a structured interview, each respondent is exposed to the same stimuli. The stimuli are often questions, but they may also be carefully constructed vignettes, lists of words, stacks of photos, clips of music or video, a table full of physical artifacts, or a garden full of plants. The idea in structured interviewing is always the same: to control the input that triggers people's responses so that their output can be reliably compared.

In the next chapter, I'll cover methods for eliciting data about cultural domains and about social networks, but we begin with questionnaires. Some of the lessons about building and administering questionnaires are unique to surveys conducted on the Internet—like exactly where to position the don't-know option in scalar questions (from agree to disagree, for example) on the screen (Christian et al. 2009; and see Dillman et al. 2009b and Shropshire et al. 2009 on web survey design). The major lessons, though, on how to ask questions in surveys apply to all formats.

QUESTIONNAIRES AND SURVEY RESEARCH

Survey research goes back over 200 years (take a look at John Howard's monumental 1973 [1792] survey of British prisons), but it really took off in the mid-1930s when quota sampling was first applied to voting behavior studies and to helping advertisers target consumer messages. Over the years, government agencies in all the industrialized countries have developed an insatiable appetite for information about various "target populations" (poor people, users of public housing, users of private health care, etc.).

Today, survey research is a major industry in all the industrialized countries of the world. Japan developed an indigenous survey research industry soon after World War II (see Passin [1951] for a discussion of this fascinating story). India, South Korea, Jamaica, Greece, Mexico, and many other countries have since developed their own survey research capabilities.

THE COMPUTER REVOLUTION IN SURVEY RESEARCH

There are four methods for collecting questionnaire data: (1) personal, face-to-face interviews, (2) self-administered questionnaires, (3) telephone interviews, and (4) web-based interviews (also called Internet-based interviews or online interviews). All of these methods—not just web-based interviews—can be assisted by, or fully automated with, computers.

CATI, CASI, and CAPI

The computer revolution in survey research began in the 1970s with the development of software for CATI (computer-assisted telephone interviewing). With CATI software, you program a set of survey questions and then let the computer do the dialing. Interviewers sit at their computers, wearing telephone headsets, and when a respondent agrees to be interviewed, they read the questions from the screen. With the kind of fixed-choice questions that are typical in surveys, interviewers only have to click a box on the screen to put in the respondent's answer to each question. For open-ended questions, respondents talk and the interviewer types in the response.

CASI stands for computer-assisted self-administered interview. People sit at a computer and answer questions on their own, just as if they received a questionnaire in the mail.

People can come to a central place to take a CASI survey or you can send them an interview (on a disk or a flash drive) in the mail that they can plug into their own computer (Van Hattum and de Leeuw 1999) . . . or you can set up the survey on the web, using a service like SurveyMonkey®, and people can take it from any Internet connection. (Box 9.1)

Box 9.1 The technology is changing quickly . . . really quickly

People take quickly to computer-based interviews and often find them to be a lot of fun. Fun is good because it cuts down on fatigue. Fatigue is bad because it sends respondents into robot mode and they stop thinking about their answers (Barnes et al. 1995; O'Brien and Dugdale 1978). I ran a computer-based interview in 1988 in a study comparing the social networks of people in Mexico City and Jacksonville, Florida. One member of our team, Christopher McCarty, programmed a laptop to ask respondents in both cities about their acquaintanceship networks. Few people in Jacksonville and almost no one in Mexico City had ever seen a computer, much less one of those clunky lug-ables that passed for laptops back then. But our respondents said they enjoyed the experience. "Wow, this is like some kind of computer game," one respondent said.

The technology is wildly better now, and researchers are running computer-assisted and web-based surveys all over the world. But remember: No matter how much fun Internet surveys are to make or take, all the rules of survey research apply—the rules for making good questions (see below, p. 230); the rules for good formatting (see below, p. 230); and the rules for sampling (see Chapter 6). Computers-as-interviewers are fine when the questions are clear and people don't need a lot of extra information. Suppose you ask: "Did you go to the doctor last week?" and the respondent asks: "What do you mean by doctor?" She may have gone to a free-standing clinic and seen a nurse practitioner or a physician's assistant. She probably wants to know if this counts as "going to the doctor."

Researchers in many fields are using audio, computer-assisted, self-administered interview (A-CASI) technology. With **A-CASI**, the respondent listens to the questions through headphones and types in his or her answers. The computer—a digitized voice—asks the questions, waits for the answers, and moves on. There doesn't appear to be any gain in response rate for audio CASI over text CASI (Couper et al. 2009), but just as with text-based CASI, respondents are more likely to answer questions about sensitive issues, like sexual behavior, drug and alcohol use, and abortion. An advantage of A-CASI is that people with little education can be included in the research.

CAPI software supports computer-assisted personal interviewing and **M-CAPI** (mobile CAPI) supports interviews done with a handheld computer. The computer prompts you (not the respondent) with each question, suggests probes, and lets you enter the data as you go. CAPI and M-CAPI make it easier for you to enter and manage the data. Easier is better, and not just because it saves time. It also reduces errors in the data. When you write down data by hand in the field, you are bound to make some errors. When you input those data into a computer, you're bound to make some more errors. The fewer times you have to handle and transfer data, the better. Clarence Gravlee (2002a) used this method to collect data on lifestyle and blood pressure from 100 people in Puerto Rico. His interviews had 268 multiple choice, yes/no, and open-ended questions, and took over an hour to conduct, but when he got home each night from his interviewing, he had the day's data in the computer.

Internet-Based Surveys

Internet surveys are very popular—and with good reason. They are easy to build (there's lots of interactive software out there for it) and easy to analyze (typically, the results come to you on a spreadsheet that you can pop into your favorite stats program). In theory, they should also be easy to administer—you just send people a link that they can click—but it can be tough getting people to actually take an Internet survey.

In 2000, my colleagues and I ran an Internet survey of people who had purchased a new car in the last two years or were in the market for a car now. There's no sampling frame of such people, so we ran a national, RDD (random-digit-dialing) screening survey. We offered people who were eligible and who said they had access to the Internet $25 to participate in the survey (about $32 in 2012). If they agreed, we gave them the link to the survey and a PIN. We made 11,006 calls and contacted 2,176 people. That's about right for RDD surveys. (The rest of the numbers either didn't answer, or were businesses, or there was only a child at home, etc.)

Of the 2,176 people we contacted, 910 (45%) were eligible for the web survey. Of them, 136 went to the survey site and entered their PIN, and of them, 68 completed the survey.

The data from those 68 people were excellent, but it took an awful lot of work for a purposive (nonrepresentative) sample of 68 people. At the time, just 45% of American adults had access to the Internet (SAUS 2000:Table 913). That number was up to 87% in 2009 (SAUS 2011:Table 1156) and it's growing. With programs like SurveyMonkey®, it's now easy to launch a web-based survey, and when people are motivated enough, web surveys can reach respondents in hard-to-reach groups.

To study gay Latino men, for example, Ross et al. (2004) placed about 47 million banner ads on gay-themed websites inviting potential respondents for a university-sponsored study. The ads produced about 33,000 clicks, 1,742 men who started the survey, and 1,026 men who finished it. Those 1,026 men were obviously not a random, representative sample, but Internet surveys aren't always meant for getting that kind of data. (For more on increasing response rates to Internet and mixed-mode surveys, see Dillman 2009a, and for research on incentives in online panels, see Bosnjak et al. 2003, Göritz 2008, and Heerwegh 2006.) (**Further Reading:** computer-aided and Internet-based interviews) (Box 9.2).

Box 9.2 How big Internet surveys are done

Increasingly, public opinion research is being done on **Internet panels** or **web panels**. In probability panels, survey companies solicit panelists by calling a representative sample of people across the country. In nonprobability panels, people join by clicking on an ad they see on some site. Companies that do web panel research may have over a million potential respondents from whom to choose for any given study.

Just before the presidential election in the United States in 2000, Chang and Krosnick (2009) asked people in these two kinds of panels and people in a random-digit dialing telephone survey the same questions: Who did people intend to vote for? What did they think of each of the candidates? What were their attitudes on some key voting issues? Then they repeated the exercise after the election. The Internet probability sample did best, overall, in terms of representing the nation and in terms of accuracy of reports. This is good news for survey organizations that have the money to build and maintain representative online panels. But it also reinforces the caution against generalizing from nonprobability samples.

ADVANTAGES AND DISADVANTAGES OF SURVEY FORMATS

Each major data-collection method—face-to-face, self-administered, telephone, and online interviews—has its advantages and disadvantages. Your choice of a method will depend on your own calculus of things like cost, convenience, and the nature of the questions you are asking

Face-to-Face Survey Interviews

Advantages of Face-to-Face Interviews

1. They can be used with people who could not otherwise provide information—respondents who are illiterate or nonliterate, blind, bedridden, or very old, for example.

2. If a respondent doesn't understand a question in a personal interview, you can fill in, and, if you sense that the respondent is not answering fully, you can probe for more complete data.

Conventional wisdom in survey research is that each respondent has to hear exactly the same question. In practice, this means not engaging in conversation with people who ask for more information about a particular item on a survey. Not responding to requests for more information might mean sacrificing validity for reliability. And there is evidence that a more conversational style produces more accurate data, especially when respondents really need to get clarifications on unclear concepts (Krosnick 1999; Schober and Conrad 1997).

So, carry a notebook that tells you exactly how to respond when people ask you to clarify an unfamiliar term. If you use more than one interviewer, be sure each of them carries a copy of the same notebook. Good interview schedules are pretested to eliminate terms that are unfamiliar to intended respondents. Still, there

is always someone who asks: "What do you mean by 'income'?" or "How much is 'a lot'?"

3. You can use several different data collection techniques with the same respondent in a face-to-face survey interview. Part of the interview can consist of open-ended questions; another part may require the use of visual aids, such as graphs or cue cards; and in still another, you might hand the respondent a self-administered questionnaire booklet and stand by to help clarify potentially ambiguous items. This is a useful technique for asking really sensitive questions in a face-to-face interview.

4. Personal interviews at home can be much longer than telephone or self-administered questionnaires. A one-hour-long personal interview is relatively easy, and even two- and three-hour interviews are common. It is next to impossible to get respondents to devote two hours to filling out a questionnaire that shows up in the mail, unless you are prepared to pay well for their time; and it requires exceptional skill to keep a telephone interview going for more than 20 minutes, unless respondents are personally interested in the topic (Holbrook et al. 2003). Note, though, that street-intercept or mall-intercept interviews (where you interview people on the fly), although face to face, usually have to be very quick (**Further Reading:** street-and mall intercept).

5. Face-to-face respondents get one question at a time and can't flip through the questionnaire to see what's coming. If you design an interview to start with general questions (how people feel about using new technologies at work, for example) and move on to specific questions (how people feel about using a particular new technology), then you really don't want people flipping ahead.

6. With face-to-face interviews, you know who answers the questions.

Disadvantages of Face-to-Face Interviews

1. They are intrusive and reactive. It takes a lot of skill to administer a questionnaire without subtly telling the respondent how you hope he or she will answer your questions. Other methods of administration of questionnaires may be impersonal, but that's not necessarily bad, especially if you've done the ethnography and have developed a set of fixed-choice questions for a questionnaire. Furthermore, the problem of reactivity increases when more than one interviewer is involved in a project. Making it easy for interviewers to deliver the same questions to all respondents is a plus.

2. Personal interviews are costly in both time and money. If you are working alone, without assistants, and assuming you can get around easily, I wouldn't plan on doing more than 150–200 face-to-face interviews in a year. It gets really, really tough to maintain a consistent, positive attitude long before you get to the 200th interview. With mailed and telephone questionnaires, you can survey thousands of respondents.

In addition to the time spent in interviewing people, locating respondents in a representative sample may require going back several times. In urban research especially, count on making up to half a dozen callbacks to get the really hard-to-find respondents. It's important to make all those callbacks to land the hard-to-get interviews. Survey researchers sometimes use the **sampling by convenient replacement** technique—going next door or down the block and picking up a replacement for an interviewee who happens not to be home when you show up.

This maintains the sample size, but as I mentioned in Chapter 5, it can produce some deadly bias. This is because, as you replace nonresponders with conveniently available respondents, you tend to homogenize your sample and make it less and less representative of all the variation in the population you're studying.

3. Personal interview surveys conducted by lone researchers over a long period of time run the risk of being overtaken by events. A war breaks out, a volcano erupts, or the government decides to cancel elections and imprison the opposition. It sounds dramatic, but these sorts of things are actually quite common across the world. Far less dramatic events can make the responses of the last 100 people you interview radically different from those of the first 100 to the same questions. If you conduct a questionnaire survey over a long period of time in the field, it is a good idea to reinterview your first few respondents and check the stability (reliability) of their reports.

Self-Administered Questionnaires

Advantages of Self-Administered Questionnaires

1. Mailed questionnaires (whether on paper or on a flash drive) puts the post office to work for you in finding respondents. If you cannot use the mail (because sampling frames are unavailable, or because you cannot expect people to respond, or because you are in a country where mail service is unreliable), you can use cluster and area sampling (see Chapter 5), combined with the **drop-and-collect technique**. This involves leaving a questionnaire with a respondent and going back later to pick it up. Ibeh and Brock (2004) used the method in their study of company managers in Nigeria. The standard response rate for mailed questionnaires to busy executives in sub-Saharan Africa is

around 36%. Using the drop-and-collect technique, Ibeh and Brock achieved a nearly 60% response rate (**Further Reading:** drop-and-collect technique).

2. All respondents get the same questions with a self-administered questionnaire. There is no worry about interviewer bias or response effects, based on features of the interviewer. As we saw in Chapter 8, questions about sexual behavior (including family planning) and about attitudes toward women or men or members of particular ethnic/racial groups are particularly susceptible to this problem. The perceived sexual orientation of the interviewer, for example, affects how supportive respondents are of homosexuality (Kemph and Kasser 1996).

3. You can ask more complex questions with a self-administered paper questionnaire than you can in a personal interview. Questions that involve a long list of response categories or that

require a lot of background data are hard to follow orally but are often interesting to respondents if worded right on paper.

For really complex questions, you're better off with CASI or a web-based survey because respondents don't have to think about any convoluted instructions at all—like: "Have you ever had hepatitis? If not, then skip to question 42." Later, after the respondent finishes a series of questions about her bout with hepatitis, the questionnaire says: "Now return to question 40." With CASI and web-based surveys, the computer does all the work and the respondent can focus on responding.

4. You can ask long batteries of otherwise boring questions on self-administered questionnaires that you just couldn't get away with in a personal interview. Look at Figure 9.1. Imagine trying to ask someone to sit still while you recited, say, 30 items and asked for their response. CASI and web-based surveys are much better at this.

Figure 9.1 A Battery Item in a Questionnaire. Batteries Can Consist of Many Items

Here is a list of things that people say they'd like to see in their high school. For each item, check how you feel this high school is doing	Well	Ok	Poorly	Don't Know
1. High-quality instruction	___	___	___	___
2. Good pay for teachers	___	___	___	___
3. Good mix of sports and academics	___	___	___	___
4. Preparation for college entrance exams	___	___	___	___
5. Safety	___	___	___	___
6. Music program	___	___	___	___
7. Good textbooks	___	___	___	___

5. In self-administered interviews, people aren't trying to impress anyone, and anonymity provides a sense of security, which produces more reports of things like premarital sexual experiences, constipation, arrest records, alcohol dependency, interpersonal violence, and so on. L. Peterson et al. (1996) randomly assigned two groups of 57 Swedish Army veterans to fill out the Beck's Depression Inventory (A. T. Beck et al. 1961). One group used the pencil-and-paper version; the other used a computer-based version. Those who used the computer-based version had significantly higher mean scores on really sensitive questions about depression (**Further Reading:** mode effects).

This does *not* mean that *more* reporting of behavior means more *accurate* reporting. We know better than that. But, as I've said before, more is usually better than less. If Chicanos report spending 12 hours per week in conversation with their families at home, and Anglos (as White, non–Hispanic Americans are known in the American Southwest) report spending four hours, I wouldn't want to bet that Chicanos *really* spend 12 hours, on average, or that Anglos *really* spend four hours, on average, talking to their families. But I'd find the fact that Chicanos reported spending three times as much time talking with their families pretty interesting.

Disadvantages of Self-Administered Questionnaires

1. You have no control over how people interpret questions on a self-administered instrument, whether the questionnaire is delivered on paper or on a home computer or over the Internet. There is always the danger that, no matter how much background work you do, no matter how hard you try to produce culturally correct questions, respondents will be forced into making culturally inappropriate choices in closed-ended questionnaires. If the questionnaire is self-administered, you can't answer people's questions about what a particular item means.

2. If you are not working in a highly industrialized nation, or if you are not prepared to use Dillman's Tailored Design Method (discussed below), you are likely to see response rates of 20%–30% from mailed questionnaires and even worse from Internet surveys. It is entirely reasonable to analyze the data from any survey statistically and to offer conclusions about the correlations among variables for those who responded to your survey. But low response means you can't draw conclusions about larger populations. CASI and A-CASI studies are based on real visits with people and response rates for those forms of self-administered questionnaires can be very high. Hewett et al. (2004) used A-CASI in a study of 1,293 adolescents in rural and urban Kenya. The survey had yes/no and multiple choice questions and people just punched in their responses on a keypad. Only 2% of the respondents had trouble with the equipment (even though most of them had never seen a computer), and the research team got an 80% response rate (Hewett et al. 2004:322–28).

3. Even if a mailed questionnaire is returned, you can't be sure that the respondent who received it is the person who filled it out, and the same is true for Internet and e-mail questionnaires.

4. Self-administered questionnaires are prone to serious sampling problems. Sampling frames of addresses are almost always flawed, sometimes very

badly. If you use a phone book to select a sample, you miss all those people who don't have phones, or who choose not to list their numbers, or who just have cell phones—a problem that is increasing rapidly. If you try to get around this with a random-digit dialing phase to recruit respondents, you add a lot of cost to any survey. Face-to-face administration of questionnaires is often based on an area cluster sample, with random selection of households within each cluster. This is a much more powerful sampling design than most mailed questionnaire surveys can muster, and better than online surveys that are based on volunteers.

5. In some cases, you may want respondents to answer a question without their knowing what's coming next. This is impossible in a self-administered paper questionnaire, but it's not a problem in CASI, and A-CASI, and web-based studies.

6. Self-administered paper, CASI, and web-based questionnaires are simply not useful for studying nonliterate or illiterate populations, or people who can't use a keyboard. When you need to read questions to people, face-to-face, telephone, or A- CASI technology is the way to go.

Telephone Interviews

Advantages of Telephone Interviews

1. Telephone interviews are inexpensive and convenient to do. By the 1970s, answers to many different kinds of questions asked over the phone in the United States were found to be as valid as those to questions asked in person or through the mail (Dillman 1978). Today, telephone interviewing is the most widely used method of gathering survey data across the industrialized world.

2. Phone interviews have the impersonal quality of self-administered questionnaires and the personal quality of face-to-face interviews. So, telephone surveys are unintimidating (like self-administered questionnaires), but allow interviewers to probe or to answer questions dealing with ambiguity of items (just like they can in personal interviews).

3. Using **random digit dialing (RDD)**, you can reach almost everyone who has a phone, including cell phones. In highly industrialized countries, that means you can reach almost everybody. One survey found that 28% of completed interviews using RDD were with people who had unlisted phone numbers (Taylor 1997:424). There are huge regional differences, though, in the availability of telephones (see below).

4. It is relatively easy to monitor the quality of telephone interviewers' work by having them come to a central place to conduct their operation. But if you don't monitor the performance of telephone interviewers, you invite cheating. (See below, in the section on the disadvantages of telephone interviewing.)

5. There is no reaction to the *appearance* of the interviewer in telephone surveys, although respondents *do* react to accents and speech patterns of interviewers. Oskenberg et al. (1986) found that telephone interviewers who had the lowest refusal rates had higher-pitched, louder, and clearer voices. And, as with all types of interviews, there are gender-of-interviewer and race-of-interviewer effects in telephone interviews, too. Respondents try to figure out the race or ethnicity of the interviewer and then tailor responses

accordingly. (See the section on response effects in Chapter 8.)

6. Telephone interviewing is safe. You can talk on the phone to people who live in urban neighborhoods where many professional interviewers (most of whom are women) would prefer not to go. Telephones also get you past doormen and other people who run interference for the rich.

Disadvantages of Telephone Interviews

1. If you are doing research in Haiti or Bolivia or elsewhere in the developing world, telephone surveys are out of the question, except for some urban centers, and then only if your research is about relatively well-off people. About 97% of all households in the United States have telephones (Belinfante 2009). This makes *national* surveys a cinch to do and highly reliable. But the distribution of telephones is uneven, which makes some *local* phone surveys questionable. In Westchester County, New York, for example, the median per capita income was about $80,000 per year in 2008 and over 98% of all households have phones (http://www.census.gov/cgi-bin/saipe/saipe.cgi). On the Rosebud Sioux Reservation—an area of about 5,000 square kilometers and home to about 10,000 tribal members—median

household income is around $25,000 and telephone penetration is about 75% (http://tinyurl.com/3h2mcvf; FCC 2007).

Also, samples of household phone numbers are increasingly unrepresentative because of the proliferation of cell-phone-only households. In 2010, 24% of adults in the United States were living in households that *only* had cell phones (Blumberg et al. 2011), and that number is sure to grow.

2. Telephone interviewing using RDD is convenient, but it's no lazy way out: It can take 1,000 calls to get 200–300 interviews—and that's starting with a list of working home phone numbers.

People are getting tired of phone surveys and are opting out (Morin 2004). In a careful study in 2003, the contact rate (the number of people you can actually talk to in a sample of working home phone numbers) was 79% (down from 90% six years earlier) and the refusal rate among people contacted was 66%. So, all in all, the final response rate was about 25% (Keeter et al. 2006).

This biases the outcome for some questions, but the good news is that it doesn't produce consistent bias in the results of surveys (Groves 2006). You can always get nearly 100% study sample completion, by replacing refusers with people who will cooperate. If you do that, make an extra effort to get at least some of the refusers to respond so you can test whether cooperators are a biased sample (Box 9.3).

Box 9.3 Samples of phone numbers

There are companies that sell telephone numbers for surveys. The numbers are chosen to represent businesses or residences and to represent the varying saturation of phone service in different calling areas. Even the best sample of phone numbers, though, may not be enough to keep you out of trouble. During the 1984 U.S. presidential election, Ronald Reagan's tracking poll used a list of registered voters, Republicans and Democrats alike. The poll showed Reagan comfortably ahead of his rival, Walter Mondale, except on Friday nights. Registered Republicans, it turned out, being wealthier than their counterparts among Democrats, were out Friday nights more than Democrats were, and simply weren't available to answer the phone (Begley et al. 1992:38).

3. Telephone interviews must be relatively short or people will hang up. There is some evidence that once people agree to give you their time in a telephone interview, you can keep them on the line for a remarkably long time (up to an hour) by developing special "phone personality" traits. Generally, however, you should not plan a telephone interview that lasts for more than 20 minutes.

4. And finally, this: It has long been known that, in an unknown percentage of occasions, hired interviewers willfully falsify data (Boyd and Westfall 1955). When an interviewer who is paid by the completed interview finds a respondent not at home, the temptation is to fill in the interview and get on to the next respondent. It's particularly easy for interviewers to cheat in telephone surveys—from failing to probe, to interviewing unqualified respondents, to fabricating an item response, and even to fabricating whole interviews. Kiecker and Nelson (1996) hired 33 survey research companies to do eight interviews each, ostensibly as "mop-up" for a larger national market survey. The eight respondents were plants—graduate students of drama, for whom this must have been quite a gig—and were the same eight for each of the surveys. Of the 33 interviewers studied, 10 fabricated an entire interview, 32 fabricated at least one item response, and all 33 failed to record responses verbatim.

You can eliminate most cheating by training and monitoring phone interviewers. Presser and Zhao (1992) monitored 40 trained telephone interviewers at the Maryland Survey Research Center. For the 5,619 questions monitored, interviewers read the questions exactly as worded on the survey 91% of the time. Training works.

Still, no matter how much you train interviewers. . . . Johnstone et al. (1992) studied 48 telephone interviews done entirely by women and found that female respondents elicited more sympathy, while male respondents elicited more joking. Men, say Johnstone et al., may be less comfortable than women are with being interviewed by women and wind up trying to subvert the interview by turning it into teasing or banter (**Further Reading:** telephone interviews).

WHEN TO USE WHAT

There is no perfect data collection method. Internet surveys are easy to build and easy to administer. If you don't need a probability sample, or if you are trying to recruit elusive populations, then online surveys are excellent. If the choice is between personal interviews and interviewer-absent written questionnaires, then mailed or dropped-off questionnaires are preferable when three conditions are met: (1) you are dealing with literate respondents; (2) you are confident of getting a high response rate (at least 70%); and (3) the questions you want to ask do not require a face-to-face interview or the use of visual aids such as cue cards, charts, and the like. Under these circumstances, you get more information for your time and money than from the other methods of questionnaire administration.

When you really need complete interviews—answers to all or nearly all the questions in a particular survey—then face-to-face interviews are the way to go. Caserta et al. (1985) interviewed recently bereaved respondents about adjustment to widowhood. They interviewed 192 respondents—104 in person, at home, and 88 by mailed questionnaire. Both groups got identical questions. On average, 82% of those interviewed at home three–four weeks after losing their husband or wife answered any given question. Just 68% of those who responded to the mailed questionnaire answered any given question. As Caserta et al. explain, the physical presence of the interviewer helped establish the rapport needed for asking sensitive and personal questions about the painful experience of bereavement (p. 640). (Use a hand-held computer and mobile-CAPI software to make sure you ask everyone the same questions. See above, page 217.)

If you are working in a highly industrialized country, and if a very high proportion of the population you are studying has their own telephones, then consider doing a phone survey whenever a self-administered questionnaire would otherwise be appropriate.

If you are working alone or in places where the mail and the phone system are inefficient for data collection, the drop-and-collect technique is a good alternative (see above, page 220).

Finally, there is no rule against using more than one type of interview. Mauritius, an island nation in the Indian Ocean, is an ethnically complex society. Chinese, Creoles, Franco-Mauritians, Hindus, Muslims, and other groups make up a population of about a million. Ari Nave (1997) was interested in how Mauritians maintain their ethnic group boundaries, particularly through their choices of whom to marry. A government office on Mauritius maintains a list of all people over 18 on Mauritius, so it was relatively easy for Nave to get a random sample of the population.

Contacting the sample was another matter. Nave got back just 347 out 930 mailed questionnaires, but he was able to interview another 296 by telephone and face to face, for a total of 643, or 69% of his original sample—a respectable completion rate.

USING INTERVIEWERS

Large surveys routinely employ lots of interviewers. In field research, multiple interviewers may not be worth the cost. If you can collect 100 interviews yourself and maintain careful quality control in your interview technique, then hiring one more interviewer would probably not improve your research by enough to

warrant both spending the extra money and worrying about quality control.

Recall that for estimating population proportions or means you have to quadruple the sample size to halve the sampling error. If you can't afford to hire three more interviewers (beside yourself), and to train them carefully so that they at least introduce the *same* bias to every interview as you do, consider running the survey yourself and saving the money for other things.

This only goes for surveys in which you interview a random sample of respondents to estimate a population parameter. If you are studying the experiences of a group of people or are after cultural data (as in "How are things usually done around here?"), then getting more interviews is better than getting fewer, whether you collect the data yourself or have it collected by others.

Training Interviewers

If you hire interviewers, be sure to train them—and monitor them throughout the research. A colleague used a doctoral student as an interviewer in a project in Atlanta. The senior researcher trained the student but listened to the interview tapes that came in. At one point, the interviewer asked a respondent: "How many years of education do you have?" "Four," said the respondent. "Oh," said the student researcher, "you mean you have four years of education?" "No," said the informant, bristling and insulted, "I've had four years of education beyond high school." The informant was affluent; the interview was conducted in his upper-middle-class house; he had already told the interviewer that he was in a high-tech occupation. So monitor interviewers.

If you hire a *team* of interviewers, you have one extra chore besides monitoring their work. You need to get them to act as a team. Be sure, for example, that they all use the same probes to the various questions on the interview schedule. Especially with open-ended questions, be sure to do random spot checks, *during the survey*, of how interviewers are coding the answers they get. The act of spot-checking keeps coders alert. When you find discrepancies in the way interviewers code responses, bring the group together and discuss the problem openly.

Narratives are coded after the interview. If you use of team of coders, be sure to train them together and get their interrater reliability coefficient up to at least 0.70. In other words, make sure that your interviewers use the same theme tags to code each piece of text. For details on how to do this, see the section on Cohen's kappa in Chapter 19.

Carey et al. (1996) studied the beliefs of 51 newly arrived Vietnamese refugees in upstate New York about tuberculosis. The interviews consisted of 32 open-ended questions on beliefs about symptoms, prevention, treatment, and the social consequences of having TB. The two interviewers in this study were bilingual refugees who participated in a three-day workshop to build their interview skills. They were told about the rationale for open-ended questions and about techniques for getting respondents to open up and provide full answers to the questions. The training included a *written manual* (this is very important) to which the interviewers could refer during the actual study. After the workshop, the trainees did 12 practice interviews with Vietnamese adults who were not in the study.

William Axinn ran the Tamang Family Research Project, a comparative study of villages in Nepal (Axinn 1991). Axinn and his coworkers trained a group of interviewers using the *Interviewer's Manual* from the Survey Research Center at the University of Michigan (University of Michigan 1976). That manual contains the distilled wisdom of hundreds of interviewer training exercises in the United States, and Axinn found the manual useful in training Nepalese interviewers, too.

Axinn recruited 32 potential interviewers. After a week of training (five days at eight hours a day, and two days of supervised field practice), the 16 best interviewers were selected, 10 men and six women. The researchers hired more

interviewers than they needed and after three months, four of the interviewers were fired. "The firing of interviewers who clearly failed to follow protocols," said Axinn et al., "had a considerable positive effect on the morale of interviewers who had worked hard to follow our rules" (1991:200). No one has accused Axinn of overstatement (**Further Reading:** interviewer training).

Who to Hire

In general, when hiring interviewers, look for professional interviewers first. Next, look for people who are mature enough to accept the need for rigorous training and who can work as part of a team. If need be, look for interviewers who can handle the possibility of going into some rough neighborhoods and who can answer the many questions that respondents will come up with in the course of the survey.

If you are running a survey based on personal interviews in a developing country, consider hiring college students, and even college graduates, in the social sciences. "Social sciences," by the way, does not mean the humanities. In Peru, sociologists Donald Warwick and Charles Lininger found that "some students from the humanities . . . were reluctant to accept the 'rigidities' of survey interviewing." Those students felt that "As educated individuals, they should be allowed to administer the questionnaire as they saw fit in each situation" (1975:222).

I would not use anyone who had that kind of attitude as an interviewer. But undergraduate social science students in the developing world may have real research experience since most of them aren't going on for graduate training. Students who are experienced interviewers have a lot to contribute to the design and content of questionnaires. Remember, you are dealing with colleagues who will be justly resentful if you treat them merely as employees of your study. By the same token, college students in developing nations are likely to be members of the elite who may find it tough to establish rapport with peasant farmers or the urban poor (Hursh-César and Roy 1976:308).

Make It Easy for Interviewers to Do Their Job

If you use interviewers, be sure to make the questionnaire booklet easy to use. Leave enough space for interviewers to write in the answers to open-ended questions—but not too much space. Big spaces are an invitation to some interviewers to develop needlessly long answers (Warwick and Lininger 1975:152).

Also, use two different type faces for questions and answers; put instructions to interviewers in capital letters and questions for respondents in normal type. Figure 9.2 is an example.

CLOSED- VERSUS OPEN-ENDED QUESTIONS

The most often-asked question about survey research is whether fixed-choice (also called closed-ended) or open-ended items are better. The answer is that the two formats produce different kinds of data, and it's your call when to use what.

A problem with fixed-choice questions is that people focus on the choices they have. If they'd like to offer a response other than those in front of them, they won't do it (Krosnick

1999:544). Daniel Hruschka and colleagues (2004) asked 227 Zimbawean women who were in HIV counseling l two questions about how they negotiated the use of condoms. The first question was open ended:

> Think back to when you discussed male condom use with [main male partner] since [the last counseling session]. What exactly did you ask/ tell him? Tell me in your own words.

The second question—which was asked immediately after the first—was fixed choice:

> Now I'm going to read you a list of things some women tell their partners to try and convince them to use male condoms. Tell me for each one whether you told your partner this to convince him to use male condoms.

1. Told him that she was worried about getting HIV/AIDS.

2. Told him that she is worried about giving HIV/AIDS to him.

3. Reminded him that many of his friends or relatives have already died of HIV/AIDS and that this makes her believe that anyone can get it and pass it on through sex.

4. Told him that if she gets sick with HIV/AIDS, she may no longer be able to take care of him and her children.

Figure 9.2 Using Two Different Type Faces in a Survey Instrument

22. Are you currently married?

    INTERVIEWER: CHECK ONE OF THE FOLLOWING

    ☐ **R IS NOT CURRENTLY MARRIED. SKIP TO Q. 24**

    ☐ **R IS CURRENTLY MARRIED. ASK Q.23 AND Q.24.**

23. How long have you been married?

24. Have you been married before?

5. Told him she wants to use male condoms to prevent pregnancy.

6. Told him about the study and that the study staff wanted you to ask him to use male condoms.

7. Showed him a brochure from the Ministry of Health/National AIDS Control Program urging everyone in Zimbabwe to use condoms.

The seven items for the fixed-choice question were developed from focus groups with staff at the University of Zimbabwe and in consultation with nurses and other women in the community (Hruschka et al. 2004:188–89). One of the themes extracted from the open-ended responses was: emphasizing that HIV is everywhere. Women who reported using that negotiation technique were about 300% more likely to report 100% condom use by their partners over the previous two months. None of the seven items in the fixed-choice question predicted 100% reported condom use (Hruschka et al. 2004:196).

Schuman and Presser (1981:89) asked a sample of people this question: "Please look at this card and tell me which thing you would most prefer in a job." The card had five items listed: (1) high income; (2) no danger of being fired; (3) working hours are short—lots of free time; (4) chances for advancement; and (5) the work is important and gives a feeling of accomplishment. Then they asked a different sample the open-ended question: "What would you most prefer in a job?" About 17% of the respondents to the fixed-choice question chose "chances for advancement," and over 59% chose "important work." Fewer than 2% of the respondents who were asked the open-ended question mentioned "chances for advancement," and just 21% said anything about "important" or "challenging" or "fulfilling" work.

When the questions get really threatening, fixed-choice questions are generally not a good idea. Masturbation, alcohol consumption, and drug use are reported with 50%–100% greater frequency in response to open-ended questions (Bradburn 1983:299). Apparently, people are least threatened when they can offer their own answers to open-ended questions on a self-administered questionnaire, rather than being forced to choose among a set of fixed alternatives (e.g., once a month, once a week, once a day, several times a day), and are most threatened by a face-to-face interviewer (Tourangeau and Smith 1996; Tourangeau and Yan 2007).

On the other hand, Ivis et al. (1997) found that at least one pretty embarrassing question was better asked in a fixed-choice format—and over the phone, at that. People in their survey were asked: "How often in the last 12 months have you had five or more drinks on one occasion?" Then, later in the interview, they were asked the same question, but were given nine fixed choices: (1) every day; (2) about once every other day; . . . (9) never in the last year. The fixed-choice format produced significantly more positive responses. The anonymity of telephone surveys provides a certain comfort level where people feel free to open up on sensitive topics. And notice that the anonymity of telephone surveys lets the *interviewer*, as well as the respondent, off the hook. You can ask people things you might be squeamish about if the interview were face to face, and respondents feel that they can divulge very personal matters to disembodied voices on the phone.

Overall, because closed-ended items are so efficient, most survey researchers prefer them to open-ended questions and use them whenever possible. There is no rule, however, that prevents you from mixing question types. Many survey researchers use the open-ended format for really intimidating questions and the fixed-choice format for everything else, even on the phone. Even if there are no intimidating questions in a survey, it's a good idea to stick in a few open-ended items. The open-ended questions break the monotony for the respondent, as do tasks that require referring to visual aids (like a graph).

The responses to fixed-choice questions are unambiguous for purposes of analysis. Be sure to take full advantage of this and precode fixed-choice items on a questionnaire. Put the codes right on the instrument so that typing the data into the computer is as easy (and as error free) as possible.

It's worth repeating that when you do computer-assisted interviews (CAPI, mobile-CAPI, CASI, A-CASI) you cut down on data entry error. The fewer times you have to touch data, the fewer opportunities there are to stick errors in them. I particularly like the fact that we can combine fixed-choice and open-ended questions on a hand-held computer in survey research.

FIFTEEN RULES FOR QUESTION WORDING AND FORMAT

There are some well-understood rules that all survey researchers follow in constructing questionnaire items. Here are 15 of them.

1. *Be unambiguous.* If respondents can interpret a question differently from the meaning you have in mind, they will. In my view, this is the source of most response error in fixed-choice questionnaires.

Even a simple question like "How often do you visit a doctor?" can be ambiguous. Are acupuncturists, chiropractors, chiropodists, and public clinics all doctors? If you think they are, you'd better tell people that, or you leave it up to them to decide. In some parts of the southwestern United States, people may be visiting native curers and herbalists. Are those practitioners doctors? In Mexico, many community clinics are staffed by nurses. Does "going to the doctor" include a visit to one of those clinics?

Here's how Cannell et al. (1989) recommend asking about doctor visits in the last year:

Have you been a patient in the hospital overnight in the past 12 months since July 1st 1987? (Not counting when you were in a hospital overnight.) During the past 12 months since July 1st, 1987, how many times did you actually see any medical doctor about your own health?

During the past 12 months since July 1st 1987, were there any times when you didn't actually see the doctor but saw a nurse or other medical assistant working for the doctor?

During the past 12 months since July 1st 1987, did you get any medical advice, prescriptions, or results of tests over the telephone from a medical doctor, nurse, or medical assistant working for a doctor? [Cannell et al. 1989:Appendix A, p. 1]

Words like "lunch," "community," "people," and hundreds of other innocent lexical items have lurking ambiguities associated with them, and phrases like "family planning" will cause all kinds of mischief. Half the respondents in the 1985 General Social Survey were asked if they agreed that there was too little spending for "assistance to the poor" and half were asked if there was too little spending for "welfare." A whopping 65% agreed with the first wording; just 19% agreed with the second (T. W. Smith 1987:77).

Even the word "you," as Payne pointed out (1951), can be ambiguous. Ask a nurse at the clinic "How many patients did you see last week?" and you might get a response like: "Who do you mean, me or the clinic?" If the nurse is filling out a self-administered questionnaire, she'll have to decide for herself what you had in mind. Maybe she'll get it right; maybe she won't.

2. *Use a vocabulary that your respondents understand, but don't be condescending.*

This is a difficult balance to achieve. If you're studying a narrow population (sugar cane cutters, midwives, race car drivers, pediatric nurses), then proper ethnography and pretesting with a few knowledgeable informants will help ensure appropriate wording of questions.

But if you are studying a more general population, even in a small town of just 3,000 people, then things are very different. Some respondents will require a low-level vocabulary; others will find that vocabulary insulting. This is one of the reasons often cited for doing personal interviews: You want the opportunity to phrase your questions differently for different segments of the population. Realize, however, that this poses risks in terms of reliability of response data.

3. *Remember that respondents must know enough to respond to your questions.* You'd be surprised at how often questionnaires are distributed to people who are totally unequipped to answer them. I get questionnaires in the mail and by e-mail all the time, asking for information I simply don't have.

Most people can't recall with any acceptable accuracy how long they spent in the hospital last year, how many miles they drive each week, or how much they've cut back on their use of air conditioning. They *can* recall whether they own a television, have *ever* been to Cairo, or voted in a recent election. And they can tell you whether they *think* they are well paid, or *believe* the current chief of police is doing a better job than his predecessor at cleaning up the staffing problem at the county jail.

4. Make sure there's a *clear purpose for every question* you ask in a survey. When I say "clear purpose," I mean clear to respondents, not just to you. And once you're on a topic, stay on it and finish it. Respondents can get frustrated,

confused, and annoyed at the tactic of switching topics and then coming back to a topic that they've already dealt with on a questionnaire. Some researchers do exactly this just to ask the same question in more than one way and to check respondent reliability. This underestimates the intelligence of respondents and is asking for trouble—I have known respondents to sabotage questionnaires that they found insulting to their intelligence.

You can (and should) ask questions that are related to one another at different places in a questionnaire, so long as each question makes sense in terms of its placement in the overall instrument. For example, if you are interviewing labor migrants, you'll probably want to get a labor history—by asking where the respondent has worked during the past few years. Later, in a section on family economics, you might ask whether a respondent has ever sent remittances and from where.

As you move from one topic to another, put in a transition paragraph that makes each shift logical to the respondent. For example, you might say: "Now that we have learned something about the kinds of food you like, we'd like to know about. . . ." The exact wording of these transition paragraphs should be varied throughout a questionnaire.

5. Pay careful attention to contingencies and filter questions. Many question topics contain several contingencies. Suppose you ask someone if they are married. If they answer "no," then you probably want to ask whether they've ever been married. You may want to know whether they have children, irrespective of whether they are married or have ever been married. You may want to know what people think is the ideal family size, irrespective of whether

they've been married, plan to be married, have children, or plan to have children.

You can see that the contingencies can get very complex. The best way to ensure that all contingencies are accounted for is to build a contingency flow chart like that shown in Figure 9.3 (Sirken 1972; Sudman and Bradburn 1982).

6. *Use clear scales.* There are some commonly used scales in survey research—things like: Excellent-Good-Fair-Poor; Approve-Disapprove; Oppose-Favor; For-Against; Good-Bad; Agree-Disagree;

Figure 9.3 Flow Chart of Filter Questions for Part of a Questionnaire

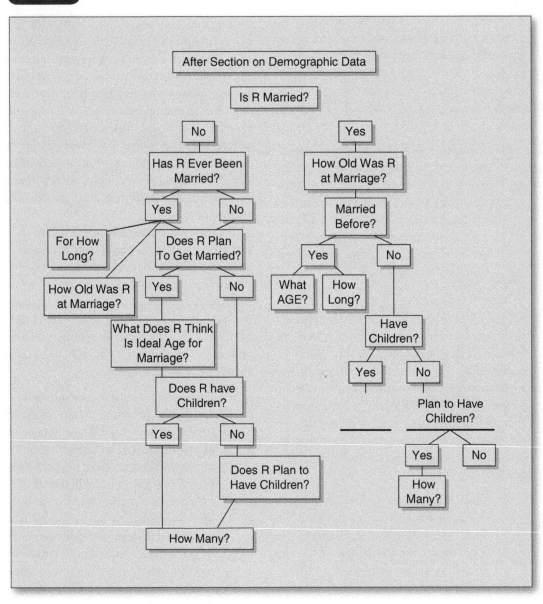

Better-Worse-About the Same; etc. Just because these are well known, however, does not mean that they are clear and unambiguous to respondents.

To cut down on the ambiguities associated with these kinds of scales, explain the meaning of each potentially ambiguous scale when you introduce it. With self-administered questionnaires, use five scale points rather than three, if you can. For example, use Strongly Approve, Approve, Neutral, Disapprove, Strongly Disapprove, rather than Approve, Neutral, Disapprove. This will give people the opportunity to make finer-grained choices. If your sample is large enough, you can distinguish during analysis among respondents who answer, say, "strongly approve" versus "approve" on some item. For smaller samples, you can aggregate the data into three categories for analysis.

Self-administered questionnaires allow the use of seven-point scales, like the semantic differential scale shown in Figure 9.4, and even longer scales. Telephone interviews often rely on three-point scales.

Notice that the semantic differential scale in Figure 9.4 has word anchors at both ends and numbers in the middle, not words. In this kind of scale, we want to let people interpret the dimension indicated by the anchors. In typical rating scales (the three- and five-point scales you see in questionnaires), we want to remove ambiguity, so we label all the points in words—like Strongly Agree, Agree, Neutral, Disagree, Strongly Disagree (Peters and McCormick 1966). (Much more on how to construct scales in Chapter 11.)

7. Try to *package questions in self-administered questionnaires*, as shown earlier in Figure 9.1. This is a way to get a lot of data quickly and easily, and, if done properly, it will prevent respondents from getting bored with a survey. For example, you might say "Please indicate how close you feel to each of the persons on this chart" and provide the respondent with a list of relatives

Figure 9.4 A 7-Point Semantic Differential Scale

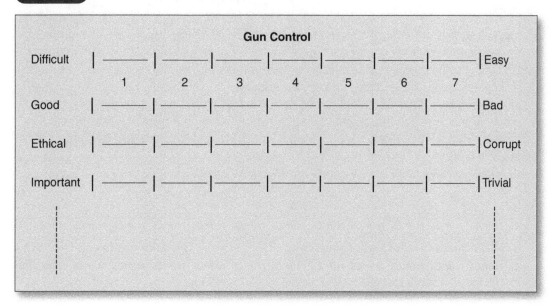

(mother, father, sister, brother, etc.) and a scale (Very Close, Close, Neutral; Distant, Very distant; etc.).

Be sure to make scales unambiguous. If you are asking how often people think they do something, don't say "regularly" when you mean "more than once a month," and limit the list of activities to no more than seven. Then introduce a question with a totally different format, to break up the monotony and to keep the respondent interested.

Packaging is best done in self-administered questionnaires. If you use these kinds of lists in a face-to-face interview, you'll have to repeat the scale for at least the first three items or activities you name, or until the respondent gets the pattern down. This can get very tiring for both interviewers and respondents.

8.   If you want respondents to check just one response, then be sure to *make the possible responses to a question exhaustive and mutually exclusive.* This may mean including a "Don't Know" option.

Here is an example (taken from a questionnaire I received) of what *not* to do:

How do you perceive communication between your department and other departments in the university? [check one]

There is much communication _____

There is sufficient communication _____

There is little communication _____

There is no communication _____

No basis for perception _____

The "no basis for perception" response took care of making the item exhaustive. The problem for me on this item was that I wanted to check both "little communication" and "sufficient communication." For me, at least, these two categories were not mutually exclusive—I didn't think there was a lot of communication, and I wasn't at all bothered by that—but the author of the survey asked me to "check one" (Box 9.4).

Box 9.4 The don't know option

You can always make questionnaire items exhaustive by giving respondents the option of saying some variant of "don't know"—like "no basis for perception." Some researchers feel that this just gives respondents a lazy way out—that people need to be made to work a bit. If there is a good chance that some of your respondents really won't have the information you ask for, then I think the "don't know" option is too important to leave out. In consumer preference surveys, though, where you actually give someone a taste of a cracker and ask them to tell you if they like it, the "don't know" option is a bad idea (**Further Reading:** don't know option).

---

9.   *Keep questions short.* Many questions require a preamble to set up a time frame or otherwise make clear what

you are asking someone to think about in answering a question. For example:

These next questions are about what your children are doing these days. You said that you have two daughters and a son. Where is your older daughter living? Your younger daughter? Your son?

Questions that are likely to intimidate respondents can have long preambles to lessen the intimidation effect. The questions themselves, however, should contain as few words as possible.

10. *Provide alternatives*, if appropriate. Suppose people are being asked to move off their land to make way for a new highway. The government offers to compensate people for the land, but people are suspicious that the government won't evaluate fairly how much compensation landowners are entitled to. If you take a survey and ask "Should the government offer people compensation for their land?" respondents can answer yes or no for very different reasons. Instead, let people check whether they agree or disagree with a set of alternatives, like: "The government should offer people compensation for their land" and "An independent board should determine how much people get for their land."

11. *Avoid loaded questions.* Any question that begins "Don't you agree that . . ." is a loaded question. Sheatsley (1983) points out, however, that asking loaded questions is a technique you can use to your advantage, on occasion, just as leading or baiting informants can be used in unstructured interviewing. A famous example comes from Kinsey's landmark study of sexual behavior of American men (Kinsey et al. 1948). Kinsey asked men "How old were you the first time you masturbated?" This made respondents feel that the interviewer already *knew* about the fact of masturbation and was only in search of additional information.

12. *Don't use double-barreled questions.* Here is a double-barreled question I found on a questionnaire: "When did you leave home and go to work on your own for the first time?" There is no reason to assume that someone had to leave home to go to work, or that they necessarily went to work if they left home.

Here is another bad question:

Please indicate if you agree or disagree with the following statement:

Marijuana is no more harmful than tobacco or alcohol, so the personal use of marijuana should be legal.

A respondent can agree (or disagree) with the first part of the statement—the assertion that marijuana is no more harmful than tobacco or alcohol—and may agree or disagree with the second part. If respondents answer "yes" or "no," how do you know if they are indicating agreement with both parts of it or just one part? Which part? How can you tell? You can't. That's why it's a bad question.

And one more—this one from a *CNN* poll on climate change:

Which of the following statements comes closest to your view of global warming: Global warming is a proven fact and is mostly caused by emissions from cars and industrial facilities like power plants and factories; global warming is a proven fact and is mostly caused by natural changes that have nothing to do with emissions from cars and industrial facilities; or, global warming is a theory that has not yet been proven.

As Jon Krosnick (2010) points out, the question lacks an option for respondents to say that they don't believe global warming is happening at all.

13. *Don't take emotional stands in the wording of questions.* Here's an example of the sort of question you see on surveys all the time—and that you should never ask: "Should the legislature raise the drinking age to 21 in order to reduce the carnage among teens on our highways?"

14. When asking for opinions *on controversial issues, specify the referent situation* as much as possible. Instead of asking: "Do you approve of abortion?" ask: "Under what conditions do you approve of abortion?" Then give the respondent as exhaustive a list of circumstances as possible to check—including the option of "under no circumstances." If the circumstances are not exclusive (rape and incest are not necessarily exclusive, for example), then let respondents check as many circumstances as they think appropriate.

15. *Don't put false premises into questions.* I once formulated the following question for a survey in Greece: "Is it better for a woman to have a house and cash as a dowry, or for her to have an education and a job that she can bring to the marriage?" This question was based on a lot of ethnographic work in a community, during which I learned that many families were sinking their resources into getting women educated and into jobs and offering this to eligible bachelors as a substitute for traditional material dowries. My question, however, was based on the false premise that all families respected the custom of dowry. The question did not allow respondents to state a third alternative—namely,

that they didn't think dowry was a custom that ought to be maintained in any form, traditional or modern. In fact, many families were deciding to reject the dowry custom altogether— something that I missed for some time. Pretest questions to avoid this problem.

Pretesting and Learning From Mistakes

There is no way to emphasize sufficiently the importance of **pretesting** any survey instrument. No matter how much you do to prepare a culturally appropriate questionnaire, it is absolutely guaranteed that you will have forgotten something important or that you will have poorly worded one or more vital element. These glitches can only be identified by pretesting.

If you are building a self-administered questionnaire, bring in a dozen or more pretest respondents and sit with them as they fill out the entire instrument (Sheatsley 1983). Encourage them to ask questions about each item. Your pretest respondents will make you painfully aware of just how much you took for granted, no matter how much ethnographic research you did or how many focus groups you ran before making up a questionnaire. There is no guarantee, by the way, that a dozen pretest respondents are enough. If you're still learning a lot after a dozen pretest respondents, then bring in some more.

For face-to-face interviews, do your pretesting under the conditions you will experience when the survey is underway for real. If respondents are going to come to your office, then pretest the instrument in your office. If you are going to respondents' homes, then go to their homes for the pretest (Box 9.5).

Box 9.5 Cognitive interviewing

Use **cognitive testing** in pretesting questions (Willis 2005; Willis and Miller 2011). This is shorthand for learning what respondents understand about each question in a survey and what they're thinking as they decide how to answer each question. In **thinkaloud interviews**, people think out loud as they decide on how to answer each question in a survey. There are three alternative outcomes with the thinkaloud technique: (1) people understand the question just as you intended them to; (2) people understand the question very well, but not the way you intended them to; and (3) people don't understand the question at all.

Don Dillman and his colleagues at the Washington State University survey research center begin thinkaloud interviews with two questions: (1) How many residences have you lived in since you were born? (2) How many windows are in your home? On the first question, some people think of cities where they've lived, while others try to think of individual residences. On the second, questions come up, like: "Is a sliding glass door a window?" These questions help respondents understand what the interview is really about: learning where the ambiguities are in questions (Dillman et al. 2009b:221–23).

Use cognitive testing when you want to make sure that your questions are culturally appropriate. Edwards et al. (2005) used the method to pretest a 28-question survey on the use of condoms by women sex workers in Mombassa, Kenya. The result was a survey with culturally appropriate vocabulary for various types of sex clients (**Further Reading:** thinkaloud and cognitive interviews).

Never use any of the respondents in a pretest for the main survey. If you are working with a small group of people, where each respondent is precious (and you don't want to use up any of them on a pretest), take the survey instrument on the road, as far away as you can get, and pretest it there. This will also prevent the pretest respondents in a small community from gossiping about the survey before it actually gets underway. A "small community," by the way, can be "the 27 students from Taiwan at your university" or the eight firefighters in a small town.

If you have a team of face-to-face interviewers, make sure they all take part in the pretest—and be sure to do some of the pretesting yourself. After the pretests, bring the interviewers together for a discussion on how to improve the survey instrument. Ask them if people found some questions hard to answer—or even refused to answer. Ask them if they would change the wording of any of the questions. Check all this yourself by watching a couple of interviews done by people on your team and note when informants ask questions and how the interviewers respond. That way, you can train interviewers to respond in the same way to questions from informants.

As you conduct the actual survey, ask people to tell you what they think of the study and of the interview they've just been through. At the end of the study, bring all the interviewers back together for an evaluation of the project. If it is wise to learn from mistakes, then the first thing to do is find out what the mistakes are. If you give them a chance, your respondents and your interviewers will tell you.

TRANSLATION AND BACK TRANSLATION

If you are trying to write good survey questions in a language other than your own, the best practice is the method of **back translation** (Brislin 1970; Werner and Campbell 1970). First, write any questionnaire in *your* native language. Then have the questionnaire translated by a bilingual person who is a native speaker of the language you a working in. Work closely with the translator, so that she or he can fully understand the subtleties you want to convey in your questionnaire items.

Next, ask another bilingual person, a native speaker of *your* language, to translate the questionnaire back into that language. This back translation should be almost identical to the original questionnaire you wrote. If it isn't, then something was lost in one of the two translations. You'd better find out which one it was and correct the problem.

Beck and Gable (2000) developed a scale for screening postpartum women for depression and then translated the scale into Spanish (Beck and Gable 2003). One item on the original scale was "I felt like my emotions were on a roller coaster." The first translator offered two options for this: "Sentí un sube y baja emocional" and "Sentí un desequilibrio emocional." The second translator translated these as "I felt like my emotions were up and down" and "I felt emotional instability" (Beck and Gable 2003:69). Not exactly the same feeling as "I felt like my emotions were on a roller coaster," but close. Do you go with one of the two Spanish translations offered? Which one? Or do you keep looking for something better in Spanish?" The answer is that you sit down with both translators, talk it through, and come to a consensus.

On-the-Fly Translation

For all its rough edges, on-the-fly translation is probably just fine for a lot of research. Since 1984, the Demographic and Health Survey (DHS) has been conducted in 75 countries across the developing world to provide data on reproductive health. Each survey is meticulously translated into local (not just national) languages.

In Kenya, for example, the DHS is produced in ten local languages, as well as in English and Swahili. Interviewers are assigned to regions where their native language is dominant. There is always some population mixing, so interviewers get a chunk of survey materials in their own language as well as a chunk in Swahili, the national language. The problem is, lots of people don't speak Swahili. So, when a Luo interviewer runs out of interviews in Luo and has to interview a Luo speaker who doesn't speak Swahili, she has to translate the questions, from a Swahili interview, on the fly. This on-the-fly translation happened in 23% of the 7,480 interviews in the 1998 DHS. Weinreb and Sana (2009) found that this made no statistical difference in the univariate data for 22 out of 24 variables in the survey, from household characteristics to reports about use of contraceptives.

Back Translation of Qualitative Data

You can use back translation to check the content of open-ended interviews, but be warned: This is tough work. Daniel Reboussin (1995) interviewed Diola women who had come from southwestern Senegal to Dakar in search of work. All the women used French at work, but they preferred Diola for interviews. Reboussin, who speaks French, spoke very little Diola, so he worked with an interpreter—a man named Antoine Badji—to develop an interview schedule in French, which Badji translated into Diola.

During the interviews, Badji asked questions in Diola and Reboussin audiotaped the responses. After each interview, Badji translated each tape (orally) into French. Reboussin transcribed the French translations, translating into English as he went.

Then he read his English transcriptions *back* to Badji, translating (orally) into French as he read. That way, Badji could confirm or disconfirm Reboussin's understanding of Badji's French rendering of the tapes.

As I said, this was tough work. It took Reboussin and Badji 17 weeks to conduct 30 interviews and get them all down into English.

Translations and the Delphi Technique

Back translation is widely used to produce multiple versions of standardized scales, but another method, called the Delphi technique, also works well. The Ennis Value Orientation Inventory was developed by Catherine Ennis and her coworkers (1990) to assess the goals of physical education teachers. Teachers who are oriented toward self-actualization, for example, argue that personal growth and the development of self-esteem are the real goals of sports in the curriculum. By contrast, teachers who are highly oriented toward social-responsibility think that students should learn to align their own needs with those of the larger group and that sports in the curriculum can help students achieve this goal. Ennis developed her inventory for use in the United States.

Chen et al. (1997) wanted to use the scale to compare the value orientation of physical education teachers in the United States and China. First, they translated the 90-item instrument into Mandarin Chinese. (There are eight major Chinese languages, but Mandarin is the lingua franca for the nation and all educated people speak and write Mandarin.) Next, they sent the English and Chinese versions of the instrument to a panel of eight experts. All eight had completed their university education and their professional training in physical education in China. All eight were also either teaching physical education at universities in the United States (and had

doctorates) or were completing their doctoral studies in the United States. These were, then, experts in the field of study (physical education) who could judge the adequacy of the Chinese translation *from* English *into* Chinese.

Each member of the panel inspected each of the 90 items on the two versions of the inventory. They rated each item on a scale of 1–5 for consistency between the English and the Chinese. Giving an item a 5 meant that they thought the Chinese and English were "highly consistent," while giving an item a 1 meant they thought the items were "inconsistent."

Panelists wrote comments and suggestions right on the rating sheet about any items they thought needed work. Then they sent the package back to Ennis and Chen. If the mean score for an item was below 4.00 (near the top of the five-point consistency scale), Ennis and Chen incorporated the panelists' suggestions and rewrote the Chinese version of the item. (They left the English version alone since that scale had already been validated.) Then they sent the package back to the panelists for another round.

The process continued for four rounds until every one of the 90 items had a consistency score of at least 4.00. Now *that's* a translation (**Further Reading:** translation and back translation).

THE RESPONSE RATE PROBLEM

Mailed questionnaires can be very effective, but there is one problem with them that all survey researchers watch for: getting enough of them back. In 1936, the *Literary Digest* sent out 10 million straw poll ballots in an attempt to predict the winner of the presidential election. They got back 2.3 million ballots and predicted Alf Landon over Franklin Delano Roosevelt in a landslide. Roosevelt got 61% of the vote.

Now, you'd think that 2.3 million ballots would be enough for anyone, but two things caused the *Digest* debacle. First, they selected their sample from automobile registries and telephone books. In 1936, this favored richer people who were more likely to be Republican.

Second, the 2.3 million ballots were only 23% of the 10 million sent out. The low response rate biased the results in favor of the Republican challenger since those who didn't respond tended to be poorer and less inclined to participate in surveys (Squire 1988) (Box 9.6).

Box 9.6 An example of nonresponse bias

Table 9.1 is from Rosnow and Rosenthal's (1997) analysis of data published by William Cochran in 1977 (p. 360). In Cochran's study, 3,116 fruit growers were sent questionnaires (about their farming practices), and one of the questions was about how many trees they owned. By luck, the real number of trees owned by each grower was known from other data.

The survey had three waves. By the end of the third wave, 1,839 (59%) of the 3,116 growers had not responded. Each successive wave produced responses from growers who owned fewer and fewer trees. The 59% of the growers who never responded had 290 trees each, compared to 456 trees for the growers who responded in the first wave. The 1,277 respondents had an average of 385 trees each—six trees more than the actual average of 329 trees for the 3,116 growers in the population.

We know, then, that the enthusiastic respondents in the first wave had a lot more trees than others who responded in the second and third waves. What about their answers to all the socioeconomic and opinion questions on the survey? Were those answers somehow affected by the number of trees they had? We don't know, and that's the problem.

Table 9.1 An Example of Nonresponse Bias in Surveys

	First Wave	Second Wave	Third Wave	Total Non-respondents	Total Population
Number of respondents	300	543	434	1,839	3,116
Proportion of the population	.10	.17	.14	.59	1.00
Mean number of trees per respondent	456	382	340	290	329

Source: R. L. Rosnow and R. Rosenthal, *People Studying People. Artifacts and Ethics in Behavioral Research*, p. 92, 1997, Freeman.

How to Adjust for Nonresponse

In 1991, the American Anthropological Association sent questionnaires to a sample of 1,229 members. The sample was stratified into several cohorts who had received their Ph.D. degrees beginning in 1971–1972 and ending in 1989–1990. The 1989–1990 cohort comprised 306 then-recent Ph.D.s. The idea was to find out what kinds of jobs those anthropologists had.

The AAA got back 840 completed questionnaires, or 68% of the 1,229, and 41% of those responding from the 1989–1990 cohort said they had academic jobs (American Anthropological

Association 1991). The AAA didn't report the response rate by cohort, but suppose that 68% of the 1989–1990 cohort—the same percentage as applies to the overall survey—sent back their questionnaires. That's 208 out of 306 responses. The 41% who said they had academic jobs would be 85 of the 208 respondents; the other 123 had nonacademic jobs.

Suppose that everyone who didn't respond (32%, or 98 out of 306) got nonacademic jobs. (Maybe that's why they didn't bother to respond.) In that case, 98 + 123 = 221 out of the 306 people in the cohort, or 72% got nonacademic jobs that year—not the 59% (100% – 41%) as reported in the survey.

It's unlikely that *all* the nonresponders were in nonacademic jobs. To handle the problem of nonresponse, the AAA might have run down a random grab of 10 of the nonresponders and interviewed them by telephone. Suppose that seven said they had nonacademic jobs. You'll recall from Chapter 6 on sampling theory that the formula for determining the 95% confidence limits of a point estimator is:

$$P(\text{the true proportion}) = \pm 1.96\sqrt{PQ/n}$$

formula 9.1

which means that

$$1.96\sqrt{(.7)(.3)/10} = 0.28$$

The probable answer for the 10 holdouts is 0.70±0.28, which means that somewhere between 42% and 98% of the 98 nonresponders from the 1989–1990 cohort probably had nonacademic jobs. All together, between

$$123 + (.42 \times 98) = 164$$

and

$$123 + (.98 \times 98) = 219$$

of the 306 people in the cohort, or 54% to 72% probably had nonacademic jobs.

Low response rate can be a disaster. People who are quick to fill out and return mailed questionnaires tend to have higher incomes and consequently tend to be more educated than people who respond later. Any dependent variables that co-vary with income and education, then, will be seriously distorted if you get back only 50% of your questionnaires. And what's worse, there is no accurate way to measure nonresponse bias. With a lot of nonresponse, all you know is that you've got bias but you don't know how to take it into account.

IMPROVING RESPONSE RATES: DILLMAN'S TOTAL DESIGN METHOD

A lot of research has been done on increasing response rates to questionnaires. Don Dillman has synthesized the research on maximizing return rates and has developed what he calls the "Total Design Method" for mail, telephone and web-based surveying (Dillman 1978; Dillman et al. 2009b). For convenience and cost effectiveness, mailed surveys are still an excellent way to collect a lot of data on a representative sample of respondents. And if you're studying hard-to-get people (like physicians or university deans), mailed surveys are the best way to go.

Professional mailed surveys on consumer behavior and political attitudes done in the United States, following Dillman's method, typically achieve a return rate of 50% to 70% (Dillman et al. 2009b:236) or higher. Converse et al. (2008) got a remarkable 82% response rate from 1500 pre-K through grade 12 teachers in Ohio and South Carolina as part of a National Board Certification evaluation program.

Dillman's method works across the world. In Spain, de Rada (2001) had a response rate of 61% in a survey of rural households about consumer habits. Jussaume and Yamdada (1990) achieved a response rate of 56% in Kobe, Japan, on a survey of food consumption, and in the Netherlands, Nederhof (1985) conducted a mail survey on attitudes toward suicide and achieved a 65% response rate. Pretty impressive.

Dillman's method is very subtle and has many well-tested components. Full instructions are in Dillman's book (Dillman et al. 2009b), but here is an overview of the main steps.

Steps in Dillman's Method

1. Professionalism: Mailed questionnaires must look thoroughly professional. Jaded, hard-bitten, oversurveyed people simply don't respond to amateurish work. Print questionnaires in booklets on standard-size paper: 8.5″ × 11″ in the United States and slightly longer A4 paper in the rest of the world. Dillman recommends using white paper. Fox et al. (1988) reported good results with light green paper, but Beebe et al. (2007), in a controlled field test, found that white paper and smaller booklet size had the best response rate.

You must be thinking: "Controlled tests of *paper color*?" Absolutely. It's because social scientists have done their homework on these little things that a response rate of over 70% is achievable—provided you're willing to spend the time and money it takes to look after all the little things. Read on and you'll see how small-but-important those "little things" are.

2. Front and back covers: Don't put any questions on either the front or back covers of the booklet. The front cover should contain a title that provokes the respondent's interest, the name and address of the survey's sponsor, and some kind of eye-catching graphic design or photo. By provoking interest, I don't mean threatening. A title like "The Greenville Air Quality Survey" is fine. "Polluted Air Is Killing Us" isn't.

Be careful in the use of photos—they contain an enormous amount of information, and you never know how respondents will interpret the information. If a respondent thinks a photo contains an editorial message (for or against some pet political position), then the survey booklet goes straight into the trash. If you don't have an appropriate photo, then use a graphic design.

The back cover should have eye-catching photos or designs, and a *brief* note thanking the respondent and inviting open-ended comments about the questionnaire. Nothing else.

3. Question order: Be sure that the first question is directly related to the topic of the study (as determined from the title on the front of the booklet); that it is interesting and easy to answer; and that it is nonthreatening. Once someone starts a questionnaire or an interview, they are likely to finish it. Introduce threatening questions well into the instrument, but don't cluster them all together.

Put general socioeconomic and demographic questions at the end of a questionnaire. These seemingly innocuous questions are threatening to many respondents who fear being identified (Sudman and Bradburn 1982). Once someone has filled out a questionnaire, they are unlikely to balk at stating their age, income, religion, occupation, etc.

4. Formatting: Mailed surveys have to look good and be easily readable or they get tossed out.

Never allow a question to break at the end of a page and continue on another page.

Use bolded letters for instructions to respondents and plain text questions themselves and line answers up vertically rather than horizontally, if possible.

Q26. During the past five years how much better or worse has Detroit become as a place to live?

_____ A lot better

_____ Somewhat better

_____ No change

_____ Somewhat worse

_____ A lot worse

_____ Not sure

5. Length: Keep mailed questionnaires down to 12 pages, with no more than 125 questions—that's three sheets of $11'' \times 17''$ folded in half and printed on both sides. Beyond that, response rates drop (Dillman 1978).

It is tempting to save printing and mailing costs and to try to get more questions into a few pages by reducing the amount of white space in a self-administered questionnaire. Don't do it. Respondents are never fooled into thinking that a thin-but-crowded questionnaire is anything other than what it seems to be: a long questionnaire that has been forced into fewer pages and is going to be hard to work through.

Use lots of open space in building schedules for personal interviews, too. Artificially short, crowded instruments only result in interviewers missing items and possibly in annoying respondents (imagine yourself sitting for 15 minutes in an interview before the interviewer flips the first page of an interview schedule).

6. The cover letter: A one-page cover letter should explain, in the briefest possible terms, the nature of the study, how the respondent was selected, who should fill out the questionnaire (the respondent or the members of the household), who is funding the survey, and why it is important for the respondent to send back the questionnaire. ("Your response to this questionnaire is very important. We need your response because....")

The one thing that increases response rate more than any other is university sponsorship (Fox et al. 1988). University sponsorship, though, is not enough. If you want a response rate that is not subject to bias, be sure to address the cover letter directly and personally to the respondent—no "Dear Respondent" allowed, unless you only have addresses, without names—and sign it using a blue ballpoint pen. Ballpoints make an indentation that

respondents can see—yes, some people do hold those letters up to the light to check. This marks the letter as having been individually signed. In Japan, Jussaume and Yamada (1990) signed all their letters with an *inkan*, or personal seal, and they wrote the address by hand on the envelope to show that they were serious.

The cover letter must guarantee confidentiality and must explain the presence of an identification number (if there is one) on the questionnaire. Some survey topics are so sensitive that respondents will balk at seeing an identification number on the questionnaire, even if you guarantee anonymity. In this case, Fowler (1984) recommends eliminating the identification number (thus making the questionnaire truly anonymous) and telling the respondents that they simply cannot be identified.

If you do this, enclose a printed postcard with the respondent's name on it and ask the respondent to mail back the postcard *separately* from the questionnaire. Explain that this will notify you that the respondent has sent in the questionnaire so that you won't have to send the respondent any reminders later on. Fowler (1984) found that people hardly ever send back the postcard without also sending back the questionnaire.

7. Packaging: Package the questionnaire, cover letter, and reply envelope and postcard in another envelope for mailing to the respondent. Print the respondent's name and address on the mailing envelope. Use first-class postage on the mailing envelope and on the reply envelope. Some people respond better to real stamps, especially bright commemorative stamps, than to metered—even first-class metered—postage (Hensley 1974).

8. Incentives: What about incentives to complete a survey? Here, the research is unambiguous: Money talks and a prepaid incentive works better than a promise of one (Church 1993; Dillman et al. 2009a:275; Warriner

et al. 1996). Mizes et al. (1984) found that offering respondents $1 to complete and return a questionnaire resulted in significantly increased returns, but offering respondents $5 did not produce a sufficiently greater return to warrant using this tactic. In 1984, $5 was close to the value of many respondents' time for filling out a questionnaire. This makes responding to a survey more like a strictly economic exchange and, as Dillman pointed out, makes it easier for people to turn down (1978:16).

In other words, despite inflation (the $5 in 1984 would be about $12 now) there is a Goldilocks solution to the problem of how much money to send people as an incentive to fill out and return a survey. If you send people too much money or too little, they may throw the survey away. If you send them just the right amount, they are likely to fill out the survey and return it. Today, except for special populations (like physicians) incentives between $1 and $5 are the norm in the United States. (On increasing response rates from physicians, see Field et al. 2002 and Edwards et al. 2009.)

9. **Contact and follow-up:** This is crucial. Send a letter, by first-class mail, to each respondent explaining the survey and informing the respondent that a questionnaire will be coming along soon. You can send people an e-mail message to tell them that a letter is coming, or you can follow up with an e-mail to ask if people have questions, but don't skimp on sending real invitation letters through the mail (Converse et al. 2008).

The pre-notice letter should arrive just a few days to a week before the actual survey shows up. A postcard thank-you/reminder to all potential respondents should arrive a week after sending out the questionnaire. The card thanks the recipient if they've already sent the survey back (and it's crossing the postcard in the mail) and reminds them to fill out the survey if they haven't yet done so.

Don't wait until the response rate drops before sending out reminders. Some people hold onto a questionnaire for a while before deciding to fill it out or throw it away. A reminder after one week stimulates response among this segment of respondents (Dillman et al. 2009b:250).

Send a second cover letter and questionnaire to everyone who has not responded three weeks later and include another copy of the questionnaire. There is no incentive sent with this packet and the tone of the letter is more urgent. For example: "We really need everyone's cooperation to make sure that the result represents people in your area." Finally, four or five weeks after the postcard, send another cover letter and copy of the questionnaire, but this time send it by courier (Fedex, UPS) or special delivery from the post office.

Does All This Really Make a Difference?

Thurman et al. (1993) used Dillman's method in a survey of attitudes and behavior of people who admit to drunk driving. They sent out questionnaires to a national sample of 1,310 and got back 765, or 58%. Not bad for a first pass, since you can usually expect about 25% to 30% from the first wave. Unfortunately, for lack of time and money, Thurman et al. couldn't follow through with all the extra mailings.

Of the 765 respondents, 237 said they were nondrinkers. This left 525 eligible questionnaires for analysis. Of the 525 respondents who said they were consumers of alcohol, 133 admitted driving while drunk in the past year. Those 133 respondents provided data of intrinsic interest, but the 765 people who responded from the nationally representative sample of 1,310 may be a biased sample on which to base any generalizations about people who drive drunk. I say "may be" a biased sample because there is no way to tell. And that's the problem.

The bottom line: The last interview you get in any survey—whether you're sending out questionnaires doing a survey by phone, or face-to-face, or on the web,—is always the most costly and it's almost always worth it. If you really care about representative data, you won't think of all the chasing around you have to do for the last interviews in a set as a nuisance but as a necessary expense of data collection. And you'll prepare for it in advance by establishing a realistic budget of both time and money (**Further Reading:** response rates).

CROSS-SECTIONAL AND LONGITUDINAL STUDIES

Most surveys are cross-sectional. The idea is to measure some variables at a single time. People's attitudes and reported behaviors change over time, however, and you never know if a single sample is truly representative of the population. Many surveys are conducted again and again to monitor changes and to ensure against picking a bad sample. Multiple cross-sectional polls use a longitudinal design. The daily—even hourly—tracking polls in U.S. presidential elections are an extreme example, but in many industrialized countries some questions have been asked of representative samples for many years.

The Gallup Poll, for example, has been asking Americans for about 70 years to list "the most important problem facing this country today." The data track the concerns of Americans about unemployment, the quality of education, drugs, street crime, the federal deficit, taxes, health care costs, poverty, racism, AIDS, abortion. . . . There are not many surprises in the data (people in the United States are more worried about the economy in recessions, less worried when the economy is clicking along) but data from the Gallup Poll, and others like it, are important because they were collected with the same instrument. People were asked the same question again and again over the years. After several generations of effort, longitudinal survey data like these have become a treasured resource in highly industrialized nations (Box 9.7).

Box 9.7 Design all research as if it were longitudinal

Longitudinal studies often start out as cross-sectional ones. As the data pile up over time, the value of the project increases. Suppose you study how married women feel about the way their husbands pitch in (or don't) with housework and parenting. Even if you study just 30 women, and even if the data are narratives, as long as you ask everyone the same question, you're doing a survey. If you ask another group of 30 women the same questions five or 10 years later, the value of the data you first collected goes way, way up because now you can make systematic comparisons across time, as well as across people. All cross-sectional studies, from term projects to senior theses, to Master's and Ph.D. theses, should be designed as if they were the start of a lifetime of research. You never know.

Panel Studies

If the results from two successive samples are very different, you don't know if it's because people's attitudes or reported behaviors have changed, or the two samples are very different, or both. The powerful panel design deals with this. In a panel study, you *interview the same people* again and again. This makes panel studies like experiments: Participants are tracked for their exposure or lack of exposure to a series of interventions in the real world.

To understand this feature of panel studies, consider the work of Jennings and his colleagues (Jennings 1987; Jennings and Markus 1984; Jennings et al. 2005). In 1965, they began what became a 32-year panel study of American high school seniors. In the first wave of the Youth Parent Socialization Panel Study (YPSPS), the researchers surveyed a nationally representative sample of 1,669 students and had 1,652 responses—a stunning 99% response rate.

In 1972, when the panelists were 25 years old, 1,348 (81%) of them were reinterviewed. In 1982, when they were 35 years old, 1,135 of them (68% of the original 1,669) were interviewed a third time. And in 1997, when the panel was 50 years old, 965 of them (55%) were interviewed a fourth time. All data from all four waves of this study are deposited with the Inter-University Consortium for Political and Social Research at the University of Michigan (Jennings et al. 2005). (The ICPSR maintains and distributes a huge archive of files from social research projects conducted all over the world.)

Many scholars have studied these data to understand, for example, how coming of age during the Civil Rights movement and the anti–Vietnam War movement affected the students' political orientation (Jennings 1987) or their participation in religion (Sherkat 1998) or their attitudes toward abortion (Killian and Wilcox 2008) as they matured.

Panel data are also useful for unmasking those mischievous, spurious correlations I mentioned in Chapter 2. Most studies on the relation between crime and housing, for example, conclude that increasing crime causes people to move out of a neighborhood. But most studies of this topic are cross-sectional. Hipp (2010), studied 2,534 census tracts (as a proxy for neighborhoods) in 13 cities over 10 years and found that, in many cases, people moved out as a consequence of other structural changes and this resulted in more crime.

It has been found repeatedly that the children of people who move around a lot are more likely to wind up in the juvenile justice system. In 1997, the National Longitudinal Survey of Youth (NLSY) built a nationally representative panel of 8,984 adolescents who were between 12 and 16 years old at the time. The panel members were interviewed every year, through 2003 and 7,755 of them (86%) were in the final wave. Gasper et al. (2010) looked at all of these data, across time, and found that yes, kids who move a lot are more likely to get into trouble with the law. But those kids were also more likely to come from poor families where the parents have little education. By the time those kids turned 12, they were already doing badly in school, which, as Gasper et al. point out (p. 473) put them at risk for delinquency.

Panel studies can be done quickly—even within a single year. Amber Wutich (2009) studied the effects of water scarcity on social interaction in an urban squatter settlement in Cochabamba, Bolivia. After a couple of months of in-depth interviewing, she and several assistants began a five-wave panel study of random sample of 72 (out of 415) households. They interviewed people in each household every two months for 10 months and found that there was significant variation in the size of personal network across the five waves.

As predicted by theory, just as the dry season began, people tried harder to mobilize their networks to get more water. Then, as the dry season advanced, people withdrew from their networks. They knew it was useless and couldn't afford the risk that they'd have to reciprocate if they did score some water. Then, as the dry season ended, people went back to their old social interaction pattern.

Attrition

People drop out between successive waves of panel surveys. If this happens, and the results of successive waves are very different, you can't tell if it's because of: (1) the special character of the drop out population; (2) real changes in the variables you're studying; or (3) both. For example, if dropouts tend to be male or poor, your results in successive waves will overrepresent the experiences of those who are female or affluent. If you run a panel study, consult a statistician about how to test for the effects of attrition.

Respondent mortality is not always a problem. Roger Trent and I did a panel study of riders on the Morgantown, West Virginia's "People Mover," an automated transport system that was meant to be a kind of horizontal elevator. You get on a little railway car (they carry only eight seated and 12 standing passengers), push a button, and the car takes you to your stop—a block away or eight miles across town. The system was brought on line a piece at a time between 1975 and 1980. Trent and I were tracking public support as the system went more places and became more useful (Trent and Bernard 1985). We established a panel of 216 potential users of the system when the system opened in 1975 and reinterviewed the members of that panel in 1976 and 1980 as more and more pieces of the system were added.

All 216 original members of the panel were available during the second wave, and 189 were available for the third wave of the survey. Note, though, that people who were unavailable had moved out of Morgantown and were no longer potential users of the system. What counted in this case was maintaining a panel large enough to represent the attitudes of people in Morgantown about the People Mover system. The respondents who stayed in the panel still represented the people whose experiences we hoped to learn about (**Further Reading:** panel studies).

SOME SPECIALIZED SURVEY METHODS

Factorial Surveys

In a factorial survey (Rossi and Berk 1997; Rossi and Nock 1982), people are presented with vignettes that describe hypothetical social situations and are asked for their judgments about those situations. The General Social Survey (http://www.norc.org/GSS+Website/) is a face-to-face survey of adults in the United States. From 1972 to 1993, it was an annual survey of 1,500 people. Since 1994, it is run every other year on two samples of 1,500 people). Figure 9.5 shows a vignette that was in the 1992 GSS.

There are 10 variables in this vignette (number of children, marital status of the mother, how much savings the family has, the total income of the family, etc.), with 1,036,800 possible combinations. That seems just about right to me. The calculus for any individual's opinion about how much money to award the deserving poor on welfare is really that complicated. Now, each of the 1,500 respondents in the GSS saw seven vignettes each, so the survey captured:

(1,500 people) (7 vignettes) (10 variables)
= 105,000

combinations, or a sample of about 10% of all the factors that probably go into people's opinion on this issue.

The results? Respondents awarded people who were looking for work a lot more than they awarded people who weren't looking for work. But mothers only got an extra $6 per week for seeking work, while fathers got over $12. And if mothers were unemployed because they wouldn't take minimum-wage jobs, they had their allotments reduced by $20 per week, on average, compared to what people were

Figure 9.5 An Example of a Vignette From a Factorial Survey

This family has four children, the youngest is 6 months old, living with their mother. The mother is divorced. The mother has a college degree and is unemployed and not looking for work because she has no ready means of transportation. The father has remarried and is permanently disabled. The family is likely to face financial difficulties for a couple of years. Her parents cannot afford to help out financially. The family has $1,000 in savings. All in all, the family's total income from other sources is $100 per week.

What should this family's weekly income be? Include both the money already available from sources other than the government, and any public assistance support you think this family should get.

Amount already received   Average U.S.
by this family   family income

```
          X                                             X
|    |    |    |    |    |    |    |    |    |    |    |    |
0    50  100  150  200  250  300  350  400  450  500  550  600
```

Source: J. A. Will, "The Dimensions of Poverty: Public Perceptions of the Deserving Poor." *Social Science Research,* 22:312–32, p. 322, 1993.

willing to give mothers who were working full time. (For comparison, it took about $270 in 2010 to buy what $100 bought in 1986.)

J. L. Miller et al. (1991) used the factorial survey method to measure perceptions of appropriate prison sentences for felons who had been convicted of 50 typical crimes, ranging from petty theft to murder. Figure 9.6 shows one of the vignettes:

The independent variables in this study combined to form 61,025 vignettes, but each of the 774 respondents in the survey only needed to see

Figure 9.6 Vignette on Punishment From Miller et al.

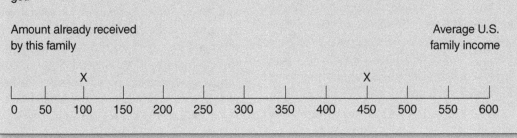

Victor J, a White, employed sewing-machine operator, was convicted of intentionally shooting his friend, Laura L., a housewife. The victim required two weeks hospitalization.

In the last five years, the offender has not been arrested or convicted. The offender claims to have been taking drugs at the time.

Victor J. was sentenced to 10 years in prison.

The sentence given was . . .

```
|---|---|---|---|---|---|---|---|---|---|---|---|---|---|---|---|---|---|---|---|---|---|---|
Much                                                                    Much
Too                                                                     Too
Low           Low              About Right            High             High
```

Source: J. L. Miller et al., "Felony Punishments: A Factorial Survey of Perceived Justice in Criminal Sentencing," *Journal of Criminal Law and Criminology* 82:396–422, p. 402, 1991. Reprinted by special permission of Northwestern University School of Law, *The Journal of Criminal Law and Criminology.*

50 randomly selected vignettes. It turns out that people's perception of the seriousness of any given crime (and what the appropriate punishment should be) depends only partly on the consequences of the crime itself. It also depends partly on characteristics of the victim, partly on characteristics of the criminal, and partly on characteristics of the respondent (like whether the respondent had been the victim of a crime).

The factorial survey combines the validity of randomized experiments with the reliability of survey research (**Further Reading:** factorial surveys and vignettes).

Time Budgets and Diaries

Time budget surveys have been done all over the world to track how ordinary human beings spend most of their days (Szalai 1972). The idea is to learn about the sequence, duration, and frequency of behaviors and about the contexts in which behaviors take place. Some researchers ask respondents to keep diaries; others conduct "yesterday interviews," in which respondents are asked to go over the last 24 hours and talk about everything they did. Some researchers combine these methods, collecting diaries from respondents and then following up with a personal interview.

Susan Shaw (1992) studied 46 middle- and working-class couples who had children living at home. All the fathers were employed full time; among the mothers, 12 were employed full time, nine were employed part time, and 25 were full-time homemakers. Both parents kept time diaries for one day during the week and for one day on a weekend. Then Shaw interviewed the parents separately for one to two hours in their homes. For each activity that they had mentioned, parents were asked if they considered the activity to be work or leisure and why.

Shaw calculated the amount of time that each parent reported spending with their children—playing with them, reading to them, and so on. The rather dramatic results are in Table 9.2. The husbands of the 12 women who were employed full time spent an average of 71 minutes per day with their children. The husbands of the 25 full-time homemakers spent just 23 minutes a day with their children. The 12 full-time employed mothers reported spending 97 minutes of each day, on average, with their children—more than the 71 minutes spent by their husbands with the children, but a lot less than the 241 minutes per day that full-time homemakers reported spending with *their* children. For these middle- and working-class families in eastern Canada, at least, fathers spend a lot more time with their children when their wives work full time. It would be very interesting to see if this finding holds up in other places.

| Table 9.2 | Average Amount of Time Fathers and Mothers Report Spending With Children, by the Mother's Employment Status |

Mother's employment status	N	Time with children per day (in minutes)	
		Mothers	Fathers
Employed full-time	12	97	71
Employed part-time	9	144	52
Full-time homemaker	25	241	23
Total	46		

Source: "Dereifying Family Leisure: An Examination of Women's and Men's Everyday Experiences and Perceptions of Family Time" by S. Shaw. 1992. *Leisure Sciences*, p. 279. Reproduced by permission or Taylor and Francis.

Like all instruments for collecting self-reports about behavior, time budgets and diaries are subject to demand characteristics and other sources of inaccuracy. Some data reported by Niemi (1993) from studies in Finland give us a taste of the problem. In one study, respondents were asked: How many hours did you work at your main work last week, possible overtime included? (Domestic work is not included in work time.) Respondents also kept diaries for two days in which they recorded all their activities at 10-minute intervals.

These data were scaled up to reflect annual rates. (To scale up the data for one week to a year, you multiply results by 52; to scale up data from one day to a year, you multiply each data point by 365. That way, you can compare the results from a week's worth of survey data to two days' worth of diary data.)

The results? Respondents recorded in their diaries working 2.4% fewer hours per week than they reported in the survey. Men reported half of 1% more hours; women reported 4.8% more. Men in agriculture reported 25% more work time than they recorded, and women in agriculture reported 43% more work time.

In a second study, Niemi compared time diary data with data from this question: How often do you engage in physical exercise during the summer/wintertime? (This included outdoor recreation, walking and bicycling, organized sports, hunting or fishing or collecting mushrooms—a broad swath of activities.)

Men reported about 7.4% more minutes per day of physical exercise than they recorded in their diaries. Women reported about 50% more. In fact, women reported exercising about 19% more minutes per day than men reported, but women recorded about 17% fewer minutes per day of physical exercise than men did.

Finally, in a third study, respondents were asked: How many times do you think you have visited the library during the past six months? The same respondents kept daily diaries and the two kinds of data were converted to annual rates.

In this case, men and women alike report over 70% more library visits than they record in their diaries.

The discrepancies, as I pointed out in Chapter 8, can be due to many things. Women in Finland may understand that question about physical exercise differently than men do and may be including a lot more of their daily activities in that category than men do. The data from the question about library visits are hardly shocking: People inflate their association with socially desirable activities to make themselves look good. And people in some occupations (like managerial positions) may be subtly trained to more accurately estimate their work time than are people in other occupations (like agriculture).

Michaelson (1985) showed that giving people a checklist increased the number of child-care behaviors they reported in "yesterday interviews." Diaries and time-budget interviews, particularly with the aid of checklists, appear to be more accurate than 24-hour recall of activities. A lot of work remains to be done on testing the accuracy of activity diaries against data from direct observation. In Chapter 14, we'll look at methods for direct observation and measurement of behavior (**Further Reading:** time budgets and diaries).

Event-History Calendar

The event-history calendar (EHC) method—also called a life history calendar or a life event calendar, or just a timeline—was developed by Balán et al. in 1969 and has since evolved into a widely used method for capturing the details of life histories. When we study the trajectory of people's lives, we want as much information as possible about transitional events—changing jobs, changing partners, migrating to a new place, changing schools, having children, getting sick, and so on. And we want more than just the outline ("I changed jobs that year") but lots of detail. ("I was really unhappy that year because my son told he wasn't going to college and was joining the Army, and so the demands of that new job kind of took my mind away from all that.")

Balán's idea was to tie series of life events to one another to help people remember those life history details. He did this systematically by setting up a grid, shown in Figure 9.7. You can set up a grid like the one in Figure 9.7 on a computer and work cooperatively with an informant on filling it all in. The grid will prompt you to ask about all the pieces and the informant will suggest new details to fill in gaps as they become apparent.

For each year in an informant's life, you would record any landmarks ("the year of my first marriage," "when I learned that my son had been killed in Iraq," "we survived Hurricane Katrina"). The landmarks then become a cueing device for eliciting specific information. So you might ask, "What job were you in when you were robbed?" or "Think about the time when you were changing jobs from Wal-Mart to K-Mart. Were you sick at all during that time?" or "How long had you lived in that particular house when your son decided to join the Army?"

Harris and Parisi (2007) interviewed 60 women in rural Mississippi about those women's decisions to go on and off welfare between October 1996 and December 2003. Instead of years, Harris and Parisi used the 87 one-month intervals during the reference time of their study and used EHC to prompt women for life changes that often precipitate the decision to go on welfare—the birth of a child, the loss of a job, dropping out of school, illness, or losing child support from a former partner, for example.

Morris and Slocum (2010) used an EHC in their interviews with 351 incarcerated women in Baltimore. They used the 35 months as their calendar period and landmarks like arrests, birthdays, anniversaries, and deaths of loved ones to prompt the women about employment, living location, intimate relationships, and brushes with violence.

Anthropologists use event calendars in societies where there are no written records. Leslie et al. (1999:375–78), for example, developed an event calendar for the Ngisonyoka section of the South Turkana pastoralists in northwestern Kenya. The Turkana name their seasons rather than their years. Based on many interviews between 1983 and 1984, Leslie et al. were able to build up a list of 143 major events associated with seasons between 1905 and 1992. Events include things like "no hump" in 1961 (it was so dry that the camels' humps shrank), "bulls" in 1942 (when their bulls were taken to pay a poll tax), and "rescue" in 1978 (when rains came). This painstaking work has since made it possible for many researchers to gather demographic and other life history data from the Ngisonyoka Turkana (**Further Reading**: event- and life-history calendars).

Randomized Response

The randomized response technique (RRT) is used in estimating the amount of some socially negative behavior in a population—things like shoplifting, extramarital sex, child abuse, being hospitalized for emotional problems, and so on. The technique was introduced by S. L. Warner in 1965 and is particularly well described by B. Williams (1978:73). It is a simple, fun, and interesting tool. Here's how it works.

First, you formulate two questions, A and B, that can be answered "yes" or "no." One question, A, is the question of interest (say, "Have you ever shoplifted?") The possible answers to this question (either "yes" or "no") do not have known probabilities of occurring. That is what you want to find out.

The other question, B, must be innocuous and the possible answers (again "yes" or "no") must have known probabilities of occurring. For example, if you ask someone to toss a fair coin and ask, "Did you toss a heads?" then the probability that they answer "yes" or "no" is

Figure 9.7 An Event History Calendar

		Migration History			Size					
Year	Age	Name of Place	State	Rural	Town	City		Educational History	Family History	Health
1940	10	San Isidro	Coahuila	x				primaria 5th grade		
41	11	"	"	"				primaria 6th grade		
42	12	Monterrey (colonia Lomas)	Nuevo Leon			x		commerce 1st grade		
43	13	"	"			"		commerce 2nd grade		
44	14	"	"			"		commerce 3rd grade		
45	15	Mexico City	Distrito Federal			"		not in school		
46	16	"	"			"		"		
47	17	"	"			"		"		
48	18	Monterrey (colonia Regina)	Nuevo Leon			"		"		
49	19	"	"			"			courtship	
1950	20	"	"			"		"		
51	21	(Colonia Modelo)	"			"		"	marriage	
52	22	"	"			"		"	first child born, male	
53	23	"	"			"		"		
54	24	"	"			"		"	second child born, female	
55	25	"	"			"		"	third child born, male	died first month
56	26	"	"			"		"	fourth child born, male	
57	27	"	"			"		"		
58	28	"	"			"			fifth child born, male	
59	29	"	"			"		"		

					Work History			
						Enterprise		
Year	Age	Name of the Occupation	Description of Duties	Position and Dependent Personnel	Type of Industry	No. of Persons Employed	Relatives	Income (in Pesos)
1940	10	farm worker	helps his father	family help	agriculture	3	yes	none
41	11	"	"	"	"	"	"	"
42	12	NOT	EMPLOYED					
43	13	"	"					
44	14	"	"					
45	15	messenger	office boy	employee 0	railroad office	350	no	300 monthly
46	16	"	"	"	"	"	"	"
47	17	"	"	"	"	"	"	"
48	18	UNEMPLOYED	FOR EIGHT	MONTHS				
49	19	clerk	types letters	employee 0	mattress factory	50	no	150 weekly
1950	20	"	"	"	"	"	"	"
51	21	"	"	"	"	"	"	180 weekly
52	22	purchasing agent	buys all materials	employee 2	"	70	"	250 weekly
53	23	"	"	"	"	"	"	"
54	24	owner of small factory	manager	employer 5	plastic toy factory	6	yes	800 monthly
55	25	"	"	"	"	"	"	"
56	26	"	"	"	"	"	"	"
57	27	"	"	"	"	"	"	"
58	28	"	"	employer 3	"	4	"	business loses about 1500 monthly
59	29	sales agent						

Source: Balán, J., H. L. Browning, E. Jelin, and L. Litzler. 1969. "A Computerized Approach to the Processing and Analysis of Life Histories Obtained in Sample Surveys." *Behavioral Science* 4:105–20.

50%. If the chances of being born in any given month were equal, then you could ask respondents: "Were you born in April, May, or June?" and the probability of getting a "yes" would be 25%. Unfortunately, births are seasonal, so the coin-toss question is preferable.

Let's assume you use the coin toss for question B. You ask someone to toss the coin and to note the result *without letting you see it*. Next, have them pick a card, from a deck of 10 cards, where each card is marked with a single integer from 1 to 10. The respondent *does not tell you what number he or she picked*, either. The genuine secrecy associated with this procedure makes people feel secure about answering question A (the sensitive question) truthfully.

Next, hand the respondent a card with the two questions, marked A and B, written out. Tell them that if they picked a number between one and four from the deck of 10 cards, they should answer question A. If they picked a number between five and 10, they should answer question B.

That's all there is to it. You now have the following: (1) each respondent knows they answered "yes" or "no" and which question they answered; and (2) you know *only* that a respondent said "yes" or "no" but not which question, A or B, was being answered.

If you run through this process with a sufficiently large representative sample of a population, and if people cooperate and answer all questions truthfully, then you can calculate the percentage of the population that answered "yes" to question A. Here's the formula:

$$P_{A \text{ or } B} = [(P_{A+} \times P_A) + (P_{B+} \times P_B)] \quad \textbf{formula 9.2}$$

The percentage of people who answer "yes" to *either* A or B = (the percentage of people who answer "yes" to question A) times (the percentage of times that question A is asked) plus (the percentage of people who answered "yes" to question B) times (the percentage of times question B is asked).

The only unknown in this equation is the percentage of people who answered "yes" to question A, the sensitive question. We know from our data the percentages of "yes" answers to *either* question. Suppose that 33% of all respondents said "yes" to *something*. Since respondents answered question A only if they chose a number from 1 to 4, then A was answered 40% of the time and B was answered 60% of the time. Whenever B was answered, there was a 50% chance of it being answered "yes" because that's the chance of getting a heads on the toss of a fair coin. The problem now reads:

$$.33 = A(.40) + .50(.60)$$

or

$$.33 = .40A + .30$$

which means that $A = 0.08$. That is, given the parameters specified in this experiment, if 33% of the sample says "yes" to either question, then 8% of the sample answered "yes" to question A.

There are two problems associated with the RRT. First, no matter what you say or do, some people will not believe that you can't identify them and will therefore not tell the truth. Bradburn, Sudman et al. (1979) report that 35% of known offenders would not admit to having been convicted of drunken driving in a randomized response survey. Second, like all survey techniques, RRT depends on large, representative samples. Because the technique is time consuming to administer, this makes getting large, representative samples difficult.

Still, the evidence is mounting that for some sensitive questions—Did you smoke dope in the last week? Have you ever bought a term paper? Have you stolen anything from your employer?—when you want the truth, the RRT is worth the effort.

Dalton et al. (1996) asked two groups of professional auctioneers six very sensitive questions about seriously illegal practices. I mean, these were *rough* questions, like: "Have you ever engaged in self-dealing without disclosure?" and "Have you ever engaged in the use of a phantom bid?" An example of self-dealing without disclosure would be getting your spouse or one of your employees to secretly bid on merchandise you wanted. Phantom bids are bids that the auctioneer acknowledges but that aren't real. You bid $50 for something; the auctioneer recognizes your bid and immediately signals that he has a bid of $60. You up your bid to $70. But the $60 bid was just a gimmick to get you to raise your bid.

One group ($n = 74$) was asked these questions straight out, in the usual way, on a written survey. The other group ($n = 67$) was asked using the randomized response technique. In the conventional survey, 15% of the auctioneers admitted to self-dealing without disclosure and 12% admitted to having engaged in phantom bids. In the randomized response survey, 46% admitted self-dealing and 36% admitted phantom bids. The results across the six questions were pretty consistent: About three times more people admitted these behaviors than did so when responding to a conventional survey.

In Germany, 6.8% of elite athletes—members of 43 national teams—admitted to doping in a randomized response test, compared to just 0.2% in a completely anonymous standard questionnaire. Even more interesting: About 0.8% of elite athletes fail randomized doping tests—or about one-eighth the percentage who admit to doping in an RRT survey (Striegel et al. 2010).

Every time I read in the newspaper that self-reported drug use among adolescents has dropped by such-and-such an amount since whenever-the-last-self-report-survey-was-done, I think about how easy it is for those data to be utter nonsense. And I wonder why the randomized response technique isn't more widely used. The answer is that it's hard work and all that work produces exactly one number: the percentage of tax cheats or drug users or whatever you're studying. But still. . . . Fortunately, it's getting easier to do RTT surveys using computer-assisted self-interviewing (Lensveldt-Mulders and Boeije 2007), although it may not be suited for web-based surveys or telephone surveys (Holbrook and Krosnik 2010) (**Further Reading:** randomized response technique).

The List Experiment

The list experiment was developed by Kuklinski et al. (1997) to unobtrusively measure socially undesirable attitudes. In this technique (which is closely related to the randomized response technique), two randomly selected samples of people—called the baseline group and the test group—are told:

> Now I'm going to read you four [five] things that sometimes make people angry or upset. After I read all four [five] statements, just tell me how many of them upset you. I don't want to know which ones, just how many.

Then, the interviewer reads four statements to the baseline group and five to the test group. The four statements that are read to both groups are:

One: the way gasoline prices keep going up.

Two: professional athletes getting million-plus salaries.

Three: requiring seat belts are used when driving.

Four: large corporations polluting the environment.

The test group gets a fifth statement, like "a Black family moving in next door" (Kuklinski et al. 1997), or "a Jewish candidate running for vice president" (J. G. Kane et al. 2004), or "a woman serving as president" (Streb et al. 2008).

If both groups are chosen at random, then the average number of items that make people angry should be more or less the same in both groups. If the number is bigger for the people in the test group, it must be because of the extra statement. So, if the average number of items that make people angry in the baseline group is 2.5 and the average number in the test group is 3.0, the percentage of people who are angered by the extra item is $(3.0 - 2.5 \times 100) = .50$, or 50%.

There are many interesting survey methods out there. Don't be afraid to experiment.

Key Concepts in This Chapter

structured interviews	sampling by convenient replacement	thinkaloud interviews
cultural domain analysis		back translation
face-to-face interviews	drop-and-collect technique	Delphi technique
self-administered questionnaires	question batteries	nonresponse bias
	mode effects	cross-sectional design
telephone interviews	random digit dialing	longitudinal design
web-based interviews	interrater reliability	panel design
Internet-based interviews	fixed-choice (closed-ended) questions	attrition
online interviews	open-ended questions	factorial survey
CATI, CASI, A-CASI, CAPI, M-CAPI	precoding of fixed choice questions	vignettes
		demand characteristics
		event history calendar
Internet surveys	contingencies	life history calendar
Internet panels	filter questions	life event calendar
web panels	contingency flow chart	timeline
response rates	loaded questions	randomized response technique
street-intercept interviews	double-barreled questions	
mall-intercept interviews	pretesting	the list experiment
reactivity	cognitive testing	

Summary

- There are two broad categories of methods for structured interviewing: questionnaires, used in survey research, and a range of methods used in cultural domain analysis. There are three methods for collecting survey questionnaire data: (1) personal, face-to-face interviews, (2) self-administered questionnaires, and (3) telephone interviews.

  - There is no perfect data collection method. Self-administered questionnaires are preferable when you are dealing with literate respondents; you are confident of getting a response rate of at least 70%; and the questions you want to ask do not require the use of visual aids such as cue cards, charts, and the like.

- o Face-to-face interviews are preferred when you need answers to all or nearly all the questions in a particular survey.
- o Telephone interviews are widely used in countries where at least 80% of the population has its own telephones.
- Multiple interviewers allow a larger sample, but any problems associated with interviewer bias are increased with more than one interviewer. If you hire interviewers, use professionals if you can. Be sure to train all interviewers—and monitor them throughout the research.
- Experiments continue on the efficacy of open- versus closed-ended questions. Since closed-ended items are so efficient, most survey researchers prefer them to open-ended questions and use them whenever possible. There is no rule against mixing question types.
- There are well-understood rules that all survey researchers follow in constructing questionnaire items. Some important rules include: Questions must be unambiguous. The vocabulary must be appropriate to the respondents. There must be a clear purpose for every question. Scales and filter questions must be clear and well packaged. Never use loaded or double-barreled questions.
- Survey instruments can be translated using the back translation method. This may be combined with the Delphi technique.
- Low response rate hurts the validity of surveys. There are ways to adjust in the data analysis phase of research for nonresponse bias, but it's much better to increase response rate in the first place.

  - o Dillman's total design method requires paying attention to many details, but it can increase response rate dramatically.
- Always pretest survey instruments, and never use any of the respondents in a pretest for the main survey.
- Surveys can be cross-sectional or longitudinal. Daily tracking polls in presidential elections in the United States are an extreme example of longitudinal surveys. Randomly selected panels are an especially powerful form of longitudinal survey. Because the same people are interviewed again and again, randomly selected panel studies share many features of true experiments.
- Some specialized methods include: factorial surveys, based on vignettes; time budgets and diaries; dietary recall; the randomized response technique; and the event calendar method.

Exercises

1. A survey research firm has landed a contract to run a statewide survey on the question "What should be done with the four billion dollars the state will receive from the tobacco settlement?" The survey will be done by mailed questionnaire. Write the cover letter for this questionnaire.

2. What's wrong with each of these questionnaire items?

Do you agree or disagree that the United States shouldn't construct the proposed new anti-ballistic-missile system?

( ) Agree   ( ) Disagree

Where do you get most of your information about current events in the nation and the world?

( ) Radio   ( ) Newspapers   ( ) Magazines

Why do you think big cars are a bad thing for America?

Why did you decide to go to college?

( ) I had a thirst for more knowledge.

( ) I wanted to get a better understanding of the world.

( ) I was too lazy to get a job.

Do you agree or disagree that the trouble with welfare is that people get too comfortable and don't want to go back to work, so the government should institute some job-training programs for people on welfare and then set a limited amount of time in which they can learn work skills and get a job?

( ) Agree   ( ) Disagree

Many people these days have come to see marijuana as being far less harmful than tobacco and they urge that its use be made legal. Do you agree or disagree with those people?

( ) Agree   ( ) Disagree

At what age were you toilet trained?

( ) Before six months

( ) Between six months old and nine months old

( ) Between nine months old and one year old

( ) Between one year old and one and a half years old

( ) Between one and a half years old and two years old

( ) Between two years old and three years old

( ) Older than three years old

( ) Not applicable

How much money do you make? $_____

3. We've all spent a good part of our lives on the phone, but good telephone interviewing skills are not easy to come by. Here's one way. Get four or five students together, all of whom agree to be part of a training group. Use any published telephone survey for this exercise.

Have each person in the group interview *one other* person on the phone. Don't allow people to interview each other.

You don't need to run a whole interview. Five minutes will do. Record each interview. Then get together in a group and listen to the interviews together. You'll quickly hear the mistakes that others make and they will quickly hear yours. Soon enough, though, you'll start hearing your own mistakes.

Be sure to have everyone sign an agreement that lays out the details of this exercise. Specify clearly that the interviews will be recorded. Specify clearly that everyone in the group will hear all the interviews. Decide among yourselves whether you want to keep or destroy the recordings when the exercise is over and put whatever you decide into the agreement. And—very important—clear the agreement with your school's Institutional Review Board. (For more on IRBs, see Chapter 4.)

Further Reading

Computer-aided and Internet-based interviews. Beach et al. (2010), Christian et al. (2009), Couper (2008), Currivan et al. (2004), De Leeuw et al. (2003), Gerich and Lehner (2006), Potdar and Koenig (2005), Renker (2008), Schonlau et al. (2002), On the ethics of research done via the Internet: Buchanan and Ess (2009), Johns et al. (2004), Joinson (2007), McKee and Porter (2009).

Street- and mall-intercept. Hammond and Parkinson (2009), Henson et al. (2010), Hornik and Ellis (1988), Poomsrikaew et al. (2010).

Drop-and-collect technique. Chikritzhs and Brady (2007), Greenfield et al. (2009), Ibeh et al. (2004), Stockwell et al. (2008).

Mode effects. Converse (1984), Dillman (2009), Dillman et al. (2009b), Foddy (1993), Fowler et al. (1999), Greenlaw and Brown-Welty (2009), Healey (2007), Kreuter et al. (2008), Maguire (2009), McCabe (2004), Reichmann et al. (2010), Schuman and Presser (1981), Schwarz (1999), Shih and Fan (2008), Toepoel et al. (2009), Tourangeau et al. (2003), van den Brakel et al (2006).

Telephone interviews. Bourque and Fielder (2003), Frey (1989), Lavrakas (1993, 2010).

Interviewer training. Billiet and Loosveldt (1988), Cannell et al. (1975), Groves and Mathiowetz (1984), Marcus at al. (1994), Mathiowetz and Cannell (1980), O'Brien et al. (2006, Olson and Peytchev (2007), Oskenberg et al. (1986).

The don't-know option. Dick (2006), Gilljam and Granberg (1993), Granberg and Westerberg (1999), Krosnick et al. (2002), Lam et al. (2002), Mondak and Davis (2001), Shoemaker et al. (2002), Sturgis et al. (2008).

Thinkaloud and cognitive interviewing. Beatty and Willis (2007), French et al. (2007), Jobe et al. (1996), Willis (2005), Willis and Miller (2011).

Translation and back translation. Abdel-Khalek (1998), Banville et al. (2002), Chen and Boore (2010), Chien and Norman (2004), Inoue et al. (2009), Kojima et al. (2002).

Response rates. Church (1993), C. Cook et al. (2000), Cycyota and Harrison (2006), Fan and Yan (2010), Fox et al. (1988), Hopkins and Gullickson (1992), Keating et al. (2008), Kropf and Blair (2005), Lynn (2001), Manfreda et al. (2008), Ryu et al. (2006), Shih and Fan (2008), Singer and Bossarte (2006), Thorpe et al. (2009), Trussell and Lavrakas (2004), van den Brakel et al. (2006), Vicente and Reis (2010), Yammarino et al. (1991).

Panel studies. For a list of panel studies across the world, see http://psidonline.isr.umich.edu/Guide/PanelStudies.aspx

Factorial surveys and vignettes. Atzmüller and Steiner (2010), Boots et al. (2003), Byers and Zeller (1998), Eifler (2010), Jasso (2006), Jasso and Opp (1997), Love and Thurman (1991), Ludwick et al. (2004), Wallander (2009).

Randomized response technique. Gingerich (2010), Lavender and Anderson (2009), Lensveldt-Mulders et al. (2005), Solomon et al. (2007).

Time budgets and diaries. Belli et al. (2009), Bishop and Syme (1995), Cheng et al. (2007), Larson et al. (2001), Mestdag (2005), Otterbach and Souza-Poza (2010), Stepanikova et al. (2010), Tiefenthaler (1997).

Event- and life-history calendars: Axinn et al. (1999), Belli (1998), Belli et al. (2009), Caspi et al. (1996), Freedman et al. (1988), Glassner and van der Vaart (2009), Kessler and Wethington (1991), Martyn and Belli (2002), Yoshihama et al. (2005).

10

Interviewing III

Relational Data—Domains and Networks

INTRODUCTION

This chapter introduces methods for collecting data about the content and structure of cultural domains and social networks. A **cultural domain** is a list of things that people in a society think somehow "go together." Those *things* can be physical and observable—kinds of wine, medicinal plants, ice cream flavors, animals you can keep at home, horror movies,

symptoms of illness—or they can be conceptual, like roles, and emotions. Networks also comprise lists—lists of people or countries or organizations—that somehow go together, and these lists, too, can be analyzed with many of the same methods used for analyzing cultural domains.

Understanding how things in any list actually do go together is to understand structure—**cognitive structure** in the case of cultural domains and **social structure** in the case of people, countries, and organizations. Getting these kinds of data is what this chapter is about. I'll show you how to analyze these kinds of data in Chapter 16 and how to analyze the data from more traditional social research projects in Chapters 20, 21, and 22.

CULTURAL DOMAINS

Interest in how human beings classify things—how they understand what goes with what—goes back a long way in the social sciences. John Stuart Mill (1898)

devoted a chapter to it in his seminal work on logic. Modern cultural domain analysis (CDA) comes from work on *cultural* systems of classification—that is, *shared* understandings of semantic relations—by anthropologists and linguists from about 1950 to 1980. Today, the methods of CDA are used in multidisciplinary fields like medical social science (including public health and nursing research), environmental social science, communications research, consumer research, criminology, and so on. For key work on the method and theory of modern CDA see Borgatti (1993/1994, 1999) and Weller and Romney (1988) (Box 10.1).

Box 10.1 Cultural domains are everywhere

James Spradley (1979) reported that he once called the St. Paul, Minnesota, police department and said he needed to find the case number of a robbery that had been committed at his house. Two bicycles had been stolen from his garage in the middle of the night while he was asleep. The police had investigated, but Spradley's insurance company needed the case number to process the claim. When Spradley told the police that he needed the case number for a robbery, they quite naturally transferred his call to the robbery unit. But the people there couldn't help him because, according to their rules, robberies involve a face-to-face encounter between the criminal and the victim and the criminal uses a gun.

Spradley was transferred to burglary, but they couldn't help him either because, they said, theft of bicycles is handled by the juvenile division in St. Paul. Eventually, Spradley got his case number, but, he said, if he had understood the police culture, he "would have begun with a simple question: What part of the police department has records of bicycles stolen from a garage when no one is present?" (1979:142). In other words, if he'd known the taxonomy for the cultural domain of crimes, he'd have asked the right question and gotten taken care of right away.

Features of Cultural Domain Analysis

There are five important features of cultural domains.

1. The elements of a cultural domain are thought by carriers of the culture to belong to a single concept and to be at the same level of contrast (Borgatti 1999; Weller and Romney 1988:9). For example, most native speakers of

English would recognize that lions and dogs belong to a conceptual category—a domain—called "animals." Lions and dogs are at the same level of contrast. If we add wolves, things change. All the elements are still in the domain of animals, but now the dogs and wolves are kinds of canines, and lions are kinds of cats.

If we work on the system of classification for a while, we'll find that most speakers of

English say that, in some culturally appropriate way, lions "go with" leopards. The lion-leopard group is culturally at the same level of contrast as the dog-wolf group. If you keep asking people about this cultural domain, you'll find that there are lots of cross-cutting rules for contrast: domestic versus wild animals, pets versus non-pets, and so on.

2. Cultural domains typically have a hierarchical structure. For many native speakers of English, lemons are a kind of citrus, which are a kind of fruit, which are a kind of food. But not for everyone. Some people skip the citrus level entirely. And people vary in what they think is the content of any cultural domain. For some native speakers of English, sharks and dolphins are kinds of fish; for others, they are not. For many native speakers of English, chimpanzees are kinds of monkeys; for others, they are kinds of apes, not kinds of monkeys.

3. Cultural domains vary in how much people agree on their content. The list of terms for members of a family (mother, father, etc.) is agreed on by most members of a culture. But not all. For some native speakers of English, a man's wife's sister's husband is the man's brother-in-law; for others, he's his wife's brother-in-law; and for others, he's no relative at all. The list of "ethnic and racial groups" shows less agreement in the United States than does the list of names for family members but more agreement than the list of "things that mothers do," which is really diffuse.

4. Many cultural domains—like the list of carpenters' tools or the list of muscles, bones, and tendons in the human leg—are the province of specialists. The list of names of major league baseball teams in the United States is agreed on by everyone who knows about this domain, but the list of greatest left-handed baseball pitchers of all time is a matter of heated debate among experts.

5. Cultural domains are, as Borgatti says, "'out there' in reality, so that, in principle,

questions about the members of a domain have a right answer" (Borgatti 1999:117). What the right answer is can vary across cultures or subcultures—or gender, for that matter.

The spectrum of visible colors, for example, is a physical reality, but around the world, women can name more colors and have a richer vocabulary for describing colors than men do (Rich 1977; Yang 2001). And people in different cultures label chunks of the color spectrum differently. For example, speakers of Navajo, Korean, Ñähñu, Welsh, and many other languages use one word to identify colors that speakers of English call green and blue.

The color is called "grue" in the linguistics literature (Kim 1985). People who have a word for grue use adjectives to express color differences within the blue-green spectrum. In Navajo, for example, the general term for grue is *dootl'izh*. Turquoise is *yáago dootl'izh*, or sky grue, and green is *tádlidgo dootl'izh*, or water scum grue (Oswald Werner, personal communication).

Cultural domain analysis, then, "is about perceptions rather than preferences" (Borgatti 1999:117). We ask people about which brand of car they prefer, which political candidate they prefer, and which features they prefer in potential mates because we want to predict their buying, voting, and marrying behaviors. We might also ask people about their income, their ethnicity, their age, and so on and then look for packages of variables about the people (single White women under 30, married Black men over 40, etc.) that predict how they will exercise their preferences—what they will buy, for whom they will vote, who they will marry.

The methods for collecting data about cultural domains include free lists, pile sorts, triad tests, and paired comparisons. The methods for analyzing cultural domain data include multidimensional scaling, cluster analysis, and correspondence analysis.

These are all computer-based visualization methods—that is, methods for reducing a welter of data to pictures that we can easily understand and interpret—and they open up many possibilities for understanding complex systems, like social networks (**Further Reading:** cultural and semantic domains).

FREE LISTING

Free listing is a deceptively simple but powerful technique. In free listing, we ask people to: "Please list all the X you can think of," where X might be teenagers' ideas about what makes a good or safe driver (Barg et al. 2009), or differences in what Hispanic and Anglo women think are causes of breast or cervical cancer (Chavez et al. 1995), or things that students and faculty think are innovative teaching (Jaskyte et al. 2009).

As in any kind of interviewing, people respond with more information if you learn how to probe for it. Brewer et al. (2002:112) found that **semantic cueing** increased the recall of items in a free list by over 40%. Ask informants to: "Think of all the kinds of X [the domain] that are like Y," where Y is that first item on their initial list. If the informant responds with more items, you take it another step: "Try to remember other types of X like Y and tell me any new ones that you haven't already said." Do this until the informant says there are no more items like Y. Then repeat the exercise for the second item on the informant's initial list, and the third, and so on.

Brewer tested three other kinds of probes for free lists: redundant questioning, nonspecific prompting, and alphabetic cueing. Here's the redundant question that Brewer and his colleagues asked a group of IV-drug users:

> Think of all the different kinds of drugs or substances people use to get high, feel good, or think and feel differently. These drugs are sometimes called recreational drugs or street drugs. Tell me the names of all the kinds of these drugs you can remember. Please keep trying to recall if you think there are more kinds of drugs you might be able to remember. [Brewer et al. 2002:347; and see Brewer and Garrett 2001]

In nonspecific prompting, after people have responded to your original question, ask them: "What other kinds of X are there?" Keep asking this question until people say they can't think of any more Xs. And in alphabetic cueing, ask informants "What kinds of X are there that begin with the letter A?" . . . "With the letter B?" And so on.

Informants who are very knowledgeable about the contents of a cultural domain usually provide longer lists than others. Some items will be mentioned over and over again, but eventually, if you keep asking people to list things, you get a lot of repeat items and all the new items are unique—that is, mentioned by only one informant. This happens pretty quickly (by the time you've interviewed 15 or 20 informants) with domains like names for animals or plants or ethnic groups, which are pretty well formed. With fuzzy domains, like "things you can do on a weekend," you might still be eliciting new items after interviewing 30 or 40 people.

You Can Learn a Lot From Free Lists

You'd be surprised at how much you can learn from free lists. Henley (1969) asked 21 students at Johns Hopkins University to name as many animals as they could in 10 minutes. The lists in this small group ranged in length from 21 to 110, with a median of 55.

The 21 people named 423 different animals, and 175 were mentioned just once. The most popular animals were: dog, lion, cat, horse, and tiger, all of which were named by more than

90% of informants. Only 29 animals were listed by more than half the informants, but 90% of those were mammals. By contrast, among the 175 animals named only once, just 27% were mammals.

But there's more. Previous research had shown that the 12 most commonly talked about animals in American speech are: bear, cat, cow, deer, dog, goat, horse, lion, mouse, pig, rabbit, and sheep. There are $n(n-1)/2$, or 66 possible unique pairs of 12 animals (dog-cat, dog-deer, horse-lion, mouse-pig, etc.). Henley examined each informant's list of animals and found the difference in the order of listing for each of the 66 pairs.

That is, if an informant mentioned goats 12th on her list, and bears 32nd, then the distance between goats and bears, for that informant, was $32 - 12 = 20$. Henley standardized these distances (that is, she divided each distance by the length of an informant's list and multiplied by 100) and calculated the average distance, over all the informants, for each of the 66 pairs of animals.

The lowest mean distance was between sheep and goats (1.8). If you named sheep, then the next thing you named was probably goats; and if you named goats, the next thing you named was probably sheep. Many speakers of English have heard the expression: "That'll separate the sheep from the goats." This part of Western culture was originally a metaphor for distinguishing the righteous from the wicked and then became a metaphor for separating the strong from the weak. The first meaning was mentioned in the Old Testament (Ezekiel 34:17), and then again around 600 years later in the New Testament (Matthew 25:31–33).

Henley's respondents were neither shepherds nor students of Western scriptural lore, but they all knew that sheep and goats somehow "go together." Free lists tell you *what goes with what*, but you need to dig to understand *why* (Box 10.2).

Box 10.2 Loose talk

Long lists don't necessarily mean that people know a lot about the things they name. In fact, in modern societies, people can often name a lot more things than they can recognize in the real world. John Gatewood (1983) interviewed 40 adult Pennsylvanians and got free lists of names of trees. He asked each informant to go through his or her list and check the trees that they thought they could actually recognize. Thirty-four out of the 40 informants listed "pine," and 31 of the 34 said that they could recognize a pine.

Orange trees were another matter. Twenty-seven people listed "orange," but only four people said they could recognize an orange tree (without oranges hanging all over it, of course). On average, these 40 Pennsylvanians said they could recognize half of the trees they listed, a phenomenon that Gatewood called **loose talk.**

Gatewood and his students (1984) asked 54 university students, half of them women and half of them men, to: (1) list all the musical instruments, fabrics, hand tools, and trees they could think of; and (2) check off the items in each of their lists that they thought they would recognize in a natural setting. Gatewood chose musical instruments, with the idea that there would be no gender difference in the number of items listed or recognized; that women might name more kinds of fabrics than would men; and that men would name more kinds of hand tools than would women. He chose the domain of trees to see if his earlier findings would replicate. There were no surprises: All the hypotheses and stereotypes were confirmed.

Free Lists and Applied Research

Finally, free listing can be used to find out where to concentrate effort in applied research. In a project on which I consulted, interviewers asked people on the North Carolina coast how they viewed the possibility of offshore oil drilling. One of the questions was: "What are the things that make life good around here?" This question cropped up after some informal interviews in seven small seaside towns. People kept saying "What a nice little town this is" and "What a shame it would be if things changed around here." Informants had no difficulty with the question, and after just 20 interviews, the researchers had a list of over 50 "things that make life good around here." The researchers chose the 20 items mentioned by at least 12 informants and explored the meaning of those items further (ICMR et al. 1993).

The humble free list has many uses. Use it a lot (**Further Reading:** free lists).

TRIAD TESTS

In a triad test, you show people three things and tell them to "Choose the one that doesn't fit" or "Choose the two that seem to go together best," or "Choose the two that are the same." The "things" can be photographs, actual plants, or 3 × 5 cards with names of people on them. (Respondents often ask "What do you mean by things being 'the same' or 'fitting together'?" Tell them that you are interested in what *they* think that means.) By doing this for all triples from a list of things or concepts, you can explore differences in cognition among individuals, and among cultures and subcultures.

Suppose you ask some native speakers of English to "choose the item that is least like the other two" in each of the following triads:

DOLPHIN	MOOSE	WHALE
SHARK	DOLPHIN	MOOSE

All three items in the first triad are mammals, but two of them are sea mammals. Some native speakers of English will choose dolphin as the odd item out because "whales and moose are both big mammals and the dolphin is smaller." In my experience, though, most people will choose moose as the most different because "whales and dolphins are both sea animals." In the second triad, many of the same people who chose moose in the first triad will choose shark because moose and dolphins are both mammals and sharks are not.

But some people who chose moose in triad 1 will choose moose again because sharks and dolphins are sea creatures, while moose are not. Giving people a judiciously chosen set of triad stimuli can help you understand interindividual similarities and differences in how people think about the items in a cultural domain.

The triad test was developed in psychology (see Kelly 1955; Torgerson 1958) and has long been used in studies of human cognition. Lieberman and Dressler (1977) used triad tests to examine variation in medical beliefs on the Caribbean island of St. Lucia. These researchers wanted to know if cognition of disease terms varied with bilingual proficiency. They used 52 bilingual English-Patois speakers and 10 monolingual Patois speakers. From ethnographic interviewing and cross-checking against various informants, they isolated nine disease terms that were important to St. Lucians.

Here's the formula for finding the number of triads in a list of n items:

$$\frac{n(n-1)(n-2)}{6} \qquad \text{formula 10.1}$$

In this case, $n = 9$ (the number of disease terms), so there are 84 possible triads. Lieberman and Dressler gave each of the 52 bilingual informants two triad tests, a week apart: one in Patois and one in English. (Naturally, they randomized the order of the items within each triad and randomized the order of presentation of the triads to informants.) They also measured how bilingual their informants were, using a standard test. The 10 monolingual Patois informants were simply given the triad test.

Next, the researchers counted the number of times that each possible pair of terms was chosen as most alike among the 84 triads. (There are $n \times (n-1)/2$ pairs or $9 \times 8/2 = 36$ pairs). They divided the total by seven (the maximum number of times that any pair appears in the 84 triads). This produced a similarity coefficient, varying between 0.0 and 1.0, for each possible pair of disease terms. The larger the coefficient for a pair of terms, the closer in meaning the two terms are. They were then able to analyze these data among English-dominant, Patois-dominant, and monolingual Patois speakers. (I'll show you how to analyze triad test data in Chapter 16.)

It turned out that when Patois-dominant and English-dominant informants took the triad test in English, their cognitive models of similarities among diseases was similar. When Patois-dominant speakers took the Patois-language triad test, however, their cognitive model was similar to that of monolingual Patois informants.

This is a very interesting finding. It means that Patois-dominant bilinguals manage to hold on to two distinct psychological models about diseases and that they switch back and forth between them, depending on what language they are speaking. By contrast, the English-dominant group displayed a similar cognitive model of disease terms, irrespective of the language in which they are tested.

Balanced Incomplete Block Designs for Triad Tests

Typically, the terms that go into a triad test are generated by a free list, and typically the list is much too long for a triad test. As you can see from formula 10.1, with just nine terms there are 84 stimuli in a triad test containing nine items. But with 15 items, just six more, the number of decisions an informant has to make jumps to 455. At 20 items, it's a mind-numbing 1,140.

Free lists of illnesses, ways to prevent pregnancy, advantages of breast-feeding, places to go on vacation, and so on easily produce 60 items or more. Even a selected, abbreviated list may be 20 items.

This led Burton and Nerlove (1976) to develop the balanced incomplete block design, or BIB, for the triad test. BIBs take advantage of the fact that there is a lot of redundancy in a triad test. Suppose you have just four items, 1, 2, 3, 4, and you ask informants to tell you something about *pairs* of these items (e.g., if the items were vegetables, you might ask "Which of these two is less expensive?" or "Which of these two is more nutritious?" or "Which of these two is easier to cook?") There are exactly six pairs of four items (1–2, 1–3, 1–4, 2–3, 2–4, 3–4), and the informant sees each pair just once.

But suppose that instead of pairs you show the informant triads and ask which two out of each triple are most similar. There are just four triads in four items (1–2–3, 1–2–4, 2–3–4, 1–3–4), but each item appears $(n-1)(n-2)/2$ times, and each pair appears $n-2$ times. For four items, there are $n(n-1)/2 = 6$ pairs; each pair appears twice in four triads, and each item on the list appears three times.

It is all this redundancy that reduces the number of triads needed in a triads test. In a complete set of 84 triads for nine items, each pair of items appears $n-2$, or seven times. If you have each pair appear just once (called a lambda 1 design), instead of seven times, then, instead of 84 triads, only 12 are needed. If you have each pair appear twice (a lambda 2 design), then 24 triads are needed. For analysis, a lambda 2 design is much better than a lambda 1. Table 10.1 shows the lambda 2 design for nine items and 10 items.

Table 10.1 Balanced Incomplete Block Designs for Triad Tests Involving 9 and 10 Items

For 9 items, 24 triads are needed, as follows: Items		For 10 items, 30 triads are needed, as follows: Items	
1, 5, 9	1, 2, 3	1, 2, 3	6, 8, 9
2, 3, 8	4, 5, 6	2, 5, 8	7, 10, 3
4, 6, 7	7, 8, 9	3, 7, 4	8, 1, 10
2, 6, 9	1, 4, 7	4, 1, 6	9, 5, 2
1, 3, 4	2, 5, 9	5, 8, 7	10, 6, 7
5, 7, 8	3, 6, 8	6, 4, 9	1, 3, 5
3, 7, 9	1, 6, 9	7, 9, 1	2, 7, 6
2, 4, 5	2, 4, 8	8, 10, 2	3, 8, 9
1, 6, 8	3, 5, 7	9, 3, 10	4, 2, 10
4, 8, 9	1, 5, 8	10, 6, 5	5, 6, 3
3, 5, 6	2, 6, 8	1, 2, 4	6, 1, 8
1, 2, 7	3, 4, 9	2, 3, 6	7, 9, 2
		2, 4, 8	8, 4, 7
		4, 9, 5	9, 10, 1
		5, 7, 1	10, 5, 4

Source: "Balanced Design for Triad Tests" by M. L. Burton and S. B. Nerlove, 1976. *Social Science Research*, p. 5.

For 10 items, a lambda 2 design requires 30 triads; for 13 items, it requires 52 triads; for 19 items, 114 triads; and for 25 items, 200 triads.

Unfortunately, there is no easy formula for choosing *which* triads in a large set to select for a BIB. Fortunately, Burton and Nerlove (1976) worked out various lambda BIB designs for up to 21 items, and Borgatti has incorporated BIB designs into Anthropac (1992a). You simply tell Anthropac the list of items you have, select a design, and tell it the number of repondents you want to interview. Anthropac then prints out a randomized triad test, one for each informant. Randomizing the order in which the triads appear to informants eliminates order-effects—possible biases that come from responding to a list of stimuli in a particular order. (See Appendix E for information on Anthropac.)

Boster et al. (1987) used a triad test and a pile sort in their study of the social network of an office. There were 16 employees, so there were 16 items in the cultural domain (the list of "all the people who work here" is a perfectly good domain). A lambda 2 test with 16 items has 80 distinct triads.

Informants were asked to "judge which of three actors was the most different from the other two."

Triad tests are easy to create with Anthropac, easy to administer, and easy to score, but they can only be used when you have relatively few items in a cultural domain. In literate societies, most people can respond to 200 triads in less than half an hour, but it can be a really boring exercise, and boring your respondents is a really bad idea. I find that people can easily handle lambda 2 triad tests with up to 15 items and 70 triads. But I also find that people generally prefer—even like—to do pile sorts (**Further Reading**: triad tasks).

FREE PILE SORTS

In 1966, John Brim put the names of 58 American English role terms (mother, gangster, stockbroker, etc.) on slips of paper. He asked 108 high school students in San Mateo, California, to spread the slips out on their desks and to "put the terms together which you feel belong together" (in Burton and Romney 1975:400). Michael Burton analyzed Brim's data using multidimensional scaling and hierarchical clustering (Burton 1968, 1972). These powerful tools were brand new at the time but are used today across all the sciences. (We'll get back to MDS and clustering in Chapter 16 on how to analyze relational data.)

I've used free pile sorts to study the social structure of institutions such as prisons, ships at sea, and bureaucracies and to map the cognitively defined social organization of small communities. I simply hand people a deck of cards, each of which contains the name of one of the people in the institution, and ask informants to sort the cards into piles, according to their own criteria. The results tell me how people in the various components of an organization (managers, production workers,

advertising people; or guards, counselors, prisoners; or seamen, deck officers, engine room personnel; or men and women in a small Greek village) think about the social structure of the group.

Instead of what goes with what, I learn who goes with whom. Then I ask informants to explain *why* people appear in the same pile. This produces a wealth of information about the cognitively defined social structure of a group.

Administering a Pile Sort

Informants often ask two questions when asked to do a pile sort: (1) "What do you mean by 'belong together'?" and (2) "Can I put something in more than one pile?" The answer to the first question is "There are no right or wrong answers. We want to learn what *you* think about these things." And although they can't put *every* item in its own pile, lots of people put *some* items in singleton piles, explaining that each item is unique and doesn't go with the others.

The easy answer to the second question is "No," because there is one card per item and a card can only be in one pile at a time. This answer cuts off a lot of information, however, because people can think of items in a cultural domain along several dimensions at once. For example, in a pile sort of consumer electronics, someone might want to put DVD recorders in one pile with TVs (for the obvious association) and in another pile with camcorders (for another obvious association), but might not want to put camcorders and TVs in the same pile.

One way to handle this problem is to have duplicate cards that you can give to people when they want to put an item into more than one pile, but be warned that this can complicate analysis of the data. An alternative is to ask the informant to do **multiple** free pile sorts of the same set of items (Box 10.3).

Box 10.3 Pile sorts with objects

Pile sorts don't have to be done with cards. You can use photographs of objects or even small objects themselves. Carl Kendall led a public health team project in El Progreso, Honduras, to study beliefs about dengue fever (Kendall et al. 1990). Part of their study involved a pile sort of the nine most common flying insects in the region. They mounted specimens of the insects in little boxes and asked people to group the insects in terms of "those that are similar."

Borgatti (1999:133), however, points out that physical stimuli, like images or objects, can produce a different kind of data than you expect. When asked to sort drawings of fish, fishermen in North Carolina sorted by shape—long thin ones, ones with a big dorsal fin, small roundish ones (Boster and Johnson 1989). "In contrast," says Borgatti (1999:133), "sorting *names* of fish allows hidden attributes to affect the sorting"—things like taste or how much of a struggle fish put up. "If you are after shared cultural beliefs," says Borgatti, "I recommend keeping the stimulus as abstract as possible" (1992b:6).

Extracting Lists From Texts

In a series of papers, John Roberts and his coworkers used pile sorts and rating tasks to study how people perceive various kinds of behaviors in games (see, e.g., Roberts and Chick 1979; Roberts and Nattress 1980). One game, studied by Roberts et al. (1980) is pretty serious: searching for foreign submarines in a P-3 airplane. The P-3 is a four-engine, turbo-prop, low-wing aircraft that can stay in the air for long periods of time and cover large patches of ocean. It is also used for search-and-rescue missions. Making errors in flying the P-3 can result in career damage and embarrassment at least, and injury or death at worst.

Through extensive, unstructured interviews with Navy P-3 pilots, Roberts et al. isolated 60 named pilot errors, through extensive unstructured interviews with navy pilots of the P-3. (This is the equivalent of extracting a free list from your interviews.) Here are a few of the errors: flying into a known thunderstorm area, taking off with the trim tabs set improperly, allowing the prop wash to cause damage to other aircraft, and inducing an autofeather by rapid movement of power level controls. The researchers asked 52 pilots to do an unrestricted

pile sort of the 60 errors and to *rate* each error on a seven-point scale of "seriousness."

They also asked the pilots to rank a subset of 13 errors on four criteria: (1) how much each error would "rattle" a pilot; (2) how badly each error would damage a pilot's career; (3) how embarrassing each error would be to commit; and (4) how much "fun" it would be to commit each error. Flying into a thunderstorm on purpose, for example, could be very damaging to a pilot's career, and extremely embarrassing if he had to abort the mission and turn back in the middle. But if the mission turned out to be successful, then taking the risk of committing a very dangerous error would be a lot of fun for pilots who are "high self-testers" (Roberts, personal communication).

Inexperienced pilots rated "inducing an autofeather" as more serious than did highly experienced pilots. Inducing an autofeather is more embarrassing than it is dangerous and is the sort of error that experienced pilots just don't make. On the other hand, as the number of air hours increased, so did pilots' view of the seriousness of "failure to use all available navigational aids to determine position." Roberts et al. (1980) suggested that inexperienced pilots might not have had enough training to assess the seriousness of this error correctly.

The Lumper-Splitter Problem

In the free pile sort method, people are told that they can make as many piles as they like, so long as they don't make a separate pile for each item or lump all the items into one pile. Like the triad test, the free pile sort presents people with a common set of stimuli, but there's a crucial difference: With free pile sorts, people can group the items together as they see fit. The result is that some people will make many piles, others will make few, and this causes the lumper-splitter problem (Weller and Romney 1988:22).

In a pile sort of animals, for example, some informants will put all the following together: giraffe, elephant, rhinoceros, zebra, wildebeest. They'll explain that these are the "African animals." Others will put giraffe, elephant, and rhino in one pile and the zebra and wildebeest in another, explaining that one is the "large African animal" pile and the other is the "medium-sized African animal pile."

It's fine to ask informants why they made each pile of items, but wait until they finish the sorting task so you don't interfere with their concentration. And don't hover over people. Find an excuse to walk away for a couple of minutes after they get the hang of it (Box 10.4).

Box 10.4 Triads versus pile sorts

Because triad tests present each respondent with exactly the same stimuli, you can compare the data across individuals. Free pile sorts tell you what the structure of the data looks like for a group of people—sort of group cognition—but you can't compare the data from individuals. On the other hand, with pile sorts, you can have as many as 50 or 60 items. All methods have their advantages and disadvantages (**Further Reading:** pile sorts).

RANKINGS

Rank ordering produces interval-level data, while ratings ("on a scale of 1-to-5, how much do you like . . . ?") produce ordinal-level data. Not all behaviors or concepts are easy to rank and there are lots of times when ratings are the best you can do, but when you can get rank-ordered data you shouldn't pass up the opportunity.

Occupations, for example, can be easily rank ordered on the basis of prestige or lucrativeness—or even accessibility. The instructions to respondents would be "Here is a list of occupations. Please rank them in order, from most likely to least likely that your daughter will have this occupation."

Then ask respondents to do the same thing for their sons. (Be sure to assign people randomly to doing the task for sons or daughters first.) Then compare the average ranking of accessibility against some independent variables and test for intracultural differences among ethnic groups, genders, age groups, and income groups.

Weller and Dungy (1986) studied breast-feeding among Hispanic and Anglo women in southern California. They asked 55 informants for a free list of positive and negative aspects of breast- and bottle-feeding. Then they selected the 20 most frequently mentioned items in this domain and converted the items to neutral, similarly worded statements. A few examples: "A way that doesn't tie you down, so you are free to do more things"; "A way that your baby feels full and satisfied"; "A way that allows you to feel closer to your baby."

Next, Weller and Dungy asked 195 women to rank the 20 statements. The women were asked which statement was most important to them in selecting a method of feeding their baby, which was the next most important to them, and so on. In the analysis, Weller and Dungy were able to relate the average rank order for Hispanics and for Anglos to independent variables like age and education (Box 10.5).

Box 10.5 The nomination technique

Use this technique to get a rank-order listing of prestige in a community. Ask: "Besides you, who are the top X [teachers] [cops] [nurses] in this [school] [precinct] [ward]," where X is some number, like five or 10, depending on the total population you're dealing with. By concatenating the nomination lists, you can test whether there is a consensus about prestige and, if there is, the rank order of the top X people.

PAIRED COMPARISONS

The method of paired comparisons is an alternative way to get rank orderings of a list of items. For any set of things, there are $n(n-1)/2$ pairs of those things. Suppose you have a list of five colors: red, green, yellow, blue, and brown. Figure 10.1 shows the paired comparison test we would use to find someone's rank-ordered preference for these five colors. In this case, the question would be: "Look at each pair of colors and, for each pair, tell me which one you like more."

In Figure 10.1, each of the five colors appears $n - 1 = 4$ times—once with each of the other four colors. To find the rank order of the colors for each informant, you count up how many times each color "wins"—that is, how many times it was circled.

Rank-order data are useful in many studies. If you are studying illnesses, for example, you can show people pairs of cards and ask: "Which of these illnesses is more life threatening?" Then you can compare the average rank order for any particular illness among men and women or across various ethnic groups. Or you might ask people to choose "the food in this pair that is better for you," or "the crime in this pair that you're more afraid of."

When you present a paired comparison test to a respondent, be sure to scramble the order of

Figure 10.1 A Paired Comparison Test for Rank-Ordered Data

In each of the following pairs of colors, please circle the one you like best:

RED	GREEN
RED	YELLOW
RED	BLUE
RED	BROWN
GREEN	YELLOW
GREEN	BLUE
GREEN	BROWN
YELLOW	BLUE
YELLOW	BROWN
BLUE	BROWN

the pairs to guard against order effects—that is, where something about the order of the items in a list influences the choices that people make.

The paired comparison technique has a lot going for it. People make one judgment at a time, so it's much easier on them than asking them to rank order a list of items by staring at all the items at once. Also, you can use paired comparisons with people who are not literate by reading the list of pairs to them, one at a time, and recording their answers.

Like triad tests, though, paired comparisons can be tedious for respondents if you use all the pairs in a set. With just 20 items, for example, informants have to make $20(19)/2 = 190$ judgments. Fortunately, there is a way to reduce this respondent burden.

Pillsworth (2008:260) collected rank-order data for 19 traits in a potential spouse—things like hard-working, physically attractive, healthy, religious, faithful, intelligent, sense of humor, reliable, and so on. She showed students at UCLA and Shuar Indians in Ecuador a randomly selected pair of traits and asked which trait was more important. Then she compared the winning trait in that pair with the other traits in the list—until it was beaten by another trait. The new winner was then compared to all the rest of the traits in the list—unless it, too, was beaten by a more preferred trait. And so on, until the list was exhausted.

This reduced respondent burden a lot. Consider a set of six things (A, B, C, D, E, and F). And suppose an informant's choices were the following (where the asterisk indicates the preferred item):

A*–B; A*–C; B*–C; A–D*; D*–E; E–A*; D–F*

With six items, there are $6(5)/2 = 15$ pairs. Yet, assuming transitivity of preference (if you like A more than B and B more than C then you like A more than C) the rank order of preference—F, D, A, E, B, C—is determined after just the seven choices shown in Pillsworth's example. The informant chose A over B and D over A, so D and B didn't have to be compared (**Further Reading:** rankings and paired comparisons).

NETWORKS

Network analysis is the study of relations among units of analysis. A network is set of things (called nodes) that are connected or related to one another in some way. If the things are resistors and capacitors and such, you have an electrical network. If the things are roads and bridges, you have a traffic network. And if the things are people, you have a social network.

There are two kinds of social networks: whole, or sociocentric networks, and personal, or egocentric networks.

Sociocentric networks are sets of links among members of closed groups. We know that groups of people are never actually closed, but we can treat the teachers in one school or employees in one firm as groups and ask questions about how they know and interact with one another—Do they ask each other for advice? Do they hang out together after work?—and the impact of these interactions—Does the structure of these relations affect their morale or how well they do their jobs?

Egocentric networks are maps, from the standpoint of individuals (called egos), of how people are connected to the people they know (their alters) (Wellman 1999). Along with information about ego's connections to his or her alters, personal networks also contain information about the attributes of alters (their sex, age, education, and anything else of interest in a particular study). Personal network data are widely used in the study of social support and social capital (Lin et al. 2001; Wellman 1999). For example, people who have good social support networks—friends and kin on whom they can rely for emotional and instrumental support—have fewer psychiatric symptoms (Lin et al. 1979:113) and recover better after a heart attack (Everson-Rose and Lewis 2005). They may even get better jobs, especially if they have network ties to people of higher status than their own (Lin, Ensel, and Vaughn 1981; Lin, Vaughn, and Ensel 1981).

COLLECTING SOCIOCENTRIC NETWORK DATA

To collect data about network ties in a group, you need: (1) a list of the members of the group; (2) one or more definitions of a tie between pairs of members; and (3) a method for finding the ties between pairs of members.

Lists of Network Members

If the group you are studying is a classroom of children, then the first names of the children might comprise the list. If the group is the set of employees in a bank, you'll probably need the first and last names. If you are studying the trade network of the members of the European Union, then the list consists of the names of the 27 countries (in 2012) of the EU. In my research on the social structure of oceanographic research vessels (Bernard and Killworth 1973), the list of the group consisted of the first names of the officers and crew (the people who operated the ship), the scientists (the people who defined the research goals), and the technicians (the people who operated the instruments for gathering the data).

Definitions of Ties

People and groups can be linked to one another in many ways. If you ask children in a classroom to name their three best friends, and then map all the links, you get a friendship network. If you ask people in an organization who they go to for advice, you get an advice network. Each definition of a tie between actors produces its own network.

Commonly used ties between actors in a social network include:

1. interaction and exchange—communicates with, gives advice to, babysits for, lends money to, shares needles with, has sex with . . .

2. affect—likes, trusts, respects, is hostile to . . .

3. kin-based ties—is the sister/brother of, is related by marriage to . . .

4. non-kin, role-based ties—is the teacher of, is the supervisor of . . .

5. cognitive ties—knows or knows about someone . . .

6. affiliations—lives in a house with, sits on a corporate board with, is a member of the same church with . . .

Each of these kinds of relations implies some form of a question for respondents. For the tie "communicates with," for example, some questions might be: (1) "Who do you exchange e-mail with in this office?" or (2) "How often do you talk to X about Y?" where X is a list of people in an organization and Y is some topic of interest in your research—like "computer problems" or "where to eat lunch" or "product design." Some questions about cognitive ties might be: (1) "Does A know B?" where A and B are all pairs of people in a group whose network you want to map; or (2) "Was A (or B, or C, etc.) at the faculty meeting yesterday?"

Methods for Finding Network Ties

Data for whole networks can be collected indirectly by asking people about their ties to others in a group or directly by observing them and recording their interactions with others in a group.

If you have a relatively small group, you can show each person a list of all the others in the group and have them check their ties with each of those others. Figure 10.2 shows an example of how to do this. Note that you can ask for more than one tie in survey instruments like these.

This kind of instrument works well for groups of 20 or 30 people. For larger groups, you can use pile sorting. Put the name of each person in a group on a card, remove the name of the respondent, and shuffle the deck. Then ask the respondent to "put these cards into piles—people in this organization who you [interact with] [communicate with on email] [see socially after work] [etc.] and people you don't." Peter Killworth and I used this method

with groups of up to 150 (Killworth and Bernard 1974).

As with Figure 10.2, this creates 1-0 (read: one-zero) data, with 1s representing ties and 0s representing the absence of ties. In several projects, I've produced valued data by asking people to make four piles (interact with all the time, sometimes, rarely, and never) and then asking them to rank order the cards in the first three piles. Recall one of the basic rules for collecting data in Chapter 2: Always measure at the highest level of measurement possible. You can turn a variable measured at the ratio level into an ordinal or a nominal variable, but you can't go the other way.

You can also produce valued data for whole networks with scaling instruments, like the one shown in Figure 10.3.

Figure 10.2 A Questionnaire for Collecting Sociocentric Network Data in a Small Group

In the form below, you'll see a list of everyone who works here at Amy's Pet Shop, including you. Next to each name, check each column that fits what you do. If you see someone socially, after work, put a check in that box. If you ask for advice from someone, then put a check in the "asks for advice from" box. If they ask you for advice, put a check in the "gets advice from box." If you both ask for and get advice from someone, you can put a check in both boxes. And if you don't get or receive advice from someone, you can just leave that blank. Of course, leave the line with your own name blank.

Person	Asks for advice from	Gets advice from	Sees socially, after work
Alexander			
Basil			
Catherine			
Doreen			
Evan			
Florence			
Gloria			
Herman			
Ingrid			
Jasper			
Kathleen			
Lauren			
Michael			
Nolan			

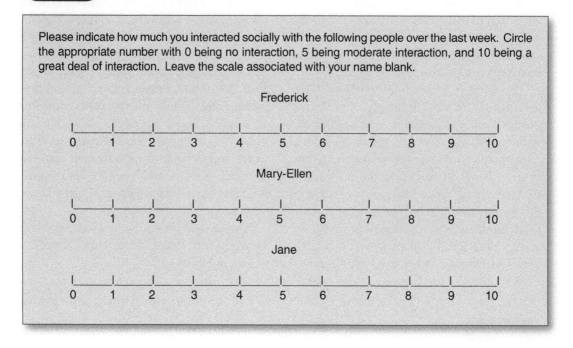

Figure 10.3 A Scaling Instrument for Collecting Valued Data About Interactions in Studies of Whole Networks

Please indicate how much you interacted socially with the following people over the last week. Circle the appropriate number with 0 being no interaction, 5 being moderate interaction, and 10 being a great deal of interaction. Leave the scale associated with your name blank.

Frederick

```
|____|____|____|____|____|____|____|____|____|____|
0    1    2    3    4    5    6    7    8    9    10
```

Mary-Ellen

```
|____|____|____|____|____|____|____|____|____|____|
0    1    2    3    4    5    6    7    8    9    10
```

Jane

```
|____|____|____|____|____|____|____|____|____|____|
0    1    2    3    4    5    6    7    8    9    10
```

COLLECTING EGOCENTRIC NETWORK DATA

To collect personal network data, you also need a list of a person's alters (a name generator) and a list of questions (a name interpreter) about each alter's attributes—things like gender, age, education and anything else that's important to the study you're doing (Marin and Hampton 2007).

To select a name generator, you have to decide what fraction of the network you're studying. Figure 10.4 shows a useful typology, laid out by Boissevain (1974:47–48).

At the center is ego, the person whose network is being mapped. Ego is surrounded by network alters in six zones of decreasing interaction:

1. First, there is a *personal cell* of a very few close relatives and ego's closest personal friends. These are people in whom ego is highly invested, both materially and emotionally.

2–3. Next, there are two *intimate zones*, comprising close friends and relatives with whom we maintain active relations (zone 2A) and passive relations (zone 2B).

4. Next, there is an *effective zone*. These are people who are useful, either because of resources that they control or because we think they know people who can help us get the resources we're after. At this level of remove, the attachment of friends is instrumental rather than emotional.

5. Next, there is a *nominal zone* comprising people we know but on whom we hardly ever call for anything. At this level of remove, there is little attachment, either instrumental or emotional.

6. Finally, there is an *extended zone* of people comprising all those people we know, but just

Figure 10.4 Boissevain's Personal Network Zones

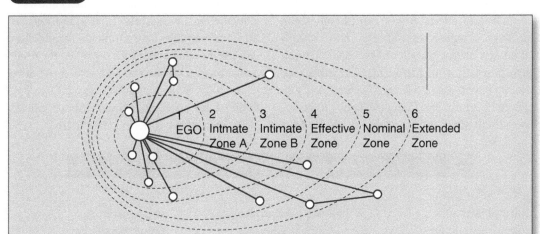

Source: J. Boissevain, *Friends of Friends. Networks, Manipulators and Coalitions,* 1974, Basil Blackwell.

barely—people whose faces we might recognize or might remember that they met us, sometime.

Researchers interested in social support study the first four zones of Figure 10.4—that is, the personal cell, the two intimate zones, and the effective zone. Marin and Hampton (2007:171) showed that the following name generator gets at all these components of personal networks:

1. From time to time, most people discuss important matters with other people. Who are the people with whom you discuss matters important to you?

2. Who from outside your home has recently helped you with tasks around the home, such as painting, moving furniture, cooking, cleaning, or major or minor repairs?

3. Suppose you need to borrow some small thing like a tool or a cup of sugar, from whom outside your household would you ask to borrow it?

4. If you need to borrow a large sum of money, say $1,000, whom would you ask for help?

5. Who are the people you really enjoy socializing with?

6. Please list anyone who is especially close to you who you have not listed in one of the previous questions (**Further Reading:** name generators).

Asking respondents these six questions can easily produce a list of 20 or more alters. Each piece of information you want about 20 alters means asking respondents 20 questions. Learning, say, the age, gender, education, occupation, and religion of 20 alters means asking respondents a total of 100 questions. And if you want information about ties among the alters, that's another $n(n-1/2)$ questions, where n is the number of alters. For 20 alters, that's *another* 190 questions, and for 40 alters it's another 780 questions.

This is why collecting personal network data is best done with software—to reduce respondent burden and to make sure that all the relevant questions get asked of each respondent. EgoNet (McCarty et al. 2011) has four modules: (1) questions about respondents; (2) questions to elicit the names of alters;

(3) questions about the alters; and (4) questions about relations among alters. All of the modules are optional, so you can ask only about network composition and skip the questions about ties among the alters if personal network structure is not of interest in your study. For example, you might ask the six questions suggested by Marin and Hampton above to generate a list of alters; or you might ask respondents to list a fixed number of people whom they know. Using a fixed number of alters allows for comparison of network content and network structure variables across individuals, and if you ask for the names of at least 30 alters, the results will represent both strong and weak ties (Lubber et al. 2007, Wutich and McCarty 2002). We'll look at how to analyze data about cultural domains and networks in Chapter 16.

Key Concepts in This Chapter

cultural domain	balanced incomplete	social network
cognitive structure	block design	whole networks
social structure	lambda-1 design	sociocentric networks
semantic relations	lambda-2 design	personal networks
level of contrast	free pile sorts	egocentric networks
hierarchical	multiple free pile sorts	egos
structure	lumper-splitter problem	alters
grue	nomination technique	social support
free listing	rank ordering	social capital
semantic cueing	paired comparisons	name generator
loose talk	order effects	name interpreter
triad test	nodes	

Summary

- Cultural, or semantic domains and networks both comprise lists of things, including people. Analysis of cultural domains and networks focuses on the content of those lists—the items— and on the structure of relations among the items.

  o There are five features of cultural domains: 1. The items are at the same level of contrast. 2. They have a hierarchical structure. 3. Agreement on the content of a domain is not uniform. 4. Some domains are widely shared while others are the province of cultural specialists. 5. There is a right answer to questions about the content and structure of a domain, but the right answer can vary by gender and other features of subgroups.

- Free listing is a method for getting the content of a domain. This requires the use of probes during interviews. Well-formed domains usually don't require more than 15 or 20 informants before the content is captured. Fuzzy domains may require 30 or 40.

  o Few people in the United States can distinguish between a first cousin, once removed and a second cousin, but they can name those things if asked to "list kinds of kin." Thus, people can name more things than they can identify, a phenomenon called "loose talk."

- Triad tests were developed in psychology and help us understand the structure of semantic domains. Informants are shown three items and are asked to pick out the one that's most different from the other two. This test is used for uncovering the cognitive structure of domains—that is, which items in a domain informants think "go together" for any reason.
  - o With nine items, there are 84 triads. Triad tests can be used with up to 25 items by employing a balanced incomplete block design.
  - o Triad tests can be made and analyzed with Anthropac software (Borgatti 1992a).
- The free pile sort is another method for testing the cognitive structure of a cultural domain. Informants sorts items (cards with the names of item or pictures, or even actual items) into piles as they see fit, putting items together that they think go together.
  - o Lists of items for a triad test of a pile sort can be extracted from texts, like interviews.
  - o Triad tests present each person with the same stimuli, so you can compare the data across individuals. With free pile sorts, people can be lumpers or splitters—making few or many piles with the same set of items. With free pile sorts, you can see the structure of a domain for a group of people but you can't compare the data from individuals. With piles sorts, though, you can have as many as 50 or 60 items and people say they are fun to do.
- Rank ordering produces interval-level data, while produce ordinal-level data. Paired comparisons produce rank-ordered data. Brands of cars can be usefully ranked in terms of prestige or how environmentally friendly they are. Like triad tests, paired comparisons can be tedious for respondents, but, like triad tests, there are ways to lower respondent burden.
- Like cultural domains, networks also comprise lists of items and the analysis involves understanding features of the content and structure of the items.
  - o There are two kinds of networks: whole, or sociocentric, and personal, or egocentric networks.
- In collecting data about personal networks, it is important to define the nature of ties. Some commonly used ties include: interaction and exchange (communicates with, gives advice to), affect (likes, trusts), is kin of, has a non-kin role (is the teacher of, is the supervisor of), cognitive ties (knows someone), and affiliations (lives in a house with, sits on a corporate board with).
  - o It is useful to think of personal networks in terms of zones (Boissevain 1974): a personal cell of a very few close relatives and friends and relatives; an intimate zone of friends and relatives with whom we maintain active and passive relations; an effective zone of people who are useful in some way; a nominal zone of people we know but on whom we hardly ever call for anything; and an extended zone of all those people we know, but just barely.

Exercises

1. Ask 10 people to list "kinds of soda" (or pop, or soda pop, depending where you live). Give them two minutes. Then ask them to list "social problems facing us today." Again, give them two minutes. Tally the results on a word processor. You should see more repeats in the list of sodas than in the list of social problems. Why is that?

2. What is the loose talk phenomenon? How does gender play a part in this phenomenon?

3. Why do we use incomplete block designs for triad tests and paired comparisons? Illustrate your answer by calculating the number of pairs and triads in a set of 25 items.

4. What is the lumper-splitter problem? How does it affect the collection of data with pile sorts?

5. Define the intimate, effective, nominal, and extended zones in a personal network.

Further Reading

Cultural and semantic domains. Boster and Johnson (1989), Brewer (1995), Conklin (1955), D'Andrade (1995), Frake (1962), Goodenough (1956), Johnson and Griffith (1996), Romney and D'Andrade (1964), Spradley (1972, 1979), Weller (1983), Weller and Romney (1988), Werner and Schoepfle (1987). Software: Anthropac (Borgatti 1992a, 1992b).

Free lists. Fennell et al. (2009), Quinlan (2005), Ryan et al. (2000), Schrauf and Sanchez (2008), K. D. Smith et al. (2007), Thompson and Juan (2006).

Triad tasks. Alvarado (1994), Callanan et al. (1994), Durrenberger and Erem (2005), Furlow (2003), Ross et al. (2005), Siar (2003).

Pile sorts. Handwerker (2001), Hines (1993), Hogan et al. (2007), Hsiao et al. (2006), Maiolo et al. (1994), Parr and Lashua (2004), Quintiliani et al. (2008), Trotter and Potter (1993), Weller and Romney (1988).

Rankings and paired comparisons. Burton (2003), Durrenberger and Doukas (2008), Kozak et al. (2008).

Name generators. Burt (1987), Fischer (1982), Marin (2004), Marsden (1987, 1990), Pustejovsky and Spillanea (2009), Wellman (1979).

11

Scales and Scaling

This chapter is about building and using composite measures. I'll cover four kinds of composite measures: (1) indexes, (2) Guttman scales, (3) Likert scales, and (4) semantic differential scales. At the end of the chapter, I'll cover a few other interesting scales. First, though, some basic concepts of scaling.

SIMPLE SCALES: SINGLE INDICATORS

A scale is a device for assigning units of analysis to categories of a variable. The assignment is usually done with numbers, and questions are used a lot as scaling devices. Here are three typical scaling questions:

1. How old are you?

You can use this question to assign individuals to categories of the variable "age." In other words, you can *scale* people by age. The number that this first question produces has ratio properties (someone who is 50 is twice as old as someone who is 25).

2. How satisfied are you with your classes this semester? Are you satisfied, neutral, or unsatisfied?

You can use *this* question to assign people to one of three categories of the variable "satisfied." That is, you can *scale* them according to how satisfied they are with their classes. Suppose we let satisfied = 3, neutral = 2, and unsatisfied = 1. Someone who is assigned the number 3 is *more* satisfied than someone who is assigned the number 1. We don't know if that means 3 times more satisfied, or 10 times, or just marginally more satisfied, so this scaling device produces numbers that have ordinal properties.

3. Do you consider yourself to be Protestant, Catholic, Jewish, Muslim, some other religion? Or do you consider yourself as having no religion?

This scaling device lets you assign individuals to—that is, *scale them* by—categories of the variable "religious affiliation." Let Protestant = 1, Catholic = 2, Jewish = 3, Muslim = 4, and no religion = 5. The numbers produced by *this* device have nominal properties. You can't add them up and find the average religion.

These three questions have different content (they tap different concepts), and they produce numbers with different properties, but they have two very important things in common. All three questions are devices for scaling people and in all three cases the respondent is the principal source of measurement error.

When you use your own judgment to assign units of analysis to categories of a scaling device, *you* are the major source of measurement error.

In other words, if you assign individuals by your own observation to the category "male" or "female," then any mistakes you make in that assignment (in scaling people by sex) are *yours*.

The same is true no matter what the unit of analysis is. Suppose you have a list of 100 countries and your job is to assign each to a category of government (parliamentary republic, constitutional monarchy, dictatorial monarchy, military dictatorship, etc.). For each country, you have some literature—scholarly books and articles, stories from the *New York Times*, reports from the U.S. State Department, and so on. You read each of these, looking for clues about the nature of governance, and assign a number (1, 2, 3, etc.) to each country. Each country is a unit of analysis and is scaled on the nominal variable called "predominant type of government."

Later, in the analysis, you might ask a question like: "Are democracies less likely to go to war with one another than, say, dictatorships?" Any mistakes you make in assigning the countries to a category of government will affect the relations you find (or don't find) in your analysis.

COMPLEX SCALES: MULTIPLE INDICATORS

A single question on a questionnaire is technically a scale if it lets you assign the people you're studying to categories of a variable. A lot of really interesting variables in social science, however, are complex and can't easily be assessed with single indicators. What single question could you ask someone to measure the amount of stress they are experiencing? Their overall political orientation, from far left to far right? How much they value physical attractiveness compared to other characteristics in potential marriage partners? How prejudiced they are against Asian immigrants on the job?

We try to measure complex variables like these with complex instruments—that is, instruments that are made up of several indicators. These complex instruments are what people commonly call scales.

A classic social science concept is "socioeconomic status" or SES. It is often measured by combining measures of income, education, and occupational prestige. Each of these measures is an operationalization of the concept SES, but none of the measures, by itself, captures the complexity of the idea of socioeconomic status. Each indicator captures a piece of the concept, and together the indicators produce a single measurement of SES (**Further Reading:** measuring SES).

Some variables are best measured by single indicators and, by Ockham's razor, we would never use a complex scale to measure something when a simple scale will do. So: The function of **single-indicator scales** is to assign units of analysis to categories of a variable. The function of composite measures, or **complex scales**, is exactly the same, but they are used when single indicators won't do the job.

INDEXES

The most common composite measure is a **cumulative index**. Indexes are made up of several items, all of which count the same. Indexes are everywhere. The Dow-Jones Industrial Average is a weighted index of the prices of 30 stocks that are traded on the New York Stock Exchange. The U.S. Consumer Price Index is a measure of how much it costs to buy a fixed set of consumer items in the United States. We use indexes to measure people's health risks: the risk of contracting HIV, of getting lung cancer, of having a heart attack, of giving birth to an underweight baby, of becoming an alcoholic, of suffering from depression, and on and on.

And we use indexes with a vengeance to measure cognitive and physical functions.

Children in industrial societies of the world begin taking intelligence tests, achievement tests, and tests of physical fitness from the first day they enter school—or even before that. Achievement indexes—like the SAT, ACT, and GRE—affect so many people in the United States that there's a thriving industry devoted to helping children and adolescents do well on them.

Indexes can be criterion referenced or norm referenced. If you've ever taken a test where the only way to get an "A" was to get at least 90%, you've had your knowledge of some subject assessed by a criterion-referenced index. If you've ever taken a test where getting an "A" required that you score in the top 10% of the class—even if the highest grade in the class were 70%—then you've had your knowledge of some subject assessed by a norm-referenced index.

Standardized tests (whether of achievement, or of performance, or of personality traits) are usually norm referenced: Your score is compared to the norms that have been established by thousands of people who took the test before you.

How Indexes Work

Multiple-choice exams are cumulative indexes. The idea is that asking just one question about the material in a course would not be a good indicator of students' knowledge of the material. Instead, students typically are asked a bunch of multiple-choice questions.

Taken together, the reasoning goes, all the questions measure how well a student has mastered a body of material. If you take a test that has 60 multiple-choice questions and you get 45 correct, you get 45 points, one for each correct answer. That number, 45 (or 75% of 60 questions), is a cumulative index of how well you did on the test.

Note that in a cumulative index, it makes no difference *which* items are assigned to you. In a test of just 10 questions, for example, there are obviously just 10 ways to get one right—but there are 45 ways to get two right, 120 ways to get three right. . . . Students can get the same score of 80% on a test of 100 questions and miss entirely different sets of 20 questions. This makes cumulative indexes robust—that is, they provide many ways to get at an underlying variable (in the case of an exam, the underlying variable is knowledge of the material).

On the other hand, stringing together a series of items to form an index doesn't guarantee that the composite measure will be useful—any more than stringing together a series of multiple-choice questions will fairly assess a student's knowledge of, say, sociology or political science.

We pretend that: (1) knowledge is a **unidimensional** variable; (2) a fair set of questions is chosen to represent knowledge of some subject; and therefore (3) a cumulative index is a fair test of the knowledge of that subject. We know that the system is imperfect, but we pretend to get on with life.

We don't have to pretend. When it comes to scaling units of analysis on complex constructs—like scaling countries on the construct of freedom or people on the construct of political conservatism—we can test the unidimensionality of an index with a technique called Guttman scaling.

GUTTMAN SCALES

In a Guttman scale, as compared to a cumulative index, the measurements for the items have a *particular pattern indicating that the items measure a unidimensional variable*. To understand the pattern we're looking for, consider the following three questions.

1. How much is 124 plus 14?

2. How much is 1/2 + 1/3 + 1/5 + 2/11?

3. If 3X = 133, then how much is X?

If you know the answer to question 3, you probably know the answer to questions 1 and 2. If you know the answer to question 2, but not to 3, it's still safe to assume that you know the answer to question 1. This means that, in general, *knowledge about basic math* is a unidimensional variable (Goodenough 1944; Guttman 1944).

Suppose you're studying worker alienation in a factory. After running a focus group and talking to some of the union leaders, you decide on three indicators of alienation, each indicating increasing alienation: (1) signing a petition against new work rules (an expression of alienation that's backed up by support from others—you're with a crowd and not out there, on your own against management); (2) calling in sick a lot (now you're making a statement on your own, but not quite challenging management directly); and (3) filing a grievance against management (now it's really you against them, nowhere to hide, winner takes all, and the loser goes home).

If your hypothesis is correct, then worker alienation—in this factory, at this moment—is a unidimensional variable. It starts with signing a petition, and as it gets stronger, it is expressed by calling in sick and finally by filing a grievance. To test this, set up a table like Table 11.1 and assign each worker one point for each of these three indicators.

Respondents 1, 2, and 3 scored positive on all three items. The next three respondents (4, 5, and 6) signed the petition and call in sick regularly, but haven't filed any grievances. Respondents 7, 8, and 9 signed the petition but did not call in sick and did not file a grievance. And respondents 10, 11, and 12 have no alienation points on this scale. They have not signed the petition, have not called in sick a lot, and have not filed a grievance. So far so good.

The next three (13, 14, 15) have filed grievances but have neither signed the petition nor called in sick a lot. Finally, respondent 16 signed the petition and filed a grievance, but does not call in sick a lot.

Table 11.1 An Index That Scales With a Guttman Coefficient of Reproducibility < 0.90

Respondent	Signed a petition	Called in sick a lot	Filed a grievance
1	+	+	+
2	+	+	+
3	+	+	+
4	+	+	−
5	+	+	−
6	+	+	−
7	+	−	−
8	+	−	−
9	+	−	−
10	−	−	−
11	−	−	−
12	−	−	−
13	−	−	+
14	−	−	+
15	−	−	+
16	+	−	+

If we had data from only the first 12 respondents, the data would form a perfect Guttman scale. For those first 12 respondents, in other words, the three behaviors (signing a petition, calling in sick, and filing a grievance) are indicators of a unidimensional variable, worker alienation.

The Coefficient of Reproducibility

Unfortunately, we've got those other four respondents to deal with. For whatever reasons, respondents 13–16 do not conform to the pattern seen in respondents 1–12. The data for respondents 13–16 are "errors" in the sense that their data diminish the extent to which the index of alienation forms a perfect

scale. To test how closely any set of index data reproduces a perfect scale, apply Guttman's (1944) coefficient of reproducibility, or CR. The formula for Guttman's CR is:

$$1 - \frac{\text{number of errors}}{\text{number of entries}} \qquad \textbf{formula 11.1}$$

Given the pattern in Table 11.1, we don't expect to see those plus signs in column 3 for respondents 13, 14, and 15. If the data scaled according to our hypothesis, then anyone who filed a grievance—anyone who has a plus in column 3—should have all pluses and a score of 3 on alienation. If we give respondents 13, 14, and 15 a scale score of 3 (for having filed a grievance), then those three cases would be responsible for *six* errors—you'd have to stick two pluses in for each of the cases to make them come out according to the hypothesis. Yes, you could make it just three, not six errors, by sticking a minus sign in column 3. Some researchers use this scoring method, but I prefer the more conservative method of scoring more errors (Goodenough 1944). It keeps you on your toes.

Finally, we don't expect that minus sign in column 2 of respondent 16's data. That case creates just one error (you only need to put in one plus to make it come out right). All together, that makes 6 + 1 = 7 errors in the attempt to reproduce a perfect scale. For Table 11.1, the CR is:

$$1 - \frac{7}{48} = .85$$

which is to say that the data come within 15% of scaling perfectly. By convention, a coefficient of reproducibility of 0.90 or greater is accepted as a significant approximation of a perfect scale. Guttman (1944) recommended a coefficient of 0.85 or better, and I'm willing to settle for that, especially with the conservative method for scoring errors.

Some Examples of a Guttman Scale

Christopher Mooney and Mei-Hsien Lee (1995) studied the history of abortion law reform. The 1973 *Roe v. Wade* decision by the U.S. Supreme Court made abortion on demand a woman's right in all 50 states. This decision didn't just happen all at once.

Before 1973, abortion was outlawed in all 50 states, but it was legal in some states when carrying the fetus to term was a threat to the woman's life. Beginning in the 1950s, various groups began working to get states to enact regulation reform and to make abortion legal under more and more circumstances. The first state in this era to enact regulation reform was Mississippi in 1966. By the time the *Roe v.*

Wade decision came down, 17 other states had enacted some kind of legislation reforming the regulation of abortion.

Mooney and Lee (1995) found that the laws in these 18 states formed a perfect Guttman scale, based on four successively more liberal conditions. In addition to cases involving threats to the woman's life, abortion would be legal: (1) when the pregnancy resulted from rape or incest; (2) when the fetus was defective or there was a risk to the woman's physical health; (3) when there was a threat to the woman's mental health; and (4) whenever a woman decided she wanted one.

Table 11.2 shows the data. When you collect data on cases, you don't know what (if any) pattern will emerge, so you pretty much grab cases and code them for traits in random order. If you grabbed cases in chronological order, for example, you wouldn't see the perfect pattern of pluses and minuses in Table 11.2.

When you have the data in a table, the first thing to do is arrange the pluses and minuses in their "best" order—the order that conforms most to the perfect Guttman scale—and compute the CR. We look for the trait that occurs most frequently (the one with the most pluses across the row) and place that one at the bottom of the matrix. Then we look for the next-most-frequent trait, and put it on the next-to-the-bottom row of the matrix.

We keep doing this until we rearrange the data to take advantage of whatever underlying pattern is hiding in the matrix. Then we count up the "errors" in the matrix and compute Guttman's coefficient of reproducibility. For these 18 states and four traits, the coefficient is a perfect 1.0, and all 18 cases can be ranked on the degree of permissiveness regarding abortion. Obviously, if a state allows abortion on demand, it allows it in all specific cases, so it gets a scale score of 4. If a state allows abortion in cases where the woman's mental health is at risk, then it allows abortion in cases where the woman's physical health is at risk and in cases of rape or incest, so it gets a scale score of 3; and so on. (The actual work of arranging

Table 11.2 A Guttman Scale of Abortion Law During the 1960s and 1970s for 18 States in the U.S.

State	Year of Reform	Rape or Incest	Defect in Fetus or Threat to Woman's Physical Health	Threat to Woman's Mental Health	On Demand	Scale Score on Permissiveness
MS	1966	+	–	–	–	1
AR	1969	+	+	–	–	2
FL	1972	+	+	–	–	2
GA	1968	+	+	–	–	2
CA	1967	+	+	+	–	3
CO	1967	+	+	+	–	3
NC	1967	+	+	+	–	3
MD	1968	+	+	+	–	3
DE	1969	+	+	+	–	3
KS	1969	+	+	+	–	3
NM	1969	+	+	+	–	3
SC	1970	+	+	+	–	3
VA	1970	+	+	+	–	3
OR	1969	+	+	+	–	3
AK	1970	+	+	+	+	4
HA	1970	+	+	+	+	4
NY	1970	+	+	+	+	4
WA	1970	+	+	+	+	4

Source: Constructed from data in C. Z. Mooney and M-H. Lee, "Legislating Morality in the American States: The Case of Pre-Roe Abortion Regulation Reform." *American Journal of Political Science* 39:599–627. Copyright © 1995.

the data and counting the errors is done by computer. (See, for example, Anthropac, Appendix E.)

What this means is that when it came to abortion, permissiveness during the 1960s and early 1970s in the United States was a unidimensional variable. That's nice to know, but there's more. The scale scores in Table 11.2

have a Spearman's rank-order correlation of 0.44 with the year of reform and this correlation was statistically significant (see Chapter 21 for more on correlation). This is support for the theory of incremental policy reform in political science. We see this process of incremental reform at work, for example, in acceptance, over time, of same-sex marriage and of medical marijuana in the various states in the United States.

According to the theory, as pressure builds for some reform, one or two states lead the way with tentative steps. Other states hang back and watch the results. Then there is a rush of states that follow and the steps are less tentative. Finally, all the states that are going to take the steps have done so and the process goes back to a slow pace again, as the remaining states hang back and assess the situation some more.

The process is evident in Table 11.2. Mississippi led off with a small step in 1966. By 1970, 17 states had enacted reform, but it would take two more years before the 18th state, Florida, would join, and that state reversed the trend to more and more liberal reform by enacting less permissive legislation than the 10 states before it had done (Box 11.1).

Box 11.1 The Bogardus Social Distance Scale

An early example of a Guttman scale is the **Bogardus Social Distance Scale**, developed by Emory Bogardus in 1925. Since Guttman didn't describe his method for testing the unidimensionality of a scale until 1944, the Bogardus scale is not usually *called* a Guttman scale, but a Guttman scale it is, nevertheless.

Bogardus showed people names of ethnic groups and asked them, for each group, which of the following seven opinions they agreed with most: "I would be willing to accept members of this group: (1) as kin through marriage; (2) as personal friends; (3) as neighbors; (4) as co-workers; (5) as citizens of their country; (6) only as visitors to their country; (7) under no condition, not even as visitors to my country."

Some version of this scale has been used in dozens of studies over the years, so there is now a substantial literature on racial and ethnic distance (**Further Reading:** Bogardus Social Distance Scale).

Data Scale, Variables Don't

Remember, *only data scale, not variables*. That is, scales like these are **sample dependent**. If the items in a cumulative index form a strong Guttman scale, we can say that, *for the sample we've tested*, the concept measured by the index is unidimensional—that the items are a composite measure of one and only one underlying concept.

Billie DeWalt (1979) used Guttman scaling to test an index of material style of life in a Mexican farming community. He scored 54 people on whether they owned eight material items (a radio, a stove, a sewing machine, etc.) and achieved a CR of 0.95. My hunch is that DeWalt's material-style-of-life scale has its analog in nearly all societies. The particular list of items that DeWalt used in rural Mexico may not scale in an African American community in the American South (Dressler et al. 1985), but *some* list of material items *will* scale there. You just have to find them.

The way to do this is to code every household in your study for the presence or absence of a list of material items. The particular list could emerge from participant observation or from informal interviews. Then you'd use a program like Anthropac to sort out the matrix, drop some material items, and build the index until it has a CR of 0.90 or better (Box 11.2).

Box 11.2 Indexes that don't scale

Indexes that do not scale can still be useful in comparing populations. Dennis Werner (1985) studied psychosomatic stress among Brazilian farmers who were facing the uncertainty of having their lands flooded by a major dam. He used a 20-item stress index developed by Berry (1976).

Since the index did not constitute a unidimensional scale, Werner could not differentiate among his *informants* (in terms of the amount of stress they were under) as precisely as DeWalt could differentiate among *his* informants (in terms of their quality of life). But farmers in Werner's sample gave a stress response to an average of 9.13 questions on the 20-item test, while Berry had found that Canadian farmers gave stress responses on an average of 1.79 questions. It is very unlikely that a difference of such magnitude between two *populations* would occur by chance (**Further Reading:** Guttman scaling).

LIKERT SCALES

Perhaps the most commonly used form of scaling is attributed to Rensis Likert (1932). Likert introduced the ever-popular five-point scale that we talked about in Chapter 9 on questionnaire construction. Recall that a typical question might read as follows:

Please consider the following statements carefully. After each statement, check the answer that most reflects your opinion. Would you say you agree a lot with the statement, agree a little, are neutral, disagree a little, or disagree a lot with each statement? Ok, here's the first statement:

Congress is doing all it can to prevent another financial crisis.

☐ Agree a lot

☐ Agree

☐ Neutral

☐ Disagree a little

☐ Disagree a lot

The five-point scale might become three points or seven points, and the agree-disagree scale may become approve-disapprove,

favor-oppose, or excellent-bad, but the principle is the same. These are all Likert-type scales.

I say "Likert-type scales" rather than just "Likert scales" because Likert did more than just introduce a format. He was interested in measuring internal states of people (attitudes, emotions, orientations) and he realized that most internal states are multidimensional. It's easy to label people as either conservatives or liberals, but the concept of political orientation is very complex. A person who is liberal on matters of domestic policy—favoring single-payer, government-run health care, for example—may be conservative on matters of foreign political policy—against involvement in any foreign military actions. Someone who is liberal on matters of foreign economic policy—favoring economic aid for all democracies that ask for it—may be conservative on matters of personal behavior—against same-sex marriage, for example.

The liberal-conservative dimension on matters of personal behavior is also complicated. There's no way to assign people to a category of this variable by asking one question. People can have live-and-let-live attitudes about sexual preference and extramarital sex and be against a woman's right to an abortion on demand.

Of course, there are packaging effects. People who are conservative on one dimension of political orientation are *likely* to be conservative on other dimensions, and people who are liberal on one kind of personal behavior are *likely* to be liberal on others. Still, no single question lets you scale people in general on a variable as complex as "attitude toward personal behavior," let alone "political orientation." That's why we need composite scales.

Steps in Building a Likert Scale

Likert's method was to take a long list of possible scaling items for a concept and find the subsets that measured the various dimensions. If the concept were unidimensional, then one subset would do. If it were multidimensional, then several subsets would be needed. Here are the steps in building and testing a Likert scale.

1. Identify and label the variable you want to measure. This is generally done by induction—that is, from your own experience (Spector 1992:13). After you work in some area of research for a while, you'll develop some ideas about the variables you want to measure. The people you talk to in focus groups, for example, may impress you with the idea that "People are afraid of crime around here," and you decide to scale people on the variable "fear of crime."

Or you may observe that some people love to poke around for hours in malls, while others prefer using the Internet to buy all their clothes, gifts, etc. Some people seem to have a black belt in shopping, while others would rather have root canal surgery than set foot in a mall. The task is then to scale (measure) people on a variable you might call "shopping orientation" with all its multidimensionality. You may need a subscale for "shopping while on vacation," another just for "car shopping," and another for "shopping for clothing that I really need." (The other way to identify variables is by deduction [see Box 1.3]. This generally involves analyzing similarity matrices, about which more in Chapters 15 and 16.)

2. Write a long list of indicator questions or statements. This is usually another exercise in induction. Ideas for the indicators can come from reading the literature on whatever research problem has captured you, from personal experience, from ethnography, from reading newspapers, from interviews with experts.

Free lists are a particularly good way to get at indicators for some variables. If you want to build a scaling device for the concept of "attitudes toward growing old," you could start by asking a large group of people to "list things that you associate with growing old" and then you could build the questions or statements in a Likert scale around the items in the list.

Be sure to use both negative and positive indicators. If you have a statement like "One of the great things about this university is the emphasis on consistently winning sports teams," then you need a negatively worded statement for balance, like "One of the bad things about this university is the emphasis they put on sports."

And don't make the indicator items extreme. Here's a badly worded item: "The emphasis on sports is the most terrible thing that has ever happened here." Let people tell *you* where they stand by giving them a range of response choices (strongly agree–strongly disagree). Don't bludgeon people with such strongly worded scale items that they feel forced to reduce the strength of their response.

In wording items, all the cautions from Chapter 9 on questionnaire design apply: Remember who your respondents are and use *their* language. Make the items as short and as uncomplicated as possible. No double negatives. No double-barreled items. Here is a terrible item:

On a scale of 1–5, how much do you agree or disagree with the following statement:

"People should speak English and give up any language they brought with them when they came to this country."

People can agree or disagree with both parts of this statement, or agree with one part and disagree with the other. When you get through, you should have four or five times the number of items as you think you'll need in your final scale. If you want a scale of, say, six items, use 25 or 30 items in the first test (DeVellis 2003:66).

3. Determine the type and number of response categories. Some popular response categories are agree-disagree, favor-oppose, helpful–not helpful, many-none, like me–not like me, true-untrue, suitable-unsuitable, always-never, and so on. Most Likert scale items have an odd number of response choices: three, five, or seven. The idea is to give people a range of choices that includes a midpoint. The midpoint usually carries the idea of neutrality—neither agree nor disagree, for example. An even number of response choices forces informants to "take a stand"; an odd number of choices lets informants "sit on the fence."

There is no best format. But if you ever want to combine responses into just two categories (yes-no, agree-disagree, like me–not like me), then it's better to have an even number of choices. Otherwise, you have to decide whether the neutral responses get collapsed with the positive answers or the negative answers—or thrown out as missing data.

4. Test your item pool on some respondents. Ideally, you need at least 100—or even 200— respondents to test an initial pool of items (Spector 1992:29). This will ensure that: (1) you capture the full variation in responses to all your items; and (2) the response variability represents the variability in the general population to which you eventually want to apply your scale.

5. Conduct an item analysis—coming right up—to find the items that form a unidimensional scale of the variable you're trying to measure.

6. Use your scale in your study and run the item analysis again to make sure that the scale is holding up. If it does, then look for relations between the scale scores and the scores of other variables for persons in your study.

ITEM ANALYSIS

This is the key to building scales. The idea is to find out which, among the many items you're testing, need to be kept and which should be thrown away. The set of items that you keep should tap a single social or psychological dimension. In other words, the scale should be unidimensional.

In the next few pages, I'm going to walk through the logic of building scales that are unidimensional. Read these pages very carefully. At the end of this section, I'll advocate using factor analysis to do the item analysis quickly, easily, and reliably. No fair, though, using factor analysis for scale construction until you understand the logic of scale construction itself.

There are three steps to doing an item analysis and finding a subset of items that constitute a unidimensional scale: (1) scoring the items; (2a) taking the interitem correlation and (2b) calculating Cronbach's coefficient alpha; and (3) taking the item-total correlation.

Scoring the Responses

The first thing to do is make sure that all the items are properly scored. Assume that we're trying to find items for a scale that measures the strength of support for lots of training in research methods among sociology students. Here are two potential scale items:

Training in multivariate statistics should be required for all undergraduate students of social science.

1	2	3	4	5
Strongly disagree	Disagree	Neutral	Agree	Strongly agree

Social science undergraduates don't need training in multivariate statistics.

1	2	3	4	5
Strongly disagree	Disagree	Neutral	Agree	Strongly agree

You can let the big and small numbers stand for any direction you want, but you must be consistent. Suppose we let the bigger numbers (4 and 5) represent support for training in multivariate statistics and let the smaller numbers (1 and 2) represent lack of support for that concept. Respondents who circle "strongly agree" on the first item get a 5 for that item. Those who circle "strongly agree" on the second item get scored as 1.

Taking the Interitem Correlation

Next, test to see which items contribute to measuring the construct you're trying to get at and which don't. This involves two calculations: the intercorrelation of the items and the correlation of the item scores with the total scores for each respondent. Table 11.3 shows the scores for three people on three items, where the items are scored from 1 to 5.

Table 11.3 The Scores for Three People on Three Likert Scale Items

Person	Item		
	1	2	3
1	1	3	5
2	5	2	2
3	4	1	3

To find the interitem correlation, we would look at all pairs of columns. These are shown in Table 11.4.

A simple measure of how much these pairs of numbers are alike or unalike involves, first, adding up their *actual differences*, Σ_d, and then dividing this by the total *possible differences*, $\max_d$.

In the first pair, the actual difference between 1 and 3 is 2; the difference between 5 and 2 is 3; the difference between 4 and 1 is 3. The sum of the differences is $\Sigma_d = 2 + 3 + 3 = 8$.

For each item, there could be as much as 4 points difference—in Pair 1, someone could have answered 1 to item 1 and 5 to item 2, for example. So for three items, the total possible difference, $\max_d$, would be $4 \times 3 = 12$. The

Table 11.4 The Data From the Three Pairs of Items in Table 11.3

Pair 1		Diff	Pair 2		Diff	Pair 3		Diff
1	3	2	1	5	4	3	5	2
5	2	3	5	2	3	2	2	0
4	1	3	4	3	1	1	3	2
Σ_d (Sum of the differences)		8			8			4
$\Sigma_d / \max_d$		0.67			0.67			0.33
$1 - \left\{ \Sigma_d / \max_d \right\}$		0.33			0.33			0.67

actual *difference* is 8 out of a possible 12 points, so items 1 and 2 are 8/12 = 0.67 *different*, which means that these two items are $1 - \Sigma_d / \max_d = 0.33$ *alike*. Items 1 and 3 are also 0.33 alike, and items 2 and 3 are 0.67 alike.

Items that measure the same underlying construct should be related to one another. If I answer "strongly agree" to the statement "Training in multivariate statistics should be required for all undergraduate students of sociology," then (if I'm consistent in my attitude and if the items that tap my attitude are properly worded) I should strongly disagree with the statement that "sociology undergraduates don't need training in multivariate statistics." If everyone who answers "strongly agree" to the first statement answers "strongly disagree" to the second, then the items are perfectly correlated.

Cronbach's Alpha

Cronbach's alpha is a statistical test of how well the items in a scale are correlated with one another. One of the methods for testing the unidimensionality of a scale is called the **split-half reliability test**. If a scale of, say, 10 items, were unidimensional, all the items would be measuring parts of the same underlying concept. In that case any five items should produce scores that are more or less like the scores of any other five items. This is shown in Table 11.5.

Split Halves and the Combinations Rule

There are many ways to split a group of items into halves and each split will give you a different set of totals. Here's the formula, known as the **combinations rule**, for selecting n elements from a set of N elements, paying no attention to the ordering of the elements:

$$\frac{N!}{n!(N-n)!} \qquad \text{formula 11.2}$$

Table 11.5	The Schematic for the Split-Half Reliability Test	
Person	Split A: Score on items 1-5	Split B: Score on items 6-10
1	X_1	Y_1
2	X_2	Y_2
3	X_3	Y_3
.	.	.
.	.	.
N	X_n	Y_n
	Total for A	Total for B

If you have 10 respondents, then there are $10!/5![(10 - 5)!] = 252$ ways to split them into halves of five each. For 20 items, there are 184,756 possible splits of 10 each. Cronbach's coefficient alpha provides a way to get the average of all these split-half calculations directly. The formula for Cronbach's alpha is:

$$\alpha = \frac{N_\rho}{1 + \rho(N-1)} \qquad \text{formula 11.3}$$

where ρ (the Greek letter *rho*) is the average interitem correlation—that is, the average correlation among all pairs of items being tested.

By convention, a good set of scale items should have a Cronbach's alpha of 0.80 or higher. Be warned, though, that if you have a long list of scale items, the chances are good of getting a high alpha coefficient. An interitem correlation of just 0.29 produces an alpha of 0.80 in a set of 10 items (DeVellis 2003:98).

Eventually, you want an alpha coefficient of 0.80 or higher for a *short* list of items, all of which hang together and measure the same thing. Cronbach's alpha will tell you if your scale hangs together, but it won't tell you which items to throw away and which to keep.

To do that, you need to identify the items that do not discriminate between people who score high and people who score low on the total set of items.

Finding the Item-Total Correlation

First, find the total score for each person. Add up each respondent's scores across all the items. Table 11.6 shows what it would look like if you tested 50 items on 200 people (each x is a score for one person on one item).

For 50 items, scored from 1 to 5, each person could get a score as low as 50 (by getting a score of 1 on each item) or as high as 250 (by getting a score of 5 on each item). In practice, each person in a survey will get a total score somewhere in between.

A rough and ready way to find the items that discriminate well among respondents is to divide the respondents into two groups, the 25% with the highest total scores and the 25% with the lowest total scores. Look for the items that the two groups have in common. Those items are *not discriminating* among informants with regard to the concept being tested. Items that fail, for example, to discriminate between people who strongly favor training in methods (the top 25%) and people who don't (the bottom 25%) are not good items for scaling people in this construct. Throw those items out.

There is a more formal way to find the items that discriminate well among respondents and the items that don't. This is the item-total correlation. Table 11.7 shows the data you need for this:

Table 11.6 Finding the Item-Total Correlation

Person	Item 1	Item 2	Item 3	.	.	Item 50
1	x	x	x	.		x
2	x	x	x	.	.	x
3	x	x	x	.	.	x
.	.	.	.	.	.	.
.	.	.	.	.	.	.
200	x	x				x

Table 11.7 The Data for the Interitem Correlation

Person	Total Score	Item 1	Item 2	Item 3	.	.	50
1	x	x	x	x	.	.	x
2	x	x	x	x	.	.	x
3	x	x	x	x	.	.	x
.	.	.	.	.	.	.	.
.	.	.	.	.	.	.	.
N	x	x	x	x	.	.	x

With 50 items, the total score gives you an idea of where each person stands on the concept you're trying to measure. If the interitem correlation were perfect, then every item would be contributing equally to our understanding of where each respondent stands. Some items do better than others. The ones that don't contribute a lot will correlate poorly with the total score for each person. Keep the items that have the highest correlation with the total scores.

You can use any statistical analysis package to find the interitem correlations, Cronbach's alpha, and the item-total correlations for a set of preliminary scale items. Your goal is to get rid of items that detract from a high interitem correlation and to keep the alpha coefficient above 0.80. (For an excellent step-by-step explanation of item analysis, see Spector 1992:43–46).

TESTING FOR UNIDIMENSIONALITY WITH FACTOR ANALYSIS

Factor analysis is a technique for data reduction. If you have 30 items in a pool of potential scale items and responses from a sample of people to those pool items, factor analysis lets you reduce the 30 items to a smaller set—say, five or six. Each item is given a score, called its factor loading. This tells you how much each item "belongs" to each of the underlying factors.

If a scale is unidimensional, there will be a single factor that underlies all the variables (items) and all the items will "load high" on that single factor. If a scale is multidimensional, then there will be a series of factors that underlie sets of variables. Scale developers get a large pool of potential scale items (at least 40) and ask a lot of people (at least 200) to respond to the items. Then they run the factor analysis and select those items that load high—typically, 0.35–0.60—on the factor or factors (the underlying concept or concepts) they are trying to understand. They also test their results—their

scale—on a new sample and refine their scale questions over time. Here's an example.

Morokoff's Sexual Assertiveness Scale for Women

Patricia Morokoff and her colleagues at the University of Rhode Island used factor analysis to develop a scale of sexual assertiveness in women (Morokoff et al. 1997). Morokoff et al. hypothesized three dimensions to this variable: (1) women varied in their ability to initiate wanted sex; (2) women varied in their ability to refuse unwanted sex; and (3) women varied in their ability to protect themselves from pregnancy and sexually transmitted disease (by demanding that the man use a condom).

Morokoff et al. made up several questionnaire items for each of nine sexual behaviors in women: kissing, touching of breasts, touching by partner of genitals, touching of partner's genitals, receiving oral sex, performing oral sex, vaginal intercourse, anal intercourse, and protecting themselves against pregnancy or disease by asking a partner to use a condom. For each behavior, the questionnaire items covered the three dimensions and the presence or absence of pressure.

For example, for kissing, when the woman was *not* under a lot of external pressure to give in, Morokoff et al. had items like: "I feel comfortable refusing to kiss a partner when I don't want to" and "If a partner wants to kiss and I don't want to, we do it anyway." For kissing when the woman *is* under a lot of external pressure to give in, they had items like: "If a partner pressures me to kiss him after I have refused, I continue to refuse" and "If I refused to kiss a partner and he continued to pressure me, I would give in."

There were similar items for touching of genitals, vaginal intercourse, demanding the use of a condom, and so on. All in all, they had 112 items about self-reported sexual behavior. The items were rated by respondents on a five-point scale: never, sometimes (about 25% of the time), about 50% of the time, usually (about 75% of the time), and always (100% of the time). Morokoff et al. also had 24 items about attitudes, and these, too, were rated on a five-point scale: disagree strongly, disagree, mixed, agree somewhat, agree strongly.

The full 136-item test was given to 260 women. The results (a matrix of 260 women by 136 responses) was factor analyzed. The analysis isolated 42 items that loaded 0.45 or higher on each of the three factors: 17 items for the *initiation* factor, 14 items for the *refusal* factor, and 11 items for the *pregnancy-STD prevention* factor (the condom factor).

Morokoff et al. next gave the 42-item questionnaire to an entirely different sample of 136 women. They used factor analysis and item-total correlation on the results of the second sample to winnow the 42 items down to just 18, with six items for each of the three subscales.

Morokoff et al. went on to test their scale on 752 more women to improve the language of the questions (they substituted the words

"begin sex" for "initiate sex," for example) and on 354 women from their original sample during a one-year follow-up to see how the subscales held up. Consistently, women reported being less assertive in refusing unwanted sex and in demanding the use of a condom when they anticipated a negative reaction from their partners (Morokoff et al. 1997:802). Morokoff et al.'s final scale is shown in Table 11.8.

All of that work gives Morokoff et al.'s sexual assertiveness scale credibility and, indeed, the scale has been used by other researchers for whom this variable is important. Jacobs and Thomlinson (2009), for example, used the scale in their study of how self-silencing increased the risk of sexually acquired HIV in women over 50. You may not develop major scales for others to use but you *should* test the unidimensionality of any composite measure you develop for your

Table 11.8 Sexual Assertiveness in Women Scale

Items that are reverse-coded are indicated by (R). Notice that in all three subscales, half the items are reverse-coded. In other words, the same concepts are tested with items that are worded positively and with items that are worded negatively. The factor loadings for each of these 18 items were all above .55 in two separate studies.

Initiation

1. I begin sex with my partner if I want to.
2. I let my partner know if I want my partner to touch my genitals.
3. I wait for my partner to touch my genitals instead of letting my partner know that's what I want. (R)
4. I wait for my partner to touch my breasts instead of letting my partner know that's what I want. (R)
5. I let my partner know if I want to have my genitals kissed.
6. Women should wait for men to start things like breast touching. (R)

Refusal

7. I give in and kiss if my partner pressures me, even if I already said no. (R)
8. I put my mouth on my partner's genitals if my partner wants me to, even if I don't want to. (R)
9. I refuse to let my partner touch my breasts if I don't want that, even if my partner insists.
10. I have sex if my partner wants me to, even if I don't want to. (R)
11. If I said no, I won't let my partner touch my genitals even if my partner pressures me.
12. I refuse to have sex if I don't want to, even if my partner insists.

Protection against pregnancy-STD
13. I have sex without a condom or latex barrier if my partner doesn't like them, even if I want to use one. (R)
14. I have sex without using a condom or latex barrier if my partner insists, even if I don't want to. (R)
15. I make sure my partner and I use a condom or latex barrier when we have sex.
16. I have sex without using a condom or latex barrier if my partner wants. (R)
17. I insist on using a condom or latex barrier if I want to, even if my partner doesn't like them.
18. I refuse to have sex if my partner refuses to use a condom or latex barrier.

Source: P. J. Morokoff et al., "Sexual Assertiveness Scale (SAS) for Women: Development and Validation." *Journal of Personality and Social Psychology* 73:790–804. Copyright © 1997 by the American Psychological Association.

own data, using factor analysis—once you understand the principles of scale development that I've laid out here. I'll show you how to do that in Chapter 22, when we get to factor analysis (**Further Reading:** Likert scaling) (Box 11.3).

Box 11.3 Scales get simpler and more widely useful over time

Notice how the scale that Morokoff and her colleagues developed got simpler as it went through a couple of tests. They started with 136 items. These were reduced to 61 (the ones that scored over 0.45 on the first factor analysis). They removed 19 of those 61 items that were redundant (they were more or less rewordings of the same thing). The remaining 42 items were reduced to 18 in the next phase of the research when they gave the test to the next sample. In building scales, researchers err on the side of using too many questions rather than too few—no sense in leaving out some items that *may* be important until you know that you can do without them. But as scales are tested and retested, researchers often find that some items are redundant and the scales get shorter.

The original **Michigan Alcoholism Screening Test (MAST)**, for example, has 25 items (Selzer 1971). Pokorny et al. (1972) showed that their 10-item **Brief-MAST** instrument was about as effective as the longer original. Shields et al. (2007) found 454 published studies that used some version of the MAST through 2005. There's a 24-question version that's just for the elderly. It's called the **MAST-G**, where G stands for "geriatric version" (Blow et al. 1992). It turns out that "Yes" answers to *just two* of the 24 questions ("When talking with others, do you ever underestimate how much you actually drink?" and "Are you drinking more now than in the past?") predict hazardous levels of drinking in old people as well as the full, 24-question test (Johnson-Green et al. 2009).

The original, 1970 version of the **Attitudes Toward Women Scale (AWS)** had 55 items (Spence and Helmreich 1972). It was down to 25 items a year later (Spence et al. 1973) and down to 15 items five years after that (Spence and Helmreich 1978). That 15-item AWS is still measuring a unidimensional variable—what people think women's rights should be—and, while attitudes are becoming more liberal/feminist all around, women are still more supportive than men are of full equality (Twenge 1997; Whatley 2008).

(Continued)

(Continued)

Besides getting shorter, scales also get validated on new populations over time. Henderson et al. (1980) developed a 50-item test of social support (called the ISSI, or **Interview Schedule for Social Interaction**) on respondents in Canberra, Australia. Undén and Orth-Gomér (1989) tested and validated a much-reduced version of the scale on Swedish men who were at risk for heart disease, and the reduced ISSI in Swedish was validated on sample of men and women in Sweden who had been diagnosed with mental illness (Eklund et al. 2007).

Revalidations and reformulations of scales are published, so it pays to do a thorough search for existing scales before launching out on your own to build new scales from scratch.

VISUAL PROPS AS SCALES

Several scales have been developed over the years with visual props. Four of them are the semantic differential, the ladder of life, the happiness stick, and the faces scale.

The Semantic Differential

I've always liked the semantic differential scaling method. It was developed in the 1950s by Charles Osgood and his associates at the University of Illinois (Osgood et al. 1957; Snider and Osgood 1969) and since then has been used by thousands of researchers across the social sciences. With good reason: The semantic differential test is easy to construct and easy to administer.

Osgood was interested in how people interpret things—inanimate things (like artifacts or monuments), animate things (like persons, or the self), behaviors (like incest, or buying a new car or shooting a deer), and intangible concepts (like gun control or literacy). This is exactly what Likert scales are designed to test, but instead of asking people to rate questionnaire items about things, Osgood tested people's feelings differently: He gave them a target item and a list of paired adjectives about the target. The adjective pairs could come from reading of the literature or from focus groups or from ethnographic interviews. Target items can be ideas (land reform, socialism, aggression), behaviors (smoking, running, collecting stamps), objects (the mall, a courtroom, horses), environmental conditions (rain, drought, jungle) . . . almost anything.

Figure 11.1 is an example of a semantic differential test. The target is the concept of "abortion on demand." If you were taking this test right now, you'd be asked to place a check on each line, depending on your reaction to each pair of adjectives.

With a Likert scale, you ask people a series of questions that get at the target concept. In a semantic differential scale, you name the target concept and ask people to rate their feelings toward it on a series of variables. The semantic differential is usually a seven-point scale, as I've indicated in Figure 11.1. Your score on this test would be the sum of all your answers to the 13 adjective pairs.

Osgood and his associates did hundreds of replications of this test, using hundreds of adjective pairs, in 26 different cultures. Their analyses showed that in every culture just three major kinds of adjectives account for most of the variation in people's responses: **adjectives of evaluation** (good-bad, difficult-easy), followed by **adjectives of potency** (strong-weak, dominant-submissive, etc.), and **adjectives of activity** (fast-slow, active-inactive, sedentary-mobile, etc.).

| Figure 11.1 | Semantic Differential Test for the Concept of a Woman's Right to Abortion on Demand. The Dimensions on This Scale Are Useful for Measuring How People Feel About Many Different Things |

Hard		——	——	——	——	——	——	——		Easy
	1	2	3	4	5	6	7	
Active		——	——	——	——	——	——	——		Passive
Difficult		——	——	——	——	——	——	——		Easy
Permanent		——	——	——	——	——	——	——		Impermanent
Warm		——	——	——	——	——	——	——		Cold
Beautiful		——	——	——	——	——	——	——		Ugly
Strong		——	——	——	——	——	——	——		Weak
Reassuring		——	——	——	——	——	——	——		Unsettling
Important		——	——	——	——	——	——	——		Trivial
Fast		——	——	——	——	——	——	——		Slow
Clean		——	——	——	——	——	——	——		Dirty
Exciting		——	——	——	——	——	——	——		Boring
Useful		——	——	——	——	——	——	——		Useless

As the target for a semantic differential scale changes, you have to make sure that the adjective pairs make sense. The adjective pair ethical-corrupt works for some targets, but you probably wouldn't use it for having a cold. Indoor-outdoor works for lots of targets—kinds of music, hobbies, even famous persons—but it's not appropriate for targets like patio furniture, preservation of wilderness, or hang gliding, which are, by definition, outdoor things.

Vincke et al. (2001) used the semantic differential scale to explore the meaning of 25 sex acts among gay men in Flanders, Belgium. Their informants scaled each act (anal insertive sex, anal receptive sex, insertive fellatio, receptive fellatio, interfemoral sex, and so on) on six paired dimensions: unsatisfying/satisfying, stimulating/dull, interesting/boring, emotional/unemotional, healthy/unhealthy, and safety/danger. Vincke et al. then compared results on the semantic differential for men who practiced safe sex (with one partner or with a condom) and men who practiced unsafe sex (multiple partners and without a condom) to see which sex acts were more gratifying for high-risk-taking and low-risk-taking men (**Further Reading:** semantic differential).

Cantril's Ladder of Life

Figure 11.2 shows Hadley Cantril's ladder of life (1965). People are asked to list their concerns in life (financial success, healthy children, freedom from war, and so on). Then they are shown the ladder and are told that the bottom rung, 0, represents the worst-possible life and the top rung, 10, represents the best-possible life. For each of their concerns they are asked to point out where they are on the ladder right now, where they were five years ago, and where they think they'll be five years from now.

Note that the ladder of life is a self-anchoring scale. Respondents are asked to explain, in their own terms, what the top and bottom rungs of the ladder mean to them.

Visual props like this can be used for interviewing nonliterate as well as literate respondents. Keith et al. (1994) used the ladder of life in a study of aging in seven cultures. In five of the sites (two in the United States, one in Hong Kong, and two in Ireland) where most informants were literate, they used a six-rung ladder. (In Hong Kong, where people were comfortable placing themselves *between* but not *on* rungs, the team redesigned the ladder into a flight of stairs.) Among the Herero and Kung of Botswana, where many people were not literate, they replaced the ladder with the five fingers of the interviewer's hand (Keith et al. 1994:xxx, 113).

Hansen and McSpadden (1993) used the ladder-of-life technique in their studies of Zambian and Ethiopian refugees in Zambia and the United States. In Zambia, Hansen actually constructed a small wooden ladder and found that the method worked well. McSpadden used several methods to explore how Ethiopian refugees adjusted to life in the United States. Even when other methods failed, McSpadden found that the ladder-of-life method got people to talk about their experiences, fears, and hopes.

Be careful to tell people exactly what you want when you use any kind of visual prop. M. Jones and Nies (1996) used Cantril's ladder to measure the importance of exercise to elderly African American women. At least Jones and Nies *thought* that's what they were measuring. The mean for the ladder rating was about 9 on a scale of 1–10. Respondents thought they were being asked *how important exercise is*, not how important exercise is *to them, personally*. The researchers failed to explain properly to their respondents what the ladder was supposed to measure, and even devout couch potatoes are going to tell you that

Figure 11.2 Cantril's Ladder of Life

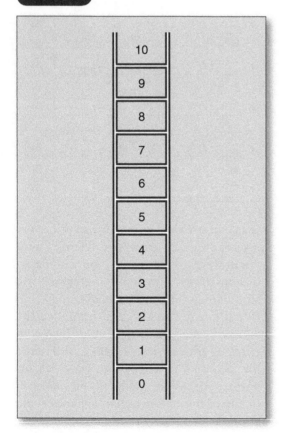

Source: H. Cantril. *The Pattern of Human Concerns.* Copyright © 1965 by Rutgers, The State University. Reprinted by permission of Rutgers University Press.

exercise is important if you ask them the general question (**Further Reading:** ladder of life).

The Faces Scale

Another interesting device is the **faces scale** shown in Figure 11.3. It's a seven-point (or five-point, or nine-point) scale with stylized faces that change from joy to gloom.

This technique was developed by Kunin in 1955 to measure job satisfaction and has been used widely for this ever since. Andrews and Withey (1976) adapted the faces scale to study well being and the device is now widely used for that. Physicians, nurses, and psychologists use this scale when they ask patients to describe pain. It's particularly good when working with children (Gulur et al. 2009; Wong and Baker 1988), but it's effective with adults as well (A. Harrison 1993) and, like the ladder of life and the semantic differential, has been used in many populations, in one form or another.

You can use the faces scale to capture people's feelings about health care, personal safety—even consumer items (brands of beer, titles of current movies, etc.). People are told: "Here are some faces expressing various feelings. Which face comes closest to how you feel about xxx?" Try using this scale with names of well-known political figures or music artists just to get a feel for how interesting it is.

If you use the faces scale, check for differences in how men and women interpret the neutral face—the one in the middle with the straight-line mouth. Elfering and Grebner (2010) found that 57% of men in their study interpreted the neutral face as sad, compared to 80% for women (**Further Reading:** faces scale).

MAGNITUDE SCALING

Most scales in the social sciences are **category scales**. The semantic differential is usually a seven-point scale. Likert-like scales are often five-point scales. These are ordinal measures, but people often have more finely graded opinions than a 1–5 scale captures. For some time, researchers have been experimenting with methods for measuring the actual magnitude of people's impressions, feelings, and attitudes.

These methods, known as **magnitude scaling** are based on the power law in psychophysics (Stevens 1957). The power law looks like this:

$$\psi = R = kS^b \qquad \text{formula 11.4}$$

Figure 11.3 The Faces Scale

Source: F. M. Andrews and S. B. Withey, *Social Indicators of Well-Being: Americans' Perceptions of Life Quality, Appendix A*, p. 13. Copyright © 1976. Plenum.

where the Greek letter ψ (psi, pronounced "sigh" in English) is perception of the magnitude of some physical stimulus (like a light or a tone); R is what people *say* is the magnitude of the stimulus; and S is the physical stimulus itself (for example, the intensity of the tone in decibels). The exponent b is the power to which you have to raise people's responses to make R and S identical, and k is some constant (Lodge 1981:13).

Suppose you tell people that the brightness value of some light is 50 points and then show them a light that's twice as bright. *If the exponent, b, in formula 11.4 were exactly 1.00*, then, averaging over a lot of people, R would be 100. Over the years, researchers have discovered the exponent—the deviation from 1.00—for various visual, auditory, and other sense stimuli, including line length.

Figure 11.4 is a visual stimulus, from Milton Lodge's book on magnitude scaling (1981:9). If you ask people to rate the lines in Figure 11.4 on a scale of 1–5 (short,

Figure 11.4 Line Lengths as a Visual Stimulus for Direct Magnitude Scaling

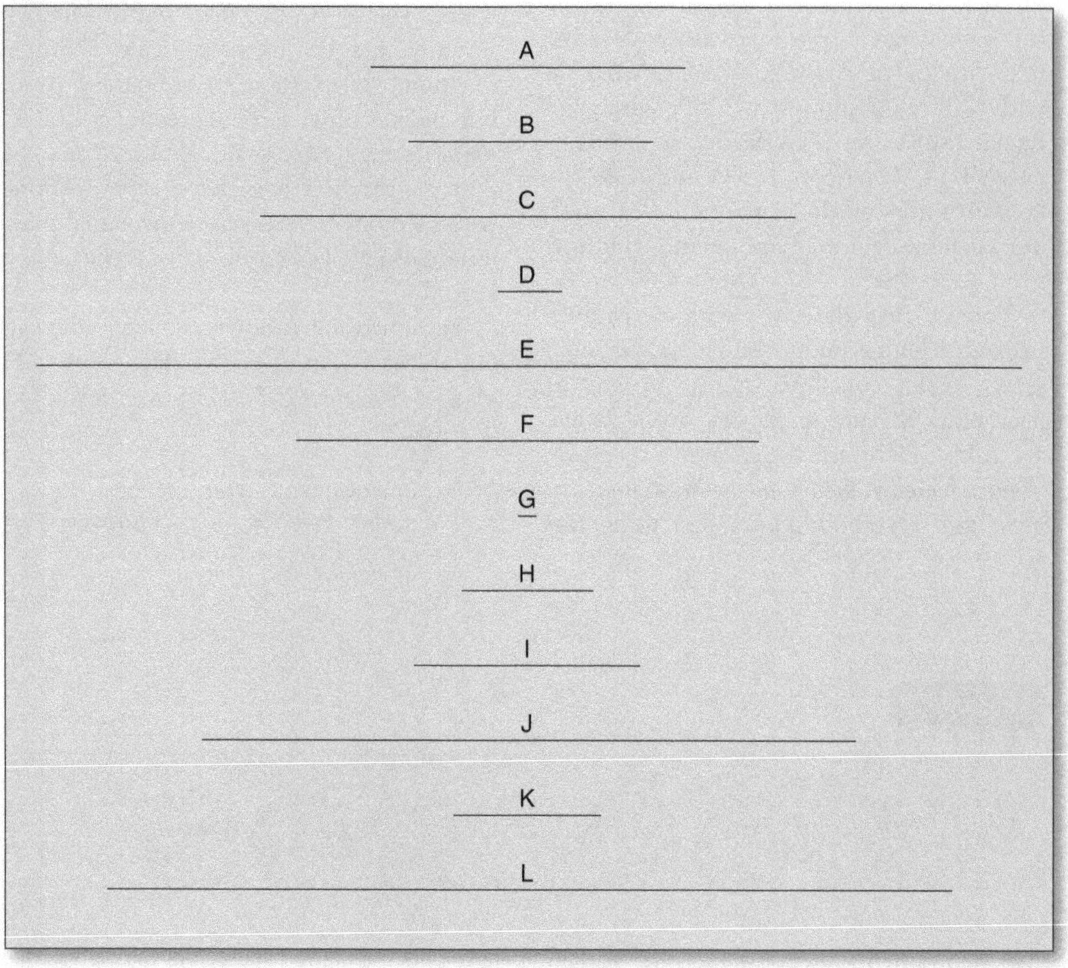

Source: M. Lodge, *Magnitude Scaling: Quantitative Measurement of Opinions*, p. 9. Copyright © 1981 by Sage Publications.

medium short, medium, medium long, long), they'll give lines D and G a 1 (short) and they'll give lines E and L (and perhaps C) a 5 (long). Instead, Lodge told 375 people that line A has a length of 50 (not 50 inches or millimeters or miles . . . just 50) and asked them to say how long they thought each of the other lines were. The correlation between the average of their guesses about the length of each line and the actual length of each line was 0.988.

Now, line A in Lodge's test was is actually about 50mm. Hardly anyone can look at line A and tell you it's 50mm, but if you tell people that line A has a value of 50, most of the time they'll tell you that line E has a value of 100. Line E was actually 98mm, or 1.96 times as long as line A, but people round off and get the proportion almost dead on (the *almost* part is why the proportionality exponent is only 0.988 and not 1.00). Line G was 2 mm long, so it was 1/49th the length of line E. Most people give line G a 1 if you tell them that line E is 50. In other words, with a little error, people mostly get the proportions right. (You can test this yourself.)

Magnitude Scaling of Constructs

Does the power law for physical stimuli, like line lengths, translate into better measurement for subjective things, like attitudes? In 1977, the possibility of magnitude scaling of opinions was tested on the National Crime Victimization Survey. The 54,000 respondents saw subsets of 25 from a list of 204 crimes. Here are the instructions to the respondents:

I would like to ask your opinion about how serious YOU think certain crimes are. The first situation is "A person steals a bicycle parked on the street." This has been given a score of 10 to show its seriousness. Use this first situation to judge all others. For example, if you think a situation is 20 TIMES MORE serious

than the bicycle theft, the number you tell me should be around 200, or if you think it is HALF AS SERIOUS, the number you tell me should be around 5, and so on. There is no upper limit. Use ANY number so long as it shows how serious YOU think the situation is. If YOU think something is not a crime, give it a zero.

The respondents then saw a list of 25 crimes . . . things like: (1) A person using force, robs a victim of $10. The victim struggles and is shot to death. (2) A person steals property worth $10,000 from outside a building. (3) A person disturbs the neighborhood with loud, noisy behavior.

And so on. As it turns out, many respondents find magnitude scaling easy to do, and it appears that, for some stimuli, subjective responses do obey some version of the power law. For example, across repeated national studies in the United States, on average, people think a crime of theft is twice as serious as another crime of theft, if the dollar amount stolen in one crime is about 13 times greater than the dollar amount stolen in another crime (Lodge 1981:22).

Magnitude Scaling of Countries' Hostility to the United States

In the 1990s, after the collapse of the Soviet Union, two political scientists, Valerie Sulfaro and Mark Crislip (1997), hypothesized that Americans would have to realign their ideas about who the enemies are out there. Sulfar and Crislip asked 145 undergraduates to rate 19 countries (including one fictitious country, the United Arab Republic) on a seven-point scale. The end points of the scale were labeled "most hostile" and "least hostile" to the United States. Respondents practiced direct magnitude estimation by doing that line-length exercise in Figure 11.4. The correlation between the students' estimation of the line lengths and the actual line lengths was more than 0.99.

With this practice session behind them, the students moved on to estimating, by direct magnitude scaling, the amount of hostility they thought various countries had toward the United States.

Sulfaro and Crislip used France as their reference point for this exercise. They showed respondents a line whose length represented the amount of hostility that France has toward the United States. Respondents then drew lines representing how much hostility they thought the other 18 countries (Britain, Iraq, Panama, etc., etc.) had toward the United States. Each country wound up with two average scores, one for the categorical estimate (on a scale from 1–7) of hostility, and one for the line-drawing exercise. Sulfaro and Crislip converted these average scores into standard scores. The results are shown in Table 11.9.

The entries in Table 11.9 are in standard deviations above and below the mean. Positive standard scores tell you how friendly each country is perceived to be toward the United States, relative to the average for all countries; negative scores tell you how hostile each country is perceived to be, relative to the average for all countries. (I'll show you how to compute standard scores in Chapter 20, when we get to quantitative data analysis.) Canada, Australia, and Britain are more than one standard deviation higher on friendliness (the opposite of hostility). Cuba and Iraq are more than one standard deviation below the mean.

The correlation between these two measures of perceived hostility to the United States is a whopping 0.96, but notice the difference in the score for France on the line lengths and categorical estimates. When France is evaluated categorically, it is not directly compared to any other country. In

Table 11.9 Standardized Hostility/Friendliness Scores for 19 Countries

Country	Line Lengths	Categorical Estimates
Canada	1.24	1.36
Australia	1.24	1.32
Britain	1.15	1.17
Mexico	.78	.65
India	.51	.76
Japan	.23	.35
Saudi Arabia	.52	.21
Israel	.38	.29
Germany	.35	.30
France	.19	.85
Panama	−.03	.03
United Arab Republic	−.29	−.41
PRC (China)	−.32	−.23
Bosnia	−.35	−.84
Russia	−.40	−.29
Nicaragua	−.52	−.72
Serbia	−.42	−.81
Cuba	−1.11	−1.29
Iraq	−3.15	−2.67

Source: V. A. Sulfaro and M. S. Crislip, "How Americans Perceive Foreign Policy Threat: A Magnitude Scaling Analysis." *Political Psychology* 18. Copyright © 1997.

this condition, France gets a very low hostility-toward-the-U.S. score: 0.85 is nearly a full standard deviation above the mean, almost the same as Britain. When France's hostility toward the United States is evaluated *relative to that of other countries*, then France scores far, far below Britain—the same as Japan (Box 11.4).

Box 11.4 Why magnitude scaling is not used more

Magnitude scaling produces some excellent results, but it is complicated to administer (respondents don't always understand what they're supposed to do) and the data are a bit harder to analyze than are categorical data. For one thing, you need to calculate geometric means rather than arithmetic means of the measure of subjective stimuli. This involves taking the natural logarithm of each measure, taking the average of the logs, and then exponentiating the result to get back to where you started. Not exactly straightforward.

With easier-to-use computer programs available for data analysis these days, I expect magnitude scaling to come into its own. It's got a lot of appeal (**Further Reading:** magnitude scaling).

AND FINALLY . . .

There are thousands of published scales. Whatever you're interested in, the chances are good that someone has developed and tested a scale to measure it. Scales are not automatically portable—a scale that measures stress among Vietnamese American women may not measure stress among Hispanic American men—but it makes sense to seek out any published scales on variables you're studying. You may be able to adapt the scales to your needs, or you may get ideas for building and testing an alternative scale.

The Handbook of Research Design and Social Measurement (D. C. Miller and Salkind 2002) always seems hopelessly out of date, yet it remains the best place to start looking for published scales. It's a treasure house full of useful information (**Further Reading:** scales and scaling).

Key Concepts in This Chapter

composite measures	robust	Likert scales
single-indicator scales	unidimensional	Likert-type scales
multiple indicators	Guttman scaling	double-barreled items
cumulative index	coefficient of reproducibility	item analysis
indexes	Bogardus Social	factor analysis
criterion referenced	Distance Scale	scoring the items
norm referenced	sample dependent	interitem correlation

Cronbach's
  coefficient alpha
item-total correlation
split-half reliability
  test
the combinations rule
factor loading
Michigan Alcoholism
  Screening Test (MAST)

Brief MAST
MAST-G
Attitudes Toward Women
  Scale (AWS)
Interview Schedule for
  Social Interaction
the semantic differential
target item
paired adjectives

adjectives of evaluation
adjectives of potency
adjectives of activity
Cantril's ladder of life
self-anchoring scale
faces scale
category scales
magnitude scaling
power law

Summary

- A scale is a device for assigning units of analysis to categories of a variable. The assignment is usually done with numbers, and questions are used a lot as scaling devices.

  o A single question on a questionnaire is technically a scale if it lets you assign the people you're studying to categories of a variable. A lot of really interesting variables in social science, however, are complex and can't easily be assessed with single indicators.
- The most common composite measure is a cumulative index. These are made up of several items, all of which count the same.

  o A test in which the only way to get an "A" is to get at least 90% is a criterion-referenced index. A test in which getting an "A" requires that you score in the top 10% of the class is a norm-referenced index.
- A Guttman scale is a unidimensional index. That is, the items are a composite measure of one, and only one underlying concept.

  o The unidimensionality of an index is sample dependent. If the items in a cumulative index form a Guttman scale, then the concept measured by the index is unidimensional, but only for the sample tested.
- Likert scales are the best-known and most widely used scales. A true Likert scale is more than just a format for asking questions. It is a series of items that have been shown to be indicators of an underlying, unidimensional concept.

  o Multidimensional concepts are often measured with complex Likert scales that have several subscales, each of which comprises indicators of a unidimensional concept.
  o Likert scales are tested through a procedure called item analysis. This involves taking the interitem correlation and calculating Cronbach's alpha as a measure of scale reliability. Computers make it easy to use factor analysis to test the unidimensionality of scales.
- With a Likert scale, you ask people a series of questions that get at the target concept. In a semantic differential scale, you name the target concept and ask respondents to rate their feelings toward it on a series of variables.

- Most scales use ordinal categories, but people have more finely graded opinions than, say, a 1–5 scale captures. Magnitude scaling adapts methods from psychophysics to measure attitudes more directly and at a higher level of measurement.

  o Other scales include Cantril's ladder of life and the faces scale.
  o Magnitude scaling is based on the power law in psychophysics.

Exercises

1. This exercise is on the history of scale development. Many scales have changed over the years. It's very instructive to pick an old scale and follow it through its evolution to a modern form. The Wilson-Patterson Conservatism Scale, for example, was developed in the 1960s in New Zealand (G. D. Wilson and Patterson 1968). It was modified for use in the United States by Bahr and Chadwick (1974). Later, Collins and Hayes tested a short version of scale (1993).

   Document the history of a widely used scale. Here are some you might choose from: the Locus of Control Scale (Rotter 1966), the Social Readjustment Scale (Holmes and Rahe 1967), the Authoritarian Personality Scale (Adorno et al. 1950), and the Bem Sex Role Inventory (Bem 1974).

2. Try building a Likert scale to test how serious college students are about their education. This may sound like an easy thing to do, but it isn't. Get together with a small group of students and work on this together. What questions would you ask students if you wanted to scale them on how serious they were about their education? Would the amount of time they claim to spend in the library, or the amount of time they claim to spend partying be useful data? How about what they want to do with their lives after they get their bachelor's degree?

   Once you have a list of questions about attitudes and behaviors, follow the rest of the steps outlined in this chapter, including the item analysis, to get your scale down to a small number of items. You can substitute any value or orientation you like for this exercise. If measuring how serious students are about their education is too close for comfort, then try that shopping orientation variable I mentioned earlier.

3. Get together with a group of other students and decide on a set of target items for a semantic differential test. The items can be types of jobs (forest ranger, family physician, insurance salesperson . . .), names of colors (blue, red, yellow, pink . . .), names of countries (France, Venezuela, Zambia . . .), kinds of music (reggae, jazz, country, classical . . .). Make copies of Figure 11.1 on your word processor and print out a series of semantic differential tests, one for each target item. Choose adjective pairs that make sense for the target items you are studying. For each target item, calculate the mean, across the respondents, of each adjective pair.

Further Reading

Measuring SES. Cirino et al. (2002), Ensminger and Fothergill (2003), Oakes and Rossi (2003).

Bogardus Social Distance Scale. McAllister and Moore (1991), Owen et al. (1981), Parillo and Donoghue (2005).

Guttman scaling. Goodenough (1963), Graves et al. (1969), Liao and Tu (2006), Maitra and Schensul (2002), Wutich and Ragsdale (2008).

Likert scaling. DeVellis (2003).

Semantic differential. Adams-Webber (1997), Arnold-Cathalifaud et al. (2008), Cooker and White (1993), Leunes et al. (1996), Montiel and Boehnke (2000), Ohanian (1990), Turnage (2008).

Ladder of life. Gallicchio et al. (2009), Suhail and Cochrane (1997).

Faces scale. Pasero (1997), Suhail and Chaudhry (2004).

Magnitude scaling. Bard et al. (1996), Goyder (2003), Ogata et al. (2004), Orth and Wegener (1983).

Scales and scaling. Beere (1990), Coombs (1964), Dunn-Rankin (2004), D. C. Miller and Salkind (2002), Netemeyer et al. (2003), Nunnally (1978), Nunnally and Bernstein (1994), Torgerson (1958).

12

Participant Observation

INTRODUCTION

This chapter is about the skills required for doing ethnography, based on **participant observation**. What I have to say about participant observation is naturally colored by my own experience as an anthropologist. That experience includes fieldwork in places that took several days to get to, where the local language has no literary tradition, and where the chances of coming down with a serious illness are nontrivial. It also includes the study of an elite blue-collar work group (the men and women who run oceanographic research vessels), acculturation among European ethnics in the United States (Greek Americans in Tarpon Springs, Florida), the effects of word processors on the organization of work in six cultures. . . .

In fact, anthropologists are more likely these days to study the impact of television on culture in Brazil (Kottak 2009), the meaning of hair styles among African American women (Dione Rosado 2007), the everyday culture of the English (Fox 2004), the formation of Croatian identity in Croatia and in Toronto (Winland 2007), how basic training in the U.S. Army transforms young people into soldiers (Bornmann 2009), consumer behavior (Sherry 1995), gay culture (Boellstorff 2007), or life on the mean streets of big cities (Bourgois 1995; Fleisher 1998) than they are to study isolated tribal or peasant peoples. In Hume and Mulcock's (2004) collection of 17 self-reflective studies of anthropologists about their fieldwork, just three cases deal with work in isolated communities.

Although participant observation in small, isolated communities has some special characteristics, the techniques and skills that are required seem to me to be pretty much the same everywhere.

WHAT *IS* PARTICIPANT OBSERVATION?

Participant observation usually involves fieldwork, but not all fieldwork is participant observation. Gomes do Espirito Santo and Etheredge (2002) interviewed 1,083 male clients of female sex workers and collected saliva specimens (to test for HIV) during 38 nights of fieldwork in Dakar, Senegal. Six people were involved in the data collection, and the lead researcher was with the team throughout the three and a half months in the field. This was serious fieldwork, but hardly participant observation.

Nor is participant observation the same thing as **ethnography**. Ethnography is, inconsiderately, both a verb and a noun. It's the *process* of collecting descriptive data about a culture and it's the *product* of all that work. The product is usually an article or a book, sometimes a film.

And there is nothing particularly qualitative about participant observation or ethnography. Yes, a lot of the data collected by participant observers are qualitative: texts of open-ended interviews that have been recorded and transcribed; field notes taken while watching and listening to people in natural settings; photographs of the content of people's houses; audio recordings of people telling stories; videos of people making lasagna, getting married, having an argument. But lots of data collected by participant observation fieldworkers are based on quantitative methods like direct observation, questionnaires, and pile sorts.

So much for what participant observation isn't. Here's what it is: Participant observation is one of those **strategic methods** I talked about in Chapter 1—like experiments, surveys, or archival research. It puts you where the action is and lets you collect data . . . any kind of data you want, narratives or numbers. It has been used for generations by positivists and interpretivists alike.

Participant observation involves going out and staying out, learning a new language (or a new dialect of a language you already know), and experiencing the lives of the people you are studying as much as you can. It's about immersing yourself in a culture and learning to remove yourself every day from that immersion so you can intellectualize what you've seen and heard, put it into perspective, and write about it convincingly. It's about stalking culture in the wild—establishing rapport and learning to act so that people go about their business as usual when you show up. If you are a successful participant observer, you will know when to laugh at what people think is funny; and when people laugh at what you say, it will be because you *meant* it to be a joke.

This makes participant observation the most ethically problematic of social research methods. If this sounds a bit raw, I mean it to come out that way. Only by confronting the stark truth about participant observation—that, like everyday life everywhere, it involves deception and constant impression management—can we hope to conduct ourselves ethically in fieldwork (More on this later.) (Box 12.1).

Box 12.1 Is participant observation science?

For many researchers, participant observation is a humanistic method, not a scientific one. It is the strategic method that produces experiential knowledge that lets you talk from the gut about what it feels like to plant a garden in the high Andes or dance all night in a street rave in Seattle.

From my traditional, positivist perspective, participant observation is also a scientific method, and a brawny one at that. It produces effective knowledge—knowledge for moving the levers of the world. Nancy Scheper-Hughes developed a nomothetic theory, based on participant observation that accounts for the tragedy of infant mortality in northeast Brazil and the direct involvement of mothers in their infants' deaths (1992). And it has long been used in understanding high-technology work operations: Brigitte Jordan reports on how she and her team of ethnographers at Xerox Corporation determined the information flow and the hierarchy of interactions in the operations room of a major airline at a metropolitan airport (Jordan 1992b).

When it's done right, participant observation turns fieldworkers into instruments of data collection and data analysis. The implication is that *better* fieldworkers are *better* data collectors and *better* data analyzers. And the implication of *that* is that participant observation is not an attitude or an epistemological commitment or a way of life. It's a craft, like designing experiments or administering questionnaire surveys. As with all crafts, becoming a skilled artisan at participant observation takes practice.

SOME HISTORY

Bronislaw Malinowski (1884–1942) didn't invent participant observation, but he is widely credited with developing it as a method of social research. A British social anthropologist (born in Poland), Malinowski went out to study the people of the Trobriand Islands, in the Indian Ocean, just before World War I. At the time, the Trobriand Islands were a German possession, so when the war broke out, Malinowski was interned and could not return to England for three

years. He made the best of the situation. Here he is describing his methods:

> Soon after I had established myself in Omarkana, Trobriand Islands, I began to take part, in a way, in the village life, to look forward to the important or festive events, to take personal interest in the gossip and the developments of the village occurrences; to wake up every morning to a new day, presenting itself to me more or less as it does to the natives. . . . As I went on my morning walk through the village, I could see intimate details of family life, of toilet, cooking, taking of meals; I could see the arrangements for the day's work, people starting on their errands, or groups

of men and women busy at some manufacturing tasks.

Quarrels, jokes, family scenes, events usually trivial, sometimes dramatic but always significant, form the atmosphere of my daily life, as well as of theirs. It must be remembered that the natives saw me constantly every day, they ceased to be interested or alarmed, or made self-conscious by my presence, and I ceased to be a disturbing element in the tribal life which I was to study, altering it by my very approach, as always happens with a newcomer to every savage community. In fact, as they knew that I would thrust my nose into everything, even where a well-mannered native would not dream of intruding, they finished by regarding me as a part and parcel of their life, a necessary evil or nuisance, mitigated by donations of tobacco. [1922:7–8]

Ignore the patronizing rhetoric about the "savage community" and "donations of tobacco." (I've learned to live with this part my discipline's history. Knowing that all of us, in every age, look quaint, politically incorrect, or just plain hopeless to those who come later, has made it easier.) Focus instead on the amazing, progressive (for that time) method that Malinowski advocated: Spend lots and lots of time in studying a culture, learn the language, hang out, do all the everyday things that everyone else does, become inconspicuous by sheer tenaciousness, and stay aware of what's really going on.

Participant observation has very deep roots in sociology as well. Beatrice Webb was doing participant observation—complete with note taking and informant interviewing—in the 1880s and she wrote in detail about the method in her 1926 memoir (Webb 1926).

Just about then, the long tradition in sociology of urban ethnography—the "Chicago School"—began at the University of Chicago under the direction of Robert Park and Ernest Burgess (see Park et al. 1925). This tradition has never paid any respect at all to disciplinary boundaries. In fact, one of Park's students was his son-in-law, Robert Redfield, the anthropologist who pioneered community studies in Mexico.

Just back from lengthy fieldwork with Aborigine peoples in Australia, another young anthropologist, William Lloyd Warner, was also influenced by Park. Warner launched one of the most famous American community-study projects of all time, the Yankee City series (Warner 1963; Warner and Hunt 1941). (Yankee City was the pseudonym for Newburyport, Massachusetts.) In 1929, sociologists Robert and Helen Lynd published the first of many ethnographies about Middletown. (Middletown was the pseudonym for Muncie, Indiana.)

Some of the classic ethnographies that came out of the early Chicago School include Harvey Zorbaugh's *The Gold Coast and the Slum* (1929) and Clifford Shaw's *The Jack Roller* (1930). In *The Jack Roller*, a 22 year old named Stanley talks about what it was like to grow up as a delinquent in early twentieth-century Chicago. It still makes great reading.

Becker et al.'s *Boys in White* (1961)—about the student culture of medical school in the 1950s—should still be required reading for anyone trying to understand the culture of medicine in the United States. The Chicago ethnography tradition continues in the pages of the *Journal of Contemporary Ethnography* (which began in 1972 under the title *Urban Life and Culture*) and in more recent books like Mitchell Duneier's *Sidewalks* (1999) (a five-year study of street vendors in New York) and Gary Fine's *Kitchens: The Culture of Restaurant Work* (1996) (**Further Reading**: history of ethnography in the social sciences).

Participant observation today is everywhere—in political science (Schatz 2009), management (Watson 2011), education (Marx and Moss 2011), nursing (Sinclair 2011), criminology (Carter 2006)—and one of the wonderful results of all this is a growing body of literature about participant observation itself. There are highly focused studies, full of practical advice, and there are poignant discussions of the overall *experience* of fieldwork. For large doses of both, see Wolcott (1995), Agar (1996), and Handwerker (2001) (**Further Reading:** participant observation).

FIELDWORK ROLES

Fieldwork can involve three very different roles: (1) **complete participant**; (2) **participant observer**; and (3) **complete observer**. The first role involves deception—becoming a member of a group without letting on that you're there to do research. The third role involves following people around and recording their behavior with little if any interaction. This is part of direct observation, which we'll take up in Chapter 14.

By far, most ethnographic research is based on the second role, that of the participant observer. Participant observers can be insiders who observe and record some aspects of life around them (in which case, they're **observing participants**); or they can be outsiders who participate in some aspects of life around them and record what they can (in which case, they're **participating observers**).

In 1965, I went to sea with a group of Greek sponge fishermen in the Mediterranean. I lived in close quarters with them, ate the same awful food as they did, and generally participated in their life—as an outsider. I didn't dive for sponges, but spent most of my waking hours studying the behavior and the conversation of the men who did. The divers were curious about what I was writing in my notebooks, but they went about their business and just let me take notes, time their dives, and shoot movies (Bernard 1987). I was a participating observer.

Similarly, when I went to sea in 1972 and 1973 with oceanographic research vessels, I was part of the scientific crew, there to watch how oceanographic scientists, technicians, and mariners interacted and how this interaction affected the process of gathering oceanographic data. There, too, I was a participating observer (Bernard and Killworth 1973).

Circumstances can sometimes overtake the role of mere participating observer. In 1979, El Salvador was in civil war. Thousands fled to Honduras where they were sheltered in refugee camps near the border. Phillipe Bourgois went to one of those camps to initiate what he hoped would be his doctoral research in anthropology. Some refugees there offered to show him their home villages and Bourgois crossed with them, illegally, into El Salvador for what he thought would be a 48-hour visit. Instead, Bourgois was trapped, along with about a thousand peasants, for two weeks, as the Salvadoran military bombed, shelled, and strafed a 40-square-kilometer area in search of rebels (Bourgois 1990). Perforce, Bourgois became an observing participant.

John Van Maanen played both of these roles, one after the other, in his dissertation research on how rookie cops in a California city become street-wise. There was nothing accidental about this, either. First, Van Maanen went through the three-month training course at the police academy. Everyone at the academy knew why he was there, but he was a full participant in training. He was an observing participant. Then, for four months, Van Maanen rode 8–10 hours a day in the back of a patrol car as a participant observer (Van Maanen 1973). His first role not only gave Van Maanen the credibility he needed for his second role to be successful, it also gave him a deep appreciation of what he was observing in his second role.

Researchers at the U.S. Federal Bureau of Prisons asked Mark Fleisher (1989) to do an ethnographic study of job pressures on guards in a maximum-security federal penitentiary in California. It costs a lot to train a guard—a correctional officer, or CO in the jargon of the profession—and there was an unacceptably high rate of them leaving the job after a year or two. Could Fleisher look into the problem?

Fleisher said he'd be glad to do the research and asked when he could start "walking the mainline"—that is, accompanying the COs on their rounds through the prison. He was told that he'd be given an office at the prison and that the guards would come to his office to be interviewed. Fleisher said he was sorry, but he was an anthropologist, he was doing participant observation, and he'd have to have the run of the prison. Sorry, they said back, only sworn correctional officers can walk the prison halls. So, swear me in, said Fleisher, and off he went to training camp for six weeks to become a sworn federal correctional officer. *Then* he began his year-long study of the U.S. Penitentiary at Lompoc, California. In other words, he became an observing participant in the culture he was studying. Like Van Maanen, Fleisher never hid what he was doing. When he went to

USP-Lompoc, Fleisher told everyone that he was doing a study of prison life.

Barbara Marriott (1991) studied how the wives of U.S. Navy male officers contributed to their husbands' careers. Marriott was herself the wife of a retired captain. She was able to bring the empathy of 30 years of full participation to her study. She, too, took the role of observing participant and, like Fleisher, she told her informants exactly what she was doing.

Holly Williams (1995) spent 14 years as a nurse, ministering to the needs of children who had cancer. When Williams did her doctoral dissertation, on how the parents of those young patients coped with the trauma, she started as a credible insider, as someone whom the parents could trust with their worst fears and their hopes against all hope. Williams was a complete participant who became an observing participant by telling the people whom she was studying exactly what she was up to and enlisting their help with the research (Box 12.2).

Box 12.2 Going native

Some fieldworkers start out as participating observers and find that they are drawn completely into their informants' lives. In 1975, Kenneth Good went to study the Yanomami in the Venezuelan Amazon. He planned on living with the Yanomami for 15 months, but he stayed on for nearly 13 years. "To my great surprise," says Good, "I had found among them a way of life that, while dangerous and harsh, was also filled with camaraderie, compassion, and a thousand daily lessons in communal harmony" (Good 1991:ix). Good learned the language and became a nomadic hunter and gatherer. He was adopted into a lineage and given a wife. (Good and his wife, Yárima, tried living in the United States, but after a few years, Yárima returned to the Yanomami.)

Marlene Dobkin de Rios did fieldwork in Peru and married the son of a Peruvian folk healer, whose practice she studied (Dobkin de Rios 1981). And Jean Gearing (1995) is another anthropologist who married her closest informant on the island of St. Vincent.

Does **going native** mean loss of objectivity? Perhaps, but not necessarily. In the industrialized countries of the West, we *expect* immigrants to go native. We expect them to become fluent in the local language, to make sure that their children become fully acculturated, to participate in the economy and politics of the nation, and so on. If some of them become anthropologists, no one questions whether their immigrant background produces a lack of objectivity. Since total objectivity is, by definition, a myth, I'd worry more about producing credible data and strong analysis and less about whether going native is good or bad.

HOW MUCH TIME DOES IT TAKE?

It's common to spend a year or more doing participant observation fieldwork. Anthropologists do this all the time, but so do sociologists and other social scientists. From 1970 to 1975, William Bainbridge (1978) studied a satanic cult called the Process Church of the Final Judgment. Bainbridge pretended to be a "depressive piano tuner" and convinced the members of the church that he himself was a believer (1992:31). (See Chapter 14 for a discussion of the ethics of disguised observation.)

Ruffing-Ruhal (1993) acted as facilitator for a wellness group of older women. As a participant observer, Ruffing-Ruhal took field notes on 75 of these weekly meetings in an attempt to identify core themes of well-being. Salisbury et al. (1993) spent two and a half years studying how disabled children were treated at one elementary school.

A lot of participant observation studies, however, are done in a matter of weeks or a few months. Norman Conti (2009) was a participant observer during a 21-week course at a police academy, documenting how recruits develop their occupational culture. Gretchen Purser (2009) spent five months studying the hiring of illegal immigrant day laborers. She divided her time each week between a street corner that had become a shape-up venue and a not-for-profit agency about a mile away that brought day laborers and potential employers together.

At the extreme low end, it is possible to do useful participant observation in just a few days. Assuming that you've wasted as much time in laundromats as I did when I was a student, you could conduct a reasonable participant observation study of one such place in a week. You'd begin by bringing in a load of wash and paying careful attention to what's going on around you.

After two or three nights of observation, you'd be ready to tell other patrons that you were conducting research and that you'd appreciate their letting you interview them. The reason you could do this is because you already speak the native language and have already picked up the nuances of etiquette from previous experience. Participant observation would help you intellectualize what you already know.

Rapid Assessment and Applications Research

Applied researchers usually don't have the luxury of doing long-term participant observation fieldwork. In fact, applied work—like needs assessment in nutrition and health care, education, conservation, and agricultural development—often has to be done in a few weeks. This doesn't leave much time for building rapport and, beginning in the 1970s, researchers in those fields developed **rapid assessment procedures**, including **rapid ethnographic assessment** and **participatory rapid assessment (PRA)**. These methods are very useful in long-term fieldwork.

In **participatory mapping**, for example, people draw maps of their communities and locate key places on the maps. Robert Chambers, a pioneer in PRA, spent two full days in 1974 trying to map the wells in an Indian village. Fifteen years later, in 1989, one of his colleagues asked people in another Indian village to map their wells. The job was done in 25 minutes, and the villagers noted which wells had water and which were dry (Chambers 2006).

In **participatory transects**, a technique that Chambers borrowed from wildlife biology, you walk through an area systematically with key informants, observing and asking for explanations of everything you see along the transect. Chambers also engages people in group discussions of key events in a community's history and asks them to identify clusters of households according to wealth. In other words, as an applied researcher, Chambers is called on to do rapid assessment of rural community needs and takes the people fully into his confidence as research partners. This strategy is just as effective in hospital or county school systems or police precincts as in rural communities.

The key to high-quality, quick ethnography, according to Handwerker (2001), is to go into a study with a clear question and to limit your study to five focus variables. If the research is exploratory, you just have to make a reasonable guess as to what variables might be important and hope for the best. Most rapid assessment studies, however, are applied research, which means that you can take advantage of earlier, long-term studies to narrow your focus.

In general, though, participant observation is not for the impatient. It took Daniel Wolf three years just to get into the Rebels, a brotherhood of outlaw bikers and another couple of years riding with them before he had the data for his doctoral dissertation (Wolf 1990).

The amount of time you spend in the field can make a big difference in what you learn. Raoul Naroll (1962) found that anthropologists who stayed in the field for at least a year were more likely to report on sensitive issues like witchcraft, sexuality, political feuds, etc. Ethnographers who have done very long-term participant observation find that they eventually get data about social change that is simply not possible to get in any other way (Foster et al. 1979) (**Further Reading:** rapid assessment) (Box 12.3).

Box 12.3 Conversations over many years

My wife Carole and I spent May 2000 on Kalymnos, the Greek island where I did my doctoral fieldwork in 1964–65. We'd been visiting that island steadily for 35 years, but something qualitatively different happened in 2000. I couldn't quite put my finger on it, but by the end of the month I realized that people were talking to me about grandchildren. The ones who had grandchildren were chiding me—very good-naturedly, but chiding nonetheless—for not having any grandchildren yet. The ones who didn't have grandchildren were in commiseration mode. They wanted someone with whom to share their annoyance that "Kids these days are in no hurry to make families" and that "All kids want today...especially girls...is to have careers."

This launched lengthy conversations about how "everything had changed" since we had been our children's ages and about how life in Greece was getting to be more and more like Europe (what many Greeks call Germany, France, and the rest of the fully industrialized nations of the European Union) and even like the United States. I suppose there were other ways I could have gotten people into give-and-take conversations about culture change, gender roles, globalization, modernization, and other big topics, but the grandchildren deficit was a terrific opener in 2000. It wasn't just age. These conversations were the result of the rapport that comes with having common history with people.

In 2004, our daughter, son-in-law, and new granddaughter Zoë came to Kalymnos for Zoë's first birthday. There is a saying in Greek that "the child of your child is twice your child." You can imagine all the conversations, late into the night, about that. By 2009, the grandchildren deficit had been resolved for many of my cohort, but not for all. By this time, people in their late 60s and early 70s were talking openly about things that could not have been imagined 40 years earlier, like: Who will take care of old people if there are no granddaughters?

The bottom line: You can do highly focused participant observation research in your own language, to answer specific questions about your own culture, in a matter of weeks or months. How do middle-class, second-generation, Mexican American women make decisions on which of several brands to select when they go grocery shopping? If you are a middle-class Mexican American woman, you can probably find the answer to that question, using participant observation, in a few weeks, because you have a wealth of personal experience to draw on.

But if you're starting out fresh, and not a member of the culture you're studying, count on taking three months or more, under the best conditions, to be accepted as a participant observer—that is, as someone who has learned enough to learn. And count on taking a lifetime to learn some things.

VALIDITY—AGAIN

There are at least five reasons for insisting on participant observation in the conduct of scientific research about cultural groups.

1. As I've stressed, participant observation makes it possible to collect different kinds of data. Participant observation fieldworkers have witnessed births, interviewed violent men in maximum-security prisons, stood in fields noting the behavior of farmers, trekked with hunters through the Amazon forest in search of game, and pored over records of marriages, births, and deaths in village churches and mosques around the world.

It is impossible to imagine a complete stranger walking into a birthing room and being welcomed to watch and record the event or being allowed to examine any community's vital records at whim. It is impossible, in fact, to imagine a stranger doing *any* of the things just mentioned or the thousands of other intrusive acts of data collection that anthropologists, sociologists, and other fieldworkers engage in all the time. What makes it all possible is participant observation.

2. Participant observation reduces the problem of reactivity, of people changing their behavior when they know that they are being studied. As you become less and less of a curiosity, people take less and less interest in your comings and goings. They go about their business and let you do such bizarre things as conduct interviews, administer questionnaires, and even walk around with a stopwatch, clipboard, and camera.

Phillipe Bourgois (1995) spent four years living in El Barrio (the local name for Spanish Harlem) in New York City. It took him a while, but eventually he was able to keep his recorder running for interviews about dealing crack cocaine and even when groups of men bragged about their involvement in gang rapes.

Bottom line: Presence builds trust. Trust lowers reactivity. Lower reactivity means higher validity of data. Nothing is guaranteed in fieldwork, though. When Le Compte told children at a school that she was writing a book about them, they started acting out in "ways they felt would make good copy" by mimicking characters on popular TV programs (Le Compte et al. 1993).

3. Participant observation helps you formulate sensible questions, in the local language. Have you ever gotten a questionnaire in the mail and said to yourself "What a dumb set of questions"? If a social scientist who is a member of your own culture can make up what you consider to be "dumb" questions, imagine the risk *you* take in making up a questionnaire in a culture different from your own. Remember, it's just as important to ask sensible questions in a face-to-face interview as it is on a survey instrument.

4. Participant observation gives you an intuitive understanding of what's going on in a

culture and allows you to speak with confidence about the meaning of data. It lets you make strong statements about cultural facts that you've collected. It extends both the internal and the external validity of what you learn from interviewing and watching people. In short, participant observation helps you understand the *meaning* of your observations (Box 12.4).

Box 12.4 The meaning of data

Here's a classic example. In 1957, N. K. Sarkar and S. J. Tambiah published a study, based on questionnaire data, about economic and social disintegration in a Sri Lankan village. They concluded that about two-thirds of the villagers were landless. The British anthropologist, Edmund Leach, did not accept that finding (Leach 1967). He had done participant observation fieldwork in the area, and knew that the villagers practiced patrilocal residence after marriage. By local custom, a young man might receive *use* of some of his father's land even though legal ownership might not pass to the son until the father's death.

In assessing land ownership, Sarkar and Tambiah asked whether a "household" had any land, and if so, how much. They defined an independent household as a unit that cooked rice in its own pot. Unfortunately, all married women in the village had their own rice pots. So Sarkar and Tambiah wound up estimating the number of independent households as very high and the number of those households that owned land as very low. Based on these data, they concluded that there was gross inequality in land ownership and that this characterized a "disintegrating village" (the title of their book).

Don't conclude from Leach's critique that questionnaires are "bad" while participant observation is "good." I can't say often enough that participant observation makes it possible to collect quantitative survey data or qualitative interview data from some sample of a population. Qualitative and quantitative data inform each other and produce insight and understanding in a way that cannot be duplicated by either approach alone. Whatever data collection methods you choose, participant observation maximizes your chances for making valid statements.

---

5. Many research problems simply cannot be addressed adequately by anything except participant observation. If you want to understand how a local court works, you can't very well disguise yourself and sit in the court room unnoticed. The judge would soon spot you as a stranger, and, after a few days, you would have to explain yourself. It is better to explain yourself at the beginning and get permission to act as a participant observer. In this case, your participation consists of acting like any other local person who might sit in on the court's proceedings. After a few days, or weeks, you would have a pretty good idea of how the court worked: What kinds of crimes are adjudicated, what kinds of penalties are meted out, and so forth. You might develop some specific hypotheses from your qualitative notes—hypotheses regarding covariations between severity of punishment and independent variables other than severity of crime. Then you could test those hypotheses on a sample of courts.

Think this is unrealistic? Try going down to your local traffic court and see whether defendants' dress or manner of speech predict variations in fines for the same infraction. The point is, getting a general understanding of how any social institution or organization works—the local justice system, a hospital, a ship, or an entire community—is best achieved through participant observation.

ENTERING THE FIELD

Perhaps the most difficult part of actually doing participant observation fieldwork is making an entry. There are five rules to follow.

1. There is no reason to select a site that is difficult to enter when equally good sites are available that are easy to enter (see Chapter 3). In many cases, you *will* have a choice—among equally good school districts, communities, hospitals, political precincts, or cell blocks. When you have a choice, take the field site that promises to provide easiest access to data.

2. Go into the field with as much written documentation as you can about yourself and your project. Whether you're going to a foreign country or to a school or a shopping center, it helps to carry one or more letters of introduction from your university, your funding agency, or your client if you are doing contract research. Letters from universities should spell out your affiliation, who is funding you, and how long you will be at the field site.

If you're going out of the country, be sure that those letters are in the language spoken where you will be working, and that they are signed by the highest academic authorities possible. Letters of introduction should not go into detail about your proposed research. Have a separate document describing your proposed work and present it to gatekeepers who ask for it, along with your letters of introduction. If you study an outlaw biker gang, like Daniel Wolf did (1991), forget about letters of introduction.

3. Don't try to wing it, unless you absolutely have to. There is nothing to be said for "getting in on your own." Use personal contacts to help you make your entry into a field site. Charles Gallmeier spent nearly a year traveling with and studying the Summit City Rockets, a pseudonym for a minor league hockey team in the U.S. Midwest. Gallmeier got permission to travel and hang out with the team because his father was a respected sports writer who had spent 25 years covering the league (Gallmeier 1991).

When I went to the island of Kalymnos, Greece, in 1964, I carried with me a list of people to look up. I collected the list from people in the Greek American community of Tarpon Springs, Florida, who had relatives on Kalymnos. When I went to Washington, DC, to study how decision makers in the bureaucracy used (or didn't use) scientific information, I had letters of introduction from colleagues at Scripps Institution of Oceanography (where I was working at the time).

If you are studying any hierarchically organized community (hospitals, police departments, universities, school systems, etc.), it is *usually* best to start at the top and work down. Find out the names of the people who are the gatekeepers and see them first. Assure them that you will maintain strict confidentiality and that no one in your study will be personally identifiable. In some cases, starting at the top can backfire, though. If there are warring factions in a community or organization, and if you gain entry to the group at the top of *one* of those factions, you will be asked to side with that faction.

Another danger is that top administrators of institutions may try to enlist you as a kind of spy. They may offer to facilitate your work if you will report back to them on what you find out about specific individuals. This is absolutely off limits in research. If that's the price of doing a study, you're better off choosing another institution. In the two years I spent doing research on communication structures in federal prisons, no one ever asked me to report on the activities of specific inmates. But other researchers have reported experiencing this kind of pressure, so it's worth keeping in mind (**Further Reading:** gatekeepers).

4. Think through in advance what you will say when ordinary people (not just gatekeepers) ask you: What are you doing here? Who sent you? Who's funding you? What good is your research and who will it benefit? Why do you want to learn about people here? How long will you be here? How do I know you aren't a spy for _____? (where the blank is filled in by whoever people are afraid of). The rules for presentation of self are simple: Be honest, be brief, and be absolutely consistent. In participant observation, if you try to play any role besides yourself, you'll just get worn out (Jones 1973).

Not everyone will be thrilled about your role as a researcher. Terry Williams studies cocaine use in after-hours clubs in New York. One club he went to turned out to be having "gay night" when he showed up. "I thought," said Williams, "I would take advantage of the situation for sociological purposes, making comparisons between heterosexual and homosexual cocaine users." He goes on:

I was wearing black leather (the fashion in New York at the time), not realizing the role of black leather in the gay community. I noticed a group of men sitting in a corner and moved toward them inconspicuously, or so I thought, until I was eight or ten feet away. One of them stared up at me and I, of course, looked toward him. His sleeves were rolled past his elbows, revealing purple and red tattoos on both arms.

After looking at me for a few seconds, he walked over and offered to buy me a drink, asking if this was my first time there. I explained that I had been there before and informed him that I was a researcher and just wanted to talk to as many people as possible. He grew red in the face and said to his companions in a loud voice, hands on hips, head cocked to one side: "Hey, get a load of this one. He wants to do research on us. You scum bag. What do we look like, pal? Fucking guinea pigs?" [T. Williams 1996:30]

After that experience, Williams became, as he said, "more selective" in whom he told about his real purpose in those after-hours clubs.

5. Spend time getting to know the physical and social layout of your field site. It doesn't matter if you're working in a small town, an urban enclave, a hospital, or a police precinct. Walk it and map it. Write down notes about how it *feels* to you. Is it crowded? Do the buildings or furniture seem old or poorly kept? Are there any distinctive odors?

You'd be surprised how much information comes from asking people about little things like these. I can still smell the distinctive blend of diesel fuel and taco sauce that's characteristic of so many bus depots in rural Mexico. Asking people about those smells opened up long conversations about what it's like for poor people, who don't own cars, to travel in Mexico and all the family and business reasons they have for traveling. If something in your environment makes a strong sensory impression, write it down.

A really good early activity in any participant observation project is to make maps and charts—kinship charts of families, chain-of-command charts in organizations, maps of offices or villages or whatever physical space you're studying, charts of who sits where at meetings, and so on.

For making maps, take a GPS (global positioning system) device to the field with you. GPS devices that are accurate to within 3 meters or less are available for under $200 (see Appendix E for more about this). A GPS tracks your path via satellite, so that if you can walk the perimeter of an area you can map it and mark its longitude and latitude accurately.

Eri Sugita (2006) studied the relation between the washing of hands by the mothers of young children and the rate of diarrheal disease among those children in Bugobero, Uganda. Sugita used a GPS device to map the position of every well and every spring in Bugobero. Then she walked to each of the water sources from each of the 51 households in her study and, wearing a pedometer, measured the travel distance to the nearest source of clean water.

If you are working in a really large area, you may not be able to map it, but you should walk as much of it as possible, as early as possible in your fieldwork. If you are studying a group that has no physical location (like a social movement), it still pays to spend time "mapping" the social scene (Schatzman and Strauss 1973). This means getting down the names of the key players and charting their relations.

Another good thing to do is to take a census of the group you're studying as soon as you can. Be careful, though. Taking a census can be a way to gain rapport in a community (walking around and visiting every household can have the effect of giving you credibility), but it can also backfire if people are afraid you might be a spy. Michael Agar reports that he was branded as a Pakistani spy when he went to India, so his village census was useless (1980b).

THE SKILLS OF A PARTICIPANT OBSERVER

To a certain extent, participant observation must be learned in the field. The strength of participant observation is that you, as a researcher, become the instrument for data collection and analysis through your own experience. Consequently, you have to experience participant observation to get good at it. Nevertheless, there are a number of skills that you can develop before you go into the field.

Learning the Language

Unless you are a full participant in the culture you're studying, being a participant observer makes you a freak. Here's how anthropologists looked to Vine Deloria (1969:78), a Sioux writer:

Anthropologists can readily be identified on the reservations. Go into any crowd of people. Pick out a tall gaunt white man wearing Bermuda shorts, a World War II Army Air Force flying jacket, an Australian bush hat, tennis shoes, and packing a large knapsack incorrectly strapped on his back. He will invariably have a thin, sexy wife with stringy hair, an I. Q. of 191, and a vocabulary in which even the prepositions have eleven syllables. . . . This creature is an anthropologist.

Now, 40-plus years later, it may be the anthropologist's husband who jabbers in 11-syllable words, but the point is still the same. The most important thing you can do to stop being a freak is to speak the language of the people you're studying—and speak it well. Franz Boas was adamant about this. "Nobody," he said, "would expect authoritative accounts of the civilization of China or Japan from a man who does not speak the languages readily, and who has not mastered their literatures" (1911:56). And yet, "the best kept secret of anthropology," says Robbins Burling, "is the linguistic incompetence of ethnological fieldworkers" (2000 [1984]:v).

That secret is actually not so much well kept as ignored. In 1933, Paul Radin, one of Franz Boas's students, complained that Margaret Mead's work on Samoa was superficial because she wasn't fluent in Samoan (Radin 1966 [1933]:179). Sixty-six years later, Derek Freeman (1999) showed that Mead was probably duped by at least some of her adolescent informants about the extent of their sexual experience because she didn't know the local language.

In fact, Mead talked quite explicitly about her use of interpreters. It was not necessary, said Mead, for fieldworkers to become what she called *virtuosos* in a native language. It was enough simply to *use* a native language, as she put it, without actually speaking it fluently:

[I]f one knows how to exclaim "how beautiful" of an offering, "how fat" of a baby, "how big" of a just shot pig; if one can say "my foot's asleep" or "my back itches" as one sits in a closely pack native group with whom one is as yet unable to hold a sustained conversation; if one can ask the simple questions: "Is that your child?" "Is your father living?" "Are the mosquitoes biting you?" or even utter culturally appropriate squeals and monosyllables which accompany fright at a scorpion, or startle at a loud noise, it is easy to establish rapport with people who depend upon affective contact for reassurance. [Mead 1939:198]

Robert Lowie would have none of it. A people's ethos, he said, is never directly observed. "It can be inferred only from their self-revelations," and this, indeed, requires the dreaded virtuosity that Mead had dismissed (Lowie 1940:84–87). The "horse-and-buggy ethnographers," said Lowie, accepted virtuosity—that is, a thorough knowledge of the language in which one does fieldwork—on principle. "The new, stream-lined ethnographers," he taunted, "renounce 'virtuosity' as superfluous" (Lowie 1940:87).

Lowie was careful to say that a thorough knowledge of a field language did not mean native proficiency. And Mead understood the benefits of being proficient in a field language. But she also understood that a lot of ethnography gets done through interpreters or through contact languages, like French, English, and pidgins . . . the not-so-well kept secret among fieldworkers all over the world (**Further Reading:** using interpreters).

Still, according to Brislin et al. (1973:70), Samoa is one of those cultures where "it is considered acceptable to deceive and to 'put on' outsiders. Interviewers are likely to hear ridiculous answers, not given in a spirit of hostility but rather sport." Brislin et al. call this the **sucker bias**, and warn fieldworkers to watch out for it. Presumably, knowing the local language fluently is one way to become alert to and avoid this problem.

When it comes to doing effective participant observation, learning a new jargon in your own language is just as important as learning a foreign language. Peggy Sullivan and Kirk Elifson studied the Free Holiness church, a rural group of Pentecostals whose rituals include the handling of poisonous snakes (rattles, cottonmouths, copperheads, and water moccasins). They had to learn an entirely new vocabulary:

> Terms and expressions like "annointment," "tongues," "shouting," and "carried away in the Lord," began having meaning for us. We learned informally and often contextually through conversation and by listening to sermons and testimonials. The development of our understanding of the new language was gradual and probably was at its greatest depth when we were most submerged in the church and its culture. . . . We simplified our language style and eliminated our use of profanity. We realized, for example, that one badly placed "damn" could destroy trust that we had built up over months of hard work. [Sullivan and Elifson 1996:36]

How to Learn a New Language

In my experience, the way to learn a new language is to learn a few words and to say them brilliantly. Yes, study the grammar and vocabulary, but the key to learning a new language is saying things right, even just a handful of things. This means capturing not just the pronunciation of words, but also the intonation, the use of your hands, and other nonverbal cues that show you are really, really serious about the language and are trying to look and sound as much like a native as possible.

Michael Herzfeld (2009s) reports that when he did his first summer's fieldwork in Bangkok, he couldn't get ordinary people in the street to respond to him in Thai. People just stared at him. On his second trip, a Thai person asked *him* for directions on the street. What had changed? Despite his White Western face, a street vendor told him, he used Thai gestures and *looked* Thai (p. 141).

When you say the equivalent of "Hey, hiya doin" in any language—Zulu or French or

Arabic—with just the right intonation, people will think you know more than you do. They'll come right back at you with a flurry of words, and you'll be lost. Fine. Tell them to slow down—again, in that great accent you're cultivating.

Consider the alternative: You announce to people, with the first, badly accented word out of your mouth, that you know next to nothing about the language and that they should therefore speak to you with that in mind. When you talk to someone who is not a native speaker of your language, you make an automatic assessment of how large their vocabulary is and how fluent they are. You adjust both the speed of your speech and your vocabulary to ensure comprehension. That's what speakers of other languages will do with you, too. The trick is to act in a way that gets people into pushing your limits of fluency and into teaching you cultural insider phrases.

A good fraction of any culture is in the idioms and especially in the metaphors (more about metaphors in Chapter 18). To understand how powerful this can be, imagine you are hired to tutor a student from Nepal who wants to learn English. You point to some clouds and say "clouds" and she responds by saying "clouds." You say "very good" and she says "no brainer." You can pick up the learning pace after that kind of response.

As you articulate more and more of those phrases like a native, people will increase the rate at which they teach you by raising the level of their discourse with you. They may even compete to teach you the subtleties of their language and culture. When I was learning Greek in 1960 on a Greek merchant ship, the sailors took delight in seeing to it that my vocabulary of obscenities was up to their standards and that my usage of that vocabulary was suitably robust.

In 1964–1965, I spent a year on the island of Kalymnos in the Aegean Sea, collecting data for my doctoral thesis, and although I studied modern Greek as part of my graduate training at the University of Illinois, my accent, mannerisms, and vocabulary were heavily influenced by the experiences I had actually using the language.

When I went to teach at the University of Athens in 1969, my colleagues there were delighted that I wanted to teach in Greek, but they had some cognitive dissonance about my accent. How to reconcile the fact that an educated foreigner spoke reasonably fluent Greek with a rural, working-class accent? It didn't scan, but they were very forgiving. After all, I *was* a foreigner, and the fact that I was making an attempt to speak the local language counted for a lot.

So, if you are going off to do fieldwork in a foreign language, try to find an intensive summer course in the country where that language is spoken. Not only will you learn the language (and the local dialect of that language), you'll make personal contacts, find out what the problems are in selecting a research site, and discover how to tie your study to the interests of local scholars.

And this goes for anyone studying Vietnamese shrimpers in Louisiana or Somalis in Minneapolis. Don't let the fact that you *can* use just English to study people in immigrant communities convince you that you *don't need to* get at least some fluency in the ancestral language of the people among whom you want to do participant observation. Knowing the language that people speak to their grandparents will open many doors.

You can study French in France, but you can also study it in Montreal, Martinique, or Madagascar. You can study Spanish in Spain, but you can also study it in Mexico, Bolivia, or Paraguay. And you'd be amazed at the range of language courses available at universities these days: Ulithi, Aymara, Quechua, Nahuatl, Swahili, Turkish, Amharic, Basque, Eskimo, Navajo, Zulu, Hausa, Amoy. . . . If the language you need is not offered in a formal course, try to find an individual speaker of the language who would be willing to tutor you in a self-paced course (**Further Reading:** language and fieldwork) (Box 12.5).

Box 12.5 When not to mimic

The key to understanding the culture of loggers, lawyers, bureaucrats, schoolteachers, or ethnic groups is to become intimately familiar with their vocabulary. Words are where the cultural action is. My rule about mimicking pronunciation changes, though, if you are studying an ethnic or occupational subculture in your own society and the people in that subculture speak a different dialect of your native language. In this situation, mimicking the local pronunciation will just make you look silly. Even worse, people may think you're ridiculing them.

Building Explicit Awareness

Another important skill in participant observation is what Spradley (1980:55) called explicit awareness of the little details in life. Try this experiment: The next time you see someone look at their watch, go right up to them and ask them the time. Chances are they'll look again because when they looked the first time they were not *explicitly aware* of what they saw. Tell them that you are a student conducting a study and ask them to chat with you for a few minutes about how they tell time.

Many people who wear analog watches look at the *relative positions* of the hands, not at the numbers on the dial. They subtract the current time (the position of the hands now) from the time they have to be somewhere (the image of what the position of the hands will look like at some time in the future), and calculate whether the difference is anything to worry about. They never have to become explicitly aware of the fact that it is 3:10 p.m. People who wear digital watches may be handling the process somewhat differently. We could test that.

Kronenfeld et al. (1972) reported an experiment in which informants leaving several different restaurants were asked what the waiters and waitresses (as they were called in those gender-differentiated days) were wearing, and what kind of music was playing. Informants agreed much more about what the waiters were wearing than about what the waitresses were wearing. The hitch: None of the restaurants had waiters at all, only waitresses.

Informants also provided more detail about the kind of music in restaurants that did not have music than they provided for restaurants that did have music. Kronenfeld speculated that, in the absence of real memories about things they'd seen or heard, informants turned to cultural norms for what must have been there (i.e., "What goes with what") (D'Andrade 1973).

You can test this yourself. Pick out a large lecture hall where a male professor is not wearing a tie. Ask a group of students on their way out of a lecture hall what color tie their professor was wearing. Or observe a busy store clerk for an hour and count the number of sales she rings up. Then ask her to estimate the number of sales she handled during that hour.

You can build your skills at becoming explicitly aware of ordinary things. Get a group of colleagues together and write separate, detailed descriptions of the most mundane, ordinary things you can think of: making a bed, doing laundry, building a sandwich, shaving (face, legs, underarms), picking out produce at the supermarket, etc. Then discuss one another's descriptions and see how many details others saw that you didn't and vice versa. If you work carefully at this exercise you'll develop a lot of respect for how complex, and how important, are the details of ordinary life.

If you want to see the level of detail you're shooting for here, read Anthony F. C. Wallace's little classic "Driving to Work" (1965). Wallace had made the 17-mile drive from his home to the University of Pennsylvania about 500 times when he drew a map of it, wrote out the details, and extracted a set of rules for his behavior. He was driving a 1962 Volkswagen Beetle in those days. It had 12 major mechanical controls (from the ignition switch to the windshield wiper—yes, there was just one of them, and you had to pull a switch on the instrument panel with your right hand to get it started), all of which had to be handled correctly to get him from home to work safely every day.

Building Memory

Even when we are explicitly aware of things we see, there is no guarantee that we'll remember them long enough to write them down. Building your ability to remember things you see and hear is crucial to successful participant observation research.

Try this exercise: Walk past a store window at a normal pace. When you get beyond it and can't see it any longer, write down all the things that were in the window. Go back and check. Do it again with another window. You'll notice an improvement in your ability to remember little things almost immediately. You'll start to create mnemonic devices for remembering more of what you see. Keep up this exercise until you are satisfied that you can't get any better at it.

Here's another one. Go to a church service, other than one you're used to. Take along two colleagues. When you leave, write up what you each think you saw, in as much detail as you can muster and compare what you've written. Go back to the church and keep doing this exercise until all of you are satisfied that: (1) you are all seeing and writing down the same things; and (2) you have reached the limits of your ability to recall complex behavioral scenes.

Try this same exercise by going to a church service with which you *are* familiar and take along several colleagues who are *not*. Again, compare your notes with theirs, and keep going back and taking notes until you and they are seeing and noting the same things. You can do this with any repeated scene that's familiar to you: a bowling alley, a fast-food restaurant, etc.

Remember, training your ability to see things reliably does not guarantee that you'll see things accurately. But reliability is a necessary but insufficient condition for accuracy. Unless you become at least a reliable instrument of data gathering, you don't stand much of a chance of making valid observations.

Bogdan (1972:41) offers some practical suggestions for remembering details in participant observation. If, for some reason, you can't take notes during an interview or at some event, and you are trying to remember what was said, *don't talk to anyone* before you get your thoughts down on paper. Talking to people reinforces some things you heard and saw at the expense of other things.

Also, when you sit down to write try to remember things in historical sequence, as they occurred throughout the day. As you write up your notes you will invariably remember some particularly important detail that just pops into memory out of sequence. When that happens, jot it down on a separate piece of paper (or tuck it away in a separate little note file on your word processor) and come back to it later, when your notes reach that point in the sequence of the day.

Another useful device is to draw a map—even a rough sketch will do—of the physical space where you spent time observing and talking to people that day. As you move around the map, you will dredge up details of events and conversations. In essence, let yourself walk through your experience. You can practice all these memory-building skills now and be much better prepared if you decide to do long-term fieldwork later.

Maintaining Naiveté

Try also to develop your skill at being a novice—at being someone who genuinely wants to learn a new culture. This may mean working hard at suspending judgment about some things. David Fetterman made a trip across the Sinai Desert with a group of Bedouins. One of the Bedouins, says Fetterman,

> Shared his jacket with me to protect me from the heat. I thanked him, of course, because I appreciated the gesture and did not want to insult him. But I smelled like a camel for the rest of the day in the dry desert heat. I thought I didn't need the jacket. . . . I later learned that without his jacket I would have suffered from sunstroke. . . . An inexperienced traveler does not always notice when the temperature climbs above 130 degrees Fahrenheit. By slowing down the evaporation rate, the jacket helped me retain water. [1989:33]

Maintaining your naiveté will come naturally in a culture that's unfamiliar to you, but it's a bit harder to do in your own culture. Most of what you do "naturally" is so automatic that you don't know how to intellectualize it.

If you are like many middle-class Americans, your eating habits can be characterized by the word "grazing"—that is, eating small amounts of food at many, irregular times during the course of a typical day, rather than sitting down for meals at fixed times. Would you have used that kind of word to describe your own eating behavior? Other members of your own culture are often better informants than you are about that culture, and if you really let people teach you, they will.

If you look carefully, though, you'll be surprised at how heterogeneous your culture is and how many parts of it you really know nothing about.

Find some part of your own culture that you don't control—an occupational culture, like long-haul trucking, or a hobby culture, like amateur radio—and try to learn it. That's what you did as a child. This time, try to intellectualize the experience. Take notes on what you learn about *how to learn*, on what it's like being a novice, and how you think you can best take advantage of the learner's role. Your imagination will suggest a lot of other nooks and crannies of our culture that you can explore as a thoroughly untutored novice (Box 12.6).

Box 12.6 When not to be naive

The role of naive novice is not *always* the best one to play. Humility is inappropriate when you are dealing with a culture whose members stand a lot to lose by your incompetence. Michael Agar (1973, 1980a) did field research on the life of heroine addicts in New York City. His informants made it plain that Agar's ignorance of their lives wasn't cute or interesting to them.

Even with the best of intentions, Agar could have given his informants away to the police by just by being stupid. Under such circumstances, you shouldn't expect your informants to take you under their wing and teach you how to appreciate their customs. Agar had to learn a lot, and very quickly, to gain credibility with his informants.

There are situations where your expertise is just what's required to build rapport with people. Anthropologists have typed documents for illiterate people in the field and have used other skills (from coaching basketball to dispensing antibiotics) to help people and to gain their confidence and respect.

If you are studying highly educated people, you may have to prove that you know a fair amount about research methods before they will deal with you. Agar (1980b:58) once studied an alternative lifestyle commune and was asked by a biochemist who was living there: "Who are you going to use as a control group?" In my study of ocean scientists (Bernard 1974), several informants asked me what computer programs I was going to use to do a factor analysis of my data.

Building Writing Skills

The ability to write comfortably, clearly, and often is one of the most important skills you can develop as a participant observer. Ethnographers who are not comfortable as writers produce few field notes and little published work. If you have any doubts about your ability to pound out thousands of words, day in and day out, then try to build that skill now, before you go into the field for an extended period.

The way to build that skill is to team up with one or more colleagues who are also trying to build their expository writing ability. Set concrete and regular writing tasks for yourselves and criticize one another's work on matters of clarity and style. There is nothing trivial about this kind of exercise. If you think you need it, do it.

Good writing skills will carry you through participant observation fieldwork, writing a dissertation and, finally, writing for publication. Don't be afraid to write clearly and compellingly. The worst that can happen is that someone will criticize you for "popularizing" your material. I think ethnographers should be criticized if they take the exciting material of real people's lives and turn it into deadly dull reading.

Hanging Out, Gaining Rapport

It may sound silly, but just hanging out is a skill, and until you learn it you can't do your best work as a participant observer. Remember what I said at the beginning of this chapter: Participant observation is *a strategic* method that lets you learn what you want to learn and apply all the data collection methods that you may want to apply.

When you enter a new field situation, the temptation is to ask a lot of questions to learn as much as possible as quickly as possible. There are many things that people can't or won't tell you in answer to questions. If you ask people too quickly about the sources of their wealth, you are likely to get incomplete data. If you ask too quickly about sexual liaisons, you may get thoroughly unreliable responses.

Hanging out builds trust, or **rapport**, and trust results in ordinary conversation and ordinary behavior in your presence. Once you know, from hanging out, exactly what you want to know more about, and once people trust you not to betray their confidence, you'll be surprised at the direct questions you can ask.

In his study of Cornerville (Boston's heavily Italian American neighborhood called North End), William Foote Whyte wondered whether "just hanging on the street corner was an active enough process to be dignified by the term 'research.' Perhaps I should ask these men questions," he thought. He soon realized that "one has to learn when to question and when not to question as well as what questions to ask" (1989:78).

The Ethical Dilemma of Rapport

Face it: "Gaining rapport" is a euphemism for impression management, one of the "darker arts" of fieldwork, in Harry Wolcott's apt phrase (1995:chap. 6). E. E. Evans-Pritchard, the great British anthropologist, made clear in 1937 how manipulative the craft of ethnography really is. He was doing fieldwork with the Azande of Sudan and wanted to study their rich tradition of witchcraft. Even with his long-term fieldwork and command of the Azande language, Evans-Pritchard couldn't get people to open up about witchcraft, so he decided to "win the good will of one or two practitioners and to persuade them to divulge their secrets in strict confidence" (1958 [1937]:151). Strict confidence? He was planning on writing a book about all this.

Progress was slow, and although he felt that he could have "eventually wormed out all their secrets" he hit on another idea: His personal servant, Kamanga, was initiated into the local group of practitioners and "became a practising witch-doctor" under the tutelage of a man named Badobo (Evans-Pritchard 1958 [1937]:151). With Badobo's full knowledge, Kamanga reported every step of his training to his employer. In turn, Evans-Pritchard used the information "to draw out of their shells rival practitioners by playing on their jealousy and vanity."

Badobo knew that anything he told Kamanga would be tested with rival witch doctors. Badobo couldn't lie to Kamanga, but he could certainly withhold the most secret material. Evans-Pritchard analyzed the situation carefully and pressed on. Once an ethnographer is "armed with preliminary knowledge," he said, "nothing can prevent him from driving deeper and deeper the wedge if he is interested and persistent" (Evans-Pritchard 1958 [1937]:152).

Still, Kamanga's training was so slow that Evans-Pritchard nearly abandoned his inquiry into witchcraft. Providence intervened. A celebrated witch doctor, named Bögwözu, showed up from another district, and Evans-Pritchard offered him a very high wage if he'd take over Kamanga's training. Evans-Pritchard explained to Bögwözu that he was "tired of Badobo's wiliness and extortion," and that he expected his generosity to result in Kamanga learning all the tricks of the witch doctor's trade (Evans-Pritchard 1958 [1937]:152).

But the really cunning part of Evans-Pritchard's scheme was that he continued to pay Badobo to tutor Kamanga. He *knew* that Badobo would be jealous of Bögwözu and would strive harder to teach Kamanga more about witch-doctoring. Here is Evans-Pritchard going on about his deceit and the benefits of this tactic for ethnographers:

> The rivalry between these two practitioners grew into bitter and ill-concealed hostility. Bögwözu gave me information about medicines and magical rites to prove that his rival was ignorant of the one or incapable in the performance of the other. Badobo became alert and showed himself no less eager to

demonstrate his knowledge of magic to both Kamanga and to myself. They vied with each other to gain ascendancy among the local practitioners. Kamanga and I reaped a full harvest in this quarrel, not only from the protagonists themselves but also from other witch-doctors in the neighborhood, and even from interested laymen. [Evans-Pritchard 1958 [1937]:153]

Objectivity

Finally, **objectivity** is a skill, like language fluency, and you can build it if you work at it. Some people build more of it, others less. More is better.

If an objective measurement is one made by a robot—that is, a machine that is not prone to the kind of measurement error that comes from having opinions and memories—then no human being can ever be completely objective. We can't rid ourselves of our experiences, and I don't know anyone who thinks it would be a good idea even to try.

We can, however, become aware of our experiences, our opinions, our values. We can hold our field observations up to a cold light and ask whether we've seen what we wanted to see, or what is really out there. The goal is not for us, as humans, to become objective machines; it is for us to achieve objective—that is, accurate—knowledge by transcending our biases. No fair pointing out that this is impossible. It *is* impossible to do completely, but it's not impossible to do at all. Priests, social workers, clinical psychologists, and counselors suspend their own biases all the time, more or less, in order to listen hard and give sensible advice to their clients.

Laurie Krieger, an American woman doing fieldwork in Cairo, Egypt, studied physical punishment against women. She learned that wife beatings were less violent than she had imagined and that the act still sickened her. Her reaction brought out a lot of information from women who were recent recipients of their husbands' wrath. "I found out," she says, "that the biased outlook of an American woman and a trained anthropologist was not always disadvantageous, as long as I was aware of and able to control the expression of my biases" (1986:120).

Colin Turnbull held objective knowledge as something to be pulled from the thicket of subjective experience. Fieldwork, said Turnbull, involves a self-conscious review of one's own ideas and values—one's self, for want of any more descriptive term. During fieldwork you "reach inside," he observed, and give up the "old, narrow, limited self, discovering the new self that is right and proper in the new context." We use the field experience, he said, "to know ourselves more deeply by conscious subjectivity." In this way, he concluded, "the ultimate goal of objectivity is much more likely to be reached and our understanding of other cultures that much more profound" (Turnbull 1986:27).

Many phenomenologists see objective knowledge as the goal of participant observation. Danny Jorgensen, for example, advocates complete immersion and becoming the phenomenon you study. "Becoming the phenomenon," Jorgensen says, "is a participant observational strategy for penetrating to and gaining experience of a form of human life. It is an objective approach insofar as it results in the accurate, detailed description of the insiders' experience of life" (1989:63). In fact, many ethnographers have become cab drivers or exotic dancers, jazz musicians, or members of satanic cults to do participant observation fieldwork.

If you use this strategy of full immersion, Jorgensen says, you must be able to switch back and forth between the insiders' view and that of an analyst. To do that—to maintain your objective, analytic abilities—Jorgensen suggests finding a colleague with whom you can talk things over regularly. That is, give yourself an outlet for discussing the theoretical, methodological, and emotional issues that

inevitably come up in full participation field research. It's good advice.

Objectivity and Value Neutrality

Objectivity does not mean (and has never meant) value neutrality. No one asks Amnesty International to be neutral in its effort to document state-sanctioned torture. We recognize that the power of the documentation is in its objectivity, in its chilling irrefutability, not in its neutrality.

Claire Sterk, an ethnographer from the Netherlands, has studied prostitutes and intravenous drug users in mostly African American communities in New York City and Newark, New Jersey. Sterk was a trusted friend and counselor to many of the women with whom she worked. In one two-month period, she attended the funeral of seven women she knew who had died of AIDS. She felt that "every researcher is affected by the work he or she does. One cannot remain neutral and uninvolved; even as an outsider, the researcher is part of the community" (1989:99, 1999).

At the end of his second year of research on street life in El Barrio, Phillipe Bourgois's friends and informants began telling him about their experiences as gang rapists. Bourgois's informants were in their mid- to late 20s then and the stories they told were of things they'd done as very young adolescents, more than a decade earlier. Still, Bourgois says, he felt betrayed by people whom he had come to like and respect. Their "childhood stories of violently forced sex," he says, "spun me into a personal depression and a research crisis" (1995:205).

In *any* long-term field study, be prepared for some serious tests of your ability to remain a dispassionate observer. One of my teachers, Hortense Powdermaker (1966), was once confronted with the problem of knowing that a lynch mob was preparing to go after a particular Black man. She was powerless to stop the mob and fearful for her own safety.

I have never grown accustomed to seeing people ridicule the handicapped, though I see it every time I'm in Mexico and Greece, and I recall with horror the death of a young man on one of the sponge diving boats I sailed with in Greece. I knew the rules of safe diving that could have prevented that death; so did all the divers and the captains of the vessels. They ignored those rules at terrible cost. I wanted desperately to *do* something, but there was nothing I could do. My lecturing them at sea about their unsafe diving practices would not have changed their behavior. That behavior was driven, as I explained in Chapter 2, by structural forces and the technology—the boats, the diving equipment—of their occupation. By suspending active judgment of their behavior, I was able to record it. "Suspending active judgment" does not mean that I eliminated my bias or that my feelings about their behavior changed. It meant only that I kept the bias to myself while I was recording their dives.

NATIVE ETHNOGRAPHY: STUDYING YOUR OWN CULTURE

Objectivity gets its biggest test in native ethnography—that is, when you study your own culture. Hodkinson (2002, 2005) joined the goth scene when he was 16 and then studied goth culture during his mid-20s. When Hodkinson interviewed goth youth face to face, his own physical appearance made his insider status clear. To gain trust in Internet discussion groups, though, he dropped hints about his identity in his online conversations, he posted photos of himself, and he met face to face with some subscribers (2005:138).

Barbara Meyerhoff worked in Mexico when she was a graduate student. Later, in the early 1970s, when she became interested in ethnicity and aging, she decided to study elderly Chicanos. The people she approached

kept putting her off, asking her "Why work with us? Why don't you study your own kind?" Meyerhoff was Jewish. She had never thought about studying her own kind, but she launched a study of poor, elderly Jews who were on public assistance. She agonized about what she was doing and, as she tells it, never resolved whether it was anthropology or a personal quest.

Many of the people she studied were survivors of the Holocaust. "How, then, could anyone look at them dispassionately? How could I feel anything but awe and appreciation for their mere presence? . . . Since neutrality was impossible and idealization undesirable, I decided on striving for balance" (Meyerhoff 1989:90).

There is no final answer on whether it's good or bad to study your own culture. Plenty of people have done it, and plenty of people have written about what it's like to do it. On the plus side, you'll know the language and you'll be less likely to suffer from culture shock. On the minus side, it's harder to recognize cultural patterns that you live every day and you're likely to take a lot of things for granted that an outsider would pick up right away.

If you are going to study your own culture, start by reading the experiences of others who have done it—like William Turner's experience (1986) in his study of Black Appalachians in Kentucky, or Marwan Kraidy's experience (1999) in his study of Maronite Christians in Lebanon—so you'll know what you're facing in the field (**Further Reading:** studying your own culture).

GENDER, PARENTING, AND OTHER PERSONAL CHARACTERISTICS

By the 1930s, Margaret Mead had already made clear the importance of gender as a variable in data collection (see Mead 1986).

Gender has at least two consequences: It limits your access to certain information; it influences how you perceive others.

In all cultures, you can't ask people certain questions because you're a [woman] [man]. You can't go into certain areas and situations because you're a [woman] [man]. You can't watch this or report on that because you're a [woman] [man]. Even the culture of social scientists is affected: Your credibility is diminished or enhanced with your colleagues when you talk about a certain subject because you're a [woman] [man] (Altorki and El-Solh 1988; Golde 1986; Scheper-Hughes 1983; Warren 1988; Whitehead and Conaway 1986).

Sara Quandt, Beverly Morris, and Kathleen DeWalt spent months investigating the nutritional strategies of the elderly in two rural Kentucky counties (Quandt et al. 1997). According to DeWalt, the three women researchers spent months interviewing key informants and never turned up a word about the use of alcohol. "One day," says DeWalt:

the research team traveled to Central County with Jorge Uquillas, an Ecuadorian sociologist who had expressed an interest in visiting the Kentucky field sites. One of the informants they visited was Mr. B, a natural storyteller who had spoken at length about life of the poor during the past sixty years. Although he had been a great source of information about use of wild foods and recipes for cooking game he had never spoken of drinking or moonshine production.

Within a few minutes of entering his home on this day, he looked at Jorge Uquillas, and said "Are you a drinking man?" (Beverly whipped out the tape recorder and switched it on.) Over the next hour or so, Mr. B talked about community values concerning alcohol use, the problems of drunks and how they were dealt with in the community, and provided a number of stories about moonshine in Central County. The presence of another man gave Mr. B the opportunity to talk about issues he found interesting, but felt would have been inappropriate to discuss with women. [DeWalt et al. 1998:280]

On the other hand, feminist scholars have made it clear that gender is a negotiated idea. What you can and can't do if you are a man or a woman is more fixed in some cultures than in others, and in all cultures there is lots of individual variation in gender roles. While men or women may be "expected" to be this way or that way in any given place, the variation in male and female attitudes and behaviors within a culture can be tremendous.

All participant observers confront their personal limitations and the limitations imposed on them by the culture they study. When she worked at the Thule relocation camp for Japanese Americans during World War II, Rosalie Wax did not join any of the women's groups or organizations. Looking back after more than 40 years, Wax concluded that this was just poor judgment.

I was a university student and a researcher. I was not yet ready to accept myself as a total person, and this limited my perspective and my understanding. Those of us who instruct future fieldworkers should encourage them to understand and value their full range of being, because only then can they cope intelligently with the range of experience they will encounter in the field. [1986:148]

Beside gender, we have learned that being a parent helps you talk to people about certain areas of life and get more information than if you were not a parent. My wife and I arrived on the island of Kalymnos, Greece, in 1964 with a two-month-old baby. As Joan Cassell says, children are a "guarantee of good intentions" (1987:260), and wherever we went, the baby was the conversation opener. But be warned: Taking children into the field can place them at risk. (More on health risks below.)

Being divorced has its costs. Nancie González found that being a divorced mother of two young sons in the Dominican Republic was just too much. "Had I to do it again," she says, "I would invent widowhood with appropriate rings and photographs" (1986:92).

Even height may make a difference: Alan Jacobs once told me he thought he did better fieldwork with the Maasai because he's 6'5" than he would have if he'd been, say, an average-sized 5'10".

Personal characteristics make a difference in fieldwork. Being old or young lets you into certain things and shuts you out of others. Being wealthy lets you talk to certain people about certain subjects and makes others avoid you. Being gregarious makes some people open up to you and makes others shy away. There is no way to eliminate the personal equation in participant observation fieldwork or in any other scientific data-gathering exercise for that matter without sending robots out to do the work. Of course, the robots would have their own problems (**Further Reading:** race and gender in fieldwork).

SEX AND FIELDWORK

It is unreasonable to assume that single, adult fieldworkers are all celibate, yet the literature on field methods was nearly silent on this topic for many years. When Evans-Pritchard was a student, just about to head off for Central Africa, he asked his major professor for advice. "Seligman told me to take ten grains of quinine every night and keep off women" (Evans Pritchard 1973:1). As far as I know, that's the last we heard from Evans-Pritchard on the subject.

Colin Turnbull (1986) tells us about his affair with a young Mbuti woman, and Dona Davis (1986) discusses her relationship with an engineer who visited the Newfoundland village where she was doing research on menopause. In Turnbull's case, he had graduated from being an asexual child in Mbuti culture to being a youth and was expected to have sexual relations. In Davis's case, she was expected not to have sexual relations, but she also learned that she was not bound by the expectation. In

fact, Davis says that "being paired off" made women more comfortable with her because she was "simply breaking a rule everyone else broke" (1986:254).

Proscriptions against sex in fieldwork are silly, because they don't work. But understand that this is one area that people everywhere take very seriously. The rule on sexual behavior in the field is this: Do nothing that you can't live with, both professionally and personally. This means that you have to be even more conscious of any fallout, for you and for your partner, than you would in your own community. Eventually, you will be going home. How will that affect your partner's status? (**Further Reading:** sex and fieldwork).

SURVIVING FIELDWORK

The title of this section is the title of an important book by Nancy Howell (1990). Even 20 years on, anyone—sociologist, anthropologist, epidemiologist, or social psychologist—who plans to do fieldwork in developing nations should read Howell's book. Howell surveyed 204 anthropologists about illnesses and accidents in the field, and the results are sobering. The maxim that "anthropologists are otherwise sensible people who don't believe in the germ theory of disease" is apparently correct (Rappaport 1990).

One hundred percent of anthropologists who did fieldwork in south Asia reported being exposed to malaria and 41% reported contracting the disease. Eighty-seven percent of anthropologists who worked in Africa reported exposure and 31% reported having had malaria. Seventy percent of anthropologists who worked in south Asia reported having had some liver disease.

Among all anthropologists, 13% reported having had hepatitis A. I was hospitalized for six weeks for hepatitis A in 1968 and spent most of another year recovering. Glynn Isaac died of hepatitis B at age 47 in 1985 after a long career of fieldwork in Africa. Typhoid fever is also common among researchers who work in developing countries, as are amoebic dysentery, giardia, ascariasis, hookworm, and other infectious diseases.

Accidents have injured or killed many fieldworkers. Fei Xiaotong, a student of Malinowski's, was caught in a tiger trap in China in 1935. The injury left him an invalid for six months. His wife died in her attempt to go for help. Michelle Zimbalist Rosaldo was killed in a fall in the Philippines in 1981. Thomas Zwickler, a graduate student at the University of Pennsylvania, was killed by a bus on a rural road in India in 1985. He was riding a bicycle when he was struck. Kim Hill was accidentally hit by an arrow while out with an Ache hunting party in Paraguay in 1982 (Howell 1990:passim).

Five members of a Russian-American team of researchers on social change in the Arctic died in 1995 when their *umiak* (a traditional, walrus-hided Eskimo boat) was overturned by a whale (see Broadbent 1995). The researchers included three Americans (two anthropologists—Steven McNabb and Richard Condon and a psychiatrist—William Richards), and two Russians (one anthropologist—Alexander Pika—and the chief Eskimo ethnographic consultant to the project—Boris Mumikhpykak). Nine other Eskimo villagers also perished in that accident. I've had my own unpleasant brushes with fate and I know many others who have had very, very close calls.

What can you do about the risks? Get every inoculation you need before you leave, not just the ones that are required by the country you are entering. Check your county health office for the latest information from the Centers for Disease Control about illnesses prevalent in the area you're going to. If you go into an area that is known to be malarial, take a full supply of antimalarial drugs with you so you don't run out while you're out in the field.

When people pass around a gourd full of *chicha* or *pulque* or palm wine, decline politely

and explain yourself if you have to. You'll probably insult a few people, and your protests won't always get you off the hook, but even if you only lower the number of times you are exposed to disease, you lower your risk of contracting disease.

After being very sick in the field, I learned to carry a supply of bottled beer with me when I would visit a house where I was sure I'd be given a gourd full of local brew. The gift of bottled beer is appreciated and heads off the embarrassment of having to turn down a drink I'd rather not have. It also makes plain that I'm not a teetotaler. If you *are* a teetotaler, you've got a ready-made get-out.

If you do fieldwork in a remote area, consult with physicians at your university hospital for information on the latest blood-substitute technology. If you are in an accident in a remote area and need blood, a nonperishable blood substitute can buy you time until you can get to a clean blood supply. Some fieldworkers carry a supply of sealed hypodermic needles with them in case they need an injection. Don't go anywhere without medical insurance and don't go to developing countries without evacuation insurance. It costs $60,000–100,000 to evacuate a person by jet from central Africa to Paris or Frankfurt. It costs a few hundred dollars a year for insurance to cover it.

Fieldwork in remote areas isn't for everyone, but if you're going to do it, you might as well do it as safely as possible. Candice Bradley, a Type-I diabetic, did long-term fieldwork in western Kenya. She took her insulin, glucagon, blood-testing equipment, and needles with her. She arranged her schedule around the predictable, daily fluctuations in her blood-sugar level. She trained people on how to cook for her and she laid in large stocks of diet drinks so that she could function in the relentless heat without raising her blood sugars (Bradley 1997:4–7).

With all this, Bradley still had close calls—near blackouts from hypoglycemia—but her close calls are no more frequent than those experienced by other field researchers who work in similarly remote areas. The rewards of foreign fieldwork can be very great, but so are the risks. (**Further Reading:** dangerous fieldwork).

THE STAGES OF PARTICIPANT OBSERVATION

In what follows, I will draw on three sources of data: (1) a review of the literature on field research; (2) conversations with colleagues during the last 40 years, specifically about their experiences in the field; and (3) five years of work, with the late Michael Kenny, directing National Science Foundation field schools in cultural anthropology and linguistics.

During our work with the field schools (1967–1971), Kenny and I developed an outline of researcher response in participant observation fieldwork. Those field schools were 10 weeks long and were held each summer in central Mexico. One school was held in the interior of the Pacific Northwest. In Mexico, students were assigned to Ñähñu-speaking communities in the vicinity of Ixmiquilpan, Mexico. In the Northwest field school, students were assigned to small logging and mining communities in the Idaho panhandle. In Mexico, a few students did urban ethnography in the regional capital of Pachuca, while in the Northwest field school, a few students did urban ethnography in Spokane, Washington.

The stages that Kenny and I identified in the 10-week field experiences of our students were more or less the same in Mexico and in the United States, in rural communities and in cities, and they had analogs in our own experiences with year-long fieldwork.

Initial Contact

During the initial contact period, many long-term fieldworkers report experiencing a kind of euphoria as they begin to move about in a new culture. It shouldn't come as any surprise that people who are attracted to the idea of living in a new culture are delighted when they begin to do so.

But not always. Here is Napoleon Chagnon's recollection of his first encounter with the Yanomamo: "I looked up and gasped when I saw a dozen burly, naked, sweaty, hideous men staring at us down the shafts of their drawn arrows . . . had there been a diplomatic way out, I would have ended my fieldwork then and there" (Chagnon 1983:10–11).

The desire to bolt and run is more common than we have admitted in the past. Charles Wagley, who would become one of anthropology's most distinguished ethnographers, made his first field trip in 1937. A local political chief in Totonicapán, Guatemala, invited Wagley to tea in a parlor overlooking the town square. The chief's wife and two daughters joined them. While they were having their tea, two of the chief's aides came in and hustled everyone off to another room. The chief explained the hurried move to Wagley:

> He had forgotten that an execution by firing squad of two Indians, "nothing but vagrants who had robbed in the market," was to take place at five p.m. just below the parlor. He knew that I would understand the feelings of ladies and the grave problem of trying to keep order among brutes. I returned to my ugly pensión in shock and spent a night without sleep. I would have liked to have returned as fast as possible to New York. [Wagley 1983:6]

Finally, listen to Rosalie Wax describe her encounter with the Arizona Japanese internment camp that she studied during World War II. When she arrived in Phoenix it was 110°. Later that day, after a bus ride and a 20-mile ride in a GI truck, across a dusty landscape that "looked like the skin of some cosmic reptile," with a Japanese American who wouldn't talk to her, Wax arrived at the Gila camp. By then it was 120°. She was driven to staff quarters, which was an army barracks divided into tiny cells, and abandoned to find her cell by a process of elimination.

> It contained four dingy and dilapidated articles of furniture: an iron double bedstead, a dirty mattress (which took up half the room), a chest of drawers, and a tiny writing table, and it was hotter than the hinges of Hades. . . . I sat down on the hot mattress, took a deep breath, and cried. . . . Like some lost two-year-old, I only knew that I was miserable. After a while, I found the room at the end of the barrack that contained two toilets and a couple of wash basins. I washed my face and told myself I would feel better the next day. I was wrong. [Wax 1971:67]

Culture Shock

Even among fieldworkers who have a pleasant experience during their initial contact period (and many do), almost all report experiencing some form of depression and shock soon thereafter—usually within a few weeks. One kind of shock comes as the novelty of the field site wears off and there is this nasty feeling that research has to get done. Some researchers (especially those on their first field trip) may also experience feelings of anxiety about their ability to collect good data.

A good response at this stage is to do highly task-oriented work: making maps, taking censuses, doing household inventories, collecting genealogies, and so on. Another useful response is to make clinical, methodological field notes about your feelings and responses in doing participant observation fieldwork.

Another kind of shock is to the culture itself. Culture shock (a term introduced in 1960 by Kalervo Oberg) is an uncomfortable stress response and must be taken very seriously. In serious cases of culture shock, nothing seems right. You may find yourself very upset at a lack of clean toilet facilities, or people's eating habits, or their child-rearing practices. The prospect of having to put up with the local food for a year or more may become frightening. You find yourself focusing on little annoyances—something as simple as the fact that light switches go side to side rather than up and down may upset you.

This last example is not fanciful, by the way. It happened to a colleague of mine, and I once became infuriated with the fact that men didn't shake hands "the way they're supposed to." You may find yourself blaming everyone in the culture, or the culture itself, for the fact that your informants don't keep appointments for interviews or don't keep them "on time."

Culture shock commonly involves a feeling that people really don't want you around (which may, in fact, be the case). You feel lonely and wish you could find someone with whom to speak your native language. Even with a spouse, the strain of using another language day after day and concentrating hard so that you can collect data in that language can be emotionally wearing.

A common personal problem in field research is not being able to get any privacy. Many people across the world find the Anglo-Saxon notion of privacy grotesque. When we first went out to the island of Kalymnos in Greece in 1964, my wife Carole and I rented quarters with a family. The idea was that we'd be better able to learn about family dynamics. Women of the household were annoyed and hurt when my wife asked for a little time to be alone. When I came home at the end of each day's work, I could never just go to my family's room, shut the door, and talk to my wife about my day, or hers, or our new baby's. If I didn't share everything during waking hours with the family we lived with, they felt rejected.

After about two months of this, we had to move out and find a house of our own. My access to data about intimate family dynamics was curtailed. But it was worth it because I felt that I'd have had to abort the whole trip if I had to continue living in what my wife and I felt was a glass bowl all the time. As it turns out, there is no word for the concept of privacy in Greek. The closest gloss translates as "being alone," and connotes loneliness.

I suspect that this privacy problem is common to all English-speaking researchers who work in developing countries. Here's what M. N. Srinivas, himself from India, wrote about his work in the rural village of Ramapura, near Mysore:

> I was never left alone. I had to fight hard even to get two or three hours absolutely to myself in a week or two. My favorite recreation was walking to the nearby village of Kere where I had some old friends, or to Hogur which had a weekly market. But my friends in Ramapura wanted to accompany me on my walks. They were puzzled by my liking for solitary walks. Why should one walk when one could catch a bus, or ride on bicycles with friends. I had to plan and plot to give them the slip to go out by myself. On my return, however, I was certain to be asked why I had not taken them with me. They would have put off their work and joined me. (They meant it.) I suffered from social claustrophobia as long as I was in the village and sometimes the feeling became so intense that I just had to get out. [1979:23]

Culture shock subsides as researchers settle in to the business of gathering data on a daily basis, but it doesn't go away because the sources of annoyance don't go away. Unless you are one of the very rare people who truly "go native" in another culture, you will cope with culture shock, not eliminate it. You will remain conscious of things annoying you, but you won't feel like they are crippling your ability to work. Like Srinivas, when things get too intense, you'll have the good sense to leave the field site for a bit rather than try to stick it out.

Discovering the Obvious

In the next phase of participant observation, researchers settle into collecting data on a more or less systematic basis (see Kirk and Miller 1986). This is sometimes accompanied by an interesting personal response—a sense of discovery where you feel as if informants are finally letting you in on the "good stuff" about their culture.

Much of this "good stuff" will later turn out to be commonplace. You may "discover,"

for example, that women have more power in the community than meets the eye or that there are two systems for dispute settlement—one embodied in formal law and one that works through informal mechanisms.

A concomitant to this feeling of discovery is sometimes a feeling of being in control of dangerous information and a sense of urgency about protecting informants' identities. You may find yourself going back over your field notes, looking for places that you might have lapsed and identified an informant and making appropriate changes. You may worry about those copies of field notes you have already sent home, and even become a little worried about how well you can trust your major professor (or whoever you sent the notes to) to maintain the privacy of those notes.

This is the stage of fieldwork when you hear anthropologists start talking about "their" village, and how people are, at last, "letting them in" to the secrets of the culture. The feeling has its counterpart among all long-term participant observers. It often spurs researchers to collect more and more data; to accept every invitation, by every informant, to every event; to fill the days with observation, and to fill the nights with writing up field notes. Days off become unthinkable, and the sense of discovery becomes more and more intense.

This is the time to take a serious break.

The Break

The mid-fieldwork break, which usually comes after three or four months, is a crucial part of the overall participant observation experience for long-term researchers. It's an opportunity to get some distance, both physical and emotional, from the field site. It gives you a chance to put things into perspective, think about what you've got so far, and what you need to get in the time remaining. Use this time to collect data from regional or national statistical services; visit with colleagues at the local university and discuss your findings; visit other communities in other parts of the country.

And be sure to leave some time to just take a vacation, without thinking about research at all.

Your informants also need a break from you. "Anthropologists are uncomfortable intruders no matter how close their rapport," wrote Charles Wagley. "A short respite is mutually beneficial. One returns with objectivity and human warmth restored. The anthropologist returns as an old friend" who has gone away and returned, and has thereby demonstrated his or her genuine interest in a community (Wagley 1983:13).

The same goes for sociologists, political scientists, or any other researchers doing participant observation. Everyone needs a break.

Focusing

After the break, you will have a better idea of exactly what kinds of data you are lacking, and your sense of problem will also come more sharply into focus. The reason to have a formally prepared design statement *before* you go to the field is to tell you what you should be looking for. Nevertheless, even the most focused research design will have to be modified in the field. In some cases, you may find yourself making radical changes in your design based on what you find when you get to the field and spend several months actually collecting data.

There is nothing wrong or unusual about this, but new researchers sometimes experience anxiety over making any major changes. The important thing at this stage is to focus the research and use your time effectively rather than agonizing over how to save components of your original design, if that design turns out to be truly unworkable.

Exhaustion, the Second Break, and Frantic Activity

After seven or eight months, some participant observers start to think that they have exhausted their informants, both literally and figuratively. That is, they may become embarrassed about continuing to ask their informants for more information. Or they may make the supreme mistake of believing that their informants have no more to tell them. The reason this is such a mistake is that the store of cultural knowledge in any culturally competent person is enormous—far more than anyone could hope to extract in a year or two.

At this point, another break is usually a good idea. You'll get another opportunity to take stock, order your priorities for the time remaining, and see both how much you've done and how little. The realization that, in fact, informants have a great deal more to teach them and that they themselves have precious little time left in the field sends many investigators into a frenetic burst of activity during this stage.

Leaving the Field

The last stage of participant observation is leaving the field. When should you leave? Steven Taylor, a sociologist at the Center for Human Policy, says that when he starts to get bored writing field notes he knows it's time to close down and go home. Taylor recognizes that writing field notes is time consuming and tedious, but it's exciting, too, when you're chasing down information that plugs directly into your research effort (Taylor 1991:243). When it stops being exciting, it's time to leave the field.

Don't neglect this part of the process. Let people know that you are leaving and tell them how much you appreciate their help. The ritual of leaving a place in a culturally appropriate way will make it possible for you to go back and even to send others.

Participant observation is an intensely intimate and personal experience. People who began as your informants may become your friends as well. In the best of cases, you come to trust that they will not deceive you about their culture and they come to trust you not to betray them—that is, not to use your intimate knowledge of their lives to hurt them. (You can imagine the worst of cases.) There is often a legitimate expectation on both sides that the relationship may be permanent, not just a one-year fling.

For many long-term participant observation researchers, there is no final leaving of the "the field." I've been working with some people, on and off, for 50 years. Like many researchers who work in Latin America, I'm godparent to a child of my closest research collaborator. From time to time, people from Mexico or from Greece will call my house on the phone, just to say "Hi" and to keep the relationship going.

Or their children, who happen to be doing graduate work at a university in the United States, will call and send their parents' regards. They'll remind you of some little event they remember when they were seven or eight and you came to their parents' house to do some interviewing and you spilled your coffee all over yourself as you fumbled with your tape recorder. People remember the darndest things. You'd better be ready when it happens.

Many fieldworkers have been called on to help the children of their informants get into a college or university. This is the sort of thing that happens 20 years after you've "left" the field. The fact is, participant observation fieldwork can be a lifetime commitment. As in all aspects of ordinary life, you have to learn to choose your relationships well. Don't be surprised if you make a few mistakes.

THE FRONT EDGE OF SOCIAL SCIENCE: COMBINING METHODS

More and more social researchers these days have learned what a powerful method participant observation is at all stages of the research process. The method stands on its own but it is also increasingly part of a mixed-methods strategy, as researchers combine qualitative and quantitative data to answer questions of interest (Box 12.7).

Box 12.7 Mixed-methods research

"Mixed methods" is short-hand for the collection and analysis of qualitative and quantitative data in the same project and the design of research that involves both from the start. The first occurrence of the term "mixed methods" in the Social Science Citation Index dates from 1993 and of the 1,867 occurrences, up to January 2012, all but 21 were earlier than the year 2000. There is a *Journal of Mixed Methods Research* and several excellent textbooks on how to do this kind of research.

This mixed-methods movement reflects the best practices of the biological and physical sciences. Among Galileo's notes about the moon was that the surface was "not smooth, uniform, and precisely spherical," as was then commonly believed, but "uneven, rough, and full of cavities and prominences," like that of the Earth (Galileo 1610:3). Galileo made many calculations in his work on heavenly bodies and on acceleration, but his observational notes were qualitative—and that combination has characterized natural science ever since.

Laura Miller (1997), for example, used a mix of ethnographic and survey methods to study gender harassment in the U.S. Army. Keeping women out of jobs that have been traditionally reserved for men is *gender* harassment; asking women for sex in return for a shot at one of those jobs is *sexual* harassment. (Gender harassment need not involve sexual harassment, or vice versa.)

Miller spent nearly two years collecting data at eight army posts and at two training centers in the United States where war games are played out on simulated battlefields. She lived in Somalia with U.S. Army personnel for 10 days, in Macedonia for a week, and in Haiti for six days during active military operations in those countries. Within the context of participant observation, she did unstructured interviewing, in-depth interviewing, and group interviewing. Her group interviews were spontaneous: over dinner with a group of high-ranking officers; sitting on her bunk at night, talking to her roommates; in vehicles, bouncing between research sites, with the driver, guide, protocol officer, translator, and guard (Miller, personal communication).

"Forms of gender harassment" in the U.S. Army turns out to be one of those cultural domains that people recognize and think about, but for which people have no ready list in their heads. You can't just ask people: "List the kinds of gender harassment." From her ethnographic interviews, though, Miller was able to derive what she felt was just such a list, including:

1. *resistance* to authority (hostile enlisted men ignore orders from women officers);

2. *constant scrutiny* (men pick up on every mistake that women make and use those mistakes to criticize the abilities of women in general);

3. *gossip and rumors* (women who date many men are labeled "sluts"; women who don't date at all are labeled "dykes"; and any woman can easily be unjustly accused of "sleeping her way to the top");

4. *outright sabotage* of women's tools and equipment on work details; and

5. *indirect threats* against women's safety (talking about how women would be vulnerable to rape if they were to go into combat).

This list emerges from qualitative research—hanging out, talking to people and gaining their trust, and generally letting people know that you're in for the long haul with them. If you are trying to develop programs to correct things that are wrong with a program, then this list, derived entirely from participant observation, is enough. An education program to counter gender harassment against women in the U.S. Army must include something about each of the problems that Miller identified.

While ethnographic methods are enough to *identify* the problems and processes, ethnography can't tell you *how much* each problem and process counts. Yes, enlisted army men can and do sabotage army women's tools and equipment on occasion. How often? Ethnography can't help with that one. Yes, men do sometimes resist the authority of women officers. How often? Ethnography can't help there, either.

Fortunately, Miller also collected questionnaire data—from a quota sample of 4,100 men and women, Whites and Blacks, officers and enlisted personnel. In those data, 19% of enlisted men and 18% of male noncommissioned officers (like sergeants) said that women should be treated exactly like men and should serve in the combat units just like men, while just 6% of enlisted women and 4% of female noncommissioned officers agreed with this sentiment. You might conclude, Miller says, that men are more supportive than women are of equality for women in combat roles. Some men with whom Miller spoke, however, said that women should be given the right to serve in combat *so that, once and for all, everyone will see that women can't cut it.*

Are men really what Miller called "hostile proponents" of equality for women? Could that be why the statistics show so many more men in favor of women serving in combat units? Miller went back to her questionnaire data: About 20% of men in her survey said that women should be assigned to combat units just like men were—but almost to a man they also said that putting women into combat units would reduce the military's effectiveness.

In other words, the numerical analysis showed that Miller's concept of "hostile proponent of equality" was correct.

This subtle concept advances our understanding considerably of how gender harassment against women plays out in the U.S. Army.

Did you notice the constant feedback between ethnographic and survey data here? The ethnography produced ideas for policy recommendations and for the content for a questionnaire. The questionnaire data illuminated and validated many of the things that the ethnographer learned during participant observation. Those same survey data produced anomalies—things that didn't quite fit with the ethnographer's intuition. More ethnography turned up an explanation for the anomalies. And so on. Ethnographic and survey data combined produce more insight than either does alone (**Further Reading:** mixed methods).

Key Concepts in This Chapter

participant observation	going native	the sucker bias
ethnography	rapid assessment	explicit awareness
strategic methods	procedures	hanging out
impression management	rapid ethnographic	rapport
rapport	assessment	objectivity
fieldwork roles	participatory rapid	becoming the
complete participant	assessment	phenomenon
participant observer	participatory	value neutrality
complete observer	mapping	indigenous research
direct observation	participatory transects	researcher response
observing participants	reactivity	culture shock
participating observers	gatekeepers	the privacy problem

Summary

- Participant observation is one of the strategic methods of the social sciences, along with experiments, surveys, and archival research.
  - Participant observation turns fieldworkers into instruments of data collection and data analysis. It involves establishing rapport and learning to act so that people go about their business as usual when you show up.
  - Participant observation involves deception and impression management. The ethical imperative looms as large for participant observers as it does for experimentalists.

- While participant observation is most associated with cultural anthropology, it has a long history and is used across the social sciences.
  - The Chicago School of sociology, beginning in the 1920s under Robert Park and Ernest Burgess, was based on an ethnographic approach. It continues today in monographs and in the pages of the *Journal of Contemporary Ethnography*.
- It's common to spend a year or more doing participant observation fieldwork. Many participant observation studies are done in a few months or even less.
  - Applied ethnographic research is often done in just a few weeks using methods known collectively as rapid assessment procedures, including participatory mapping and participatory transects. These methods are effective in villages or in organizations.
- One of the strengths of participant observation is its emphasis on validity. Participant observation lowers the reactivity problem in the collection of observational data.
- Participant observation requires certain skills. These include learning the local language, dialect, or jargon; developing explicit awareness; building memory; maintaining naiveté; learning to hang out and build rapport; maintaining objectivity; and learning to write clearly.
  - Learning to hang out and develop rapport involves skills that are highly manipulative. This raises special ethical concerns for participant observers.
  - Objectivity does not mean value neutrality. When Amnesty International documents state-sanctioned torture, we recognize the power of the documentation in its objectivity, not in the neutrality of the data collectors.
- Personal characteristics are important variables in participant observation. Gender, sexual orientation, race, ethnicity, and marital status all color our access to data and the way we interpret data in some way.
  - Feminist scholars have made it clear that gender is a negotiated idea. What you can and can't do if you are a man or a woman is more fixed in some cultures than in others, and in all cultures there is lots of individual variation in gender roles.
- There are seven stages of emotional response in projects based on participant observation fieldwork. These are: (1) initial contact; (2) culture shock; (3) discovering the obvious; (4) the break; (5) focusing; (6) exhaustion, the second break, and frantic activity; and (7) leaving.
- Participant observation is a powerful method that stands on its own, but it is also increasingly part of a mixed-method strategy, as researchers combine qualitative and quantitative data to answer questions of interest.

Exercises

1. This exercise is designed to help you develop skills in taking field notes and in intellectualizing the idea of participant observation. For the next two weeks, take field notes about going to class. Eventually, you want to be able to write a descriptive paper about the act of going to class and the meaning of going to class to different kinds of people. Do men and women act differently in class? Do they sit differently? Do they position themselves in the lecture hall differently? Do people act differently at 8 a.m. and at 3 p.m.? How about in large lecture classes versus small classes?

You'll find that there's a *lot* to this little exercise. You'll have to interview students who attend a variety of classes, including classes that you'd never consider taking, and you'll have to do some observing of classes in which you aren't enrolled. This will require asking professors for permission to sit in and to sign informed consent forms. Be sure you code your field notes from your observations. If several students in your class are doing this exercise, get together with them and compare your note-taking and note-coding tactics.

2. This next exercise is designed to help you build your skills at becoming explicitly aware of everyday things. Get a group of three or more students together and make a list of some mundane, everyday activities—like making a bed, doing laundry, building a sandwich, shaving (face, legs, underarms), picking out produce at the supermarket, etc. Pick three things and have everyone in the group write one-page descriptions of those things. The idea is to just sit down and think through the details and write up, from memory, how you go about, say, doing your laundry. Then, get the group together to read and discuss each other's descriptions. Look specifically for details that everyone writes down about a particular activity and for details that only one person writes down about the same activity.

3. Tomorrow night you're going to write down a simple list of your day's activities, so tomorrow when you wake up, remember to think about everything you do all day. The idea is to remember as many details as you can about what you did, what you ate, where you went, and whom you met all day.

The day after tomorrow, carry a little notepad with you and jot down everything you do, what you eat, where you go, whom you meet. The object of this exercise is to make you painfully aware of the limitations of memory and why it's a good idea to jot down notes, even if they're just reminders and not full of detail.

4. Make a map of some physical space where you spend time. It can be the cafeteria, a lounging area, your apartment, a laundromat, a public park, whatever. The idea is to learn to make maps to scale. This involves, among other things, learning to walk so that your pace is constant. My pace is 30.5 inches on flat ground. Your pace will tend to increase when you walk downhill and to decrease when you walk uphill, but with practice, you can learn to adjust for these differences and keep your pace constant.

5. The object of this next exercise is to write a paper on a specialized craft by interviewing one key informant. The craft can be computer repair or shoe repair. Harriers and glaziers have very specialized knowledge. The problem in a complex society is not finding people who have specialized craft knowledge. The problem is finding people who will talk to you openly about their knowledge. Pick one area of specialized craft knowledge and interview at least three people who control that knowledge.

Take careful *methodological* notes during the interview about the dynamics of the interaction. Some people are better cultural informants than are others. How can you tell?

Further Reading

History of ethnography in the social sciences. Adler and Adler (1987), Bulmer (1984), Chapoulie (2004), Cunliffe (2010), Hallett and Fine (2000), Levine (1995), Lofland (1983), Platt (1994), Stocking (1983, 1991, 1992), Zickar and Carter (2010).

Participant observation. Behar (1996), Bruyn (1966), Cassell and Symon (1994), Denzin and Lincoln (1994), DeWalt and DeWalt (2011), Fenno (1990), Fetterman (1998), Fielding (1993), Gummesson (1991), Hammersley (1990), Junker (1960), Spradley (1980),

Stewart (1998), Taylor and Bogdan (1998), Whyte (1984), Wolcott (2008), Woods (1986).

Rapid assessment. Baker et al. (2008), Beebe (2001), Chambers (1991), Gittelsohn et al. (1998), Mignone et al. (2009), Scrimshaw and Gleason (1992), Scrimshaw and Hurtado (1987).

Gatekeepers. Harrington (2003), Magolda (2000), Rashid (2007), Reeves (2010), Wanat (2008).

Using interpreters. Borchgrevnik (2003), Jentsch (1998), Larrison et al. (2010), Phillips (1959), Temple (2002).

Language and fieldwork. Burling (2000 [1984]), Levy and Hollan (1998), Owusu (1978), Werner and Fenton (1973), Winchatz (2006, 2010).

Studying your own culture. Altorki and El-Sohl (1988), Chock (1986), Fahim (1977, 1982), Jones (1970), Kerra and Phillips (2008), Kim (1990), Kuwayama (2003), Messerschmidt (1981), Narayan (1993), Peirano (1998), Shami (1989), Stephenson and Greer (1981), Tahir (2010), Zaman (2008).

Race and gender in fieldwork. Brown and De Casanova (2009), Harrington (2003), Henderson (2009), McKeganey and Bloor (1991). Volume 11, issue 2 of *Men and Masculinities* (special section on men doing anthropology of women).

Sex and fieldwork. Cupples (2002), Kulick and Wilson (1995), La Pastina (2006), Whitehead and Conaway (1986), M. Wilson (1997), Wolcott (2002).

Dangerous fieldwork. Belousov et al. (2007), Kovats-Bernat (2008), Lee (1995), Nordstrom and Robben (1995), Paterson et al. (1999), Sharp and Kremer (2006).

Mixed methods. Axinn and Pearce (2006), Creswell and Plano Clark (2011), Mertens (2010), Tashakkori and Teddlie (2010). And see the *Journal of Mixed Methods Research*.

13

Field Notes and Database Management

Those who want to use qualitative methods because they seem easier than statistics are in for a rude awakening

—[Taylor and Bogdan 1984:53]

The difference between field *experience* and field *work* is field *notes*. In this chapter, I focus on how to write field notes and how to handle other kinds of material—like newspaper clippings and photos—that ethnographers accumulate during fieldwork. The lessons about coding and analyzing field notes apply just as well to transcripts of interviews and to other textual data, which we'll take up in Chapter 19.

ABOUT FIELD NOTES

Plan to spend two–three hours every working day of a participant observation study writing up field notes, working on your diary, and coding interviews and notes. Ralph Bolton asked 34 ethnographers about their field note practices; they reported spending anywhere from one and a half hours to seven hours a day on write-up (1984:132).

Remember that it takes twice as long to write up notes about a recorded interview as it does to conduct an interview in the first place. You have to listen to a recorded interview at least once before you can write up the essential notes from it, and then it takes as long again to get the notes down. If you need full transcriptions of interviews, plan to spend around six hours for each hour of interview, assuming that the recording is clear, the interview is in your own language, and you have a transcribing machine with a foot pedal. You can cut transcription time in half by using voice recognition software (more about this back in Chapter 8, and see Appendix E).

Every colleague with whom I've ever discussed this agrees that it's best to set aside a time each day for working on your notes. And don't sleep on your notes. It's easy to forget material that you want in your notes if you don't write them up in the afternoon or evening each day. The same goes for your own thoughts and impressions of events. If you don't write them up every day, while they are fresh, they'll vanish into the night.

This means that you shouldn't get embroiled in a lot of activities that prevent you from writing up field notes. There are plenty of exceptions to this rule. Here's one. You are studying how families create culture by telling and retelling certain stories. You sit down to write up the day's field notes and you get a call from a key informant who tells you to come right on over to meet her father who is leaving on a trip in the morning and wants to tell you himself the story she had told you earlier about his experience as a refugee during World War II. You couldn't possibly turn that one down. But remember, it's easy to let doing anything except writing notes become the norm rather than the exception.

Create many small notes rather than one long, running commentary. Make many separate note files, rather than adding to the same humongous file day after day. (With text management software, you won't lose track of anything. More about that later.) You can have one file for each day, or you can have files for each interview or each event you attend.

HOW TO WRITE FIELD NOTES

The method I present here for writing and coding field notes was developed and tested by the late Michael Kenny and me, between 1967 and 1971, when we ran those NSF-supported field schools in cultural anthropology that I described in Chapter 12. Kenny and I relied initially on our own experience with field notes, and we borrowed freely from the experience of many colleagues. The method we developed involves jottings, a diary, a daily log, and three kinds of formal notes: methodological notes, descriptive notes; and analytic notes.

Two things can be said about the method I'm going to lay out here: (1) it works; and (2) it's not the only way to do things. If you do field research, you'll develop your own style of writing notes and you'll add your own little tricks as you go along. Still, the method described here will help you work systematically at taking field notes and will allow you to search through them quickly and easily to look for relations in your data. I wish I had used this method when I was doing my own M.A. and Ph.D. fieldwork—and I wish that computers and database management systems had been available then, too.

FOUR TYPES OF FIELD NOTES

You'll write four kinds of notes in fieldwork: jottings, a diary, and a log, which I'll discuss first, and field notes proper, which I'll take up in the section that follows.

Jottings

Field jottings—what Roger Sanjek calls **scratch notes** (1990:96)—are what get you through the day. Human memory is a very poor recording device, especially for the kind of details that make the difference between good and so-so ethnographic research. Keep a little note pad with you at all times and make field jottings on the spot. This applies to both formal and informal interviews in bars and cafés, in homes and on the street.

It also applies to things that just strike you as you are walking along. Jottings will provide you with the trigger you need to recall a lot of details that you don't have time to write down while you're observing events or listening to an informant. Even a few key words will jog your memory later. Remember: *If you don't write it down, it's gone* (Box 13.1).

Box 13.1 Little computers, bigger computers, and field notes

Some ethnographers like to use notebooks and take their jotting notes by hand; others like to use PDA's or smartphones for this task during the day and then write up their field notes on a larger computer at night. Anything you're comfortable with is fine.

Clearly, there are times when you just can't take notes. Morris Freilich did research in the 1950s with the Mohawks in Brooklyn, New York, and on the Caughnanaga Reservation, 10 miles south of Montreal. He did a lot of participant observation in a bar and, as Freilich tells it, every time he pulled out a notebook his audience became hostile. So, Freilich kept a small notebook in his hip pocket and would periodically duck into the men's room at the bar to scribble a few jottings (Freilich 1977:159).

William Sturtevant used stubby little pencils to take furtive notes; he found the technique so useful, he published it (1959). When Hortense Powdermaker did her research on race relations in Mississippi in 1932, she took surreptitious notes on sermons at African American churches. "My pocketbook was large," she said, "and the notebook in it was small" (1966:175).

Every fieldworker runs into situations where it's impossible to take notes. It is always appropriate to be sensitive people's feelings, and it is sometimes a good idea to just listen attentively and leave your notebook in your pocket. You'd be surprised, though, how few of these situations there are. Don't talk yourself into not jotting down a few notes on the incorrect assumption that people won't like it if you do.

The key is to take up the role of researcher immediately when you arrive at your field site, whether that site is a corporate office in Chicago or a village in a developing nation. Let people know from the first day you arrive that you are there to study their way of life. Don't try to become an inconspicuous participant rather than what you really are: an observer who wants to participate as much as possible. Participant observation means that you try to *experience* the life of your informants to the extent possible; it doesn't mean that you try to melt into the background and *become* a fully accepted member of a culture other than your own.

It's often impossible to do that anyway. After decades of coming and going in Indian villages in Mexico, I never became the slightest bit inconspicuous. Be honest with people and keep your note pad out as much of the time as possible. Ask your informants for their permission to take notes while you are talking with them. If people don't want you to take notes, they'll tell you.

Or they may tell you to take notes when you don't want to. Paul Killworth studied the social organization of the British Army. Because notebooks are, as he says, "part of Army uniform," he was able to go anywhere with his notebook in hand and take notes freely. But if he put his notebook aside for more than a few minutes, soldiers would ask him if he was getting lazy. "More than one relaxing moment," he says, "was stopped by someone demanding that I write something down" (1997:5).

Or they may ask to see your notes. A student researcher in one of our field schools worked in a logging camp in Idaho. He would write up his notes at night from the jottings he took all day. Each morning at 6:00 a.m. he nailed the day's sheaf of notes (along with a pen on a string) to a tree for everyone to look at. Some of the men took the time to scribble helpful (or amusing or rude) comments on the notes. If you use this technique, watch out for the CNN effect. That's when people tell you things they want to tell everyone because they know you're going to broadcast whatever they say. This is a disaster if you're trying to make everybody around you feel confident that you're not going to blab about them.

Even when people get accustomed to your constant jottings, you can overdo it. Emerson et al. (1995:23) cite the following field note from an ethnographer who was studying divorce negotiations:

On one occasion when finishing up a debriefing . . . [the mediator] began to apply some eye make-up while I was finishing writing down some observations. She flashed me a mock disgusted look and said, "Are you writing *this* down too" indicating the activity with her eye pencil.

The Diary

Notes are based on observations that will form the basis of your publications. A diary, on the other hand, is personal. It's a place where you can run and hide when things get tough. You absolutely need a diary in any ethnography project. It will help you deal with loneliness, fear, and other emotions that make fieldwork difficult.

A diary chronicles how you feel and how you perceive your relations with others around you. If you are really angry at someone, you should write about it—in your diary. Jot down emotional highs and lows while they're happening, if you can, and write them up in your diary at the end of the day. During data analysis, your diary will become an important professional document. It will give you information that will help you interpret your field notes and will make you aware of your personal biases.

Dennis McGilvray (1989) did fieldwork in Akkaraipattu, Sri Lanka in 1969–71. Here is an excerpt from his diary:

January 7, 1970. Akkaraipattu. A miserable night indeed. Slight fever, humidity, and mosquitos. Abuthahir doesn't come at 5:00 AM as he promised. But at 6:00 AM, just as I was finally getting to sleep, he came to slaughter the cow to inaugurate the house. The whole spectacle was quite bloody and aroused deep sympathy from me for the poor cow. A mob of 75 children plus various old adults assemble to watch the butchering and to watch me. Mainly me. What little appetite I had soon vanished, and I basically felt sick, but nonetheless I had to endure endless questions and invasions of my morning bathing and shaving ritual. It seems that word of my camera, typewriter, and tape recorder has spread for miles around. And everyone also knows I am getting a jeep, and they all want reservations for rides. In a more healthy state, I would be able to tolerate the speechless scrutiny of my every action, but this morning I came close to blowing my lid.

February 18, 1970. Akkaraipattu. For the first time, really, since being in Akk, I would love to have a drink. Just a nice highball with ice, nothing too powerful. I am weary. It was another of those days when people grab me by the tongue and won't let go. It's what I need to learn Tamil,

I know, but it is often mindwracking and definitely like brainwashing. Right now, after everyone has finally gone and I am alone at last, I wish I could take a hot bath and crawl into a soft cool bed (dry, too) with clean sheets. But I can't: everything, my sleeping bag included, is slightly damp from the rain. The mosquitos and sundry bugs are waiting for me, and the bed still has no mattress so I sleep on planks.

What a drag. I still feel as if I am not well-enough coordinated in studying Tamil: it is all just bits and pieces. "The Tamil Chef," latest installment. Samitamby, my Barber neighbor, hailed me to the back fence again for another culinary delicacy. This time it was tortoise eggs and a bunch of green leaves. "Vitamin A and calcium" he exhorted, brandishing the clump of leaves. Palani (my Tamil cook), under strong pressure from Samitamby, laced every item for lunch with these damn leaves, which have zero taste whatsoever. As for the eggs, I tried the omelet but couldn't take the boiled eggs: they are still soft when cooked and look like rancid cheese fondue inside.

Franz Boas got engaged to Marie Krackowizer in May 1883, just three weeks before beginning his first field trip. It was a grueling 15 months on Baffin Island and at sea. Boas missed German society terribly and, although he couldn't mail the letters, he wrote about 500 pages to his fiancée. Here is an excerpt from his diary:

December 16, north of Pangnirtung. My dear sweetheart. . . . Do you know how I pass these long evenings? I have a copy of Kant with me, which I am studying, so that I shall not be so completely uneducated when I return. Life here really makes one dull and stupid. . . . I have to blush when I remember that during our meal tonight I thought how good a pudding with plum sauce would taste. But you have no idea what an effect privations and hunger, real hunger, have on a person. Maybe Mr. Kant is a good antidote! The contrast is almost unbelievable when I remember that a year ago I was in society and observed all the rules of good taste, and tonight I sit in this snow hut with Wilhelm and an Eskimo eating a piece of raw, frozen seal meat which had first to be hacked up with an axe, and greedily gulping my coffee. Is that not as great a contradiction as one can think of? [Cole 1983:29]

When Malinowski was trapped in the Trobriand Islands during World War I, he, too, missed his fiancée and European society and occasionally lashed out at the Trobrianders in his diary (Malinowski 1967:253–54). Fieldwork in another culture is an intense experience, but don't think that you have to be stranded in Sri Lanka or the Arctic or Melanesia for things to get intense.

Your diary will give you an outlet for writing things that you don't want to become part of a public record. Publication of Malinowski's and Boas's diaries have helped make all fieldworkers aware that they are not alone in their frailties and self-doubts.

The Log

A log is a running account of how you plan to spend your time, how you actually spend your time, and how much money you spent. A good log is the key to doing systematic fieldwork and to collecting both qualitative and quantitative data on a systematic basis.

A field log should be kept in bound books of blank, lined pages or, if you are working in an area where you have continuous access to the Internet, on a scheduling app. The advantage of a big, clunky logbook (say, 6″ × 8″ in size) is that you can see at a glance what your agenda is as you have that first cup of coffee in the morning.

Each day of fieldwork, whether you're out for a year or a week, should be represented by a double page of the log or the equivalent in an app. The pages on the left should list what you *plan* to do on any given day. The facing pages will recount what you *actually* do each day.

If you use a book, begin your log on pages 2 and 3. Put the date on the top of the even-numbered page to the left. Then, go through the entire notebook and put the successive dates on the even-numbered pages. By doing this in advance, even the days on which you "do nothing," or are away from your field site, will have double log pages devoted to them.

The first day or two that you make a log you will use only the right-hand pages where you keep track of where you go, who you see, and what you spend. Some people like to carry their logs around with them. Others prefer to jot down the names of the people they run into or interview and enter the information into their logs when they write up their notes in the evening.

Keep a file of 25-word profiles on as many people you meet as you can. Start by jotting profiles on index cards (one for each person you meet) or on a phone app and then moving the profile to your computer when you write your field notes. If you are doing network analysis, put the connections for each person—who people know and how they know them—into the profile as you learn those things. Before you go into any second or third interview, look up the key biographical information you have about the person. During the first couple of minutes of the interview, work in a comment that shows you remember some of those key bio-facts. You'll be surprised how far that'll take you.

Jot down the times that you eat and what you eat, and write down who you eat with and how much you spend on meals away from your house. You'll be surprised at how much you learn from this, too.

After a day or two, you will begin to use the left-hand sheets of the log. As you go through any given day, you will think of many things that you want to know but can't resolve on the spot. Write those things down in your jot book or in your log. When you write up your field notes, think about who you need to interview or what you need to observe about each of the things you wondered about that day.

Right then and there, open your log and commit yourself to finding each thing out at a particular time on a particular day. If finding something out requires that you talk to a particular person, then put that person's name in the log, too. If you don't know the person to talk to, then put down the name of someone whom you think can steer you to the right person.

Suppose you're studying a school system. It's September 5 and you are talking to MJR, a fifth-grade teacher. She tells you that since the school adopted a new curriculum, including sex education for grades 4 and up, some children are very uncomfortable. Write a note to yourself in your log to ask mothers of some of the children about this issue and to interview the school principal.

Later on, when you are writing up your notes, you may decide not to interview the principal until after you have accumulated more data about how mothers in the community feel about the new curriculum. On the left-hand page for September 6 you note: "need interviews with mothers about new curriculum." On the left-hand page of September 10 you note: "make appointment for interview on 23rd with school principal." On the left-hand page for September 23 you note: "target date for interview with school principal."

As soon as it occurs to you that you need to know how many people in an organization work on flex time, or the difference in price of vegetables bought from a local supermarket and the same vegetables bought from a farmer's market, commit yourself *in your log to a specific time* when you will try to get answers to your questions. Whether the question you think of requires a formal appointment, or a direct, personal observation, or an informal interview in a bar, write the question down in one of the left-hand pages of your log.

Don't worry if the planned activity log you create for yourself winds up looking nothing like the activities you actually engage in from day to day. Frankly, you'll be lucky to do half the things you think of to do, much less do them when you want to. The important thing is to fill those left-hand pages, as far out into the future as you can, with specific information that you need and specific tasks you need to perform to get that information.

This is not just because you want to use your time effectively, but because the process of building a log forces you to think hard about the questions you really want to answer in your research and the data you really need. You will start any field research project knowing some of the questions you are interested in. But those questions may change; you may add some and drop others—or your entire emphasis may shift.

The right-hand pages of the log are for recording what you actually accomplish each day. As I said, you'll be appalled at first at how little resemblance the left-hand and the right-hand pages have to one another. You'll get over it. Just keep reminding yourself that good fieldwork does not depend on the punctuality of informants or on your ability to do all the things you want to do. It depends on your systematic work over a period of time. If some informants do not show up for appointments (and often they won't), you can evaluate whether you really need the data you thought you were going to get from them. If you do need the data, put a note on the left-hand page for that same day, or for the next day, to contact the informant and reschedule the appointment.

If you still have no luck, you may have to decide whether it's worth more of your time to track down a particular person or a particular piece of information. Your log will tell you how much time you've spent on it already and will make the decision easier. There's plenty of time for everything when you think you've got months stretching ahead of you. But you only have a finite amount of time in any fieldwork project to get useful data, and the time goes very quickly.

FIELD NOTES

And now, about field notes. . . . Let's face it: After a hard day trekking all over [town] [the

jungle] [the hospital] [the desert] interviewing people, hanging out, and recording behavior, it's hard to sit down and write up field notes. Sometimes, it's downright intimidating. We know this much about field notes for sure: The faster you write up your observations, the more detail you can get down. More is better. Much more is much better (except, of course, when data are systematically biased, in which case more is decidedly worse).

There are three kinds of field notes: methodological notes, descriptive notes, and analytic notes.

Methodological Notes

Methodological notes deal with technique in collecting data. If you work out a better way to keep a log than I've described here, don't just *use* your new technique: Write it up in your field notes and publish a paper about your technique so others can benefit from your experience. (See Appendix E for a list of professional journals that publish articles on research methods in the social and behavioral sciences.) If you find yourself spending too much time with marginal people in the culture, make a note of it, and discuss how that came to be. You'll discover little tricks of the trade, like the "uh-huh" technique discussed in Chapter 8. (Remember that one? It's where you learn how and when to grunt encouragingly to keep an interview going.) Write up notes about your discoveries. Mark all these notes with a big "M" at the top—M for "method."

Methodological notes are also about your own growth as an instrument of data collection. Collecting data is always awkward when you begin a field project, but it gets easier as you become more comfortable in a new culture. During this critical period of adjustment, you should intellectualize what you're learning about doing fieldwork by taking methodological notes.

When I first arrived in Greece in 1960, I was invited to dinner at "around 7 p.m." When I arrived at around 7:15 (which I thought was a polite 15 minutes late), I was embarrassed to find that my host was still taking a bath. I should have known that he really meant "around 8 p.m." when he said "around 7." My methodological note for the occasion simply stated that I should not show up for dinner before 8 p.m. in the future.

Some weeks later, I figured out the general rules for timing of evening activities, including cocktails, dinner, and late-night desserts in the open squares of Athens. Robert Levine has studied the psychology of time by asking people around the world things like "How long would you wait for someone who was late for a lunch appointment?" On average, Brazilians say they'd wait 62 minutes. On average, says Levine, "Americans would need to be back at their office two minutes *before*" the late Brazilian lunch was just getting underway (Levine 1997:136).

When I began fieldwork with the Ñähñu people of central Mexico in 1962, I was offered *pulque* everywhere I went. I tried to refuse politely; I couldn't stand the stuff. But people were very insistent and seemed offended if I didn't accept the drink. Things were particularly awkward when I showed up at someone's house and there were other guests there. Everyone enjoyed *pulque* but me, and most of the time people were too poor to have beer around to offer me.

At that time, I wrote a note that people "felt obliged by custom to offer *pulque* to guests." I was dead wrong. As I eventually learned, people were testing me to see if I was affiliated with the Summer Institute of Linguistics (SIL), an evangelical missionary group (and nondrinkers of alcohol) that had its regional headquarters in the area where I was working.

The SIL is comprised of many excellent linguists who produce books and articles on the grammar of the nonwritten languages of the world and translations of the Bible into those languages. There was serious friction between the Indians who had converted to Protestantism and those who remained Catholic. It was important for me to disassociate myself from the SIL, so my methodological note discussed the importance of conspicuously consuming alcohol and tobacco to identify myself as an anthropologist and not as a missionary.

Nine years later, in 1971, I still couldn't stand *pulque*—and I was sure that drinking out of those common gourds that were passed around was what sent me to the hospital in 1968. I started carrying a couple of six packs of beer in the car and offering it to people who offered me *pulque*. This worked and the methods lesson was clear: Beer kept my reputation of independence from the SIL intact and was universally accepted because beer was costly and prestigious compared to *pulque*.

Eight years later, in 1979, I read that William Partridge had a similar predicament during his work in Colombia (Kimball and Partridge 1979:55). Everywhere Partridge went, it seems, people offered him beer, even at 7:00 a.m. He needed an acceptable excuse, he said, to avoid spending all his waking hours getting drunk.

After a few months in the field, Partridge found that telling people "*Estoy tomando una pastilla*" ("I'm taking a pill") did the trick. Locally, the pill referred to in this phrase was used in treating venereal disease. Everyone knew that you didn't drink alcohol while you were taking this pill, and the excuse was perfect for adding a little virility boost to Partridge's reputation. Partridge used his knowledge of local culture to get out of a tough situation.

Methodological notes, then, have to do with the conduct of field inquiry itself. You will want to make methodological notes especially when you do something silly that breaks a cultural norm. If you are feeling particularly sheepish, you might want to write those feelings into your diary where no one else will see what you've written; but you don't want to waste the opportunity to make a straightforward methodological note on such occasions, as well.

Descriptive Notes

Descriptive notes are the meat and potatoes of fieldwork. Most notes are descriptive and are from two sources: watching and listening. Interviews with informants produce acres of notes, especially if you use a recorder and later write down large chunks of what people say or even transcribe the interviews completely.

Observations of processes, like feeding children, building a house, hanging out at the water cooler, and so on, also produce a lot of notes. Descriptive field notes may contain birth records that you've copied out of a local church registry, or they may consist of summary descriptions of a community center or police station or a shopping mall, or any environmental features that you think are important.

The best way to learn to write descriptive field notes is to practice doing it with others who are also trying to learn. Get together with one or more partners and observe a process that's unfamiliar to all of you. It could be a church service other than one you've seen before, or it could be an occupational process that you've not witnessed. (I remember the first time I saw plasterers hang ceilings: They do it on stilts.)

Whatever you observe, try to capture in field notes the details of the behavior and the environment. Try to get down "what's going on." Then ask people who are watching the ceremony or process to explain what's going on and try to get notes down on their explanation. Later, get together with your research partner(s) and discuss your notes with one another. You'll find that two or three people see much more than just one sees. You might also find that you and your partners saw the same things but wrote down different subsets of the same information.

Analytic Notes

You will write up fewer analytic notes than any other kind. This is where you lay out your ideas about how you think the culture you are studying is organized. Analytic notes can be about relatively minor things. When I finally figured out the rules for showing up on time for evening functions in Greece, that was worth an analytic note. And when I understood the rules that governed the naming of children that was worth an analytic note, too.

As I said in Chapter 2, in the section on theory, it took me almost a year to figure out why the casualty rate among Kalymnian sponge divers was going up, while the worldwide demand for natural sponges was going down. When it finally made sense, I sat down and wrote a long, long analytic field note about it. After thinking about the problem for many years, I finally understood why bilingual education in Mexico does not result in the preservation of Indian languages (it's a long story; see Bernard 1992). As the ideas developed, I wrote them up in a series of notes.

Analytic notes are the product of a lot of time and effort and may go on for several pages. They are often the basis for published papers or for chapters in dissertations and books. They will be the product of your understanding and will come about through your organizing and working with descriptive and methodological notes over a period of time. Don't expect to write a great many analytic notes, but write them all your life, even (especially) after you are out of the field.

CODING FIELD NOTES

Gene Shelley (1992) studied people who suffer from end-stage kidney disease. Most patients are on hemodialysis. Some are on peritoneal dialysis. The "hemo" patients go to a dialysis center, several times a week, while the "pero" patients perform a dialysis (called continuous ambulatory peritoneal dialysis, or CAPD) on themselves several times a day.

Figure 13.1 shows three descriptive notes from Shelley's research. First, there's a delimiter (she used the dollar sign) that marks the beginning of each note. This lets you pack all the notes together in one big file so a word processor or text analysis program knows where notes begin and end. Next is a unique number that identifies the note in a continuing sequence, starting with 0001. Next is the date.

Then come some numbers that refer to theme codes. In note 3, this is preceded by a location indicator. Finally, at the end of the codes at the top of each field note, there's a cryptic indicator of the person to whom Shelley attributes the information—except for note 3, which was based on observation

Coding Versus Indexing

I want to make clear the three different uses of the word "code." When I say: "Use codes for places and informant names," the word "code" means an encryption device. The object is to hide information, not dispense it. When William Partridge interviewed cannabis growers in Colombia, he identified the texts by

Figure 13.1 Field Notes From Gene Shelley's Study of Kidney Disease Patients (1992)

$ 615 8B16B89: 757.3; Dr. H
Dr. H explains that in peritoneal dialysis you exchange 2 liters of fluid several times a day (based on body size). Women do it about 3 times and men about 4 times because of larger body size. People mostly do a "dwell" for about 8 hours overnight while they sleep (fluid is inflowed into peritoneal cavity and allowed to sit there overnight). Then they do peritoneal dialysis when they wake up and another time or two during the day. Peritoneal dialysis patients are pretty close to being healthy. They have to take medication but you cannot tell them from healthy people, he says.

$ 742 8B30B89: 57.3, 757.5; Nurse Ralph B.
CAPD training takes about a week to 10 days. During this time, the patients comes in every day and receives training. Ralph thinks that when the whole family comes in for the training, the patients do better. They have about 20 CAPD patients right now. Ralph said there are 3 types of CAPD patients: (1) those patients who are already on hemo and in pretty good shape, usually well-motivated. (2) those who are late getting started and are in trouble (medically) and are hurriedly trying to learn the procedure. (It takes 2 weeks to get a catheter inserted and then have it heal. Since this surgery is viewed as "elective surgery," it can be bumped and rescheduled.) Only after surgery and healing can the training take place. (3) those who have lost a kidney which was transplanted. They are just waiting for another kidney and they view CAPD as temporary and are not that motivated to learn it because they think they won't be on it long.

$ 876 12B6B89: Waiting Room 571; 580; 580.7; 580.1; 264; 12;
While waiting to talk to Dr. H, I sat in the hemodialysis waiting room. I watched and listed to patients (and waiting family) who were waiting to get on the dialysis machines. They were talking about how sometimes the staff is rough with them when putting the needles in to get the vein access. One guy said the needle went once "right into his bone." Another guy said "the girl had to try 7 times" to get his blood and he was about to hit her. (The nurse said at the time, "I know this hurts.") Another woman threatened physical harm to technicians who draw blood roughly. One patient mentioned that sometimes they have to get different vein access sites (i.e., the groin or the top of the foot). They were all talking, not always to anyone in particular (but sometimes they were). They were talking in a way so that everyone in the room could be in the conversation if they wanted to.

Source: G. A. Shelley, "The Social Networks of People with End-Stage Renal Disease: Comparing Hemodialysis and Peritoneal Dialysis Patients." Ph.D. dissertation, University of Florida, Gainesville. 1992.

a letter code and kept the only copy of his notes in a locked trunk (Kimball and Partridge 1979:174).

You don't have to be interviewing cannabis growers to be paranoid about keeping your informants' identity secret. You never know what seemingly innocuous information might embarrass or hurt someone if your data fall into the wrong hands. (Box 13.2)

Box 13.2 Sometimes, even your best isn't enough . . .

Cora Du Bois did her fieldwork in the vilalge of Atimelang on the Indonesian island of Alor in 1937–39, when Indonesia was a Dutch colony. Du Bois's classic book on Alor appeared in 1944, but in the meantime, the Japanese had taken territory from the Dutch in 1942, during World War II. When the war ended in 1945, Du Bois learned that village leaders in Atimelang had said publicly that they thought Hamerica (the Alorese word for America and the name that they had given the house they'd helped Du Bois build) would win the war. The Japanese, fearing rebellion by the people of Atimelang beheaded five of Du Bois's friends in the village. As Du Bois put it, when her book was re-issued in 1960: "there is no end to the intricate chain of responsibility and guilt that the pursuit of even the most arcane social research involves" (p. xiv).

When I say: "Code your notes for the themes you develop in your analysis," the word "code" means an indexing device. Suppose you do 100 interviews with women about their birthing experience. If you stick the code PAIN into the text whenever a woman mentions anything about pain or about feeling hurt, you'd be using the code PAIN as an indexing device—that is, as a way to find your way back to all the places in the text where anything about pain is mentioned. It's just like an index to a book. It says that "sampling" is on page 237 and sure enough, when you go to page 237, you find you're reading about sampling.

The third meaning of the word "code" is a measurement device. Suppose you make judgments about the amount of pain—by counting words like "agony" as indicating more pain than words like "distress" or by looking at the content and meaning of the text and counting "It was painful, but I got through it" as indicating less pain than "I prayed I would die." You might use codes like LO-PAIN, MID-PAIN, or HI-PAIN, and in this case, you'd be using codes for actual measurement.

Theme Codes: The OCM

Shelley used a modified version of the **Outline of Cultural Materials (OCM)**, to code her field notes. The OCM was developed originally by G. P. Murdock in 1950 as a way to index and organize ethnographic materials in the Human Relations Area Files. The OCM has gone through several editions over the years, and the latest edition is available online at http://www.yale.edu/hraf/outline.htm (Murdock et al. 2004 [1961]).

There are 91 big cultural domains in the OCM, in blocks of 10, from 10 to 91. Block 58, for example, covers marriage with codes for nuptials (585), divorce (586), and so on. Other major domains are things like kinship, entertainment, social stratification, war, health, sex, and religious practices. Every project is unique, so you'll need codes that aren't in the OCM, but you can add decimals (or words) and extend the codes forever. Table 13.1 shows Shelley's adaptation of the OCM code 757 (medical therapy):

Don't be put off by the lengthiness of the OCM coding list. That's its strength. Many field researchers have used the OCM over the years to code their field notes and other materials. You'll only use a fraction of the codes on any given project, but if you do use the OCM in the field, you'll quickly find yourself building supplemental coding schemes to fit your particular needs.

Figure 13.2 shows how Gordon Gibson used the OCM to code a series of ethnographic

| Table 13.1 | Shelley's (1992) Adaptation of the OCM Code 757 on Medical Therapy |

| 757.1 Transplantation |
| 757.2 Hemodialysis |
| 757.3 CAPD (peritoneal dialysis) |
| 757.4 Home dialysis |
| 757.5 Adjustment to dialysis |
| 757.6 Compliance with medical regime |
| 757.7 Machinery involved in dialysis |
| 757.8 Medicines |
| 757.9 Medical test results |
| 757.91 HIV test results |

| Figure 13.2 | Gibson's Coding of the Himba Films |

13 GIBSON (film)		E-5 (1961) 1969 HIMBA	
11:09:29	Picture	Bride and companion walk toward hut, then bride and unmarried girl drop to their knees and crawl into hut. People are seen sitting in front of hut as the two disappear inside.	585* 342
	Sound	The bride and their companions solemnly return to the hut in Vesenga's village where she has been staying, and she and the unmarried girl enter the hut.	
11:29:30	Picture	People sitting and standing near hut.	585*
	Sound	Women and children of the village, and those visiting, from other villages, have gathered to sit near the bride.	342 574 857
11:42:22	Picture	Boys seated eating meat.	585*
	Sound	Young boys eat together.	262 857
11:45:10	Picture	Meat in basket and men seated, eating. A man standing and eating meat off a bone, places the bone on a bush. The groom is seated, his arms folded on his knees. He takes a piece of meat from a pail on the ground between his feet.	585* 264 574
	Sound	The bridegroom and his friends are still seated by the bower, where they are finishing.	

Source: L. Kreiss and E. Stockton, "Using the Outline of Cultural Materials as a Basis for Indexing the Content of Ethnographic Films." *Behavior Science Research* 15:281–93, table on p. 280, 1980.

films on the Himba, a cattle-herding society in Namibia (in Kreiss and Stockton 1980:287). The film coded in Figure 13.2 is about a wedding, so each piece is coded 585, the OCM code for nuptials. Where the hut is seen, the code for dwellings (342) is inserted. Where the film shows people eating meat, the codes 262 (diet) and 264 (eating) are inserted. In the frame at 11:45:10, the code for visiting (574) appears, and in the two earlier frames, the code for childhood activities (857) is inserted. When Gibson did this work in the 1970s, the database was held on a mainframe. Today, you would just watch a video on your computer and enter codes as you go.

Theme Codes: In Vivo

Many people find the use of number codes distracting. Matthew Miles and Michael Huberman (1994), authors of a classic book on qualitative data analysis, advocated the use of words or mnemonics that look like the original concept. Like many researchers, they find that mnemonic codes (like ECO for economics, DIV for divorce, and so on) are easier to remember than numbers. Figure 13.3 shows an example of how to do this.

Another value of using your own codes is that they develop naturally from your study and you'll find it easy to remember them as you code your notes each day. Strauss and Corbin (1990:68) recommend in vivo codes as

names for things. In vivo codes are catchy phrases or words used by informants. In his study of Alaskan fishermen, Jeffrey Johnson heard people talking about a "clown." The word turned out to be a terrific label for a type of person found in many organizations. The term emerged in vivo from the mouths of Johnson's informants (Johnson and Miller 1983).

If you use your own coding scheme, or if you modify an existing scheme (like the OCM), be sure to write up a verbose codebook in case you forget what "A5" or "EMP" or whatever cute abbreviations you dreamed up at the time you did the coding mean.

And don't get too picky when you make up your own codes. Coding is supposed to be data reduction, not data proliferation. Mathew Miles was involved in a big ethnographic project to evaluate six schools. All the researchers developed their own codes and the code list quickly grew to 202 categories of actors, processes, organizational forms, and efforts. Each of the six researchers insisted that his or her field site was unique and that the highly specialized codes were all necessary. It became impossible for anyone to use the unwieldy system, and they just stopped coding altogether (Miles 1983:123).

The important thing is not which coding scheme you use, it's that you code your notes and do it consistently. In most projects, the coding scheme takes shape as the notes are written. The scheme is revised a lot before it becomes stable. Even if you use the OCM, it will take a while before you see how your field

Figure 13.3 Coding Field Notes With Mnemonics

412 MA XOR 101210 MIG WOM ECO

This is note number 412. It's about an informant named MA in these notes. She is from a community you label XOR.

The date is October 12, 2010 and the note is about migration in search of work. The note is coded using abbreviations for themes as being about migration (MIG), about women (WOM), and about economics (ECO).

notes are shaping up and think about making specific changes to the codes.

ANALYZING FIELD NOTES

Until about 1980, field notes were all written on cards or sheets of paper and then hand marked with codes indicating themes. Some people still like to write field notes on paper, but most fieldworkers type up their notes on a computer and then use a text analysis program to code those notes. Text analysis programs don't analyze anything, but they do take a lot of the drudgery out of coding and they make it easier to analyze your notes (Box 13.3).

Box 13.3 Using a word processor to analyze field notes

If all you want to do is **code and retrieve** notes about particular topics whenever you want, then a word processor is all you need. Just create a symbol that will never be used for anything except codes—perhaps the ampersand followed by a backslash, &\. Then use that symbol to tag material in your notes. For example, you might tuck the phrase "&\marriage" into your notes as an indicator that you're talking about marriage "about here." Then, when you want to look for chunks of text that deal with marriage, you just look for the code &\marriage.

Tucking tags like this into your notes lets you mark text that is about marriage, even though the word "marriage" might not be mentioned (as might be the case, say, in a description of a wedding ceremony).

You can also use the font features (bold, italics, color) of a word processor to code your notes. You'd be surprised at what you can do with a simple word processor. For more, see Ryan (2004) and La Pelle (2004). And lots more about finding and coding themes in texts in Chapter 19 (**Further Reading:** field notes and field diaries).

I think it's best to start analyzing with the ocular scan method, or eyeballing. In this low-tech method, you go through your notes, reading them, one at a time. You live with them, read them over and over again, and eventually get a feel for what's in them. This is followed by the interocular percussion test, in which patterns jump out and hit you between the eyes. For some, nothing is more fun or efficient at this early stage of analysis than pawing through a sheaf of printed notes, moving them around on the floor, putting them into piles, and thinking about them. For others, printing notes is a waste of time and trees. They like to read through their notes on a screen and code on the fly. There is no single best way to analyze field notes. Figure out what you like and stay with it.

For me, a text analysis program is the way to go. You can ask questions like: "Find every note in which I used the word *woman* but only if I also used the word *migration* within three lines of the word *woman*." If you code your notes with themes, you can look for any combination of those, too. The mechanics are simple. The important thing is to decide what the themes are then to use those themes in coding your notes. We'll get the problem of finding themes in Chapter 19.

DATABASE MANAGEMENT

What do you do if you have physical things, like photos or news clippings, rather than notes? Local newspapers are a great source of data about communities, but once you start clipping all the interesting stories, you quickly wind up with hundreds of pieces. And the same goes for photos. They are full of information, but—especially with digital photos—it's easy to accumulate a huge number of them.

Database management is the way to handle these kinds of data. Number your clippings or photos, starting with 00001, and set up a database using any of the popular programs, like Microsoft Access® or FileMaker Pro®. The records of the database will be the numbered items, from 1 to *n*. The fields of the database will include things like the name of the informant associated with each item, the place where you collected it, the date, and the topics associated with it, and so on. Some items may get one or two topical codes; others may need 10, so build at least 10 code spaces into the database.

When you ask the database "Which clippings are about sexual harassment?" or "Which photos are about old men?" or "Which photos are about servants making purchases for others?" you'll get back answers like: "The information you want is on records 113, 334, 376, 819, 820, and 1,168."

Once you get accustomed to setting up databases, you'll wonder how you ever got along without them.

Key Concepts in This Chapter

jottings
scratch notes
the CNN effect
the diary
the log
methodological notes

descriptive notes
analytic notes
encryption device
indexing device
measurement
   device

Outline of Cultural
   Materials (OCM)
in vivo codes
code and retrieve
DBM: database
   management

Summary

- The difference between field *work* and field *experience* is field *notes*.
  - There are four types of field notes: jottings, the diary, the log, and formal notes.
  - Diaries are essential. Your diary will give you an outlet for writing things that you don't want to become part of a public record. The log is the key to collecting both qualitative and quantitative data on a systematic basis.
  - The log lets you record what you did each day, where you went, who you saw, and what you spent on each activity.
- Interviews can be transcribed, but it takes around six hours to fully transcribe each hour of interview. This can be cut in half using voice recognition software.
- Write three kinds of formal notes: methodological notes, descriptive notes, and analytic notes.
  - Put what you learn about actually doing field research in the methodological notes.
  - Write lots of descriptive notes about what you see and hear.
  - Write occasional analytic notes as you come to understand how something works.

- Don't be inconspicuous about writing jottings unless you have to. Better to assume the role of researcher from the start so that people expect to see you taking notes.
- Don't worry if people don't show up for interviews or you can't get everything done you wanted to get done right away. Field research takes lots of patience.
- Write brief (25-word) profiles of people you meet. Transfer those profiles to your computer with your field notes at night.
- Code your field notes as you go. Most ethnographers prefer *in vivo* codes, but any coding scheme will do, as long as you're consistent.
  - Coding will be the first step in analysis of your data. Most codes are tags, or indexing devices. They let you retrieve notes on single themes or on themes that co-occur.
- Use database management software to organize physical materials like newspaper clippings, photos, and artifacts.

Exercises

1. The best way to learn about field notes is to write them and code them. This exercise requires at least three people. Take one or more colleagues to a religious service with which you are all unfamiliar, plus another colleague who knows the service intimately. Take notes about the service individually, without consulting one another. Then later, code your notes separately. Finally, come together to discuss the notes and the codes. Have the person familiar with the service go over your notes and tell what he or she thinks you got wrong, what you got right, and what you missed entirely. Come up with a coding scheme—a set of themes and mnemonics for those themes. Wait at least a week and repeat the exercise at the same place. Your notes and the codes you apply to those notes should start to converge.

   Do this exercise with a function, like a parade, or an outdoor event, like a party.

Further Reading

Field notes and field diaries. Atkinson (1992), Creese et al. (2008), Montgomery and Bailey (2007), Radaelli (2009), Rapport (1990), Roldán (2002), Sanjek (1990), Wolfinger (2002).

14

Direct and Indirect Observation

INTRODUCTION

Interviewing is a great way to learn about attitudes and values. And it's a great way to find out what people think they do. When you want to know what people *actually do*, however, there is no substitute for watching them or studying the physical traces their behavior leaves behind. This chapter is about direct observation (watching people and recording their behavior on the spot) and indirect observation (the archeology of human behavior).

There are two big strategies for direct observation of behavior. You can be blatant about it and reactive, or you can be unobtrusive and nonreactive. In reactive observation, people know that you are watching them and may play to their audience—you. You can wind up with data about what people want you to see and learn little about what people do when you're not around. In unobtrusive observation, you study people's behavior *without their knowing it*. This stops people from playing to an audience, but it raises tough ethical questions.

We begin with the two most important methods for direct observation, continuous monitoring and spot sampling of behavior. Then we take up unobtrusive observation (and the ethical issues associated it), and, finally, indirect observation.

CM—CONTINUOUS MONITORING

In continuous monitoring, or CM, or focal follows, you watch a person or group of people and record the behavior as faithfully as possible. CM is widely used in assessing the quality of human interactions—between, for example, adolescent girls and their mothers (Baril et al. 2009), workers and employers (Sproull 1981), the police and civilians (Sykes and Brent 1983), clinical professors and young physicians (Graffam et al. 2008). CM is a mainstay in behavioral psychology for assessing anxieties and phobias (Harb et al. 2003), and it has been used to study how people eat (Stunkard and Kaplan 1977; Zive et al. 1998) and how people use architectural space (Bechtel 1977). CM is one of the all-around varsity methods.

Assessing Work

The technique of CM was first applied in the field of management by Charles Babbage, the nineteenth-century mathematician who invented the computer. Babbage studied the behavior of workers in a factory and determined that a pound of number 11 straight pins (5,546 of them) should take exactly 7.6892 hours to make (Niebel 1982:4; original: Babbage 1835:184). The method was developed further by two industrial engineers.

In 1911, Frank B. Gilbreth published a landmark study on bricklayers, looking at things like where masons set up their pile of bricks and how far they had to reach to retrieve each brick. From these studies, he was able to make recommendations on how to raise productivity through conservation of motion while lowering worker fatigue and increasing morale.

Before Gilbreth, the standard in the trade was 120 bricks per hour. After Gilbreth published, the standard reached 350 bricks per hour (Niebel 1982:24). Not all bricklayers were thrilled with these new standards, but studies like those of Gilbreth were the beginning of what is today called scientific management, time and motion research, and human factors engineering.

This field was earlier called "Taylorism," named for studies by Frederick W. Taylor (1911). Taylorism now connotes a kind of ruthless extraction of productivity by regulating every second of a worker's time (see Jurgens et al. 1993; Waring 1991), but the methods of CM are still used today in assessing work. Devine et al. (2010), for example, show that e-prescribing (where physicians enter prescriptions electronically) takes, on average, 69 seconds compared to 45 seconds to write prescriptions by hand, but, as Devine et al. say, "improvements in safety and quality may be worth the investment of time" (p. 152) (**Further Reading:** time and motion studies and direct observation of work).

CM and Children

Continuous monitoring is particularly useful in studying children—in classrooms and playgrounds, in clinical settings and in homes. Self-administered questionnaire surveys are practically useless with children: The young ones can't read them or fill them out, and the older ones won't put up with them. Personal interviews are useful but don't tell you what children actually do with their time.

You can do *participant* observation with children (see Fine and Sandstrom [1988] for tips on how to do this), but the attractive thing about studying children by CM is that, unlike adults, children seem not to be bothered by the presence of researchers. Children don't usually change their behavior when they're being studied, and when they do, they're pretty obvious about it. Most researchers report that, after a time, children go about their business and ignore researchers, note pads, stopwatches, video cameras, and other gadgets (**Further Reading:** direct observation of children in the field).

One Boy's Day

On April 26, 1949, eight observers took 30-minute turns following Raymond Birch, a seven year old, as he went through his day—from the time he got up at 7:00 a.m. until he

was asleep again at 8:33 p.m. Raymond lived in a small town—population 725—in the Midwest. Roger Barker and Herbert Wright (1951) called this a "field study in psychological ecology." As part of a larger community study of children, the eight fieldworkers spent six months observing grades 1 and 2 in the local public school before following Raymond.

By then, the observers were well known around town. In fact, four of them were *from* the town. At approximately one-minute intervals, they recorded Raymond's vocalizations and body movements as well as their own on-the-spot impressions of Raymond's perceptions, motives, and feelings. As Barker and Wright recognized, "behavior without motives, feelings, and meanings is of little significance" (1951:8). Some of the behavior was interaction with the observer. No sense pretending the observer wasn't part of the picture. They got everything.

At the end of each 30-minute session, the fieldworkers used their notes and dictated to a tape recorder, getting down as much detail as they could remember. (Remember, this was 1949. Tape recorders weighed around 30 pounds then and were anything but portable.) Another member of the team listened to the narrative and made notes on ambiguities in the record. The listener queried the observer about any points in question.

Both the queries and the answers were recorded and the final narrative—the book *One Boy's Day*—reflects everything the team could come up with. They're never going to make a movie of this book, but it's a phenomenal piece of naturalistic research. Figure 14.1 shows an excerpt from Barker and Wright's study—an excerpt that covers just five minutes of Raymond Birch's day.

The Zapotec Children Study

Douglas Fry used CM to study aggressive play among Zapotec children. From 1981 to 1983, Fry did 18 months of participant

Figure 14.1 Five Minutes of Observation

After school

3:15. Raymond climbed on his bicycle.

Very slowly he started to ride away from the school with Roy holding onto the carrier over the back wheel.

Roy called out to Jimmy Olson, who was going by, "Look at Jimmy's old, big, long raincoat."

Raymond asked, A What you got your raincoat on for, Jimmy?"

Jimmy immediately took the raincoat off and said, "There," rather self-satisfied and as if to please Raymond.

Roy slowed down a little and Raymond sped up, leaving Roy behind with Jimmy and some of the others.

3:16. Raymond continued on his way alone. He rode slowly and carefully down to the corner of the square.

He saw Mr. Howard coming.

He got off his bike.

He stepped off the curb and started pushing his bike across the street.

About in the middle of the street he met Mr. Howard and said, "Hello, Mr. Howard," in a pleasant way.

Mr. Howard responded warmly, "Well, hi, sir. How are you getting along?"

He passed Raymond and went on his way.

3:17. Raymond remounted his bike.

He rode on across the intersection to the sidewalk in front of the courthouse.

He kicked the front wheel of the bike up over the curb. He bit his lower lip as he made the effort.

He walked the bicycle to the bottom of the front steps leading up to the courthouse lawn.

Raymond practically carried the bicycle up the steps (See Plate 21.) The bicycle was heavy and it took many grunts, groans, and puffs to get it up the flight of six or eight steps. Raymond did this efficiently and quickly.

He immediately mounted the bike, almost before he had gotten past the top step.

3:19. He rode back and forth near the top of the steps on the walk.

Without dismounting, he paused momentarily.

Looking very intent, he rode around the trees, between benches, crisscrossing the sidewalk.

It looked as if he were putting on a performance for me.

He scrutinized the pedals as he rode by me.

Raymond began to ride somewhat faster as he zigzagged along the sidewalk.

Then he rode up the sidewalk to the main courthouse entrance, using only one hand to steer.

With a sidelong glance, he looked at me shyly but proudly. The restrained smile that came and went fleetingly seemed to indicate that he was quite proud of his one-hand riding but did not want to show it.

He barely missed some trees and benches as he made a very sharp turn.

Source: R. Barker and H. F. Wright, *One Boy's Day. A Specimen Record of Behavior,* Copyright © 1951, Harper & Brothers.

observation fieldwork in La Paz and San Andrés, two small Zapotec-speaking villages just four miles apart in the Valley of Oaxaca, Mexico. During the last five months of his research, Fry did direct CM of 24 children (three–eight years old) in each village. Before that, he visited almost all the households in the villages several times so that children had become accustomed to him when he began his intensive observation.

Fry describes his data collection procedures clearly:

The formal focal sampling observations were conducted between May and September of 1983. They represent each day of the week and encompass the daylight hour. Most observations (84%) were conducted within family compounds, although children were also observed in the streets, town squares, school yards, fields, and hills. I alternated sampling between the two communities on a weekly to biweekly basis. A total of 588 observations were conducted, resulting in an average of approximately 12 observations for each focal child (M = 12.25, sd = 6.21). On average, each focal child was observed for just over 3 hours (M = 3.13 hours, sd = 1.39 hours), resulting in a total of 150 hours of observation time for the entire sample.

Focal observations were narrated into a tape recorder carried in a small backpack or recorded on paper using a shorthand system. I recorded a running commentary of the behaviors engaged in by the focal child, using behavior elements defined in the previously developed ethogram. I moved with a focal child in order to maintain continuous visual contact (Altmann 1974), but did not remain so close as to interfere with actions or unduly attract the child's attention. Whenever a focal child engaged in any type of antagonistic behavior, the specifics of the interaction were noted, including identity of the interactant(s) and any facial expressions or gestures. For instance, interactions such as the following were recorded: Focal boy punches, pushes sister of 3 year old while laughing (sister does nothing in response). [Fry 1990:326–27]

Like Barker and Wright's study of a single focal child, Fry's study is in the tradition of ethology, or behavioral biology. Most ethologists study nonhuman animals (everything from moths to fish to chimpanzees), but there is increasing interest across the social sciences in the study of natural human behavior and in the methods of ethology. In tests on treadmills, for example, men walk faster than women; but in malls, women walk faster than men (Hangland and Cimbalo 1997). Measuring behavioral differences like these tells us nothing about why those differences exist, but they do suggest hypotheses for testing in the natural world.

It is standard practice in ethology to develop an ethogram, or list of behaviors, for a species being studied. Fry developed his ethogram of Zapotec children by watching them in public places before beginning his study of focal individuals. Based on 150 hours of focal child observation, Fry's data contain 764 episodes of what he calls "play aggression" and 85 episodes of "serious aggression."

Play aggression is a punch, kick, tackle, etc., accompanied by smiles, laughs, and playfaces. Serious aggression is episodes accompanied by low frowns, bared teeth, fixated gazes and crying. Fry found that when girls initiated serious aggression, it was almost always with other girls (93% of cases). But when boys initiated serious aggression, it was just as likely to be with girls as with other boys (**Further Reading:** ethology and human ethology).

Observing Grownups in the Field

I don't want to give the impression that direct observation is only for watching kids. A lot of really interesting research is done across the social sciences by following adults around and watching what they do. Kneidinger et al. (2001) studied touching behavior in 119 mostly White, male baseball players and 52 mostly White, female softball players in six major universities in the southeastern United States. Kneidigner et al. developed an ethogram of 37 touching behaviors before they even launched their main study. The touching behaviors included things like tapping gloves, high fives, butt slaps, and chest grabs ("one participant grabs the front of the other participant's shirt").

The main study involved watching and recording 1,961 touching behaviors across

99 innings of baseball for the men and 1,593 touching behaviors across 63 innings of softball for the women. Among the interesting results: Men and women touched each other the same amount after winning games, but women touched each other more than men touched each other after losing games (Kneidinger et al. 2001:52).

Pearson (1990) studied the energy expenditure of 145 Samoan men and women in Western Samoa, American Samoa, and Honolulu. He wanted to know if urbanization changed the Samoans' lifestyle as measured by their energy intake and expenditure. He interviewed his informants and asked them to recall their activities over the past 24 hours, noting each activity and probing during the interview to help people remember them.

To check the 24-hour recall data, he did continuous monitoring of 47 men, while a female assistant monitored 43 women. They accumulated a total of 825 hours of observation, with their subjects in direct view 92% of the time. The estimates of active energy expenditure from direct observation data of men were 33%–80% lower than the estimates from the recall data. The estimates for women were 27%–53% lower. Women did better than men in recalling their activities, but both men and women were way off the mark, particularly in recalling their light-to-moderate work of the previous day. Pearson's work makes it clear that recall is not a good substitute for observation (**Further Reading**: direct observation of adults in the field).

Studying Shoppers

Martin Murtaugh (1985) used CM to study the use of arithmetic by grocery shoppers. He recruited 24 adults in Orange County, California. Accompanied by two observers, each informant wore a small tape recorder while shopping at a supermarket. As the informants went about their shopping, they talked into the tape recorder about how they were deciding which product to buy, what size to choose, and so on.

One observer mapped the shopper's route through the store and recorded the prices and amounts of everything purchased. The other researcher kept up a running interview with the shopper, probing for details. Murtaugh was aware of the potential for reactivity in his study. But he was interested in understanding the way people thought through ordinary, everyday arithmetic problems, and his experiment was a good way to generate those problems under natural conditions.

In a similar experiment, Titus and Everett (1996) gave 63 people a list of 21 actual items to buy in a grocery store. The shoppers wore small tape recorders and talked about their experiences and their decisions as they went through the store, finding the items on the list. Here are a few actual snippets of the shoppers' monologues as they went through the store, putting the 21 items into their grocery carts:

> Shopper #42. Picnic supplies, plastic wrap, dog food. I don't think we need anything here. I see bread, candy. Doesn't look like I need that. Bleaches, liquid detergents. I need some dishwashing detergent.

> Shopper #31. Boullion cubes. . . . Let's try with soup. It's a soup base.

> Shopper #02. The powdered milk. I'm going to go right up here to baking needs. It may be there. But it's not. [Titus and Everett 1996:272, 274, 276]

Titus and Everett transcribed and analyzed the recorded monologues of the shoppers. This is a case of continuous monitoring of behavior by the subjects themselves, and it yielded some very interesting findings. As they went through the store, consumers made a lot of errors— they would go down this aisle or that, thinking they'd find a particular product and soon realize that they were on the wrong track. A lot of these errors were the result of consumers simply not sharing the culture of the store managers regarding what goes with what (**Further Reading:** observing shoppers).

RECORDING AND CODING BEHAVIORAL DATA

Many CM researchers record their observations orally. It's less tedious than writing; it lets you focus your eyes on what's going on; it lets you record details later that might be left out of a on-the-spot written description; it avoids the limitations of a check list; and it lets you get information about context as well as about the behavior you're studying. Moreover, you can easily transcribe your recorded observations, once you've got your voice recognition software trained (see above, Chapter 8, and Appendix E). Here's what a transcription looks like:

Alex has turned left down the aisle for paper products. The next item on his list is dinner napkins. He stops and looks down the aisle. Around midway down the aisle there are four people stopped, all looking at products on the shelves. They are blocking the aisle. Alex stares at this for a few seconds, like he's trying to assess the situation. He does a 180 and heads back this way, skipping the napkins and going on to the pork roast.

But there are trade-offs. If you want measurements from this kind of data, you have to code them. You have to listen to the recordings over and over again and decide what behaviors to code for each of the people you observe. Coding on the spot (by using a behavioral checklist or by inputting codes into a handheld computer) produces immediate quantitative data. It's very difficult to code *and* talk into a recorder at the same time, so you need to decide what kind of data you need and why you need them before you choose a method.

If you are trying to understand a behavioral *process*, then focus on qualitative data. If you need measurements of *how much* or *how often* people engage in this or that behavior, then focus on quantitative data. And as always, who says you can't do both?

Coding Schemes

Just as with surveys and attitude scales (Chapters 9 and 11), there's no point in reinventing the wheel. Over the years, researchers have developed coding schemes for using direct observation in many different situations—in studies of interactions between married couples, in studies of teacher effectiveness, in worker-management negotiations, and so on. If others have developed and tested a good system for coding behaviors of interest to you, use it. Don't feel that it's somehow more prestigious or morally better for you to make up everything from scratch. Knowledge grows when researchers can compare their data to the data others have collected using the same or similar instruments.

Figure 14.2 shows the basic coding scheme for **Interaction Process Analysis (IPA)**, a system developed over 60 years ago by Robert F. Bales in his research on communications in small groups (Bales 1950).

Despite its age, the Bales coding scheme continues to be used in the study of classrooms (Koivusaari 2002) and work teams (Nam et al. 2009)—in fact, in any situation where people interact with one another, like doctor's offices. Stewart (1984), for example, audiotaped 140 doctor-patient interactions in the offices of 24 family physicians and assessed the interactions with Bales's Interaction Process Analysis. Ten days later, Stewart interviewed the patients at their homes to assess satisfaction and compliance. That is, were the patients satisfied with the care they'd gotten and were they taking the pills they'd been told to take? Sure enough, when physicians are coded as engaging in many patient-centered behaviors, patients report higher compliance and satisfaction.

| Figure 14.2 | Categories for Direct Observation |

Problem Areas			Observation Categories
Positive Reactions	A	1	Shows solidarity, raises other's status, gives help, rewards
		2	Shows tension release, jokes, laughs, shows satisfaction
		3	Agrees, shows passive acceptance, understands, concurs, complies
Attempted Answers	B	4	Gives suggestions, direction, implying autonomy for other
		5	Gives opinion, evaluation, analysis, expresses feelings, wishes
		6	Gives orientation, information, repeats, clarifies, confirms
Questions	C	7	Asks for orientation, information, repetition, confirmation
		8	Asks for opinion, evaluation, analysis, expression of feeling
		9	Asks for suggestions, direction, possible ways of action
Negative Reactions	D	10	Disagrees, shows passive rejection, formality, withholds help
		11	Shows tension, asks for help, withdraws out of field
		12	Shows antagonism, deflates other's status, defends or asserts self

Source: Adapted from R. F. Bales, "Some Uniformities of Behavior in Small Social Systems." In *Readings in Social Psychology*, rev. ed., E. L. Hartley et al., eds. pp. 146–159. (1952 Holt, Rinehart & Winston).

One of the best things about the IPA system is that the 12 behaviors shown in Figure 14.2 are recognizable in practically any culture. Any act of communication can be identified as being one of those 12 categories. A detailed outline for coding interpersonal relations was developed by Bales and Cohen (1979) in their book, aptly titled *SYMLOG*, which stands for "systematic multiple level observation of groups" (**Further Reading:** IPA and Bales's coding scheme).

CM is used widely in educational research to track student-teacher interactions and to assess teacher effectiveness. Amidon and Flanders (Amidon and Hough [1967]; Flanders [1967]) developed a coding scheme for this kind of work that has been used and adapted ever since (Devet 1990; Hagekull and Hammarber 2004). Figure 14.3 shows the original Amidon/Flanders scheme.

Make no mistake about this: CM is tough to do. It can take several months of training for observers to become adept at using complex coding schemes. It used to be that observers had to code behaviors with pen and paper and

this, I think, is what made direct observation relatively rare in social research outside of labs. These days, behavioral coding is being done with hand-held computers and software that lets you program any key to mean "initiates conversation," "reciprocates affect," or whatever. (See Gravlee et al. [2006], Ice [2004], and Koster [2006] for details about using this technology, and see Appendix E.) As it becomes easier for fieldworkers to observe and code behavior at the same time, I think we'll see renewed interest in continuous monitoring and in the use of complex coding schemes.

COMPARATIVE RESEARCH—THE SIX CULTURE STUDY

Broad, general coding schemes are particularly useful for comparative research. Whether you're comparing sessions of psychotherapy groups, interaction sessions in laboratory

Figure 14.3 The Armidon/Flanders Scheme for Coding Categories of Interaction in the Classroom

Teacher Talk	**Indirect Influence**	1. *Accepts feeling:* accepts and clarifies the feeling tone of the students in a nonthreatening manner. Feelings may be positive or negative. Predicting and recalling feelings are included. 2. *Praises or encourages:* praises or encourages student action or behavior. Jokes that release tension, not at the expense of another individual, nodding head or saying "uh huh?" or "go on" are included. 3. *Accepts or uses ideas of student:* clarifying, building, or developing ideas or suggestions by a student. As teacher brings more of his or her own ideas into play, shift to category five. 4. *Asks questions:* asking a question about content or procedure with the intent that a student answer.
	Direct Influence	5. *Lectures:* giving facts or opinions about content or procedure; expressing his or her own ideas; asking rhetorical questions. 6. *Gives directions:* directions, commands, or orders with which a student is expected to comply. 7. *Criticizes or justifies authority:* statements, intended to change student behavior from nonacceptable to acceptable pattern; bawling someone out; stating why the teacher is doing what he or she is doing, extreme self-reference.
Student Talk		8. *Student talk-response:* talk by students in response to teacher. Teacher initiates the contact or solicits student statement. 9. *Student talk-initiation:* talk by students, which they initiate. If "calling on" student is only to indicate who may talk next, observer must decide whether student wanted to talk. If he or she did, use this category.
		10. *Silence or confusion:* pauses, short periods of silence, and periods of confusion in which communication cannot be understood by the observer.

Source: E. J. Amidon and J. B. Hough, *Interaction Analysis: Theory. Research. and Application*, 1967, Addison-Wesley.

experiments, or the natural behavior of people in field studies, using a common coding scheme really pays off because you can make direct comparisons across cases and look for generalization.

A classic comparative study of children was run by Beatrice and John Whiting between 1954 and 1956. In the Six Culture Project, field researchers spent from six to 14 months in Okinawa, Kenya, Mexico, the Philippines, New England, and India. They made a total of some 3,000 five-minute (CM) observations on 67 girls and 67 boys between the ages of three and 11.

Observations were limited to just five minutes because they were so intense, produced so much data, and required so much concentration and effort that researchers would have become fatigued and lost a lot of data in longer sessions. The investigators wrote out, in clear sentences, everything they saw children doing during the observation periods and also recorded data about the physical environment and others with whom children were interacting.

The data were sent from the field to Harvard University for coding according to a scheme of 12 behavior categories that had been worked out in research going back some 15 years before the Six Culture Study began. The behavioral categories included: seeks help, seeks attention, seeks dominance, suggests, offers support, offers help, acts socially, touches, reprimands, assaults sociably, assaults not sociably, symbolic aggression (frightens, insults, threatens with gesture, challenges to compete). (Full details on the use of the Whiting scheme are published in Whiting et al. [1966]. See Whiting and Whiting [1973] for a discussion of their methods for observing and recording behavior.)

On average, every 10th observation was coded by two people, and these pairs of "coding partners" were rotated so that coders could not slip into a comfortable pattern with one another. Coders achieved 87% agreement on childrens' actions; that is, given a list of 12 kinds of things a child might be doing, coders agreed 87% of the time. They also agreed 75% of the time on the act that precipitated a child's actions, and 80% of the time on the effects of a child's actions (Whiting and Whiting 1975:55).

The database from the Six Culture Study consists of approximately 20,000 recorded acts, for 134 children, or about 150 acts per child, on average.

Very strong conclusions can be drawn from this kind of robust database. For example, Whiting and Whiting (1975:179) note that nurturance, responsibility, success, authority, and casual intimacy "are types of behavior that are differentially preferred by different cultures." They conclude that "these values are apparently transmitted to the child before the age of six." They found no difference in amount of nurturant behavior among boys and girls three–five years of age. After that,

however, nurturant behavior by girls increases rapidly with age, while boys' scores on this trait remain stable.

By contrast, reprimanding behavior starts out low for both boys and girls and increases with age equally for both sexes, across six cultures. The older the children get, the more likely they are to reprimand anyone who deviates from newly learned cultural rules. "Throughout the world," the Whitings concluded, "two of the dominant personality traits of children between seven and eleven are self-righteousness and bossiness" (1975:184). Anyone who grew up with an older sibling already knows that, but the Whitings' demonstration of this cross-cultural fact is a major scientific achievement (**Further Reading:** other interaction coding systems).

USING VIDEO FOR CONTINUOUS MONITORING

Even with a fixed coding scheme, an observer in a CM situation has to decide among alternatives when noting behavior—whether someone is acting aggressively or just engaging in rough play, for example. Recording behavior on film or video lets several analysts study the behavior stream and decide at leisure how to code it. It also makes your data available for coding by others, now and in the future. (Human ethologists, like Irenäus Eibl-Eiblsfeldt [1989], have amassed hundreds of miles of film and videotape of ordinary people doing ordinary things across the world.)

In the 1970s, Marvin Harris and his students installed videotape cameras in the public rooms of several households in New York City. Families gave their permission and were guaranteed legal control over the cameras during the study and of the videotapes after the cameras were removed. Teams of observers monitored the equipment from remote locations. Later, the continuous verbal and nonverbal data were coded to study regularities in interpersonal relations in families.

Anna Lou Dehavenon (1978), for example, studied two Black and two White families for three weeks and coded their nonverbal behavior for such things as compliance with requests and the distribution and consumption of foods in the households. Dehavenon's data showed that the amount of authoritarianism in the four families correlated perfectly with income differences. The lower the family income, the more superordinate behavior in the home (1978:3).

One would hypothesize, from participant observation alone, that this was the case. But *testing* this kind of hypothesis requires the sort of quantified data that straightforward, direct observation provides. (See Sharff [1979] and Reiss [1985] for two more studies of households using the Harris videotapes.)

By the 1980s, social scientists were using video in studies of consumer behavior. Observers at Planmetrics, a marketing research firm, videotaped 70 volunteer parents for over 200 hours as the volunteers diapered their babies. The research was done on contract with Kimberly-Clark, manufacturer of "Huggies," a brand of disposable diapers. The cameras were not hidden, and after a while people just went about their business as usual, according to Steven Barnett, the anthropologist who led the study.

Close observation showed that many parents could not tell whether their babies needed a diaper change, so the researchers recommended that the diapers contain an exterior chemical strip that changed color when the baby was wet. The observers also noticed that parents were powdering their babies' legs and that parents were treating the red marks left by the diaper gathers as if the marks were diaper rash. The firm recommended that the gathers be redesigned so that there would be no more red marks (Kilman 1985; Lewin 1986). Today, video is used routinely in research on product design and use (Wasson 2000) (Box 14.1).

Box 14.1 Video is easier than ever

As video cameras have gotten smaller, easier to use, and less expensive, more field researchers have been using this technology for close examination of behavior streams. Brigitte Jordan, for example, used videotape in her study of birthing events across cultures (Jordan 1992a; see also Jordan and Henderson 1993) and Kremer-Sadlik and Paugh (2007) documented the emergence of what their middle-class informants in Los Angeles called "quality time" in everyday family life. You can code digital video today as easily as you can code written text. Look for lots more use of systematically recorded and coded video in social research.

CM and Reactivity

There are two ways to lower reactivity in continuous monitoring. One of them is participant observation. Once you've built up rapport and trust in a field situation, people are less likely to change their behavior when you're around. Even if they do change their behavior, you're more likely to notice

the change and take that into account (S. A. Harvey et al. 2009).

The second way to lower reactivity is training. We can't eliminate observer bias entirely, but lots of evidence shows that training helps make people better—more reliable and more accurate—observers (Hartmann and Wood 1990; Kent et al. 1977). We do the best we can. Just because a "perfectly aseptic environment is impossible," Clifford Geertz (1973:30) reminds us (paraphrasing the economist Robert Solow 1970:101), doesn't mean we "might as well conduct surgery in a sewer."

Joel Gittelsohn and his coworkers (1997) tested the effects of participant observation and training on reactivity in their study of child-care practices in rural Nepal. Over the course of a year, 10 trained fieldworkers observed behavior in 160 households. Each home was visited seven times. Except for a three–four-hour break in the middle of the day, the fieldworkers observed a focal child, two–five years of age, and all the caregivers of that child, from 6:00 a.m. until 8:00 p.m. This study, then, involved both children and adults.

The observers coded for over 40 activities, including health-related behaviors, feeding activities, and various kinds of social interactions (punishment, affection, and so on). The rate of some behaviors changed a lot over the course of the year. On average, across 1,101 observations, the number of times per day that a caregiver served food to a child without asking the child if he or she wanted it fell by half.

The observers also coded *each time they were interrupted* by one of the people whom they were observing (and what the interruption was about: e.g., light conversation, being asked for favors or medicine). This allowed Gittelsohn et al. to track reactivity across the seven household visits. Reactivity was noticeable during the first visit and then fell off dramatically. This study shows clearly that: (1) reactivity exists; and (2) it goes away quickly when indigenous observers stay on the job over time (Gittelsohn et al. 1997).

Still, reactivity bias is something to watch for in any study that involves intrusive, direct observation. Police often react to direct observation of their behavior by showing off the more exciting sides of their work (a small percentage react by trying to shelter observers from the sordid aspects of their work). In one

study, seven observers accompanied patrol officers and documented 7,443 encounters between the police and citizens over 729 shifts (Spano 2007:456).

Police were more proactive—taking fewer breaks, going out of their way to show the observer scenes of violence and death, and so on—in 21% of the shifts during the first quarter of the study. This dropped to 14% in the later three quarters of the study. There was also a strong gender component: For male observers, reactivity was documented in just 8% of interactions during the early stages of the fieldwork, compared to 36% for female observers. By the later stages of the study, male observers documented proactive reactivity in 11% of interactions, compared to 17% for female observers (**Further Reading:** reactivity in observational research).

SPOT SAMPLING (SCAN SAMPLING) AND TIME ALLOCATION STUDIES

Instantaneous spot sampling, or scan sampling, or time sampling, was developed in behavioral psychology, in the 1920s, and is widely used in ethology today. Influenced by John B. Watson's (then) revolutionary behaviorist approach to psychology, W. C. Olson (1929) sought to measure the behavior of nervous habits in normal children by taking repeated short samples under the most natural conditions possible. Leonard H. C. Tippett introduced spot sampling of the behavior stream in 1935 in his study of the fraction of time that textile workers actually spent working at their machines (and see Rosander et al. 1958).

In time allocation (TA) studies, which are based on time sampling, an observer appears at randomly selected places, and at randomly selected times, and records what people are doing when they are first seen (Gross 1984). The idea behind the TA method is simple and appealing: If you sample a sufficiently large number of representative acts, you can use the percentage of *times* people are seen doing things (working, playing, resting, eating) as a proxy for the percentage of *time* they spend in those activities.

Beck and Arnold (2009), for example, used this method in their study of 32 two-earner couples in Los Angeles who had school-age children. On average, when they are home, the couples spend 16.4% of their time in some kind of leisure activity—watching TV, sleeping in, reading. This turns out to be more than any other activity, including child care and household chores (Graesch 2009:85), yet the parents all felt pressed for time. As with so many modern, dual-earner families, these families felt obligated to enroll their children in many after-school activities. Taking kids to and from all these activities; communicating with activity leaders (coaches, tutors, etc.), networking with the parents of other kids in each program; attending events (games, recitals, etc.)—all made enormous demands on the parents' time and attention.

Reactivity in TA Research

In CM, getting around the reactivity problem involves staying with the program long enough to get people accustomed to your being around. Eventually, people just get plain tired of trying to manage your impression and they act naturally. In TA research, the trick is to catch a glimpse of people in their natural activities before they see you coming on the scene—before they have a chance to modify their behavior. Richard Scaglion, an anthropologist, studied the Abelam of New Guinea. "It is not easy," he says, "for an anthropologist in the field to come upon an Abelam unawares. Since I did not want to record 'greeting anthropologist' as a frequent activity when people were first observed, I often had to reconstruct what they were doing immediately before I arrived" (1986:540).

Borgerhoff-Mulder and Caro (1985) coded the observer's judgment of whether people saw

the observer first, or vice versa, and compared that to whether the Kipsigis (in Kenya) they were studying were observed to be active or idle. People were idle significantly more often when they spied the observer coming before the observer saw them.

Did people become idle when they saw an observer approaching? Or was it easier for idle folks to see an observer before the observer saw them? Borgerhoff-Mulder and Caro found that people who were idle were sitting or lying down much more often than were people who were active. People at rest may be more attentive to their surroundings than those who are working and would be judged more often to have seen the researcher approaching.

Sampling Problems in TA Research

There are five questions to ask when drawing a sample for a TA study:

1. Who do I watch?

2. Where do I go to watch them?

3. When do I go there?

4. How often do I go there?

5. How long do I spend watching people when I get there? [Gross 1984]

Regina Smith Oboler (1985) did a TA study among the Nandi of Kenya. She was interested in differences in the activities of adult men and women. The Nandi, Oboler said, "conceptualize the division of labor as sex segregated. Is this true in practice as well? Do men and women spend their time in substantially different or similar types of activities?" (p. 203).

Oboler selected 11 households, comprising 117 people, for her TA study. Her sample was not random. "Selecting a random sample," she said, "even for one *kokwet* (neighborhood) would have made observations impossibly difficult in terms of travel time" (Oboler

1985:204). Instead, Oboler chose a sample of households that were matched to social and demographic characteristics of the total population and within half an hour's walking distance from the compound where she lived.

Oboler divided the daylight hours of the week into 175 equal time periods and gave each period (about two hours) a unique three-digit number. Then, using a table of random numbers, she chose time periods to visit each household. She visited each household four times a week (on different days of the week) during two weeks each month and made nearly 1,500 observations on those households during her nine months in the field.

Oboler found that, for her sample of observations, adult men spend around 38% of their time "in activities that might reasonably be considered 'work' by most commonly used definitions of that term" (Oboler 1985:205). Women in her sample spent over 60% of their time working.

Table 14.1 shows the number of spot observations necessary to estimate the frequency of an activity to within a fractional accuracy. It also tells you how many observations you need if you want to see an activity at least once with 95% probability.

Here's how to read the table. Suppose people spend about 5% of their time eating. This is shown in the first column as a frequency, f, of 0.05. If you want to estimate the frequency of the activity to within 20%, look across to the column in the center part of the Table 14.1 under 0.20. If you have 1,825 observations, and your data say that people eat 5% of the time, then you can safely say that the true

Table 14.1 Number of Observations to Estimate the Frequency of an Activity to Within a Fractional Accuracy

True Frequency of Activity	Number of Observations Needed to See the Activity at a Particular Fraction of Accuracy							To See Activities at Least Once with 95% Probability
f	0.05	0.1	0.15	0.2	0.3	0.4	0.5	
0.01	152127	38032	16903	9508	4226	2377	1521	299
0.02	75295	18824	8366	4706	2092	1176	753	149
0.03	49685	12421	5521	3105	1380	776	497	99
0.04	36879	9220	4098	2305	1024	576	369	74
0.05	29196	7299	3244	1825	811	456	292	59
0.06	24074	6019	2675	1505	669	376	241	49
0.07	20415	5104	2268	1276	567	319	204	42
0.08	17671	4418	1963	1104	491	276	177	36
0.09	15537	3884	1726	971	432	243	155	32
0.10	13830	3457	1537	864	384	216	138	29
0.15	8708	2177	968	544	242	136	87	19
0.20	6147	1537	683	384	171	96	61	14
0.25	4610	1152	512	288	128	72	46	11
0.30	3585	896	398	224	100	56	36	9
0.40	2305	576	256	144	64	36	23	6
0.50	1537	384	171	96	43	24	15	5

Source: H. R. Bernard and P. D. Killworth, "Sampling in Time Allocation Research." *Ethnology* 32:211, 1993.

percentage of time spent eating is between 4% and 6%. (Twenty percent of 5% is 1%. Five percent, plus or minus 1%, is 4%–6%.) (For the formula used to derive the numbers in Table 14.1, see Bernard and Killworth 1993.)

Suppose you do a study of the daily activities of families in a community and your data show that men eat 4% of the time, while women eat 6% of the time. If you have 300 observations, then the error bounds of the two estimates overlap considerably (about 0.02–0.06 for the men and 0.04–0.08 for the women).

You need about 1,800 observations to tell whether 0.06 is really bigger than 0.04 comparing across groups. It's the same for other activities: If women are seen at leisure 20% of their time and caring for children 25% of their time, then 1,066 observations are required to tell if women really spend more time caring for children than they do at leisure.

Oboler had 1,500 observations. It is clear from Table 14.1 that her findings about men's and women's leisure and work time are not accidents. An activity seen in a sample of just 256 observations to occur 40% of the time can be estimated actually to occur between 40%, plus or minus 15% of 40%, or between 34% and 46%. Since men are seen working 38% of the time and about half of Oboler's 1,500 observations were of men, her finding is solid.

Night-Time Sampling

Virtually all spot sampling studies of behavior are done during the daylight hours, between 6 a.m. and 7 p.m.

We know that life doesn't stop when the sun goes down. Richard Scaglion (1986) showed the importance of night-time observations in TA studies. When he did his study of the Abelam in New Guinea, there were 350 people in the village, living in 100 households. He randomly selected two households each day and visited them at randomly selected times, throughout the day *and night*.

Scaglion didn't get much sleep during the month that he did this work, but his findings

were worth the sacrifice. He coded his 153 observations into 13 categories of activities: sleeping, gardening, idle, cooking and food preparation, ritual, visiting, eating, hunting, construction, personal hygiene, child care, cleansing and washing, and craftwork. Only 74% of Abelam activities during night-time hours were coded as "sleeping." Seven of the nine observations that he coded as "ritual" occurred after dark. Half of all observations coded as "hunting" occurred at night, and six out of eight observations coded as "visiting" were nocturnal.

Had he done his TA study only during the day, Scaglion would have overestimated the amount of time that Abelam people spend gardening by about a fourth. His data show that gardening takes up about 26% of the Abelam's daylight hours, but only 20% of their total waking time in each 24-hour period. If you did a TA study of undergraduates in the United States and you only observed them during daylight hours, you'd miss a lot.

Coding and Recording TA Data

Sampling is one of two problems in TA research. The other is measurement. How do we know that when Oboler recorded that someone was "working," we would have recorded the same thing? If you were with Oboler when she recorded that someone was engaged in "cooking behavior," would you have agreed with her assessment? Every time? You see the problem.

It gets even thornier. Suppose you work out a coding scheme that everyone agrees with. And suppose you train other observers to see just what you see. Or, if you are doing the research by yourself, suppose you are absolutely consistent in recording behaviors.

Even if all these reliability problems are taken care of, what about observation validity? What do you do, for example, when you see people engaged in multiple behaviors? A woman might be holding a baby and stirring a pot at the same time. Do you code her as engaged in child care or in cooking (Gross 1984:542)? If someone saw that you were lying down reading, and you were studying for an exam, should they record that you were working or relaxing?

Do you record all behaviors? Do you mark one behavior as primary? This last question has important implications for data analysis. There are only so many minutes in a day, and the percentage of people's time that they allocate to activities has to add up to just 100%. If you code multiple activities as equally important, then there will be more than 100% of the day accounted for. Most TA researchers use their intuition, based on participant observation, to decide which of the multiple simultaneous activities they witness to record as the primary one and which as secondary.

The best solution is to record *all* possible behaviors you observe in the order of their primacy, according to your best judgment at the time of observation. Use a check sheet, programmed into a hand-held computer, to record behaviors (see Appendix E). Digital media make backup easier, but be sure to store your data in several places (Box 14.2).

Box 14.2 Back up your data. Really.

Tapping observational codes directly into a hand-held computer lets you focus on the behavior; reduces data error (transferring data from paper to computer introduces an inevitable source or error); and lets you back up your data quickly. Be paranoid about data. Those horror stories you've heard about lost data? They're true. Read M. N. Srinivas's account [1979:xiii] of how he lost all three copies of his field notes, compiled over a period of 18 years, in a fire at Stanford.

EXPERIENCE SAMPLING

In experience sampling (ES), people respond at random times during a day or a week to questions about what they're doing, or who they're with, or what they're feeling at the moment. The method was originally developed for use with beepers (Csikszentmihaly et al. 1977). When the beeper went off, people would jot an entry into a paper diary or talk about their actions, feelings, and surroundings into a small recorder (Box 14.3).

Box 14.3 Experience sampling and modern technology

As with many other data collection methods, ES has been made easier with better technology. These days, researchers ask informants to respond to random cell-phone calls to fill out a form on a smartphone or PDA (Foo et al. 2009; Wenze et al. 2007). For some populations—people checking Facebook or taking web-based courses or playing games—informants can be asked to respond online to random requests.

ES offers two big advantages. First, it combines the power of random spot checks with the relative ease of having people report on their own behavior. Csikszentmihalyi and Larson (1987) demonstrated the reliability of ES in a number of studies. Validity is another matter, but when people record or talk about what they're doing and how they're feeling on the spot, this should lessen the inherent inaccuracy of recall data.

The second advantage is that, working on your own, you can only be in one place at a time, but with cell phones and the Internet, you can collect spot-observation data from lots of people at once.

Wong and Csikszentmihalyi (1991) used ES in their study of gender differences in affiliation motivation—that is, differences in how men and women establish and maintain relationships with others. They recruited 170 high-achiever students from two suburban high schools in Chicago. The students (68 boys and 102 girls) filled out a background questionnaire about demographic information and family relationships. They also filled out the *Personality Research Form* which, among other things, measures "affiliateveness"—how motivated people are to "win friendships and maintain association with others" (D. N. Jackson 1984:6).

Each student carried around a beeper for a week and received seven–nine random pages per day, between 7:00 a.m. and 10:p.m. on weekdays and between 9:00 a.m. and 12:00 noon on weekends. Whenever the beeper went off, students filled out an ES form that asked them: (1) If you had a choice, who would you be with? (2) Who are you with? (3) What are you thinking about? (4) What are the main things you're doing?

Three experienced coders tackled the open-ended questions (questions 3 and 4). They coded 20 forms each and discussed the differences in their codes. Then they coded 60 forms and had interrater agreement between 90% and 95%. After that, they just coded the forms and kept checking regularly with one another to make sure that they were able to keep up the high level of agreement.

This study yielded a lot of interesting results. Girls reported about twice as many thoughts about interpersonal relations as did boys. Regardless of how high students scored on the affiliation scale, the female students spent more time with friends and less time alone than did boys. Just as you'd expect, girls who scored higher on the affiliation scale (meaning they liked being with others) actually spent more time in social interactions (talking and hanging out with friends, going to parties, etc.) than did girls who scored low on that scale.

No surprise there. But differences in affiliation orientation had no effect on the amount of time that boys spent in social interactions. Boys were more likely than girls to be loners, no matter how much they liked being with others.

And even more interesting: Boys who scored high on the affiliation scale felt worse than boys who scored low, regardless of whether they were with friends or alone. According to Wong and Csikszentmihalyi, if boys like to develop interpersonal relationships, they are ambivalent about themselves. Highly affiliative girls think of themselves as influential, while influential boys are more likely to be aggressive than affiliative. These findings emerge from data about how people actually spend their time and about how people feel about themselves and others. The combination is tough to beat (**Further Reading:** experience sampling).

A FEW FINAL WORDS ON REACTIVE OBSERVATION

Where does all this leave us? Well, first of all, I don't want to give the impression that direct observation data are automatically accurate. Lots of things can clobber the accuracy of directly observed behavior. Observers may be biased by their own expectations of what they are looking for or by expectations about the behavior of women or men or any ethnic group (Kent et al. 1977; Spano 2007).

On balance, though, direct observation does provide more accurate results than do reports of behavior. McCann et al. (1997) studied 12 behaviors of Alzheimer's patients in a nursing home. The staff reported on the amount of each behavior for each of 177 patients, while trained observers actually counted a sample of the behaviors using time sampling.

You can guess the result: Reports by the staff were way off the mark. If you want to know, say, whether, wandering happens *more often* than, say, unconnected speech among Alzheimer's patients, then staff reports might be enough. But if you want to know *how often* those behaviors actually occur, then nothing short of direct observation will do.

If you are unfamiliar with the direct, reactive-observation approach to data gathering, you may feel awkward about walking around with a clipboard (and perhaps a stopwatch) and writing down what people are doing—or with beeping people and asking them to interrupt what they're doing to help you get some data.

This is a reasonable concern, and direct observation is not for everyone. It's not a detached method, like sending out questionnaires and waiting for data to be delivered to your doorstep or to your computer. It is not a fun method, either. Hanging out, participating in normal daily activities with people, and writing up field notes at night is more enjoyable than monitoring and recording what people are doing.

But many fieldworkers find that direct observation allows them to address issues that are not easily studied by any other method. Grace Marquis (1990) studied a shanty town in Lima, Peru. Children in households that kept chickens were at higher risk for getting diarrhea than were other children. The chickens left feces in the homes and the feces contained an organism that causes diarrhea. Continuous monitoring showed that children touched the chicken droppings and, inevitably, touched their mouths with their hands. It was hard, tedious work, but the payoff was serious.

Direct observation may also seem overly time consuming. Actually, random spot checking of behavior is a cost effective and productive way to use *some* of your time in any field project. When you're studying a group that has clear boundaries (an organization, like a hospital or a police precinct, or a public school), you can get very fine-grained data about people's behavior from a TA study, based on random spot checks. More important, as you can see from Table 14.1, with proper sampling you can generalize to large

populations (whole school districts, an entire aircraft manufacturing plant, even cities) from spot checks of behavior in ways that no other method allows.

You may be concerned that a strictly observational approach to gathering data about human behavior fails to capture the *meaning* of data for the actors. This, too, is a legitimate concern. A classic example is Geertz's (1973:6) observation that a wink can be the result of getting a speck of dust in your eye or a conscious act of conspiracy. And that's just a wink. People can engage in any of thousands of behaviors (skipping a class, wearing a tie, having their navel pierced . . .) for many, many different reasons. Knowing the meaning of behavior is essential to understanding it.

On the other hand, one of our most important goals in science is to constantly challenge our own ideas about what things mean. That's how theories develop, are knocked down, and gain in their power to explain things. Why shouldn't we also challenge the theories—the explanations—that the people we study give us for their own behavior?

Ask people who are coming out of a church, for example, why they just spent two hours there. Some common responses include "to worship God," "to be a better person," "to teach our children good values." Hardly anyone says "to dress up and look good in front of other people," "to meet potential golf partners for Sunday afternoon," "to maximize my ability to meet potential mates whose ethnic and social backgrounds are compatible with my own." Yet, we know that these last three reasons are what *some* people would say if they thought others wouldn't disapprove.

Finally, you may have some qualms about the ethics of obtrusive observation. It cannot be said too often that *every single data collection act* in the field has an ethical component, and a fieldworker is obliged every single time to think through the ethical implications of data collection acts. Personally, I have less difficulty with the potential ethical problems of obtrusive, reactive observation than I do with any other data collection method, including participant observation. In obtrusive observation, people actually *see* you (or a camera) taking down their behavior, and they can ask you to stop. Nothing is hidden.

In participant observation (the method you might think of as the least problematic from an ethical perspective), we try to put people at ease, make them forget we're really listening hard to what they're telling us, and get them to "open up." In ethnographic fieldwork, I'm acutely aware that people are taking me into their confidence and I'm always a bit nervous about the responsibility that puts on me not to abuse that confidence.

On the other hand, the method that presents the *most* ethical problems is unobtrusive, nonreactive–that is, disguised—direct observation.

DISGUISED FIELD OBSERVATION

Disguised field observation is the ultimate in participant observation—you join, or pretend to join, some group and secretly record data about people in the group.

In 1960, John H. Griffin, a White journalist went through some drug treatment to temporarily turn his skin black. He traveled the southern United States for about a month, taking notes on how he was treated. His book, *Black Like Me* (1961) was a real shocker. It galvanized a lot of support by Whites in the North for the then fledgling Civil Rights movement. Clearly, Griffin engaged in premeditated deception in gathering the data for his book. But Griffin was a journalist; scientists don't deceive their informants, right?

Pseudopatients Check Into a Psychiatric Hospital

Wrong. Everyone knows that you can get psychiatrists to disagree in court with one another

about the diagnosis and prognosis of a defendant. David Rosenhan was interested in this instability of psychological diagnoses and particularly in the possibility that mental hospitals might create an environment conducive to certain kinds of diagnoses. He recruited seven confederates who, like him, would check themselves into mental hospitals and observe how they were treated.

The eight pseudopatients (three woman and five men) called a total of 12 mental hospitals in the United States and asked for an appointment to be evaluated for admission. (After they were released from one hospital, some of the researchers checked into another; hence the 12 hospitals for eight patients.) During their admission interviews, the pseudopatients reported hearing voices. The voices said "empty," "hollow," and "thud."

That was it. No other symptoms. The putative patients gave false names and occupations (they couldn't very well mention their real occupations since three of them were psychologists and one was a psychiatrist), but otherwise acted normally and answered questions about themselves truthfully. In the end, these fieldworkers were all admitted to the various hospitals. One of the pseudopatients was diagnosed as manic-depressive, but all the rest were diagnosed as schizophrenics.

They were model patients. They accepted medications—which they secretly flushed down the toilet—and obeyed orders from the staff. This was tough work. The pseudopatients were not allowed to divulge what they were up to just because they were tired of (or exasperated with) the experiment. If they wanted out, they had to convince the hospital staff to release them. The idea was to act normally long enough to be diagnosed as ready for release. And eventually, they *were* released (it took them between one week and seven weeks of confinement to achieve this)—diagnosed as "schizophrenia in remission" or as "asymptomatic" or as "improved" (Rosenhan 1973, 1975). The common implication in all these release diagnoses is not that the patient has been cured, but that she or he is still a schizophrenic.

Rosenhan's study still makes wonderful reading. The "patients" took notes. Some staff members wrote this up as "note-taking behavior"—a clear sign of schizophrenia. A nurse at one hospital unbuttoned her blouse to adjust her bra—in front of a room full of male patients. The researcher who reported this incident said he felt that the nurse just didn't think of the men in that room as human beings. To her, those men were patients, with no humanity, sexual or otherwise.

A senior psychiatrist, with a group of young physicians, pointed to some patients who were waiting outside the cafeteria. It was half an hour before lunch. The senior psychiatrist explained that this was an example of the "oral-acquisitive" behavior one expects in patients with schizophrenia. It hadn't occurred to these psychiatrists, said Rosenhan, that there isn't much else to do in a mental institution beside eat (Rosenhan 1973:253).

While none of the doctors, nurses, and attendants at these hospitals had a clue about what was going on, some of the real patients saw through the charade. One actually accused the fieldworker of being an undercover journalist.

Critiques of Rosenhan's Study

Rosenhan's study met with fierce criticism. Spitzer (1976) pointed out that the diagnosis "in remission" is hardly ever used in the discharge of real schizophrenics. Of 300 schizophrenic patients discharged at the New York State Psychiatric Institute in 1974, Spitzer found that not one was released with a diagnosis of "in remission." He corroborated this by checking with 12 other hospitals in New York, California, and Georgia. Only a handful of patients were

ever released from those hospitals as schizophrenics in remission.

In Rosenhan's study, the staff were fooled into letting people into the hospitals . . . but, asked Spitzer, so what? Wouldn't people showing up at an emergency room complaining of intense stomache pains be diagnosed as suffering from gastritis? The duped psychiatrists, said Spitzer, had no way of knowing that the pseudopatients were lying. Eventually, those same duped psychiatrists diagnosed that rarest of events, "schizophrenia in remission" (Spitzer 1976:461). Rosenhan's data, said Spitzer, are a testimony to the diagnostic skills of the staff at the hospitals where Rosenhan and his fellow pseudopatients did their fieldwork.

Are These Pseudopatient Studies Ethical?

Was it ethical to dupe the hospital workers like that? Rosenhan's study made mental health workers—from psychiatrists to nurses, to social workers—conscious of the power of labeling. Once you get tagged officially as "crazy," the label tends to stick. People start treating you the way they think people in your condition ought to be treated. But the price of this knowledge was deceit. The use of deception in field experiments is still being discussed (Riach and Rich 2004).

Since Rosenhan's groundbreaking work, the simulated-client (or mystery-shopper) method has been used in dozens of studies to evaluate the performance of pharmacists (F. Smith 2009), family-planning clinics (Katz and Naré 2002; Sykes and O'Sullivan 2006), and other health care providers (Madden et al. 1997) and to uncover discrimination in markets.

Ayres (1991), for example, sent fake buyers to car dealerships in the Chicago area. Across more than 400 attempts to buy cars, Whites got lower final offers than African Americans; White men got lower final offers than White women; and African American men got lower final offers than African American women.

U.S. government agencies send fake clients to apply for jobs, to rent apartments, or to buy homes and to uncover discrimination (Sharpe 1998). The U.S. Supreme Court ruled that this practice is legal in the pursuit of fair housing (Ayres 1991:823), and the U.S. Equal Employment Opportunity Commission has used data from these field experiments to sue offending businesses.

People across the political spectrum have quite different ideas about whether this is just a dose of the same medicine that offenders dish out (which seems fair), or entrapment (which seems foul). Does this mean that ethics are simply a matter of political orientation and opinion? In the abstract, most people answer this question with a strong "no." When things get concrete—when the fortunes and reputations of real people are at stake—the answer becomes less clear (van den Borne 2007).

But if you think deceiving landlords or realtors or the staff of mental hospitals is something, read on (**Further Reading:** pseudopatients and simulated clients).

The Tearoom Trade Study

Without telling his subjects that he was doing research, Laud Humphreys (1975) observed hundreds of homosexual acts among men in St. Louis, Missouri. Humphreys's study produced important results. The men involved in this "tearoom trade" came from all walks of life, and many were married and living otherwise straight lives. Humphreys made it clear that he did not engage in homosexual acts himself, but played the role of the "watch queen," or lookout, warning his informants when someone approached the restroom. This deception and unobtrusive observation, however, did not cause the storm of criticism that accompanied the first publication of Humphreys's work in 1970.

That was caused by Humphreys having taken his research a step further. He jotted down the license plate numbers of the men who used the restroom for quick, impersonal sex, and got their names and addresses from motor vehicle records. He waited a year after doing his observational work, and then, on the pretext that they had been randomly selected for inclusion in a general health survey, he interviewed 100 of his research subjects in their homes.

Humphreys was careful to change his car, his hair style, and his dress. According to him, his informants did not recognize him as the man who had once played watch queen for them in public toilets. *This* is what made Humphreys's research the focus of another debate that is still going on about the ethics of disguised field observation.

Five years after the initial study was published, Humphreys himself said that he had made a mistake. He had endangered the social, emotional, and economic lives of his research subjects. Had his files been subpoenaed, he could not have claimed immunity. He decided at the time that he would go to jail rather than hurt his informants (Humphreys 1975).

Everyone associated with Humphreys agreed that he was totally committed to protecting his informants. He was very concerned with the ethics of his research, as any reader of his monograph can tell. Humphreys was an ordained Episcopal priest who had held a parish for more than a decade before going to graduate school. He was active in the Civil Rights movement in the early 1960s and spent time in jail for committing crimes of conscience. His credentials as an ethical person, conscious of his responsibilities to others, were in good order.

But listen to what Arlene Kaplan Daniels had to say about all this, in a letter to Myron Glazer, a sociologist and ethnographer:

> In my opinion, no one in the society deserves to be trusted with hot, incriminating data. Let me repeat, *no one.* . . . We should not have to rely on the individual strength of conscience which may be required. Psychiatrists, for example, are notorious gossipers [about their patients]. . . . O. K.,

so they mainly just tell one another. But they *sometimes* tell wives, people at parties, you and me. [Daniels had done participant observation research on psychiatrists.] And few of them would hold up under systematic pressure from government or whatever to get them to tell. . . . The issue is not that a few brave souls *do* resist. The issue is rather what to do about the few who will not. . . . There is *nothing* in our training—any more than in the training of psychiatrists, no matter what they say—to prepare us to take up these burdens. [Quoted in Glazer 1975:219–20; emphasis in the original.]

Researchers who conduct the kinds of studies that Humphreys did invoke several arguments to justify their use of deception.

1. It is impossible to study such things as homosexual encounters in public rest rooms in any other way.

2. Disguised field observation is a technique that is available only to researchers who are physically and linguistically indistinguishable from the people they are studying. In other words, to use this technique, you must be a member of the larger culture, and thus, there is no real ethical question involved, other than whether you, as an individual, feel comfortable doing this kind of research.

3. Public places, like restrooms, are, simply, public. The counterargument is that people have a right to expect that their behavior in public toilets will not be recorded, period. [Koocher 1977]

My own position is that the decision to use deception is up to you, provided that the *risks of detection are your own risks and no one else's.* When Jack Weatherford (1986) took a job as manager of a porn shop in Washington, DC, the people who came to the store to watch the movies or connect with prostitutes didn't know they were being studied by a participant observer, but neither were they in any danger that their identities would be divulged.

Similarly, when Wendy Chapkis became a licensed massage therapist and became a participant observer in her secret research on prostitution (1997), she assumed risks, but the risks were hers. If detection risks harm to others, don't even consider disguised participant observation.

Recognize, too, that it may not be possible to foresee the potential harm that you might do using disguised observation. This is what leads scholars like Kai Erikson (1967, 1996) to the conclusion that research that requires deception is never justified.

THE ETHICS OF DECEPTION

But is all deception equally deceitful? Aren't there grades of deception? In the 1960s, Edward Hall and others (Hall 1963, 1966; Watson and Graves 1966) showed how people in different cultures use different "body language" to communicate—that is, they stand at different angles to one another, or at different distances when engaging in serious versus casual conversation.

Hall called this different use of space proxemics. He noted that people learn this proxemic behavior as part of their early cultural learning, and he hypothesized that subcultural variations in spatial orientation often leads to breakdowns in communication, isolation of minorities, and so on.

This observation established a tradition of research—one that continues today—on how people use space. Early on, Aiello and Jones (1971) studied the proxemic behavior of middle-class White and lower-class Puerto Rican and Black school children. They trained a group of elementary school teachers to observe and code the distance and orientation of pairs of children to one another during recess periods.

Sure enough, there were clear cultural and gender differences. White children stand much farther apart in ordinary interaction than do either Black or Puerto Rican children. The point here is that the teachers were natural participants in the system. The researchers trained these natural participants to be observers to cut out any reactivity that outsiders might have caused in doing the observation.

Scherer (1974) studied pairs of children in a schoolyard in Toronto. He used only lower-class Black and lower-class White children in his study, to control for socioeconomic effects. Scherer adapted techniques from photogrammetry (making surveys by using photographs). He mounted a camera in a park adjacent to the schoolyard. Using a telephoto lens, he took unobtrusive shots of pairs of children who were at least 30 meters away.

Then Scherer measured the average distance between two children, and did his analysis on the quantitative data. Scherer found no significant differences in the distance between pairs of White or Black children (**Further Reading:** proxemics).

Unobtrusive observation is used in environmental studies to assess the walking speed of people in cities as opposed to rural areas (Levine and Bartlett 1984), indoors versus outdoors (Rotton et al. 1990), in cities of various sizes (Walmsley and Lewis 1989; Levine 1997), and so on. Rotton et al. (1990), for example, timed 80 men and 80 women who were walking in either a climate-controlled mall that contained 46 stores or in an open-air shopping center of 44 stores.

As in most studies of this type, they marked off 50-foot strips of pavement or floor space and stationed themselves where they could watch and time people who were traversing those strips. Contrary to popular wisdom, heat didn't slow down urban shoppers of either sex. And Sykes et al. (1993) sat unobtrusively in bars, counting the number of drinks people consumed. Confirming popular wisdom, people drink faster and spend less time in bars

when they are in groups of two or more than when they're alone.

I don't consider these field studies of shoppers, children, pedestrians, and drinkers in bars to be unethical. The people being studied were observed in the course of their ordinary activities, out in the open, in truly public places. Despite making unobtrusive observations or taking surreptitious pictures, the deception involved was passive—it didn't involve duping the subjects of the research, making them believe one thing to get them to do another. I don't think that any real invasion of privacy occurred.

The Micturition Study

You can't say that about the work of Middlemist et al. (1976). They wanted to measure the length of time it takes for men to begin urinating, how long men continue to urinate, and whether these things are affected by how close men stand to each other in public toilets. (*Why* they wanted to know these things is another story.)

At first, the investigators simply pretended to be grooming themselves at the sink in a public toilet at a university. They tracked the time between the sound of a fly being unzipped and urine hitting the water in the urinal as the time for onset; they also noted how long it took for the sound of urine to stop hitting the water in the urinal, and counted this as the duration of each event. They noted whether subjects were standing alone, next to someone, or one or two urinals away from someone.

In general, the closer a man stood to another man, the longer it took him to begin urinating and the shorter the duration of the event. This confirmed laboratory research showing that social stress inhibits relaxation of the urethral sphincter in men, thus inhibiting the flow of urine.

Middlemist et al. decided to control the independent variable—how far away another man was from each subject. They placed "BEING CLEANED" signs on some urinals, and forced unsuspecting men to use a particular urinal in a public toilet. Then a confederate stood next to the subject, or one urinal away, or did not appear at all. The observer hid in a toilet stall next to the urinals and made the measurements. The problem was, the observer couldn't hear flies unzipping and urine hitting the water from inside the stall—so the researchers used a periscopic prism, trained on the area of interest, to make the observations directly.

Personally, I doubt that many people would have objected to the study if Middlemist and his colleagues had just lurked in the rest room and done simple, unobtrusive observation. But when they contrived to make men urinate in a specific place, when they contrived to manipulate the dependent variable (urination time), and, above all, when they got that periscope into the act, that changed matters. This is a clear case of invasion of privacy by researchers, in my view.

In a critique of the research, Koocher (1977:120) said that "at the very least, the design seems laughable and trivial." Middlemist et al. (1977:123) defended themselves, saying that "we believe . . . that the pilot observation and the experiment together constitute an example of well-controlled field research, adequate to test the null hypothesis that closeness has no effect" on the duration of urination among men in public rest rooms.

Actually, Middlemist et al.'s study *design* was anything but trivial. In fact, it was quite elegant. And the results of their research have been cited many times in articles on the stress of crowding—like why many people prefer to stand in commuter trains rather than sit in middle seats between other passengers (Evans and Wener 2007)—and on paruresis, an anxiety disorder that inhibits urination in the presence of, or anticipated presence of, others (Boschen 2008). The question that is still debated today is whether knowing what they found out was worth using the method they chose?

Passive Deception

Passive deception involves no experimental manipulation of informants to get them to act in certain ways. Humphreys's first, strictly observational study (not the one where he used a pretext to interview people in their homes) involved passive deception. He made his observations in public places where he had every right to be in the first place. He took no names down, and no data could be traced to any particular individual. Humphreys observed felonies, and that makes the case more complex. But in my mind, at least, he had the right to observe others in public places, irrespective of whether those observed believed that they would or would not be observed.

Many social scientists, including sociologists, social psychologists, and anthropologists, use passive deception in their field research. I have spent hours pretending to be a shopper in a large department store and have observed mothers who are disciplining their children. I have played the role of a strolling tourist on Mexican beaches (an easy role to play, since that was exactly what I was), and recorded how American and Mexican families occupied beach space. I have surreptitiously clocked the time it takes for people who were walking along the streets of Athens (Greece), New York City, Gainesville (Florida), and Ixmiquilpan (Mexico) to cover 10 meters of sidewalk at various times of the day. I have stood in crowded outdoor bazaars in Mexico, watching and recording differences between Indians and non-Indians in the amount and kinds of produce purchased.

I have never felt the slightest qualm about having made these observations. In my opinion, passive deception is ethically aseptic. Ultimately, however, the responsibility for the choice of method, and for the practical, human consequences of using a particular method, rests with you, the individual researcher. Are you disturbed by the fact that Humphreys did his research at all, or only by the fact that he came close to compromising his informants? As you answer that question for yourself, you'll have a better idea of where *you* stand on the issue of disguised field observation (**Further Reading:** deception in field studies).

BEHAVIOR TRACE STUDIES: THE ARCHEOLOGY OF BEHAVIOR

Think of behavior trace studies as behavioral archeology. Do people in different cultures really have a different sense of time? Levine and Bartlett (1984) went to 12 cities in six countries and noted the time on 15 randomly chosen bank clocks in each city. Then they measured the difference between the time shown on the clocks and the time reported by the local telephone company in each city. The most accurate public clocks were Japanese—off by an average of just 34 seconds. U.S. clocks were next (off by an average of 54 seconds), followed by the clocks in Taiwan, England, and Italy (71 sec., 72 sec., and 90 sec., respectively). Indonesia came in last, at 189 sec.

Here you have hard, archeological evidence of clock-setting behavior across six countries. Real people had set those 15 clocks in each city, and real people were responsible for making sure that the clocks were adjusted from time to time. Levine and Bartlett looked at whether differences in the average deviation of the clocks from the real time predicted differences in the rate of heart disease.

They don't. The country with the lowest rate of heart disease, Japan, has the

most accurate clocks and the fastest overall pace of life (as measured by several other indicators). Apparently, according to Levine and Bartlett, it's possible in some cultures to be hard *working* without being hard *driving*.

Sechrest and Flores (1969) recorded and analyzed bathroom graffiti in a sample of men's public toilets in Manilla and Chicago. They wanted to examine attitudes toward sexuality in the two cultures. The results were striking. There was no difference in the percentage of graffiti in the two cities that dealt with heterosexual themes. But fully 42% of the Chicago graffiti dealt with homosexuality, while only 2% of the Manilla graffiti did, showing a clear difference in the two cultures regarding level of concern with homosexuality. (For other studies of bathroom graffiti, see Green 2003 and Otta et al. 1996.)

Gould and Potter (1984) did a survey of used up (not smashed up) automobiles in five Providence, Rhode Island, junkyards. They calculated that the average use-life of American-made cars is 10.56 years, irrespective of how many times cars change hands. This is a good deal longer than most Americans would guess. Gould also compared use-life against initial cost and found that paying more for a car doesn't affect how long it will last. Interesting and useful findings.

In their classic book on *Unobtrusive Measures*, Webb et al. (1966, 2000) identified a class of measures based on erosion. Administrators of Chicago's Museum of Science and Industry had found that the vinyl tiles around an exhibit showing live, hatching chicks needed to be replaced about every six weeks. The tiles around other exhibits lasted for years without having to be replaced. Webb et al. 2000 (p. 37) suggested that this erosion measure (the rate of wear on vinyl tiles) might be a proxy for a direct measure of the popularity of exhibits. The faster the tiles wear out, the more popular the exhibit (Box 14.4).

Box 14.4 Weighing the evidence

Dean Archer and Lynn Erlich (1985) had a hypothesis that sensational crimes (with a lot of press coverage) result in increased sales of handguns. The police would not allow them to see the handgun applications, so they asked a member of the police staff to put the permits into envelopes, by month, for three months before and three months after a particular sensational crime. Then they weighed the envelopes and converted the weight to handgun applications. To do this, they got a chunk of blank applications and found out how many applications there were per ounce.

The technique is very reliable. The correlation between the estimates of researchers and the actual weights of the envelopes was 0.99, and in a controlled experiment, researchers were able to tell the difference of just one sheet of paper in 15 out of 18 tries. Real data can be messy, though. Lots of handgun applications have addenda attached, for example. Still, the correlation between researchers' estimates and the true number of handgun applications across six months was 0.94.

As Archer and Erlich suggest, the weight method can be used to study confidential records when you want to know only aggregate outcomes—about things like drunk driving arrests, the influx of psychiatric patients to a clinic, the number of grievance filings in a company, the number of abortion referrals, and the number of complaints against agencies—and don't need data about individuals.

ARCHIVAL RESEARCH

Archival research is truly nonreactive. Whether you're studying archival records of births, migrations, visits to a hospital, or consumer purchases, people can't change their behavior after the fact. The original data might have been collected reactively, but that's one reason why historians demand such critical examination of sources.

Another advantage of doing what Caroline Brettell calls "fieldwork in the archives" (1998) is that you can study things using archival data that would be too politically "hot" to study any other way. And archival research is inexpensive. Be on the lookout for interesting archival materials: government reports, personal diaries or photo collections, industrial data, medical records, school records, wills, deeds, records of court cases, tax rolls, and land-holding records.

Measuring Trends in Women's Fashion

Using fashion magazines going back to 1844, Alfred Kroeber made eight separate measurement of women's clothing in the United States and France (Kroeber 1919). He measured things like the diameter of the skirt at the hem, the diameter of the waist, the depth of decolletage (measured from the mouth to the middle of the corsage edge in front), and so on. After analyzing the data, Kroeber claimed to have found "an underlying pulsation in the width of civilized women's skirts, which is symmetrical and extends in its up and down beat over a full century; and an analogous rhythm in skirt length, but with a period of only about a third the duration" (p. 257). Kroeber offered his finding as evidence for long-cycle behavior in civilization.

Allport and Hartman (1931) criticized Kroeber for having been insufficiently critical of his sources. They found, for example, that the range in width of skirts for one year, 1886, was greater than the range Kroeber reported for 1859–1864 and that some years had very few cases on which to base measurements. If the data are suspect, Allport and Hartman concluded, then so are the regularities Kroeber claimed to have found (1931:342–43).

Richardson scoured the archives of fashion and extended the database from 1605 to 1936 (J. Richardson and Kroeber 1940). Before making measurements for all the new years included in the study, Richardson redid Kroeber's measurements for 1844–1846 and for 1919 and assured herself that she was coding each plate the same way Kroeber had done in 1919 (J. Richardson and Kroeber 1940).

More than 40 years later, Lowe and Lowe (1982) reanalyzed the Richardson-Kroeber data for the 150 years from 1787 to 1936, using all the firepower of modern statistics and computers. Kroeber's first analysis was vindicated: Stylistic change in women's dress is in stable equilibrium (changing with patterned regularity), and is driven by "inertia, cultural continuity, a rule system of aesthetic proportions, and an inherently unpredictable element" (Lowe and Lowe 1982:521).

Mulcahy and Herbert (1990) added data for the years 1937–1982 and found more variability in those 46 years than in the 150 years before 1937. For example, a plot of the moving average for skirt width from 1811 to 1926 has the same shape as the plot for 1926–1976. In other words, the cycle of skirt length had been cut by more than half in 1976.

Still, Allport and Hartman's critique was right on target in 1931. You can't be too critical of your sources. Archival data may appear clean, especially if they come packaged on computer files and are coded and ready to be analyzed. But they may be riddled with error. Consider carefully all the possible sources of bias (informant error, observer error, etc.) that might have been at work in the setting down of the data. Ask how, why, and under what conditions a particular set of archival data was collected. Ask who collected the data and what biases she or he might have had (**Further Reading:** unobtrusive measures of behavior).

AND FINALLY . . .

No data are free of error. In some parts of Mexico, the number of consensual unions is greater than the number of formal marriages, making court records about marriages problematic. In the United States, statistics for some kinds of crime are untrustworthy. Many crimes go unreported and those that are reported may not be recorded at all or may be recorded in the wrong category. In some countries, rural people may wait as long as six months to report a birth, and a significant fraction of their children may die within that period. It is almost always better to understand distortion in data than to throw them out.

Key Concepts in This Chapter

direct observation	focal follows	24-hour recall
indirect observation	scientific management	Interaction Process Analysis
reactive observation	time and motion research	(IPA)
nonreactive observation	human factors engineering	instantaneous spot sampling
unobtrusive observation	ethology	scan sampling
continuous monitoring	behavioral biology	time sampling
spot sampling	ethogram	time allocation (TA) studies

experience sampling   simulated-client method   proxemics
disguised field observation   mystery-shopper method   passive deception
pseudopatients   grades of deception   behavior trace studies

Summary

- When you want to know what people actually do, there is no substitute for watching them or studying the physical traces their behavior leaves behind. Direct observation involves watching people and recording their behavior on the spot; indirect observation involves gathering the archeological residue of human behavior.
- In continuous monitoring, or CM, you watch a person, or group of people, and record their behavior. The technique was developed in the field of management and is used today across the social sciences.
    - CM is particularly useful in studying children—in classrooms and playgrounds, in clinical settings and in homes.
    - CM is widely used in clinical research. Field researchers also use CM to track shopping behavior and work behavior.
    - CM is hard work and is highly reactive, but it produces very important data about behavior. The database from the Six Culture Study, for example, consists of about 20,000 recorded acts for 134 children. Strong conclusions can be drawn from this kind of robust database.
- Data from CM must be coded. Researchers have developed coding schemes for interactions between married couples, for studies of teacher-pupil interaction, for worker-management negotiations, and so on.
    - Video has made CM easier. As video cameras have gotten smaller, easier to use, and less expensive, more field researchers are using this technology for close examination of behavior streams.
- Time allocation, or TA, studies are based on spot sampling. The researcher simply appears at randomly selected places, at randomly selected times, and records what people are doing when they are first seen.
    - If you sample a large, unbiased number of acts, then the percentage of *times* people are seen doing things is an unbiased estimated of the percentage of *time* they spend in those activities.
    - Nearly all spot sampling studies of behavior are done during the daylight hours, between 6 a.m. and 7 p.m.
- Besides issues of sampling, TA studies have special coding problems. If someone saw that you were lying down reading, and you were studying for an exam, should they record that you were working or relaxing?
    - Record *all* possible behaviors you observe in the order of their primacy, according to your best judgment at the time of observation and use a separate check sheet for each observation.
- Experience sampling, or ES, combines the power of random spot checks with the relative ease of having people report on their own behavior.
    - People respond to beepers or calls or texts and fill in a form about what they're doing, or who they're with, or what they're feeling at the moment the beeper goes off or they get a call or text message. For some behaviors, like online learning or online game playing, people respond to a random request on their screen.
    - A single investigator can only be in one place at a time, but with beepers, you can collect spot-observation behavioral data from lots of people at once.

- In disguised field observation, a researcher pretends to actually join a group, and proceeds to record data about people in the group.
  - Some of the most interesting and important studies in the social sciences have been done using disguised field observation, but this method raises very serious ethical concerns.
  - There are grades of deception in research. Unobtrusive observation is used in environmental studies to measure the walking speed of people in cities and rural areas. Compare this passive deception to sending pseudopatients to a hospital to test the diagnostic skills of the staff.
- You can observe behavior indirectly by examining the traces of it that people leave behind. Everything from telephone bills to garbage creates indirect indicators of real human behavior. Think of this as behavioral archeology.
  - Behavioral trace studies are nonreactive and often yield enormous amounts of data that can be standardized, quantified, and compared across groups and over time.

Exercises

1. To learn continuous monitoring, go to a shopping mall and record the interaction behavior of 30 mother-child pairs for two minutes each. Record carefully the number of children each mother has and her interaction with each child. Try to find out whether interaction patterns are predictable from: (1) the number of children a mother has to cope with; (2) the ages of the children; (3) the socioeconomic class or ethnicity of the family; or (4) some other factors.

   This exercise is instructive, if not humbling. It's a real challenge to code for socioeconomic class and ethnicity when you can't talk to the people you observe. Do this with at least one colleague so you can both check the reliability of your coding.

2. Give some shoppers a recorder and ask them to go around a grocery store looking for the following list of items. These are the same items that Titus and Everett (1996) used in their study of shoppers:

Cooking oil	Apple juice
Tomato paste	Maple syrup
Household dyes	Whipped nondairy topping
Dishwashing liquid	
Grated cheese	Frozen waffles
Powdered soft drink mix	Peanut butter
Furniture polish	Cream cheese
Charcoal	Limes
Powdered milk	Canned tuna
Vinegar	Marshmallows
Bouillon cubes	Frozen turkey

Analyze the results to see if there are global strategies that people use to find their way through an unfamiliar environment.

Repeat this in a different kind of store—like an office supply store—to see how different products might produce different finding strategies. Be sure to get permission from the manager of any store in which you want to do systematic observation. Offer to provide the manager with a copy of your report. And be sure that the shoppers you work with have given written, informed consent regarding their participation in this exercise.

3. There's a lot of research on vigilance behavior in humans. David Barash (1972) found that students who eat alone in a cafeteria are more likely to choose a table next to a wall, while students in groups are equally likely to sit at a wall table or a table in the middle of the room. He also found that loners look up about twice as much as do people in groups. Freidenberg and Cimbalo (1996) repeated and confirmed the results of Barash's experiment.

Now it's your turn. As they did, make your observations between 11:30 a.m. and 1:30 p.m. on seven consecutive weekdays. Map the tables in a cafeteria (you'll be able to do this if you've completed the map-making exercise in Chapter 12) and record whether singles or groups (count the number of people in groups) choose a wall or a center table. To count people looking up, choose a random person from each group and do continuous monitoring for five minutes. Think of wall tables and middle tables as being conditions in an experiment. If there are more wall tables (or middle tables), then remember to weight your counts when you do the analysis.

For more on human ethology research on how people use and manage personal space, see **Further Reading**: ethology and human ethology.

4. There are 1,440 minutes in a day, so there are 10,080 minutes in a week. If you sleep eight hours a day, then cut the 10,080 minutes down by a third, or 3,360 minutes. If you sleep 7.5 hours a day, then cut the 10,080 minutes down by 3,150 minutes, and so on.

Take a random sample of 204 minutes from the minutes of all nonsleeping time in your week. Then, on each of those 204 minutes, jot down what you're doing. Nobody else is going to see this, so be ruthlessly honest about the exercise. As Table 14.1 shows, with 204 observations you can say, with great confidence, that an activity that occurs 7% of the time in your data, actually occurred between 3.5% and 10.5% of the time in your life during those seven days.

One of the problems you'll face in this exercise is deciding how to code all the different activities you write down. You'll wind up with things like "getting a candy bar from the vending machine at Arbuth Hall" and "having breakfast." Do you code both of those observations as "eating behavior" or do you code the first as "snacking" and the second as "eating"? Or do you code the first one as "acquiring food" and only the second as eating?

Further Reading

Time and motion studies and direct observation of work. Adler (1993), Coutts and Reaburn (2000), Razmi and Shakhs-Niyae (2008), Tipping et al. (2010), Toupin et al. (2007).

Direct observation of children. Aspland and Gardner (2003), Blurton-Jones (1972), , Borich and Klinzing (1984), Guilmet (1979), Harvey et al. (2009), McGrew (1972), Medley and

Mitzel (1958), Meh (1996), Mileski (1971), Pellegrini (1996), Raver and Peterson (1988), Ridgers et al. (2010), Rosenshine and Furst (1973), Sit et al. (2010).

Direct observation of adults. Campos et al. (2009), O'Brian (1998), Saudargas and Zanolli (1990), Schneider (2009), Weigl et al. (2009), M. E. Young et al. (2009).

Ethology and human ethology. Barash (1973, 1974, 1977), Beck (2007), Eibl-Eiblsfeldt (1989), Hutt and Hutt (1970), Lehner (1979), Schmitt (1997).

Observing shoppers. Gram (2010), Sharkey et al. (2010), Spilkova and Hochel (2009).

IPA and Bales's coding scheme. Allen et al. (1989), Atwal and Caldwell (2005), Bell (2001), Hynsook and White-Traut (2005), Koskinen (2010), Nam et al. (2009), Poole and Folger (1981).

Other interaction coding systems. Bakeman and Gottman (1997), Bakeman and Quera (1995), W. H. Brown et al. (1996), Greenwood et al. (1985), Longabaugh (1963), Matsumoto et al. (1991), Mustonen and Pulkkinen (1997), Rimal (2001), Sorensen et al. (1989).

Reactivity in observational research. Cousens et al. (1996), Gardner (2000), Harvey et al. (2009), Spano (2006).

Experience sampling. Asakawa and Csikszentmihalyi (1998), Christensen et al. (2003), Csikszentmihalyi and Hunter (2003), Pearce et al. (2005), Rusting and Larsen (1998), Scollon et al. (2009), Shumow et al. (2008), Verkasalo (2010), Weisner et al. (2001).

Pseudopatients and simulated clients. Chalker et al. (2004), Huntington and Schuler (1993), Igun (1986), Kafle et al. (1996), Katz and Naré (2002), Marsh et al. (2004), G. D. Smith and Mertens (2004), Tuladhar et al. (1998), Viber et al. (2009).

Deception in field studies. Brymer (1998), Bulmer (1991), Lauder (2003), Lugosi (2006), Rynkiewick and Spradley (1976). See **Further Reading** in Chapter 4 for readings on deception and debriefing.

Proxemics. Albas (1991), Ardener (1981), Evans and Wener (2007), Hashimoto and Borders (2005), Høgh-Olesen (2008), Kendon (1981), Kenner and Katsimaglis (1993), Low and Lawrece-Zúñiga (2003).

Unobtrusive measures of behavior. Bridges et al. (2002), Cialdini and Baumann (1981), Marques et al. (2003), Page (1997), Sagberg et al. (1997), G. D. Smith and Merten (2004).

PART IV
Data Analysis

15

Introduction to Qualitative and Quantitative Analysis

INTRODUCTION

This is the first of eight chapters about analyzing data. In this chapter, we begin with the basics—what analysis is and how to use matrices, tables, and flow charts to present the results of data analysis. We move on, in Chapter 16, to analyzing cultural domain data and proximity data. Those are the kinds of data we first encountered in Chapter 10 . . . and more about this in a minute.

This is followed by three chapters on analyzing qualitative data. There is growing interest in the social sciences in the

analysis of qualitative data. Little wonder. Most of the recoverable information about human thought and behavior in complex societies is naturally occurring text: books, magazines, and newspapers, diaries, property transactions, recipes, correspondence, song lyrics, billboards. . . .

Other qualitative data include artifacts (toys, clothing, buildings, computers, furniture), images (television ads, slasher films, family photo albums), behaviors (crossing a busy street, giving a university lecture, laying out a garden), narratives (folk tales, life histories, open-ended responses to interview questions), and events (church ceremonies, homecoming games, blind dates).

Chapter 17 is on ethnographic decision modeling, folk taxonomies, componential analysis, and analytic induction—methods based on principles of systematic logic applied to qualitative data. Chapter 18 covers methods for studying grammar beyond the sentence—narrative analysis, performance analysis, schema analysis, and discourse analysis. Chapter 19 covers the two major methods in the social sciences that involve coding text: grounded theory and content analysis.

Finally, Chapters 20, 21, and 22 are on methods for analyzing profile data. These chapters cover univariate, bivariate, and multivariate analysis.

Some of these chapters about analysis are quantitative in orientation; some are qualitative; and some are a blend of qualitative and quantitative approaches. It's fair to say that there are qualitative and quantitative data and that these different types of data need to be analyzed with different methods. But, in my view, forcing people in the social sciences to choose between qualitative and quantitative approaches results in trained incapacity.

QUALITATIVE/ QUANTITATIVE

By a quirk of English grammar, the phrase "qualitative data analysis" is mischievously ambiguous. Unless someone spells it out in lots of words, you never know if the phrase means "the qualitative analysis of data" or the "analysis of qualitative data." And the same goes for "quantitative data analysis." Figure 15.1 lays out the possibilities.

Cell *a* is the qualitative analysis of qualitative data. Interpretive studies of texts are of this kind. You focus on and name themes in texts. You tell the story, as you see it, of how the themes are related to one another and how characteristics of the speaker or speakers account for the existence of certain themes and the absence of others. You may deconstruct the text, look for hidden subtexts, and, in general, try to let your audience know—using the power of good rhetoric—the deeper meaning or the multiple meanings of the text.

Looking diagonally from cell *a*, cell *d* refers to the quantitative analysis of quantitative data. Lots of useful data about human behavior come to us as numbers. Direct observation of behavior, village censuses, time allocation

Figure 15.1 Qualitative-Quantitative Data and Analysis

Analysis	Data	
	Qualitative	Quantitative
Qualitative	(a) Interpretive text studies. Hermeneutics, Grounded Theory	(b) Search for and presentation of meaning in results of quantitative processing
Quantitative	(c) Turning words into numbers. Classic Content Analysis, Word Counts, Free Lists, Pile Sorts, etc.	(d) Statistical and mathematical analysis of numeric data

Source: H. R. Bernard 1996. "Qualitative Data, Quantitative Analysis." *Cultural Anthropology Methods Journal* 8:9–11.

studies, close-ended questions in surveys—all produce numerical data.

Cell *b* is the qualitative analysis of quantitative data. This can involve the search for patterns using visualization methods, like multidimensional scaling and hierarchical clustering. (We'll get to these methods next, in Chapter 16.) Cell *b* is also about the search for, and the presentation of, *meaning* in the results of quantitative data processing. It's what quantitative analysts do after they get through doing the work in cell *d*. Without the work in cell *b*, cell *d* studies are sterile and superficial.

Which leaves cell *c*, the quantitative analysis of qualitative data. This involves turning the data from words or images into numbers. Scholars in communications, for example, tag a set of television ads from Mexico and the United States to test whether consumers are portrayed as older in one country than in the other. Political scientists code the rhetoric of a presidential debate to look for patterns and predictors of policies. Archeologists code a set of artifacts to produce emergent categories or styles or to test whether some intrusive artifacts can be traced to a source.

WHAT ARE DATA?

Data—qualitative and quantitative alike—are reductions of experience. Electrons and DNA are things. We experience those things with the help of instruments and record what we experience. Whatever we record—their shape, their size, their weight, their speed—are data. If we record numbers to represent our experience of electrons, we get quantitative data. If we record sounds, words, or pictures, we get qualitative data.

In the social sciences, we are interested in people's behavior, thoughts, emotions, and artifacts (the physical residue of people's thoughts, emotions, and behavior) and the environmental conditions in which people behave, think, feel, and make things. We experience these things mostly by watching and listening. When we reduce that experience to numbers, the result is quantitative data. And when we reduce people's thoughts, behaviors, emotions, artifacts, and environments to sounds, words, or pictures, the result is qualitative data.

Each kind of data—qualitative and quantitative—and each kind of data reduction—qualitative and quantitative—is useful for answering certain kinds of questions. Skilled social researchers can do it all.

WHAT'S ANALYSIS?

Analysis is the search for patterns in data and for ideas that help explain why those patterns are there in the first place. The way I see it, analysis is ultimately all qualitative. It starts before you collect data—you have to have some ideas about what you're going to study—and it continues throughout any research effort. As you develop ideas, you test them against your observations: Your observations may then modify your ideas, which then need to be tested again, and so on. Don't look for closure in the process. If you're doing it right, it never stops (Box 15.1).

Box 15.1 Data processing and data analysis

Most methods for quantitative analysis—things like factor analysis, cluster analysis, regression analysis, and so on—are really methods for **data processing** and for finding patterns in data. Interpreting those patterns is up to you. Interpretation—**data analysis**—involves telling us what findings mean and linking your findings to the findings of other research. This all starts with ideas in your head and comes out in words on paper. It's a pretty qualitative exercise.

Don't worry about getting ideas. Once you have data in your hands, either words or numbers, your hardest job will be to sort through all the ideas you get and decide which ones to test. And don't worry about seeing patterns in your data or about not being able to come up with causal explanations for things you see. It can happen very fast, often in a matter of hours or days after starting any research project, so be suspicious of your pet ideas and continually check yourself to make sure you're not inventing or at least not embellishing patterns.

Seeing patterns that aren't there happens all the time in research, qualitative or quantitative, just from eagerness and observer expectations. If you are highly self-critical, your tendency to see patterns everywhere will diminish as the research progresses.

The Constant Validity Check

The problem can also get worse, though, if you accept uncritically the folk analyses of articulate or prestigious informants. It's important to seek the emic perspective and to document folk analyses (Lofland 1971), but as your interviews and notes pile up, try consciously to switch back and forth between the emic and etic perspectives. Check yourself from either buying into folk explanations or rejecting them without considering their possible validity. The constant validity check is not hard to do. It's just hard to remember to do it systematically. Here are some guidelines.

1. If you are interviewing people, look for consistencies and inconsistencies among knowledgeable informants and find out why those informants disagree about important things.

2. Whenever possible, check people's reports of behavior or of environmental conditions against more objective evidence. If you were a journalist at a good newspaper or magazine and you submitted a story based on informants'

reports without checking the facts, you'd never get it past your editor's desk. I see no reason not to hold social scientists to the standard that the best journalists face every day.

3. Be open to negative evidence rather than annoyed when it pops up. When you run into a case that doesn't fit your theory, ask yourself whether it's the result of: (a) normal **intracultural variation**; (b) your lack of knowledge about the range of appropriate behavior; or (c) a genuinely unusual case.

4. As you come to understand how something works, seek out alternative explanations from key informants and from colleagues, and listen to them carefully. American folk culture, for example, holds that women left home for the work force because of something called "feminism" and "women's liberation." That's a popular emic explanation. An alternative, etic explanation is that feminist values and orientations are supported, if not caused, by women being *driven* out of their homes and into the work force by the hyperinflation during the 1970s that drove down the purchasing power of their husbands' incomes (Margolis 1984). Both the emic, folk explanation and the etic explanation are interesting for different reasons.

5. Try to fit extreme cases into your theory, and if the cases won't fit, don't be too quick to throw them out. It is always easier to throw out cases than it is to reexamine your own ideas, but the easy way out is hardly ever the right way in research.

DATA MATRICES

One of the most important concepts in all data analysis—whether we're working with quantitative or qualitative data—is the data matrix. There are two basic kinds of data matrices: profile matrices and proximity matrices. Figure 15.2 shows what these two kinds of matrices look like.

Profile Matrices

Most analysis in the social sciences is about *how properties of things are related to, or predict other properties of those things.* We ask, for example: Does having been sexually molested as a child influence whether a woman will remain in a physically abusive marriage? Does family wealth affect the SAT scores of the family's children? Does the per capita gross national product of a nation affect the probability that it will go to war with its neighbors?

This is called profile analysis. You start with series of *things*—units of analysis—and you measure a series of *variables* for each of those things. This produces a profile matrix, or, simply, a data matrix. *A data matrix is a table of cases and their associated variables.* Figure 15.2(a) shows the shape of a profile matrix. Each unit of analysis—each row—is

Figure 15.2 Two Kinds of Matrices: Profiles and Proximities

a. Profile matrix persons by variables					
Respondent	**Age**	**Sex**	**Education**	**Natal Household Size**	**Current Household Size**	**Ethnicity**
1	27	2	3	6	4	3
2	31	1	2	3	2	1
3	+	+	+	+	+	+
4	+	+	+	+		

b. Proximity matrix of the variables (columns)					
	Age	**Sex**	**Education**	**Natal Household Size**	**Current Household Size**	**Ethnicity**
Age	___					
Sex		___				
Education			___			
Natal Household Size				___		
Current Household Size					___	
Ethnicity						___

profiled by a particular set of measurements on some variables—the columns. Matrices of this shape are also called two-mode because the things in the rows (the cases) and the things in the columns (properties of the cases) are different.

The rows of a profile matrix are often respondents to a questionnaire, but they can be marriage records, folk tales, interview texts, churches—even time periods (1980, 1981, 1982 . . . 2011).

Figure 15.2(b) shows a proximity matrix of variables. Matrices of this shape are also called one-mode because the things in the rows and the things in the columns are the same and cells represent how proximate— that is, how close or how far—they are to one another. Imagine the list of variable names stretching several feet to the right, off the right-hand margin of the page, and several feet down, off the lower margin. That is

what would happen if you had, say, 100 variables about each of your respondents. For each and every pair of variables in the matrix of data, you could ask: Are these variables related?

Proximity Matrices

Profile matrices contain measurements of variables for a set of items. Proximity matrices contain measurements of relations, or proximities, between items. If the measurements in a proximity matrix tell how alike or close things are to each other, then you have a similarity matrix. If the measurements in a proximity matrix tell how far apart or unalike things are from each other, then you have a dissimilarity matrix. We'll need the concept of a proximity matrix for several kinds of analyses coming up in the chapters that follow (Box 15.2).

Box 15.2 Similarity and dissimilarity matrices

If you've had a course in statistics and seen a correlation matrix, you've had experience with a similarity matrix. The bigger the number in each cell—the higher the correlation—the more alike two things are.

If you've ever read one of those tables of distances between cities that you see on road maps, you've had experience with a dissimilarity matrix. The bigger the numbers in the cells, the more "dissimilar" two cities are. In other words, the larger the number in any cell, the further apart two cities are on the map.

You can convert a profile matrix into two kinds of proximity matrix—one for the correlation between all pairs of rows and one for the correlation between all pairs of columns. If you compare rows, you find out how similar the units of analysis are to one another. If you compare columns, you find out how similar the variables are to one another.

PRESENTING RESULTS IN MATRICES AND TABLES

An important part of all analysis, qualitative and quantitative, is the production of visual displays. Laying out your data in table or matrix form and drawing your theories out in the form of a flow chart or map helps you understand what you have and helps you communicate your ideas to others (Miles and Huberman 1994). Learning to build and use qualitative data matrices and flow charts requires practice, but you can get started by studying examples published in research journals.

Donna Birdwell-Pheasant (1984), for example, wanted to understand how differences in interpersonal relations change over time in the village of Chunox, Belize. She questioned 216 people about their relations with members of their families over the years and simulated a longitudinal study with data from a cross-sectional sample. She checked the retrospective data with other information gathered by questionnaires, direct observations, and semistructured interviews. Table 15.1 shows the analytic framework that emerged from Birdwell-Pheasant's work.

Birdwell-Pheasant identified five kinds of relations: absent, attenuated, coordinate, subordinate, and superordinate. These represent the rows of the matrix in Table 15.1. The columns in the matrix are the four major types of family relations: ascending generation (parents, aunts, uncles, etc.), siblings, spouse, and descending generation (children, nephews, and nieces, etc.).

Birdwell-Pheasant then went through her data and "examined all the available data on Juana Fulana (In Latin America, Juan Fulano and Juana Fulana are the male and female equivalents of "so-and-so"—as in "Is so-and-so married?") and decided whether, in 1971, she had a coordinate or subordinate relationship with her mother (e.g., did she have her own kitchen? her own wash house?).

Birdwell-Pheasant repeated the process, for *each* of her 216 informants, for *each* of the four relations in Table 15.1, and for *each* of the years 1965, 1971, 1973, 1975, and 1977. This required 216(4)(5) = 4,320 decisions. Birdwell-Pheasant didn't have data on all possible informant-by-year-by-relation combinations, but by the time she was through, she had a database of 742 "power readings" of family relations over time and was able to make some very strong statements about patterns of domestic structure over time in Chunox. This is an excellent example of the use of qualitative data to develop a theory and the conversion of qualitative data to a set of numbers for testing that theory.

Stephen Fjellman and Hugh Gladwin (1985) studied the family histories of Haitian migrants to the United States. Fjellman and Gladwin found an elegant way to present a lot of information about those histories in a simple chart. Table 15.2 shows one chart for a family of four people in 1982.

This Haitian American family began in 1968 when Jeanne's father sent her to Brooklyn, New York, to go to high school. The single plus sign for 1968 shows the founding of the family by Jeanne. Jeanne's father died in 1971, and her mother, sister, and brother joined her in New York. Jeanne adopted Marc in 1975, and in 1976 she and her mother moved with Marc to Miami. Lucie and Charles remained together in New York. The two minus signs in the row for 1976 indicate that Jeanne's sister and brother were no longer part of the household founded by Jeanne.

Two years later, in 1978, Lucie got married and Charles joined Jeanne's household in Miami. Also in 1978, Jeanne began saving money and applying for visas to bring her cousins Hughes and Valerie to Miami. The asterisks show that these two people are in the process of joining the household. In 1979, Anna's sister, Helen joined the family, and in 1982 Charles went back to New York to live again with Lucie.

There is a lot of information in this chart, but the detail is gone. We don't know *why* Jeanne went to the United States in 1968; we don't know *why* Charles left Jeanne's household in 1976 or *why* he rejoined the group in 1978. Fjellman and Gladwin present seven of these family history charts in their article and provide the historical detail in vignettes below each chart. Their purpose in reducing all the historical detail to a set of pluses and minuses, however, is to allow us to see at a glance the patterns of family growth, development, and decay.

Table 15.1 Birdwell-Pheasant's Matrix of Criteria for Assigning Values to Major Relationships Between People in Her Study

	Major Types of Relationships			
Values of Relationships	Ascending Generation	Siblings	Spouse	Descending Generation
Absent	parents deceased, migrated permanently, or estranged	only child; siblings deceased, migrated permanently, or estranged	single or widowed; spouse migrated or permanently estranged	no mature offspring; all offspring deceased, or migrated permanently, or estranged
Attenuated	does not live with parents or participate in work group with parent; does visit and/or exchange food	does not live with siblings or participate in work groups with them; does visit and/or exchange food	separation, but without final termination of union; e.g., temporary migration	offspring do not live with parents or participate in work group with them; do visit and/or exchange food
Coordinate	participates in work group with parents sharing decision-making authority	participates in work group with siblings under parents' authority; or works with siblings only, sharing decision making	married; in charge of own sex specific domain with minimal interference from partner	participates in a work group with offspring, sharing decision-making authority
Subordinate	participates in work group with parent; parent makes decisions	participates in work group of siblings; other sibling(s) make decisions	individual's normal control within sex-specific domain is interfered with by spouse	dependent, elderly parent, unable to work
Super-ordinate	makes decisions for dependent, elderly parent who is unable to work	participates in work group with siblings; makes decisions for group	interferes with spouse's normal controls within sex-specific domain	heads work group that includes one or more mature offspring; makes decisions for group

Source: D. Birdwell-Pheasant, "Personal Power Careers and the Development of Domestic Structure in a Small Community." *American Ethnologist* 11 (4), 1984.

Table 15.2 Family History of Haitian Migrants to Miami

Year	Jeanne	Anna (mother)	Lucie (sister)	Charles (brother)	Marc (adopted son)	Helen (aunt)	Hughes & Valerie (cousins)	Number in Household
1968	+							1
1971	+	+	+	+				4
1975	+	+	+	+	+			5
1976	+	+	−	−	+			3
1978	+	+	−	+	+		+	4
1979	+	+	−	+	+	+	+	5
1982	+	+	−	−	+	+	+	4

Source: S. M. Fjellman and H. Gladwin, "Haitian Family Patterns of Migration to South Florida." *Human Organization* 44:307, 1985.

PRESENTING RESULTS: CAUSAL FLOW CHARTS

Causal maps represent theories about how things work. They are visual representations of ideas that emerge from studying data, seeing patterns, and coming to conclusions about what causes what. Causal maps do not have to have numbers attached to them, although that is where causal modeling eventually leads. After all, it is better to know *how much* one thing causes another than to know simply that one thing *does* cause another. With or without numbers, though, causal models are best expressed as a flow chart.

A causal flow chart consists of a set of boxes connected by a set of arrows. The boxes contain descriptions of states (like being the youngest child, or owning a tractor, or being Catholic, or feeling angry), and the arrows tell you how one state leads to another. The simplest causal map is a visual representation of the relation between two variables

$$A \rightarrow B$$

which reads: "A leads to or causes B."

Real life is usually much, much more complicated than that. Look at Figure 15.3. It is Stuart Plattner's algorithm, based on intensive interviews and participant observation at produce markets in St. Louis, for how merchants decide what stock to buy. *An algorithm is a set of ordered rules that tell you how to solve a problem*—like "find the average of a list of numbers," or, in this case, "determine the decisions of produce merchants." (The capital letter Q in Figure 15.3 stands for "quantity.")

Read the flow chart from top to bottom and left to right, following the arrows. At the beginning of each week, the merchants seek information on the supply and cost of produce items. After that, the algorithm gets complicated. Plattner notes that the model may seem "too complex to represent the decision process of plain folks at the marketplace." However, Plattner says, the chart "still omits consideration of an enormous amount of knowledge pertaining to qualities of produce at various seasons from various shipping areas" (Plattner 1982:405).

Now, on to the nuts and bolts of data analysis.

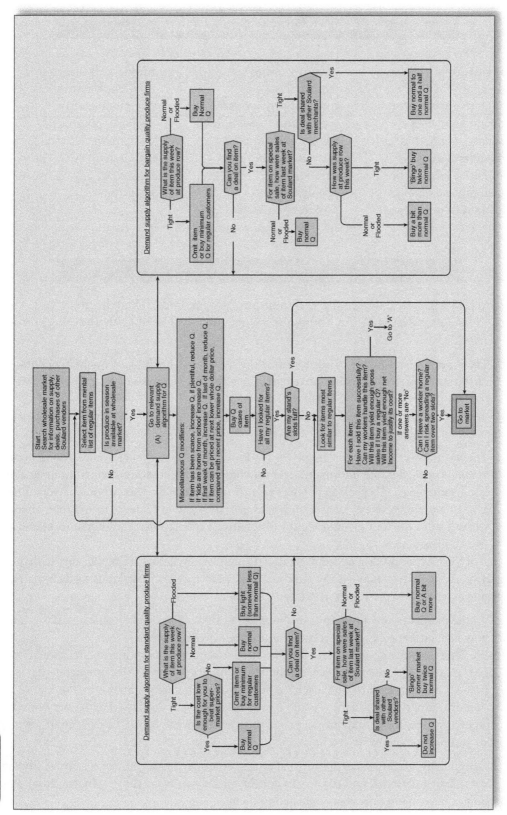

Source: S. Plattner, "Economic Decision Making in a Public Marketplace." *American Ethnologist* 9:404, 1982.

401

Key Concepts in This Chapter

qualitative analysis of
   qualitative data
quantitative analysis of
   quantitative data
qualitative analysis of
   quantitative data
quantitative analysis of
   qualitative data
reductions of experience

data processing
data analysis
constant validity check
intracultural variation
emic explanation
etic explanation
data matrix
profile matrices
proximity matrices

profile analysis
two-mode matrix
one-mode matrix
similarity matrix
dissimilarity matrix
causal map
flow chart
algorithm

Summary

- Different kinds of data require different analytic methods. The adjectives "quantitative" and "qualitative" are ambiguous when they are used with the phrase "data analysis."

  o There are four meanings to account for: the qualitative analysis of qualitative data, the quantitative analysis of quantitative data, the qualitative analysis of quantitative data, and the quantitative analysis of qualitative data.

- Analysis is the search for patterns in data and for ideas that help explain why those patterns are there in the first place.

  o The constant validity check involves: (1) looking for consistencies and inconsistencies among knowledgeable informants and finding out why those informants disagree about important things; (2) checking people's reports of behavior or of environmental conditions against more objective evidence; (3) being open to negative evidence rather than annoyed when it pops up; and (4) looking for alternative explanations from key informants and from colleagues.

- One of the most important concepts in all data analysis—whether we're working with quantitative or qualitative data—is the data matrix. There are two basic kinds of data matrices: profile matrices and proximity matrices.

  o Profile matrices show properties (in columns) of things (in rows). Profile analysis is about how properties of things are related to and predict one another.
  o Proximity matrices contain measurements of relations between items. Measurements of how close things are to each other produce a similarity matrix. Measurements that show how far apart things are from each other form a dissimilarity matrix.

- An important part of all analysis is the production of visual displays. Laying out your data in table or matrix form, and drawing your theories out in the form of a flow chart, or map, helps you understand what you have.

  o Causal maps, or flow charts, are visual representations of ideas that emerge from studying data, seeing patterns, and coming to conclusions about what-causes-what. Causal maps do not have to have numbers attached to them.

Exercises

1. Write a brief essay on the idea that quantitative analysis in social research involves reducing people to numbers, while qualitative analysis involves reducing people to words.

2. Why are the phrases "qualitative data analysis" and "quantitative data analysis" ambiguous?

3. What is a causal flow chart? How is it different from a matrix display of relations among variables?

Further Reading

The methods mentioned in this chapter are covered in detail in the next seven chapters. For example, you'll find further reading about content analysis and grounded theory in the **Further Reading** section at the end of Chapter 19, along with exercises in text analysis. You'll find further reading about proximity matrices at the end of Chapter 16, and exercises for multivariate analysis and further reading on causal modeling at the end of Chapter 22.

16

Analyzing Cultural Domains and Proximity Matrices

INTRODUCTION

In Chapter 10, I introduced you to methods for collecting data about the content and structure of cultural domains and social networks. The content of any domain or a personal network is a list. The structure of any domain, or any network, requires examining proximity matrices—that is, matrices of relations among the constituent items in a list. In this chapter, I'll show you how to analyze these kinds of data.

Why start with cultural domains and proximity matrices? Actually, we could begin our tour of data analysis anywhere, with any kind of data, because all data analysis, whether we're talking about the qualitative or quantitative kind, requires the same set of big skills. Here's a list of those big skills: (1) logical reasoning; (2) ways to test the results of logical reasoning. That's it. That's the whole list of big skills. All the other skills (and there are hundreds of them) are in one of the two big-skill categories.

The ability to engage in **constant comparison**, for example, is a really nice skill to develop. It's part of the logical reasoning set of tools and it means being able to hold some ideas in your head so you can compare them to new ones that emerge as you analyze data. For qualitative data, this means holding onto themes in some narratives and comparing them to new themes that pop into your head as you read the narratives a second and a third and a fourth time. For quantitative data, constant comparison means looking for patterns in many small findings as you run, say, correlations or chi-squared tests to examine hypotheses about what goes with what.

The point is, any of the skills you learn about how to analyze any data—qualitative or quantitative—are going to serve you well as you work with more and different kinds of data. In fact, having lots of skills in analyzing data will make you fearless about collecting different kinds of data. Once you master multidimensional scaling and cluster analysis, for example—two methods of analysis we'll cover in this chapter—you'll be able to analyze network data and once you can do that, you can do semantic network analysis, which will dramatically extend your capacity to analyze text, and . . . you get the idea.

We begin with free lists.

ANALYZING FREE LISTS

Gery Ryan and I told 34 people: "Please write down the names of all the fruits you can think of" (Bernard and Ryan 2010:167). Because free list data are texts, they have to be cleaned up before you can analyze them. Only 10 people listed grapes, but another 22 (for a total of 32 out of 34 people) listed grape (in the singular). Before counting up the frequency for each item in the free lists, we had to combine all mentions of grapes and grape. It doesn't matter whether you change grapes into grape or vice versa, so long as you make all the required changes.

It takes some work to clean up the spelling in free lists. In our data, three people listed bananna (wrong spelling), and 27 people listed banana (right spelling); three people listed avacado (wrong), one listed avocato (wrong), and six people listed avocado (right). Cantaloupe was hopeless, as was pomegranate. We got eight cantaloupes (the preferred spelling in the dictionary), six cantelope, two cantelopes, and three canteloupes. We got 17 listings for guava and one for guayaba, which happens to be the Spanish term for guava. We got 10 listings for passion fruit and one for passion-fruit, with a hyphen (when computers list word frequencies, they see those two listings as different).

Once the data were cleaned, we plotted how often each fruit was mentioned. The

Figure 16.1 Scree Plot of Free List of 143 Fruits From 34 Informants

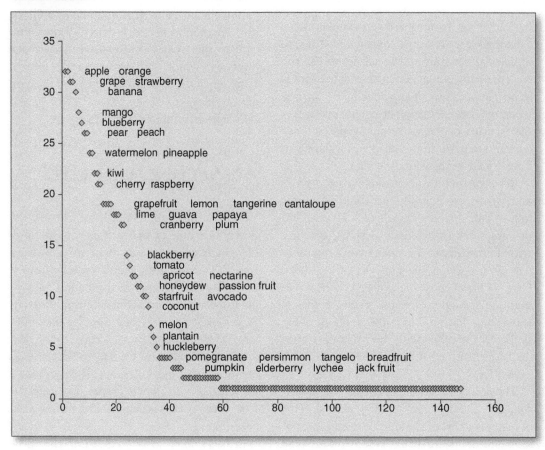

Source: H. R. Bernard and G. W. Ryan, *Analyzing Qualitative Data: Systematic Approaches.* Thousand Oaks, CA: Sage Publications. 2010. p. 169.

result is the scree plot in Figure 16.1. ("Scree" refers to the rocks that pile up at the base of a cliff and the telltale L-shape of the pile.)

The shape of the curve in Figure 16.1 is typical for a well-defined domain, like fruits: The 34 informants named a total of 147 different fruits, but 88 of those fruits were named by just one person (prickly pear and quince, for example) and almost everyone named a few items (apple and orange, for example). Compare that to the results for lists of "things that mothers do." For this domain, our 34 informants named 554 items, of which 515 were named by just one person, and only a handful (love, clean, cook) were named by five or more people.

Many domains—like fruits or animals or emotions or racial/ethnic groups—are well defined. Others are fuzzier, but many of the most interesting domains—like things that mothers do or things that people might do on a weekend, or things that you can do to stay healthy—are also things that people don't have easy lists for. (For more about free lists, see **Further Reading,** Chapter 10.)

Measuring the Salience of Free-List Items

Ryan and I asked 42 American adolescents (20 boys and 22 girls) to list "things they were worried about" concerning their health (Bernard and Ryan 2010:170). Table 16.1 shows the results.

Over three-quarters of the informants (76.2%) mentioned sexually transmitted diseases (STDs), and over one-third (35.7%) specifically mentioned HIV/AIDS. This is what we expect from adolescents but, surprisingly, nearly half (45.2%) of the respondents (all under age 20) were worried about cancer—a worry usually associated with older people.

Just six of the 20 boys (30% of the sample) mentioned cancer, compared to 13 of the 22 girls (59%). And when the boys mentioned cancer at all, they ranked it fifth, on average, of the illnesses they were worried about, compared to second for the girls. The girls, it turned out, were very worried about breast cancer, but when the data from both genders were combined, this wasn't noticeable.

The frequency of items in a set of free lists is one indicator of the importance—or

Table 16.1 Free List Results From 42 Adolescents About Their Health Concerns

	Total Sample (N = 42)		Girls (n = 22)			Boys (n = 20)			Difference Women%-Men%
	Freq	%	Rank	Freq	%	Rank	Freq	%	
Cold/Flu	12	28.6	3	10	45.5	9	2	10.0	35.5
Cancer	19	45.2	2	13	59.1	5	6	30.0	29.1
Eating Disorders	10	23.8	4	8	36.4	9	2	10.0	26.4
HIV/AIDS	15	35.7	3	10	45.5	6	5	25.0	20.5
Mono	10	23.8	5	7	31.8	8	3	15.0	16.8
Stress	8	19.0	7	5	22.7	8	3	15.0	7.7
Weight-Obesity	10	23.8	6	6	27.3	7	4	20.0	7.3
Skin-related	13	31.0	5	7	31.8	5	6	30.0	1.8
Hygiene	8	19.0	8	4	18.2	7	4	20.0	−1.8
Disease	8	19.0	8	4	18.2	7	4	20.0	−1.8
Eating Right	7	16.7	9	3	13.6	7	4	20.0	−6.4
STDs	32	76.2	1	16	72.7	1	16	80.0	−7.3
Fitness	12	28.6	7	5	22.7	4	7	35.0	−12.3
Drug Abuse	9	21.4	9	3	13.6	5	6	30.0	−16.4
Alcohol-related	16	38.1	6	6	27.3	2	10	50.0	−22.7
Smoking-related	11	26.2	9	3	13.6	3	8	40.0	−26.4

Source: H. R. Bernard and G. W. Ryan, *Analyzing Qualitative Data: Systematic Approaches.* Thousand Oaks, CA: Sage Publications. 2010. p. 171.

salience—of those items to informants. Another indicator is how early, on average, an item gets mentioned. If you ask native speakers of American English to list animals, you'll find that: (1) cat and dog are mentioned a lot; and (2) they are mentioned early (Henley 1969). In fact, those two animals are typically the first two animals that get mentioned.

Charismatic megafauna—elephants, whales, lions, and so on—also get mentioned a lot, but usually after the common household animals get named. Thus, in addition to frequency, we can measure the average rank that each item appears in a set of lists. J. J. Smith (1993) observed that a simple, average rank can be misleading. If you mention ocelot first on your list but no one else mentions it at all, then the average rank for ocelot is 1. Also, free listing produces lists of varying length. It's one thing to name elephants fifth in a list of 30 animals and quite another to name elephants fifth in a list of 10 animals.

Smith's S (J. J. Smith and Borgatti 1997) takes into account both the frequency of an item and how early in each list it is mentioned and is a popular measure of item cognitive salience. The formula for Smith's S is

$$S = ((\sum (L - R_j + 1) / L) / n \qquad \text{formula 16.1}$$

"where S is the average rank of an item across all lists in the sample, weighted by the length of the lists in which the item actually occurs; L = length of (number of items in) a list; R_j = rank of item j in the list (first = 1); and n is the number of lists in the sample" (Smith and Borgatti 1997:208–209). This measure is also "highly correlated with simple frequency" (Borgatti 1999:149) and so, for most analyses, simple frequency counts of free list data are all that's needed. Anthropac (Borgatti

1992a) makes short work of free lists (see Appendix E) (**Further Reading:** measuring salience).

Selecting Items From a Free List for Further Study

Researchers use scree plots to choose a set of items to study in more depth. For example, by counting the dots in Figure 16.1, we see that: (1) 14 fruits were mentioned by 20 or more of our 34 informants; and (2) 58 items were mentioned by at least two people. All the other fruits were mentioned just once.

How many items should we choose from these data as representing the contents of the domain? There is no formal rule here, but a good general rule is to select items that are mentioned by at least 10% of informants. If you have 40 informants, then choose items that were mentioned by at least four of them. If this still produces too many items, then move up to 15% of informants or more.

There is nothing forcing you to take every item that's mentioned a lot, especially if you already know something about the domain you're studying. If you want to study, say, 40 items in depth, you can choose some that are mentioned frequently and others that are mentioned less frequently—or even by no one at all. I'll show you an example of this later.

An item mentioned once is usually not a good candidate to include for further work on the structure of the domain. The whole idea of a cultural domain, as contrasted with an individual cognitive domain is that the content is shared (Borgatti 1999). On the other hand, we often want to know where a particular item fits within a cultural domain.

Once we have identified the items in a cultural domain, the next step is to examine how the items are related to each other. To do this, we ask people to make similarity judgments—to tell us what goes with what.

Pile sorts are an effective method for collecting these judgments.

ANALYZING PILE SORT DATA: INDIVIDUAL MATRICES

Begin a pile sort task by writing the name of each item on a single card (index cards cut in thirds work nicely). Label the back of each card with the number from 1 to n (where n is the total number of items in the domain). Spread the cards out randomly on a large table with the item-side up and the number-side down. (Be sure to shuffle the deck between informants.) Ask people to sort the cards into piles according to which items they think belong together.

Figure 16.2 shows the pile sort data for one male informant who sorted the names of 18 fruits. It also shows the format for recording the pile sort data. Pile #1 contained items 2, 11, and 13. In other words, this informant put the cards for orange, lemon, and grapefruit into one pile.

Table 16.2 shows the data from Figure 16.2 in the form of a similarity matrix, similar to the one you saw in Chapter 15.

When the informant put items 2, 11, and 13 (orange, lemon, grapefruit) into a pile, he did so because he thought the items were similar. To indicate this, there is a 1 in the matrix where items 2 and 11 intersect; another 1 in the cell where items 2 and 13 intersect; and another 1 in the cell where 11 and 13 intersect.

Similarly for Pile #2: There is a 1 in the 1-5 cell, the 1-9 cell, the 1-14 cell, and so on. There are 0s in all the cells that represent no

| Figure 16.2 | Pile Sort Data for One Person for 18 Fruits |

1. Apple	7. Watermelon	13. Grapefruit
2. Orange	8. Pineapple	14. Plum
3. Papaya	9. Pear	15. Banana
4. Mango	10. Strawberry	16. Avocado
5. Peach	11. Lemon	17. Fig
6. Blueberry	12. Cantaloupe	18. Cherry

One Person's Sorting of 18 Fruits

Pile #1: 2, 11, 13

Pile #2: 1, 5, 9, 14, 17, 18

Pile #3: 3, 4, 8, 15, 16

Pile #4: 6, 10

Pile #5: 7, 12

Source: H. R. Bernard and G. W. Ryan, *Analyzing Qualitative Data: Systematic Approaches.* Thousand Oaks, CA: Sage Publications. 2010. p. 173. Used by permission.

Table 16.2 Similarity Matrix from One Person's Pile Sorting of the 18 Fruits

		1 AP	2 OR	3 PA	4 MA	5 PE	6 BL	7 WA	8 PI	9 PE	10 ST	11 LE	12 CA	13 GR	14 PL	15 BA	16 AV	17 FI	18 CH
1	Apple	1	0	0	0	1	0	0	0	1	0	0	0	0	1	0	0	1	1
2	Orange	0	1	0	0	0	0	0	0	0	0	1	0	1	0	0	0	0	0
3	Papaya	0	0	1	1	0	0	0	1	0	0	0	0	0	0	1	1	0	0
4	Mango	0	0	1	1	0	0	0	1	0	0	0	0	0	0	1	1	0	0
5	Peach	1	0	0	0	1	0	0	0	1	0	0	0	0	1	0	0	1	1
6	Blueberry	0	0	0	0	0	1	0	0	0	1	0	0	0	0	0	0	0	0
7	Watermelon	0	0	0	0	0	0	1	0	0	0	0	1	0	0	0	0	0	0
8	Pineapple	0	0	1	1	0	0	0	1	0	0	0	0	0	0	1	1	0	0
9	Pear	1	0	0	0	1	0	0	0	1	0	0	0	0	1	0	0	1	1
10	Strawberry	0	0	0	0	0	1	0	0	0	1	0	0	0	0	0	0	0	0
11	Lemon	0	1	0	0	0	0	0	0	0	0	1	0	1	0	0	0	0	0
12	Canteloupe	0	0	0	0	0	0	1	0	0	0	0	1	0	0	0	0	0	0
13	Grapefruit	0	1	0	0	0	0	0	0	0	0	1	0	1	0	0	0	0	0
14	Plum	1	0	0	0	1	0	0	0	1	0	0	0	0	1	0	0	1	1
15	Banana	0	0	1	1	0	0	0	1	0	0	0	0	0	0	1	1	0	0
16	Avocado	0	0	1	1	0	0	0	1	0	0	0	0	0	0	1	1	0	0
17	Fig	1	0	0	0	1	0	0	0	1	0	0	0	0	1	0	0	1	1
18	Cherry	1	0	0	0	1	0	0	0	1	0	0	0	0	1	0	0	1	1

similarity of a pair of items (for this inform-ant) and 1s down the diagonal (since items are similar to themselves). Notice that if 11 is similar to 13, then 13 is similar to 11, so

this particular matrix is also symmetric. In a symmetric matrix, the bottom and top halves (above and below the diagonal of 1s) are identical (Box 16.1).

Box 16.1 Getting pile-sort data into a computer

Anthropac is a DOS program, so it takes some learning of commands, but it's still the easiest way I know to import pile sort data into a computer for analysis. Once you have pile sort data into a computer, you can use any major statistical package to analyze the matrices. I use Ucinet, a Windows program, because it shares files with Anthropac. Any data you import with Anthropac is available to Ucinet for analysis. Ucinet also can export data as an Excel® file, so you can use the data in your favorite statistics program.

MULTIDIMENSIONAL SCALING

If you examine it carefully, you'll see that, despite the 1s and 0s, there is not a shred of math in Table 16.2. It contains nothing more than the information in the bottom half of Figure 16.2, displayed as 1s and 0s, and there is nothing numerical about those 1s and 0s. They simply stand for oranges and papayas and so on. But by substituting 1s and 0s for the names of the items, we can use a computer to look for patterns in the informant's pile sort data.

Figure 16.3 is a multidimensional scaling, or MDS, of these data. MDS is one of several visualizations methods now widely used in all

the sciences—methods that look for patterns in numerical data and display those patterns graphically. The MDS in Figure 16.3 shows the pattern in Table 16.2. That is, it shows how one informant sees the similarities among the 18 fruits.

Look carefully at Table 16.2. There are 1s in the cells 2-11, 2-13, and 11-13. This is because the informant put orange (2), lemon (11), and grapefruit (13) in one pile and noth-ing else in that pile. This behavior is presented graphically in Figure 16.3 with the orange-lemon-grapefruit cluster shown separated from other clusters. (And notice that, since Table 16.2 is a symmetric similarity matrix, there are 1s in cells 11-2, 13-2, and 13-11.) (For more on pile sorts, see the **Further Reading** section in Chapter 10.) (Box 16.2).

Box 16.2 MDS scaling is everywhere

Multidimensional scaling was developed by psychologists and anthropologists (Kruskal and Wish 1978; Romney et al. 1972; Shepard 1966), but it was quickly picked up in marketing research (P. E. Green and Carmone 1970), criminology (Sherman and Dowdle 1974), political science (Rabinowitz 1975), and many other fields. Today, MDS is used across the social sci-ences and in the biological and physical sciences as well (**Further Reading:** multidimen-sional scaling).

Figure 16.3 Two-Dimensional MDS for 18 Fruits Sorted by One Informant

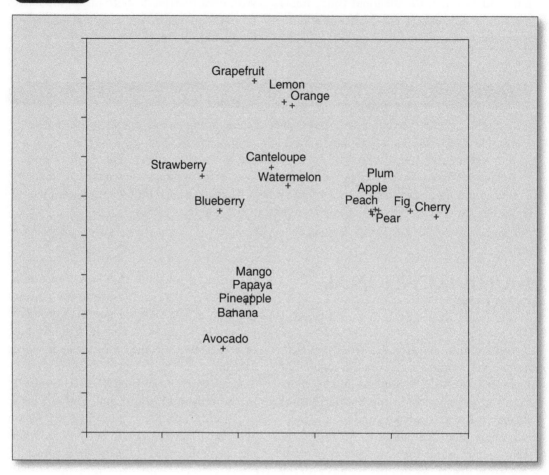

How MDS Works

You'll sometimes see multidimensional scaling called smallest-space analysis. That's because MDS programs work out the best spatial representation of a set of objects that are represented by a set of similarities. Suppose, for example, that you measure the distance, in miles, among three cities, A, B, and C. The matrix for these cities is in the inside box of Table 16.3.

Table 16.3 Distances Among Four Cities

	A	B	C	D
A	X	50	40	110
B		X	80	45
C			X	115
D				X

Figure 16.4 Two-Dimensional Plot of the Distance Among Three Cities (a) and Among Four Cities (b)

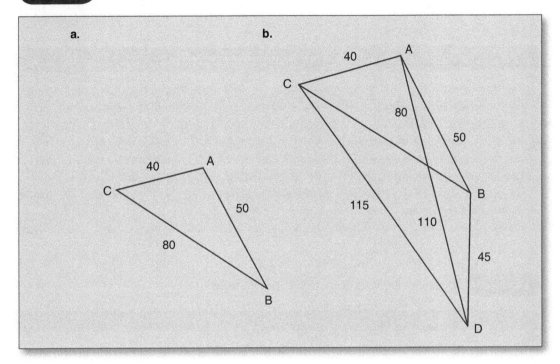

Clearly, cities A and C are closer to one another than are A and B, or B and C. You can represent this with a triangle, as in Figure 16.4a.

In other words, we can place points A, B, and C on a plane in some position relative to each other. The distance between A and B is longer than that between A and C (reflecting the difference between 50 and 80 miles); and the distance between B and C is longer than that between A and C (reflecting the difference between 40 and 80 miles).

A rule in graph theory says that you can plot the relations among any set of relations in $n - 1$ dimensions, where n is the number relations. With three cities, there are three relations: AB, AC, and BC, so it's easy to plot all the distances in proper proportion to one another in a two-dimensional graph. In fact, Figure 16.4a contains precisely the same information as the inside box of Table 16.3, but in graphic form. You can see in Figure 16.4a that

the physical distance (in inches) between B and C is twice that of A and C.

If we add a fourth city, things get considerably more complicated. With four items, there are six relations to cope with: AB, AC, AD, BC, BD, and CD. These relations are shown in the complete set of numbers in Table 16.3. We can plot the relations among these six pairs perfectly in a graph of $n - 1 = 5$ dimensions, but what would we do with a five-dimensional graph? Instead, we try two dimensions and see if the distortion is acceptable.

MDS programs produce a statistic that measures this distortion, or stress, as it's called, which tells us how far off the graph is from one that would be perfectly proportional. The lower the stress, the better the solution. Table 16.4 shows the road distance, in miles, between all pairs of nine cities in the United States. Most researchers will accept a stress of ≤0.15 (read: equal to or less than 0.15) in an MDS graph. The MDS graph produced from the set of relations in Table 16.4, and shown in Figure 16.5, has a stress of close to zero because

Table 16.4 contains metric data—reasonably accurate measures of a physical reality. In this case, it's distance between points on a map (Box 16.3).

Box 16.3 Two kinds of proximities

The numbers in Table 16.4 are dissimilarities, not similarities. Recall from Chapter 15 that in a **similarity matrix**, bigger numbers mean that pairs of things are closer to each other—more like each other—and smaller numbers mean that things are farther apart—less like each other. In a **dissimilarity matrix**, bigger numbers means that pairs of things are farther apart—less like each other—and smaller numbers mean that things are closer to each other—more like each other. (Recall from Chapter 15 that similarity and dissimilarity matrices are called, collectively, **proximity matrices** because they tell you how close or far apart things are.)

Table 16.4 Distances Between Nine U.S. Cities (in miles)

	BOS	NY	DC	MIA	CHI	SEA	SF	LA	DEN
Boston	0								
NY	206	0							
DC	429	233	0						
Miami	1504	1308	1075	0					
Chicago	963	802	671	1329	0				
Seattle	2976	2815	2684	3273	2013	0			
SF	3095	2934	2799	3053	2142	808	0		
LA	2979	2786	2631	2687	2054	1131	379	0	
Denver	1949	1771	1616	2037	996	1037	1235	1059	0

Source: AnthroPac 4.0 and AnthroPac 4.0 Methods Guide, by S. P. Borgatti, 1992a, 1992b.

Figure 16.5 looks suspiciously like a map of the United States. All nine cities are placed in proper juxtaposition to one another, but the map looks sort of upside-down and backward. If we could only flip the map over from left to right and from bottom to top. . . .

Multidimensional scaling programs are notoriously unconcerned with details like this. So long as they get the juxtaposition right, they're finished. Figure 16.5 shows that the program got it right. (Obviously, you can rotate any MDS graph through some angle

about any axis and it will still have the same meaning. Think about a map of the surface of the Earth from the perspective of someone who is looking out from 100 miles inside the Earth. It would be the same map that you're accustomed to, but flipped.)

This means that you can use MDS to create outline maps of your own. To make a map to scale of a classroom, for example, you would measure the distance between all pairs of some set of points, like the teacher's desk, the door, the closet, one or more windows, and so on. A

Figure 16.5 Two-Dimensional MDS Solution for the Numbers in Table 16.4

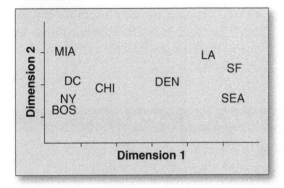

(and 36 measurements) gets you a basic outline map of the United States.

Interpreting MDS Graphs

It's convenient to think of the MDS graph in Figure 16.3 as a sort of mental map. That is, it represents what the informant was thinking when he pile sorted those fruits. I say "sort of mental map" because MDS graphs of pile-sort data are not one-to-one maps of what's going on inside people's heads. We treat them, however, as a rough proxy for what people were thinking when they made piles of cards or words or whatever.

Looking at Figure 16.3, it looks like there's a citrus cluster, a berry cluster, a melon cluster, a fruit tree cluster, and a tropical cluster. We can check our intuition about these clusters by running a cluster analysis, shown in Figure 16.6.

Read Figure 16.6 as follows: At the first level of clustering, the informant put #7

set of 10 points means 45 pairs and 45 measurements. The more pairs of points you measure the more accurate the map will be—that is, the more correctly the points will be placed in relation to one another—but, as you can see from Figure 16.5, even a set of nine points

Figure 16.6 Cluster Analysis of 18 Fruits From One Pile Sort

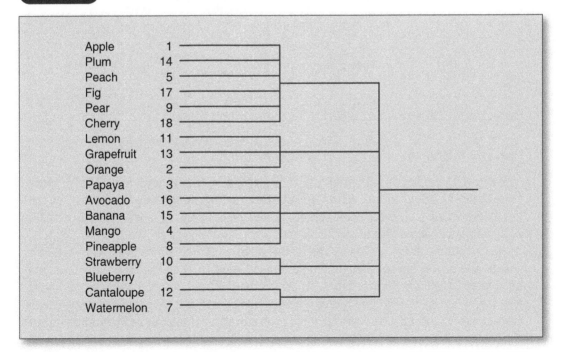

Source: H. R. Bernard and G. W. Ryan, *Analyzing Qualitative Data: Systematic Approaches.* Thousand Oaks, CA: Sage Publications. 2010. p. 177.

(watermelon) and #12 (cantaloupe) together, and he put #6 (blueberry) and #10 (strawberry) together. These two clusters together form a cluster at the second level. And the same goes for the other clusters: They come together at the second level and all form one big cluster.

Because there is just one informant, there can only be two levels. The first level is the level at which the informant made the separate piles. The second is the entire set of fruits. I've taken you what looks like a trivial exercise to show you how to read the cluster diagram (or dendrogram) and the MDS picture. As we'll see next, things get more interesting when we add informants (Box 16.4).

Box 16.4 Dimensions and clusters in MDS

Susan Weller (1983) asked 24 Guatemalan women—some urban, some rural—to do a pile sort of 27 illness names. Figure 16.7 shows the MDS graph of the illnesses for Weller's urban sample.

Figure 16.7 MDS Representation of 27 Illnesses for Urban Guatemalan Women

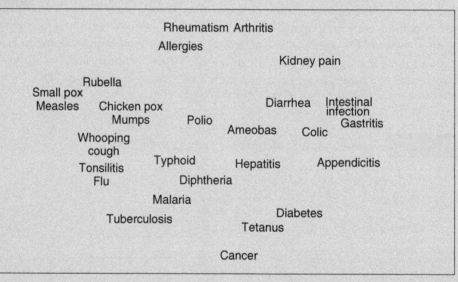

Source: S. Weller, "New Data on Intracultural Variability: The Hot-Cold Concept of Medicine and Illness," *Human Organization,* Vol. 42, pp. 249–257. © 1983.

When you interpret an MDS graph, look for **arrays** or **dimensions** as well as for **clusters**. There is a clump on the right that might be called "gastrointestinal disorders." On the left there is a clump of "childhood disorders." Those, at least, are the labels that struck Weller as appropriate. I agree with her intuition about this. What do *you* think?

How about the arrays or dimensions? To me, it looks like informants distinguish between chronic and acute illnesses (from top to bottom in Figure 16.7) and between infectious and noninfectious illnesses (from left to right). But remember: Interpretation of numerical results is always a brazen, flat-out qualitative exercise, a Rorschach test for social scientists—which is why I like it so much. Use every technique you can think of in data analysis, and let your experience guide your interpretation. Interpretation of results is where data analysis in all science ultimately becomes a humanistic activity.

ANALYZING PILE SORT DATA: AGGREGATE MATRICES

To test whether this pattern holds up, Ryan and I asked five more informants to do the pile sort exercise (Bernard and Ryan 2010:179). Each informant's data produce an individual similarity matrix of 1s and 0s, like the matrix shown in Table 16.2. Table 16.5 shows the aggregate similarity matrix for the six informants.

To produce Table 16.5, just stack the six individual matrices on top of one another, count the number of 1s down the column for each cell, and divide by six. (This is all done instantly with a computer program, like Anthropac or Ucinet). That tells you the percentage of people who put each pair of fruits together in a pile. Because there are six informants here, the numbers in the cells of Table 16.5 can be 0.00 (none out of six), 0.17 (one out of six), 0.33 (two out of six), 0.50 (three out of six), 0.67 (four out of six), 0.83 (five out of six), and 1.00 (six out of six).

For example, reading across the top row in Table 16.5, we see that five out of six informants (83%) put apple and pear in the same pile. Reading across the third row, we see that four out of six people (67%) put papaya and mango in the same pile. And so on. Just like Table 16.2, Table 16.5 is symmetric (check it and see for yourself).

CLUSTER ANALYSIS

Figure 16.8 shows the MDS plot of the data in Table 16.5. It looks pretty much like Figure 16.3, but there are some differences. Averaging across the six informants, figs and cherries now appear to be in a separate cluster and to be a bridge between the berry group (strawberries and blueberries) and the major tree-fruit group (apples, plums, peaches, and pears). Furthermore, banana, which was in the tropical fruit cluster for our first informant, now appears to be a bridge between the tropical fruit cluster (mangos, papayas, pineapples, and avocados) and the traditional tree fruit cluster (apples, plums, peaches, and pears) (Box 16.5).

Box 16.5 Clusters and bridges

What does it mean to say that "figs and cherries appear to be a bridge between the berry group and major tree-fruit group" or that "banana appears to be a bridge between tropical fruits and traditional tree fruits"?

When we interviewed people about why they put various fruits together, some people who put figs and cherries with apples and pears said "These all grow on trees." People who put figs and/or cherries into other piles said things like "Figs are more exotic, but not like mangoes" or "Cherries grow on trees, but they are small and clumpy." Some informants said that banana was a tropical fruit and "went with papaya," but others said it was unique and belonged in a group by itself. One person said it belonged with apples and pears "because you can mix them together to make fruit salad."

Always ask people to explain their pile choices. Later, when you see figs and cherries in an MDS graph lying between a berries cluster and traditional tree-fruit cluster, you'll have some basis for interpreting the graph.

Table 16.5 Aggregate Similarity Matrix From Six Pile Sorts of the 18 Fruits in Figure 16.2

	ap	or	Pap	Man	pea	blu	wat	pin	per	str	lem	can	gpf	plu	ban	avc	fig	chr
Apple	1.00	0.00	0.00	0.00	0.83	0.00	0.17	0.00	0.83	0.00	0.00	0.00	0.00	0.83	0.17	0.00	0.17	0.33
Orange	0.00	1.00	0.17	0.17	0.00	0.00	0.17	0.17	0.00	0.00	0.83	0.17	1.00	0.00	0.00	0.17	0.00	0.00
Papaya	0.00	0.17	1.00	0.67	0.17	0.00	0.17	0.50	0.17	0.00	0.00	0.17	0.17	0.17	0.33	0.67	0.17	0.00
Mango	0.00	0.17	0.67	1.00	0.00	0.00	0.17	0.50	0.00	0.00	0.00	0.33	0.17	0.00	0.33	0.67	0.00	0.00
Peach	0.83	0.00	0.17	0.00	1.00	0.00	0.00	0.00	1.00	0.00	0.00	0.00	0.00	1.00	0.17	0.17	0.17	0.33
Blueberry	0.00	0.00	0.00	0.00	0.00	1.00	0.00	0.00	0.00	0.83	0.00	0.00	0.00	0.00	0.00	0.00	0.50	0.67
Watermelon	0.17	0.17	0.17	0.17	0.00	0.00	1.00	0.17	0.00	0.00	0.00	0.83	0.17	0.00	0.00	0.17	0.00	0.00
Pineapple	0.00	0.17	0.50	0.50	0.00	0.00	0.17	1.00	0.00	0.00	0.00	0.17	0.17	0.00	0.50	0.50	0.00	0.00
Pear	0.83	0.00	0.17	0.00	1.00	0.00	0.00	0.00	1.00	0.00	0.00	0.00	0.00	1.00	0.17	0.17	0.17	0.33
Strawberry	0.00	0.00	0.00	0.00	0.00	0.83	0.00	0.00	0.00	1.00	0.00	0.00	0.00	0.00	0.00	0.00	0.50	0.50
Lemon	0.00	0.83	0.00	0.00	0.00	0.00	0.00	0.00	0.00	0.00	1.00	0.00	0.83	0.00	0.00	0.00	0.00	0.00
Cantaloupe	0.00	0.17	0.17	0.33	0.00	0.00	0.83	0.17	0.00	0.00	0.00	1.00	0.17	0.00	0.00	0.17	0.00	0.00
Grapefruit	0.00	1.00	0.17	0.17	0.00	0.00	0.17	0.17	0.00	0.00	0.83	0.17	1.00	0.00	0.00	0.17	0.00	0.00
Plum	0.83	0.00	0.17	0.00	1.00	0.00	0.00	0.00	1.00	0.00	0.00	0.00	0.00	1.00	0.17	0.17	0.17	0.33
Banana	0.17	0.00	0.33	0.33	0.17	0.00	0.00	0.50	0.17	0.00	0.00	0.00	0.00	0.17	1.00	0.33	0.00	0.00
Avocado	0.00	0.17	0.67	0.67	0.17	0.00	0.17	0.50	0.17	0.00	0.00	0.17	0.17	0.17	0.33	1.00	0.00	0.00
Fig	0.17	0.00	0.00	0.00	0.17	0.50	0.00	0.00	0.17	0.50	0.00	0.00	0.00	0.17	0.00	0.00	1.00	0.50
Cherry	0.33	0.00	0.00	0.00	0.33	0.67	0.00	0.00	0.33	0.50	0.00	0.00	0.00	0.33	0.00	0.00	0.50	1.00

Source: H. R. Bernard and G. W. Ryan, *Analyzing Qualitative Data: Systematic Approaches.* Thousand Oaks, CA: Sage Publications. 2010. p. 179.

Figure 16.8 Multidimensional Scaling of the Data in Table 16.5

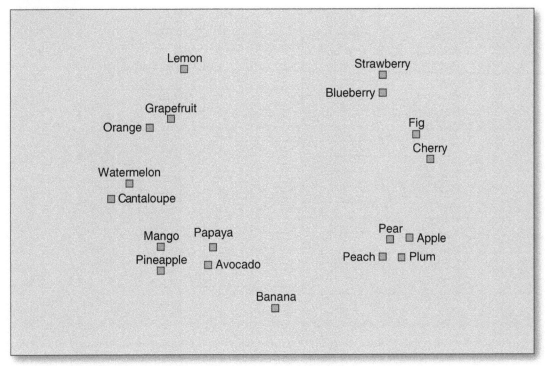

Source: H. R. Bernard and G. W. Ryan, *Analyzing Qualitative Data: Systematic Approaches*. Thousand Oaks, CA: Sage Publications. 2010. p. 181.

The cluster analysis on the data in Table 16.5 is shown in Figure 16.9. It confirms that, despite some expected intracultural variation, these informants saw cherries and figs as related to strawberries and blueberries and saw all four of these fruits as more closely related to apples, plums, peaches, and pears than to all the other fruits.

How Cluster Analysis Works

Consider the following example from de Ghett (1978:121):

1   3   7   9   14   20   21   25

This set of numbers has no meaning at all, so we can concentrate on the method of clustering them, without any interpretation getting in the way. When we get through with this example, we'll move on to a set of numbers that does have meaning. The distance between 1 and 3 is 2. The distance between 21 and 25 is 4. So, in a numerical sense, 1 and 3 are twice as similar to one another as 21 and 25 are to one another. Table 16.6 shows the dissimilarity matrix for these numbers.

There are several ways to find clusters in this matrix. Two of them are called single-link or closest-neighbor analysis and complete-link or farthest-neighbor analysis (there are others, but I won't go into them here). In single-link clustering, we use only the numbers adjacent to the diagonal: 2, 4, 2, 5, 6, 1, 4. The two clustering solutions (done with Ucinet) are shown in Figure 16.10.

In the single-link solution, the two closest neighbors are 20 and 21. They are exactly one

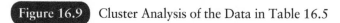

Figure 16.9 Cluster Analysis of the Data in Table 16.5

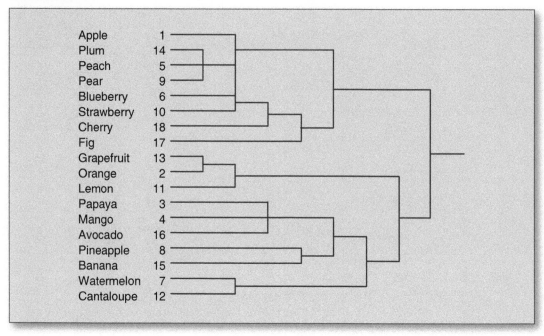

Source: H. R. Bernard and G. W. Ryan, *Analyzing Qualitative Data: Systematic Approaches.* Thousand Oaks, CA: Sage Publications. 2010. p. 182.

Table 16.6 Dissimilarity Matrix for Clustering

	1	3	7	9	14	20	21	25
1	0							
3	2	0						
7	6	4	0					
9	8	6	2	0				
14	13	11	7	5	0			
20	19	17	13	11	6	0		
21	20	18	14	12	7	1	0	
25	24	22	18	16	11	5	4	0

Source: J. V. de Ghett, "Hierarchical Cluster Analysis." In *Quantitative Ethology*, ed. by P. W. Colgan, 1978, Wiley.

unit of distance apart, and there is a 1 adjacent to the diagonal of the original matrix where 20 and 21 come together. In Figure 16.10a, 20 and 21 are shown joined at level 1. The numbers 1–3 and the numbers 7–9 are the next closest neighbors. They are both two units

Figure 16.10 | Cluster Analysis of the Data in Table 16.6

a. SINGLE LINK							
Level	1	3	7	9	14	20	21	25
1						×	×	×
2	×	× ×	× ×	×		×	×	×
4	×	× × × × × ×			×	×	× × ×
5	×	× × × × × × ×	×		×	×	× × ×
6	×	× × × × × × × ×	×		× ×	×	× × ×

b. COMPLETE LINK							
Level	1	3	7	9	14	20	21	25
1						×	×	×
2	×	× ×	× ×	× ×		×	×	×
5	×	× ×	× ×	×		×	× × × × ×
7	×	× ×	× × × × ×		×	× × × × ×
13	×	× × × × × ×	× × × × × ×	×	× × ×
24	×	× × × × ×	× × × × × ×	×	× × ×

apart. Figure 16.10a shows them joined at level 2.

Once a pair is joined, it is considered a unit. The pairs 1–3 and 7–9 are joined together at level 4 because they are four units apart (the nearest neighbor to the pair 1–3 is 7, which is four units from 3). The pair 21–25 are also four units apart. However, 20–21 are already joined, so 25 joins this pair at level 4. The connections are built up to form a tree.

Figure 16.10b shows the complete-link (or farthest neighbor) clustering solution for the data in Table 16.6. In complete-link clustering, all the numbers in Table 16.6 are used. Once again, the pair 20–21 is joined at level 1 because the pair is just one unit apart. The pairs 1–3 and 7–9 join at level 2.

At this point, the complete-link and single-link solutions are identical. At the next level, though, things change. The neighbors of 20–21 are 14 and 25. The farthest neighbor from 14 to 20–21 is 21. The distance is seven units. The farthest neighbor from 25 to 20–21 is 20. The distance is five units. Since five is less than seven, 25 joins 20–21 at level 5. But the two pairs 1–3 and 7–9 are not joined at this level.

The only number not yet joined to some other number is 14. It is compared to its farthest neighbors in the adjacent clusters: 14 is 11 units away from 25 (which is now part of the 20–21–25 cluster) and it's seven units away

from the 7–9 cluster. So, at level 7, 14 is joined to 7–9. The same game is played out with all the clusters to form the tree in Figure 16.10b.

Clusters of Cities

The complete-link method tends to create more discrete clusters; the single-link method tends to clump things together more. The method you choose determines the results you get. Look at Figure 16.11a and b to see what happens when we use the single-link and complete link clustering methods on the data in Table 16.6.

To me, the complete-link method seems better with these data. Denver "belongs" with San Francisco and Los Angeles more than it belongs with Boston and New York. But that may be my own bias. Coming from New York, I think of Denver as a western U.S. city, but I've heard people from San Francisco talk about "going *back east* to Denver for the weekend" (**Further Reading:** cluster analysis).

Green Behavior and Electric Cars in the United States

OK, now that you know how MDS and cluster analysis work, here's an example from some research. In the mid-1990s, under a contract

Figure 16.11   Complete Link and Single Link Solutions for the Data in Table 16.4

```
a. SINGLE LINK
              S                       C
              E           B           H   D
      M       A           O           I   E
      I       T           S           C   N
      A       T           T           A   V
      M   L   S   L       O   N   D   G   E
Level I   E   F   A       N   Y   C   O   R
 206                    × × ×
 233                    × × × × ×
 379          × × ×     × × × × ×
 671            × × ×     × × × × × × × ×
 808      × × × × ×     × × × × × × × ×
 996      × × × × ×     × × × × × × × × × ×
1037      × × × × × × × × × × × × × × × × ×
1075  × × × × × × × × × × × × × × × × × × ×
```

```
b. COMPLETE LINK
                      C   S
              B       H   E           D
      M       O       I   A           E
      I       S       C   T           N
      A       T       A   T           V
      M       O   N   D   G   L   S   L   E
Level I       N   Y   C   O   E   F   A   R
 206      × × ×
 379      × × ×           × × ×
 429      × × × × ×       × × ×
 963      × × × × × × ×   × × ×
1037      × × × × × × ×   × × × × ×
1235      × × × × × × ×   × × × × × × ×
1504  × × × × × × × × ×   × × × × × × ×
3273  × × × × × × × × × × × × × × × × × × ×
```

from a U.S. automobile manufacturer, Gery Ryan, Steve Borgatti, and I studied the domain of green behaviors in the United States—that is, things people believe they can do to help the environment (Bernard et al. 2009). Using free lists, we generated 85 "things people can to do help the environment" Then, 44 people pile-sorted those 85 items. This produced an aggregate, 85×85 similarity matrix of the items.

Figure 16.12 shows the MDS for that matrix. With all the labels for the behaviors, it's hard to see the pattern, but if we cut the labels down to three- and four-letter abbreviations and superimpose the results of a cluster analysis (Figure 16.13), a strong pattern emerges.

MDS and cluster analysis *display* clusters but researchers *name* them. We named the five clusters of green behaviors in Figure 16.13 "household," "lawn and garden," "recycling," "advocacy," and "transportation." I said earlier that you can insert items into a domain analysis even if nobody mentions it in free lists.

See the label "Elec" in the transportation cluster? It stands for "buy an electric car." When we did this research, in 1996, electric and hybrid cars were still in the design stage. Our client wanted to know where Americans might place the behavior of "buying an electric car" within the domain of green behaviors, so we stuck that item into the pile sort task of the study, even though none of our informants mentioned this behavior in the free list of "things people can do for the environment."

ANALYZING TRIAD DATA

Triad tests produce similarity matrices and these can also be analyzed using MDS and clustering. When you finish reading this section, you should have a better understanding of how MDS works on a matrix of similarities or dissimilarities.

Figure 16.12 MDS of 85 Green Behaviors

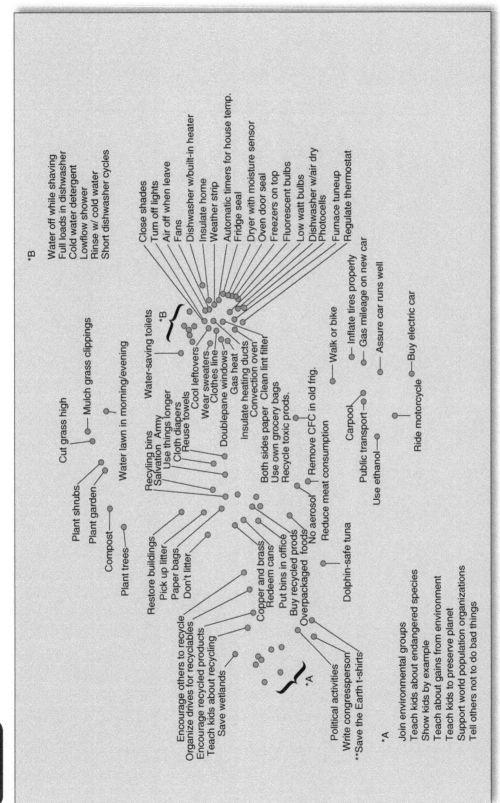

Source: H. R. Bernard et al. "Green Cognition and Behavior: A Cultural Domain Analysis." In *Networks, Resources and Economic Action. Ethnographic Case Studies in Honor of Hartmut Lang,* Dietrich Reimer Verlag, 2009.

Figure 16.13 MDS of 85 Green Behaviors

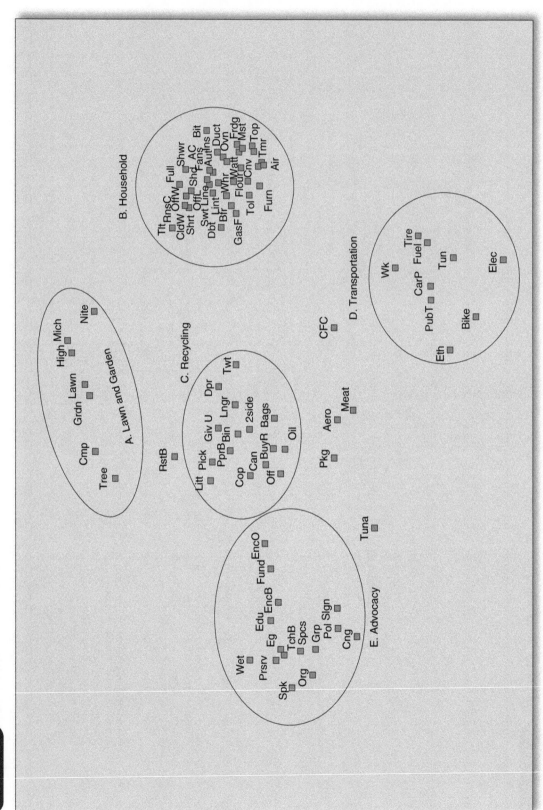

Source: H. R. Bernard et al. "Green Cognition and Behavior: A Cultural Domain Analysis." In *Networks, Resources and Economic Action. Ethnographic Case Studies in Honor of Hartmut Lang,* Dietrich Reimer Verlag, 2009.

Recall from Chapter 10 how triad tests work. Figure 16.14 shows the instructions and first 10 lines of a typical triad test. In this case, the domain is a list of 15 emotions: love, anger, disgust, shame, fear, anguish, envy, anxious, tired, happy, sad, lonely, bored, hate, and excitement. The data come from a class project where we interviewed 40 people and used a lambda-2 design. In a complete design with 15 items, there are $n(n-1)$ $(n-2)/6 = 455$ triads, but that's because every pair of items shows up $(n-2) = 13$ times. Using a lambda-2, balanced incomplete block design (see Chapter 10 for details on these), each pair of items shows up twice and this cuts the number of triads down to just 70. Since each pair of items shows up twice, each cell in the item-by-item similarity matrix for each informant can contain just three numbers: 0.00, 0.50, or 1.00.

Figure 16.15 shows the individual similarity matrices from two informants who took the

Figure 16.14 Instructions for a Triad Test

Thank you for participating in this study. On the next page, you will find a set of three words on each line. For each set, please mark the item that is MOST DIFFERENT from the other two. For example, for the set

CHERRY	APPLE	DOG

you would circle DOG, since cherries and apples are very similar, at least when compared to dogs. Here is another example:

DOG	CAT	ROCK

In this case, you would probably circle ROCK. Please give an answer for EVERY set of three, even if you are not sure of the answer. DO NOT SKIP ANY SETS: if you don't know the answer, just guess. Thank you.

[PUT THE ACTUAL TEST ON A SEPARATE PAGE FROM THE INSTRUCTIONS]

ANGER	SAD	ENVY
BORED	ANGUISH	SAD
LONELY	FEAR	ENVY
SAD	LOVE	ANGUISH
ANXIOUS	HATE	HAPPY
TIRED	ANXIOUS	BORED
HATE	LOVE	ANGUISH
ANGER	LOVE	HAPPY
FEAR	LOVE	ANXIOUS
TIRED	HAPPY	LONELY

Figure 16.15 Two Matrices From a Triad Test

Matrix #1:		1	2	3	4	5	6	7	8	9	10	11	12	13	14	15
		LOVE	ANGR	DISG	SHAM	FEAR	ANGU	ENVY	ANXI	TIRE	HAPP	SAD	LONE	BORE	HATE	EXCI
1	LOVE	0.00	0.00	0.00	0.00	0.50	0.00	0.00	0.00	0.00	1.00	0.00	0.00	0.00	0.50	1.00
2	ANGER	0.00	0.00	1.00	0.00	0.50	0.50	0.00	0.50	0.00	0.00	0.00	0.00	0.00	1.00	0.00
3	DISGUST	0.00	1.00	0.00	1.00	1.00	1.00	0.50	1.00	0.00	0.00	0.50	0.50	0.00	1.00	0.00
4	SHAME	0.00	0.00	1.00	0.00	0.50	1.00	1.00	0.00	0.00	0.00	0.00	0.50	0.00	0.50	0.00
5	FEAR	0.50	0.50	1.00	0.50	0.00	0.50	1.00	1.00	0.00	0.00	0.00	0.50	0.00	1.00	0.00
6	ANGUISH	0.00	0.50	1.00	1.00	0.50	0.00	1.00	1.00	0.00	0.00	1.00	0.00	0.00	0.50	0.00
7	ENVY	0.00	0.00	0.50	1.00	1.00	1.00	0.00	0.50	0.00	0.00	0.50	0.50	0.50	0.50	0.00
8	ANXIOUS	0.00	0.50	1.00	0.00	1.00	1.00	0.50	0.00	0.00	0.00	0.00	0.00	0.00	0.00	0.50
9	TIRED	0.00	0.00	0.00	1.00	0.00	0.00	0.00	0.00	0.00	0.00	1.00	0.50	1.00	0.00	0.00
10	HAPPY	1.00	0.00	0.00	0.00	0.00	0.00	0.00	0.00	0.00	0.00	0.50	0.00	0.00	0.50	1.00
11	SAD	0.00	0.00	0.50	0.00	0.00	1.00	0.50	0.00	1.00	0.50	0.00	1.00	0.50	0.00	0.00
12	LONELY	0.00	0.00	0.00	0.50	0.50	0.00	0.50	0.00	0.50	0.00	1.00	0.00	0.50	0.00	0.00
13	BORED	0.00	0.00	0.00	0.00	0.00	0.00	0.50	0.00	1.00	0.00	0.50	0.50	0.00	0.00	0.50
14	HATE	0.50	1.00	1.00	0.50	1.00	0.50	0.00	0.00	0.00	0.50	0.50	0.00	0.00	0.00	0.00
15	EXCITEMENT	1.00	0.00	0.00	0.00	0.00	0.00	0.00	0.50	0.00	1.00	0.00	0.00	0.50	0.00	0.00

		1	2	3	4	5	6	7	8	9	10	11	12	13	14	15
		LOVE	ANGR	DISG	SHAM	FEAR	ANGU	ENVY	ANXI	TIRE	HAPP	SAD	LONE	BORE	HATE	EXCI
1	LOVE	0.00	0.00	0.00	0.00	0.00	0.00	0.50	0.00	0.00	1.00	0.00	0.00	0.00	1.00	1.00
2	ANGER	0.00	0.00	1.00	0.00	1.00	0.50	1.00	0.50	0.00	0.00	0.00	0.00	0.00	1.00	0.00
3	DISGUST	0.00	1.00	0.00	1.00	1.00	1.00	1.00	1.00	0.00	0.00	0.50	0.00	0.00	0.50	0.00
4	SHAME	0.00	0.00	1.00	0.00	0.00	0.50	0.00	1.00	1.00	0.00	1.00	0.50	0.00	0.50	0.00
5	FEAR	0.00	1.00	1.00	0.00	0.00	1.00	1.00	0.50	0.00	0.00	0.50	0.00	0.00	1.00	0.00
6	ANGUISH	0.00	0.50	1.00	0.50	1.00	0.00	1.00	1.00	0.00	0.00	1.00	0.00	0.00	0.50	0.00
7	ENVY	0.50	1.00	1.00	0.00	1.00	1.00	0.00	0.50	0.00	0.00	0.00	0.50	0.00	0.50	0.00
8	ANXIOUS	0.00	0.50	1.00	1.00	0.50	1.00	0.50	0.00	0.50	0.00	0.50	0.00	0.00	0.50	0.50
9	TIRED	0.00	0.00	0.00	1.00	0.00	0.00	0.00	0.00	0.00	0.00	1.00	0.50	0.50	0.00	0.00
10	HAPPY	1.00	0.00	0.00	0.00	0.00	0.00	0.00	0.00	0.00	0.00	0.00	0.00	0.00	0.00	1.00
11	SAD	0.00	0.00	0.50	1.00	0.50	1.00	0.00	0.50	1.00	0.00	0.00	1.00	0.00	0.00	0.00
12	LONELY	0.00	0.00	0.00	0.00	0.50	0.00	0.50	0.00	0.50	0.00	1.00	0.00	0.50	0.00	0.00
13	BORED	0.00	0.00	0.00	0.00	0.00	0.00	0.00	0.00	0.50	0.00	0.00	0.50	0.00	0.00	0.00
14	HATE	1.00	1.00	0.50	0.50	1.00	0.50	0.50	0.50	0.00	0.00	0.00	0.00	0.00	0.00	0.50
15	EXCITEMENT	1.00	0.00	0.00	0.00	0.00	0.00	0.00	0.50	0.00	1.00	0.00	0.00	0.00	0.50	0.00

triad test about emotions. Looking across the first row of Matrix #1, we see a 0.00 in the first cell for love-love, and then zeros down the diagonal since the matrix is symmetric. Next, we see that both times the informant saw the pair love-anger, she circled one of them, making the other member of the love-anger pair similar to the third item in that triad.

The same thing happened for love-disgust and love-shame. When she saw the pair love-fear, though, she circled one of them once and she circled the third item in the triad once. That is, half the time she kept the pair together (as similar) and half the time she kept them apart (as dissimilar, compared to a third item), so there's a 0.50 in that cell. She did the same thing for love-hate. She kept the pairs love-happy and love-excitement together both times they showed up in the triad test, and we see 1.00 in those cells.

Compare this to informant #2. He also kept the love-happy and love-excitement pairs together both times they show up in his triad test, but he never kept love-fear together; he kept love-envy together once; and he kept love-hate together twice.

To aggregate the 40 individual matrices from this triad test, we stack them on top of each other, sum down each cell and divide by 40 to get an average similarity for each pair of items. Figure 16.16 shows this aggregate similarity matrix.

Reading across the first line, we see that 82% of the time, these 40 informants put love and happy together but they put love and bored together only 8% of the time. Reading down the second column, we see that informants put hate and anger together 95% of the time but never put anger and tired together.

Figure 16.17 shows the multidimensional scaling, in two dimensions, for the aggregate similarity matrix in Figure 16.16.

Moore et al. (1999) studied these same emotions, using a triad test, in Japanese speakers, Chinese speakers, and American English speakers. Figure 16.18 shows the shared model for these emotion terms in all three languages. (Moore et al. used correspondence analysis to produce the display in Figure 16.18. Correspondence analysis is another method for visualizing relations among sets of items.) Naturally, there is some part of the model that is unique to each language and some part that is unique to each individual. But what stands out to me is the overlap—the sharing of the model in Figures 16.17 and 16.18. Using triad tests, pile sorts, and other systematic methods lets you make these kinds of comparisons (For more on triad tests, see **Further Reading** in Chapter 10).

ANALYZING SENTENCE FRAMES

James Young and Linda Garro (1994 [1981]) studied illness beliefs and illness behaviors in two communities in Mexico. In the 1970s, when Young and Garro did their work there, the people of Uricho had good access to Western medicine—good roads, nearby clinics with medical staff, etc.—and the people of Pichátaro had little access. In fact, the people of Pichátaro went to Western doctors half as much as did the people of Uricho. Young and Garro wanted to test whether this difference in behavior was reflected in a different set of beliefs about the causes and symptoms of illness.

One of the methods they used for this test was **frame substitution**, or item-by-feature matrices. Tables 16.7 and 16.8 show the illnesses and sentence frames in their research with 20 respondents. Each respondent was asked 396 (18 x 22) questions: Can dysentery come from anger? (illness 5, frame 1) Does dysentery come from walking about without shoes? (illness 5, frame 19) Can you get fever sores from eating lots of cold things? (illness 17, frame 12) . . . and so on.

Figure 16.16 Aggregate Proximity Matrix for Triads: 40 Informants, 15 Emotions

Aggregate Proximity Matrix		1	2	3	4	5	6	7	8	9	10	11	12	13	14	15
		LOVE	ANGR	DISG	SHAM	FEAR	ANGU	ENVY	ANXI	TIRE	HAPP	SAD	LONE	BORE	HATE	EXCI
1	LOVE	0.00	0.09	0.08	0.21	0.10	0.08	0.35	0.16	0.10	0.82	0.20	0.14	0.08	0.41	0.74
2	ANGER	0.09	0.00	0.85	0.19	0.59	0.64	0.46	0.32	0.00	0.17	0.40	0.09	0.04	0.95	0.11
3	DISGUST	0.08	0.85	0.00	0.76	0.76	0.66	0.55	0.63	0.08	0.08	0.38	0.08	0.14	0.70	0.13
4	SHAME	0.21	0.19	0.76	0.00	0.22	0.75	0.51	0.38	0.57	0.10	0.57	0.39	0.09	0.47	0.06
5	FEAR	0.10	0.59	0.76	0.22	0.00	0.57	0.40	0.71	0.05	0.11	0.55	0.59	0.08	0.86	0.21
6	ANGUISH	0.08	0.64	0.66	0.75	0.57	0.00	0.85	0.47	0.20	0.10	0.70	0.31	0.08	0.69	0.09
7	ENVY	0.35	0.46	0.55	0.51	0.40	0.85	0.00	0.44	0.06	0.08	0.08	0.30	0.28	0.47	0.11
8	ANXIOUS	0.16	0.32	0.63	0.38	0.71	0.47	0.44	0.00	0.16	0.29	0.30	0.17	0.20	0.39	0.40
9	TIRED	0.10	0.00	0.08	0.57	0.05	0.20	0.06	0.16	0.00	0.14	0.63	0.44	0.73	0.04	0.13
10	HAPPY	0.82	0.17	0.08	0.10	0.11	0.10	0.08	0.29	0.14	0.00	0.34	0.09	0.04	0.08	0.85
11	SAD	0.20	0.40	0.38	0.57	0.55	0.70	0.08	0.30	0.63	0.34	0.00	0.71	0.31	0.24	0.19
12	LONELY	0.14	0.09	0.08	0.39	0.59	0.31	0.30	0.17	0.44	0.09	0.71	0.00	0.59	0.06	0.06
13	BORED	0.08	0.04	0.14	0.09	0.08	0.08	0.28	0.20	0.73	0.04	0.31	0.59	0.00	0.14	0.19
14	HATE	0.41	0.95	0.70	0.47	0.86	0.69	0.47	0.39	0.04	0.08	0.24	0.06	0.14	0.00	0.28
15	EXCITEMENT	0.74	0.11	0.13	0.06	0.21	0.09	0.11	0.40	0.13	0.85	0.19	0.06	0.19	0.28	0.00

Figure 16.17 MDS in Two Dimensions of the Data in Figure 16.16

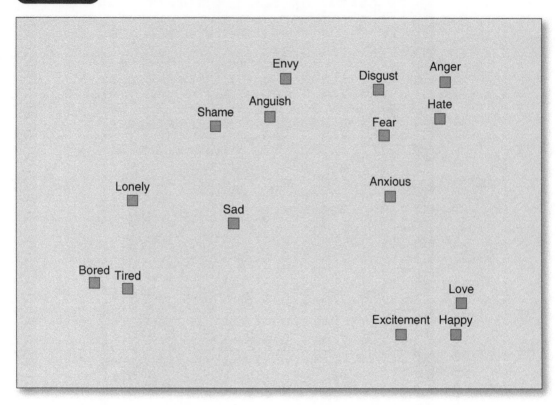

Table 16.9 shows the format for the profile matrix that would result from each person's responses. Each illness could have from 0 to 22 properties (causes or symptoms) and there are 18(17)/2 = 153 pairs of the 18 illnesses. Each time an informant said that a pair of illnesses had the same cause or symptom, that pair of illnesses got a point. There were 20 informants, so each pair of illnesses could have from 0 to (20 × 22) = 440 points.

The MDS for the two 18 x 18 similarity matrices (one for Pichátaro and one for Uricho) that result from all this is shown in Figures 16.19a and 16.19b. The circles indicate the clusters found by cluster analysis of the same data. Recall that any MDS can be rotated 360 degrees in any plane with no loss of information. Bottom line: Young and Garro got the same results

about illness *beliefs* in both villages, even though the people in one village had better access to Western medicine and took advantage of that access (**Further Reading:** frame substitution or item-by-feature matrices).

ANALYZING PAIRED COMPARISONS

Pile sorts, sentence frames, and triad tests all help us understand the semantic structure of items in a cultural domain. We also want to understand how people evaluate the items in a domain on a particular attribute. The most common way to evaluate items on an attribute is with a rating scale, like the one in Figure 16.20. Ratings are

Figure 16.18 A Shared Model of the Semantic Structure of 15 Emotions for Chinese, English, and Japanese

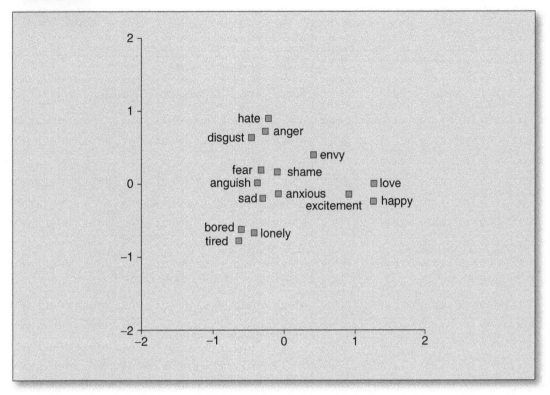

Source: Adapted from A. K. Romney et al. "Cultural Universals: Measuring the Semantic Structure of Emotion Terms in English and Japanese. *PNAS* 94:5489–94, Fig. 1, p. 5490, 1997.

fine when you have lots of items, but they produce a lot of ties because people can give the same rating number to many items. With rank-ordered data, there are no ties: You can only put one item first, one second, and so on. If you have 15 or fewer items in a domain, then try to get rank-ordered data.

One way to do that is to spread a set of cards out on a table, each with the name of an item, and ask people to pick up their top ranked one (most good-natured dog; most scary illness; most difficult musical instrument to play) . . . then the next most, and the next most, and so on. If people have a hard time with this, then paired comparisons is the answer.

In paired comparisons, people put all pairs of items in a list, one pair at a time, and are asked to evaluate each pair, separately, on an attribute. Instead of asking "On a scale of 1 to 5, please rate these emotions on their intensity," we would ask "For each pair of emotions, circle the one that you think has more intensity." For the studies of 15 emotions, there would be

$$n(n-1)/2 = 15(14)/2 = 105$$

pairs: anxious-bored, hate-fear, disgust-excitement, tired-shame, etc., etc.

Each item in a set appears $n-1$ times in the set of all pairs, so in the case of the 15 emotions, informants would see hate, for example, paired with each of the other 14 emotions. This gives each emotion 14 chances to win—to be circled as having

Table 16.7 Illness Terms Used in Term-Frame Interviews

1. *Enfermedad de corazón*	Heart illness
2. *Empacho*	Blocked digestion
3. *Cólico*	Colic, sharp stomach pains
4. *Mollera caida*	Fallen fontanel, displacement of a section of the top of the skull
5. *Disenteria*	Dysentery
6. *Calor subido*	Risen heat
7. *Gripa*	Grippe, cold, flu
8. *Desposiciones*	Diarrhea
9. *Sofoca del estomago*	Bloated stomach
10. *Latido*	Palpitations, brought on by eating delay
11. *Broncomonia*	Bronchopneumonia
12. *Anginas*	Swollen glands in the neck
13. *Bilis*	Bile, illness resulting from a fright or other strong emotional experience
14. *Punzadas*	Sharp headache around the temples
15. *Pulmonio*	Pneumonia
16. *Mal de ojo*	Evil eye; also *eratikua* or *tzitiparata*
17. *Fogazo*	Fever sores
18. *Bronquitis*	Bronchitis

Source: J. C. Young and L. Y. Garro, "Variation in the Choice of Treatment in Two Mexican Communities." *Social Science and Medicine* 16:1453–63, Table 3, 1982.

higher intensity, in this case. The number of times an item wins in this game is its rank order. Ranking data can be analyzed with various statistical methods, *including the cultural consensus model* (For more on paired comparisons, see **Further Reading**, Chapter 10).

CULTURAL CONSENSUS ANALYSIS

Historically, sociologists and anthropologists described cultures in terms of norms—the Navajo are matrilocal, the Yakö practice

Table 16.8 Belief Frames Used in Term-Frame Interviews

1. Can _____ come from anger? (¿Puede venir _____ por un coraje?)

2. Does _____ come from the "heat"? (¿Viene _____ por el calor?)

3. Are there pains in the chest with _____? (¿Hay dolores en el pecho con _____?)

4. When you leave a warm place and enter into the cold air, can you get _____? (¿Cuando sale de un lugar caliente y entra en el aire frio, se puede agarrar _____?)

5. Can you get _____ from eating lots of "hot" things? (¿Se puede agarrar _____ por comer muchas cosas calientes?)

6. Does _____ come from an "air"? (¿Vien _____ por un aire?)

7. With _____ does the head hurt? (¿Con _____ duele la cabeza?)

8. Can you cure _____ with folk remedies? (¿Puede curar _____ con remedios caseros?)

9. Does _____ come from germs? (¿viene _____ por los microbios?)

10. Does _____ come from not eating "by the hours"? (¿Viene _____ por no comer a las horas?)

11. With _____ do you lose your appetite? (¿Con _____ se quita la hambre?)

12. Can you get _____ from eating lots of "cold" things? (¿Se puede agarrar _____ por comer muchas cosas frescas?)

13. With _____ is there a temperature? (¿Con _____ hay calentura?)

14. When you get wet, can you get _____? (¿Cuando se moja uno, se puede agarrar _____?)

15. With _____ is there pain in the stomach? (¿Con _____ hay dolar en el estómago?)

16. Does _____ come from the "cold"? (¿Viene _____ por el frio?)

17. Does _____ come by contagion from other people? (¿Viene _____ por contagio de otras personas?)

18. Can _____ come from witchcraft? (¿Puede venir _____ por la brujeria?)

19. Does _____ come from walking about without shoes? (¿Viene _____ por pisar sin zapatos?)

20. When you have _____ do you have to take "hot" remedies to be cured? (¿Cuando uno tiene _____ tiene que tomar cosas calientes para curarse?)

21. Can you cure _____ with "doctors" remedies? (¿Puede curar _____ con remedies médicos?)

22. Can _____ come from a fright? (¿Puede venir _____ por un susto?)

Note: Spanish frames reflect local usage.

Source: J. C. Young and L. Y. Garro, "Variation in the Choice of Treatment in Two Mexican Communities." *Social Science and Medicine* 16:1453–63, Table 4, 1982.

Table 16.9 Profile Matrix for One Informant's Responses to the 396 Questions in Young and Garro's Test of Illness Beliefs

	1	2	3	4	5	6	7	8	9	10	11	12	13	14	15	16	17	18
1																		
2																		
3																		
4																		
5																		
6																		
7																		
8																		
9																		
10																		
11																		
12																		
13																		
14																		
15																		
16																		
17																		
18																		
19																		
20																		
21																		
22																		

double descent—but a landmark paper in 1975 by Pertti and Gretel Pelto made clear that intracultural variation—based on things like gender, age, economic status, occupational specialization, and so on—was the norm in all societies.

Some cultural knowledge, like the names of the months, is widely shared but much of it is distributed unevenly. We hear, for example, that women know more about fashion than men do in the United States and that men know more about cars than women do. We hear that young people in rural Appalachia aren't learning the names and uses of medicinal plants as

much as their elders did. How can we test if competence in particular cultural domains varies by gender or age?

Cultural consensus analysis gives us a way to measure the extent to which people agree about the contents of a cultural domain—to measure domain-specific cultural competence.

Cultural Competence

Consensus analysis is based on a long and distinguished intellectual history on the power of collective wisdom, going back to a paper by the Marquis de Condorcet (1785) on the probability

Figure 16.19a MDS of Pichátaro Term-Frame Data

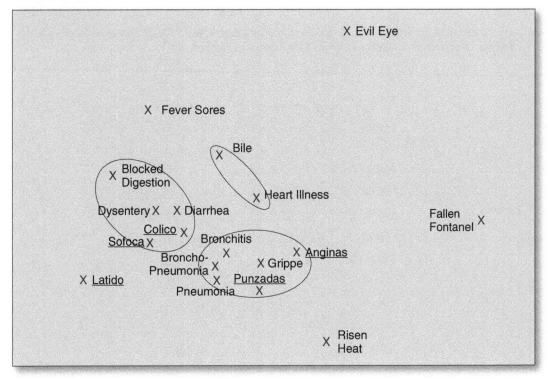

Source: J. C. Young and L. Y. Garro, "Variation in the Choice of Treatment in Two Mexican Communities." *Social Science and Medicine* 16:1453–63, Fig. 2, p. 1460, 1982.

Figure 16.19b MDS of Uricho Term-Frame Data

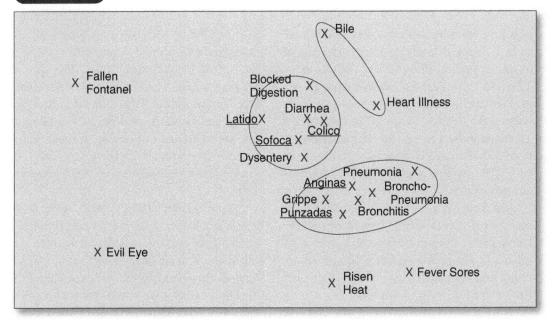

Source: J. C. Young and L. Y. Garro, "Variation in the Choice of Treatment in Two Mexican Communities." *Social Science and Medicine* 16:1453–63, Fig. 3, p. 1460, 1982.

Figure 16.20 An Example of a Rating Scale

Please rate the following emotions in terms of their intensity, where "1" indicates the least amount of intensity, and where "5" indicates the greatest amount of intensity.

ANXIOUS	1___	2___	3___	4___	5___
ENVY	1___	2___	3___	4___	5___
LONELY	1___	2___	3___	4___	5___
BORED	1___	2___	3___	4___	5___
ANGUISH	1___	2___	3___	4___	5___
HATE	1___	2___	3___	4___	5___
DISGUST	1___	2___	3___	4___	5___
FEAR	1___	2___	3___	4___	5___
EXCITEMENT	1___	2___	3___	4___	5___
SHAME	1___	2___	3___	4___	5___
TIRED	1___	2___	3___	4___	5___
LOVE	1___	2___	3___	4___	5___
ANGER	1___	2___	3___	4___	5___
SAD	1___	2___	3___	4___	5___
HAPPY	1___	2___	3___	4___	5___

of a jury reaching a correct decision in legal cases as opposed to relying on the judgment of a single person (Batchelder and Romney 1986). In 1907, Francis Galton attended a fair in Plymouth, England where 800 people guessed the weight of an ox. The ox weighed 1,198 pounds. The spread of guesses went from 1,074 to 1,293 pounds, but the mean was 1,196 pounds (Galton 1907a, 1907b)—almost dead on.

And Robyn Dawes (1977) asked 25 male members of the faculty in psychology at the University of Oregon to rate the height of all other 24 colleagues using five scales, like those I discussed in Chapter 11: semantic differential (from short to tall), Likert-like (extremely short to extremely tall), and so on. The first factor scores for the five scales—the score on

the underlying variable with which all the scales were associated—correlated 0.98 with the actual height of the men. The title of Dawes's article was "Suppose We Measured Height with Rating Scales Instead of Rulers?" Well, the answer is: As long as you take the average of a bunch of people on those scales, you can lose the rulers and do pretty well. (For a review of collective wisdom, see Surowiecki 2004).

James Boster (1985, 1986) walked 58 Aguaruna Jívaro women (in Peru) through a garden that had 61 varieties of manioc. He asked the women *waji mama aita?* ("What kind of manioc is this?") and calculated the likelihood that all possible pairs of women agreed on the name of a plant. Boster had planted the garden himself, so he *knew* the true identification of each plant. Sure enough, *the more women agreed* on the identification of a plant, *the more likely they were to know* what the plant actually was. In other words, people who know lot about—are highly competent in—a cultural domain tend to agree with each other about the content of the domain and people who know little tend to disagree.

When Agreement Equals Knowledge: Equation 1

Romney et al. (1986) took all this a step further by showing exactly how, and under what conditions, agreement among a set of people equals knowledge. (For details of the proof, see the original article by Romney et al. [1986]. See Borgatti and Carboni [2007] and Weller [2007] for clear, nonmathematical explanations of the theory. Weller [2007] is a key resource for instructions on how to run consensus analysis and how to interpret the results.)

In brief, there are two equations: one expressing the probability that a person answers a question correctly and one expressing the probability that two people agree on the answer to a question. The first equation comes from classical test theory—the kind that produces all those standardized tests you've taken all your life.

$$m_i = d_i + 1 - d_i / L \qquad \textbf{formula 16.2}$$

Adjusting for Guessing

This equation says that the probability of getting the answer to a question right (m_i) is the probability that you know the answer (d_i) plus the probability $(1 - d_i / L)$ that you guess right if you don't know the answer, where L is the number of choices available for guessing. In a true-false question, for example, there is a 0.50 probability of guessing the right answer at random. In a question with three answers, the probability of guessing right is 0.33. In a test where each question has five answers, it's 0.20. The formula for adjusting a test score for guessing is:

$$K = [S - 1 / L] / [1 - 1 / L] \qquad \textbf{formula 16.3}$$

where K = actual knowledge, S is the original test score, and L is the number of choices available when a student has to guess the answer (see Borgatti 1997; Weller 2007).

Table 16.10 shows the answers by one student to 25 multiple choice questions on one of my exams. The questions on this exam each had five possible answers, so the student made 25 choices of a number between 1 and 5. To find out how well the student did on the whole exam, we count up the number of matches between the student's vector of numbers and the vector that represents the correct answers and we divide by the total number of questions. This student got 19 matches, or $19/25 = 0.76$.

Table 16.10 Grading a Test With an Answer Key for 25 Multiple-Choice Questions

Questions																								
1	2	3	4	5	6	7	8	9	10	11	12	13	14	15	16	17	18	19	20	21	22	23	24	25
Answers																								
3	3	2	3	2	1	4	3	2	2	5	5	2	2	5	5	1	3	1	4	2	1	5	4	1
Answer key																								
3	3	2	2	2	4	4	3	2	2	5	4	2	1	5	2	1	3	1	4	3	1	5	4	1

The student's adjusted knowledge score would be:

$$K = \frac{.76 - .20}{1 - .20} = .70$$

In other words, d_i for this student—the probability that she actually *knows* the answer to any question on the test—is 0.70.

When Agreement Equals Knowledge: Equation 2

The second equation in the consensus model is the probability that two people, i and j, agree on the answer to a question. There are four ways for this to happen: (1) i and j both know the answer with probability d; (2) i knows the answer and j guesses correctly; (3) j knows the answer and i guesses correctly; and (4) neither i nor j know the answer but they make the same guess, which may or may not be the correct one. The combined probability here is:

$$m_{ij} = d_i d_j + \frac{1 - d_i d_j}{L} \qquad \textbf{formula 16.4}$$

which, as Borgatti and Carboni (2007:454) say, in a marvelous understatement, is "pleasingly analogous to" the first equation.

Assumptions of the Model

In other words, under certain conditions, "we can estimate the amount of knowledge of each person by knowing only the pattern of agreement among persons in the group" (Borgatti and Carboni 2007:455). Here are the conditions:

1. The culturally correct answer might be incorrect from an outsider's perspective (as often happens when we compare folk knowledge about illnesses or plants or climate to scientific knowledge). Any variation you find among informants is the result of *individual* differences in their knowledge, not the result of being members of subcultures.

2. Informants give their answers to your test questions independently of one another. Consensus analysis is not for focus group data.

3. All the questions in your test come from the same cultural domain and are more-or-less of equal difficulty. No fair asking about things you can do to help your child get into college and things you can do to make a successful dinner party in the same test.

Running Consensus Analysis

If these assumptions are met, we can run a factor analysis of the corrected-for-guessing, people-by-question matrix. The results tell us if our informants share a single culture about the domain we're testing and, if they do, what their knowledge of that domain is.

Factor analysis, remember, is a set of statistical techniques for reducing a data matrix to a set of underlying variables. It is used in the development of attitude scales to look for packages of specific items (like how you feel about gun control or abortion or single-sex marriage) that measure different aspects of big, underlying variables (like rightish or leftish political orientation). (More about factor analysis in Chapter 22.)

In consensus analysis, factor analysis is used to test whether there is a single, underlying component, or culture. If there is, then there will be one major factor—knowledge of the domain—and each person's score on that factor is their competence in the domain. One major factor—a single culture—is indicated when: (1) the first factor is large relative to the second (a rule of thumb for this is that the first eigenvalue in the factor analysis is at least three times the size of the second); and (2) no informant has a negative score on the first factor (if there is a single culture, people shouldn't have negative knowledge of it).

If the ratio of the first to the second eigenvalue is less than three-to-one or if there are negative scores on the first factor, then there may be more than one culture in the group of informants who took the test. For example, men and women may represent different cultural subgroups for some domains, as might members of different ethnic or religious groups. You can test this by running a consensus analysis on the subgroups separately.

There are two other possibilities. First, one group of people may be competent in a domain while another group knows little about it. For example, Romney et al. (1987) asked 26 undergraduates (13 men and 13 women) about the effectiveness of 15 kinds of birth control. Seven of the men had negative scores on the first factor of the analysis, so Romney et al. ran the analysis separately on the men and the women. For the women, the ratio of the first to the second eigenvalue was more than four-to-one, so there was one big underlying factor (knowledge about the effectiveness of birth control methods) and the women's factor scores were all positive. For the men, the ratio was about one-to-one, and six of the 13 had negative scores on the first factor. In other words, for those 13 men, it wasn't just that they didn't share a culture about the domain, they had little or no knowledge of the domain at all.

Another possibility is that you've got a shaman, or the equivalent, in your sample. If you run a consensus analysis and find one or two negative first-factor (knowledge) scores out of a large sample, it may be that you've included people whose knowledge about the domain is so specialized it doesn't jibe with that of others in the mainstream. It is to the advantage of shamans everywhere, whether their knowledge is about curing illness or making money on the stock market, to protect that knowledge by keeping it maximally different from mainstream knowledge. Use consensus analysis to find highly knowledgeable informants but never pass up the chance to interview a shaman.

Retrieving the Answer Key to a Test

If there is a single culture—if there is one major factor representing knowledge of the domain and if there are no negative scores on that factor—then informant scores on the first factor represent their knowledge about—their cultural competence in—the domain. And because of the relationship between formulas 16.2 and 16.4—that is, the relation between agreement and knowledge—we can retrieve the answer key to the set of questions on the test by looking at the most common answers—that wisdom-of-crowds thing again—and by giving more weight to the answers of the high scorers on the test when the crowd is split on the answers to a particular culture.

I tested this, using Ucinet (Borgatti et al. 2002) on data from a 1995 class I taught on intro to anthropology. There were 168 students in the class and the exam had 60 questions. Recall that the ratio of the first eigenvalue to the second should be at least three-to-one to conclude that there is a consensus. In this case, the ratio was more than 20-to-one, so there was, indeed, one big underlying factor associated with the answers that students gave to the questions on the test. Because the purpose of the test was to gauge students' knowledge of the material, the factor can be interpreted as *knowledge*, and each student's score on that big factor can be interpreted as his or her score on the test.

Figure 16.21 shows the correlation between the first factor score for each student and the score that each student actually got on the test. The correlation is 0.96—almost perfect. It's so close, in fact, that had I lost the answer key I could have given every student his or her factor score as the grade for the test with no impact on the final grade for the course. And this is no fluke: Borgatti and Carboni (2007:458) ran this analysis on a test of 91 students in an organizational behavior class and got a 0.95 correlation—again, almost perfect.

Figure 16.21 Plot of Raw Grades and Scores From a Cultural Consensus Analysis on an Intro to Anthropology Test. The Correlation Is 0.96

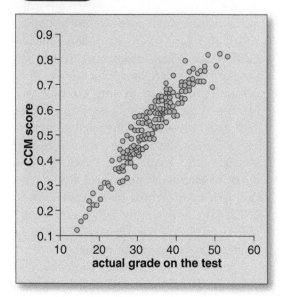

The answer key for my test that was derived from the analysis was also almost perfect. Taking the majority answers to the 60 questions and adjusting for guessing, the analysis got 58 right. Here are the two questions that it missed:

"Natural selection" selects for:

(1) reproductive success.

(2) survival of the fittest.

(3) survival of the species.

(4) adaptive radiation.

(5) random mutations.

The first hominid to live in regions with cold winters was:

(1) Homo erectus.

(2) Homo hablis.

(3) Homo sapiens neandertalensis.

(4) archaic Homo sapiens.

(5) Australopithecus afarensis.

For the first question, 70 students picked (1), reproductive success (the correct answer), but 79 students picked (2), survival of the fittest. For the second question, 49 students picked (1), Homo erectus (the correct answer), but 90 students picked (3), Homo sapiens neandertalensis. (In those days, Neanderthals were still classified as a subspecies of modern humans. Today, they would be classified as a separate species.) Popular culture—about Neanderthal Man and about the phrase "survival of the fittest"—was just too powerful to be overcome fully by some anthropology lectures (Box 16.6).

Box 16.6 Cultural consensus and multiple answer keys

Hruschka et al. (2008) used frame elicitation in interviews with women in Bangladesh, about the causes and symptoms of postpartum hemorrhage. Of the 149 people in their sample, 98 were lay women, 37 were traditional birth attendants (TBAs), and 14 were skilled birth attendants (SBAs)—that is, women who had been trained in modern medical techniques for midwifery.

When Hruschka et al. ran the data through consensus analysis, the ratio of the first to the second eigenvalue was nearly 6-to-1 and there were no negative competencies. This indicated a single cultural model. But when they picked the data apart, *none* of the SBAs agreed with the statement "*alga* (evil spirits) is a cause of excessive, life-threatening bleeding," whereas 84% of TBAs and 78% of lay women agreed.

(Continued)

(Continued)

This turned out to indicate a pattern: The SBAs agreed among themselves about many of the items in the cultural knowledge test; the lay women and the TBAs agreed with each other; and the two groups disagreed. In other words, the two groups of women were drawing their answers to test questions from different answer keys.

What this means is that if you can retrieve an etically correct answer key, you can apply the model (cautiously, always cautiously . . . see Box 16.6) to tests of emic data—like people's ideas about who hangs out with whom in an organization or what people think are good ways to cure a cold, avoid getting AIDS, take care of a baby, etc. It still takes knowledge of the local culture to fully understand the distribution of knowledge about a cultural domain. But when we ask people to list holidays or to rate the social status of others in a community we don't want to know only their opinions. We want to know the holidays and the social status of people. We never had an answer key to tell whether informants were reporting this information accurately. Now we do.

Making Up Questions for a Formal Consensus Test

The key to running a formal consensus analysis is building good test items. This takes work. Start with systematic and indepth interviews with knowledgeable informants about the domain you're investigating and do a close analysis of those qualitative data so that you can create sensible questions—that is, questions that reflect the content of the domain. We expect professors who make up course exams to know the material cold, and you should expect no less of yourself when you make up questions for a formal consensus analysis. About half the questions should be positive (true, yes, agree) and about half should be negative (false, no, disagree).

Jeffrey Johnson and David Griffith (1996) studied what people in North Carolina know about the link between seafood safety and coastal pollution using the formal cultural consensus model. First, they asked some expert informants to free list: (1) the kinds of pollution along the Atlantic coast (examples included acid rain, chemical runoff as the result of coastal erosion, and so on); (2) the species (clams, crabs, tuna) that might be affected by the various types of pollution; and (3) problems that might arise, like diseases in fish. From these data, Johnson and Griffith identified 12 types of pollution, 11 causes of pollution, and 10 species. Next, they asked a convenience sample of commercial fishermen and local residents of various ethnic backgrounds to: (1) pile sort the types of pollution; (2) link each pollutant to the problems they cause; and (3) identify the species that each pollutant affected the most.

Johnson and Griffith asked the informants to explain why they made all these linkages and transcribed the results. Then, three coders went through the transcripts, tagging statements about how the seafood, pollutants, and various risks to health and the environment were related. There were 53 statements identified by at least two of the three coders. The researchers turned these into a true-false knowledge test, with half the statements positive (true) and half being negative. For example, "heavy metals cause sores on both fish and people" is true (positive), but "heavy metals are necessary nutrients for both fish and people" is false (negative).

Finally, Johnson and Griffith gave the test to 142 people in the area including: (1) a representative sample of 122 people, stratified by residence (rural-urban), income (high and low), and ethnicity (White and Black);

(2) 10 students from their university; and (3) 10 marine scientists. They analyzed the 142(people)-by-53(statement) matrix using the formal consensus model. The first eigenvalue in the analysis of the agreement matrix was over seven times bigger than the second. Those 142 people, despite coming from such different backgrounds, drew from a single culture in answering the 53 questions on the test about seafood and pollution.

Fine-grained analysis, though, turned up some interesting differences. The consensus was that the following statement was true: "Much of the pollution dumped into coastal and ocean waters has no effect on the flavor or seafood." The scientists, however, disagreed.

The Informal Model

When you have ordinal or ratio or rank-ordered data, including data from pile sorts and triad tests, use the informal model of consensus analysis (Weller 2007) (Box 16.7).

Box 16.7 Lumpers and splitters

Be careful, though: With free pile sorts, some people make just a few piles and others make many. **Lumpers and splitters** are technically not responding to the same cues when you ask them to sort items freely into piles. This means you can test whether there is a single culture—whether most people see the relations among a set of items in a pile sort similarly—and you can look for informants who are most representative of the culture, but you wouldn't put much stock in individual factor scores or use those scores as input into any other analysis.

In this model, you create a people-by-people similarity matrix from the original people-by-item test and factor the similarity matrix. You can do this in most statistical packages, but Anthropac and Ucinet will do it automatically. Here's an example.

Adam Kiš (2007) found that people in the village of Njolomole, Malawi, had stopped going to every funeral because, with AIDS, there were just too many to go to. Kiš asked 23 people to: "Name all of the reasons you can think of for attending a funeral." He listed the 12 reasons cited most often on a piece of paper and asked 30 people: "If there were too many funerals in your village so that you could not attend each one, which of the following reasons would be the most important in helping you decide which funerals to attend?" Then he asked people to mark the next most important reason, and the next, and so on down the list. Table 16.11 shows his data.

These are rank-ordered data, so the informal consensus model is appropriate. To do this, correlate all pairs of rows in Table 16.11 and turn it into a 30-by-30, people-by-people similarity matrix (any statistical package will do; and for more about correlation, see Chapter 21). The result for the first 10 rows is shown in Table 16.12.

Read Table 16.12 as follows: Informants 4 and 9 are highly and positively correlated (0.741); informants 6 and 2 are hardly correlated at all (0.070); informants 2 and 3 are weakly and negatively correlated (–0.364); and so on. The negative correlation for informants 2 and 3 means that they tended to rank the reasons for going to a funeral in some opposite ways. For example, looking across rows 2 and 3 of Table 16.11, informant 2 ranked HEL (helping the family of the deceased with funeral preparations) last on his list, and informant 3 ranked it third.

Table 16.11	Rankings of 12 Reasons for Attending a Funeral (1 Is Most Important, 12 Is Least Important)

| | Reason | | | | | | | | | | | |
Informant	REC	SOR	HEL	CUS	REL	EAT	FRI	GIF	CON	GOO	CHU	COF
1	4	1	2	7	6	12	11	8	5	10	3	9
2	1	5	12	4	11	7	3	2	8	9	10	6
3	4	5	3	9	2	12	11	8	6	2	10	7
4	3	4	2	10	5	12	6	7	1	11	9	8
5	2	11	3	10	4	12	5	6	1	7	8	9
6	3	8	9	2	7	12	10	6	5	1	4	1
7	1	8	10	6	5	12	7	4	2	9	3	11
8	3	7	5	8	1	9	2	11	4	10	6	12
9	3	2	4	11	1	12	8	5	7	10	9	6
10	1	5	3	2	10	12	11	8	4	7	6	9
11	2	4	7	1	5	12	11	6	3	8	9	10
12	1	2	4	6	9	12	8	5	7	3	10	11
13	3	4	1	5	11	9	7	6	8	2	12	10
14	4	10	2	6	1	12	7	9	3	8	5	11
15	2	5	3	1	11	12	10	9	4	6	8	7
16	5	3	6	4	11	12	8	7	1	2	9	10
17	7	4	8	6	9	12	10	3	5	1	2	11
18	1	8	3	6	5	12	4	11	2	7	9	10
19	5	4	1	8	9	12	3	7	10	11	2	6
20	1	10	2	11	8	12	5	4	6	3	9	7
21	2	5	8	7	6	12	1	11	4	9	3	10
22	3	4	2	1	6	12	7	9	5	11	8	10
23	1	3	5	11	7	12	10	2	4	6	8	9
24	12	10	5	8	1	11	2	7	3	4	6	9
25	2	1	7	3	4	12	8	10	5	9	6	11
26	1	7	3	2	5	9	8	6	4	10	12	11
27	1	4	2	9	5	12	8	3	11	7	6	10
28	1	7	4	2	5	12	9	11	10	8	3	6
29	3	4	9	5	1	12	2	8	6	10	7	11
30	1	2	4	6	5	12	11	8	3	7	9	10

The list of reasons are: REC = reciprocity (attending a specific person's funeral so that his or her family members will attend your family's funerals), SOR = sorrow, HEL = to help the family of the deceased with funeral preparations, CUS = going out of custom, REL = going because ego is a relative of the deceased, EAT = to eat the requisite funeral feast, FRI = attending because ego is a friend of the deceased, GIF = to bring gifts to the family of the deceased, CON = to console the family of the deceased, GOO = to say good-bye to the deceased, CHU = going because ego is a member of the same church as the deceased, COF = to carry the coffin.

Source: A. Kiš, "An Analysis of the Impact of AIDS on Funeral Culture in Malawi." *NAPA Bulletin* 27:129–40, Table 1, 2007.

Table 16.12 Correlation Matrix for the First 10 Rows of Table 16.11

	1	2	3	4	5	6	7	8	9	10
1	1.000	−0.231	0.399	0.650	0.273	0.245	0.406	0.336	0.601	0.699
2	−0.231	1.000	−0.364	−0.028	−0.098	0.070	0.273	−0.147	−0.007	0.105
3	0.399	−0.364	1.000	0.420	0.462	0.378	0.084	0.175	0.587	0.364
4	0.650	−0.028	0.420	1.000	0.748	−0.049	0.441	0.601	0.741	0.455
5	0.273	−0.098	0.462	0.748	1.000	0.245	0.587	0.622	0.448	0.336
6	0.245	0.070	0.378	−0.049	0.245	1.000	0.608	0.042	−0.112	0.622
7	0.406	0.273	0.084	0.441	0.587	0.608	1.000	0.483	0.280	0.469
8	0.336	−0.147	0.175	0.601	0.622	0.042	0.483	1.000	0.406	0.140
9	0.601	−0.007	0.587	0.741	0.448	−0.112	0.280	0.406	1.000	0.196
10	0.699	0.105	0.364	0.455	0.336	0.622	0.469	0.140	0.196	1.000

Next, factor analyze the 30-by-30 matrix of informant agreements using a variant of factor analysis called minimal residuals (or MINRES). I did this with SYSTAT®, but you can use SPSS® or any major statistical package. The results are in Figure 16.22. The first factor is large, relative to the second (the ratio is 3.157), which means that there is a single culture at work, despite the differences in the way people ranked their reasons for going to a funeral. There is a nice range of scores—from 0.07 (for informant 2) to 0.92 (for informant 30)—and there are no negative scores, but some people (like informants 10, 11, 22, 25, and 30) are clearly more knowledgeable about the reasons for going to a funeral than others.

Kiš interviewed these knowledgeable informants in depth and asked them why reciprocity (attending someone's funeral so that his or her family will attend your family's funerals) was the runaway most-important reason given and why carrying the coffin and partaking of the traditional funeral feast were ranked so low. It turned out that carrying coffins was only for young

men, and his sample of 30 informants did not have that many young men in it. If he'd had more young men in his sample, this might have resulted in a higher overall ranking of eating as a reason for attending a funeral, since coffin bearers get generous portions of food.

Selecting Domain-Specific Informants

This brings up a really interesting use of consensus analysis: Selecting domain-specific informants. Table 16.13, from Weller and Romney (1988), shows the number of people you need to produce valid and reliable data about particular cultural domains, given that the three conditions of the model are more-or-less met. (I say "more-or-less" because the model is very robust, which means that it produces very similar answers even when its conditions are more-or-less, not perfectly, met.) Just 10 informants, with an average competence of 0.7 have a 99% probability of answering each question on a true-false test correctly, with a confidence level of 0.95. Only 13

Figure 16.22 Factor Analysis of the Complete 30 × 30 Matrix Implied by Table 16.12

FACTOR ANALYSIS

Method of extraction: Maximum likelihood

Method of rotation: NONE

Minimum eigenvalue to retain: 1.0

EIGENVALUES

FACTOR	VALUE	PERCENT	CUM %	RATIO
1:	12.709	42.4	42.4	3.157
2:	4.026	13.4	55.8	1.444
3:	2.788	9.3	65.1	1.177
4:	2.368	7.9	73.0	1.253
5:	1.889	6.3	79.3	1.038
6:	1.820	6.1	85.3	1.295
7:	1.405	4.7	90.0	1.181
8:	1.190	4.0	94.0	1.254

Individual scores on the first factor:

1 0.750	11 0.815	21 0.506
2 0.070	12 0.774	22 0.826
3 0.589	13 0.514	23 0.712
4 0.756	14 0.707	24 0.090
5 0.645	15 0.722	25 0.824
6 0.539	16 0.633	26 0.739
7 0.633	17 0.380	27 0.666
8 0.542	18 0.803	28 0.577
9 0.594	19 0.365	29 0.606
10 0.820	20 0.501	30 0.922

informants, with a relatively low average competence of 0.5 are needed if you want a 90% probability of answering each question on a test correctly, with a confidence level of 0.95.

And, as Table 16.14 shows, when you have interval level data, if you interview 10 people whose responses correlate 0.49, then the aggregate of their answers are likely to correlate 0.95 with the true answers.

Consensus analysis shows that: (1) only a relatively small sample of informants is needed for studying particular cultural domains; and (2) there will be variation in knowledge among informants who are competent in a cultural domain.

Consensus analysis is great for finding top people who can talk about well-defined areas of cultural knowledge. But if you are doing

Table 16.13	Minimal Number of Informants Needed to Classify a Desired Proportion of Questions With a Specified Confidence Level for Different Levels of Cultural Competence

| Proportion of Questions | Average Level of Cultural Competence | | | | |
	.5	.6	.7	.8	.9
.95 confidence level					
0.80	9	7	4	4	4
0.85	11	7	4	4	4
0.90	13	9	6	4	4
0.95	17	11	6	6	4
0.99	29	19	10	8	4
.99 confidence level					
0.80	15	10	5	4	4
0.85	15	10	7	5	4
0.90	21	12	7	5	4
0.95	23	14	9	7	4
0.99	>30	20	13	8	6

Source: S. C. Weller and A. K. Romney, *Systematic Data Collection*, p. 77, 1988, Sage Publications.

Table 16.14	Agreement Among Individuals and Estimated Validity of Aggregating Their Responses for Different Samples

| Agreement | Validity | | | | |
	0.80	0.85	0.90	0.95	0.99
0.16	10	14	22	49	257
0.25	5	8	13	28	148
0.36	3	5	8	17	87
0.49	2	3	4	10	51

Source: S. C. Weller and A. K. Romney, *Systematic Data Collection,* p. 77, 1988, Sage Publications.

general descriptive ethnography and you're looking for all-around good informants, consensus analysis is *not* a substitute for the time-honored way that ethnographers have always chosen key informants: luck, intuition, and hard work by both parties to achieve a working relationship based on trust (**Further Reading:** consensus analysis).

Cultural Consonance

An important development in the use of consensus analysis is the **cultural consonance model** by William Dressler and his colleagues (Dressler, Balierio et al. 2007; Dressler et al. 1996) and the application of the consonance model to the study of lifestyle and health. Here, lifestyle is defined as *having things* and *doing things* that one needs to have and do so as to have a good life as an X, where X is whatever people you're working with. Material things might be anything from a bicycle to a Ferrari, while behavioral things might be anything from visiting the district capital at least once a year to only flying first class, depending on where you're working.

To get a material-style-of-life scale, you need a list of, material goods and leisure activities. The list can come from inventorying homes, from open-ended interviews about leisure, from free lists, from the *Style* section of the local newspaper. . . . You can create a Guttman scale of the items, as Pollnac et al. (1975) and DeWalt (1979) did, or you can ask people, as Dressler did (1996) to rate each item from 1-to-3 for its importance to living a good life (1 = not at all important, 2 = somewhat important, and 3 = very important). If you have 20 or fewer items, you can ask people to rank order them in terms of importance. A trick here is to ask people to divide the items first into three piles (unimportant to very important) and then to rank the items within each pile. This is easier for people to do than to rank order a lot of items in one go.

The informants-by-lifestyle-items matrix can then be analyzed to see if the pattern of responses indicates a cultural consensus about what it takes to be living well. Dressler did this in Brazil and found that 22 of 39 material and behavioral items were considered somewhat important or very important for an ideal lifestyle. He also found that the percentage of those 22 culturally important things that people had accounted for a significant amount of the variation in blood pressure. In other words, Dressler tested the existence of a shared cultural model for a good life and showed that dissonance from that model produced stress and other unhealthy outcomes.

ANALYZING NETWORK DATA

As we saw in Chapter 10, network analysis involves the study of both lists and the structure of relations among items in lists. When the items are people, the set of relations is a social network.

The nodes in a whole network don't have to be people. Aggregates of people (like countries or firms or schools) can also be treated as things that have connections to one another. For example, if you analyze trade among the 200-or-so countries of the world, you'll discover Wallerstein's core-periphery structure of the world system, with the rich countries in the middle, all linked strongly through trade, and the poorer countries around the edge, liked weakly, both to the core counties and to one another (Wallerstein 1974, 2004).

Corporations are linked by people who sit on multiple boards of directors. Universities are linked by competition in sports. Hospitals in a city are linked by doctors who practice in more than one institution. If you analyze networks like these, you'll discover cliques of corporations, universities, and hospitals, and the links between the cliques.

Books and other consumer items are related to one another through co-purchasing. When Amazon.com tells you that "customers who bought this item also bought . . . ," they are pulling that information from a co-purchasing network (Krebs 1999, 2003). Articles in scholarly journals are tied to one another through co-citation, or who cites who. If you analyze co-citation networks, you'll discover what are called invisible colleges—groups of scholars who studied at the same schools, publish in the same journals, and so on (Gmür 2003).

One-Mode and Two-Mode Data

Table 16.15 shows the general form of a sociomatrix. It is a matrix of who-to-whom data where the cells indicate links between pairs of people. Table 16.15 is a one-mode matrix because the things in the rows and the columns are the same. The typical data matrix in social research, shown in Table 16.16, is a two-mode matrix, in which the rows are cases (people, countries, marriage contracts) and the columns are attributes of the cases, including independent and dependent variables. (See Chapter 2 if you need to brush up on these terms.)

The cells of a one-mode matrix, like the one in Table 16.15, can be filled with 1s and 0s or they can be filled with valued data.

A 1/0 matrix (read: one-zero matrix, also called an adjacency matrix) indicates whether a tie exists between any two actors—like whether A asks B for advice. In a valued-data matrix, the numbers in the cells indicate the strength of a tie between pairs of actors—like how much people say they like or trust each other or how much they say they go to one another for advice.

Graphs and Matrices

Table 16.17 shows hypothetical data for seven people in a work group. We show each of them a list of the names of the other six and ask them to indicate whether they go to each of those six for advice about some matter at work. We see that Barbara goes to Colleen for advice (there's a 1 in the cell where Barbara's row meets Colleen's

Table 16.15 A Sociomatrix, or One-Mode, Who-to-Whom Matrix

	A	B	C	D	E	F	G
A	–						
B		–					
C			–				
D				–			
E					–		
F						–	
G							–

Table 16.16 Classical Data Matrix: Rows Are Cases and Columns Are Attributes of Cases

ID	Independent variables				Dependent variable
	Age	Gender	Income	Education	
1					
2					
3					
4					
5					
6					
7					

Table 16.17 A 7 × 7 Advice Network

	Alan	Barbara	Colleen	David	Eileen	Faye	Gary
Alan	–	1	1	0	0	1	0
Barbara	0	–	1	0	1	0	1
Colleen	1	0	–	1	0	0	0
David	1	1	1	–	1	1	0
Eileen	0	1	1	1	–	0	0
Faye	1	0	1	1	0	–	0
Gary	0	0	1	0	0	1	–
totals	3	3	6	3	2	3	1

column) but Colleen does not go to Barbara (there's a 0 in the cell where Colleen's row meets Barbara's column).

Advice networks are often **asymmetric,** as are affection networks (A says he or she likes B, but B doesn't reciprocate), exchange networks (A lends money to B, but not vice versa), and communication networks (A initiates email contact with B but not vice versa). In the study of disease transmission, sexual networks are usually treated as symmetric.

Any matrix of ties between actors can be expressed as a graph. Figure 16.23 displays the data in Table 16.17 as a graph. Figure 16.23 is a directed graph. The arrows show the direction of each tie. Undirected graphs just show the existence of a tie, but without any indication of direction. Figure 16.23 is, of course, an asymmetric graph (Box 16.8).

Box 16.8 Spring embedders and tutorials

One of the most important methods for analyzing network data is to visualize them as graphs so that their structure can more easily apprehended. Figures 16.23 was made with a **spring embedder** in a program called Netdraw, available free from analytictech.com. The name "spring embedder" reflects the idea that the points in a graph are like springs that push and pull on each other. People or other actors who are like one another—who have high similarity in a proximity matrix—will tend to pull each other closer, while people who are very different from one another will push each other apart. Like MDS, spring embedders arrange the members of a group—the nodes in a graph—in a way that reduces the stress of all that pulling and pushing (Freeman 2000:10).

Netdraw is also part of Ucinet (Borgatti et al. 2002), a suite of programs for analyzing relational data, especially social network data. A good introduction to network analysis is a free, online book by Robert Hanneman and Mark Riddle (2005). The book provides many examples, using Ucinet to demonstrate the measurement of network properties. (See Appendix E for more about software for network analysis.)

| Figure 16.23 | The Structure of an Advice Network: A Graph of the Data in Table 16.17 |

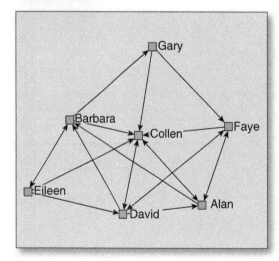

One-Mode Matrices From Two-Mode Matrices

You can also create one-mode, interaction data from two-mode data about people and events or artifacts with which people are associated. The result is an **affiliation matrix**.

Table 16.18 shows a famous two-mode, people-by-event matrix: White women in Natchez, Mississippi, in 1936 (in the rows) by 14 social events they attended, over a period of nine months, as reported in the newspapers of the time (Davis et al. 1941:148). The events included things like a church supper, a bridge party, a supper party, a meeting of the Parent-Teachers Association, or the meeting of a women's club (L. C. Freeman 2003; Homans 1951:82).

Table 16.19 shows the two, one-mode matrices that can be produced from Table 16.18: The woman-by-woman matrix in Table 16.19a shows the *number of events that each pair of women attended together* (the diagonal shows the number of events that each woman attended), while Table 16.19b shows the *number of women who attended any pair of events* (and the diagonal shows the number of women who were at each event).

NETWORK STRUCTURE

Once we have a matrix of relations among a set of objects or people, we can analyze that matrix

Table 16.18 A Two-Mode Matrix of Women by Social Events They Attended

Event day/month Name	1 6/27	2 3/2	3 4/12	4 9/26	5 2/25	6 5/19	7 3/15	8 9/16	9 4/8	10 6/10	11 2/23	12 4/7	13 11/21	14 8/3
Mrs. Evelyn Jefferson	1	1	1	1	1	1	0	1	1	0	0	0	0	0
Miss Laura Mandeville	1	1	1	0	1	1	1	1	0	0	0	0	0	0
Miss Theresa Anderson	0	1	1	1	1	1	1	1	1	0	0	0	0	0
Miss Brenda Rogers	1	0	1	1	1	1	1	1	0	0	0	0	0	0
Miss Charlotte McDowd	0	0	1	1	1	0	1	0	0	0	0	0	0	0
Miss Frances Anderson	0	0	1	0	1	1	0	1	0	0	0	0	0	0
Miss Eleanor Nye	0	0	0	0	1	1	1	1	0	0	0	0	0	0
Miss Pearl Oglethorpe	0	0	0	0	0	1	0	1	1	0	0	0	0	0
Miss Ruth DeSand	0	0	0	0	1	0	1	1	1	0	0	0	0	0
Miss Verne Sanderson	0	0	0	0	0	0	1	1	1	0	0	1	0	0
Miss Myra Lidell	0	0	0	0	0	0	0	1	1	1	0	1	0	0
Miss Katherine Rogers	0	0	0	0	0	0	0	1	1	1	0	1	1	1
Mrs. Sylvia Avondale	0	0	0	0	0	0	1	1	1	1	0	1	1	1
Mrs. Nora Fayette	0	0	0	0	0	1	1	0	1	1	1	1	1	1
Mrs. Helen Lloyd	0	0	0	0	0	0	1	1	0	1	1	1	0	0
Mrs. Dorothy Murchison	0	0	0	0	0	0	0	1	1	0	0	0	0	0
Mrs. Olivia Carleton	0	0	0	0	0	0	0	0	1	0	1	0	0	0
Mrs. Flora Price	0	0	0	0	0	0	0	0	1	0	1	0	0	0

Source: Data from Davis et al. *Deep South*, p. 148, 1941, University of Chicago Press.

Table 16.19a One-Mode, Affiliation Matrix for the Women (rows) in Table 16.18

Woman	EJ	LM	TA	BR	CM	FA	EN	PO	RD	VS	ML	KR	SA	NF	HL	DM	OC	FP
Evelyn Jefferson	8	6	7	6	3	4	3	3	3	2	2	2	2	2	1	2	1	1
Laura Mandeville	6	7	6	6	3	4	4	2	3	2	1	1	2	2	1	1	0	0
Theresa Anderson	7	6	8	6	4	4	4	3	4	3	2	2	3	3	2	2	1	1
Brenda Rogers	6	6	6	7	4	4	4	2	3	2	1	1	2	2	2	1	0	0
Charlotte McDowd	3	3	4	4	4	2	2	0	2	1	0	0	1	1	1	0	0	0
Frances Anderson	4	4	4	4	2	4	3	2	2	1	1	1	1	1	1	1	0	0
Eleanor Nye	3	4	4	4	2	3	4	2	3	2	1	1	2	2	1	1	0	0
Pearl Oglethorpe	3	2	3	2	0	2	2	3	2	2	2	2	2	2	1	2	1	1
Ruth DeSand	3	3	4	3	2	2	3	2	4	3	2	2	3	2	2	2	1	1
Verne Sanderson	2	2	3	2	1	1	2	2	3	4	3	3	4	3	3	2	1	1
Myra Lidell	2	1	2	1	0	1	1	2	2	3	4	4	4	3	3	2	1	1
Katherine Rogers	2	1	2	1	0	1	1	2	2	3	4	6	6	5	3	2	1	1
Sylvia Avondale	2	2	3	2	1	1	2	2	3	4	4	6	7	6	4	2	1	1
Nora Fayette	2	2	3	2	1	1	2	2	2	3	3	5	6	8	4	1	2	2
Helen Lloyd	1	2	2	2	1	1	2	1	2	3	3	3	4	4	5	1	1	1
Dorothy Murchison	2	1	2	1	0	1	1	2	2	2	2	2	2	1	1	2	1	1
Olivia Carleton	1	0	1	0	0	0	0	1	1	1	1	1	1	2	1	1	2	2
Flora Price	1	0	1	0	0	0	0	1	1	1	1	1	1	2	1	1	2	2

Table 16.19b One-Mode, Affiliation Matrix for the Events (columns) in Table 16.18

Event	E1	E2	E3	E4	E5	E6	E7	E8	E9	E10	E11	E12	E13	E14
E1	3	2	3	2	3	3	2	3	1	0	0	0	0	0
E2	2	3	3	2	3	3	2	3	2	0	0	0	0	0
E3	3	3	6	4	6	5	4	5	2	0	0	0	0	0
E4	2	2	4	4	4	3	3	3	2	0	0	0	0	0
E5	3	3	6	4	8	6	6	7	3	0	0	0	0	0
E6	3	3	5	3	6	8	5	7	4	1	1	1	1	1
E7	2	2	4	3	6	5	10	8	5	3	2	4	2	2
E8	3	3	5	3	7	7	8	14	9	4	1	5	2	2
E9	1	2	2	2	3	4	5	9	12	4	3	5	3	3
E10	0	0	0	0	0	1	3	4	4	5	2	5	3	3
E11	0	0	0	0	0	1	2	1	3	2	4	2	1	1
E12	0	0	0	0	0	1	4	5	5	5	4	6	3	3
E13	0	0	0	0	0	1	2	2	3	3	2	3	3	3
E14	0	0	0	0	0	1	2	2	3	3	1	3	3	3

for its structural properties. Network **structure** refers to the pattern of ties among the nodes in a network and where any particular node is in that pattern. The number of possible patterns is essentially infinite, but Figure 16.24 shows five for illustration (from Bandyopadhyay et al. 2011:8).

The dots in each structure are the nodes, and the arcs, or lines are the network connections or ties. Arrows at the end of lines tell you which way a tie goes. In pattern 1, there are five people in the group and everyone is connected, although the ties are asymmetric. Person 3, for example, is tied to person 1, but person 1 does not reciprocate.

In pattern 2 of Figure 16.24, there are 10 people in the network but, despite the fact that the ties are symmetric, the network is fragmented into four **components**, including one component with just one person in it. (When

all the ties are reciprocated, there is no need to show any arrows.)

Pattern 3 has five people. There is only one component and all members of the network have reciprocal ties, but the structure is fragile. If you remove person 1 from pattern 3, the network fragments into singleton components. This makes person 1 pretty powerful.

Pattern 4 is a circle with perfectly asymmetric ties. Everyone in pattern 4 can get to everyone else, but only by going through intermediaries.

Finally, pattern 5 is a large network of 13 people. It's connected, but very hierarchical. All the connections flow from the bottom up.

Centrality

One of the most important concepts in network analysis is the idea that structural

---

Figure 16.24 Some Types of Networks

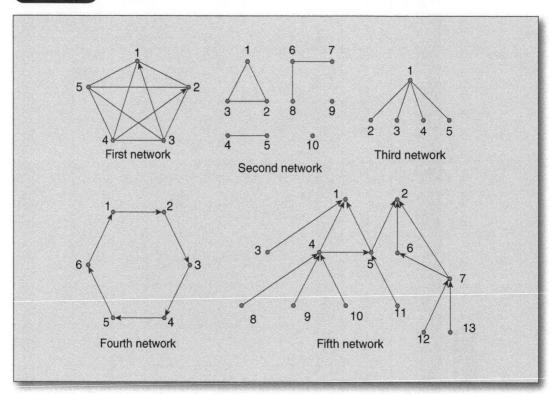

Source: Adapted from S. Bandyopadhyay et al. *Models for Social Networks with Statistical Applications,* 2011, Sage Publications.

position—where a node is in a network—limits or enhances access to information and other resources. There are several ways to measure centrality, including **degree centrality**, **closeness centrality**, and **betweenness centrality**. Figure 16.25 shows David Krackhardt's (1990) kite network for illustrating the various ways to measure centrality.

Degree centrality is the number of direct connections (ties, links, relations) any node has to all the other nodes in a network. In Figure 16.25, node D is connected to nodes A, B. C, E, F, and G. Node D has the most connections to others of anyone in the network and has a degree centrality of 6.

Nodes F and G have the shortest average paths to all the other nodes in the network and thus, the highest closeness centrality. There are 10 nodes in the network, so each node has a path to each of the other 9. Node D, with the highest degree centrality, has a path of 1 to nodes A, B, C, E, F, and G, but has a path of 2 to node H, a path of 3 to node I, and a path of 4 to node J.

The sum of those paths is 15 and the average is 15/9 = 1.67. Node F has a path of 1 to A, C, D, G, and H, a path of 2 to B, E, and

I, and a path of 3 to J. The sum of those paths is 14 and the average is 14/9 = 1.56. Node F, then (and G, which is equivalent to F) is closest to all the other nodes. In practical terms, nodes F and G are in the best position to know what everyone else in the network is doing.

The concept of betweenness centrality was developed by Linton Freeman (1979) and involves counting the number of times any node is on the shortest path between all pairs of nodes in a network. In Figure 16.25, node H has the highest betweenness centrality. Betweenness is power. H can block communication between parts of the network that are otherwise unconnected. As Krackhardt (1990:352) says: "D, F, and G are 'better connected' (have more connections) than H, but their connections are connected to each other, so that the information contained within these various parts tends to be redundant."

This might be a good thing for H, but if the people in Figure 16.25 depend on H for too much, the network is fragile.

STUDYING WHOLE NETWORKS

Among its many uses, whole network analysis is used in the study of organizations to help explain outcomes like the flow and concentration of money, power, and information.

Figure 16.26 shows a graph of links among 37 small towns in Russia in the twelfth and thirteenth centuries. The lines of the graph are the rivers that connected the towns and facilitated trade. Node number 35 on the graph was a tiny little place called Moscow. It had the highest betweenness centrality of any of the towns in the network: It was the place through which more traders had to pass to connect with all the other nodes in the network (Pitts 1979).

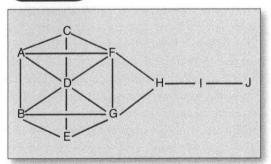

Figure 16.25 The Kite Network Illustrating Centrality

Source: D. Krackhardt, "Assessing the Political Landscape: Structure, Cognition, and Power in Organizations." *Administrative Science Quarterly* 35:342–69, p. 351, 1990.

Figure 16.26 Graph of Russian Trade Routes in the 12th and 13th Centuries

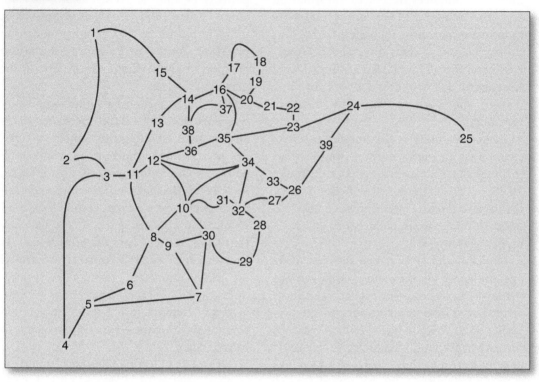

Source: F. Pitts, "The Medieval River Trade Network of Russia Revisited." *Social Networks* 1:285–92, p. 286, 1979.

Whole network analysis is also widely used in management and communications studies to lay out the structure of organizations—particularly, the hidden structure, the one not displayed on the official organization charts in managers' offices—and to determine the role of individuals within organizations (Borgatti and Foster 2003; Valente 2008).

Cross et al. (2001) asked each of the 20 top managers of an oil company to go through the list of the other 19 and indicate those with whom they exchanged information frequently. The executives worked in three divisions of the company—exploration, drilling, and production—and there was some question about the ability of the managers in those divisions to share knowledge as they worked on new projects. Figure 16.27, comparing the official organizational chart with the real network

of information exchange, shows that the concern was well placed.

The production division had been moved recently and its members had become isolated from their colleagues. Institutionalizing meetings among the division members solved that problem. The linchpin of the network, Cole, had developed a reputation for his willingness to share technical information with others. He was overwhelmed with requests to participate on projects and had become a bottleneck in the information flow. The solution was to examine the requests that Cole got for input and to allocate some of them to executives. This not only made Cole feel less burdened—it also made his potentially leaving the firm less of a problem (Cross et al. 2001) (Box 16.9) (**Further Reading:** whole, sociocentric, networks).

Figure 16.27 Formal and Informal Structure in an Organization

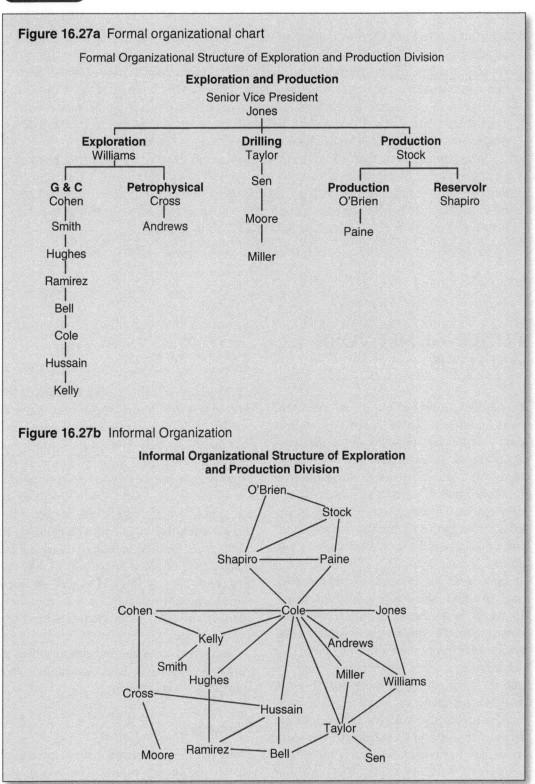

Figure 16.27a Formal organizational chart

Formal Organizational Structure of Exploration and Production Division

Exploration and Production
Senior Vice President
Jones

Figure 16.27b Informal Organization

Informal Organizational Structure of Exploration and Production Division

Source: R. Cross, "Knowing What We Know: Supporting Knowledge Creation and Sharing in Social Networks." *Organizational Dynamics* 30:100–20, p. 107, 2001.

Box 16.9 You never know what a network analysis will turn up

In another case, Peter Killworth and I (1974) mapped the communications of the inmates and staff in a federal prison. One thing you can do with a network map is look for cliques—people who tend to hang out with or talk to one another, to the exclusion of other cliques. We presented the map to the warden and his staff and asked them to interpret the cliques. Most of it was easy: "This group is all the guards who were MPs in the Army, while this one is the college–kid guards with degrees in criminology." "This group is White inmates from cities in the North, and this one is Black inmates from small towns in the South." "This one is mixed-race, but they're all in here for drug crimes." You get the idea.

There was one group that made no ethnographic sense to the staff. The group had just three people in it: two northern Whites and one southern Black, all of whom had committed different kinds of crime. Two weeks later, the three of them escaped together. We were careful to explain that network analysis can uncover hidden groups, but it cannot predict the behavior of people in those groups (Bernard and Killworth 1997).

PERSONAL NETWORK ANALYSIS

In the classic recipe for social research, shown earlier in Table 16.16, you collect data on the variables, compare the variables across the cases, and see if variation in one or more independent variables predicts variation in outcomes, like consumer preferences, adjusting to widowhood, using alternative medicine, leaving a gang, moving up successfully in a company . . . and so on.

Egocentric, or personal social network analysis adds to this classic recipe for research by asking the question: How much of the outcome variables in which we're interested is the result of *who people know* and *how people are related to each other*, not just who people are and the environment in which they live? In analyzing personal networks, then, we're interested as much in network content (the characteristics of people in an individual's network) as we are in network structure (things like centrality) (McCarty 2002; McCarty and Bernard 2003).

"It's Not What You Know, It's Who You Know"

This old saying sums up the wisdom of the ages about the importance of personal networks. Making good contacts while you're in school can help you later in life when you're looking for a job, and knowing the right people can steer you to better health care when you get sick. When people move to a new town, they find people they trust—a relative or friend who came there first, or people who belong to their church, or members of some organization, like the Rotary or Elks or Junior League—to learn which neighborhoods have the best schools and which supermarkets have the best produce.

Everyone knows this and everyone does it. And network analysts have learned some very interesting things about it.

Homophily

Homophily, for example, is the formation of social ties among people who are similar in some way, like age, gender, skin color, ethnicity, wealth, religion, occupation, or education. The power of this principle has been known since ancient times. In *The Republic* (Book I), written in 380 BCE, Plato (n.d.) quotes Cephalus as saying to Socrates: "Men of my age flock together; we are birds of a feather, as the old proverb says."

Today, after many systematic network studies, we have learned a lot about homophily. It "limits people's social worlds," as McPherson et al. (2001:415) put it, "in a way that has powerful implications for the information they receive, the attitudes they form, and the interactions they experience." Interracial-interethnic marriage in the United States has increased steadily over the last few decades, but counting all combinations of White, Black, Asian, Native American, and Asian marriages, is still only about 8% of all marriages (Lewis and Ford-Robertson 2010:13).

Weak Ties and Strong Ties

Another key finding about network content is the remarkable "strength of weak ties," as Mark Granovetter called it (1973, 1995). For example, people in managerial, technical, and professional fields who have lots of weak network ties—acquaintances—have more success in landing new jobs than do people who have to rely on fewer, stronger ties. Strong network ties—close friends, partners or relatives—have more-or-less the same information that you have. In a job search, the strength of weak ties is the result of tapping into information from *outside* your circle of close ties. In many cases, Granovetter found, people learned about job opportunities from network contacts who they had long forgotten (1973:1371–72).

While weak ties are important for information flow, strong ties—kin and friends or acquaintances with whom you have an emotional rather than simply an instrumental

tie—turn out to be better than for social support. When you really need help—getting a ride to the grocery store or having someone check on your house while you're out of town—or when you really need someone to lean on emotionally, it's the close ties that do the heavy lifting for you.

ADDING NETWORK DATA TO THE CLASSIC RECIPE

To measure things like the fraction of strong versus weak ties in a network, we need information about the members of people's networks. Table 16.20 shows two kinds of information about personal networks. Ego—the person whose network we're studying—is Kylie. Kylie has listed some people she knows—her network alters.

In Table16.20a, we see some attributes of Kylie's alters—their age, their education, their gender. From the data in this table, we can calculate the percentage of Kylie's same-sex alters. It's 67%. Table 16.21 shows how we add that information to the classic data matrix in Table 16.16. In Table 16.21, the new column is labeled "Percent Same Sex Alters."

We can also calculate the mean age of Kylie's alters (it's 26.67) and the percentage of Kylie's alters who are, like her, smokers (it's 50%). These numbers, too, can be added to Table 16.21 as new *attributes of Kylie.*

Table 16.20b shows Kylie's answer to the question: "When you're not around, do A and B talk to each other?"—where A and B are all pairs of the alters Kylie named as being in her network. From Table 16.20b, we can calculate the density of Kylie's network and other measures of network structure, like the centrality of each of Kylie's alters. Density is the number of ties in a network divided by the number of possible ties. (Very dense personal networks

Table 16.20 Two Kinds of Data About the Alters in a Network

Table 16.20a. Alter Attribute Data for Kylie

Alter	Age	Education	Gender	Smokes
Jeanette	24	12	0	0
Alexander	25	16	1	1
Dylan	48	12	1	0
Maria	19	12	0	1
Ashley	31	18	0	1
Leah	25	14	0	0

Table 16.20b. Alter-by-Alter Relation Matrix for Kylie

Alter	Jeanette	Alexander	Dylan	Maria	Ashley	Leah
Jeanette	–	1	0	0	1	1
Alexander	1	–	1	0	1	0
Dylan	0	1	–	0	0	0
Maria	0	0	0	–	1	1
Ashley	1	1	0	1	–	0
Leah	1	0	0	1	0	–

Table 16.21 Adding Network Variables to the Classic Data Matrix in Social Research

	Independent Variables				Dependent Variable	Network Variables			
	Gender	Age	Income	Education	Smokes Cigarettes	Network Density	Average Age of Alters	Percent Same Sex Alters	Percent Alters Who Smoke
Kylie	1	24		16	1	0.47	26.67	0.67	0.50
Frank	0	22		14	0				
Maria	1	38		12	0				
Shawn	0	19		13	1				
Allison	1	42		18	0				
Karen	1	26		14	0				

indicate greater reliance on strong ties rather than on weak ties.) In Table 16.20b, there are 14 ties out of a possible 30, so the density is 14/30 = 0.47. That number is added to Table 16.21 in a column labeled "Network Density."

Once we add these variables to the profiles of the other respondents in Table 16.21

(Frank, Maria, Shawn, Allison, and Karen), we can test whether, and to what extent, knowing things about the content (Table 16.20a) and structure (Table 16.20b) of each person's network adds explanatory power to the classic recipe for social research (Box 16.10).

Box 16.10 Why there are more studies of network content than of network structure

From the start, one of most profound questions in social science has been whether the pattern of relations in which people are embedded–the social structure–has an impact on what people think and what they do. Many researchers have found an association between structural features of personal networks–features like density–and some outcome variable. But there's a problem.

If you ask a respondent to list just 10 network alters, then getting the network interaction matrix in Table 16.20b means that the respondent has to make 45 judgments about alter-alter interactions or relations. At 20 alters, that number rises to 190. At 30 alters, it's 435.

McCarty et al. (2007) showed that a random sample of 20 pairs of alters from 40 is sufficient to determine the structural features of a person's network. Still, that's a lot of work for both respondents and researchers to do, so most studies of personal network structure are done on seven or fewer alters.

In a classic study, Elizabeth Bott (1957/1971) found a correlation between the density of social networks among 20 working-class couples in London and the degree of their conjugal role segregation. Couples that had tightly knit (high-density) networks had more traditional roles–they didn't share household chores, for example. Does the hypothesis hold for upper-middle-class couples? How about in rural areas of England? In other cities of the world?

To test Bott's hypothesis requires a much larger sample of respondents than Bott studied and you have to determine whether all pairs of each respondent's network alters know each other or interact in some way.

Collecting this kind of data is a lot easier these days with software, like EgoNet (McCarty et al. 2011. For more on EgoNet, see p. 277 at the end of Chapter 10.) (**Further Reading:** personal, egocentric, networks).

SEMANTIC NETWORKS

A central lesson of this chapter is that any set of relations among actors in a matrix can be represented in a matrix or in a graph. If we have a series of texts, like transcribed interviews, we can treat the words as actors (Schnegg and Bernard 1996). We can produce a two-mode, profile matrix where the rows are texts and the columns are all the substantive words (or tagged themes) in those texts. We can then correlate the rows and produce a one-mode matrix in which the rows and columns both refer to the texts and in which the cells contain a single number that expresses how similar pairs of texts are to one another. This is the basis for semantic network analysis.

Ha-Yong Jang (1995) did this to examine whether there is a national culture discernible in the annual letters to stockholders from the CEOs of U.S. and Japanese corporations. He selected 35 Fortune 500 companies, including 18 U.S. and 17 Japanese firms, matched by type of business. For example, Ford was matched with Honda, Xerox with Canon, and so on. All of these firms are traded on the New York Stock Exchange, and each year stockholders receive an annual message from either the CEO or the president of these companies. (Japanese firms that trade on the New York Exchange send the annual letters in English to their U.S. stockholders.)

Jang downloaded the 1992 annual letters to shareholders and isolated 94 words that occurred at least 26 times across the corpus of 35 letters (Jang 1995:49). Then Jang created a 94(word)-by-35(company) matrix, where the rows are the 94 words and the columns are the 35 companies and the cells contained a number from 0 to 25, 25 being the largest number of times any word ever occurred in one of the letters (the word was "company" and it occurred 25 times in the letter from General Electric).

Figure 16.28 Multidimensional Scaling of Jang and Barnett's Company-by-Company Data

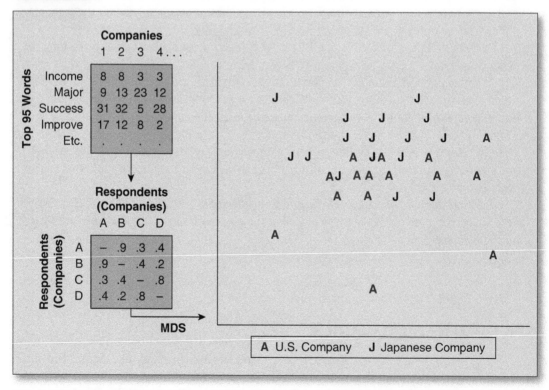

Source: H-J. Jang and G. Barnett. "Cultural Differences in Organizational Communication: A Semantic Network Analysis." *Bulletin de Méthodologie Sociologique* 44:31–59, 1994.

Next, Jang created a 35(company)-by-35(company) similarity matrix of companies based on the co-occurrence of words in their letters to stockholders. Figure 16.28 shows the result of running multidimensional scaling on Jang's 35 × 35 matrix of similarities between companies (from Jang and Barnett 1994). The results of this visualization are clear: There are, indeed, two sets of corporate letters to stockholders, one American and one Japanese.

Jang and Barnett found that 13 words were most associated with the American group of companies: board, chief, leadership, president, officer, major, position, financial, improved, good, success, competitive, and customer. From their close reading of all the texts and their knowledge of corporate culture, Jang and Barnett saw these 13 words as representing two themes: financial information and organizational structure. Six words were more associated with the Japanese companies: income, effort, economy, new, development, and quality. To Jang and Barnett, these words represented organizational operations and reflected Japanese concern for the development of new, quality products to compete in the U.S. business environment (**Further Reading**: semantic network analysis).

AND FINALLY . . .

As I said at the beginning of this chapter, once you understand proximity matrix methods like multidimensional scaling and cluster analysis, you'll be able to analyze any kind of relational data, including social network and even networks of words.

Key Concepts in This Chapter

constant comparison
scree plot
salience
pile sorts
symmetric matrix
multidimensional scaling
smallest space analysis
stress
similarity matrix
dissimilarity matrix
proximity matrices
mental map
cluster analysis
arrays
dimensions
clusters
aggregate similarity matrix
single-link analysis
closest-neighbor analysis
complete-link analysis

farthest-neighbor analysis
triad tests
lambda-2
balanced incomplete block
  design
frame substitution
item-by-feature matrices
sentence frames
paired comparisons
cultural consensus analysis
cultural competence
collective wisdom
factor analysis
shaman
lumpers and splitters
domain-specific
  informants
cultural consonance
nodes
core-periphery structure

sociomatrix
one-mode matrix
two-mode matrix
valued data
one-zero (1/0)
  matrix
adjacency matrix
asymmetric
symmetric
directed graph
undirected graph
spring embedder
affiliation matrix
network structure
arcs
components
degree centrality
closeness centrality
betweenness centrality
network content

support networks	ego	semantic network
homophily	alters	analysis
strength of weak ties	density	words as actors

Summary

- This chapter is about analyzing lists and proximity matrices or matrices of relations. We begin with free lists.

  o Free lists must be cleaned before they can be analyzed.

  o Once data are cleaned, analysis begins with counting the number of times each item is mentioned and plotting the results. Well-defined domains, like names for racial and ethnic groups, have relatively few items with a large fraction of items mentioned by many people. Loosely defined domains, like things that mothers do, will comprise many items mentioned just once.

  o Salience can be measured in several ways. The frequency of items in a set of free lists is one indicator of salience. Another is how early, on average, an item gets mentioned, taking the varying length of lists into account.

  o Free lists can be used to help select items in a cultural domain for further study.

- Pile sorts produce symmetric, one-mode matrices, one for each person. Multidimensional scaling (MDS) is used to visualize the relations among items in a proximity matrix.

  o Matrices can be aggregated to get an overall picture of how people, collectively, think about the items in a domain.

  o MDS is also called smallest-space analysis because MDS programs work out the best spatial representation of a set of objects that are represented by a set of similarities.

  o To interpret MDS graphs, look for arrays—dimensions—and clusters.

- Cluster analysis can also be applied to the one-mode matrices.

  o Two ways to find clusters in relational matrices are single-link (or closest neighbor) and complete link (or farthest neighbor) analysis.

  o When you analyze matrices with different algorithms, you get different results that require researcher interpretation. This involves naming clusters and dimensions.

  o Triad data can also be analyzed with MDS and cluster analysis.

  o With a lambda-2 design, each pair of items shows up twice in the matrix. This cuts the number of triads down to just 70 from 455 for a 15-item triad test.

- In frame substitution, respondents are asked n-times-m questions, where n is some item (like an illness) and m is a property of the item (like a symptom or a cause or a cure). This produces an n-by-m profile matrix for each person. Each time a respondent says that, say, a pair of illnesses has the same property, that pair of illnesses gets a point. With 20 respondents, each pair of illnesses could have from 0 to 20-times-m points. The aggregate matrix can be analyzed with MDS and clustering.

- Pile sorts, sentence frames, and triad tests help us understand the semantic structure of items in a cultural domain. We also want to understand how people evaluate the items in a domain on a particular attribute.

  o The most common way to evaluate items on an attribute is with a rating scale. Rating scales produce a lot of ties because people can give the same rating number to many items.

With 15 or fewer items in a domain, it is possible to get rank-ordered data using paired comparisons.

- With cultural consensus analysis, we can measure the extent to which people agree about the contents of a cultural domain and to assess people's domain-specific cultural competence.

  o The method is grounded in a tradition of research on collective wisdom.
  o There are two equations that specify how agreement among a set of people equals knowledge—one expressing the probability that a person answers a question correctly and one expressing the probability that two people agree on the answer to a question.
  o In building consensus model tests, about half the questions should be positive (true, yes, agree) and about half should be negative (false, no, disagree).
  o You can use the consensus model to identify experts in cultural domains.

- Methods for analyzing relational data can be used to analyze network data
- A sociomatrix is a one-mode matrix of who-to-whom data where the cells indicate links between pairs of people. The typical data matrix in social research is a two-mode matrix in which the rows are cases (people, countries, marriage contracts) and the columns are attributes of the cases, including independent and dependent variables.

  o Matrices of relations can be symmetric or asymmetric and graphs of networks can be directed or undirected.

- Many specific measures have been developed for studying networks. Three measures of centrality in networks are closeness centrality, degree centrality, and betweenness centrality.
- Whole network analysis is used in the study of organizations to help explain outcomes like the flow and concentration of money, power, information, and to determine the role of individuals.
- Personal, or egocentric, network analysis is widely used in the study of social support and social capital.

  o Personal social network analysis adds to the classic recipe for research by asking the question: How much of the outcome variables in which we're interested is the result of *who people know* and *how people are related to each other*, not just who people are and the environment in which they live?

- In analyzing personal networks, we're interested in network content as well as in network structure.

  o Homophily is seen in many personal networks. That is, people tend to associate with others who share attributes like age, sex, ethnicity, and so on.
  o Weak network ties (acquaintances) are important for information flow but strong ties (kin and friends or acquaintances with whom you have an emotional rather than simply an instrumental tie) are important for social support.

- Network thinking, and network analysis, can be applied to the study of any set of relations. In semantic network analysis, for example, we treat words as actors.

Exercises

1. Get a group of two or three students together and replicate Henley's (1969) study: Ask 30–40 people to free list all the animals they can think of in one minute. Clean and analyze the lists to discover the most popular animals and also to see if there are clear packaging effects in

how people remember animals. Look for clumpings of domestic animals, pets, wild animals, birds, fishes, and so on.

Use Anthropac (Borgatti 1992a, 1992b, free at analytictech.com) to import and analyze the lists. (You can use Excel® to produce a scree plot.)

2. Choose 30 animals from the free lists in Exercise 1. Write the names of the animals on cards and collect pile sort data from 30 to 40 people. Use Anthropac to import the data and either Anthropac or Ucinet to analyze the data with multidimensional scaling and cluster analysis.

3. Interview six people about what causes people to catch a cold, how you know you have a cold and not some other illness, and how to deal with a cold once you have it. From the interview data, build a test of 40 true-false questions about colds—causes, symptoms, and cures. Give the test to 30 or more people and run consensus analysis on the data. If you can do it, try to get data from doctors, nurses, and pharmacists, so you can compare the results with those from people who are not health professionals.

4. Here is a multidimensional scaling plot of similarity data about 15 animals. These data come from pile sorts. The stress in this two-dimensional plot is less than 0.10. Interpret this graph. Point out and name the clusters. Interpret the position of dog and cat and interpret the position of alligator.

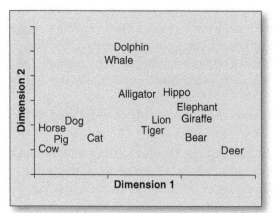

5. Map your own social network. First, list 40 people you know, in any order that comes to mind. Then, for every pair of those 40 people (40 × 39/2 = 780 pairs), answer the question: Does A know B? Then, build a 40-by-40 matrix with 1s in the cells of all the pairs who you think know each other and 0s in the cells of the pairs whom you think don't know each other. Finally, draw a map of this network. This would be a really tedious exercise if you had to do it by hand, but you can do it easily with EgoNet (McCarty et al. 2011), free at http://sourceforge.net/projects/egonet/.

Further Reading

Measuring salience: Quinlan (2005), Robbins and Nolan (2000), J. J. Smith and Borgatti (1997), J. J. Smith et al. (1995), Sutrop (2001), Thompson and Juan (2006).

Multidimensional scaling. Bolton and Vincke (1996), McWhirter et al. (2000), Mugavin (2008), Pinkley et al (2005), Schmelkin et al. (2010), Sturdisson et al. (2006), Sturrock and Rocha (2000), Weisner (1973), Whaley and Longoria (2009).

Cluster analysis. Aldenderfer and Blashfield (1984), Doreian (2004), Subhash and Kumar (2006).

Frame substitution or item-by-feature matrices. D'Andrade et al. (1972), Hruschka et al. (2008), Stefflre (1972), Young (1978).

Consensus analysis. Caulkins (2001), Chavez et al. (1995), Garro (2000), Handwerker (2002), S. M. Harvey and Bird (2004), Jaskyte and Dressler (2004), M. L. Miller et al. (2004), C. S. Smith et al. (2010), Swora (2003).

Whole, sociocentric, networks. Burt and Minor (1983), Coleman et al. (1957), Freeman (1979, 2004), Freeman et al. (1992), Hanneman and Riddle (2005), Knoke and Yang (2008), Scott (2000), Wasserman and Faust (1994), Wasserman and Galaskiewicz (1994).

Personal, egocentric networks. Boissevain and Mitchell (1973), Cross and Parker (2004), Gottlieb (1981), Lin (2001), Lin et al. (2001), Marsden (2002), Marsden and Lin (1982), McKether et al. (2009), Mitchell (1969), Padgett and Ansell (1993), Schneider and Huber (2008), Wellman (1999, 2007).

Semantic network analysis. Cepela and Danowski (2009), Doerfel (1998), Nolan and Ryan (2000).

17

Analyzing Qualitative Data I

Applying Logic to Text

In this chapter, we'll examine four methods for analyzing qualitative data: ethnographic decision modeling, folk taxonomies (taxonomic analysis), componential analysis, and analytic induction (including Boolean analysis). These methods are all based on the application of logic. More about this as we move along. Let's get right to the first method: ethnographic decision modeling.

ETHNOGRAPHIC DECISION MODELING (EDM)

Ethnographic decision models (EDMs) predict the choices that people make under specific circumstances. Any recurring decision—to buy or not to buy a car, to use or not use a condom during sex, to take a sick child to the doctor—can be modeled with this method. The method was developed by Christina Gladwin (1989) and is based on asking questions, sorting out some logical rules about how the questions have to be ordered, and laying out the order in a picture (like a tree diagram) or in writing.

As with all cognitive research methods, we don't know if EDMs just predict behavior or if they also reflect the way people think about things. The jury is still out on that one. But EDMs get the prediction right 80 to 90% of the time and that's as good as it gets in the social sciences (Box 17.1).

Box 17.1 Decision making and decision models in the social sciences

Ethnographic decision modeling was developed in anthropology, but the study of decision making and the statistical modeling of decisions are major areas of research across the social sciences. For leads into this literature, consult Fischoff (2010).

How to Build EDMs

There are four main steps in doing decision modeling. (1) Select a specific behavioral choice to model and elicit decision criteria from a convenience sample of respondents. (2) Further elaborate and verify the decision criteria on a purposive, heterogeneous sample of informants. (3) Use the ethnographic data from step 1 and the survey data from step 2 to build a hierarchical decision model. (4) Test the model on an independent and, if possible, representative sample from the same population. We'll take these in turn.

Step 1. First, decide on the decision you are studying and what the alternatives are in that decision. EDMs are not limited to binary decisions but are easiest to build for questions about behaviors that can be answered yes or no. I'll use the decision "to make your 8 a.m. class or not" as an example. The alternatives are yes and no.

Step 2. A grand tour ethnographic question like "Tell me about why people go to class or skip 8 a.m. classes" will get you a lot of information about the alternatives and the reasons for the alternatives, especially from expert informants. The major alternatives are: Get up and go to class, get up and do something else, sleep in. The "get up and do something else" alternative consists of a list: lounge around, watch old soaps on the tube, study for an exam later in the day, and so on.

Step 3. To make your ethnographic knowledge about the decision more formal—that is, to build an EDM—track down Alex, a respondent who has an 8 a.m. class and ask: "Did you make your 8 a.m. class today?" When he answers, ask him: "Why [did you] [didn't you] go to that class?" Suppose he says "I went to class today because I *always* go to class unless I'm sick." Ask him: "Were you sick this morning?" Record his answer and draw a tree diagram (also called a dendrogram), like the one in Figure 17.1, to represent his decision.

| Figure 17.1 | An Ethnographic Decision Model After Interviewing One Informant (Alex) |

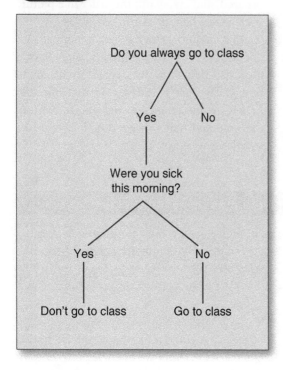

Do you always go to class

Yes   No

Were you sick
this morning?

Yes   No

Don't go to class   Go to class

| Figure 17.2 | An Ethnographic Decision Model After Interviewing Two Informants (Alex and Sheila) |

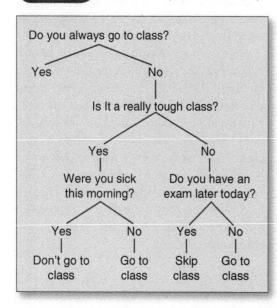

Do you always go to class?

Yes   No

Is It a really tough class?

Yes   No

Were you sick   Do you have an
this morning?   exam later today?

Yes   No   Yes   No

Don't go to   Go to   Skip   Go to
class   class   class class

Figure 17.1 accounts perfectly for Alex's decision. It has to; it contains nothing more than the information from the ethnographic interview with Alex.

Now go to your second respondent, Sheila, who says that yes, she went to her 8 a.m. class. Why? "It's a really tough class," she says, "If I miss one of those classes, I'll never catch up."

Every reason for your respondents' decisions becomes a question you can ask. Use what you learned from your interview with Alex and ask Sheila: "Do you *always* go to class?" Sheila says that she sometimes skips early classes if those classes are really easy and she needs to study for an exam in another class later in the day. Ask her: "Were you sick this morning?" If she says, "no," draw the diagram in Figure 17.2.

Your third respondent, Brad, says that no, he didn't go to class this morning; no, he doesn't always go to class; yes, he skips class when he's sick; no, he wasn't sick this morning; no, he didn't have an exam later in the day; no, his 8 a.m. class isn't tough; but he was out very late last night and just didn't feel like going to class this morning. Figure 17.3 combines all the information we have for Alex, Sheila, and Brad.

In fact, we don't know if Sheila was out late last night, and if she had been, whether that would have affected her decision to go to class early this morning. We can find out by going back and asking Sheila the new question. We could also go back and ask Alex if he had an exam later in the day and if he'd been out late last night.

But we won't. In practice, it is very difficult to go back to informants and ask them all the questions you accumulate from EDM interviews. Instead, the usual practice is to build a composite diagram, like the one in Figure 17.3, and push on. We also won't ask Brad what he *would* have done if he'd had a really tough 8:00 a.m. class and had been out late the night before. In building EDMs, *we deal only with people's reports of their actual, most recent behavior.*

Figure 17.3 An Ethnographic Decision Model After Interviewing Three Informants (Alex, Sheila, and Brad)

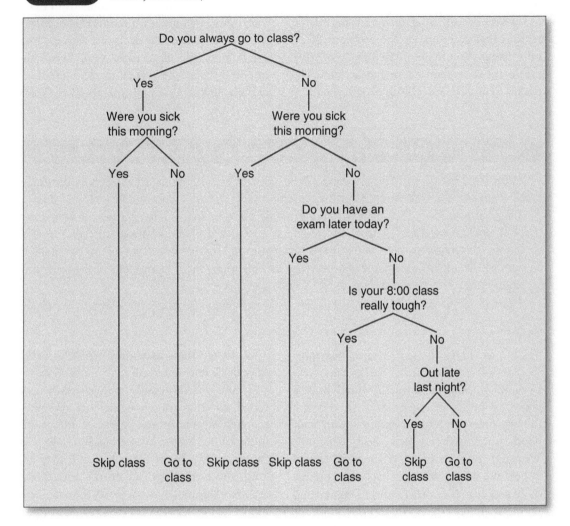

Eventually, you'll stop getting new decisions, reasons, and constraints. Building a model for the decision on a single campus to attend or not attend early classes probably won't require more than 20 informants. Building an EDM that accounts for this decision on two very different campuses—say, a small, private college and a huge state school—may take twice that many informants. As the culture gets more heterogeneous, the sample size needed to find a stable decision model goes up. Accounting for the decisions of students in New York City and Sussex, England, will require more interviews. Add Mexico City and the number may double again. Add Cameroon. . . .

Step 4. Figure 17.3 may account for all the decisions of your next several informants, but eventually you'll run into an informant who says she doesn't always go to class, she wasn't sick this morning, she doesn't have a tough class at 8 a.m., she wasn't out late last night, and she still didn't make her early class today. Why? Because she just didn't feel like it.

If you add enough constraints, you can always build a model to account for every decision of every respondent. But what's the use of a model with 20 different sets of ordered reasons that accounts for the decisions of 20 informants? You might as well just ask every informant to explain his or her actions. The trick is to model the decisions of, say, 18 out of 20 informants (90% prediction) with just a handful of ordered rules. So, when you stop getting new reasons or constraints from EDM interviews, try building a model that accounts for at least 80% of the decisions with the fewest number of rules. Then—and here's the important part—test your model against an entirely new group of informants (Box 17.2).

Box 17.2 The interview for the second group of informants is different

It's different because you do ask them all the questions in your model (that is, you probe for all the reasons and constraints for the decision that your first group taught you) and then you guess what their decision was. In our example, you'd interview 20 or 30 new informants, all of whom have 8 a.m. classes, and you'd ask each one: Do you always go to class? Were you sick this morning? Were you out late last night? and so on, exhausting all the questions from your model. If your model works, you'll be able to *predict* the decisions of the second group from their answers to the model's questions.

Testing an EDM on a National Sample

Gery Ryan, Stephen Borgatti, and I built a decision model for this question: "Think about the last time you had an empty can in your hand—juice, iced tea, soda, beer, whatever. What did you do with it?" (Ryan and Bernard 2006). We interviewed a convenience sample of 70 people in California, North Dakota, and Florida and asked them 31 questions about the event, but we were able to predict 90% of reported decisions with just the questions in Figure 17.4.

Read Figure 17.4 as follows: Start by asking informants if they were at home when they made the most recent decision about what to do with that can. If they were at home, then ask if they recycle other products besides cans. If they were, then guess that they claimed to have recycled the can. This will result in two errors. That is two out of 23 people in this condition claim not to have recycled. Read the rest of Figure 17.4 similarly. The whole model gets 63 out of 70, or 90% right—and that's

77% better than assigning people a result (recycle or not) randomly.

Figure 17.5 shows what happened when we tested our ethnographic model in a nationally representative telephone survey of 386 people in the United States. We got 84.5% right, and that was 59% better than chance. It may not work for everything, but on this model, the ethnographic model was a proxy for a national model of the decision on what to do with an empty can.

Representing Complicated Models With Tables: Young and Garro's EDM

James Young and Linda Garro studied how Tarascan people in Pichátaro, Mexico, choose one of four ways to treat an illness: Use a home remedy, go to a native curer, see a *practicante* (a local, nonphysician practitioner of modern medicine), or go to a physician (see Garro 1986; Young 1980; Young and Garro 1982, 1994 [1981]). From their ethnographic work, Young and Garro believed that the decision to

Figure 17.4 Ethnographic Decision Model for Recycling Cans

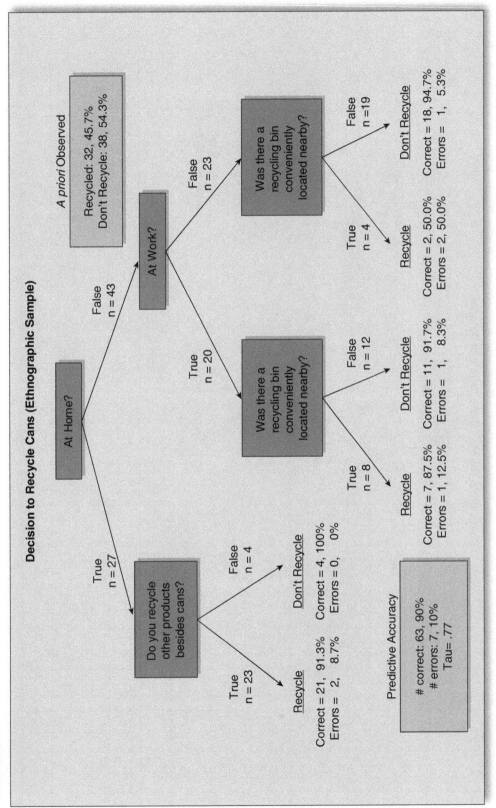

Source: G. W. Ryan and H. R. Bernard, "Testing an Ethnographic Decision Tree Model on a National Sample: Recycling Beverage Cans," *Human Organization* Vol. 65, pp. 103–114, 2006.

Figure 17.5 National Test of an Ethnographic Decision Model

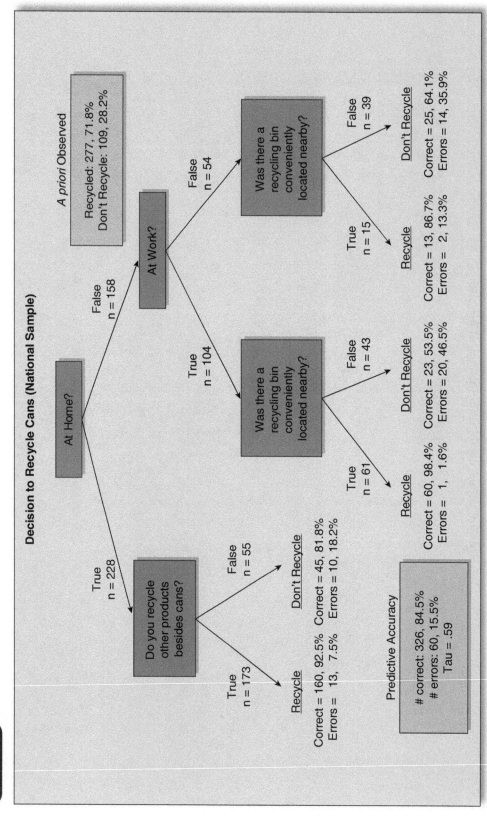

Decision to Recycle Cans (National Sample)

A priori Observed

Recycled: 277, 71.8%
Don't Recycle: 109, 28.2%

At Home?

False
n = 158

True
n = 228

At Work?

Do you recycle
other products
besides cans?

False
n = 54

True
n = 104

True
n = 173

False
n = 55

Was there a
recycling bin
conveniently
located nearby?

Was there a
recycling bin
conveniently
located nearby?

Recycle   Don't Recycle

Correct = 160, 92.5%   Correct = 45, 81.8%
Errors = 13, 7.5%   Errors = 10, 18.2%

False
n = 39

True
n = 15

False
n = 43

True
n = 61

Don't Recycle

Correct = 25, 64.1%
Errors = 14, 35.9%

Recycle

Correct = 13, 86.7%
Errors = 2, 13.3%

Don't Recycle

Correct = 23, 53.5%
Errors = 20, 46.5%

Recycle

Correct = 60, 98.4%
Errors = 1, 1.6%

Predictive Accuracy

# correct: 326, 84.5%
# errors: 60, 15.5%
Tau = .59

Source: G.W. Ryan and H. R. Bernard, "Testing an Ethnographic Decision Tree Model on a National Sample: Recycling Beverage Cans," *Human Organization* Vol. 65, pp. 103–114, 2006.

use one or another of these treatments depended on four factors:

1. how serious an illness was perceived to be (gravity);

2. whether a home remedy for the illness was known;

3. whether the informant had confidence in the general efficacy of a mode of treatment for a particular illness; and

4. accessibility (in terms of cost and transportation) of a particular mode of treatment.

The choice situations emerged from structured interviews with eight men and seven women who were asked:

Если you or another person in your household were ill, when—for what reasons—would you [consult] [use] _____ instead of [consulting] [using] _____? [Young and Garro 1994 (1981):132]

Young and Garro used this question frame to elicit responses about all six possible pairs of treatment alternatives: home remedy vs. a physician, curer vs. home remedy, and so on. To check the validity of the statements made in the interviews, Young and Garro collected case histories of actual illnesses and their treatments from each of the 15 informants.

Next, the researchers completed interviews with 20 informants using a series of "What if . . ." questions to generate decisions, under various combinations of circumstances, regarding the selection of treatments for illnesses. For example, informants were asked:

Let's say there is a person who has a very grave illness. In this family, money is scarce—sure, they're eating, but there is just not anything left over. They have had this illness in the family before, and they now know of the remedy that benefited the illness on the previous occasion.

What do you think they are going to do? [Young and Garro 1994 (1981):137]

This vignette combines the condition of a serious illness (level 3 on gravity in Tables 17.1 and 17.2), with lack of accessibility (no money), and a known remedy that can be applied at home. Young and Garro used the three levels of gravity, two possible conditions of knowing a remedy (yes and no), and two possible conditions of accessibility (yes and no) in making up the vignettes, which meant that they had to make up eight of them. Each vignette was presented to each informant for a response. Tables 17.1 and 17.2 show the decision tables for Young and Garro's data.

From these qualitative data, collected in structured interviews, Young and Garro developed their decision model, for the initial choice of treatment. The model, containing nine decision rules, is shown in Table 17.1.

Rule number 1, for example, says that if the illness is not serious and there is a known home remedy, then treat the illness yourself. Rule number 9 says that for grave illnesses there is an implicit understanding that physicians are better (hence the M in parentheses), so if there is money, then go to a physician. Rule number 9 also says that for the few cases of very grave illnesses where physicians are commonly thought not to be effective, apply rule number 7 and go to a curer. The blank spaces in the top part of Table 17.1 indicate irrelevant conditions. In rule number 1, for example, there is no question about accessibility for home remedies because they cost little or nothing and everyone has access to them.

Sometimes the treatment selected for an illness doesn't work and another decision has to be made. Table 17.2, with 11 decision rules, shows Young and Garro's analysis of this second stage of decision making. Their entire two-stage model is based on their sense of emerging patterns in the data they collected about decision making. The question is: Does it work?

Table 17.1 Young and Garro's Decision Table for How Pichatareños Choose an Initial Method of Treating an Illness

Rules:	1	2	3	4	5	6	7	8	9
Conditions									
gravity[a]	1	1	1	2	2	2	3	3	3
known home remedy[b]	Y	N	N	Y	N				
faith[c]		F	M	(F)	F	M	F	M	(M)
Accessibility[d]								N	Y
Choices									
self-treatment	X			X					
curer		X			X		X		
practicante			X			X		X	
physician									X

a. 1 = nonserious 2 = moderately serious 3 = grave
b. Y = yes N = no
c. F = favors folk treatment M = favors medical treatment
d. Y = money and transportation available N = either money or transportation not available
Source: J. C. Young and L. C. Garro, *Medical Choice in a Mexican Village*, 1981 (reissued 1994), p. 154, Waveland.

Young and Garro tested their model against 444 treatment choices gathered from 62 households over a six-month period. To make the test fair, none of the informants in the test were among those whose data were used in developing the model. Table 17.3 shows the results of the test. There were 157 cases covered by rule number 1 from Table 17.1 (first-stage decision), and in every single case informants did what the rule predicted. In Table 17.3, errors (informants' choices that are not predicted by the model) are in parentheses, so informants did what rule number 6 predicted 20 out of 29 times.

Overall, for the first stage, Young and Garro's decision rules predict about 94% of informants' reported behavior. After removing the cases covered by rules 1 and 4 (which account for half the cases in the data, but which could be dismissed as common-sense,

routine decisions and not in need of any pretentious "analysis"), their model still predicts almost 83% of reported behavior. Even for the second stage, after first-stage decisions fail to result in a cure, and decisions get more complex and tougher to predict, the model predicts an impressive 84% of reported behavior.

Representing Complicated Models With IF-THEN Charts: Ryan and Martínez's EDM

Gery Ryan and Homero Martínez (1996) built an EDM for how mothers in San José, Mexico, treated children who have diarrhea. Ryan and Martínez knew, from living in the village, that mothers there use seven different treatments in treating their children's diarrhea. Five of the treatments consist of giving the child one or

<table>
| Table 17.2 | Young and Garro's Decision Table Showing How Pichatareños Choose a Method of Treating an Illness When Their First Choice Doesn't Work |
</table>

Rules: Conditions	1	2	3	4	5	6	7	8	9	10	11
preceding choice[a]	ST	ST	ST	ST	C-P	C-P	C	P	Dr	Dr	Dr
current gravity[b]		1–2	3	3	1	2–3	2–3	2–3			
faith[c]	F	M	M	(M)							M
accessibility[d]			N	Y		Y	N	N		N	Y
choices											
self-treatment					X						
curer	X								X	X	X
practicante		X	X					X			
physician				X		X					X

a. ST = self-treatment C = curer P = *practicante* Dr = physician

b. 1 = nonserious 2 = moderately serious 3 = grave

c. F = favors folk treatment M = favors medical treatment

d. Y = money and transportation available N = either money or transportation not currently available

Source: J. C. Young and L. C. Garro, *Medical Choice in a Mexican Village,* 1981 (reissued 1994), p. 156, Waveland.

more of the following: (1) tea; (2) homemade rice water; (3) medication from the pharmacy (their informants told them "If you can say it, you can buy it"); (4) a carbonated beverage; or (5) a commercially produced oral rehydration solution. The other two treatments are: (6) manipulating the child's body (massaging the child's body, pinching the child's back) or (7) taking the child to the doctor.

Ryan and Martínez asked 17 mothers in San José who had children under age five what they did the last time their children had diarrhea. Then they went systematically through the treatments, asking each mother why she had used X instead of A, X instead of B, X instead of C, and so on down through the list.

Mothers in San José listed the following factors for choosing one treatment over another:

duration of the episode

perceived cause (from worms, from *empacho*, from food, etc.)

whether there was mucous in the stool

whether there was blood in the stool

whether the stools smelled bad

whether the stools were frequent or not

whether the stools were loose or not

whether the child had fever

color of the stool

whether the child had a dry mouth

whether the child had dry eyes

whether the child was vomiting

whether the child had swollen glands

Table 17.3 Test Results of Young and Garro's Decision Model of How Pichatareños Choose a Treatment Method When They Are Ill[a]

Table	Rule	Self-Treatment	Curer	*Practicante*	Physician	Totals	Percentage Correct
18.1	1	157				157	
	2		4			4	
	3			5		5	
	4	67			(1)	68	
	5		8			8	
	6	(2)		20	(7)	29	
	7		8			8	
	8		(2)	4	(2)	8	
	9			(2)	11	13	
					Subtotal	300	94.7%
18.2	1		19			19	
	2		(1)	28	(6)	35	
	3		(3)	6		9	
	4			(2)	22	24	
	5	3	(1)			4	
	6	(2)	(2)	(1)	24	29	
	7	(1)		3	(2)	6	
	8		2	(1)		3	
	9	(1)	7			8	
	10					0	
	11				7	7	
					Subtotal	144	84.0%
					Total	444	91.2%

[a]*Note:* Young and Garro collected data on 489 illness incidents but had complete decision data for 444 of those incidents.

Source: J. C. Young and L. C. Garro, *Medical Choice in a Mexican Village,* 1981 (reissued 1994) p. 165, Waveland.

Table 17.4 shows the data from the 17 women in Ryan and Martínez's original sample and the decision to take the child to the doctor. Read the table like this: Mother #1 said that her child's last episode of diarrhea lasted two days and was caused by bad food. The stools contained mucous, but did not contain blood. The stools smelled bad, were frequent and loose. The child had fever, the stools were yellow. The child had dry mouth and dry eyes, but was not vomiting and did not have swollen glands. In the end, Mother #1 did not take her child to the doctor. (The codes for cause and color are from Spanish; see the legend just below the table.)

Table 17.4 makes it clear that mothers took their children to the doctor if the child had blood in the stool, had swollen glands, or was vomiting, or if the diarrhea had lasted *more than* seven days. None of the other factors played a part in the final decision to take the child to the doctor.

But remember: There were seven different treatments, and mothers often try several treatments in any given episode. Ryan and Martínez looked at the pattern of circumstances for all seven treatments and built a model that accounted for the treatment decisions made by the 17 mothers. Their model had just six rules and three constraints.

Figure 17.6 shows the model as a series of **IF-THEN statements**. Notice the constraints: For a woman to choose a modern medication, she has to know about it and it has to be easy to get and cheap. The constraints to the rules are derived from ethnographic interviews. So was the observation that mothers distinguished between curative and palliative treatments—treatments that stop diarrhea and treatments that simply make the child feel better until the episode is over. The model postdicted (accounted for) 89% of the treatments that the 17 mothers had reported.

Next, Ryan and Martínez tested their model. They interviewed 20 more mothers, but this time they asked each woman every question in the model. In other words, they asked each woman: "In your child's last episode of diarrhea, did the stools have blood in them? Did the child have swollen glands? What caused the diarrhea?" and so on. The IF-THEN model in Figure 17.6 accounted for 84% of the *second* group's treatment decisions (**Further Reading:** ethnographic decision models).

I expect to see ethnographic decision models applied to lots of important social behaviors—behaviors like using or not using a condom.

FOLK TAXONOMIES

There are about 6,000 languages spoken in the world today. Speakers of all those languages name things in the natural world. In 1914, Henderson and Harrington published a monograph on the ethnozoology of the Tewa Indians of New Mexico. Scholars ever since have been interested in understanding the variety of ways in which people organize their knowledge of the natural world.

In the 1950s, anthropologists began systematically producing folk taxonomies—that is, hierarchical, taxonomic graphs to represent how people organize their knowledge of plants and animals. These ethnobotanical and ethnozoological taxonomies don't necessarily mirror scientific taxonomies, but the whole point of what became known as ethnoscience is to understand cultural knowledge on its own terms.

Scientific taxonomies for plants and animals recognize six primary levels of distinction (phylum, class, order, family, genus, and species) and lots of in-between levels, as well (infraorder, superorder, subclass, etc.), but folk taxonomies of plants and animals across the world are generally limited to five or, at most, six levels. Figure 17.7 (from D'Andrade 1995) shows part of the folk taxonomy of *creatures* for native speakers of English.

Covert Categories

There are six culturally appropriate levels of hierarchical distinction identified in Figure 17.7: (1) First, there is the unique beginner, a single label that identifies the cultural domain. (2) Next is a relatively small set of life

Table 17.4   Decision to Take the Child to the Doctor

mother	doctor	days	cause	muc.	blood	smell	freq	loose	fever	color	mouth	eyes	vomit	gland
1	N	2	C	Y	N	Y	Y	Y	Y	A	Y	Y	N	N
2	N	20	E	Y	N	Y	Y	Y	N	A	Y	Y	N	N
3	Y	8	T	N	N	Y	Y	Y	Y	N	Y	Y	N	N
4	Y	8	C	Y	N	Y	N	Y	Y	V	.	.	Y	Y
5	N	3	P	Y	N	Y	Y	Y	Y	A	Y	Y	N	Y
6	N	3	L	N	N	Y	Y	Y	N	B	Y	Y	N	N
7	Y	8	D	Y	N	Y	Y	Y	N	A	Y	Y	N	N
8	N	1	D	N	N	Y	Y	Y	N	A	.	.	N	N
9	N	.	C	Y	N	N	Y	Y	N	B	Y	Y	N	N
10	N	3	O	N	N	N	Y	Y	N	A	Y	Y	N	N
11	N	2	C	N	N	N	N	N	N	A	.	.	N	N
12	N	.	C	N	N	Y	Y	Y	N	A	Y	Y	N	N
13	N	4	C	N	N	Y	N	N	N	A	Y	Y	N	N
14	Y	4	E	N	N	Y	Y	Y	Y	V	Y	.	N	N
15	Y	3	I	Y	Y	Y	Y	Y	Y	A	Y	Y	Y	N
16	N	2	C	Y	N	N	Y	Y	N	V	Y	Y	N	N
17	N	7	E	N	N	N	Y	Y	N	A	N	N	N	N

Cause
C = food
L = worms
E = empacho
I = indigestion

D = teething
T = dirt
P = parasites
O = other

Color
A = yellow
V = green
B = white
N = black

Source: G. W. Ryan and H. Martínez, "Can We Predict what Mothers Do? Modeling Childhood Diarrhea in Rural Mexico." *Human Organization* 55:47–57, 1996.

Figure 17.6 Ryan and Martinez's Decision Model as a Series of IF-THEN Rules

Rule 1	
IF	Child has blood stools OR child has swollen glands OR child is vomiting
THEN	take child to doctor.
Rule 2	
IF	diarrhea is caused by *empacho*
THEN	give physical treatment.
Rule 3	
IF	previous rules do not apply OR there is no cure with *empacho* treatment
THEN	give the highest preferred curing treatment that meets constraints.
Rule 4	
IF	previous treatment did not stop diarrhea
THEN	compare the two highest treatments of remaining options.
Rule 4.1	
IF	one is a curing remedy AND meets its constraints
THEN	give this treatment.
Rule 4.2	
IF	both or neither are curing remedies AND each meets its respective constraints
THEN	give the highest raked preference.
Rule 5	
IF	the previous treatment did not stop the diarrhea AND the episode is less than 1 week
THEN	repeat rule 4
Rule 6	
IF	the episode has lasted more than 1 week
THEN	take the child to a doctor.
Constraints	
IF	you know how to make ORS (oral rehydration solution) AND your child will drink ORS
THEN	give ORS
IF	you know a medication that works for diarrhea AND you have it in the house
THEN	give the pill or liquid medication.
IF	you know a medication that works for diarrhea AND it is cheap AND it is easy to obtain.
THEN	give the pill or liquid medication.

Source: G. W. Ryan and H. Martinez, "Can We Predict What Mothers Do? Modeling Childhood Diarrhea in Rural Mexico," *Human Organization* 55:47–57, 1996.

forms (animals, fish, insects, etc.). (3) Then there is an intermediate level, which includes covert categories, if any exist in a particular taxonomy (Berlin et al. 1968). Folk genera (level 4), folk species (level 5), and folk varieties (level 6) round out the picture.

There is a covert, unnamed category in Figure 17.7 comprising wolves, foxes, dogs, coyotes, and some other things (the dashed line extending down from coyote, indicates that the covert category contains more than what's listed in the figure). In a scientific taxonomy, foxes are not in the same genus with dogs and wolves. The latter are in the genus *Canis*, while foxes are in the genus *Vulpes*. Many speakers of English, however, classify foxes and wolves in the category of "things in the dog family," or "canines," and a folk taxonomy of English animal terms respects that.

The intermediate category of "cat" is not covert. How can you tell? As D'Andrade says, you can say "Look at that cat" if you're talking about a tiger, but it's weird to say "Look at that dog" if you're pointing to a fox, so "cat" is a named intermediate category and "dog" isn't.

There are two more things about Figure 17.7. Note how we use words for generic animals in English that would be at the species level in a scientific taxonomy (wolf, coyote, and dog are all members of the genus *Canis*, species *lupus*, *latrans*, and *familiaris*, respectively) and how the species level in the folk taxonomy comprises names for subspecies in a scientific taxonomy.

Also, look at how D'Andrade has placed octopus and snake in Figure 17.7. The horizontal lines show that D'Andrade has classified these creatures as nonaffiliated generics. They might be classified as life forms, but, as D'Andrade points out, there are many nonaffiliated generics in the ocean, including clams, lobsters, seahorses, jellyfish, and octopi.

Cultural Domains and Folk Taxonomies

It was quickly recognized that folk taxonomies could be developed for *any* cultural domain,

not just for ethnobotanical and ethnozoological knowledge. In fact, we use folk taxonomies all the time to order our experience and guide our behavior.

Take someone to a supermarket—one they've never been to before—and ask them to find peanut butter. Follow them as they make their way around the store and get them to talk about what they think they're doing. Here's a typical response:

> Well, let's see, milk and eggs are over there by that wall, and the meat's usually next to that, and the canned goods are kind of in the middle, with the soaps and paper towels and stuff on the other side, so we'll go right in here, in the middle. No, this is the soap aisle, so let's go over to the right. . . . Sure, here's the coffee, so it's got to be on this aisle or the next, with cans of things like ravioli.

Any competent member of U.S. or Canadian culture will find the peanut butter in a hurry, but not everything is so clear. Shredded coconut and walnuts are often shelved with flour in the United States because they are used in baking, but other nuts—cashews and peanuts, for example—may be shelved somewhere else, like with the snacks. Lychee nuts (a Chinese dessert food) and matzohs (unleavened bread boards eaten primarily by Jews) are sometimes shelved in U.S. supermarkets together under "ethnic foods," but may be shelved in separate "Oriental foods" and "Jewish foods" sections if local populations of those groups are sufficiently large.

How to Make a Taxonomy: Pile Sorts

Pile sorting is an efficient method for generating taxonomic trees (Werner and Fenton 1973). Simply hand informants the familiar pack of cards, each of which contains some term in a cultural domain. Informants sort the cards into piles, according to whatever criterion makes sense to them. After the first sorting, informants are handed each pile and asked

Figure 17.7 Partial Taxonomy for Creatures in English

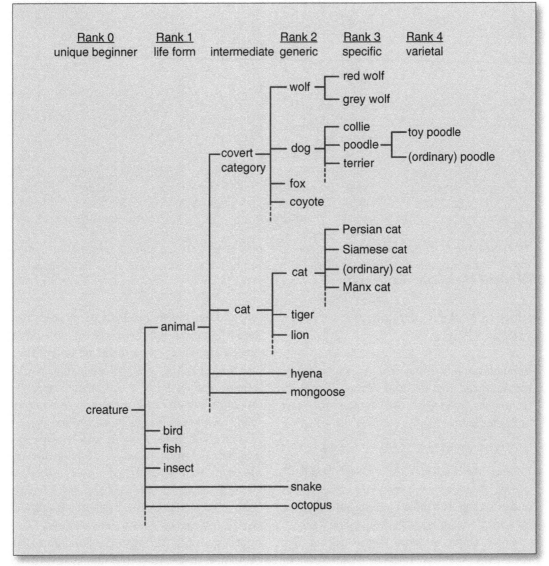

Source: R. G. D'Andrade. *The Development of Cognitive Anthropology.* p. 99. Copyright 1995 Cambridge University Press.

to go through the exercise again. They keep doing this until they say that they cannot subdivide piles any further. At each sorting level, informants are asked if there is a word or phrase that describes each pile.

Perchonock and Werner (1969) used this technique in their study of Navajo animal categories. After an informant finished doing a pile sort of animal terms, Perchonock and Werner built a branching tree diagram, like the one in Figure 17.8. They would ask the informant to make up sentences or phrases that expressed some relation between the nodes. They found that informants intuitively grasped the idea of tree representations for taxonomies.

Figure 17.8 Part of the Navajo Animal Kingdom, Derived From a Pile Sort

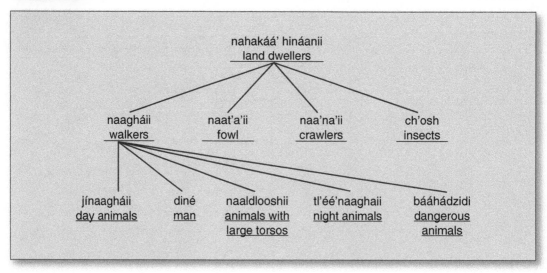

Source: N. Perchonock and O. Werner, "Navaho Systems of Classification: Some Implications for Ethnoscience." *Ethnology* 8:229–242. Copyright © 1969.

How to Make a Taxonomy: Lists and Frames

In building a folk taxonomy, many researchers combine the free-list and frame elicitation techniques I described in Chapter 10. Start with the frame:

What kinds of _____ are there?

where the blank is "cars," "trees," "saddles," "snow," "soldiers"—whatever you're interested in understanding. This frame is used again and again, until an informant says that the question is silly.

For example, suppose you asked a native speaker of American English "What kinds of foods are there?" You might get a list like: pasta, meat, fish, fruits, vegetables, snacks. . . ." (You'll probably get a slightly different set of labels if you ask a native speaker of British English this same question.)

Next, you ask: "What kinds of pasta [meats] [fish] [etc.] are there?" The answer for meats might be: beef, lamb, chicken, pork, venison. . . .

So you extend the search: "What kinds of beef [lamb] [chicken] [etc.] are there?" For some people, at least, you'll find that beef is divided into steak, chops, hamburger, and so

on, and that chicken is divided into dark meat and white meat. But if you ask "What kinds of steaks are there?" you might be told: "There are no kinds; they just are what they are." If you're dealing with a real steak lover, you might be told about Porterhouse, T-bone, rib eye, Delmonico, filet mignon, and so on.

Once you have a list of lexical items in a domain, and once you've got the basic divisions down, the next step is to find out about overlaps. Some foods, like peanuts, get classified as snacks and as protein sources by different people—or even by the same person at different times.

The point is, although the Food and Drug Administration may have codified foods in the United States, there is no codified set of folk rules for a taxonomy of foods in U.S. culture. The only way to map this is to construct folk taxonomies from information provided by a number of people and to get an idea of the range of variation and areas of consistency in how people think about this domain. You can learn about the possible overlaps in folk categories by using the substitution frames:

Is _____ a kind of _____ ?

Is _____ a part of _____ ?

Once you have a list of terms in a domain, and a list of categories, you can use this substitution frame for all possible combinations. Are marshmallows a kind of meat? A kind of fish? A kind of snack? This can get really tedious, but discovering levels of contrast—that *magenta* is a kind of *red*, that *cashews* are a kind of *nut*, that *alto* is a kind of *sax*, or that *ice cream* is a kind of *dessert*—just takes plain hard work. Unless you're a child, in which case all this discovery is just plain fun.

A common way to display folk taxonomies is with a branching tree diagram. Figure 17.9 shows a tree diagram for part of a folk taxonomy of passenger cars. I elicited this taxonomy in Morgantown, West Virginia, from Jack in 1976.

Things to Look for in Folk Taxonomies

There are five points to make about the taxonomy shown in Figure 17.9:

1. Interinformant variation is common in folk taxonomies. That is, different people may use different words to refer to the same category of things. Sometimes, in fact, terms can be almost idiosyncratic. Jack distinguished among what he called "regular cars," "station wagons," and "vans." The term "regular cars" is not one you normally see in automobile ads, or hear from a salesperson on a car lot.

2. Category labels do not necessarily have to be simple lexical items, but may be complex phrases. The category labeled "4-wheel drive" vehicles in Figure 17.9 was sometimes called "off-road vehicles" in 1976, or even "vehicles you can go camping in or tow a horse trailer with." Jack said that Jeep station wagons were both wagons *and* 4-wheel-drive cars you can go camping in.

3. Labels change over time. By the 1990s, those cars that Jack had called "vehicles you can go camping in or tow a horse trailer with" were being called "utes" by some people—short for "sport utility vehicle." Today, the term widely used is SUV, though small SUVs are sometimes called "cute utes."

4. There are those covert categories I mentioned—categories for which people have no label at all, or at least not one they find easily accessible. Some people insist that Corvettes, Camaros, Maseratis, and MGs are part of a single category, which they find difficult to name (one informant suggested "sporty cars" as a label). Others, like Jack, separate "performance cars" from "sports cars" and even subdivide sports cars into "true sports cars" and "rally cars." Be on the lookout for unlabeled categories (that is, unlabeled nodes in a branching tree diagram) in any folk taxonomy.

5. Even when there are consistent labels for categories, the categories may represent multiple dimensions, each of which has its own levels of contrast. For example, many native speakers of American English recognize a category of "foreign cars" that cuts across the taxonomy in Figure 17.9. There are foreign sports cars, foreign luxury cars, and foreign regular cars.

Folk taxonomies can be very, very complex. One way to get at the complexity is through multidimensional scaling (see Chapter 16). Another is a technique known as componential analysis (**Further Reading:** folk taxonomies).

COMPONENTIAL ANALYSIS

Componential analysis is a formal, qualitative technique for studying meaning. There are two objectives: (1) to specify the conditions under which a native speaker of a language will call something (like a plant, a kinsman, a car) by a particular term; and (2) to understand the cognitive process by which native speakers decide which of several possible terms they should apply to a particular thing.

The first objective is descriptive, but the second is a kind of causal analysis and is what the developers of the technique had in mind in the 1950s and 1960s (see Conklin 1955; Frake 1962; Goodenough 1956; Wallace 1962). Charles Frake,

Figure 17.9 Part of Jack's Taxonomy of Cars and Trucks

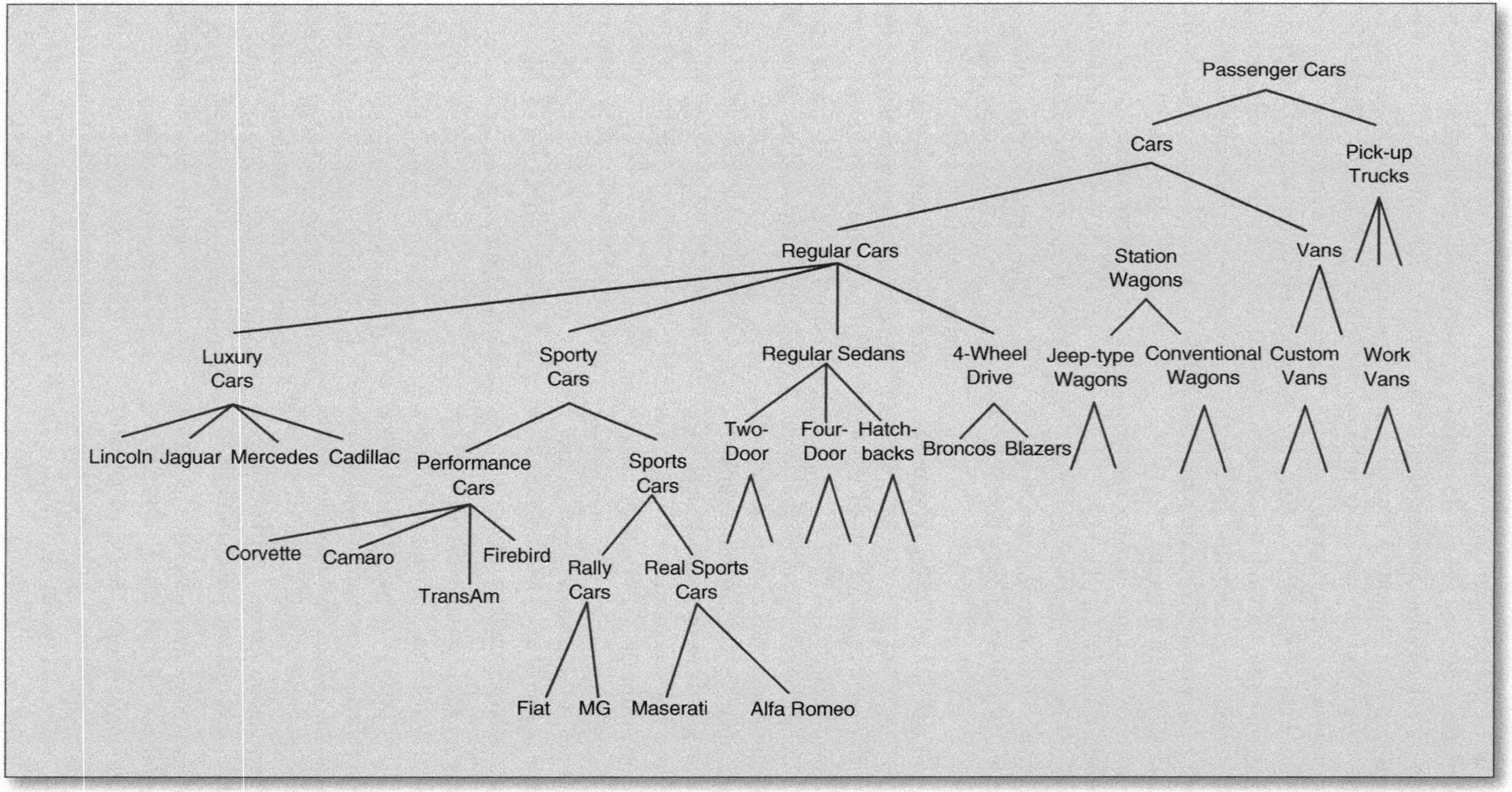

for example, described componential analysis as a step toward "the analysis of terminological systems in a way which reveals the conceptual principles that generate them" (1962:74). This created a lot of criticism, but more on that later.

Componential analysis is based on the principle of distinctive features in phonology, the branch of linguistics devoted to the study of the sounds of a language. To understand the principle, think about the difference in the sounds represented by P and B in English. Both are made by twisting your mouth into the same shape. This is a *feature* of the P and B sounds called "bilabial" or "two-lipped."

Another feature is that they are both "stops." That is, they are made by stopping the flow of air for an instant as it moves up from your lungs and releasing the flow suddenly. An S sound, by contrast, also requires that you restrict the air flow, but not completely. You kind of let the air slip by in a hiss. The only difference between a P and a B sound is that the P is voiceless while the B is voiced—you vibrate your vocal cords while making a P.

If you add up all the phonological features of the words "bit" and "pit," the only feature that differentiates them is voicing on the first sound in each word. The "pitness" of a pit and the "bitness" of a bit are clearly not in the voicelessness or voicedness of the sounds P and B, but any native speaker of English will distinguish the two words, and their meanings, and can trace the difference between them to that little feature of voicing if you push them a bit.

There is a unique little bundle of features that define each of the consonantal sounds in English. The only difference between the words "mad" and "bad" is that the bilabial sound M is nasal, and not a stop. These distinctive features carry meaning for native speakers of a language.

This principle can be adapted to the study of other domains of culture. Any two "things" (sounds, kinship terms, names of plants, names of animals, etc.) can be distinguished by exactly one binary feature that either occurs (+) or

Table 17.5	A Componential Analysis of Four Things With Two Features	
	Feature 1	Feature 2
Thing 1	+	+
Thing 2	+	−
Thing 3	−	+
Thing 4	−	−

doesn't occur (−). Table 17.5 shows that with two features you can distinguish four things: Thing 1 can be (++), thing 2 can be (+ −), thing 3 can be (− +), and thing 4 can be (− −). Each bundle of features is different and defines each of the four things. With three binary features, you can distinguish eight things; with four, 16; with five, 32; and so on.

When componential analysis was introduced, it was applied to the set of English kinship terms (Goodenough 1956) and it continues to be used for understanding kinship systems (Kronenfeld 2009; Pericliev and Valdez-Perez 1998). A "daughter" in English, for example, is a *consanguineal, female, descending generation* person. So is a niece, but a niece is *through a sibling or a spouse.*

Table 17.6 shows the distinctive feature principle applied to a list of 22 barnyard animals. (This example was first suggested by Hjelmslev 1961:70). Stallions are adult male horses and foals are baby horses. Notice that there is no column in Table 17.6 labeled "male" and no column labeled "juvenile." A parsimonious set of features for distinguishing among these animals does not require all that information. A stallion is a nonfemale, gendered (that is, not neutered), adult horse. Any horse that is not female and gendered and not an adult must be a colt. A barrow is a neutered, adult hog, and a wether is a neutered, adult sheep.

Actually, if we wanted the most parsimonious set of features we would drop one of the last four columns in Table 17.6. Those columns identify the general class of animals—horses, cattle, sheep, and swine—to which each named animal

Table 17.6 A Componential Analysis of 17 Barnyard Animals

Feature Animal	Female	Neuter	Adult	Horses	Cattle	Sheep	Swine
Cow	+	−	+	−	+	−	−
Bull	−	−	+	−	+	−	−
Steer	−	+	+	−	+	−	−
Calf	−	+	−	−	+	−	−
Heifer	+	−	−	−	+	−	−
Mare	+	−	+	+	−	−	−
Stallion	−	−	+	+	−	−	−
Gelding	−	+	+	+	−	−	−
Foal	−	+	−	+	−	−	−
Filly	+	−	−	+	−	−	−
Colt	−	−	−	+	−	−	−
Sow	+	−	+	−	−	−	+
Boar	−	−	+	−	−	−	+
Barrow	−	+	+	−	−	−	+
Piglet	−	+	−	−	−	−	+
Gilt	+	−	−	−	−	−	+
Shoat	−	−	−	−	−	−	+
Sheep	−	−	+	−	−	+	−
Ram	−	−	+	−	−	+	−
Ewe	+	−	+	−	−	+	−
Wether	−	+	+	−	−	+	−
Lamb	−	−	−	−	−	+	−

belongs. If the domain of barnyard animals comprised *just* those four classes, then a not-horse, not-cattle, not-sheep animal *must* be a swine. I've left all four animal classes in Table 17.6 because there are other classes of barnyard animals not yet represented (chickens, rabbits, goats, etc.).

Componential analysis can be applied to any domain of a language where you are interested in understanding the semantic features that make up the domain. Table 17.7 shows a componential analysis of seven cars, using three features elicited from Jack (he of the taxonomy shown in Figure 17.9).

A Corvette is an expensive car, not very practical, and not foreign; a Mercedes is an expensive, practical, foreign car; and so on. Each of the seven cars is uniquely defined by the three features Jack mentioned.

Faris's Study of Cat Harbour: Componential Analysis From Ethnography

James Faris (1968) studied the lexicon of social events in Cat Harbour, a small fishing community on the northeast coast of

| Table 17.7 | Minimal Componential Analysis for Seven Cars, According to Jack |

Car	1 Expensive	2 Practical	3 Foreign
Corvette	+	−	−
Firebird	−	−	−
MG	−	−	+
Maserati	+	−	+
Mercedes	+	+	+
Jeep	−	+	−
Dodge Van	+	+	−

Newfoundland. During his research, Faris asked about the different kinds of social events and learned that some were classified as "occasions" and others were not. The occasions included weddings, funerals, birthdays, scoffs, and events at which mummers (troupes of actors) could be present. The nonoccasions included meetings of fishermen (called "union meetings"), church services, christenings, teas, banquets, socials, concerts, suppers, and evening gatherings of men (p. 120). To understand what separated occasions from nonoccasions, Faris looked at the features of the events. Some were fun, other not. Some were public, others limited to a few families. All occasions involve serving food, but so do some of the nonoccasions.

By systematically examining the features of each social event and the meaning of each event to the people of Cat Harbour, Faris solved the puzzle. All of the so-called occasions involved approved deviation from the rules of everyday behavior. Scoffs, for example, involve a few couples who get together to dance, play cards, and eat a meal to which they all contribute. The men (and occasionally, the women) drink, and there is a lot of sexual banter—something that would not be tolerated in other situations. All the ingredients for the scoff, or

dinner, are stolen. Under any other circumstance, this would not be tolerated, but one is allowed to "buck" (a euphemism for stealing) the makings of a scoff from neighbors and friends. A scoff, Faris tells us, is "an occasion of sanctioned license, a legitimization of behavior and action normally considered 'sin'" (p. 228).

Likewise, weddings involved dancing "jigs and reels with heavy sexual overtone" and men drinking to excess. "After having heard from several persons of the evils of sexual license and excessive drink," Faris says, "I observed these same people participating with gusto in these activities at a 'wedding'—only to be told again by them the following day of the evils of sexual license and excessive drinking" (p. 228). At funerals, the mourners are removed from everyday roles, and birthdays are excuses for scoffs. At Christmas, people dress in costumes and masks and go around to houses where they are given food and alcohol. Men may dress as women and women as men. All in all, Faris concluded, the feature that distinguished the so-called occasions from other social events was the sanctioned deviance.

Problems With Componential Analysis

There are two problems with componential analysis. First of all, it seems a bit shallow to say that a Corvette is an expensive, impractical, American car and nothing more, or that a Mercedes is an expensive, practical, foreign car and nothing more. You can get so caught up in finding the minimal analytic combination of features in this type of analysis that you forget you're interested in the meaning that people assign to different objects in a domain. On the other hand, if you know the most parsimonious set of distinctive features for an item in a domain, you can predict how someone will label new things in the domain that they haven't encountered before.

The second problem with componential analysis is the same one we run into with all cognitive research methods: We have no idea if it reflects how people actually think. This problem was raised early in the development of cognitive studies by Robbins Burling (1964), who noted that, in a folk taxonomy of trees, he could not tell the essential cognitive difference between hemlock and spruce. "Is it gross size, type of needle, form of bark, or what?" If an ethnographer could not answer this question, Burling observed, then no componential analysis could claim to be "more than an exercise of the analyst's imagination" (p. 27).

This same critique could apply to any social research that "imputes the presence of something inside people" (like values and attitudes) and must be balanced with a positive perspective on what *can* be done (Hymes 1964:119).

In fact, what can be done is impressive, intuitively compelling analysis of the meanings that people attach to terms in their languages: Decision analysis allows us to predict which of several behavioral options people will take, under specific circumstances; taxonomic analysis lets us predict which class of things some new thing will be assigned to; componential analysis lets us predict what classification label will be assigned to some object. These methods produce effective knowledge that finds application in practical fields like health care delivery and advertising (**Further Reading:** componential analysis).

ANALYTIC INDUCTION AND BOOLEAN TESTS

Analytic induction is a formal, qualitative method for building up causal explanations of phenomena from a close examination of cases and the application of rules of logic. The rules for this kind of inductive exercise were formalized by John Stuart Mill (1898:259). Two of Mill's rules—what he called "the method of agreement" and the "method of difference"—are the foundation of analytic induction.

The method of agreement states that if two or more cases of a phenomenon are different in every way but have one thing in common, then that thing has to be the cause or the effect of the phenomenon. The method of difference states that if two cases of something are alike in every respect, except for one thing, then that thing is at least part of the cause of the phenomenon (Mill 1898:255, 256).

The term, "analytic induction" was introduced to the social science literature by Florian Znaniecki in 1934, in his book on sociological method (pp. 235ff). Observing that the method had a long history, especially in the physical sciences, Znaniecki contrasted analytic induction with what he called enumerative, or statistical induction (pp. 221ff) (Box 17.3).

Box 17.3 Statistical induction

By the 1920s, with the development of things like the correlation coefficient and the t-test, statistical induction had become very popular in the social sciences. In **statistical induction**, you see if the distribution of two things (like age and weight) are related and you try to infer cause and effect.

Social scientists were quick to notice the flaw in this logic: Just because the number of hours of daylight and the number of drownings per day are associated doesn't mean that one of those things causes the other. They're both caused by summer, nice weather, and lots of people at the beach. In other words, the correlation between the number of daylight hours and the number of drownings is spurious. Still, with proper precaution, statistical induction is an excellent start in the search for rules governing social phenomena (see above p. 52).

The Steps in Analytic Induction

The idea of analytic induction is to formulate ironclad rules about the causes and effects of social phenomena—with none of the wishy-washy tendencies and associations that are the product of statistical analysis. (Think of the difference between saying: "Whenever you see X you will see Y" and "Whenever you see X, there is a 62% chance that you'll see Y"). Several qualitative methods—including grounded theory, schema analysis, and decision modeling—are based on the logic of analytic induction.

W. S. Robinson (1951) laid out the rules for the method. Here's the algorithm:

1. Start with a single case and develop a theory to account for that one case.

2. Look at a second case and see if the theory fits.

3. If it does, go on to a third case.

4. Keep doing this until you run into a case that doesn't fit your theory. (If you see something called **negative case analysis**, or **deviant case analysis**, this is what it means; see Emigh 1997.)

5. At this point, you have two choices: Modify the theory or redefine the phenomenon you're trying to explain.

6. Repeat the process until your theory is stable—that is, until it explains every new case you try (W. S. Robinson 1951:813). No fair explaining cases by declaring them all unique. That's an easy way out, but not an option of the method.

How many cases in a row do you need to explain before declaring victory? As in any science, the answer is that you're never home free. No matter how many cases your theory explains, there's always the possibility that the next one will fail the test. Still, if a theory is built on 10–20 cases, and it goes on to explain another, independent sample of 10–20 cases, that's strong evidence in any field that the theory should be accepted.

Cressey's Study of Embezzlers

Among the best-known studies to use analytic induction is Donald Cressey's classic on embezzlers. Cressey (1950, 1953) interviewed 133 prisoners at the Illinois State Penitentiary at Joliet—men who had been convicted of stealing money from their employers. This is the part of analytic induction where you define and redefine the phenomenon you want to study. Cressey could have defined the phenomenon as simply "stealing from employers," but he decided to focus only on men who had taken their jobs with no intention of becoming embezzlers. During a screening interview to find prisoners who were eligible for his study, Cressey listened carefully and chose men who said they had never intended to steal—that it just sort of happened (1950:740).

Cressey began with the hypothesis that men who were in positions of financial trust—like accountants—would become embezzlers if they came to believe, on the job, that taking money from their employers was just a "technical violation" and not really illegal (1950:741). Unfortunately, as soon as he started doing his interviews, real-life embezzlers told Cressey that they knew all along that what they were doing was illegal. So Cressey formulated a second hypothesis: Men will embezzle when they have some need—like a family emergency or a gambling debt—that they can interpret as an emergency and that they can't see being met legally.

This hypothesis was abandoned when Cressey ran into two kinds of negative cases: men who reported having emergencies that did not drive them to steal and men who stole when they had no financial emergency. One of the prisoners told Cressey that no man would steal if he always confided in his wife about financial problems, but Cressey had to reject this hypothesis, too (1950:741).

Cressey was getting closer, though. His next hypothesis was that men who have the technical skill to embezzle would do so if they had any kind of problem (financial or otherwise) that they felt: (1) could *not* be shared with anyone; and (2) *could* be solved with an infusion of money.

Some men told Cressey that they had been in this situation and had not embezzled because the circumstances were not sufficiently clear to make stealing something they could reconcile with their values. That's when Cressey added the final piece of the theory: Men had to be able to square "their conceptions of themselves as trusted persons with conceptions of themselves as users of the entrusted funds or property" (1950:742).

This theory explained all 133 cases that Cressey collected. In fact, it also explained about 200 cases that had been collected by others in the 1930s (1950:740).

Critique of Analytic Induction

Social scientists in the 1950s were quick to notice the flaws in analytic induction (W. S. Robinson 1951; R. Turner 1953). The most obvious is that the method accounts for data you've already collected but does not allow prediction about individual cases. Cressey could not predict, *a priori*—that is, without data about actual embezzlers who had been arrested and jailed for their crime—which bank workers would violate the trust of their employers. His theory, however, was superb, *a posteriori*—explaining the cases he had in hand.

The critique, then, is that, much as in grounded theory, theories derived from analytic induction explain what's already known. This is not as strong a critique as it may appear. Retrospective understanding of a small set of cases, especially if achieved with systematic methods of data collection and analysis, allows us to make strong predictions about the set of uncollected cases yet to come. In other words,

analytic induction does not produce perfect knowledge for the prediction of individual cases, but it can do as well as statistical induction—the standard in social science—in predicting the outcome in aggregates of cases, and it does so with a relatively small number of cases.

It's true that collecting and analyzing case histories of phenomena is much more labor intensive than, say, collecting questionnaire data by telephone. But if you want and need context to derive a theory in the first place or to understand the complexity of a phenomenon, then case histories, analytic induction, and patience produce powerful results.

Finally, one of the critiques of analytic induction is that it is based on simple, binary input and output variables. In Cressey's case, the men either rationalized having violated their employer's trust or they didn't. Like all methods, analytic induction is useful for some problems and not useful for others. It's not very good at handling shades of grey. But for many phenomena, simple black-and-white explanations are enough.

QUALITATIVE COMPARATIVE ANALYSIS—QCA

In any event, with all the critiques, analytic induction fell out of favor for several decades. It has enjoyed a revival, though, since Charles Ragin (1987, 1994) formalized the logic of the method using a Boolean approach. Boolean algebra involves two states: true or false, present or absent, one or zero. With two dichotomous conditions, A and B, there are four possible combinations: (A and B), (A and not-B), (not-A and B), and (not-A and not-B). With three dichotomous variables, A, B, and C, there are eight combinations; with four, there are sixteen combinations; and so on. Ragin called the method he developed qualitative comparative analysis, or QCA.

An example will make this clear.

Haworth-Hoeppner's Study of Eating Disorders

Susan Haworth-Hoeppner (2000) used QCA in her study of why White, middle-class women develop eating disorders. She interviewed 30 of those women, 21 of whom were either anorexics or bulimics, for 2 hours each about their body image and eating problems. She used open coding to find major themes in these interviews (see Chapter 19 on open coding); four themes emerged as factors in the development of eating disorders:

1. A family in which the woman was constantly criticized, by one or both parents as she was growing up about almost everything—her weight, her looks, her personality, her appearance, her performance. In the analysis that follows, this is called C, for "critical family environment."

2. Parents who tried to control everything the woman did by yelling and hitting and by laying down rules, particularly rules about food. This is called R, for "coercive parental control."

3. Parents who made the woman feel unaccepted and unloved. This is called U, for "unloved."

4. A family in which all the conversations seemed to revolve around weight or appearance. This is called D, for "main discourse on weight" (Haworth-Hoeppner 2000:216).

Next, Haworth-Hoeppner coded each of the 30 transcripts for these four concepts. Did the woman live in a family where she was always being criticized for her appearance? Were her parents controlling? Unloving? Always going on about weight and appearance? Finally, she coded for the dependent variable: Was the woman herself bulimic or anorexic? The resulting data are shown in Table 17.8.

Look at Table 17.8 carefully. It has 30 lines, one for each person in the study, and

five columns. The four independent variables (the hypothesized causes) are coded (1 or 0) in the first four columns (after the case number) and the one dependent variable, the outcome, is coded (also 1 or 0) in the last column. Consider case number 3. This woman's narrative was coded as having the themes of C and U present (she reported growing up in a critical family environment and having unloving parents) but was not coded for R and D (coercive parental control and a main discourse on weight). From the narrative, there was no evidence that woman #3 was a bulimic or an anorexic, so there is a 0 in the column on the far right.

In fact, nine of the 30 women showed no evidence of an eating disorder. Six of the nine had *none* of the four factors identified by Haworth-Hoeppner. You can see that in Table 17.8 by looking for the six cases that are in the 0000 condition. Nine women (cases 22–30) reported growing up in families where *all four* hypothesized causes were present. In every one of those nine cases there was evidence of either bulimia or anorexia.

Arranging Data in a Truth Table

Next, Haworth-Hoeppner arranged her data in the form of what's called a Boolean truth table in logic. This is shown in Table 17.9. This table has only 16 rows, not 30, because here the rows are the combinations of conditions, not the profiles of individual people. As there are four hypothesized causal variables, and each one can be present or absent, there are 2^4, or 16 possible combinations, so there are 16 rows in the table.

Five of the 16 conditions in Table 17.9—0101, 0010, 0011, 0111, and 0110—though logically possible did not occur in Haworth-Hoeppner's 30 informants. For example, the 0101 condition involves: (1) the absence of a critical family environment; (2) the presence of coercive parental control; (3) the absence of unloving parents; and (4) a main family discourse on weight. In other words, it involves a loving, supportive family in which the parents exert coercive control and are

Table 17.8 Data Matrix for Haworth-Hoeppner's Study

Case	Critical family Environment	Coercive Parental Control	Unloving Parent-Child Relationship	Main Discourse on Weight	Suffers From Eating Disorder
1	1	0	0	0	0
2	0	1	0	0	0
3	1	0	1	0	0
4	0	0	0	0	0
5	0	0	0	0	0
6	0	0	0	0	0
7	0	0	0	0	0
8	0	0	0	0	0
9	0	0	0	0	0
10	1	1	1	0	1
11	1	1	0	0	1
12	0	0	0	1	1
13	0	0	0	1	1
14	1	0	0	1	1
15	1	0	0	1	1
16	1	1	0	1	1
17	1	1	0	1	1
18	1	1	0	1	1
19	1	1	0	1	1
20	1	0	1	1	1
21	1	0	1	1	1
22	1	1	1	1	1
23	1	1	1	1	1
24	1	1	1	1	1
25	1	1	1	1	1
26	1	1	1	1	1
27	1	1	1	1	1
28	1	1	1	1	1
29	1	1	1	1	1
30	1	1	1	1	1

Source: Susan Haworth-Hoeppner, "The Critical Shapes of Body Image: The Role of Culture and Family in the Production of Eating Disorders." *Journal of Marriage and the Family* 62:212–27, p. 218, 2000 (and personal communication).

always going on about weight. It's an unlikely combination and, indeed, it did not occur in Haworth-Hoeppner's data.

These logical conditions that did not occur in the data are shown as Xs in Table 17.9. A truth table forces us to consider all logical possibilities, even though some combinations of features are unlikely to occur in real data.

Four conditions—1000, 0100, 1010, and 0000—were present in Haworth-Hoeppner's informants but did not produce an eating disorder. The first three of these conditions produced

a single case each (of absence of an eating disorder) and the 0000 condition produced six cases in which eating disorders were absent. These nine cases—shown in parentheses in Table 17.9—do not get explained in analysis. QCA (and analytic induction in general) is best used for explaining the cases where factors lead to a phenomenon (Haworth-Hoeppner 2000:218).

Still, if we can explain the existence of a phenomenon like eating disorders among a set of White, middle-class women that would be quite a lot.

Table 17.9 Truth Table for Haworth-Hoeppner's Data

Critical Family Environment	Coercive Parental Control	Unloving Parent-Child Relationship	Main Discourse on Weight	Outcomes: Presence of Eating Disorders (# of cases)
1	0	0	0	1 (0)
0	1	0	0	1 (0)
0	1	0	1	X
0	0	1	0	X
1	0	1	0	1 (0)
0	0	1	1	X
0	1	1	1	X
0	1	1	0	X
0	0	0	0	6 (0)
1	1	1	0	1 (1)
1	1	0	0	1 (1)
0	0	0	1	1 (2)
1	0	0	1	1 (2)
1	1	0	1	1 (4)
1	0	1	1	1 (2)
1	1	1	1	1 (9)

Note: X = condition not observed; 1= condition observed; ( ) = # of cases.

Source: Susan Haworth-Hoeppner, "The Critical Shapes of Body Image: The Role of Culture and Family in the Production of Eating Disorders." *Journal of Marriage and the Family* 62:212–27, p. 218, 2000.

*Finding the Simplest Set, or
Prime Implicants*

The next step in QCA is to simplify the truth table—to cut it down to its prime implicants. The last seven lines of Table 17.9 show the configurations that produce eating disorders:

1110

1100

0001

1001

1101

1011

1111

Letters are easier to comprehend than 1s and 0s. Haworth-Hoeppner used upper-case C, R, U, and D to represent the presence of the four factors that produce eating disorders and lower-case c, r, u, and d to represent the absence of those factors. The configurations that produced eating disorders (the bottom seven lines in Table 17.9) are shown in the top panel of Table 17.10.

To find the simplest set of features—the prime implicants—that account for the dependent variable (eating disorders) requires a systematic comparison of all pairs of configurations that produce eating disorders.

There are $n(n - 1)/2$ pairs of anything, so, with three elements in a set—A, B, and C—there are $3(2) = 6/2 = 3$ pairs. Here they are: AB, AC, BC. With four elements (cars, people, countries, whatever), there are $4(3) = 12/2 = 6$ pairs. There are, then, $7(6)/2 = 21$ pairs of the seven configurations in the top panel of Table 17.10.

Pair 1 and 2, for example, is: CRUd and CRud

Pair 1 and 3 is: CRUd and cruD

And so on, down to pair 6 and 7: CrUD and CRUD

The method here is to examine all pairs of conditions and see if we can reduce the number of combinations that account for the outcomes in the truth table. Then we see if we can

reduce the number of combinations again until we find the minimum number of variables and their combinations that account for a set of cases in a truth table. These are called the prime implicants in Boolean logic.

Using Ragin's method, Haworth-Hoeppner simplified the configurations in Table 17.10 by examining pairs of configurations and looking for terms that are unnecessary. Notice that both C R U D and C r U D produce the same outcome (an eating disorder). This makes R superfluous. On the other hand, R is needed for the pair C R U d and C R u D, but in that case, U is superfluous (Haworth-Hoeppner 2000:219–20). On the first pass, Haworth-Hoeppner found that she could reduce the 21 configurations to just eight combinations of the four variables, in sets of three. These are shown on the left-hand side of the bottom panel in Table 17.10.

Haworth-Hoeppner gave these eight configurations new numbers and repeated the process. There are $8(7)/2 = 28$ pairs of eight configurations, but in the end, Haworth-Hoeppner found that only three combinations of variables (CD, CR, and ruD) were needed to account for the 21 cases of eating disorders in her data. Those configurations are shown in the right-hand column of the bottom panel of Table 17.10. The final result—the prime implicants for eating disorders—is expressed in the Boolean formula:

Eating disorders = CR + CD + ruD

We read this as: "Eating disorders are caused by the simultaneous presence of C AND R, AND by the simultaneous presence of C AND D, AND by the presence of D in the absence of R and U" (Haworth-Hoeppner 2000:219–20).

Note how U dropped out of the picture entirely. From the literature about eating disorders, Haworth-Hoeppner expected to find that unloving parents were a prime factor in creating the problem for women. But from the QCA, she learned that this feature was simply not needed to explain the cases in her sample. This sets up an entire agenda for future research.

Table 17.10 Simplifying Haworth-Heoppner's Data

The Seven Configurations That Produce Eating Disorders

Configurations in Table 17.8 That Produced Eating Disorders	C Critical Family Environment	R Coercive Parental Control	U Unloving Relationship With Parents	D Main Discourse on Weight in Family
1	C	R	U	d
2	C	R	u	d
3	c	r	u	D
4	C	r	u	D
5	C	R	u	D
6	C	r	U	D
7	C	R	U	D

Simplifying to Eight Pairs of the Seven Configurations Above

		Call These	Simplifying Again	
1+2	CRd	1	1+7	CR
1+7	CRU	2	2+3	CR
2+5	CRu	3	5+8	CD
3+4	ruD	4	6+7	CD
4+5	CuD	5	4	ruD
4+6	CrD	6		
5+7	CRD	7		
6+7	CUD	8		

Summary: Eating disorders = CR + CD + ruD

Source: Susan Haworth-Hoeppner, "The Critical Shapes of Body Image: The Role of Culture and Family in the Production of Eating Disorders." *Journal of Marriage and the Family* 62:212–227, p. 219, 2000.

AND FINALLY . . .

Like many methods for analyzing qualitative data, QCA requires that human coders read and code text and produce a matrix. The object of the analysis, however, is not to show the relationships between all codes, but to find the minimal set of logical relationships among the concepts that account for a single dependent variable. With four binary independent variables, as in Haworth-Hoeppner's data, there are 16 configurations to simplify. With each additional variable, the analysis becomes much more difficult. Fortunately, computer programs are available for this kind of analysis (**Further Reading:** QCA. And see Appendix E for QCA software).

ethnographic decision
   models
folk taxonomies
componential analysis
analytic induction
Boolean analysis
tree diagram or dendrogram
decision table
IF-THEN statements

postdiction
folk taxonomies
ethnoscience
covert categories
nonaffiliated generics
taxonomic tree
levels of contrast
componential analysis
causal analysis

distinctive feature
analytic induction
statistical induction
negative case analysis
deviant case analysis
qualitative comparative
   analysis (QCA)
truth table
prime implicants

Summary

- Ethnographic decision models are qualitative, causal analyses that predict what kinds of choices people will make under specific circumstances.

  o The first thing to do is decide which decision you are studying and what the alternatives are in that decision. Every alternative becomes a question you can ask of the next respondent.

  o You can always build a model that accounts for the actual decisions of a group of people. The real test is whether the model works on a new group of people.

  o Complicated models can be represented with tables and IF-THEN charts.

- Folk taxonomies are hierarchical graphs that represent how people organize their knowledge of plants, animals, and other cultural domains. The object is to understand cultural knowledge on its own terms. We use folk taxonomies all the time to order our experience and guide our behavior.

  o Scientific taxonomies for plants and animals recognize six primary levels of distinction. Folk taxonomies of plants and animals across the world are generally limited to five or, at most, six levels.

  o The process of building a folk taxonomy involves getting a list of the items in a domain and then using the frame elicitation technique to sort out the hierarchical arrangement of the items in the domain.

  o Interinformant variation is common in folk taxonomies: Different people may use different words to refer to the same category of things. Some domains have covert categories and category labels may be complex phrases, not just simple lexical items.

- Componential analysis is a formal technique for studying meaning. The objectives are to specify the conditions under which a native speaker of a language will call something by a particular term and to understand how people choose among alternative terms.

  o Componential analysis is based on the principle of distinctive features in phonology, the branch of linguistics devoted to the study of the sounds of a language. The principle was first extended to kinship terminology, but can be applied to many cultural domains.

- Analytic induction is a formal, qualitative method for building up causal explanations of phenomena from a close examination of cases. The method involves developing and explanation for something and examining cases until the explanation doesn't fit. As cases are added, the explanation becomes more inclusive.

  o The method of analytic induction can be formalized in terms of Boolean logic. Boolean variables are dichotomous: true or false, present or absent.

o With three dichotomous variables, there are eight possibilities; with four there are 16 . . . and so on. Using logical operators, complex phenomena can often be explained with just a few well-chosen binary variables.

Exercises

1. This exercise can be done by individuals, but it's more productive if several students work together. Replicate the study on the decision to attend an early morning class. Begin by asking students who *have* an early class if they went to the most recent one of those classes. Whatever their answer, ask for the reason: Why did they go or why did they not go? Keep asking people and continue to build a list of reasons until two people in a row give you *no new reasons*—that is, reasons you haven't heard before.

   Next, ask a sample of 40 students who have an early class if they went to the most recent of those classes. (If you have five students in your group, that's only eight interviews each.) Whatever their answer, ask them *all* the questions that can be based on the list of reasons you've accumulated for going or not going to an early morning class. Use data from 20 of the interviews to build a decision model—one of those tree diagrams—and then use the data from the other 20 interviews to test the model.

2. Choose any cultural domain and build a folk taxonomy of that domain. Some interesting domains include: things you can major in as an undergraduate; kinds of music; kinds of sports; tools you're likely to find in somebody's garage; things that students eat for lunch. Here again, the first thing to do is get several people to free list the items in the domain. Then, use the frame-elicitation technique to find the taxonomic relations among the items in the domain.

3. Make a list of all the kinship terms in English. The basic set of terms is shared by most speakers of American English, but there are regional differences and ethnic differences in the content of this domain. Using a small set of distinctive features, do a componential analysis of this list of terms. Consult Romney and D'Andrade (1964) or D'Andrade (1995) for hints about the components of meaning in the list of English kin terms.

   Try to get lists of kin terms in several other languages. Some dialects of Spanish have a word (*concuñado*, *concuñada*) for "the nonblood relation between the two men who marry a pair of sisters or two women who marry a pair of brothers." There is no analog for this kinship term in English, where the men in this structural relation optionally refer to one another as a brother-in-law—if they use any kin term at all.

Further Reading

Ethnographic decision modeling. Bauer and Wright (1996), Dash and Gladwin (2007), Dy et al. (2005), Edmonds (2010), Fairweather (1999), Fang et al. (2009), Montbriand (1994), Ruiz-Casere and Heymann (2009).

Folk taxonomies. Atran (1998), Berlin (1992), Bruner et al. (1956), Conklin (1962), Hupka et al. (1999), Kay (1971), Keil (1989), G. A. Miller (1956), Raven et al. (1971), Rosch (1975).

Componential analysis. Goodenough (1956), Hage (1987 [1972]), Lounsbury (1956), Spradley (1987 [1972]), Sturtevant (1964), Taub and Leger (1984), Wallace (1962).

Analytic induction and Boolean tests. Basurto and Speer (2012), Benoit and Ragin (2009), Bulmer (1979), Manning (1982), Ragin (1998), Roscigno and Hodson (2004), Schneider and Wagemann (2006), Vink and Van Vliet (2009).

18

Analyzing Qualitative Data II

Grammar Beyond the Sentence

INTRODUCTION

All native speakers of human languages know the rules of grammar for their language. We hear sentences every day that we've never heard before and somehow we manage to decode them. We don't have a list of sentences in our heads. Instead, we learn a list of rules for making words and for putting words together into sentences.

Some rules are phonological. Consider this sentence: "He worked for two bosses at the same time." We don't pronounce the word "bosses" as if it were "bossiss" (where the iss rhymes with the second syllable in "practice"). That would violate the phonological rule that demands voicing of sibilants (like the final s in "bosses") after vowels like the ə, or schwa (the second vowel in "bosses"). When you add voice to the s sound, it becomes a z sound.

Some rules are syntactic—that is, about building sentences. We don't say "He is writing book" because that violates the English syntactic rule that requires an article (either "the" or "a") before the noun "book."

And some rules are semantic. We don't say "busy, purple forests dream indignantly" because, even though the syntax is correct, that would violate semantic rules about the kinds of things that can be busy or purple or that can dream. It is, however, the prerogative—even the mandate—of poets to concoct new images by violating just these rules.

Phonology, syntax, and semantics are increasingly complex sets of rules for building sensible utterances. This chapter covers methods for studying grammar beyond the sentence, including narrative analysis, performance analysis, schema analysis, conversation analysis, language in use, and language and power.

NARRATIVE ANALYSIS

Human beings are natural story tellers. You can ask people anything about their personal experience, from the extraordinary—like what it's like to survive hand-to-hand combat—to the mundane—like how they make breakfast, and you'll get a narrative. Narrative analysis is the search for regularities in how people, within and across cultures, tell stories.

One major genre of narratives involves recounting an event: What happened? How did it happen? Why did it happen? What was the result? The object is to discover themes and recurring structures.

Rubinstein's Study of the Death of Mothers

Robert Rubinstein, for example, asked 103 middle-class, married women in Philadelphia, ages 40–62, to describe how they reacted to the recent death of their widowed mothers. In the lengthy interviews, one question that Rubinstein asked was: "Can you tell me the story of your mother's death? What happened? How did she die?" (1995:259).

The stories of these women ranged from short, chronological sequences (mostly from women who had light or no caregiving duties during their mother's terminal illness or whose mother died suddenly or who lived at least two hours away from their mother by car) to long, complex stories about their mothers' illness and death (mostly from women who had heavy caregiving responsibilities and whose mother's terminal illness lasted more than six months).

Despite the differences in story length, Rubinstein found strong structural regularities. Most informants began their stories with what Rubinstein calls a "medical preamble" (p. 262) and a "narrative of decline element" (p. 263):

And she even began to notice, you know, something wasn't quite right. All the testing they had done, they said, you know, her mental ability isn't that impaired. And I kinda laughed because in January they had said that she was kinda, like, not too bad for a woman who had seen multiple decline in systems. And I kinda laughed because I wanted to come [back for testing] this year. And they said, "Well, bring her back next year and we'll, you know, assess her. This will be a relative point from which we can determine how gradual her decline is becoming." [So] I call them a year later to say she's dead.

Most women "medicalized the stories of their mothers' deaths" (p. 263), with details about visits to emergency rooms and about decisions to have surgery, for example. Most informants also mentioned their mother's personality traits:

So, we didn't push her to move in [with me]. You know, we let her make the decision. And then in May she, uh, we closed up her apartment. She never actually went back and she liked it that way. Yeah, she liked leaving there when she was able to walk [out]. [There's some people for whom] it's almost an insult to their dignity and their independence to be seen that way [starting to physically slide downhill], you know to end up being carted out in a wheel chair. You know, people were noticing that she [mother] wasn't herself, and she was a pretty forceful individual, very dominant, very independent, very outspoken, and her mental abilities had begun to slip a little, but her physical decline was becoming more noticeable. [p. 268]

Notice the transcription. The author selectively uses "kinda" instead of "kind of" to convey the conversational tone of the story, but he also inserts brackets to indicate things that were implied, but not said, in the narrative. There is only the barest attempt to include the kind of detailed information about false starts and tokens (like umm and uhh) that are required in transcriptions for conversation analysis (coming up later).

Finally, if women were present at their mother's death, they often described the death scene. Here are two contrasting scenes that Rubinstein counts as similar parts of these narratives:

1. . . . And she kept on talking. And a lot of it was about things from the past. But whatever it was, even when my brother and sister got there, we couldn't, umm, none of us got through to her. Her eyes were just moving around . . . and she even suffered to the very end, I mean, in her own way. It wasn't a peaceful death, really. [p. 270]

2. Most of the family was there, and my mother was having more difficulty breathing and I had her in my arms trying to talk to her, reassuring her that I loved her and one thing and another. And she died. . . . Yes, right in my arms, which was a

beautiful way to die. It was like my mother's gift of peace to me, knowing that I could not have been any closer. [p. 271]

Rubinstein's analysis, in the best tradition of narrative analysis, focuses on the stories themselves, on the themes—like the medicalization of death, the impossible dilemmas that arise in deciding on medical care for the terminally ill, the emotional pain for daughters of not being able to find the "mother-who-was" in mothers who were demented—and on how themes are combined and ordered in predictable ways.

Bletzer and Koss's Study: Comparing Narratives

Systematic comparison is a hallmark of analysis in the social sciences, whether the data are text or numbers. Keith Bletzer and Mary Koss (2006) analyzed 62 narratives by poor women in the southwestern United States who had survived rape, including 25 Cheyenne women, 24 Anglo women, and 13 Mexican American women. The women in all three groups were, on average, about the same age (mid-30s) and were recruited at health clinics that served their respective communities. In particular, the women recruited had mentioned on a screening survey that they had had an "'unwanted sexual experience' that involved force" (Bletzer and Koss 2006:10).

This is an exemplary sampling design for getting at the research question in the project: How do low-income women of different cultural backgrounds—holding region of the country and socioeconomic status constant—tell the story of being victims of sexual violence? Notice especially that the researchers had participants from the majority culture (Anglo women) so that useful comparisons could be made and that they limited their sample of Mexican American women to those who had been raised at least to adolescence in Mexico.

During the interview, each woman was asked to tell her own story of rape, in her own words. The researchers looked at the stories in terms familiar to students of sexual violence: initial reaction, long-term consequences, mourning, and attempts at recovery. In addition to themes, they looked for narrative structuring devices.

For example, Anglo women used nested stories in their narratives; the Mexican American women made less use of this device; and the Cheyenne women didn't use it at all but typically ordered the phases of their stories more than did the Anglo or Mexican American women (Bletzer and Koss 2006:18). Anglo women also used narrative markers (like "so, then. . . ." "so, anyways. . . ." "and then. . . ." etc.) more than did the women in the other two groups (p. 21).

All the women used the metaphor of feeling soiled and dirty after being raped, and the Anglo women sometimes used triplets in their descriptions (Bletzer and Koss 2006:22):

"Angry, scared, degraded. Felt like I was worthless." (Anglo)

"Then when I got pregnant out of it, it just made me feel dirty." (Anglo)

"I just felt dirty and degraded. I wanted to hide so nobody could see me." (Anglo)

"I felt low, I felt raunchy." (Cheyenne)

"I felt sick, dirty. I wanted to kill myself." (Cheyenne)

"It made me feel like I was dirty, nasty. . . . Made me feel real dirty." (Cheyenne)

"Anguish, very strong. Desperation, and sadness, painful sadness." (*Angustia, muy grande. Una desesperación, y tristeza, dolorosa*) (Mexican). [Bletzer and Koss 2006:16]

Bletzer and Koss also note what *isn't* in the narratives: Many of the Anglo and Mexican American women, they say, expressed thoughts of revenge against their assailants, but none of Cheyenne women did (Bletzer and Koss 2006:17). In fact, the Cheyenne women almost never named men in their accounts of rape; Mexican women named people with whom they had good relations; and the Anglo women named intimates as well as people with whom they had troubled relations (p. 14) (**Further Reading:** narrative analysis).

PERFORMANCE ANALYSIS: ETHNOPOETICS

Performance analysis involves the search for regularities in the delivery of highly stylized narratives, like folk tales, sermons, and political speeches. Ethnopoetics is performance analysis applied to oral literature (Rothenberg 1975 [1969]; Tedlock 1977).

Hymes's Discovery of Universal Ethnopoetics

In 1977, Dell Hymes reported that "the narratives of the Chinookan peoples of Oregon and Washington can be shown to be organized in terms of lines, verses, stanzas, scenes, and what many call acts." Hymes felt that this discovery might be relevant to many indigenous languages of the Americas (1977:431). That turned out to be an understatement: Hymes's work on the ethnopoetics of Native American oral literature offered a method for studying the regularities of oral literature anywhere in the world. Let me take you through some details of Hymes's study of Chinookan and you'll see what I mean.

Chinookan is a family of American Indian languages from the northwest coast of North America. Shoalwater Chinook and Kathlamet Chinook are two mutually unintelligible languages (related in the way French and Spanish are both Romance languages), but Franz Boas, the founder of American anthropology, had run into an informant who was fluent in both

Shoalwater and Kathlamet and had collected texts in both languages between 1890 and 1894. Hymes examined those texts as well as texts from Clackamas Chinook (collected in 1930 and 1931 by Melville Jacobs) and in Wasco-Wishram Chinook (collected by Sapir in 1905, by Hymes in the 1950s, and by Michael Silverstein in the 1960s and 1970s).

What Hymes found was that features of Chinook that might have seemed idiosyncratic to the speakers of those three Chinook languages—Shoalwater, Kathlamet, and Clackamas Chinook—were actually "part of a common fabric of performance style," so that the three languages "share a common form of poetic organization" (Hymes 1977:431) (Box 18.1).

Box 18.1 A theory of ethnopoetics

Hymes's discovery made clear once and for all that Native American texts have something to contribute to a general theory of poetics and literature. Hymes discovered the existence of verses, by recognizing repetition within a block of text. "Covariation between form and meaning," said Hymes, "between units with a recurrent Chinookan pattern of narrative organization, is the key" (1977:438).

In some texts, Hymes found recurrent linguistic elements that made the task easy. Linguists who have worked with precisely recorded texts in Native American languages have noticed the recurrence of elements like "Now," "Then," "Now then," and "Now again" at the beginning of sentences. These kinds of things often signal the separation of verses. The trick is to recognize them and the method is to look for "abstract features that co-occur with the use of initial particle pairs in the narratives" of other speakers who use initial particle pairs. The method, then, is a form of controlled comparison (1977:439) and it applies to the study of oral literature everywhere.

In a series of articles and books (1976, 1977, 1980a, 1980b, 1981), Hymes showed that most Native American texts of narrative performance (going back to the early texts collected by Boas and his students and continuing in today's narrative performance by American Indians as well) are organized into verses and stanzas that are aggregated into groups of either fives and threes or fours and twos. Boas and his students organized the narratives of American Indians into lines.

According to Virginia Hymes, this hid from view "a vast world of poetry waiting to be released by those of us with some knowledge of the languages" (1987:65). Dell Hymes's method, according to Virginia

Hymes, involves "working back and forth between content and form, between organization at the level of the whole narrative and at the level of the details of lines within a single verse or even words within a line" (1987:67–68). Gradually, an analysis emerges that reflects the analyst's understanding of the larger narrative tradition and of the particular narrator.

This emergent analysis doesn't happen miraculously. It is, Virginia Hymes reminds us, only through close work with many narratives by many narrators that you develop an understanding of the narrative devices that people use in a particular language and the many ways they use those little devices (1987).

Tedlock's Study of the *Popol Vuh*

Dennis Tedlock (1987) showed the exegetical power that linguistic methods can bring to the text analysis. He had translated the *Popol Vuh*, a sixteenth-century Quiché Maya manuscript that had been written out by Francisco Ximénez, a missionary of the time. The *Popol Vuh* is one of those big epics, like the *Iliad* or *Beowulf* that were meant to be recited aloud. Is it possible, Tedlock asked, to analyze the text and figure out how to narrate it today as performers would have done in ancient times?

In doing his translation of the *Popol Vuh*, Tedlock had relied on Andrés Xiloj, a modern speaker of Quiché. Xiloj had not been trained to read Maya, but he was literate in Spanish and made the transition very quickly. "When he was given his first chance to look at the Popol Vuh text, he produced a pair of spectacles and began reading aloud, word by word" (p. 145).

Like many medieval manuscripts in Europe, Ximénez's rendition of the *Popol Vuh* was more or less an undifferentiated mass of text with almost no punctuation. In other words, Tedlock had no clues about how a performer of the narrative 500 years ago might have varied his timing, emphasized this or that segment, used different intonations, and so forth.

Tedlock's solution was to study stylized oral narratives (not just casual speech) of modern speakers of Quiché. He recorded speeches, prayers, songs, and stories and looked for phrases and patterns in the wording that had analogs in the *Popol Vuh* (p. 147). He devised special punctuation symbols for marking pauses, accelerations, verse endings, and so on and applied them to the *Popl Vuh*. It's in the use of those written marks that we see Tedlock's analysis—his understanding of how a performance went.

Tedlock then made systematic comparison across other ancient texts to look for recurrent sound patterns that signify variations in meaning. (Think of how we use rising intonation at the end of sentences in English to signify a question and how some people in our society use the same intonation in declarative sentences at the beginning of phone conversations when the object is to jar someone's memory, as in: "Hi, this is Mary? I was in your intro class last semester?") What Tedlock found was that Quiché verse has the same structure as ancient Middle Eastern texts—texts that, he points out, predate Homer. In fact, Tedlock concluded, it is the same structure found in all living oral traditions that have not yet been influenced by writing (p. 146; and see Tedlock 1977).

We turn next to schema analysis—the discovery of cultural models, or grammars of behavior (**Further Reading:** ethnopoetics and performance analysis).

SCHEMAS, MODELS, AND METAPHORS

Schema analysis is based on the observation that everyday life—to say nothing of special situations, like major rituals—is too complex for people to learn one scene at a time. Just as we don't learn a list of sentences, we don't learn a list of behaviors or scenes. There must, the reasoning goes, be some rules—a grammar—that help us make sense of so much information.

These rules comprise schemas (Casson 1983:430), or **scripts**, as Schank and Abelson (1977) called them. Schemas enable culturally skilled people to fill in the details of a story. We often hear things like "Fred lost his data because he forgot to save his work." We know that Fred's forgetting to save his work didn't actually *cause* him to lose his data. A whole set of links are left out, but they are easily filled in by listeners who have the background to do so (Box 18.2).

Box 18.2 Goffman's breaking frame

When you buy a car, you expect to bargain on the price, but when you order food in a restaurant you expect to pay the price on the menu. You know that you are supposed to tip in certain kinds of restaurants and that you don't tip at fast-food counters. When someone you hardly know says, "Hi, how's it going?" they don't expect you to stop and give them a complete run-down on how your life is going these days. If you did launch into a peroration about your life, you'd be acting outside the prevailing schema—**breaking frame**, as Erving Goffman put it (1974). When people do that, we react viscerally and wonder "How the heck did they get in here?"

When many people in a society share a schema, then the schema is cultural. We can learn about **cultural schemas** by analyzing narratives. Willett Kempton (1987), for example, asked people to tell him about how they adjusted the thermostats for the furnaces in their homes. He found that Americans have two quite different schemas for how thermostats work.

Some people hold to a **feedback theory**: The thermostat senses the temperature and turns the furnace on or off to keep the room at some desired temperature. This theory produces set-it-and-forget-it behavior. You set the thermostat at some temperature and let the system do its job. Other people hold to a **valve theory**. You set the thermostat at some much higher temperature than what you really want. This forces the furnace to pour out lots of heat, fast. When the temperature is where you want it, you turn the dial down. The first theory is etically correct and the second is etically incorrect, but the second is widely held and is responsible for a lot of wasted energy.

People who push the elevator button over and over again probably subscribe to a valve theory. We could test that.

Quinn's American Marriage Schema

Naomi Quinn interviewed 11 American couples about marriage. The couples came from different parts of the country. Some were recently married; others were married a long time. And they represented various occupations, education levels, and ethnic and religious groups. Each of the 22 people were interviewed separately for 15 to 16 hours, and the interviews were transcribed.

Quinn analyzed this body of text to discover the concepts underlying American marriage and to show how these concepts are tied together—how they form a cultural schema, shared by people from different backgrounds about what constitutes success and failure in marriage (Quinn 1982, 1987, 1992, 1996, 1997).

Quinn's method is to look for metaphors in rhetoric—as proxies for themes—and to deduce the schemas, or underlying principles, that could produce those metaphors. For instance, Quinn's informants often compared marriages (their own and those of others) to manufactured and durable products ("It was put together pretty good") and to journeys ("We made it up as we went along; it was a sort of do-it-yourself project"). And when people were surprised at the breakup of a marriage, they would say things like "That marriage was like the Rock of Gibraltar" or "It was nailed in cement." People use these metaphors because they assume that their listeners know that cement and the Rock of Gibraltar are things that last forever.

The method of looking at metaphors as indicators of schemas was developed by George Lakoff and Mark Johnson (2003 [1980]), but Quinn goes further. She reasons that if schemas are what make it possible for people to fill in around the bare bones of a metaphor, then the metaphors must be surface phenomena and cannot themselves be the basis for shared understanding. She tries to understand how metaphors group together and finds that the hundreds of metaphors in her enormous corpus of text all fit into just eight classes: lastingness, sharedness, compatibility, mutual benefit, difficulty, effort, success (or failure), and risk of failure.

The classes of metaphors, the underlying concepts, are linked together in a schema that guides the discourse of ordinary Americans about marriage. Here is Quinn's understanding of that schema:

> Marriages are ideally lasting, shared and mutually beneficial. . . . Benefit is a matter of fulfillment. . . . Fulfillment and, more specifically, the compatibility it requires, are difficult to realize but this difficulty can be overcome, and compatibility and fulfillment achieved, with effort. Lasting marriages in which difficulty has been overcome by effort are regarded as successful ones. Incompatibility, lack of benefit, and the resulting marital difficulty, if not overcome, put a marriage at risk of failure. [1997:164]

Mathews's Mexican Folktale Schema

Holly Mathews (1992) collected 60 tellings of *La Llorona* (the weeping woman), a morality tale told across Mexico. Here is one telling, which Mathews says is typical:

> La Llorona was a bad woman who married a good man. They had children and all was well. Then one day she went crazy and began to walk the streets. Everyone knew but her husband. When he found out he beat her. She had much shame. The next day she walked into the river and drowned herself. And now she knows no rest and must forever wander the streets wailing in the night. And that is why women must never leave their families to walk the streets looking for men. If they are not careful they will end up like La Llorona. [p. 128]

In another telling, La Llorona kills herself because her husband becomes a drunk and loses all their money. In yet another, she kills herself because her husband is seen going with other women and La Llorona, in disbelief, finally catches him paying off a woman in the streets.

Mathews found that men and women tended to emphasize different things in the story, but the woman always winds up killing herself, no matter who tells it. The morality tale succeeds in shaping people's behavior, she says, because the motives of the characters in the story conform to a schema, shared by men and women alike, about how men and women see each other's fundamental nature (Mathews 1992:129).

Men, according to Mathews's understanding of the cultural model in rural Mexico, view women as sexually uncontrolled. Unless they are controlled, or control themselves, their true nature will emerge and they will begin (as the story says) to "walk the streets" in search of sexual gratification. Men, for their part, are viewed by women as sexually insatiable. Men are driven, like animals, to satisfy their desires, even at the expense of family obligations. In her grammar of the La Llorona tales, Mathews shows that women have no recourse but to kill themselves when they cannot make their marriages work.

Mathews goes beyond identifying the schema and tries to explain where the schema comes from. Most marriages in the village where Mathews did her research (in the state of Oaxaca) are arranged by parents and involve some exchange of resources between the families. Once resources like land are exchanged there's no turning back, which means that parents can't or won't take back a daughter if she wants out of a marriage. Then, as Mathews explains, the only way a woman can end her marriage is suicide (Mathews 1992:150). And that, Mathews, says, is why suicide is part of virtually all tellings of the La Llorona tale (**Further Reading:** schema analysis, mental models, metaphor analysis).

CONVERSATION ANALYSIS

Conversation analysis is the search for the grammar of ordinary discourse, or talk-in-interaction. It is the study of how people take turns in ordinary discourse—who talks first (and next, and next), who interrupts, who waits for a turn.

If you listen carefully to ordinary conversations between equals, you'll hear a lot of sentence fragments, false starts, interruptions, overlaps (simultaneous speech), and repeating of words and phrases. As students of conversation have learned, however, there is order in all that seeming chaos as participants respond to each other (even in strong disagreements and shouting matches) and take turns (Goodwin 1981:55ff).

The grammatical rules of turn taking are, like the rules that govern the formation of sentences, known to native speakers of any language. But unlike the other rules of grammar, the rules for taking turns are flexible and allow turn taking to be negotiated, on the fly, by participants in a conversation. At the molecular level, then, every conversation is unique, but the study of many conversational exchanges can expose the general rules, within and across cultures, that govern how conversations start, evolve, and end (Box 18.3).

Box 18.3 Turn-taking rules in institutions

In many institutional settings, turn taking in meetings is regulated by someone acting as leader. Even these rules can be subtle. At a convention of Alcoholics Anonymous in Southeast Asia, a meeting described by O'Halloran (2005:541) operated on an unspoken, but apparently well-understood rule: A member would rise and go to the microphone at the speaker's table. This simple act was sufficient to claim a turn.

And pilots all over the world have a special turn-taking rule: They absolutely must learn to let each other finish each sentence before jumping in with the next one (Nevile 2007).

Transcriptions

To identify turns and other features of conversations (like adjacency pairs and repair sequences, which we'll take up later), you need detailed records of actual talk-in-interaction. The tactic for signaling the intention to take a turn or to repair a broken turn sequence may be a word or a phrase, or it may be prosodic features of speech (intonation, length of vowels, stress, and so on), or breaths, tokens (like er, ummm, eh), gestures, body language, or gazes (R. Gardner 2001; Goodwin 1994).

Table 18.1 shows one widely used system, developed by Gail Jefferson (1983, 2004), for transcribing speech, including some of the basic prosodic features (**Further Reading:** transcribing conversation).

Taking Turns and Repair Tactics

We've known for a long time that there are regularities in conversations (Aristotle observed in Poetics IV that "conversational speech runs into iambic lines more frequently than into any other kind of verse"), but Harvey Sacks and his colleagues, Emmanuel Schegloff and Gail Jefferson, are widely credited for developing the systematic study of order in conversations (Jefferson 1973; Sacks et al. 1974; Schegloff 1968; Schegloff and Sacks 1973). Among the basic rules they discovered are that the

| Table 18.1 | Conventions for Transcribing Conversations |

Symbol	Definition
:	Indicates length. More colons indicate more length.
>text<	Speech between angle brackets is faster than normal speech.
(text) ( )	Text in parentheses means that the transcriber had doubts about it. Parens with no text means that transcriber could not make it out at all.
(1.6) (.)	Numbers in parens indicate pauses, in seconds and tenths of a second. A period in parens indicates an untimed and quick pause.
((text))	Double parens contain comments by the researcher about people's gestures, gazes, and so on. Often in italics.
[ ]	Square brackets indicate where one person interrupts another or talks simultaneously.
–	An en-dash (longer than a hyphen) indicates an abrupt end in the middle of a word.
?	A question mark indicates rising intonation. It does not necessarily mean that a question is being asked.
.	A period indicates falling intonation. It does not necessarily mean the end of a sentence.
=	The equal sign indicates that a person takes a turn immediately as the previous turn ends.
°text°	Text between degree symbols is quieter than the rest of the text.
TEXT	Text in caps is louder than the rest of the text.
Text	Underlining means that the text is emphasized.
.hh and hh	These indicate inhaled (with period first) and exhaled (no period) breaths, as often occurs in natural conversation.

Source: Adapted from Jefferson, G. 1983. Issues in the Transcription of Naturally-Occurring Talk. Caricature Versus Capturing Pronunciation Particulars. Tilburg Papers on Language and Literature. Tilburg, Netherlands: University of Tilburg. http://www.liso.ucsb.edu/Jefferson/Caricature.pdf.

person who is speaking may (but does not have to) identify the next speaker to take a turn (Sacks et al. 1974:700ff). This is done with conversational devices—like "So what do you think, Jack?"—or with gazes or body language (Goodwin 1986, 1994). If the person speaking does not select the next speaker, then any other person in the conversation can self-select to take a turn.

Alternatively, the next speaker may jump in before a speaker has completed a turn, by

anticipating the end of a turn—a supportive gesture—or by interrupting and trying to take away the speaker's turn by force—a hostile gesture. Big gaps occur so rarely in real conversations because speakers anticipate the end of turns so well. For example:

1. A: what a cute <u>no::se</u>.

2. B: all [babies ha-

3. A: [no they don't

A takes a turn; B responds and then A says "No they don't" just as the syllable "ba" in "baby" registers. There is no gap at the end of B's turn because the end of B's turn is predictable to A. And even though A contradicts B, the interruption is supportive, in grammatical terms—that is, it doesn't violate any rules—because it keeps the conversation going.

If the turn taking runs out of steam in a conversation, either because it becomes unpredictable or the content gets used up and no one jumps in to take a turn at the appropriate time, then the current speaker may (but does not have to) continue talking. If none of these things happen, there will be a gap in the conversation. Gaps don't usually last very long if the rules of conversation are followed.

How Repair Tactics Work

The rules are often broken in real conversations. People often do interrupt each other unsupportively and don't wait to take their turns. People who get interrupted don't always push on, trying to finish their turn, but relinquish their turn instead, without finishing. On the other hand, people usually recognize when the preferred order of turn taking has not been adhered to and engage in what are called repair tactics. For example, Sacks et al. (1974) noted that when two people start talking over each other, one of them might just stop and let the other finish. Here's an example:

1. A: [It's not like we–

2. B: [Some people are–

3. B: Sorry.

4. A: No, g'head

5. B: .hhhh I wus jus gonna say that some people aren't innerested in sports [at all.

6. A:　　　　[right

This is a simple repair tactic that doesn't involve any serious content. Other repair tactics can be more complex. The result of this repair sequence could have come out differently. But in the study of hundreds of natural conversations between equals, we can uncover the rules governing how people open and close conversations, how they repair mistakes (when they break the rules of turn taking, for example), and how they segue from one theme to another.

The turn-taking sequence rules can be suspended, of course, in the telling of jokes and stories. If you ask someone "Did you hear the one about . . . ?" and they say "No, tell me," then this suspends turn taking until you're finished with the joke. If they interrupt you in telling the joke, this breaks the rule for this conversation element.

And the same thing goes for story-telling. If you say "I was on the flight from hell coming back from Detroit last week" and the person you're talking to responds by saying "What happened?" then you get to tell the story all the way through. Certain kinds of interruptions are permitted—in fact, you expect people to say "Uh, huh" and other such supportive interruptions when you're on a roll—but sidetracking you completely from the story is not expected.

It's not expected, but it happens, and when sidetracking happens, one of several repair sequences might kick in. "Sorry, I got you off track. Then what happened?" is a repair sequence. We've all experienced the pain of never getting back to a story from which we were sidetracked in a conversation. When that happens, we might think badly of the person who did it or we might shrug it off—depending on the context and what's at stake. If you're in a job interview and the interviewer sidetracks you, you'd probably think twice about insisting that the interviewer let you finish the story you were telling.

Adjacency Pairs

Among the first things that conversation analysts noticed when they started looking carefully at conversations was ordered pairs of expressions, like questions and greetings (Schegloff and Sacks 1973). Once the first part of a pair occurs, the second part is expected.

For example, as Schegloff pointed out (1968, 1979), if you say "Hello" and you get silence in return, you might take the absence of response as meaningful. If someone asks "How're you doing?" and you respond by saying "Great" but don't follow up with "And how about you?" then the other person might look for meaning in your tone of voice. Did you say "Great" with enthusiasm or with sarcasm? If the former, you might hear "I'm so glad to hear that," in return. But if it was the latter, you might hear "Sorry I asked" or "Excuse me for asking" with equal sarcasm. In other words, other people's interpretation of the content in your turn leads them to adjust the content of their next turn.

Sacks (1992:3ff) noticed that workers at a psychiatric hospital's emergency telephone line greeted callers by saying something like, "Hello. This is Mr. Smith. May I help you?" Most of the time, the response was "Hello, this is Mr. Brown," but on one occasion, the caller responded, "I can't hear you." When the worker repeated his greeting, "This is Mr. *Smith*," with an emphasis on Smith, the caller responded "Smith."

In this case, the rule for an **adjacency pair** was not really being broken. It was being negotiated by both parties, on the fly, during the conversation. Mr. Smith, the suicide prevention worker, was trying to get the caller to give his name, and the caller was trying not to give his name.

Dynamic Sequences

If conversations are dynamic things, with constant negotiation, then to understand the rules of conversations, you can't interview people about the rules of, say, greetings. You have to study real conversations in which greetings occur. Here is an example of an adjacency pair—a question-answer pair—that's broken up between its parts:

1. A: is it good? the Szechuan pork?

2. B: y'like spicy, [uh–

3. A: [yeah

4. B: it's kinda, y'know, hot.

5. A: <u>great</u>

6. B: yeah, me too.

There is a lot going on here. A asks B if a particular dish is good. This is the first part of a question pair, which calls for an answer. B responds with another question, which creates a new expectation for an answer. A anticipates this and answers "yeah" (line 3) before B finishes her thought (which presumably was "y'like spicy, uh, food?").

B doesn't want to give up her turn just yet, so she completes the thought, in line 4. This gives A the opportunity to reaffirm that he does, in fact like spicy food (that her "yeah" in line 3 was not just an acknowledgment of B's question) before B answers A's first question. A reaffirms his "yeah" response with "great" in line 5. The segment ends with B agreeing that he, too, likes spicy food.

Looking at this segment, it seems like the first adjacency pair, the question about whether the Szechuan pork is good, has never been answered. But it has. The answer is implied in the inserted question in line 2 and the retesting in line 4, all of which is shorthand for: "Yes, if you like spicy food, then the Szechuan pork is good, otherwise it isn't."

If this seems complicated, it's because it is. It's very, very complicated. Yet, every native speaker of English understands every piece of this analysis because: (1) the segment of conversation is rule based; (2) we understand the rules; and (3) we understand that the outcome is the result of cooperation by both speakers, A and B, as they (4) attend to each other's words; (5) draw on cultural knowledge that they share about being out on a date and about Chinese restaurants; and (6) build a conversation dynamically. In this case, two people, in a conversation among equals, have worked together to make everything come out right.

And if you think this is complicated, just add more speakers. With two people in a conversation, A and B, there are two pairs of people—AB (as seen from A's perspective) and BA (as seen from B's perspective)—figuring out each other's motives and behaviors and negotiating their way through the interaction. With three people in a conversation (A, B, and C), there are three pairs (AB, AC, BC) doing the negotiating. With six people, there are 30 such pairs. Deborah Tannen (1984) analyzed two hours and 40 minutes of conversation among six friends at a Thanksgiving dinner. The analysis is a 170-page book, and that doesn't include the hundreds of pages of transcripts on which the analysis is based.

Dinner parties often start out as conversations among six or eight simultaneous participants, but they soon break up into smaller conversations that are easier to manage. Some conversations among large groups of people, however, require special rules so that they don't break up into conversations among shifting subgroups.

Manzo's Study of Taking Turns in a Jury

Juries in the United States are composed of six, nine, or 12 members (depending on the kind of trial), and have special kinds of conversation. They have a leader (the jury foreman or forewoman), and people work hard to make sure that the cultural rules for such formal conversations (written down nowhere, but widely understood) are followed. Among other things, the rules require that no one gets completely drowned and sidelined, unless they deserve to be (by breaking the cultural rules themselves).

John Manzo (1996) studied how jurors for a criminal trial managed turn taking in their deliberations. The case was against a man who was charged with possessing a handgun in violation of his parole. The deliberations were videotaped for a PBS documentary. Figure 18.1 shows the layout of the jury table, and Table 18.2 contains the data for one turn-taking sequence. At the start of the deliberations, the foreperson, juror 1,

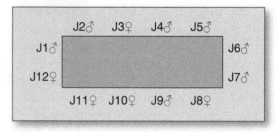

Figure 18.1 Layout of a Jury Table

Source: J. Manzo, "Taking Turns and Taking Sides: Opening Scenes from Two Jury Deliberations." *Social Psychology Quarterly* 59:107–125, p. 110, 1996.

at the head of the table, on the left, proposed that each juror talk about how she or he felt about the case.

Manzo noticed that, at lines 10 and 12, both juror 2 and juror 12 chime in and support juror 1's suggestion about everyone making an opening statement. It takes 2.5 seconds for juror 2 to respond after juror 12 does, but the foreperson, juror 1, chooses juror 2 (to his left), rather than juror 12. Juror 2 launches right in, down to line 27.

Now, look closely at what happens next. At this juncture, it is still possible for juror 12 to be the next speaker. After all, she had signaled her interest back in line 10. But at the end of his statement, juror 2 turns his gaze toward juror 3, to his left, and then down to the table. Juror 3 cranes her head to see what the foreperson will do next. He nods to juror 3 and she launches into her statement (down to line 39).

The first turn for an opening statement was decided entirely by juror 1, who chose juror 2 over juror 12. The *second* turn, however, is a joint operation, involving three people: the foreperson and jurors 2 and 3. Juror 3's gaze, at the end of his statement, toward juror 1 sets things up; juror 3's craning her neck to see the foreperson is part of the operation; and juror 1's gaze toward juror 3 nails down that it is her turn.

By the time juror 3 completes her turn (at line 39), she only has to shift her weight to her left, for juror 4 to take up the next turn. At this point, the rule is established. No more gazes or

Table 18.2 Excerpts From a Jury Deliberation

Line	Speaker	Text
1	J1	If I may make a suggestion? rather than- I know that
2		juries uh um >like Mr. ( ) mentioned< like to take a
3		vote right off the bat and … hh I think if we do::
4		that we'll probably end up discussing it anyhow so
5		let's:: just go around the table discuss the case?
6		and your: .hh views? and uh after:: everybody's said
7		their piece us (.5)we can uh. take a vote on u
8		what we think. if::: that's agreeable to everybody?
9		(1.8)
10	J12	uh huh
11		(2.5)
12	J2	sounds good=
13	J1	=so. ((turns to and smiles at)2))you wanna start?
14	J2	mm okay? .hh I found three:: points. that the
15		prosecutor. hadda prove? he proved .hh that the
16		defendant did possess the gun >the defendant
17		<u>knew</u> he possessed a gun< .hh and that uh: the
18		defendant knew he was (.) a convicted felon at the
19		time he uh: possessed a gun .. hh however uh::.
20		because of this case and because of uhm: (1.6)
21		because of the:: record of the defendant uh I'd have
22		a re- I'd have a real <u>tough</u> time .h uh voting him
23		guilty on this a:nduh:- I haven't made up my <u>mind</u>
24		yet .hhh but I see <u>both</u> sides of- both sides of uhm::
25		<u>both</u> the cases BOTH of the cases as they've been
26		laid out. and uh: rinow? I haven't made up my mind
27		one uh >how I'm goin ta vote.
28		(2.3) ((J2 *directs gaze toward J3 and then down to*
29		*table. J7 then nods in the direction of J3, and J3*
30		*cranes her neck in order to meet J1's gaze))*
31	J3	>Okay I feel the defendant is .< guilty. uh. on
32		all three accusations <u>technically</u>. (.) but I I guess
33		I feel that we should also take into consideration
34		the fact that. .h he du::z have a reading disability.
35		as well as maybe some <u>other</u> disabilities >I'm not
36		trying to play on your <u>sympathies</u> or anything but.
37		.h it is <u>something</u> that I have to consider tch and
38		right now I haven't (.) determined whether I should
39		name the defendant guilty or innocent.
40		(3.0) ((*juror 3 produces a postural shift toward J4*
41		*without eye contact))*
42	J4	.hh I fee:1 that …

Source: J. Manzo, "Taking Turns and Taking Sides: Opening Scenes From Two Jury Deliberations." *Social Psychology Quarterly* 59:107–125, p. 110, 1996.

instructions from juror 1 are needed (**Further Reading:** conversation analysis).

LANGUAGE IN USE

Language in use is about how people use language to get things done. Studies in this area of discourse analysis involve detailed analysis of interaction—much like conversation analysis, but paying attention to the content and the motivations of speakers, not just to the structure of their interaction.

People around the world are very adept at using just the right language to find marriage partners (Gal 1978), at using jokes to engage in forbidden political discourse (Van Boeschoten 2006), at adjusting their language to get children to behave in classrooms (De Fina 1997; Morine-Dershima 2006); at using subtle language cues to bribe border officials while giving everyone plausible deniability (Mele and Bello 2007). . . .

One area of interest is situational ethnicity, or ethnic identity switching. This phenomenon—where people adopt different ethnicity markers, depending on the situation—has fascinated social scientists for years (Gluckman 1958 [1940]; Nagata 1974; Okamura 1981). People switch ethnicity by telling jokes, or by choosing particular foods when offered a choice, or by casually dropping cultural-insider phrases that signal ethnicity to others. They may do this to land a job, to get a better price in a bargaining situation, or to get a better table in a restaurant.

Negrón's Study of Situational Ethnicity in New York

Rosalyn Negrón (2007, 2012) studied situational ethnicity among Puerto Rican American and other Hispanics in New York. Her work focused on how Spanish-English bilinguals use code switching—moving back and forth between two languages—as a marker for ethnic identity switching and for getting things they wanted in various interactions. (Box 18.4)

Box 18.4 Getting audio of real conversations

It's not easy getting uninterrupted audio of real conversations, but technology makes it a lot easier today than it used to be. In 1958, William Soskin, a psychologist, and Vera John, an anthropologist, got several pairs of people—young married couples at a resort—to wear big, clunky voice transmitters 14–16 hours a day for two weeks. The contraptions were 1.5" × 2.5" × 5" and were worn on a shoulder strap. A 1'-long antenna, attached to the strap, stuck up from the shoulder blade, and the couples carried a battery pack that was changed daily. The couples' conversations were picked up on radio receiver and recorded on tape. Luckily, the resort manager not only gave permission for the experiment; he announced at dinner one night why the couples were wearing the conspicuous apparatus (Soskin 1963; Soskin and John 1963).

To get her data on situational ethnicity, Negrón had 11 informants wear small voice recorders for two weeks. She got 578 hours of audio recordings of everyday interactions—people talking to each other at work, at school, at home, in church, shopping, and in social gatherings. The little recorders fit into cell phone cases that could be clipped to people's pants waists or pockets. The recorders had remote control mic's that could be clipped to shirt pockets, collars, or lapels. People could turn off the recordings whenever they wanted to, but after a while, the participants in Negrón's study just left the recorders on—even during bathroom breaks (Negrón 2012).

One of Negrón's informants was Roberto, a 36-year-old Venezuelan who grew up in New York in a neighborhood of Whites, Blacks, and Latinos. Roberto has blue eyes and white skin. He's married to a Puerto Rican women and his step-mother is a Black Haitian. He is completely fluent in Venezuelan Spanish, two dialects of Puerto Rican Spanish (standard and nonstandard), African American Vernacular English, and New York English.

Roberto sells equipment for street fairs—tables, chairs, canopies, and so on. In the interaction below, Roberto goes into a cell phone store and gives James, the store manager, a flyer about the street-fair business. Like Roberto, James is a Latino who looks European and who speaks English with no Spanish accent at all.

Dropping Hints and Doing Business

As they start to talk, neither one knows that the other is Latino, but both of them have business interests to pursue—Roberto to sell his street-fair merchandise; James to sell his cell phones. Listen:

1 R: H'you doing.

2 J: Alright.=

3 R: =You guys ah participating in the street fai(-r)z?

4   (0.7)

5 J: Yeah.

6 R: You are? (0.5) 'K. Just in case you need, ah, in

7   case you need canopies tables and chai(-r)z,

8   (1.0)

9   j's gimee a call.

10 J: Yeah. I don't know when the next one is I

11   haven't got [any-]

12 R: [May twenty-secon(-d).]

13 J: Rea:.lly?

14 R: That's the one with the Chamber and <Broadview

15   is in deh:: fawl>.

16   (1.0)

17 J: Mm, well I do the Broadview one over at at my

18   other store.

19 R: Ah, which store is [that-

20 J: [(By the), ah, Junction Boulevard.

21 R: On Junction?, yeah?

22 J: Yeah.

23 R: Well, I got the canopies, tables and chairs. I

24   used to work for Broadview. I worked for Broadview

25   for 8 yea(-r)z.

26 J: [°Ok.°]

27 R: [An'] um I started a canopy company (0.5)

28   that's (0.8) direct contact with dem, so whenever you

29   need one or if you need tables, chai(r)z whatever

30   you need,[j's give me a cawl ahead of time, let=

31 J: [°Ok.°

32 R: =me know what event, give me your spot nuhmbuh and

33   it will be there before you get der.

34   (1.0)

35 J: Ok.=

36 R: =And [it'll already be set up.

37 J: [( )=

38 R: =>Yah.<

[Negrón 2011:87–88]

Roberto is dropping clues all over the place that he's a New Yorker. There's the aw sound (fawl and cawl in lines 15 and 30, instead of fall and call); the use of deh, der and dem instead of the, there and them (lines 15, 28, 33); and the dropped r's in chairs, fairs, years, and numbers (lines 3, 7, 25, 29, 32). So, far, though, there's no hint that either of them is Latino. That soon changes. James looks at the flyer that Roberto gave him:

39 J: Let me give you some information.

40   (5.0)

41 J: *Roberto?*

42 R: Yeah.

43 J: I had a couple of other customers that that(.) do

44   fairs and stuff.

45 R: O?k.

46   (2.0)

47 J: °Try to give you some info.°

48   (2.0)

49   ((James searches for business card))

50 J: °(Ok)° ((James hands Roberto business card))

[Negrón 2011:89]

In line 41, James reads Roberto's name from the flyer, using perfect Spanish pronunciation of the name. He then hands Roberto his own business card.

51   (3.0)

52   ((Roberto reads business card))

53 R: *Cuchifrito* for Thought.

       'Puerto Rican soul food'

54   ((Roberto laughs))

55 R: I like that [That's hot.]

56   ((Roberto looking at business card))

57 J: [(Yeah I),] I own an online magazine

58   called *Cuchifrito* for Thought, it's been around for 8

59   years.

60 R: O?k.

61 J: Ahm, (2.0) I'm working with a company called

62   *Asamblea Latina?*

       'Latino Assembly'

63   (.5)

64 J: They did something really big in, ah, Flushing

65   Meadow Park last year.

66 R: *No me diga/h/.*=

       'You don't say?'

67 J: =Yeah and >it's all *Latino*(-s)< and [and from 21 countries?]

68 R: [*O:h, coño, e(-s)ta (bien).*]

       'Oh, damn, that's good.'

69 J: >and they used a bunch [of canopies and stuff like that.]<=

70 R: [°Mm::::h, o?k.°]

[Negrón 2011:90–91]

There's a Lot Going on Here, Too

In line 53, when Roberto reads James's card aloud, he uses perfect Spanish pronunciation for the word *cuchifrito*. *Cuchifritos* are small cubes of fried pork (usually tails, ears, stomach, and tongue) and are a famous Spanish Caribbean dish. Any speaker of Spanish who lives in a Puerto Rican or Dominican neighborhood in New York City would know the word and its ethnic implications. In line 58, when James repeats the word, he, too, uses the Spanish pronunciation. He follows up by telling Roberto that he works for *Alianza Latina*, again code switching from perfect English in line 61 to perfect Spanish in line 62.

A few lines later, in lines 66 and 68, Roberto nails it all down, by responding in Spanish to James's discussion in English about an event in Flushing Meadow Park. And it's not just any old Spanish. In lines 66 and 68, Roberto uses an unmistakably Puerto Rican dialect.

In Negrón's work, we see again how important it is to be steeped in a culture to do this kind of analysis. You have to know, for example, about *cuchifritos*, and you have to know that the aspiration at the end of *diga/h/* in the expression *No me diga/h/* in line 66 is a replacement for an s and that this is characteristic of Caribbean Spanish (**Further Reading:** code switching and ethnic identity).

LANGUAGE AND POWER: CRITICAL DISCOURSE ANALYSIS

The critical perspective in social science is rooted in Antonio Gramsci's discussion (1994; Forgacs 2000) in the 1930s of what he called **cultural hegemony**. Modern states, Gramsci observed, control the mass media and the schools, the structural mechanisms for shaping and transmitting culture. Marxist theory predicts that the culture (the superstructure) follows the structure, and so the lower and middle classes in modern states come to believe in— even advocate—the entrenched differences in power that keep them subservient to the elite.

Everyone in a society knows the rules for these power differences. These rules—another instance of grammar beyond the sentence—are played out in discourse and can be observed. Critical discourse analysis is the study of language and power: how men and women, doctors and patients, employers and employees, and so on, either work together to maintain and reinforce those rules or how they resist them.

Gender and Discourse

Mattei (1998), for example, counted the number of times male and female witnesses in a U.S. Senate hearing were interrupted. These were panel hearings in the nomination of David H. Souter to the U.S. Supreme Court. There were 30 question periods in these panels, and Mattei counted 76 cases of overlap in the testimony. Thirteen cases of overlap were simply to ask the witness to speak louder or to ask a senator to clarify a question. The other 63 cases were interruptions—that is, cutting off a speaker and trying to take over a turn.

The distribution of these 63 cases is revealing. As we expect, senators (who are in a position of power) interrupted witnesses 41 times; witnesses interrupted senators 22 times. Also as expected, of the 41 interruptions by senators, 34 were against women and seven were against men. Women, however, were more assertive than men were when it came to interrupting senators: Of the 22 interruptions against senators by witnesses, 17 were by women (see Box 18.5).

Box 18.5 Gendered interruption

Pioneering research by Zimmerman and West (1983 [1975]) showed that, in ordinary conversations, men interrupted women more often than women interrupted men. Later research by these same scholars and by many others has shown how complex the patterns are. Kennedy and Camden (1983), for example, showed that women sometimes interrupt more than men, and Kendall and Tannen (2001:552) showed that not all interruptions are equal: Some are better characterized as overlapping, where the purpose is really "to show support rather than to gain the floor." And West (1995:116) showed that in conversations with men, it is often women's response efforts that enable men to "produce 'something worth listening to' in the first place" (**Further Reading:** gendered interruption).

Doctor-Patient Interaction

Dozens of studies have established the asymmetry in the doctor-patient relation: Doctors use their knowledge to establish their authority and patients adopt a meek, accepting role.

Maynard (1991) analyzed how a doctor delivers bad news to a mother and father of a child who has developmental problems (particularly in language and speech). The parents tell the doctor that their child, J, doesn't seem to be progressing normally in speaking. The doctor says that J is having a problem with language, which, he says, is different from speaking.

The parents don't understand the distinction, and the doctor says:

> Language are (*sic*) the actual words. Speech is how the words sound. Okay? J's speech is a very secondary consideration. It's the language which is her problem. When language goes into her brain, it gets garbled up, and doesn't make sense. . . . It has something to do with the parts of her brain that control speech, that control language, and it doesn't work. [Maynard 1991:454]

What's going on here? The parents are being taught that they don't control certain kinds of information and must therefore accept a subservient role in the interaction. Talcott Parsons had observed this patient-doctor dynamic in his discussion of roles (1951), but Maynard shows that patients don't necessarily come into the doctor's office with that role in mind. Instead, they develop the subservient role, *in cooperation with doctors*, during conversations about the illness.

Borges and Waitzkin's Study: Coding Doctor-Patient Interactions

Howard Waitzkin and his colleagues (Borges and Waitzkin 1995; Waitzkin et al. 1994) analyzed transcripts of 50 encounters between older patients and primary care internists.

Analysis begins by coding the text for elements of interest in the research. In this case, coders were told to "flag instances when either doctors or patients made statements that conveyed ideologic content or expressed messages of social control" and nonverbal elements in the text—like interruptions or shifts in tone of voice or unresponsiveness to questions by patients—"that might clarify a deeper structure lying beneath the surface elements of discourse" (Borges and Waitzkin 1995:35).

When the coders finished their work, they produced a "preliminary structural outline or diagram that depicted how the medical discourse . . . processed contextual issues" (Borges and Waitzkin 1995:35). Then members of the research group met together for several months to review annotated transcripts and preliminary outlines or diagrams. They looked at all the coded instances of ideology and social control—the main topics that they had told the coders to flag—and chose texts to illustrate those and other themes, like gender roles and aging.

There were plenty of instances in which the members of the team disagreed about the meaning of a text. In those cases, they report, "we brainstormed to resolve our disagreements and tried to avoid the discussion's being dominated by one person's views" (Borges and Waitzkin 1995:35).

Recognizing that readers can have different interpretations of the same text, the researchers made all their original data available for reanalysis by filing them at University Microfilms International. Then they present their results, which consist of a series of excerpts from the texts and an analysis of the meaning of each excerpt (**Further Reading**: doctor-patient interaction).

Presenting the Results

This is a common method for presenting results of interpretive analysis: laying out conclusions that are instantiated by prototypical quotes from the transcripts.

For example, a woman visits her doctor complaining of multiple symptoms. The doctor reaches a diagnosis of what's called "suburban syndrome," an illness that affects women who try to do too much outside the home while maintaining all their responsibilities at home as well. The doctor prescribes rest; the patient says that she wants a prescription for tranquilizers. The doctor resists at first, but then relents—and not only gives the patient a prescription, but a renewable one, at that. He tries to reassure the patient that there is nothing wrong with her that withdrawing from a few activities wouldn't fix. Still, the patient returns to her concern about organic disease and the doctor cuts her off:

P: That's what I thought maybe you
    would give me a blood test today,
        see if I was anemic

D: [For what? Nah (words)

P: [I sometimes feel

    light-headed

D: I know.

P: And my mother, and my mother tends
   to be anemic.

D: Don't choose a diagnosis out of the
   blue. Buy a medical book and get a
   real *nice* diagnosis. Well, and you,
   I'll order them (referring to the tranquilizers). Which drug store do you
   use?
[Borges and Waitzkin 1995:40–41]

Borges and Waitzkin comment on this section of text:

From the doctor's viewpoint, a search for an underlying physical disorder is fruitless. Such patients with diverse somatic symptoms can present diagnostic and therapeutic challenges for primary care physicians. The doctor concludes that the patient's physical symptoms reflect troubles in her social context, more than pathophysiology. Yet his attempts to persuade her on this point never quite succeed. . . . A college graduate with young children at home, the patient does not refer at any time to her own work aspirations or to her children, nor does the doctor ask. For the present and the indefinite future, one assumes, her work consists of the housewife's duties. Although the doctor gives a contextual diagnosis, suburban syndrome, potentially important contextual issues arise in the conversation either marginally (brief allusions to the patient's husband) or not at all (work aspirations, child care arrangements, and social support network). Nevertheless, the doctor manages the patient's contextual difficulties by encouraging rest and prescribing a tranquilizer. Presumably the patient continues to accept the ideologic assumption that her social role as suburban homemaker is the proper one for her. She thus returns and consents to same social context as before, now with the benefit of medical advice and pharmacologic assistance. [Borges and Waitzkin 1995:41]

Here's another example from the same project—a snippet of interaction between a doctor (D) and his patient (P), an elderly woman who has come in for a follow-up of her heart disease:

P: Well I should—now I've got birthday
   cards to buy.

   I've got seven or eight birthdays this
   week—month. Instead of that I'm just
   gonna write 'em and wish them a
   happy birthday. Just a little note, my
   grandchildren.

D: Mm hmm.

P: But I'm not gonna bother. I just can't
   do it all, Dr. —

D: Well.

P: I called my daughters, her birthday was
   just, today's the third.

D: Yeah.

P: My daughter's birthday in Princeton was the uh first, and I called her up and talked with her. I don't know what time it'll cost me, but then, my telephone is my only indiscretion.
[Waitzkin et al. 1994:330]

Then, the researchers comment:

At no other time in the encounter does the patient refer to her own family, nor does the doctor ask. The patient does her best to maintain contact, even though she does not mention anything that she receives in the way of day-to-day support. Compounding these problems of social support and incipient isolation, the patient recently has moved from a home that she occupied for 59 years. [Waitzkin et al. 1994:330]

And finally, Waitzkin et al. interpret the discourse:

This encounter shows structural elements that appear beneath the surface details of patient-doctor communication. . . . Contextual issues affecting the patient include social isolation; loss of home, possessions, family, and community; limited resources to preserve independent function; financial insecurity; and physical deterioration associated with the process of dying. . . . After the medical encounter, the patient returns to the same contextual problems that trouble her, consenting to social conditions that confront the elderly in this society.

That such structural features should characterize an encounter like this one becomes rather disconcerting, since the communication otherwise seems so admirable. . . . The doctor manifests patience and compassion as he encourages a wide-ranging discussion of socioemotional concerns that extend far beyond the technical details of the patient's physical disorders. Yet the discourse does nothing to improve the most troubling features of the patient's situation. To expect differently would require redefining much of what medicine aims to do. [1994:335–36]

AND FINALLY . . .

Talk in interaction is governed by rules, but, like all of culture, those rules change with economic, political, demographic, and technological conditions. In 1985, for example, 14% of physicians in the United States were women and hardly anyone used e-mail. In 2008, 48% of medical school students were women and e-mail was being replaced by Facebook and Twitter as the main means of communication for millions of people. Do these demographic and technological changes influence the dynamics of doctor-patient interaction? Do the same dynamics of interaction hold true in economically developed societies, like Japan and Australia, where doctors earn a third to a half of what they earn in the United States? We could test that, too.

Key Concepts in This Chapter

narrative analysis	breaking frame	ordered pairs
performance analysis	cultural schemas	adjacency pairs
schema analysis	feedback theory	language in use
conversation analysis	valve theory	situational ethnicity
language in use	morality tale	ethnic identity switching
language and power	talk-in-interaction	code switching
medicalization of death	prosodic features of	critical perspective
nested stories	speech	cultural hegemony
ethnopoetics	turn taking	critical discourse analysis
scripts	repair tactics	language and power

Summary

- All native speakers of human languages know the rules of grammar for their language. There are rules for making words, for putting words together into sentences, and for using words correctly to convey meaning. There are also rules for grammar beyond the sentence.

  o Methods for studying grammar beyond the sentence, include narrative analysis, performance analysis, schema analysis, conversation analysis, language in use, and critical discourse analysis.
- Human beings are natural story tellers. You can ask people anything about their personal experience and you'll get a narrative. Narrative analysis is the search for regularities in how people, within and across cultures, tell stories.

  o One major genre of narratives involves recounting an event: What happened? How did it happen? Why did it happen? What was the result? The object is to discover themes and recurring structures.

  o Like any empirical data, narratives can be systematically compared in the search for themes.
- Performance analysis involves the search for regularities in the delivery of highly stylized narratives, like folk tales, sermons, and political speeches.

  o Ethnopoetics is performance analysis applied to oral literature. It involves the study of many narratives by many different narrators in order to understand the devices that people use in a particular language.
- Schema analysis is based on the observation that everyday life is too complex for people to learn one scene at a time. Just as we don't learn a list of sentences, we don't learn a list of behaviors or scenes. There must be rules—a grammar—that help us make sense of so much information.

  o Schemas let culturally skilled people to fill in the details of a story. We often hear things like "Fred lost his data because he forgot to save his work." We know that Fred's forgetting to save his work didn't actually *cause* him to lose his data. A whole set of links are left out in ordinary conversations, but they are easily filled in by listeners who have the background to do so.
- Conversation analysis is the search for the grammar of ordinary discourse, or talk-in-interaction.

  o Unlike the other rules of grammar, the rules for taking turns, repair tactics and other aspects of talk-in-interaction are negotiated, on the fly, by participants in a conversation. Every conversation is unique, but they are also subject to rules, within and across cultures, that govern how they start, evolve, and end.

  o Detailed transcriptions are required to identify when and how people take turns and other features of conversations.
- Language in use is about how people use language to get things done. Like conversation analysis, this involves detailed transcriptions, but the focus is on the motivations of speakers, not just the structure of their interaction.

  o One area of interest is situational ethnicity, or ethnic identity switching, where people adopt different ethnicity markers, depending on the situation by casually dropping cultural-insider phrases that signal ethnicity to others.

- The critical perspective in social science is represented in discourse analysis in the study of language and power: How men and women, doctors and patients, employers and employees, and so on work together to maintain and reinforce the rules of power distinctions or how they resist them.
  - o In general, men interrupt women more often than women interrupt men, but the pattern is complex. Women sometimes interrupt more than men; some interruptions are designed to support rather than undermine interaction.
  - o Studies also show the asymmetry in the doctor-patient relation: Doctors use their knowledge to establish their authority, and patients adopt a meek, accepting role. Here, too, the patterns can be complex, and they may change over time or across cultures.

Exercises

1. Ask people to tell you a commonly known fairy tale: Cinderella, Little Red Riding Hood, The Three Little Pigs, etc. (See Dundes [1982] for an example of how folklorists compare renditions of the same tale.) The fairy tales of Hans Christian Andersen, Charles Perrault, and the Brothers Grimm have been translated into many languages and are widely known in Spanish. Work in whatever language you want, but record the six tellings of one story and transcribe them using the Jefferson method in Table 18.1. This will give you an appreciation for what transcription really takes, and it will give you six replications of a narrative cultural artifact.

   Examine the transcripts for consistencies and inconsistencies in prosodic and other features of performance.

   If possible, form a research group. With five students in a group, each collecting five or six tellings of a single tale, you'll wind up with a corpus of 25–30 tellings. If you have a class of 15–20 students, you could each collect just two tellings and have data for several kinds of analysis.

2. Video a five-minute dialog between any two people. A good way to generate the data is to give two people a hot political or other topic to discuss. The topic can be local (something going on at your school), national, or international. It just has to be something that both parties know about and want to talk about. In particular, analyze the turn-taking behavior of the two parties.

   Use the Jefferson method in Table 18.1 to transcribe the conversation in minute detail. (Doing one five-minute conversation will show you what it takes to get all the detail.)

   If you can work with colleagues and record six–10 conversations, you can analyze the data for regularities in turn-taking and repair tactics. If you have conversations between men and women, two women, and two men, you can analyze the data for gendered differences in turn-taking and repair tactics. Do they give each other equal time? Does one party interrupt more often than the other? Does one party use put-down language more than the other?

Further Reading

Narrative analysis. Andrews et al. (2004), Atkinson and Delamont (2006, especially vols. 1 and 2), Baker-Ward et al. (2005), Bloom (2003), Blum-Kulka (1993), Boje (2001), Coffey and Atkinson (1996), Franzosi (2010), Hanks (1989), Riessman (1993), Roy (2006), Schiffrin (2003), Simons et al. (2008), Sosulski et al. (2010).

Ethnopoetics and performance analysis. Bauman (1984, 1986), Blommaert (2006), Foster (1989), Goh (2010), D. Hymes (1981, 2003), Juzwik (2004), Kataoka (2009), Koven (2004), Norrick (2010), Poveda (2002), Quick (1999), Sammons and Sherzer (2000).

Schema analysis, mental models, and metaphor analysis. Schemas: Bem (1981, 1983, 1985), Brewer (1999, 2000), D'Andrade (1991), D'Andrade and Strauss (1992), Holland and Quinn (1987), Hudak (1993), Izquierdo and Johnson (2007), Mandler (1984), Nishida (1999), Paolisso (2007), Saito (2000), Shore (2009), Strauss and Quinn (1997). Mental models: Atran et al. (2005), Bang et al. (2007), Bennardo (2002), Carley and Palmquist (1992), D'Andrade and Strauss (1992), Gentner and Stevens (1983), Halford (1993), Johnson-Laird (1983), Ross (2002), Wierzbicka (2004). Metaphor analysis. Allan (2007), Bennardo (2008); Bialostok (2002), Cornell (1984), Dunn (2004), Ignatow (2004), Lakoff and Kövecses (1987), Rees et al. (2007), Saban et al. (2007), Santa Ana (1999), Schmitt (2005), Slaughter (2005), Steger (2007).

Transcribing conversation. Atkinson and Heritage (1984), Bucholz (2000, 2007), Davidson (2010), Dressler and Kreuz (2000), J. A. Edwards and Lampert (1993), Ochs (1979), Powers (2005), Psathas (1979), Psathas and Anderson (1990).

Conversation analysis. Drew and Heritage (2006), Gafaranga (2001), Goodwin and Heritage (1990), Psathas (1995), Silverman (1993, 1998), Zeitlyn (2004).

Code switching and ethnic identity. Auer (2005), De Fina (2007), Fung and Carter (2007), Gafaranga (2001), Schilling-Estes (2004), Shin (2010), Wei and Milroy (1995).

Gendered interruption. K. J. Anderson and Leaper (1998), James and Clarke (1993), Okamoto et al. (2002), Smith-Lovin and Brody (1989), Tannen (1984, 1994), ten Have (1991), Menz and Al-Roubaie (2008), Werner-Wilson et al. (1997).

Doctor-patient interaction. Heath (1989), Maynard and Heritage (2005), McHoul and Rapley (2005), J. D. Robinson (1998), Robinson and Heritage (2005), ten Have (1991), West (1984), West and Zimmerman (1983).

19

Analyzing Qualitative Data III

Grounded Theory and Content Analysis

INTRODUCTION

This chapter is about two very different kinds of text analysis: grounded theory and content analysis. The two methods reflect the two great epistemological approaches for all research: induction and deduction (see Box 1.3).

Grounded theory research is mostly based on inductive or open coding. The idea is to

become grounded in the data and to allow understanding to emerge from close study of the texts.

Content analysis is mostly based on deductive coding. In doing deductive analysis of text, you start with a hypothesis *before* you start coding. The idea is to test whether your hypothesis is correct.

All research is, ultimately, a combination of inductive and deductive effort, and there is no point in talking about whether induction or deduction is better. They're both terrific if you use them to answer appropriate questions. But when you're in the exploratory and discovery stage of any research project, whether your data are words or numbers, the work is mostly inductive; when you're in the confirmatory stage of any research project—again, no matter what kind of data you have—the work is mostly deductive.

GROUNDED THEORY

Human experience is endlessly interesting because it is endlessly unique. A migrant from Mexico who crosses the U.S. border one step ahead of the authorities lives through a unique experience and has a unique story to tell, but 20 such stories will reveal similarities and patterns. Discovering pattern in human experience requires close, inductive examination of unique cases plus the application of deductive reasoning. Grounded theory is a set of systematic techniques for doing this. The method was developed by two sociologists, Barney Glaser and Anslem Strauss, in a seminal book titled *The Discovery of Grounded Theory: Strategies for Qualitative Research* (1967). As the title implies, the aim is to discover theories—causal explanations—grounded in empirical data, about how things work.

The original method of grounded theory was in the positivist tradition of social science. Glaser (2002) remained committed to the original, mostly inductive approach, while Strauss—first in 1987 on his own and then with Julie Corbin (Corbin and Strauss 2008; Strauss and Corbin 1998)—allowed for more use of deduction. And, in an influential series of books and articles, Kathy Charmaz (1995, 2000, 2002) has developed an alternative method, called constructivist grounded theory. This brand of the method—in which respondents and researchers create data together, interactively, during an interview—is in the interpretivist tradition of the social science.

Whichever tradition you favor, there are three steps in grounded theory: coding the texts for themes; linking themes into theoretical models; and displaying and validating the models.

Coding Texts for Themes

Actually coding themes in a text is a relatively simple, if time-consuming, affair—once you know what the themes are. Four methods for discovering themes are: (1) highlighting, (2) pile sorts, (3) word counts, and (4) key-word-in-context (KWIC) tables.

1. *Highlighting.* When you start to work with a corpus of written text, just read it and if you see something that you think might be important, highlight it, either with markers or on a computer. Some of the words and phrases you highlight will turn into names for themes. In fact, Corbin and Strauss (2008:65) recommend explicitly using actual phrases from your text—the words of real people—to name themes, a technique they call in vivo coding (and see Chapter 13 on coding field notes).

Willms et al. (1990) and Miles and Huberman (1994) suggest starting with some general themes derived from reading the literature and adding more themes and subthemes as you go. This is somewhere between inductive and deductive coding. You have a general idea of what you're after and know what at least some of the big themes are, but you're still in a discovery mode, so you let new themes emerge from the texts as you go along.

Look for repetitions. "Anyone who has listened to long stretches of talk," says Roy D'Andrade, "knows how frequently people circle through the same network of ideas"

(1991:287). In my study of how ocean scientists interact with the people in Washington, DC, who are responsible for ocean policy (Bernard 1974), I kept hearing the word "brokers." Scientists and policymakers alike used this word to describe people whom they trusted to act as go-betweens, so "broker" became one of the code themes for my work.

Look for unusual terms or common words that are used in unusual ways. James Spradley (1972) recorded conversations among homeless men (they were called tramps in those days) at informal gatherings, meals, and card games. Spradley kept hearing the men talk about "making a flop," which was their jargon for finding place to sleep each night. Spradley went through his material and isolated everything he could find about flops: ways to make a flop, kinds of people who bother you when you flop, and so on. Then Spradley went back to his informants and asked them for more information about each of these subthemes.

And, said Spradley (1979:199–201), look for evidence of social conflict, cultural contradictions, informal methods of social control, things that people do in managing impersonal social relationships, methods by which people acquire and maintain achieved and ascribed status, and information about how people solve problems. Each of these arenas is likely to yield major themes in cultures.

2. *Pile sorts*. To use the pile-sorting method—what Lincoln and Guba (1985: 347–49) call cutting and sorting—look for real quotes from the interviews you do with informants that represent what you think are important topics in the data. Cut out each quote (making sure to leave some of the context in which the quote occurs) and paste it onto a 3 × 5 index card. On the back of the card, note who said it and where it appeared in the text. Then, lay out the cards on a big table, sort them into piles of similar quotes, and *name each pile*. These are the themes (Ryan and Bernard 2003:94).

Check your reliability by asking several friends or colleagues (the more the better) to sort the cards into piles of "what goes with what." Sayles et al. (2007) analyzed 300 pages of transcripts from seven focus groups about the experience of stigma among people living with HIV. First, they read the transcripts and picked out 500 statements that represented what they thought were themes. Next, they printed the statements on slips of paper and sorted the slips into piles of more general themes, or domains. Then, other team members went through the material and decided, by consensus, if each of the slips belonged in its original pile or in one of the other piles—or a brand new pile.

3. *Word counts*. Ryan and Weisner (1996) told fathers and mothers of adolescents: "Describe your children. In your own words, just tell us about them." In looking for themes in these rich texts, Ryan and Weisner did a word count. Mothers were more likely than fathers to use words like as "friends," "creative," and "honest"; fathers were more likely than were mothers to use words likely "school," "student," and "independent." These counts became clues about the themes that Ryan and Weisner eventually used in coding the texts.

4. *KWIC tables*. The classic KWIC method is a concordance, which is a list of every substantive word in a text with its associated sentence. Concordances have been done on sacred texts from many religions and on famous works of literature from Euripides (Allen and Italie 1954), to Beowulf (Bessinger and Smith 1969), to Dylan Thomas (Farringdon and Farringdon 1980). These days, KWIC lists are generated by asking a computer to find all the places in a text where a particular word or phrase appears and printing it out in the context of some number of words (say, 30) before and after it. You (and others) can sort these instances into piles of similar meaning to assemble a set of themes.

No matter how you actually *do* inductive coding—whether you start with paper and highlighters or use a computer to paw through your texts; whether you use in vivo codes, or use numbers, or make up little mnemonics of your own; whether you have some big themes in mind to start or let all the themes emerge from your reading—by the time you identify the themes and refine them to the point where

they can be applied to an entire corpus of texts, a lot of interpretive analysis has already been done. Miles and Huberman say simply: "Coding is analysis" (1994:56) (Box 19.1).

Box 19.1 Where do you stop?

Coding turns free-flowing texts into a set of nominal variables. In a set of texts about the experience of divorce, people do or do not talk about what to do about pension funds; they do or do not talk about how their children are taking it; they do or do not talk about their relations with their former in-laws; and so on.

Where do you stop? There is practically no end to the number of themes you can isolate for any text. When I was in high school, my science teacher put a bottle of Coca-Cola on his desk and challenged our class to come up with interesting ways to describe that bottle. Each day for weeks that bottle sat on his desk as new science lessons were reeled off, and each day new suggestions for describing that bottle were dropped on the desk on the way out of class.

I don't remember how many descriptors we came up with, but there were dozens. Some were pretty lame (pour the contents into a beaker and see if the boiling point was higher or lower than that of sea water) and some were pretty imaginative (cut off the bottom and test its magnifying power), but the point was to show us that there was no end to the number of things we could describe (measure) about that Coke bottle, and the point sunk in. I remember it every time I try to code a text (**Further Reading:** the mechanics of coding texts).

Kurasaki's and Nyamongo's Codebooks

Here are two examples to illustrate the analytic power of coding text.

Karen Kurasaki (1997) studied the ethnic identity of *sansei*, third-generation Japanese Americans. She interviewed 20 people and used a grounded theory approach to do her analysis. She started with seven major themes: (1) a sense of history and roots; (2) values and ways of doing things; (3) biculturality; (4) sense of belonging; (5) sense of alienation; (6) self-concept; and (7) worldview. As the analysis progressed, she split the major themes into subthemes. So, for example, she split the first theme into (1) sense of having a Japanese heritage and (2) sense of having a Japanese American social history.

As the coding progressed further, she eventually decided to combine two of the

major themes (sense of belonging and sense of alienation) and wound up with six major themes and a total of 18 themes. Kurasaki assigned her own numerical codes to each of the themes—1.1 for the first subtheme in macrotheme 1, 7.2 for the second subtheme in macrotheme 7, and so on—and used those numbers to actually code her transcribed interviews. Her codebook is shown in Table 19.1.

Isaac Nyamongo (1998) did semistructured interviews with 35 Gusii people in Kenya about how they responded to various symptoms associated with malaria. In addition to using a grounded theory approach to develop the theme codes, Nyamongo wanted to do statistical analysis of his data. Table 19.2 shows his codebook. (Nyamongo did all the interviewing in Gusii—a language spoken by about two million people in Kenya—and all

Table 19.1 Kurasaki's Coding Scheme for Her Study of Ethnic Identity Among Sansei in California

First-Order Category	Second-Order Category	Numeric Code
Sense of history and roots	Sense of having a Japanese heritage	1.1
	Sense of having a Japanese American social history	1.2
Values and ways of doing things	Japanese American values and attitudes	2.1
	Practice of Japanese customs	2.2
	Japanese way of doing things	2.3
	Japanese American interpersonal or communication styles	2.4
	Japanese language proficiency	2.5
Biculturality	Integration or bicultural competence	3.1
	Bicultural conflict or confusion	3.2
Sense of belonging	Sense of a global ethnic or racial community	4.1
	Sense of interpersonal connectedness with same ethnicity or race of others	4.2
	Sense of intellectual connectedness with other ethnic or racial minorities	4.3
	Searching for a sense of community	4.4
Sense of alienation	Sense of alienation from ascribed ethnic or racial group	5.1
Self-concept	Sense of comfort with one's ethnic or racial self	6.1
	Searching for a sense of comfort with one's ethnic or racial self	6.2
Worldview	Social consciousness	7.1
	Sense of oppression	7.2

Source: K. S. Kurasaki, "Ethnic Identity and Its Development Among Third-Generation Japanese Americans." Ph.D. diss., Department of Psychology, DePaul University.

the interviews were transcribed in Gusii, but he coded the transcripts using English themes and English-looking mnemonics.)

Notice the difference between Nyamongo's and Kurasaki's codebooks. In addition to some basic information about each respondent (in columns 1–33), Nyamongo coded for 24 themes. Those 24 themes, however, were nominal variables. He coded occupation, for example, as one of eight possible types. And notice that he used words, not numbers for those occupations, and that one possible entry was "information not available" (columns 19–32, 33, 121).

The code SYM1, in column 75, stands for "symptom #1" and refers to whether or not an

Table 19.2 Nyamongo's (1998) Codebook: How Gusii Respond to Malaria

Column	Code	Variable Description and Variable Values
1–3	RESP_ID	Informant number, from 001–035
4–11	NAME	Name of the informant
12–13	AGE	Age in years as reported by the informant.
14–18	GENDER	1 = female, 2 = male
19–32	OCC	Occupation of the informant. This is a nominal variable. The possible scores are housewife (1), farmer (2), retired worker (3), security guard (4), teacher (5), student (6), artisan (7), village elder (8), and n.a. if the informant reported no occupation
33 :	SES	Socioeconomic status is an ordinal variable measured by presence of the following in the homestead. 1= grass-thatched house, 2 = iron-sheet-roofed, dirt-floor house, 3 = iron-sheet-roofed, cemented-floor house, 4 = semipermanent house, 5 = permanent house, 9 = information not available
41	CAUSE1	If mosquito is mentioned by informant as the cause of malaria. 1 = yes, 0 = no
42	CAUSE2	If eating sugarcane, ripe bananas, and roast green maize are mentioned by informant as the cause of malaria. 1 = yes, 0 = no
43 :	CAUSE3	If causes other than CAUSE1 and CAUSE2 are given. 1 = yes, 0 = no
48	CTRL1	What should be done to reduce malaria cases? 1 = keep compound clean, 0 = other
49	CTRL2	What should be done to reduce malaria cases? 1 = take medicine for prophylaxis, 0 = other
50	CTRL3	What should be done to reduce malaria cases? 1 = use net or spray or burn coil, 0 = other
51	CTRL4	What should be done to reduce malaria cases? 1 = nothing can be done, 0 = other
52	DIAG	Diagnosis of illness by the informant. 1 = malaria, 0 = other illness
53	FACTOR1	Does cost influence whether people use home management or hospital-based care? 1 = yes, 0 = no
54	FACTOR2	Does duration of sickness influence whether people use home management or hospital-based care? 1 = yes, 0 = no
55	FACTOR3	Is intensity (severity) a factor influencing whether people use home management or hospital-based care? 1 = yes, 0 = no

(Continued)

(Continued)

Column	Code	Variable Description and Variable Values
56 :	HELP1	Type of support given to informant by family or friends. 1 = buying medicine, 0 = other
75	SYM1	If the informant mentions headache as a symptom. 1 = yes, 0 = no
80	SYM14	If the informant mentions child has unusual cries as a symptom. 1 = yes, 0 = no
81	SYM15	Other—if not one of SYM1 through SYM14. 1 = yes, 0 = no.
91 :	TREAT11	Did the informant report using pills bought over the counter as the first treatment resort? 1 = yes, 0 = no
96 :	TREAT21	Second treatment resort. The values are the same as for TREAT11, COLUMN 91
119	WITCH	If the informant mentions that witchcraft may be implicated if patient has malaria. 1 = yes, 0 = no
120	YESDIAG	Does the coder think the informant made the right diagnosis based on the informant's stated symptoms? 1 = yes, 0 = no
121	COST	Cost of receiving treatment from private health care provider in Kenyan shillings, from 0001–9999, 9999 = information not available

Source: Data reproduced with permission of the author.

informant mentioned headache in his or her narrative as a symptom of malaria. Nyamongo coded for whether people mentioned any of 14 symptoms, and he added a 15th code, SYM15 (in column 81) for "other." When you break up a list of things into a series of yes/no, present/absent variables, like Nyamongo did with CAUSE and SYM and so on, it turns nominal variables into a series of dummy variables. Thus, Nyamongo's codebook has a total of 88 theme *variables* (including all the dummy variables), even though he coded for just 24 *themes* (like symptoms, treatments, and so on).

Table 19.3 shows a piece of the **data matrix** produced by Nyamongo's coding of the 35 narratives. This kind of matrix can be analyzed statistically (see Chapters 20–22) (**Further Reading:** codebooks).

Linking Themes Into Theoretical Models

Once you have a *set of themes* coded in a *set of texts*, the next step in grounded theory is to identify *how themes are linked to each other* in a theoretical model (Miles and Huberman 1994:134–37). Memoing is one of the keys to doing this. In memoing, you continually write down your thoughts about what you're reading. These thoughts become information on which to develop theory. Memoing is taking "field notes" on

Table 19.3 Part of the Data Matrix From Nyamongo's Analysis of 35 Gusii Texts

person	age	sex	occupation	SES	A A A	CTRL1	A A A	CAUSE1	A A A	HELP1	A A A	WITCH	A A A
1	48	M	retired worker	2		1		1		0		0	
2	58	M	farmer	1		0		1		0		1	
3	68	M	clan elder	1		1		1		0		1	
•			•	•		•		•		•		•	
•			•	•		•		•		•		•	
•			•	•		•		•		•		•	
33	54	F	teacher	2		1		1		0		0	
34	57	F	artisan	2		0		0		0		0	
35	26	F	housewife	1		1		1		0		1	

531

observations about texts. The observations can be about the themes that you see emerging or your ideas about how the themes are connected. The important thing is, just as with ethnographic field notes, to get your thoughts down as you have them (Corbin and Strauss 2008:117–41).

Once a model starts to take shape, start shopping for negative cases—ones that don't fit the pattern. This is another key to theory building. Negative cases either disconfirm parts of a model or suggest new connections that need to be made. In either case, negative cases need to be accommodated when you present your results.

Suppose you comb through a set of narratives from women in the labor market. Some women say that they got upset with their last job and quit. You find that most of the women who did this have husbands who earn a pretty good living. Now you have a take-this-job-and-shove-it category. Is there a case in which a woman says "You know, I'd be outta this crummy job in a minute if I didn't have two kids at home to take care of all by myself"? Don't wait for that case to come to you. Go looking for it. This is theoretical sampling, another key element of grounded theory research.

In theoretical sampling, you decide what cases to study based on the content of the developing theory so that sampling, coding and theory building all develop together. In a true grounded theory study, you begin coding with the first interview and select cases for study as concepts emerge and the theory develops (Glaser and Strauss 1967:45–77) (**Further Reading:** theoretical sampling and negative case analysis) (Box 19.2).

Box 19.2 Grounded theory and the grounded theory approach

Many studies today follow a grounded theory approach that does not involve theoretical sampling. Instead, scholars who use inductive methods to discover and code themes interviews may say that they are using a grounded theory *approach* without doing a grounded theory *study*. Scholars who follow a general grounded theory approach may develop a theory on half their data and then check it on the other half. This adds an element of verification to the method as well.

Displaying and Validating the Models

So, how do you actually build theoretical models and what do they look like? In grounded theory research, the search for theory begins with the very first line of the very first interview you code.

How to get started? Begin with a small chunk of text and code line by line. Identify potentially useful concepts. Mark key phrases "because," as Sandelowski's (1995b:373) says, "they make some as yet inchoate sense." Name the concepts. Move on to another chunk and do this again. And again. And again. This is what Strauss and Corbin (1998:101–21) call open coding and Charmaz (2002) calls initial coding. The process here is one of fragmenting text into conceptual components.

The next step involves defragments a lot more theorizing, but now it's in service to defragmenting text. As you code, pull examples of all concepts together and think about how each concept might be related to larger, more inclusive concepts—called categories in the language of grounded theory—that you can look for in texts. This involves the constant comparative method (Glaser and Strauss 1967:101–15; Strauss and Corbin 1998:78–85, 93–99), and it goes on throughout the GT process, right up through the development of complete theories. Coding for categories is variously called focused coding (Charmaz 2002:686) or theoretical coding or axial coding (Strauss and Corbin 1998: 123–42).

Kearney's Study of Pregnant Women Who Use Cocaine

Margaret Kearney and her colleagues (1995) interviewed 60 women who reported using crack cocaine an average of at least once weekly during pregnancy. The semistructured interviews lasted from one to three hours and covered childhood, relationships, life context, previous pregnancies, and actions during the current pregnancy related to drug use, prenatal care, and self-care. Kearney et al. coded and analyzed the transcripts as they went. As new topics emerged, investigators asked about the topics in subsequent interviews. In this way, they linked data collection and data analysis in one continuous effort.

Kearney et al. (1995) coded the data first for the general topics they used to guide the interviews. Later, they would use these codes to search for and retrieve examples of text related to various interview topics. Next, team members reread each transcript searching for examples of social psychological themes in the women's narratives. Each time they found an example, they asked: "What is this an example of?" The answers suggested substantive categories that were refined with each new transcript.

Kearney et al. (1995) looked at how substantive categories were related. They recorded their ideas about these interactions in the forms of memos and developed a preliminary model. With each subsequent transcript, they looked for negative cases and pieces of data that challenged their emerging model. They

adjusted the model to include the full range of variation that emerged in the transcripts.

To begin with, Kearney et al. (1995) identified five major categories, which they called: VALUE, HOPE, RISK, HARM REDUCTION, and STIGMA MANAGEMENT. (Capital letters are often used for code names in grounded theory research, just as in statistical research.) Women valued their pregnancy and the baby-to-be in relation to their own life priorities (VALUE); women expressed varying degrees of hope that their pregnancies would end well and that they could be good mothers (HOPE) and they were aware that cocaine use posed risks to their fetus but they perceived that risk differently (RISK). Women tried in various ways to minimize the risk to the fetus (HARM REDUCTION) and they used various stratagems to reduce social rejection and derision (STIGMA MANAGEMENT).

By the time they had coded 20 interviews, Kearney et al. (1995) realized that the categories HARM REDUCTION and STIGMA MANAGEMENT were components of a more fundamental category that they labeled EVADING HARM. After about 30 interviews had been coded, they identified and labeled an overarching psychological process they called SALVAGING SELF that incorporated all five of the major categories. By the time they'd done 40 interviews, Kearney et al. felt they had reached theoretical saturation, which means that they were not discovering new categories or relations among categories. Just to make sure, they conducted another 20 interviews and confirmed the saturation.

Figure 19.1 shows the graphic model that Kearney et al. (1995) produced to represent their understanding of how the process worked. Kearney et al. described in rich detail each of the major categories that they discovered, but notice how each of the substantive themes in their model is succinctly defined by a quote from a respondent.

Figure 19.1   The Relation of Themes/Categories in Kearney et al.'s Analysis of How Pregnant Drug Users Viewed Their Own Behavior

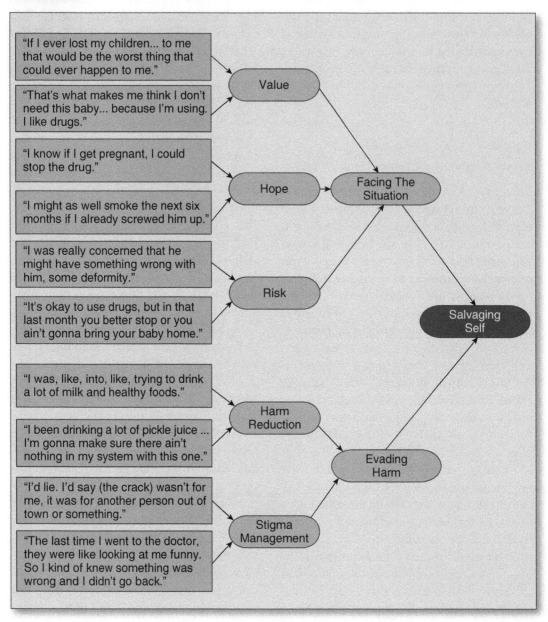

Source: M. H. Kearney et al., "Salvaging Self—A Grounded Theory of Pregnancy on Crack Cocaine." *Nursing Research* 44:208–13. © 1995.

When the steps of the grounded theory approach are followed, models or theories are produced that are, indeed, *grounded* in the text. These models, however, are not the final product of the grounded theory approach. In their original formulation, Glaser and Strauss (1967) emphasized that the building of grounded theory models is a step in the research process. The next is to confirm the validity of a model by testing it on an independent sample of data. Kearney et al. (1995) checked the validity of their model by presenting it to knowledgeable respondents (pregnant drug users), to members of the project staff, and to health and social service professionals who were familiar with the population (**Further Reading:** grounded theory).

Using Exemplar Quotes

Besides displaying models, one of the most important methods in text analysis is the presentation of direct quotes from respondents—quotes that lead the reader to understand quickly what it took you months or years to figure out. You choose segments of text—verbatim quotes from respondents—as exemplars of concepts and theories or as exemplars of exceptions to your theories (those superimportant negative cases).

This technique looks easy, but it's not. You have to choose the exemplars very carefully because your choices constitute your analysis, as far as the reader is concerned, and you have to avoid what Lofland (1971) called the two great sins of qualitative analysis to use the exemplar quote technique effectively.

The first sin, excessive analysis, involves the all-too-familiar practice of jargony writing and the avoidance of plain English to say plain things. If you analyze a batch of data and conclude that something simple is going on, don't be afraid to say so. There is absolutely nothing of scientific value to be gained from making straightforward things complicated.

Compare these two sentences: (1) "The more generations that people from various ethnic groups are in the United States, the less likely they are to speak anything but English." (2) "Over an expanding number of generations, people of ethnic heritage in the United States become, probabilistically, less likely to adhere to

their traditional linguistic symbol systems." The best word to describe the second sentence is yucky.

The second sin consists of avoiding doing any analysis on your own—being so gun-shy of theory and jargon that you simply fill up your papers and books with lengthy quotes from people and offer no analysis at all. Data do not speak for themselves. I've been in rooms full of data and never heard a sound. You have to develop your ideas (your analysis) about what's going on, state those ideas clearly, and illustrate them with selected quotes from your respondents.

Katherine Newman (1986), for example, collected life history material from 30 White, middle-class American women, ages 26–57, who had suffered severe losses of income as a result of divorce. Newman discovered and labeled two groups of women, according to her informants' own accounts of which period in their lives had the greatest effect on how they viewed the world. Women whose adolescent and early married years were in the 1960s and early 1970s seemed to be very different from "women of the Depression" who were born between 1930 and 1940.

These women had grown up in two very different socioeconomic and political environments; the differences in those environments had a profound effect on the shaping of people's subjective, interpretive, and symbolic views of the world, and, according to Newman's analysis, this accounted for differences in how her informants responded to the economic loss of divorce. Newman illustrated her analytic finding with quotes from her informants.

One woman said:

I grew up in the '30s on a farm in Minnesota, but my family lost the farm during the Depression. Dad became a mechanic for the WPA, after that, but we moved around a lot. I remember that we never had any fresh fruits or vegetables during that whole time. At school there were soup lines and food handouts. . . . You know, I've been there. I've seen some hard times and it wasn't pleasant. Sometimes when I get low on money now, I get very nervous remembering those times.

By contrast, "women of the '60s" felt the economic loss of divorce but tended to stress the value of having to be more self-reliant and the importance of friends, education, and personal autonomy over dependence on material things. Newman illustrated this sentiment with quotes like the following:

Money destroyed my marriage. All my husband wanted was to accumulate more real estate. We had no emotional relationship. Everything was bent toward things. Money to me now is this ugly thing.

Newman found differences in the way women in the two age cohorts dealt with kin support after divorce, the way they related to men in general, and a number of other things that emerged as patterns in her data. For each observation of a patterned difference in response to life after divorce, Newman used selected quotes from her informants to make the point.

Here's another example, from the study I did with Ashton-Vouyoucalos (1976) on Greek labor migrants. Everyone in the population we were studying had spent five years or more in West Germany and had returned to Greece to reestablish their lives. We were interested in how these returned migrants felt about the Greece they returned to, compared with the Germany they left.

Before doing a survey, however, we collected life histories from 15 people, selected because of their range of experiences. Those 15 returned migrants were certainly no random sample, but the consistency of their volunteered observations of differences between the two cultures was striking. Once we noticed the pattern emerging,

we laid out the data in tabular form, as shown in Table 19.4. The survey instrument that we eventually built reflected the concerns of our informants.

In reporting our findings, Ashton-Vouyoucalos and I referred to the summary table and illustrated each component with selected quotes from our informants. The issue of gossip, for example (under "negative aspects of Greece" in Table 19.4), was addressed by Despina, a 28-year-old woman from Thrace. Despina was happy to be back in Greece, but she said:

Look, here you have a friend you visit. Sooner or later you'll wear or do something she doesn't like. We have this habit of gossiping. She'll gossip behind your back. Even if it's your sister. In Germany, they don't have that, at least. Not about what you wear or what you eat. Nothing like that. That's what I liked.

By the way, the translation of Despina's comment has been doctored to make it sound a bit more seamless than it did in the original. I've seen thousands of really interesting quotes in ethnographic reports, and common sense says that most of them were fixed up a bit. I don't see anything wrong with this. In fact, I'm grateful to writers who do it. Unexpurgated speech is terrible to read. It's full of false starts, run-ons, fragments, pauses, filler syllables (like "uh" and "y'know"), and whole sentences whose sole purpose is to give speakers a second or two while they think of what to say next. If you are doing conversation analysis, you need *all* the detail. But if you're doing whole text analysis and you don't edit that stuff, you'll bore your readers to death.

CONTENT ANALYSIS

Content analysis is a set of methods for systematically coding and analyzing qualitative data

Table 19.4 Summary of Repatriates' Ambivalent Statements About Greece

Negative aspects of Greece

Economic

1. Wages are low.
2. Few jobs are available, especially for persons with specialized skills.
3. Working conditions are poor.
4. Inflation is high, especially in the prices of imported goods.

Sociocultural

1. People in general (but especially public servants) are abrupt and rude.
2. The roads are covered with rubbish.
3. Everyone, even friends and relatives, gossips about each other and tries to keep each other down.
4. People of the opposite sex cannot interact easily and comfortably.

Political

1. The government is insecure and might collapse with ensuing chaos or a return to dictatorship.
2. Fear of actual war with Turkey creates a climate of insecurity.

Negative aspects of Germany

Economic

1. Economic opportunities are limited because a foreigner cannot easily open up a private business.
2. People are reluctant to rent good housing at decent prices to migrant workers.

Sociocultural

1. One feels in exile from one's home and kin.
2. Life is limited to house and factory.
3. The weather seems bitterly cold and this furthers the sense of isolation.
4. Migrants are viewed as second-class citizens.
5. Children may be left behind in Greece, to the sometimes inadequate care of grandparents.
6. Lack of fluency in German puts Greek workers at a disadvantage.
7. Parents must eventually choose between sending their children to German schools (where they will grow away from their parents) or to inadequate Greek schools in German cities.
8. Factory routines are rigid, monotonous, and inhuman and sometimes the machinery is dangerous.

Political

1. Migrants have no political voice in Germany or in their home country while they are abroad.

Source: H. R. Bernard and S. Ashton_Vouyoucalos, "Return Migration to Greece." *Journal of the Steward Anthropological Society* 8:31–51, 1976. Table reproduced with permission from the *Journal of the Steward Anthropological Society.*

and for testing hypotheses about texts, usually statistically. Content analysis has very deep roots in studies of the media, going back over a hundred years (Krippendorff 2004a:5). The systematic application of scientific methods for analyzing text got a real boost with the study of political propaganda, particularly in the period before and during World War II (Box 19.3). (See Krippendorff [2004a:6–12] and Neuendorf [2002:23–45] for excellent reviews.)

> ### Box 19.3 How content analysis became admissible in court
>
> When the Nazis came to power in the 1930s, the U.S. Government Communications Commission began monitoring short-wave radio broadcasts from Germany. Analysts established 14 major propaganda themes in the Nazi media. In 1942, the U.S. Department of Justice accused William Dudley Pelley of sedition, claiming that Pelley was publishing pro-Nazi propaganda while the United States was at war with Germany.
>
> The government asked independent coders to classify 1,240 items in Pelley's publications as belonging or not belonging to one of those 14 Nazi propaganda themes. Harold Lasswell, a political scientist and expert in propaganda analysis, testified that 1,195 of the items (96.4%) "were consistent with and suggested copying from the German propaganda themes" (*United States v. Pelley 1942*). Pelley was convicted. The conviction was upheld by the U.S. Circuit Court of Appeals, and the admissibility in court of evidence based on this simple method of content analysis was established (Goldsen 1947).

Steps in Content Analysis

There are seven big steps in content analysis—and a lot of little ones:

1. Formulate a research question or a hypothesis based on existing theory or on prior research.

2. Select a set of texts to test the question or hypothesis.

3. Create a set of codes (variables, themes) in the research question or hypothesis.

4. Pretest the variables on a few of the selected texts. Fix any problems that turn up with regard to the codes and the coding so that the coders become consistent in their coding.

5. Apply the codes to the rest of the texts.

6. Create a case-by-variable matrix from the texts and codes.

7. Analyze the matrix using whatever level of analysis is appropriate.

We'll go over these, in turn, using a now-classic study on people as products.

Hirschman's Study of People as Products

1. *Formulate a research question or hypothesis, based on existing theory or on prior research.*

In social exchange theory (Homans 1961), human interaction is seen as a series of exchanges of goods and services; in studies of human mate selection, women tend to prefer men of higher social and economic status and men tend to prefer women of greater physical beauty (Buss 1985; Pawlowski and Jasienska 2008).

Drawing on this literature, Elizabeth Hirschman (1987) reasoned that men and women would offer and seek the 10 resources shown in Table 19.5. For example, Hirschman expected that men would seek physical beauty and love more than women do in personal ads; conversely, women would offer physical attractiveness and love more than men do. To test her hypotheses, Hirschman needed a corpus of personal ads . . . which brings us to step 2.

2. *Select a set of texts to test the question or hypothesis.*

Table 19.5 The Expected Pattern of Resource Exchange in Personal Ads

Women Are Expected to Offer and Men to Seek	Men Are Expected to Offer and Women to Seek
Physical attractiveness	Money
Love	Educational status
Entertainment	Intellectual status
Information about their demographic characteristics (age, marital status, residence)	Occupational status
Ethnicity	
Personality	

Source: Adapted from E. C. Hirschman, "People as Products: Analysis of a Complex Marketing Exchange." *Journal of Marketing* 51:98–108, p. 103, 1987.

Hirschman randomly sampled 100 female-placed ads and 100 male-placed ads in *New York Magazine* and *The Washingtonian* from May 1983 to April 1984. (In those days, sexual traits and services were less than 1% of resources sought or offered.)

3. *Create a set of codes (variables, themes) in the research question or hypothesis.*

In this case, the variables, or themes, are the 10 resources in Table 19.5. The real work here is building a coding scheme—deciding on how to code the text in the ads. For example, "NYU grad" would count as "educational status." "Tall," "thin," "shapely," "good looking," "handsome," and so on, would count as "physical features." "Shy" and "young at heart" would count as personality traits. "Small-town girl" would be coded as demographic information (residence).

4. *Pretest the variables on a few of the selected texts. Fix any problems that turn up with regard to the codes and the coding so that the coders become consistent in their coding.*

Hirschman gave 10 men and 11 women the list of ten resource categories and a list of 100 resource items taken from 20 additional ads.

The 21 test respondents were able to categorize all 100 test items.

5. *Apply the codes to the rest of the texts.*

Next, two coders—a man and a woman, neither of whom knew the hypotheses that Hirschman was testing—coded all the resources in the ads. Of 3,782 resource items coded, the coders differed on 636 (16.8%) and in another 480 cases (12.7%) one coder neglected to categorize an item that the other coder had tagged. Hirschman resolved the 636 coding discrepancies—that is, she decided which coder was right. For the 480 coding omissions, Hirschman checked the ad and made sure that the resource item was correctly coded by the one coder who saw it. If this was the case (as it always was, apparently), then the resource was assigned to the ad by both coders.

6. *Create a case-by-variable matrix from the texts and codes.*

In this case, the data matrix would have looked something like Table 19.6: The first column is the number of the ad. Column 2 is for the name of the magazine. The cells in column 3 would have a 1 or a 0 to indicate whether the ad had been placed by a man or a

Table 19.6 The Data Matrix for Hirschman's Study of Personal Ads

Ad #	Mag	Female Placed	Physical Features Offered	Physical Features Sought	Money Offered	Money Sought	Educ Status Offered	Educ Status Sought	Occup Status Offered	Occup Status Offered	Etc.
1											
2											
3											
4											
•											
•											
•											
•											
•											
405											

woman. Next would come 20 columns, two for each of the 10 resource categories. For each of the ads, these columns would indicate how many of each of the 10 resource categories had been sought or offered.

7. *Analyze the matrix using whatever level of analysis is appropriate.*

First, Hirschman ran an analysis of variance, or ANOVA (see Chapter 21) and found that, whatever differences there were by gender in the content of the ads, those differences weren't affected by the city of origin. For the rest of the analyses, Hirschman could combine all her data, from both cities. Then she tested for gender effects. The ads were of different length (some people included three or four of the 10 resources in their ad; some included six or seven . . . or even 10; and some repeated resources two or more times), so Hirschman used percentages rather than raw

counts. If an ad listed six resources and two of them were about physical characteristics (tall, wavy hair), then physical characteristics were counted in that ad as 2/6, or 33%. Now Hirschman had a set of percentages, shown in Table 19.7.

Four of Hirschman's hypotheses were confirmed by a statistical test: (1) Men seek physical attractiveness more than women do. (2) Women offer physical attractiveness more than men do. (3) Women seek money more than men do. (4) Men offer money more than women do.

In 1983–1984, the way men and women wrote their own personal ads conformed to traditional gender role expectations. By 1995–1996, though, things were changing. Lance (1998) studied 1,433 personal ads from that year in four newspapers and magazines in the southeastern United States. Men continued to seek good looks and women continued to seek

Table 19.7 Summary of Hirschman's Findings

Resource	Mean Offered by Women	Mean Sought by Women	Mean Offered by Men	Mean Sought by Men
Physical status	.221	.090	.151	.223
Money	.018	.080	.059	.010
Educational status	.013	.008	.013	.009
Occupational status	.067	.032	.086	.011
Intellectual status	.048	.050	.030	.059
Love	.061	.168	.063	.158
Entertainment services	.107	.071	.080	.103
Demographic info	.217	.219	.283	.195
Ethnicity info	.091	.007	.090	.053
Personality info	.144	.200	.131	.150

Source: E. C. Hirschman, "People as Products: Analysis of a Complex Marketing Exchange." *Journal of Marketing* 51:98–108, p. 104, 1987.

financial stability—but second on their list of preferences. Men and women alike mentioned personality characteristics as their most preferred traits in potential mates. In Spain, Gil-Burman et al. (2002) found that, although men of all ages sought physical attractiveness in women, women under 40 sought physical attractiveness in men (Box 19.4) (**Further Reading:** content analysis of personal ads).

Box 19.4 The "texts" for content analysis don't have to be written

Cowan and O'Brien (1990) had some ideas about the roles of men and women in slasher films. They wanted to know, for example, whether men or women were more likely to be survivors, and what other personal characteristics accounted for those who got axed and those who lived. The corpus of text in this case was 56 slasher movies. These movies contained a total of 474 victims, who were coded for gender and survival. Conventional wisdom about slasher films holds that victims are mostly women, and slashers are mostly men.

While slashers in these films were, in fact, mostly men, it turned out that victims were equally likely to be male or female. Surviving as a female slasher victim, however, was strongly associated with the absence of sexual behavior and with being less physically attractive than nonsurviving females. The male nonsurvivors were cynical, egotistical, and dictatorial. Cowan and O'Brien conclude that, in slasher films, sexually pure women survive and that "unmitigated masculinity" ends in death (1990:195) (**Further Reading:** content analysis).

Intercoder Reliability

It is quite common in content analysis to have more than one coder mark up a set of texts. The idea is to test for intercoder or interrater reliability—that is, whether multiple coders reckon that the same constructs apply to the same chunks of text. There is a simple way to measure agreement between a pair of coders: you just line up their codes and calculate the percentage of agreement. This is shown in Table 19.8 for two coders who have coded 20 texts for a single theme, using a binary code, 1 or 0.

Both coders have a 0 for texts 1, 4, 5, 7, and 10, and both coders have a 1 for text 2. These two coders agree a total of six times out of 10—five times that the theme, whatever it is, does not appear in the texts, and one time that

Table 19.8 Measuring Simple Agreement Between Two Coders on a Single Theme

Units of Analysis (Documents/Observations)										
	1	2	3	4	5	6	7	8	9	10
Coder 1	0	1	0	0	0	0	0	0	1	0
Coder 2	0	1	1	0	0	1	0	1	0	0

the theme does appear. On four out of 10 texts, the coders disagree. On text 9, for example, coder 1 saw the theme in the text, but coder 2 didn't. Overall, these two coders agree 60% of the time.

Cohen's Kappa

The total observed agreement is a popular method for assessing reliability, but it has long been recognized that coders can agree on the presence or absence of a theme just by chance. **Cohen's kappa** (Cohen 1960), or k measures *how much better than chance* is the agreement between a pair of coders on the presence or absence of binary (yes/no) themes in texts and is a popular measure of reliability. Here is the formula for kappa:

$$k = \frac{\text{Observed} - \text{Chance}}{1 - \text{Chance}} \quad \textbf{formula 19.1}$$

When k is 1.0, there is perfect agreement between coders. When k is zero, agreement is what might be expected by chance. When k is negative, the observed level of agreement is less than what you'd expect by chance. And when k is positive, the observed level of agreement is greater than what you'd expect by chance. Table 19.9

shows the data in Table 19.8 rearranged so that we can calculate kappa.

The *observed agreement* between Coder 1 and Coder 2 is:

$$\frac{a+d}{n}$$

Here, Coder 1 and Coder 2 agreed that the theme was present in the text once (cell a) and they agreed that the theme was absent five times (cell d), for a total of 6, or 60% of the 10 texts.

The probability that Coder 1 and Coder 2 agree by chance is:

$$\frac{a+b}{n} + \frac{a+c}{n} + \frac{c+d}{n} + \frac{b+d}{n}$$

Here, the probability that Coder 1 and Coder 2 agreed by chance is $.08 + .48 = .56$. Using formula 19.1, we calculate kappa:

$$k = \frac{.60 - .56}{1 - .56} = .0909$$

In other words, the 60% observed agreement between the two coders for the data in Table 19.9 is about 9% better than we'd expect by chance—nothing to write home about (Box 19.5).

Table 19.9 The Coder-by-Coder Agreement Matrix for the Data in Table 19.5

		Coder 2		
		Yes	No	Coder 1 totals
Coder 1	Yes	1 (*a*)	1 (*b*)	2
	No	3 (*c*)	5 (*d*)	8
	Coder 2 totals	4	6	10 (*n*)

Box 19.5 Problems with measuring reliability

There is a substantial literature about statistical issues associated with measures of reliability and which measure of reliability is best under various conditions (see Lombard et al. [2005] for a review). For example, with kappa, the more units of analysis being coded, the harder it is to get a high kappa score (Krippendorf 2004b).

The most versatile measure of reliability is **Krippendorff's alpha** (2004a:221ff). It can be used with nominal, ordinal, and interval variables; it can be used with any number of coders; and it corrects for missing data (which occurs when coders mark up overlapping but not exactly the same sets of texts).

Krippendorff recommends that analysts rely only on variables that attain an alpha coefficient of 0.80 or better, but would allow variables with coefficients between 0.667 and 0.800 to be used for "drawing tentative conclusions" (2004a:241). Kappa is easily calculated in some of the most widely known statistical packages, like SPSS°, SAS°, Systat°, and Stata°. (See Kang et al. [1993] for a macro that calculates alpha and other statistics in SAS.)

Carey et al.'s Use of Kappa

Carey et al. (1996) asked 51 newly arrived Vietnamese refugees in New York State 32 open-ended questions about tuberculosis. Topics included knowledge and beliefs about TB symptoms and causes as well as beliefs about susceptibility to the disease, prognosis for those who contract the disease, skin-testing procedures, and prevention and treatment methods. The researchers read the responses and built a code list based simply on their own judgment. The initial codebook contained 171 codes.

Then Carey et al. (1996) broke the text into 1,632 segments. Each segment was the response by one of the 51 respondents to one of the 32 questions. Two coders independently coded 320 of the segments, marking as many of the themes as they thought appeared in each segment. Segments were counted as reliably coded if both coders used the same codes on it. If one coder left off a code or assigned an additional code, then this was considered a coding disagreement.

On their first try, only 144 (45%) out of 320 responses were coded the same by both coders. The coders discussed their disagreements and found that some of the 171 codes were redundant, some were vaguely defined, and some were not mutually exclusive. In some cases, coders simply had different understandings of what a code meant. When these problems were resolved, a new, streamlined codebook was issued, with only 152 themes, and the coders marked up the data again. This time they were in agreement 88.1% of the time.

To see if this apparently strong agreement was a fluke, Carey et al. tested intercoder reliability with kappa. The coders agreed perfectly ($k = 1.0$) on 126 out of the 152 codes that they'd applied to the 320 sample segments. Only 17 (11.2%) of the codes had final k values ≥0.89. As senior investigator, Carey resolved any remaining intercoder discrepancies himself (Carey et al. 1996).

How Much Intercoder Agreement Is Enough?

As with so much in real life, the correct answer is: It depends. It depends, for example, on the level of inference required. If you have texts from single mothers about their efforts to juggle home and work, it's easier to code for the theme "works full time" (a low-inference theme) than it is to code for the theme "enjoys her job" (a high-inference theme).

It also depends on what's at stake. X-rays are texts, after all, and I'd like a pretty high level of intercoder agreement if a group of physicians were deciding on whether a particular anomaly meant my going in for surgery or not. In text analysis, the standards are still evolving. Many researchers are satisfied with kappa values of around .70; others like to shoot for .80 and higher (Gottschalk and Bechtel 1993; Krippendorf 2004b) (**Further Reading:** interrater/intercoder reliability).

HRAF: Cross-Cultural Content Analysis

The Human Relations Area Files (HRAF) at Yale University is the world's largest archive of ethnography, with about a million pages of text, collected from some 8,000 books and articles, on almost 400 cultural groups around the world. The archive is growing at about 40,000 pages a year, and more than half the material is online through the 400-plus libraries at institutions that subscribe. (Go to: http://www.yale.edu/hraf/.)

Pages of the HRAF database are indexed by professional coders, following the *Outline of Cultural Materials*, or OCM, a comprehensive system for classifying material about cultures and societies around the world (Murdock et al. 2004 [1961]). There are 82 main domains in the OCM, in blocks of 10, from 10 to 91. Block 16, for example, is about demography. Within this block there are eight subdomains labeled 161, 162, ... 168. These domains cover specific topics like mortality (code 165), external migration (code 167), and so on.

HRAF turns the ethnographic literature into a database for content analysis and cross-cultural tests of hypotheses because you can search the archive for every reference to any of the codes across the more than 400 cultures that are covered.

Doing Cross-Cultural Text-Based Research

The steps for doing an HRAF study are analogous to those for doing any content analysis (Otterbein 1969):

1. State a hypothesis that requires cross-cultural data.

2. Draw a representative sample of the world's cultures.

3. Find the appropriate OCM codes in the sample or develop new codes.

4. Code the variables according to whatever conceptual scheme you've developed in forming your hypothesis.

5. Run the appropriate statistical tests and see if your hypothesis is confirmed.

For example, Barber (1998) found that the frequency of male homosexual activity was low in hunting and gathering societies and increased with the complexity of agricultural production. Ethnographic reports of male homosexuality were also more likely for societies in which women did not control their own sexuality—a well-known correlate of increased reliance on complex agriculture.

Landauer and Whiting (1964) coded 65 societies for the practice of physical stress on male infants—things like piercing (lips, nose, scarification, circumcision) or molding of arms or legs or head. Adult men in societies with these practices are significantly taller than their counterparts in which these practices are absent (about 2 or 3 inches taller). The researchers controlled for, and ruled out, variations in sunlight (and hence in the body's production of vitamin D) and variations in population genetics—two factors that are well known to cause variations in height.

But they could not rule out the possibility that parents who put their infants through this kind of stress give those children more food or better medical care, which supports growth, or that boys who are stressed during infancy become more aggressive and only the tallest survive. As the researchers themselves acknowledged, correlation doesn't mean cause (Landauer and Whiting 1964:1018) (**Further Reading:** cross-cultural studies of ethnographic text).

Computers and Text Analysis

Anyone who collects mountains of text will want to take advantage of modern text analysis software. Don't take the phrase "text analysis software" literally. Computer programs do a lot, but in the end, *you* do the analysis; *you* make the connections and formulate hypotheses to test; *you* draw conclusions and point them out to your readers.

The two broad approaches in text analysis—inductive, hypothesis-generating research and deductive, hypothesis-testing research—are reflected in the available software. Programs for automated content analysis are based on the concept of a computerized, contextual dictionary. You feed the program a piece of text; the program looks up each word in the dictionary and runs through a series of disambiguation rules to see what the words mean—for example, whether the word "concrete" is a noun (stuff you pave your driveway with) or an adjective, as in "I need a concrete example of this or I won't believe it."

Work on automated text analysis began in the 1960s. Philip Stone and others (1966) developed a program for doing automated content analysis called the *General Inquirer*. They tested it on 66 suicide notes—33 written by men who had actually taken their own lives, and 33 written by men who were asked to produce simulated suicide notes. The program parsed the texts and picked the actual suicide notes 91% of the time (Ogilvie et al. 1966). The latest version of the system (which runs with a dictionary called the Harvard 4–4) has a 13,000-word dictionary and over 6,000

rules. It can tell whether the word "broke" means "fractured," or "destitute," or "stopped functioning," or (when paired with "out") "escaped" (Rosenberg et al. 1990:303).

Over the years, computer-assisted content analysis has developed into a major industry. When you hear "This call may be monitored for quality assurance purposes," it's likely that the conversation will be turned into text that will be submitted to a high-end data-mining program for analysis.

Programs for Doing Text Analysis

Programs are widely available that support both grounded theory–type research and content analysis (see Appendix E). They allow you to code themes on the fly, as you read the text on the screen. Then the program will produce a visual model of how themes are associated (the grounded theory tradition) or it will produce a text-by-theme matrix that you can import into your favorite stats package—SPSS®, SAS®, SYSTAT®, etc.—(the content analysis tradition).

No program does everything, so do your homework before deciding on what to buy. A good place to start is the CAQDAS Networking Project (http://caqdas.soc.surrey.ac.uk/). CAQDAS (pronounced cactus) stands for computer-assisted qualitative data analysis software.

The CAQDAS site is continually updated with information on tools for analyzing qualitative data. Those tools are getting more sophisticated, with more features added all the time. Were transcription not such a nuisance, social science would have focused long ago on the wealth of qualitative data that describe life and history across the globe. But with voice-recognition software coming on strong (see Chapter 8), and transcription becoming less and less intimidating, all forms of text analysis—narrative analysis, discourse analysis, grounded theory, content analysis—will become more and more attractive.

Text analysis is only just beginning to come into its own. It's going to be very exciting.

Key Concepts in This Chapter

grounded theory
content analysis
open coding
exploratory and discovery
    stage
confirmatory stage
positivist tradition of
    grounded theory
constructivist grounded
    theory
interpretivist tradition of
    grounded theory
highlighting
pile sorts

word counts
key-word-in-context
    (KWIC)
in vivo coding
concordance
dummy variables
data matrix
memoing
negative cases
theoretical
    sampling
fragmenting text
defragmenting text
focused coding

theoretical coding
axial coding
theoretical
    saturation
exemplars of concepts
social exchange
    theory
intercoder or interrater
    reliability
Cohen's kappa
Krippendorff's alpha
cross-cultural tests of
    hypotheses
data-mining

Summary

- Two of the major traditions of text analysis are the grounded theory approach and content analysis.
- The grounded theory approach is a set of techniques for identifying categories and concepts that emerge from text and linking the concepts into substantive and formal theories. Grounded theory is mostly in the inductive tradition of social science and is practiced by scholars in both the positivist and interpretivist epistemological traditions. Content analysis is mostly in the deductive and positivist traditions.

  o The heart of grounded theory is identifying themes in texts and coding the texts for the presence or absence of those themes.

  o Grounded theory research is mostly based on inductive or "open" coding. The idea is to become grounded in the data and to allow understanding to emerge from close study of the texts. Theme codes should be easy to remember and easy to use.

  o Themes in grounded theory are linked to one another in a theoretical model. This is achieved through constant memoing and negative case analysis. Memoing is continually writing down your thoughts about what you're reading—taking "field notes" on observations about texts.

  o True grounded theory involves theoretical sampling—sampling for cases as a theory takes shape.

  o The results of grounded theory research are presented through exemplars and in visual displays.

- While grounded theory is concerned with the discovery of hypotheses from texts, content analysis is concerned with testing hypotheses, usually statistically.

  o The texts used in content analysis may be movies or television ads or other image-based data.

- o Sampling is an important issue in content analysis since the idea to generalize to a corpus of texts.
- o It is common in content analysis to have more than one coder mark up a set of texts. The results are tested for intercoder reliability.
- o Comparative research, using the Human Relations Area Files, is the application of content analysis to a corpus of ethnographic literature.
- Increasingly, social researchers are combining the inductive power of grounded theory and the deductive power of content analysis.
- Text-processing software is developing quickly. New technologies, like voice-recognition software, are making text analysis an increasingly important component of social research.

Exercises

1. Using the data from exercise 1 in Chapter 18, develop a codebook and analyze the data using an in vivo coding approach or a content analysis approach. It's easier if multiple students analyze the same tale. (You can't do a true grounded theory study on a set of transcripts since you don't have the opportunity to do on-the-fly, theoretical sampling, but you can do open coding to find themes and you can build a model from the themes.) For the content analysis approach, test hypotheses about differences in the themes emphasized by men and women telling the same story.

2. Working together in a group of five or more students, collect 25–30 narratives from people about what it's like to have a cold. Ask each respondent to tell you about what causes colds; how they treat colds; how they prevent colds. Ask all respondents to tell you about the consequences of having a cold and how they feel when they have a cold. Working together, develop a codebook and analyze these data using an in vivo coding approach or a content analysis approach. For the content analysis approach, test hypotheses about differences in the themes emphasized by men and women telling the same story.

3. Use the data from Exercise 2 in Chapter 18. Ask a colleague to code the video of the same dialog, using the codebook you've developed. Use Cohen's kappa to measure the difference between the two codings of the same dialog.

4. Replicate one of the classical content analysis studies described in this chapter. For example, replicate Hirschman's (1987) study of personal ads or Cowan and O'Brien's (1990) study of slasher films. Replicating one of these studies (or any published study based on classical content analysis) is an excellent way to learn about sampling and coding issues.

Further Reading

The mechanics of coding texts. Agar (1996), Auerbach and Silverstein (2003), Bogdan and Biklen (1992), Lincoln and Guba (1985), Lofland and Lofland (1995), Miles and Huberman (1994), Olszewski et al. (2006), Strauss and Corbin (1990), S. J. Taylor and Bogdan (1998).

Codebooks. Dey (1993), Fonteyn et al. (2008), Weston (2001), Winters et al. (2010).

Theoretical sampling and negative case analysis. Becker (1998), Boeije (2002), Dey (1993), Draucker et al. (2007), Duchscher and Morgan (2004), Lincoln and Guba (1985), McCreaddie (2010), Miles and Huberman (1994).

Grounded theory. Bryant and Charmaz (2007), Charmaz (1990), Dey (1993), Glaser (1992), Lincoln and Guba (1985), Lonkila (1995), Strauss (1987). Examples: Churchill et al. (2007), Ekins (1997), Fox-Wolfgramm et al. (1998), Hunt and Ropo (1995), Irurita (1996), Kearney et al. (1994), Sohier (1993), Strauss and Corbin (1997), Van Vliet (2008), H. S. Wilson and Hutchinson (1996), Wright (1997), H. M. Young (1998).

Content analysis of personal ads. Badahdah and Tiemann (2005), Dawson and McIntosh (2006), de Sousa Campos et al. (2002), Groom and Pennebaker (2005), Gudelunas (2005), Kaufman and Voon Chin (2003), Parekh and Berisin (2001), Phua (2002), C. A. Smith and Stillman (2002a, 2002b), Yancey and Yancey (1997).

Content analysis: Divakaran (2008), Franzosi (2008), Holsti (1969), Krippendorf (2004a), Krippendorf and Bock (2009), Weber (1990).

Intercoder/interrater reliability. Krippendorf (2004b), Kurasaki (2000), Popping and Roberts (2009), Ryan (1999).

Cross-cultural studies of ethnographic text. Ember (2007), Jankowiak and Fischer (1995), Levinson (1978, 1990), Rohner et al. (1973), Sanderson and Roberts (2008).

20

Univariate Analysis

INTRODUCTION

The next three chapters are about quantitative data analysis. We begin here with descriptive and inferential univariate analysis and move on, in Chapters 21 and 22, to bivariate and multivariate analyses. Descriptive analysis involves understanding data through graphic displays, through tables, and through summary statistics.

Descriptive analysis is about the data you have in hand. **Inferential analysis** involves making statements—inferences—about the world beyond the data you have in hand. When you say that the average age of a group of telephone survey respondents was 44.6 years, that's a descriptive analytic statement. When you say that there is a 95% statistical probability that the true mean of the population from which you drew your sample of respondents is between 42.5 and 47.5 years, *that's* an inferential statement. You infer something about the rest of the world from data in your sample.

Univariate analysis involves getting to know data intimately by examining variables precisely and in detail. **Bivariate analysis** involves looking at associations between pairs of variables and trying to understand how those associations work. **Multivariate analysis** involves, among other things, understanding the effects of more than one independent variable at a time on a dependent variable.

Suppose you're interested in the causes of variation in the income of women. You measure income as the dependent variable and some independent variables like: age, marital status, employment history, number of children, ages of children, education, and so on. The first thing to do is examine carefully the data about all the variables. That's the univariate part of the analysis.

Next, you'd look at the association between each independent variable and the dependent variable—age and income, education and income, number of children and income, etc. You'd also look at the association between pairs of independent variables—education and number of children, age and marital status, and so on. That's the bivariate part.

Finally, you'd look at the simultaneous effect of the independent variables on the dependent variables. That's the multivariate part.

You can see that there's no way to get to the multivariate part of analysis without having a real grip on the relations among pairs of variables. And there's no way to get to the bivariate part of the analysis without a solid understanding of what you've got in your data in the first place. So, on to univariate analysis (**Further Reading:** univariate analysis).

RAW DATA

The first thing to do, before you try any fancy statistical operations on your data, is to lay them out and get a feel for them. How many cases are there of people over 70? What is the average number of children in each household? How many people in your sample have extreme views on some key attitude questions?

Table 20.1 shows the raw data for five variables and 30 respondents. These data come from a telephone survey that Gery Ryan, Stephen Borgatti, and I did of 609 adults in the United States (Bernard et al. 2009). Part of the survey was about people's attitudes toward environmental activism. (The 30 respondents in Table 20.1 are a random sample of the 609.)

The first variable, gender, is a nominal, or **qualitative variable**. The respondents were men and women over the age of 18, selected randomly from across the 48 continental states of the United States. Men were coded as 1 (GENDER = male), women were coded as 2 (GENDER = female) (Box 20.1).

Box 20.1 On codes and codebooks and naming of variables

Naming variables is something of an art. For tables and other displays, you want short names for variables—six–eight characters, at most. MARSTAT (for marital status) and EDUC (for education) are obvious, but what about LONGMIGR (how long has it been since the respondent immigrated here?). Be as clever as you like with variable names, but keep a good, verbose description of each variable in your codebook so that you'll know what all those clever names mean a year later. Here's an example:

PQOL = Perceived quality of life. This was measured using an index consisting of the six items which follow. Each item is scored separately, but the items were tested and can be added to form an index. Since each item is scored from 1 to 5, the index of perceived quality of life can vary from 6 to 30 for any respondent.

Specify carefully the values that each variable can take. For example:

MARSTAT = marital status. 1 = married, 2 = divorced, 3 = separated, 4 = widowed, 5 = never married, 6 = unknown

If you use an established index or scale, then name it and provide a citation to the source. If you *adapt* a published technique to meet your particular needs, be sure to mention that, too, in the codebook. And *always file a copy of any survey instrument with your codebook*. That means *both* hard copy *and* digital copy.

In statistics, qualitative description entails assigning numbers to classes of things. Those numbers, though—like 1 for male and 2 for female—are just substitute names for "male" and "female." They are not quantities. You can count the number of 1s and 2s, but you can't add up the numbers and take their average. The average of the 1s and 2s in the column for GENDER in Table 20.1 is 1.4, but that's no more helpful than knowing the average telephone number in New York City.

The second two variables are ordinal. They are responses, on a scale of 1–5, to two statements. Here are the two items from the survey:

Americans are going to have to drastically reduce their level of consumption over the next few years.

<1> strongly disagree

<2> disagree

<3> neutral

<4> agree

<5> strongly agree

Environmentalists wouldn't be so gungho if it were their jobs that were threatened.

<1> strongly disagree

<2> disagree

<3> neutral

<4> agree

<5> strongly agree

These are items that Kempton et al. (1995) used in their study of environmental values in America. My colleagues and I wanted to see if we could replicate their results.

I've labeled the responses to the two items REDUCE and GUNGHO in Table 20.1. Notice that these two items are sort of opposites. The more you agree with REDUCE, the

Table 20.1 30 Records From Bernard et al.'s (2009) Study of Green Attitudes

			Variable		
Respondent	GENDER	REDUCE	GUNGHO	AGE	EDUC
1	2	5	1	46	18
2	2	4	2	56	12
3	1	4	3	25	18
4	1	5	4	24	12
5	1	4	2	60	5
6	1	2	4	51	18
7	1	2	4	53	14
8	2	5	4	25	13
9	1	2	4	21	15
10	2	4	4	67	13
11	2	2	1	34	16
12	1	5	3	47	18
13	1	4	1	35	12
14	2	4	3	67	12
15	1	4	4	20	12
16	2	4	2	24	15
17	1	5	2	38	16
18	2	5	2	53	14
19	1	4	2	38	12
20	2	4	3	31	14
21	1	5	4	54	15
22	2	5	4	52	14
23	1	4	2	37	14
24	1	2	1	53	14
25	1	5	5	49	18
26	1	3	3	46	16
27	2	5	4	78	14
28	2	5	2	41	12
29	1	4	2	57	12
30	1	4	4	69	10

stronger your support for environmentalist issues is likely to be. But the more you agree with GUNGHO, the *weaker* your support for environmentalist issues is likely to be. If we want bigger numbers, like 4 and 5, always to stand for support of environmentalism and smaller numbers, like 1 and 2, always to stand for lack of support, then we have to transform the data for GUNGHO so that they run in the same direction as the data for REDUCE.

This is an important part of univariate analysis. Fortunately, it's easy to do in any statistics package.

Variables 4 and 5, AGE (the respondent's age) and EDUC (the respondent's level of education), are interval. (They are really ratio variables, but recall from Chapter 2 that ratio variables are conventionally referred to as interval.) For AGE, we simply asked respondents "How old are you?" Here is the question from the survey that produced the data for EDUC:

What is the highest grade of school or year in college you yourself completed?

None	0
Elementary	01
Elementary	02
Elementary	03
Elementary	04
Elementary	05
Elementary	06
Elementary	07
Elementary	08
High School	09
High School	10
High School	11
High School	12
College–one year	13
College–two years	14
College–three years	15
College–four years	16
Some Graduate School	17
Graduate/Prof. Degree	18

FREQUENCY DISTRIBUTIONS

Table 20.2a–e shows the raw data from Table 20.1 transformed into a set of frequency distributions. I used SYSTAT® to produce Table 20.2, but any program will do.

Using a Frequency Table

One thing to look for in a frequency distribution is variability. If a variable has no variability, then it is simply not of any further interest. If everyone in this sample of respondents were the same gender, for instance, we wouldn't use GENDER in any further analysis. Looking carefully at the frequency distribution is your first line of defense against wasting a lot of time on variables that don't vary.

We see from the frequency table in Table 20.2a that 60% of the sample are men. Table 20.2d shows that age is pretty evenly distributed. Table 20.2e shows that two-thirds of the sample (20 out of 30) had more than a high school education and that five of the 30 had graduate degrees. Most people (24 out of 30) agreed or strongly agreed with the statement that Americans are going to have to reduce consumption drastically in the coming years (Table 20.2b).

People were pretty evenly split, though, on whether environmentalists would be so gung-ho if their jobs were threatened (Table 20.2c): 13 people either disagreed or strongly disagreed with that sentiment, and 12 people either agreed or strongly agreed (five were neutral).

Frequency distributions give you hints about how to collapse variables. With 609 respondents in the full survey, we had plenty of responses to all possible answers for the

Table 20.2 Frequency Distribution for the Raw Data on the Five Variables in Table 20.1

\multicolumn{5}{c}{a. Frequency Table of the Variable GENDER}
Count	Cum. Count	Percentage	Cum. Percentage	Variable GENDER
18	18	60.0	60.0	Male
12	30	40.0	100.0	Female

\multicolumn{5}{c}{b. Frequency Table of the Variable REDUCE}
Count	Cum. Count	Percentage	Cum. Percentage	Variable REDUCE
5	5	16.7	16.7	2
1	6	3.3	20.0	3
13	19	43.3	63.3	4
11	30	36.7	100.0	5

\multicolumn{5}{c}{c. Frequency Table of the Variable GUNGHO}
Count	Cum. Count	Percentage	Cum. Percentage	Variable GUNGHO
4	4	13.3	13.3	1
9	13	30.0	43.3	2
5	18	16.7	60.0	3
11	29	36.7	96.7	4
1	30	3.3	100.0	5

\multicolumn{5}{c}{d. Frequency Table of the Variable AGE}
Count	Cum. Count	Percentage	Cum. Percentage	Variable AGE
1	1	3.3	3.3	20
1	2	3.3	6.7	21
2	4	6.7	13.3	24
2	6	6.7	20.0	25
1	7	3.3	23.3	31
1	8	3.3	26.7	34
1	9	3.3	30.0	35
1	10	3.3	33.3	37
2	12	6.7	40.0	38
1	13	3.3	43.3	41
2	15	6.7	50.0	46

(Continued)

(Continued)

| | d. Frequency Table of the Variable AGE | | | |
Count	Cum. Count	Percentage	Cum. Percentage	Variable AGE
1	16	3.3	53.3	47
1	17	3.3	56.7	49
1	18	3.3	60.0	51
1	19	3.3	63.3	52
3	22	10.0	73.3	53
1	23	3.3	76.7	54
1	24	3.3	80.0	56
1	25	3.3	83.3	57
1	26	3.3	86.7	60
2	28	6.7	93.3	67
1	29	3.3	96.7	69
1	30	3.3	100.0	78
	e. Frequency Table of the Variable EDUC			
Count	Cum. Count	Percentage	Cum. Percentage	Variable EDUC
1	1	3.3	3.3	5
1	2	3.3	6.7	10
8	10	26.7	33.3	12
2	12	6.7	40.0	13
7	19	23.3	63.3	14
3	22	10.0	73.3	15
3	25	10.0	83.3	16
5	30	16.7	100.0	18

question about reducing consumption. But with a sample of just 30 responses, we didn't get anyone who said they strongly disagreed with the statement that Americans are going to have to drastically reduce their consumption in the coming years.

If all we had were these 30 cases, we'd want to create a three-category variable—disagree, neutral, and agree—by collapsing the data for REDUCE into: (1) the five people who answered 2 (disagree); (2) the one person who answered 3 (neutral); and (3) the 24 people who answered 4 or 5 (agree and strongly agree). Notice that in collapsing this variable from five categories to three, we haven't changed the level of measurement. It's still an ordinal variable (Box 20.2).

Box 20.2 More about grouped data

It's not always obvious how to create **grouped data**. In fact, it's often better not to. Look at Table 20.2e. Only two people in our sample of 30 had less than 12 years of education. We could conveniently group those two people into a category called "less than high school." There is a bulge of eight people who had 12 years of education (they completed high school), but then we see just two people who reported a year of college and seven people who reported two years of college. That bulge of seven respondents might be people who went to a community college. We might group those two sets of people into a category called "up to two years of college."

Those three people in Table 20.2e who reported four years of college (16 years of education) form an obvious class ("finished college"), and so do the five people who reported having a graduate or professional degree that required more than four years of college. But what do we do with those three people who reported three years of college? We could lump them together with the three respondents who finished college, but we could also lump them with the nine people who reported one or two years of college.

The problem is, we don't have any iron-clad decision rule that tells us how to lump data into categories. We don't want to maintain a separate category of just three respondents (the people who reported three years of college), but we don't know if they "belong" (in some socially important sense) with those who had some college or with those who completed college.

I recommend *not* grouping interval-level data unless you really have to. No matter which decision you make about those three people who reported three years of college in Table 20.2e, you're turning an interval-level variable (years of education) into an ordinal-level variable (less than high school, high school, etc.). There are times when this might be a good idea, but trading interval for ordinal measurement means throwing away data. You need a really good reason to do that.

MEASURES OF CENTRAL TENDENCY

Once we have the data laid out and have a feel for what's in there, we can start describing the variables. The first thing to do is get some overall measure of the "typical" value for each variable. This is called a measure of central tendency.

The three most widely used measures of central tendency are the mode, the median, and the mean. All these get packaged together in everyday speech as some kind of "average," but we have to be more precise in data analysis. Each measure of central tendency carries important information about the values of a variable.

Here are the definitions for each of these measures of central tendency:

1. *The mode is the attribute of a variable that occurs most frequently.* The mode can be found for nominal, ordinal, and interval-level variables, but it is the only measure of central tendency available for nominal variables.

2. *The median is the point in a distribution above and below which there are an equal number of scores in a distribution.* The median can be found for ordinal and interval-level variables.

3. *The mean, or the average, is the sum of the individual scores in a distribution, divided by the number of scores.* The mean can be found for ordinal and interval-level variables.

Central Tendency I: The Mode

The mode is the attribute of a variable that occurs most frequently. Technically, the mode is not calculated; it is observed. You find it by simply looking at the data and seeing which attribute of a variable occurs the most.

In Table 20.2d, we see that three out of 30 respondents said they were 53 years old, so 53 is the modal age. This doesn't tell us much, but in Table 20.2e we see that the modal value for education is 12 years (there are eight out of 30 cases), and this does tell us something: Finishing high school is the most common level of education in our sample of 30 respondents.

All variables (nominal, ordinal, and interval) have modal values, but nominal variables can *only* have modal values. In Table 20.2a, for example, we see that there are 18 men (GENDER = 1) and 12 women (GENDER = 2). The mode, then, is male for this sample of 30. (The mode,

by the way, was female for the full survey of 609 respondents. When you work with small samples, fluctuations of this magnitude are normal.)

Many distributions have more than one mode, and bimodal distributions are quite common. In a rural community that has experienced a lot of out-migration, for example, the age structure is likely to be bimodal: There are young people hanging around who aren't old enough to leave, and old people who can't find work in the city because of their age.

Bimodal distributions can turn up in unexpected places and when they do, they are often clues to something important going on. In 1986, 66% of cases of violent assault in Tallin (the capital of Estonia) involved one–five injuries; 28% involved 10 or more injuries; and in between, just 6% of cases involved six–nine injuries. The pattern was stable. In 1996, the figures were 63% and 33% for one–five injuries and more than 10 injuries, with just 5% involving six–nine injuries. Kompus (2006) found that this pattern—either a small or a large number of injuries inflicted on a victim during an assault—was best predicted by whether the person convicted of the crime in 1986 had been arrested for another crime over the next 15 years (Box 20.3).

Box 20.3 Using the mode

The mode is often said to be the weakest measure of central tendency, but it's very useful when you want to make a statement about a prominent qualitative attribute of a group. "More people profess to be Buddhist in this city in Japan than profess any other religion" is such a statement.

The mode is also a good common-sense alternative to the sometimes unrealistic quality of the mean. Saying that "the modal family size is four people" makes a lot more sense than saying that the "average family size is 3.81 people"—even if both statements are true.

You'll often see the mode reported as a percentage: "In this survey, 60% of the respondents were men."

The mode can also be reported in terms of **ratios**. Of the 30 respondents in Table 20.1, 12 were women and 18 were men, so the modal value for the variable GENDER in Table 20.1 is male. The ratio of men to women among these respondents is 18/12 = 1.5, while the ratio of women to men is 12/18 = .67. Reporting that "there were 1.5 men for every woman in this survey" is the same as saying that "60% of the respondents were men." Reporting that "there were .67 women for every man in this survey" is the same as saying that "40% of the respondents were women."

Central Tendency II: The Median

The median is the point in a distribution above and below which there are an equal number of scores in a distribution. It can be used with ranked or ordinal data and with interval- or ratio-level data. For an *odd number* of unique observations on a variable, the median score is $(n + 1)/2$, where n is the number of cases in a distribution.

Suppose we ask nine people to tell us how many brothers and sisters they have and we get the following answers:

0 0 1 1 1 1 2 2 3

The median observation is 1 because it is the middle score—there are four scores on either side of it, $(n + 1)/2 = 5$, and we see that the median is the fifth case in the series, once the data are arranged in order.

Often as not, though, as with the data on those 30 respondents in the green survey, you'll have an *even number* of cases. Then the median is the average of $n/2$ and $n/2 + 1$, or the midpoint between the *two* middle observations. I asked 16 undergraduate students "How long do you think you'll live?" Here are the responses:

70 73 75 75 79 80 80 83 85 86 86 87 87 90 95 96

$n/2 = 8$ and $n/2 + 1 = 9$, so the median is midway between 83 and 85, or 84. (By the way, if the two middle observations had been, say, 83, then the midpoint between them would be 83.)

The Median of Grouped Data

A lot of data in the social sciences are reported in intervals, or groups. For example, some people are uncomfortable with a straightforward question like "How much money do you make?" so researchers often ask something like:

Now we'd like to get an idea of about how much you earn each year. Do you earn:

(1) less than $20,000 per year?

(2) $20,000 or more but less than $30,000 per year?

(3) $30,000 or more but less than $40,000 per year?

(4) $40,000 or more but less than $50,000 per year?

(5) $50,000 or more but less than $60,000 per year?

and so on. This produces grouped data right from the start (see Box 20.2). Table 20.3 shows the data on AGE from Table 20.2e, grouped into 10-year intervals. To find the median in grouped data, use the formula for finding percentiles.

The formula for finding *any* percentile score in a distribution of grouped data scores is:

$$PS = L + i\left\{\frac{n - C}{f}\right\}$$ **formula 20.1**

where:

PS is the percentile score you want to calculate;

L is the real lower limit of the interval in which the percentile score lies;

n is the case number that represents the percentile score;

C is the cumulative frequency of the cases up to the interval *before* the one in which the percentile score lies;

i is the interval size; and

f is the count, or *frequency*, of the interval in which the median lies.

Ten percent of scores in a list are below the 10th percentile and 90% are above it. If you've ever taken a standardized test like the ACT or the SAT or the GRE and so on, you might have

Table 20.3	Frequency Table of the Grouped Variable AGE	
Count	Cum. Count	Variable AGE
6	6	20–29
6	12	30–39
5	17	40–49
8	25	50–59
5	30	60+

been told that you scored in the 14th percentile, or the 31st percentile, or whatever. If you scored in the 14th percentile, then 86% of the scores were lower than yours $(1.0 - .14 = .86)$.

The 25th percentile is called the first quartile and the 75th percentile is the third quartile. The difference between the values for the 25th and 75th percentiles is the inter-quartile range and is a measure of dispersion for ordinal and interval-level variables. (More on measures of dispersion later.) *The median is the 50th percentile.*

In applying formula 20.1 to the data in Table 20.3, the first thing to do is calculate *n*. There are 30 cases and we are looking for the score at the 50th percentile (the median), so *n* is (30)(.50) = 15. We are looking, in other words, for a number *above which* there are 15 cases and *below which* there are 15 cases. Looking at the data in Table 20.3, we see that there are 12 cases up to 39 years of age and 17 cases up to 49 years of age. So, *C* is 12, and the median case lies somewhere in the 40–49 range.

The real lower limit, *L*, of this interval is 39.5 (midway between 39 and 40, the boundary of the two groups) and the interval, *i*, is 10 years. Putting all this into the formula, we get:

$$PS = 39.5 + 10\left(\frac{15 - 12}{5}\right)$$
$$= 39.5 + 10(.6) = 45.5$$

So, the median age for this group of 30 people is 45.5 years. Notice that none of the respondents actually got a score of 45.5. Still, 15 of the 30 scores are above 45.5 and 15 are below it.

I've given you this grand tour of the median as a specific percentile score because I want you to understand the conceptual basis for this statistic. I'm going to do the same thing for all the statistical procedures I introduce here and in the next two chapters. You only need to work through these detailed examples once. When you understand the concepts behind the median, the standard deviation, *z*-scores, chi-square, *t*-tests, and regression, you can do all the calculations by computer.

Central Tendency III: The Mean

The arithmetic mean, or the average, is the *sum of the individual scores in a distribution, divided by the number of scores*. Means are everywhere. We see statistics on the average age at marriage, on the average price of a gallon of gas, on the average mortgage rate, on the average number of days people miss work because of illness each year, and so on.

The formula for calculating the mean is:

$$\bar{x} = \sum x / n \qquad \text{formula 20.2}$$

where $\bar{x}$ (read: x-bar) is the mean, $\sum x$ means "sum all the values of *x*" and *n* is the number of values of *x*. (Reminder: We use $\bar{x}$ when we refer to the mean of a sample of data; we use the Greek letter μ when we refer to the mean of an entire population.)

To calculate the mean age of the 30 respondents whose data are shown in Table 20.1, we add up the 30 ages and divide by 30. The mean age of these 30 respondents is 45.033 years. The formula for calculating the *mean of a frequency distribution* is:

$$\bar{x} = \sum fx / n \qquad \text{formula 20.3}$$

where $\sum fx$ is the sum of the attributes of the variable, times their frequencies.

Table 20.4 shows the calculation of the mean age for the frequency distribution shown in Table 20.2d.

Table 20.4 Calculating the Mean for the Data in Table 20.2d

Count f	AGE x	fx
1	20	20
1	21	21
2	24	48
2	25	50
1	31	31
1	34	34
1	35	35
1	37	37
2	38	76
1	41	41
2	46	92
1	47	47
1	49	49
1	51	51
1	52	52
3	53	159
1	54	54
1	56	56
1	57	57
1	60	60
2	67	134
1	69	69
1	78	78
		$\Sigma fx = 1351$ $\Sigma fx / n =$ 1351/30 = 45.033

Table 20.5 Frequency Table of the Grouped Variable AGE

x = AGE	MID-POINT	f	fx
20–29	25	6	150
30–39	35	6	210
40–49	45	5	225
50–59	55	8	440
60+	65	5	325

$n = 30$

$\sum fx = 1350$

$\bar{x} = \dfrac{1350}{30} = 45.00$

Table 20.5 shows the calculation of the mean for the grouped data on AGE in Table 20.3. When variable attributes are presented in ranges, as in the case here, we take the midpoint of the range.

Why It's Better to Collect Interval Data as Intervals

Note the problem in taking the mean of the grouped data in Table 20.5. If you go back to Table 20.2d, you'll see that all six of the people who are between 20 and 29 are really between 20 and 25. Counting them all as being 25 obviously distorts the mean.

Also, there are five people over 60 in this data set: one who is 60, two who are 67, and one each who are 69 and 78. In calculating the mean for these grouped data, I've assigned the midpoint to be 65, *as if the range were 60–69,* even though the actual range is 60–78. The real midpoint of the 60+ category is

$$(60 + 67 + 67 + 69 + 78)/5 = 68.2$$

but they are all counted as being just 60+ in Table 20.3.

If you have grouped data, however, it will almost certainly be because the data were collected in grouped form to begin with. In that case, there is no way to know what the real range or the real midpoint is for any grouped category, so you have to assign a midpoint that conforms to the midpoints of the other ranges. That's what I've done in Table 20.5 in assigning the midpoint for the 60+ category as 65.

Obviously, all this distorts the mean: the grouped data have a mean of 45.00, while the ungrouped data have a calculated mean of 45.033. In this case, the difference is teeny, but it won't always be that way. If you collect data in groups about interval variables like age, you can never go back and see how much you've distorted things. It's always better to collect interval data at the interval level, if you can, rather than in grouped form. You can always group the data later, during the analysis, but you can't "ungroup" them if you collect data in grouped form to begin with.

A Mathematical Feature of the Mean

The arithmetic mean has an important feature: *The sum of the deviations from the mean of all the scores in a distribution is zero.* Table 20.6 shows this feature with data from 10 U.S. states on the percentage of people who are on welfare.

These data are a random sample of the data in Table 20.7, showing some social

Table 20.6 Data on Temporary Aid to Needy Families in 10 U.S. States (from Table 20.7) Showing How the Sum of the Deviations From the Mean of a Distribution Is Zero

STATE	WELF06 x	Score – Mean $x - \bar{x}$
Alabama	1.0	$1.0 - 2.00 = -1.00$
California	3.3	$3.3 - 2.00 = 1.30$
Colorado	0.8	$0.8 - 2.00 = -1.20$
Washington, DC	6.8	$6.8 - 2.00 = 4.80$
Idaho	0.2	$0.2 - 2.00 = -1.80$
Minnesota	1.6	$1.6 - 2.00 = -0.40$
New York	2.4	$2.4 - 2.00 = 0.40$
North Dakota	1.1	$1.1 - 2.00 = -0.90$
Washington	2.1	$2.1 - 2.00 = 0.10$
Wisconsin	0.7	$0.7 - 2.00 = -1.30$
	$\sum x = 20.00$	$\sum x - \bar{x} = 0.00$
	$\bar{x} = \dfrac{20.00}{10} = 2.00$	

Table 20.7 Some Social Indicators for the 50 U.S. States and Washington, DC

STATE	VIOL07	WELF06	OV6508	URB08	SCH06	DOC07	OWNHOME08	INC07
AL	448	1.0	13.8	71.4	94.3	218	73.0	32,419
AK	661	1.5	7.3	67.4	90.3	228	66.4	40,042
AZ	483	1.4	13.3	92.7	99.6	210	69.1	32,833
AR	529	0.6	14.3	59.8	92.3	203	68.9	30,177
CA	523	3.3	11.2	97.7	91.4	269	57.5	41,805
CO	348	0.8	10.4	86.2	91.5	260	69.0	41,192
CN	256	1.4	13.7	91.3	90.4	376	70.7	54,981
DE	689	1.5	13.9	78.5	86.3	251	76.2	40,112
DC	1,414	6.8	11.9	100.0	100.6	807	44.1	62,484
FL	723	0.5	17.4	94.1	91.7	248	71.1	38,417
GA	493	0.7	10.1	81.4	94.6	217	68.2	33,499
HI	273	2.1	14.8	70.3	87.6	317	59.1	39,242
ID	239	0.2	12.0	65.6	95.5	169	75.0	31,804
IL	533	0.7	12.2	87.1	88.5	280	68.9	41,012
IN	334	2.1	12.8	78.2	91.2	217	74.4	33,215
IA	295	1.7	14.8	56.4	92.1	189	74.0	34,916
KS	453	1.6	13.1	63.7	91.0	223	68.8	36,525
KY	295	1.7	13.3	57.4	92.5	232	72.8	30,824
LA	730	0.6	12.3	74.3	87.1	263	73.5	35,100
ME	118	2.4	15.1	58.5	94.5	278	73.9	33,991
MD	642	1.0	12.1	94.6	89.5	421	70.6	46,471

(Continued)

(Continued)

STATE	VIOL07	WELF06	OV6508	URB08	SCH06	DOC07	OWNHOME08	INC07
MA	432	1.5	13.4	99.6	89.7	469	65.7	48,995
MI	536	2.2	13.0	81.5	87.9	250	75.9	34,423
MN	289	1.6	12.5	73.1	90.5	293	73.1	41,105
MS	291	1.0	12.7	44.1	91.7	178	75.4	28,541
MO	505	1.9	13.6	73.5	85.9	246	71.4	33,964
MT	288	1.0	14.2	35.3	92.0	221	70.3	33,225
NE	302	1.9	13.5	58.3	87.9	245	69.6	36,372
NV	751	0.7	11.4	89.8	96.0	188	63.6	39,853
NH	137	1.1	12.9	62.4	88.1	275	75.0	41,639
NJ	329	1.3	13.3	100.0	86.9	316	67.3	49,511
NM	664	2.2	13.1	66.2	88.2	244	70.4	30,706
NY	414	2.4	13.4	92.1	89.2	396	55.0	46,364
NC	466	0.7	12.4	70.3	92.0	254	69.4	33,735
ND	142	1.1	14.7	48.6	92.6	244	66.6	36,082
OH	343	1.5	13.7	80.7	88.2	267	70.8	34,468
OK	500	0.6	13.5	63.8	95.1	173	70.4	34,997
OR	288	1.1	13.3	77.9	91.0	274	66.2	35,143
PA	417	2.0	15.4	84.1	84.8	305	72.6	38,793
RI	227	3.0	14.1	100.0	87.4	376	64.5	38,829
SC	788	1.0	13.3	76.3	94.6	230	73.9	31,103
SD	169	0.8	14.4	46.0	92.9	219	70.4	35,760
TN	753	3.0	13.2	73.3	93.0	264	71.7	33,395

STATE	VIOL07	WELF06	OV6508	URB08	SCH06	DOC07	OWNHOME08	INC07
TX	511	0.7	10.2	87.7	98.3	214	65.5	37,083
UT	235	0.7	9.0	89.1	96.1	208	76.2	29,831
VT	124	1.9	14.0	33.6	99.6	374	72.8	37,483
VA	270	1.1	12.1	85.7	93.4	274	70.6	41,727
WA	333	2.1	12.0	87.7	92.2	270	66.2	41,203
WV	275	1.5	15.7	55.5	96.5	232	77.8	29,385
WI	291	0.7	13.3	72.9	86.0	259	70.4	36,272
WY	239	0.1	12.3	30.2	97.2	184	73.3	47,047

VIOL07   The violent crime rate in 2007, per 100,000 population. Table 297, Statistical Abstract of the United States, 2010.

WELF06   Total recipients of Temporary Aid to Needy Families (TANF), as a percent of the resident population in 2006. Indicators of Welfare Dependence. Annual Report to Congress 2008. U.S. Department of Health and Human Services. http://aspe.hhs.gov/hsp/indicators08/

OV6508   Percent of the resident population 65 years and older in 2008. Table 16, Statistical Abstract of the United States, 2010.

URB08   Percent of the resident population in metropolitan areas in 2008. Table 24, Statistical Abstract of the United States, 2010.

SCH06   Percent of persons 5–17 years old in public elementary and secondary schools in 2006. Some states show slightly more than 100%, presumably because students under 5 and over 17 are counted there. Table 239, Statistical Abstract of the United States, 2010.

DOC07   The number of physicians per 100,000 population in 2007. Table 159, Statistical Abstract of the United States, 2010.

HOME08   Percentage of families that owned their own home in 2008. Table 958, Statistical Abstract of the United States, 2010.

INC07   Personal income per capita in 2007. Table 665, Statistical Abstracts of the United States, 2010.

indicators for the 50 U.S. states and Washington, DC, in recent years. These data are from various editions of the Statistical Abstract of the United States. We'll be using the data in Table 20.7, as well as some other data from the SAUS as we go along in the next few chapters.

While both the median and the mean are midpoints in sets of scores, the mean has the additional feature: It is the point in a distribution at which the two halves balance each other out. Table 20.8 shows that the sum of the differences between the scores and the mean of a set of scores is zero. This feature of the mean figures prominently in the calculation of variance, which is coming right up in the section on measures of dispersion.

The Outlier Problem

The mean is one of the all-time great statistics, but it has one very important drawback: In small samples, it's heavily influenced by special cases, called **outliers**, and even in large samples, it's heavily influenced by big gaps in the distribution of cases.

For example, in Chad, some people live to 75 or 80 years of age. The mean life expectancy of people in Chad, however, is about 49 years, partly because Chad has one of the highest rates of infant mortality in the world. Of every 1,000 babies born, about 130 of them die in their first year of life. The average of three people who die at one year of age and three who die at 75 years of age is 38.

You can see this problem yourself by calculating the mean rate of violent crimes in the United States in 2007, from the data in Table 20.7. There were, on average, 427.2 violent crimes per 100,000 people that year in the United States. But if you take away Washington, DC, the mean for the rest of the United States was 407.5 violent crimes per 100,000 population. The data from DC raise the mean rate of violence for the entire United States by about 5%, even though DC has only two-tenths of 1% of the population of the United States.

The *median* rate of violent crime in the United States in 2007 was 348 per 100,000 population, *including* the data from Washington, DC, and 345.5, *excluding* DC. When data are normally distributed, the mean is the best indicator of central tendency. When interval data are highly skewed, the median is often a better indicator of central tendency. You absolutely must get a feel for the *shape* of distributions to understand what's going on.

SHAPE: VISUALIZING DISTRIBUTIONS

A good first cut at understanding whether data are normal or skewed is to lay them

| Table 20.8 | The Sum of the Differences Between the Scores and the Mean of a Set of Scores Is Zero |

Scores Below the Mean of 2.00 in Table 20.6	Scores Above the Mean of 2.00 in Table 20.6
− 1.0	1.3
− 1.2	4.8
− 1.8	0.4
− 0.4	0.1
− 0.9	
− 1.3	
Total below the mean	Total above the mean
− 6.6	6.6
−6.6 and +6.6 sum to 0	

out graphically. This is easy to do with any full-featured statistics program. I'll show you six ways to lay out your data: bar graphs and pie charts for nominal and ordinal variables; stem-and-leaf plots, box-and-whisker plots, histograms, and frequency polygons for interval variables (**Further Reading:** visualizing data).

Bar Graphs and Pie Charts

Bar graphs and pie charts are two popular ways to graph the distribution of nominal and ordinal variables. Figure 20.1 shows bar graphs for two of the variables in Table 20.1: GENDER and GUNGHO. Figure 20.2 shows the pie charts for the same variables.

Figure 20.1 Bar Charts for the Variables GENDER and GUNGHO in Tables 20.2(a) and (c)

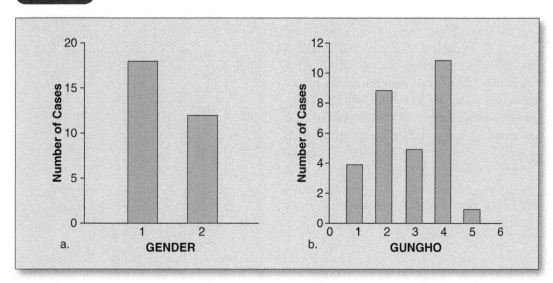

Figure 20.2 Pie Charts for the Variables GENDER and GUNGHO in Tables 20.2(a) and (c)

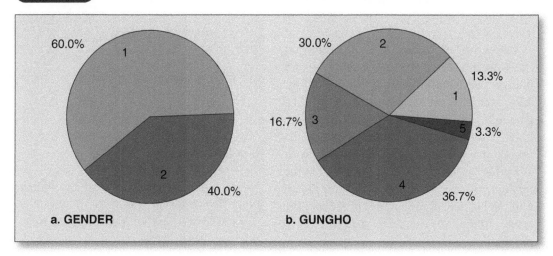

Notice that in the bar charts, the bars don't touch one another. This indicates that the data are nominal or ordinal and not continuous.

The categories of the variables are shown along the horizontal axis of the bar graph. The horizontal, or x-axis, is also called the abcissa. The number of each category is shown on the left vertical axis. The vertical, or y-axis, is also called the ordinate. You can, of course, show the percent of each category on the y-axis.

In Figure 20.1a, men are labeled 1 and women are labeled 2. Notice that it makes no difference whether we put the bar for men or the bar for the women on the left or the right when we graph GENDER. There is no order implied in the attributes of a nominal variable. When we graph ordinal variables, however, like GUNGHO, the order of the bars becomes important. The bars don't still touch, however, reflecting the fact that ordinal variables are not continuous.

Stem-and-Leaf Plots

I like to start visualizing interval data by running stem-and-leaf plots. Figure 20.3 shows a stem-and-leaf plot for the variable DOC07 in Table 20.7.

Inspection of Table 20.7 confirms that the lowest value for this variable is 169 doctors per 100,000 population (in Idaho). The "stem" in the stem-and-leaf plot is 16 (the first two digits of 169) and the "leaf" is 9. There are two cases in the 170s: Oklahoma with 173 and Mississippi with 178. The M in Figure 20.3 stands for the median, or the 50th percentile (it's 249), and the Hs indicate the upper hinge and the lower hinge, or the 25th and the 75th percentiles.

Figure 20.3 Stem and Leaf Plot of Variable DOC07 in Table 20.7

Stem and Leaf Plot of variable:		DOC07, N = 51
Minimum:		169.000
Lower hinge:		218.500
Median:		250.000
Upper hinge:		276.500
Maximum:		807.000
16		9
17		38
18		489
19		
20		38
21	H	047789
22		138
23		022
24		44568
25	M	0149
26		03479
27	H	04458
28		0
29		3
30		5
31		67
Outside Values		
37		466
39		6
42		1
46		9
80		7

Box-and-Whisker Plots

Next, I like to produce box-and-whisker plots for interval variables. Figure 20.4 shows the box-and-whisker plots for four of the variables in Table 20.7. Box-and-whisker

Box Plot of the Percentage of Urban Population in 2008 for the 50 U.S. States and the District of Columbia

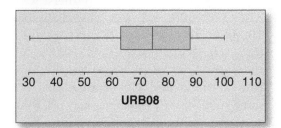

Box Plot of the Percentage of People Over 65 in 2008 for the 50 U.S. States and the District of Columbia

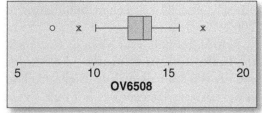

Box Plot of the Number of Violent Crimes per 100,000 Population in 2007 for the 50 U.S. States and the District of Columbia

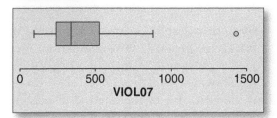

Box Plot of the Number of Physicians per 100,000 People in 2007 for the 50 U.S. States and the District of Columbia

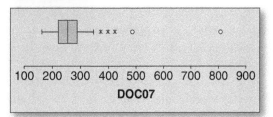

plots are chock-full of information. The boxes themselves show you the middle 50% of the cases—that is, the interquartile range. The vertical line that marks off the box at the left is the 25th percentile (the lower hinge) of the plot; the vertical line that marks off the box at the right is the 75th percentile (the upper hinge).

The vertical line inside the box is the median, or the 50th percentile. Fifty percent of the cases in the distribution fall to the right of the median line and 50% fall to the left.

The whiskers in these box plots extend one-and-a-half times the interquartile range from the lower and the upper hinges of the box. When data are normally distributed, this will be about 2.7 standard deviations from the mean. Cases outside that range are outliers and are marked by an asterisk. Cases that are more than *three times the interquartile range* from the hinges are marked by a little circle. Outliers can be quite instructive as we'll see in a minute.

Figure 20.4a shows that the percentage of urban population is pretty evenly distributed across the United States. If you were to apply formula 20.1 to the data for URB08 in Table 20.7 (or run a stem-and-leaf plot for those data), you'd find the 25th percentile (the lower hinge in the stem-and-leaf plot) to be 63.05% and the 75th percentile (the upper hinge) to be 87.7%. That is, half the states in the United States had between 63.05% and 87.7% urban population in 2007.

Notice, though, that *none* of the states in Table 20.7 are exactly 63.05% or exactly 88.7% urban. Just as the median is an abstract concept, so is every single percentile. Wyoming, with 30.2% of its population concentrated in urban areas, is the least urbanized of the states. Washington, DC, is 100% urbanized, but so are Rhode Island and New Jersey, and Massachusetts is 99.6% urbanized. There's rural land in Rhode Island, New Jersey, and Massachusetts, but, compared to the concentration of people in the urban areas, hardly anyone lives in the rural zones. ("Urban," by the way, as far as the U.S. Census is concerned, means concentrations of at least 2,500 people in a town.)

Now look at Figure 20.4b. This, too, is pretty evenly distributed. In 50% of the states, the percentage of people over 65 was between 12.25% and 13.85% in 2008—a pretty tight interquartile range. The full range, however, is much wider: Just 7.3% of the population of Alaska was over 65 and fully 17.4% of the population of Florida was over 65 in 2008.

Figure 20.4c shows that 50% of the states had between 281.5 and 526 violent crimes per 100,000 population in 2007. Maine had the lowest violent crime rate—118 per 100,000. Except for one really isolated outlier, South Carolina had the highest rate of violent crime in the United States, with 788 crimes per 100,000. The true outlier is Washington, DC, with an astounding 1,414 violent crimes per 100,000.

Figure 20.4d shows that half the states had between 218.5 and 276.5 physicians per 100,000 population in 2007. That's a narrow interquartile range, but there are real outliers here. Four states— Connecticut, Rhode Island, New York, and Maryland—are relative outliers, with 376, 376, 396, and 421 physicians per 100,000, respectively. (There are only three asterisks in Figure 20.4d even though there are four relative outliers because Rhode Island and Connecticut had the same number of physicians per 100,000, and two of the asterisks overlap.) One state, Massachusettes, with 469 physicians per 100,000, is two standard deviations above the mean. And then there's Washington, DC, with 807 physicians per 100,000.

Histograms and Frequency Polygons

Two other graphic methods are useful in univariate analysis: histograms and frequency polygons. Frequency polygons are line drawings made by connecting the tops of the bars of a histogram and displaying the result without the bars. What you get is a pure shape—less information than box plots or stem-and-leaf plots, but these graphics have a certain appeal because they are easily interpreted. Figure 20.5 shows the histogram and frequency polygon for the variable SCH06 in Table 20.7. Figure 20.6 shows the histogram and frequency polygon for WELF06 in Table 20.7. And Figure 20.7 shows the histogram and frequency polygon for HOME08 in Table 20.7.

In Figure 20.5, we see that the variable SCH06 (the percentage of five–17 year olds in each state in the United States who are in school) is more-or-less evenly distributed (between 84.8% and 100.6% of those children are in school). The distribution is symmetric, approaching the normal distribution (Box 20.4).

Figure 20.5a Histogram and Frequency Polygon for SCH06 in Table 20.7

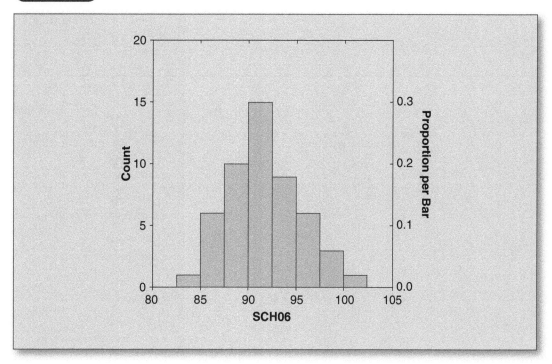

Note: The percentage of school-age children attending school is normally distributed.

Figure 20.5b Histogram and Frequency Polygon for SCH06 in Table 20.7

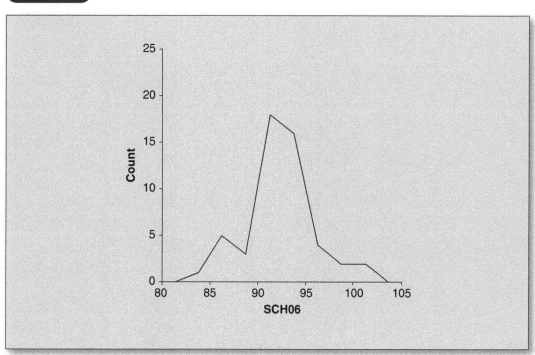

Figure 20.6a Histogram for WELF06 in Table 20.7

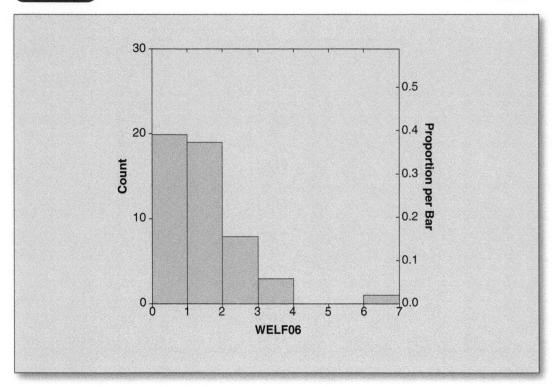

Note: The percentage of people on welfare is positively skewed.

Figure 20.6b Frequency Polygon for WELF06 in Table 20.7

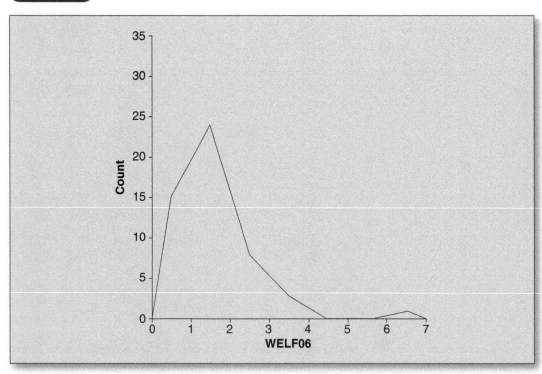

Figure 20.7a Histogram for HOME08 in Table 20.7

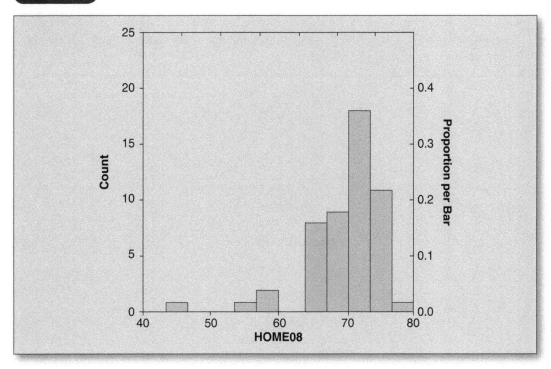

Note: The percentage of people who own their own homes is negatively skewed.

Figure 20.7b Frequency Polygon for HOME08 in Table 20.7

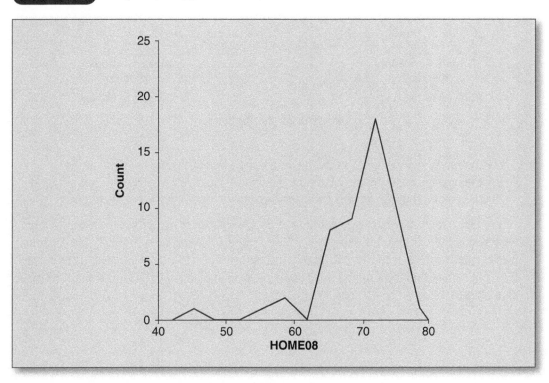

Box 20.4 Distributions again

Back in Chapter 6, on sampling, we looked at some basic *shapes* of distributions: skewed to the right, skewed to the left, bimodal, and normal. Here they are again, but this time notice the mode, the median, and the mean:

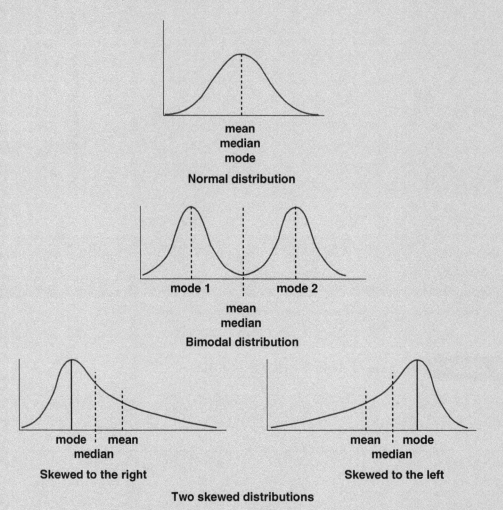

mean
median
mode

Normal distribution

mode 1   mode 2

mean
median

Bimodal distribution

mode   mean
median

Skewed to the right

mean   mode
median

Skewed to the left

Two skewed distributions

(1) the mode, the median, and the mean are the same in the normal distribution;
(2) the mean is pulled to the left of the median in negatively skewed distributions; and
(3) the mean is pulled to the right of the median in positively skewed distributions.

The mean for WELF06 (the percentage of people in each state in the United States who were receiving welfare), for example, is 1.49, while the median is 1.40; this is a slight **positive skew**. The mean for HOME08 (the percentage of families in each state in the U.S. that owned their own home) is 69.56, while the median is 70.4; this is a slight **negative skew**.

Getting a visual understanding of distributions is a great first step, but we need more information to decide whether variables are more-or-less normally distributed. As we saw in Chapter 6, the use of statistics like the z distribution and Student's t depends on the population from which samples are drawn being normal. In a normal distribution, the mean, the median, and the mode are the same and the shape of the curve is perfectly symmetrical on both sides of the mean (see Figure 6.3).

On the other hand, you won't find many perfectly normal distributions in the messy world of real social science data. Since virtually all distributions of real data are skewed, what really matters is *how much*. If the amount of skew is slight, then we can still use statistics that assume normality in the population distributions.

Figure 20.5 looks more-or-less like a normal distribution, but we can do better than just visually inspect the distribution and actually check. Figure 20.8 shows the box plot for SCH06. The plot shows that there are some outliers, but the overall distribution of cases is more or less normal. The clincher is that the median (92.2) and the mean (92.3) are practically identical.

Bimodal Distributions

Be on the lookout for **bimodal and multimodal distributions**. If you try to calculate the median or mean for a bimodal variable, you won't get a realistic picture of the central tendency in your data. Figure 20.9 shows the distribution of female life expectancy for 196 countries around the world. The mean for the distribution is 66.5 years, but the distribution is multimodal.

The two big leptokurtic bulges on the right comprise a bimodal distribution of countries in which women live from about 70 to 79 years and countries in which women live from about 80 to 86 years. The mean for these 131 countries is about 78 years. The mean of the 65 countries in which women live less than 70 years is about 58, but even in this group, there are several modes, including a group of 13 countries where life expectancy for women is between 44 and 49 years.

The moral is: Examine the frequency distribution for each of your variables. For interval and ordinal variables, find out if the distributions around the mean or median are symmetrical. If the distributions *are* symmetrical, then the mean is the measure of choice for central tendency. If the distributions are skewed, then the median is the measure of choice. And if the distributions are bimodal (or multimodal), then do a much closer examination and find out what's going on.

Figure 20.8 SCH06, the Percentage of Children Ages 5–17 in school in Each of the 50 States and Washington, DC, in 2006, Was More-or-Less Normally Distributed

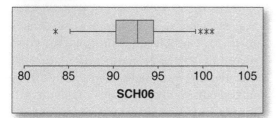

SCH06

MEASURES OF DISPERSION

After central tendency and shape, the next thing we want to know about data is something about how homogeneous or heterogeneous they are—that is, something

Figure 20.9 Female Life Expectancy Is Multimodal

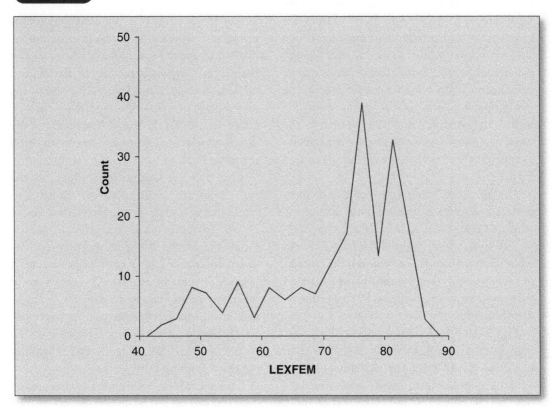

about their dispersion. For example, from the data in Table 20.7 we can calculate that there were, on average, 270.94 physicians in the United States in 2007 for every 100,000 people in the population. We'd like some measure of the variation in mean number of physicians across the 50 states and Washington, DC.

Measures of Dispersion I: Range and Interquartile Range

One measure is the range. Inspecting the third column from the right of Table 20.7, we see that Idaho had a low of 169 physicians per 100,000 population in 2007, while Washington, DC, had a high of 807. The range is 807–169 = 638. The range is a useful statistic, but it is affected strongly by

extreme scores. After Washington, DC, the next-highest concentration of physicians in 2007 was 469 in Massachusetts, and the range is 469–169 = 300, a drop of more than 50%.

The interquartile range avoids extreme scores, either high or low. The 75th percentile is 276.5 for DOC07 in Table 20.7, and the 25th percentile is 218.5, so the interquartile range is 276.5 – 218.5 = 58. This tightens the range of scores, but it is often the extreme scores that are of greatest interest. The interquartile range of freshmen SAT scores at major universities tells you about the majority—the middle 50%—of students' scores. It doesn't tell you if the university is recruiting athletes whose SAT scores are more likely to be in the bottom 25%, the middle 50%, or the top 25% of scores at those universities (see Klein 1999).

Measures of Dispersion II: Variance and the Standard Deviation

The best-known measure of dispersion for a sample of interval data is the standard deviation, usually written just *sd* or SD or *s*. The *sd* is a *measure of how much, on average, the scores in a distribution deviate from the mean score*. It gives you a feel for how homogeneous or heterogeneous a population is. (Reminder: We use *sd* for the standard deviation of a *sample*; we use the lower-case Greek sigma, σ, for the standard deviation of a population.)

The *sd* is calculated from the variance, written s^2, which is the *average squared deviation from the mean* of the measures in a set of data. To find the variance in a distribution: (1) subtract the mean of a set of observations from each observation; (2) square the difference, thus getting rid of negative numbers; (3) sum the differences; and (4) divide that sum by the sample size minus one.

Here is the formula for calculating the variance:

$$s^2 = \frac{\sum (x - \bar{x})^2}{n - 1} \qquad \text{formula 20.4}$$

where s^2 is the variance, x represents the raw scores in a distribution of interval-level observations, $\bar{x}$ is the mean of the distribution of raw scores, and n is the total number of observations.

Notice that we need to square the difference of each observation from the mean and *then* take the square root later to get the *sd*. As we saw in calculating the mean, $\sum (x - \bar{x}) = 0$. That is, the simple sum of all the deviations from the mean is zero. Squaring each $(x - \bar{x})$ gets rid of the negative numbers (Box 20.5).

Box 20.5 Variance is what you want to explain

Variance is a very important concept in statistics. It describes in a single statistic how homogeneous or heterogeneous a set of data is, and by extension, how similar or different are the units of analysis described by those data.

Variance is so important that many researchers see it as the thing you want to explain when you do statistical analysis of data. I'll explain in detail what "accounting for variance" means when we get to Chapter 21. If you can explain 100% of the variance in a distribution, that means you can predict 100% of the scores on a dependent variable by knowing the scores on some independent variable.

Consider the original set of scores in Table 20.1 on the variable, REDUCE. These scores show people's support for the idea that "Americans are going to have to drastically reduce their consumption over the next few years." Suppose that for each level of education you could predict the level of support for that attitudinal item about cutting back on consumption. If you could do this in 100% of all cases, then you would speak of "explaining all the variance" in the dependent variable.

I've never encountered this strength of association between two variables in the social sciences, but some things come pretty close, and in any event, the principle is what's important, so it's important to understand formula 20.4 on calculating variance. Variance is the basis for many of the statistics coming up in Chapter 21 on bivariate analysis.

The standard deviation, sd, is the square root of the variance, s^2. The formula for the standard deviation is:

$$sd = \sqrt{\frac{s(x - \bar{x})^2}{n-1}} \qquad \text{formula 20.5}$$

Table 20.9 shows how to calculate the standard deviation for the data on WELF06 in Table 20.6:

Substituting in the formula for standard deviation, we get:

$$sd = \sqrt{33.24/.9} = \sqrt{3.6933} = 1.92$$

If we were reporting these data, we would say that "the average percentage of adults on welfare is 2.00, sd 1.92."

For grouped data, we take the midpoint of each interval as the raw score. Table 20.10 shows the procedure for calculating the standard deviation for the grouped data in Table 20.3. We know from Table 20.5 that $\bar{x} = 45$ for the data in Table 20.3.

Substituting in the formula for sd, we get:

$$\sqrt{\frac{1000}{29}} = \sqrt{34.483} = 5.872$$

Table 20.9 Calculating the Standard Deviation for the Data in Table 20.6

State	WELF06 x	$x - \bar{x}$	$x - \bar{x}^2$
Alabama	1.0	1.0–2.00 = –1.00	1.00
California	3.3	3.3–2.00 = 1.30	1.69
Colorado	0.8	0.8–2.00 = –1.20	1.44
Washington, DC	6.8	6.8–2.00 = 4.80	23.04
Idaho	0.2	0.2–2.00 = –1.80	3.24
Minnesota	1.6	1.6–2.00 = –0.40	0.16
New York	2.4	2.4–2.00 = 0.40	0.16
North Dakota	1.1	1.1–2.00 = –0.90	0.81
Washington	2.1	2.1–2.00 = 0.10	0.01
Wisconsin	0.7	0.7–2.00 = –1.30	1.69
$n = 10$	$\Sigma x = 20$		$\sum (x - \bar{x})^2 = 33.24$

$\sum x = 20$

$\bar{x} = \dfrac{20}{10} = 2.0$

$\sum (x - \bar{x})^2 = 33.24$

$s = \sqrt{33.24/.9} = 1.92$

Table 20.10 Calculating the Standard Deviation for the Grouped Data in Table 20.3

AGE x	fx	Mid-point	$x - \bar{x}$	$x - \bar{x}^2$
20–29	6	25	$25 - 45 = -20$	400
30–39	6	35	$35 - 45 = 10$	100
40–49	5	45	$45 - 45 = 0$	0
50–59	8	55	$55 - 45 = 10$	100
60+	5	65	$65 - 45 = 20$	400
	$\sum x = 30$		$\sum x - \bar{x} = 0$	$\sum (x - \bar{x})^2 = 1000$

and we report that "the mean age (from Table 20.5) is 45.00, *sd* 5.872." For comparison, the mean and *sd* of the 30 ages (the ungrouped data) in Table 20.2d are 45.033 and 15.52.

Are these numbers describing ages and welfare rates large, or small, or about normal? There is no way to tell except by comparison across cases. By themselves, numbers such as means and standard deviations simply describe a set of data. But in comparative perspective, they help us produce theory; that is, they help us develop ideas about what causes things, and what those things, in turn, cause.

THE LOGIC OF HYPOTHESIS TESTING

One thing we can do, however, is test whether the *mean of a sample of data*, $\bar{x}$ is likely to represent the *mean of the population*, μ from which the sample was drawn. We'll test whether the mean of WELF06 in Table 20.9 is likely to represent the mean of the population of 50 states and Washington, DC. To do this, we will use the logic of hypothesis testing. This

logic is used widely—not just in the social sciences, but in all probabilistic sciences, like meteorology and genetics.

The key to this logic is the statement that we can test whether the mean of the sample *is likely to represent* the mean of the population. Here's how the logic works.

1. First, we set up a **null hypothesis**, written H_0, which states that there is no difference between the sample mean and the mean of the population from which the sample was drawn.

2. Then we set up the **research hypothesis** (also called the **alternative hypothesis**), written H_1, which states that, in fact, the sample mean and the mean of the population from which the sample was drawn are different.

3. Next, we decide whether the research hypothesis is only about **magnitude** or **directional**. If H_1 is only about magnitude—that is, it's **nondirectional**—then it can be stated just as it was in (2) above: The sample mean and the mean of the population from which the sample was drawn are different. Period.

If H_1 is directional, then it has to be stated differently: The sample mean is [bigger than] [smaller than] the mean of the population from which the sample was drawn.

This decision determines whether we will use a one-tailed or a two-tailed test of the null hypothesis.

To understand the concept of one-tailed and two-tailed tests, suppose you have a bell curve that represents the distribution of means from many samples of a population. Sample means are like any other variable. Each sample has a mean, and if you took thousands of samples from a population you'd get a distribution of means (or proportions). Some would be large, some small, and some exactly the same as the true mean of the population. The distribution would be normal and form a bell curve like the one in Box 20.4 and in Figure 6.3.

The unlikely means (the very large ones and the very small ones) show up in the narrow area under the tails of the curve, while the likely means (the ones closer to the true mean of the population) show up in the fat, middle part. In research, the question you want to answer is whether the means of variables from one, particular sample (the one *you've* got) probably represent the tails or the middle part of the curve.

Hypothesis tests are one tailed when you are interested only in whether the magnitude of some statistic is significant—that is, whether you would have expected that magnitude by chance. When the direction of a statistic is not important, then a two-tailed test is called for.

As we'll see in Chapter 21, when you predict that one of two means will be higher than the other another (like two tests taken a month apart), you would use a one-tailed test. After all, you'd be asking only whether the mean was likely to fall in one tail of the normal distribution. Look at Appendix A carefully. Scores significant at the .10 level for a two-tailed test are significant at the .05 level for a one-tailed test.

4. Finally, we determine the alpha level, written α, which is the level of significance for the hypothesis test. Typically, alpha is set at the .05 level or at the .01 level of significance. What this means is that if a mean or a proportion from a sample is likely to occur more than alpha—say, more than 5% of the time—then we *fail to reject the null hypothesis* (Box 20.6).

Box 20.6 On being significant

By custom—and only by custom—social researchers generally accept as statistically significant any outcome that is not likely to occur by chance more than five times in a hundred tries. This **p-value**, or **probability value**, is called the **.05 level of significance**. A p-value of .01 is usually considered *very* significant, and .001 is often labeled *highly* significant.

But remember: **Statistical significance** is one thing, and **substantive significance** is another matter entirely. In exploratory research, you might be satisfied with a .10 level of significance. In evaluating the side effects of a medical treatment, you might demand a .001 level—or even more.

Many researchers use asterisks instead of p-values in their writing. A single asterisk signifies a p-value of .05; a double asterisk signifies a value of .01 or less; and a triple asterisk signifies a value of .001 or less. If you read: "Men were more likely than women** to report dissatisfaction with local schoolteacher training," you'll know that the double asterisk means that the difference between men and women on this variable was significant at the .01 level or better. (**Further Reading:** statistical significance. And see the discussion on significance tests in Chapter 21.)

And conversely: If the mean or a proportion of a sample is likely to occur by chance less than alpha, then we *reject the null hypothesis*. Alpha defines the critical region of a sampling distribution—that is, the fraction of the sampling distribution small enough to reject the null hypothesis.

In neither case do we prove the research hypothesis, H_1. We either reject or we fail to reject the null hypothesis. Failing to reject the null hypothesis is the best we can do, since, in a probabilistic science, we can't ever really prove any research hypothesis beyond any possibility of being wrong.

Type I and Type II Errors

There is one more piece to the logic of hypothesis testing. The choice of an alpha level lays us open to making one of two kinds of error—called, conveniently, **Type I errors** and **Type II errors**. If we reject the null hypothesis when it's really true, that's a Type I error. If we fail to reject the null hypothesis when it is, in fact, false, that's a Type II error.

Suppose we set alpha at .05 and make a Type I error. Our particular sample produced a mean or a proportion that happened to fall in one of the 2.5% tails of the distribution (2.5% on either side accounts for 5% of all cases), but 95% of all cases would have resulted in a mean that let us reject the null hypothesis.

Consider a program to teach restaurant workers to wash their hands after going to the bathroom and returning to work. A successful program would increase public safety by decreasing the probability of transmitting disease.

We'll set this up as a field experiment, assigning some restaurants in a large chain to the experimental condition (the workers get the new program) and some to the control condition (their workers are not exposed to the new program). We'll use a chain because chains tend to hire workers at the same level of education. This will keep education from being a confound to the validity of our findings. We'll take some before and after measures for both groups. We might, for example, use an unobtrusive trace measure, like whether the paper towel dispenser had been used after each employee returned from the bathroom.

The null hypothesis is that the proposed program is useless. If you try the program out and the results show, at the .05 level of significance, that you can reject the null hypothesis, that would be great news. But suppose that H_0 is true (the program is useless) but is rejected at the .05 level. This Type I error sets off a flurry of activity: The health department proposes regulations; the city passes legislation requiring restaurant owners to shell out for the program; and so on. And for what?

The obvious way to guard against this Type I error is to raise the bar and set alpha at, say, .01. That way, a Type I error would be made once in a hundred tries, not five times in a hundred. But you see immediately the cost of this little ploy: It increases dramatically the probability of making a Type II error—not rejecting H_0 when we should do exactly that. Failing to reject the null hypothesis, we conclude that the clean-hands program is useless. This places the public at greater risk.

In a probabilistic science, we are always in danger of making one or the other of these errors. Do we try to avoid one kind more than the other? It depends on what's at stake. A Type I error in testing the clean-hands program protects the public, but puts strain on employers and the health department for increased oversight. A Type II error does more-or-less the opposite.

The correct choice here is not so obvious. Suppose the clean-hands program works, but costs, say, $10,000,000 to eliminate six additional cases per year of low-level food poisoning in a city of half a million people. How about $10,000 to eliminate 50 cases? A Type I error at the .01 level for an HIV test means that one person out of 100 is declared HIV-free when they are really HIV-positive. How many dollars are you willing to spend to get that level down to one out of 1,000?

So, What About the Mean of WELF06?

As you know from Chapter 6, statistics (like the mean) vary from sample to sample and how much they vary depends on: (1) the size of the sample; and (2) the amount of actual variation in the population from which you take your sample. The average amount of error we make in estimating a parameter from sample statistics is called the **standard error**, or **SE**, of the statistic. The SEM, or standard error of the mean, is the standard deviation, *sd*, divided by the square root of the sample size, *n*

$$SEM = sd / \sqrt{n} \qquad \text{formula 20.6}$$

We can calculate the SEM for the sample of 10 states on the variable WELF06. From Table 20.9, we know that:

$$\bar{x} = 2.00 \text{ and}$$

$$sd = 1.92$$

so:

$$SEM = 1.92 / \sqrt{10} = 0.61$$

Now, knowing the SEM, we can ask whether the random sample of 10 cases in Table 20.9 represents the total population (shown in Table 20.7) from which it was drawn. In other words: Does $\bar{x} = 2.00$ in Table 20.9 represent the real mean of the population in Table 20.7?

Testing the Means of Small Samples: The Univariate t-Test

Since this is a small sample, we can test this using Student's *t* distribution, which I introduced in Chapter 6 (see Figure 6.7). If we use all 51 data points in Table 20.7, we can calculate the true mean of WELF06: In 2006, on average, 1.49% of the people across the United States were receiving support from the Temporary Assistance to Needy Families program.

This produces a strong null hypothesis: Based on our sample of data, the mean of the population (those 50 states, plus Washington, DC) from which we drew the sample is, *in fact*, 2.00%. And here is the equally strong alternative, or research hypothesis: Based on our sample of data, the mean of the population (those 50 states, plus Washington, DC) from which we drew the sample is *not* 2.00%.

The formula for calculating *t*, when the parameter, μ, is known, is:

$$t = \frac{\bar{x} - \mu}{SEM} \qquad \text{formula 20.7}$$

So, for the sample of 10 states on WELF in 2006

$$\frac{2.00 - 1.49}{0.61} = 0.84$$

Test whether *t* is statistically significant by referring to the *t*-table in Appendix B. To use Appendix B you need to know two things: how many degrees of freedom you have and whether you want a one-tailed test or a two-tailed test (Box 20.7).

Box 20.7 On degrees of freedom

To understand the concept of degrees of freedom, suppose I give you a jar filled with thousands of beans numbered from one to nine and ask you to pick two that sum to 10. If you pick a 4 on the first draw, then you must pick a 6 on the next; if you pick a 5 on the first draw, then you must pick another 5; and so on. This is an example of one degree of freedom, because after the first draw you have no degrees of freedom left.

Suppose, instead, that I ask you to pick four beans that sum to 25. In this example, you have three degrees of freedom. No matter what you pick on the first draw, there are lots of combinations you can pick on the next three draws and still have the beans sum to 25. But if you pick a 6, a 9, and a 7 on the first *three* draws, then you must pick a 3 on the last draw. You've run out of degrees of freedom.

For a one-sample, or univariate *t*-test, the degrees of freedom, or df, is simply $n - 1$. For the sample of 10 representing WELF06, there are $10 - 1 = 9$ degrees of freedom.

Testing the Value of t

We'll use a two-tailed test for the problem here because we are only interested in whether our sample mean, 2.00, is significantly *different from*, not *bigger than*, the population mean of 1.49. Looking at the values in Appendix B, we see that any *t*-value above 2.262 is statistically significant at the .05 level with 9 degrees of freedom. With a *t*-value of 0.84, *we cannot reject the null hypothesis* that the mean of the population (those 50 states, plus Washington, DC) from which we drew the sample is 1.49.

In other words, reaching in and grabbing samples of 10 from the 51 cases of WELF06 in Table 20.7, we could get the sample mean of 2.00 more than five times out of 100 tries just by chance. *Our sample mean is not statistically different from the population mean.*

TESTING THE MEANS OF LARGE SAMPLES: USING Z-SCORES

Another way to see this is to apply what we learned about the normal distribution in Chapter 6. We know that in any normal distribution for a large population, 68.26% of the statistics for estimating parameters will fall within one standard error of the actual parameter; 95% of the estimates will fall between the mean and 1.96 standard errors; and 99% of the estimates will fall between the mean and 2.58 standard errors.

In Table 20.1, I showed you a small sample of the data from the study that Ryan, Borgatti, and I did on attitudes about environmental activism. In that study, we interviewed a random sample of 609 adults from across the United States. The mean age of respondents in our sample was 44.21, *sd* 15.75. Only 591 respondents agreed to tell us their age, so the standard error of the mean is:

$$\frac{15.75}{\sqrt{591}} = 0.648$$

Since we have a large sample, we can calculate the 95% confidence limits using the *z* distribution (Appendix A):

$$44.21 \pm 1.96(0.648) = 44.21 - 1.27 = 42.94$$

and

$$44.21 + 1.27 = 45.28$$

In other words, we expect that 95% of all samples of 591 taken from the 89 million adults in the United States in 1997, when we did our survey, are between the ages of 42.94 and 45.48. As we saw in Chapter 6, these numbers are the 95% confidence limits of the mean. As it happens, we know from the U.S. Census Bureau that the real average age of the adult (over-18) population in the United States in 1997 was 44.98.

Thus: (1) the sample statistic ($\bar{x} = 44.21\%$) and (2) the parameter ($\mu = 44.98\%$) *both* fall within the 95% confidence limits, and we *cannot reject the null hypothesis* that our sample comes from a population whose average age is equal to our sample mean.

More About z-Scores

As we saw also in Chapter 6 on sampling, every real score in a distribution has a z-score, also called a **standard score**. A z-score tells you how far, in standard deviations, a real score is from the mean of the distribution. The formula for finding a z-score is:

$$z = \frac{raw\ score - \bar{x}}{sd}$$
formula 20.8

The mean for the welfare (WELFF06) data in Table 20.9 is 2.00 and the standard deviation is 1.92. To find the z-scores of the data on welfare in Table 20.9, subtract 2.00 from each raw score and divide the result by 1.92. Table 20.11 shows these z-scores.

Why Use Standard Scores?

There are several advantages to using standard scores rather than raw scores. First of all, while raw scores are always in specialized units (percentages of people, kilos of meat, hours of time, etc.), standard scores measure the difference, in standard deviations, between a raw score and the mean of the set of scores. A z-score close to zero means that the raw score was close to the average. A z-score that is close to plus-or-minus 1 means that the raw score was about one *sd* deviation from the mean, and so on.

What this means, in practice, is that when you standardize a set of scores, you create a scale that lets you make comparisons *within* chunks of your data.

For example, we see from Table 20.11 that the welfare rates for Minnesota and Washington,

| Table 20.11 | z-Scores for the Data in Table 20.9 on Welfare Rates |

STATE	WELF06 x	z-score
Alabama	1.0	−0.5208
California	3.3	0.6771
Colorado	0.8	−0.6250
Washington, DC	6.8	2.5000
Idaho	0.2	−0.9375
Minnesota	1.6	−0.2083
New York	2.4	0.2083
North Dakota	1.1	−0.4688
Washington	2.1	0.10417
Wisconsin	0.7	−0.6771

DC, are 1.6% and 6.8%, respectively. One of these raw numbers (6.8%) is about four times the other (1.6%). But the z-scores tell us more: The rate for Minnesota is two-tenths of a *sd* below the mean, while the rate for Washington, DC, is two-and-a-half *sd* above the mean. Similarly, the raw welfare rate for California (3.3%) is three times the rate for North Dakota (1.1%), but the rates for North Dakota and California are about half a *sd* below and two-thirds of a *sd* above the mean, respectively.

A second advantage of standard scores over raw measurements is that standard scores are independent of the units in which the original measurements are made. This means that you can compare the relative position of cases across different variables.

Medical social scientists measure variables called "weight-for-length" and "length for age" in the study of nutritional status of infants across cultures. Linda Hodge and Darna Dufour (1991) studied the growth and development of Shipibo Indian children in Peru. They weighed and measured 149 infants, from newborns to 36 months in age.

By converting all measurements for height and weight to *z*-scores, they were able to compare their measurements of the Shipibo babies against standards set by the World Health Organization (Frisancho 1990) for healthy babies. The result: By the time Shipibo children are 12 months old, 77% of boys and 42% of girls have *z*-scores of –2 or more on *length-for-age*. In other words, by a year old, Shipibo babies are more than two standard deviations under the mean for healthy babies on this measure.

By contrast, only around 10% of Shipibo babies (both sexes) have *z*-scores of –2 or worse on weight-for-length. By a year, then, most Shipibo babies are clinically "stunted" but they are not clinically "wasted." This does not mean that Shipibo babies are just small-but-healthy. Infant mortality is as high as 50% in some villages, and the *z*-scores on all three measures are similar to scores found in many developing countries where children suffer from malnutrition (Box 20.8).

Box 20.8 The unintuitive *z*-score problem

There is one disadvantage to *z*-scores: Imagine trying to explain to people who have not had any instruction in statistics why you are so proud of scoring a 1.96 on one of the SATs. That *z*-score—not quite two standard deviations above the average—means that just 2.5% of all test takers scored higher than you did. The fact that *z*-scores are negative as well as positive doesn't make things any easier. A *z*-score of –0.50 on an SAT test means that about 33% of all test takers scored lower than you did.

This is why **T-scores** were invented. *T*-scores are **linear transformations** of *z*-scores. The mean of a set of *z*-scores is always 0 and its standard deviation is always 1. For the SAT, GRE, and some other achievement tests, the mean is set at 500 and the standard deviation is set at 100. A score of 400 on these tests, then, is one standard deviation below the mean; a score of 740 is 2.4 standard deviations above the mean (Friedenberg 1995:85).

THE UNIVARIATE CHI-SQUARE TEST

Chi-square (often written χ^2) is a test of whether the distribution of a series of counts is likely to be a chance event. We'll see it again in Chapter 21, on bivariate analysis, but it's also important in univariate analysis. The formula for χ^2 is:

$$\chi^2 = \sum \frac{(O - E)^2}{E} \qquad \text{formula 20.9}$$

where O represents the observed number of cases and E represents the number of cases

you'd expect, *ceteris paribus*, or "all other things being equal."

Suppose that among 14 families there is a total of 42 children. If children were distributed equally among the 14 families, we'd expect each family to have three of them. Table 20.12, on the univariate chi-square, shows what we would expect and what we found. The χ^2 value for this distribution is 30.65.

Finding the Significance of χ^2

To determine whether this value of χ^2 is significant, first calculate the degrees of freedom (abbreviated df) for the problem.

Table 20.12 Chi-Square for a Univariate Distribution

Family #														
1	2	3	4	5	6	7	8	9	10	11	12	13	14	
Expected number of children per family														
3	3	3	3	3	3	3	3	3	3	3	3	3	3	Total = 42
Observed number of children per family														
0	0	5	5	5	6	6	0	0	3	1	0	6	5	Total = 42
(Observed – Expected)^2														
9	9	4	4	4	9	9	9	9	0	4	9	9	4	
$\dfrac{(Observed - Expected)^2}{Expected}$														
3	3	1.33	1.33	1.33	3	3	3	3	0	1.33	3	3	1.33	

$$\chi^2 = \sum \frac{(O-E)^2}{E} = 3 + 3 + 1.33 + 1.33\ldots + 1.33 = 30.65$$

For a univariate table: df = the number of cells, minus one, or $14 - 1 = 13$ in this case.

Next, go to Appendix C, which is the distribution for χ^2, and read down the left-hand margin to 13 degrees of freedom and across to find the *critical value* of χ^2 for any given level of significance. The levels of significance are listed across the top of the table.

The greater the significance of a χ^2 value, the less likely it is that the distribution you are testing is the result of chance. A χ^2 value of 22.362 for the problem in Table 20.12, with 13 degrees of freedom, is significant at the .05 level; a value of 27.688 is significant at the .01 level; and a value of 34.528 is significant at the

.001 level. With a χ^2 of 30.65, we can say that the distribution of the number of children across the 14 families is statistically significant at better than the .01 level, but not at the .001 level.

Statistical significance here means only that the distribution of number of children for these 14 families is not likely to be a chance event. Perhaps half the families happen to be at the end of their fertility careers, while half are just starting. Perhaps half the families are members of a high-fertility ethnic group, and half are not. The *substantive* significance of these data requires interpretation, based on your knowledge of what's going on, on the ground.

AND FINALLY . . .

Univariate numerical analysis—frequencies, means, distributions, and so on—and univariate graphical analysis—histograms, box plots, frequency polygons, and so on—tell us a lot. Begin all analysis this way and let all your data and your experience guide you in their interpretation. It is not always possible, however, to simply scan your data and use univariate, descriptive statistics to understand the subtle relations that they harbor. That will require more complex techniques, coming up in the next two chapters.

Key Concepts in This Chapter

descriptive analysis
inferential analysis
univariate analysis
bivariate analysis
multivariate analysis
qualitative variable
frequency distributions
frequency table
grouped data
central tendency
mode
median
mean
ratios
percentiles
first quartile
third quartile
interquartile range
social indicators
outliers
bar graphs
pie charts
stem-and-leaf plots
box-and-whisker plots
histograms

frequency polygons
abcissa
ordinate
lower hinge
upper hinge
positive skew
negative skew
bimodal distribution
multimodal distribution
dispersion
range
measure of dispersion
standard deviation
variance
logic of hypothesis
    testing
null hypothesis
research hypothesis
alternative hypothesis
magnitude
directional hypotheses
nondirectional
    hypotheses
one-tailed test
two-tailed test

alpha level
level of significance
p-value (probability value)
.05 level of significance
statistical significane
substantive
    significance
critical region
Type I errors
Type II errors
standard error
standard error of
    the mean
univariate t-test
Student's t distribution
degrees of freedom
confidence limits
z-scores
standard scores
linear transformation
T-scores
linear transformations
chi-square (χ^2)
ceteris paribus
univariate chi-square test

Summary

- Quantitative data analysis involves univariate, bivariate, and multivariate analysis.
  - Univariate analysis involves getting to know data intimately by examining variables precisely and in detail.

- o Bivariate analysis involves looking at associations between pairs of variables and trying to understand how those associations work.
- o Multivariate analysis involves understanding the effects of more than one independent variable at a time on a dependent variable.
- The first thing to do in dealing with quantitative data is to lay them out in tables and in graphs and get a feel for them.
- Good codebooks are indispensable.

  - o Naming variables is something of an art, but research projects typically have dozens, even hundreds of variables. You can be as clever as you like with variable names, but include a verbose description of each variable in your codebook so you'll know what all those clever names mean a year later.
- Frequency distributions show the frequency of each attribute of a variable.
  - o If a variable has no variability, then it is of no further interest for data analysis.
  - o Frequency distributions give you hints about how to collapse variables.
- The first thing to do is get some overall measure of the "typical" value for each variable. This is called a measure of central tendency. Social researchers rely on three main measures of central tendency: the mode, the median, and the mean.

  - o The mode is the attribute of a variable that occurs most frequently. The mode can be found for nominal, ordinal, and interval-level variables, but it is the only measure of central tendency available for nominal variables. The mode is often reported in terms of percentages or ratios.
  - o The median is the point in a distribution above and below which there are an equal number of scores in a distribution. The median can be found for ordinal and interval-level variables. The median is the 50th percentile in a distribution.
  - o The mean, or the average, is the sum of the individual scores in a distribution, divided by the number of scores. The mean can be found for ordinal and interval-level variables. The sum of the deviations from the mean of all the scores in a distribution is zero.
  - o The mean is heavily influenced by special cases, called outliers, and even in large samples, it's heavily influenced by big gaps in the distribution of cases. When data are normally distributed, the mean is the best indicator of central tendency. When interval data are highly skewed, the median is often a better indicator of central tendency.
- A good first cut at understanding whether data are normally distributed or skewed is to lay them out graphically. Among the most widely used methods for graphing data are: bar charts and pie charts for nominal and ordinal variables; stem-and-leaf plots, box-and-whisker plots, histograms, and frequency polygons for interval variables.

  - o In bar charts, the bars do not touch one another. This indicates that the data are nominal or ordinal and not continuous.
  - o Stem-and-leaf plots and box plots show the median (the 50th percentile) and the lower and upper hinges (the 25th and 75th percentiles). The whiskers in box plots extend one-and-a-half times the interquartile range from the lower and the upper hinges of the box. When data are normally distributed, this will be about 2.7 standard deviations from the mean. Cases outside that range are outliers.

- o Histograms are bar charts, but the bars touch one another, indicating that the data are continuous. Frequency polygons are continuous line drawings of the same data that produce histograms. You connect the tops of the bars of a histogram and display the result without the bars. Frequency polygons and box plots help you see whether a distribution is normal or skewed to the right or to the left.
  - o Bimodal distributions are everywhere. Be on the lookout for them.
- After central tendency and shape, the next thing we want to know about data is something about how homogeneous or heterogeneous they are—that is, something about their dispersion.

  - o For interval scale variables, the most important measures of dispersion are variance and the standard deviation.
  - o The standard deviation is calculated from the variance, written s^2, which is the average squared deviation from the mean of the measures in a set of data.
- Testing whether a sample mean is likely to represent the true mean of a population involves testing a hypothesis.

  - o The logic of hypothesis testing involves setting up a null hypothesis, H_0, and an alternative hypothesis, H_1, and then trying to falsify the null hypothesis.
  - o This, in turn, involves establishing a probability level—the so-called critical region—for rejecting the null hypothesis and deciding whether to use a one- or a two-tailed test.
  - o If we reject the null hypothesis when it's really true, that's a Type I error. If we fail to reject the null hypothesis when it is, in fact, false, that's a Type II error. In a probabilistic science, we are always in danger of making one or the other of these errors. Deciding which to avoid depends on what's at stake and the resources available.
- For small samples, we can test whether the mean of a sample is likely to represent the mean of the population from which it was drawn using a t-test. For large samples, we use the z distribution.

  - o Standardized scores, or z-scores, let us compare the relative position of cases across different variables.
- The univariate chi-square tests whether the distribution of actual cases conforms statistically to the distribution we expect in a set of cases.

Exercises

1. Table 20.E.1 shows suicide rates for the 50 states of the United States in 2006:

Calculate the mean and standard deviation for these data. What happens if you don't count the data for Nevada and New Mexico? How much does that change the mean and the standard deviation?

Group these data into four chunks: (1) less than 10 per 100,000; (2) from 10 to 12 per 100,000; (3) from 12.1 to 15; and (4) more than 15 per 100,000. Calculate the median and the mean of these grouped data.

Draw a histogram and a frequency polygon (you can do this by hand or use a computer program) for the 50 data points. If you use a program, draw a stem-and-leaf plot and a box plot for these data. What is the range and the interquartile range?

Take a random sample of 15 data points and calculate the mean for the sample. Using alpha = .05, test whether the mean of the sample reflects the mean of the population of 50 elements.

2. Suppose you are participating in the development of a new program to prepare prison inmates for parole into the community. The null hypothesis is that the program doesn't work. Discuss the consequences of making a Type I or a Type II error in assessing the null hypothesis. Consider the consequences if the recipients of the program were originally incarcerated for violent or for nonviolent crimes.

3. Use the *t*-distribution to find the 95% and 99% confidence limits for $\bar{x} = 30$, $sd = 6$, $n = 18$. What happens to the confidence limits if $n = 40$?

Table 20.E.1 Suicide Rates for the 50 U.S. States, per 100,000 Population, 2006

Alabama	12.4	Hawaii	9.2	Massachusetts	6.7	New Mexico	18.0	S. Dakota	16.0
Alaska	20.0	Idaho	15.6	Michigan	11.1	New York	6.6	Tennessee	14.2
Arizona	16.0	Illinois	7.8	Minnesota	10.6	N. Carolina	12.2	Texas	10.3
Arkansas	13.3	Indiana	13.0	Mississippi	11.4	N. Dakota	13.6	Utah	15.8
California	9.2	Iowa	11.1	Missouri	13.5	Ohio	11.2	Vermont	12.0
Colorado	15.2	Kansas	13.8	Montana	19.7	Oklahoma	15.0	Virginia	11.1
Connecticut	8.0	Kentucky	14.6	Nebraska	11.2	Oregon	15.2	Washington	12.3
Delaware	10.4	Louisiana	11.6	Nevada	19.5	Pennsylvania	10.8	W. Virginia	14.1
Florida	12.6	Maine	11.0	New Hampshire	11.0	Rhode Island	8.1	Wisconsin	11.9
Georgia	10.0	Maryland	8.6	New Jersey	6.5	S. Carolina	11.9	Wyoming	21.7

Source: U.S. Statistical Abstracts, Table 118, 2006.

Further Reading

Univariate analysis. All the methods described in this chapter and the next two chapters are treated more fully in texts on statistical methods. A general text on research methods is only meant as an introduction to the range of methods available.

Visualizing data. Carr (2008), Chen et al. (2008), Friendly (2000), Jacoby (1997), Klanten et al. (2008), Tufte (1997, 2001, 2006), Wallgren et al. (1996), Ward et al. (2010).

Statistical significance. Chow (1996), Harlow et al. (1997), Hyat (2010), Leahy (2005), Lempert (2009). And see the discussion on significance testing in Chapter 21.

21

Bivariate Analysis
Testing Relations

INTRODUCTION

This chapter is about describing relations between pairs of variables—covariations—and testing the significance of those relations.

The *qualitative* concept of covariation shows up in everday conversation all the time: "If kids weren't exposed to so much TV violence, there would be less crime." Or: "If more cops were on the street, we wouldn't have so much crime." In these assertions, the rate of crime is said to covary positively with the exposure of children to violence on TV (the more exposure, the more crime) and negatively with the rate of cops on the street (the more cops, the less crime).

The concept of *statistical* covariation, however, is more precise than that used in ordinary conversation. There are two primary and two secondary things we want to know about a statistical relation between two variables:

The primary questions are these:

1. How big is it? In other words, how much better could we predict the score of a dependent variable in our sample if we knew the score of some independent variable? Statistics of various kinds answer this question.

2. Is the covariation due to chance, or is it likely to exist in the overall population to which we want to generalize? In other words, is it statistically significant? Statistical tests answer this question.

For many problems, we also want to know:

3. What is its direction? Is it positive or negative?

4. What is its shape? Is it linear or nonlinear?

Answers to these questions about qualities of a relationship are best sought by looking at graphs.

Testing for **statistical significance** is a mechanical affair—you look up, in a table, whether a statistic showing covariation between two variables is or is not significant. I'll discuss how to do this for several of the commonly used statistics that I introduce below. As you already know, statistical significance does not necessarily mean substantive or theoretical importance. Interpreting the substantive and theoretical importance of statistical significance is anything but mechanical. It requires thinking, and that's *your* job.

THE *t*-TEST: COMPARING TWO MEANS

We begin our exploration of bivariate analysis with the two-sample *t*-test. In Chapter 20, we saw how to use the one-sample *t*-test to evaluate the probability that the mean of a sample reflects the mean of the population from which the sample was drawn. The two-sample *t*-test evaluates whether the means of two independent groups differ on some variable. Table 21.1 shows data

Table 21.1 Number of Children Wanted (CW) by College Students in the U.S. and Liberia, 1977

No.	CW	REGION	SEX	No.	CW	REGION	SEX	No.	CW	REGION	SEX
1	1	U.S.	M	29	0	U.S.	F	57	12	Liberia	M
2	3	U.S.	M	30	0	U.S.	F	58	12	Liberia	M
3	3	U.S.	M	31	0	U.S.	F	59	8	Liberia	M
4	3	U.S.	M	32	0	U.S.	F	60	6	Liberia	M
5	3	U.S.	M	33	1	U.S.	F	61	4	Liberia	M
6	3	U.S.	M	34	1	U.S.	F	62	4	Liberia	M
7	2	U.S.	M	35	2	U.S.	F	63	2	Liberia	M
8	2	U.S.	M	36	2	U.S.	F	64	3	Liberia	M
9	2	U.S.	M	37	2	U.S.	F	65	3	Liberia	M
10	2	U.S.	M	38	2	U.S.	F	66	4	Liberia	M
11	2	U.S.	M	39	2	U.S.	F	67	4	Liberia	M
12	2	U.S.	M	40	2	U.S.	F	68	4	Liberia	M
13	1	U.S.	M	41	2	U.S.	F	69	4	Liberia	M
14	6	U.S.	M	42	2	U.S.	F	70	3	Liberia	F
15	1	U.S.	M	43	2	U.S.	F	71	3	Liberia	F
16	1	U.S.	M	44	6	Liberia	M	72	3	Liberia	F
17	4	U.S.	M	45	4	Liberia	M	73	3	Liberia	F
18	0	U.S.	M	46	4	Liberia	M	74	7	Liberia	F
19	5	U.S.	F	47	4	Liberia	M	75	2	Liberia	F
20	4	U.S.	F	48	5	Liberia	M	76	4	Liberia	F
21	4	U.S.	F	49	5	Liberia	M	77	6	Liberia	F
22	4	U.S.	F	50	5	Liberia	M	78	4	Liberia	F
23	3	U.S.	F	51	5	Liberia	M	79	4	Liberia	F
24	2	U.S.	F	52	5	Liberia	M	80	4	Liberia	F
25	3	U.S.	F	53	7	Liberia	M	81	4	Liberia	F
26	0	U.S.	F	54	12	Liberia	M	82	4	Liberia	F
27	2	U.S.	F	55	6	Liberia	M	83	4	Liberia	F
28	0	U.S.	F	56	6	Liberia	M	84	4	Liberia	F

Source: Data supplied by P. W. Handwerker.

collected in the 1960s by W. Penn Handwerker from American and Liberian college students on how many children they wanted.

Table 21.2 shows the relevant statistics for the data in Table 21.1. I generated the stats in Table 21.2 with SYSTAT®, but you can use any statistics package.

There are 43 American students and 41 Liberian students. The Americans wanted, on average, 2.047 children, *sd* 1.396, SEM 0.213. The Liberians wanted, on average, 4.951 children, *sd* 2.387, SEM 0.373.

The null hypothesis, H_0, is that these two means, 2.047 and 4.951, come from random samples of the *same* population—that there is no difference, except for sampling error, between the two means. Stated another way, these two means come from random samples of two populations with identical averages. The research hypothesis, H_1, is that these two means, 2.047 and 4.951, come from random samples of truly different populations.

The formula for calculating *t* for two independent samples is:

$$t = \frac{\bar{x}_1 - \bar{x}_2}{\sqrt{\sigma^2 \left(\frac{1}{n_1} + \frac{1}{n_2} \right)}} \quad \text{formula 21.1}$$

| Table 21.2 | Descriptive Statistics for Data in Table 21.1 |

	CW-USA	CW-W.A.
N of cases	43	41
Minimum	0	2
Maximum	6	12
Mean	2.047	4.951
95% CI Upper	2.476	5.705
95% CI Lower	1.617	4.198
Std. Error	0.213	0.373
Standard Dev	1.396	2.387

That is, *t* is the difference between the means of the samples, divided by the fraction of the standard deviation σ, of the total population, that comes from each of the two separate populations from which the samples were drawn. (Remember, we use Roman letters, like *s*, for sample statistics, and Greek letters, like σ, for parameters.) Since the standard deviation is the square root of the variance, we need to know the variance, σ^2, of the parent population.

The parent population is the general population from which the two samples were pulled. Our best guess at σ^2 is to pool the standard deviations from the two samples:

$$\sigma^2 = \frac{(n_1 - 1)s_1^2 + (n_2 - 1)s_2^2}{n_1 + n_2 - 2} \quad \text{formula 21.2}$$

which is very messy, but just a lot of arithmetic. For the data on the two groups of students, the pooled variance is:

$$\sigma^2 = \frac{(43 - 1)1.396^2 + (41 - 1)2.387^2}{43 + 41 - 2}$$

$$= \frac{81.85 + 227.91}{82} = 3.778$$

Now we can solve for *t*:

$$t = \frac{2.047 - 4.951}{\sqrt{3.778(.0477)}} = \frac{-2.904}{\sqrt{.180}}$$

$$= \frac{-2.904}{.4243} = 6.844$$

Testing the Value of *t*

We can evaluate the statistical significance of *t* using Appendix B. Recall from Chapter 20 that we need to calculate the degrees of freedom and decide whether we want a one-tailed or a two-tailed test to find the critical region for rejecting the null hypothesis. For a two-sample t-test, the degrees of freedom equal $(n_1 + n_2) - 2$, so there are $43 = 41 - 2 = 82$ degrees of freedom in this particular problem.

If you test the possibility that one mean will be higher than another, then you need a one-tailed test. After all, you're only asking whether the mean is likely to fall in one tail of the t-distribution (see Figure 6.7). If you want to test only whether the two means are different, and not that one will be higher than the other, then you need a two-tailed test. Notice in Appendix B that scores significant at the .10 level for a two-tailed test are significant at the .05 level for a one-tailed test; scores significant at the .05 level for a two-tailed test are significant at the .025 level for a one-tailed test, and so on.

We'll use a two-tailed test for the problem here because we are only interested in the magnitude of the difference between the means, not its direction or sign (plus or minus). We are only interested here, then, in the **modulus**, or absolute value of t, 6.844.

Looking at the values in Appendix B, we see that any t-value above 3.291 is significant for a two-tailed test at the .001 level. Assuming that our samples represent the populations of American students and Liberian students, we'd expect the observed difference in the means of how many children they want to occur by chance less than once every thousand times we run this survey.

An Example: The Bem Sex Role Inventory

Sandra Bem (1974) used the simple t-test to select items for the famous BSRI (the Bem Sex Role Inventory). She compiled a list of about 400 personality traits: about 100 positive traits that seemed feminine in tone, according to normative standards at the time (expressive, nurturing, etc.); another 100 positive traits that seemed masculine in tone (instrumental, take charge, etc.); about 100 positive, gender neutral traits; and about 100 negative, gender neutral traits.

Bem asked 100 Stanford University undergraduates to rate each of the 400 traits on a scale of 1–7, from "not at all desirable" to "extremely desirable." For example, two of the items were: "In American society, how desirable is it for a woman to be sincere?" and "In American society, how desirable is it for a man to be truthful?" If a trait were judged by both men and women to be significantly more desirable for a man than for a woman, then the trait was selected as a masculine trait; the same was done to select for feminine traits.

Bem used two-tailed t-tests to assess whether traits were significantly (alpha = .05) more masculine or more feminine and selected 10 positive and 10 negative traits, all of which scored high as either appropriately masculine or appropriately feminine, for the BSRI.

ANOVA—ANALYSIS OF VARIANCE

A t-test measures the difference between two means. Analysis of variance, or ANOVA, is a technique that applies to a set of k means.

Suppose you want to know whether a new method for teaching reading skills to fifth graders really makes a difference. You divide the fifth-grade classes in a school district into two groups—one group that uses the new teaching method and one group that does

Table 21.3	A Typical Experiment in Education	
	Average Score on the Pretest	Average Score on the Posttest
Classes using the new program	X_1	X_2
Classes using the old program	X_3	X_4

not. Both groups get tested before the program gets under way, and after the program is finished. (You'll recognize this method from Chapter 4 on experimental design.) Then the scores are compared. Table 21.3 is a schematic of the scores you'd be working with.

X_1, X_2, X_3, and X_4 in Table 21.3 are average scores. The question is: Are all the differences in these scores significant? Put another way (the null hypothesis): Despite differences in the scores, are they really from identical populations? Does it make any real difference in their reading skills if fifth graders are exposed to the new program?

This is where the *F* statistic for analysis of variance, comes in. Table 21.4 shows the scores for four groups of states in the United States (not including Washington, DC) on the percentage of teenage births in 2007. Each group of states has a mean percentage of teenage births. The question we want to answer is: Are the differences among the means significantly different, at say, the .05 level?

To answer this question we will calculate the ratio of the between-group variance, $S^2_{between}$ to the within-group variance, S^2_{within} The between-group and within-group

variances sum to the total variance, S^2. We already know, from Chapter 20, the formula for the total variance. Here it is again:

$$s^2 = \frac{\sum(x - \bar{x})^2}{n-1} \qquad \text{formula 21.3}$$

where *x* represents the raw scores in a distribution of interval-level observations, $\bar{x}$ is the mean of the distribution of raw scores, and *n* is the total number of observations. So, to find the variance in a distribution: (1) subtract each observation from the mean of the set of observations; (2) square the difference (thus getting rid of negative numbers); (3) sum the squared differences (this is called the **sum of the squares**); and (4) divide that sum by the sample size, minus 1.

The variance is calculated from the sum of the squares, $\sum(x - \bar{x})^2$. Here is the formula for calculating the sum of the squares directly from the data in Table 21.4:

$$\sum x^2 - \frac{\left(\sum x\right)^2}{n} \qquad \text{formula 21.4}$$

At the bottom of Table 21.4, I've calculated the four separate, or within-group, variances, using formula 21.3 above. Applying formula 21.4, the total sums of squares for the data in Table 21.4 is:

$$530.99 + 1,122.30 + 2,596.01 + 1,396.54$$
$$- \frac{(68.3 + 115 + 201.1 + 131.8)^2}{50}$$

$$= 5,645.84 - \frac{266,462.24}{50}$$

$$= 5,645.84 - 5,329.24 = 316.60$$

Table 21.4 Percentage of Teenage Births in the 50 U.S. States, 2007

Northeast X_1		X_1^2	Midwest X_2		X_2^2	South X_3		X_3^2	West X_4		X_4^2
NY	7.0	49	KS	10.3	106.09	FL	10.9	118.81	NM	15.7	246.49
VT	7.6	57.76	SD	9.8	96.04	AR	14.6	213.16	OR	8.9	79.21
NJ	6.4	40.96	WI	8.7	75.69	KY	12.9	166.41	ID	9.1	82.81
PA	9.3	86.49	IA	8.7	75.69	LA	13.7	187.69	HI	8.5	72.25
MA	6.4	40.96	IN	11.2	125.44	MD	8.9	79.21	NV	10.8	116.64
NH	6.6	43.56	OH	11.0	121.00	MS	17.1	292.41	CO	9.7	94.09
ME	8.4	70.56	ND	8.0	64.00	AL	13.6	334.89	UT	6.9	47.61
CN	6.9	47.61	MI	10.1	102.01	DE	10.4	108.16	CA	9.5	90.25
RI	9.7	94.09	MN	7.1	50.41	GA	12.2	148.84	WY	11.8	139.24
			MO	11.4	129.96	OK	13.9	193.21	WA	8.4	70.56
			NB	8.6	73.96	VA	8.6	73.96	AZ	12.7	161.29
			IL	10.1	102.01	NC	11.7	136.89	AK	10.1	102.01
						WV	12.5	156.25	MT	9.7	94.09
						TN	13.2	174.24			
						SC	13.4	179.56			
						TX	13.5	182.25			

$n = 9$	$n = 12$	$n = 16$	$n = 13$
$\bar{x}_1 = 7.589$	$\bar{x}_2 = 9.583$	$\bar{x}_3 = 12.862$	$\bar{x}_4 = 10.138$
$s_1^2 = 1.584$	$s_2^2 = 1.838$	$s_3^2 = 6.589$	$s_4^2 = 5.024$

$$\bar{x}_t = 10.324$$

The formula for calculating the sum of the squares between groups is:

$$\sum \frac{\sum(x_{1...2...n})^2}{n_{1...2...n}} - \frac{(\sum x_{total})^2}{n_{total}} \quad \text{formula 21.5}$$

Thus, the between-group sum of the squares is:

$$(68.3^2/9) + (115^2/12) + (211.1^2/16)$$
$$+ (131.8^2/13) - 5,329.24$$
$$= 518.32 + 1,102.08 + 2,785.20 + 1,336.25$$
$$- 5,329.24 = 154.99$$

And since:

within – group sum of square
= total sum of square – between-group
sum of square

the within-group sums of square is:

$$316.60 - 154.99 = 161.61$$

We can now calculate $s_{between}^2$, the between-group variance, and s_{within}^2, the within-group variance.

$$s_{between}^2 = \frac{\text{total between} - \text{group sums of squares}}{\text{the degrees of freedom between groups}}$$

and

$$s^2_{within=} \frac{\text{total between} - \text{group sums of squares}}{\text{the degrees of freedom within groups}}$$

We compute the degrees of freedom between groups and the degrees of freedom within groups as follows:

df between groups = the number of groups − 1

df within groups = n − the number of groups

So, for the data in Table 21.4, the df between groups is 4 − 1 = 3, and the df within groups is 50 − 4 = 46. Then:

the between-group variance = 154.99 / 3 = 51.66

and

the within-group variance = $\dfrac{161.61}{46}$ = 3.51

We now have all the information we need to calculate the F-ratio, which is:

$$\frac{s^2_{between}}{s^2_{within}}$$

(The F statistic was named for Sir Ronald Fisher, who developed the idea for the ratio of the between-group and the within-group variances as a general method for comparing the relative size of means across many groups.) We calculate the ratio of the variances:

$$F = \frac{51.66}{3.51} = 14.78$$

Well, is 14.78 a statistically significant number? (Box 21.1).

Box 21.1 Rounding error versus computer calculations

If you run the ANOVA on a computer, using SYSTAT® or SPSS®, you'll get a slightly different answer: 14.70. The difference (0.08) is due to **rounding error** from all the calculations we just did. Computer programs may hold on to 12 decimal places all the way through before returning an answer. In doing these calculations by hand, I've rounded each step of the way to just two decimal places. Rounding error doesn't affect the results of the ANOVA calculations in this particular example because the value of the F statistic is so big. But when the value of the F statistic is below 5, then relatively small rounding errors can lead to errors of interpretation.

The moral is: Learn how to do these calculations by hand, once. Then, use a computer program to do the work for you.

To find out, we go to Appendix D, which shows the values of F for the .05 and the .01 level of significance. The values for the between-group df are shown across the top of Appendix D, and the values for the within-group df are shown along the left side. Looking across the top of the table, we find the column for the between-group df. We come down that column to the value of the within-group df. In other words, we look down the column labeled 3 and come down to the row for 46.

There is no row for exactly 46 degrees of freedom for the within-group value, so we use the nearest value, which is for 40 df. We see that any F value greater than 2.84 is statistically significant at the .01 (that is, the 1%) level. The F value we got for the data in Table 21.4 was a colossal 14.78. It is very unlikely that the difference in the mean rate of births to teenage mothers across the four regions of the United States is the result of sampling error (Box 21.2).

Box 21.2 The relative rate of births to teenagers

Births to teenagers in the United States dropped by 20%, from 13% to 10.4% between 1996 and 2007. This drop reflects larger social forces, including an increase in education for women—about 86% of women in the United States graduate from high school and about 30% graduate from college, compared to 82% and 20% in the mid-1990s. The earning power that comes with increased education translates into postponement of fertility and part of this postponement is reflected in a lower percentage of births to teens.

Despite this, the correlation between the percentage of births to teens across the 50 U.S. states in 1996 and 2007 is 0.96. The rate of teen births is dropping, but the differences among the regions shown in this ANOVA example have remained remarkably stable.

An Example of ANOVA: Rating the Performance of Job Candidates

Prewett-Livingston et al. (1996) studied 86 African American and 67 White patrol officers (including 124 men and 29 women) who were candidates for promotion to the rank of sergeant in a city police force. As part of the regular promotion process, each candidate is interviewed by a panel of four people: three officers at the rank of sergeant or above and a psychologist, who is the panel leader. Prewett-Livingston et al. created six panels: two that were predominantly African American, comprised of one White and three African American interviewers; two that were predominantly White, comprised of one African American and three White interviewers; and two that were racially balanced. Then they assigned the 153 candidates randomly to one of the six panels.

Each panelist rated each candidate from 0 to 10 on 14 items (knowledge of procedure, communication skills, etc.). The 14 items were summed to form a single score for each candidate by each panelist. Then, the scores of the White panelists were averaged together and the scores of the African American panelists were averaged. Each candidate then had: (1) an average score by Whites on his or her panel; and (2) an average score by African Americans on his or her panel.

Prewett-Livingston et al. (2007) tested each of the three pairs of panels to make sure that the overall ratings were not statistically different from one another. Since the panels were reliable, Prewett-Livingston et al. combined the data from the two panels in each panel type. This set up a $3 \times 2 \times 2$ analysis of variance test: There are three panel types (primarily White, primarily African American, and racially balanced); two races for the candidates (African American and White); and two races for the interviewers (African American and White). Panel type and race of candidate are between-group variables, while race of interviewer is a within-group variable.

Analysis of variance showed evidence that the rated performance of candidates is affected by the race of the candidate and the racial composition of the panels. The effects, however, were not stereotypical. White and African American raters on majority White panels *both* tended to score White candidates higher than they scored African American candidates. Similarly, White and African American raters on majority African American panels *both* tended to score African American candidates higher than they scored White candidates (Box 21.3).

Box 21.3 More complex forms of ANOVA

Dependent variables in which social scientists are interested, and that are amenable to ANOVA, are things like: scores on tests of knowledge or attitudes, scores on personality tests, number of interpersonal contacts, blood pressure, number of minutes per day spent in various activities, number of grams of various nutrients consumed per day . . . to name just a few.

When there is one dependent variable (such as a test score) and one independent variable (a single intervention like the reading program), then no matter how many groups or tests are involved, a **one-way analysis of variance** is needed.

If more than one independent variable is involved (say, several competing new housing programs and several socioeconomic backgrounds), and a single dependent variable (like the scores on tests of attitudes toward welfare), then **multiple-way ANOVA** is called for.

If there are multiple dependent variables, then **MANOVA**, is called for. When two or more dependent variables are correlated with one another, then **analysis of covariance (ANCOVA)** techniques are used. Multiple-way ANOVA allows you to determine if there are interaction effects among independent variables. That is, with interval-level scores on independent variables, we can use ANOVA to measure the interaction effects among variables—to determine if a variable has different effects under different conditions.

DIRECTION AND SHAPE OF COVARIATIONS

As you can tell from my discussion of box plots and frequency polygons and such in Chapter 20, I like to look at things like shape and direction—qualitative things—in connection with numerical results. The direction of covariation refers to whether a covariation is positive or negative; the shape of covariation refers to whether a relation is linear or nonlinear.

For example, the amount of cholesterol you have in your blood and the probability that you will die of a heart attack at any given age are positive covariants: The *more* cholesterol, the *higher* the probability. Similarly, *the more violence* that children are exposed to on television and in video games, *the more aggressive* they are likely to be (C. A. Anderson et al. 2010; Huesmann et al. 2003).

By contrast, *the more education* you have, *the lower the probability that you smoke cigarettes*. Education and the probability of smoking cigarettes are **negative covariants**.

Some shapes and directions of bivariate relations are shown in the five scatterplots (also called scattergrams) of Figure 21.1. Figure 21.1a is a plot of the percentage of children, ages 5–17, in each of the 50 states in the United States (without Washington, DC) who were in public schools in 2006, and the percentage of adults in each of the 50 states who were in prison the following year. The dots are scattered haphazardly, and it's pretty obvious that there is *no relation*

Figure 21.1a

A Random Plot. There Is No Relation Between the Proportion of the Adult Population in Prison in 2007 and the Proportion of the School-Age Children Enrolled in School in the 50 States of the U.S. in 2006

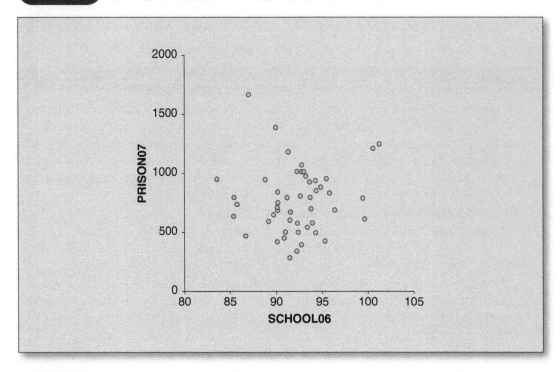

Figure 21.1b

A Linear, Negative Relation Between the Life Expectancy for Women and the Rate of Infant Mortality in Countries of the World, 2005–2010

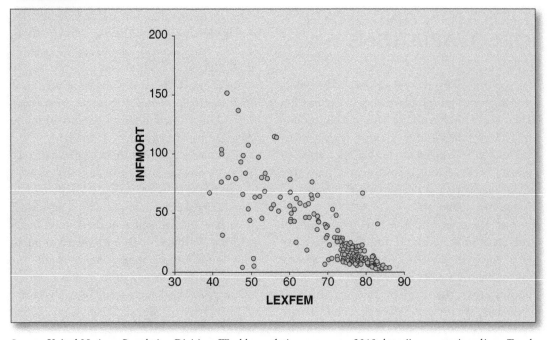

Source: United Nations, Population Division. World population prospects, 2010. http://esa.un.org/unpd/wpp/Excel-Data/mortality.htm. Accessed January 7, 2012.

Figure 21.1c A Linear, Positive Relation Between the Average per Capita Income and the Number of Physicians per Hundred Thousand Population for the 50 States of the U.S. in 2007

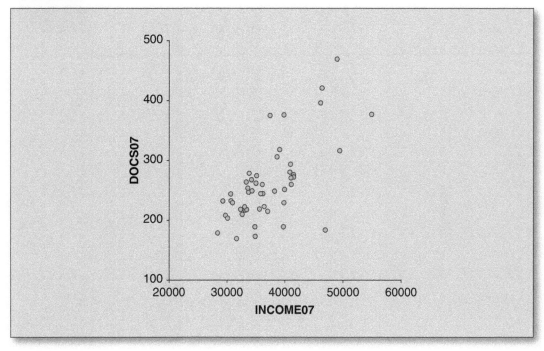

Source: Statistical Abstracts of the United States 2010, Tables 159, 664.

Figure 21.1d A Nonlinear Relation Between the per Capita Gross Domestic Product and the Rate of Infant Mortality in Countries of the World

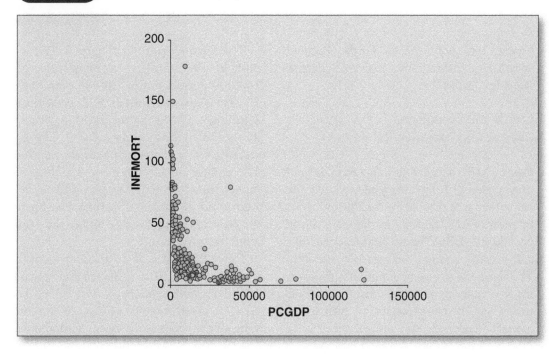

Source: The World Factbook. Central Intelligence Agency 2010. https://www.cia.gov/library/publications/the-world-factbook/rankorder/2091rank.html and https://www.cia.gov/library/publications/the-world-factbook/rankorder/2004rank.html

Figure 21.1e A Nonlinear Relation Between Age and the Number of Friends or Acquaintances People Have

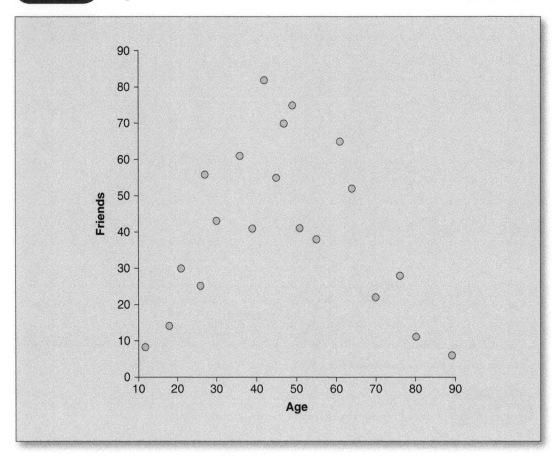

between these two variables (**Further Reading:** visualizing covariations. Also see **Further Reading,** Chapter 20).

Linear and Nonlinear, Positive and Negative Relations

Figure 21.1b is a plot of the infant mortality rate (the number of babies, per thousand, who die before they are a year old) by the life expectancy, for each of 225 countries in the world in the period 2005–2010. This is a clear case of a *linear and negative relation* between two variables: The higher the score on one variable, the lower the score tends to be on the other. So, in countries where the life expectancy is high, infant mortality tends to be low, and vice versa.

The third scatterplot, Figure 21.1c, is a plot of the number of physicians per 100,000 population in 2007 in each of the 50 states in the United States (without Washington, DC), by the average per capita income in those states in 2007. This is a clear case of a *linear and positive relation:* The higher the score on one variable, the higher the score tends to be on the other. Across the United States, then, the higher the per capita income, the higher the availability of physicians.

Figure 21.1d is a plot, for countries of the world in 2009–2010, of the relation between infant mortality and per capita GDP. The GDP, or gross domestic product, is the total value of the goods and services produced in a country. The per capita GDP at this time ranged from about $300 per person, for Burundi and the Republic of Congo, to $122,000 person in Lichtenstein. The dots in Figure 21.1d are not scattered around randomly—*something* is clearly going on between these two variables. As the per capita GDP rises, the rate of infant mortality falls, but the *shape* of the relation is *nonlinear*. (More on this later.)

Figure 21.1e shows another kind of nonlinear relation. The relation between age and the number of people one knows has this peaked shape. Early in life the number of friends, kin, and acquaintances is small, but that number grows as you get older. This relation is linear and positive. The longer you live, the more people you get to know.

Up to a point. If you live long enough, a lot of the people you know start dying, and your network shrinks. There is a strong, negative relation between age and number of people in your network after age 70. A special kind of correlation coefficient, called *eta*, measures the strength of this kind of nonlinear covariation, and I'll discuss it at the end of this chapter when we deal with regression.

CROSS-TABS OF NOMINAL VARIABLES

Now that we've looked at shape and direction, let's get down to actually looking for relations between variables. We begin with nominal variables and move on to ordinal and then interval variables.

Table 21.5 is an example of a cross-tab, or cross-tabulation table of two nominal variables. It's a 2 × 2 (read: two-by-two) cross-tabulation of household types (married-couples-with-children and single-female-parents-with-children) by so-called racial groups (White and African American) in the United States in 2008 (Box 21.4).

Table 21.5 Distribution of Family Types, by Race, in the U.S. in 2008

A 2 × 2 Table of Household Type by Race in the U.S. in 2008 (in Thousands)

	White	African American	Row Total
Married parents	21,165 (80%)	1,990 (43%)	23,155
Single female parent	5,298 (20%)	2,639 (57%)	7,937
Column total	26,463 (100%)	4,629 (100%)	31,092

Source: Table 66, Statistical Abstract of the United States (2010).

Box 21.4 About the social concept of race

I say so-called-race here because, as an anthropologist, I know how problematic that word *race* is. For most English speakers, race has a biological meaning, even though it is essentially a social concept, with hardly any biological utility when applied to humans.

I'm tempted to use the phrase *ethnic group* to refer to African Americans and Whites, but there are serious problems associated with that seemingly innocuous phrase, too. Applied to people whom the U.S. Census calls African Americans and Whites, the term *ethnic group*

(Continued)

(Continued)

implies that people who have similar skin color and who share common historical roots (their ancestors either arrived in North America from Africa or came from Europe) share an ethnicity. Italian Americans from New York, Hassidic Jews from Denver, Mennonites from rural Minnesota, Polish Americans from Detroit. . . . Do all these people really share the same ethnicity because they are white skinned and have ancestors who came from some place in Europe?

Consider the differences in the cultural content of people who are black-skinned, Cajun-English bilinguals from rural Louisiana; black-skinned, Gullah-English bilinguals of coastal South Carolina; and black-skinned residents of, say, New York City. Do all *these* people really share an ethnicity because they are black skinned and have ancestors who came from some place on the continent of Africa? The mind boggles at the thought of trying to force all these cultural groups into some kind of cookie-cutter mold because of such arbitrary characteristics as skin color and historical ancestry.

I use the word *race*, then, with all the qualifications it deserves. The data in Table 21.5 show pretty clearly that there is an association between skin color and family type. What *that* association is really about is worthy of serious investigation by social scientists.

Reading Percentage Tables

A 2 × 2 table is also called a four-fold table. Any table comparing data on two variables is called a **bivariate table**. Not all bivariate tables are 2 × 2, since variables can take more than just two values. Table 21.6 shows a 3 × 2 (read: three-by-two) table of marital status by sex in the United States in 2009. In these tables, the numbers are in thousands and the numbers in parentheses are *column percentages*. In Table 21.5, we see that there were 26,463,000 households in the United States in 2008 with children under the age of 18 and classified by the Bureau of the Census as White. Of those, 21,165,000, or 80% of the 26,463,000, had two parents, and 5,298,000 (20%) had one parent.

Many researchers display only the column percentages in a bivariate table, along with the column totals, or Ns, and a summary statistic that describes the table. This convention is shown in Table 21.7. Tables are less cluttered this way, and you get a better understanding of what's going on from percentages than from raw numbers in a bivariate table. As long as

Table 21.6 A 3 × 2 Table of Marital Status by Sex in 2009 (in thousands)

	Male	Female	Row Total
Married and living together	60,844 (36.7%)	60,844 (68.5%)	121,688
Widowed	2,813 (1.7%)	11,441 (12.9%)	14,254
Divorced or separated	101,916 (61.6%)	16,486 (18.6%)	118,402
Column total	165,573 (100%)	88,771 (100%)	254,344

Source: U.S. Census Bureau. America's Families and Living Arrangements, Table A2. http://www.census.gov/population/www/socdemo/hh-fam/cps2009.html

the row totals and column totals are given, the interested reader can easily reconstruct the Ns for each cell.

Table 21.7

A 2 × 2 Table of Household Type by Race in the U.S. in 2008 (in thousands), With Percentages in the Cells and Ns in the Margins

	White	African American	Row Total
Married parents	(80%)	(43%)	23,155
Single female parent	(20%)	(57%)	7,937
Column total	26,463 (100%)	4,629 (100%)	31,092

Source: Table 66, Statistical Abstract of the United States (2010).

Numbers along the right side and below a table—that is, the numbers in the margins—are called, unsurprisingly, the marginals. The marginal in the lower-right-hand corner of Tables 21.5 and 21.7 (31,092) is the total frequency of elements in the table. The sum of the marginals down the right-hand side and the sum of the marginals across the bottom are identical.

CORRELATION AND CAUSE: ANTECEDENT AND INTERVENING VARIABLES

Note that the column percentages sum to 100% and that since we have percentaged the tables down the columns, it makes no sense to total the percentages in the right margin. In constructing bivariate tables, no matter what size (2 × 2, 3 × 2, or larger tables), we put the dependent variable in the rows and the independent variable in the columns. Then there's an easy rule to follow in reading a table: *percentage down the columns and interpret across the rows* (Box 21.5).

Box 21.5 Where do X and Y go?

By convention, the values of dependent variables make up the rows of tables and the values of independent variables make up the columns. Also by convention, the values of dependent variables are plotted on the Y axis, or **abcissa** of a scatterplot and the values of independent variables are plotted on the X axis, or **ordinate**. It is important to be consistent in data analysis, and it's much easier to be consistent if you follow a convention in setting up tables and scatterplots.

There are exceptions to these conventions in the literature—they are, after all, conventions and not laws—for example, when the independent variable (the columns) has too many categories to fit on a narrow page.

Try doing this for Table 21.5. I've put the independent variable (White or African American) in the columns and the dependent variable (single-female-parent and married-parent families) in the rows. *Percentaging down*, see that 80% of White households had two parents and 20% had one female parent (the small number of single-father households is not shown). For African American households, 43% had two parents and 57% had one parent. *Interpreting across*, we see that 80% of White households had two parents compared to 43% of African American households, and that 20% of White households had single parents compared to 57% for African American households.

There's no getting around it: When we do cross-tab analysis like this, we're trying to *understand* something about cause and effect. But as I explained in Chapter 2, there is absolutely *no assumption* that an independent variable actually *causes* a dependent variable.

I know this sounds a little convoluted, but look at Table 21.5 carefully and you can see how it works. Clearly, the probability in 2008 of belonging to a one-parent family was much higher for African Americans than it was for Whites in the United States. It was, in fact, almost three times more likely (20% compared to 57%). Clearly, the dependent variable here is family type, and not race. Nobody's skin color (which is, after all, what the so-called race variable is about) depends on whether they are a member of a two-parent or a one-parent family.

And clearly—and I mean absolutely, positively, no-fooling, clearly—*being* an African American *did not cause anyone*, not one single person, to be part of a single-parent household. There is definitely a relation between the independent and dependent variable, but *it's not a cause-and-effect relation*.

To understand the relation between these variables, we need to ask some questions about **antecedent variables** and **intervening variables**.

In Figure 21.2a, A and B appear to be related, but a third variable, C, is related to and prior to both of them. The association between A and B is not an illusion. It's a real association, but they are related to one or more antecedents—like poverty.

In Figure 21.2b, the dependent variable, C, is the consequence of one or more intervening

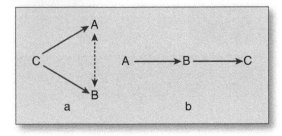

Figure 21.2 Antecedent and Intervening Variables

variables. In this case, we know that people in poverty are forced, because of where they live, to attend underfunded schools. We also know that this lowers opportunities for the the kind of employment that sustain two-parent families. The apparent relation between race and family structure in the United States is the consequence of many antecedent and intervening variables.

Forty years ago, Tidball (1973) found that women who graduate from women's colleges were more likely to turn up in lists like Who's Who of American Women than were women who graduated from coed schools and attributed the correlation to the fact that women's self-esteem is enhanced in the supportive environment of an all-women's school.

A generation later, Ledman et al. (1995) found provisional support for the existence of an intervening variable: Women who graduate from all-women's schools, they said, are more likely to go on for graduate work—and advanced degrees are a pretty good predictor of success. Since then, more research has corroborated that women's colleges do create a supportive environment that enhances self-esteem (Kinzie et al. 2007). Perhaps the development of self-esteem is the intervening variable that produces more participation in graduate school by women who attend women's colleges. A lot more research on this will illuminate the complex relations of antecedent and intervening variables at work here.

LAMBDA AND THE PRE PRINCIPLE

Look at Table 21.5 again. Suppose that, for each of the 31,092,000 households with children under 18, you were asked to guess whether they were single-parent families or two-parent families and that you didn't know anything about their race. Since the mode for the dependent variable in this table is "married parents" (i.e., 23,155,000 compared to 7,937,000), you should guess that all families have two parents.

If you did that, you'd make 7,937,000 mistakes out of the 31,092,000 choices, for an error rate of 7,937,000/31,092,000, or 25.5%. Call this the old error.

Now suppose you knew the mode for each independent variable (each column) in Table 21.5. The mode for African Americans is single-parent households and the mode for Whites is two-parent households. Knowing this, your best guess would be that *every* White household has two parents and *every* African American household has one parent. You would still make some mistakes, but fewer than if you just guessed that all families have two parents.

How many fewer? When you guess that every one of the 4,629,000 African American families in the United States has one parent, you make 1,990,000 mistakes. And when you guess that every one of the 26,463,000 White families in the United States has two parents, you make 5,298,000 mistakes. The total new error is: 1,990,000 + 5,298,000 = 7,288,000 mistakes, which is 23.4% of 31,092,000.

The *difference* between the old error (25.5%) and the new error (23.4%), divided by the old error (25.5%) is the proportionate reduction of error, or PRE. Thus:

$$PRE = \frac{Old\ Error - New\ Error}{Old\ Error}$$

formula 21.6

$$PRE = \frac{7,937,000 - 7,288,000}{7,937,000} = 0.082$$

This PRE measure of association for nominal variables is called lambda, written either L or λ. A lambda of 0.082 (or 8.2%) means that if you know the distribution of the independent variable, you can guess the scores on the dependent variable 8.2% more of the time than if you didn't know the distribution of the independent variable.

The PRE principle is the basis for many of the most commonly used measures of association.

CHI-SQUARE

With bivariate data on nominal variables, many researchers use a statistic called chi-square, often written as χ^2, to test the null hypothesis that differences in the table exist solely by chance. As we saw in Chapter 14, χ^2 is easy to compute, and there are standardized tables for determining whether a particular χ^2 value is statistically significant.

Chi-square tells you whether or not a relation *exists* between or among variables. It tells you the *probability* that a relation is the result of chance. But it is not a PRE measure of correlation, so it doesn't tell you the *strength* of association among variables.

The principal use of χ^2 is for testing the hypothesis that there is *no relation* between two nominal variables—that is, for testing the null hypothesis. Looking at Table 21.5, we suspect that there is a relation between race and household type. Using the null-hypothesis strategy, we try as hard as we can to prove that our suspicion is dead wrong—that, in fact, no such relation exists at all.

If, after a really good faith effort, we *fail to accept* the null hypothesis, we can reject it. Using this approach, we never prove anything using statistical tests like χ^2. We just fail to disprove things. As it turns out, that's quite a lot.

Calculating χ^2

The formula for calculating χ^2 for a bivariate table is the same as the one we saw in Chapter 20 for a univariate distribution. Here it is again:

$$\chi^2 = \sum \frac{(O - E)^2}{E} \qquad \text{formula 21.7}$$

where O represents the observed number of cases in a particular cell of a bivariate table and E represents the number of cases you'd expect for that cell *if there were no relation* between the variables in that cell.

For each cell in a bivariate table, simply subtract the expected frequency from the observed and square the difference. Then divide by the expected frequency and sum the calculations for all the cells. Clearly, if all the observed frequencies equal all the expected frequencies, then χ^2 will be zero; that is, there will be no relation between the variables.

Although χ^2 can be zero, it can never have a negative value. The more the Os differ from the Es (i.e., something nonrandom is going on), the bigger χ^2 gets.

Calculating the Expected Frequencies in Bivariate Tables

The expected frequencies are calculated *for each cell* with the formula:

$$F_e = \frac{(R_t)(C_t)}{n} \qquad \text{formula 21.8}$$

where F_e is the expected frequency for a particular cell in a table; R_t is the frequency total for the row in which that cell is located; C_t is the frequency total for the column in which that cell is located; and n is the total sample size (the lower-right-hand marginal).

Remember: It is inappropriate to use χ^2 if F_e for any cell is less than 5, and be sure to run χ^2 on tables of raw frequencies, not on tables of percentages.

The test for χ^2 can be applied to any size bivariate table. Table 21.8 shows a hypothetical census of observed adherents, in four Native American tribes, of three competing religions and the expected number of adherents to each religion. Reading across the top of the table, in tribe #1, there are 150 Catholics, 104 Protestants, and 86 members of the Native American Church. For Tribe #1, we expect:

$$\frac{(340)(590)}{2,011} = 99.75$$

Catholics (the cell in the upper-left-hand corner of Table 21.8). We expect 119.03 Protestants and 121.22 members of the Native American Church for Tribe #1, and so on.

Chi-square for this table is a walloping 162.08. To determine the number of degrees of freedom for a bivariate χ^2 table, we calculate:

$$df = (r - 1)(c - 2) \qquad \text{formula 21.9}$$

Table 21.8 A Hypothetical Census of Religious Belief in Four Groups of Native Americans

	Observed frequencies			
Tribe	Catholic	Protestants	Native American Church	Total
1	150	104	86	340
2	175	268	316	759
3	197	118	206	521
4	68	214	109	391
Total	590	704	717	2,011
	Expected frequencies			
1	99.75	119.03	121.22	
2	222.68	265.71	270.61	
3	152.85	182.39	185.76	
4	114.71	136.88	139.41	

which means: Multiply the number of rows, minus one, by the number of columns, minus one. For Table 21.8, there are:

$$(4 - 1 \text{ rows})(3 - 1 \text{ columns}) = 6 \ df$$

Without even looking it up in Appendix C (the χ^2 distribution), it's clear that the competing religions are not evenly distributed across the groups. If you had collected these data, you'd now be faced with the problem of interpreting them—that is, telling the story of how the various religions gain adherents at the expense of the others in various places.

Suppose that instead of a census, we take a 10% random sample of the groups—one that turns out to reflect almost perfectly the religious preferences of the population. The results, and the expected frequencies, would look like Table 21.9.

Chi-square for Table 21.9 is 15.44. This is about 10% of the $\chi^2 = 162.08$ that we got for Table 21.8. It's still significant at the .02 level, but if we'd taken a 5% sample, χ^2 would be around 7 or 8, and with six degrees of freedom it would no longer be statistically significant, even at the .10 level. Sample size makes a real difference here.

Chi-Square for Multiple Comparisons

Like ANOVA, you can use χ^2 to make multiple comparisons across complex tables. Table 21.10 is an example. Researchers have identified five value orientations among physical education teachers: disciplinary mastery (DM), learning process (LP), self-actualization (SA), social responsibility (SR), and ecological integration (EI) (Chen et al. 1997:136).

So, for example, teachers who score high on the DM scale focus their attention on helping students gain proficiency with sports skills. SA-oriented teachers believe that their job is to help students attain personal growth. Teachers who score high on the SR scale believe that

Table 21.9 Observed and Expected Frequencies for a 10% Sample of the Data in Table 21.8

| | Observed frequencies Religion | | | |
| | Catholic | Protestants | Native American Church | Total |
Tribe				
1	15	10	9	34
2	18	27	32	77
3	20	12	21	53
4	7	21	11	39
Total	60	70	73	203
Expected frequencies				
1	10.04926	11.72414	12.23	
2	22.75862	26.55172	27.69	
3	15.66502	18.27586	19.06	
4	11.52709	11.52709	14.02	

their job is to help children recognize the needs of society and to become team players. Teachers with a high LP value orientation focus on helping children "learn how to learn," with the expectation that this is what does children the most good. And the EI-oriented folks believe in an approach that integrates the other four values into the curriculum.

Ang Chen and his colleagues (1997) wanted to see if there were strong differences in these value perspectives among physical education teachers in the United States and China. The 854 participants in the study came from six American school districts ($n = 495$) and four Chinese school districts ($n = 359$). All the participants took the Revised Ennis Value Orientation Inventory (Ennis et al. 1992), which was designed to measure educational value orientations. (To understand how these researchers translated the scale into Chinese, see the section on "back translation" in Chapter 9.) The 90

items in the inventory are divided into five subscales of 18 items each. Each item is ranked on a scale of 1–5, with 5 being "most valued" and 1 being "least valued."

A teacher is given a score of "high value orientation" on a subscale if she or he scores 0.6 standard deviations above the mean, across all respondents, for that 18-item subscale. Chen et al. calculated the mean, *across all 854 respondents* in both countries for each of the five value orientations. If a teacher's score on a particular value orientation was ≥ (equal to or greater than) 0.6 standard deviations above the mean for all teachers (irrespective of country), then they counted that teacher's score on that value orientation as "high." Otherwise, the teacher's score was "low." Table 21.10 shows the distribution of the results, and the χ^2 scores, for both countries on all five subscales.

There are five two-by-two tables in Table 21.10. Each of the five has a χ^2 value, shown

Table 21.10 Five Value Orientations Among Teachers in the USA and China

Value Country	DM USA	DM China	LP USA	LP China	SA USA	SA China	EI USA	EI China	SR USA	SR China
Low										
n	337	242	374	202	332	253	384	193	259	343
%	68.1	67.4	75.6	56.3	67.1	70.5	77.6	53.8	52.3	95.5
High										
n	158	117	121	157	163	106	111	166	236	16
%	31.9	32.6	24.4	43.7	32.9	29.5	22.4	46.2	47.7	4.5
Chi-square	0.02		28.85		0.74		43.79		147.08	
p	0.89		0.001		0.39		0.001		0.001	

Source: A. Chen et al., "Universality and Uniqueness of Teacher Educational Value Orientations: A Cross-Cultural Comparison between the USA and China." *Journal of Research and Development in Education* 30:135–143, Copyright © 1997.

in the next-to-last row, and a *p*-value, or probability, shown in the last row. The data for the first table, regarding the DM scale, show that about two-thirds of Americans and Chinese teachers think disciplinary mastery is very important in the physical education curriculum. The difference between them (68.1% vs. 67.4%) is insignificant. Chi-square is .02, and the *p*-value for this χ^2 is .89. If you ran this particular test a thousand times, you'd expect to get a distribution like the one in this table about 89% of the time.

Just because a χ^2 value is statistically insignificant doesn't mean it's uninteresting. The third χ^2 table across Table 21.10 is for SA, or self-actualization. There is no difference between the Chinese and American teachers on valuing self-actualization. Now, this is a trait that we usually associate with the "rugged individualist" American culture, so finding no real difference between Americans and Chinese on this value orientation captures our attention.

The real shocker, though is in the subtable on social responsibility (labeled SR over on the right of Table 21.10). This is a trait we associate with the "collective mentality" of schooling in communist countries, yet it is valued far more by

Americans in the physical education curriculum than by their Chinese counterparts. What's going on here?

According to Chen (personal communication), the Chinese education system, along with other components of the communist society, does, indeed, emphasize the value of aligning one's individual needs with those of the society. Chen speculates that by the time children get to high school, they have acquired this norm so completely (and their social behavior is under so much control) that physical education teachers don't need to give it any priority in the curriculum.

The Special Case of the 2 × 2 Table

When you have a 2 × 2 cross-tab (read: two-by-two cross tab) of nominal data, there is an easy formula to follow for computing χ^2. Here it is:

$$\chi^2 = \frac{n\left(|ad-bc|-\frac{n}{2}\right)^2}{(a+b)(c+d)(a+c)(b+d)}$$

formula 21.10

where a, b, c, and d are the individual cells shown in Figure 21.3, and *n* is the total of all the cells (the lower-right-hand marginal).

The straight bars inside the parentheses mean that you take the absolute value of the operation ad – bc (that is, you ignore a negative sign, if bc is bigger than ad), and you subtract *n*/2 from *it*. Then you square that number and multiply it by *n* and divide that by the denominator.

Carol Boyd and her colleagues (1993) in the School of Nursing at the University of Michigan examined a random sample of 80 medical records for African American men and women who were enrolled in an urban, community-based drug abuse treatment facility. The idea was to take gender differences into account in developing therapeutic programs for men and for women in recovery from drug abuse. There were no differences among the 37 men and 43 women in mean age, sibling order, or marital status.

There was, however, one variable on which men and women appeared to differ a

Table 21.11	Data From Boyd et al.'s Study of Child Abuse

	Women	Men	Total
Reported having been sexually abused as a child	25	2	27
Reported not having been sexually abused as a child	18	35	53
Total	43	37	80

Source: C. J. Boyd et al., "Gender Differences Among African-American Substance Abusers." *Journal of Psychoactive Drugs*, 25:301–305, Copyright © 1993.

lot: the probability of having experienced sexual abuse as a child. Table 21.11 shows the distribution of self-reported data from the sample.

Table 21.12 shows the traditional calculation of χ^2 for Boyd's data. Notice that the numerator in each of the four above calculations is the same: $(2 - 12.49)^2 = 110.04$. So is $(25 - 14.51)^2$ and so are the rest of the numerators. It is this property that allows computation of χ^2 for 2 × 2 tables using formula 21.10. Chi-square for the data in Table 21.12 is 24.74, which is statistically significant at better than the $p = .001$ level.

Figure 21.3	Cells in a 2 × 2 table

a	b	a + b
c	d	c + d
a + c	b + d	*n*

Table 21.12	Calculating χ^2 for the Data in Table 21.11

Observed	Expected	O – E	$(O - E)^2$	$(O - E)^2/E$
2	27 × 37/80 = 12.49	–10.49	110.04	8.81
25	27 × 43/80 = 14.51	10.49	110.04	7.58
35	53 × 37/80 = 24.51	10.49	110.04	4.49
18	53 × 43/80 = 28.49	–10.49	110.04	3.86
				3 = 24.74 $p < .001$

About Low Cell Counts

The conclusion we should draw from Table 21.11 seems pretty clear: Women are more likely to have experienced childhood sexual abuse than are men. Notice that there are only two cases in one of the cells in Table 21.11. When there are fewer than five cases *expected* in any cell, χ^2 can be distorted and there is a danger of drawing the wrong conclusion from the data. In this case, that would mean concluding incorrectly that women are more likely than are men to experience childhood sexual abuse.

But notice from Table 21.12 that there are 12.49 cases *expected* of men who report having been sexually abused as a child. The fact that only two cases actually turned up in this cell is thus evidence, not a cause for worry. Also, in this particular case, the researchers had a lot more to go on than just the χ^2 value. There are hundreds of studies, statistical and ethnographic, documenting the fact that women take the brunt of childhood sexual abuse.

Watch out, however, for situations in which the expected number of cases falls below five. When this is the case, consider using Fisher's exact test, which is described next (Box 21.6).

Box 21.6 Cramer's *V* and phi

Cramer's *V* is based on χ^2 and is a measure of the association between two nominal variables. The formula is:

$$V = \sqrt{\frac{\chi^2}{n(k-1)}} \qquad \text{formula 21.11}$$

where *k* is the number of rows or columns in your table, whichever is less. If you have three rows and four columns, then $k = 3$ and $k-1 = 2$. Multiply the number of cases in your sample by $k-1$. Next, divide χ^2 by that number. Finally, take the square root of *that* number. Cramer's *V* will give you an idea of how strong the association is between nominal variables.

For a 2 x 2 table, $k-1 = 1$, and so the denominator becomes, simply, *n*. This is the **phi coefficient**, sometimes written with the Greek letter φ. Thus:

$$\varphi = \sqrt{\frac{\chi^2}{n}} \qquad \text{formula 21.12}$$

Fisher's Exact Test

Fisher's exact probability test is used for 2×2 tables whenever the *expected* number of frequencies for any cell is less than five. With fewer than five expected occurrences in a cell, χ^2 values are generally not trustworthy.

Table 21.13 shows hypothetical data on the attitudes of 15 American students toward spending a year overseas as part of their undergraduate program. Eight of the students grew up in families where at least one parent had served in the military; the other seven grew up in families where neither parent had ever served in the military.

| Table 21.13 | Hypothetical Data on Students' Attitudes Toward Studying Abroad |

Attitude	Parent(s) in Military	Parent(s) Not in Military	Total
Positive	7 [4.8]	2 [4.2]	9
Negative	1 [2.8]	5 [2.8]	6
Total	8	7	15

Of the eight students who had at least one parent who had served in the military, seven were positive toward the idea of a year abroad and one was negative. Of the seven students who had no parent who had served in the military, five were positive about the study-abroad option and two were negative. The *expected* values for each cell are shown in brackets in Table 21.13.

Since the cells have expected values of less than five, we apply Fisher's exact text. There are thousands of ways to throw the expected cases (5, 3, 4, 3) into four cells, but there are fewer ways to do it if you have to make the right-hand marginals add up to the observed values. Given a set of fixed marginals in a 2×2 table, the probability of seeing any distribution of cases is:

$$p = \frac{(a+b)!(c+d)!(a+c)!(b+d)!}{n!a!b!c!d!}$$

formula 21.13

where a, b, c, and d are the actual contents of the four cells in the 2×2 table (see Figure 21.3 above) and n is the total number of cases. (An exclamation point signifies the factorial of a number, or the product of a sequence of numbers. So, 5! is five-factorial, or $5 \times 4 \times 3 \times 2 \times 1 = 120$). The exact probability of

observing the particular distribution of cases in Table 21.13 is:

$$p = \frac{(362,880)(720)(40,320)(5,040)}{(1,307,674,368,000)(5,040)(2)(1)(120)}$$
$$= 0.033566434$$

For a one-tailed test of the null hypothesis, we need to add this probability to the probability of finding any other distributions that are more extreme than the one in the actual data. There is one configuration of these data that is more extreme: $a = 8$, $b = 1$, $c = 0$, and $d = 6$ (where a, b, c, and d are the cells in Figure 21.3). The exact probability of that distribution is 0.001398601. For a one-tailed test, we add these probabilities:

$$0.033566434 + 0.001398601 = 0.034965$$

For a two-tailed test, the probability is .041. It's not just double the one-tailed probability because the distribution of the elements in Table 21.13 is uneven, but it's easy to calculate using any major stats package.

The Odds Ratio

The exact probability of getting the particular distribution of the 80 cases in Table 21.11 is 0.000000304. That value—and the 24.74 value of χ^2 for Table 21.11—is interesting, but it doesn't say anything about the strength of the relation between the variables. A nice, intuitive statistic for this is the odds ratio or **OR**.

The odds, across the 80 respondents represented in Table 21.11, of having been sexually abused as a child are $27/53 = 0.5094$, or about 51%. That is, these respondents are twice as likely (the reciprocal of 0.51) to report that they *weren't* sexually abused as a child as they were to report that they had been abused.

We can go further. The odds of men in this sample of respondents reporting that they were abused as a child are 2/35 = 0.057. When the odds of something happening are less than 1.0, this indicates a negative association—in this case between sex of respondent and the reporting of having experienced sexual abuse as a child. The odds of women in this sample of respondents reporting that they were abused as a child are 25/18 = 1.388.

For 2 × 2 tables, like the one in Table 21.11, the odds ratio is:

$$\frac{a\,/\,c}{b\,/\,d} \qquad \textbf{formula 21.14}$$

The odds ratio for the data in 21.11 is:

$$\frac{25\,/\,18}{2\,/\,35} = \frac{1.388}{0.057} = 24.35$$

The odds of women reporting having been sexually abused as children are more than 24 times the odds of men doing so. The odds ratio has a lot of appeal because it can be generalized for looking at the interactions among complex sets of nominal variables.

TESTING THE ASSOCIATION BETWEEN ORDINAL VARIABLES

Once you understand the PRE principle, a lot of things in statistics fall into place. Kempton et al. (1995) surveyed intentionally selected samples of people in the United States whom they thought would show pro- and anti-environmentalist attitudes. (Members of the Sierra Club, for example, are people you'd anticipate would be proenvironmental activism, while loggers are people you'd think would be against that kind of activity.) Figure 21.4 shows two questions from Kempton et al.'s study: Gery Ryan, Stephen Borgatti, and I used these items in a survey, and Table 21.14 shows the results. Notice that these items are reverse scored, so that a higher number indicates support for environmentalism.

If the two variables were perfectly related, then every respondent who agreed with one statement would agree with the other; every respondent who disagreed with one statement would disagree with the other; and so on. Things never work out so neatly, but if you knew the proportion of matching pairs among your respondents, you'd have a PRE measure of association for ordinal variables. The measure would tell you how much more correctly you could guess the rank of one ordinal variable for each respondent if you knew the score for the other ordinal variable in a bivariate distribution.

Gamma

What we want is a PRE measure of association that tells us whether knowing the ranking of pairs of people on one variable increases our ability to predict their ranking on a second variable and by how much. To do this, we need to understand the ways in which pairs of ranks can be distributed. This will not appear obvious at first, but bear with me.

The number of possible pairs of observations (on any given unit of analysis) is:

$$\textit{Number of pairs of observations} = \frac{n(n-1)}{2}$$

formula 21.15

where n is the sample size. There are (149)(148)/2 = 11,026 pairs of observations in Table 21.14.

There are several ways that pairs of observations can be distributed if they are ranked on two ordinal variables.

1. They can be ranked in the same order on *both* variables. We'll call these "same."

Figure 21.4 Two Questions From Kempton et al.'s (1995) Study of Attitudes About the Environment

You shouldn't force people to change their lifestyle for the sake of the environment

    1. Disagree   2. Neutral   3. Agree

Environmentalists wouldn't be so gung-ho if it were their jobs that were threatened.

    1. Disagree   2. Neutral   3. Agree

Source: W. Kempton et al., *Environmental Values in American Culture*, 1995, MIT Press.

Table 21.14 Distribution of Responses on Two Ecological Attitude Items

| | Gung Ho | | | |
Force change in lifestyle	Agree	Neutral	Disagree	Row totals
Disagree	16	7	61	84
Neutral	7	7	7	21
Agree	13	4	27	44
Column totals	36	18	95	149

2. They can be ranked in the opposite order on both variables. We'll call these "opposite."

3. They can be tied on either the independent or dependent variables, or on both. We'll call these "ties."

In fact, in almost all bivariate tables comparing ordinal variables, there are going to be a lot of pairs with tied values on both variables. Gamma, written G or g, is a popular measure of association between two ordinal variables because it *ignores* all the tied pairs. The formula for gamma is:

$$G = \frac{\text{No. of same-ranked pairs} - \text{No. of opposite-ranked pairs}}{\text{No. of same-ranked pairs} + \text{No. of opposite-ranked pairs}}$$

formula 21.16

Gamma is an intuitive statistic; it ranges from −1.0 (for a perfect negative association), to +1.0 (for a perfect positive association), through 0 in the middle for complete independence of two variables.

If there are just two ordinal ranks in a measure, and if the number of opposite-ranked pairs is 0, then gamma would equal 1. Suppose we measured income and education ordinally, such that: (1) anyone with less than a high school diploma is counted as having low education, and anyone with at least a high school diploma is counted as having high education; and (2) anyone with an income of less than $30,000 dollars a year is counted as having low income, while anyone with at least $30,000 a year is counted as having high income.

Now suppose that *no one* who had at least a high school diploma earned less than $30,000 dollars a year. There would be no pair of observations, then, in which low income and high education (an opposite pair) co-occurred.

If the number of same ranked pairs is zero, then gamma would equal +1.0. Suppose that *no one* who had a high school diploma also had a high income. This would be a perfect negative association, and gamma would be –1.0. Both +1.0 and –1.0 are perfect correlations.

Calculating the Pairs for Gamma

The number of same-ranked pairs in a bivariate table is calculated by multiplying each cell by the sum of all cells *below it and to its right*. The number of opposite-ranked pairs is calculated by multiplying each cell by the sum of all cells *below it and to its left*. This is diagrammed in Figure 21.5.

Gamma for Table 21.14, then, is:

$$G = \frac{1,364 - 2,241}{1,364 + 2,241} = \frac{-877}{3,605} = -.24$$

Gamma tells us that the variables are associated negatively—people who agree

with either of the statements tend to disagree with the other, and vice versa—but it also tells us that the association is relatively weak.

Testing the Significance of Gamma

How weak? If you have more than 50 elements in your sample, you can test for the probability that gamma is due to sampling error using a procedure developed by Goodman and Kruskal (1963). A useful presentation of the procedure is given by Loether and McTavish (1993:598, 609). First, the gamma value must be converted to a *z*-score, or standard score. The formula for converting gamma to a *z*-score is:

$$z = (G - \gamma)\sqrt{n_s + n_o \; / \; 2n(1 - G^2)}$$

formula 21.17

where G is the *sample* gamma, γ is the gamma for the *population*, n is the size of your sample, n_s is the number of same-ranked pairs, and n_o is the number of opposite-ranked pairs.

Figure 21.5 Calculating Gamma

In Table 21.14, the number of same-ranked pairs is:		The number of opposite-ranked pairs is:	
16 (7 + 7 + 4 + 27) =	720	61 (7 + 7 + 13 + 4) =	1,891
+ 7 (7 + 27)	= 238	+ 7 (7 + 13)	= 140
+ 7 (4 + 27)	= 217	+ 7 (4 + 13)	= 119
+ 7 (27)	= 189	+ 7 (13)	= 91
Total	1,364	Total	2,241

Note: To calculate the same-ranked pairs in this 3 × 3 table, multiply each score by the sums of all scores below it and to the right. Then sum the totals. To calculate the opposite-ranked pairs, multiply each score by the sums of the scores below it and to the left. Then sum the totals.

As usual, we proceed from the null hypothesis and assume that γ for the entire population is zero—that is, that there really is no association between the variables we are studying. If we can reject that hypothesis, then we can assume that the gamma value for our sample probably approximates the gamma value, γ, for the population. Using the data from Figure 21.5 and the gamma value for Table 21.14:

$$z = (-.24 - 0)\sqrt{(1,364 + 2,241 / 2(149)(1 - (-.24)^2}$$
$$= -.86$$

You'll recall that Appendix A—the z-score table—lists the proportions of area under a normal curve that are described by various z-score values. To test the significance of gamma, look for the z-score in column 1 of the table. Column 2 shows the area under a normal curve between the mean (assumed to be zero for a normal curve) and the z-score. We're interested in column 3, which shows the area under the curve that is *not* accounted for by the z-score.

A z-score of −.86 accounts for all but .1949 of the area under a normal curve. This means that we *cannot* reject the null hypothesis. The gamma score of −.24 is not sufficiently strong to confirm that there is a significant association between responses to the two attitudinal questions about environmental activism.

Kendall's Tau-b

Some researchers prefer a statistic called Kendall's tau–b (written T_b or τ_b) instead of gamma for bivariate tables of ordinal data

because gamma ignores tied pairs in the data. The formula for τ_b is:

$$\tau_b = \frac{n_s - n_o}{\sqrt{(n_s + n_o + n_{td})(n_s + n_o + n_{ti})}} \quad \text{formula 21.18}$$

where n_s is the number of same-ranked pairs, n_o is the number of opposite-ranked pairs, n_{td} is the number of pairs tied on the dependent variable, and n_{ti} is the number of pairs tied on the independent variable. You can calculate the tied pairs as follows:

$$n_{td} = \sum R(R-1)/2$$

$$n_{ti} = \sum C(C-1)/2$$

where R refers to the row marginals (the dependent variable) and C refers to the column marginals (the independent variable). In Table 21.14:

$$n_{td} = 84(83) + 21(20) + 44(43)/2 = 4,642$$

$$n_{ti} = 36(35) + 18(17) + 95(94)/2 = 5,248$$

We already have the numerator for τ_b in this case (we calculated the number of same-ranked and opposite-ranked pairs in Figure 21.5), so:

$$\tau_b = \frac{1,364 - 2,241}{\sqrt{(1,364 + 2,241 + 4,642)(1,364 + 2,241 + 5,248)}}$$
$$= -0.10$$

This confirms the weak, negative association we saw from the results of the gamma test. Kendall's τ_b will usually be smaller than gamma because gamma ignores tied pairs, while τ_b uses almost all the data (it ignores the relatively few pairs that are tied on both variables).

Yule's Q

Yule's Q is the equivalent of gamma for 2×2 tables of ordinal variables, like high versus low prestige, salary, education, religiosity, and so on. Yule's Q can be calculated on frequencies or on percentages. The formula is:

$$Q = \frac{(ad) - (bc)}{(ad) + (bc)}$$ **formula 21.19**

Yule's Q is another of those handy, easy-to-use statistics. A good rule of thumb for interpreting Q is given by J. A. Davis (1971): When Q is 0, the interpretation is naturally that there is no association between the variables. When Q ranges between from 0 to –.29, or from 0 to +.29, you can interpret this as a negligible or small association. Davis interprets a Q value of ±.30 to ±.49 as a "moderate" association; a value of ±.50 to ±.69 as a "substantial" association; and a value of ±.70 or more as a "very strong" association.

Rutledge (1990) was interested in the effect of one-parent or two-parent families on children's relations with their mothers and fathers. She surveyed African American college-aged women, mostly from Chicago. One of the questions she asked was: "When you were growing up, how close were you to your father? Were you considerably close, moderately close, or not close at all?" I've collapsed Rutledge's data into two response categories, close and not close, in Table 21.15.

Here is the calculation of Yule's Q for these data:

$$Q = \frac{(135)(31) - (36)(13)}{(135)(31) + (36)(13)}$$

$$= \frac{4185 - 468}{4185 + 468} = \frac{3717}{4653}$$

$$= .80$$

| Table 21.15 | Family Structure With Self-Reported Closeness to Parents |

Close to father?	Two Parents	One Parent	Total
Yes	135	36	171
No	13	31	44
Total	148	67	215

Source: E. M. Rutledge, "Black Parent-Child Relations: Some Correlates." Abstracted from data in Table 2. *Journal of Comparative Family Studies* 21:369–78, Copyright © 1998.

Yule's Q for these data is .80. Most of the women who come from two-parent homes are close to their fathers, while 46% (31/67) who come from one-parent homes are not. The reason is obvious: Overwhelmingly, one-parent homes are headed by mothers, not by fathers.

WHAT TO USE FOR NOMINAL AND ORDINAL VARIABLES

In general:

1. Use x^2 to see how often you could expect to find the differences you see in the table just by chance. In appropriate situations, calculate odds ratios to measure the strength of relationships.

2. Use gamma (or tau, or—in the case of 2×2 tables—Yule's Q) to measure the association between two ordinal variables.

In actual practice, ordinal variables with seven ranks are treated if they were interval variables. In practice, many researchers treat ordinals with just five ranks as if they were intervals, because association between interval-level variables can be analyzed by the most powerful statistics—which brings us to correlation and regression.

CORRELATION: THE POWERHOUSE STATISTIC FOR COVARIATION

When at least one of the variables in a bivariate relation is interval or ratio level, we use a measure of correlation: Spearman's *rho* (*rho* is the Greek letter ρ), also called Spearman's *r*, or r_s, when the data are rank ordered; Pearson's product moment correlation, written simply as *r*, to measure the strength of linear relations; or *eta* squared (*eta* is the Greek letter η, pronounced either eat-a or ate-a) to measure the strength of certain kinds of nonlinear relations. (Go back to the section on "shape of relations" at the beginning of this chapter if you have any doubts about the concept of a nonlinear relation.)

Spearman's *r*

Brenner and Tomkiewicz (1982) studied expectations among young African Americans and Whites entering the labor force out of college. They surveyed 342 graduating business majors about the importance (on a scale of 1–5) of 25 job characteristics. The sample comprised 51 African American men, 53 African American women, 121 White men, and 117 White women. The results are shown in Table 21.16.

Notice that only two of the job characteristics (#20: Has clear-cut rules and procedures to follow and #22: Permits a regular routine in time and place of work) have mean scores below 3.0. Virtually all the characteristics are at least moderately desirable, but some are much more desirable than others.

The scale is ordinal (1–5), so, strictly speaking, you can't tell if a score of 4 is one-third greater than a score of 3 or twice as big as a score of 3. Pearson's correlation coefficient is designed specifically to take advantage of the information in interval variables, so with ordinal scales you need some other measure of correlation. Spearman's coefficient of rank-ordered correlation is an excellent choice for sets of 30 or fewer rank-ordered objects.

Brenner and Tomkiewicz ranked the job characteristics and applied the following formula:

$$r_s = 1 - \frac{6 \sum d^2}{n(n^2 - 1)} \qquad \text{formula 21.20}$$

where *d* is the difference between the ranks on all pairs of objects. Table 21.17 shows the computation of d^2 for the data on men and women.

For these graduating business majors, at least, men and women have essentially the same (rather high) expectations for the jobs they hope to land: $r_s = .852$. The Spearman correlation for African Americans and Whites is nearly as strong (.829), with just a couple of items accounting for most of the difference in ranks. Item #10 (Involves working with congenial associates) is ranked much higher by Whites and item #19 (Satisfies your cultural and aesthetic interests) is ranked much higher by African Americans.

Pearson's *r*

Pearson's product moment correlation—typically called Pearson's *r*—measures how much of the time changes in one variable correspond with equivalent changes in the other variables. It can also be used as a measure of association between an interval and an ordinal variable, or between an interval and a dummy variable. (Dummy variables are nominal variables coded as 1 or 0, present or absent. See Chapter 19 on text analysis.) The square of

Table 21.16 Mean Scores and Item Rank by Race and Sex of 25 Job Characteristics

Job Characteristics	White $n = 238$		Black $n = 104$		Male $n = 172$		Female $n = 170$	
How important is it to you to have a job which:	Mean	rank	Mean	rank	Mean	rank	Mean	rank
1. Requires originality and creativity	3.91	12	3.98	11	4.00	10.5	3.84	9
2. Makes use of your specific educational background	3.89	11	4.48	22.5	4.00	10.5	4.13	15
3. Encourages continued development of knowledge skills	4.40	23.5	4.48	22.5	4.33	22.5	4.52	23
4. Is respected by other people	4.17	18	4.26	17	4.15	17.5	4.26	17
5. Provides job security	4.40	23.5	4.60	24	4.44	24	4.47	22
6. Provides the opportunity to earn a high income	4.22	19	4.27	18.5	4.33	22.5	4.14	16
7. Makes a social contribution by the work you do	3.52	6	4.22	15	3.77	8	3.68	6
8. Gives you the responsibility for taking risks	3.42	5	3.48	4	3.59	5	3.27	4
9. Requires working on problems of central importance to the organization	3.70	8	3.89	7	3.83	9	3.69	7
10. Involves working with congenial associates	4.24	20.5	3.97	10	4.03	12	4.29	19
11. Provides ample leisure time off the job	3.99	13	3.94	9	4.07	14	4.87	25
12. Provides change and variety in duties and activities	4.24	20.5	4.27	18.5	4.18	19	4.31	20

(Continued)

Table 21.16 (Continued)

Job Characteristics	White n = 238		Black n = 104		Male n = 172		Female n = 170	
How important is it to you to have a job which:	Mean	rank	Mean	rank	Mean	rank	Mean	rank
13. Provides comfortable working conditions	4.31	22	4.47	21	4.28	21	4.44	21
14. Permits advancement to high administrative responsibility	4.16	17	4.24	16	4.26	20	4.11	14
15. Permits working independently	3.80	9.5	4.06	12	4.09	15	3.96	11
16. Rewards good performance with recognition	4.13	15	4.12	13	4.15	17.5	4.10	13
17. Requires supervising others	3.37	3	3.39	2	3.56	4	3.18	3
18. Is intellectually stimulating	4.14	16	4.21	14	4.06	13	4.27	18
19. Satisfies your cultural and aesthetic interests	3.40	4	3.93	8	3.48	3	3.63	5
20. Has clear-cut rules and procedures to follow	2.80	1	3.41	3	3.00	1	2.95	1
21. Permits you to work for superiors you admire and respect	3.80	9.5	3.72	5	3.63	6	3.93	10
22. Permits a regular routine in *time and place of work	2.86	2	3.37	1	3.02	2	3.01	2
23. Requires meeting and speaking with many other people	3.68	7	3.88	6	3.75	7	3.74	8
24. Permits you to develop your own methods of doing the work	4.01	14	4.28	20	4.14	16	4.04	12
25. Provides a feeling of accomplishment	4.74	25	4.72	25	4.68	25	4.79	24

Source: O. C. Brenner and J. Tomkiewicz, "Job Oorientation of Black and White College Graduates in Business." *Personnel Psychology,* Table 1, Copyright © 1982.

| Table 21.17 | Computing Spearman's Rank Order Correlation Coefficient for the Data on Men and Women in Table 21.16 |

Rank for Men	Rank for Women	Difference in the Ranks (d)	d²
10.5	9	1.5	2.25
10.5	15	−4.5	20.25
22.5	23	−0.5	0.25
17.5	17	0.5	0.25
24.0	22	2.0	4.00
22.5	16	6.5	42.25
8.0	6	2.0	4.00
5.0	4	1.0	1.00
9.0	7	2.0	4.00
12.0	19	−7.0	49.00
14.0	25	−11.0	121.00
19.0	20	−1.0	1.00
21.0	21	0.0	0.00
20.0	14	6.0	36.00
15.0	11	4.0	16.00
17.5	13	4.5	20.25
4.0	3	1.0	1.00
13.0	18	−5.0	25.00
3.0	5	−2.0	4.00
1.0	1	0.0	0.00
6.0	10	−4.0	16.00
2.0	2	0.0	0.00
7.0	8	−1.0	1.00
16.0	12	4.0	16.00
25.0	24	1.0	1.00
		Total	385.50

$$Spearman's\ r = 1 - \frac{6(385.5)}{25(25^2 - 1)}$$
$$= 1 - 2,313/15,600 = .852$$

Pearson's r is a PRE measure of association for linear relations between interval variables. That statistic, called r-squared, tells us how much better we could predict the scores of a dependent variable, if we knew the scores of some independent variable.

Table 21.18 shows data for a random sample of 10 cases for two variables in Table 20.7: (1) the number of physicians per 100,000 population; and (2) the average per capita income.

To give you an idea of where we're going with this example, the correlation between per capita income and the availability of physicians across the United States is around .763, and this is reflected in the sample of 10 states, for which the correlation is $r = .836$.

| Table 21.18 | Physicians and Per Capita Income for 10 U.S. States (2007) |

State	Per capita income in thousands of dollars (x)	Physicians/100,000 population (y)
Mississippi	28.541	178
South Carolina	31.103	230
North Dakota	36.082	244
Iowa	34.916	189
Kansas	36.525	223
Michigan	34.423	250
Delaware	40.112	251
Maryland	46.471	421
Oklahoma	34.997	173
Arizona	32.833	210
	$\bar{x} = 35.600$	$\bar{y} = 236.9$

Source: Tables 159, 665, Statistical Abstract of the United States (2010).

Now, suppose you had to predict the number of doctors per 100,000 population for each of the 10 states in Table 21.18 *without knowing anything about the average per capita income for those states*. Your best guess—the one where you'd make the smallest errors—would be the mean, 236.9 physicians per 100,000. You can see this in Figure 21.6, where I've plotted the distribution of physician availability per 100,000 and per capita income for the 10 states shown in Table 21.18.

The Sums of the Squared Distances to the Mean

The dotted line across Figure 21.6 is the mean: 236.9. Each dot in Figure 21.6 is physically distant from the dotted mean line by a certain amount. The sum of the squares of these distances to the mean line is the smallest sum possible (that is, the smallest cumulative

prediction error you could make), given that you *only* know the mean of the dependent variable. The distances from the dots *above* the line to the mean are positive; the distances from the dots *below* the line to the mean are negative. The sum of the actual distances is zero. Squaring the distances gets rid of the negative numbers.

But suppose you *do* know the data in Table 21.18 regarding the per capita income of people in those 10 states. Can you reduce the prediction error in guessing the availability of physicians for those 10 states? Could you draw another line through Figure 21.6 that "fits" the dots better and reduces the sum of the distances from the dots to the line?

You bet you can. The solid line that runs diagonally through the graph in Figure 21.6 minimizes the prediction error for these data. This line is called the best fitting line, or the least squares line, or the regression line. When you understand how this regression line is derived, you'll understand how correlation works.

Figure 21.6	A Plot of the Data in Table 21.19. The Dotted Line Is the Mean. The Solid Line Is Drawn From the Regression Equation $y = -189.983 + 11.991(x)$

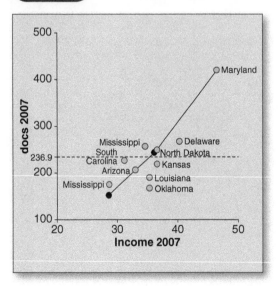

REGRESSION

The formula for the regression line is

$$y = a + bx \qquad \text{formula 21.21}$$

where y is the variable value of the dependent variable, a and b are some constants (which you'll learn how to derive in a moment), and x is the variable value of the independent variable. The constant, a, is computed as

$$a = \bar{y} - b(\bar{x}) \qquad \text{formula 21.22}$$

and b is computed as

$$b = \frac{n\left(\sum xy\right) - \left(\sum x\right)\left(\sum y\right)}{n\left(\sum x^2\right) - \left(\sum x\right)^2} \qquad \text{formula 21.23}$$

Table 21.19 shows the data needed for finding the regression equation for the raw data in Table 21.18.

The constant b is:

$$b = \frac{10(86969.759) - (356.003)(2369)}{10(12893.364) - (126738.136)}$$

$$= 11.991$$

and the constant a is then

$$a = 236.9 - 11.991(35.6) = -189.983$$

The **regression equation** for any pair of scores on income (x) and physician availability (y), then, is:

$$y = a + bx = -189.983 + 11.991(x)$$

Table 21.19 Computation of Pearson's r Directly From Data in Table 21.18

State	x Per capita Income, in Thousands of Dollars	y Physicians/ 100,000 Population	xy	x^2	y^2
Mississippi	28.541	178	5080.298	814.589	31684
South Carolina	31.103	230	7153.690	967.397	52900
North Dakota	36.082	244	8804.008	1301.911	59536
Iowa	34.916	189	6599.124	1219.127	35721
Kansas	36.525	223	8145.075	1334.076	49729
Michigan	34.423	250	8605.75	1184.943	62500
Delaware	40.112	251	10068.112	1608.973	63001
Maryland	46.471	421	19564.291	2159.554	177241
Oklahoma	34.997	173	6054.481	1224.790	29929
Arizona	32.833	210	6894.930	1078.006	44100
	$\bar{x} = 35.600$	$\bar{y} = 236.9$			

$\sum x = 356.003 \qquad \sum y = 2369 \qquad \sum xy = 86969.759$

$\bar{x} = 35.600 \qquad \bar{y} = 236.9 \qquad \sum x^2 = 12893.364 \qquad \sum y^2 = 606341$

$$r_{xy} = \frac{n\sum xy - \sum x \sum y}{\sqrt{[n\sum x^2 - (\sum x)^2][n\sum y^2 - (\sum y)^2]}} \qquad \text{formula 21.24}$$

$$r_{xy} = \frac{10(86969.759) - [(356.003)(2369)]}{\sqrt{[10(12893.364) - 356^2][10(606341) - 2369^2]}} = .836$$

Drawing the Regression Line

To draw the regression line in Figure 21.6, find the expected y coordinate for two of the actual data points on the independent variable, x. For example, for Mississippi in Table 21.18, the expected number of physicians per 100,000 population is:

$$y = -189.983 + 11.991(28.541) = 152.252$$

and for Kansas, the expected number of physicians is:

$$y = -189.983 + 11.991(36.525) = 247.988$$

Put a dot on Figure 21.6 at the intersection of

$$x = 28.541, \ y = 152.252$$

and

$$x = 36.525, \ y = 247.988$$

and connect the dots. Extend the line through the entire graph. That's the regression line.

The squared deviations (the distances from any dot to the line, squared) add up to less than they would for any other line we could draw through that graph. The mean, then, is the least squares point for a *single* variable. The regression line is the least squares line for a plot of *two* variables. That's why the regression line is also called the "best fitting" line.

Suppose we want to predict the dependent variable y (physician availability) when the independent variable x (per capita income) is $33,000 dollars per year. In that case,

$$y = -189.983 + 11.991(33.0)$$
$$= 395.703 - 189.983 = 205.720$$

physicians per 100,000 population. In other words, the regression equation lets us estimate the availability of physicians for income levels that are not even represented in our sample.

How Regression Works

To give you an absolutely clear idea of how the regression formula works, Table 21.20 shows all the predictions along the regression line for the data in Table 21.18.

We now have two predictors of the availability of physicians: (1) the mean number of physicians available, which is our best guess when we have no data about some independent variable like per capita income; and (2) the values produced by the regression equation when we *do* have information about something like per capita income.

Each of these predictors produces a certain amount of error, or *variance*, which is the difference between the predicted number for the dependent variable and the actual measurement. This is also called the residual—that is, what's left over after making your prediction using the regression equation. To anticipate the discussion of multiple regression in Chapter 22: The idea is to use two or more independent variables to reduce the size of the residuals.

You'll recall from Chapter 20, in the section on variance and the standard deviation, that in the case of the mean, the total variance is the average of the squared deviations of the observations from the mean, $1/n[\sum(x - \bar{x})^2]$. In the case of the regression line predictors, the variance is the sum of the squared deviations from the regression line. Table 21.21 compares these two sets of errors, or variances, for the data in Table 21.18.

We now have all the information we need for a true PRE measure of association between two interval variables. Recall the formula for a PRE measure: the old error minus the new

Table 21.20 Regression Predictions for the Dependent Variable in Table 21.18

For the state of	Where the Average per Capita Income in Thousands of Dollars in 2007 Was	Predict That the Number of Physicians per 100,000 Population Will Be	and Compare That to the Actual Number of Physicians That Year
Mississippi	28.541	$-189.9832 + 11.991(28.541) = 152.252$	178
South Carolina	31.103	$-189.9832 + 11.991(31.103) = 182.973$	230
North Dakota	36.082	$-189.983 + 11.991(36.082) = 242.676$	244
Iowa	34.916	$-189.9832 + 11.991(34.916) = 228.695$	189
Kansas	36.525	$-189.9832 + 11.991(36.525) = 247.988$	223
Michigan	34.423	$-189.9832 + 11.991(34.423) = 222.783$	250
Delaware	40.112	$-189.9832 + 11.991(40.112) = 291.000$	251
Maryland	46.471	$-189.9832 + 11.991(46.471) = 367.251$	421
Oklahoma	34.997	$-189.9832 + 11.991(34.997) = 229.666$	173
Arizona	32.833	$-189.9832 + 11.991(32.833) = 203.717$	210

Table 21.21 Comparison of the Error Produced by Guessing the Mean Number of Physicians per 100,000 Population in Table 21.18 and the Error Produced by Applying the Regression Equation for Each Guess

State	y Physicians	Old Error $(y - \bar{y})^2$	Prediction Using the Regression Equation	New Error $(y -$ the prediction using the regression equation$)^2$
Mississippi	178	3469.10	152.252	662.960
S. Carolina	230	47.61	182.973	2211.539
N. Dakota	244	50.41	242.676	1.753
Iowa	189	2294.41	228.695	1575.693
Kansas	223	193.21	247.988	624.400
Michigan	250	171.61	222.783	740.765
Delaware	251	198.81	291.003	1600.000
Maryland	421	33892.81	367.251	2888.955
Oklahoma	173	4083.21	229.666	3211.036
Arizona	210	723.61	203.721	39.476
		$\Sigma = 45{,}124.90$		$\Sigma = 13{,}556.576$

error, divided by the old error. For our example in Table 21.18:

$$PRE = \frac{45,124.9 - 13,556.576}{45,124.9} = .69957$$

In other words: The proportionate reduction of error in guessing the relative availability of physicians for the sample of states shown in Table 21.18—given that you know the distribution of per capita income for those states and can apply a regression equation—compared to just guessing the mean of physician availability, is .69957, or about 70%.

This quantity is usually referred to as *r*-squared (written r^2), or the amount of variance accounted for by the independent variable. It is also called the **coefficient of determination** because it tells us how much of the variance in the dependent variable is predictable from the scores of the independent variable. Pearson's *r* is the square root of this measure, or, in this instance, .836—which is just what we calculated in Table 21.19 by applying formula 21.24.

CALCULATING *r* AND r^2

I've given you this grand tour of regression and correlation because I want you to see that Pearson's *r* is not a direct PRE measure of association: its *square*, r^2, is.

So, what's better, Pearson's *r* or r^2 for describing the relation between interval variables? Pearson's *r* is easy to compute from raw data and it varies from –1 to +1, so it has direction and an intuitive interpretation of magnitude. It's also almost always bigger than r^2. By contrast, r^2 is a humbling statistic. A correlation of .30 looks impressive until you square it and see that it explains just 9% of the variance in what you're studying.

The good news is that if you double a correlation coefficient, you quadruple the variance accounted for. For example, if you get an *r* of .25, you've accounted for 6.25% of the variance, or error, in predicting the score of a dependent variable from a corresponding score on an independent variable. An *r* of .50 is twice as big as an *r* of .25, but four times as good, because 50^2 means that you've accounted for 25% of the variance (Box 21.7).

Box 21.7 Tracking variables over time

By the way, in case you're wondering, the correlation between the average per capita income and the availability of physicians has remained steady at between *r* = .75 and *r* = .77 for the last several years in the United States. Physicians in the United States earn a lot of money but there are very few of them, relative to the whole population, so their earnings have no noticeable effect on the average income of people across the 50 states in the United States. Average state income predicts the number of physicians so well because physicians, like any other occupational group, go where the money is for their services.

Testing the Significance of *r*

Just as with gamma, it is possible to test whether or not any value of Pearson's *r* is the result of sampling error, or reflects a real covariation in the larger population. In the case of *r*, the null hypothesis is that, within certain confidence limits, we should predict that the real coefficient of correlation in the population of interest is actually zero—that there is no relation between the two variables.

We need to be particularly sensitive to the possible lack of significance of sample statistics when we deal with small samples—which is a lot of the time, it turns out. The procedure for testing the confidence limits of r is a bit complex. To simplify matters, I have constructed Table 21.22, which you can use to get a ball-park reading on the significance of Pearson's r. The top half of Table 21.22 shows the 95% confidence limits for representative samples of 30, 50, 100, 400, and 1,000, where the Pearson's r values are .1, .2, .3, etc. The bottom half of Table 21.22 shows the 99% confidence limits.

Table 21.22   Confidence Limits for Pearson's r for Various Sample Sizes

	Sample Size				
Pearson's r	30	50	100	400	1,000
99% confidence limits					
.10	ns	ns	ns	ns	.04–.16
.20	ns	ns	.004–40	.10–.29	.14–.26
.30	ns	.02–.54	.11–.47	.21–.39	.24–.35
.40	.05–.67	.14–.61	.21–.55	.32–.48	.35–.45
.50	.17–.73	.25–.68	.31–.63	.42–.57	.45–.54
.60	.31–.79	.39–.75	.45–.71	.53–.66	.56–.64
.70	.45–.85	.52–.82	.59–.79	.65–.75	.67–.73
.80	.62–.90	.67–.88	.72–.86	.76–.83	.78–.82
.90	.80–.95	.83–.94	.85–.93	.88–.92	.89–.91
95% confidence limits					
.10	ns	ns	ns	ns	.02–.18
.20	ns	ns	ns	.07–.32	.12–.27
.30	ns	ns	.05–.51	.18–.41	.23–.45
.40	ns	.05–.80	.16–.59	.28–.50	.33–.46
.50	.05–.75	.17–.72	.28–.67	.40–.59	.44–.56
.60	.20–.83	.31–.79	.41–.74	.51–.68	.55–.65
.70	.35–.88	.46–.85	.55–.81	.63–.76	.66–.74
.80	.54–.92	.62–.90	.69–.88	.75–.84	.77–.83
.90	.75–.96	.80–.95	.84–.94	.87–.92	.88–.91

Reading the top half of Table 21.22, we see that at the 95% level, the confidence limits for a correlation of .20 in a random sample of 1,000 are .14 and .26. This means that in fewer than five tests in 100 would we expect to find the correlation smaller than .14 or larger than .26. In other words, we are 95% confident that the true r for the population (written ρ, which is the Greek letter *rho*) is somewhere between .14 and .26.

By contrast, the 95% confidence limits for an r of .30 in a random sample of 30 is not significant at all; the true correlation could be 0, and our sample statistic of .30 could be the result of sampling error.

The 95% confidence limits for an r of .40 in a random sample of 30 is statistically significant. We can be 95% certain that the true correlation in the population (ρ) is no less than .05 and no larger than .67. This is a statistically significant finding, but not much to go on insofar as external validity is concerned. You'll notice that with large samples (like 1,000), even very small correlations are significant at the .01 level. On the other hand, just because a statistical value is significant doesn't mean that it's important or useful in understanding how the world works.

Looking at the lower half of Table 21.22, we see that even an r value of .40 is statistically insignificant when the sample is as small as 30. If you look at the spread in the confidence limits for both halves of Table 21.22, you will notice something very interesting: A sample of 1,000 offers *some* advantage over a sample of 400 for bivariate tests, but the difference is small and the costs of the larger sample could be very high, especially if you're collecting all your own data.

Recall from Chapter 6, on sampling, that to halve the confidence interval you have to quadruple the sample size. Where the unit cost of data is high—as in research based on direct observation of behavior or in face-to-face interviews—the point of diminishing returns on sample size is reached quickly. Where the unit cost of data is low—as it is with mailed questionnaires or with telephone or Internet surveys—a larger sample is worth trying for.

NONLINEAR RELATIONS

And now for something different. All the examples I've used so far have been for linear relations where the best-fitting "curve" on a bivariate scatterplot is a straight line. A lot of really interesting relations, however, are nonlinear. Consider political orientation over time. The Abraham Lincoln Brigade was a volunteer, battalion-strength unit of Americans who fought against the rightist forces of Francisco Franco during the Spanish Civil War, 1936–1939. The anti-Franco forces were supported by leftist groups and by the Soviet Union, which existed from 1922 until 1991. In 1986, on the 50th anniversary of the start of the Spanish Civil War, surviving members of the Lincoln Brigade gathered at Lincoln Center in New York City.

Covering the gathering for the *New York Times*, R. Shepard (1986) noted that "While some veterans might still be inspired by their youthful Marxism," many had "broken with early orthodoxies" and had become critical of the Soviet Union since their youth. There are many examples of leftist activists in modern society who are born into relatively conservative, middle-class homes, become radicals in their 20s, and become rather conservative after they "settle down" and acquire family and debt obligations. Later in life, when all these obligations are over, they may once again return to left-wing political activity.

This back-and-forth swing in political orientation probably looks something like Figure 21.7.

Nonlinear Relations Are Everywhere

Beginning with −5° F and continuing up to 75° F, the mean number of assaults rises steadily with the average daily temperature in U.S. cities. Then it begins to drop. Figure 21.8, from Cohn and Rotton (1997) shows the dramatic

Figure 21.7   A Nonlinear Relation: Political Orientation Through Time

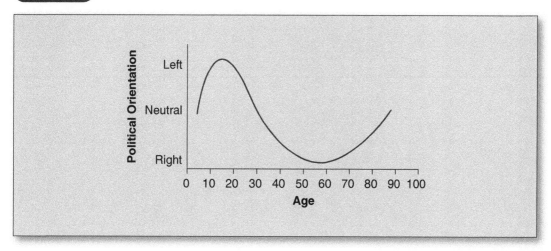

pattern. The reasons for this pattern are very complex (and controversial), but it is clear from Figure 21.8 that a simple, linear correlation is inadequate to describe what's going on.

Smits et al. (1998) measured the strength of association between the educational level of spouses in 65 countries and how that relates to industrialization. Figure 21.9 shows what they found. It's the relation between per capita energy consumption (a measure of industrialization and hence of economic development) and the amount of educational homogamy in those 65 countries. (Homogamy means marrying someone who is similar to you, so educational homogamy means marrying someone who has the same level of education as you do.) The relation between the two variables is very clear: It's an inverted U.

You might think that the relation between these two variables would be linear—people of similar education would be attracted to each other—but it isn't. Here's how Smits et al. reckon the inverted U happens: People in non-industrialized countries rely mostly on agriculture, so family background (which determines wealth) tends to be the main criterion for selecting mates. As industrialization takes off, education becomes more and more important and family background becomes less important for building wealth. Educated people seek each other out to maximize their life chances.

Eventually, though, when countries are highly industrialized, education is widespread, people have high wages, and there are social security systems. People in *those* countries don't have to rely on their children for support in old age, so romantic love becomes the dominant force in mate selection and the level of educational homogamy drops like a stone.

If you get a very weak r or r^2 for two variables that you believe, from theory or from field research are strongly related, then draw a scatterplot and check it out. Scatterplots are available in all the major statistical packages and they are, as you saw in Figure 21.1, packed with information. For sheer intuitive power, there is nothing like them.

Figure 21.10a, for example, is the same plot we saw in Figure 21.1d of infant mortality and per capita gross domestic product in 2009 for 210 countries of the world. I've repeated the figure here because I want you to see it next to Figure 21.10b, which is a plot of infant mortality and the natural logarithm of PCGDP. The correlation between the two original variables is −0.489, indicating a moderate negative relation.

Transforming each value of PCGDP into its natural logarithm has the effect of making the distribution more normal, but it changes the interpretation of the graph. In Figure 21.10b,

Figure 21.8 The Relationship Between Temperature and the Rate of Assault Is Nonlinear

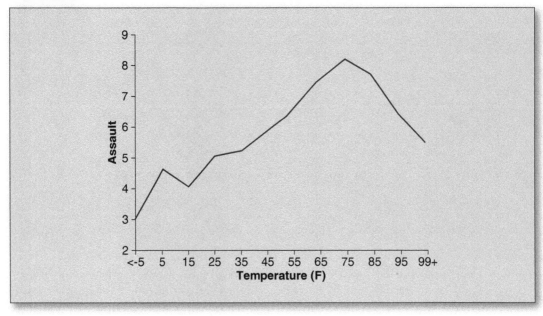

Source: E. G. Cohn and J. Rotton, "Assault as a Function of Time and Temperature: A Moderator-Variable Time-Series Analysis," *Journal of Personality and Social Psychology* 72:1322–1334, Copyright © 1997.

Figure 21.9 The Relation Between per Capita Energy Consumption and Educational Homogamy Is Nonlinear

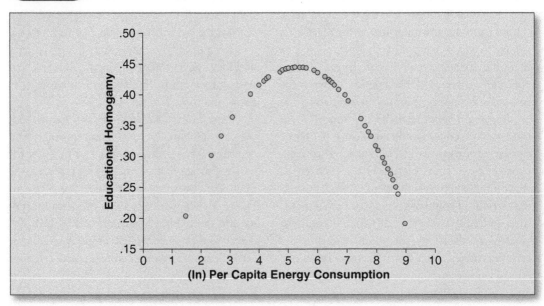

Source: J. Smits et al., "Educational Homogamy in 65 Countries: An Explanation of Differences in Openness Using Country-Level Explanatory Variables." *American Sociological Review* 63:264–285, Copyright ©1998.

Figure 21.10a Infant Mortality by per Capita Gross Domestic Product for 220 Countries

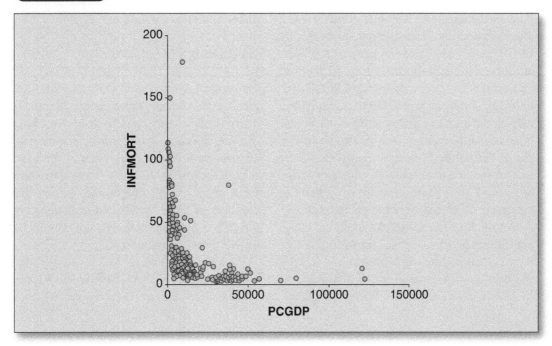

Source: The World Factbook. Central Intelligence Agency 2010. https://www.cia.gov/library/publications/the-world-factbook/rankorder/2091rank.html and https://www.cia.gov/library/publications/the-world-factbook/rankorder/2004rank.html

Figure 21.10b Log of Infant Mortality by per Capita Gross Domestic Product for 220 Countries

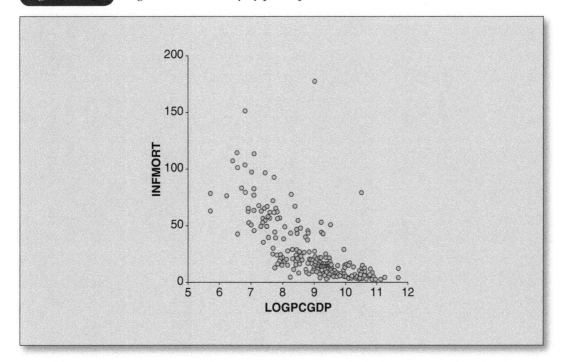

Source: The World Factbook. Central Intelligence Agency 2010. https://www.cia.gov/library/publications/the-world-factbook/rankorder/2091rank.html and https://www.cia.gov/library/publications/the-world-factbook/rankorder/2004rank.html

the correlation is now a strong –0.737, but we know from Figure 21.10a that the relation between the log of PCGDP and informant mortality is not linear. At the bottom, doubling the PCGDP, from $300 to $600 per year has little effect on the infant mortality rate. At the top end, it takes less than a doubling of PCGDP to halve infant mortality rate. On the other hand, halving the infant mortality at the bottom end means the difference between about 150 deaths per 1,000 babies born and about 75, while halving the infant mortality of countries at the top means the difference between about six deaths per 1,000 babies born and about three.

Bottom line: If a scatterplot looks anything like Figure 21.10a, consider transforming the data by "taking the logs" (that is, converting the data to their logarithms). If a scatterplot looks like the shapes in Figure 21.7, 21.8, or 21.9, then consider using eta-squared, a statistic for nonlinear regression.

Calculating Eta-Squared

Eta-squared, written η^2 or eta^2, is a PRE measure that tells you how much better you could do if you predicted the separate means for *chunks* of your data than if you predicted the mean for all your data. Figure 21.11 graphs the hypothetical data in Table 21.23. These data show, for a sample of 20 people ages 12–89, their "number of close friends and acquaintances" (i.e., not counting people who are only friends on social networking sites).

The dots in Figure 21.11 are the data points from Table 21.23. Respondent #10, for

Figure 21.11 Number of Friends by Age

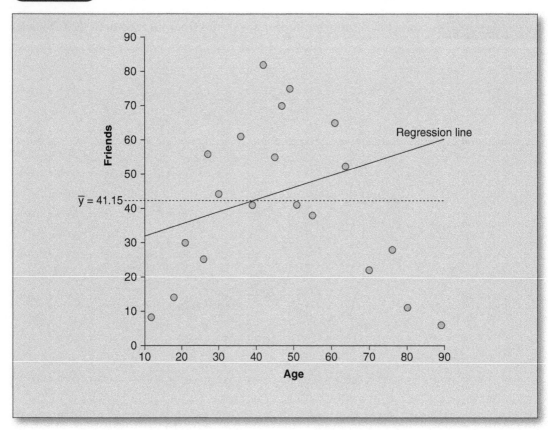

	Hypothetical Data on
Table 21.23	Number of Friends by Age

Person	Age	Number of Friends	
1	12	8	
2	18	14	$\bar{y}_1 = 19.25$
3	21	30	
4	26	25	
5	27	56	
6	30	43	
7	36	61	
8	39	41	
9	42	82	$\bar{y}_2 = 57.00$
10	45	55	
11	47	70	
12	49	75	
13	51	41	
14	55	38	
15	61	65	
16	64	52	
17	70	22	
18	76	28	$y_3 = 23.80$
19	80	11	
20	89	6	
		$\bar{y} = 41.15$	

example, is 45 years of age and was found to have approximately 55 friends and acquaintances. The horizontal dashed line in Figure 21.11 is the global average for these data, 41.15. Clearly: (1) the global average is not of much use in predicting the dependent variable; (2) knowing a person's age *is* helpful in predicting the size of his or her social network; but (3) the linear regression equation is hardly any better than the global mean at reducing error in predicting the dependent variable. You can see this by comparing the mean line and

the regression line (the slightly diagonal line running from lower left to upper right in Figure 21.11). They are not that different.

What that regression line depicts is the correlation between age and size of network, which is a puny –.099. But if we inspect the data visually, we find that there are a couple of natural "breaks." It looks like there's a break in the late 20s, and another somewhere in the 60s. We'll break these data into three age chunks from 12 to 26, 27 to 61, and 64 to 89, take separate means for each chunk, and see what happens. I have marked the three chunks and their separate means on Table 21.23.

Like *r*, which must be squared to find the variance accounted for, *eta*² is a measure of this and is calculated from the following formula:

$$\eta^2 = 1 - \frac{\sum(y - \bar{y}_c)^2}{\sum(y - \bar{y})^2} \qquad \text{formula 21.25}$$

where y_c is the average for each chunk and *y* is the overall average for the dependent variable. For Table 21.23, eta-squared is:

$$1 - \frac{3,871.55}{10,058.55} = .62$$

which is the proportionate reduction of error in predicting the number of friends people have from the three separate averages of their age rather than from the global average of their age. This shows a pretty strong relation between the two variables, despite the very weak Pearson's *r*.

STATISTICAL SIGNIFICANCE, THE SHOTGUN APPROACH, AND OTHER ISSUES

To finish this chapter, I want to deal with four thorny issues in social science data analysis:

(1) measurement and statistical assumptions; (2) significance tests; (3) eliminating the outliers; and (4) the shotgun method of analysis.

Measurement and Statistical Assumptions

By now you are comfortable with the idea of nominal, ordinal, and interval-level measurement. This seminal idea was introduced into social science in a classic article by S. S. Stevens in 1946. Stevens said that statistics like *t* and *r*, because of certain assumptions that they made, required interval-level data, and this became an almost magical prescription.

Thirty-four years later, Gaito (1980) surveyed the (by then voluminous) mathematical statistics literature and found no support for the idea that measurement properties have anything to do with the selection of statistical procedures. Social scientists, said Gaito, confuse measurement (which focuses on the meaning of numbers) with statistics (which doesn't care about meaning at all) (p. 566). So, treating ordinal variables as if they were interval, for purposes of statistical analysis, is often a safe thing to do, especially with five or more ordinal categories (Boyle 1970; Harwell and Gatti 2001; Labovitz 1971a). Not everyone agrees, though, and the discussion continues (Kampen and Swyngedouw 2000).

The important thing is measurement, not statistics. As I pointed out in Chapter 2, many concepts, such as gender, race, and class are much more subtle and complex than we give them credit for being. Instead of measuring them qualitatively (remember that assignment of something to a nominal category is a qualitative act of measurement), we ought to be thinking hard about how to measure them ordinally.

Emil Durkheim was an astute theorist. He noted that the division of labor became more complex as the complexity of social organization increased (Durkheim1933 [1893]). But he, like other theorists of his day, divided the world into a series of dichotomous categories (*gemeinschaft* vs. *gesellschaft*, or mechanical vs. organic solidarity).

Today, social theorists want to know how degrees of differences in aspects of social organization (like the division of labor in society) are related to social complexity. This requires some hard thinking about how to measure these two variables with more subtlety. The meaning of the measurements is crucial (**Further Reading:** measurement in social science).

Eliminating the Outliers

Another controversial practice in data analysis is called eliminating the outliers, which means removing extreme values from data analysis. If there are clear indications of measurement error (a person with a score of 600 on a 300-point test turns up in your sample), you can throw out the data that are in error.

The problem comes when outliers (so-called freak cases) are eliminated just to smooth out data—to achieve better fits of regression lines to data. A single wealthy household might be ignored in calculating the average household income in a community on the theory that it's a "freak case." But what if it isn't? What if it represents a small, but substantively significant proportion of cases in the community? Eliminating it only prevents the discovery of that fact.

Trivially, you can always achieve a perfect fit to a set of data if you reduce it to just two points. After all, two points are always connected by a straight line. But is creating a good fit what you're after? Don't you really want to understand what makes the data messy in the first place? In general, you cannot achieve understanding of messiness by cleaning things up. Still, as in all aspects of research, be ready to break this rule, too, when you think you'll learn something by doing so.

Figure 21.12a shows the relation between the number of violent crimes per 100,000 population and the average annual pay for people in the 50 U.S. states and Washington, DC, in 2007. Figure 21.12b shows exactly the same thing, but without including the data from Washington, DC. The correlation between the two variables *with* DC in the picture is 0.28. When we leave out the data for DC, the correlation sinks to −0.06.

That's because the violent crime rate in Washington, DC, was an appalling 1,414 per 100,000 in 2007, and the average annual pay there was $62,484. For the 50 states in the United States, the next highest violent crime rate, in Florida, was half that of DC, and the next highest average pay, in Connecticut, was just 12% lower than that in DC.

The sizes of the dots in Figures 21.12a and b indicate the influence each data point has on the correlation—that is, how much the correlation would change if you took each data point out of the calculation. That huge circle in the upper-right-hand corner of Figure 21.12a is DC. Now, *that's* an outlier.

What to do with outliers? Try using the median to describe the central tendency rather than eliminating cases. Or report the results of your analysis with and without outliers, as I just did with Figures 21.12a and b (**Further Reading:** dealing with outliers).

Tests of Significance

This is a hot topic in social science. Fifty years ago, researchers began arguing that statistical tests of significance are virtually useless (Rozeboom 1960), and the drumbeat has continued ever since (see Ziliak and McCloskey [2008] for a review).

I wouldn't go that far. Consider the hypothesis that the universe is expanding. As Wainer (1999) points out, being able to reject the hull hypothesis at $p < .05$ would be quite a contribution. Will Dr. X be denied tenure a year from now? Lots of people, says Wainer, would be happy to know that they could reject the null hypothesis at, say, $p < .001$. It's true that if you don't have a representative sample, then a test of statistical significance doesn't allow you to generalize beyond your particular sample of data.

On the other hand, if you get significant results on a nonrandom sample, at least you can rule out the operation of random properties *in your sample* (Blalock 1979:238–39).

Use tests of significance but remember that they aren't magical and that the .01 and .05 levels of significance, although tribal customs, are not sacred. They are simply conventions that have developed for convenience over the years. Greenwald et al. (1996:181–82) offer some useful advice about reporting p values.

1. In many situations, it's enough to use simple asterisks in your prose to indicate statistical significance. But if you need to report p values, then do so with an = sign, not with a < or > sign. If a p value is .042, don't report it as $p < .05$ ("the probability is less than .05"). Just report it as $p = .042$ and be done with it. Probability, just like the confidence we have in probabilistic results, is a continuous variable. Why cut out all that information with arbitrary cutoffs?

2. A single p value of .05 is as an indicator of a relation, but is not convincing support for a hypothesis. By tradition, researchers almost never report probabilities that are greater than .05. Five *repeated results* of $p = .06$, or even .10, are more convincing than a single result of $p = .05$ that something's really going on.

The Bonferroni Correction

If you want to be especially cautious in reporting correlations, you can apply a test known as the **Bonferroni correction**. There are two kinds of spurious correlation. One happens when the correlation between two variables is caused by a third, independent, variable. Another occurs when two variables covary because of sheer accident. It happens all the time. In fact, it occurs with a known probability.

Take a random sample of, say, 30 variables in the world, measure them, and correlate all

Figure 21.12a — Violent Crimes in the United States (for all states and Washington, DC) per 100,000 Population, by Average Annual Personal Income, 2007

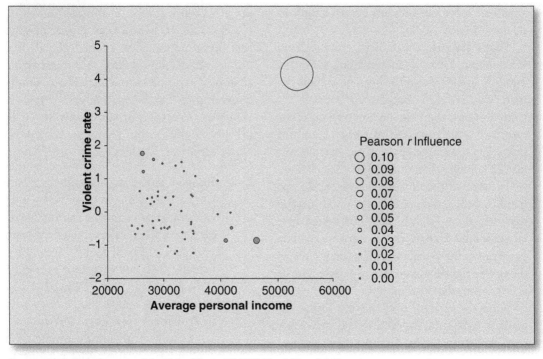

Source: Statistical Abstracts of the United States 2010 Tables 297 and 665.

Figure 21.12b — Violent Crimes in the United States (for all states, without Washington, DC) per 100,000 Population, by Average Annual Personal Income, 2008

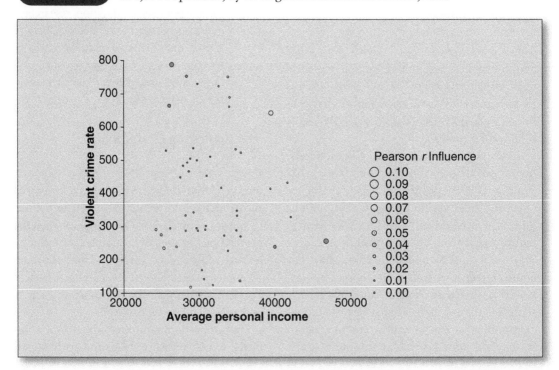

pairs of those variables. (There are $(30 \times 29) / 2$ = 435 pairs of 30 anything.) According to the Bonferroni rule, you should get a correlation, significant at the $p = < .05$ level, in 5% of all cases—in 22 out of 435 pairs—just by chance. So, if you build a matrix with 435 pairs of correlations and find that 20 of them are significant at the .05 level or better, you can't be sure that this is not simply a random event.

You *always* have to explain why any two variables are correlated, since correlation, by itself, never implies cause and effect. But when you go fishing for significant correlations in a big matrix of them, and find fewer than you'd expect by chance alone, things are even tougher.

How tough? Pick a level of significance for reporting findings in your data—say, .05. If you have 30 variables in your analysis and 435 tests of covariations in your matrix, divide .05 by 435 = .0001. If you report these correlations as significant at the 5% level (the level you chose originally), then, according to the Bonferroni rule, your report will be valid (see Kirk 1982; Koopmans 1981). This is a very, very conservative test, but it will prevent you from making those dreaded Type I errors and reporting significant relations that aren't really there.

On the other hand, this will increase your chance of making Type II errors—rejecting some seemingly insignificant relations when they really *are* important. You might fail to show, for example, that certain types of exposure are related to contracting a particular disease, and this would have negative public health consequences. There's no free lunch.

Consider a study by Dressler (1980). He studied a sample of 40 people in the Caribbean island of St. Lucia, all of whom had high blood pressure. Dressler measured nine variables having to do with his respondents' ethnomedical beliefs and their compliance with a physician-prescribed treatment regimen. He reported the entire matrix of $(9 \times 8)/2 = 36$ correlations, 13 of which were significant at the 5% level or better.

Dressler might have expected just $36 \times .05$ = 1.8 such correlations by chance. Three of the 13 correlations were significant at the .001 level. According to the Bonferroni rule, correlations at the .05/36 = .0014 level would be reportable at the .05 level as valid. Under the circumstances, however (13 significant correlations with only about two expected by chance), Dressler was quite justified in reporting all his findings and was not being overly conservative.

I feel that if you are doing fieldwork, and using small data sets, you should be comfortable with tests of significance at the $p < .10$ level, especially if you can repeat your finding in independent tests. Two or three repeated experiments that produce similar results in the same direction at the .10 level of significance are more convincing evidence of something going on than is one experiment that just barely pans out at the .05 level.

On the other hand, you can always find significant covariations in your data if you lower alpha (the level of significance) enough, so be careful. Remember, you're using statistics to get hints about things that are going on in your data. I cannot repeat often enough the rule that real analysis (building explanations and suggesting plausible mechanisms that make sense out of covariations) is what you do *after* you do statistics.

I also can't stress enough the difference between **statistical significance** and **practical significance**. If you have a large enough n (in the thousands), you will surely find significant statistical relations in your data. Each of those relations may account for a small amount of the variance in what you're interested in understanding, but that doesn't mean that the relations are of practical use.

Suppose you come up with a new curriculum for teaching high school students about the dangers of smoking cigarettes. You implement the program in a classic experimental design, so that, of the 2,000 students in the district, 1,000 are exposed to the curriculum and another 1,000 are exposed to the curriculum you hope to replace.

At the end of the experiment, students in the treatment group score significantly higher on their tests of knowledge about the dangers of smoking than do students who were exposed to the old curriculum. With that many students, a few points of difference on the test might be statistically significant, indicating that the new curriculum is better.

But suppose it costs $30 more per student to implement the new curriculum. Will the school board shell out $30 × 2,000 = $60,000 to put in the new curriculum and achieve a very small, but statistically significant, improvement in students' knowledge about smoking? The statistical level of significance in the results may play *some* role in the board's decision, but I'll bet that other things will weigh even more heavily in their deliberations.

Even if the difference in test results is spectacular—students who take the new curriculum learn, say, twice as much about the dangers of smoking as do the students who study the old curriculum—it doesn't mean that the board will implement the new curriculum. Someone on the board may have the audacity to ask you whether you can prove that a spectacular difference in *knowledge* among students translates into safer *behavior* (**Further Reading:** statistical significance).

Statistical Power

The power of a statistical test is the probability of *correctly accepting your research hypothesis*. If you're thinking: "You mean it's the probability of taking 'yes' for an answer?" then you're right on track. As you know, the traditional way to conduct research is to: (1) formulate a hypothesis; (2) turn the hypothesis around into a null hypothesis; and then (3) try as hard as we can to prove the null hypothesis.

This is *not* perverse. All of us positivists out here know that it's impossible to absolutely, positively, prove any hypothesis to be forever unfalsifiably true. So we do the next best thing. We try our very best to disprove our best ideas (our research hypotheses) and hope that we fail, leaving us with the right to say that our best guess is that we were right to begin with.

What this means in the real life of researchers is that statistical power is the probability of avoiding *both* Type I *and* Type II errors: rejecting the null hypothesis when it's really true (Type I error) or accepting a null hypothesis when it's really false (Type II error).

This probability depends on two things: (1) the minimum size of the difference between two outcomes that you will accept as a *real* difference; and (2) the size of the sample. So, to achieve a given amount of statistical power in any experiment or survey, you need to calculate the size of the sample required, given the minimum size of the difference between two outcomes—the effect size—that you will accept as a real difference (Cohen 1988; Kraemer and Thiemann 1987).

This is a very important and subtle issue. Suppose you ask 100 men and 100 women, matched for socioeconomic status, race, and religion, to take the Attitudes Toward Women Scale (AWS). The null hypothesis is that there is no difference between the mean scores of the men and the mean scores of the women on this scale. How big a difference do you need between the mean of the men and the mean of the women on this scale to reject the null hypothesis and conclude that, in fact, the difference is real—that men and women really differ on their attitudes toward women as expressed in the AWS?

The answer depends on the power of the test of the difference in the means. Suppose you analyze the difference between the two means with a *t*-test, and suppose that the test is significant at the .05 level. Statistical power is the probability that you are wrong to report this result as an indicator that you can reject the null hypothesis.

The result, at the $p = .05$ level, indicates that the difference you detected between the mean for the men and the mean for the women would be expected to occur by chance fewer than five times in 100 runs of the same experiment. It does *not* indicate that you are $1-p$, or 95% confident that you have correctly rejected the null hypothesis. The power of the finding of $p = .05$ depends on the size of the sample and on the size of the difference that you expected to find before you did the study.

In the case of the AWS, there are 40 years of data available. These data make it easy to say how big a difference you expect to find if the men and women in your sample are really different in their responses to the AWS. Many surveys are done without this kind of information available. You can offer a theory to explain the results from one experiment or survey. But you can't turn around and use those same data to *test* your theory. As replications accumulate for questions of importance in the social sciences, the question of statistical power becomes more and more important.

So, what's the right amount of statistical power to shoot for? Cohen (1992) recommends that researchers plan their work—that is, set the effect size they recognize as important, set the level of statistical significance they want to achieve (.05, for example, or .01), and calculate the sample size—to achieve a power of .80.

A power value of .80 would be an 80% chance of recognizing that our original hypothesis is really true and a 20% chance of rejecting our hypothesis when it's really true. If you shoot for a power level of much lower than .80, says Cohen, you run a big risk of making a Type II error.

On the other hand, power ratings much higher than .80 might require such large Ns that researchers couldn't afford them (Cohen 1992:156). If you want 90% power for a .01 (1%) two-tailed test of, say, the difference between two Pearson's rs, then, you'd need

364 participants (respondents, subjects) to detect a difference of .20 between the scores of the two groups. If you were willing to settle for 80% power and a .05 (5%) two-tailed test, then the number of participants drops to 192 (**Further Reading:** statistical power).

The Shotgun Approach

A closely related issue concerns shotgunning. This involves constructing a correlation matrix of all combinations of variables in a study, and then relying on tests of significance to reach substantive conclusions. It is quite common for field researchers in anthropology or sociology to acquire measurements on as many variables as they have informants—and sometimes even *more* variables than informants.

There is nothing wrong with this. If you are doing field research, after a very short time in the field you will think up lots and lots of variables that appear potentially interesting to you. Include as many of them as you have time to ask on a survey without boring your informants. The result of effective data collection is a large profile matrix of items-by-variables (if this is unfamiliar to you, see the section on profile matrices and proximity matrices in Chapter 15).

Even a small matrix of 20 variables contains 190 unique pairs. It would take forever to go through each pair and: (1) decide whether it was worth spending the time to test for covariation in each case; (2) decide on the proper test to run (depending on the level of measurement involved in each case); (3) run the test; and (4) inspect and interpret the results.

There are two ways out of this fix. One way is to think hard about data and ask only those questions about covariation that seem plausible on theoretical grounds. It may not be important, for example, to test whether a respondent's rank in a sibling set (first child, second child, etc.) covaries with his or her blood pressure. On the other hand, maybe it does. You can decide whether to test the relation between these two particular variables based on your knowledge of prior research, theory, and hunches.

The other way out of the fix is the shotgun strategy. You simply use a computer to transform your profile matrix into a similarity matrix in which each cell is occupied by an appropriate measure of association—percentage of matched pairs, Pearson's r, gamma—depending on whether the variables were measured as nominals, ordinals, or intervals. Then you scan the similarity matrix in search of significant covariations.

Kunitz et al. (1981) studied the determinants of hospital utilization and surgery in 18 communities on the Navajo Indian Reservation during the 1970s. They measured 21 variables in each community, including 17 independent variables (the average education of adults, the percentage of men and women who worked full time, the average age of men and women, the percentage of income from welfare, the percentage of homes that had bathrooms, the percentage of families living in traditional houses, etc.), and four dependent variables (the rate of hospital use—variable 21—and the rates for the three most common types of surgery—variables 18, 19, 20). Table 21.24 shows the correlation matrix of all 21 variables in this study.

Kunitz et al. (1981) point out in the footnote to their matrix that, for $n = 18$, the 0.05 level of probability corresponds to $r = 0.46$ and the 0.01 level corresponds to $r = 0.56$. By the Bonferroni correction, they could have expected:

$$[(21 \times 20) / 2](.05) = 10.5$$

correlations significant at the 0.05 level and

$$[(21 \times 20) / 2](.01) = 2.1$$

correlations significant at the 0.01 level by chance. There are 73 correlations significant at the 0.05 level or better in Table 21.24, and 42

of those correlations are significant at the 0.01 level.

Kunitz et al. (1981) examined these correlations and were struck by the strong association of the hysterectomy rate to all the variables that appear to measure acculturation. I'm struck by it, too. This interesting finding was not the result of deduction and testing; it was the result of shotgunning. The finding is not proof of anything, but it sure seems like a strong clue to me. I'd want to follow this up with research on how acculturation affects the kind of medical care that women receive and whether all those hysterectomies are necessary.

The Problem With the Shotgun Approach

The problem with shotgunning is that you might be fooled into thinking that *statistically* significant correlations are also *substantively* significant. This is a real danger, and it should not be minimized (Labovitz 1972). It results from two problems.

1. You have to be very careful about choosing a statistical measure of association, depending on how the variables were measured in the first place. A significant correlation in a matrix may be an artifact of the statistical technique used and not be of any substantive importance. Running a big correlation matrix of all your variables may produce some statistically significant results that would be insignificant if the proper test had been applied.

2. There is a known probability that any correlation in a matrix might be the result of chance. The number of expected significant correlations in a matrix is equal to the level of significance you choose, times the number of variables. If you are looking for covariations that are significant at the 5% level, then you only need 20 tests of covariation to find one such covariation by chance. If you are looking for covariations that are significant at the 1% level, you should expect to find one, by chance,

Table 21.24 Correlation Matrix of All 21 Variables in Kunitz et al's (1981) Study of Hostpital Use on the Navajo Reservation

	1	2	3	4	5	6	7	8	9	10	11	12	13	14	15	16	17	18	19	20
1. Near hospital																				
2. Near surgery	.67																			
3. Wage work	-.24	-.09																		
4. Welfare	.52	.46	-.54																	
5. Education of men	-.42	-.43	.73	-.49																
6. Education of women	.01	-.21	.67	-.32	.81															
7. Hogans	.07	.37	-.26	.72	-.28	-.40														
8. Bathrooms	-.44	-.57	.63	-.63	.70	.64	-.47													
9. Household size	.01	-.16	-.48	.24	-.34	-.07	.04	.12												
10. Working women	-.35	-.36	.68	-.65	.65	.57	.48	.62	-.22											
11. Working men	-.24	-.18	.73	-.37	.73	.63	-.16	.41	-.45	.45										
12. Vehicles	.34	-.08	.40	-.17	.22	.52	-.53	.29	-.06	.31	.40									
13. Median income	-.45	-.51	.66	-.60	.67	.60	-.38	.79	-.07	.83	.48	.27								
14. Per capita income	-.25	-.20	.68	-.46	.61	.40	-.15	.29	-.68	.48	.51	.30	.47							
15. Age of women	-.23	-.03	-.47	-.15	-.36	.66	-.02	-.46	-.30	-.37	-.32	.56	-.43	-.04						
16. Age of men	.28	.15	-.77	.31	-.60	-.55	.01	-.67	.06	-.51	-.68	-.35	-.63	-.45	.60					
17. Age of patients	.13	.47	.13	-.14	-.21	-.15	-.18	-.22	-.36	-.04	-.26	-.15	-.26	-.02	.29	32				
18. Hysterectomies	-.41	-.48	.62	-.55	.57	.46	-.23	.75	-.09	.45	.46	39	.62	.59	-.37	-.62	.28			
19. Appendectomies	-.31	-.40	.32	-.14	.44	.33	.16	.51	.13	.07	.27	.01	.42	.35	-.31	-.49	-.56	-.62		
20. Cholesystectomies	-.23	-.70	.15	-.43	.35	.34	.46	.68	.22	.19	.12	.31	.40	.14	-.17	-.17	-.35	.70	.49	
21. Hospital rate	-.49	.24	.02	-.26	.02	-.25	-.09	.16	-.19	-.04	-.34	-.33	.01	.22	.43	.16	.45	.17	.10	.18

$n = 18$; 0.46. $p = .05$; 0.56 $p = .01$

Source: Reprinted from *Social Science and Medicine.* 15B. S. J. Kunitz et al., "Determinants of Hospital Utilization and Surgery on the Navajo Indian Reservation, 1972–1978," 71–79. Copyright © 1981. with permission of Elsevier Science.

in every 100 tries. In a matrix of 100 variables with 4,950 correlations, you might find around 50 significant correlations at the 1% level by chance.

This does not mean that 50 correlations at the 1% level in such a matrix *are* the result of chance. They just *might* be. There could be 100 or more significant correlations in a symmetric matrix of 100 variables. If 50 of them (4950/100) might be the result of chance, how can you decide which 50 they are? You can't. You can never know for sure whether any particular correlation is the result of chance. You simply have to be careful in your interpretation of *every* correlation in a matrix.

Use the shotgun. Be as cavalier as you can in looking for statistically significant covariations, but be very conservative in interpreting their substantive importance. Correlations are hints to you that something is going on between two variables. Just keep in mind that the leap from correlation to cause is often across a wide chasm.

If you look at Table 21.22 again, you can see just how risky things can be. A correlation of .60 is significant at the 1% level of confidence with a sample as small as 30. Notice, however, that the correlation in the population is 99% certain to fall between .20 and .83, which is pretty widespread. You wouldn't want to build too big a theory around a correlation that just might be down around the .20 level, accounting for just 4% of the variance in what you're interested in.

Remember these rules:

1. Not all significant findings at the 5% level of confidence are equally important. A very weak correlation of .10 in a sample of a million people would be statistically significant, even if it were substantively trivial. By contrast, in small samples, substantively important relations may show up as statistically insignificant.

2. Don't settle for just one correlation that supports a pet theory; insist on several, and be on the lookout for artifactual correlations.

Fifty years ago, before statistical packages were available, it was a real pain to run any statistical tests. It made a lot of sense to think hard about which of the thousands of possible tests one really wanted to run by hand on an adding machine. It still makes a lot of sense. Even though computers have eliminated the drudge work in data analysis, they haven't eliminated the need to think critically about your results. If anything, computers have made it more important than ever to be self-conscious about the interpretation of statistical findings. But if you *are* self-conscious about this issue, and dedicated to thinking critically about your data, then I believe you should take full advantage of the power of the computer to produce a mountain of correlational hints that you can follow up.

Finally, by all means, use your intuition in interpreting correlations; common sense and your personal experience in research are powerful tools for data analysis. If you find a correlation between the number of times that men have been arrested for drug dealing and the number of younger siblings they have, you'd suspect that this correlation might be just a chance artifact.

On the other hand, maybe it isn't. There is just as much danger in relying slavishly on personal intuition and common sense as there is in placing ultimate faith in computers. What appears silly to you may, in fact, be an important signal in your data. The world is filled with self-evident truths that aren't true and self-evident falsehoods that aren't false. The role of science, based on solid technique and the application of intuition, is to sort those things out.

Key Concepts in This Chapter

covariations
statistical significance
t-test
parent population
pooled variance
modulus
absolute value
the Bem Sex Role Inventory
  (BSRI)
Analysis of variance
  (ANOVA)
F-statistic
between-group variance
within-group variance
total variance
sum of the squares
F-ratio
rounding error
one-way analysis of
  variance
multiple-way ANOVA
  MANOVA
analysis of covariance
  ANCOVA
direction of covariation
shape of covariation
linear relation

nonlinear relation
positive covariants
negative covariants
scatterplots (scattergrams)
cross-tabulation table
  (cross-tabs)
four-fold table
bivariate table
marginals
abcissa
ordinate
antecedent variables
intervening variables
old error
new error
proportionate reduction of
  error (PRE)
lambda
chi-square
expected frequencies
2×2 cross-tab
Cramer's V
phi coefficient
Fisher's exact probability
  test
odds ratio (OR)
proportion of matching pairs

gamma (G, g)
Kendall's tau-b (T_b, τ_b)
Yule's Q
Spearman's rho
  (Spearman's r, r_s)
Pearson's product moment
  correlation
Pearson's r
dummy variable
best-fitting line
least squares line
regression line
regression equation
residual
r-squared (r^2)
coefficient of
  determination
natural logarithm
Eta-square (η^2, eta^2)
eliminating the
  outliers
the Bonferroni
  correction
statistical significance
practical significance
statistical power
shotgun strategy

Summary

- Statistical covariation involves four questions: (1) How much better can we predict the score of a dependent variable in our sample if we knew the score of some independent variable? (2) Is the covariation due to chance, or is it likely to exist in the overall population to which we want to generalize? (3) Is it positive or negative? (4) Is it linear or nonlinear?
- The two-sample t-test evaluates whether the means of two independent groups differ on some variable.
  - The null hypothesis, H_0, is that the two means come from random samples of the *same* population—that there is no difference, except for sampling error, between the two means. The research hypothesis, H_1, is that the two means come from random samples of truly different populations.
  - We evaluate the statistical significance of t using Appendix B. Testing the possibility that one mean is higher than another requires a one-tailed test. Use a two-tailed test when you

are only interested in the magnitude of the difference between the means, not its direction or sign (plus or minus).

- A t-test measures the difference between two means. Analysis of variance, or ANOVA, is a technique that applies to a set of K means.

  o Within-group variance is a measure of how much the scores of individual units of analysis are different from one another. Between-group variance expresses the amount that the scores between groups are different from one another.

  o To find whether the means of several groups are significantly different from one another, calculate the ratio between the mean of the between-group variance and the mean of the within-group variance. Use Appendix D to determine the statistical significance of the ratio.

- The concept of direction refers to whether a covariation is positive or negative. The concept shape refers to whether a relation is linear or nonlinear. Scatterplots help us see whether covariations are positive or negative, linear or nonlinear.

- Cross-tabulation tables, or cross-tabs, display the relations among two or more nominal or ordinal variables. The values for dependent variable are displayed in the rows and the values for independent variable are in the columns. Then the rule is: *percentage down the columns and interpret across the rows*.

- Covariation does not necessarily mean cause and effect.

  o To understand the relation between two variables, we need to ask about antecedent and intervening variables: (1) Is there some variable that is *related to, and prior to*, both the independent and dependent variables? (2) Is there some variable that enters the picture *between* the independent and dependent variables?

- The PRE principle (proportionate reduction of error) is the foundation for many statistical tests. A PRE measure tells you how much better you can guess the scores on a dependent variable by knowing the distribution of an independent variable. Chi-square tells you the probability that a relation between or among variables is the result of chance. But it is not a PRE measure of correlation, so it doesn't tell you the strength of association among variables. The principle use of χ^2 is for testing the hypothesis that there is no relation between two nominal variables—that is, for testing the null hypothesis.

  o Fisher's exact probability test is used for 2×2 tables whenever the expected number of frequencies for any cell is less than five. With fewer than five expected occurrences in a cell, χ^2 values are generally not trustworthy.

  o A direct and intuitive measure of strength for understanding the relation between nominal variables is the odds ratio.

- Gamma is a PRE measure for ordinal variables. Gamma tells you how much more correctly you could guess the rank of one ordinal variable for each unit of analysis if you knew the score for the other ordinal variable in a bivariate distribution.

  o Some researchers prefer a statistic called Kendall's tau–b (written t_b or τ_b) instead of gamma for bivariate tables of ordinal data because gamma ignores tied pairs in the data.

  o Yule's Q is the equivalent of gamma for 2×2 tables of ordinal variables.

- When at least one of the variables in a bivariate relation is interval or ratio level, we use a measure of correlation: Spearman's *rho*, when the data are rank ordered; Pearson's product moment correlation, written simply as r, to measure the strength of linear relations; or *eta* squared (the Greek letter η^2) to measure the strength of certain kinds of nonlinear relations.

o Pearson's r measures how much of the time changes in one variable correspond with equivalent changes in the other variables. The square of Pearson's r is a PRE measure of association for linear relations between interval variables. r-squared tells us how much better we can predict the scores of a dependent variable, if we know the scores of some independent variable.

- Correlation is best understood in the context of regression. The regression equation for any pair of scores on two variables is $y = a + bx$. To draw the regression line, find the expected y coordinate for two of the actual data points on the independent variable, x, and connect the dots.

o The values produced by the regression equation produces a certain amount of error, which is the difference between the predicted number for the dependent variable and the actual measurement. This residual is what's left over after making your prediction using the regression equation.

o r-squared, or the coefficient of determination, is the amount of variance accounted for by the independent variable. It tells us how much of the variance in the dependent variable is predictable from the scores of the independent variable. The Pearson product moment correlation, written as r, is the square root of this measure.

- In linear relations, the best-fitting "curve" on a bivariate scattergram is a straight line. A lot of really interesting relations, however, are nonlinear. A few such relations include: political orientation and age, the size of personal networks and age, the mean number of assaults and mean daily temperature, and the educational level of marriage partners and the mean level of industrialization.

- Data analysis is a complex intellectual exercise. Four important issues that continue to be debated include: (1) measurement and statistical assumptions; (2) significance tests; (3) eliminating the outliers; and (4) the shotgun method of analysis.

o Measurement and statistical assumptions. As I pointed out in Chapter 2, many concepts, such as gender, race, and class are much more subtle and complex than we give them credit for being. Instead of measuring them qualitatively (remember that assignment of something to a nominal category is a qualitative act of measurement), we ought to be thinking hard about how to measure them ordinally.

o Eliminating the outliers is always a temptation because doing so produces higher correlations. But is creating a good statistical fit what you're after? Don't you really want to understand what makes the data messy in the first place? In general, you cannot achieve understanding of messiness by cleaning things up.

o Statistical tests of significance are not magical. In particular the .05 and .01 levels of significance are arbitrary. Test the power of any statistical test to guard against failing to see that your research hypothesis should be accepted.

o Shotgunning involves constructing a correlation matrix of all combinations of variables in a study, and then relying on tests of significance to reach substantive conclusions. The problem with shotgunning is that you might be fooled into thinking that statistically significant correlations are also substantively significant.

Exercises

1. Marlene Dobkin de Rios (1981) studied the clientele of a Peruvian folk healer. She suspected that women clients were more likely to have had personal experience with witchcraft (or to have a close family member who has had personal contact with witchcraft) than were men clients. The following table shows Dobkin de Rios's data.

Table E21.1 Dobkin de Rios's Data on Experience With Witchcraft, by Gender

	Personal experience with witchcraft or close family with personal contact	No personal experience with witchcraft	Totals
Male clients	12	15	27
Female clients	63	5	68
Total	75	20	95

Source: M. Dobkin de Rios, "Socioeconomic Characteristics of an Amazon Urban Healer's Clientele." *Social Science and Medicine*, 15B:51–63, Copyright ©1981.

In how many cases out of 1,000 would you expect this distribution of cases by chance? To answer this question, find the value of χ^2 for this table. How many degrees of freedom does this table have? Using the proper number of df, consult Appendix C to find the level of significance for χ^2.

2. Hunfield et al. (1996) tested the level of grief in 13 couples in Rotterdam, Holland, six months after the couples had lost an infant. The couples were all relatively young and all the babies had died of major congenital anomalies less than a year after birth. Hunfield et al. tested the men and women separately on three separate measures of grief: amount of active grief, difficulty coping with the loss, and level of despair. For men, the mean total grief score was $\bar{x} = 72.8 \; sd \, 11.2$. For women, $\bar{x} = 73.6 \; sd \, 16.1$. Hunfield et al. report that was no significant difference between men and women on this grief scale. Test their conclusion using the t-distribution.

3. Philipp (1998) asked 101 African American and 280 White high school students to rate their preferences for 20 leisure activities. Here are the results:

Table E21.2 Preferences Among 281 High School Students for 20 Leisure Activities

Activity	African American Males n = 47		African American Females n = 54		White Males n = 140		White Females n = 140	
	rank	mean	rank	mean	rank	mean	rank	mean
Going to the beach	3	2.15	2	1.60	1	1.67	1	1.37
Playing basketball	1	1.41	5	2.36	4	2.41	13	3.29
Going to the mall	2	1.78	1	1.45	6	2.51	2	2.00
Reading for pleasure	15	4.30	10	3.55	18	4.50	14	3.37
Playing video games	5	2.76	9	3.21	9	3.09	17	3.62
Bowling	9	3.61	8	2.74	8	3.08	9	2.81
Watching TV	4	2.59	4	2.04	7	2.63	7	2.47
Playing soccer	20	4.98	18	4.44	15	3.88	11	3.15
Using a computer	10	3.63	7	2.72	12	3.39	10	3.08
Horseback riding	16	4.41	14	3.96	10	3.23	3	2.07
Waterskiing	14	4.26	17	4.30	5	2.42	5	2.13
Singing in a choir	13	4.07	6	2.37	19	4.51	16	3.47
Collecting stamps/coins	18	4.78	19	4.68	20	4.99	20	4.65
Camping	11	3.94	15	4.00	3	2.25	4	2.08
Jogging	8	3.49	11	3.57	11	3.31	8	2.74
Fishing	7	3.48	13	3.81	2	2.17	12	3.16
Playing a musical instrument	12	3.98	12	3.68	14	3.85	15	3.38
Golfing	19	4.89	20	4.92	16	4.15	19	4.58
Dancing	6	2.80	3	2.04	13	3.79	6	2.38
Going to a museum	17	4.52	16	4.02	17	4.47	18	3.68

Source: S. E. Philipp, "Race and Gender Differences in Adolescent Peer Group Approval of Leisure Activities." *Journal of Leisure Research* 30:214–232, Copyright © 1998.

Use Spearman's rank order correlation to test whether the leisure preferences of the White males are statistically different from those of the White females. What other comparisons can you make?

4. Rusting and Larsen (1998) used the experience sampling method to assess the mood of 19 men and 27 women three times a day (morning, noon, and evening) for 60 days. At each

rating time, participants rated, on a scale of 0 (not at all) to 6 (extremely), whether they felt depressed, unhappy, frustrated, worried, or angry. They also assessed, on a scale of 1–9: (1) whether they felt that *they* were responsible for their current mood or that others were responsible (this variable was scored 1 = *due to me* to 9 = *due to others* and is called EXTERNAL in the table below); (2) whether their moods were controllable or uncontrollable (1 = *controllable*, called CONTROLLABLE); (3) whether they felt their moods were stable or unstable (1 = *unstable*, and is called STABLE); and (4) whether their moods were the result of a particular situation or something that was a big part of their life in general (1 = *particular situation*, called GLOBAL).

Here are the results, across 46 people and 180 ratings. Test the hypothesis (using *t*-tests) that things get worse for people as the day goes along.

Table E21.3 Assessment of Mood Changes Across 60 Days

	Morning		Afternoon		Evening	
	M	SD	M	SD	M	SD
External	1.60	0.95	1.94	1.06	2.66	1.28
Uncontrollable	1.43	0.91	1.63	0.97	2.02	1.02
Stable	1.29	0.68	1.51	0.72	2.06	0.96
Global	1.16	0.76	1.36	0.79	1.84	1.10

Source: C. L. Rusting and R. J. Larsen, "Diurnal Patterns of Unpleasant Mood: Associations with Neuroticism, Depression, and Anxiety." *Journal of Personality* 66:85–103, Copyright © 1998.

5. Make a list of 20 items that you normally buy at the supermarket (or use the list of 21 items from Titus and Everett's [1996] study; see Exercise 2, Chapter 14). The next time you go shopping, note the cost of these items. Ask two people who shop at markets other than yours to do the same. You should have a 20 (or 21) × 3 table of items-by-supermarkets. Using ANOVA, test the hypothesis that there is no difference in the overall cost of shopping at the three markets. (If the brand is important in determining the price, then note the brand as well as the item. The price of soap, for example, is quite sensitive to brand differences, while the cost of bananas is much less so.)

As an alternative to this project, find the average price of renting an apartment in three or more different parts of your city and use ANOVA to test the hypothesis that it costs about the same to live anywhere.

6. Here are the average 2008 salaries of public school teachers for the 50 states of the United States. Each state is identified as being in one of four regions: Northeast = 1, Midwest = 2, West = 3, and South = 4. Use ANOVA to test the hypothesis that, statistically speaking, there really isn't much difference in teachers' salaries across the United States.

Table E21.4 Public Elementary and Secondary Schoolteachers' Average Salaries in the 50 U.S. States, 2008

State	Area	Salary	State	Area	Salary	State	Area	Salary	State	Area	Salary
CT	1	62.0	IL	2	60.5	AL	3	46.6	AK	4	56.8
ME	1	43.4	IN	2	49.2	AR	3	45.8	AZ	4	45.8
MA	1	63.8	IA	2	45.7	DE	3	56	CA	4	65.8
NH	1	48.3	KS	2	44.8	FL	3	46.9	CO	4	47.5
NJ	1	61.3	MI	2	56.1	GA	3	51.5	HI	4	53.4
NY	1	65.5	MN	2	50.6	KY	3	47.2	ID	4	44.1
PA	1	56.1	MO	2	43.2	LA	3	47	MT	4	42.9
RI	1	57.2	NB	2	43.6	MD	3	60.1	NV	4	47.7
VT	1	46.6	ND	2	40.3	MS	3	42.4	NM	4	45.1
			OH	2	53.4	NC	3	47.4	OR	4	52.7
			SD	2	36.7	OK	3	43.6	UT	4	41.6
			WI	2	49.1	SC	3	45.8	WA	4	49.9
						TN	3	44.8	WY	4	53.0
						TX	3	46.2			
						VI	3	46.7			
						WV	3	42.5			

Source: Table 252, *Statistical Abstract of the United States* (2011).

Further Reading

Visualizing covariations. Cleveland (1994), Doherty and Anderson (2009), Jacoby (1997), Wallgren et al. (1996).

Measurement in the social sciences. Bartholomew (2006), Blalock (1982), Coombs (1964), Kempf-Leonard (2005), Norman (2010), Nunnally (1978).

Dealing with outliers. Barnett and Lewis (1994), Flowers et al. (1997), Lewis-Beck (1995), Wilcox (1998).

Statistical significance. Carver (1978, 1993), Cohen (1994), Harlow et al. (1997), Labovitz (1971b), Leahy (2005), Lempert (2009), Zuckerman et al. (1993).

Statistical power. Hedges and Rhoads (2010), Murphy and Myors (1998).

22

Multivariate Analysis

INTRODUCTION

Most of the really interesting dependent variables in the social world—things like personality type, amount of risk-taking behavior, level of wealth accumulation, attitudes toward women or men—appear to be caused by a large number of independent variables, many of which are dependent variables themselves. The goal of multivariate analysis is to test hypotheses about *how* variables are related, based on a theory of causation. This is called **causal modeling.**

Multivariate analysis involves an array of statistical procedures. You will run into these procedures again and again as you read journal articles and monographs—things like multiple regression, partial regression, factor analysis, multidimensional scaling, analysis of variance, and so on. I'll introduce you to the conceptual basis of some of these methods here. I hope that this will give you an idea of the range of tools available and enough information so you can read and understand research articles in which these techniques are used. I also hope that this will arouse your curiosity enough so that you'll study these methods in more advanced classes. This is the fun part (Box 22.1).

Box 22.1 Courses on multivariate analysis

Once you have mastered the logic of multivariate analysis, seek out courses that take you more deeply into the use of these powerful tools. Courses on multivariate analysis are offered in stats departments, but many departments of sociology, psychology, education, and public health also offer courses in multivariate analysis to their students. The examples used in those courses are usually from whatever academic discipline in which the instructor was trained, but by now you've gathered that *that* doesn't make much difference.

All multivariate techniques require caution in their use. It is easy to be impressed with the elegance of multivariate analysis and to lose track of the theoretical issues that motivated your study in the first place. On the other hand, multivariate techniques are important aids to research, and I encourage you to experiment and learn to use them. Try out several of these techniques; learn to read the computer output they produce when used on your data.

But don't be afraid to play and have a good time. If you hang around social scientists who use complex statistical tools in their research, you'll hear people talk about "massaging" their data with this or that multivariate technique, or about "teasing out signals" from their data, and "separating the signals from the noise." These are not the sort of phrases used by people who are bored with what they're doing.

ELABORATION: CONTROLLING FOR INDEPENDENT VARIABLES

We begin with the elaboration method developed by Paul Lazarsfeld and his colleagues (1972) for analyzing data from surveys. This method involves teasing out the complexities in a bivariate relation by controlling for the effects of a third variable.

It's going to take you a while to get through the next half dozen pages on the elaboration method. There's nothing more complicated than a chi-square (χ^2), so they're not tough going. They're just plain tedious. Bear with me though. Eventually, you'll give a computer a list of independent variables, specify a dependent variable, and let the machine do the heavy lifting. But the next few pages will give you an appreciation of what a multivariate analysis does. So be patient, pay close attention to the tables, and stay with it.

Men and Women Voters

In 1996, just after the presidential election, the Bureau of Business and Economic Research at the University of Florida conducted a statewide poll. Respondents were asked, among other things, who they voted for plus some socio-demographic information (sex, age, income, marital status, race-ethnicity). Respondents were also asked the following questions:

Would you say that you (and your family living there) are better off or worse financially than you were a year ago?

1. Better off

2. Same

3. Worse off

4. Don't know

Looking ahead, which would you say is more likely—that in the country as a whole we'll have continuous good times during the next five years or so, or that we will have periods of widespread unemployment or depression, or what?

1. Good times

2. Uncertain; good and bad

3. Bad times

4. Don't know

The first question is designed to measure current and personal financial optimism or pessimism. The second is designed to measure long-term and general optimism or pessimism. Table 22.1 shows the relation between the answers to the question about the short term (labeled YEAR-AGO) and income (labeled INCOME). Income was originally coded into 9 categories, but I've cut it into two chunks: Low = up to $40,000 (which was the median for the sample) and High = above $40,000.

Table 22.1a shows that, across all 435 respondents who answered both questions, the relation between current optimism and level of income is statistically very significant. Chi-square is 14.326, with 2 degrees of freedom and $p = 0.001$. Unsurprisingly, if you had high income, you were far more likely to see things as having gotten better over the past year.

When we control for sex, though, the picture changes. Table 22.1b shows that for women, the original relation continues to hold, but Table 22.1c shows that the statistically significant relation between current financial optimism and current income vanishes for men. The antecedent variable, sex, influences the relation between current financial optimism and current income.

Table 22.2 shows the relation between the answers to the question about the long term (labeled NEXT5) and income. This

| Table 22.1a | Bivariate Relation Between Current Financial Optimism and Current Income |

	INCOME		
YEAR-AGO	High	Low	Total
Better off	74	102	176
Same	89	63	152
Worse off	67	40	107
Total	230	205	435
χ^2 = 14.326 2 degrees of freedom, $p = 0.001$.			

Source: Bureau of Business and Economic Research, University of Florida.

| Table 22.1b | Same as 22.1a, but for Women Only |

	INCOME		
YEAR-AGO	High	Low	Total
Better off	37	49	86
Same	51	23	74
Worse off	38	20	58
Total	126	92	218
χ^2 = 12.865 with 2 degrees of freedom, $p = 0.002$.			

Source: Bureau of Business and Economic Research, University of Florida.

| Table 22.1c | Same as 22.1a, but for Men Only |

	INCOME		
YEAR-AGO	Low	High	Total
Better off	37	53	90
Same	38	40	78
Worse off	29	20	49
Total	104	113	217
χ^2 = 4.183, with 2 degrees of freedom, $p = 0.124$ n.s.			

Source: Bureau of Business and Economic Research, University of Florida.

table shows how the same antecedent variable—sex—can play a different role. Across the full sample of respondents (Table 22.2a), there is no statistically significant relation between long-term optimism/pessimism and current level of income. Controlling for sex, we see that the relation *remains* statistically nonsignificant for men (Table 22.2b) but *emerges* as significant for women (Table 22.2c).

In Table 22.1, controlling for the antecedent variable had the effect of trouncing a statistically significant relation in one of the subtables. In Table 22.2, controlling for the same antecedent variable had the effect of turning a statistically nonsignificant relation into a significant one in one of the subtables.

PARTIAL CORRELATION

I haven't proved anything by all this laying out of tables. Don't misunderstand me. Elaboration tables are a great start—they test whether your ideas about some antecedent or intervening variables are plausible by showing what *could* be going on—but they don't tell you *how things work* or *how much* those antecedent or intervening variables are contributing to a correlation you want to understand. For that, we need something a bit more . . . well, elaborate.

Partial correlation is a *direct* way to control for the effects of a third (or fourth or fifth . . .) variable on a relation between two variables.

Car Wrecks and Teenage Births

Here's an interesting case. Across the 50 states in the United States, there is a stunning correlation ($r = .778$) between the percentage of live births to teenage mothers

| Table 22.2a | Bivariate Relation Between Long-Term Optimism and Current Income |

	INCOME		
NEXT5	Low	High	Total
Good times	107	85	192
Good and bad	31	36	67
Bad times	70	81	151
Total	208	202	410
$\chi^2 = 3.608$, with 2 degrees of freedom, $p = 0.165$			

Source: Bureau of Business and Economic Research, University of Florida.

| Table 22.2b | Same as 16.2a, but for Men Only |

	INCOME		
NEXT5	Low	High	Total
Good times	52	54	106
Good and bad	14	21	35
Bad times	34	36	70
Total	100	111	211
$\chi^2 = 0.924$ with 2 degrees of freedom, $p = 0.630$			

Source: Bureau of Business and Economic Research, University of Florida.

| Table 22.2c | Same as 16.2a, but for Women Only |

	INCOME		
NEXT5	Low	High	Total
Good times	55	31	86
Good and bad	17	15	32
Bad times	36	45	81
Total	108	91	199
$\chi^2 = 6.417$ with 2 degrees of freedom, $p = 0.040$			

Source: Bureau of Business and Economic Research, University of Florida.

(15–19 years of age) and the number of motor vehicle deaths per hundred million miles driven. States that have a high rate of road carnage also have a high rate of births to teenagers.

This one's a real puzzle. Obviously, there's no *direct* relation between these two variables. There's no way that the volume of highway carnage causes the number of teenage mothers or vice versa, so we look for something that might cause both of them.

I have a hunch that these two variables are correlated because they are both the consequence of the fact that certain regions of the country are poorer than others. I know from my own experience, and from having read a lot of research reports, that the western and southern states are poorer, overall, than are the industrial and farming states of the Northeast and the Midwest. My hunch is that poorer states will have fewer miles of paved road per million people, poorer roads overall, and older vehicles. All this might lead to more deaths per miles driven.

Table 22.3 shows the zero order correlation among three variables: motor vehicle deaths per hundred million miles driven (it's labeled MVD in Table 22.3), the percentage of live births to young women 15–19 years of age (TEENBIRTH), and average personal income (INCOME). Zero-order correlations do not take into account the influence of other variables (Box 22.2).

Box 22.2 The correlation is stable

The data in Table 22.3 are for 1995–96, when I wrote the first edition of this book. Between 1995 and 2007, the rate of teenagers giving birth in the United States dropped from about 56.7 to about 42.5 babies per 1,000 and the rate of births to unmarried women rose from 45 to 52.3 per 1,000 women. Despite these dramatic changes in fertility patterns over just 12 years, the correlation between the rate of teenage births and the rate of death in car wrecks remained almost identical (0.778 in 1995–96 and 0.781 in 2007). The strong correlations between INCOME and MVD (−0.662 in the mid-1990s, −0.649 in 2007) and between TEENBIRTH and INCOME (−0.700 and −0.636) were also little changed.

Table 22.3 Correlation Matrix for Three Variables

	TEENBIRTH	INCOME	MVD
TEENBIRTH	1.000		
INCOME	−.700	1.000	
MVD	.778	−.662	1.000

Source: MVD for 1995, *Statistical Abstract of the United States*, Table 1018, 1997. TEENBIRTH for 1996, *Statistical Abstract of the United States*, Table 98, 1997. INCOME for 1996, *Statistical Abstract of the United States*, Table 706, 1997.

With interval-scale variables we can use the formula for partial correlation to test directly what effect, if any, income has on the correlation between TEENBIRTH and MVD. The formula for partial correlation is:

$$r_{12\cdot3} = \frac{r_{12} - [r_{32} \times r_{13}]}{\left[\sqrt{1 - r_{32}^2}\right] \times \left[\sqrt{1 - r_{13}^2}\right]} \qquad \text{formula 22.1}$$

where $r_{12\cdot3}$ = means "the correlation between variable 1 (MVD) and variable 2 (TEENBIRTH), *controlling* for variable 3 (INCOME) is . . ." (Partial correlation can be done on ordinal variables by substituting a statistic like tau or gamma for *r* in the formula above.)

Table 22.4 shows the calculation of the partial correlations for the entries in Table 22.3.

So, the partial correlation between MVD and TEENBIRTH, controlling for INCOME is:

$$\frac{.778 - [(.700)(-.662)]}{(.714143)(.749504)} = \frac{.3146}{.535253}$$

$$= .58774594$$

which we can round off to .59. (Remember, we have to use a *lot* of decimal places during the calculations to keep the rounding error in check. When we get through with the calculations we can round off to two or three decimal places.) In other words, when we partial out the effect of income, the correlation between MVD and TEENBIRTH drops from about .78 to about .59. That's because income is correlated with motor vehicle deaths ($r = -.662$) *and* with teenage births ($r = .49$).

If a partial correlation of .59 between the rate of motor vehicle deaths and the rate of teenage births still seems high, then perhaps other variables are at work. You can "partial out" the effects of two or more variables at once, but as you take on more variables, the formula naturally gets more complicated (Box 22.3).

Or you can work out and test a model of how several independent variables influence a dependent variable all at once. This is the task of multiple regression, which we'll take up next.

Table 22.4 Calculating the Partial Correlations for the Entries in Table 22.3

Pairs	Pearson's *r*	r^2	$1 - r^2$	$\sqrt{1-r^2}$
r_{12} (MVD and TEENBIRTH)	.778	.605284	.394716	.628264
r_{13} (MVD and INCOME)	−.662	.438244	.561756	.749504
r_{32} (TEENBIRTH and INC)	−.700	.4900	.5100	.714143

Box 22.3 Higher order partials

A simple correlation is a zero-order correlation. Formula 22.1 is for a **first-order correlation**. The formula for a **second-order correlation** (controlling for two variables at the same time) is

$$r_{12\cdot34} = \frac{r_{12\cdot3} - [r_{14\cdot3}r_{24\cdot3}]}{\left[\sqrt{1 - r_{14\cdot3}^2}\right] \times \left[\sqrt{1 - r_{24\cdot3}^2}\right]} \qquad \textbf{formula 22.2}$$

For more on partial correlation, see Gujarati and Porter (2008).

MULTIPLE REGRESSION

Partial correlation tells us how much a third (or fourth . . .) variable contributes to the relation between two variables. Multiple regression puts all the information about a series of variables together into a single equation that takes account of the interrelation among independent variables. The result of multiple regression is a statistic called multiple-R, which is the combined correlation of a set of independent variables with the dependent variable, taking into account the fact that each of independent variables might be correlated with each of the *other* independent variables.

Even more interesting is multiple-R squared, or R^2. Remember that little-r-squared, r^2 (the square of the Pearson product moment correlation coefficient) is the amount of variance in the dependent variable accounted for by the independent variable in a simple regression? Big R-squared, R^2, is the amount of variance in the dependent variable accounted for by two or more independent variables simultaneously.

Now, if the predictors of a dependent variable were all uncorrelated with each other, we could just add together the pieces of the variance in the dependent variable accounted for by each of the independent variables. That is, it would be nice if: $R^2 = r_1^2 + r_2^2 + r_3^2 \ldots$

It's a real annoyance, but independent variables *are* usually correlated with one another. We need a method for figuring out how much variance in a dependent variable is accounted for by a series of independent variables after taking account of all the overlap in variances accounted for across the independent variables. That's what multiple regression does.

The Multiple Regression Equation

Recall from Chapter 21 that the regression equation expresses how an independent variable is related to a dependent variable. On the left-hand side of the equation, we have the unknown score for y, the dependent variable. On the right-hand side we have the y-intercept, called a. It's the score for y if the independent variable were zero. We have another coefficient, called b, that tells by *how much* to multiply the score on the independent variable for each unit change in that variable.

The general form of the equation

$$y = a + bx$$

which means that the dependent variable, y, equals some constant plus another constant times the independent variable x. So, for example, a regression equation like

Starting Annual Income
$$= \$26,000 + (\$5,000 \times \text{Years of College})$$

predicts that, on average, someone with a high school education will start out earning \$26,000 a year; those with a year of college will earn \$31,000; and so on. From this equation nine years of university education (what it takes to get a Ph.D. in most fields) would be predicted to start at \$71,000:

Starting Annual Income = \$26,000
$$+ (\$5,000 \times 9) = \$71,000$$

Now suppose that the average starting salary for someone who has a Ph.D. is \$85,000. Several things could account for the discrepancy between our prediction and the reality. Sampling problems could be the culprit. Or it could be that there is just a lot of variability in starting salaries of people who have the Ph.D. English teachers who go to work in small, liberal arts colleges might start at \$45,000, while chemists who go to work for major oil companies might start at \$145,000.

No amount of fixing the sample will do anything to get rid of the variance of starting salaries. In fact, the better the sample, the better it will reflect the enormous variance in those salaries.

In simple regression, if starting salary and years of education are related variables, we want to know "How accurately can we predict a person's starting salary if we know how many years of education they have beyond high school?" In multiple regression, we build more complex equations that tell us how much each of *several* independent variables contributes to predicting the score of a single dependent variable.

A typical question for a multiple regression analysis might be "How well can we predict a person's starting salary if we know how many years of college they have, *and* their major, *and* their gender, *and* their age, *and* their ethnic background?" Each of those independent variables contributes something to predicting a person's starting salary after high school.

The regression equation for two independent variables, called x_1 and x_2, and one dependent variable, called y, is:

$$y = a + b_1 x_1 + b_2 x_2 \qquad \text{formula 22.3}$$

which means that we need to find a separate constant—one called b_1 and one called b_2—by which to multiply each of the two independent variables. The general formula for multiple regression is:

$$y = a + b_1 x_1 + b_2 x_2 \ldots b_n x_n \quad \text{formula 22.4}$$

Recall that simple regression yields a PRE measure, r^2. It tells you how much better you can predict a series of measures of a dependent variable than you could by just guessing the mean for every measurement. Multiple regression is also a PRE measure. It, too, tells you how much better you can predict measures of a dependent variable than you could if you guessed the

mean—but using all the information available in a series of independent variables.

The key to regression are those b coefficients in formula 22.4. We want weights that, when multiplied by the independent variables, produce the best possible prediction of the dependent variable. That is, we want predictions that result in the smallest possible residuals. Those coefficients, by the way, are not existential constants. They change with every sample you take and with the number of independent variables in the equation.

The MVD-TEENBIRTH Puzzle

Let's try to solve the puzzle of the relation between teenage births and the rate of motor vehicle deaths. We can take a stab at this using multiple regression by trying to predict the rate of teenage births *without* the data from motor vehicle deaths.

From our previous analyses with elaboration tables and with partial correlation, we already had an idea that income might have something to do with the rate of teen births. We know from the literature (Handwerker 1998) that poverty is associated with violence and with teenage pregnancy and that this is true across ethnic groups, so in Table 22.5, I've added a variable on violent crimes (in 1995) to the three variables in Table 22.3.

We see right away that the mean per capita income predicts the rate of births to teenagers ($r = -.700$) almost as well as does the rate of motor vehicle deaths ($r = .778$) and that mean income *also* predicts the rate of motor vehicle deaths rather well ($r = -.662$).

This is a clue about what might be going on: An antecedent variable, the level of income, might be responsible for the rate of motor vehicle deaths *and* the rate of teenage births. (By the way, did you notice that the strong correlations above were *negative*? The greater the mean income in the state, the lower the rate of

Table 22.5   Correlation Matrix for Variables Associated With the Percentage of Teenage Births in the U.S.

	TEENBIRTH	INCOME	VIOLRATE	MVD
TEENBIRTH	1.000			
INCOME	−.700	1.000		
VIOLRATE	.340	.190	1.000	
MVD	.778	−.662	.245	1.000

teenage births and the lower the rate of motor vehicle deaths. Remember, correlations can vary from −1.0 to +1.0 and that the strength of the correlation has nothing to do with its direction.)

The task for multiple regression is to see how the independent variables predict the dependent variable *together*. If the correlation between mean per capita income and the rate of births to teenagers is −.700, that means that the independent variable accounts for 49% ($-.700^2$) of the variance in the dependent variable. And if the correlation between the rate of violent crimes and the rate of births to teenagers is .340 in Table 22.5, then the independent variable accounts for 11.56% ($.340^2$) of the variance in the dependent variable.

We can't just add these variances-accounted-for together, though, because the two independent variables are related to each other—each of the independent variables accounts for some variance in the other.

Figure 22.1 shows what the output looks like from SYSTAT® when I asked the program to calculate the multiple correlation, R, for INCOME and VIOLRATE on TEENBIRTH.

Figure 22.1 tells us that the regression equation is:

$$TEENBIRTH = 28.096$$
$$+ (.006 \times VIOLRATE)$$
$$+ (-.001 \times INCOME)$$

For example, the violence rate for Wisconsin was 281 crimes per 100,000 residents in 1995 and the average income in

Figure 22.1   Multiple Regression Output From SYSTAT[7]

```
Dep Var: TEENBIRTH  N: 50  Multiple R: 0.850  Squared multiple R: 0.722

Adjusted squared multiple R: 0.710  Standard error of estimate: 1.829

Effect Coefficient  Std Error  Std Coef  Tolerance    t     P(2 Tail)

CONSTANT  28.096    1.822      0.0         .        15.423   0.000

VIOLRATE   0.006    0.001      0.491     0.964       6.269   0.000

INCOME    -0.001    0.000     -0.793     0.964     -10.130   0.000
```

Wisconsin was $21,184 in 1996. The regression equation predicts that the teenage birth rate for Wisconsin will be 8.6. The actual rate was 10.6 in 1996. The mean rate of teenage births for the 50 U.S. states was 12.9. The multiple regression, then makes a better prediction than the mean: The difference between 10.6 and 12.9 is 2.3, while the difference between 8.6 and 10.6 is 2.0 (Box 22.4).

Box 22.4 The regression coefficients

There are three **regression coefficients** in this equation. They are the a, b_1, and b_2 coefficients in formula 22.3. Each of the b coefficients is the product of the standardized regression coefficient for each independent variable with the ratio of the standard deviation of the independent variable to the standard deviation of the dependent variable.

The standardized coefficient for the relation between x_1 (TEENBIRTH) and x_2 (INCOME) is

$$\beta(x_1 x_2) = \frac{r_{12} - (r_{13})(r_{23})}{1 - (r_{23})^2}$$

so, for INCOME(x_2), $\beta = -.793$ and for VIOLRATE (x_3), $\beta = -.491$

These figures are given in Figure 22.1 as the standardized coefficients.
The standard deviation for the mean of INCOME is: 3074.969.
The standard deviation for the mean of TEENBIRTH is: 3.399.
The standard deviation for the mean of VIOLRATE is: 269.225

Thus $b_1 = -.793 \times \dfrac{3.399}{3,074.969} = -.001$ and $b_2 = .491 \times \dfrac{3.399}{269.225} = .006$

These figures are given in Figure 22.1 as the unstandardized regression coefficients. The method for calculating the value for a in the multiple regression equation is beyond the scope of this book. For details, see Pedhazur (1997).

If you work out all the differences between the predictions from the *multiple* regression equation and the predictions from the *simple* regression equation involving *just* the effect of income on teenage births, the difference in the predictions will be the difference between accounting for 49% of the variance vs. accounting for 72.2% of the variance in the dependent variable (Box 22.5).

Box 22.5 Some details about this regression example

In this example, y is TEENBIRTH, x_1 is INCOME and x_2 is VIOLRATE. $R^2_{1 \cdot 23}$ is the relation of TEENBIRTH (the 1 in the subscript) to both INCOME and VIOLRATE (the 2 and 3 in the postscript). This relation is:

$$R^2_{1 \cdot 23} = R^2_{12} + R^2_{1 \cdot (3 \cdot 2)}$$

(Continued)

(Continued)

which is the relation between TEENBIRTH and VIOLRATE once you partial out the contribution of INCOME. Calculating $R^2_{1\cdot23}$ then:

$$R^2_{1\cdot23} = r_{13} - (r_{12})(r_{32}) = .340 - (-.700)(.19)$$
$$= .473$$

Taking the partial contribution of this relation to the dependent variable:

$$\frac{.473}{\sqrt{1-19^2}} = .481776$$

The contribution of this correlation to the variance of TEENBIRTH is $.481776^2$, or .23211. INCOME accounts for 49% of the variance in TEENBIRTH. Adding contributions, we get .49 + .23211, or 72.2%, which is the squared multiple-R in Figure 22.1. For more about deriving multiple regression equations, consult Pedhazur (1997) or Gujarati and Porter (2008).

But there's more. If we add up the variances accounted for by the zero-order correlations of INCOME and VIOLRATE on TEENBIRTH, we get 49% + 11.56% = 60.56%. According to the results in Figure 22.1 and Box 22.4, however, the income in a state and the rate of violent crimes *together* account for 72.2% of the variance in teenage births. In other words, the two variables acting together account for *more* than they do separately, and this is the case despite the fact that the independent variables are moderately correlated ($r = .340$) with each other.

In fact, INCOME explains 43.82% of the variance in motor vehicle deaths ($r = -.662$ and $r^2 = .4382$) and VIOLRATE explains 6% of the variance in motor vehicle deaths ($r = .245$ and $r^2 = .0600$). *Together,* though, INCOME and VIOLRATE have a multiple-R of .762 and an R^2 of .581. Here again, the two variables explain more variance working together than they explain working separately.

In other words, it's the complex association of per capita income *and* the level of violence that explains so much variance in *both* the rate of teenage births and the rate of motor vehicle deaths. It turns out that lots of things are best explained by a series of variables acting together.

Two Examples of Multiple Regression

Scott Myers (2010) tested the impact of predictor variables on the academic achievement of third-grade public school students in Kansas. Myers's dependent variable—his proxy for academic achievement—was the percentage of students in the 295 school districts across the state who scored "Proficient" or better on the 2008 Third Grade Kansas Reading Assessment.

For each superintendent, Myers had data on: (1) longevity (how many years he or she had served in the district); (2) years of experience being a superintendent; and (3) years of experience in education. And for each district,

Myers knew (4) the number of students and the (5) the percentage of students who qualified for free or reduced meals. A superintendent's total years of experience in education had no statistically significant impact on student achievement, but the other four independent variables together accounted for 9.9% of the variance in students' performance on the 2008 Third Grade Kansas Reading Assessment.

Korsching et al. (1980) used a shotgun or shopping technique in their multivariate study of a group of families who were relocated when the land they lived on in Kentucky became part of a reservoir project. Their multiple regression found seven social and economic factors that accounted for at least some of the variance in relative satisfaction with new and old residences among those relocated.

Those factors were: change in social activities (accounting for 18%); education (accounting for 4%); total family income before relocation (another 4%); change of financial situation (3%). Three other variables (satisfaction with resettlement payments, tenure status on the land, and length of residence in the old house) each accounted for 1% or less. All together, the seven independent variables accounted for 31% of the variance in satisfaction with the move (Box 22.6).

Box 22.6 On explaining just a little of something

In social science research, multiple regression (including path analysis, which is coming up next) typically accounts for between 10% and 50% of the variance in any dependent variable, using between two and eight independent variables. It is customary not to include independent variables that account for less than 1% of the variance in a multiple regression equation, but there is no law against doing so.

Does accounting for 10%–50% of the variance in what you're interested in seem feeble? Consider these two facts:

1. In 2007, the average White male had a life expectancy at birth of 75.9 years in the United States, or 27,721 days. The life expectancy at birth for the average African American male was 70.0 years, or 25,567 days. The *difference* is 2,204 days (SAUS 2011:Table 102. See http://www.census.gov/compendia/statab/2011/tables/11s0102.pdf).

2. There were approximately 2.2 million births in Mexico in 2010 and around 39,000 infant deaths—that is, about 18 infant deaths per 1,000 live births. Compare these figures to the United States, where there were 4.2 million births and approximately 26,000 infant deaths, or about 6.14 per 1,000 live births. If the infant mortality rate in Mexico were the same as that in the United States, the number of infant deaths would be about 13,000 instead of 39,000. The *difference* would be 26,000 infant deaths.

Suppose you could account for 10% of the *difference* in longevity among White and African American males in the United States (220 days) or 10% of the *difference* between the United States and Mexico in infant deaths (2,600 children). Would that be worthwhile? Because knowledge about phenomena leads to more effective control over those phenomena, the most important contribution a scientist can make to solving a human problem is to be right about what causes it. I'd try to account for every percent I could.

Some Cautions in Doing Multiple Regression

Caution 1: Automated regression is very easy.

Many statistics programs do what is called a stepwise multiple regression. You specify a dependent variable and a series of independent variables that you suspect play some part in determining the scores of the dependent variable.

The program looks for the independent variable that correlates best with the dependent variable and then adds in the variables one at a time, accounting for more and more variance, until all the specified variables are analyzed, or until variables fail to enter because incremental explained variance is lower than a preset value, say, 1%.

Stepwise multiple regression is another one of those controversial hot topics in data analysis. Some people feel strongly that it is mindless and keeps you from making your own decisions about what causes what in a complex set of variables. It's rather like the significance test controversy and the shotgun controversies I discussed in Chapter 21.

And my take on it is the same: Learn to use all the tools and make your own decisions about the meaning of your findings. It's your responsibility to do the data processing and it's your responsibility to determine the meaning of your findings. Don't let robots take over any of your responsibilities. And don't be afraid to use all the hot tools, either.

Caution 2: Lurking multicollinearity.

Multivariate models are subject to a problem that simply can't exist when you have one independent variable: Independent variables can be correlated. In fact, when two variables both strongly predict a third, you'd expect the first two to be correlated. This **multicollinearity** means that you may not be able to tell the influence of one independent variable *free from the influence of the independent variables with which it is correlated.*

One way to avoid this problem is to conduct true experiments and nothing but true experiments. By assigning research participants randomly to control and experimental groups, we ensure that any correlation between independent variables is the result of chance. Nice work if you can get it, but much of what we want to study in social science requires survey research or ethnography and simply isn't the stuff of lab experiments.

Fortunately, multicollinearity distorts the findings of multiple regression only occasionally, and multicollinearity problems show up very clearly. The most dramatic sign of a multicollinearity problem is when your statistical program tells you that it cannot solve the equation. Some statistical programs calculate condition indexes that diagnose problematical multicollinearity. Conditions indexes higher than 30 signal a multicollinearity problem.

But basic regression output shows the most common sign of a multicollinearity problem: Low probabilities for zero-order correlations between a series of independent variables and one dependent variable remain low in multivariate models when the variables are entered separately, but the probabilities for all the variables rise when you put them in the model together.

PATH ANALYSIS

Path analysis is a particular application of multiple regression. In multiple regression, we know: (1) which independent variables help predict some dependent variable; and (2) how much variance in the dependent variable is explained by each independent variable. But multiple regression is an inductive technique: It does not tell us which are the antecedent variables, which are the intervening variables, and so on.

Path analysis is the application of multiple regression for testing conceptual models of multivariate relations—that is, for testing specific theories about how the independent variables in a multiple regression equation may be influencing each other—and how this ultimately leads to the dependent variable outcome.

The method was developed by the geneticist Sewall Wright in 1921 and became very popular in the social sciences in the 1960s (see Duncan 1966). It fell out of favor for a while (isn't it nice to know that there are fads and fashions even in statistics?), but it's making a strong comeback now that statistics packages make it easier to test complex models.

I rather like the method because it depends crucially on the researcher's best guess about how a system of variables really works. It is, in other words, a nice combination of quantitative and qualitative methods.

An Example of Path Analysis: Why Some Patients Wind Up Back in the Hospital

Lockery et al. (1994) studied the rehospitalization of people over 60. These days, people are discharged as quickly as possible from hospitals to keep down costs. For old people in frail health, if they are discharged too quickly, or don't get the right posthospitalization therapy, they can quickly wind up back in the hospital.

Figure 22.2 shows Lokery et al.'s conceptual model of the process: Some sociodemographic factors associated with patients and their families influence the extent to which patients are involved in the decision about their own discharge from the hospital. This decision leads to patients being sent directly home or to some other, intermediate institution, like a nursing home or a rehabilitative hospital, for continued therapy. The dependent variable is whether the patient winds up back in the original hospital within 30 days of discharge.

The input variable, ADL (the Activities of Daily Living scale), is a measure of how independent people are in feeding, bathing, and dressing themselves; going to the bathroom; and so on. The higher the ADL score, the less people can do for themselves. SES is socioeconomic class, with higher scores meaning lower SES. Marital status was coded as 1 = married and 0 = unmarried. Depression was measured with one of the standard checklists (Derogatis and Melisaratos 1983), so that the higher the score, the higher the level of depression.

Locus of control is the famous scale developed by Rotter (1966) to measure how much people feel they are in control of their own lives. Higher scores mean higher internal control; lower scores mean that people feel that others are in charge of their lives.

Family conflict, control, and independence refer to how much family members: (1) discuss their feeling openly; (2) boss each other around; and (3) encourage each other to make their own decisions. These things were hypothesized to influence whether family members or hospital staff participated in the decision about where the patient would go after leaving the hospital and these, in turn, were thought to influence the extent of the patient's own involvement in the decision.

Patient involvement in the discharge was scored from 1 to 5, with 1 = no involvement to 5 = full involvement. Patients were asked whether their families and/or the hospital staff had been involved in the process and these were scored 1 or 0. Discharge placement was scored 1 if the patient went to another institution or 0 if the patient was sent home, and rehospitalization was scored 1 or 0, depending on whether the patient was back in the hospital 30 days later.

Of the 264 patients whom Lockery et al. (1994) interviewed, 45 wound up back in the hospital 30 days later. Figure 22.3 shows the

Figure 22.2 Lockery et al.'s (1994) Conceptual Model of Rehospitalization of Elders

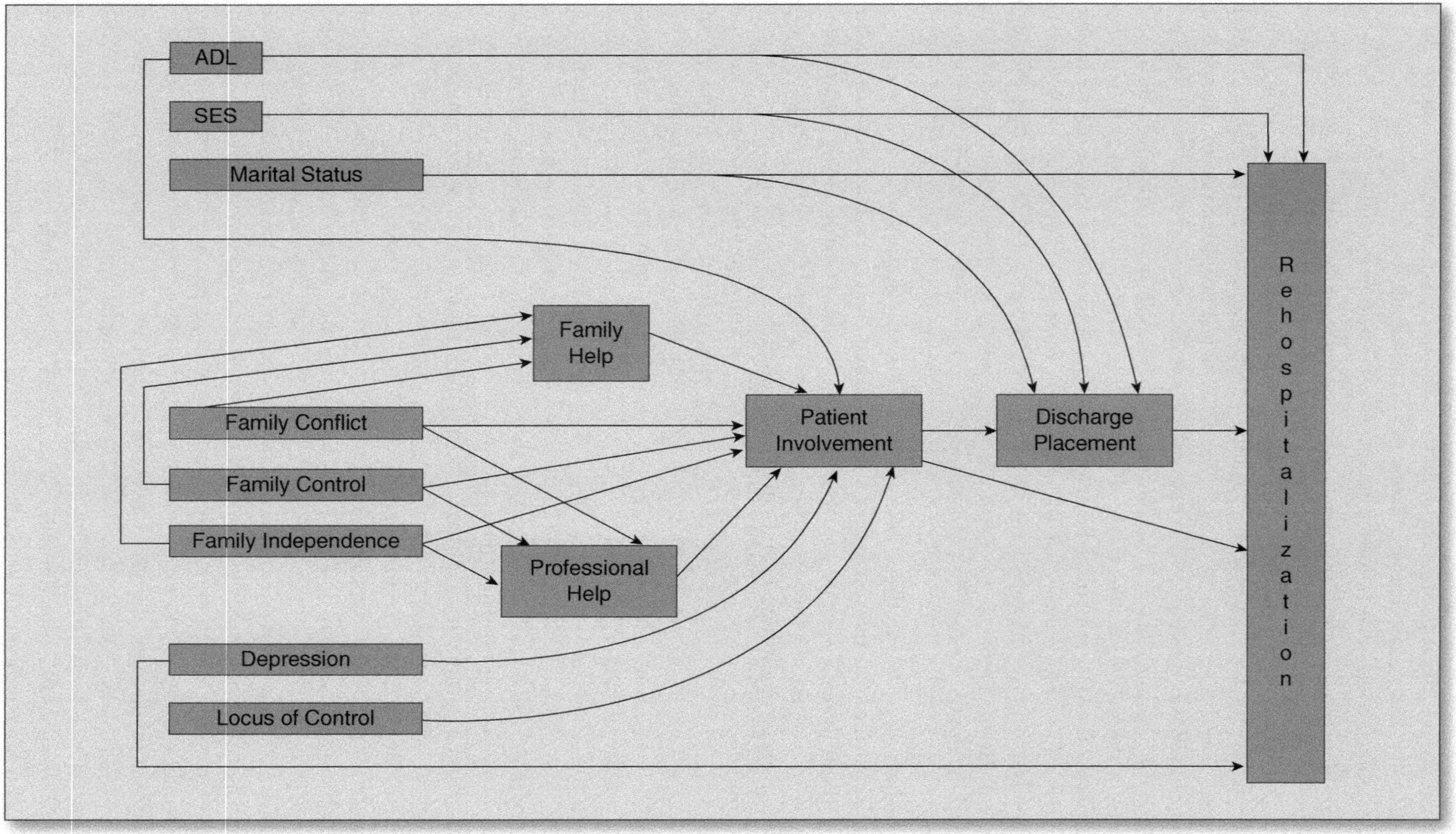

Note: ADLs = activities of daily living; SES = socioeconomic status.

Source: S. A. Lockery et al., "Factors Contributing to the Early Rehospitalization of Elderly People." *Health and Social Work* 19:182–191, Copyright © 1994. National Association of Social Workers, Inc., Health & Social Work

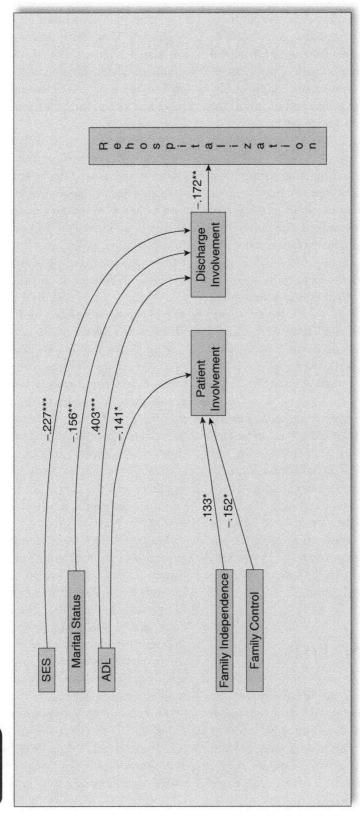

Figure 22.3 Lockery et al.'s (1994) Final Path Model of Rehospitalization of Elders

Notes: Only relations between exogenous variables significant at *p* = .05 or less (**p* ≤ .05, ***p* ≤ .01, ****p* ≤ .001) are shown in figure. SES = socioeconomic status; ADLs = activities of daily living.

Source: S. A. Lockery et al., "Factors Contributing to the Early Rehospitalization of Elderly People." *Health and Social Work* 19:182–191, Copyright © 1994. National Association of Social Workers, Inc., Health & Social Work

path analysis from their data. Notice how much cleaner it is. Depression is gone. Locus of control is gone. Family help and professional help had no influence on patient involvement in the decision. Even more importantly, whether a patient was involved or not in the discharge decision had no impact on whether he or she was back in the hospital a month later.

The way it worked out was simply this: Lower socioeconomic status patients (those with higher scores on the SES variable) were more likely to be discharged directly to their homes (low SES patients have less money to pay for expensive nursing and rehabilitative care); married patients were more likely to be sent home, but when they got there, they had someone to help take care of them; patients who scored high on the ADL scale—that is, those who could not take care of themselves very well—were much more likely to be sent to a nursing home or a rehabilitation center.

In the end, those who wound up in nursing homes or rehab care were less likely to be back in the hospital a month later. Home is nice, but frail elderly people—especially those who are poor and who have no spouse at home—need care and they won't get it there.

Path analysis is often used to test which of several plausible theories is most powerful, but in the end, you're left out there, all by yourself, defending your theory on the basis of whatever data are available right now.

FACTOR ANALYSIS

Factor analysis is a set of techniques for information packaging and data reduction. The data are often about items for building scales (more about this in a minute), but can just as well be about artifacts (movies, songs, buildings, cars, brands of beer . . .), people (movie stars, politicians, fashion models, criminals, classical musicians . . .), or even countries.

Factor analysis is based on the simple and compelling idea that if things we observe are correlated with each other, they must have some underlying variable in common. Factor analysis refers to a set of techniques for identifying and interpreting those underlying variables, or factors.

For example, people in the United States who are in favor of gun control are likely (but not guaranteed) to be in favor of: (1) a woman's right to an abortion; (2) participation by the U.S. military in overseas peacekeeping missions of the United Nations; and (3) affirmative action in college admissions. People who are against gun control are likely to favor: (1) restrictions on abortion; (2) less involvement of the United States in UN peacekeeping missions; and (3) curbs on affirmative action.

People are free to mix and match their opinions on any of these issues, but overall, there is a strong association of opinions across these issues. Factor analysis assumes that this association is the result of an underlying, hypothetical variable, a general attitude orientation. We can use a set of statistical techniques to identify both the existence and the content of this underlying variable. Naming the variable is a strictly qualitative exercise.

Many studies have demonstrated the existence of an underlying value orientation usually called "liberal versus conservative." Liberals and conservatives exhibit packages of attitudes about things like personal freedom (as with the right to own a hand gun or the right to an abortion), about foreign policy (as with involvement in peacekeeping missions), and about domestic policies (as with affirmative action).

This idea of multidimensional supervariables that underlie a set of observations was first articulated in 1904 by Charles E. Spearman (he for whom Spearman's rank-order correlation coefficient is named—see Chapter 21). Spearman noticed that the scores of students on various exams (classics, French, English, math, etc.) were correlated. He suggested that the exam scores were correlated with each other because they were all correlated with an underlying factor, which he labeled g, for general intelligence.

The single-factor theory of intelligence has been repudiated and defended over the years and continues to be the focus of scholarly and political debate, but the idea of factors—multidimensional variables—that underlie and give rise to a set of correlated events is one of the most important developments in all the social sciences. It is used across the social sciences in data reduction—to explore large data sets with dozens or even hundreds of variables to extract a few variables that tell a big story.

In political science, for example, Lieske (1993) partitioned the 3,164 counties in the United States into 10 distinctive regional subcultures by looking for common, underlying factors in the correlations among 45 racial, ethnic, religious, and social structural variables. In social psychology, Stein et al. (1991) used factor analysis to test the influence of ethnicity, socioeconomic status, and various anxieties as barriers to the use of mammography among White, African American, and Hispanic women. Factor analysis confirmed the influence of five kinds of anxiety: fear of radiation, fear of pain, embarrassment about breast exams, anxiety about what might be found, and concerns about cost.

Factor Analysis and Scales

As I mentioned in Chapter 11, factor analysis is used widely across the social sciences in building reliable, compact scales for measuring social and psychological variables. Suppose, for example, you are interested in attitudes toward gender role changes among women. You suspect that the underlying forces of role changes are related to premarital sexuality, working outside the home, and the development of an independent social and economic life among women. You make up 50 attitudinal items and collect data on those items from a sample of respondents.

Factor analysis will help you decide whether the 50 items you made up really test for the underlying forces you think are at work. If they do, then you could use a few benchmark items—the ones that "load high" on the factors—and this would save you from having to ask every respondent about all 50 items you made up. You would still get the information you need—or much of it, anyway. How much? The amount would depend on how much variance in the correlation matrix each of your factors accounted for.

The notion of variance is very important here. Factors account for chunks of variance—the amount of dispersion or correlation in a correlation matrix. Factors are extracted from a correlation matrix in the order of the amount of variance that they explain in the matrix. Some factors explain a lot of variance; others may be very weak and are discarded by researchers as not being useful. In a dense matrix, only one or a few factors may be needed to account for a lot of variance, while in a dispersed matrix, many factors may be needed.

The most common statistical solution for identifying the underlying factors in a correlation matrix is called the orthogonal solution. In orthogonal factor analyses, factors are found that have as little correlation with each other as possible. Other solutions that result in intercorrelated factors are also possible (the various solutions are options that you can select in all the major statistical packages, like SAS®, SYSTAT®, and SPSS®). Some researchers say that these solutions, although messier than orthogonal solutions, are more like real life.

So-called factor loadings are the correlations between the factors and the variables that are subsumed by, or appear to be components of, factors. All the old variables "load" on each new factor. The idea is to establish some cutoff below which you would not feel comfortable accepting that an old variable "loaded onto" a factor. Many researchers use 0.50 as the cutoff, and look at loadings of 0.30–49 as worth considering. Some researchers insist that a variable should load at least 0.60 before accepting it as an unambiguous component of a factor and look at variables that load between 0.30 and 0.59 as worth considering.

Once you have a list of variables that load high on a factor (irrespective of sign, plus or minus), you look at the list and decide what the factor *means*. An example should make all this a lot clearer.

Handwerker's Domestic Activities Scale

Penn Handwerker (1996a, 1998) used factor analysis to test whether the construct of "domestic cooperation" on Barbados was unidimensional. He asked a random sample of 428 Barbadian women whether their husband or boyfriend helped with any of the following: cooking, washing clothes, washing dishes, bathing children, taking children places, and caring for children. To put these items of domestic cooperation in context, he also asked each woman whether her husband or boyfriend was *expected* to treat her as an equal and whether her husband or boyfriend *did, in fact*, treat her as an equal.

Table 22.6 is a schematic of Handwerker's data matrix. The eight variables are labeled COOK, WASH, DISH, BATH, TAKE, CARE, EQUAL1, and EQUAL2.

Table 22.6 is a profile matrix (see Figure 15.2a), but factor analysis is done on a similarity matrix (see Figure 15.2b). If Handwerker had asked the women: "On a scale of 1–10, how much does your husband or boyfriend help you with the cooking?" the entries in Table 22.6 would have been 1–10. With that kind of data, a factor analysis program would turn the profile matrix into a similarity matrix by calculating Pearson's r for all possible pairs of columns. But Handwerker asked the women Yes/No questions (that's why Table 21.6 contains only 0s and 1s).

One way to turn a 1/0 profile matrix into a similarity matrix is to calculate the percentage of matches for all possible pairs of columns. That is, when two columns have a 1 or a 0 in the same row, count that as a hit. When two columns have different entries in the same row, count that as a miss. Then, count up all the hits and divide by the number of possible hits (that is, the number of respondents)—in this case, 428.

This results in what's called a simple matching coefficient. (There are other kinds of

---

Table 22.6 Schematic of Handwerker's Profile Matrix

ID	COOK	WASH	DISH	BATH	TAKE	CARE	EQUAL1	EQUAL2
1	1	0	1	1	1	0	1	0
2	0	1	0	0	1	0	1	1
3	1	0	0	0	1	1	1	0
.								
.								
.								
428	1	1	0	1	1	0	1	1

Source: Adapted from "Constructing Likert Scales: Testing the Validity and Reliability of Single Measures of Multidimensional Variables" by W. P. Handwerker, 1996a, *Cultural Anthropology Methods Journal* 8(1):2.

matching coefficients, but I won't go into them here.) The result is an 8×8 similarity matrix. Table 22.7 shows the results of Handwerker's factor analysis of that matrix.

In reading the output from factor analysis, we look for items that load high on each factor. For me, that means loadings of at least .60, although others may use .50 or .40. From Table 22.7, it's clear that the domain of "domestic cooperation" is *not* unidimensional. In fact, it has three dimensions. Interpreting the results in Table 22.7, it seemed to Handwerker that Factor 1 had something to do with "household chores." He labeled that factor "Domestic." Factor 2, he thought, comprised "chores associated with children," so he labeled it "Children." In open-ended interviews, Barbadian women interpreted the third factor as being about affection and empowerment within families, so Handwerker labeled it "Affection."

Over the next few years, Handwerker had the opportunity to refine and test his scale on two more Caribbean islands, Antigua and

St. Lucia. He dropped EQUAL1 because it was redundant with EQUAL2 and he dropped the question about "caring for children in other ways" (CARE) because respondents told him that it was ambiguous.

Handwerker also added four new questions—things that had come up in open-ended interviews as important to women: (1) Does your partner take responsibility for the children for an evening or an afternoon when you have something to do? (2) Does your partner take time off from work to share responsibility for children who are sick? (3) Does your partner talk with you and respect your opinion? (4) Does your partner spend his free time with you?

These new questions are labeled TIME, SICK, FREET, and TALK in Table 22.8, which shows the results for Antigua and St. Lucia.

There are at least four things to notice about Table 22.8:

1. Despite the subtraction of some variables and the addition of others, the results from all

Table 22.7   Factor Loadings for Handwerker's Data From Barbados

Variable	Factor 1 Domestic	Factor 2 Children	Factor 3 Affection
COOK	0.893	0.232	0.161
WASH	0.895	0.121	0.058
DISH	0.824	0.329	0.191
BATH	0.795	0.324	0.194
TAKE	0.291	0.929	0.159
CARE	0.307	0.922	0.175
EQUAL1	0.188	0.203	0.734
EQUAL2	0.091	0.066	0.854
Explained Variance	39.150	25.516	17.841

Source: "Constructing Likert Scales: Testing the Validity and Reliability of Single Measures of Multidimensional Variables" by W. P. Handwerker, 1996a, *Cultural Anthropology Methods Journal* 8(1):2.

Table 22.8 Factor Loadings for Handwerker's Data From Antigua and St. Lucia

	Antigua			St. Lucia		
Variable	Domestic	Children	Affection	Domestic	Children	Affection
COOK	0.793	0.317	0.106	0.783	0.182	0.161
WASH	0.845	0.163	0.090	0.818	0.056	0.018
DISH	0.791	0.32	0.203	0.781	0.197	0.173
*BATH	0.493	0.654	0.207	0.596	0.584	0.090
TAKE	0.271	0.738	0.289	0.246	0.790	0.196
TIME	0.253	0.820	0.258	0.228	0.833	0.061
SICK	0.210	0.786	0.151	0.121	0.742	−0.067
FREET	0.10	0.299	0.802	−0.010	0.691	0.319
EQUAL	0.147	0.155	0.898	0.177	0.117	0.883
TALK	0.142	0.20	0.883	0.113	0.112	0.909
Explained variance	26.46	26.459	25.051	24.188	27.905	18.191

Source: "Constructing Likert Scales: Testing the Validity and Reliability of Single Measures of Multidimensional Variables" by W. P. Handwerker, 1996a, *Cultural Anthropology Methods Journal* 8(1):3.

three islands are very stable. COOK, WASH, and DISH are components of a single large factor across all three Caribbean countries.

2. Although BATH loads relatively or high on the domestic chore factor across all three islands, it also loads high or relatively high on the children factor for two of the islands. The asterisk for BATH in Table 22.8 indicates that item should be dropped in the future because it does not reliably distinguish the two factors.

3. FREET loads on the children factor for St. Lucia, but it loads on the affection factor for Antigua. It turns out that Handwerker's assistant changed the wording for the FREET question slightly when she did the interviews on Antigua. Instead of asking: "Does your partner spend his free time with you?" she asked "Does your partner spend his free time with you or with your children?" (Handwerker 1996a:3). That little change apparently made enough of a difference in the responses to change the factor loading.

4. Across all three replications, the three factors in Tables 22.7 and 22.8 account for 70%–80% of the variance in the original data matrix. That is, about three-fourths to four-fifths of the variance in the original data is accounted for by just three underlying variables (the three factors) rather than the full list of original variables. For women across the Caribbean, the construct of domestic cooperation is multidimensional and comprised of three subconstructs: sharing of everyday domestic chores, sharing of responsibilities for children, and affection from men as defined by being treated as an equal.

DISCRIMINANT FUNCTION ANALYSIS (DFA)

Discriminant function analysis (DFA) is used to classify cases into categorical variables from ordinal and interval variables. For example, we may want to classify which of two (or more) groups an individual belongs to: male or female; those who have been labor migrants versus those who have not; those who are high, middle, or low income; those in favor of something and those who are not; and so on.

DFA is a statistical method developed for handling this problem. It has been around for a long time (Fisher 1936) but, like most multivariate techniques, DFA has become more popular since user-friendly computer programs have made it easier to do.

Lambros Comitas and I used DFA in our study of two groups of people in Athens, Greece: those who had returned from having spent at least five years in West Germany as labor migrants and those who had never been out of Greece. We were trying to understand how the experience abroad might have affected the attitudes of Greek men and women about traditional gender roles (Bernard and Comitas 1978). Our sample consisted of 400 persons: 100 male migrants, 100 female migrants, 100 male nonmigrants, and 100 female nonmigrants. Using DFA, we were able to predict with 70% accuracy whether an informant had been a migrant on the basis of just five variables.

There are some things you need to be careful about in using DFA, however. Notice that our sample in the Athens study consisted of half migrants and half nonmigrants. That was because we used a disproportionate, stratified sampling design to ensure adequate representation of returned migrants in the study. Given our sample, we could have guessed whether one of our informants was a migrant with 50% accuracy without any information about the informant at all.

Only a very small fraction of the population of Athens in 1977, when we did the study, consisted of former long-term labor migrants to West Germany. The chances of stopping an Athenian at random on the street at that time and grabbing one of those returned labor migrants was less than 5%.

Suppose that, armed with the results of the DFA that Comitas and I did, I asked random Athenians five questions, the answers to which allow me to predict 70% of the time whether any respondent had been a long-term labor migrant to West Germany. No matter what the answers were to those questions, I'd be better off predicting that the random Athenian was *not* a returned migrant. I'd be right more than 95% of the time.

Furthermore, why not just ask the random survey respondent straight out: "Are you a returned long-term labor migrant from West Germany?" With such an innocuous question, presumably I'd have gotten a correct answer at least as often as our 70% prediction based on knowing five pieces of information. What DFA did for us, though, was help us understand the factors that distinguished returned migrants from their compatriots who had stayed home. So, while DFA is not a prediction device, it's a powerful classification device.

In fact, many social science research problems are about understanding things so you can classify them correctly. Livingstone and Lunt (1993) surveyed 217 people in Oxford, England, and divided them into six types, based on whether or not people were in debt, whether or not people had savings, and people who live exactly within their income (with neither savings nor debt). DFA, using a variety of variables (age, class, education, income, expenses, attitudes toward debt, etc.) correctly classified almost 95% of the cases into one of the six groups that Livingstone and Lunt had identified.

Gans and Wood (1985) used DFA technique for classifying Samoan women as traditional or modern with respect to their ideal family size. If women stated that they wanted three or fewer children, Gans and Wood placed them in a category they labeled "modern." Women who said they wanted four or more children were labeled "traditional." DFA showed that just six of the many variables that Gans and Wood had collected allowed them to classify correctly which category a woman belonged to in 75% of all cases. The variables were such things as age, owning a car, level of education, etc.

It would have been ridiculous for Gans and Wood to have asked women straight out: "Are you traditional or modern when it comes to the number of children you'd like?" DFA (combined with on-the-ground ethnography) gave them a good picture of the variables that go into Samoan women's desired family size.

Similarly, Comitas and I were able to describe the attitudinal components of gender role changes by using DFA, and our prediction rate of 70% was significantly better than the 50% we'd have gotten by chance, given our sampling design. If you're careful about how you interpret the results of a discriminant function analysis, it can be a really important addition to your statistical tool kit.

AND FINALLY . . .

In a world of thousands of variables and millions of combinations of variables, how do you decide what to test? There is no magic formula. My advice is to follow every hunch you get. Some researchers insist that you have a good theoretical reason for including variables in your design and that you have a theory-driven reason to test for relations among variables once you have data. They point out that anyone can make up an explanation for any relation or lack of relation

after seeing a table of data or a correlation coefficient.

This is very good advice, but I think it's a bit too restrictive, for three reasons:

1. Data analysis should be lots of fun, and it can't be unless it's based on following your hunches. Most relations are easy to explain, and peculiar relations beg for theories to explain them. You just have to be very careful not to conjure up support for every statistically significant relation, merely because it happens to turn up. There is a delicate balance between being clever enough to explain an unexpected finding and just plain reaching too far. As usual, there is no substitute for thinking hard about your data.

2. It is really up to you during research design to be as clever as you can in thinking up variables to test. You're entitled to include some variables in your research just because you think they might come in handy. Just don't overdo it. There is nothing more tedious than an interview that drones on for hours without any obvious point other than that the researcher is gathering data on as many variables as possible.

3. The source of ideas has no necessary effect on their usefulness. You can get ideas from an existing theory or from browsing through data tables—or from talking about research problems with your friends. The important thing is not *how* you get a hunch, it's *whether you can test* your hunches and create plausible explanations for whatever findings come out of those tests. If others disagree with your explanations, then let them demonstrate that you are wrong, either by reanalyzing your data or by producing new data. But stumbling onto a significant relation between some variables does nothing to invalidate the relation.

So, when you design your research, try to think about the kinds of variables that might be useful in testing your hunches. Use the principles in Chapter 3 and consider internal state variables (e.g., attitudes, values, beliefs); external state variables (e.g., age, height, gender, race, health status, occupation, wealth status); physical and cultural environmental variables (e.g., rainfall, socioeconomic class of a neighborhood); and time or space variables (Have attitudes changed over time? Do the people in one community behave differently from those in another otherwise similar community?).

In applied research, important variables are the ones that let you target a policy—that is, focus intervention efforts on subpopulations of interest (the rural elderly, victims of violent crime, overachieving third graders, etc.)—or that are more amenable to policy manipulation (knowledge is far more manipulable than attitudes or behavior, for example). No matter what the purposes of your research, or how you design it, the two principle rules of data analysis are:

1. If you have an idea, test it.

2. You can't test it if you don't have data on it.

Enjoy.

Key Concepts in This Chapter

causal modeling
elaboration method
controlling for the effects of
    a third variable
subtables
partial correlation
zero-order correlation
partial out
first-order correlation

second-order correlation
multiple regression
multiple R
multiple R-squared, R^2
residuals
regression coefficients
stepwise multiple regression
multicollinearity
condition indexes

path analysis
factor analysis
factors
orthogonal solution
factor loadings
simple matching coefficient
discriminant function
    analysis (DFA)

Summary

- Most social phenomena are complex. The goal of multivariate analysis is to explain how variables are related and to develop a theory of causation that accounts for the fact that variables are related to one another.

  o Multivariate analysis is not a single method but involves an array of statistical procedures.

- The elaboration method involves teasing out the complexities in a bivariate relation by controlling for the effects of antecedent or intervening variables.

  o When we control for antecedent variables like sex, a bivariate relation may continue to hold, but it may also vanish for members of one sex.

  o Alternatively, when we control for antecedent variables like sex, a nonexistent bivariate relation may emerge for members of one sex.

- Partial correlation is a direct way to control for the effects of a third (or fourth or fifth . . .) variable on a relation between two variables.

  o For example, when we partial out the effect of a third variable, a zero-order bivariate relation may change dramatically, one way or the other. And when we partial out the effect of income, the correlation between the rate of motor vehicle deaths and teenage births across the 50 states of the United States drops from about .78 to about .67. This is because income is correlated strongly with motor vehicle deaths and with teenage births.

- Multiple regression puts all the information about a series of variables together into a single equation that takes account of the interrelation among independent variables.
  - ○ The result of multiple regression is a statistic called multiple-R, which is the combined correlation of a set of independent variables with the dependent variable, taking into account the fact that each of independent variables might be correlated with each of the other independent variables.
  - ○ Multiple-R-squared, or R^2, is the amount of variance in the dependent variable accounted for by two or more independent variables simultaneously.
  - ○ A typical question for a multiple regression analysis might be "How well can we predict a person's starting salary if we know how many years of college they have, *and* their major, *and* their gender, *and* their age, *and* their ethnic background?"
  - ○ Multiple regression typically accounts for 10%–50% of the variance in any dependent variable, using between two and eight independent variables. This may seem like a small amount, but the implications, both theoretical and practical, of really understanding a piece of complex social research puzzle can be very important.
- Path analysis is a method for testing theories about how the independent variables in a multiple regression equation may be influencing each other.
  - ○ Path analysis lets you test a particular theory about the relations among a system of variables, but it doesn't produce the theory. *You* have to do that.
  - ○ Path coefficients are standardized values. They show the influence of multiple independent variables on the dependent variables in terms of standard deviations.
- In multivariate models, independent variables can be correlated. This multicollinearity means that you can't tell the influence of an independent variable free from influence by other independent variables with which it is correlated.
- Factor analysis is a set of techniques for information packaging and data reduction. The idea is that if some things are correlated with each other, they must have something in common. That thing in common is called a factor.
  - ○ Factor analysis is used across the social sciences in the construction of personality and achievement test and in exploring large data sets to extract a few variables that tell a big story.
  - ○ Factors account for chunks of variance in a data matrix. The most common method for finding the underlying factors in a matrix is called the orthogonal solution, in which factors are found that have as little correlation with each other as possible.
  - ○ Factor loadings are the correlations between the new factors and the old variables that are replaced by factors. All the old variables "load" on each new factor. By convention, variables that load at least 0.60 on a factor unambiguously represent that factor, and variables between 0.30 and 0.59 are worth considering.
- Discriminant function analysis (DFA) is used to classify cases into categorical variables from ordinal and interval variables.
  - ○ While DFA is a powerful classification device, it is not a prediction device. Still, many problems in the social sciences are essentially about understanding things so you can classify them correctly.
- Finally, it's good to remember that anyone can make up an explanation for any relation or lack of relation after seeing a table of data or a correlation coefficient.
  - ○ This means that you have to be very careful not to conjure up support for every statistically significant relation, merely because it happens to turn up.
  - ○ It doesn't mean that you have to back off. Conjuring up ideas and testing them is great fun and very productive.

Exercises

1. Immediately following the presidential election of 1996, the Bureau of Business and Economic Research at the University of Florida surveyed Florida's voters. Median annual income for the sample of 438 respondents was $40,000. In the following tables, INCOME=1 is at or below the median. INCOME=2 is above the median. VOTE=1 means the respondent voted for Bill Clinton. VOTE=2 means the respondent voted for George Bush or Ross Perot.

   Interpret the following tables:

Table A Who People Voted for by Median Income

	INCOME		
VOTE	Equal to or Less Than $40,000 per Year	More Than $40,000 per Year	Total
Clinton	141	94	235
Bush or Perot	92	111	203
Total	233	205	438

$\chi^2 = 9.427, p < .002$

Table B Who People Voted for by Median Income (Men Only)

	INCOME		
VOTE	Equal to or Less Than $40,000 per Year	More Than $40,000 per Year	Total
Clinton	55	47	102
Bush or Perot	51	66	117
Total	106	113	219

$\chi^2 = 2.329, p < .127$

Table C Who People Voted for by Median Income (Women Only)

	INCOME		
VOTE	Equal to or Less Than $40,000 per Year	More Than $40,000 per Year	Total
Clinton	86	47	133
Bush or Perot	41	45	86
Total	127	92	219

$\chi^2 = 6.187, p < .013$

Source: Bureau of Business and Economic Research, University of Florida.

Of the 499 original respondents, 438 provided data for both variables and were eligible for this cross-tab. Perot voters comprise 6.8% of the sample. How could you test whether combining them accounts for the results in these tables?

2. Here is the output of a multiple regression. The dependent variable, TFR, is the estimated total fertility rate for 1995–2000 of women in 187 countries around the world. The independent variables are: the life expectancy of women in those countries (LEXFEM); the log of the per capita gross domestic product (LOGPCGDP); and the log of the informant mortality rate for those countries (LOGINFMORT). These data are from the United Nations Statistics Division Internet site on social indicators for countries of the world (http://www.un.org/Depts/unsd/social/main.htm).

```
Adjusted squared multiple R: 0.753 Standard error of estimate: 0.871

Effect      Coefficient  Std Error  Std Coef   Tolerance  t       P(2 Tail)

CONSTANT      6.713        1.510      0.000        .       4.445   0.000

LEXFEM       -0.102        0.013     -0.643      0.196    -7.823   0.000

LOGPCGDP      0.196        0.068      0.185      0.328     2.907   0.004

LOGINFMORT    0.673        0.163      0.392      0.147     4.136   0.000
```

Write the regression equation for predicting TFR. The standardized coefficient for LEXFEM is negative. Explain what this means.

Further Reading

There are two things you can do to follow up on the discussion in this chapter. First, take courses in statistics, including multivariate methods. There is no substitute for this. And second, read articles in scientific journals that involve the application of multivariate methods, including multiple regression and path analysis, as well as multidimensional scaling, cluster analysis, and others.

Appendix A
Table of Areas Under a Normal Curve

(A) z	(B) area between mean and z	(C) area beyond z	(A) z	(B) area between mean and z	(C) area beyond z	(A) z	(B) area between mean and z	(C) area beyond z
0.00	.0000	.5000	0.37	.1554	.3446	0.80	.2881	.2119
0.01	.0040	.4960	0.41	.1591	.3409	0.81	.2910	.2090
0.02	.0080	.4920	0.42	.1628	.3372	0.82	.2939	.2061
0.03	.0120	.4880	0.43	.1664	.3336	0.83	.2967	.2033
0.04	.0160	.4840	0.44	.1700	.3300	0.84	.2995	.2005
0.05	.0199	.4801	0.45	.1736	.3264	0.85	.3023	.1977
0.06	.0239	.4761	0.46	.1772	.3228	0.86	.3051	.1949
0.07	.0279	.4721	0.47	.1808	.3192	0.87	.3078	.1922
0.08	.0319	.4681	0.48	.1844	.3156	0.88	.3106	.1894
0.09	.0359	.4641	0.49	.1879	.3121	0.89	.3133	.1867
0.10	.0398	.4602	0.50	.1915	.3085	0.90	.3159	.1841
0.11	.0438	.4562	0.51	.1950	.3050	0.91	.3186	.1814
0.12	.0478	.4522	0.52	.1985	.3015	0.92	.3212	.1788
0.13	.0517	.4483	0.53	.2019	.2981	0.93	.3238	.1762
0.14	.0557	.4443	0.54	.2054	.2946	0.94	.3264	.1736
0.15	.0596	.4404	0.55	.2088	.2912	0.95	.3289	.1711
0.16	.0636	.4364	0.56	.2123	.2877	0.96	.3315	.1685
0.17	.0675	.4325	0.57	.2157	.2843	0.97	.3340	.1660
0.18	.0714	.4286	0.58	.2190	.2810	0.98	.3365	.1635
0.19	.0753	.4247	0.59	.2224	.2776	0.99	.3389	.1611
0.20	.0793	.4207	0.60	.2257	.2743	1.00	.3413	.1587
0.21	.0832	.4168	0.61	.2291	.2709	1.01	.3438	.1562
0.22	.0871	.4129	0.62	.2324	.2676	1.02	.3461	.1539
0.23	.0910	.4090	0.63	.2357	.2643	1.03	.3485	.1515
0.24	.0948	.4052	0.64	.2389	.2611	1.04	.3508	.1492
0.25	.0987	.4013	0.65	.2422	.2578	1.05	.3531	.1469
0.26	.1026	.3974	0.66	.2454	.2546	1.06	.3554	.1446
0.27	.1064	.3936	0.67	.2486	.2514	1.07	.3577	.1423
0.28	.1103	.3897	0.68	.2517	.2483	1.08	.3599	.1401
0.29	.1141	.3859	0.69	.2549	.2451	1.09	.3621	.1379
0.30	.1179	.3821	0.70	.2580	.2420	1.10	.3643	.1357
0.31	.1217	.3783	0.71	.2611	.2389	1.11	.3665	.1335
0.32	.1255	.3745	0.72	.2642	.2358	1.12	.3686	.1314
0.33	.1293	.3707	0.73	.2673	.2327	1.13	.3708	.1292
0.34	.1331	.3669	0.74	.2704	.2296	1.14	.3729	.1271
0.35	.1368	.3632	0.75	.2734	.2266	1.15	.3749	.1251
0.36	.1406	.3594	0.76	.2764	.2236	1.16	.3770	.1230
0.37	.1443	.3557	0.77	.2794	.2206	1.17	.3790	.1210
0.38	.1480	.3520	0.78	.2823	.2177	1.18	.3810	.1190
0.39	.1517	.3483	0.79	.2852	.2148	1.19	.3830	.1170

(A) z	(B) area between mean and z	(C) area beyond z	(A) z	(B) area between mean and z	(C) area beyond z	(A) z	(B) area between mean and z	(C) area beyond z
1.20	.3849	.1151	1.61	.4463	.0537	2.02	.4783	.0217
1.21	.3869	.1131	1.62	.4474	.0526	2.03	.4788	.0212
1.22	.3888	.1112	1.63	.4484	.0516	2.04	.4793	.0207
1.23	.3907	.1093	1.64	.4495	.0505	2.05	.4798	.0202
1.24	.3925	.1075	1.65	.4505	.0495	2.06	.4803	.0197
1.25	.3944	.1056	1.66	.4515	.0485	2.07	.4808	.0192
1.26	.3962	.1038	1.67	.4525	.0475	2.08	.4812	.0188
1.27	.3980	.1020	1.68	.4535	.0465	2.09	.4817	.0183
1.28	.3997	.1003	1.69	.4545	.0455	2.10	.4821	.0179
1.29	.4015	.0985	1.70	.4554	.0446	2.11	.4826	.0174
1.30	.4032	.0968	1.71	.4564	.0436	2.12	.4830	.0170
1.31	.4049	.0951	1.72	.4573	.0427	2.13	.4834	.0166
1.32	.4066	.0934	1.73	.4582	.0418	2.14	.4838	.0162
1.33	.4082	.0918	1.74	.4591	.0409	2.15	.4842	.0158
1.34	.4099	.0901	1.75	.4599	.0401	2.16	.4846	.0154
1.35	.4115	.0885	1.76	.4608	.0392	2.17	.4850	.0150
1.36	.4131	.0869	1.77	.4616	.0384	2.18	.4854	.0146
1.37	.4147	.0853	1.78	.4625	.0375	2.19	.4857	.0143
1.38	.4162	.0838	1.79	.4633	.0367	2.20	.4861	.0139
1.39	.4177	.0823	1.80	.4641	.0359	2.21	.4864	.0136
1.40	.4192	.0808	1.81	.4649	.0351	2.22	.4868	.0132
1.41	.4207	.0793	1.82	.4656	.0344	2.23	.4871	.0129
1.42	.4222	.0778	1.83	.4664	.0336	2.24	.4875	.0125
1.43	.4236	.0764	1.84	.4671	.0329	2.25	.4878	.0122
1.44	.4251	.0749	1.85	.4678	.0322	2.26	.4881	.0119
1.45	.4265	.0735	1.86	.4686	.0314	2.27	.4884	.0116
1.46	.4279	.0721	1.87	.4693	.0307	2.28	.4887	.0113
1.47	.4292	.0708	1.88	.4699	.0301	2.29	.4890	.0110
1.48	.4306	.0694	1.89	.4706	.0294	2.30	.4893	.0107
1.49	.4319	.0681	1.90	.4713	.0287	2.31	.4896	.0104
1.50	.4332	.0668	1.91	.4719	.0281	2.32	.4898	.0102
1.51	.4345	.0655	1.92	.4726	.0274	2.33	.4901	.0099
1.52	.4357	.0643	1.93	.4732	.0268	2.34	.4904	.0096
1.53	.4370	.0630	1.94	.4738	.0262	2.35	.4906	.0094
1.54	.4382	.0618	1.95	.4744	.0256	2.36	.4909	.0091
1.55	.4394	.0606	1.96	.4750	.0250	2.37	.4911	.0089
1.56	.4406	.0594	1.97	.4756	.0244	2.38	.4913	.0087
1.57	.4418	.0582	1.98	.4761	.0239	2.39	.4916	.0084
1.58	.4429	.0571	1.99	.4767	.0233	2.40	.4918	.0082
1.59	.4441	.0559	2.00	.4772	.0228	2.41	.4920	.0080
1.60	.4452	.0548	2.01	.4778	.0222	2.42	.4922	.0078
2.43	.4925	.0075	2.74	.4969	.0031	3.05	.4989	.0011
2.44	.4927	.0073	2.75	.4970	.0030	3.06	.4989	.0011

(A)	(B) area between mean and	(C) area beyond	(A)	(B) area between mean and	(C) area beyond	(A)	(B) area between mean and	(C) area beyond
z	z	z	z	z	z	z	z	z
2.45	.4929	.0071	2.76	.4971	.0029	3.07	.4989	.0011
2.46	.4931	.0069	2.77	.4972	.0028	3.08	.4990	.0010
2.47	.4932	.0068	2.78	.4973	.0027	3.09	.4990	.0010
2.48	.4934	.0066	2.79	.4974	.0026	3.10	.4990	.0010
2.49	.4936	.0064	2.80	.4974	.0026	3.11	.4991	.0009
2.50	.4938	.0062	2.81	.4975	.0025	3.12	.4991	.0009
2.51	.4940	.0060	2.82	.4976	.0024	3.13	.4991	.0009
2.52	.4941	.0059	2.83	.4977	.0023	3.14	.4992	.0008
2.53	.4943	.0057	2.84	.4977	.0023	3.15	.4992	.0008
2.54	.4945	.0055	2.85	.4978	.0022	3.16	.4992	.0008
2.55	.4946	.0054	2.86	.4979	.0021	3.17	.4992	.0008
2.56	.4948	.0052	2.87	.4979	.0021	3.18	.4993	.0007
2.57	.4949	.0051	2.88	.4980	.0020	3.19	.4993	.0007
2.58	.4951	.0049	2.89	.4981	.0019	3.20	.4993	.0007
2.59	.4952	.0048	2.90	.4981	.0019	3.21	.4993	.0007
2.60	.4953	.0047	2.91	.4982	.0018	3.22	.4994	.0006
2.61	.4955	.0045	2.92	.4982	.0018	3.23	.4994	.0006
2.62	.4956	.0044	2.93	.4983	.0017	3.24	.4994	.0006
2.63	.4957	.0043	2.94	.4984	.0016	3.25	.4994	.0006
2.64	.4959	.0041	2.95	.4984	.0016	3.30	.4995	.0005
2.65	.4960	.0040	2.96	.4985	.0015	3.35	.4996	.0004
2.66	.4961	.0039	2.97	.4985	.0015	3.40	.4997	.0003
2.67	.4962	.0038	2.98	.4986	.0014	3.45	.4997	.0003
2.68	.4963	.0037	2.99	.4986	.0014	3.50	.4998	.0002
2.69	.4964	.0036	3.00	.4987	.0013	3.60	.4998	.0002
2.70	.4965	.0035	3.01	.4987	.0013	3.70	.4999	.0001
2.71	.4966	.0034	3.02	.4987	.0013	3.80	.4999	.0001
2.72	.4967	.0033	3.03	.4988	.0012	3.90	.49995	.00005
2.73	.4968	.0032	3.04	.4988	.0012	4.00	.49997	.00003

Source: Statistical Tables and Formulas, Table 1, p. 3. New York: John Wiley, 1981. Reprinted by permission of A. Hald.

Appendix B
Student's *t* Distribution

	Level of Significance for one-tailed test					
	.10	.05	.025	.01	.005	.0005
	Level of Significance for two-tailed test					
df	.20	.10	.05	.02	.01	.001
1	3.078	6.314	12.706	31.821	63.657	636.619
2	1.886	2.920	4.303	6.965	9.925	31.598
3	1.638	2.353	3.182	4.541	5.841	12.941
4	1.533	2.132	2.776	3.747	4.604	8.610
5	1.476	2.015	2.571	3.365	4.032	6.859
6	1.440	1.943	2.447	3.143	3.707	5.959
7	1.415	1.895	2.365	2.998	3.499	5.405
8	1.397	1.860	2.306	2.896	3.355	5.041
9	1.383	1.833	2.262	2.821	3.250	4.781
10	1.372	1.812	2.228	2.764	3.169	4.587
11	1.363	1.796	2.201	2.718	3.106	4.437
12	1.356	1.782	2.179	2.681	3.055	4.318
13	1.350	1.771	2.160	2.650	3.012	4.221
14	1.345	1.761	2.145	2.624	2.977	4.140
15	1.341	1.753	2.131	2.602	2.947	4.073
16	1.337	1.746	2.120	2.583	2.921	4.015
17	1.333	1.740	2.110	2.567	2.898	3.965
18	1.330	1.734	2.101	2.552	2.878	3.922
19	1.328	1.729	2.093	2.539	2.861	3.883
20	1.325	1.725	2.086	2.528	2.845	3.850
21	1.323	1.721	2.080	2.518	2.831	3.819
22	1.321	1.717	2.074	2.508	2.819	3.792
23	1.319	1.714	2.069	2.500	2.807	3.767
24	1.318	1.711	2.064	2.492	2.797	3.745
25	1.316	1.708	2.060	2.485	2.787	3.725
26	1.315	1.706	2.056	2.479	2.779	3.707
27	1.314	1.703	2.052	2.473	2.771	3.690
28	1.313	1.701	2.048	2.467	2.763	3.674
29	1.311	1.699	2.045	2.462	2.756	3.659
30	1.310	1.697	2.042	2.457	2.750	3.646
40	1.303	1.684	2.021	2.423	2.704	3.551
60	1.296	1.671	2.000	2.390	2.660	3.460
120	1.289	1.658	1.980	2.358	2.617	3.373
∞	1.282	1.645	1.960	2.326	2.567	3.291

Source: R. A. Fisher and F. Yates, *Statistical Tables for Biological, Agricultural and Medical Research,* Table III. London: Longman, 1974. Reprinted by permission of Pearson Education Limited.

Appendix C
Chi-Square Distribution Table

			Probabilities			
df	*.99*	*.95*	*.90*	*.80*	*.70*	*.50*
1	.000157	.00393	.0158	.0642	.148	.455
2	.0201	.103	.211	.446	.713	1.386
3	.115	.352	.584	1.005	1.424	2.366
4	.297	.711	1.064	1.649	2.195	3.357
5	.554	1.145	1.610	2.343	3.000	4.351
6	.872	1.635	2.204	3.070	3.828	5.348
7	1.239	2.167	2.833	3.822	4.671	6.346
8	1.646	2.733	3.490	4.594	5.527	7.344
9	2.088	3.325	4.168	5.380	6.393	8.343
10	2.558	3.940	4.865	6.179	7.267	9.342
11	3.053	4.575	5.578	6.989	8.148	10.341
12	3.571	5.226	6.304	7.807	9.034	11.340
13	4.107	5.892	7.042	8.634	9.926	12.340
14	4.660	6.571	7.790	9.467	10.821	13.339
15	5.229	7.261	8.547	10.307	11.721	14.339
16	5.812	7.962	9.312	11.152	12.624	15.338
17	6.408	8.672	10.085	12.002	13.531	16.338
18	7.015	9.390	10.865	12.857	14.440	17.338
19	7.633	10.117	11.651	13.716	15.352	18.338
20	8.260	10.851	12.443	14.578	16.266	19.337
21	8.897	11.591	13.240	15.445	17.182	20.337
22	9.542	12.338	14.041	16.314	18.101	21.337
23	10.196	13.091	14.848	17.187	19.021	22.337
24	10.865	13.848	15.659	18.062	19.943	23.337
25	11.524	14.611	16.473	18.940	20.867	24.337
26	12.198	15.379	17.292	19.820	21.792	25.336
27	12.879	16.151	18.114	20.703	22.719	26.336
28	13.565	16.928	18.939	21.588	23.647	27.336
29	14.256	17.708	19.768	22.475	24.577	28.336
30	14.953	18.493	20.599	23.364	25.508	29.336

			Probabilities				
df	.30	.20	.10	.05	.025	.01	.001
1	1.074	1.642	2.706	3.841	5.024	6.635	10.827
2	2.408	3.219	4.605	5.991	7.378	9.210	13.815
3	3.665	4.624	6.251	7.815	9.348	11.345	16.268
4	4.878	5.989	7.779	9.488	11.143	13.277	18.465
5	6.064	7.289	9.236	11.070	12.832	15.086	20.517
6	7.231	8.588	10.645	12.592	14.449	16.812	22.457
7	8.383	9.803	12.017	14.067	16.013	18.475	24.322
8	9.524	11.030	13.362	15.507	17.535	20.090	26.125
9	10.656	12.242	14.684	16.919	19.023	21.666	27.877
10	11.781	13.442	15.987	18.307	20.483	23.209	29.588
11	12.899	14.631	17.275	19.675	21.920	24.725	31.264
12	14.011	15.812	18.549	21.026	23.337	26.217	32.909
13	15.119	16.985	19.812	22.362	24.736	27.688	34.528
14	16.222	18.151	21.064	23.685	26.119	29.141	36.123
15	17.322	19.311	22.307	24.996	27.488	30.578	37.697
16	18.418	20.465	23.542	26.296	28.845	32.000	39.252
17	19.511	21.615	24.769	27.587	30.191	33.409	40.790
18	20.601	22.760	25.989	28.869	31.526	34.805	42.312
19	21.689	23.900	27.204	30.144	32.852	36.191	43.820
20	22.775	25.038	28.412	31.410	34.170	37.566	45.315
21	23.858	26.171	29.615	32.671	35.479	38.932	46.797
22	24.939	27.301	30.813	33.924	36.781	40.289	48.268
23	26.018	28.429	32.007	35.172	38.076	41.638	49.728
24	27.096	29.553	33.196	36.415	39.364	42.980	51.179
25	28.172	30.675	34.382	37.652	40.646	44.314	52.620
26	29.246	31.795	35.563	38.885	41.923	45.642	54.052
27	30.319	32.912	36.741	40.113	43.194	46.963	55.476
28	31.391	34.027	37.916	41.337	44.461	48.278	56.893
29	32.461	35.139	39.087	42.557	45.722	49.588	58.302
30	33.530	36.250	40.256	43.773	46.979	50.892	59.703

Source: R. A. Fisher and F. Yates, *Statistical Tables for Biological, Agricultural and Medical Research,* Table IV. London: Longman, 1974. Reprinted by permission of Pearson Education Limited.

Appendix D

F Table for the .05 Level of Significance

df₁ / df₂	Numerator Degrees of Freedom							
	1	*2*	*3*	*4*	*5*	*6*	*8*	*10*
1	161.4	199.5	215.7	224.6	230.2	234.0	238.9	241.9
2	18.51	19.00	19.16	19.25	19.30	19.33	19.37	19.40
3	10.13	9.55	9.28	9.12	9.01	8.94	8.85	8.79
4	7.71	6.94	6.59	6.39	6.26	6.16	6.04	5.96
5	6.61	5.79	5.41	5.19	5.05	4.95	4.82	4.74
6	5.99	5.14	4.76	4.53	4.39	4.28	4.15	4.06
7	5.59	4.74	4.35	4.12	3.97	3.87	3.73	3.64
8	5.32	4.46	4.07	3.84	3.69	3.58	3.44	3.35
9	5.12	4.26	3.86	3.63	3.48	3.37	3.23	3.14
10	4.96	4.10	3.71	3.48	3.33	3.22	3.07	2.98
11	4.84	3.98	3.59	3.36	3.20	3.09	2.95	2.85
12	4.75	3.89	3.49	3.26	3.11	3.00	2.85	2.75
13	4.67	3.81	3.41	3.18	3.03	2.92	2.77	2.67
14	4.60	3.74	3.34	3.11	2.96	2.85	2.70	2.60
15	4.54	3.68	3.29	3.06	2.90	2.79	2.64	2.54
16	4.49	3.63	3.24	3.01	2.85	2.74	2.59	2.49
17	4.45	3.59	3.20	2.96	2.81	2.70	2.55	2.45
18	4.41	3.55	3.16	2.93	2.77	2.66	2.51	2.41
19	4.38	3.52	3.13	2.90	2.74	2.63	2.48	2.38
20	4.35	3.49	3.10	2.87	2.71	2.60	2.45	2.35
21	4.32	3.47	3.07	2.84	2.68	2.57	2.42	2.32
22	4.30	3.44	3.05	2.82	2.66	2.55	2.40	2.30
23	4.28	3.42	3.03	2.80	2.64	2.53	2.37	2.27
24	4.26	3.40	3.01	2.78	2.62	2.51	2.36	2.25
25	4.24	3.39	2.99	2.76	2.60	2.49	2.34	2.24
26	4.23	3.37	2.98	2.74	2.59	2.47	2.32	2.22
27	4.21	3.35	2.96	2.73	2.57	2.46	2.31	2.20
28	4.20	3.34	2.95	2.71	2.56	2.45	2.29	2.19
29	4.18	3.33	2.93	2.70	2.55	2.43	2.28	2.18
30	4.17	3.32	2.92	2.69	2.53	2.42	2.27	2.16
40	4.08	3.23	2.84	2.61	2.45	2.34	2.18	2.08
60	4.00	3.15	2.76	2.53	2.37	2.25	2.10	1.99
80	3.96	3.11	2.72	2.48	2.33	2.21	2.05	1.95
120	3.92	3.07	2.68	2.45	2.29	2.17	2.02	1.91
∞	3.84	3.00	2.60	2.37	2.21	2.10	1.94	1.83

Degrees of Freedom for the Denominator

				Numerator Degrees of Freedom				
df_1 df_2	12	15	20	30	40	60	120	∞
1	243.9	245.9	248.0	250.1	251.1	252.2	253.3	254.3
2	19.41	19.43	19.45	19.46	19.47	19.48	19.49	19.50
3	8.74	8.70	8.66	8.62	8.59	8.57	8.55	8.53
4	5.91	5.86	5.80	5.75	5.72	5.69	5.66	5.63
5	4.68	4.62	4.56	4.50	4.46	4.43	4.40	4.36
6	4.00	3.94	3.87	3.81	3.77	3.74	3.70	3.67
7	3.57	3.51	3.44	3.38	3.34	3.30	3.27	3.23
8	3.28	3.22	3.15	3.08	3.04	3.01	2.97	2.93
9	3.07	3.01	2.94	2.86	2.83	2.79	2.75	2.71
10	2.91	2.85	2.77	2.70	2.66	2.62	2.58	2.54
11	2.79	2.72	2.65	2.57	2.53	2.49	2.45	2.40
12	2.69	2.62	2.54	2.47	2.43	2.38	2.34	2.30
13	2.60	2.53	2.46	2.38	2.34	2.30	2.25	2.21
14	2.53	2.46	2.39	2.31	2.27	2.22	2.18	2.13
15	2.48	2.40	2.33	2.25	2.20	2.16	2.11	2.07
16	2.42	2.35	2.28	2.19	2.15	2.11	2.06	2.01
17	2.38	2.31	2.23	2.15	2.10	2.06	2.01	1.96
18	2.34	2.27	2.19	2.11	2.06	2.02	1.97	1.92
19	2.31	2.23	2.16	2.07	2.03	1.98	1.93	1.88
20	2.28	2.20	2.12	2.04	1.99	1.95	1.90	1.84
21	2.25	2.18	2.10	2.01	1.96	1.92	1.87	1.81
22	2.23	2.15	2.07	1.98	1.94	1.89	1.84	1.78
23	2.20	2.13	2.05	1.96	1.91	1.86	1.81	1.76
24	2.18	2.11	2.03	1.94	1.89	1.84	1.79	1.73
25	2.16	2.09	2.01	1.92	1.87	1.82	1.77	1.71
26	2.15	2.07	1.99	1.90	1.85	1.80	1.75	1.69
27	2.13	2.06	1.97	1.88	1.84	1.79	1.73	1.67
28	2.12	2.04	1.96	1.87	1.82	1.77	1.71	1.65
29	2.10	2.03	1.94	1.85	1.81	1.75	1.70	1.64
30	2.09	2.01	1.93	1.84	1.79	1.74	1.68	1.62
40	2.00	1.92	1.84	1.74	1.69	1.64	1.58	1.51
60	1.92	1.84	1.75	1.65	1.59	1.53	1.47	1.39
80	1.88	1.80	1.70	1.60	1.54	1.49	1.41	1.32
120	1.83	1.75	1.66	1.55	1.50	1.43	1.35	1.25
∞	1.75	1.67	1.57	1.46	1.39	1.32	1.22	1.00

Degrees of Freedom for the Denominator

F TABLE FOR THE .01 LEVEL OF SIGNIFICANCE

df_1 / df_2	Numerator Degrees of Freedom							
	1	*2*	*3*	*4*	*5*	*6*	*8*	*10*
1	4052	4999.5	5403	5625	5764	5859	5982	6056
2	98.50	99.00	99.17	99.25	99.30	99.33	99.37	99.40
3	34.12	30.82	29.46	28.71	28.24	27.91	27.49	27.23
4	21.20	18.00	16.69	15.98	15.52	15.21	14.80	14.55
5	16.26	13.27	12.06	11.39	10.97	10.67	10.29	10.05
6	13.75	10.92	9.78	9.15	8.75	8.47	8.10	7.87
7	12.25	9.55	8.45	7.85	7.46	7.19	6.84	6.62
8	11.26	8.65	7.59	7.01	6.63	6.37	6.03	5.81
9	10.56	8.02	6.99	6.42	6.06	5.80	5.47	5.26
10	10.04	7.56	6.55	5.99	5.64	5.39	5.06	4.85
11	9.65	7.21	6.22	5.67	5.32	5.07	4.74	4.54
12	9.33	6.93	5.95	5.41	5.06	4.82	4.50	4.30
13	9.07	6.70	5.74	5.21	4.86	4.62	4.30	4.10
14	8.86	6.51	5.56	5.04	4.69	4.46	4.14	3.94
15	8.68	6.36	5.42	4.89	4.56	4.32	4.00	3.80
16	8.53	6.23	5.29	4.77	4.44	4.20	3.89	3.69
17	8.40	6.11	5.18	4.67	4.34	4.10	3.79	3.59
18	8.29	6.01	5.09	4.58	4.25	4.01	3.71	3.51
19	8.18	5.93	5.01	4.50	4.17	3.94	3.63	3.43
20	8.10	5.85	4.94	4.43	4.10	3.87	3.56	3.37
21	8.02	5.78	4.87	4.37	4.04	3.81	3.51	3.31
22	7.95	5.72	4.82	4.31	3.99	3.76	3.45	3.26
23	7.88	5.66	4.76	4.26	3.94	3.71	3.41	3.21
24	7.82	5.61	4.72	4.22	3.90	3.67	3.36	3.17
25	7.77	5.57	4.68	4.18	3.85	3.63	3.32	3.13
26	7.72	5.53	4.64	4.14	3.82	3.59	3.29	3.09
27	7.68	5.49	4.60	4.11	3.78	3.56	3.26	3.06
28	7.64	5.45	4.57	4.07	3.75	3.53	3.23	3.03
29	7.60	5.42	4.54	4.04	3.73	3.50	3.20	3.00
30	7.56	5.39	4.51	4.02	3.70	3.47	3.17	2.98
40	7.31	5.18	4.31	3.83	3.51	3.29	2.99	2.80
60	7.08	4.98	4.13	3.65	3.34	3.12	2.82	2.63
80	6.96	4.88	4.04	3.56	3.25	3.04	2.74	2.55
120	6.85	4.79	3.95	3.48	3.17	2.96	2.66	2.47
∞	6.63	4.61	3.78	3.32	3.02	2.80	2.51	2.32

Degrees of Freedom for the Denominator

			Numerator Degrees of Freedom					
df_1 df_2	12	15	20	30	40	60	120	∞
1	6106	6157	6209	6261	6287	6313	6339	6366
2	99.42	99.43	99.45	99.47	99.47	99.48	99.49	99.50
3	27.05	26.87	26.69	26.50	26.41	26.32	26.22	26.13
4	14.37	14.20	14.02	13.84	13.75	13.65	13.56	13.46
5	9.89	9.72	9.55	9.38	9.29	9.20	9.11	9.02
6	7.72	7.56	7.40	7.23	7.14	7.06	6.97	6.86
7	6.47	6.31	6.16	5.99	5.91	5.82	5.74	5.65
8	5.67	5.52	5.36	5.20	5.12	5.03	4.95	4.86
9	5.11	4.96	4.81	4.65	4.57	4.48	4.40	4.31
10	4.71	4.56	4.41	4.25	4.17	4.08	4.00	3.91
11	4.40	4.25	4.10	3.94	3.86	3.78	3.69	3.60
12	4.16	4.01	3.86	3.70	3.62	3.54	3.45	3.36
13	3.96	3.82	3.66	3.51	3.43	3.34	3.25	3.17
14	3.80	3.66	3.51	3.35	3.27	3.18	3.09	3.00
15	3.67	3.52	3.37	3.21	3.13	3.05	2.96	2.87
16	3.55	3.41	3.26	3.10	3.02	2.93	2.84	2.75
17	3.46	3.31	3.16	3.00	2.92	2.83	2.75	2.65
18	3.37	3.23	3.08	2.92	2.84	2.75	2.66	2.57
19	3.30	3.15	3.00	2.84	2.76	2.67	2.58	2.49
20	3.23	3.09	2.94	2.78	2.69	2.61	2.52	2.42
21	3.17	3.03	2.88	2.72	2.64	2.55	2.46	2.36
22	3.12	2.98	2.83	2.67	2.58	2.50	2.40	2.31
23	3.07	2.93	2.78	2.62	2.54	2.45	2.35	2.26
24	3.03	2.89	2.74	2.58	2.49	2.40	2.31	2.21
25	2.99	2.85	2.70	2.54	2.45	2.36	2.27	2.17
26	2.96	2.81	2.66	2.50	2.42	2.33	2.23	2.13
27	2.93	2.78	2.63	2.47	2.38	2.29	2.20	2.10
28	2.90	2.75	2.60	2.44	2.35	2.26	2.17	2.06
29	2.87	2.73	2.57	2.41	2.33	2.23	2.14	2.03
30	2.84	2.70	2.55	2.39	2.30	2.21	2.11	2.01
40	2.66	2.52	2.37	2.20	2.11	2.02	1.92	1.80
60	2.50	2.35	2.20	2.03	1.94	1.84	1.73	1.60
80	2.41	2.28	2.11	1.94	1.84	1.75	1.63	1.49
120	2.34	2.19	2.03	1.86	1.76	1.66	1.53	1.38
∞	2.18	2.04	1.88	1.70	1.59	1.47	1.32	1.00

Degrees of Freedom for the Denominator

Source: C. M. Thompson, "Tables of the Percentage Points of the Inverted Beta (F) Distribution," *Biometrika* 33 (1943), pp. 73–88. Reprinted by permission of Oxford University Press.

Appendix E
Resources for Social Researchers

CODES OF ETHICS

American Sociological Association Code of Ethics: http://www.asanet.org/about/ethics.cfm

A Guide to Professional Ethics in Political Science (3rd ed.): http://www.apsanet.org/imgtest/ethicsguideweb.pdf

Ethical Principles of Psychologists and Code of Conduct: http://www.apa.org/ethics/code2002.html

Society for Applied Anthropology. The Statement of Professional and Ethical Responsibilities: http://www.sfaa.net/sfaaethic.html

Code of Ethics of the American Anthropological Association: http://www.aaanet.org/_cs_upload/issues/policy-advocacy/27668_1.pdf

National Association for the Practice of Anthropology. Ethical Guidelines for Practitioners: http://practicinganthropology.org/ethical-guidelines/

DIRECT OBSERVATION AND SURVEY RESEARCH

For information on using a hand-held computer or smartphone in the field to input data from direct observation of behavior, see Gravlee et al. (2006). These researchers used Entryware®, MCAPI (mobile computer assisted personal interview) software from Techneos (www.techneos.com). Ice (2004) used The Noldus Observer®, in her field research (http://www.noldus.com/), as did Koster (2006). These and other products turn a PDA or smartphone into a data-entry and data-management device. You program the keys (or use a mouse or stylus as the input device) to record events according to your own codes. This eliminates the need for checklists and coding sheets when you do direct observation, which lets you keep your eyes on the action.

Many programs let you build screens—on mobile devices or on desktop computers or on the web—for running survey interviews. New products are being developed quickly. To find these, search for software for CAPI (computer assisted personal interview), MCAPI (mobile CAPI), CASI (computer assisted self-interview), and ACASI (audio CASI). With ACASI, people hear the interview and respond on a computer rather than read the interview. The advantage is that the interview can be entirely private. For an example of this software, go to: http://www.tufts.edu/med/nutrition-infection/acasi/acasisoftware.html.

A popular program for building and running web-based surveys is SurveyMonkey® at http://www.surveymonkey.com.

STATISTICS PACKAGES

There are many excellent packages available. Before buying a stat package, find out if your campus has a site license for one or more of the following programs. If you do have to buy a program of your own, check the Internet sites for student prices. Here are the URLs for widely used stats packages:

SAS® http://www.sas.com/technologies/analytics/statistics/stat/index.html

SPSS® http://www.spss.com/. For students, go to: http://www.academicsuperstore.com/ and search for SPSS Grad Pack.

SYSTAT® http://www.systat.com. Students can download MYSTAT, a smaller version of SYSTAT, at no cost. http://www.systat.com/MystatProducts.aspx

WINKS® http://www.texasoft.com/. For student pricing, go here: http://www.texasoft.com/Student_Order.htm.

STATA® http://www.stata.com/

There are many online courses offered in statistics, including commercial courses and freeware. The R-Project for Statistical Computing offers a wide variety of routines for statistical analysis. The software is free, here: http://www.r-project.org/.

VOICE RECOGNITION SOFTWARE

Two popular programs are Dragon Naturally Speaking® (http://www.nuance.com/naturallyspeaking) and the VR software that comes with Windows 7. (http://windows.microsoft.com/en-US/windows7/What-can-I-do-with-Speech-Recognition). For the Mac: Dragon Dictate for Mac http://www.macspeech.com/pages.php?pID=143.

ANTHROPAC

This free software contains a suite of programs for collecting and analyzing data on cultural domains. There are routines for collecting and analyzing free lists, piles sorts, triads, paired comparisons, and ratings. Tools for analysis include multidimensional scaling, hierarchical clustering, property fitting (PROFIT), factor analysis, correspondence analysis, and quadratic assignment. All of these tools for analysis are also available in Ucinet. Files produced in Anthropac and Ucinet are compatible with one another and can be exported from Ucinet to Excel. Anthropac, however, is the only program that imports data from free lists, triad tests, and paired comparisons. Ucinet and Anthropac are also the only programs that run the formal model of consensus analysis. Both programs are available from http://www.analytictech.com/.

SOFTWARE FOR TEXT ANALYSIS

For information on many of the programs available, go to: http://caqdas.soc.surrey.ac.uk. For a tutorial on choosing the right software for you, go to: http://caqdas.soc.surrey.ac.uk/softwareoptions.html. Software is developing fast. A recent web-based addition to the field is Dedoose (http://www.dedoose.com/).

There is no such thing as a best program. Some are designed especially for video and some will let you treat documents and images alike as text that you can code. Many programs have free, downloadable demos. Try before you buy and remember: If you don't know how to write, a word processor won't help you. If you don't know anything about statistics, a stats package won't help you. In the same way, text analysis software will *facilitate* text analysis, but it won't *do* text analysis. That's a job that only you can do.

Many commercial programs are being developed to do automatic theme extraction and text analysis. Free academic programs include Kathleen Carley's program, AutoMap (http://www.casos.cs.cmu.edu/projects/automap). And see James Danowski's program, WORDij, for semantic network analysis: http://freewordij.net.

WordStat is a versatile program that combines statistics and text analysis. Info here: http://www.provalisresearch.com/wordstat/wordstat.html

For information on workshops and conferences on text analysis, as well as training programs:

http://www.surrey.ac.uk/sociology/research/researchcentres/caqdas/trainingandevents/

http://www.asu.edu/clas/polisci/cqrm/institute.html

http://www.uofaweb.ualberta.ca/iiqm/Conferences.cfm http://www.iiqm.ualberta.ca/

http://www.esourceresearch.org/tabid/380/default.aspx

SOFTWARE FOR NETWORK ANALYSIS

Collecting and analyzing network data is supported today by an array of accessible software. The most widely used packages for analyzing and visualizing network data are Ucinet (Borgatti et al. 2002) and Pajek (Batagelj and Mrvar n.d.). For personal network data, EgoNet (McCarty et al. 2007) lets you build a network survey that respondents take on a computer (or you can ask the questions on the survey yourself and enter the data on the computer as you go). EgoNet has analysis and visualization modules, for drawing network diagrams, but you can also export the data and analyze them with Ucinet and Pajek.

GPS

The Global Positioning System, or GPS, was developed by the Department of Defense in the United States. It relies on a system of satellites with world-wide coverage. A simple GPS unit, for under $200, can access the system and tell you, within 3 meters, your position on the Earth's surface. For more on the GPS, go to: http://www.gps.gov and http://tycho.usno.navy.mil/gps.html. For reviews of GPS units, go to: http://reviews.cnet.com/gps.

HAND-HELD COMPUTERS-PDAS

This technology is converging rapidly with smartphones. For reviews of PDAs and smart phones, go to: http://reviews.cnet.com/bestsmartphones/.

AIDS FOR TRANSCRIBING

For reviews of digital recorders and transcribers, http://reviews.cnet.com/1770-5_7-.html?query=transcriber&tag=srch. There are several transcriber systems available that will handle both audio and video data, including Transana® (open source): http://www.transana.org and HyperTranscribe: http://www.researchware.com.

JOURNALS THAT PUBLISH ARTICLES ABOUT RESEARCH METHODS

There are dozens of journals that publish articles on research methods in the social sciences. The journals listed here are devoted *primarily* to research methods.

Qualitative Methods

Forum: Qualitative Sozialforschung

This journal publishes in English and is free at http://www.qualitative-research.net/index.php/fqs.

Qualitative Research, Qualitative Inquiry, and Qualitative Health Research

These three journals from SAGE Publications are devoted exclusively to the discussion of and the promotion of qualitative methods in social science. Go to: http://www.qrj.sagepub.com/, http://qix.sagepub.com/, and http://qhr.sagepub.com/.

Journal of Contemporary Ethnography

Not a methods journal, but I browse this one regularly. It began in 1972 and publishes research based on qualitative methods. Many articles contain information about the methods and techniques used in the research. Go to: http://jce.sagepub.com/.

Qualitative and Quantitative Methods

Administrative Science Quarterly

ASQ is published by the Johnson Graduate School of Management at Cornell University. The journal has a long history of publishing articles on qualitative research methods, beginning with a now classic special issue in 1979, edited by John Van Maanen. The special issue was published as a book and is a valuable resource (Van Maanen 1983). Go to: http://www.johnson.cornell.edu/publications/asq.

Bulletin de Méthodologie Sociologique

This multidisciplinary quarterly publishes articles in French or English. All articles have abstracts in both English and French. To see the contents of current and back issues, go to: http://bms.sagepub.com.

Field Methods

This interdisciplinary journal is devoted to articles about methods for collecting, analyzing, and presenting data about human thought and human behavior in the natural world. Go to: http://fmx.sagepub.com.

Organizational Research Methods

This journal focuses entirely on research methods for studies of organizations. Go to: http://orm.sagepub.com/

Journal of Mixed Methods Research

This journal started in 2007. The title reflects the recognition, across the social sciences, of the importance of mixing qualitative and quantitative methods in many studies. Go to: http://mmr.sagepub.com/

Quantitative Methods

Public Opinion Quarterly

POQ began in 1937 and is published by Oxford University Press for the American Association for Public Opinion Research. This is where you go to learn the latest on writing good questionnaires, on techniques for interviewing, on training interviewers, and so on. Go to: http://poq.oxfordjournals.org/

Sociological Methodology

This is a book-length, once-a-year publication, sponsored by the American Sociological Association and published by Wiley-Blackwell. Go to: http://www.wiley.com/bw/journal.asp?ref=0081-1750

Sociological Methods and Research

This is a quarterly, interdisciplinary journal that publishes articles by methodologists from across the spectrum of social science. Go to: http://smr.sagepub.com/.

Psychological Methods

This journal, devoted to methods in research design and measurement, has been published by the American Psychological Association since 1996. Go to: http://www.apa.org/pubs/journals/met/index.aspx.

Social Science Research

SSR is an interdisciplinary journal that publishes papers in all areas of quantitative social research and has many papers on research methods. Go to: http://www.elsevier.com/locate/ssresearch.

World Cultures Journal

Published since 1985, this journal is devoted to cross-cultural studies—that is, the use of cultures as units of analysis. Go to: http://eclectic.ss.uci.edu/~drwhite/worldcul/world7.htm.

QCA: QUALITATIVE COMPARATIVE ANALYSIS

The COMPASS site is devoted to small-*n* analysis and has information about QCA, including programs that do this kind of Boolean analysis. Go to:

http://www.compasss.org. For information about QCA software, see

http://www.compasss.org/pages/resources/software.html and

http://www.u.arizona.edu/~cragin/fsQCA. In addition, Anthropac has a routine for analyzing truth tables.

HUMAN RELATIONS AREA FILES

The main site for HRAF is at: http://www.yale.edu/hraf. It has tutorials for doing and teaching cross-cultural research. It also has the latest (2004) version of the *Outline of Cultural Materials* at: http://www.yale.edu/hraf/Ocm_xml/newOcm.xml.

References

Abbot, A. 1998. The causal devolution. *Sociological Methods and Research* 27:148–81.

Abdel-Khalek, A. M. 1998. Internal consistency of an Arabic adaptation of the Depression Inventory in four Arab countries. *Psychological Reports* 82:264–66.

Abdul-Rahman, M. S. 2003. *Islam: Questions and answers*. Vol. 4, *The Hadeeth and its sciences*. London: MSA Publications Ltd.

Abdul-Raof, H. 2010. *Schools of Qur'anic exegesis: Genesis and development*. New York: Routledge.

Ackerman, R. J., and E. W. Gondolf. 1991. Adult children of alcoholics: The effects of background and treatment on ACOA symptoms. *The International Journal of the Addictions* 26:1159–72.

Adams-Webber, J. 1997. Self-reflexion in evaluating others. *American Journal of Psychology* 110:527–41.

Addams, J. 1926. *Twenty years at Hull House*. New York: Macmillan.

Adler, P. A., and P. Adler. 1987. The past and future of ethnography. *Journal of Contemporary Ethnography* 16:4–24.

Adler, P. S. 1993. Time-and-motion regained. *Harvard Business Review* 71:97–108.

Adorno, T. W., E. Frenkel-Brunswick, D. J. Levinson, and R. N. Sanford. 1950. *The authoritarian personality*. New York: Harper & Row.

Agar, M. 1973. *Ripping and running*. New York: Academic Press.

Agar, M. 1980a. Getting better quality stuff: Methodological competition in an interdisciplinary niche. *Urban Life* 9:34–50.

Agar, M. 1980b. *The professional stranger*. New York: Academic Press.

Agar, M. 1996. *The professional stranger: An informal introduction to ethnography*. 2d ed. San Diego: Academic Press.

Agresti, A., and C. A. Franklin. 2007. *Statistics: The art and science of learning from data*. Upper Saddle River, NJ: Pearson Prentice Hall.

Ahmed, A. M. 2010. Muslim discrimination: Evidence from two lost-letter experiments. *Journal of Applied Social Psychology* 40:888–98.

Ahmed, A. M., and M. Hammarstedt. 2008. Discrimination in the rental housing market: A field experiment on the Internet. *Journal of Urban Economics* 64:362–72.

Ahrentzen, S., D. W. Levine, and W. Michelson. 1989. Space, time, and activity in the home: A gender analysis. *Journal of Environmental Psychology* 9:89–101.

Aiello, J. R., and S. E. Jones. 1971. Field study of the proxemic behavior of young school children in three subcultural groups. *Journal of Personality and Social Psychology* 19:351–56.

Albas, C. 1991. Proxemic behavior: A study of extrusion. *The Journal of Social Psychology* 131:697–702.

Aldenderfer, M. S., and R. K. Blashfield 1984. *Cluster analysis*. Beverly Hills, CA: Sage.

Alexandre, G. C., P. Nadonovsky, C. L. Moraes, and M. Reichenheim. 2010. The presence of a stepfather and child physical abuse, as reported by a sample of Brazilain mothers in Rio de Janeiro. *Child Abuse and Neglect* 34:959–66.

Allan, C. 2007. Exploring natural resource management with metaphor analysis. *Society and Natural Resources* 20:351–62.

Allen, J. T., and G. Italie. 1954. *A concordance to Euripides*. Berkeley: University of California Press.

Allen, W. R., R. A. Comerford, and J. A. Ruhe. 1989. Factor analytic study of Bales' interaction process analysis. *Educational and Psychological Measurement* 49:701–707.

Allport, F. H., and D. A. Hartman. 1931. The prediction of cultural change: A problem illustrated in studies by F. Stuart Chapin and A. L. Kroeber. In *Methods in social science*, S. A. Rice, ed., 307–52. Chicago: University of Chicago Press.

Allport, G. 1979 [1954]. *The nature of prejudice*. Reading, MA: Addison-Wesley.

Al-Nuaim, A. A., E. A. Bamgboye, K. A. Al-Rubeaan, and Y. Al-Mazrou. 1997. Overweight and obesity in Saudi Arabian adult population. Role of sociodemographic variables. *Journal of Community Health* 22:211–23.

Altmann, J. 1974. Observational study of behavior: Sampling methods. *Behaviour* 49:227–67.

Altorki, S., and C. F. El-Solh, eds. 1988. *Arab women in the field: Studying your own society*. Syracuse, NY: Syracuse University Press.

Alvarado, N. 1994. Empirical validity of the Thematic Apperception Test. *Journal of Personality Assessment* 63:59–79.

American Anthropological Association (AAA). 1991. 1990 PhD survey results. *Anthropology Newsletter* 32:1, 44.

Amidon, E. J., and J. B. Hough. 1967. *Interaction analysis: Theory, research, and application*. Reading, MA: Addison-Wesley.

Anderson, C. A. 1989. Temperature and aggression: Ubiquitous effects of heat on occurrence of human violence. *Psychological Bulletin* 106:74–96.

Anderson, C. A., A. Shibuya, N. Ihori, E. L. Swing, B. J. Bushman, A. Sakamoto, H. R. Rothstein, and M. Saleem. 2010. Video violent game effects on aggression, empathy, and prosocial behavior in Eastern and Western countries: A meta-analytic review. *Psychological Bulletin* 136:151–73.

Anderson, K. J., and C. Leaper. 1998. Meta-analyses of gender effects on conversational interruption: Who, what, when, where, and how. *Sex Roles* 39:225–52.

Anderson, M. S., E. A. Ronning, R. De Vries, and B. C. Martinson. 2010. Extending the Mertonian norms: Scientists' subscription to norms of research. *Journal of Higher Education* 81:366–93.

Anderson, S. 2003. Why dowry payments declined with modernization in Europe but are rising in India. *The Journal of Political Economy* 111:269–310.

Andrews, F. M., and S. B. Withey. 1976. Social indicators of well-being: Americans' perceptions of life quality. New York: Plenum.

Andrews, M., S. D. Sclater, C. Squire, and M. Tamboukou. 2004. Narrative research. In *Qualitative research practice*, C. Seale, G. Gobo, J. F. Gubrium, and D. Silverman, eds., 109–24. Thousand Oaks, CA: Sage.

Aquilino, W. S. 1993. Effects of spouse presence during the interview on survey responses concerning marriage. *Public Opinion Quarterly* 57:358–76.

Aquilino, W. S. 1994. Interview mode effects in surveys of drug and alcohol use: A field experiment. *Public Opinion Quarterly* 58:210–40.

Aquilino, W. S., D. L. Wright, and A. J. Supple. 2000. Response effects due to bystander presence in CASI and paper-and-pencil surveys of drug use and alcohol use. *Substance Use and Misuse* 35:845–67. Special issue: *Methodological Issues in the Measurement of Drug Use.*

Archer, D., and L. Erlich. 1985. Weighing the evidence: A new method for research on restricted information. *Qualitative Sociology* 8:345–58.

Ardener, S., ed. 1981. *Women and space: Ground rules and social maps.* New York: St. Martin's Press.

Ardilly, P., and Y. Tillé. 2006. *Sampling methods: Exercises and solutions.* New York: Springer.

Arnold-Cathalifaud, M., D. Thumala, A. Urquiza, and A. Ojeda. 2008. Young people's images of old age in Chile: Exploratory research. *Educational Gerontology* 34:105–23.

Aronson, E., and J. Mills. 1959. The effect of severity of initiation on liking for a group. *Journal of Abnormal and Social Psychology* 59:177–81.

Asakawa, K., and M. Csikszentmihalyi. 1998. The quality of experience of Asian American adolescents in activities related to future goals. *Journal of Youth and Adolescence* 27:141–63.

Asimov, I. 1989. *Asimov's chronology of science and discovery.* New York: Harper & Row.

Aspland, H., and F. Gardner. 2003. Observational measures of parent-child interaction: An introductory review. *Child and Adolescent Mental Health* 8:136–43.

Atkinson, J. M., and J. Heritage, eds. 1984. *Structures of social action: Studies in conversation analysis.* New York: Cambridge University Press.

Atkinson, P. 1992. The ethnography of a medical setting: Reading, writing, and rhetoric. *Qualitative Health Research* 2:451–74.

Atkinson, P., and S. Delamont, eds. 2006. *Narrative methods,* 4 vols. London: Sage.

Atran, S. 1998. Folk biology and the anthropology of science: Cognitive universals and cultural particulars. *Behavioral and Brain Sciences* 21:547–609.

Atran, S., D. L. Medin, and N. O. Ross. 2005. The cultural mind: Environmental decision making and cultural modeling within and across populations. *Psychological Review* 112:744–76.

Atwal, A., and K. Caldwell. 2005. Do all health and social care professionals interact equally: A study of interactions in multidisciplinary teams in the United Kingdom. *Scandinavian Journal of Caring Sciences* 19:268–73.

Atzmüller, C., and P. M. Steiner. 2010. Experimental vignette studies in survey research. *European Journal of Research Methods for the Behavioral and Social Sciences* 6:128–38.

Auer, P. 2005. A postscript: Code-switching and social identity. *Journal of Pragmatics* 37:403–10.

Auerbach, C. F., and L. B. Silverstein. 2003. *Qualitative data: An introduction to coding and analysis.* New York: New York University Press.

Aunger, R. 1992. Sources of variation in ethnographic interview data: The case of food avoidances in the Ituri forest, Zaire. Paper presented at the annual meeting of the American Anthropological Association, San Francisco, California.

Aunger, R. 2004. *Reflexive ethnographic science.* Walnut Creek, CA: AltaMira.

Axinn, W. G. 1991. The influence of interviewer sex on responses to sensitive questions in Nepal. *Social Science Research* 20:303–19.

Axinn, W. G., and L. D. Pearce. 2006. *Mixed method data collection strategies.* New York: Cambridge University Press.

Axinn, W. G., L. D. Pearce, and D. Ghimire. 1999. Innovations in life history calendar applications. *Social Science Research* 28:243–64.

Ayres, I. 1991. Fair driving: Gender and race discrimination in retail car negotiations. *Harvard Law Review* 104:817–72.

Babbage, C. 1835. *On the economy of machinery and manufactures.* 4th ed. London: Charles Knight.

Babbie, E. 1983. *The practice of social research.* 3d ed. Belmont, CA: Wadsworth.

Bachman, R., H. Zaykowski, C. D. Lanier, M. Poteyeva, and R. Kallmyer. 2010. Estimating the magnitude of rape and sexual assault against American Indian and Alaska Native (AIAN) women. *The Australia and New Zealand Journal of Criminology* 43:199–222.

Bacon, F. 1902 [1620]. *Novum organum.* Ed. by J. Devey. New York: American Home Library Company.

Badahdah, A. M., and K. A. Tiemann. 2005. Mate selection criteria among Muslims living in America. *Evolution and Human Behavior* 26:432–40.

Baert, P. 1998. *Social theory in the twentieth century.* New York: New York University Press.

Bahr, H. M., and B. A. Chadwick. 1974. Conservatism, racial intolerance, and attitudes toward racial assimilation among Whites and American Indians. *Journal of Social Psychology* 94:45–56.

Bainbridge, W. S. 1978. *Satan's power: A deviant psychotherapy cult.* Berkeley: University of California Press.

Bainbridge, W. S. 1992. *Social research methods and statistics: A computer-assisted introduction.* Belmont, CA: Wadsworth.

Bakeman, R., and J. M. Gottman. 1997. *Observing interaction. An introduction to sequential analysis.* Cambridge: Cambridge University Press.

Bakeman, R., and V. Quera. 1995. *Analyzing interaction. Sequential analysis with SDIS and GSEQ.* Cambridge: Cambridge University Press.

Baker, J., M. Levy, and D. Grewal. 1992. An experimental approach to making retail store environmental decisions. *Journal of Retailing* 68:445–60.

Baker, J. B., A. W. Bazemore, and C. J. Jacobson. 2008. Rapid assessment of access to primary care in remote parts of the developing world. *Field Methods* 20:296–309.

Baker, R. 1996a. PRA with street children in Nepal. *PLA Notes* 25:56–60. London: International Institute for Environment and Development.

Baker, R. (with C. Panter-Brick and A. Todd). 1996b. Methods used in research with street children in Nepal. *Childhood* 3:171–93.

Baker, R., S. J. Blumberg, J. M. Brick, M. P. Couper et al. 2010. Research synthesis. AAPOR report on online panels. *Public Opinion Quarterly* 74:711–81.

Baker-Ward, L. E., K. L. Eaton, and J. B. Banks. 2005. Young soccer players' reports of a tournament win or loss: Different emotions, different narratives. *Journal of Cognition and Development* 6:507–27.

Balán, J., H. L. Browning, E. Jelin, and L. Litzler. 1969. A computerized approach to the processing and analysis of life histories obtained in sample surveys. *Behavioral Science* 4:105–20.

Bales, R. F. 1950. *Interaction process analysis. A method for the study of small groups.* Cambridge, MA: Addison-Wesley.

Bales, R. F., and S. P. Cohen. 1979. *SYMLOG: A system for the multiple level observation of groups.* New York: The Free Press.

Bamberg, S., and G. Moser. 2007. Twenty years after Hines, Hungerford, and Tomera: A new meta-analysis of psycho-social determinants of pro-environmental behavior. *Journal of Environmental Psychology* 27:14–25.

Bandura, A., C. Barbaranelli, G. V. Caprara, and C. Pastorelli. 1996. Mechanisms of moral disengagement in the exercise of moral agency. *Journal of Personality and Social Psychology* 71:364–74.

Bandyopadhyay, S., A. R. Rao, and B. K. Sinha. 2011. *Models for social networks with statistical applications.* Thousand Oaks, CA: Sage.

Bang, M., D. L. Medin, and S. Atran. 2007. Cultural mosaics and mental models of nature. *Proceedings of the National Academy of Sciences* 104:13868–74.

Banville, D., P. Desrosiers, and Y. Genet-Volet 2002. Comparison of value orientations of Quebec and American teachers: A cultural difference? *Teaching and Teacher Education* 18:469–82.

Barabási, A. L. 2002. *Linked: The new science of networks.* Cambridge, MA: Perseus.

Barash, D. P. 1972. Human ethology: The snack-bar security syndrome. *Psychological Reports* 31:577–78.

Barash, D. P. 1973. Human ethology: Personal space reiterated. *Environment and Behavior* 5:67–72.

Barash, D. P. 1974. Human ethology: Displacement activities in a dental office. *Psychological Reports* 34:947–49.

Barash, D. P. 1977. Human ethology: Exchanging cheetahs for Chevrolets? *Environment and Behavior* 9:487–90.

Barber, N. 1998. Ecological and psychosocial correlates of male homosexuality: A cross-cultural investigation. *Journal of Cross-Cultural Psychology* 29:387–401.

Barchard, K. A., and J. Williams. 2008. Practical advice for conducting ethical online experiments and questionnaires for United States psychologists. *Behavior Research Methods* 40 4:1111–28.

Bard, E. G., D. Robertson, and A. Sorace. 1996. Magnitude estimation of linguistic acceptability. *Language* 72:32–68.

Barg, F. K., S. Keddem, K. R. Ginsburg, and F. K. Winston. 2009. Teen perceptions of good drivers and safe drivers: Implications for reaching adolescents. *Injury Prevention* 15:24–29.

Baril, H., J. Danielle, E. Chartrand, and M. Dubé. 2009. Females' quality of relationships in adolescence and friendship support in adulthood. *Canadian Journal of Behavioural Science* 41:161–68.

Barker, B., L. Degenhardt, and L. Topp. 2004. The external validity of results derived from ecstasy users recruited using purposive sampling strategies. *Drug and Alcohol Dependence* 73:33–40.

Barker, R., and H. F. Wright. 1951. *One boy's day. A specimen record of behavior.* New York: Harper & Brothers.

Barnard, M. 2009. "You could take this topic and get a fistfight going": Communicating about feminism in interviews. *Discourse and Communication* 3:427–47.

Barnes, B. 1995. *The elements of social theory.* Princeton, NJ: Princeton University Press.

Barnes, J. H., B. F. Banahan, III, and K. E. Fish. 1995. The response effect of question order in computer-administered questioning in the social sciences. *Social Science Computer Review* 13:47–63.

Barnett, V., and T. Lewis. 1994. *Outliers in statistical data.* 3d. ed. West Sussex, UK: John Wiley and Sons.

Barroso, J. 1997. Reconstructing my life: Becoming a long-term survivor of AIDS. *Qualitative Health Research* 7:57–74.

Bartholomew, D. J., ed. 2006. *Measurement.* London: Sage.

Bartlett, F. C. 1937. Psychological methods and anthropological problems. *Africa* 10:401–19.

Basurto, X., and J. Speer. 2012. Structuring the calibration of qualitative data as assets for Qualitative Comparative Analysis (QCA). *Field Methods* (in press).

Batagelj, V., and A. Mrvar. n.d. Pajek. Program for large network analysis. http://pajek.imfm.si/doku.php (accessed June 24, 2011).

Batchelder, W. H., and A. K. Romney. 1986. The statistical analysis of a general Condorcet model for dichotomous choice situations. In *Information pooling and decision making*, B. Grofman and G. Owen, eds., 103–12. Greenwich, CT: JAI.

Bauer, M., and A. L. Wright 1996. Integrating qualitative and quantitative methods to model infant feeding behavior among Navajo mothers. *Human Organization* 55:183–92.

Bauman, R.1984. *Verbal art as performance*. Prospect Heights, IL: Waveland Press.

Bauman, R. 1986. *Story, performance, and event. Contextual studies of oral narrative*. New York: Cambridge University Press.

Beach, S. R., R. Schulz, H. B. Degenholtz, N. G. Castle, J. Rosen, A. R. Fox, and R. K. Morycz. 2010. Using audio computer-assisted self-interviewing and interactive voice response to measure elder mistreatment in older adults: Feasibility and effects on prevalence estimates. *Journal of Official Statistics* 26:507–33.

Beatty, P. C., and G. B. Wiilis. 2007. Research synthesis: The practice of cognitive interviewing. *Public Opinion Quarterly* 71:287–311.

Bechtel, R. B. 1977. *Enclosing behavior*. Stroudsburg, PA: Dowden, Hutchinson, & Ross.

Beck, A. T., C. H. Ward, M. Mendelson, J. E. Mock, and J. Erbaugh. 1961. An inventory for measuring depression. *Archives of General Psychiatry* 4:561–71.

Beck, C. T., and R. K. Gable. 2000. Postpartum Depression Screening Scale: Development and psychometric testing. *Nursing Research* 49:272–82.

Beck, C. T., and R. K. Gable. 2003. Postpartum Depression Screening Scale: Spanish version. *Nursing Research* 52:296–306.

Beck, M. E. 2007. Dinner preparation in the United States. *British Food Journal* 109:531–47.

Beck, M. E., and J. E. Arnold. 2009. Gendered time use at home: An ethnographic examination of leisure time in middle-class families. *Leisure Studies* 28:121–42.

Becker, H. S. 1998. *Tricks of the trade: How to think about your research while you're doing it*. Chicago: University of Chicago Press.

Becker, H. S. 2004. Comment on Kevin D. Haggerty, Ethics creep: Governing social science research in the name of ethics. *Qualitative Sociology* 27:415–16.

Becker, H. S., B. Geer, E. C. Hughs, and A. L. Strauss. 1961. *Boys in white. Student culture in medical school*. Chicago: University of Chicago Press.

Beebe, J. 2001. *Rapid assessment: An introduction*. Walnut Creek, CA: AltaMira.

Beebe, T. J., S. M. Stoner, K. J. Anderson, and A. R. Williams. 2007. Selected questionnaire size and color combinations were significantly related to survey response rates. *Journal of Clinical Epidemiology* 60:1184–89.

Beere, C. A. 1990. *Gender roles: A handbook of tests and measures*. New York: Greenwood Press.

Begley, S., H. Fineman, and V. Church. 1992. The science of polling. *Newsweek*, September 28, pp. 38–39.

Behar, R. 1996. *The vulnerable observer: Anthropology that breaks your heart*. Boston: Beacon Press.

Belansky, E. S., and A. K. Boggiano. 1994. Predicting helping behaviors: The role of gender and instrumental/expressive self-schemata. *Sex Roles* 30:647–61.

Belinfante, A. 2009. Telephone subscribership in the United States. Federal Communications Commission Report, August. http://hraunfoss.fcc.gov/edocs_public/attachmatch/DOC-292759A1.pdf (accessed August 23, 2009).

Bell, D. C. 2009. *Constructing social theory*. Lanham, MD: Rowman & Littlefield.

Bell, L. 2001. Patterns of interaction in multidisciplinary child protection teams in New Jersey. *Child Abuse and Neglect* 25:65–80.

Belli, R. F. 1998. The structure of autobiographical memory and the event history calendar: Potential improvements in the quality of retrospective reports in surveys. *Memory* 6:383–406.

Belli, R. F., F. P. Stafford, and D. F. Alwin, eds. 2009. *Calendar and time diary methods in life course research*. Thousand Oaks, CA: Sage.

Belousov, K., T. Horlick-Jones, M. Bloor, Y. Gilinsky, V. Golbert, Y. Kostikovsky, M. Levi, and D. Pentsov. 2007. Any port in a storm: Fieldwork difficulties in dangerous and crisis-ridden settings. *Qualitative Research* 7:155–75.

Bem, S. L. 1974. The measurement of psychological androgyny. *Journal of Consulting and Clinical Psychology* 42:155–62.

Bem, S. L. 1979. Theory and measurement of androgyny: A reply to the Pedhazur-Tetenbaum and Locksley-Colten critiques. *Journal of Personality and Social Psychology* 37:1047–54.

Bem, S. L. 1981. Gender schema theory: A cognitive account of sex typing. *Psychological Review* 88:354–64.

Bem, S. L. 1983. Gender schema theory and its implications for child development: Raising gender-aschematic children in a gender-schematic society. *Signs* 8:598–616.

Bem, S. L. 1985. Androgyny and gender schema theory: A conceptual and empirical integration. In *Psychology and gender*, T. B. Sonderegger, ed., 179–226. Lincoln: University of Nebraska Press.

Ben-David, J., and T. A. Sullivan. 1975. Sociology of science. *Annual Review of Sociology* 1:203–22.

Benham, B. 2008. Moral accountability and debriefing. *Kennedy Institute of Ethics Journal* 18:253–73.

Benjamin, L. T., Jr., and J. A. Simpson. 2009. The power of the situation: The impact of Milgram's obedience studies on personality and social psychology. *American Psychologist* 64:12–19.

Bennardo, G. 2002. Map drawing in Tonga, Polynesia: Accessing mental representations of space. *Field Methods* 14:390–417.

Bennardo, G. 2008. Metaphors, source domains, and key words in Tongan speech about social relationships: 'Ofa "love" is giving. *Anthropological Linguistics* 50:174–204.

Bennett, C. A., A. M. de Silva-Sanigorski, M. Andrea, M. Nichols, A. C. Bell, and B. A. Swinburn. 2009. Assessing the intake of obesity-related foods and beverages in young children: Comparison of a simple population survey with 24 hr-recall. *International Journal of Behavioral Nutrition and Physical Activity* 6: Article Number 71. doi: 10.1186/1479-5868-6-71.

Benoit, R., and C. Ragin. 2009. *Configurational comparative methods. Qualitative Comparative Analysis (QCA) and related techniques.* Thousand Oaks, CA: Sage.

Berg, D. N., and K. K. Smith, eds. 1985. *Exploring clinical methods for social research.* Beverly Hills, CA: Sage.

Berinsky, A. J. 2004. Can we talk? Self-presentation and the survey response. *Political Psychology* 25:643–59.

Berlin, B. 1992. *Ethnobotanical classification: Principles of categorization of plants and animals in traditional societies.* Princeton, NJ: Princeton University Press.

Berlin, B., D. E. Breedlove, and P. H. Raven. 1968. Covert categories and folk taxonomies. *American Anthropologist* 70:290–99.

Bermant, G. 1982. Justifying social research in terms of social benefit. In *Ethical issues in social science research*, T. L. Beauchamp et al., eds., 125–43. Baltimore: The Johns Hopkins University Press.

Bernard, H. R. 1967. Kalymnian sponge diving. *Human Biology* 39:103–30.

Bernard, H. R. 1974. Scientists and policymakers: A case study in the ethnography of communications. *Human Organization* 33:261–75.

Bernard, H. R. 1987. Sponge fishing and technological change in Greece. In *Technology and social change,* 2d ed., H. R. Bernard and P. J. Pelto, eds., 167–206. Prospect Heights, IL: Waveland.

Bernard, H. R. 1992. Preserving language diversity. *Human Organization* 41:82–88.

Bernard, H. R. 1996. Qualitative data, quantitative analysis. *Cultural Anthropology Methods Journal* 8:9–11.

Bernard, H. R., and S. Ashton-Vouyoucalos. 1976. Return migration to Greece. *Journal of the Steward Anthropological Society* 8:31–51.

Bernard, H. R., and L. Comitas. 1978. Greek return migration. *Current Anthropology* 19:658–59.

Bernard, H. R., E. Johnsen, P. Killworth, and S. Robinson. 1989. Estimating the size of an average personal network and of an event population. In *The small world,* M. Kochen, ed., 159–75. Norwood, NJ: Ablex Publishing.

Bernard, H. R., and P. D. Killworth. 1973. On the social structure of an ocean-going research vessel and other important things. *Social Science Research* 2:145–84.

Bernard, H. R., and P. D. Killworth. 1974. Scientists and crew. *Maritime Studies and Management* 2:112–25.

Bernard, H. R., and P. D. Killworth. 1979. Review of the small world literature. *Sociological Symposium* 28l:15–24.

Bernard, H. R., and P. D. Killworth. 1993. Sampling in time allocation research. *Ethnology* 32:211.

Bernard, H. R., and P. D. Killworth. 1997. The search for social physics. *Connections* 20:16—34. http://www.analytictech.com/connections/v20(1)/keynote.htm (accessed September 20, 2010).

Bernard, H. R., P. D. Killworth, C. McCarty, and G. A. Shelley. 1990. Estimating the size of personal networks. *Social Networks* 23:289–312.

Bernard, H. R., P. D. Killworth, L. Sailer, and D. Kronenfeld. 1984. The problem of informant accuracy: The validity of retrospective data. *Annual Review of Anthropology* 13:495–517.

Bernard, H. R., and P. J. Pelto. 1987. Technology and anthropological theory. In *Technology and social change,* rev. 2d ed., H. R. Bernard and P. J. Pelto, eds., 359–76. Prospect Heights, IL: Waveland.

Bernard, H. R., and G. W. Ryan. 2010. *Analyzing qualitative data: Systematic approaches.* Thousand Oaks, CA: Sage.

Bernard, H. R., G. Ryan, and S. Borgatti. 2009. Green cognition and behavior: A cultural domain analysis. In *Networks, resources and economic action. Ethnographic case studies in honor of Hartmut Lang,* C. Greiner and W. Kokot, eds., 189–215. Berlin: Dietrich Reimer Verlag.

Bernard, H. R., and J. Salinas Pedraza. 1989. *Native ethnography: A Mexican Indian describes his culture.* Newbury Park, CA: Sage.

Berry, J. 1976. *Human ecology and cognitive style.* New York: Wiley.

Bessinger, J. B., and P. H. Smith. 1969. *A concordance to Beowulf.* Ithaca, NY: Cornell University Press.

Bialostok, S. 2002. Metaphors for literacy: A cultural model of white, middle-class parents. *Linguistics and Education* 13:347–71.

Bickel, R., S. Weaver, T. Williams, and L. Lange.1997. Opportunity, community, and teen pregnancy in an Appalachian state. *Journal of Educational Research* 90:175–81.

Biernacki, P., and D. Waldorf. 1981. Snowball sampling: Problems, techniques, and chain referral sampling. *Sociological Methods and Research* 10:141–63.

Billiet, J., and G. Loosveldt. 1988. Improvement of the quality of responses to factual survey questions by interviewer training. *Public Opinion Quarterly* 52:190–211.

Bingham, W. Van Dyke, B. V. Moore, and J. W. Gustad. 1959. *How to interview.* 4th rev. ed. New York: Harper.

Birdwell-Pheasant, D. 1984. Personal power careers and the development of domestic structure in a small community. *American Ethnologist* 11:699–717.

Bishop, B., and G. J. Syme. 1995. The social costs and benefits of urban consolidation: A time budget/contingent valuation approach. *Journal of Economic Psychology* 16:223–45.

Blair, E. 1979. Interviewing in the presence of others. In *Improving interview method and questionnaire design: Response effects to threatening questions in survey research*, N. M. Bradburn and S. Sudman, eds., 134–46. San Francisco: Jossey-Bass.

Blair, E., S. Sudman, N. M. Bradburn, and C. B. Stocking. 1977. How to ask questions about drinking and sex: Response effects in measuring consumer behavior. *Journal of Marketing Research* 14:316–21.

Blalock, H. M., ed. 1974. *Measurement in the social sciences: Theories and strategies*. Chicago: Aldine.

Blalock, H. M. 1979. *Social statistics*. Rev. 2d ed. New York: McGraw-Hill.

Blalock, H. M. 1982. *Conceptualization and measurement in the social sciences*. Beverly Hills, CA: Sage.

Blass, T. 1999. The Milgram paradigm after 35 years: Some things we no know about obedience to authority. *Journal of Applied Social Psychology* 29:955–78.

Blass, T. 2004. *The man who shocked the world. The life and legacy of Stanley Milgram*. New York: Basic Books.

Bleek, W. 1987. Lying informants: A fieldwork experience from Ghana. *Population and Development Review* 13:314–22.

Bletzer, K., and M. P. Koss. 2006. After-rape among three populations in the Southwest. *Violence Against Women* 12:5–29.

Blommaert, J. 2006. Applied ethnopoetics. *Narrative Inquiry* 16:181–90.

Bloom, D. 2003. Narrative discourse. In *Handbook of discourse processes*, A. C. Graesser, M. A. Gernsbacher, and S. Goldman, eds., 287–320. Mahwah, NJ: L. Erlbaum Associates.

Bloom, G., D. Stevens, and T. Wickwire. 2003. Expert coaches' perceptions of team building. *Journal of Applied Sport Psychology* 15:129–43.

Bloor, M., F. Frankland, M. Thomas, and K. Robson. 2001. *Focus groups in social research*. Thousand Oaks, CA: Sage.

Blow, F. C., K. J. Brower, J. E. Schulenberg, L. M. Demo-Dananberg, J. P. Young, and T. P. Beresford. 1992. The Michigan Alcohol Screening Test—Geriatric Version (MAST-G): A new elderly specific screening instrument. *Alcoholism: Clinical and Experimental Research* 16:372.

Blumberg, S. J., J. V. Luke, G. Nadarajasundaram, M. E. Davern, M. H. Boudreaux, and K. Soderberg. 2011. Wireless substitution: State-level estimates from the National Health Interview Survey, January 2007–June 2010. National health statistics reports; no 39. Hyattsville, MD: National Center for Health Statistics. http://www.cdc.gov/nchs/data/nhsr/nhsr039.pdf (accessed June 26, 2011).

Blum-Kulka, S. 1993. "You gotta know how to tell a story": Telling, tales, and tellers in American and Israeli narrative events at dinner. *Language in Society* 22:361–402.

Blurton-Jones, N. G., ed. 1972. *Ethological studies of child behaviour*. Cambridge: Cambridge University Press.

Boas, F., ed. 1911. *Handbook of American Indian languages*. Washington, DC: Bureau of American Ethnology, Bulletin No. 40.

Bocchiaro, P., and P. G. Zimbardo. 2010. Defying unjust authority: An exploratory study. *Current Psychology* 29:155–170.

Bochner, S. 1971. The use of unobtrusive measures in cross-cultural attitudes research. In *A question of choice: An Australian Aboriginal dilemma*, R. M. Berndt, ed., 107–15. Nedlands, Australia: University of Western Australia Press.

Bochner, S. 1972. An unobtrusive approach to the study of housing discrimination against Aborigines. *Australian Journal of Psychology* 24:335–37.

Bochner, S. 1980. Unobtrusive observation in cross-cultural experimentation. In *Handbook of cross-cultural psychology*, Vol. 2, *Methodology*, H. C. Triandis and J. W. Berry, eds., 319–88. Boston: Allyn & Bacon.

Boeije, H. R. 2002. A purposeful approach to the constant comparative method in the analysis of qualitative interviews. *Quality and Quantity* 36:391–409.

Boeije, H. R. 2004. And then there were three: Why third persons are present in interviews and the impact on the data. *Field Methods* 16:3–32.

Boelen, W. A. M. 1992. Street corner society. Cornerville revisited. *Journal of Contemporary Ethnography* 21:11–51.

Boellstorff, T. 2007. Queer studies in the house of anthropology. *Annual Review of Anthropology* 36:17–35.

Boellstorff, T. 2008. *Coming of age in Second Life*. Princeton, NJ: Princeton University Press.

Bogdan, R. 1972. *Participant observation in organizational settings*. Syracuse, NY: Syracuse University Press.

Bogdan, R., and S. K. Biklen. 1992. *Qualitative research for education: An introduction to theory and methods*. 2d ed. Boston: Allyn & Bacon.

Boissevain, J. 1974. *Friends of friends. Networks, manipulators and coalitions*. Oxford, UK: Basil Blackwell.

Boissevain, J., and J. C. Mitchell, eds. 1973. *Network analysis: Studies in human interaction*. The Hague: Mouton.

Boje, D. M. 2001. *Narrative methods for organizational and communication research*. Thousand Oaks, CA: Sage.

Bokowski, K., and S. Buetow. 2011. Making the invisible visible: A photovoice exploration of homeless women's health and lives in central Auckland. *Social Science and Medicine* 72:739–46.

Bolton, R. 1984. We all do it, but how? A survey of contemporary fieldnote procedure. In *Final report: Computers in ethnographic research*. ERIC, no. ED 1. 310/2:248173, App. IV, pp. 119–43. Washington, DC: National Institute of Education.

Bolton, R., and J. Vincke. 1996. Risky sex and sexual cognition: The cartography of eros among Flemish gay men. *Journal of Quantitative Anthropology* 6:171–208.

Bonham, C., E. Fujii, E. Im, and J. Mak. 1992. The impact of the hotel room tax: An interrupted time series approach. *National Tax Journal* 45:433–41.

BonJour, L. 1985. *The structure of empirical knowledge*. Cambridge, MA: Harvard University Press.

Booth, C., ed. 1902. *Life and labor of the people of London*. New York: Macmillan.

Boots, D. P., J. K. Cochran, and K. M. Heide. 2003. Capital punishment preferences for special offender populations. *Journal of Criminal Justice* 31:553–65.

Borchgrevnik, A. 2003. Silencing language: Of anthropologists and interpreters. *Ethnography* 4:95–121.

Borgatti, S. P. 1992a. *Anthropac 4.98*. Columbia, SC: Analytic Technologies. http://www.analytictech .com/ (accessed May 13, 2009).

Borgatti, S. P. 1992b. *Anthropac 4.0 methods guide*. Columbia, SC: Analytic Technologies.

Borgatti, S. P. 1993/1994. Cultural domain analysis. *Journal of Quantitative Anthropology* 4:261–78.

Borgatti, S. P. 1997. Consensus analysis. http://www .analytictech.com/borgatti/consensu.htm (accessed March 8, 2010).

Borgatti, S. P. 1999. Elicitation techniques for cultural domain analysis. In *Enhanced ethnographic methods*, J. J. Schensul, M. D. LeCompte, B. K. Natasi, and S. P. Borgatti, eds., 115–51. Walnut Creek, CA: AltaMira.

Borgatti, S. P., and I. Carboni. 2007. On measuring individual knowledge in organizations. *Organizational Research Methods* 10:449–62.

Borgatti, S. P., M. G. Everett, and L. C. Freeman 2002. *Ucinet for Windows. Software for social network analysis*. Harvard, MA: Analytic Technologies. http://www.analytictech.com/ (accessed June 20, 2010).

Borgatti, S. P., and P. C. Foster. 2003. The network paradigm in organizational research: A review and typology. *Journal of Management* 29:991–1013.

Borgerhoff Mulder, M. B., and T. M. Caro. 1985. The use of quantitative observational techniques in anthropology. *Current Anthropology* 26:323–36.

Borgers, N., J. Hox, and D. Sillel. 2004. Response effects in surveys on children and adolescents: Options, negative wording, and neutral mid-point. *Quality and Quantity* 38:17–33.

Borges, S., and H. Waitzkin 1995. Women's narratives in primary care medical encounters. *Women and Health* 23:29–56.

Borich, G., and G. Klinzing. 1984. Some assumptions in the observation of classroom process with suggestions for improving low inference measurement. *Journal of Classroom Interaction* 20:36–44.

Bornmann, J. W. 2009. Becoming soldiers: Army basic training and the negotiation of identity. Ph.D. dissertation, George Washington University.

Boruch, R. F., and J. S. Cecil, eds. 1983. *Solutions to ethical and legal problems in social research*. New York: Academic Press.

Boschen, M. J. 2008. Paruresis (psychogenic inhibition of micturition): Cognitive behavioral formulation and treatment. *Depression and Anxiety* 25:903–12.

Bosk, C. 2004. The ethnographer and the IRB: Comment on Kevin D. Haggerty, Ethics creep: Governing social science research in the name of ethics. *Qualitative Inquiry* 27:417–20.

Bosnjak, M., and T. L. Tuten. 2003. Prepaid and promised incentives in web surveys: An experiment. *Social Science Computer Review* 21:208–17.

Boster, J. S. 1985. Requiem for the omniscient informant: There's life in the old girl yet. In *Directions in cognitive anthropology*, J. Dougherty, ed., 177–97. Urbana: University of Illinois Press.

Boster, J. S. 1986. Exchange of varieties and information between Aguaruna manioc cultivators. *American Anthropologist* 88:428–36.

Boster, J. S., and J. C. Johnson. 1989. Form or function: A comparison of expert and novice judgments of similarity among fish. *American Anthropologist* 91:866–89.

Boster, J. S., J. C. Johnson, and S. C. Weller. 1987. Social position and shared knowledge: Actors' perceptions of status, role, and social structure. *Social Networks* 9:375–87.

Bott, E. 1957/1971. *Family and social network*. London: Tavistock.

Bourgois, P. I. 1990. Confronting anthropological ethics: Ethnographic lessons from Central America. *Journal of Peace Research* 27:43–54.

Bourgois, P. I. 1995. *In search of respect: Selling crack in El Barrio*. New York: Cambridge University Press.

Bourque, L., and E. P. Fielder. 2003. *How to conduct telephone surveys*. Vol. 4, *The survey kit*. 2d ed. Thousand Oaks, CA: Sage.

Bowman, S. A. 2006. A comparison of the socioeconomic characteristics, dietary practices, and health status of women food shoppers with different food price attitudes. *Nutrition Research* 26:318–24.

Boyd, C. J., F. Blow, and L. S. Orgain. 1993. Gender differences among African-American substance abusers. *Journal of Psychoactive Drugs* 25:301–305.

Boyd, H. W., Jr., and R. Westfall. 1955. *The Journal of Marketing* 19:311–24.

Boyle, E., Jr. 1970. Biological patterns in hypertension by race, sex, body weight, and skin color. *Journal of the American Medical Association* 213:1637–43.

Bradburn, N. M. 1983. Response effects. In *Handbook of survey research*, P. H. Rossi, J. D. Wright, and A. B. Anderson, eds., 289–328. New York: Academic Press.

Bradburn, N. M., and S. Sudman et al. 1979. *Improving interview method and questionnaire design: Response effects to threatening questions in survey research*. San Francisco: Jossey-Bass.

Bradley, C. 1997. Doing fieldwork with diabetes. *Cultural Anthropology Methods Journal* 9:1–7.

Braunsberger, K., H. Wybenga, and R. Gates. 2007. A comparison of reliability between telephone and web-based surveys. *Journal of Business Research* 60:758–64.

Braunstein, M. S. 1993. Sampling a hidden population: Noninstitutionalized drug users. *AIDS Education and Prevention* 5:131–40.

Brenner, O. C., and J. Tomkiewicz. 1982. Job orientation of black and white college graduates in business. *Personnel Psychology* 35:89–103.

Brettell, C. B. 1998. Fieldwork in the archives: Methods and sources in historical anthropology. In *Handbook of methods in cultural anthropology*, H. R. Bernard, ed., 513–46. Walnut Creek, CA: AltaMira.

Brewer, D. D. 1995. Cognitive indicators of knowledge in semantic domains. *Journal of Quantitative Anthropology* 5:107–28.

Brewer, D. D., and S. B. Garrett. 2001. Evaluation of interviewing techniques to enhance recall of sexual and drug injection partners. *Sexually Transmitted Diseases* 28:666–77.

Brewer, D. D., S. B. Garrett, and G. Rinaldi. 2002. Free-listed items are effective cues for eliciting additional items in semantic domains. *Applied Cognitive Psychology* 16:343–58.

Brewer, D. D., and B. L. Yang. 1994. Patterns in the recall of persons in a religious community. *Social Networks* 16:347–79.

Brewer, W. F. 1999. Schemata. In *The MIT encyclopedia of the cognitive sciences*, R. A. Wilson and F. C. Keil, eds., 729–30. Cambridge, MA: MIT Press.

Brewer, W. F. 2000. Bartlett's concept of the schema and its impact on theories of knowledge representation in contemporary cognitive psychology. In *Bartlett, culture and cognition*, A. Saito, ed., 69–89. Hove, UK: Psychology Press.

Bridges, F. S., D. A.Anzalone, S. W. Ryan, and F. L. Anzalone. 2002. Extensions of the lost letter technique to divisive issues of creationism, Darwinism, sex education, and gay and lesbian affiliations. *Psychological Reports* 90:391–400.

Bridgman, P. W. 1927. *The logic of modern physics*. New York: Macmillan. (Reprinted 1980, New York: Arno.)

Briggs, C. L. 1986. *Learning how to ask: A sociolinguistic appraisal of the role of the interview in social science research*. New York: Cambridge University Press.

Brim, J. A., and D. H. Spain. 1974. *Research design in anthropology: Paradigms and pragmatics in the testing of hypotheses*. New York: Holt, Rinehart, and Winston.

Brink, P. J., and M. J. Wood, eds. 1998. *Advanced design in nursing research*. 2d ed. Thousand Oaks, CA: Sage.

Brislin, R. W. 1970. Back-translation for cross-cultural research. *Journal of Cross-Cultural Psychology* 1:185–216.

Brislin, R. W., W. J. Lonner, and R. M. Thorndike. 1973. *Cross-cultural research methods*. New York: Wiley.

Broadbent, N. 1995. Accident claims lives of researchers in Russian Far East. *Anthropology Newsletter*, November, pp. 39–40.

Broeder, A. 1998. Deception can be acceptable. *American Psychologist* 53:805–806.

Brown, J. R. 2010. *The laboratory of the mind. Thought experiments in the natural sciences*. 2d ed. New York: Routledge.

Brown, T. M., and E. M. De Casanova. 2009. Mothers in the field: How motherhood shapes fieldwork and researcher-subject relations. *Women's Studies Quarterly* 37:42–62.

Brown, W. H., S. L. Odom, and A. Holcombe. 1996. Observational assessment of young children's social behavior with peers. *Early Childhood Research Quarterly* 11:19–40.

Bruner, J. S., J. J. Goodnow, and G. A. Austin. 1956. *A study of thinking*. New York: Wiley.

Bruwer, J. D., and N. E. Haydam. 1996. Reducing bias in shopping mall-intercept surveys: The time-based systematic sampling method. *South African Journal of Business Management* 27:9–17.

Bruyn, S. T. H. 1966. *The human perspective in sociology. The methodology of participant observation*. Englewood Cliffs, NJ: Prentice-Hall.

Bryant, A., and K. Charmaz, eds. 2007. *The SAGE handbook of grounded theory*. London: Sage.

Bryant, C. 1985. *Positivism in social theory and research*. New York: St. Martin's Press.

Brymer, R. A. 1998. Hanging out with the good 'ole boys, gangsters, and other disreputable characters: Field research, quantitative research, and exceptional events. In *Doing ethnographic research: Fieldwork settings*, S. Grills, ed., 143–61. Thousand Oaks, CA: Sage.

Buchanan, E. A., and C. Ess. 2009. Internet research ethics: The field and its critical issues. In *The handbook of information and computer ethics*, K. E. Himma and H. T. Tavani, eds., 273–92. Hoboken, NJ: John Wiley & Sons. doi: 10.1002/9780470281819.

Bucholtz, M. 2000. The politics of transcription. *Journal of Pragmatics* 32:1439–65.

Bucholz, M. 2007. Variations in transcription. *Discourse Studies* 9:784–808.

Bulmer, M. 1979. Concepts in the analysis of qualitative data. *Sociological Review* 27:651–77.

Bulmer, M. 1984. *The Chicago School of Sociology: Institutionalization, diversity, and the rise of sociological research*. Chicago: University of Chicago Press.

Bulmer, M., ed. 1991. *Social research ethics: An examination of the merits of covert participant observation*. New York: Holmes and Meier.

Burdette, A. M., C. G. Ellison, T. D. Hill, and N. D. Glenn. 2009. "Hooking up" at college: Does religion make a difference? *Journal for the Scientific Study of Religion* 48:535–51.

Burger, J. 2009. Replicating Milgram. Would people still obey today? *American Psychologist* 64:1–11.

Burgess, R. G. 1989. *The ethics of educational research*. London: Falmer.

Burling, R. 1964. Cognition and componential analysis: God's truth or hocus-pocus? *American Anthropologist* 66:20–28.

Burling, R. 2000 [1984]. *Learning a field language*. Prospect Heights, IL: Waveland.

Burnham, K. P., D. R. Anderson, and J. L. Laake. 1980. Estimation of density from line transect sampling of biological populations. *Wildlife Monographs* 72: 3–202.

Burt, R. S.1987. A note on strangers, friends and happiness. *Social Networks* 9:311–31.

Burt, R. S., and M. J. Minor. 1983. *Applied network analysis: A methodological introduction*. Beverly Hills, CA: Sage.

Burton, M. L. 1968. Multidimensional scaling of role terms. Ph.D. dissertation, Stanford University.

Burton, M. L. 1972. Semantic dimensions of occupation names. In *Multidimensional scaling: Applications in the behavioral sciences*, Vol. 2, *Applications*, A. K. Romney, R. N. Shepard, and S. B. Nerlove, eds., 55–72. New York: Seminar Press.

Burton, M. L. 2003. Too many questions? The uses of incomplete cyclic designs for paired comparisons. *Field Methods* 15:115–30.

Burton, M. L., and S. B. Nerlove. 1976. Balanced designs for triad tests. *Social Science Research* 5:247–67.

Burton, M. L., and A. K. Romney. 1975. A multidimensional representation of role terms. *American Ethnologist* 2:397–407.

Bush, A. J., and J. F. Hair, Jr. 1985. An assessment of the mall intercept as a data collection method. *Journal of Marketing Research* 22:158–67.

Bushman, B. J., and A. M. Bonacci. 2004. You've got mail: Using e-mail to examine the effect of prejudiced attitudes on discrimination against Arabs. *Journal of Experimental Social Psychology* 40:753–59.

Buss, D. M. 1985. Human mate selection. *American Scientist* 73:47–51.

Byers, B., and R. A. Zeller. 1998. Measuring subgroup variation in social judgment research: A factorial survey approach. *Social Science Research* 27: 73–84.

Cabassa, L. J. 2003. Measuring acculturation: Where we are and where we need to go. *Hispanic Journal of Behavioral Sciences* 25:127–46.

Cahnman, W. J. 1948. A note on marriage announcements in the *New York Times*. *American Sociological Review* 13:96–97.

Cahyanto, I., L. Pennington-Gray, and B. Thapa. 2009. Reflections from utilizing reflexive photography to develop rural tourism in Indonesia. *Tourism Analysis* 14:721–36.

Calabro, M.A., G. J. Welk, A. L. Carriquiry, S. M. Nusser, N. K. Beyler, and C. E. Matthews. 2009. Validation of a computerized 24-hour physical activity recall (24PAR) instrument with pattern-recognition activity monitors. *Journal of Physical Activity and Health* 6:211–20.

Calder, N. 1993. *Studies in early Muslim jurisprudence*. New York: Oxford University Press.

Callanan, M. A., A. N. Repp, M. G. McCarthy, and M. A. Latzke. 1994. Children's hypotheses about word meanings: Is there a basic level constraint? *Journal of Experimental Child Psychology* 57:108–38.

Cambon de Lavalette, B. C. Tijus, S. Poitrenaud, C. Leproux, J. Bergeronc, and J-P. Thouez. 2009. Pedestrian crossing decision-making: A situational and behavioral approach. *Safety Science* 47: 1248–53.

Camp, R., M. E. Vielhaber, and J. L. Simonetti. 2001. *Strategic interviewing: How to hire good people*. San Francisco: Jossey-Bass.

Campbell, D. T. 1957. Factors relevant to the validity of experiments in social settings. *Psychological Bulletin* 54:297–312.

Campbell, D. T. 1974. Evolutionary epistemology. In *The library of living philosophers*, P. A. Schlipp, ed., Vol. 14, *The philosophy of Karl Popper*, Book 1, 413–63. La Salle, IL: Open Court Publishing.

Campbell, D. T. 1975. Degrees of freedom and the case study. *Comparative Political Studies* 8:178–93.

Campbell, D. T. 1979. Degrees of freedom and the case study. In *Qualitative and quantitative methods in evaluation research*, T. D. Cook and C. S. Reichart, eds., 49–67. Beverly Hills, CA: Sage.

Campbell, D. T. 1988. Qualitative knowing in action research. In *Methodology and epistemology for social science: Selected papers*, E. S. Overman, ed., 360–76. Chicago: University of Chicago Press.

Campbell, D. T., and R. F. Boruch. 1975. Making the case for randomized assignment to treatments by considering the alternatives: Six ways in which quasi-experimental evaluations in compensatory education tend to underestimate effects. In *Evaluation and experiment: Some critical issues in assessing social programs*, C. A. Bennett and A. A. Lumsdaine, eds., 195–296. New York: Academic Press.

Campbell, D. T., and D. W. Fiske. 1959. Convergent and discriminant validation by the multitrait-multimethod matrix. *Psychological Bulletin* 56:81–105.

Campbell, D. T., and E. S. Overman. 1988. *Methodology and epistemology for social science: Selected papers*. Chicago: University of Chicago Press.

Campbell, D. T., and H. L. Ross. 1968. The Connecticut crackdown on speeding: Time-series data in quasi-experimental analysis. *Law and Society Review* 3:33–53.

Campbell, D. T., and J. C. Stanley. 1963. *Experimental and quasi-experimental designs for research*. Boston: Houghton Mifflin.

Campbell, D. T., and J. C. Stanley. 1966. *Experimental and quasi-experimental designs for research*. Chicago: Rand McNally.

Campos, B., A. P. Graesch, R. Repetti, T. Bradbury, and E. Oths. 2009. Opportunity for interaction? A naturalistic observation study of dual-earner families after work and school. *Journal of Family Psychology* 23:798–807.

Cannell, C. F., G. Fisher, and T. Bakker. 1961. Reporting of hospitalization in the Health Interview Survey. *Health Statistics*. Series D, no. 4. USDHEW, PHS. Washington, DC: U.S. Government Printing Office.

Cannell, C. F., and F. J. Fowler. 1965. Comparison of hospitalization reporting in three survey procedures. *Vital and health statistics*. Series 2, no. 8. Washington, DC: U.S. Government Printing Office.

Cannell, C. F., and R. L. Kahn. 1968. Interviewing. In *The handbook of social psychology*. Vol. 2, *Research methods*, G. Lindzey and E. Aronson, eds., 526–95. Reading, MA: Addison-Wesley.

Cannell, C. F., S. Lawson, and D. Hausser. 1975. *A technique for evaluating interviewer performance*. Ann Arbor: Institute for Social Research, University of Michigan.

Cannell, C. F., L. Oksenberg, and J. M. Converse. 1979. *Experiments in interview techniques. Field experiments in health reporting 1971–1977*. Ann Arbor: Institute for Social Research, University of Michigan.

Cannell, C. F., L. Oksenberg, G. Kalton, K. Bischoping, and F. J. Fowler. 1989. *New techniques for pretesting survey questions*. Final Report, Grant No. HS 05616. National Center for Health Services Research and Health Care Technology Assessment. Ann Arbor: Survey Research Center, University of Michigan.

Cantril, H. 1965. *The pattern of human concerns*. New Brunswick, NJ: Rutgers University Press.

Caplan, P. J., M. Crawford, J. S. Hyde, and J. T. E. Richeardson. 1997. *Gender differences in human cognition*. London: Oxford University Press.

Carey, J. W., M. Morgan, and M. J. Oxtoby. 1996. Intercoder agreement in analysis of responses to open-ended interview questions: Examples from tuberculosis research. *Cultural Anthropology Methods Journal* 8:1–5.

Carley, K., and M. Palmquist. 1992. Extracting, representing, and analyzing mental models. *Social Forces* 70:601–36.

Carneiro, R. L. 2010. *The evolution of the human mind: From supernaturalism to naturalism—An anthropological perspective*. New York: Eliot Werner Publications.

Carr, N. T. 2008. Using Microsoft Excel® to calculate descriptive statistics and create graphs. *Language Assessment Quarterly* 5:43–62.

Carter, T. J. 2006. Police use of discretion: A participant observation study of game wardens. *Deviant Behavior* 27:591–627.

Carver, R. P. 1978. The case against statistical significance testing. *Harvard Educational Review* 48:378–99.

Carver, R. P. 1993. The case against statistical significance testing, revisited. *Journal of Experimental Education* 61:287–92.

Caserta, M. S., D. A. Lund, and M. F. Dimond. 1985. Assessing interviewer effects in a longitudinal study of bereaved elderly adults. *Journal of Gerontology* 40:637–40.

Caspi, A., T. E. Moffitt, A. Thornton, D. Freedman, J. W. Amell, H. Harrington, J. Smeijers, and P. A. Silva. 1996. The life history calendar: Research and clinical assessment method for collecting retrospective event-history data. *International Journal of Methods in Psychiatric Research* 6:101–14.

Cassell, C., and G. Symon, eds. 1994. *Qualitative methods in organizational research: A practical guide*. Thousand Oaks, CA: Sage.

Cassell, J., ed. 1987. *Children in the field*. Philadelphia: Temple University Press.

Casson, R. 1983. Schemata in cultural anthropology. *Annual Review of Anthropology* 12:429–62.

Casterline, J. B., and V. C. Chidambaram. 1984. The presence of others during the interview and the reporting of contraceptive knowledge and use. In *Survey analysis for the guidance of family planning programs*, J. A. Ross and R. McNamara, eds., 267–98. Liege, Belgium: Ordina Editions.

Catania, J. A., D. Binson, J. Canchola, L. M. Pollack, W. Hauck, and T. J. Coates. 1996. Effects of interviewer gender, interviewer choice, and item wording on responses to questions concerning sexual behavior. *Public Opinion Quarterly* 60:345–75.

Caulkins, D. D. 2001. Consensus, clines, and edges in Celtic cultures. *Cross-Cultural Research* 35:109–26.

Cepela, N. T., and J. A. Danowski. 2009. Automatic mapping of social networks of political actors from large collections of news stories. SONAM '09. International Conference on Advances in Social Network Analysis and Mining, IEEE. Pp. 212–18.

Chagnon, N. 1983. *Yanomamo. The fierce people*. 3d ed. New York: Holt, Rinehart & Winston.

Chalker, J., S. Ratanawijitrasin, N. T. K Chuc, M. Petzold, and G. Tomson. 2004. Effectiveness of a multi-component intervention on dispensing practices at private pharmacies in Vietnam and Thailand—A randomized controlled trial. *Social Science and Medicine* 60:131–41.

Chambers, R. 1991. Shortcut and participatory methods for gaining social information for projects. In *Putting people first: Sociological variables in rural development*, M. Cernea, ed., 515–37. New York: World Bank. http://repository.forcedmigration.org/show _metadata.jsp?pid=fmo:3802 (accessed December 19, 2010).

Chambers, R. 2006. Participatory mapping and geographic information systems: Whose map? Who is empowered and who is disempowered? Who gains and who loses? *The Electronic Journal on Information Systems in Developing Countries* 25:1–11. http://www.ejisdc.org/ojs2/index.php/ ejisdc/article/viewFile/239/160 (accessed March 8, 2010).

Chang, L., and J. A. Krosnick. 2009. National surveys via RDD telephone interviewing versus the Internet. Comparing sample representativeness amd response quality. *Public Opinion Quarterly* 73:641–78.

Chapkis, W. 1997. *Live sex acts: Women performing erotic labor*. New York: Rutledge.

Chapman, P., R. B. Toma, R. V. Tuveson, and M. Jacob. 1997. Nutrition knowledge among adolescent high school female athletes. *Adolescence* 32:437–46.

Chapoulie, J-M. 2004. Using the history of the Chicago tradition of sociology for empirical research. *Annals of the American Academy of Political and Social Science* 595:157–67.

Charmaz, K. 1990. "Discovering" chronic illness: Using grounded theory. *Social Science and Medicine* 30:1161–72.

Charmaz, K. 1995. Grounded theory. In *Rethinking methods in psychology*, J. A. Smith, R. Harré, and L. van Langenhove, eds., 27–49. London: Sage.

Charmaz, K. 2000. Grounded theory: Objectivist and constructivist methods. In *The handbook of qualitative research*, N. K. Denzin and Y. S. Lincoln, eds., 507–35. Thousand Oaks, CA: Sage.

Charmaz, K. 2002. Qualitative interviewing and grounded theory analysis. In *Handbook of interview research*, J. F. Gubrium and J. A. Holstein, eds., 675–94. Thousand Oaks, CA: Sage.

Chavez, L. R., F. A. Hubbell, J. M. McMullin, R. G. Martinez, and S. I. Mishra. 1995. Structure and meaning in models of breast and cervical cancer risk factors: A comparison of perceptions among Latinos, Anglo women, and physicians. *Medical Anthropology Quarterly* 9:40–74.

Chen, A., Z. Liu, and C. D. Ennis. 1997. Universality and uniqueness of teacher educational value orientations: A cross-cultural comparison between the USA and China. *Journal of Research and Development in Education* 30:135–43.

Chen, C-H., W. Härdle, and A. Unwin, eds. 2008. *Handbook of data visualization*. Berlin: Springer.

Chen, H-Y., and J. R. P. Boore. 2010. Translation and back-translation in qualitative nursing research: Methodological review. *Journal of Clinical Nursing* 19:234–39.

Cheng, S-L., W. Olsen, D. Southerton, and A. Warde. 2007. The changing practice of eating: Evidence from UK time diaries, 1975 and 2000. *British Journal of Sociology* 58:39–61.

Chien, W. T., and I. Norman. 2004. The validity and reliability of a Chinese version of the family burden interview schedule. *Nursing Research* 53:314–22.

Chikritzhs, T., and M. Brady. 2007. Postscript to "Fact or Fiction: A Critique of the National Aboriginal and Torres Strait Islander Social Survey 2002." *Drug and Alcohol Review* 26:221–22.

Cho, W. K. T., and J. H. Fowler. 2010. Legislative success in a small world: Social network analysis and the dynamics of congressional legislation. *Journal of Politics* 72:124–35.

Chock, P. P. 1986. Irony and ethnography: On cultural analysis of one's own culture. *Anthropological Quarterly* 59:87–96.

Choi, N., and D. R. Fuqua. 2003. The structure of the Bem Sex Role Inventory: A summary report of 23 validation studies. *Educational and Psychological Measurement* 63:872–87.

Choi, T-M., S-C. Liu, K-M. Pang, and P-S. Chow. 2008. Shopping behaviors of individual tourists from the Chinese Mainland to Hong Kong. *Tourism Management* 29:811–20.

Chomsky, N. 1959. Review of *Verbal Behavior* by B. F. Skinner. *Language* 35:26–58.

Chow, S. L. 1996. *Statistical significance: Rationale, validity and utility*. Thousand Oaks, CA: Sage.

Christensen, T. C., L. Feldman Barrett, E. Bliss-Moreau, K. Lebo, and C. Kaschub. 2003. A practical guide to experience-sampling procedures. *Journal of Happiness Studies* 4:53–78.

Christian, L. M., N. L. Parsons, and D. A. Dillman. 2009. Designing scalar questions for web surveys. *Sociological Methods and Research* 37:393–425.

Christianson, G. E. 1984. *In the presence of the creator: Isaac Newton and his times*. New York: Free Press.

Christie-Mizell, C. A., and R. L. Peralta. 2009 The gender gap in alcohol consumption during late adolescence and young adulthood: Gendered attitudes and adult roles. *Journal of Health and Social Behavior* 50:410–26.

Church, A. H. 1993. Estimating the effect of incentives on mail survey response rates: A meta-analysis. *Public Opinion Quarterly* 57:62–79.

Churchill, S. L., V. L. Plano Clark, K. Prochaska-Cue, J. W. Creswell, and L. Ontai-Grzebik. 2007. How rural low-income families have fun: A grounded

theory study. *Journal of Leisure Research* 39: 271–94.

Cialdini, R. B., and D. J. Baumann. 1981. Littering—A new unobtrusive measure of attitude. *Social Psychology Quarterly* 44:254–59.

Cialdini, R. B., R. J. Borden, A. Thorne, M. R. Walker, S. Freeman, and L. R. Sloan. 1976. Basking in reflected glory: Three (football) field studies. *Journal of Personality and Social Psychology* 34:366–75.

Cirino, P. T., C.E. Chin, R. A. Sevcik, M. Wolf, M. Lovett, and R. D. Morris. 2002. Measuring socioeconomic status: Reliability and preliminary validity for different approaches. *Assessment* 9:145–55.

Citro, C. F., D. R. Ilgen, and C. B. Marrett, eds. 2003. *Protecting participants and facilitating social and behavioral sciences research*. Panel on institutional review boards, surveys, and social science research, Committee on National Statistics and Board on Behavioral, Cognitive, and Sensory Sciences, Division on Behavioral Sciences and Education, National Research Council of the National Academies. Washington, DC: National Academies Press.

Claiborne, W. 1984. Dowry killings show social stress in India. *Washington Post*, September 22, p. A1.

Clancy, K. J., P. D. Berger, and T. L. Magliozzi. 2003. The ecological fallacy: Some fundamental research misconceptions corrected. *Journal of Advertising Research* 43:370–80.

Clark, L. D. Vincent, L. Zimmer, and J. Sanchez. 2009. Cultural values and political economic contexts of diabetes among low-income Mexican Americans. *Journal of Transcultural Nursing* 20:382–94.

Clark-Ibañez, M. 2004. Framing the social world with photo-elicitation interviews. *American Behavioral Scientist* 47:1507–27.

Cleveland, W. S. 1994. *The elements of graphing data*. 2d ed. Summit, NJ: Hobart.

Cochran, W. G. 1977. *Sampling techniques*. 2d ed. New York: Wiley.

Coffey, A., and P. Atkinson. 1996. *Making sense of qualitative data: Complementary research strategies*. Thousand Oaks, CA: Sage.

Cohen, D. A., T. A. Farley, and K. Mason. 2003. Why is poverty unhealthy? Social and physical mediators. *Social Science and Medicine* 57:1631–41.

Cohen, J. 1960. A coefficient of agreement for nominal scales. *Educational and Psychological Measurement* 20:37–48.

Cohen, J. 1988. *Statistical power analysis for the behavioral sciences*. 2d ed. Hillsdale, N.J.: Lawrence Erlbaum Associates.

Cohen, J. 1992. A power primer. *Psychological Bulletin* 112:155–59.

Cohen, J. 1994. The earth is round ($p < .05$). *American Psychologist* 49:997–1003.

Cohen, L. E., and M. Felson. 1979. Social change and crime rate trends: A routine activity approach. *American Sociological Review* 44:588–608.

Cohen-Kettenis, P. T., and L. J. G. Gooren. 1999. Transsexualism. A review of etiology, diagnosis and treatment. *Journal of Psychosomatic Research* 46:315–33.

Cohn, E. G. 1990. Weather and crime. *British Journal of Criminology* 30:51–64.

Cohn, E. G., and J. Rotton. 1997. Assault as a function of time and temperature: A moderator-variable time-series analysis. *Journal of Personality and Social Psychology* 72:1322–34.

Cole, D. 1983. The value of a person lies in his *herzen-bildung*: Franz Boas' Baffin Island letter-diary, 1883–1884. In *Observers observed*, G. W. Stocking, ed., 13–52. Madison: University of Wisconsin Press.

Coleman, J. S. 1966. *Equality of educational opportunity*. Washington, DC: U.S. Dept. of Health, Education, and Welfare, Office of Education/National Center for Education Statistics.

Coleman, J., E. Katz, and H. Menzel. 1957. The diffusion of an innovation among physicians, *Sociometry* 20:253–70.

College Board. 2008. SAT Reasoning Test: Mean scores by gender within ethnicity. Table 8. http://professionals.collegeboard.com/profdownload/Total_Group_Report.pdf (accessed March 13, 2009).

Collier, J., Jr. 1957. Photography in anthropology: A report on two experiments. *American Anthropologist* 59:843–59.

Collings, P. 2009. Participant observation and phased assertion as research strategies in the Canadian Arctic. *Field Methods* 21:133–53.

Collins, D. M., and P. F. Hayes. 1993. Development of a short-form conservatism scale suitable for mail surveys. *Psychological Reports* 72:419–22.

Coluccia, E., and G. Louse. 2004. Gender differences in spatial orientation: A review. *Journal of Environmental Psychology* 24:329–40.

Comte, A. 1875–1877. *System of positive polity*. 4 vols. Trans. by J. H., F. Harrison, E. S. Beeseley, R. Gongreve, and H. D. Hutton. London: Longmans, Green.

Comte, A. 1974 [1855]. *The essential Comte*. Ed. by S. Andreski. Trans. by M. Clarke. New York: Barnes & Noble.

Comte, A. 1975. *Auguste Comte and positivism: The essential writings*. Ed. by G. Lenzer. New York: Harper & Row.

Comte, A. 1988. *Cours de philosophie positive. Introduction to positive philosophy*. Trans. by F. Ferre. Indianapolis: Hackett Publishing.

Conklin, H. C. 1955. Hanuóo color categories. *Southwestern Journal of Anthropology* 11:339–44.

Conklin, H. C. 1962. Lexicographical treatment of folk taxonomies. In *Problems in lexicography*, F. W. Householder and S. Saporta, eds., 119–41. Bloomington: Indiana University Research Center in Anthropology, Folklore, and Linguistics Publication 21.

Connolly, M. 1990. Adrift in the city: A comparative study of children in Bogota, Colombia, and Guatemala City. *Child and Youth Services* 14:129–49.

Constable, N. 2003. *Romance on a global stage. Pen pals, virtual ethnograpohy, and "mail order" marriages*. New York: Shapiro, Bernstein & Co.

Conti, N. 2009. A Visigoth system: Shame, honor, and police socialization. *Journal of Contemporary Ethnography* 38:409–32.

Converse, J. M. 1984. Strong arguments and weak evidence: The open/closed question controversy of the 1940s. *Public Opinion Quarterly* 48:267–82.

Converse, J. M., and H. Schuman. 1974. *Conversations at random: Survey research as the interviewers see it*. New York: John Wiley.

Converse, P. D., E. W. Wolfe, X. Huang, and F. L. Oswald. 2008. Response rates for mixed-mode surveys using mail and e-mail/web. *American Journal of Evaluation* 29:99–107.

Cook, C., F. Heath, and R. L. Thompson. 2000. A meta-analysis of response rates in web- or Internet-based surveys. *Educational and Psychological Measurement* 60:821–36.

Cook, K. S., and T. Yamagishi. 2008. A defense of deception on scientific grounds. *Social Psychology Quarterly* 71:215–21.

Cook, S. W. 1975. A comment on the ethical issues involved in West, Gunn, and Chernicky's "Ubiquitous Watergate": An attributional analysis. *Journal of Personality and Social Psychology* 32:66–68.

Cook, T. D., and D. T. Campbell. 1979. *Quasi-experimentation: Design and analysis issues for field settings*. Chicago: Rand McNally College Publishing.

Cook, T. D., H. Cooper, and D. S. Cordray et al. 1992. *Meta-analysis for explanation. A casebook*. New York: Russell Sage Foundation.

Cook, T. D., W. R. Shadish, W. R., and V. C. Wong. 2008. Three conditions under which experiments and observational studies produce comparable causal estimates: New findings from within-study comparisons. *Journal of Policy Analysis and Management* 27:724–50.

Cooke, C. A. 2004. Young people's attitudes towards guns in America, Great Britain, and Western Australia. *Aggressive Behavior* 30:93–104.

Cooker, M., and W. F. White. 1993. Influence of personal beliefs and attitudes on certification of pre-service teachers. *Education* 114:284–92.

Coombs, C. H. 1964. *A theory of data*. New York: Wiley.

Cooper, H., L. V. Hedges, and J. C. Valentine, eds. 2009. *The handbook of research synthesis and meta-analysis*. New York: Russell Sage Foundation.

Corbin, J., and A. Strauss. 2008. *Basics of qualitative research: Techniques and procedures for developing grounded theory*. 3d ed. Thousand Oaks, CA: Sage.

Cornell, L. L. 1984. Why are there no spinsters in Japan? *Journal of Family History* 9:326–39.

Corrion, K., T. Long, A. L. Smith, and F. d'Arripe-Longueville. 2009. "It's not my fault; it's not serious": Athlete accounts of moral disengagement in competitive sport. *The Sport Psychologist* 23:388–404.

Cottingham, J. 1988. *The rationalists*. Oxford, UK: Oxford University Press.

Couper, M.P., R. Tourangeau, and T. Marvin. 2009. Taking the audio out of audio-CASI. *Public Opinion Quarterly* 73:281–303.

Couper, M. P. 2008. *Designing effective web surveys*. New York: Cambridge University Press.

Couper, M. P., E. Singer, and R. Tourangeau. 2003. Understanding the effects of audio-CASI on self-reports of sensitive behavior. *Public Opinion Quarterly* 67:385–95.

Cousens, S., B. Kanki, S. Toure, I. Diallo, and V. Curtis. 1996. Reactivity and repeatability of hygiene behaviour: Structured observations from Burkina Faso. *Social Science and Medicine* 43:1299–308.

Cowan, G., and M. O'Brien. 1990. Gender and survival vs. death in slasher films: A content analysis. *Sex Roles* 23:187–96.

Coutts, A. J., and P. R. Reaburn. 2000. Time and motion analysis of the AFL field umpire. Australian Football League. *Journal of Science and Medicine in Sport* 3:132–39.

Craib, I. 1997. *Classical social theory*. New York: Oxford University Press.

Creese, A., A. Bhatt, N. Bhojani, and P. Martin. 2008. Fieldnotes in team ethnography: Researching complementary schools. *Qualitative Research* 8:197–215.

Cressey, D. R. 1950. The criminal violation of financial trust. *American Sociological Review* 15:738–43.

Cressey, D. R. 1953. *Other people's money: A study in the social psychology of embezzlement*. Glencoe, IL: The Free Press.

Creswell, J. W. 2003. *Research design: Qualitative, quantitative, and mixed methods strategies*. Thousand Oaks, CA: Sage.

Creswell, J. W. 2009. *Research design: Qualitative, quantitative, and mixed methods approaches*. 3rd ed. Thousand Oaks, CA: Sage.

Creswell, J. W., and V. L. Plano-Clark. 2007. *Designing and conducting mixed methods research*. Thousand Oaks, CA: Sage.

Creswell, J. W., and V. L. Plano Clark. 2011. *Designing and conducting mixed methods research*. 2d. ed. Thousand Oaks, CA: Sage.

Cross, R., and A. Parker. 2004. *The hidden power of social networks*. Boston: Harvard Business School Press.

Cross, R., A. Parker, L. Prusak, and S. P. Borgatti. 2001. Knowing what we know: Supporting knowledge creation and sharing in social networks. *Organizational Dynamics* 30:100–20.

Crossley, N. 2005. The new social physics and the science of small world networks. *The Sociological Review* 53:351–59.

Crume, T. L., C. DiGiuseppe, T. Byers, A. P. Sirotnak, and C. J. Garrett. 2002. Underascertainment of child maltreatment fatalities by death certificates, 1990–1998. *Pediatrics* 110:e18. http://pediatrics.aappublications.org/cgi/reprint/110/2/e18 (accessed June 28, 2009).

Cruz, T. H., S. W. Marshall, J. M. Bowling, and A. Villaveces. 2008. The validity of a proxy acculturation scale among U.S. Hispanics. *Hispanic Journal of Behavioral Sciences* 30:425–46.

Csikszentmihalyi, M., and J. Hunter. 2003. Happiness in everyday life: The uses of experience sampling. *Journal of Happiness Studies* 4:185–99.

Csikszentmihalyi, M., and R. Larson. 1987. Validity and reliability of the experience-sampling method. Special issue: Mental disorders in their natural settings: The application of time allocation and experience-sampling techniques in psychiatry. *Journal of Nervous and Mental Disease* 175:526–36.

Csikszentmihalyi, M., R. Larson, R., and S. Prescott. 1977. The ecology of adolescent activity and experience. *Journal of Youth and Adolescence* 6:281–94.

Cullen, F. T., and P. Wilcox, eds. 2010. *Encyclopedia of criminological theory*. Thousand Oaks, CA: Sage.

Cummings, L. L., and C. J. Berger. 1976. Organization structure: How does it influence attitude and performance? *Organizational Dynamics* 5:34–49.

Cunliffe, A. L. 2010. Retelling tales of the field in search of organizational ethnography 20 years on. *Organizational Research Methods* 13:224–39.

Cupples, J. 2002. The field as a landscape of desire: Sex and sexuality in geographical fieldwork. *Area* 34:382–90.

Currivan, D. B., A. L. Nyman, C. F. Turner, and L. Biener. 2004. Does telephone audio computer-assisted self-interviewing improve the accuracy of prevalence estimates of youth smoking? Evidence from the UMass Tobacco Study. *Public Opinion Quarterly* 68:542–64.

Curtice, J., and N. Sparrow. 1997. How accurate are traditional quota opinion polls? *Journal of the Market Research Society* 39:433–48.

Cycyota, C. S., and D. A. Harrison. 2006. What (not) to expect when surveying executives: A meta-analysis of top manager response rates and techniques over time. *Organizational Research Methods* 9:133–60.

Czaja, R., and J. Blair. 2005. *Designing surveys: A guide to decisions and procedures*. 2d ed. Thousand Oaks, CA: Pine Forge Press.

Daley, W. R., A. Karpati, and M. Shelk. 2001. Needs assessment of the displaced population following the August 1999 earthquake in Turkey. *Disasters* 25:67–75.

Dalton, D. R., J. C. Wimbush, and C. M. Daily. 1996. Candor, privacy, and "legal immunity" in business ethics research: An empirical assessment of the randomized response technique (RTT). *Business Ethics Quarterly* 6:87–99.

Daly, M., and M. Wilson. 1988. *Homicide*. New York: Aldine de Gruyter.

Daly, M., and M. Wilson. 1998. *The truth about Cinderella*. New Haven, CT: Yale University Press.

Dancy, J. 1985. *An introduction to contemporary epistemology*. Oxford, UK: Blackwell.

D'Andrade, R. G. 1973. Cultural constructions of reality. In *Cultural illness and health*, L. Nader and T. W. Maretzki, eds., 115–27. Washington, DC: American Anthropological Association.

D'Andrade, R. G. 1974. Memory and the assessment of behavior. In *Measurement in the social sciences*, H. M. Blalock, Jr., ed., 159–86. Chicago: Aldine.

D'Andrade, R. G. 1991. The identification of schemas in naturalistic data. In *Person schemas and maladaptive interpersonal patterns*, M. Horowitz, ed., 279–301. Chicago: University of Chicago Press.

D'Andrade, R. G. 1995. *The development of cognitive anthropology*. Cambridge: Cambridge University Press.

D'Andrade, R. G., N. R. Quinn, S. B. Nerlove, and A. K. Romney. 1972. Categories of disease in American-English and Mexican-Spanish. In *Multidimensional scaling: Theory and applications in the behavioral sciences*, Vol. 2., A. K. Romney, R. N. Shepard, and S. B. Nerlove, eds., 9–54. New York: Seminar Press.

D'Andrade, R. G., and C. Strauss, eds. 1992. *Human motives and cultural models*. New York: Cambridge University Press.

Dash, N., and H. Gladwin. 2007. Evacuation decision making and behavioral responses: Individual and household. *Natural Hazards Review* 8:69–77.

Dattalo, P. 2008. *Determining sample size: Balancing power, precision, and practicality*. New York: Oxford University Press.

Dattalo, P. 2010. *Strategies to approximate random sampling and assignment*. New York: Oxford University Press.

Davidson, C. 2010. Transcription matters: Transcribing talk and interaction to facilitate conversation analysis of the taken-for-granted in young children's interactions. *Journal of Early Childhood Research* 8: 115–31.

Davis, A., B. B. Gardner, and M. R. Gardner. 1941. *Deep South*. Chicago: The University of Chicago Press.

Davis, D. 1986. Changing self-image: Studying menopausal women in a Newfoundland fishing village. In *Self, sex and gender in cross-cultural fieldwork*, T. L. Whitehead and M. E. Conaway, eds., 240–62. Urbana: University of Illinois Press.

Davis, D. W. 1997. The direction of race of interviewer effects among African-Americans: Donning the black mask. *American Journal of Political Science* 41:309–23.

Davis, J. A. 1971. *Elementary survey analysis*. Englewood Cliffs, NJ: Prentice-Hall.

Davis, K., and S. Weller. 1999. The effectiveness of condoms in reducing heterosexual transmitted HIV. *Family Planning Perspectives* 31:272–79.

Davis, N. Z. 1981. Printing and the people. In *Literacy and social development in the West*, H. J. Graf, ed., 69–95. Cambridge: Cambridge University Press.

Dawes, R. M. 1977. Suppose we measured height with rating scales instead of rulers. *Applied Psychological Measurement* 1:267–73.

Dawson, B. L., and W. D. McIntosh. 2006. Sexual strategies theory and Internet personal advertisements. *CyberPsychology and Behavior* 9:614–17.

De Fina, A. 1997. An analysis of Spanish bien as a marker of classroom management in teacher-student interaction. *Journal of Pragmatics* 28:337–54.

De Fina, A. 2007. Code-switching and the construction of ethnic identity in a community of practice. *Language and Society* 36:371–92.

de Ghett, V. J. 1978. Hierarchical cluster analysis. In *Quantitative ethology*, P. W. Colgan, ed., 115–44. New York: Wiley.

Dehavenon, A. L. 1978. Superordinate behavior in urban homes: A video analysis of request-compliance and food control behavior in two black and two white families living in New York City. Ph.D. dissertation, Columbia University.

De Leeuw, E., J. Hox, and S. Kef. 2003. Computer-assisted self-interviewing tailored for special populations and topics. *Field Methods* 15:223–51.

Dellino, D. 1984. Tourism: Panacea or plight. Impacts on the quality of life on Exuma, Bahamas. Master's thesis, University of Florida.

Deloria, V. 1969. *Custer died for your sins: An Indian manifesto*. New York: Macmillan.

Denzin, N. K., and Y. S. Lincoln, eds. 1994. *Handbook of qualitative research*. Thousand Oaks, CA: Sage.

de Rada, V. D. 2001. Mail surveys using Dillman's TDM in a southern European country: Spain. *International Journal of Public Opinion Research* 13:159–72.

Derogatis, L. R., and N. Melisaratos. 1983. The Brief Symptom Inventory: An introductory report. *Psychological Medicine* 13:595–605.

Descartes, R. 1960 [1637]. *Discourse on method; and meditations*. New York: Liberal Arts Press.

Descartes, R. 1993 [1641]. *Discourse on method and meditations on first philosophy*. Trans. by Donald A. Cress. 3d ed. Indianapolis: Hackett Publishing.

De Smith, M. J., M. F. Goodchild, and P. A. Longley. 2007. *Geospatial analysis: A comprehensive guide to principles, techniques, and software tools*. Leicester, UK: Matador.

de Solla Price, D. J. 1975. *Science since Babylon*. New Haven, CT: Yale University Press.

de Sousa Campos, L. O. Emma, and J. de Oliveira Siqueira. 2002. Sex differences in mate selection strategies: Content analyses and responses to personal advertisements in Brazil. *Evolution and Human Behavior* 23:395–406.

Deutscher, I. 1973. *What we say, what we do*. Glenview, IL: Scott Foresman.

DeVellis, F. F. 2003. *Scale development: Theory and applications*. 2d ed. Newbury Park, CA: Sage.

Devet, B. 1990. A method for observing and evaluating writing lab tutorials. *Writing Center Journal* 10:75–83.

Devine, E. B., W. Hollingworth, R. H. Hansen, N. M. Lawless, J. L. Wilson-Norton, D. P. Martin, D. K. Blough, and S. D. Sullivan. 2010. Electronic prescribing at the point of care: A time–motion study in the primary care setting. *Health Services Research* 45:152–71.

DeWalt, B. R. 1979. *Modernization in a Mexican ejido*. New York: Cambridge University Press.

DeWalt, K. M., and B. R. DeWalt. 2011. *Participant observation. A guide for fieldworkers*. Lanham, MD: AltaMira.

DeWalt, K. M., B. R. DeWalt, and C. B. Wayland. 1998. Participant observation. In *Handbook of methods in cultural anthropology*, H. R. Bernard, ed., 259–99. Walnut Creek, CA: AltaMira.

Dey, I. 1993. *Qualitative data analysis: A user friendly guide for social scientists*. London: Routledge and Kegan Paul.

Dick, H. P. 2006. What to do with "I don't know:" Elicitation in ethnographic and survey interviews. *Qualitative Sociology* 29:87–102.

Dickerson, S. S., M. A. Neary, and M. Hyche-Johnson. 2000. Native American graduate nursing students' learning experiences. *Journal of Nursing Scholarship* 32:89–196.

Dijkstra, W., and J. van der Zouwen. 1982. *Response behaviour in the survey-interview*. New York: Academic Press.

Dillman, D. A. 1978. *Mail and telephone surveys: The total design method*. New York: Wiley.

Dillman, D. A. 2009. Some consequences of survey mode changes in longitudinal surveys. In *Methodology of longitudinal surveys*, P. Lynn, ed., 127–40. Chichester, UK: Wiley.

Dillman, D. A., G. Phelps, R. Totora, K. Swift, J. Kohrell, J. Berck, and B. L. Messer. 2009a. Response rate and measurement differences in mixed-mode surveys using mail, telephone, interactive voice response (IVR) and the Internet. *Social Science Research* 38:1–18.

Dillman, D. A., J. D. Smyth, and L. M. Christian. 2009b. *Internet, mail, and mixed-mode surveys: The tailored design method*. New York: Wiley.

Dilthey, W. 1989 [1883]. *Introduction to the human sciences*. Princeton, NJ: Princeton University Press.

Dilthey, W. 1996. *Hermeneutics and the study of history*. Ed. by R. A. Makkreel and F. Rodi. Princeton, NJ: Princeton University Press.

DiMaggio, P. J. 1995. Comments on "What theory is not." *Administrative Science Quarterly* 40:391–97.

Dione Rosado, S. 2007. Nappy hair in the Diaspora: Exploring the cultural politics of hair among women of African descent. Ph.D. dissertation, University of Florida.

Dittmar, H. 1991. Meanings of material possessions as reflections of identity: Gender and socio-material position in society. *Journal of Social Behavior and Personality* 6:165–86.

Divakaran, A., ed. 2008. *Multimedia content analysis: Theory and applications*. New York: Springer.

Dobkin de Rios, M. 1981. Socioeconomic characteristics of an Amazon urban healer's clientele. *Social Science and Medicine* 15B:51–63.

Doerfel, M. L. 1998. What constitutes semantic network analysis? A comparison of research methodologies. *Connections* 21:16–26.

Doherty, M. E., and R. B. Anderson. 2009. Variation in scatterplot displays. *Behavior Research Methods* 41:55–60.

Dohrenwend, B. S., and S. A. Richardson. 1965. Directiveness and nondirectiveness in research interviewing: A reformulation of the problem. *Psychology Bulletin* 63:475–85.

Doob, A. N., and A. E. Gross. 1968. Status of frustrator as an inhibitor of horn honking responses. *Journal of Social Psychology* 76:213–18.

Dordick, G. A. 1996. More than refuge. *Journal of Contemporary Ethnography* 24:373–404.

Doreian, P. 2004. Cluster analysis. In *The SAGE encyclopedia of social science research methods*, M. Lewis-Beck, A. Bryman, and T. F. Liao, eds., 128–30. Thousand Oaks, CA: Sage.

Dotinga, A. R., J. J. M. van den Eijndem, W. Bosveld, and H. F. L. Garretsen. 2005. The effect of data collection mode and ethnicity of interviewer on response rates and self-reported alcohol use among Turks and Moroccans in the Netherlands: An experimental study. *Alcohol and Alcoholism* 40:242–48.

Douglas, K. B. 1998. Impressions: African American first-year students' perceptions of a predominantly white university. *The Journal of Negro Education* 67:416–31.

Drake, S. 1978. *Galileo at work: His scientific biography*. Chicago: University of Chicago Press.

Draucker, C. B., D. S. Martsolf, R. Ross, and T. B. Rusk. 2007. Theoretical sampling and category development in grounded theory. *Qualitative Health Research* 17:1137–48.

Dressler, R. A., and R. J. Kreuz. 2000. Transcribing oral discourse: A survey and a model system. *Discourse Processes* 29:25–36.

Dressler, W. W. 1980. Ethnomedical beliefs and patient adherence to a treatment regimen: A St. Lucian example. *Human Organization* 39:88–91.

Dressler, W. W. 1996. Culture and blood pressure: Using consensus analysis to create a measurement. *Cultural Anthropology Methods Journal* 8:6–8.

Dressler, W. W. 2005. What's cultural about biocultural research? *Ethos* 33:20–45.

Dressler, W. W., M. C. Balieiro, and J. E. dos Santos. 1997. The cultural construction of social support in Brazil: Associations with health outcomes. *Culture, Medicine and Psychiatry* 21:303–35.

Dressler, W. W., M. C. Balieiro, and J. E. dos Santos. 2002. Cultural consonance and psychological distress. *Paidéia: Cadernos de Psicologia e Educação* 12:5–18.

Dressler, W. W., M. C. Balieiro, R. P. Ribeiro, and J. E. dos Santos. 2007. A prospective study of cultural consonance and depressive symptoms in urban Brazil. *Social Science and Medicine* 65:2058–69.

Dressler, W. W., J. E. dos Santos, and M. C. Balieiro. 1996. Studying diversity and sharing in culture: An example of lifestyle in Brazil. *Journal of Anthropological Research* 52:331–53.

Dressler, W. W., S. Haworth Hoeppner, and B. J. Pitts. 1985. Household structure in a southern Black community. *American Anthropologist* 87:853–62.

Dressler, W. W., R. P. Ribeiro, M. C. Balieiro, K. S. Oths, and J. E. dos Santos. 2004. Eating, drinking and being depressed: The social, cultural and psychological context of alcohol consumption and nutrition in a Brazilian community. *Social Science and Medicine* 59:709–20.

Drew, P., and J. Heritage, eds. 2006. *Conversation analysis*. Thousand Oaks, CA: Sage.

Du Bois, C. 1961. *The people of Alor. A social-psychological study of an East Indian island*. With analyses by Abraham Kardiner and Emil Oberholzer. Vol. 1. New York: Harper Torchbooks.

Ducanes, G., and M. Abella. 2008. Labor shortage responses in Japan, Korea, Singapore, Hong Kong, and Malaysia: A review and Evaluation. ILO Asian Regional Programme on Governance of Labour Migration Working Paper No.2. Bangkok: International Labor Organization. http://www.ilo.org/wcmsp5/groups/public/---asia/---ro-bangkok/documents/publication/wcms_099166.pdf (accessed March 9, 2010).

Duchscher, J. E. B, and D. Morgan. 2004. Grounded theory: Reflections on the emergence vs. forcing debate. *Journal of Advanced Nursing* 48:605–12.

Dukes, R. L, J. B. Ullman, and J. A. Stein. 1995. An evaluation of D.A.R.E. (Drug Abuse Resistance Education) using a Solomon four-group design with latent variables. *Evaluation Review* 19:409–35.

Duncan, O. D. 1966. Path analysis: Sociological examples. *American Journal of Sociology* 72:1–16.

Dundes, A., ed. 1982. *Cinderella. A folklore casebook.* New York: Garland.

Duneier, M. 1999. *Sidewalk.* New York: Farrar, Straus & Giroux.

Duneier, M. 2006. Ethnography, the ecological fallacy, and the 1995 Chicago heat wave. *American Sociological Review* 71:679–88.

Dunn, C. D. 2004. Cultural models and metaphors for marriage: An analysis of discourse at Japanese wedding receptions. *Ethos* 32:348–73.

Dunn-Rankin, P. 2004. *Scaling methods.* 2d ed. Mahwah, NJ: Lawrence Erlbaum.

Durand, C., A. Blais, and M. Larochelle. 2004. The polls in the 2002 French presidential election: An autopsy. *Public Opinion Quarterly* 68:602–22.

Duranleau, D. 1999. Random sampling of regional populations: A field test. *Field Methods* 11:61–67.

Durkheim, E. 1933 [1893]. *The division of labor in society.* Trans. by George Simpson. Glencoe, IL: The Free Press.

Durkheim, E. 1958. *Socialism and Saint-Simon.* Ed. by A. Gouldner. Trans. by C. Sattler. Yellow Springs, OH: Antioch Press.

Durkheim, E. 1933 [1893]. *The division of labor in society.* Trans. by George Simpson. Glencoe, IL: The Free Press.

Durkheim, E. 1951 [1897]. *Suicide. A study in sociology.* Glencoe, IL: The Free Press.

Durrenberger, E. P., and D. Doukas. 2008. Gospel of wealth, gospel of work: Counter hegemony in the U.S. working class. *American Anthropologist* 110:214–25.

Durrenberger, E. P., and S. Erem. 2005. Checking for relationships across domains measured by triads and paired comparisons. *Field Methods* 17:150–69.

Dy, S. M., H. R. Rubin, and H. P. Lehman 2005. Why do patients and families request transfers to tertiary care? A qualitative study. *Social Science and Medicine* 61:1846–53.

Dyl, J., and S. Wapner. 1996. Age and gender differences in the nature, meaning, and function of cherished possessions for children and adolescents. *Journal of Experimental Child Psychology* 62:340–77.

Easlea, B. 1980. *Witch hunting, magic, and the new philosophy.* Atlantic Highlands, NJ: Humanities Press.

Edgerton, R. B. 1966. Conceptions of psychosis in Four East African societies. *American Anthropologist* 68(Part 1):408–25.

Edgerton, R. B., and A. Cohen. 1994. Culture and schizophrenia: The DOSMD challenge. *British Journal of Psychiatry* 164:222–31.

Edmonds, J. K. 2010. Social networks, decision making and use of skilled birth attendants to prevent maternal mortality in Matlab, Bangladesh. Ph.D. dissertation, Emory University.

Edwards, J. A., and M. D. Lampert, eds. 1993. *Talking data: Transcription and coding in discourse research.* Hillsdale, NJ: Lawrence Erlbaum Associates.

Edwards, M., S. Thomsen, and C. Toroitich-Ruto. 2005. Thinking aloud to create better condom-use questions. *Field Methods* 17:183–99.

Edwards, P. J., I, Roberts, M. J. Clarke, C. DiGiuseppi, R. Wentz, I. Kwan, R. Cooper, L. M. Felix, and S. Pratap 2009. Methods to increase response to postal and electronic questionnaires. *Cochrane Database of Systematic Reviews* 2009, Issue 3. Art. No.: MR000008. DOI: 10.1002/14651858.MR000008.pub4. http://tinyurl.com/235kvjk (accessed June 14, 2010).

Edwards, S. L., M. L. Slattery, and K-N. Ma. 1998. Measurement errors stemming from nonrespondents present at in-person interviews. *Annals of Epidemiology* 8:272–77.

Eibl-Eiblsfeldt, I. 1989. *Human ethology.* New York: Aldine de Gruyter.

Eifler, S. 2010. Validity of a factorial survey approach to the analysis of criminal behavior. *European Journal of Research Methods for the Behavioral and Social Sciences* 6:139–46.

Eisenstein, E. 1979. *The printing press as an agent of change: Communications and cultural transformations in early modern Europe,* 2 vols. Cambridge: Cambridge University Press.

Ekins, R. 1997. *Male femaling: A grounded theory approach to cross-dressing and sex-changing.* New York: Routledge.

Eklund, M., A. Bengtsson-Tops, and H. Lindstedt. 2007. Construct and discriminant validity and dimensionality of the Interview Schedule for Social Interaction (ISSI) in three psychiatric samples. *Nordic Journal of Psychiatry* 61:182–88.

Elfering, A., and S. Grebner. 2010. A smile is just a smile: But only for men. Sex differences in meaning of faces scales. *Journal of Happiness Studies* 11:179–91.

El Guindi, F. 2004. *Visual anthropology.* Walnut Creek, CA: AltaMira.

Elliott, M. N., D. Golinelli, K. Hambarsoomian, J. Perlman, and S. L. Wenzel. 2006. Sampling with field burden constraints: An application to sheltered homeless and low-income housed women. *Field Methods* 18:43–58.

Elliott, M. N., D. McCaffrey, J. Perlman, G. N. Marshall, and K. Hambarsoomians. 2009. Use of expert ratings as sampling strata for a more cost-effective probability sample of a rare population. *Public Opinion Quarterly* 73:56–73.

Ember, C. R. 2007. Using the HRAF collection of ethnography in conjunction with the standard cross-cultural sample and the ethnographic atlas. *Cross-Cultural Research* 41:396–427.

Emerson, R. M., R. I. Fretz, and L. L. Shaw. 1995. *Writing ethnographic fieldnotes.* Chicago: University of Chicago Press.

Emigh, R. J. 1997. The power of negative thinking: The use of negative case methodology in the development of sociological theory. *Theory and Society* 5:649–84.

Ennis, C. D., A. Chen, and J. Ross. 1992. Educational value orientations as a theoretical framework for experienced urban teachers' curricular decision making. *Journal of Research and Development in Education* 25:156–64.

Ennis, C. D., L. K. Mueller, and L. M. Hooper. 1990. The influence of teacher value orientations on curriculum planning within the parameters of a theoretical framework. *Research Quarterly for Exercise and Sport* 61:360–68.

Ensminger, M. E., and K. Fothergill. 2003. A decade of measuring SES: What it tells us and where to go from here. In *Socioeconomic status, parenting, and child development*, M. H. Bornstein and R. H. Bradley, eds., 13–27. Mahwah, NJ: Lawrence Erlbaum.

Erikson, K. T. 1967. A comment on disguised observation in sociology. *Social Problems* 14:366–73.

Erikson, K. T. 1996. A response to Richard Leo. *The American Sociologist* 27:129–30.

Evans, G. W., H. N. Ricciuti, S. Hope, I. Schoon, R. H. Bradley, R. F. Corwyn, and C. Hazan. 2010. Crowding and cognitive development: The mediating role of maternal responsiveness among 36-month-old children. *Environment and Behavior* 42:135–48.

Evans, G. W., and R. E. Wener. 2007. Crowding and personal space invasion on the train: Please don't make me sit in the middle. *Journal of Experimental Psychology* 27:90–94.

Evans-Pritchard, E. E. 1958 [1937]. *Witchcraft, oracles, and magic among the Azande*. Oxford, UK: Oxford University Press.

Evans-Pritchard, E. E. 1973. Some reminiscences and reflections on fieldwork. *Journal of the Anthropological Society of Oxford* 4:1–12.

Everson-Rose, S. A., and T. T. Lewis. 2005. Psychosocial factors and cardiovascular disease. *Annual Review of Public Health* 26:469–500.

Fahim, H. M. 1977. Foreign and indigenous anthropology: The perspectives of an Egyptian anthropologist. *Human Organization* 36:80–86.

Fahim, H. M. 1982. *Indigenous anthropology in non-Western societies: Proceedings of a Burg-Wartenstein symposium*. Durham: University of North Carolina Press.

Fairweather, J. R. 1999. Understanding how farmers choose between organic and conventional production: Results from New Zealand and policy implications. *Agriculture and Human Values* 16:5–63.

Fan, W., and Z. Yan. 2010. Factors affecting response rates of the web survey: A systematic review. *Computers in Human Behavior* 26:132–39.

Fang, K., Y-C. Lin, and T. L. Chuang. 2009. Why do Internet users play massively multiplayer online role-playing games? A mixed method. *Management Decision* 47:1245–60.

Faris, J. C. 1968. Validation in ethnographical description: The lexicon of "occasions" in Cat Harbour. *Man*, New Series, 3:112–24.

Farley, J. U., and D. R. Lehmann. 1986. *Meta-analysis in marketing. Generalization of response models*. Lexington, MA: D.C. Heath.

Farringdon, J. M., and M. G. Farringdon. 1980. *A concordance and word-lists to the poems of Dylan Thomas*. Swansea, UK: Ariel House.

Feagin, J. R., A. M. Orum, and G. Sjoberg. 1991. *A case for the case study*. Chapel Hill: University of North Carolina Press.

Feigl, H. 1980. Positivism. In *Encyclopaedia brittanica*, Vol. 14. Chicago: Encyclopaedia Brittanica, Inc.

Feldman, R. E. 1968. Response to compatriot and foreigner who seek assistance. *Journal of Personality and Social Psychology* 10:202–14.

Feng, J-Y., T-Y. Huang, and C-J. Wang. 2010. Kindergarten teachers' experience with reporting child abuse in Taiwan. *Child Abuse and Neglect: The International Journal* 34:124–28.

Fennell, D., A. S. Q. Liberato, and B. Zsembik. 2009. Definitions and patterns of CAM use by the lay public. *Complementary Therapies in Medicine* 17:71–77.

Fenno, R. 1990. *Watching politicians: Essays on participant observation*. Berkeley: Institute of Governmental Studies, University of California at Berkeley.

Fermi, L., and B. Bernardin. 1961. *Galileo and the scientific revolution*. New York: Basic Books.

Festinger, L. A. 1957. *A theory of cognitive dissonance*. Stanford, CA: Stanford University Press.

Fetterman, D. 1989. *Ethnography Step-by-Step*. Newbury Park, CA: Sage.

Fetterman, D. 1998. *Ethnography Step-by-Step*. 2d ed. Newbury Park, CA: Sage.

Field, T. S., C. A. Cadoret, M. L. Brown, M. Ford, S. M. Greene, D. Hill, M. C. Hornbrook, R. T. Meenan, M. J. White, and J. M. Zapka. 2002. Surveying physicians. Do components of the "Total Design Approach" to optimizing survey response rates apply to physicians? *Medical Care* 40:596–605.

Fielding, N. 1993. Ethnography. In *Researching social life*, N. Gilbert, ed., 154–71. London: Sage.

Fielding, N. 2008. Grid computing and qualitative social science. *Social Science Computer Review* 26:301–16.

Fine, G. A. 1996. *Kitchens: The culture of restaurant work*. Berkeley: University of California Press.

Fine, G. A., and K. L. Sandstrom. 1988. *Knowing children: Participant observation with minors*. Newbury Park, CA: Sage.

Finkel, S. E., Guterbock, T. M., and M. J. Borg. 1991. Race-of-interviewer effects in a preelection poll: Virginia 1989. *Public Opinion Quarterly* 55:313–30.

Finocchiaro, M. A. 2005. *Retrying Galileo, 1633–1992*. Berkeley: University of California Press.

Fischer, C. 1982. *To dwell among friends: Personal networks in town and city*. Chicago: University of Chicago Press.

Fischhoff, B. 2010. *Judgment and decision making*. Wiley Interdisciplinary Reviews: Cognitive Science. New York: Oxford University Press.

Fisher, C. B. 2005. Deception research involving children: Ethical practices and paradoxes. *Ethics and Behavior* 15:271–87.

Fisher, D. 1993. *Fundamental development of the social sciences: Rockefeller Philanthropy and the United States Social Science Research Council*. Ann Arbor: University of Michigan Press.

Fisher, R. A. 1936. The use of multiple measurements in taxonomic problems. *Annals of Eugenics* 7:179–88.

Fiske, D. W. 1982. Convergent-discriminant validation in measurements and research strategies. *New Directions for Methodology of Social and Behavioral Science* 12:77–92.

Fjellman, S. M., and H. Gladwin. 1985. Haitian family patterns of migration to South Florida. *Human Organization* 44:301–12.

Flanagan, T. J., and D. R. Longmire, eds. 1996. *Americans view crime and justice: A national public opinion survey.* Newbury Park, CA: Sage.

Flanders, N. A. 1970. *Analyzing teaching behavior.* Reading, MA: Addison-Wesley.

Fleisher, M. 1989. *Warehousing violence.* Newbury Park, CA: Sage.

Fleisher, M. 1998. *Dead end kids: Gang girls and the boys they know.* Madison: University of Wisconsin Press.

Flowers, J. H., D. C. Buhman, and D. D. Turnage. 1997. Cross-modal equivalence of visual and auditory scatterplots for exploring bivariate data samples. *Human Factors* 39:341–51.

Fluehr-Lobban, C. 1996. Rejoinder to Wax and Herrera. *Human Organization* 55:240. (See also entries for Wax [1996] and for Herrera [1996].)

Fluehr-Lobban, C. 2008. Anthropology and ethics in America's declining imperial age. *Anthropology Today* 24:18–22.

Foddy, W. 1993. *Constructing questions for interviews and questionnaires: Theory and practice in social research.* New York: Cambridge University Press.

Fonteyn, M. E., M. Vettese, D. R. Lancaster, and S. Bauer-Wu. 2008. Developing a codebook to guide content analysis of expressive writing transcripts. *Applied Nursing Research* 21:165–68.

Foo, M-D., M. A. Uy, and R. A. Baron. 2009. How do feelings influence effort? An empirical study of entrepreneurs' affect and venture effort. *Journal of Applied Psychology* 94:1086–94.

Forgacs, D., ed. 2000. *The Gramsci reader: Selected writings 1916–1935, 2000.* New York: New York University Press.

Forte, M. C. 2011. The Human Terrain System and anthropology: A review of ongoing public debates. *American Anthropologist* 113:149–53.

Foster, G. M., Scudder, T., Colson, E., and R. V. Kemper, eds. 1979. *Long-term field research in social anthropology.* New York: Academic Press.

Foster, M. 1989. "It's cookin' now": A performance analysis of the speech events of a Black teacher in an urban community college. *Language in Society* 18:1–29.

Fowler, F. J. 1984. *Survey research methods.* Newbury Park, CA: Sage.

Fowler, F. J., P. M. Gallagher, and S. Nederend. 1999. Comparing telephone and mail responses to the CAHPS™ Survey Instrument. *Medical Care* 37, No. 3, Supplement: Consumer Assessment of Health Plans Study: MS41–MS49.

Fowler, F. J., A. M. Roman, and Z. X. Di. 1998. Mode effects in a survey of Medicare prostate surgery patients. *Public Opinion Quarterly* 62:29–46.

Fox, K. 2004. *Watching the English.* London: Hodder and Stoughton.

Fox, R. J., M. R. Crask, and J. Kim. 1988. Mail survey response rate: A meta-analysis of selected techniques for inducing response. *Public Opinion Quarterly* 52:467–91.

Fox-Wolfgramm, S. J., K. B. Boal, and J. G. Hunt. 1998. Organizational adaptation to institutional change: A comparative study of first-order change in prospector and defender banks. *Administrative Science Quarterly* 43:87–126.

Frake, C. O. 1962. The ethnographic study of cognitive systems. In *Anthropology and human behavior,* T. Gladwin and W. Sturtevant, eds., 72–85. Washington, DC: The Anthropological Society of Washington.

Franzosi, R., ed. 2008. *Content analysis.* Four volumes. London: Sage.

Franzosi, R. 2010. *Quantitative narrative analysis.* Thousand Oaks, CA: Sage.

Freedman, D., A. Thornton, D. Camburn, D. Alwin, and L. Young-DeMarco. 1988. The life history calendar: A technique for collecting retrospective data. *Sociological Methodology* 18:37–68.

Freeman, D. 1999. *The fateful hoaxing of Margaret Mead: A historical analysis of her Samoan research.* Boulder, CO: Westview.

Freeman, L. C. 1979. Centrality in social networks: Conceptual clarification. *Social Networks* 1:215–39.

Freeman, L. C. 2000. Visualizing social networks. *Journal of Social Structure.* http://www.cmu.edu/joss/content/articles/volume1/Freeman.html (accessed March 3, 2011).

Freeman, L. C. 2003. Finding social groups: A meta-analysis of the southern women data. In *Dynamic social network modeling and analysis,* R. Breiger, K. Carley, and P. Pattison, eds., 37–77. Washington, DC: The National Academies Press.

Freeman, L. C. 2004. *The development of social network analysis: A study in the sociology of science.* Vancouver, BC: Empirical Press.

Freeman, L. C., A. K. Romney, and S. C. Freeman. 1987. Cognitive structure and informant accuracy. *American Anthropologist* 89:310–25.

Freeman, L. C., D. R. White, and A. K. Romney, eds. 1992. *Research methods in social network analysis.* New Brunswick, NJ: Transaction Publishers.

Freeman, S., M. R. Walker, R. Borden, and B. Latané. 1975. Diffusion of responsibility and restaurant tipping: Cheaper by the bunch. *Personality and Social Psychology Bulletin* 1:584–87.

Freidenberg, B. M., and R. S. Cimbalo. 1996. Human ethology: Eating, security, and curiosity. *Perceptual and Motor Skills* 83:489–90.

Freilich, M., ed. 1977. *Marginal natives at work: Anthropologists in the field.* 2d ed. Cambridge, MA: Schenkman.

French, D. P., R. Cooke, N. Mclean, M. Williams, and S. Sutton. 2007. What do people think about when they answer theory of planned behavior questionnaires? A "think aloud study." *Journal of Health Psychology* 12:672–87.

Frenk, S. M., S. L. Anderson, M. Chaves, and N. Martin. 2011. Assessing the validity of key informant reports about congregations' social composition. *Sociology of Religion* 72:78–90.

Freud, S. 1962. *Three essays on the theory of sexuality.* Trans. by J. Strachey. New York: Basic Books.

Frey, J. H. 1989. *Survey research by telephone.* 2d ed. Newbury Park, CA: Sage.

Friedenberg, L. 1995. *Psychological testing. Design, analysis, and use.* Needham Heights, MA: Allyn & Bacon.

Friendly, M. 2000. *Visualizing categorical data.* Cary, NC: SAS Institute.

Frisancho, A. R. 1990. *Anthropometric standards for the assessment of growth and nutritional status.* Ann Arbor: University of Michigan Press.

Fry, D. P. 1990. Play aggression among Zapotec children: Implications for the practice hypothesis. *Aggressive Behavior* 16:321–40.

Fuller, S. 2004. *Kuhn vs. Popper: The struggle for the soul of science.* New York: Columbia University Press.

Fung, L., and R. Carter 2007. Cantonese e-discourse: A new hybrid variety of English. *Multilingua* 26:35–66.

Furlow, C. 2003. Comparing indicators of knowledge within and between cultural domains. *Field Methods* 15:51–62.

Gafaranga, J. 2001. Linguistic identities in talk-in-interaction: Order in bilingual conversation. *Journal of Pragmatics* 33:1901–25.

Gaito, J. 1980. Measurement scales and statistics: Resurgence of an old misconception. *Psychological Bulletin* 87:564–67.

Gal, S. 1978. Peasant men can't get wives: Language change and sex roles in a bilingual community. *Language in Society* 7:1–16.

Galileo Galilei. 1610. The starry messenger. http://www .bard.edu/admission/forms/pdfs/galileo (accessed March 5, 2011).

Galilei, Galileo. 1997 [1632]. *Galileo on the world systems: A new abridged translation and guide.* Trans. by M. A. Finocchiaro. Berkeley: University of California Press.

Gallicchio, L., S. Miller, H. Zacur, and J. A. Flaws. 2009. Race and health-related quality of life in midlife women in Baltimore, Maryland. *Maturitas* 63:67–72.

Gallmeier, C. P. 1991. Leaving, revisiting, and staying in touch: Neglected issues in field research. In *Experiencing fieldwork*, W. B. Shaffir and R. A. Stebbins, eds., 224–31. Newbury Park, CA: Sage.

Galton, F. 1907a. Vox populi. *Nature* 75:450–51.

Galton, F. 1907b. Reply to Hooker. *Nature* 75:509–10.

Gans, L. P., and C. S. Wood. 1985. Discriminant analysis as a method for differentiating potential acceptors of family planning: Western Samoa. *Human Organization* 44:228–33.

Gardner, F. 2000. Methodological issues in the direct observation of parent-child interaction: Do observational findings reflect the natural behavior of participants? *Clinical Child and Family Psychology Review* 3:185–98.

Gardner, R. 2001. *When listeners talk. Response tokens and listener stance.* Philadelphia: John Benjamins Publishing Co.

Garot, R. 2007. "Where you from!": Gang identity as performance. *Journal of Contemporary Ethnography* 36:50–84.

Garro, L. C. 1986. Intracultural variation in folk medical knowledge: A comparison between curers and non-curers. *American Anthropologist* 88:351–70.

Garro, L. C. 2000. Remembering what one knows and the construction of the past: A comparison of cultural consensus theory and cultural schema theory. *Ethos* 28:275–319.

Gasper, J., S. DeLuca, and A. Estacion. 2010. Coming and going: Explaining the effects of residential and school mobility on adolescent delinquency. *Social Science Research* 39:459–76.

Gates, R., and P. Solomon. 1982. Research using the mall intercept: State of the art. *Journal of Advertising Research* 22:43–49.

Gatewood, J. B. 1983. Loose talk: Linguistic competence and recognition ability. *American Anthropologist* 85:378–87.

Gatewood, J. B. 1984. Familiarity, vocabulary size, and recognition ability in four semantic domains. *American Ethnologist* 11:507.

Gazioglu, A. E. I. 2008. Gender, gender roles affecting mate preferences in Turkish college students. *College Student Journal* 42:603–16.

Gearing, J. 1995. Fear and loving in the West Indies: Research from the heart. In *Taboo: Sex, identity, and erotic subjectivity in anthropological fieldwork*, D. Kulick and M. Willson, eds., 186–218. London: Routledge.

Geertz, C. 1973. *The interpretation of cultures. Selected essays.* New York: Basic Books.

Gelardi, A. M. G. 1996. The influence of tax law changes on the timing of marriages: A two-country analysis. *National Tax Journal* 49:17–30.

Gentner, D., and A. L. Stevens, eds. 1983. *Mental models.* Hillsdale, NJ: L. Erlbaum Associates.

Gerard, H. B., and G. C. Mathewson. 1966. The effects of severity of initiation on liking for a group: A replication. *Journal of Experimental Social Psychology* 2:278–87.

Gerich, J. 2008. Real or virtual? Response behavior in video-enhanced, self-administered computer interviews. *Field Methods* 20:356–76.

Gerich, J., and R. Lehner. 2006. Video computer-assisted self-interviews for deaf respondents. *Field Methods* 18:267–83.

Gerring, J. 2007. *Case study research: Principles and practices.* New York: Cambridge University Press.

Giddens, A. 1974. *Positivism and sociology.* London: Heinemann.

Gil-Burman, C., F. Peláez, and S. Sánchez. 2002. Mate choice differences according to sex and age: An analysis of personal advertisements in Spanish newspapers. *Human Nature* 13:493–508.

Gilljam, M., and D. Granberg. 1993. Should we take don't know for an answer? *Public Opinion Quarterly* 57:348–57.

Gilovich, T., R. Vallone, and A. Tversky. 1985. The hot hand in basketball—on the misperception of random sequences. *Cognitive Psychology* 17:295–314.

Gingerich, D. W. 2010. Understanding off-the-books politics: Conducting inference on the determinants of sensitive behavior with randomized response surveys. *Political Analysis* 18:349–80.

Giorgi, A. 1986. Theoretical justification for the use of descriptions in psychological research. In *Qualitative research in psychology: Proceedings of the International Association for Qualitative Research*, P. D. Ashworth, A. Giorgi, and J. J. de Koning, eds., 6–46. Pittsburgh, PA: Duquesne University Press.

Gittelsohn, J., P. J. Pelto, M. E. Bentley, K. Bhattacharyya, and J. L. Jensen. 1998. *Rapid assessment procedures. Ethnographic methods to investigate women's health*. Boston: International Nutrition Foundation. http://unu.edu/unupress/food2/UIN01E/UIN01E00.HTM (accessed December 19, 2010).

Gittelsohn, J., A. V. Shankar, K. P. West, and R. M. Ram. 1997. Estimating reactivity in direct observation studies of health behaviors. *Human Organization* 56:182–89.

Gladwin, C. H. 1989. *Ethnographic decision tree modeling*. Newbury Park, CA: Sage.

Glaser B. G. 1992. *Basics of grounded theory*. Mill Valley, CA: Sociology Press.

Glaser, B. G. 2002. Constructivist grounded theory? FQS. Forum: *Qualitative Social Research* 3(3). http://www.qualitative-research.net/index.php/fqs/index (accessed March 7, 2010).

Glaser, B. G., and A. Strauss. 1967. *The discovery of grounded theory: Strategies for qualitative research*. New York: Aldine.

Glass, G. V. 1976. Primary, secondary, and meta-analysis of research. *Educational Researcher* 5:3–8.

Glass, G. V., V. L. Willson, and J. M. Gottman. 1979. *Design and analysis of time-series experiments*. Boulder, CO: Associated University Press.

Glassner, T., and W. van der Vaart. 2009. Applications of calendar instruments in social surveys: A review. *Quality and Quantity* 43:333–49.

Glazer, M. 1975. Impersonal sex. In *Tearoom trade: Impersonal sex in public places*, L. Humphreys, ed., 213–22. Enl. ed. with a retrospect on ethical issues. Chicago: Aldine.

Gluckman, M. 1958 [1940]. The analysis of a social situation in modern Zululand. *African Studies* 14:1–30, 147–74. Reprinted as Rhodes-Livingston Paper No. 28. Manchester, UK: Manchester University Press, 1958.

Gmür, M. 2003. Co-citation analysis and the search for invisible colleges: A methodological evaluation. *Scientometrics* 57:27–57.

Godoy, G., P. Kostishack, D. Wilkie, and K. O'Neill. 1998. The socioeconomic correlates of error in the estimation of agricultural field size: An experimental study among the Tawahka Indians of Honduras. *Field Methods* 10:48–53.

Godoy, R., V. Reyes-Garcia, S. Tanner, W. R. Leonard, T. McDade, and T. Huanca. 2009. Can we trust an adult's estimate of parental school attainment?

Disentangling social desirability bias and random measurement error. *Field Methods* 20:26–45.

Goffman, E. 1974. *Frame analysis*. New York: Harper & Row.

Goh, A. 2010. A Japanese ritual performance of laughter. *Society* 47:31–34.

Goins, J., J. Jellema, and H. Zhang. 2010. Architectural enclosure's effect on office worker performance: A comparison of the physical and symbolic attributes of workspace. *Building and Environment* 45:944–48.

Goldberg, J., M. S. Richards, R. J. Anderson, and M. B. Rodin. 1991. Alcohol consumption in men exposed to the military draft lottery: A natural experiment. *Journal of Substance Abuse* 3:307–13.

Golde, P., ed. 1986. *Women in the field: Anthropological experiences*. 2d ed. Berkeley: University of California Press.

Goldman, A. E., and S. S. McDonald. 1987. *The group depth interview: Principles and practice*. Englewood Cliffs, NJ: Prentice-Hall.

Goldman, L. K., and S. A. Glantz. 1998. Evaluation of antismoking advertising campaigns. *Journal of the American Medical Association* 279:772–77.

Goldsen, J. M. 1947. Analyzing the contents of mass communication: A step toward inter-group harmony. *International Journal of Opinion & Attitude Research* 1:81–92.

Gölge, Z. B., M. F. Yavuz, S. Mudderisoglou, and M. S. Yavuz. 2003. Turkish university students' attitudes toward rape. *Sex Roles* 49:653–61.

Gomes do Espirito Santo, M. E., and G. D. Etheredge. 2002. How to reach clients of female sex workers: A survey "by surprise" in brothels in Dakar, Senegal. *Bulletin of the World Health Organization* 80:709–13.

Gomm, R., M. Hammersley, and P. Foster, eds. 2000. *Case study method: Key issues, key texts*. Thousand Oaks, CA: Sage.

González, N. S. 1986. The anthropologist as female head of household. In *Self, sex and gender in cross-cultural fieldwork*, T. L. Whitehead and M. E. Conaway, eds., 84–102. Urbana: University of Illinois Press.

González, R. J. 2007. Towards mercenary anthropology? The new U.S. Army counterinsurgency manual *FM 3-24* and the military-anthropology complex. *Anthropology Today* 23:14–19.

Good, K. (with D. Chanoff). 1991. *Into the heart*. New York: Simon & Schuster.

Goode, W. J., and P. K. Hatt. 1952. *Methods in social research*. New York: McGraw-Hill.

Goodenough, W. H. 1944. A technique for scale analysis. *Educational Psychological Measurement* 4:179–90.

Goodenough, W. H. 1956. Componential analysis and the study of meaning. *Language* 32:195–216.

Goodenough, W. H. 1963. Some applications of Guttman scale analysis to ethnography and culture theory. *Southwestern Journal of Anthropology* 19:235–50.

Goodman, L., and W. Kruskal. 1963. Measures of association for cross classifications III: Approximate sampling theory. *Journal of the American Statistical Association* 58:302–22.

Goodwin, C. 1981. *Conversational organization: Interaction between speakers and hearers.* New York: Academic Press.

Goodwin, C. 1986. Gesture as a resource for the organization of mutual orientation. *Semiotica* 62:29–49.

Goodwin, C. 1994. Recording human interaction in natural settings. *Pragmatics* 3:181–209.

Goodwin, C., and J. Heritage. 1990. Conversation analysis. *Annual Review of Anthropology* 19:283–307.

Gorden, R. L. 1975. *Interviewing: Strategy, techniques, and tactics.* Homewood, IL: Dorsey.

Gorden, R. L. 1987. *Interviewing: Strategy, techniques, and tactics.* 4th ed. Chicago: Dorsey Press.

Gordon, S. 1991. *The history and philosophy of social science.* New York: Routledge.

Göritz, A. S. 2008. The long-term effect of material incentives on participation in online panels. *Field Methods* 20:211–25.

Gotschi, E., R. Delve, and B. Freyer. 2009. Participatory photography as a qualitative approach to obtain insights into farmer groups. *Field Methods* 21:290–308.

Gottlieb, B. H., ed. 1981. *Social networks and social support.* Beverly Hills, CA: Sage.

Gottschalk, L. A., and R. J. Bechtel. 1993. *Psychologic and neuropsychiatric assessment. Applying the Gottschalk-Gleser content analysis method to verbal sample analysis using the Gottschalk-Bechtel computer scoring system.* Palo Alto, CA: Mind Garden.

Gould, R. A., and P. B. Potter. 1984. Use-lives of automobiles in America: A preliminary archaeological view. In *Toward an ethnoarchaeology of modern America,* R. A. Gould, ed., 69–93. Brown University: Department of Anthropology, Research Papers in Anthropology (No. 4).

Goyder, J. 2003. Measuring social identities: Problems and progress. *International Journal of Public Opinion Research* 15:180–91.

Graesch, A. P. 2009. Material indicators of family busyness. *Social Indicators Research* 93:85–94.

Graffam, B., L. Bowers, and K. N. Keene. 2008. Using observations of clinicians' teaching practices to build a model of clinical instruction. *Academic Medicine* 83:768–74.

Gram, M. 2010. Self-reporting vs. observation: Some cautionary examples from parent/child food shopping behavior. *International Journal of Consumer Studies* 34:394–99.

Gramsci, A. 1994. *Letters from prison.* Ed. by F. Rosengarten. Trans. by R. Rosenthal. New York: Columbia University Press.

Granberg, D., and C. Westerberg. 1999. Inclusion of don't know respondents, reliability of indexes and representatives in survey research. *Sociological Focus* 32:401–11.

Granovetter, M. 1973. The strength of weak ties. *American Journal of Sociology* 78:1360–80.

Granovetter, M. 1995. *Getting a job.* 2d ed. Chicago: University of Chicago Press.

Graves, T. D., N. B. Graves, and M. J. Korbin. 1969. Historical inferences from Guttman scales: The return of age-area magic? *Current Anthropology* 10:317–38.

Gravlee, C. C. 2002a. Mobile computer-assisted personal interviewing with handheld computers: The Entryware System 3.0. *Field Methods* 14:322–36.

Gravlee, C. C. 2002b. Skin color, blood pressure, and the contextual effect of culture in southeastern Puerto Rico. Ph.D. dissertation, University of Florida.

Gravlee, C. C., and W. W. Dressler. 2005. Skin pigmentation, self-perceived color, and arterial blood pressure in Puerto Rico. *American Journal of Human Biology* 17:195–206.

Gravelee, C. C., W. W. Dressler, and H. R. Bernard. 2005. Skin color, social classification, and blood pressure in Puerto Rico. *American Journal of Public Health* 95:2191–97.

Gravlee, C. C., S. N. Zenk, S. Woods, Z. Rowe, and A. J. Schulz. 2006. Handheld computers for direct observation of the social and physical environment. *Field Methods* 18:382–97.

Grayling, A. C. 1996. Epistemology. In *The Blackwell companion to philosophy,* N. Bunnin and E. P. Tsui-James, eds., 38–63. Oxford, UK: Blackwell.

Green, B. L., and D. T. Kenrick, 1994. The attractiveness of gender-typed traits at different relationship levels: Androgynous characteristics may be desirable after all. *Personality and Social Psychology Bulletin* 20:244–53.

Green, J. A. 2003. The writing on the stall. Gender and graffiti. *Journal of Language and Social Psychology* 22:282–96.

Green, P. E., and F. J. Carmone. 1970. *Multidimensional scaling and related techniques in marketing analysis.* Boston: Allyn & Bacon.

Greenbaum, T. L. 1998. *The handbook for focus group research.* 2d ed., rev. and expanded. Thousand Oaks, CA: Sage.

Greenbaum, T. L. 2000. *Moderating focus groups. A practical guide for group facilitation.* Thousand Oaks, CA: Sage.

Greenfield, T. K., W. C. Kerr, J. Bond, Y. Ye, and T. Stockwell. 2009. Improving graduated frequencies alcohol measures for monitoring consumption patterns: Results from an Australian national survey and US diary validity study. *Contemporary Drug Problems: An Interdisciplinary Quarterly* 36:705–33.

Greenlaw, C., and S. Brown-Welty. 2009. Testing assumptions of survey mode and response cost: A comparison of web-based and paper-based survey methods. *Evaluation Review* 33:464–80.

Greenwald, A. G., R. González, R. J. Harris, and D. Guthrie. 1996. Effect sizes and *p* values: What should be reported and what should be replicated? *Psychophysiology* 33:175–83.

Greenwood, C. R., J. C. Delquadri, S. O. Stanley, B. Terry, and R. V. Hall. 1985. Assessment of ecobehavioral interaction in school settings. *Behavioral Assessment* 7:331–47.

Gregory, B. T., S. G. Harris, A. A. Armenakis, and C. L. Shook. 2009. Organizational culture and effectiveness: A study of values, attitudes, and organizational outcomes. *Journal of Business Research* 62:673–79.

Grieco, E. M., and R. C. Cassidy. 2001. Overview of race and Hispanic origin. Census 2000 Brief C2KBR/01–1.

Washington, DC: U.S. Bureau of the Census. March 2001. http://www.census.gov/prod/2001pubs/c2kbr01-1.pdf (accessed March 8, 2010).

Griffin, J. H. 1961. *Black like me.* Boston: Houghton-Mifflin.

Groom, C. J., and J. W. Pennebaker. 2005. The language of love: Sex, sexual orientation, and language use in online personal advertisements. *Sex Roles: A Journal of Research* 52:447–61.

Gross, D. R. 1984. Time allocation: A tool for the study of cultural behavior. *Annual Review of Anthropology* 13:519–58.

Gross, D. R. 1992. *Discovering anthropology.* Mountain View, CA: Mayfield.

Groves, R. M. 2006. Nonresponse rates and nonresponse bias in household surveys. *Public Opinion Quarterly* 70:646–75.

Groves, R. M., and N. A. Mathiowetz. 1984. Computer assisted telephone interviewing: Effects on interviewers and respondents. *Public Opinion Quarterly* 48:356–69.

Gubrium, J. F., and J. A. Holstein. 1997. *The new language of qualitative method.* New York: Oxford University Press.

Gudelunas, D. 2005. Online personal ads: Community and sex, virtually. *Journal of Homosexuality* 49:1–33.

Guest, G., A. Bunce, and L. Johnson. 2006. How many interviews are enough? An experiment with data saturation and variability. *Field Methods* 18:59–82.

Guilmet, G. M. 1979. Instructor reaction to verbal and nonverbal-visual behavior in the urban classroom. *Anthropology and Education Quarterly* 10:254–66.

Gujarati, D. N., and D. Porter. 2008. *Basic econometrics.* 5th ed. New York: McGraw-Hill.

Gulur, P., S. W. Rodi, T. A. Washington, J. P. Cravero, G. J. Fanciullo, G. J. McHugo, and J. C. Baird. 2009. Computer face scale for measuring pediatric pain and mood. *The Journal of Pain* 10:173–79.

Gummesson, E. 1991. *Qualitative methods in management research.* Newbury Park, CA: Sage.

Gunter, B., A. Furnham, and C. Beeson. 1997. Recall of television advertisements as a function of program evaluation. *The Journal of Psychology* 131:541–43.

Guttman, L. 1944. A basis for scaling qualitative data. *American Sociological Review* 9:139–50.

Guzzo, R. A., S. E. Jackson, and R. E. Katzell. 1987. Meta-analysis. In *Research in organizational behavior*, B. M. Staw and L. L. Cummings, eds., vol. 9. Greenwich, CT: JAI Press

Hadaway, C. K., and P. L. Marler. 2005. How many Americans attend worship each week? An alternative approach to measurement. *Journal for the Scientific Study of Religion* 44:307–22.

Hadaway, C. K., P. L. Marler, and M. Chaves. 1998. Overreporting church attendance in America: Evidence that demands the same verdict. *American Sociological Review* 63:122–30.

Hage, P. 1987 [1972]. München beer categories. In *Culture and cognition*, J. P. Spradley, ed., 263–78. Prospect Heights, IL: Waveland.

Hagekull, B., and A. Hammarberg. 2004. The role of teachers' perceived control and children's characteristics in interactions between 6-year olds and their teachers. *Scandinavian Journal of Psychology* 45:301–12.

Haggerty, K. 2004. Ethics creep: Governing social science research in the name of ethics. *Qualitative Sociology* 27:391–414.

Halford, G. S. 1993. *Childrens's understanding: The development of mental models.* Hillsdale, NJ: L. Erlbaum Associates.

Hall, E. T. 1963. A system of notation of proxemic behavior. *American Anthropologist* 65:1003–26.

Hall, E. T. 1966. *The hidden dimension.* New York: Doubleday.

Hallett, T., and G. A. Fine. 2000. Ethnography 1900: Learning from the field research of an old century. *Journal of Contemporary Ethnography* 29:593–617.

Hamlet, J. D. 1994. Religious discourse as cultural narrative: A critical analysis of African-American sermons. *The Western Journal of Black Studies* 18:11–17.

Hammersley, M. 1990. *Classroom ethnography. Empirical and methodological essays.* Philadelphia: Open University Press.

Hammersley, M. 2009. Against the ethicists: On the evils of ethical regulation. *International Journal of Social Research Methodology* 12:211–25.

Hammond, D., and C. Parkinson. 2009. The impact of cigarette package design on perceptions of risk. *Journal of Public Health* 31:345–53.

Handwerker, W. P. 1989. *Women's power and social revolution: Fertility transition in the West Indies.* Newbury Park, CA: Sage.

Handwerker, W. P. 1993. Simple random samples of regional populations. *Cultural Anthropology Methods Journal* 5:12.

Handwerker, W. P. 1996a. Constructing Likert scales: Testing the validity and reliability of single measures of multidimensional variables. *Cultural Anthropology Methods Journal* 8:1–6.

Handwerker, W. P. 1996b. Power and gender: Violence and affection experienced by children in Barbados, W. I. *Medical Anthropology* 17:101–28.

Handwerker, W. P. 1998. Why violence? A test of hypotheses representing three discourses on the roots of domestic violence. *Human Organization* 57:200–208.

Handwerker, W. P. 2001. *Quick ethnography: A guide to rapid multi-method research.* Walnut Creek, CA: AltaMira.

Handwerker, W. P. 2002. The construct validity of cultures: Cultural diversity, cultural theory, and a method for ethnography. *American Anthropologist* 104:106–22.

Handwerker, W. P. 2003. Sample design. In *Encyclopedia of social measurement*, K. Kempf-Leonard, ed., 429–36. San Diego: Academic Press.

Handwerker, W. P., J. Hatcherson, and J. Herbert. 1997. Sampling guidelines for cultural data. *Cultural Anthropology Methods Journal* 9:7–9.

Handwerker, W. P., and D. F. Wozniak. 1997. Sampling strategy for the collection of cultural data: An extension of Boas's answer to Galton's problem. *Current Anthropology* 38:869–75.

Haney, C., C. Banks, and P. Zimbardo. 1973. Interpersonal dynamics in a simulated prison. *International Journal of Criminology and Penology* 1:69–97.

Hangland, A., and R. S. Cimbalo. 1997. Human ethology: Age and sex differences in mall walking. *Perceptual and Motor Skills* 85:845–46.

Hanks, W. F. 1989. Texts and textuality. *Annual Review of Anthropology* 18:95–127.

Hanneman, R. A., and M. Riddle. 2005. *Introduction to social network methods*. Riverside: University of California Press, Riverside. http://faculty.ucr.edu/~hanneman/ (accessed December 17, 2010).

Hansen, A., and L. A. McSpadden. 1993. Self-Anchoring Scale, or ladder of life: A method used with diverse refugee populations. Unpublished manuscript.

Harari, H., O. Harari, and R. V. White. 1985. The reaction to rape by American male bystanders. *Journal of Social Psychology* 125:653–58.

Harb, G. C., W. Eng, T. Zaider, and R. G. Heimberg. 2003. Behavioral assessment of public-speaking anxiety using a modified version of the Social Performance Rating Scale. *Behaviour Research and Therapy* 41:1373–80.

Harburg, E., L. Gleibermann, P. Roeper, M. A. Schork, and W. J. Schull. 1978. Skin color, ethnicity and blood pressure I: Detroit Blacks. *American Journal of Public Health* 68:1177–83.

Harlow, L. L., S. A. Mulaik, and J. H. Steiger, eds. 1997. *What if there were no significance tests?* Mahwah, NJ: L. Erlbaum Associates.

Harper, D. 2002. Talking about pictures: A case for photo-elicitation. *Visual Studies* 17:13–26.

Harrington, B. 2003. The social psychology of access in ethnographic research. *Journal of Contemporary Ethnography* 32:592–625.

Harris, D. A., and D. M. Parisi. 2007. Adapting life history calendars for qualitative research on welfare transitions. *Field Methods* 19:40–58.

Harris, M. 1968. *The rise of anthropological theory*. New York: Thomas Crowell.

Harris, M. 1979. *Cultural materialism: The struggle for a science of culture*. New York: Random House.

Harris, M., J. G. Consorte, J. Lang, and B. Byrne. 1993. Who are the Whites? Imposed census categories and the racial demography of Brazil. *Social Forces* 72:451–62.

Harrison, A. 1993. Comparing nurses' and patients' pain evaluations: A study of hospitalized patients in Kuwait. *Social Science & Medicine* 36:683–92.

Harshbarger, C. L. 1995. Farmer-herder conflict and state legitimacy in Cameroon. Ph.D. dissertation, University of Florida.

Hartman, J. J. 1978. Social demographic characteristics of Wichita, Sedwick County. In *Metropolitan Wichita—Past, present, and future*, G. Miller and J. Skaggs, eds., 22–37. Lawrence: Kansas Regents Press.

Hartman, J. J., and J. Hedblom. 1979. *Methods for the social sciences: A handbook for students and non-specialists*. Westport, CT: Greenwood.

Hartmann, D. P., and D. D. Wood. 1990. Observational methods. In *International handbook of behavior modification therapy*. 2d ed., A. S. Bellack, M. Hersen, and A. E. Kazdin, eds., 107–38. New York: Plenum.

Harvey, D. L., and M. H. Reed. 1996. The culture of poverty: An ideological analysis. *Sociological Perspectives* 39:465–95.

Harvey, E. A., J. L. Friedman-Weieneth, A. L. Miner, R. J. Bartolomei, S. D. Youngwirth, R. L. Hashim, and D. H. Arnold. 2009. The role of ethnicity in observers' ratings of mother-child behavior. *Developmental Psychology* 45:1497–508.

Harvey, S. A., M. P. Olortegui, E. Leontsini, and P. J. Winch. 2009. "They'll change what they're doing if they know that you're watching": Measuring reactivity in health behavior because of an observer's presence—A case from the Peruvian Amazon. *Field Methods* 21:3–25.

Harvey, S. M., and S. T. Bird. 2004. What makes women feel powerful? An exploratory study of relationship power and sexual decision-making with African Americans at risk for HIV/STDs. *Women and Health* 39:1–18.

Harwell, M. R., and G. G. Gatti. 2001. Rescaling ordinal data to interval data in educational research. *Review of Educational Research* 71:105–31.

Hashimoto, K., and A. L. Borders. 2005. Proxemics and its affects on travelers during the sales contact in hotels. *Journal of Travel and Tourism Marketing* 18:49–61.

Hatch, D., and M. Hatch. 1947. Criteria of social status as derived from marriage announcements in the *New York Times*. *American Sociological Review* 12:396–403.

Hausman, D. B., and A. Hausman. 1997. *Descartes's legacy: Minds and meaning in early modern philosophy*. Toronto: University of Toronto Press.

Haworth-Hoeppner, S. 2000. The critical shapes of body image: The role of culture and family in the production of eating disorders. *Journal of Marriage and the Family* 62:212–27.

Hayek, F. A. von. 1952. *The counter-revolution of science*. Glencoe, IL: The Free Press.

Hays, J. A. 1984. Aging and family resources: Availability and proximity of kin. *Gerontologist* 24:149–53.

Healey, B. 2007. Drop downs and scroll mice: The effect of response option format and input mechanism employed on data quality in web surveys. *Social Science Computer Review* 25:111–28.

Healey, M.. F. Jordan, B. Pell, and C. Short. 2010. The research–teaching nexus: A case study of students' awareness, experiences, and perceptions of research. *Innovations in Education and Teaching International* 47:235–46.

Heath, C. 1989. Pain talk: The expression of suffering in the medical consultation. *Social Psychology Quarterly* 52:113–25.

Heath, S. B. 1972. *Telling tongues*. New York: Columbia University Press.

Heckathorn, D. D. 1997. Respondent-driven sampling: A new approach to the study of hidden populations. *Social Problems* 44:174–99.

Heckathorn, D. D. 2002. Respondent-driven Sampling II: Deriving valid population estimates from chain-referral samples of hidden populations. *Social Problems* 49:11–34.

Heckathorn, D. D. 2007. Extensions of respondent-driven sampling: Analyzing continuous variables and controlling for differential recruitment. *Sociological Methodology* 37:151–207.

Hedges, L. V., and I. Olkin. 1985. *Statistical methods for meta-analysis*. Orlando, FL: Academic Press.

Hedges, L. V., and C. Rhoads. 2010. *Statistical power analysis in education research*. Washington, DC: National Center for Special Education Research. NCSER 2010-3006. http://www.eric.ed.gov/PDFS/ED509387.pdf (accessed January 16, 2011).

Heerwegh, D. 2006. An investigation of the effect of lotteries on web survey response rates. *Field Methods* 18:205–20.

Hektner, J. M., J. A. Schmidt, and M. Csikszentmihalyi. 2007. *Experience sampling method: Measuring the quality of everyday life*. Thousand Oaks, CA: Sage.

Hemphill, S. A., G. Munro, and S. Oh. 2007. Adolescents' expenditure on alcohol: A pilot study. *Australian Journal of Social Issues* 42:623–35.

Henderson, F. B. 2009. "We thought you would be white": Race and gender in fieldwork. *Political Science and Politics* 42:291–94.

Henderson, J., and J. P. Harrington. 1914. *Ethnozoology of the Tewa Indians*. Smithsonian Institution, Bureau of American Ethnology, Bulletin 56. Washington, DC: Government Printing Office.

Henderson, S., D. G. Byrne, and P. Duncan-Jones. 1980. Measuring social relationships: The Interview Schedule for Social Interaction. *Psychological Medicine* 10:723–34.

Henley, N. M. 1969. A psychological study of the semantics of animal terms. *Journal of Verbal Learning and Verbal Behavior* 8:176–84.

Henriksen, K., and E. Dayton. 2006. Organizational silence and hidden threats to patient safety. *Health Services Research* 41:1539–54.

Henry, G. T. 1990. *Practical sampling*. Newbury Park, CA: Sage.

Hensley, W. E. 1974. Increasing response rates by choice of postage stamps. *Public Opinion Quarterly* 38:280–83.

Henson, S., J. Cranfield, and D. Herath. 2010. Understanding consumer receptivity towards foods and non-prescription pills containing phytosterols as a means to offset the risk of cardiovascular disease: An application of protection motivation theory. *International Journal of Consumer Studies* 34:28–37.

Herrera, C. D. 1996. Informed consent and ethical exemptions. *Human Organization* 55:235–37. (See entries for Wax [1996] and for Fluehr-Lobban [1996].)

Herrera, C. D. 2001. Ethics, deception, and "those Milgram experiments." *Journal of Applied Philosophy* 18:245–56.

Herszenhorn, D. M. 2009. Census nominee tries to ease Republican senators' fears on 2010 count. *New York Times* (May 15). http://www.nytimes.com/2009/05/16/us/politics/16census.html?_r=1 (accessed June 10, 2009).

Hertwig, R., and A. Ortmann. 2008. Deception in experiments: Revisiting the arguments in its defense. *Ethics and Behavior* 18:59–92.

Herzfeld, M. 2009. The cultural politics of gesture. *Ethnography* 10:131–52.

Hew, M. L. A., and S. C. Wesley. 2007. Tourist shoppers' satisfaction with regional shopping mall experiences. *International Journal of Culture, Tourism, and Hospitality Research*. 1:82–96.

Hewett, P. C., A. S. Erulkar, and B. S. Mensch. 2004. The feasibility of computer-assisted survey interviewing in Africa: Experience from two rural districts in Kenya. *Social Science Computer Review* 22:319–34.

Hine, C. 2000. *Virtual ethnography*. London: Sage.

Hines, A. M. 1993. Linking qualitative and quantitative methods in cross-cultural survey research: Techniques from cognitive science. *American Journal of Community Psychology* 21:729–46.

Hipp, J. 2010. A dynamic view of neighborhoods: The reciprocal relationship between crime and neighborhood structural characteristics. *Social Problems* 57:205–30.

Hirschman, E. C. 1987. People as products: Analysis of a complex marketing exchange. *Journal of Marketing* 51:98–108.

Hjelmslev, L. 1961. *Prolegomena to a theory of language*. Tran. By F. J. Whitfield. Rev. English edition. Madison: University of Wisconsin Press.

Hodge, L. G., and D. Dufour. 1991. Cross-sectional growth of young Shipibo Indian children in eastern Peru. *American Journal of Physical Anthropology* 84:35–41.

Hodkinson, P. 2002. *Goth: Identity, style and subculture*. Oxford: Berg.

Hodkinson, P. 2005. "Insider research" in the study of youth cultures. *Journal of Youth Studies* 8:131–49.

Hoeyer, K. 2006. "Ethics wars": Reflections on the antagonism between bioethicists and social science observers of biomedicine. *Human Studies* 29:203–27.

Hogan, B., J. A. Carrasco, and B. Wellman. 2007. Visualizing personal networks: Working with participant-aided sociograms. *Field Methods* 19:116–44.

Høgh-Olesen, H. 2008. Human spatial behavior: The spacing of people, objects and animals in six cross-cultural samples. *Journal of Cognition and Culture* 8:245–80.

Holbrook, A. L., M. C. Green, and J. A. Krosnick. 2003. Telephone versus face-to-face interviewing of national probability samples with long questionnaires. Comparisons of respondent satisficing and social desirability response bias. *Public Opinion Quarterly* 67:79–125.

Holbrook, A. L., and J. A. Krosnick. 2010. Social desirability bias in voter turnout reports. *Public Opinion Quarterly* 74:37–67.

Holland, D., and N. Quinn. 1987. *Cultural models in language and thought*. Cambridge: Cambridge University Press.

Holland, D., and D. Skinner. 1987. Prestige and intimacy: The cultural models behind Americans' talk about gender types. In *Cultural models in language and thought*, D. Holland and N. Quinn, eds., 78–111. New York: Cambridge Univesity Press.

Hollinger, R. 1994. *Postmodernism and the social sciences: A thematic approach*. Thousand Oaks, CA: Sage.

Hollis, M. 1996. Philosophy of social science. In *The Blackwell companion to philosophy*, N. Bunnin and E. P. Tsui-James, eds., 358–87. Oxford, UK: Blackwell.

Holmes, T. H., and R. H. Rahe. 1967. The Social Readjustment Rating Scale. *Journal of Psychosomatic Research* 11:213–18.

Holsti, O. R. 1969. *Content analysis for the social sciences and humanities*. Reading, MA: Addison-Wesley.

Homans, G. C. 1961. Social behavior as exchange. *American Journal of Sociology* 63:597–606.

Hopkins, K. D., and A. R. Gullickson. 1992. Response rates in survey research: A meta-analysis of the effects of monetary gratuities. *The Journal of Experimental Education* 61:52–62.

Horn, W. 1960. Reliability survey: A survey on the reliability of response to an interview survey. *Het PTT-Bedriff* (The Hague) 10:105–56.

Hornik, J. 1992. Tactile stimulation and consumer response. *Journal of Consumer Research* 19:449–58.

Hornik, J., and S. Ellis. 1988. Strategies to secure compliance for a mall intercept interview. *Public Opinion Quarterly* 52:539–51.

Horowitz, T., and G. J. Massey, eds. 1991. *Thought experiments in science and philosophy*. Savage, MD: Rowman & Littlefield.

Howard, J. 1973 [1792]. *Prisons and lazarettos*. Vol. 1. *The state of the prisons in England and Wales: With preliminary observations, and an account of some foreign prisons and hospitals*. Montclair, NJ: Patterson Smith.

Howell, N. 1990. *Surviving fieldwork*. Washington, DC: American Anthropological Association.

Hoyle, R. H., ed. 1999. *Statistical strategies for small sample research*. Thousand Oaks, CA: Sage.

Hruschka, D. J., B. Cummings, D. C. St. John, J. Moore, G. Khumalo-Sakutukwa, and J. W. Carey. 2004. Fixed-choice and open-ended response formats: A comparison from HIV prevention research in Zimbabwe. *Field Methods* 16:184–202.

Hruschka, D. J., L. M. Sibley, N. Kalim, and J. K. Edmonds. 2008. When there is more than one answer key: Cultural theories of postpartum hemorrhage in Matlab, Bangladesh. *Field Methods* 20:315–37.

Hsiao, A. F., G. W. Ryan, R. D. Hays, I. D. Coulter, R. M. Andersen, and N. S. Wenger. 2006. Variations in provider conceptions of integrative medicine. *Social Science and Medicine* 62:2973–87.

Hudak, M. A. 1993. Gender schema theory revisited: Men's stereotypes of American women. *Sex Roles: A Journal of Research* 28:279–93.

Hudson, H. F. 2004. *The great betrayal: Fraud in science*. Orlando, FL: Harcourt.

Huesmann, L. R., J. Moise, C. P. Podolski, and L. D. Eron. 2003. Longitudinal relations between childhood exposure to media violence and adult aggression and violence: 1977–2002. *Developmental Psychology* 39:201–21.

Hull, C. L. 1934. The rats' speed of locomotion gradient in the approach to food. *Journal of Comparative Psychology* 17:393–422.

Hultsch, D. F., S. W. S. MacDonald, M, A. Hunter, S. B. Maitland, and R. A. Dixon. 2002. Sampling and generalisability in developmental research: Comparison of random and convenience samples of older adults. *International Journal of Behavioral Development* 26:345–59.

Hume, D. 1978 [1739–40]. *A treatise on human nature*. 2d ed. Ed. by L. A. Selby-Bigge and P. N. Nidditch. New York: Oxford University Press.

Hume, L., and J. Mulcock, eds. 2004. *Anthropologists in the field*. New York: Columbia University Press.

Humphreys, L. 1975. *Tearoom trade: Impersonal sex in public places*. Enl. ed. with a retrospect on ethical issues. Chicago: Aldine.

Hunfield, J. A., M. M. Mourik, J. Passchier, and D. Tibboel. 1996. Do couples grieve differently following infant loss? *Psychological Reports* 79:407–10.

Hunt, J. G., and A. Ropo. 1995. Multi-level leadership: Grounded theory and mainstream theory applied to the case of General Motors. *Leadership Quarterly* 6:379–412.

Hunt, M. M. 1997. *How science takes stock: The story of meta-analysis*. New York: Russell Sage Foundation.

Hunter, J. E., and F. L. Schmidt. 2004. *Methods of meta-analysis: Correcting error and bias in research findings*. 2d ed. Thousand Oaks, CA: Sage.

Huntington, D., and S. R. Schuler. 1993. The simulated client method: Evaluating client-provider interactions in family planning clinics. *Studies in Family Planning* 24:187–93.

Hupka, R. B., A. P. Lenton, and K. A. Hutchison. 1999. Universal development of emotion categories in natural language. *Journal of Personality and Social Psychology* 77:247–78.

Hursh-César, G., and P. Roy, eds. 1976. *Third World surveys: Survey research in developing nations*. Delhi: Macmillan.

Husserl, E. 1964 [1907]. *The idea of phenomenology*. Trans. by W. P. Alston and G. Nakhnikian. The Hague: Nijhoff.

Husserl, E. 1999. *The essential Husserl: Basic writings in transcendental phenomenology*. Ed. by D. Welton. Bloomington: Indiana University Press.

Hutt, S. J., and C. Hutt. 1970. *Direct observation and measurement of behavior*. Springfield, IL: C. C. Thomas.

Hyman, H. H. 1954. *Survey design and analysis*. New York: The Free Press.

Hyman, H. H., and W. J. Cobb. 1975. *Interviewing in social research*. Chicago: University of Chicago Press.

Hymes, D. H. 1964. Discussion of Burling's paper. *American Anthropologist* 66:116–19.

Hymes, D. H. 1976. Louis Simpson's "The Deserted Boy." *Poetics* 5:119–55.

Hymes, D. H. 1977. Discovering oral performance and measured verse in American Indian narrative. *New Literary History* 8:431–57.

Hymes, D. H. 1980a. Verse analysis of a Wasco text: Hiram Smith's "At'unaqa." *International Journal of American Linguistics* 46:65–77.

Hymes, D. H. 1980b. Particle, pause, and pattern in American Indian narrative verse. *American Indian Culture and Research Journal* 4:7–51.

Hymes, D. H. 1981. *In vain I tried to tell you: Essays in ethnopoetics*. Philadelphia: University of Pennsylvania Press.

Hymes, D. H. 2003. *Now I know only so far: Essays in ethnopoetics*. Lincoln: University of Nebraska Press.

Hymes, V. 1987. Warm Springs Sahaptin narrative analysis. In *Native American discourse: Poetics and rhetoric*, J. Sherzer and A. Woodbury, eds., 62–102. Cambridge: Cambridge University Press.

Hynsook, S., and R. White-Traut. 2005. Nurse-child interaction on an inpatient paediatric unit. *Journal of Advanced Nursing* 52:56–62.

Ibeh, K. I. N., and J. K.-U. Brock. 2004. Conducting survey research among organisational populations in developing countries: Can the drop and collect technique make a difference? *International Journal of Marketing Research* 46:375–83.

Ibeh, K. I. N., J. K.-U. Brock, and Y. J. Zhou. 2004. The drop and collect survey among industrial populations: Theory and empirical evidence. *Industrial Marketing Management* 33:155–65.

Ice, G. 2004. Technological advances in observational data collection: The advantages and limitations of computer-assisted data collection. *Field Methods* 16:352–75.

ICMR (Institute for Coast and Marine Resources) and East Carolina University. 1993. *Coastal North Carolina socioeconomic study*. Vol. 4. Pile Sort and Data Analysis. Performer: East Carolina University, Greenville, NC. Institute for Coastal and Marine Resources; Impact Assessment, Inc., La Jolla, CA. Sponsor: Minerals Management Service, Herndon, VA. Atlantic OCS Region. September 30, 1993. Report: OCS/MMS93/0055.

Ignatow, G. 2004. Speaking together, thinking together? Exploring metaphor and cognition in a shipyard union dispute. *Sociological Forum* 19:405–33.

Igun, U. A. 1986. Reported and actual prescription of oral rehydration therapy for childhood diarrhoeas by retail pharmacists in Nigeria. *Social Science and Medicine* 39:797–806.

Inoue, A., N. Kawakami, A. Tsutsumi, A. Shimazu, M. Tsuchiya, M. Ishizaki, M. Tabata, M. Akiyama, A. Kitazume, M. Kuroda, and M. Kivimaki. 2009. Reliability and validity of the Japanese version of the Organizational Justice Questionnaire. *Journal of Occupational Health* 51:74–83.

International Monetary Fund (IMF). 2009. World Economic Outlook Database, April 2009. http://tinyurl.com/c2rwdh (accessed June 21, 2009).

Irurita, V. F. 1996. Hidden dimensions revealed— Progressive grounded theory study of quality care in the hospital. *Qualitative Health Research* 6:331–49.

Israel, B. A., E. Eng., A. J. Schulz, and E. A. Parker, eds. 2005. *Methods in community-based participatory research for health*. San Francisco: Jossey-Bass.

Ivis, F. J., S. J. Bondy, and E. M. Adlaf. 1997. The effect of question structure on self-reports of heavy drinking: Closed-ended versus open-ended questions. *Journal of Studies on Alcohol* 58:622–24.

Izquierdo, C., and A. Johnson. 2007. Desire, envy and punishment: A Matsigenka emotion schema in illness narratives and folk stories. *Culture, Medicine, and Psychiatry* 31:419–44.

Jackson, D. N. 1984. *Personality research form manual*. Goshen, NY: Research Psychologists Press.

Jackson, H., and R. L. Nuttall. 1997. *Childhood abuse: Effects on clinicians' personal and professional lives*. Thousand Oaks, CA: Sage.

Jackson, S., and S. Gee. 2005. "Look Janet," "No you look John": Constructions of gender in early school reader illustrations across 50 years. *Gender and Education* 17:115–28.

Jacob, M. C. and L. Stewart. 2004. *Practical matter: Newton's science in the service of industry and empire: 1687–1851*. Cambridge, MA: Harvard University Press.

Jacobs, L. 1995. *The Jewish religion: A companion*. New York: Oxford University Press.

Jacobs, R. J., and B. Thomlinson. 2009. Self-silencing and age as risk factors for sexually acquired HIV in midlife and older women. *Journal of Aging and Health* 21:102–28.

Jacoby, W. G. 1997. *Statistical graphics for univariate and bivariate data*. Sage University Papers Series. Quantitative applications in the social sciences, no. 117. Thousand Oaks, CA: Sage.

Jaeger, R. M. 1984. *Sampling in education and the social sciences*. New York: Longmans, Green.

James, D., and S. Clarke. 1993. Women, men and interruptions: A critical review of research. In *Gender and conversational interaction*, D. Tannen, ed., 281–312. New York: Oxford University Press.

Jamieson, P. E., and D. Romer. 2010. Trends in U.S. movie tobacco portrayal since 1950: A historical analysis. *Tobacco Control* 19:179–84.

Jang, H-Y. 1995. Cultural differences in organizational communication and interorganizational networks: A semantic network analysis. Ph.D. dissertation, State University of New York at Buffalo.

Jang, H-Y., and G. A. Barnett 1994. Cultural differences in organizational communication: A semantic network analysis. *Bulletin de Methodologie Sociologique* 44:31–59.

Jankowiak, W. R., and E. F. Fischer. 1995. A cross-cultural perspective on romantic love. *Ethnology* 31:149–55.

Jaranson, J. M., J. Butcher, L. Halcón, D. R. Johnson, C. Robertson, K. Savik, M. Spring, and J. Westermeyer. 2004. Somali and Oromo refugees: Correlates of torture and trauma history. *American Journal of Public Health* 94:591–98.

Jargowsky, P. A. 2005. The ecological fallacy. In *The encyclopedia of social measurement*, Vol. 1, A–E, K. Kempf-Leonard, ed., 715–22. Oxford, UK: Elsevier/Academic Press.

Jasanoff, S., G. E. Markle, J. C. Petersen, and T. Pinch. 1995. *The handbook of science and technology studies*. Thousand Oaks, CA: Sage.

Jaskyte, K., and W. W. Dressler. 2004. Studying culture as an integral aggregate variable: Organizational culture and innovation in a group of nonprofit organizations. *Field Methods* 16:265–84.

Jaskyte, K., H. Taylor, and R. Smariga. 2009. Student and faculty perceptions of innovative teaching. *Creativity Research Journal* 21:111–16.

Jasso, G. 2006. Factorial survey methods for studying beliefs and judgments. *Sociological Methods and Research* 34:334–423.

Jasso, G., and K-D. Opp. 1997. Probing the character of norms: A factorial survey analysis of the norms of political action. *American Sociological Review* 62:947–64.

Jefferson, G. 1973. A case of precision timing in ordinary conversation: Overlapped tag-positioned address terms in closing sequences. *Semiotica* 9:47–96.

Jefferson, G. 1983. Issues in the transcription of naturally-occurring talk. Caricature versus capturing pronunciation particulars. Tilburg Papers on Language and Literature. Tilburg, Netherlands: University of Tilburg. http://www.liso.ucsb.edu/Jefferson/Caricature.pdf (accessed February 9, 2010).

Jefferson, G. 2004. Glossary of transcript symbols with an introduction. In *Conversation analysis*, G. H. Lerner, ed., 13–31. Philadelphia: John Benjamins.

Jemielniak, J., and P. Mikłaszewicz, eds. 2010. *Interpretation of law in the global world: From particularism to universal approach*. New York: Springer.

Jenkins, J. H., and R. J., Barrett, eds. 2004. *Schizophrenia, culture, and subjectivity: The edge of experience*. New York: Cambridge University Press.

Jennings, M. K. 1987. Residues of a movement: The aging of the American protest generation. *American Political Science Review* 81:367–82.

Jennings, M. K., and G. B. Markus. 1984. Partisan orientations over the long haul: Results from the three-wave political socialization study. *American Political Science Review* 78:1000–18.

Jennings, M. K., G. B. Markus, R. G. Niemi, and L. Stoker. 2005. Youth-Parent Socialization Panel Study, 1965–1997: Four Waves Combined [computer file]. ICPSR04037-v1. Ann Arbor, MI: Inter-university Consortium for Political and Social Research [distributor], 2005-11-04. doi:10.3886/ICPSR04037.

Jentsch, B. 1998. The "interpreter effect": Rendering interpreters visible in cross-cultural research and methodology. *Journal of European Social Policy* 8:275–89.

Jobe, J. B., D. M. Keler, and A. F. Smith. 1996. Cognitive techniques in interviewing older people. In *Answering questions: Methodology for determining cognitive and communicative processes in survey research*, N. Schwarz and S. Sudman, eds., 197–219. San Francisco: Jossey-Bass.

Johns, G. 1994. How often were you absent? A review of the use of self-reported absence data. *Journal of Applied Psychology* 79:574–91.

Johns, M. D., S. C. Shing-Ling, and G. J. Hall, eds. 2004. *Online social research: Methods, issues and ethics*. New York: Peter Lang.

Johnson, A. 1978. *Quantification in anthropology*. Stanford, CA: Stanford University Press.

Johnson, J. C. 1990. *Selecting ethnographic informants*. Newbury Park, CA: Sage.

Johnson, J. C., and D. C. Griffith. 1996. Pollution, food safety, and the distribution of knowledge. *Human Ecology* 24:87–108.

Johnson, J. C., and M. L. Miller. 1983. Deviant social positions in small groups: The relation between role and individual. *Social Networks* 5:51–69.

Johnson, R. K., P. Driscoll, and M. I. Goran. 1996. Comparison of multiple-pass 24-hour recall estimates of energy intake with total energy expenditure determined by the doubly labeled water method in young children. *Journal of the American Dietetic Association* 96:1140–44.

Johnson-Green, D., M. E. McCaul, and P. Roger. 2009. Screening for hazardous drinking using the Michigan Alcohol Screen Test–Geriatric Version (MAST-G) in elderly persons with acute cerebrovascular accidents. *Alcoholism: Clinical and Experimental Research* 33:1555–61.

Johnson-Laird, P. N. 1983. *Mental models: Toward a cognitive science of language, inference, and consciousness*. Cambridge, MA: Harvard University Press.

Johnston, L. G., A. Trummal, L. Lohmus, and A. Ravalepik. 2009. Efficacy of convenience sampling through the Internet versus respondent driven sampling among males who have sex with males in Tallinn and Harju County, Estonia: Challenges reaching a hidden population. *AIDS Care* 21:1195–202.

Johnstone, B., K. Ferrara, and J. M. Bean. 1992. Gender, politeness, and discourse management in same-sex and cross-sex opinion-poll interviews. *Journal of Pragmatics* 18:405–30.

Joinson, A. N., K. McKenna, T. Postmes, and U.-D. Reips, eds. 2007. *The Oxford handbook of Internet psychology*. New York: Oxford University Press.

Jones, D. J. 1970. Towards a native anthropology. *Human Organization* 29:251–59.

Jones, D. J. 1973. The results of role-playing in anthropological research. *Anthropological Quarterly* 46:30–37.

Jones, M., and M. A. Nies. 1996. The relationship of perceived benefits of and barriers to reported exercise in older African American women. *Public Health Nursing* 13:151–58.

Jordan, B. 1992a. *Birth in four cultures: A cross-cultural investigation of childbirth in Yucatan, Holland, Sweden, and the United States*. 4th exp. ed. Rev. by R. Davis-Floyd. Prospect Heights, IL: Waveland.

Jordan, B. 1992b. *Technology and social interaction: Notes on the achievement of authoritative knowledge in complex settings*. Technical report #IRL92–0027. Palo Alto, CA: Institute for Research on Learning.

Jordan, B., and A. Henderson. 1993. Interaction analysis: Foundations and practice. Xerox Palo Alto Research Center and Institute for Research on Learning. Working paper.

Jorgensen, D. 1989. *Participant observation*. Newbury Park, CA: Sage.

Junker, B. H. 1960. *Field work: An introduction to the social sciences*. Chicago: University of Chicago Press.

Jurgens, U., T. Malsch, and K. Dohse. 1993. *Breaking from Taylorism: Changing norms of work in the automobile industry*. New York: Cambridge University Press.

Jussaume, R. A., Jr., and Y. Yamada. 1990. A comparison of the viability of mail surveys in Japan and the United States. *Public Opinion Quarterly* 54:219–28.

Juzwik, M. M. 2004. What rhetoric can contribute to an ethnopoetics of narrative performance in teaching: The significance of parallelism in one teacher's narrative. *Linguistics and Education* 15:359–86.

Kadushin, C. 1968. Power, influence and social circles: A new methodology for studying opinion makers. *American Sociological Review* 33:685–99.

Kadushin, C. 1972. *The social work interview*. New York: Columbia University Press.

Kafle, K. K., J. M. Madden, A. D. Shresta, S. B. Karkee, P. L. Das, Y. M. S. Pradhan, and J. D. Quick. 1996. Can licensed drug sellers contribute to safe motherhood? A survey of the treatment of pregnancy-related anaemia in Nepal. *Social Science and Medicine* 42:1577–88.

Kahn, M. E., and E. A. Morris. 2009. Walking the walk. The association between community environmentalism and green travel behavior. *Journal of the American Planning Association* 75:389–405.

Kahn, R. L., and C. F. Cannell. 1957. *The dynamics of interviewing*. New York: Wiley.

Kail, B. L., D. D. Watson, S. Ray, and National AIDS Research Consortium. 1995. Needle-using practices within the sex industry. *American Journal of Drug and Alcohol Abuse* 21:241–55.

Kalton, G. 2009. Methods for oversampling rare subpopulations in social surveys. *Survey Methodology* 35:125–41.

Kampen, J. L., and M. Swyngedouw. 2000. The ordinal controversy revisited. *Quality and Quantity* 34: 87–102.

Kamper, G. D., and M. G. Steyn. 2011. Black students' perspectives on learning assets at a former White university. *Journal of Asian and African Studies* 46:278–92.

Kane, E. W., and L. J.Macaulay. 1993. Interviewer gender and gender attitudes. *Public Opinion Quarterly* 57:1–28.

Kane, J. G., S. C. Craig, and K. D. Wald. 2004. Religion and presidential politics in Florida: A list experiment. *Social Science Quarterly* 85:281–93.

Kang, N., A. Kara, H. A. Laskey, and F. B. Seaton. 1993. A SAS macro for calculating intercoder agreement in content analysis. *Journal of Advertising* 23:17–28.

Kant, I. 1966 [1787]. *Critique of pure reason*. Trans. by F. Max Muller. New York: Anchor Books.

Kataoka, K. 2009. A multi-modal ethnopoetic analysis (Part 1): Text, gesture, and environment in Japanese spatial narrative. *Language and Communication* 29:287–311.

Katsurada, E, and Y. Sugihara. 1999. A preliminary validation of the Bem Sex Role Inventory in Japanese culture. *Journal of Cross-Cultural Psychology* 30:641–45.

Katz, D. 1942. Do interviewers bias polls? *Public Opinion Quarterly* 6:248–68.

Katz, K., and C. Naré. 2002. Reproductive health knowledge and use of services among young adults in Dakar, Senegal. *Journal of Biosocial Science* 34:215–31.

Kaufman, G., and P. Voon Chin. 2003. Is ageism alive in date selection among men? Age requests among gay and straight men in Internet personal ads. *Journal of Men's Studies* 11:225–35.

Kaufman, J. S., and C. Poole. 2000. Looking back on "causal thinking in the social sciences." *American Review of Public Health* 21:101–19.

Kay, P. 1971. Taxonomy and semantic contrast. *Language* 47:866–87.

Kazdin, A. E. 1998. *Methodological issues and strategies in clinical research*. 2d ed. Washington, DC: American Psychological Association.

Kearney, M. H., S. Murphy, K. Irwin, and M. Rosenbaum. 1995. Salvaging self—A grounded theory of pregnancy on crack cocaine. *Nursing Research* 44:208–13.

Kearney, M. H., S. Murphy, and M. Rosenbaum. 1994. Mothering on crack cocaine—A grounded theory analysis. *Social Science and Medicine* 38:351–61.

Keating, N. L., A. M. Zaslavsky J. Goldstein, D. W. West, and J. Z. Ayanian. 2008. Randomized trial of $20 versus $50 incentives to increase physician survey response rates. *Medical Care* 46:878–81.

Keeter, S., C. Kennedy, M. Dimock, J. Best, and P. Craighillo. 2006. Gauging the impact of growing nonresponse on estimates from a national RDD telephone survey. *Public Opinion Quarterly* 70:759–79.

Keil, F. 1989. *Concepts, kinds, and cognitive development*. Cambridge, MA: MIT Press.

Keil, J. E., S. H. Sandifer, C. B. Loadholt, and E. Boyle, Jr. 1981. Skin color and education effects on blood pressure. *American Journal of Public Health* 71:532–34.

Keil, J. E., H. A. Tyroler, S. H. Sandifer, and E. Boyle, Jr. 1977. Hypertension: Effects of social class and racial admixture. *American Journal of Public Health* 67:634–39.

Keith, J., C. L. Fry, A. P. Glascock, C. Ikels, J. Dickerson-Putnam, H. Harpending, and P. Draper. 1994. *The aging experience: Diversity and commonality across cultures*. Thousand Oaks, CA: Sage.

Keith-Spiegel, and G. P. Koocher. 2005. The IRB paradox: Could the protectors also encourage deceit? *Ethics and Behavior* 15:339–49.

Keller, J. F., and A. Rivera. 2007. Visual methods in the assessment of diet intake in Mexican American women. *Western Journal of Nursing Research* 29:758–73.

Kellstedt, P. M., D. A. M. Peterson, and M. D. Ramirez. 2010. The macro-politics of a gender gap. *Public Opinion Quarterly* 74:477–98.

Kelly, G. A. 1955. *The psychology of personal constructs*. New York: Norton.

Kempf-Leonard, K., ed. 2005. *Encyclopedia of social measurement*. Amsterdam: Elsevier Academic Press.

Kemph, B. T., and T. Kasser. 1996. Effects of sexual orientation of interviewer on expressed attitudes toward male homosexuality. *The Journal of Social Psychology* 136:401–403.

Kempton, W. 1987. Two theories of home heat control. In *Cultural models in language and thought*,

D. Holland and N. Quinn, eds., 222–42. Cambridge: Cambridge University Press.

Kempton, W., J. S. Boster, and J. A. Jartley. 1995. *Environmental values in American culture*. Cambridge, MA: MIT Press.

Kendall, C., E. Leontsini, E. Gil, F. Cruz, P. Hudelson, and P. Pelto. 1990. Exploratory ethnoentomology. Using Anthropac to design a dengue fever control program. *Cultural Anthropology Methods Journal* 2:11–12.

Kendall, S., and D. Tannen. 2001. Discourse and gender. In *The handbook of discourse analysis*, D. Schiffrin, D. Tannen, and H. E. Hamilton, eds., 548–67. Oxford, UK: Blackwell.

Kendon, A. 1981, ed. *Nonverbal communication, interaction, and gesture: Selections from semiotica*. The Hague: Mouton.

Kennedy, C. W., and C. Camden. 1983. A new look at interruptions. *Western Journal of Speech Communication* 47:45–58.

Kenner, A. N., and G. Katsimaglis. 1993. Gender differences in proxemics: Taxi-seat choice. *Psychological Reports* 72:625–26.

Kent, R. N., J. Kanowitz, K. D. O'Leary, and M. Cheiken. 1977. Observer reliability as a function of circumstances of assessment. *Journal of Applied Behavioral Analysis* 10:317–24.

Kerlinger, F. N. 1973. *Foundations of behavioral research*. New York: Holt, Rinehart & Winston.

Kerra, N., and N. Phillips. 2008. Researching "back home": International management research as autoethnography. *Organizational Research Methods* 11:541–61.

Kessler, R. C., and E. Wethington. 1991. The reliability of life event reports in a community survey. *Psychological Medicine* 21:723–38.

Kiecker, P., and J. E. Nelson. 1996. Do interviewers follow telephone instructions? *Journal of the Market Research Society* 38:161–176.

Kilcullen, D. 2007. Ethics, politics and nonstate warfare. A response to González in this issue. *Anthropology Today* 23:20.

Kilduff, M., C. Crossland, W. Tsai, and D. Krackhardt. 2008. Organizational network perceptions versus reality: A small world after all? *Organizational Behavior and Human Decision Processes* 107: 15–28.

Killian, M., and C. Wilcox. 2008. Do abortion attitudes lead to party switching? *Political Research Quarterly* 61:561–73.

Killworth, P. D., and H. R. Bernard. 1974. CATIJ: A new sociometric technique and its application to a prison living unit. *Human Organization* 33:335–50.

Killworth, P. D., and H. R. Bernard. 1976. Informant accuracy in social network data. *Human Organization* 35:269–96.

Killworth, P. R. P. 1997. Culture and power in the British army: Hierarchies, boundaries and construction. Ph.D. dissertation, University of Cambridge.

Kilman, L. 1985. Anthropological studies help sell U.S. products. *Pittsburgh Post Gazette*, September 30, p. 15.

Kim, A. I. 1985. Korean color terms: An aspect of semantic fields and related phenomena. *Anthropological Linguistics* 27:425–36.

Kim, C. S. 1990. The role of the nonwestern anthropologist reconsidered: Illusion versus reality. *Current Anthropology* 31:196–201.

Kim, J., J. H. Kang, S. Kim, T. Smith, J. Son, and J. Berktold. 2010. Comparison between self-administered questionnaire and computer-assisted self-interview for supplemental survey nonresponse. *Field Methods* 22:57–69.

Kimball, S. T., and W. T. Partridge. 1979. *The craft of community study: Fieldwork dialogues*. Gainesville: University of Florida Press.

Kimmel, A. J. 1998. In defense of deception. *American Psychologist* 53:803–805.

Kincaid, H. 1996. *Philosophical foundations of the social sciences: Analyzing controversies in social research*. New York: Cambridge University Press.

King, G. 1997. *A solution to the ecological inference problem: Reconstructing individual behavior from aggregate data*. Princeton, NJ: Princeton University Press.

King, G., O. Rosen, and M. A. Tanner. 2004. *Ecological inference. New methodological strategies*. New York: Cambridge University Press.

King, N. 1994. The qualitative research interview. In *Qualitative methods in organizational research: A practical guide*, C. Cassell and G. Symon, eds., 14–36. Thousand Oaks, CA: Sage.

Kinsey, A. C., W. B. Pomeroy, and C. E. Martin. 1948. *Sexual behavior in the human male*. Philadelphia: Saunders.

Kinzie, J., A. D. Thomas, M. M. Palmer, P. D. Umbach, and G. D. Kuh. 2007. Women students at coeducational and women's colleges: How do their experiences compare? *Journal of College Student Development* 48:145–65.

Kirk, J., and M. Miller. 1986. *Reliability and validity in qualitative research*. Newbury Park, CA: Sage.

Kirk, R. E. 1982. *Experimental design*. 2d ed. Monterey, CA: Brooks/Cole.

Kirk, R. E. 1995. *Experimental design: Procedures for the behavioral sciences*. 3d ed. Pacific Grove, CA: Brooks/Cole.

Kiš, A. D. 2007. An analysis of the impact of AIDS on funeral culture in Malawi. *NAPA Bulletin* 27:129–40.

Kish, L. 1995 [1965]. *Survey sampling*. New York: Wiley.

Kivetz, R., O. Urminsky, and Y. Zheng. 2006. The goal-gradient hypothesis resurrected: Purchase acceleration, illusionary goal progress, and customer retention. *Journal of Marketing Research* 43:39–58.

Klanten, R., N. Bourquin, S. Ehmann, T. Tissot, and F. van Heerden, eds. 2008. *Data flow: Visualizing information in graphic design*. Berlin: Gestalten.

Klein, F. C. 1999. On sports: Academic dilemma. *The Wall Street Journal*, April 2, p. W4.

Kleinman, A. 1980. *Patients and healers in the context of culture: An exploration of the borderland between anthropology, medicine, and psychiatry*. Berkeley: University of California Press.

Kluckhohn, K. 1945. The personal document in anthropological science. In *The use of personal documents in history, anthropology, and sociology*, L. Gottschalk, C. Kluckhohn, and R. Angell, eds., 79–176. New York: Social Science Research Council, Bulletin 53.

Kneidinger, L. M., T. L. Maple, and S. A. Tross. 2001. Touching behavior in sport: Functional components, analysis of sex differences, and ethological considerations. *Journal of Nonverbal Behavior* 25:43–62.

Knoke, D., and S. Yang. 2008. *Social network analysis*. 2d ed. Thousand Oaks, CA: Sage.

Kochen, M., ed. 1989. *The small world*. Norwood, NJ: Ablex.

Kohut, A. 2008. Getting it wrong. *New York Times*, January 10. http://www.nyt.com (accessed August 23, 2009).

Koivusaari, R. 2002. Horizontal and vertical interaction in children's computer-mediated communications. *Educational Psychology* 22:235–47.

Kojima, M., T. A. Furukawa, H. Takahashi, M. Kawai, T. Nagaya, and S. Tokudome. 2002. Cross-cultural validation of the Beck Depression Inventory-II in Japan. *Psychiatry Research* 110:291–99.

Kompus, T. 2006. Bimodal distribution of violent assaults. *Forensic Science International* 160:17–26.

Koocher, G. P. 1977. Bathroom behavior and human dignity. *Journal of Personality and Social Psychology* 35:120–21.

Koopmans, L. H. 1981. *An introduction to contemporary statistics*. Boston: Duxbury.

Korsching, P., J. Donnermeyer, and R. Burdge. 1980. Perception of property settlement payments and replacement housing among displaced persons. *Human Organization* 39:332–33.

Koskinen, H. I. 2010. Social interactions between veterinary medical students and their teachers in an ambulatory clinic setting in Finland. *Journal of Veterinary Medical Education* 37:159–64.

Koster, J. M. 2006. The use of the The Observer 5.0 and a Psion handheld computer in a remote fieldwork setting. *Field Methods* 18:430–36.

Kottak, C. 2009. *Prime-time society: An anthropological analysis of television and culture*. Updated ed. Walnut Creek, CA: Left Coast.

Kovats-Bernat, J. C. 2008. Negotiating dangerous fields: Pragmatic strategies for fieldwork amid violence and terror. *American Anthropologist* 104:208–22.

Koven, M. 2004. Getting "emotional" in two languages: Bilinguals' verbal performance of affect in narratives of personal experience. *Text* 24:471–515.

Kozak, R. A., W. C. Spetic, H. W. Harshaw, T. C. Maness, and S. R. J. Sheppard. 2008. Public priorities for sustainable forest management in six forest dependent communities in British Columbia. *Canadian Journal of Forest Research* 38:3071–74.

Kozinets, R. V. 2010. *Netnography: Doing ethnographic research online*. London: Sage.

Krackhardt, D. 1990. Assessing the political landscape: Structure, cognition, and power in organizations. *Administrative Science Quarterly* 35:342–69.

Kraemer, H. C., and S. Thiemann. 1987. *How many subjects? Statistical power analysis in research*. Newbury Park, CA: Sage.

Kraidy, M. M. 1999 The global, the local, and the hybrid: A native ethnography of glocalization. *Critical Studies in Media Communication* 16:456–76.

Krebs, V. 1999. The social life of books. http://www.orgnet.com/booknet.html (accessed August 29, 2010).

Krebs, V. 2003. Divided we stand? http://www.orgnet.com/leftright.html (accessed August 29, 2010).

Kreiss, L., and E. Stockton. 1980. Using the outline of cultural materials as a basis for indexing the content of ethnographic films. *Behavior Science Research* 15:281–93.

Kremer-Sadlik, T., and A. L. Paugh. 2007. Everyday moments: Finding "quality time" in American working families. *Time and Society* 16:287–308.

Kreuter, F., S. Presser, and R. Tourangeau. 2008. Social desirability bias in CATI, IVR, and web surveys: The effects of mode and question sensitivity. *Public Opinion Quarterly* 72:847–65.

Krieger, L. 1986. Negotiating gender role expectations in Cairo. In *Self, sex and gender in cross-cultural fieldwork*, T. L. Whitehead and M. E. Conaway, eds., 117–28. Urbana: University of Illinois Press.

Krippendorff, K. 2004a. *Content analysis: An introduction to its methodology*. 2d ed. Thousand Oaks, CA: Sage.

Krippendorff, K. 2004b. Reliability in content analysis. Some common misconceptions and recommendations. *Human Communication Research* 30:411–33.

Krippendorff, K., and M. A. Bock, eds. 2009. *The content analysis reader*. Thousand Oaks, CA: Sage.

Kroeber, A. L. 1919. On the principle of order in civilization as exemplified by changes in women's fashions. *American Anthropologist* 21:235–63.

Kronenfeld, D. B. 2009. *Fanti kinship and the analysis of kinship terminologies*. Urbana: University of Illinois Press.

Kronenfeld, D. B., J. Kronenfeld, and J. E. Kronenfeld. 1972. Toward a science of design for successful food service. *Institutions and Volume Feeding* 70:38–44.

Kropf, M. E., and J. Blair. 2005. Eliciting survey cooperation—Incentives, self-interest, and norms of cooperation. *Evaluation Review* 29:559–75.

Krosnick, J. A. 1999. Survey research. *Annual Review of Psychology* 50:537–67.

Krosnick, J. A. 2010. The climate majority. *New York Times*, June 9. http://www.nytimes.com/2010/06/09/opinion/09krosnick.html?scp=1&sq=jon%20krosnick&st=cse (accessed June 9, 2010).

Krosnick, J. A., A. L. Holbrook, M. K. Berent, R. T. Carson, W. M. Hanemann, R. J. Kopp, R. C. Mitchell, S. Presser, P. A. Ruud, V. K. Smith, W. R. Moody, M. C. Green, and M. Conaway. 2002. The impact of "no opinion" response options on data quality. Non-attitude reduction or an invitation to satisfice? *Public Opinion Quarterly* 66:371–403.

Krueger, R. A. 1994. *Focus groups: A practical guide for applied research*. 2d ed. Thousand Oaks, CA: Sage.

Kruskal, J. B., and M. Wish. 1978. *Multidimensional scaling*. Beverly Hills, CA: Sage.

Kubota, Y., K. Maruyama, S. Sato, Y. Ishikawa, T. Shimamoto, M. Inagawa, M. Ohshima, S. Murai, and H. Iso. 2010. Reproducibility of 24-hour dietary recall for vitamin intakes by middle-aged Japanese men and women. *Journal of Nutrition Health and Aging* 14:196–200.

Kuhn, T. S. 1970. *The structure of scientific revolutions*. 2d ed. Chicago: University of Chicago Press.

Kuklinski, J. H., M. D. Cobb, and M. Gilens. 1997. Racial attitudes and the "New South." *The Journal of Politics* 59:323–49.

Kulick, D., and M. Willson, eds. 1995. *Taboo: Sex, identity, and erotic subjectivity in anthropological fieldwork*. London: Routledge.

Kunin, T. 1955. The construction of a new type of attitude measure. *Personnel Psychology* 8:65–77.

Kunitz, S. J., H. Temkin-Greener, D. Broudy, and M. Haffner. 1981. Determinants of hospital utilization and surgery on the Navajo Indian Reservation, 1972–1978. *Social Science and Medicine* 15B:71–79.

Kunovich, R. S., and R. G. Rashid. 1992. Mirror training in three dimensions for dental students. *Perceptual and Motor Skills* 75:923–28.

Kurasaki, K. S. 1997. Ethnic identity and its development among third-generation Japanese Americans. Ph.D. dissertation, Department of Psychology, DePaul University.

Kurasaki, K. S. 2000. Intercoder reliability for validating conclusions drawn from open-ended interview data. *Field Methods* 12:179–94.

Kuwayama, T. 2003. "Natives" as dialogic partners. Some thoughts on native anthropology. *Anthropology Today* 19:8–13.

Kvale, S. 2009. *InterViews: Learning the craft of qualitative research interviewing*. 2d. ed. Thousand Oaks, CA: Sage.

Kvalem, I. L., J. M. Sundet, K. I. Rivo, and D. E. Eilertsen. 1996. The effect of sex education on adolescents' use of condoms: Applying the Solomon four-group design. *Health Education Quarterly* 23:34–47.

Kwon, H. Y. 2010. Economic perceptions and electoral choice in South Korea: The case of the 2007 presidential election. *Pacific Review* 23:183–201.

Labovitz, S. 1971a. The assignment of numbers to rank order categories. *American Sociological Review* 35:515–24.

Labovitz, S. 1971b. The zone of rejection: Negative thoughts on statistical inference. *Pacific Sociological Review* 14:373–81.

Labovitz, S. 1972. Statistical usage in sociology. *Sociological Methods and Research* 3:14–37.

Lakoff, G., and M. Johnson. 2003 [1980]. *Metaphors we live by*. Chicago: University of Chicago Press.

Lakoff, G., and Z. Kövecses. 1987. The cognitive model of anger in American English. In *Cultural models in language and thought*, D. Holland and N. Quinn, eds., 195–221. New York: Cambridge University Press.

Lam, T .C. M., K. Green, and C. Bordignon. 2002. Effects of item grouping and position of the "don't know" option on questionnaire response. *Field Methods* 14:418–32.

Lance, L. M. 1998. Gender differences in heterosexual dating. A content analysis of personal ads. *Journal of Men's Studies* 6:297–305.

Landauer, T. K., and J. W. M. Whiting. 1964. Infantile stimulation and adult stature of human males. *American Anthropologist* 66:1007–28.

La Pastina, A. C. 2006. The implications of an ethnographer's sexuality. *Qualitative Inquiry* 12:724–35.

La Pelle, N. 2004. Simplifying qualitative data analysis using general purpose software tools. *Field Methods* 16:85–108.

LaPiere, R. T. 1934. Attitudes versus actions. *Social Forces* 13:230–37.

Larrison, C. R., D. Velez-Ortiz, P. M. Hernandez, L. M. Piedera, and A. Goldberg. 2010. Brokering language and culture: Can ad hoc interpreters fill the language gap at community health centers? *Social Work in Public Health* 25:387–407.

Larson, R. W., M. H. Richards, B. Sims, and J. Dworkin. 2001. How urban African American young adolescents spend their time: Time budgets for locations, activities, and companionship. *American Journal of Community Psychology* 29:565–97.

Lastrucci, C. L. 1963. *The scientific approach*. Cambridge, MA: Schenkman.

Latané, B., and J. M. Darley. 1968. Group inhibition of bystander intervention in emergencies. *Journal of Personality and Social Psychology* 10:215–21.

Lauder, M. 2003. Covert participant observation of a deviant community: Justifying the use of deception. *Journal of Contemporary Religion* 18:185–96.

Laurent, C., K. Seck, N. Coumba, T. Kane, N. Samb, A. Wade, F. Liégeois, S. Mboup, I. Ndoye, and E. Delaporte. 2003. Prevalence of HIV and other sexually transmitted infections, and risk behaviours in unregistered sex workers in Dakar, Senegal. *AIDS* 17:1811–16.

Lavender, J. M., and D. A. Anderson. 2009. Effect of perceived anonymity in assessments of eating disordered behaviors and attitudes context sensitive. *International Journal of Eating Disorders* 42:546–51.

Lavrakas, P. 1993. *Telephone survey methods: Sampling, selection, and supervision*. Newbury Park, CA: Sage.

Lavrakas, P. 2010. Telephone surveys. In *Handbook of survey research*, 2d ed., P. V. Marsden and J. D. Wright, eds., 471–98. Bingley, UK: Emerald Group Publishing.

Lazarsfeld, P. F. 1954. *Mathematical thinking in the social sciences*. Glencoe, IL: The Free Press.

Lazarsfeld, P. F. 1982. *The varied sociology of Paul F. Lazarsfeld: Writing*. New York: Columbia University Press.

Lazarsfeld, P. F. 1993. *On social research and its language*. Ed. by R. Boudon. Chicago: University of Chicago Press.

Lazarsfeld, P. F., A. Pasanella, and M. Rosenberg, eds. 1972. *Continuities in the language of social research*. New York: The Free Press.

Lazarsfeld, P. F., and M. Rosenberg. 1955. *The language of social research: A reader in the methodology of social research*. Glencoe, IL: The Free Press.

Lea, K. L. 1980. Francis Bacon. *Encyclopaedia britannica*, Vol. 2. Chicago: Encyclopaedia Britannica, Inc.

Leach, E. R. 1967. An anthropologist's reflection on a social survey. In *Anthropologists in the field*, D. C. Jongmans and P. C. Gutkind, eds., 75–88. Assen, The Netherlands: Van Gorcum.

Leahy, E. 2005. Alphas and asterisks: The development of statistical significance testing standards in sociology. *Social Forces* 84:1–24.

Le Compte, M. D., and J. Preissle (with R. Tesch). 1993. *Ethnography and qualitative design in educational research*. 2d ed. San Diego: Academic Press.

Ledman, R. E., M. Miller, and D. R. Brown. 1995. Successful women and women's colleges: Is there an intervening variable in the reported relationship? *Sex Roles: A Journal of Research* 33:489–97.

Lee, R. M. 1995. *Dangerous fieldwork*. Thousand Oaks, CA: Sage.

Lee, R. M. 2010. The secret life of focus groups: Robert Merton and the diffusion of a research method. *The American Sociologist* 41:115–41.

Lehner, P. N. 1979. *Handbook of ethological methods*. New York: Garland STPM.

Leith, L. M. 1988. Choking in sports: Are we our own worst enemies? *International Journal of Sport Psychology* 19:59–64.

Lempert, R. 2009. The significance of statistical significance: Two authors restate an incontrovertible caution. Why a book? *Law and Social Inquiry* 34:225–49.

Lenski, G. E., and J. C. Leggett. 1960. Caste, class and deference in the research interview. *American Journal of Sociology* 65:463–67.

Lensvelt-Mulders, G. J. L. M., and H. R. Boeije. 2007. Evaluating compliance with a computer assisted randomized response technique: A qualitative study into the origins of lying and cheating. *Computers in Human Behavior* 23:591–608.

Lensveldt-Mulders, G. J. L. M., J. J. Hox, P. G. M. van der Heuden, and C. J. M. Maas. 2005. Meta-analysis of randomized response research: Thirty-five years of validation. *Sociological Methods and Research* 33:319–48.

Leslie, P. W., R. Dyson-Hudson, E. A. Lowoto, and J. Munyesi. 1999. Appendix 1. Ngisonyoka event calendar. In *Turkana herders of the dry savanna: Ecology and biobehavioral response of nomads to an uncertain environment*, M. A. Little and P. W. Leslie, eds., 375–78. New York: Oxford University Press.

Lester, P. E., and L. K. Bishop. 1997. *Handbook of tests and measurement in education and the social sciences*. Lancaster, PA: Technomic Publishing.

Leunes, A., A. Bourgeois, and R. Grajales. 1996. The effects of two types of exposure on attitudes toward aspects of juvenile delinquency. *The Journal of Social Psychology* 136:699–708.

Levine, D. N. 1995. *Visions of the sociological tradition*. Chicago: University of Chicago Press.

Levine, R. V. 1997. *A geography of time*. New York: Basic Books.

Levine, R. V., and K. Bartlett. 1984. Pace of life, punctuality, and coronary heart disease in six countries. *Journal of Cross-Cultural Psychology* 15:233–55.

Levine, R. V., A. Norenzayan, and K. Philbrick. 2001. Cross-cultural differences in helping strangers. *Journal of Cross-Cultural Psychology* 32:543–60.

Levinson, D., ed. 1978. *A guide to social theory: Worldwide cross-cultural tests*. New Haven, CT: HRAF Press.

Levinson, D. 1990. Bibliography of substantive worldwide cross-cultural studies. *Behavior Science Research* 24:105–40.

Levy, P. S., and S. Lemeshow. 1999. *Sampling of populations: Methods and applications*. 3d ed. New York: Wiley.

Levy, R., and D. Hollan. 1998. Person-centered interviewing and observation. In *Handbook of methods in cultural anthropology*, H. R. Bernard, ed., 333–64. Walnut Creek, CA: AltaMira.

Levy-Storms, L., and S. P. Wallace. 2003. Use of mammography screening among older Samoan women in Los Angeles County: A diffusion network approach. *Social Science and Medicine* 57:987–1000.

Lewin, T. 1986. Cultural consultant: Steve Barnett. Casting an anthropological eye on American consumers. *New York Times*, May 11, p. A6.

Lewis, O. 1961. *The children of Sánchez*. New York: Random House.

Lewis, O. 1965. *La Vida: A Puerto Rican family in the culture of poverty—San Juan and New York*. New York: Random House.

Lewis, R., Jr., and J. Ford-Roberston. 2010. Understanding the occurrence of interracial marriage in the United States through differential assimilation. Journal of Black Studies (published online March 8, 2010 (accessed March 5. 2011).doi:10.1177/0021934709355120.

Liao, P-S, and H-H Tu. 2006. Examining the scalability of sexual permissiveness in Taiwan. *Social Indicators Research* 76:207–32.

Lichtenstein, B. 2004. Caught at the clinic. African American men, stigma, and STI treatment in the Deep South. *Gender and Society* 18:369–88.

Lieber, M. J., and K. C. Fox. 2005. Race and the impact of detention on juvenile justice decision making. *Crime and Delinquency* 51:470–97.

Lieberman, D., and W. W. Dressler. 1977. Bilingualism and cognition of St. Lucian disease terms. *Medical Anthropology* 1:81–110.

Lieske, J. 1993. Regional subcultures of the United States. *The Journal of Politics* 55:888–913.

Lightcap, J. L., J. A. Kurland, and R. L. Burgess. 1982. Child abuse: A test of some predictions from evolutionary theory. *Ethology and Sociobiology* 3:61–67.

Likert, R. 1932. A technique for the measurement of attitudes. *Archives of Psychology* 22:1–55.

Lin, N. 2001. *Social capital: A theory of social structure and action*. New York: Cambridge University Press.

Lin, N., K. Cook, and R. S. Burt, eds. 2001. *Social capital: Theory and research*. New York: Aldine de Gruyter.

Lin, N., W. M. Ensel, R. S. Simeone, and W. Kuo. 1979. Social support, stressful life events, and illness: A model and an empirical test. *Journal of Health and Social Behavior* 2:108–19.

Lin, N., W. M. Ensel, and J. C. Vaughn. 1981. Social resources and strength of ties: Structural factors in occupational status attainment. *American Sociological Review* 46:393–405.

Lin, N., J. C. Vaughn, and W. M. Ensel. 1981. Social resources and occupational status attainment. *Social Forces* 59:1163–81.

Lincoln, Y. S., and E. G. Guba. 1985. *Naturalistic inquiry.* Beverly Hills, CA: Sage.

Lindberg, S. M., J. S. Hyde, J. L. Petersen, and M. C. Linn 2010. New trends in gender and mathematics performance: A meta-analysis. *Psychological Bulletin* 136:1123–35.

Lippa, R. 1991. Some psychometric characteristics of gender diagnosticity measures: Reliability, validity, consistency across domains and relationship to the Big Five. *Journal of Personality and Social Psychology* 61:1000–11.

Livingstone, S., and P. Lunt. 1993. Savers and borrowers: Strategies of personal financial management. *Human Relations* 46:963–85.

Locke, J. 1996 [1690]. *An essay concerning human understanding.* Ed. by K. P. Winkler. Abridged. Indianapolis: Hackett Publishing.

Lockery, S. A., R. E. Dunkle, C. S. Kart, and C. J. Coulton. 1994. Factors contributing to the early rehospitalization of elderly people. *Health and Social Work* 19:182–91.

Lodge, M. 1981. *Magnitude scaling. Quantitative measurement of opinions.* Beverly Hills, CA: Sage.

Loether, H. J., and D. G. McTavish. 1993. *Descriptive and inferential statistics.* Boston: Allyn & Bacon.

Lofland, J. H. 1971. *Analyzing social settings. A guide to qualitative observation and analysis.* Belmont, CA: Wadsworth.

Lofland, J. H. 1976. *Doing social life.* New York: Wiley.

Lofland, J. H., and L. H. Lofland. 1995. *Analyzing social settings.* 3d ed. Belmont, CA: Wadsworth.

Lofland, L. H. 1983. Understanding urban life: The Chicago legacy. *Urban Life* 11:491–511.

Loftus, E. F., and W. Marburger. 1983. Since the eruption of Mt. St. Helens, has anyone beaten you up? Improving the accuracy of retrospective reports with landmark events. *Memory and Cognition* 11:114–20.

Lombard, M., J. Snyder-Duch, and C. Campanella Bracken. 2005. Practical resources for assessing and reporting intercoder reliability in content analysis research projects. http://www.temple.edu/sct/mmc/reliability/ (accessed March 31, 2008).

Longabaugh, R. 1963. A category system for coding interpersonal behavior as social exchange. *Sociometry* 26:319–44.

Lonkila, M. 1995. Grounded theory as an emerging paradigm for computer-assisted qualitative data analysis. In *Computer-aided qualitative data analysis,* U. Kelle, ed., 41–51. Thousand Oaks, CA: Sage.

Loo, R., and K. Thorpe. 1998. Attitudes toward women's roles in society: A replication after 20 years. *Sex Roles* 39:903–12.

Loo, R., and K. Thorpe 2005. Relationships between attitudes towards women's roles in society, and work and life values. *Social Science Journal* 42:367–74.

Lounsbury, F. 1956. A semantic analysis of the Pawnee kinship usage. *Language* 32:158–94.

Love, M. B., and Q. Thurman. 1991. Normative beliefs about factors that affect health and longevity. *Health Education Quarterly* 18:183–94.

Low, S. M., and D. Lawrence-Zúñiga. 2003. *The anthropology of space and place: Locating culture.* Malden, MA: Blackwell.

Lowe, J. W. G., and E. D. Lowe. 1982. Cultural pattern and process: A study of stylistic change in women's dress. *American Anthropologist* 84:521–44.

Lowie, R. H. 1940. Native languages as ethnographic tools. *American Anthropologist* 42:81–89.

Lubbers, M., J. L. Molina, and C. McCarty. 2007. Personal networks and ethnic identifications: The case of migrants in Spain. *International Sociology* 22:720–40.

Lubbers, M. J., J. L Molina, J. Lerner, U. Brandes, J. Avila, and C. McCarty. 2010. Longitudinal analysis of personal networks. The case of Argentinean migrants in Spain, *Social Networks* 32: 91–104.

Ludwick, R., M. E. Wright, R. A. Zeller, D. W. Dowding, W. Lauder, and J. Winchell. 2004. An improved methodology for advancing nursing research: Factorial surveys. *Advances in Nursing Science* 27:224–38.

Lueptow, L. B., S. L. Moser, and B. F. Pendleton. 1990. Gender and response effects in telephone interviews about gender characteristics. *Sex Roles* 22:29–42.

Lugosi, P. 2006. Between overt and covert research: Concealment and disclosure in an ethnographic study of commercial hospitality. *Qualitative Inquiry* 12:541–61.

Lundberg, G. A. 1942. *Social research. A study in methods of gathering data.* 2d ed. New York: Longmans, Green.

Lundberg, G. A. 1964. *Foundations of sociology.* New York: David McKay.

Lyman, S. M. 1989. *The seven deadly sins: Society and evil.* Rev. and expanded ed. Dix Hills, NY: General Hall.

Lynd, R. S., and H. M. Lynd. 1929. *Middletown. A study in contemporary American culture.* New York: Harcourt, Brace & Company.

Lynn, P. 2001. The impact of incentives on response rates to personal interview surveys: Role and perceptions of interviewers. *International Journal of Public Opinion Research* 13:326–36.

Mach, E. 1976. *Knowledge and error: Sketches on the psychology of enquiry.* Ed. by B. McGuiness. Trans. by T. J. McCormack and P. Foulkes. Boston: D. Reidel.

Machamer, P., ed. 1998. *The Cambridge companion to Galileo.* New York: Cambridge University Press.

Madden, J. M., J. D. Quick, and D. Ross-Degnan. 1997. Undercover careseekers: Simulated clients in the study of health provider behavior in developing countries. *Social Science and Medicine* 45:1465–82.

Madrigal, M., and J. Chen. 2008. Moderating and mediating effects of team identification in regard to causal attributions and summary judgments following a game outcome. *Journal of Sport Management* 22:717–33.

Magolda, P. M. 2000. Accessing, waiting, plunging in, wondering, and writing: Retrospective sense-making of fieldwork. *Field Methods* 12:209–34.

Maguire, K. B. 2009. Does mode matter? A comparison of telephone, mail, and in-person treatments in contingent valuation surveys. *Journal of Environmental Management* 90:3528–33.

Mahaffy, K. A. 1996. Cognitive dissonance and its resolution: A study of lesbian Christians. *Journal for the Scientific Study of Religion* 35:392–402.

Maiolo, J. R. M. M. Young, E. W. Glazier, M. A. Downs, and J. S. Petterson. 1994. Pile sorts by phone. *Field Methods* 6:1–2.

Maitra, S., and S. L. Schensul. 2002. Reflecting diversity and complexity in marital sexual relationships in a low-income community in Mumbai. *Culture, Health, and Sexuality* 4:133–51.

Malinowski, B. 1967. *A diary in the strict sense of the term*. New York: Harcourt, Brace & World.

Mandler, J. M. 1984. *Stories, scripts, and scenes: Aspects of schema theory*. Hillsdale, NJ: L. Erlbaum Associates.

Manfreda, K. L., M. Bosniak, J. Berzelak, I. Haas, and V. Vehovar. 2008. Web surveys versus other survey modes. A meta-analysis comparing response rates. *International Journal of Market Research* 50:79–104.

Manning, P. K.1982. Analytic induction. In *Handbook of social science methods*, Vol. 2, *Qualitative methods*, R. Smith and P. K. Manning, eds., 273–302. New York: Harper.

Manning, R., M. Levine, and A. Collins. 2007. The Kitty Genovese murder and the social psychology of helping. The parable of the 38 witnesses. *American Psychologist* 62:555–62.

Mantzavinos, C. 2005. *Naturalistic hermeneutics*. Trans. by D. Arnold. New York: Cambridge University Press.

Manza, J., and C. Brooks. 1998. The gender gap in U.S. presidential elections: When? Why? Implications? *American Journal of Sociology* 103:1235–66.

Manzo, J. 1996. Taking turns and taking sides: Opening scenes from two jury deliberations. *Social Psychology Quarterly* 59:107–25.

Marcus, S. E., S. L. Emont, R. D. Corcoran, G. A. Giovino, J. P. Pierce, M. N. Waller, and R. M. Davis. 1994. Public attitudes about cigarette smoking: Results from the 1990 Smoking Activity Volunteer Executed Survey. *Public Health Reports* 109:125–34.

Marczyk, G., D. DeMatteo, and D. Festinger. 2005. *Essentials of research design and methodology*. Hoboken, NJ: John Wiley and Sons.

Margolis, M. 1984. *Mothers and such*. Berkeley: University of California Press.

Marin, A. 2004. Are respondents more likely to list alters with certain characteristics?: Implications for name generator data. *Social Networks* 26:289–307.

Marin, A., and K. N. Hampton. 2007. Simplifying the personal network name generator: Alternatives to traditional multiple and single name generators. *Field Methods* 19:163–93.

Markie, P. J. 1986. *Descartes' gambit*. Ithaca, NY: Cornell University Press.

Marques, P. R. R. B. Voas, and A. S. Tippetts. 2003. Behavioral measures of drinking: Patterns from the alcohol interlock record. *Addiction* 98 Supplement 2:13–19.

Marquis, G. S. 1990. Fecal contamination of shanty town toddlers in households with non-corralled poultry, Lima, Peru. *American Journal of Public Health* 80:146–50.

Marquis, K. H., and C. Cannell. 1969. *A study of interviewer-respondent interaction in the urban employment survey*. Ann Arbor: Survey Research Center, University of Michigan.

Marriott, B. 1991. The use of social networks by naval officers' wives. Ph.D. dissertation, University of Florida.

Marsden, P. V. 1987. Core discussion networks of Americans. *American Sociological Review* 52:122–31.

Marsden, P. V. 1990. Network data and measurement. *Annual Review of Sociology* 16:435–63.

Marsden, P. V. 2002. Egocentric and sociocentric measures of centrality. *Social Networks* 24:407–22.

Marsden, P. V., and N. Lin, eds. 1982. *Social structure and network analysis*. Beverly Hills, CA: Sage.

Marsh, C., and E. Scarborough. 1990. Testing nine hypotheses about quota sampling. *Journal of the Market Research Society* 32:485–506.

Marsh, V. M., W. M. Mutemi, A. Willetts, K. Bayah, S. Were, A. Ross, and K. Marsh. 2004. Improving malaria home treatment by training drug retailers in rural Kenya. *Tropical Medicine and International Health* 9:451–60.

Martin, J. 1981. Relative deprivation: A theory of distributive injustice for an era of shrinking resources. In *Research in organizational behavior*, Vol. 3, L. L. Cummings and B. M. Staw, eds. 53–107. Greenwich, CT: JAI Press.

Martínez, I. L., and O. Carter-Pokras. 2006. Assessing health concerns and barriers in a heterogeneous Latino community. *Journal of Health Care for the Poor and Underserved* 17:899–909.

Martyn, K. K., and R. F. Belli. 2002. Retrospective data collection using event history calendars. *Nursing Research* 51:270–74.

Marx, H., and D. M. Moss. 2011. Please mind the culture gap: Intercultural development during a teacher education study abroad program. *Journal of Teacher Education* 62:35–47.

Matarazzo, J. 1964. Interviewer mm-humm and interviewee speech duration. *Psychotherapy: Theory, Research and Practice* 1:109–14.

Mathews, H. F. 1992. The directive force of morality tales in a Mexican community. In *Human motives and cultural models*, R. D'Andrade and C. Strauss, eds., 127–62. New York: Cambridge University Press.

Mathiowetz, N., and C. Cannell. 1980. Coding interviewer behavior as a method of evaluating performance. In *Proceedings of the section on survey research methods*, 525–28. Washington, DC: American Statistical Association. http://www.amstat .org/sections/srms/proceedings/papers/1980_108.pdf (acessed March 5, 2011).

Matland, R. E., and D. T. Studlar. 1996. The contagion of women candidates in single-member district and proportional representation electoral systems: Canada and Norway. *Journal of Politics* 58:707–33.

Matsumoto, D., P. Ekman, and A. Fridlund. 1991. Analyzing nonverbal behavior. In *Practical guide to using video in the behavior sciences*, P. W. Dowrick, ed., 153–65. New York: Wiley.

Matt, G. E., and A. M. Navarro. 1997. What meta-analyses have and have not taught us about psychotherapy effects: A review and future directions. *Clinical Psychology Review* 17:1–32.

Mattei, L. R. W. 1998. Gender and power in American legislative discourse. *The Journal of Politics* 60:440–61.

Max-Planck Institute. 2002. The human life table database 2002. http://www.lifetable.de (accessed March 5, 2011).

Maxwell, J. A. 2005. *Qualitative research design: An interactive approach*. 2d ed. Thousand Oaks, CA: Sage.

Maynard, D. W. 1991. Interaction and asymmetry in clinical discourse. *American Journal of Sociology* 97:448–95.

Maynard, D. W., and J. Heritage. 2005. Conversation analysis, doctor-patient interaction, and medical communication. *Medical Education* 39:428–35.

McAllister, I., and R. Moore. 1991. Social distance among Australian ethnic groups. *Social Science Research* 75:95–100.

McCabe, S. E. 2004. Comparison of web and mail surveys in collecting illicit drug use data: A randomized experiment. *Journal of Drug Education* 34:61–72.

McCann, J. J., D. W. Gilley, L. E. Hebert, L. A. Beckett, and D. A. Evans. 1997. Concordance between direct observation and staff rating of behavior in nursing home residents with Alzheimer's disease. *The Journals of Gerontology*, Series B 52:63–74.

McCarroll, J. E., A. S. Blank, and K. Hill. 1995. Working with traumatic material: Effects on Holocaust Memorial Museum staff. *American Journal of Orthopsychiatry* 65:66–75.

McCarty, C. 2002. Measuring Structure in Personal Networks. *Journal of Social Structure*, 3. http://www.cmu.edu/joss/content/articles/volume3/McCarty.html (accessed August 29, 2011).

McCarty, C., and H. R. Bernard. 2003. Social network analysis. In *Encyclopedia of community: From the village to the virtual world*, Vol. 3, K. Christensen and D. Levinson, eds., 1321–25. Thousand Oaks, CA: Sage.

McCarty, C., C. Collins, E. Lavigne, M. Smith, and P. Schoaff. 2011. EgoNet. Sourceforge. http://sourceforge.net/projects/egonet/ (accessed March 5, 2010).

McCarty, C., P. D. Killworth, and J. Rennell. 2007. Impact of methods for reducing respondent burden on personal network structural measures. *Social Networks* 29:300–15.

McCombie, S. C., and J. K. Anarfi. 2002. The influence of sex of interviewer on the results of an AIDS survey in Ghana. *Human Organization* 61:51–57.

McCracken, G. D. 1988. *The long interview*. Newbury Park, CA: Sage.

McCreaddie, M. 2010. Harsh humour: A therapeutic discourse. *Health and Social Care in the Community* 18:633–42.

McDonald, D. D., and R. G. Bridge. 1991. Gender stereotyping and nursing care. *Research in Nursing and Health* 14:373–78.

McDonald, L. 1993. *The early origins of the social sciences*. Montreal: McGill-Queen's University Press.

McDonald, L. 1994. *The women founders of the social sciences*. Ottawa: Carleton University Press.

McFate, M. 2005. Anthropology and counterinsurgency: The strange story of their curious relationship. *Military Review* 85:24–38.

McFaul, M. 2007. Ukraine imports democracy: External influences on the Orange Revolution. *International Security* 32:45–83.

McGarva, A, R., M. Ramsey, and S. A. Shear. 2006. Effects of driver cell-phone use on driver aggression. *Journal of Social Psychology* 146:133–46.

McGilvray, D. 1989. A few selected excerpts from my Sri Lanka diary, 1969–1971. *Field Methods* [Cam Newsletter] 1:6–7.

McGrew, W. C. 1972. *An ethological study of children's behavior*. New York: Academic Press.

McHoul, A., and R. Rapley. 2005. A case of attention-deficit/hyperactivity disorder diagnosis: Sir Karl and Francis B. slug it out on the consulting room floor. *Discourse and Society* 16:419–49.

McKee, H. A., and J. E. Porter. 2009. *The ethics of Internet research: A rhetorical, case-based process*. New York: Peter Lang.

McKeganey, N., and M. Bloor. 1991. Spotting the invisible man. The influence of male gender on fieldwork relations. *British Journal of Sociology* 42:195–210.

McKether, W. L., J. C. Gluesing, and K. Riopelle. 2009. From interviews to social network analysis: An approach for revealing social networks embedded in narrative data. *Field Methods* 21:154–80.

McMahon, E. M., R. Reulbach, P. Corcoran H. S. Keeley, I. J. Perry, and E. Arensman. 2010. Factors associated with deliberate self-harm among Irish adolescents. *Psychological Medicine* 40:1811–19.

McNamara, M. S. 2005. Knowing and doing phenomenology: The implications of the critique of "nursing phenomenology" for a phenomenological inquiry: A discussion paper. *International Journal of Nursing Studies* 42:695–704.

McPherson, M., L. Smith-Lovin, and J. M. Cook. 2001. Birds of a feather: Homophily in social networks. *Annual Review of Sociology* 27:415–44.

McWhirter, B. T., B. Palombi, and C. P. Garbin. 2000. University employees' perceptions of university counseling center services and consultation activities: A multidimensional scaling analysis. *Journal of College Counseling* 3:142–57.

Mead, M. 1939. Native languages as field-work tools. *American Anthropologist* 41:189–205.

Mead, M. 1986. Fieldwork in Pacific islands, 1925–1967. In *Women in the field: Anthropological experiences*, 2d ed., P. Golde, ed., 293–332. Berkeley: University of California Press.

Medley, D. M., and H. E. Mitzel. 1958. A technique for measuring classroom behavior. *Journal of Educational Psychology* 49:86–92.

Meh, C. C. 1996. SOCRATES streamlines lesson observations. *Educational Leadership* 53:76–78.

Mehta, R., and R. W. Belk. 1991. Artifacts, identity, and transition: Favorite possessions of Indians and Indian immigrants to the United States. *Journal of Consumer Research* 17:398–411.

Mele, M. M., and B. M. Bello. 2007. Coaxing and coercion in roadblock encounters on Nigerian highways. *Discourse and Society* 18:437–52.

Menz, F., and A. Al-Roubaie. 2008. Interruptions, status and gender in medical interviews: The harder you brake, the longer it takes. *Discourse and Society* 19:645–66.

Merli, M. G., and A. E. Rafferty. 2000. Are births underreported in rural China? Manipulation of statistical records in response to China's population policies. *Demography* 37:109–26.

Mertens, D. M. 2010. *Research and evaluation in education and psychology: Integrating diversity with qualitative, quantitative, and mixed methods.* 3d. ed. Thousand Oaks, CA: Sage.

Mertens, D. M., and P. E. Ginsberg, eds. 2009. *The handbook of social research ethics.* Thousand Oaks, CA: Sage.

Merton, R. K. 1938. Science and the social order. *Philosophy of Science* 5:323–37.

Merton, R. K. 1970. *Science technology and society in seventeenth century England.* New York: Harper and Row.

Merton, R. K. 1973. *The sociology of science: Theoretical and empirical investigations.* Chicago: University of Chicago Press.

Merton, R. K. 1987. The focused interview and focus groups. *Public Opinion Quarterly* 51:550–66.

Merton, R. K., M. Fiske, and P. L. Kendall. 1956. *The focused interview: A manual of problems and procedures.* Glencoe, IL: The Free Press.

Merton, R. K., and P. F. Lazarsfeld. 1950. *Continuities in social research: Studies in the scope and method of "The American soldier."* Glencoe, IL: The Free Press.

Messerschmidt, D. A., ed. 1981. *Anthropologists at home in North America: Methods and issues in the study of one's own society.* New York: Cambridge University Press.

Mestdag, I. 2005. Where has family time gone? In search of joint family activities and the role of the family meal in 1966 and 1999. *Journal of Family History* 30:304–23.

Meyerhoff, B. 1989. So what do you want from us here? In *In the field: Readings on the field research experience,* C. D. Smith and W. Kornblum, eds., 83–90. New York: Praeger.

Mhurchu, C. N., R. Maddison, Y. Jiang, A. Jull, H. Prapavessis, and A. Rodgers. 2008. Couch potatoes to jumping beans: A pilot study of the effect of active video games on physical activity in children. *International Journal of Behavioral Nutrition and Physical Activity* 5:8 doi:10.1186/1479-5868-5-8.

Michaelson, W. 1985. *From sun to sun. Daily obligations and community structure in the lives of employed women and their families.* Totowa, NJ: Rowman & Allanheld.

Middlemist, R. D., E. S. Knowles, and C. F. Matter. 1976. Personal space invasion in the lavatory: Suggestive evidence for arousal. *Journal of Personality and Social Psychology* 33:541–46.

Middlemist, R. D., E. S. Knowles, and C. F. Matter. 1977. What to do and what to report: A reply to Koocher. *Journal of Personality and Social Psychology* 35:122–24.

Mignone, J., G. M. Hiremath, V. Sabnis, Laxmi, J., S. Halli, J. O'Neil, B. M. Ramesh, J. Blanchard, and S. Moses. 2009. Use of rapid ethnographic methodology to develop a village-level rapid assessment tool predictive of HIV infection in rural India. *The International Journal of Qualitative Methods* 8:68–83.

Miles, M. B. 1983. *Qualitative data as an attractive nuisance: The problem of analysis.* Beverly Hills, CA: Sage.

Miles, M. B., and A. M. Huberman. 1994. *Qualitative data analysis.* 2d ed. Thousand Oaks, CA: Sage.

Mileski, M. 1971. Courtroom encounters: An observation study of a lower criminal court. *Law and Society Review* 5:473–538.

Milgram, S. 1963. Behavioral study of obedience. *Journal of Abnormal and Social Psychology* 67:371–78.

Milgram, S. 1965. Some conditions of obedience and disobedience to authority. *Human Relations* 18:57–76.

Milgram, S. 1967. The small-world problem. *Psychology Today* 1:60–67.

Milgram, S. 1969. The lost-letter technique. *Psychology Today* 3:30–33, 66–68.

Milgram, S. 1974. *Obedience to authority.* New York: Harper & Row.

Milgram, S., L. Mann, and S. Harter. 1965. The lost-letter technique: A tool for social research. *Public Opinion Quarterly* 29:437–38.

Mill, J. S. 1866. *Auguste Comte and positivism.* Philadelphia: Lippincott.

Mill, J. S. 1869. *The subjection of women.* New York: D. Appleton & Co.

Mill, J. S. 1898. *A system of logic, ratiocinative and inductive. Being a connected view of the principles of evidence and the methods of scientific investigation.* New York: Harper & Brothers.

Miller, D. C., and N. J. Salkind. 2002. *Handbook of research design and social measurement.* 6th ed. Newbury Park, CA: Sage.

Miller, F. G., J. P. Gluck, and D. Wendler. 2008. Debriefing and accountability in deceptive research. *Kennedy Institute of Ethics Journal* 18:235–51.

Miller, G. A. 1956. The magical number seven, plus or minus two: Some limits on our capacity for processing information. *Psychological Review* 63:81–97.

Miller, J. L., P. H. Rossi, and J. E. Simpson. 1991. Felony punishments: A factorial survey of perceived justice in criminal sentencing. *Journal of Criminal Law and Criminology* 82:396–422.

Miller, K. W., L. B. Wilder, F. A. Stillman, and D. M. Becker. 1997. The feasibility of a street-intercept survey method in an African-American community. *The American Journal of Public Health* 87:655–58.

Miller, L. L. 1997. Not just weapons of the weak: Gender harassment as a form of protest for Army men. *Social Psychology Quarterly* 60:32–51.

Miller, M. L., J. Kaneko, P. Bartram, J. Marks, and D. D. Brewer. 2004. Cultural consensus analysis and environmental anthropology: Yellowfin tuna fishery management in Hawaii. *Cross-Cultural Research* 38:289–314.

Milliman, R. 1986. The influence of background music on the behavior of restaurant patrons. *Journal of Consumer Research* 13:286–89.

Mills, A. J., E. Wiebe, and G. Durepos, eds. 2009. *Encyclopedia of case study research.* Thousand Oaks, CA: Sage.

Minadeo, R. 1969. *The lyre of science: Form and meaning in Lucretius' De Rerum Natura.* Detroit: Wayne State University Press.

Mishra, S. I., P. H. Luce, and C. R. Baquet. 2009. Increasing Pap smear utilization among Samoan women: Results from a community based participatory randomized trial. *Journal of Health Care for the Poor and Underserved* 20 (supplement to issue 2):85–101.

Mitchell, C., ed. 1969. *Social networks in urban situations: Analyses of personal relationships in central African towns.* Manchester, UK: Manchester University Press.

Mitchell, R. 1965. Survey materials collected in the developing countries: Sampling, measurement, and interviewing obstacles to intra- and international comparisons. *International Social Science Journal* 17:665–85.

Miyazaki, A. D., and K. A. Taylor. 2008. Researcher interaction biases and business ethics research: Respondent reactions to researcher characteristics. *Journal of Business Ethics* 81:779–95.

Mizes, J. S., E. L. Fleece, and C. Ross. 1984. Incentives for increasing return rates: Magnitude levels, response bias, and format. *Public Opinion Quarterly* 48:794–800.

Mondak, J. J., and B. C. Davis. 2001. Asked and answered: Knowledge levels when we will not take "don't know" for an answer. *Political Behavior* 23:199–224.

Montbriand, M. J. 1994. Decision heuristics of patients with cancer: Alternative and biomedical choices. Ph.D. dissertation, University of Saskatchewan.

Montgomery, P., and P. H. Bailey. 2007. Field notes and theoretical memos in grounded theory. *Western Journal of Nursing Research* 29:65–79.

Montiel, C. J., and K. Boehnke. 2000. Preferred attributes of effective conflict resolvers in seven societies: Culture, development level, and gender differences. *Journal of Applied Social Psychology* 30:1071–79.

Mooney, C. Z., and M-H. Lee. 1995. Legislating morality in the American states: The case of pre-Roe abortion regulation reform. *American Journal of Political Science* 39:599–627.

Moore, C. C., A. K. Romney, T.-L. Hsia, and C. D. Rusch. 1999. The universality of the semantic structure of emotion terms: Methods for the study of inter- and intra-cultural variability. *American Anthropologist* 101:529–46.

Moore, R. S., J. P. Lee, S. E. Martin, M. Todd, and C. Bong. 2099. Correlates of persistent smoking in bars subject to smokefree workplace policy. *International Journal of Environmental Research and Public Health* 6:1341–57.

Morgan, D. L. 1989. Adjusting to widowhood: Do social networks make it easier? *The Gerontologist* 29:101–107.

Morgan, D. L., and R. Krueger. 1998. *The focus group kit,* 6 vols. Thousand Oaks, CA: Sage.

Morgan, L. H. 1877. *Ancient society. Or researches in the lines of human progress from savagery, through barbarism, to civilization.* New York: H. Holt.

Morgan, L. H. 1997 [1870]. *Systems of consanguinity and affinity of the human family.* Lincoln: University of Nebraska Press.

Morgan, M. G., B. Fischoff, A. Bostrom, and C. J. Atman. 2002. *Risk communication: A mental models approach.* New York: Cambridge University Press.

Morin, R. 2004. Don't ask me: As fewer cooperate on polls, criticism and questions mount. *The Washington Post,* October 28, p. C01.

Morine-Dershimer, G. 2006. Classroom management and classroom discourse. In *Handbook of classroom management: Research, practice, and contemporary issues,* C. M. Evertson and C. S. Weinstein, eds., 127–56. Mahwah, NJ: L. Erlbaum Associates.

Morokoff, P. J., K. Quina, L. L. Harlow, L. Whitmire, D. M. Grimley, P. R. Gibson, and G. J. Burkholder. 1997. Sexual Assertiveness Scale (SAS) for women: Development and validation. *Journal of Personality and Social Psychology* 73:790–804.

Morris, M. 1993. Telling tales explain the discrepancy in sexual partner reports. *Nature* 365:437–40.

Morris, M. 1996. Culture, structure, and the underclass. In *Myths about the powerless: Contesting social inequalities,* M. B. Lykes, A. Banuazizi, R. Liem, and M. Morris, eds., 34–49. Philadelphia: Temple University Press.

Morris, N. A., and L. A. Slocum. 2010. The validity of self-reported prevalence, frequency, and timing of arrest: An evaluation of data collected using a life event calendar. *Journal of Research in Crime and Delinquency* 47:210–40.

Morrison, F. J., E. M. Griffith, and J. A. Frazier. 1996. Schooling and the 5 to 7 shift: A natural experiment. In *The five to seven year shift: The age of reason and responsibility,* A. J. Sameroff and M. M. Haith, eds., 161–86. Chicago: University of Chicago Press.

Morrow, K. M., S. Vargas, R. K. Rosen, A. L. Christensen, L. Salomon, L. Shulman, C. Barroso, and J. L. Fava. 2007. The utility of non-proportional quota sampling for recruiting at-risk women for microbicide research. *AIDS and Behavior* 11:586–95.

Morse, J. M., ed. 1994. *Critical issues in qualitative research methods.* London: Sage.

Moustakas, C. E. 1994. *Phenomenological research methods.* Thousand Oaks, CA: Sage.

Mugavin, M. E. 2008. Multidimensional scaling: A brief overview. *Nursing Research* 57:64–68.

Mulcahy, F. D., and S. Herbert. 1990. Women's formal evening wear, 1937–1982. *Journal of Social Behavior and Personality* 5:481–96.

Mumford, M., S. Connelly, S. T. Murphy, L. D. Davenport, A. L. Antes, R. P. Brown, J. H. Hill, and E. P. Waples. 2009. Field and experience influences on ethical decision making in the sciences. *Ethics and Behavior* 19:263–89.

Murdock, G. P., C. S. Ford, A. E. Hudson, R. Kennedy, L. W. Simmons, and J. W. Whiting. 2004 [1961]. *Outline of cultural materials.* 5th rev. ed., modified in 2004. New Haven, CT: Human Relations Area Files, Inc.

Murphy, G., L. B. Murphy, and T. M. Newcomb. 1937. *Experimental social psychology.* New York: Harper & Brothers.

Murphy, K. R., and B. Myors. 1998. *Statistical power analysis: A simple and general model for traditional and modern hypothesis tests.* Mahwah, NJ: L. Erlbaum Associates.

Murray, T. 1980. Learning to deceive. *The Hastings Center Report* 10:11–14.

Murtaugh, M. 1985. The practice of arithmetic by American grocery shoppers. *Anthropology and Education Quarterly* 16:186–92.

Mustonen, A., and L. Pulkkinen. 1997. Television violence: A development of a coding scheme. *Journal of Broadcasting and Electronic Media* 41:168–89.

Myers, S. 2010. A multiple regression analysis of six factors concerning school district demographics and superintendent tenure and experience in 2007–2008 schools relative to student achievement on the third grade Kansas reading assessments. Ph.D. dissertation, Kansas State University.

Nachman, S. R. 1984. Lies my informants told me. *Journal of Anthropological Research* 40: 536–55.

Nachmias, D., and C. Nachmias. 1976. *Research methods in the social sciences.* New York: St. Martin's Press.

Nagata, J. 1974. What is Malay? Situational selection of ethnic identity in a plural society. *American Ethnologist* 1:331–50.

Nam, C. B., and M. Boyd. 2004. Occupational status in 2000—Over a century of census-based measurement. *Population Research and Policy Review* 23:327–58.

Nam, C. S., J. B. Lyons, H-S Hwang, and S. Kim. 2009. The process of team communication in multi-cultural contexts: An empirical study using Bales' interaction process analysis (IPA). *International Journal of Industrial Ergonomics* 39:771–82.

Narayan, K. 1993. How native is a "native" anthropologist? *American Anthropologist* 95:671–86.

Narayan, S., and J. A. Krosnick. 1996. Education moderates some response effects in attitude measurement. *Public Opinion Quarterly* 60:58–88.

Nardi, P. M. 2003. *Doing survey research: A guide to quantitative methods.* Boston: Allyn and Bacon.

Naroll, R. 1962. *Data quality control.* New York: The Free Press.

National Cancer Institute. 1997. *Risks of cigarette smoking for women on the rise.* NIH news release. http://www.nih.gov/news/pr/apr97/nci-23.htm (accessed March 8, 2010).

Nave, A. 1997. Conducting a survey in a newly developed country. *Cultural Anthropology Methods Journal* 9:8–12.

Nederhof, A. J. 1985. A survey on suicide: Using a mail survey to study a highly threatening topic. *Quality and Quantity* 19:293–302.

Negrón, R. 2011. *Ethnic Identification Among Urban Latinos: Language and Flexibility.* El Paso, TX: LFB Scholarly Publishing LLC.

Negrón, R. 2012. Audio recording everyday talk. *Field Methods* (in press).

Netemeyer, R. G., W. O. Bearden, and S. Sughash. 2003. *Scaling procedures: Issues and applications.* Thousand Oaks, CA: Sage.

Neuendorf, K. A. 2002. *The content analysis guidebook.* Thousand Oaks, CA: Sage.

Neurath, O. 1973. *Empiricism and sociology.* Ed. by M. Neurath and R. S. Cohen. Trans. by P. Foulkes and M. Neurath. Dordrecht, The Netherlands: Reidel.

Nevile, M. 2007. Talking without overlap in the airline cockpit: Precision timing at work. *Text and Talk* 27:225–49.

Newman, K. S. 1986. Symbolic dialects and generations of women: Variations in the meaning of post-divorce downward mobility. *American Ethnologist* 13: 230–52.

Newsham, G., J. Brand, C. Donnelly, J. Veitch, M. Aries, and K. Charles. 2009. Linking indoor environment conditions to job satisfaction: A feld study. *Building Research and Information* 37:129–47.

Nicks, S. D., J. H. Korn, and T. Mainieri. 1997. The rise and fall of deception in social psychology and personality research, 1921 to 1994. *Ethics and Behavior* 7:69–77.

Niebel, B. W. 1982. *Motion and time study.* 7th ed. Homewood, IL: Irwin.

Niemi, I. 1993. Systematic error in behavioural measurement: Comparing results from interview and time budget studies. *Social Indicators Research* 30:229–44.

Nightingale, F. 1871. *Introductory notes on lying-in institutions.* London: Longmans, Green.

Nisbet, R. A. 1980. *The history of the idea of progress.* New York: Basic Books.

Nishida, H. 1999. Cognitive approach to intercultural communication based on schema theory. *International Journal of Intercultural Relations* 5:753–77.

Nolan, J. M., and G. W. Ryan. 2000. Fear and loathing at the cineplex: Gender differences in descriptions and perceptions of slasher films. *Sex Roles* 42:39–56.

Nordstrom, C., and A. C. G. M. Robben, eds. 1995. *Fieldwork under fire: Contemporary studies of violence and survival.* Berkeley: University of California Press.

Norman, G. 2010. Likert scales, levels of measurement and the "laws" of statistics. *Advances in Health Science Education* 15:625–32.

Norrick, N. R. 2010. Laughter before the punch line during the performance of narrative jokes in conversation. *Text and Talk* 30:75–95.

Nunnally, J. C. 1978. *Introduction to psychological measurement*. Rev. ed. New York: McGraw-Hill.

Nunnally, J. C., and I. H. Bernstein. 1994. *Psychometric theory*. 3d ed. New York: McGraw-Hill.

Nyamongo, I. K. 1998. Lay people's responses to illness: An ethnographic study of anti-malaria behavior among the Abagusii of southwestern Kenya. Ph.D. dissertation, University of Florida.

Oakes, J. M., and P. H. Rossi. 2003. The measurement of SES in health research: Current practice and steps toward a new approach. *Social Science and Medicine* 56:769–84.

Oboler, R. S. 1985. *Women, power, and economic change: The Nandi of Kenya*. Stanford, CA: Stanford University Press.

O'Brian, R. 1998. Stationary spot behavior checks and extended observation: Adapting time allocation to marketplaces. *Field Methods* 10:57–59.

O'Brien, E. M., M. C. Black, L. R. Carley-Baxter, and T. R. Simon. 2006. Sensitive topics, survey non-response, and considerations for interviewer training. *American Journal of Preventive Medicine* 31:419–26.

O'Brien, T. O., and V. Dugdale. 1978. Questionnaire administration by computer. *Journal of the Market Research Society* 20:228–37.

Ochs, E. 1979. Transcription as theory. In *Developmental pragmatics*, E. Ochs and B. B. Schieffelin, eds., 43–72. New York: Academic Press.

O'Donnell, D. A., W. C. Roberts, and M. E. Schwab-Stone. 2011. Community violence exposure and post-traumatic stress reactions among Gambian youth: The moderating role of positive school climate. *Social Psychiatry and Psychiatric Epidemiology* 46:59–67.

Ogata, Y., Y. Kobayashi, T. Fukuda, K. Mori, M. Hashimoto, and K. Otosaka. 2004. Measuring relative work values for home care nursing services in Japan. *Nursing Research* 53:145–53.

Ogburn, W. F. 1930. The folk-ways of a scientific sociology. *Publication of the American Sociological Society* 25:1–10.

Ogilvie, D. M., P. J. Stone, and E. S. Schneidman. 1966. Some characteristics of genuine versus simulated suicide notes. In *The General Inquirer: A computer approach to content analysis*, P. J. Stone et al., eds., 527–35. Cambridge, MA: MIT Press.

O'Halloran, S. 2005. Symmetry in interaction in meetings of Alcoholics Anonymous: The management of conflict. *Discourse and Society* 16:535–60.

Ohanian, R. 1990. Construction and validation of a scale to measure celebrity endorsers' perceived expertise, trustworthiness, and attractiveness. *Journal of Advertising* 19:39–52.

Okamoto, D. G., L. S. Rashotte, and L. Smith-Lovin 2002. Measuring interruption: Syntactic and contextual methods of coding conversation. *Social Psychology Quarterly* 65:38–55.

Okamura, J. Y. 1981. Situational ethnicity. *Ethnic and Racial Studies* 4:452–65.

Oliffe, J. L., and J. L. Bottorff. 2007. Further than the eye can see? Photo elicitation and research with men. *Qualitative Health Research* 17:850–58.

Olson, K., and A. Peytchev. 2007. Effect of interviewer experience on interview pace and interviewer attitudes. *Public Opinion Quarterly* 71:273–86.

Olson, M. E., D. Diekema, B.A. Elliott, and C. M. Renier. 2010. Impact of income and income inequality on infant health outcomes in the United States. *Pediatrics* 126:1165–73.

Olson, W. C. 1929. *The measurement of nervous habits in normal children*. Minneapolis: University of Minnesota Press.

Olszewski, B., D. Macey, and L. Lindstrom. 2006. The practical work of <coding>: An ethnomethodological inquiry. *Human Studies* 29:363–80.

Onwuegbuzie, A. J., and K. M. Collins. 2007. A typology of mixed methods sampling designs in social science research. *Qualitative Report* 12:281–316.

Orlando, R. A. 1992. Boelen may know Holland, Boelen may know Barzini, but Boelen "doesn't know diddle about the North End!" *Journal of Contemporary Ethnography* 21:69–79.

Ormiston, G. L., and A. D. Schrift, eds. 1990. *The hermeneutic tradition: From Ast to Ricoeur*. Albany: State University of New York Press.

Orth, B., and B. Wegener. 1983. Scaling occupational prestige by magnitude estimation and category rating methods: A comparison with the sensory domain. *European Journal of Social Psychology* 13:417–31.

Ortmann, A., and R. Hertwig. 1997. Is deception acceptable? *American Psychologist* 52:746–47.

Ortmann, A., and R. Hertwig 1998. The question remains: Is deception acceptable? *American Psychologist* 53:806–807.

Osgood, C. E., D. J. Suci, and P. H. Tannenbaum. 1957. *The measurement of meaning*. Urbana: University of Illinois Press.

Oskenberg, L., L. Coleman, and C. F. Cannell. 1986. Interviewers' voices and refusal rates in telephone surveys. *Public Opinion Quarterly* 50:97–111.

Ostrander, S. A. 1980. Upper-class women: Class consciousness as conduct and meaning. In *Power structure research*, G. W. Domhoff, ed., 73–96. Beverly Hills, CA: Sage.

Otani, H., and H. L. Whiteman. 1994. Cued recall hypermnesia is not an artifact of response bias. *American Journal of Psychology* 107:401–21.

Otta, E. P. R. Santana, L. M. Lafraia, R. L. Hoshino, R. P. Texeira, and S. L. Vallochi. 1996. Musa latrinalis: Gender differences in restroom graffiti. *Psychological Reports* 78:871–80.

Otterbach, S., and A. Sousa-Poza. 2010. How accurate are German work-time data? A comparison of time-diary reports and stylized estimates. *Social Indicators Research* 97:325–39.

Otterbein, K. 1969. Basic steps in conducting a cross-cultural study. *Behavior Science Notes* 4:221–36.

Owen, C. A., H. C. Eisner, and T. R. McFaul. 1981. A half-century of social distance research: National replication of the Bogardus studies. *Sociology and Social Research* 66:80–98.

Owusu, M. 1978. Ethnography of Africa: The usefulness of the useless. *American Anthropologist* 80:310–34.

Oxford, J., M. Johnson, and B. Purser. 2004. Drinking in second generation Black and Asian communities in the English Midlands. *Addiction Research and Theory* 12:11–30.

Ozkan, T., and T. Lajunen 2005. Masculinity, femininity, and the Bem Sex Role Inventory in Turkey. *Sex Roles* 52:103–10.

Packer, D. J. 2008. Identifying systematic disobedience in Milgram's obedience experiments: A meta-analytic review. *Perspectives on Psychological Science* 3: 301–304.

Padgett, J. F., and C. K. Ansell. 1993. Robust action and the rise of the Medici, 1400–1434. *American Journal of Sociology* 98:1259–319.

Page, S. 1997. An unobtrusive measure of racial behavior in a university cafeteria. *Journal of Applied Social Psychology* 27:2172–76.

Paik, H., and G. Comstock. 1994. The effects of television violence on antisocial behavior: A meta-analysis. *Communication Research* 21:516–46.

Palys, T. 2008. Purposive sampling. In *The SAGE encyclopedia of qualitative research methods*, Vol. 2, L. M. Given, ed., 697–98. Thousand Oaks, CA: Sage.

Pan, M. L. 2008. *Preparing literature reviews: Qualitative and quantitative approaches*. Glendale, CA: Pyrczak Publishers.

Paolisso, M. 2007. Taste the traditions: Crabs, crab cakes, and the Chesapeake Bay blue crab fishery. *American Anthropologist* 109:654–55.

Papadopoulos, F. C., E. Petridou, C. E. Frangakis, T. Farmakakis, H. Moller, and G. Rider. 2004. Switching to the euro: Still hard to swallow. *Archives of Disease in Childhood* 89:382–83.

Papineau, D. 1996. Philosophy of science. In *The Blackwell companion to philosophy*, N. Bunnin and E. P. Tsui-James, eds., 290–324. Oxford, UK: Blackwell.

Parekh, R., and E. V. Beresin. 2001. Looking for love? Take a cross-cultural walk through the personals. *Academic Psychiatry* 25:223–33.

Park, R. E., E. W. Burgess, and R. D. McKenzie. 1925. *The city*. Chicago: University of Chicago Press.

Parr, M. G., and B. D. Lashua. 2004. What is leisure. The perceptions of recreation practitioners and others. *Leisure Sciences* 26:1–17.

Parrillo, V. N., and C. Donoghue 2005. Updating the Bogardus social distance studies: A new national survey. *The Social Science Journal* 42:257–71.

Parsons, T. 1951. *The social system*. Glencoe, IL: The Free Press.

Pasero, C. L. 1997. Using the faces scale to assess pain. *American Journal of Nursing* 97:19–20.

Passin, H. 1951. The development of public opinion research in Japan. *International Journal of Opinion and Attitude Research* 5:20–30.

Paterson, B. L., D. Gregory, and S. Thorne. 1999. A protocol for researcher safety. *Qualitative Health Research* 9:259–69.

Pausewang, S. 1973. *Methods and concepts of social research in a rural and developing society*. Munich: Weltforum Verlag.

Pawlowski, B., and G. Jasienska. 2008. Women's body morphology and preferences for sexual partners' characteristics. *Evolution and Human Behavior* 29:19–25.

Payne, S. L. 1951. *The art of asking questions*. Princeton, NJ: Princeton University Press.

Pearce, J. M., M. Ainley, and S. Howard. 2005. The ebb and flow of online learning. *Computers in Human Behavior* 21:745–71.

Pearson, J. 1990. Estimation of energy expenditure in Western Samoa, American Samoa, and Honolulu by recall interviews and direct observation. *American Journal of Human Biology* 2:313–26.

Pedhazur, E. J. 1997. *Multiple regression in behavioral research: Explanation and prediction*. 3d ed. Fort Worth, TX: Harcourt Brace College Publishers.

Peirano, M. G. S. 1998. When anthropology is at home: The different contexts of a single discipline. *Annual Review of Anthropology* 27:105–28.

Pellegrini, A. D. 1996. *Observing children in their natural worlds: A methodological primer*. Mahwah, NJ: L. Erlbaum Associates.

Pelto, P. J., and G. H. Pelto. 1975. Intracultural diversity: Some theoretical issues. *American Ethnologist* 2:1–18.

Pelto, P. J., and G. H. Pelto. 1978. *Anthropological research: The structure of inquiry*. Cambridge: Cambridge University Press.

Peng, T. K. 2006. Construct validation of the Bem Sex Role Inventory in Taiwan. *Sex Roles* 55:843–51.

Perchonock, N., and O. Werner. 1969. Navajo systems of classification: Some implications of food. *Ethnology* 8:229–42.

Pericliev, V., and R. E. Valdes-Perez. 1998. Automatic componential analysis of kinship semantics with a proposed structural solution to the problem of multiple models. *Anthropological Linguistics* 40:272–317.

Peters, D. L., and E. J. McCormick. 1966. Comparative reliability of numerically anchored versus job-task anchored rating scales. *Journal of Applied Psychology* 50:92–96.

Peterson, L., V. Johannsson, and S. G. Carlsson. 1996. Computerized testing in a hospital setting: Psychometric and psychological effects. *Computers in Human Behavior* 12:339–50.

Peterson, M., and B. M. Johnstone. 1995. The Atwood Hall health promotion program, Federal Medical Center, Lexington, Ky.: Effects on drug-involved federal offenders. *Journal of Substance Abuse Treatment* 12:43–48.

Peterson, R. A. 1984. Asking the age question. *Public Opinion Quarterly* 48:379–83.

Petty, Sir W. 1899 [1690]. *The economic writings of Sir William Petty*. Ed. by C. H. Hull. Cambridge: The University Press.

Philipp, S. F. 1998. Race and gender differences in adolescent peer group approval of leisure activities. *Journal of Leisure Research* 30:214–32.

Phillips, D. L., and K. J. Clancy. 1972. Effects of "social desirability" in survey studies. *American Journal of Sociology* 77:921–40.

Phillips, H. P. 1959. Problems of translation and meaning in field work. *Human Organization* 18:184–92.

Phua, V. C. 2002. Sex and sexuality in men's personal advertisements. *Men and Masculinities* 5:178–91.

Piaget, J. 1952. *The origins of intelligence in children.* New York: W. W. Norton and Co.

Piliavin, I. M., J. Rodin, and J. A. Piliavin. 1969. Good samaritanism: An underground phenomenon? *Journal of Personality and Social Psychology* 13: 289–99.

Pillsworth, E. G. 2008. Mate preferences among the Shuar of Ecuador: Trait rankings and peer evaluations. *Evolution and Human Behavior* 29: 256–67.

Pinker, S. 2003. *The blank slate: The modern denial of human nature.* London: Penguin.

Pinkley, R. L., M. J. Gelfand, and L. Duan. 2005. Where, when and how: The use of multidimensional scaling methods in the study of negotiation and social conflict. *International Negotiation* 10:79–96.

Pitts, F. 1979. The medieval river trade network of Russia revisited. *Social Networks* 1:285–92.

Plato. N.d. *The Republic.* Trans. by B. Jowett. *The Internet Classic Archive.* http://classics.mit.edu/Plato/republic.2.i.html (accessed August 20, 2010).

Platt, J. 1994. The Chicago School and firsthand data. *History of the Human Sciences* 7:57–80.

Plattner, S. 1982. Economic decision making in a public marketplace. *American Ethnologist* 9:399–420.

Poggie, J. J. 1972. Toward quality control in key informant data. *Human Organization* 31:23–30.

Pokorny, A. D., B. A. Miller, and M. B. Kaplan. 1972. The brief MAST: A shortened version of the Michigan Alcoholic Screening Test. *American Journal of Psychiatry* 129:342–45.

Pollnac, R. B., C. Gersuny, and J. J. Poggie. 1975. Economic gratification patterns of fishermen and mill workers in New England. *Human Organization* 34:1–7.

Poole, M. S., and J. P. Folger. 1981. A method for establishing the representational validity of interaction coding systems: Do we see what they see? *Human Communication Research* 8:26–42.

Poomsrikaew, O., C. J. Ryan, and J. Zerwic. 2010. Knowledge of heart attack symptoms and risk factors among native Thais: A street-intercept survey method. *International Journal of Nursing Practice* 16:492–98.

Popper, K. R. 1966. *The open society and its enemies.* 5th ed. Princeton, NJ: Princeton University Press.

Popper, K. R. 1968. *The logic of scientific discovery.* 2d ed. New York: Harper & Row.

Popping, R., and C. W. Roberts. 2009. Coding issues in modality analysis. *Field Methods* 1:244–64.

Porter, R., ed. 2003–2008. *The Cambridge history of science,* 8 vols. New York: Cambridge University Press.

Porter, T. M., and D. Ross, eds. 2003. *The modern social sciences.* Vol 7, *The Cambridge history of sciences.* New York: Cambridge University Press.

Potdar, R., and M. A. Koenig. 2005. Does audio-CASI improve reports of risky behavior? Evidence from a randomized field trial among young urban men in India. *Studies in Family Planning* 36:107–16.

Poulin, M. 2010. Reporting on first sexual experience: The importance of interviewer-respondent interaction. *Demographic Research* 22 (article 11). FOI:10.4054/DemRes.2010.22.11.

Poveda, D. 2002. Quico's story: An ethnopoetic analysis of a Gypsy boy's narratives at school. *Text* 22: 269–300.

Powdermaker, H. 1966. *Stranger and friend: The way of an anthropologist.* New York: Norton.

Powers, W. R. 2005. *Transcription techniques for the spoken word.* Lanham, MD: AltaMira.

Pozzulo, J. D., J. Dempsey, E. Maeder, and L. Allen. 2010. The effects of victim gender, defendant gender, and defendant age on juror decision making. *Criminal Justice and Behavior* 37:47–63.

Prebisch, R. 1984. *Power relations and market laws.* Notre Dame, IN: The Helen Kellogg Institute for International Studies, University of Notre Dame.

Prebisch, R. 1994. Latin American periphery in the global system of capitalism. In *Paradigms in economic development: Classic perspectives, critiques, and reflections,* R. Kanth, ed., 165–76. Armonk, NY: M. E. Sharpe.

Press, J. E., and E. Townsley. 1998. Wives' and husbands' housework reporting: Gender, class, and social desirability. *Gender and Society* 12:188–218.

Presser, S., and L. Stinson. 1998. Data collection mode and social desirability bias in self-reported religious attendance. *American Sociological Review* 63: 137–45.

Presser, S., and S. Zhao. 1992. Attributes of questions and interviewers as correlates of interviewing performance. *Public Opinion Quarterly* 56:236–40.

Prewett-Livingston, A. J., H. S. Feild, J. G. Veres III, and P. M. Lewis. 1996. Effects of race on interview ratings in a situational panel interview. *Journal of Applied Psychology* 2:178–86.

Price, D. H. 2003. Subtle means and enticing carrots. The impact of funding on American Cold War anthropology. *Critique of Anthropology* 23:373–41.

Price, L. 1987. Ecuadorian illness stories: Cultural knowledge in natural discourse. In *Cultural models in language and thought,* D. Holland and N. Quinn, eds., 313–42. Cambridge: Cambridge University Press.

Pridemore, W. A., M. B. Chamlin, and J. K. Cochran. 2007. An interrupted time-series analysis of Durkeim's social deregulation thesis: The case of the Russian Federation. *Justice Quarterly* 24:272–90.

Pruchno, R. R. A., J. E. Brill, Y. Shands, J. R. Gordon, M. W. Genderson, M. Rose, and F. Cartwright. 2008. Convenience samples and caregiving research: How generalizable are the findings? *Gerontologist* 48:820–27.

Psathas, G., ed. 1979. *Everyday language.* New York: Irvington Publishers.

Psathas, G. 1995. *Conversation analysis: The study of talk in interaction.* Thousand Oaks, CA: Sage.

Psathas, G., and T. Anderson. 1990. The "practices" of transcription in conversation analysis. *Semiotica* 78:75–99.

Purser, G. 2009. The dignity of job seeking men: Boundary work among immigrant day laborers. *Journal of Contemporary Ethnography* 38:117–39.

Pustejovsky, J. E., and J. P. Spillanea. 2009. Question-order effects in social network name generators. *Social Networks* 31:221–29.

Quandt, S., M. Z. Vitolins, K. M. DeWalt, and G. Roos. 1997. Meal patterns of older adults in rural communities: Life course analysis and implications for undernutrition. *Journal of Applied Gerontology* 16:152–71.

Quas, J. A., B. L. Bottoms, T. M. Haegerich, and K. L Nysse-Carris. 2002. Effects of victim, defendant, and juror gender on decisions in child sexual assault cases. *Journal of Applied Social Psychology* 32:1993–2021.

Quételet, A. 1969 [1842]. *Physique sociale, ou, essai sur le développement des facultés de l'homme*. Paris: J.-B. Bailliere et fils. Reprinted in trans. in 1969 from the 1842 ed. as *A treatise on man and the development of his faculties*. Gainesville, FL: Scholars' Facsimiles and Reprints.

Quick, C. S. 1999. Ethnopoetics. *Folklore Forum* 30: 95–105.

Quinlan, M. 2005. Considerations for collecting freelists in the field: Examples from ethnobotany. *Field Methods* 17:219–34.

Quinn, N. 1982. Commitment in American marriage: A cultural analysis. *American Ethnologist* 9: 775–98.

Quinn, N. 1987. Convergent evidence for a cultural model of American marriage. In *Cultural models in language and thought*, D. Holland and N. Quinn, eds., 173–92. Cambridge: Cambridge University Press.

Quinn, N. 1992. The motivational force of self-understanding: Evidence from wives' inner conflicts. In *Human motives and cultural models*, R. D'Andrade and C. Strauss, eds., 90–126. New York: Cambridge University Press.

Quinn, N. 1996. Culture and contradiction: The case of Americans reasoning about marriage. *Ethos* 24: 391–425.

Quinn, N. 1997. Research on shared task solutions. In *A cognitive theory of cultural meaning*, C. Strauss and N. Quinn, eds., 137–88. New York: Cambridge University Press.

Quinnipiac University. 2009 (May 14). Report on the Qunnipiac Poll. http://www.quinnipiac.edu/x1295.xml?ReleaseID=1298 (accessed August 5, 2009).

Quintiliani, L. M., M. K. Campbell, P. S. Haines, and K. H. Webber. 2008. The use of the pile sort method in identifying groups of healthful lifestyle behaviors among female community college students. *Journal of the American Dietetic Association* 108:1503–507.

Rabinowitz, G. B. 1975. An introduction to nonmetric multidimensional scaling. *American Journal of Political Science* 19:343–90.

Radaelli, C. 2009. Desperately seeking regulatory impact assessments: Diary of a reflective researcher. *Evaluation* 15:31–48.

Radin, P. 1966 [1933]. *The method and theory of ethnology*. New York: Basic Books.

Ragin, C. C. 1987. *The comparative method: Moving beyond qualitative and quantitative strategies*. Berkeley: University of California Press.

Ragin, C. C. 1994. Introduction to qualitative comparative analysis. In *The comparative political economy of the welfare state*, T. Janowski and A. M. Hicks, eds., 299–317. Cambridge: Cambridge University Press.

Ragin, C. C. 1998. The logic of qualitative comparative analysis. *International Review of Social History* 43(suppl. 6):105–24.

Rappaport, R. 1990. Forward. In *Surviving fieldwork*, N. Howell, ed., vii–viii. Washington, DC: American Anthropological Association.

Rapport, N. 1990. Surely everything has already been said about Malinowski's diary! *Anthropology Today* 6:5–9.

Rashid, S. F. 2007. Accessing married adolescent women: The realities of ethnographic research in an urban slum environment in Dhaka, Bangladesh. *Field Methods* 19:369–83.

Raven, P., B. Berlin, and D. Breedlove. 1971. The origins of taxonomy. *Science* 174:1210–13.

Raver, S. A., and A. M. Peterson. 1988. Comparison of teacher estimates and direct observation of spontaneous language in preschool handicapped children. *Child Study Journal* 18:277–84.

Razmi, J., and M. Shakhs-Niyaee. 2008. Developing a specific predetermined time study approach: An empirical study in a car industry. *Production Planning and Control* 19:454–60.

Reason, P., and H. Bradbury, eds. 2001. *Handbook of action research: Participative inquiry and practice*. Thousand Oaks, CA: Sage.

Reboussin, D. 1995. From Affiniam-Boutem to Dakar: Migration from the Casamance, life in the urban environment of Dakar and the resulting evolutionary changes in local Diola organizations. Ph.D. dissertation, University of Florida.

Redfield, R. 1948. The art of social science. *American Journal of Sociology* 54:181–90.

Reed, T. W., and R. J. Stimson, eds. 1985. *Survey interviewing. Theory and techniques*. Sydney: Allen & Unwin.

Rees, C. E., L. V. Knight, and C. E. Wilkinson. 2007. Doctors being up there and we being down here: A metaphorical analysis of talk about student/doctor-patient relationships. *Social Science and Medicine* 65:725–37.

Reese, S. D., W. A. Danielson, P. J. Shoemaker, T-K. Chang, and Huei-ling Hsu. 1986. Ethnicity-of-interviewer effects among Mexican-American and Anglos. *Public Opinion Quarterly* 50:563–72.

Reeves, C. L. 2010. A difficult negotiation: Fieldwork relations with gatekeepers. *Qualitative Research* 10:315–31.

Reichmann, W. M., E. Losina, G. R. Seage III, C. Arbelaez, S. A. Safren, J. N. Katz, A. Hetland, and R. P. Walensky. 2010. Does modality of survey administration impact data quality: Audio computer assisted self interview (ACASI) versus self-administered pen and paper? *PLoS ONE* 5,1:e8728.

Reiss, N. 1985. *Speech act taxonomy as a tool for ethnographic description: An analysis based on videotapes of continuous behavior in two New York households.* Philadelphia: John Benjamins.

Renker, P. R. 2008. Breaking the barriers: The promise of computer-assisted screening for intimate partner violence. *Journal of Midwifery and Women's Health* 53:496–503.

Resnik, D. B. 2007. *The price of truth: How money affects the norms of science.* New York: Oxford University Press.

Rhodes, T., M. Simić, S. Baroš, L. Platt, and Z. Bojan. 2008. Police violence and sexual risk among female and transvestite sex workers in Serbia: Qualitative study. *British Medical Journal BMJ* 2008; 337:a811 doi: 10.1136/bmj.a811.

Riach, P. A., and J. Rich. 2004. Deceptive field experiments of discrimination: Are they ethical? *Kyklos* 57:457–70.

Ricci, J. A., N. W. Jerome, N. Megally, and O. Galal. 1995. Assessing the validity of information recall: Results of a time use pilot study in peri-urban Egypt. *Human Organization* 54:304–308.

Rich, E. 1977. Sex-related differences in color vocabulary. *Language & Speech* 20:404–409.

Richardson, A., and T. Uebel, eds. 2007. *The Cambridge companion to logical empricism.* New York: Cambridge University Press.

Richardson, J., and A. L. Kroeber. 1940. Three centuries of women's dress fashions: A quantitative analysis. *Anthropological Records* 5:111–53.

Richardson, L. 1988. Secrecy and status: The social construction of forbidden relationships. *American Sociological Review* 53:209–19.

Ricoeur, P. 1981. *Hermeneutics and the human sciences: Essays on language, action, and interpretation.* Trans. by J. B. Thompson. New York: Cambridge University Press.

Ricoeur, P. 2007. *From text to action.* New ed. Evanston, IL: Northwestern University Press.

Ridgers, N. D., G. Stratton, and T. L. McKenzie. 2010. Reliability and validity of the system for observing children's activity and relationships during play (SOCARP). *Journal of Physical Activity and Health* 7:17–25.

Riessman, C. K. 1993. *Narrative analysis.* Newbury Park, CA: Sage.

Rifon, N. J., R. LaRose, and S. M. Choi. 2005. Your privacy is sealed: Effects of web privacy seals on trust and personal disclosure. *The Journal of Consumer Affairs* 39:339–62.

Rimal, R. N. 2001. Analyzing the physician-patient interaction: An overview of six methods and future research directions. *Health Communication* 13: 89–99.

Rindfleisch, A., J. E. Burroughs, and F. Denton. 1997. Family structure, materialism, and compulsive consumption. *Journal of Consumer Research* 23:312–25.

Robbins, M. C., and J. M. Nolan 2000. A measure of semantic category clustering in free-listing tasks. *Field Methods* 12:18–28.

Robbins, M. C., A. V. Williams, P. L. Killbride, and R. B. Pollnac. 1969. Factor analysis and case selection in complex societies. *Human Organization* 28:227–34.

Roberts, J., E. P. Mulvey, and J. Horney. 2005. A test of two methods of recall for violent events. 2005. *Journal of Quantitative Criminology* 21:175–93.

Roberts, J. M., and G. E. Chick. 1979. Butler County eight-ball: A behavioral space analysis. In *Sports, games, and play: Social and psychological viewpoints*, J. H. Goldstein, ed., 65–100. Hillsdale, NJ: Lawrence Erlbaum Associates.

Roberts, J. M., T. V. Golder, and G. E. Chick. 1980. Judgment, oversight, and skill: A cultural analysis of P-3 pilot error. *Human Organization* 39:5–21.

Roberts, J. M., and S. Nattrass. 1980. Women and trap-shooting: Competence and expression in a game of physical skill with chance. In *Play and culture*, H. B. Schwartzman, ed., 262–90. West Point, NY: Leisure Press.

Robinson, D., and S. Rhode. 1946. Two experiments with an anti-Semitism poll. *Journal of Abnormal and Social Psychology* 41:136–44.

Robinson, J. D. 1998. Getting down to business—Talk, gaze, and body orientation during openings of doctor-patient consultations. *Human Communication Research* 25:97–123.

Robinson, J. D., and J. Heritage 2005. The structure of patients' presenting concerns: The completion relevance of current symptoms. *Social Science and Medicine* 61:481–93.

Robinson, M. B., and C. E. Robinson. 1997. Environmental characteristics associated with residential burglaries of student apartment complexes. *Environment and Behavior* 29:657–75.

Robinson, W. S. 1950. Ecological correlations and the behavior of individuals. *American Sociological Review* 15:351–57.

Robinson, W. S. 1951. The logical structure of analytic induction. *American Sociological Review* 16:812–18.

Rohde, D. 2007. Army enlists anthropology in war zones. *New York Times*, October 5. http://www.nytimes.com/2007/10/05/world/asia/05afghan.html (accessed June 11, 2009).

Rohner, R. 1969. *The ethnography of Franz Boas.* Chicago: University of Chicago Press.

Rohner, R., B. R. DeWalt, and R. C. Ness. 1973. Ethnographer bias in crosscultural research. *Behavior Science Notes* 8:275–317.

Roldán, A. V. 2002. Writing ethnography. Malinowski's fieldnotes on Baloma. *Social Anthropology* 10:377–93.

Romer, D., P. E. Jamieson, and K. H. Jamieson. 2006. Are news reports of suicide contagious? A stringent test in six U.S. cities. *Journal of Communication* 56:253–70.

Romney, A. K., W. H. Batchelder, and S. C. Weller. 1987. Recent applications of cultural consensus theory. *American Behavioral Scientist* 31:163–77.

Romney, A. K., and R. G. D'Andrade, eds. 1964. Cognitive aspects of English kin terms. In *Transcultural studies in cognition. American Anthropologist* 66 (3, part 2, entire issue):146–70.

Romney, A. K., C. C. Moore, and C. D. Rusch. 1997. Cultural universals: Measuring the semantic structure of emotion terms in English and Japanese. *Proceedings of the National Academy of Sciences* 94:5489–94.

Romney, A. K., R. N. Shepard, and S. B. Nerlove, eds. 1972. *Multidimensional scaling: Applications in the behavioral sciences*, Vol. 2, *Applications*. New York: Seminar Press.

Romney, A. K., S. C. Weller, and W. H. Batchelder. 1986. Culture as consensus: A theory of culture and informant accuracy. *American Anthropologist* 88:313–38.

Rosander, A. C., H. E. Guterman, and A. J. McKeon. 1958. The use of random work sampling for cost analysis and control. *Journal of the American Statistical Association* 53:382–97.

Rosch, E. 1975. Cognitive representations of semantic categories. *Journal of Experimental Psychology* 104:192–233.

Roscigno, V. J., and R. Hodson. 2004. The organizational and social foundations of worker resistance. *American Sociological Review* 69:14–39.

Rosenau, P. M. 1992. *Post modernism and the social sciences: Insights, inroads, and intrusions*. Princeton, NJ: Princeton University Press.

Rosenberg, S. D., P. P. Schnurr, and T. E. Oxman. 1990. Content analysis: A comparison of manual and computerized systems. *Journal of Personality Assessment* 54:298–310.

Rosenhan, D. L. 1973. On being sane in insane places. *Science* 179:250–58.

Rosenhan, D. L. 1975. The contextual nature of psychiatric diagnosis. *Journal of Abnormal Psychology* 84:462–74.

Rosenshine, B., and N. Furst. 1973. The use of direct observation to study teaching. In *Second handbook of research on teaching*, R. W. Travers, ed., 122–83. Chicago: Rand McNally.

Rosenthal, R. 1984. *Meta-analytic procedures for social research*. Beverly Hills, CA: Sage.

Rosenthal, R., and L. Jacobson. 1968. *Pygmalion in the classroom*. New York: Holt, Rinehart & Winston.

Rosenthal, R., and D. B. Rubin. 1978. Interpersonal expectancy effects: The first 345 studies. *The Behavioral and Brain Sciences* 3:377–415.

Rosnow, R. L., and R. Rosenthal. 1997. *People studying people. Artifacts and ethics in behavioral research*. New York: Freeman.

Ross, M. W., E. J. Essien, and I. Torres. 2006. Conspiracy beliefs about the origin of HIV/AIDS in four racial/ethnic groups. *Journal of Acquired Immune Deficiency Syndrome* 41:342–44.

Ross, M. W., B. R. Simon Rosser, J. Stanton, and J. Konstan. 2004. Characteristics of Latino men who have sex with men on the Internet who complete and drop out of an Internet-based sexual behavior survey. *AIDS Education and Prevention* 16:526–37.

Ross, N. 2002. Cognitive aspects of intergenerational change: Mental models, culture change, and environmental behavior among the Lancandon Maya of southern Mexico. *Human Organization* 61:125–38.

Ross, N., T. Barrientos, and A. Esquit-Choy. 2005. Triad tasks, a multipurpose tool to elicit similarity judgments: The case of Tzotzil Maya plant taxonomy. *Field Methods* 17:269–82.

Rossi, P. H., and R. Berk. 1997. *Just punishments: Federal guidelines and public views compared*. New York: Aldine de Gruyter.

Rossi, P. H., and S. L. Nock. 1982. *Measuring social judgments: The factorial survey approach*. Beverly Hills, CA: Sage.

Rothenberg, J. 1975 [1969]. Total translation. In *Literature of the American Indians: Views and interpretations*, A. Chapman, ed., 292–308. New York: New American Library.

Rothschild, R. F. 1981. What happened in 1780? *Harvard Magazine* 83:20–27.

Rotter, J. B. 1966. Generalized expectancies for internal versus external control of reinforcement. *Psychological Monographs* 30 (entire No. 609).

Rotter, J. B. 1990. Internal versus external control of reinforcement: A case history of a variable. *American Psychologist* 45:489–93.

Rotton, J., and M. Shats. 1996. Effects of state humor, expectancies, and choice on postsurgical mood and self-medication: A field experiment. *Journal of Applied Social Psychology* 26:1775–94.

Rotton, J., M. Shats, and R. Standers. 1990. Temperature and pedestrian tempo. Walking without awareness. *Environment and Behavior* 22:650–74.

Rousseau, J.-J. 1988 [1762]. *On the social contract*. Trans. and ed. by D. A. Cress. Indianapolis: Hackett Publishing.

Roy, K. M. 2006. Father stories: A life course examination of paternal identity among low-income African American men. *Journal of Family Issues* 27:31–54.

Ruback, R. B., and D. Juieng. 1997. Territorial defense in parking lots: Retaliation against waiting drivers. *Journal of Applied Social Psychology* 27:821–34.

Rubel, A. J., C. W. O'Nell, and R. Collado-Adrdón. 1984. *Susto. A folk illness*. Berkeley: University of California Press.

Rubin, D. B. 1974. Estimating causal effects of treatments in randomized and nonrandomized studies. *Journal of Educational Psychology* 66:688–701.

Rubin, H. J., and I. S. Rubin. 2005. *Qualitative interviewing: The art of hearing data*. 2d ed. Thousand Oaks, CA: Sage.

Rubinstein, R. L. 1995. Narratives of elder parental death: A structural and cultural analysis. *Medical Anthropology Quarterly* 9:257–76.

Ruffing-Rahal, M. A. 1993. An ecological model of group well-being: Implications for health promotion with older women. *Health Care for Women International* 14:447–56.

Ruffing-Rahal, M. A., L. J. Barin, and C. J. Combs. 1998. Gender role orientation as a correlate of perceived health, health behavior, and qualitative well-being in older women. *Journal of Women and Aging* 10:3–19.

Ruiz-Caseres, M., and J. Heymann. 2009. Children home alone unsupervised: Modeling parental decisions and associated factors in Botswana, Mexico, and Vietnam. *Child Abuse and Neglect* 33:312–23.

Rusting, C. L., and R. J. Larsen. 1998. Diurnal patterns of unpleasant mood: Associations with neuroticism, depression, and anxiety. *Journal of Personality* 66:85–103.

Rutledge, E. M. 1990. Black parent-child relations: Some correlates. *Journal of Comparative Family Studies* 21:369–78.

Ryan, G. W. 1999. Measuring the typicality of text: Using multiple coders for more than just reliability and validity checks. *Human Organization* 58:313–22.

Ryan, G. W. 2004. Using a word processor to tag and retrieve blocks of text. *Field Methods* 16:109–30.

Ryan, G. W., and H. R. Bernard. 2000. Data management and analysis methods. In *Handbook of qualitative research*, 2d ed., N. K. Denzin and Y. S. Lincoln, eds., 769–802. Thousand Oaks, CA: Sage.

Ryan, G. W., and H. R. Bernard. 2003. Techniques to identify themes. *Field Methods* 15:85–109.

Ryan, G. W., and H. R. Bernard. 2006. Testing an ethnographic decision tree model on a national sample: Recycling beverage cans. *Human Organization* 65:103–14.

Ryan, G. W., and H. Martínez. 1996. Can we predict what mothers do? Modeling childhood diarrhea in rural Mexico. *Human Organization* 55:47–57.

Ryan, G. W., J. M. Nolan, and P. S. Yoder. 2000. Successive free listing: Using free lists to generate explanatory models. *Field Methods* 12: 83–107.

Ryan, G. W., and T. Weisner. 1996. Analyzing words in brief descriptions: Fathers and mothers describe their children. *Cultural Anthropology Methods Journal* 8:13–16.

Rynkiewick, M., and J. P. Spradley, eds. 1976. *Ethics and anthropology: Dilemmas in fieldwork*. New York: John Wiley.

Ryu, E., M. P. Couper, and R. W. Marans. 2006. Survey incentives: Cash vs. in-kind; face-to-face vs. mail; Response rate vs. nonresponse error. *International Journal of Public Opinion Research* 18:89–106.

Saban, A., B. N. Kocbecker, and A. Saban. 2007. Prospective teachers' conceptions of teaching and learning revealed through metaphor analysis. *Learning and Instruction* 17:123–39.

Sacks, H. 1992. *Lectures on conversation*. Cambridge, MA: Basil Blackwell.

Sacks, H., E. A. Schegloff, and G. Jefferson. 1974. A simplest systematics for the organization of turn-taking conversation. *Language* 50:696–735.

Sagberg, F., S. Fosser, and I-A. F. Saetermo. 1997. An investigation of behavioural adaptation to airbags and antilock brakes among taxi drivers. *Accident Analysis and Prevention* 29:293–302.

Saito, A., ed. 2000. *Bartlett, culture and cognition*. Hove, UK: Psychology Press.

Salamone, F. 1977. The methodological significance of the lying informant. *Anthropological Quarterly* 50:117–24.

Salganik, M. J., and D. D. Heckathorn. 2004. Sampling and estimation in hidden populations using respondent-driven sampling. *Sociological Methodology* 34:193–239.

Salisbury, C. L., M. M. Palombaro, and T. M. Hollowood. 1993. On the nature and change of an inclusive elementary school. *Journal of the Association for Persons with Severe Handicaps* 18:75–84.

Salmon, M. H. 1997. Ethical considerations in anthropology and archaeology; or, relativism and justice for all. *Journal of Anthropological Research* 53:47–63.

Sammons, K., and J. Sherzer, eds. 2000. *Translating Native American verbal art: Ethnopoetics and ethnography of speaking*. Washington, DC: Smithsonian Institution Press.

Sandelowski, M. 1995a. Sample size in qualitative research. *Research in Nursing and Health* 18: 179–83.

Sandelowski, M. 1995b. Qualitative analysis: What it is and how to begin. *Research in Nursing and Health* 18:371–75.

Sanderson, S. K., and W. W. Roberts. 2008. The evolutionary forms of the religious life: A cross-cultural, quantitative analysis. *American Anthropologist* 110:454–66.

Sanghavi, P., K. Bhalla, and V. Das. 2009. Fire-related deaths in India in 2001: A retrospective analysis of data. *Lancet* 373:1282–88.

Sanjek, R. 1990. *Fieldnotes*. Ithaca, NY: Cornell University Press.

Santa Ana, O. 1999. "Like an animal I was treated": Anti-immigrant metaphor in U. S. public discourse. *Discourse and Society* 10:191–224.

Sarkar, N. K., and S. J. Tambiah. 1957. *The disintegrating village*. Colombo, Sri Lanka: Ceylon University Socio-Economic Survey of Pata Dumbara.

Sarton, G. 1935. Quételet (1796–1874). *Isis* 23:6–24.

Sarton, G. 1952–1959. *A history of science*. Cambridge, MA: Harvard University Press.

Saudargas, R. A., and K. Zanolli. 1990. Momentary time sampling as an estimate of percentage time: A field validation. *Journal of Applied Behavior Analysis* 23:533–37.

SAUS. 1947. Statistical abstract of the United States. Washington, DC: U.S. Census Bureau. http://www .census.gov/prod/www/abs/statab1901_1950.htm (accessed March 8, 2009).

SAUS. 1997. Statistical abstract of the United States. Washington, DC: U.S. Census Bureau. http://www .census.gov/prod/www/abs/statab1995_2000.html (accessed January 30, 2011).

SAUS. 2000. Statistical abstract of the United States. Washington, DC: U.S. Census Bureau. http://www .census.gov/prod/www/abs/statab1995_2000.html (accessed August 23, 2009).

SAUS. 2010. Statistical abstract of the United States. Washington, DC: U.S. Census Bureau. http://www .census.gov/compendia/statab/2010edition.html (accessed September 27, 2010).

SAUS.2011 Statistical abstract of the United States. Washington, DC: U.S. Census Bureau. http://www .census.gov/prod/2011pubs/11statab/infocomm.pdf (accessed June 14, 2011).

Sayles, J. N., G. W. Ryan, J. S. Silver, and W. E. Cunningham. 2007. Experiences of social stigma and implications for healthcare among a diverse population of HIV positive adults. *Journal of Urban Health* 84:814–28.

Scaglion, R. 1986. The importance of nighttime observations in time allocation studies. *American Ethnologist* 13:537–45.

Schank, R. C., and R. P. Abelson. 1977. *Scripts, plans, goals, and understanding: An inquiry into human knowledge structures.* Hillsdale, NJ: Lawrence Erlbaum.

Schatz, E. 2009. *Political ethnography: What immersion contributes to the study of power.* Chicago: University of Chicago Press.

Schatzman, L., and A. Strauss. 1973. *Field research. Strategies for a natural sociology.* Englewood Cliffs, NJ: Prentice-Hall.

Schegloff, E. A. 1968. Sequencing in conversational openings. *American Anthropologist* 70:1075–95.

Schegloff, E. A. 1979. Identification and recognition in telephone conversation openings. In *Everyday language: Studies in ethnomethodology*, G. Psathas, ed., 23–78. New York: Irvington.

Schegloff, E. A., and H. Sacks. 1973. Opening up closings. *Semiotica* 7:289–327.

Scheper-Hughes, N. 1983. Introduction: The problem of bias in androcentric and feminist anthropology. In *Confronting problems of bias in feminist anthropology*, N. Scheper-Hughes, ed., 109–16. *Women's Studies* 10 (special issue).

Scheper-Hughes, N. 1992. *Death without weeping. The violence of everyday life in Brazil.* Berkeley: University of California Press.

Scherer, S. E. 1974. Proxemic behavior of primary-school children as a function of the socioeconomic class and subculture. *Journal of Personality and Social Psychology* 29:800–805.

Schiffrin, D. 2003. We knew that's it: Retelling the turning point of a narrative. *Discourse Studies* 5:535–61.

Schiller, F. C. S. 1969 [1903]. *Humanism. Philosophical essays.* Freeport, NY: Books for Libraries Press.

Schilling-Estes, N. 2004. Constructing ethnicity in interaction. *Journal of Sociolinguistics* 8:163–95.

Schlegel, A., and H. Barry, III. 1986. The cultural consequences of female contribution to subsistence. *American Anthropologist* 88:142–50.

Schmelkin, L. P., K. A. Gilbert, and R. Silva. 2010. Multidimensional scaling of high school students' perceptions of academic dishonesty. *High School Journal* 93:156–65.

Schmitt, A., ed. 1997. *New aspects of human ethology.* New York: Plenum Press.

Schmitt, R. 2005. Systematic metaphor analysis as a method of qualitative research. *Qualitative Report* 10:358–94.

Schnegg, M., and H. R. Bernard. 1996. Words as actors: A method for doing semantic network analysis. *Cultural Anthropology Methods Journal* 8:7–10.

Schneider, B. L. 2009. Method differences in measuring working families' time. *Social Indicators Research* 93:105–110.

Schneider, C. Q., and C. Wagemann. 2006. Reducing complexity in Qualitative Comparative Analysis (QCA): Remote and proximate factors and the consolidation of democracy. *European Journal of Political Research* 45:751–86.

Schneider, H. L., and L. M. Huber, eds. 2008. *Social networks: Development, evaluation and influence.* New York: Nova Science Publishers.

Schnettler, S. 2009. A structured overview of 50 years of small-world research. *Social Networks* 31: 165–78.

Schober, M. F., and F. G. Conrad. 1997. Does conversational interviewing reduce survey measurement error? *Public Opinion Quarterly* 61:576–602.

Scholte, R. H. J., E. A. P. Poelen, G. Willemsen, D. I. Boomsma, and R. C. M. E. Engels. 2008. Relative risks of adolescent and young adult alcohol use: The role of drinking fathers, mothers, siblings, and friends. *Addictive Behaviors* 33:1–14.

Schonlau, M., R. D. Fricker, Jr., and M. N. Elliott. 2002. *Conducting research surveys via e-mail and the web.* Santa Monica, CA: Rand.

Schrauf, R. W., and J. Sanchez. 2008. Using freelisting to identify, assess, and characterize age differences in shared cultural domains. *Journal of Gerontology: Social Sciences* 63B:S385–S393.

Schuman. H. 2008. *Method and meaning in polls and surveys.* Cambridge, MA: Harvard University Press.

Schuman, H. 2009. Context effects and social change. *Public Opinion Quarterly* 73:172–79.

Schuman, H., and S. Presser. 1981. *Questions and answers in attitude surveys.* San Diego, CA: Academic Press.

Schuster, J. A. 1977. *Descartes and the scientific revolution.* Princeton, NJ: Princeton University Press.

Schutte, J. W., and H. M. Hosch. 1997. Gender differences in sexual assault verdicts: A meta-analysis. *Journal of Social Behavior and Personality* 12:759–72.

Schutz, A. 1962. *Collected papers I: The problem of social reality.* The Hague: Martinus Nijhoff.

Schwadel, P. 2010. Age, period, and cohort effects on U. S. religious service attendance: The declining impact of sex, southern residence, and Catholic affiliation. *Sociology of Religion* 71:2–24.

Schwarcz, S. H. Spindler, S. Scheer, L. Valleroy, and A. Lansky 2007. Assessing representativeness of sampling methods for reaching men who have sex with men: A direct comparison of results obtained from convenience and probability samples. *AIDS and Behavior* 11:596–602.

Schwarz, N. 1999. Self-reports. How the questions shape the answers. *American Psychologist* 54:93–105.

Schwarz, N., H.-J. Hippler, B. Deutsch, and F. Strack. 1985. Response scales: Effects of category range on reported behavior and comparative judgments. *Public Opinion Quarterly* 49:388–95.

Schweizer, T. 1998. Epistemology: The nature and validation of anthropological knowledge. In *Handbook of methods in cultural anthropology*, H. R. Bernard, ed., 39–87. Walnut Creek, CA: AltaMira.

Science. 1972. *The Brawling Bent.* March 24, pp. 1346–47.

Scollon, C. N., E. Diener, and S. Oishi. 2005. An experience sampling and cross-cultural investigation of the relation between pleasant and unpleasant affect. *Cognition and Emotion* 19:27–52.

Scott, G. 2008. "They got their program, and I got mine": A cautionary tale concerning the ethical implications of using respondent-driven sampling to study injection drug users. *International Journal of Drug Policy* 19:42–51.

Scott, J. 2000. *Social network analysis: A handbook.* 2d. ed. London: Sage.

Scrimshaw, N. S., and G. R. Gleason, eds. 1992. *Rapid assessment procedures. Qualitative methodologies for planning and evaluation of health related programmes.* Boston: International Nutrition Foundation for Developing Countries (INFDC). http://unu.edu/unupress/food2/UIN08E/UIN08E00.HTM (accessed December 19, 2010)

Scrimshaw, S. C. M., and E. Hurtado. 1987. *Rapid assessment procedures for nutrition and primary health care.* Los Angeles: University of California at Los Angeles, Latin American Center Publications.

Sechrest, L., and L. Flores. 1969. Homosexuality in the Philippines and the United States: The handwriting on the wall. *Journal of Social Psychology* 79:3–12.

Seiter, J. S. 2007. Ingratiation and gratuity: The effect of complimenting customers on tipping behavior in restaurants. *Journal of Applied Social Psychology* 37:478–85.

Selin, H., ed. 2008. *Encyclopaedia of the history of science, technology, and medicine in non-Western cultures.* New York: Springer.

Selzer, M. L. 1971. The Michigan Alcoholism Screening Test: The quest for a new diagnostic instrument. *American Journal of Psychiatry* 127:1653–58.

Shadish, W. R., T. D. Cook, and D. T. Campbell. 2002. *Experimental and quasi-experimental designs for generalized causal inference.* Boston: Houghton Mifflin.

Shami, S. 1989. Socio-cultural anthropology in Arab universities. *Current Anthropology* 30:649–54.

Sharf, R. H. 2002. *Coming to terms with Chinese Buddhism: A reading of the Treasure Store Treatise.* Honolulu: University of Hawaii Press.

Sharff, J. W. 1979. Patterns of authority in two urban Puerto Rican households. Ph.D. dissertation, Columbia University.

Sharkey, J. R., W. R. Dean, J. A. St. John, and J. C. Huber. 2010. Using direct observations on multiple occasions to measure household food availability among low-income Mexicano residents in Texas colonias. *BMC Public Health* 10: Number: 445. doi:10.1186/1471-2458-10-445.

Sharp, G., and E. Kremer. 2006. The safety dance: Confronting harassment, intimidation, and violence in the field. *Sociological Methodology* 36:317–27.

Sharpe, D., and C. Faye. 2009. A second look at debriefing practices: Madness in our method? *Ethics and Behavior* 19:432–47.

Sharpe, R. 1998. EEOC backs away from filing race-bias suit. *The Wall Street Journal,* June 24, p. A4.

Shaw, C. R. 1930. *The jack-roller. A delinquent boy's own story.* Chicago: University of Chicago Press.

Shaw, S. 1992. Dereifying family leisure: An examination of women's and men's everyday experiences and perceptions of family time. *Leisure Studies* 14:271–86.

Sheatsley, P. B. 1983. Questionnaire construction and item wording. In *Handbook of survey research,*

P. H. Rossi, J. D. Wright, and A. B. Anderson, eds., 195–230. New York: Wiley.

Sheets, J. W. 1982. Nonleptokurtic marriage distances on Colonsay and Jura. *Current Anthropology* 23: 105–106.

Shelley, G. A. 1992. The social networks of people with end-stage renal disease: Comparing hemodialysis and peritoneal dialysis patients. Ph.D. dissertation, University of Florida.

Shelley, G. A., H. R. Bernard, P. D. Killworth, E. Johnsen, and C. McCarty. 1995. Who knows your HIV status? What HIV+ patients and their network members know about each other. *Social Networks* 17:189–217.

Shepard, R. N. 1966. Metric structures in ordinal data. *Journal of Mathematical Psychology* 3:287–315.

Sherkat, D. E. 1998. Counterculture or continuity? Competing influences on baby boomers' religious orientations and participation. *Social Forces* 76:1087–14.

Sherma, R. D., and A. Sharma, eds. 2008. *Hermeneutics and Hindu thought: Toward a fusion of horizons.* New York: Springer.

Sherman, E., A. Mathur, and R. B. Smith. 1997. Store environment and consumer purchase behavior: Mediating role of consumer emotions. *Psychology and Marketing* 14:361–78.

Sherman, R. C., and M. D. Dowdle. 1974. The perception of crime and punishment: A multidimensional scaling analysis. *Social Science Research* 3:109–26.

Sherry, J. F., Jr. 1995. *Contemporary marketing and consumer behavior: An anthropological sourcebook.* Thousand Oaks, CA: Sage.

Shields, A. L., R. T. Howell, J. S. Potter, and R. D. Weiss. 2007. The Michigan Alcoholism Screening Test and its shortened form: A meta-analytic inquiry into score reliability. *Substance Use and Misuse* 42:1783–1800.

Shih, T-H., and X. Fan. 2008. Comparing response rates from web and mail surveys: A meta-analysis. *Field Methods* 20:249–71.

Shin, S-Y., 2010. The functions of code-switching in a Korean Sunday school. *Heritage Language Journal* 7:91–116.

Shoemaker, P. J., M. Eichholz, and E. A. Skewes. 2002. Item nonresponse: Distinguishing between don't know and refuse. *International Journal of Public Opinion Research* 14:193–201.

Shore, B. 2009. Making time for family: Schemas for long-term family memory. *Social Indicators Research* 93:95–103.

Shostack, A. L., and G. P. Campagna. 1991. Daily living patterns, human relations, and community services in a sample of New Jersey board and care homes: Report of an exploratory survey. *Adult Residential Care Journal* 5:7–28.

Shotland, R. L. 1976. *University communication networks: The small world method.* New York: Wiley.

Shotland, R. L., and M. K. Straw. 1976. Bystander response to an assault: When a man attacks a woman. *Journal of Personality and Social Psychology* 34:990–99.

Shrader-Frechette, K. 1994. *Ethics of scientific research.* Lanham, MD: Rowman & Littlefield.

Shropshire, K. O., J. E. Hawdon, and J. C. Witte. 2009. Web survey design: Balancing measurement, response, and topical interest. *Sociological Methods Research* 37:344–70.

Shumow, L., J. A. Schmidt, and H. Kackar. 2008. Reading in class and and out of class: An experience sampling method study. *Middle Grades Research Journal* 3:97–120.

Shweder, R., and R. G. D'Andrade. 1980. The systematic distortion hypothesis. In *Fallible judgment in behavioral research*, R. Shweder, ed., 37–58. San Francisco: Jossey-Bass.

Siar, S. V. 2003. Knowledge, gender, and resources in small-scale fishing: The case of Honda Bay, Palawan, Philippines. *Environmental Management* 31:569–80.

Sieber J. E., R. Iannuzzo, and B. Rodriguez. 1995. Deception methods in psychology: Have they changed in 23 years? *Ethics and Behavior* 5:67–85.

Silver, B. L. 1998. *The ascent of science*. New York: Oxford University Press.

Silverman, D. 1993. *Interpreting qualitative data: Methods of analyzing talk, text, and interaction.* Thousand Oaks, CA: Sage.

Silverman, D. 1998. *Harvey Sacks: Social science and conversation analysis.* New York: Oxford University Press.

Simons, L., J. Lathlean, and C. Squire. 2008. Shifting the focus: Sequential methods of analysis with qualitative data. *Qualitative Health Research* 18:120–32.

Sinclair, S. 2011. Impact of death and dying on the personal lives and practices of palliative and hospice care professionals. *CMAJ: Canadian Medical Association Journal* 183:180–87.

Singer, E., and R. M. Bossarte. 2006. Incentives for survey participation—When are they "coercive"? *American Journal of Preventive Medicine* 31: 411–18.

Singer, E., and S. Presser. 1989. *Survey research methods: A reader.* Chicago: University of Chicago Press.

Sirken, M. G. 1972. *Designing forms for demographic surveys.* Chapel Hill: Laboratories for Population Statistics, University of North Carolina.

Sit, C. H. F., J. W. K. Lam, and T. L. McKenzie. 2010. Direct observation of children's preferences and activity levels during interactive and online electronic games. *Journal of Physical Activity and Health* 7:484–89.

Skinner, B. F. 1938. *The behavior of organisms: An experimental analysis.* New Jersey: Prentice Hall.

Skinner, B. F. 1957. *Verbal behavior.* New York: Appleton-Century-Crofts.

Slater, M., S. Antley, A. Davison, D. Swapp, C. Guger, C. Baker, N. Pistrang, and M. V. Sanchez-Vives. 2006. A virtual reprise of the Stanley Milgram obedience experiments. *PLoS ONE* 1(1):e39. doi: 10.1371/journal.pone.0000039.

Slaughter, V. 2005. Young children's understanding of death. *Australian Psychologist* 40:179–86.

Smith, C. A., and S. Stillman. 2002a. Butch/femme in the personal advertisements of lesbians. *Journal of Lesbian Studies* 6:45–51.

Smith, C. A., and S. Stillman. 2002b. What do women want? The effects of gender and sexual orientation on the desirability of physical attributes in the personal ads of women. *Sex Roles* 46:337–42.

Smith, C. S., M. Morris, F. Langois-Winkle, W. Hill, and C. Francovich. 2010. A pilot study using cultural consensus analysis to measure systems-based practice performance. *International Journal of Medical Education* 1:15–18.

Smith, F. 2009. The quality of private pharmacy services in low and middle-income countries: A systematic review. *Pharmacy World and Science* 31:351–61.

Smith, G. D., and T. Mertens. 2004. What's said and what's done: The reality of sexually transmitted disease consultations. *Public Health* 118:96–103.

Smith, J. J. 1993. Using Anthropac 3.5 and a spreadsheet to compute a free-list salience index. *Cultural Anthropology Methods (Field Methods)* 5:1–3.

Smith, J. J., and S. P. Borgatti. 1997. Salience counts—and so does accuracy: Correcting and updating a measure for free-list item salience. *Journal of Linguistic Anthropology* 7:208–209.

Smith, J. J., L. Furbee, K. Maynard, S. Quick, and L. Ross. 1995. Salience counts: A domain analysis of English color terms. *Journal of Linguistic Anthropology* 5:203–16.

Smith, K. D., S. T. Smith, and J. C. Christopher. 2007. What defines the good person? Cross-cultural comparisons of experts' models with lay prototypes. *Journal of Cross-Cultural Psychology* 38:333–60.

Smith, L. D. 1986. *Behaviorism and logical positivism.* Stanford, CA: Stanford University Press.

Smith, M. L., and G. V. Glass. 1977. Meta-analysis of psychotherapy outcome studies. *American Psychologist* 32:752–60.

Smith, R. 1997. *The Norton history of the human sciences.* New York: W. W. Norton.

Smith, T. W. 1987. That which we call welfare by any other name would smell sweeter. An analysis of the impact of question wording on response patterns. *Public Opinion Quarterly* 51:75–83.

Smith, T. W. 1989. The hidden percent: An analysis of nonresponse on the 1980 General Social Survey. In *Survey research methods*, E. Singer and S. Presser, eds., 50–68. Chicago: University of Chicago Press.

Smith, T. W. 1998. A review of church attendance measures. *American Sociological Review* 63:131–36.

Smith-Lovin, L., and C. Brody. 1989. Interruptions in group discussions: The effect of gender and group composition. *American Sociological Review* 54: 424–35.

Smits, J., W. Ultee, and J. Lammers. 1998. Educational homogamy in 65 countries: An explanation of differences in openness using country-level explanatory variables. *American Sociological Review* 63:264–85.

Snider, J. G., and C. E. Osgood, eds. 1969. *Semantic differential technique.* Chicago: Aldine.

Snow, C. P. 1964. *The two cultures: And a second look.* Cambridge: Cambridge University Press.

Sohier, R. 1993. Filial reconstruction: A theory on development through adversity. *Qualitative Health Research* 3:465–92.

Solomon, J., S. K. Jacobson, K. D. Wald, and M. Gavin. 2007. Estimating illegal resource use at a Ugandan park with the randomized response technique. *Human Dimensions of Wildlife* 12:75–88.

Solomon, R. L. 1949. An extension of control group design. *Psychological Bulletin* 46:137–50.

Solomon, R. L., and M. S. Lessac. 1968. A control group design for experimental studies of developmental processes. *Psychological Bulletin* 70:145–50.

Solow, R. M. 1970. Science and ideology in economics. *Public Interest* 21:94–107.

Sommers-Flanagan, J., and R. Sommers-Flanagan. 2003. *Clinical interviewing*. New York: John Wiley & Sons.

Sorensen, G., T. G. Plax, and P. Kearney. 1989. The strategy selection-construction controversy: A coding scheme for analyzing teacher compliance-gaining message constructions. *Communication Education* 38:102–18.

Sorensen, R. A. 1992. *Thought experiments*. New York: Oxford University Press.

Soskin, W. F. 1963. *Verbal interaction in a young married couple*. Lawrence: University of Kansas Press.

Soskin, W. F., and V. John. 1963. The study of spontaneous talk. In *The stream of behavior: Explorations of its structure and content*, R. G. Barker, ed., 228–82. New York: Appleton-Century Crofts.

Sosulski, M. R., N. T. Buchanan, and C. M. Donnell. 2010. Life history and narrative analysis: Feminist methodologies contextualizing Black women's experiences with severe mental illness. *Journal of Sociology and Social Welfare* 37:29–58.

Spano, R. 2006. Observer behavior as a potential source of reactivity: Describing and quantifying observer effects in a large-scale observational study of police. *Sociological Methods and Research* 34:521–53.

Spano, R. 2007. How does reactivity affect police behavior? Describing and quantifying the impact of reactivity as behavioral change in a large-scale observational study of police. *Journal of Criminal Justice* 35:453–65.

Spearman, C. 1904. "General intelligence," objectively determined and measured. *American Journal of Psychology* 15:201–93.

Spector, P. E. 1992. *Summated rating scale construction*. Newbury Park, CA: Sage.

Spence, J. T. 1991. Do the BSRI and the PAQ measure the same or different concepts? *Psychology of Women Quarterly* 15:141–65.

Spence, J. T., and E. D. Hahn. 1997. The Attitudes Toward Women Scale and attitude change in college students. *Psychology of Women Quarterly* 21:17–34.

Spence, J. T., and R. L. Helmreich. 1972. The Attitudes Toward Women Scale: An objective instrument to measure attitudes toward the rights and roles of women in contemporary society. *Catalog of Selected Documents in Psychology* 2:66–67.

Spence, J. T., and R. L. Helmreich. 1978. *Masculinity and femininity: Their psychological dimensions, correlates, and antecedents*. Austin: University of Texas Press.

Spence, J. T., R. L. Helmreich, and J. Stapp. 1973. A short version of the Attitudes Toward Women Scale (AWS). *Bulletin of the Psychonomic Society* 2:219–20.

Spence, J. T., R. L. Helmreich, and J. Stapp. 1974. The Personal Attributes Questionnaire: A measure of

sex-role stereotypes and masculinity-femininity. *Catalog of Selected Documents in Psychology* 4:43–44.

Spencer, S. 2011. *Visual research methods in the social sciences: Awakening visions*. New York: Routledge.

Spiegelberg, H. 1980. *Phenomenology. Encyclopaedia brittanica*, 15th ed., Vol. 14. Chicago: Encyclopaedia Brittanica, Inc.

Spilkova, J., and M. Hochel. 2009. Toward the economy of pedestrian movement in Czech and Slovak shopping malls. *Environment and Behavior* 41:443–55.

Spitzer, R. L. 1976. More on pseudoscience in science and the case for psychiatric diagnostics. *Archives of General Psychiatry* 33:459–70.

Spradley, J. P. 1972. Adaptive strategies of urban nomads. In *Culture and cognition: Rules, maps, and plans*, J. P. Spradley, ed., 235–78. New York: Chandler.

Spradley, J. P. 1979. *The ethnographic interview*. New York: Holt, Rinehart &Winston.

Spradley, J. P. 1980. *Participant observation*. New York: Holt, Rinehart & Winston.

Spradley, J. P. 1987. Adaptive strategies of urban nomads. In *Culture and cognition*, J. P. Spradley, ed., 235–62. Prospect Heights, IL: Waveland. Orig. pub. in 1972 in *The anthropology of urban environments*, T. Weaver and D. J. White, eds.. Boulder, CO: Society for Applied Anthropology. Monograph, no. 11.

Spring, M., J. Westermeyer, L. Halcon, K. Savik, C. Robertson, D. R. Johnson, J. N. Butcher, and J. Jaranson. 2003. Sampling in difficult to access refugee and immigrant communities. *Journal of Nervous and Mental Disease* 191:813–19.

Sproull, L. S. 1981. Managing education programs: A micro-behavioral analysis. *Human Organization* 40:113–22.

Squire, P. 1988. Why the 1936 "Literary Digest" poll failed. *Public Opinion Quarterly* 52:125–33.

Srinivas, M. N. 1979. The fieldworker and the field: A village in Karnataka. In *The fieldworker and the field*, M. N. Srinivas, A. M. Shah, and E. A. Ramaswamy, eds., 19–28. Delhi: Oxford University Press.

Steblay, N. M. 1997. Social influence in eyewitness recall: A meta-analytic review of lineup instruction effects. *Law and Human Behavior* 21:283–97.

Stefflre, V. J. 1972. Some applications of multidimensional scaling to social science problems. In *Multidimensional scaling: Theory and applications in the behavioral sciences*, Vol. 2, A. K.Romney, R. N. Shepard, and S. B. Nerlove, eds., 211–43. New York: Seminar Press.

Steger, T. 2007. The stories metaphors tell: Metaphors as a tool to decipher tacit aspects in narratives. *Field Methods* 19:3–23.

Stein, J., S. A. Fox, and P. J. Murata. 1991. The influence of ethnicity, socioeconomic status, and psychological barriers on the use of mammography. *Journal of Health and Social Behavior* 32:101–13.

Stein, R. H. 1987. *The synoptic problem*. Grand Rapids, MI: Baker Book House.

Steinmetz, G., ed. 2005. *The politics of method in the human sciences: Positivism and its epistemological others*. Durham, NC: Duke University Press.

Stemmer, N. 2004. Has Chomsky's argument been refuted? A reply to Skinner, Cautilli, and Hantula. *The Behavior Analyst Today* 4:376–82.

Stepanikova, I., N. H. Nie, and X. He. 2010. Time on the Internet at home, loneliness, and life satisfaction: Evidence from panel time-diary data. *Computers in Human Behavior* 26:329–38.

Stephenson, J. B., and L. S. Greer. 1981. Ethnographers in their own cultures: Two Appalachian cases. *Human Organization* 30:333–43.

Sterk, C. E. 1989. Prostitution, drug use, and AIDS. In *In the field: Readings on the field research experience*, C. D. Smith and W. Kornblum, eds., 91–100. New York: Praeger.

Sterk, C. E. 1999. *Tricking and tripping: Prostitution in the era of AIDS*. Putnam Valley, NY: Social Change Press.

Stern, S. E., and J. E. Faber. 1997. The lost e-mail method: Milgram's lost-letter technique in the age of the Internet. *Behavior Research Methods Instruments and Computers* 29:260–63.

Stevens, S. S. 1946. On the theory of scales and measurement. *Science* 103:677–80.

Stevens, S. S. 1957. On the psychophysical power law. *Psychological Review* 64:153–81.

Steward, J. H. 1955. *The theory of culture change. The methodology of multilinear evolution*. Urbana: University of Illinois Press.

Stewart, A. 1998. *The ethnographer's method*. Thousand Oaks, CA: Sage.

Stewart, D. W., P. N. Shamdasani, and D. W. Rook. 2007. *Focus groups: Theory and practice*. 2d ed. Thousand Oaks, CA: Sage.

Stewart, E. A., and R. L. Simons. 2010. Race, code of the street, and violent delinquency: A multilevel investigation of neighborhood street culture and individual norms of violence. *Criminology* 48: 569–605.

Stewart, M. A. 1984. What is a successful doctor-patient interview? A study of interactions and outcomes. *Social Science and Medicine* 19:167–75.

Stinchcombe, A. L. 1968. *Constructing social theories*. New York: Harcourt, Brace & World.

Stine, R. 1990. An introduction to bootstrap methods. *Sociological Methods and Research* 18:243–91.

Stocking, G. W., Jr. 1983. *Observers observed: Essays on ethnographic fieldwork*. Madison: University of Wisconsin Press.

Stocking, G. W., Jr., ed. 1991. *Colonial situations: Essays on the contextualization of ethnographic knowledge*. Madison: University of Wisconsin Press.

Stocking, G. W., Jr., ed. 1992. *The ethnographer's magic and other essays in the history of anthropology*. Madison: University of Wisconsin Press.

Stockwell, T. J. Zhao, T. Chikritzhs, and T. K. Greenfield. 2008. What did you drink yesterday? Public health relevance of a recent recall method used in the 2004 Australian National Drug Strategy Household Survey. *Addiction* 103:919–28.

Stone, P. J., D. C. Dunphy, M. S. Smith, and D. M. Ogilvie. 1966. *The General Inquirer: A computer approach to content analysis*. Cambridge, MA: MIT Press.

Storer, N. W. 1966. *The social system of science*. New York: Holt, Rinehart & Winston.

Storosum, J. G., B. J. van Zwieten, and T. Wohlfarth. 2003. Suicide risk in placebo vs. active treatment in placebo-controlled trials for schizophrenia. *Archives of General Psychiatry* 60:365–68.

Stouffer, S., A., E. A. Suchman, L. C. DeVinney, S. A. Star, and R. M. Williams. 1949. *The American soldier: Adjustment during army life*. Princeton, NJ: Princeton University Press.

Strauss, A. 1987. *Qualitative analysis for social scientists*. Cambridge: Cambridge University Press.

Strauss, A., and J. Corbin. 1990. *Basics of qualitative research. Grounded theory procedures and techniques*. Thousand Oaks, CA: Sage.

Strauss, A., and J. Corbin, eds. 1997. *Grounded theory in practice*. Thousand Oaks, CA: Sage.

Strauss, A., and J. Corbin. 1998. *Basics of qualitative research: Grounded theory procedures and techniques*. 2d ed. Thousand Oaks, CA: Sage.

Strauss, C., and N. Quinn. 1997. *A cognitive theory of cultural meaning*. New York: Cambridge University Press.

Stray, S. 2009. Lies, damned lies, and statistics: The accuracy of survey responses. *Quality and Quantity* 43:161–71.

Streb, M. J., B. Burrell, B. Frederick, and M. A. Genovese. 2008. Social desireability effects and support for a female president. *Public Opinion Quarterly* 72:76–89.

Streib, G. F. 1952. Use of survey methods among the Navaho. *American Anthropologist* 54:30–40.

Striegel, H., R. Ulrich, and P. Simon. 2010. Randomized response estimates for doping and illicit drug use in elite athletes. *Drug and Alcohol Dependence* 106:230–32.

Stunkard, A., and D. Kaplan. 1977. Eating in public places: A review of reports of the direct observation of eating behavior. *International Journal of Obesity* 1:89–101.

Sturidsson, K., N. Långström, M. Grann, G. Sjöstedt, U. Åsgård, and E-M. Aghede. 2006. Using multidimensional scaling for the analysis of sexual offence behaviour: A replication and some cautionary notes. *Psychology, Crime and Law* 12:221–30.

Sturgis, P., N. Allum, and P. Smith. 2008. An experiment in the measurement of political knowledge. *Public Opinion Quarterly* 72:90–102.

Sturrock, K., and J. Rocha. 2000. A multidimensional scaling stress evaluation table. *Field Methods* 12:49–60.

Sturtevant, W. C. 1959. A technique for ethnographic note-taking. *American Anthropologist* 61:677–78.

Sturtevant, W. C. 1964. Studies in ethnoscience. In *Transcultural studies in cognition*, K. A. Romney and R. G. D'Andrade, eds., 99–131. *American Anthropologist* 66(3, pt. 2).

Subhash, S., and K. A. Kumar. 2006. Cluster analysis and factor analysis. In *The handbook of marketing research: Uses, misuses, and future advances*, R. Grover and M. Vriens, eds., chap. 18. Thousand Oaks, CA: Sage. http://www.sage-ereference.com/hdbk_mktgresearch/Article_n18.html (accessed March 5, 2011).

Sudman, S. 1976. *Applied sampling*. New York: Academic Press.

Sudman, S., E. Blair, N. M. Bradburn, and C. Stocking. 1977. Estimates of threatening behavior based on reports of friends. *Public Opinion Quarterly* 41:261–64.

Sudman, S., and N. M. Bradburn. 1974. *Response effects in surveys: Review and synthesis.* Chicago: Aldine.

Sudman, S., and N. M. Bradburn. 1982. *Asking questions.* San Francisco: Jossey-Bass.

Sudman, S., N. M. Bradburn, and N. Schwarz. 1996. *Thinking about answers: The application of cognitive processes to survey methodology.* San Francisco: Jossey-Bass.

Sudman, S., and N. Schwarz 1989. Contributions of cognitive psychology to advertising research. *Journal of Advertising Research* 29:43–53.

Sugita, E. W. 2006. Increasing quantity of water: Perspectives from rural households in Uganda. *Water Policy* 8:529–37.

Suhail, K., and H. R. Chaudhry. 2004. Predictors of subjective well-being in an eastern Muslim culture. *Journal of Social and Clinical Psychology* 3: 359–76.

Suhail, K., and R. Cochrane. 1997. Seasonal changes in affective state in samples of Asian and white women. *Social Psychiatry and Psychiatric Epidemiology* 32:149–57.

Sulfaro, V., and M. N. Crislip. 1997. How Americans perceive foreign policy threat: A magnitude scaling analysis. *Political Psychology* 18:103–26.

Sullivan, P., and K. Elifson. 1996. In the field with snake handlers. In *In the field. Readings on the research experience*, C. D. Smith and W. Kornblum, eds., 33–38. New York: Praeger.

Sundvik, L., and M. Lindeman. 1993. Sex-role identity and discrimination against same-sex employees. *Journal of Occupational and Organizational Psychology* 66:1–11.

Surowiecki, J. 2004. *The wisdom of crowds: Why the many are smarter than the few and how collective wisdom shapes business, economies, societies and nations.* New York: Doubleday.

Sussman, S., P. Sun, and C. W. Dent. 2006. A meta-analysis of teen cigarette smoking cessation. *Health Psychology* 25:549–57.

Sutrop, U. 2001. List task and a cognitive salience index. *Field Methods* 13:263–76.

Suttles, G. D. 1968. *The social order of the slum: Ethnicity and territory in the inner city.* Chicago: University of Chicago Press.

Sutton, R. I., and B. M. Staw. 1995. What theory is *not. Administrative Science Quarterly* 40:371–84.

Swaen, G., and L. van Amelsvoort. 2009. A weight of evidence approach to causal inference. *Journal of Clinical Epidemiology* 62:270–77.

Swora, M. G. 2003. Using cultural consensus analysis to study sexual risk perception: A report on a pilot study. *Culture, Health, and Sexuality* 5:339–52.

Sykes, R. E., and E. E. Brent. 1983. *Policing: A social behaviorist perspective.* New Brunswick, NJ: Rutgers University Press.

Sykes, R. E., R. D. Rowley, and J. M. Schaefer. 1993. Effects of group participation on drinking behaviors in public bars: An observational survey. *Journal of Social Behavior and Personality* 5(special issue): 385–402.

Sykes, S., and K. O'Sullivan. 2006. A "mystery shopper" project to evaluate sexual health and contraceptive services for young people in Croydon. *Journal of Family Planning and Reproductive health Care* 32:25–26.

Szalai, A., ed. 1972. *The use of time. Daily activities of urban and suburban populations in twelve countries.* The Hague: Mouton.

Tabuchi, H. 2009. Japan pays foreign workers to go home. *New York Times*, April 22. http://www.nytimes.com/2009/04/23/business/global/23immigrant.html (accessed January 31, 2011).

Tahir, A. 2010. Muslim-on-Muslim social research: Knowledge, power, and religo-cultural identities. *Social Epistemology* 24:137–43.

Tannen, D. 1984. *Conversational style: Analyzing talk among friends.* Norwood, NJ: Ablex.

Tannen, D. 1994. *Gender and discourse.* New York: Oxford University Press.

Tanur, J. M. 1992. *Questions about questions: Inquiries into the cognitive bases of surveys.* New York: Russell Sage Foundation.

Tashakkori, A., and C. Teddlie. 2003. *Handbook of mixed methods in social and behavioral research.* Thousand Oaks, CA: Sage.

Tashakkori, A., and C. Teddlie, eds. 2010. *SAGE handbook of mixed methods in social and behavioral research.* 2d ed. Thousand Oaks, CA: Sage.

Taub, D. E., and R. G. Leger. 1984. Argot and the creation of social types in a young gay community. *Human Relations* 37:181–89.

Taylor, F. W. 1911. *The principles of scientific management.* New York: Harper.

Taylor, H. 1997. The very different methods used to conduct telephone surveys of the public. *Journal of the Marketing Research Society* 37:421–32.

Taylor, K. M., and J. A. Shepperd. 1996. Probing suspicion among participants in deception research. *American Psychologist* 51:886–87.

Taylor, S. J. 1991. Leaving the field: Relationships and responsibilities. In *Experiencing fieldwork: An inside view of qualitative research*, W. B. Shaffir and R. A. Stebbins, eds., 238–45. Newbury Park, CA: Sage.

Taylor, S. J., and R. Bogdan. 1998. *Introduction to qualitative research methods.* 3d ed. New York: Wiley.

Teddlie, C., and F. Yu. 2007. Mixed methods sampling: A typology with examples. *Journal of Mixed Methods Research* 1:77–100.

Tedlock, D. 1977. Toward an oral poetics. *New Literary History* 8:507–19.

Tedlock, D. 1987. Hearing a voice in an ancient text: Quiché Maya poetics in performance. In *Native American discourse: Poetics and rhetoric*, J. Sherzer and A. Woodbury, eds., 140–75. Cambridge: Cambridge University Press.

Temple, B. 2002. Crossed wires: Interpreters, translators, and bilingual workers in cross-language research. *Qualitative Health Research* 12: 844–54.

Templeton, J. F. 1994. *The focus group: A strategic guide to organizing, conducting and analyzing the focus group interview.* Revised ed. Chicago: Probus Publishing Co.

ten Have, P. 1991. Talk and institution: A reconsideration of the "asymmetry" of doctor-patient interaction. In *Talk and social structure. Studies in ethnomethodology and conversation analysis,* D. Boden and Z. H. Zimmerman, eds., 138–63. Berkeley: University of California Press.

Thompson, E. C., and Z. Juan. 2006. Comparative cultural salience: Measures using free-list data. *Field Methods* 18:398–412.

Thompson, S. K. 2002. *Sampling.* 2d ed. New York: John Wiley and Sons.

Thornberg, R. 2008. "It's not fair!"—Voicing pupils' criticisms of school rules. *Children and Society* 22:418–28.

Thorpe, C., B. Ryan, S. L. McLean, A. Burt, M. Stewart, J. B. Brown, G. J. Reid, and S. Harris. 2009. How to obtain excellent response rates when surveying physicians. *Family Practice* 26:65–68.

Thurman, Q., S. Jackson, and J. Zhao. 1993. Drunk-driving research and innovation: A factorial survey study of decisions to drink and drive. *Social Science Research* 22:245–64.

Tidball, M. E. 1973. Perspectives on academic women and affirmative action. *Educational Record* 54:130–35.

Tiefenthaler, J. 1997. Fertility and family time allocation in the Philippines. *Population and Development Review* 23:377–97.

Timm, J. R., ed. 1992. *Texts in context. Traditional hermeneutics in South Asia.* Albany: State University of New York Press.

Tindale, R. S., and D. A. Vollrath. 1992. "Thought experiments" and applied social psychology. In *Methodological issues in applied social psychology,* F. B. Bryant et al., eds., 219–38. New York: Plenum.

Tinsley, H. E., D. J. Tinsley, and C. E. Croskeys. 2002. Park usage, social milieu, and psychosocial benefits of park use reported by older urban park users from four ethnic groups. *Leisure Sciences* 24:199–218.

Tippett, L. H. C. 1935. Statistical methods in textile research. *Transactions, The Journal of the Textile Institute* 26:T51–T70.

Tipping, M. D., V. E. Forth, D. B. Magill, K. Englert, and M. V. Williams. 2010. Systematic review of time studies evaluating physicians in the hospital setting. *Journal of Hospital Medicine* 5:353–59.

Titus, P. A., and P. B. Everett. 1996. Consumer wayfinding tasks, strategies, and errors: An exploratory field study. *Psychology and Marketing* 13:265–90.

Toepoel, V., D. Corrie, and M. van Soest. 2009. Design of Web questionnaires: An information-processing perspective for the effect of response categories. *Sociological Methods and Research* 37:371–92.

Tong, Y. 2010. Place of education, gender disparity, and assimilation of immigrant scientists and engineers earnings. *Social Science Research* 39:610–26.

Tooker, E. 1997. Introduction. In *Systems of consanguinity and affinity of the human family,* L. H. Morgan, ed., vii–xx. Lincoln: University of Nebraska Press.

Torgerson, W. S. 1958. *Theory and methods of scaling.* New York: Wiley.

Toulmin, S. E. 1980. Philosophy of science. *Encyclopaedia brittanica,* Vol. 16. Chicago: Encyclopaedia Brittanica, Inc.

Toupin, D., L. Lebel, D. Dubeau, D. Imbeau, and L. Bouthillier. 2007. Measuring the productivity and physical workload of brushcutters within the context of a production-based pay system. *Forest Policy and Economics* 9:1046–55.

Tourangeau, R., M. P. Couper, and D. M. Steiger. 2003. Humanizing self-administered surveys: Experiments on social presence in web and IVR surveys. *Computers in Human Behavior* 19:1–24.

Tourangeau, R., and T. W. Smith. 1996. Asking sensitive questions: The impact of data collection, question format, and question context. *Public Opinion Quarterly* 60:275–304.

Tourangeau, R., and T. Yan. 2007. Sensitive questions in surveys. *Psychological Bulletin* 133:859–83.

Tremblay, M. 1957. The key informant technique: A non-ethnographic application. *American Anthropologist* 59:688–701.

Trent, R., and H. R. Bernard. 1985. Local support for an innovative transit system. *Journal of Advanced Transportation Research* 19:237–39.

Trochim, W. M. K. 1986. *Advances in quasi-experimental design and analysis.* San Francisco: Jossey-Bass.

Trotter, R. T., III, and J. M. Potter. 1993. Pile sorts, a cognitive anthropological model of drug and AIDS risks for Navajo teenagers: Assessment of a new evaluation tool. *Drugs and Society* 7:23–39.

Trussell, N., and P. J. Lavrakas. 2004. The influence of incremental increases in token cash incentives on mail survey response—Is there an optimal amount? *Public Opinion Quarterly* 68:349–67.

Tsang, J-A, and W. C. Rowatt. 2007. *International Journal for the Psychology of Religion* 17:99–120.

Tufte, E. R. 1997. *Visual explanations: Images and quantities, evidence and narrative.* Cheshire, CT: Graphics Press.

Tufte, E. R. 2001. *The visual display of quantitative information.* 2d ed. Cheshire, CT: Graphics Press.

Tufte, E. R. 2006. *Beautiful evidence.* Cheshire, CT: Graphics Press.

Tuladhar, S. M., S. S. Acharya, M. Pradhan, J. Pollock, and G. Dallabetta. 1998. The role of pharmacists in HIV/STD prevention: Evaluation of an STD syndromic management intervention in Nepal. *AIDS* 12(Suppl. 2):S81–S87.

Turnage, A. K. 2008. Email flaming behavior and organizational conflict. *Journal of Computer-Mediated Communication* 13:43–59.

Turnbull, C. 1986. Sex and gender: The role of subjectivity in field research. In *Self, sex and gender in cross-cultural fieldwork,* T. L. Whitehead and M. E. Conaway, eds., 17–29. Urbana: University of Illinois Press.

Turner, C. F., A. Al-Tayyib, S. M. Rogers, E. Eggleston, M. A. Villaroel, A. M. Roman, J. R. Chromy, and P. C. Cooley. 2009. Improving epidemiological surveys of sexual behaviour conducted by telephone. *International Journal of Epidemiology* 38:1118–27.

Turner, R. 1953. The quest for universals in sociological research. *American Sociological Review* 18:604–11.

Tversky, A., and D. Kahneman. 1971. Belief in the law of small numbers. *Psychological Bulletin* 76:105–10.

Twenge, J. M. 1997. Attitudes towards women, 1970–1995. *Psychology of Women Quarterly* 21:35–51.

Undén, A-L., and K. Orth-Gomér. 1989. Development of a social support instrument for use in population surveys. *Social Science and Medicine* 29:1387–92.

United Nations, Dept. of Economic and Social Affairs, Economic and Social Development. 2009. http://unstats.un.org/unsd/demographic/products/socind/inc-eco.htm (accessed August 14, 2009).

United States v. Pelley; Same v. Brown; Same v. Fellowship Press, Inc. Nos. 8086-8088. United States Court of Appeals for the Seventh Circuit. 132 F.2d 170; 1942 U.S. App. LEXIS 2559. December 17, 1942.

University of Michigan. Survey Research Center. 1976. *Interviewer's Manual*. Rev. ed. Ann Arbor: Institute for Social Research, University of Michigan.

Uriell, A. A., and C. M. Dudley. 2009. Sensitive topics: Are there modal differences? *Computers in Human Behavior* 25:76–87.

U. S. Bureau of the Census. 2009. *Design and Methodology. American Community Survey.* http://www.census.gov/acs/www/methodology/methodology_main/ (accessed August 21, 2011).

U.S. Bureau of the Census. n.d. Statement by William G. Barron Jr. on the current status of results of Census 2000 Accuracy and Coverage Evaluation Survey. CB01-CS.06. http://www.census.gov/Press-Release/www/releases/archives/census_2000/000710.html (accessed March 8, 2010).

Vadez, V., V. Reyes-García, R. Godoy, L. Williams, L. Apaza, E. Byron, T. Huanca, W. R. Leonard, E. Pérez, and D. Wilkie. 2003. Validity of self-reports to measure deforestation: Evidence from the Bolivian highlands. *Field Methods* 15:289–304.

Valente, T. W. 2008. Communication network analysis. In *The SAGE sourcebook of advanced data analysis methods for communication research*, A. F. Hayes, M. D. Slater, and L. B. Snyder, eds., 247–74. Thousand Oaks, CA: Sage.

Van Boeschoten, R. 2006. Code-switching, linguistic jokes and ethnic identity: Reading hidden transcripts in a cross-cultural context. *Journal of Modern Greek Studies* 24:347–77.

van den Borne, F. 2007. Using mystery clients to assess condom negotiation in Malawi: Some ethical concerns. *Studies in Family Planning* 38:322–30.

van den Brakel, J. A., R. Vis-Visschers, and J. J. G. Schmeets. 2006. An experiment with data collection modes and incentives in the Dutch Family and Fertility Survey for Young Moroccans and Turks. *Field Methods* 18: 321–34.

van den Hoonaard, W. C., ed. 2002. *Walking the tightrope: Ethical issues for qualitative researchers.* Toronto: University of Toronto Press.

van den Mortel, T. 2007. Faking it: Social desirability response bias in self-report research. *Australian Journal of Advanced Nursing* 25:40–48.

van der Vaart, W. 2009. Testing a cue-list to aid attitude recall in surveys: A field experiment. *Journal of Official Statistics* 25:363–78.

van der Vaart, W., Y. Ongena, A. Hoogendoorn, and W. Dijkstra. 2006. Do interviewers' voice characteristics influence cooperation rates in telephone surveys? *International Journal of Public Opinion Research* 18:488–99.

Van Hattum, M. J. C., and E. D. de Leeuw. 1999. A disk-by-mail survey of pupils in primary schools: Data quality and logistics. *Journal of Official Statistics* 15:413–29.

Van Maanen, J. 1973. Observations on the making of a policeman. *Human Organization* 32:407–18.

Van Maanen, J. ed. 1983. *Qualitative methodology.* Beverly Hills, CA: Sage.

van Poppel, F., and L. H. Day. 1996. A test of Durkheim's theory of suicide—Without committing the "ecological fallacy." *American Sociological Review* 61: 500–507.

Van Ryzin, G. G. 1995. Cluster analysis as a basis for purposive sampling of projects in case study evaluations. *Evaluation Practice* 16:109–19.

van Straaten, I., R. C. M. E. Engels, C. M. E. Rutger, C. Finkenauer, and R. W. Holland. 2008. Sex differences in short-term mate preferences and behavioral mimicry: A semi-naturalistic experiment. *Archives of Sexual Behavior* 37:902–11.

Van Vliet, K. J. 2008. Shame and resilience in adulthood: A grounded theory study. *Journal of Counseling Psychology* 55:233–45.

Van Willigen, J., and V. C. Channa. 1991. Law, custom, and crimes against women: The problem of dowry death in India. *Human Organization* 50:369–77.

Verkasalo, H. 2010. Analysis of smartphone user behavior. IEEE. Ninth International Conference on Mobile Business 2010 Ninth Global Mobility Roundtable. doi:10.1109/ICMB-GMR. 2010.74

Viberg, N., P. Mujinja, W. Kalala, L. Kumaranayake, S. Vyas, G. Tomson, and C. S. Lundborg. 2009. STI management in Tanzanian private drugstores: Practices and roles of drug sellers. *Sexually Transmitted Infections* 85:300–307.

Vicente, P., and E. Reis. 2010. Using questionnaire design to fight nonresponse bias in web surveys. *Social Science Computer Review* 28:251–67.

Villarroel, M., C. F. Turner, S. Rogers, A. Roman, P. C. Cooley, A. B. Steinberg, E. Eggleston, and J. R. Chromy. 2008. T-ACASI reduces bias in STD measurements: The National STD and Behavior Measurement Experiment. *Sexually Transmitted Diseases* 35:499–506.

Vincke, J., R. Bolton, and P. De Vleeschouwer. 2001. The cognitive structure of the domain of safe and unsafe gay sexual behavior in Belgium. *AIDS CARE* 13:57–70.

Vink, M. P., and O. Van Vliet. 2009. Not quite crisp, not yet fuzzy? Assessing the potentials and pitfalls of multi-value QCA. *Field Methods* 21:265–89.

Virués-Ortega, J. 2006. The case against B. F. Skinner 45 years later: An encounter with N. Chomsky. *The Behavior Analyst* 29:243–51.

Viswanathan M. A. A., E. Eng, G. Gartlehner, K. N. Lohr, D. Griffith , S. Rhodes, C. Samuel-Hodge, S. Maty, L. Lux, L. Webb, S. F. Sutton, T. Swinson, A. Jackman, and L. Whitener. 2004. Community-based participatory research: Assessing the evidence. Evidence Report/Technology Assessment No. 99 (Prepared by RTI–University of North Carolina Evidence-based Practice Center under Contract No. 290-02-0016). AHRQ Publication 4–E022–2. Rockville, MD: Agency for Healthcare Research and Quality. http://www.ahrq.gov/downloads/pub/evidence/pdf/cbpr/cbpr.pdf (accessed June 23, 2011).

Voltaire. 1967 [1738]. *The elements of Sir Isaac Newton's philosophy*. Trans. by John Hanna. London: Cass.

Wagley, C. 1983. Learning fieldwork: Guatemala. In *Fieldwork: The human experience*, R. Lawless, V. H. Sutlive, and M. D. Zamora, eds., 1–18. New York: Gordon & Breach.

Wainer, H. 1999. One cheer for null hypothesis significance testing. *Psychological Methods* 4:212–13.

Waitzkin, H., T. Britt, and C. Williams. 1994. Narratives of aging and social problems in medical encounters with older persons. *Journal of Health and Social Behavior* 35:322–48.

Walden, G. R. 2008. *Focus groups: A selective annotated bibliography*. Lanham, MD: Scarecrow Press.

Walker, I. 2006. Drivers overtaking bicyclists: Objective data on the effects of riding position, helmet use, vehicle type, and apparent gender. *Accident Analysis and Prevention* 39:417–25.

Walker, I. 2007. Drivers overtaking bicyclists: Objective data on the effects of riding position, helmet use, vehicle type, and apparent gender. *Accident Analysis and Prevention* 39:417–25.

Wallace, A. F. C. 1962. Culture and cognition. *Science* 135:352–57.

Wallace, A. F. C. 1965. Driving to work. In *Context and meaning in cultural anthropology*, M. E. Spiro, ed., 277–96. New York: The Free Press.

Wallander, L. 2009. 25 years of factorial surveys in sociology: A review. *Social Science Research* 38:505–20.

Wallerstein, I. M. 1974. *The modern world-system; capitalist agriculture and the origins of the European world-economy in the sixteenth century*. New York: Academic Press.

Wallerstein, I. M. 2004. *World-systems analysis: An introduction*. Durham, NC: Duke University Press.

Wallgren, A., B. Wallgren, R. Persson, U. Jorner, and J-A. Haaland. 1996. *Graphing statistics and data: Creating better charts*. Thousand Oaks, CA: Sage.

Walmsley, D. J., and G. J. Lewis. 1989. The pace of pedestrian flows in cities. *Environment and Behavior* 21:123–50.

WalterMaurer, E. M., C. A. Ortega, and L-A. McNutt. 2003. Issues in estimating the prevalence of intimate-partner violence: Assessing the impact of abuse status on participation bias. *Journal of Interpersonal Violence* 18:959–74.

Walther, F. J. 2005. Withholding treatment, withdrawing treatment, and palliative care in the neonatal intensive care unit. *Early Human Development* 81: 965–72.

Wanat, C. L. 2008. Getting past the gatekeepers: Differences between access and cooperation in public school research. *Field Methods* 20:191–208.

Wang, C., and M. A. Burris. 1997. Photovoice: Concept, methodology, and use for participatory needs assessment. *Health Education and Behavior* 24:369–87.

Ward, M., G. Grinstein, and D. Keim. 2010. *Interactive data visualization: Foundations, techniques, and applications*. Natick, MA: A. K. Peters.

Ward, V. M., J. T. Bertrand, and L. F. Brown. 1991. The comparability of focus group and survey results— 3 case-studies. *Evaluation Review* 15:266–83.

Waring, S. P. 1991. *Taylorism transformed: Scientific management theory since 1945*. Chapel Hill: University of North Carolina Press.

Wark, G. R., and D. L. Krebs. 1996. Gender and dilemma differences in real-life moral judgment. *Developmental Psychology* 1996 32:220–30.

Warner, S. L. 1965. Randomized response: A survey technique for eliminating evasive answer bias. *Journal of the American Statistical Association* 60:63–69.

Warner, W. L., ed. 1963. *Yankee City*. New Haven, CT: Yale University Press.

Warner, W. L., and P. S. Hunt. 1941. *The social life of a modern community*. New Haven, CT: Yale University Press.

Warren, C. A. B. 1988. *Gender issues in field research*. Newbury Park, CA: Sage.

Warriner, K., J. Goyder, H. Gjertsen, P. Hohner, and K. McSpurren. 1996. Charities, no; lotteries, no; cash, yes. Main effects and intereactions in a Canadian incentives experiment. *Public Opinion Quarterly* 60:542–62.

Warwick, D. P., and C. A. Lininger. 1975. *The sample survey: Theory and practice*. New York: McGraw-Hill.

Wasserman, S., and K. Faust. 1994. *Social network analysis: Methods and applications*. Cambridge: Cambridge University Press.

Wasserman, S., and J. Galaskiewicz, eds. 1994. *Advances in social network analysis: Research in the social and behavioral sciences*. Thousand Oaks, CA: Sage.

Wasson, C. 2000. Ethnography in the field of design. *Human Organization* 59:377–88.

Watkins, N., F. Cole, and S. Weidemann. 2010. The War Memorial as healing environment: The psychological effect of Vietnam Veterans Memorial on Vietnam War combat veterans' posttraumatic stress disorder symptoms. *Environment and Behavior* 42:351–75.

Watson, O. M., and T. D. Graves. 1966. Quantitative research in proxemic behavior. *American Anthropologist* 68:971–85.

Watson, T. J. 2011. Ethnography, reality, and truth: The vital need for studies of "how things work" in organizations and management. *Journal of Management Studies* 48:202–17.

Watters, J. K., and P. Biernacki. 1989. Targeted sampling: Options for the study of hidden populations. *Social Problems* 36:416–30.

Watts, D. J. 1999. Networks, dynamics, and the small-world phenomenon. *American Journal of Sociology* 105:493–527.

Watts, D. J. 2003. *Six degrees: The science of a connected age.* New York: W. W. Norton.

Watts, D. J. 2004. The "new" science of networks. *Annual Review of Sociology* 30:243–70.

Watts, D. J,. and S. H. Strogatz. 1998. Collective dynamics of "small-world" networks. *Nature* 393:440–42

Waugh, I. M., E. V. Plake, and B. M. Rienzi. 2000. Assessing attitudes toward gay marriage among selected Christian groups using the lost-letter technique. *Psychological Reports* 86:215–18.

Wax, R. 1971. *Doing fieldwork: Warnings and advice.* Chicago: University of Chicago Press.

Wax, R. 1986. Gender and age in fieldwork and fieldwork education: "Not any good thing is done by one man alone." In *Self, sex and gender in cross-cultural fieldwork,* T. L. Whitehead and M. E. Conaway, eds., 129–50. Urbana: University of Illinois Press.

Weatherford, J. M. 1986. *Porn row.* New York: Arbor House.

Webb, B. 1926. *My apprenticeship.* London: Longmans, Green.

Webb, C. 1984. Feminist methodology in nursing research. Women's perceptions of having a hysterectomy. *Journal of Advanced Nursing* 9:249–56.

Webb, E. J., D. T. Campbell, R. D. Schwartz, and L. Sechrest. 1966. *Unobtrusive measures: Nonreactive research in the social sciences.* Chicago: Rand McNally.

Webb, E. J., D. T. Campbell, R. D. Schwartz, and L. Sechrest. 2000. Unobtrusive measures. Rev. 2d ed. Thousand Oaks, CA: Sage.

Webb, E. J., and K. E. Weick. 1983. Unobtrusive measures in organizational theory: A reminder. In *Qualitative research,* J. van Mannen, ed., 209–24. Beverly Hills, CA: Sage.

Webb, S., and B. P. Webb. 1910. *The state and the doctor.* New York: Longmans, Green.

Weber, M. 1978. *Economy and society: An outline of interpretive sociology.* Ed. by G. Roth and C. Wittich. Berkeley: University of California Press.

Weber, R. P. 1990. *Basic content analysis.* Newbury Park, CA: Sage.

Webster, C. 1990. Attitudes toward marketing practices: The effects of ethnic identification. *Journal of Applied Business Research* 7:107–16.

Wei, L., and L. Milroy 1995. Conversational code-switching in a Chinese community in Britain: A sequential analysis. *Journal of Pragmatics* 23:281–99.

Weigl, M., A. Müller, A. Zupanc, and P. Angerer. 2009. Participant observation of time allocation, direct patient contact, and simultaneous activities in hospital physicians. *BMC Health Services Research* 9:110. http://www.biomedcentral.com/1472-6963/9/110 (accessed March 6, 2011).

Weik, K. E. 1995. What theory is not, theorizing is. *Administrave Science Quarterly* 40:385–90.

Weinberger, J. 1985. *Science, faith, and politics: Francis Bacon and the utopian roots of the modern age.* Ithaca, NY: Cornell University Press.

Weinberger, M., J. A. Ferguson, G. Westmoreland, L. A. Mamlin, D. S. Segar, G. J. Eckert, J. Y. Greene, D. K. Martin, and W. M. Tierney. 1998. Can raters consistently evaluate the content of focus groups? *Social Science and Medicine* 46:929–33.

Weinreb, A. 2006. The limitations of stranger-interviewers in rural Kenya. *American Sociological Review* 71:1014–39.

Weinreb, A., and M. Sana. 2009. The effects of questionnaire translation on demographic data and analysis. *Population Research and Policy Review* 28:429–54.

Weisner, T. 1973. The primary sampling unit: A nongeographical based rural-urban sample. *Ethos* 1:546–59.

Weisner, T. 2002. The American dependency conflict: Continuities and discontinuities in behavior and values of countercultural parents and their children. *Ethos* 29:271–95.

Weisner, T., G. W. Ryan, L. Reese, K. Kroesen, L. Bernheimer, and R. G. Allimore. 2001. Behavior sampling and ethnography: Complementary methods for understanding home-school connections among Latino immigrant families. *Field Methods* 13:20–46.

Weisstub, D. N., ed. 1998. *Research on human subjects: Ethics, law, and social policy.* Kidlington, Oxford, UK: Pergamon.

Weisstub, D. N., and G. Diaz Pintos, eds. 2007. *Autonomy and human rights in health care: An international perspective.* New York: Springer.

Weller, S. C. 1983. New data on intracultural variability: The hot-cold concept of medicine and illness. *Human Organization* 42:249–57.

Weller, S. C. 2007. Cultural consensus theory: Applications and frequently asked questions. *Field Methods* 19:339–68.

Weller, S. C., and C. I. Dungy. 1986. Personal preferences and ethnic variations among Anglo and Hispanic breast and bottle feeders. *Social Science and Medicine* 23:539–48.

Weller, S. C., and A. K. Romney. 1988. *Structured interviewing.* Newbury Park, CA: Sage.

Wellman, B. 1979. The community question. *American Journal of Sociology* 84:1201–31.

Wellman, B., ed. 1999. *Networks in the global village: Life in contemporary communities.* Boulder, CO: Westview.

Wellman, B. 2007. Challenges in collecting personal network data. The nature of personal network analysis. *Field Methods* 19:111–15.

Wells, G. L., E. A. Olson, and S. D. Charman. 2003. Distorted retrospective eyewitness reports as functions of feedback and delay. *Journal of Experimental Psychology: Applied* 9:42–52.

Wentland, E. J., and K. W. Smith. 1993. *Survey responses: An evaluation of their validity.* San Diego: Academic Press.

Wenze, S. J., K. C. Gunthert, and N. R. Forand. 2007. Influence of dysphoria on positive and negative cognitive reactivity to daily mood fluctuations. *Behaviour Research and Therapy* 45:915–27.

Werblow, J. A., H. M. Fox, and A. Henneman. 1978. Nutrition knowledge, attitudes and patterns of women athletes. *Journal of the American Dietetic Association* 73:242–45.

Werner, D. 1985. Psycho-social stress and the construction of a flood-control dam in Santa Catarina, Brazil. *Human Organization* 44:161–66.

Werner, O., and D. T. Campbell. 1970. Translating, working through interpreters, and the problem of decentering. In *Handbook of method in cultural anthropology*, R. Naroll and R. Cohen, eds., 398–420. New York: Natural History Press.

Werner, O., and J. Fenton. 1973. Method and theory in ethnoscience or ethnoepistemology. In *A handbook of method in cultural anthropology*, R. Naroll and R. Cohen, eds., 537–78. New York: Columbia University Press.

Werner, O., and G. M. Schoepfle. 1987. *Systematic fieldwork*, 2 vols. Newbury Park, CA: Sage.

Werner-Wilson, R. J., S. J. Price, T. S. Zimmerman, and M. J. Murphy. 1997. Client gender as a process variable in marriage and family therapy: Are women clients interrupted more than men clients? *Journal of Family Psychology* 11:373–77.

Wertz, R. T. 1987. Language treatment for aphasia is efficacious, but for whom? *Topics in Language Disorders* 8:1–10.

West, C. 1984. *Routine complications: Troubles with talk between doctors and patients.* Bloomington: University of Indiana Press.

West, C. 1995. Women's competence in conversation. *Discourse and Society* 6:107–31.

West, C., and D. Zimmerman. 1983. Small insults: A study of interruptions in cross-sex conversations between unacquainted persons. In *Language, gender, and society*, B. Thorne, C. Kramarae, and N. Henley, eds, 102–17. Rowley, MA: Newbury House Publishers.

West, S. G., S. P. Gunn, and P. Chernicky. 1975. Ubiquitous Watergate: An attributional analysis. *Journal of Personality and Social Psychology* 32:55–65.

Westermeyer, J. 1996. Alcohol and older American Indians. *Journal of Studies on Alcohol* 57: 117–18.

Westfall, R. S. 1993. *The life of Isaac Newton.* New York: Cambridge University Press.

Weston, C., T. Gandell, J. Beauchamp, L. McAlpine, C. Wiseman, and C. Beauchamp. 2001. Analyzing interview data: The development and evolution of a coding system. *Qualitative Sociology* 24: 381–400.

Whaley, A. L., and R. A. Longoria. 2009. Preparing card sort data for multidimensional scaling analysis in social psychological research: A methodological approach. *The Journal of Social Psychology* 149: 105–15.

Whatley, M. A. 2008. The dimensionality of the 15 item Attitudes Toward Women Scale. *Race, Gender and Class* 15:265–71.

White, L. A. 1949. *The science of culture. A study of man and civilization.* New York: Farrar, Strauss.

Whitehead, T. L., and M. E. Conaway, eds. 1986. *Self, sex and gender in cross-cultural fieldwork.* Urbana: University of Illinois Press.

Whiting, B. W., and J. W. M. Whiting. 1973. Methods for observing and recording behavior. In *Handbook of method in cultural anthropology*, R. Naroll and R. Cohen, eds., 282–315. New York: Columbia University Press.

Whiting, B. W., and J. W. M. Whiting (with R. Longabaugh). 1975. *Children of six cultures: A psycho-cultural analysis.* Cambridge, MA: Harvard University Press.

Whiting, J. W. M., I. L. Child, and W. W. Lambert et al. 1966. *Field guide for a study of socialization.* New York: Wiley.

Whyte, W. F. 1960. Interviewing in field research. In *Human organization research*, R. W. Adams and J. J. Preiss, eds., 299–314. Homewood, IL: Dorsey.

Whyte, W. F. 1981 [1943]. *Street corner society: The social structure of an Italian slum.* 3d ed. Chicago: University of Chicago.

Whyte, W. F. 1984. *Learning from the field: A guide from experience.* Beverly Hills, CA: Sage.

Whyte, W. F. 1989. Doing research in Cornerville. In *In the field: Readings on the field research experience*, C. D. Smith and W. Kornblum, eds., 69–82. New York: Praeger.

Whyte, W. F. 1996a. Qualitative sociology and deconstructionism. *Qualitative Inquiry* 2:220–26.

Whyte, W. F. 1996b. Facts, interpretations, and ethics in qualitative inquiry. *Qualitative Inquiry* 2:242–44.

Whyte, W. F., and K. K. Whyte. 1984. *Learning from the field: A guide from experience.* Beverly Hills, CA: Sage.

Wiederman, M., D. Weis, and E. Algeier. 1994. The effect of question preface on response rates in a telephone survey of sexual experience. *Archives of Sexual Behavior* 23:203–15.

Wierzbicka, A. 2004. The English expression good boy and good girl and cultural models of child rearing. *Culture and Psychology* 10:251–78.

Wilcox, R. R. 1998. How many discoveries have been lost by ignoring modern statistical methods? *American Psychologist* 53:300–14.

Wilk, R. R. 1990. Household ecology: Decision making and resource flows. In *The ecosystem approach in anthropology. From concept to practice*, E. F. Moran, ed., 323–56. Ann Arbor: University of Michigan Press.

Wilke, J. R. 1992. Supercomputers manage holiday stock. *The Wall Street Journal*, December 23, B1:8.

Will, J. A. 1993. The dimensions of poverty: Public perceptions of the deserving poor. *Social Science Research* 22:312–32.

Williams, B. 1978. *A sampler on sampling*. New York: Wiley.

Williams, H. A. 1995. Social support, social networks and coping of parents of children with cancer: Comparing White and African American parents. Ph.D. dissertation, University of Florida.

Williams, T. 1996. Exploring the cocaine culture. In *In the field. Readings on the research experience*, C. D. Smith and W. Kornblum, eds., 27–32. New York: Praeger.

Willis, G. B. 2005. *Cognitive interviewing*. London: Sage.

Willis, G. B., ed. 2011. Advances in cognitive interviewing: Applications to cross-cultural surveys. *Field Methods* 23. Special issue on cognitive interviewing.

Willis, G. B., and K. Miller. 2011. Cross-cultural applications of cognitive interviewing. *Field Methods* 23. Special issue.

Willms, D. G., J. A. Best, D. W. Taylor, J. R. Gilbert, D.M.C. Wilson, E. A. Lindsay, and J. Singer. 1990. A systematic approach for using qualitative methods in primary prevention research. *Medical Anthropology Quarterly* 4:391–409.

Wilson, D., J. McMaster, R. Greenspan, L. Mboyi, T. Ncube, and B. Sibanda. 1990. Cross-cultural validation of the Bem Sex Role Inventory in Zimbabwe. *Personality and Individual Differences* 11:651–56.

Wilson, G. D., and J. R. Patterson. 1968. A new measure of conservatism. *British Journal of Social and Clinical Psychology* 7:264–69.

Wilson, H. S., and S. A. Hutchinson. 1996. Methodologic mistakes in grounded theory. *Nursing Research* 45:122–24.

Wilson, M. 1997. Playing the dance, dancing the game: Race, sex, and stereotype in anthropological fieldwork. *Ethnos* 62:24–48.

Wilson, M. D. 1991. *Descartes*. London: Routledge.

Winch, P. 1990. *The idea of a social science and its relation to philosophy*. 2d ed. London: Routledge.

Winchatz, M. 2006. Fieldworker or foreigner? Ethnographic interviewing in nonnative languages. *Field Methods* 18:83–97.

Winchatz, M. 2010. Participant observation and the nonnative ethnographer: Implications of positioning on discourse-centered fieldwork. *Field Methods* 22: 340–56.

Windelband, W. 1998 [1894]. History and natural science. *Theory and Psychology* 8:5–22.

Winland, D. 2007. *We are now a nation. Croats between "home" and "homeland."* Toronto: University of Toronto Press.

Winters, C. A., S. Cudney, and T. Sullivan. 2010. The evolution of a coding schema in a paced program of research. *Qualitative Report* 15:1415–30.

Wolcott, H. F. 1995. *The art of fieldwork*. Walnut Creek, CA: AltaMira.

Wolcott, H. F. 2002. *Sneaky kid and its aftermath. Ethics and intimacy in fieldwork*. Walnut Creek, CA: AltaMira.

Wolcott, H. F. 2008. *Ethnography: A way of seeing*. 2d ed. Walnut Creek, CA: AltaMira.

Wolf, D. R. 1990. *The Rebels: A brotherhood of outlaw bikers*. Toronto: University of Toronto Press.

Wolf, D. R. 1991. High-risk methodology. Reflections on leaving an outlaw society. In *Experiencing fieldwork*, W. B. Shaffir and R. A. Stebbins, eds., 211–23. Newbury Park, CA: Sage.

Wolf, F. M. 1986. *Meta-analysis: Quantitative methods for research synthesis*. Beverly Hills, CA: Sage.

Wolfinger, N. 2002. On writing fieldnotes: Collection strategies and background expectancies. *Qualitative Research* 2:85–95.

Wong, D., and C. Baker. 1988. Pain in children: Comparison of assessment scales. *Pediatric Nursing* 14:9–17.

Wong, M. M-H., and M. Csikszentmihalyi. 1991. Affiliation motivation and daily experience: Some issues on gender differences. *Journal of Personality and Social Psychology* 60:154–64.

Woods, P. 1986. *Inside schools: Ethnography in educational research*. New York: Routledge and Kegan Paul.

Woodside, A. G., and E. J. Wilson. 2002. Respondent inaccuracy. *Journal of Advertising Research* 42:7–18.

Woolhouse, R. S. 1996. Locke. In *The Blackwell companion to philosophy*, N. Bunnin and E. P. Tsui-James, eds., 541–54. Oxford, UK: Blackwell.

World Factbook, The. Central Intelligence Agency 2010. https://www.cia.gov/library/publications/the-world-factbook/rankorder/2091rank.html and https://www.cia.gov/library/publications/the-world-factbook/rankorder/2004rank.html (accessed March 6, 2011).

Wormald, B. H. G. 1993. *Francis Bacon: History, politics and science*. New York: Cambridge University Press.

Wright, J. D., and P. W. Marsden. 2010. Social research and social science: History, current practice, and future prospects. In *Handbook of survey research*, 2d ed., P. V. Marsden and J. D. Wright, eds., 3–25. Bingley, UK: Emerald Group Publishing.

Wright, K. B. 1997. Shared ideology in Alcoholics Anonymous: A grounded theory approach. *Journal of Health Communication* 2:83–99.

Wright, S. 1921. Correlation and causation. *Journal of Agricultural Research* 20:557–85.

Wuthnow, R. 1976. A longitudinal, cross-national indicator of societal religious commitment. *Journal for the Scientific Study of Religion* 16:87–99.

Wutich, A. 2009. Water scarcity and the sustainability of a common pool resource institution in the Andes. *Human Ecology* 37:179–92.

Wutich, A., and C. McCarty. 2008. Social networks and infant feeding in Oaxaca, Mexico. *Maternal and Child Nutrition* 4:121–35.

Wutich, A., and K. Ragsdale. 2008. Water insecurity and emotional distress: Coping with supply, access, and seasonal variability of water in a Bolivian squatter settlement. *Social Science and Medicine* 67:2116–25.

Yammarino, F. J., S. J. Skinner, and T. L. Childers. 1991. Understanding mail survey response behavior. A meta-analysis. *Public Opinion Quarterly* 55:613–39.

Yancey, G. A., and S.W. Yancey. 1997. Black-White differences in the use of personal advertisements for individuals seeking interracial relationships. *Journal of Black Studies* 27:650–67.

Yang, L., and G. Zhiyong. 2010. Internet's impact on expert-citizen interactions in public policymaking. A meta analysis. *Government Information Quarterly* 27:431–41.

Yang, R. K., K. S. Burrola, and C. H. Bryan. 2009. Suicide ideation among participants in an after-school program: A convenience sample. *Child and Youth Services* 31:3–13.

Yang, Y. 2001. Sex and language proficiency level in color naming performance: An ESL/EFL perspective. *International Journal of Applied Linguistics* 11:238–56.

Yarrow, D., A. S. Baron, and M. R. Benaji. 2006. From American city to Japanese village: A cross-cultural investigation of implicit race attitudes. *Child Development* 77:1268–81.

Ybarra, M. L., J. Langhinrichsen-Rohling, J. Friend, and M. Diener-West. 2009. Impact of asking sensitive questions about violence to children and adolescents. *Journal of Adolescent Health* 45:499–507.

Yin, R. K. 2003. *Case study research: Design and methods*. 3d ed. Thousand Oaks, CA: Sage.

Yoshihama, M., B. Gillespie, A. C. Hammock, R. F. Belli, and R. M. Tolman. 2005. Does the life history calendar method facilitate the recall of intimate partner violence? Comparison of two methods of data collection. *Social Work Research* 29:151–63.

Young, F. W., and K. Minai. 2001. The structural determinants of mortality in Japanese prefectures. *International Journal of Japanese Sociology* 10:45–55.

Young, H. M. 1998. Moving to congregate housing: The last chosen home. *Journal of Aging Studies* 12:149–65.

Young, J. C. 1978. Illness categories and action strategies in a Tarascan town. *American Ethnologist* 5:81–97.

Young, J. C. 1980. A model of illness treatment decisions in a Tarascan town. *American Ethnologist* 7:106–31.

Young, J. C., and L. Y. Garro. 1982. Variation in the choice of treatment in two Mexican communities. *Social Science and Medicine* 16:1453–63.

Young, J. C., and L. C. Garro. 1994 [1981]. *Medical choice in a Mexican village*. Prospect Heights, IL: Waveland.

Young, M. E., M. Madison, N. T. Mai, A. Sirisegaram, and M. Wilson. 2009. Food for thought. What you eat depends on your sex and eating companions. *Appetite* 53:268–71.

Zaman, S. 2008. Native among the natives. *Journal of Contemporary Ethnography* 37:135–54.

Zehner, R. B. 1970. Sex effects in the interviewing of young adults. *Sociological Focus* 3:75–84.

Zeitlyn, D. 2004. The gift of the gab: Anthropology and conversation analysis. *Anthropos* 99:452–68.

Zickar, M. J., and N. T. Carter. 2010. Reconnecting with the spirit of workplace ethnography: A historical review. *Organizational Research Methods* 13:304–19.

Ziliak, S. T., and D. N. McCloskey. 2008. *The cult of statistical significance: How the standard error costs us jobs, justice, and lives*. Ann Arbor: University of Michigan Press.

Zimbardo, P. G. 1973. On the ethics of intervention in human psychological research: With special reference to the Stanford prison experiment. *Cognition* 2: 243–56.

Zimbardo, P. G. 2007. *The Lucifer effect: Understanding how good people turn evil*. New York: Random House.

Zimbardo, P. G. 2009. The Stanford prison experiment. A simulation study of the psychology of imprisonment conducted at Stanford University. http://www.prisonexp.org/ (accessed January 18, 2011).

Zimmerman, D. H., and C. West. 1983 [1975]. Sex roles, interruptions, and silences in conversation. In *Language and sex: Difference and dominance*, B. Thorne and N. Henley, eds., 105–29. Rowley, MA: Newbury House.

Zipp, J. F., and J. Toth. 2002. She said, he said, they said: The impact of spousal presence in survey research. *Public Opinion Quarterly* 66:177–208.

Zive, M. M., G. C. Frank-Spohrer, J. F. Sallis, T. L. McKenzie, J. P. Elder, C. C. Berry, S. L. Broyles, and P. R. Nader. 1998. Determinants of dietary intake in a sample of white and Mexican-American children. *Journal of the American Dietetic Association* 98:1282–89.

Znaniecki, F. 1934. *The method of sociology*. New York: Farrar and Rinehart.

Zocalli, R., M. R. Muscatello, A. Bruno, D. Serrano, D. Campolo, G. Pandolfo, C. Gianluca, C. Cedro, D. La Torre, and M. Meduri. 2008. Gender role identity in a sample of Italian male homosexuals. *Journal of Homosexuality* 55:265–73.

Zorbaugh, H. W. 1929. *The Gold Coast and the slum. A sociological study of Chicago's near North Side*. Chicago: The University of Chicago Press.

Zuckerman, M., H. S. Hodgins, A. Zuckerman, and R. Rosenthal. 1993. Contemporary issues in the analysis of data: A survey of 551 psychologists. *Psychological Science* 4:49–53.

Author Index

Subject Index

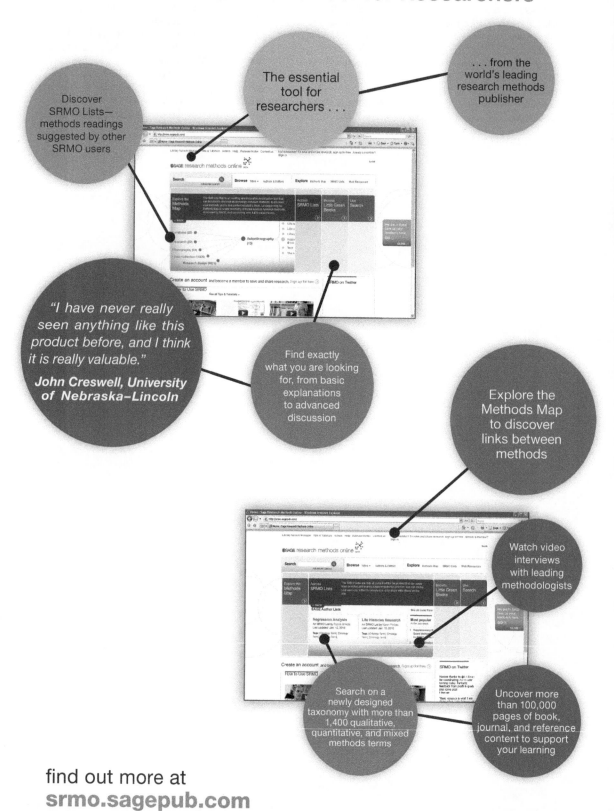